S0-ADD-228

The Complete Guide to the Art of Modern Cookery

Auguste Escoffier in his 80th year, New York, 1926

A. ESCOFFIER

The Complete Guide to the Art of Modern Cookery

the first translation into English
in its entirety of

LE GUIDE CULINAIRE

Translated by

H. L. Cracknell and R. J. Kaufmann

Superseding A GUIDE TO MODERN COOKERY,
first published in 1907

VNR VAN NOSTRAND REINHOLD
New York

Published in the United States of America by
Van Nostrand Reinhold
115 Fifth Avenue
New York, New York 10003

First published 1979
Reprinted 1981, 1983, 1984, 1985, 1986, 1987, 1989, 1990

ISBN 0-831-75478-8

Filmset in 'Monophoto' Times 9 on 10 pt
Printed in Great Britain by
Richard Clay Ltd, Norwich, Norfolk

CONTENTS

	Page
Frontispiece Portrait	
Translators' Preface	vii
Author's Foreword to the First Edition	ix
Introduction to the Second Edition of the *Guide Culinaire*	xi
Introduction to the Third Edition of the *Guide Culinaire*	xv
Introduction to the Fourth Edition of the *Guide Culinaire*	xvii
Biographical Note by Pierre P. Escoffier	xix
Weights, Measures and Temperatures—Abbreviations and Conversions	xxiii

Chapter 1 SAUCES 1
Stocks—Roux—Basic Sauces—Small Compound Brown and White Sauces—Cold Sauces—English Sauces—Butters—Marinades—Brines—Savoury Jellies.

Chapter 2 GARNISHES 42
Panadas—Forcemeats—Quenelles—Preparations for Hot and Cold Garnishes—List of Garnishes.

Chapter 3 SOUPS 65
Classification—Bouillons—Clarifications—Garnishes—Royales—Consommés—Cold Consommés —Thick Soups—Foreign Soups

Chapter 4 HORS-D'OEUVRE 120
Cold and Hot Hors-d'oeuvre.

Chapter 5 EGGS
Sur le Plat—Poached—Soft-boiled—Moulded—en Cocotte—Fried—Hard-boiled—Scrambled—Cold—Omelettes—Plovers' Eggs. 155

Chapter 6 FISH 180
Court-bouillons—Methods of Cooking—Forcemeats—Mousses and Mousselines—Fresh Water Fish—Salt Water Fish—Shellfish—Snails—Frogs' Legs.

Chapter 7 RELEVES AND ENTREES OF BUTCHERS' MEAT 257
Principles of Cooking. Beef—Veal—Mutton and Lamb—Pork.

Chapter 8 RELEVES AND ENTREES OF POULTRY 363
Chicken—Turkey—Goose—Duck—Guinea Fowl—Pigeon—Foie gras.

Chapter 9 RELEVES AND ENTREES OF GAME 425
Furred Game—Venison—Boar—Hare—Rabbit. Feathered Game—Pheasant—Partridge—Quail—Woodcock—Snipe etc.—Water-Fowl.

Chapter 10 COMPOSITE ENTREES 456
Hot Pies—Timbales—Tourtes—Vols-au-Vent.

Chapter 11 COLD PREPARATIONS 457
Galantines—Pâtés—Terrines—Simple and Composed Salads.

Chapter 12 ROASTS 469
Principles of Roasting. Butcher's Meat—Poultry—Game.

Chapter 13 VEGETABLES AND FARINACEOUS PRODUCTS 476
Methods of Cooking and Finishing. Vegetables—Potatoes—Farinaceous Products.

Chapter 14 SWEETS, PUDDINGS AND DESSERTS 512
Pastes—Hot and Cold Sauces—Hot and Cold Sweet Dishes.

Chapter 15 ICES 562
Mixtures—Cream and Fruit Ices—Coupes—Biscuits—Bombes—Parfaits—Mousses—Poudings Glacés—Soufflés Glacés—Punchs—Sorbets.

Chapter 16 SAVOURIES 577
Various Savouries and Sandwiches.

Chapter 17 POACHED FRUITS, JAMS AND DRINKS 582
Poached Fruits—Jams—Jellies—Hot and Cold Drinks.

GLOSSARY 589

MENUS 593

INDEX 610

TRANSLATORS' PREFACE

It is our privilege to have had the honour of translating Escoffier's *Le Guide Culinaire* from the original French and it is our great pleasure to present to the English speaking public this, the first complete English translation of his great work.

The task of translating has been long and arduous but at the same time most rewarding; as practising chefs we can only say without appearing to be immodest, that it has confirmed in our minds what we have always felt, that this book is indeed a masterpiece—that its basic principles are as valid today as when it was first published in 1903.

It should not be thought that this work is an old and out of date one; Escoffier was directly concerned with each new edition right up until 1921 when the fourth edition appeared. He kept on altering and improving it over the years in keeping with his ideas of modification and adaptations. It is this fourth edition which has been translated.

That Escoffier was a forward-thinking man ever prepared to adapt to and accept new ideas, can be evinced by a perusal of his Introductions to the succeeding editions. He speaks of the changes brought about in his lifetime by the changing social trends and he stresses the need to modify and up-date traditional working methods and forms of service. In 1907 he said that cooking would become more scientific and his words have been proved correct.

But despite all the changes that he experienced in his lifetime there was one thing that had never changed and, as he says, never will change, and that is that the fundamental methods are soundly based and unalterable and will endure.

Although he up-dated accepted formulas and created many new ones, on the fundamentals of cooking he never compromised. He undertook the task of formulating them so as to inform his colleagues and to hand them on to us and to future generations. If it were not for him and this monumental work we have no hesitation in saying that these fundamentals would have been lost in the welter of opposing and often uninformed views.

And yet this book is a guide only, it does not go into minute details of preparation. Escoffier assumes that his readers will have a sound basic knowledge of food and cooking as without this the reader would flounder in the dark and the results could be less than perfect. He says it is for those who practise the art of cookery whether they be the professional chef or manager, the housewife or the gourmet. As a guide then, it should be read and studied and referred to constantly; a book to be kept somewhere in the kitchen and not relegated to the library shelf to gather dust.

Escoffier was perhaps the last in a long line of great chefs who not only wrote a cookery book but had the integrity and force of character to change with the times, to introduce new ideas and to stamp these with the weight of his authority. His devotion to duty and to his art is epitomised in the fact that he managed to write this monumental work in the short space of some five years whilst still directing the kitchens of the places where he worked; it still remains to be seen whether another of his calibre will appear and don his mantle.

We firmly believe then that the English speaking world should have recourse to this book and that the Complete Guide to the Art of Modern Cookery is the work which will help to maintain standards and will guide the destiny of the culinary world for years to come.

So we have tried to make a faithful translation of the *Guide Culinaire* leaving it as close to what Escoffier wrote as possible. As is well known, many French culinary technical terms are difficult to translate precisely and because of this some have been left untranslated in the body of the work. Some of the ingredients he mentions are no longer available and it is, of course, left to the reader to find a substitute, which is quite in keeping with his principle of adaptation and modification. The Glossary at the end of the book will help in explaining some of these.

The weights and measures used in this book are given first in the original metric units together with their approximate equivalents in Imperial units as well as equivalent U.S. cup measurements for liquids. To assist the American readers a few selected cup measurements for solid and dry commodities are given in a short selection of conversion tables at the beginning of the book. We feel that the capable housewife and the dedicated gourmet as well as the professional chef will thus be able to cope with the demands of the recipes.

This book is a repository (not a mausoleum) of all that is best in Classical French and International cookery consisting as it does of more than 5,000 recipes with a great deal of theory on the principles of cookery. The recipes themselves are not necessarily complicated and protracted, in fact many are beautifully simple; thus we think that this book will also be of great value to the young who aspire to achieve high standards and to students on catering courses who need to understand something of the intricacies of *Haute Cuisine*.

Our earnest hope then is that this work will be favourably received by the public and will meet with the success which it deserves.

H. L. CRACKNELL
R. J. KAUFMANN

FOREWORD TO THE FIRST EDITION

It is twenty years since I first put the idea of writing this book to our dear now departed master, Urban Dubois, who greatly encouraged me to realize the project. But being engaged on so many other duties it was not until 1898 that, with the collaboration of Monsieur Philéas Gilbert, I began the first stages of the book. Shortly after this, recalled to London for the opening of the Carlton Hotel and kept extremely busy by the organizing of the kitchens of this great hotel, I was forced to put off my writing to a less busy time.

At the insistence of my many colleagues and with the assurance of the devoted assistance of my friends, Philéas Gilbert and Emile Fétu, the work was again taken up where it had been left off in 1898. I owe it to the encouragement of many people and especially to the tenacity and perseverance of both my collaborators that this enormous task was brought to a successful conclusion.

I wanted to create a useful tool rather than just a recipe book whilst leaving the reader free to decide on the way to carry out the work according to his own personal views; I tried by drawing on my experience of more than forty years of practice, to lay down, at least in principle, the traditional methods of operation.

If this work is not yet exactly what I dreamed of or what it will one day become, it can nevertheless render a useful service to my colleagues. To this end I have kept it within reach of most people's pockets, especially for those with only limited means because it is for the younger generation that I have mainly written it and particularly for those who, starting work today, will in twenty years' time be at the top of their profession in charge of a large organization.

I did not want to make this a work of luxury and just a book for the library but rather a constant guide and companion that would always be at hand to use and of which the advice would always be of value.

Although it contains more than 5000 recipes I have no pretentions that this guide is exhaustive; even if it were today, it would no longer be so tomorrow, because progress marches on and each day brings forth new recipes and new methods. All that I can do to overcome this drawback is to keep the work up-to-date by noting any new recipes and ideas and remedying inevitable omissions by including them in each new edition.

As a friend of theirs for many years I wish to place this book under the posthumous patronage of Messieurs Urban Dubois and Emile Bernard whose great shadows still fill the culinary horizon. And I am happy to be able to reaffirm here and with renewed emphasis, my admiration for them as being the ones who, since the days of Carême, have carried the glory of the art of cookery to its greatest heights.

Force of circumstances have reserved for me the honour of bringing to the type of service they introduced, some very important changes brought about mainly by the demands of the ever-increasing pace of life of the times we are living in. I was the first to curtail the use of fancy bases and create new and simpler ways of presenting food and, in order to be able to apply these methods, at the same time to create new equipment. Now I can say in all sincerity, just as much today as in the days when I produced the sumptuous presentations as prescribed by Dubois and Bernard, that I believe myself to be in perfect agreement with them. These men of genius, although admirers of the great Carême, nevertheless did not hesitate to change those parts of his work which no longer agreed with current trends, and were the first to realize that sooner or later necessity would compel the adoption of the recommendations made here in this book. At a time when all is undergoing modification and change, it would be foolish to claim to establish the future of an art which is connected in so many ways to fashion and is just as changeable.

But what already existed at the time of Carême, which exists today and which will continue to exist for as long as cooking itself, are the fundamentals of this art of cookery; they may become simpler on the surface but do not lose their value; on the contrary. And if tastes are constantly being refined, these fundamentals must be continuously refined to satisfy them; to counteract the disastrous effects of the modern pace of living on peoples' nerves, they must become even more exact and scientific.

I hereby affirm then that the more the art of cookery progresses in this manner, the greater grows the respect of present-day chefs for these three men of the nineteenth century who have had such an influence on their destinies. For Carême, Dubois and Bernard, whom we all too often regard from the point of view of their artistry, were just as outstanding in their dedication to the actual basics of the culinary art. We certainly owe works of unchallenged value to Gouffé, to Favre, to Hélouis and to Reculet, to name only a few of those who are no longer with us, but not one of their books can be compared with that masterpiece, the *Cuisine Classique*.

In presenting this new work to my colleagues, it is my duty to recommend the need to study carefully the immortal works of the great masters as well as other culinary books and publications. As the popular saying goes 'One can never know too much'; the more one learns the more one sees the need to learn more and that study, as well as broadening the mind of the craftsman, provides an easy way of perfecting himself in the practice of our art.

The only profit I wish to draw from this book and the only reward I crave, is to see, in this respect, my advice listened to and followed by those for whom it was written.

1st November 1902 A. ESCOFFIER

INTRODUCTION TO THE SECOND EDITION OF THE *GUIDE CULINAIRE*

On the occasion of the appearance of this the second edition of a work whose favourable reception by our colleagues has assured a success far surpassing our most ambitious hopes, we feel it our bounden duty to express our deep gratitude and to thank all our readers. Our thanks must go as much to those from whom we have received welcoming approval as to those who have done us the honour of making useful criticisms of which we are forced to take account where they appear to us to be justified.

In order to acknowledge the warm reception received from the public, no effort has been spared to increase the technical value of this work and to correct various errors caused by the wish to produce a logical classification of the recipes and also to condense them as much as possible, though without detracting from the clarity of the methods and recipes of which our layout necessitated such brevity. We have added a number of new recipes to the revised text, most of them in the way they are made and served being inspired by the demands of today's clientele whilst taking account where reasonable and possible of the increasing tendency for even quicker forms of service. These tendencies have increased so much over the past few years that they deserve our close attention and a serious study of their influence on modern food service would not be out of place here.

The art of cookery depends on the psychological state of society for the way it manifests itself; it follows closely the dictates of society without being able to separate itself from its impact. Where the steady, even pace of life is not troubled by any preoccupations, where the future seems assured and safe from the vagaries of fortune, the art of cookery always flourishes because it contributes to one of the most agreeable of the pleasures given to man to enjoy.

On the other hand, when life is hectic and where the countless cares of business and industry worry the spirit of man, good living can only play a minor role. More often the need to eat appears to those caught in the throes of business, as no longer a pleasurable occasion but an unnecessary chore. They consider the time spent in eating as wasted and what they demand above all else from those whose duty it is to cater for them, is not to be kept waiting.

Such habits can and must be condemned, if only from the point of view of the health of customers whose stomachs have to put up with their consequences; such habits are utterly deplorable. However, it is not within our power to restrain them; all that culinary science can do is to palliate man's imprudence where possible by the excellence of its products.

For the customer who demands quick service, we have no alternative but to satisfy him or to lose his custom; what we refuse in this respect, our competitors will supply.

We are therefore, obliged to go along with his whims. If our normal system of operation and type of service does not lend itself to this commitment then we must resolutely change it. Only one thing must remain unchanged and untouched and that is the quality of the dishes—the flavour value that comes from the fundamentals of cookery on which our work is built. We have already introduced reforms in the manner of presentation; a whole host of presentation pieces have already disappeared and are still disappearing from use such as pedestals, borders and ornamental skewers. One can go even further in this direction as will be explained further on in this Introduction. Simplicity of presentation will be taken to its ultimate limits but at the same time the nutritive and taste values of dishes will be increased. We will make them lighter and more easily digestible for delicate stomachs. We will condense them and remove much of the waste matter. In a word, cookery whilst continuing to be an art will become scientific and will have to submit its formulas which very often are still too empirical, to a method and precision which leaves nothing to chance.

From a culinary point of view we are in a state of transition; the old ways of working still have their fervent adherants whom we understand and with whom in our hearts we share their ideas. How not to lament the passing of those days when a meal was both a ceremony and a celebration, when our traditional French cookery displayed its wonders to the great delight of lovers of good food? How not to seize joyfully every occasion that presents itself to pay homage to Comus the joyous god of good living and feasting? And so we have made a point of keeping in this work which is really a collection of the traditions of French cookery rather than a personal work, a whole host of dishes that have been discarded from the modern repertoire but which any cook worthy of his name should know about in order to be able to satisfy as the occasion arises, the most princely of guests as well as the average person; as well for the contented gourmet for whom time spent at the table is never too long as for the business man to whom it means everything. So we cannot be accused of bias towards the new methods; we have simply wished to follow the forward march of our art, to be up-to-date and to obey the express desires of our guests, hosts or customers before whose wishes we must bow.

We maintain that we render our colleagues a service by causing them to search hard—though without sacrificing any of their personal preferences—for means of improving the speed of service without detracting from their standards. Generally speaking, our methods of working are still largely determined by custom. Under pressure from the customer whose demands have to be met, we have already had to simplify our working methods; but it seems as though we are pursuing this course reluctantly. We defend our ground step by step and yield only with bad grace. So although we have almost totally done away with pedestals we have hung on to complicated garnishes; they are arranged at enormous cost of time, they are cumbersome and their elaborateness is a mistake from the gastronomic point of view and should only be reserved, if the wishes of the guests or hosts are to be met for the rare occasions when it is possible to make use of them without affecting the quality of the dishes; that is to say, when one has at his disposal large quantities of the three essentials: time, money and vast, well-equipped kitchens.

Under ordinary working conditions we must try to produce a considerable simplification of garnishes and to reduce the items to three or four at most, whether for Entrées or Relevés and whether they be meat, poultry or fish. When a quick service is called for, these garnishes must always be served separately as must the sauce. In this way the arranging of the dish for presentation is greatly simplified and the food is served hotter, more quickly and more neatly. The form of service, whether it be directly on to the customer's plate or from a serving dish is quick and easy because the size of the dish is not so large and the various items arranged on it are easily handled.

With the present system of service a considerable amount of time is lost in preparing the bases and the garnished ornamental skewers which raise up or adorn the item of food, as well as in arranging the garnish around it. These presentations require large service dishes even for an item which is small in itself and intended for a small number of guests. The result is that if the dish is to be served, the size of the dish makes it as awkward for the guest as it is for the waiter. And these are not the least among the many snags with complicated garnishes; to it must be added the loss of quality which results from arranging the garnish on the dish in advance, unavoidable when there is a large number of people to be served, with the result that the food gets cold whilst it is being served and so on. All these disadvantages just for one effect—that of presenting the dish for a moment before the gaze of the guests who have scarcely the time to catch a glimpse of a dish more or less richly and correctly dressed. In fact, only habit can explain the continued existence of these bad practices outside of those circles which are becoming ever more rare, where the sumptuous cooking of bygone days can still be carried on.

To ensure quick service we cannot recommend too highly to our colleagues the use where possible of a deep rectangular dish for the arrangement and presentation of food; except of course where a large item is to be served. Whether for hot or cold foods it offers such advantages that no other kind of dish can be compared with it.

Yet again we wish to declare that in recommending new methods we do not intend the out of hand condemnation of old ones; we simply want to persuade our colleagues to study the habits and tastes of guests and to adapt their efforts to these habits and tastes. Our illustrious master, Carême, was talking one day to one of his colleagues who was complaining bitterly of the unrefined habits and uncouth tastes of his master, habits and tastes which shocked him to the extent that he had made up his mind to leave his post rather than go on ignoring the principles of high class cookery which he had followed all his working life. 'You would be quite wrong to behave thus,' replied Carême, 'in matters of cookery there are not a number of principles, there is only one and that is to satisfy the person you are serving.'

It is for us to ponder on this reply. It is absolutely ridiculous to try to impose our own habits and methods on those whom we serve; we must convince ourselves that the first and most essential of our duties is to conform to their wishes.

We might be critized for falling in so willingly to the whims of our guests and that by going to the extreme in simplifying our methods of presentation and service we are debasing our art and turning it into a craft. This is not so because simplicity does not necessarily rule out beauty.

May we be allowed to repeat here what we said in the first edition of this work as regards the presentation of dishes: 'We are convinced that the ability to give the highest possible distinction to the most humble item by presenting it in an elegant and correct form will always be the result of technical knowledge.

'But the result that the cook has in mind when executing a fine presentation can only be achieved by the appropriate and sober use of edible ingredients arranged in harmony. We must accept as a strict rule that in future all presentations that include inedible items will be avoided and that a simplicity of good taste will be the outstanding characteristic.

'To attain this result there are a very large number of means. By use of only edible ingredients such as truffles, mushrooms, egg whites, vegetables, salt ox-tongue, he can combine and endlessly vary some very attractive decorations.

'The time has gone for those complicated presentations made fashionable by cooks in the time of the Restoration. However, for a very special occasion, the cook has to comply with the requirements of the old methods and he must, above all, relate the intricate arrangement of the dish to the amount of time and resources at his disposal, never sacrificing the means to the end and not forgetting that the over-elaborateness of the decoration cannot make up for the lack of or the weakness of the flavour.'

This has always been our belief. Cookery will evolve—as society itself does—without ever ceasing to be an art.

It has to be admitted that customs and the way we live have changed since 1850 so cookery too must change. The great works of Dubois and Bernard met the needs of their time but even if they last for ever as documents and as a basis for our methods of working, the pattern which they made so respected no longer meets the requirements of our day.

We must respect, love and study these great works—they together with the works of Carême must be the basis of our methods of working. But instead of copying them servilely, we ourselves should seek new approaches so that we too may leave behind us methods of working that have been adapted to the customs and needs of our time.

1st February 1907

INTRODUCTION TO THE THIRD EDITION OF THE *GUIDE CULINAIRE*

In offering this the third edition of the *Guide Culinaire* to our colleagues, we have a duty to renew our thanks for the interest that they have never ceased to surround this book with, and also for the kind encouragement that so many people have offered.

There is nothing we wish to add to the Introduction to the second edition because what we said then concerning the profession is as true today as it was in 1907 and will be for many years to come. Nevertheless, we wish to state that this, the third edition, carefully edited and considerably modified, justifies the forecasts and keeps the promise contained in the following passage by M. Escoffier from the Introduction to the first edition; 'Although it contains more than 5000 recipes I have no pretentions that this guide is exhaustive; even if it were today, it would no longer be so tomorrow, because progress marches on and each day brings forth new recipes and new methods. All that I can do to overcome this drawback is to keep the work up-to-date by noting any new recipes and ideas and remedying inevitable omissions by including them in each new edition.'

These lines explain the increase in size by more than 300 pages in this edition and justify the important changes we believed it to be necessary to make to the previous one, such as:

(1) The change in the lay-out of the book which it is calculated will make it less crowded and easier to handle.

(2) The re-casting of the Index which was a summary before, as a complete list of the contents in alphabetical order; and

(3) The exclusion of a number of recipes which seemed to be no longer used and their replacement by new recipes which have appeared over the last few years and have gained public approval.

To bring about these various improvements without increasing the already large size of the book, we have had to omit the menus from the back of the book where they had been in previous editions.

These menus have been revised and reproduced along with many other carefully chosen ones, in a special book entitled *Le Livre des Menus* which will be on sale to the public at the same time as this edition. In it will also be found the chart showing the correct allocation of duties for a large kitchen together with the corresponding menus and information.

In this way we have been able to give the important matter of menu writing a logical treatment and to expand it in the way it deserves.

This new book will be indispensable not only to our colleagues but also to head waiters, managers and housewives for whom it will fill a long felt need. We dare to hope that the improvements made to this present edition will receive the approval of the culinary world from whom we have already received so many marks of goodwill and that our art, to the glory of which we have attempted to build a lasting memorial, will likewise benefit from our humble efforts.

1st May 1912

INTRODUCTION TO THE FOURTH EDITION OF THE *GUIDE CULINAIRE*

Since the time when the third edition of the *Guide Culinaire* was published (May 1912), cooking, like all other professions and industries, has gone through a difficult period and even now is experiencing its disastrous effects.

Nevertheless, it resists them successfully and we believe that the time is not far off when post-war restrictions will come to an end and progress will be resumed. Meanwhile, the continuous steep rise in the price of foodstuffs is making the task of those who are in charge of the work of the kitchen even more difficult; and because, through experience, we understand the difficulties of this task, in this edition we have concentrated on simplifying a large number of the recipes, especially the garnishes without, however, altering any of the basic principles.

In addition we have eliminated all those recipes which seemed of minor interest and replaced them with new ones most of which are of recent origin.

In presenting this fourth edition of the *Guide Culinaire* to our colleagues and to those members of the general public who are interested in cookery, we hope and believe that it will receive the same warm welcome as its predecessors.

January 1921

BIOGRAPHICAL NOTE BY PIERRE P. ESCOFFIER

I have been asked to give a brief account of my grandfather's life. It is no easy matter to do so about a man who lived to be eighty-eight and was active until the very last years. Much must be omitted which could be significant. He died over forty years ago. Those who knew him personally are becoming few indeed. For the others, I hope these notes may give an idea of the man he was and the change his profession underwent during his lifetime.

Georges Auguste Escoffier was born in 1846 in Villeneuve Loubet, a village which nestles peacefully below its mediaeval castle, in the neighbourhood of Nice. His father was a congenial blacksmith who read the newspaper, with comments, to his neighbours and at seventy-five walked briskly to the city seven miles away to sell the tobacco he grew. In these happy family surroundings, Auguste spent his first years and schooldays until the age of thirteen.

Time then came for him to learn a trade. His inclination would have led him to painting or sculpture, but his father saw little future in such activities and sent him to his brother who owned the Restaurant Français, one of the better restaurants in Nice, then at the start of its fame as a winter resort. Life was hard in the kitchens in those days—all the more so for an apprentice—and his uncle granted Auguste no special favours. However, in this way he experienced all facets of cooking and catering, but the working conditions were such that improving them would remain his life-long concern.

When he was nineteen, the owner of the Petit Moulin Rouge, the most fashionable restaurant in Paris, noticed him during a stay in Nice and invited him to join his team. There he stayed but for a brief military training, until 1870 when the Franco-Prussian war broke out and he was recalled to the army.

His 'Souvenirs d'un Cuisinier de l'Armée du Rhin' published in the *Revue de l'Art Culinaire* gives a lively account of his experiences, first in charge of catering for a section of the Imperial H.Q., and then as *chef de cuisine* in Mainz on the Rhine, adding his personal views about food supply to the marching troops. He recalls menus in time of scarcity, including some staggering ones during the siege of Paris, when the zoo and stray animals were the only source of protein.

Once the war was over, Auguste Escoffier returned to the Petit Moulin Rouge, now as *chef de cuisine*, and from time to time was called upon at the opening of new restaurants in the provinces. There is no doubt, however, that for him the main event of this period was his wedding with Delphine Daffis, the daughter of a publisher. Writing poetry herself, she contributed to his first publication in book form entitled *Les Fleurs en Cire*, a neat little guide to a field in which he had become quite an expert. They had two sons and a daughter, and though circumstances later kept them apart for long periods, they remained profoundly devoted to one another until the very end, 55 years later.

In 1884 they left Paris for Monte Carlo where the gambling casino was enjoying rapidly growing fame. He was *Directeur de Cuisine* of the Grand Hotel and during the next six years divided his time between the Grand Hotel in winter and the Hotel National in Lucerne, Switzerland, in the summer. It was here in 1884 that he met César Ritz who came from a small village in the Swiss Valais. Ritz started as a hotel groom and rapidly worked his way up to head waiter and into hotel management. Their mutual understanding and teamwork was to bring about the most significant changes and modern development in the hotel industry.

In 1890 they were called to the Savoy Hotel in London as general manager and head of restaurant services respectively. Their success was beyond expectation. The Duc d'Orléans established his headquarters at the Savoy; French and British aristocracy, foreign princes and U.S. 'kings', artists Sarah Bernhardt and Melba were regular patrons. When Ritz left the Savoy in 1898, Escoffier declined to break the team and together they opened the Ritz Hotel in Paris, soon the meeting place of 'La Belle Epoque.'

With the turn of the century they came back to London to launch the Carlton Hotel in the Haymarket—where New Zealand House now stands since the Carlton was bombed in World War II—and where they planned the inner layout and arrangements. The response was tremendous. Sponsored by the Prince of Wales, the Carlton became the first public restaurant where a gentleman could take his wife for supper after the theatre. Everyone who was anyone had to be seen at the Carlton. The name was used the world over, like the Savoy and the Ritz, as a symbol of perfection.

Escoffier remained at this post until 1919. This was a period of great personal achievement. Running firmly every side of the restaurant's services, appearing every evening in the dining-room with a word for each of the many familiar patrons among the daily 500 guests he also managed to find time for plenty of other activities. With the assistance and contribution of devoted professional experts like Philéas Gilbert and Emile Fétu, the long preparation of the *Guide Culinaire* was finalized and its first edition published. Then by means of a contract between the Hamburg–Amerika Line and the Carlton, he planned and organized the first installation of *à la carte* restaurants on board transatlantic liners, an example soon followed by all other shipping companies. A firm called A. Escoffier Ltd was also set up, its line of sauces and products receiving immediate acclaim; the firm, however, was sold in 1915 after his second son was killed in action and his first son (my father) who was managing the firm had enlisted, and had been transferred to the British Forces where he was in charge of E.F.C. services in Boulogne.

During this period, all enterprising young chefs came to the Carlton for training and later found places the world over, expanding the reputation of French cooking and establishing its supremacy. The 1914 war brought other preoccupations: safeguarding the best standards at the Carlton, making do with the shortage of personnel and products, preparing foodstuffs and Christmas puddings for the troops, and setting up committees for the assistance of families of enlisted staff.

In 1919 the President of France, R. Poincaré, on an official visit to London, conferred upon him the cross of the Chevalier de la Légion d'Honneur. Soon after, at the age of seventy-three, he left London to settle in Monte Carlo. But it was scarcely a retirement. During the next twelve years he was indefatigable; he was invited and took part in numerous professional demonstrations, culinary exhibitions, inaugurations, and received honours in numerous cities including Copenhagen, Stockholm, Frankfurt, Zurich, Prague and New York where he sailed in 1926 to celebrate his eightieth birthday and again later to inaugurate the Hotel Pierre.

In March 1928 Edouard Herriot, ex-Prime Minister, then Minister for *Instruction Publique*, presided at a banquet in the Palais d'Orsay where some 350 friends —colleagues, journalists, writers—were gathered to celebrate Auguste Escoffier's promotion to Officier de la Légion d'Honneur.

Despite a long and hard-working life, he never enjoyed affluence and never had the time or inclination to look after his investments. By the time of his death in February 1935 his financial circumstances were precarious. His wife had died a few weeks earlier.

Quite apart from the words of official tributes and the fond memories of those with whom he worked, his life's work is preserved in his articles and books and the writings of others, including the biography by E. Herbodeau and P. Thalamas. Two associations founded in his memory, *Les Amis d'Escoffier* and *Les Disciples d'Escoffier*, form active groups in Europe, America and Japan. In recent years, the Musée d'Art Culinaire was opened in the house where he was born in Villeneuve Loubet, and the Foundation A. Escoffier was set up to promote the careers of chefs. Both are due to the relentless and generous determination of Joseph Donon, one of the last Carlton trainees whom Escoffier launched on to a successful career in America.

And now H. L. Cracknell and R. J. Kaufmann have devoted considerable time and effort in translating with great care and accuracy the last French edition of *Le Guide Culinaire*, adding useful information which will no doubt be much welcomed by the reader.

To his family, Auguste Escoffier was a gentle, understanding and encouraging man, the very grandfather one would wish for, and much loved. The contribution to his memory by colleagues, disciples and friends is gratefully received and appreciated.

PIERRE P. ESCOFFIER

WEIGHTS, MEASURES AND TEMPERATURES—ABBREVIATIONS AND CONVERSIONS

To facilitate ease of working from this book it has been felt necessary to use several different sets of measurements. There are the original metricated quantities which are mostly for ten portions, followed by the nearest Imperial conversions of these weights and measures and their equivalent U.S. cup measurements for liquids only; the U.S. cup is taken as having a capacity of 8 fluid ounces.

In all cases it is recommended that the best method of measuring quantities of solids is by weighing but for those who still want to use the U.S. cup measurement a short list is given here of the more commonly used commodities.

The following equivalent temperatures for the descriptive oven heats given in the text should be taken as approximate and adjusted as felt necessary in accordance with the type of equipment being used and in certain cases the degree of cooking required, especially for roast meats. Experience in baking and roasting etc. is after all the best guide.

The abbreviations given here are those used in the text.

ABBREVIATIONS

Metric		Imperial and American	
g	gram	oz	ounce
kg	kilogram	lb	pound
dl	decilitre	fl oz	fluid ounce
litre	this is always given in full	pt	pt
mm	millimetre	gal	gallon
cm	centimetre	in	inch
		tsp	teaspoon
		tbs	tablespoon

°C °Celsius or Centigrade
°F °Fahrenheit

The U.S. cup = 8 fluid ounces, the U.S. pint = 2 cups or 16 fl oz and the U.S. gallon = 8 U.S. pints or 128 fl oz.

WEIGHTS

Metric	Imperial
5 g	$\frac{1}{6}$ oz
10 g	$\frac{1}{3}$ oz
20 g	$\frac{2}{3}$ oz
25 g	1 oz
30 g	1 oz
50 g	2 oz
60 g	2 oz
75 g	$2\frac{1}{2}$ oz
100 g	$3\frac{1}{2}$ oz
125 g	$4\frac{1}{2}$ oz
150 g	5 oz
200 g	7 oz
250 g ($\frac{1}{4}$ kg)	9 oz
300 g	11 oz
400 g	14 oz
450 g	1 lb
500 g ($\frac{1}{2}$ kg)	1 lb 2 oz
750 g ($\frac{3}{4}$ kg)	1 lb 10 oz
1000 g (1 kg)	$2\frac{1}{4}$ lb

Note: Fractions of a kilogram are used in recipes where the ingredients measure a $\frac{1}{4}$ kg, $\frac{1}{2}$ kg, or $\frac{3}{4}$ kg, otherwise the number of grams are written out in full, i.e. 1 kg 400 g.

LIQUID MEASURES

Metric	Imperial	U.S.A.
$\frac{1}{4}$ dl	1 fl oz	$\frac{1}{8}$ cup
$\frac{1}{2}$ dl	2 fl oz	$\frac{1}{4}$ cup
$\frac{3}{4}$ dl	3 fl oz	$\frac{3}{8}$ cup
1 dl	$3\frac{1}{2}$ fl oz	$\frac{1}{2}$ cup
$1\frac{1}{2}$ dl	5 fl oz	$\frac{5}{8}$ cup
2 dl	7 fl oz	$\frac{7}{8}$ cup
$2\frac{1}{2}$ dl	9 fl oz	$1\frac{1}{8}$ cups
3 dl	$\frac{1}{2}$ pt	$1\frac{1}{4}$ cups
4 dl	14 fl oz	$1\frac{3}{4}$ cups
5 dl	18 fl oz	$2\frac{1}{4}$ cups
6 dl	1 pt	$2\frac{5}{8}$ cups
7 dl	$1\frac{1}{4}$ pt	3 cups
$7\frac{1}{2}$ dl	$1\frac{1}{3}$ pt	$3\frac{1}{4}$ cups
8 dl	$1\frac{2}{5}$ pt	$3\frac{1}{2}$ cups
9 dl	$1\frac{3}{5}$ pt	4 cups
1 litre	$1\frac{3}{4}$ pt	$4\frac{1}{2}$ cups
$1\frac{1}{4}$ litres	$2\frac{1}{5}$ pt	$5\frac{1}{2}$ cups
$1\frac{1}{2}$ litres	$2\frac{5}{8}$ pt	$6\frac{1}{2}$ cups
$1\frac{3}{4}$ litres	3 pt	$7\frac{1}{2}$ cups
2 litres	$3\frac{1}{2}$ pt	9 cups
3 litres	$5\frac{1}{4}$ pt	$6\frac{1}{2}$ pt
4 litres	7 pt	$8\frac{3}{4}$ pt
5 litres	$8\frac{3}{4}$ pt	$1\frac{3}{8}$ gal
10 litres	$2\frac{1}{4}$ gal	$2\frac{3}{4}$ gal
15 litres	$3\frac{1}{4}$ gal	4 gal

LENGTH

Metric	Imperial and U.S.
1 mm	$\frac{1}{25}$ in
2 mm	$\frac{1}{12}$ in
3 mm	$\frac{1}{8}$ in
5 mm	$\frac{1}{5}$ in
8 mm	$\frac{1}{3}$ in
1 cm	$\frac{2}{5}$ in
2 cm	$\frac{4}{5}$ in
$2\frac{1}{2}$ cm	1 in
5 cm	2 in
6 cm	$2\frac{1}{2}$ in
7 cm	$3\frac{1}{4}$ in
8 cm	$3\frac{1}{2}$ in
10 cm	4 in

OVEN TEMPERATURES

The following is a guide to the approximate temperatures of the descriptive oven heats given in this book.

Description	°Celsius (Centigrade)	°Fahrenheit
Cool	140	275
Warm	150	300
Moderate	170–190	325–375
Moderately Hot	200	400
Hot	220	425
Very Hot	230–240	450–500

SOME USEFUL U.S. CUP MEASURES

Ingredient	Imperial Equivalent	Metric Equivalent
ground almonds	4½ oz	125 g
dried fruit	6 oz	175 g
lentils, yellow split peas etc.	8 oz	225 g
rice, tapioca etc.	8 oz	225 g
flour	5 oz	150 g
sifted flour	4½ oz	125 g
sugar: caster, granulated	7 oz	200 g
icing sugar	4 oz	110 g
cornflour (cornstarch)	4½ oz	125 g
cheese: grated Parmesan	8 oz	225 g
butter, lard, dripping	8 oz	225 g
tomato: roughly chopped flesh only	7 oz	200 g
spinach: cooked and chopped	12 oz	325 g
beef kidney suet, chopped	5 oz	150 g

Each measure is equivalent to 1 U.S. cup.

CHAPTER 1

SAUCES

Foreword to the Basic Culinary Preparations

This book is written for all who practise the art of cookery, but nevertheless at the very outset it is felt necessary to say something about the basic culinary preparations which play such an important part in the work of the kitchen.

These culinary preparations define the basic fundamentals and the requisite ingredients without which nothing of importance can be attempted. It is for this reason that they are so important and why they occupy such a place in the work of the cook who wishes to be successful.

It is not sufficient merely to have the desire to do well nor even to possess the necessary skills for making these basic preparations to which constant recourse has to be made—the means to create these basic preparations must also be present and they must be provided for the cook by placing at his disposal everything required in the way of commodities of the best possible quality.

However profligate extravagance is as bad as a restrictive economy which puts the brake on the full extent of the talents of a cook, causing the conscientious worker to become discouraged and even leading directly to failure.

The most skilled cook in the world cannot attempt anything if given nothing and it would be totally inconsistent to expect him to produce work of a high standard from imperfect or insufficient ingredients. The most important point concerning these basic culinary preparations is that it is necessary to provide everything needed as regards quantity and quality.

Understandably, what is possible in one establishment may not be possible in another and the means fashion the end. The type of work is determined by the requirements of the guest and the means of producing this work is, naturally, determined by his requirements. Everything is relative but there is a standard which must not be deviated from, especially with reference to the basic culinary preparations. The person in charge of an establishment who allows any exception to this and who adheres too strictly to the hard and fast rule of economy taken to its uttermost limit where it becomes incompatible with the order of conduct of a good kitchen, forfeits the right to criticize the person who he has put in charge of running his kitchen. If he does this he should realize that such criticisms are untenable and unjust and he should understand that it is just as impossible to produce first class results from imperfect or insufficient commodities as it is absurd to expect that a second-rate draught wine, by being put into a bottle, will transform it into a great wine.

If, however, the cook has at his disposal all the ingredients required, the processing of these basic culinary preparations must then be given very special attention. The ingredients must be handled in such a way that being given every possible care, they will be above reproach when finished. Thus by means of this careful processing and in accordance with the accepted methods of preparation, he will achieve the desired results.

THE PRINCIPAL BASIC CULINARY PREPARATIONS

The principal basic culinary preparations include:

Bouillons or *stocks* specifically made for soups.
Consommés which are the same Bouillons or stocks specially clarified.
Brown stocks and *white stocks*—beef, veal, chicken, game and fish; these are the basis for making the thickened gravies and basic sauces.
Fumets and *Essences*—these are the complementary adjuncts used to enhance the quality of the small sauces.
Glazes—meat, chicken, game and fish.
Roux—brown, blond and white.
Foundation or *Basic* sauces—Espagnole (brown sauce), Velouté, Béchamel, tomato.
Savoury or *Aspic Jellies*—meat and fish.

Also included under this heading are:

Mirepoix and *Matignons*—aromatic flavouring materials.
Courts-bouillons and *Blancs*—cooking liquors for fish, meat and vegetables.

Marinades and *Brines*.
Various *Forcemeats* and *Stuffings*.
Various ancillary preparations for use in garnishing etc.

The layout of this book does not permit these principal preparations to be dealt with in the same order as they are listed. The basic methods of roasting, grilling, gratinating etc. are not dealt with under one comprehensive heading but will be found in the various sections of the book where the method actually deals with a commodity. For example, the preparation of Stocks, Fumets, Essences, Glazes, Marinades, Jellies and Compound Butters are all included in the Chapter on Sauces,

the preparation of Consommés, Clarifications and Garnishes for soups are included in the Chapter on Soups,

the preparation of Forcemeats and ancillary preparations are in the Chapter on Garnishes,

the preparation of Courts-bouillons and special stuffings for fish are included in the Chapter on Fish, and

the theory of the methods of cooking for Grills, Braisings and Poêlés are included in the Chapter entitled Relevés and Entrées.

GENERAL PRINCIPLES GOVERNING THE PREPARATION OF SAUCES

Sauces represent one of the most important components of cookery. It is they that have inspired and sustained the universal predominance of the French Cuisine; it is therefore impossible to devote too much care and attention to their preparation.

The basic component used in the production of sauces is a stock or gravy; it can be brown stock or Estouffade for making brown sauces, or clear gravy or white stock for making Veloutés. It is to the production of perfect stocks that the sauce cook should devote himself—the sauce cook who is, as the Marquis de Cussy remarked, 'the enlightened chemist, the creative genius and the cornerstone of the edifice of superlative cookery'.

In traditional French cookery all the recipes with the exception of roasts, were based upon braises and stews. Even at that time, stocks were the keynote of the culinary structure and the amount of ingredients needed for their production may now appear excessive in this age of false economy. In fact the introduction of Roux into French cookery by the Spanish cooks of Anne of Austria, must have passed almost unnoticed so insignificant was their role at the time—the stocks being sufficient in their own right. It was only when a period of economic retrenchment arrived that Espagnole came into its own as a necessary substitute for poor quality stocks.

It was gradually perfected but its use very quickly overtook the purpose for which it had been created and it is no exaggeration to suggest that during the latter part of the nineteenth century, the use of Espagnole became excessive. To this misuse can be attributed the appearance of an indifferent cookery, bereft of any well-defined flavour and where the entire range of tastes become lost in one single insipid level.

After a lapse of several years a strenuous reactionary movement was launched against this uniformity of flavour which was so repugnant to the chefs of that time. In the most important kitchens veal stocks that were both clear and translucent as well as of a clearly defined flavour, resumed their rightful place and the use of Espagnole because of this, declined in importance. After all, what is the reason for using this basic sauce? The strength and taste are not its own, rather it is the stock which provides these and it is in this stock that its value lies. The addition to the stock, the Roux, has a supporting role in the making of sauces in the form of a thickening agent but it provides very little in the way of actual flavour and it is necessary, if the sauce is to be perfect, for the flavour of the Roux to be almost eliminated during the cooking of the sauce.

When a sauce has been properly prepared by careful simmering and skimming, only the thickening properties of the starchy base are left behind. But if it is absolutely necessary to give a smooth texture to the sauce it would be much easier to provide this by using a more pure form of starch which would allow it to be finished in as short a space of time as possible, thus avoiding the need for a too long cooking time. It is therefore highly likely that before long a starch similar to cornflour or arrowroot but in the purest possible form, will be used to replace flour in the making of Roux.

In the present state of cookery there are several reasons why the use of the two sauces, Espagnole and Jus lié continue to be necessary. In the preparation of large braised items and in stews, excepting for those using lamb and mutton, Espagnole combined with tomato and brought to perfection with the juices which come from the commodity being cooked is completely in accordance with its role. In the form of Demi-glace, Espagnole also fills an indispensable role for many of the Sautés.

Even so, small, light, meat and poultry dishes can benefit from the use of Jus lié especially if it is used with discretion and in association with the process of deglazing and if the stock is in accordance with the preparation it is to accompany.

Modern cookery has established this formal and logical rule so that there is accordance between the meats and their sauces. Thus a piece of game must be served with sauces made from game stock or from a neutral-flavoured stock and not with meat stock. It is true that game stock is not so strong but the fundamental and proper flavour is fully retained. The same is true as regards the preparation of fish which because of the neutral flavour of the sauces normally used with it, require the addition of *fumets* which give their particular flavour to each individual preparation.

It is recognized that the dictates of economy are frequently an obstacle to the observance of these rules but at least the diligent cook who is mindful of his reputation will adhere to them as closely as possible so that he may achieve, if not a perfect result, at least a satisfactory one.

BASIC PREPARATIONS USED IN THE MAKING OF SAUCES

STOCKS

1 Estouffade—Brown Stock

To make 10 litres ($2\frac{1}{4}$ gal or $2\frac{3}{4}$ U.S. gal)

Nutritive Ingredients:

6 kg (13 lb) shin of beef on the bone
6 kg (13 lb) knuckle of veal (or lean veal trimmings)
1 knuckle of raw ham (blanched)
650 g (1 lb 7 oz) fresh pork rind (blanched)

Flavouring Ingredients:

650 g (1 lb 7 oz) roughly chopped carrot
650 g (1 lb 7 oz) roughly chopped onion
1 Bouquet garni—comprising:
  100 g ($3\frac{1}{2}$ oz) parsley stalks
  10 g ($\frac{1}{3}$ oz) thyme
  5 g ($\frac{1}{6}$ oz) bay leaves
  1 clove garlic

Liquid:

14 litres (3 gal or $3\frac{3}{4}$ U.S. gal) water

Preparation:

Bone out the meats. Break the bones small and lightly brown them in the oven. Fry the carrot and onion brown in a little fat. Prepare the stock by placing these bones, vegetables, ham, pork rind and Bouquet garni into a stockpot, add the cold water, bring to the boil, skim and simmer very gently for at least 12 hours keeping the liquid at the same level throughout this time by adding boiling water as required. Cut the meat into very large dice, fry brown in hot fat and place in a pan. Cover with some of the prepared stock and boil until it is reduced to a glaze; repeat this process two or three times. Add the remainder of the stock, bring to the boil, skim to remove all fat and allow to simmer gently until all the flavour has been extracted from the meat. Pass through a strainer and reserve for use.

Note: When preparing brown stock which includes bones, especially those from beef, it is recommended that the procedure should be in accordance with the above recipe by first preparing a stock from the bones, simmering it gently for 12–15 hours and using it as the liquid for moistening the meat.

It is incorrect to place all the ingredients in the stockpot and fry them together in fat before adding the water as there will be a danger of overcolouring the ingredients thus spoiling the flavour of the stock. In practice the principle of diffusion is sufficient in itself to colour the stock; this is the most natural and suitable method of obtaining the required colour.

2 Ordinary White Stock

To make 10 litres ($2\frac{1}{4}$ gal or $2\frac{3}{4}$ U.S. gal)

Nutritive Ingredients:

10 kg (22 lb) shin of veal, veal trimmings and veal bones
4 raw chicken giblets or carcasses

Flavouring Ingredients:

800 g ($1\frac{3}{4}$ lb) carrots
400 g (15 oz) onions
300 g (11 oz) leek
100 g ($3\frac{1}{2}$ oz) celery
4 cloves
1 Bouquet garni—comprising:
  100 g ($3\frac{1}{2}$ oz) parsley stalks
  a sprig of thyme
  1 bay leaf

Liquid and Seasoning:

12 litres ($2\frac{5}{8}$ gal or $3\frac{1}{4}$ U.S. gal) water
60 g (2 oz) salt

Preparation:

Bone out the shin and chop the bones very small; tie the meat. Place all the bones and meat into a stockpot, cover with the water and add the salt. Bring to the boil. Skim carefully and add the vegetables and flavouring. Allow to simmer very gently and evenly for 3 hours. Pass through a strainer and reserve for use.

Note: This stock should be kept clear by continuous, even simmering and by removing the scum and fat with great care.

White stock can also be made in the same way as brown stock by placing the broken bones alone in the stockpot with the water and simmering gently for 5 hours; then straining it and adding the stock to the meat, vegetables and flavourings and proceeding as for brown stock. This method has the advantage of extracting all the gelatinous properties of the bones. It is, however, necessary to use more water to compensate for the added length of time of cooking the bones. There should still be 12 litres (2⅝ gal or 3¼ U.S. gal) of liquid left to add to the meat.

3 White Chicken Stock

This stock is prepared in the same way and with the same ingredients as basic white stock but with the addition of extra chicken giblets and carcasses and three boiling fowls.

4 Brown Veal Stock or Gravy

To make 10 litres (2¼ gal or 2¾ U.S. gal)

Nutritive Ingredients:
6 kg (13 lb) boned shin or shoulder of veal, tied
5 kg (11 lb) veal bones, chopped very small

Flavouring Ingredients:
600 g (1 lb 5 oz) carrots
400 g (14 oz) onions
2 bay leaves
2 sprigs of thyme
100 g (3½ oz) parsley stalks

Liquid:
12 litres (2⅗ gal or 3¼ U.S. gal) water or ordinary white stock
40 g (1½ oz) salt—only if using water

Preparation:
Cover the base of a thick bottomed pan or stockpot with the carrots and onions cut into slices; add the rest of the flavouring ingredients and the meat and bones which have been previously browned in the oven.

Cover the pan, place on top of the stove and sweat the ingredients for 10 minutes. Add a little of the stock or water and cook rapidly to reduce it to a glaze. Repeat this operation once or twice more then add the remainder of the stock or water; bring to the boil, skim carefully and allow to simmer gently and evenly for 6 hours. Pass through a strainer and reserve for use. This stock may be reduced before being used, according to requirements.

5 Game Stock

To make 5 litres (8¾ pt or 1⅜ U.S. gal)

Nutritive Ingredients:
3 kg (7 lb) neck, breast and trimmings of venison, old if possible but fresh
1 kg (2¼ lb) hare trimmings
2 old partridges
1 old pheasant
2 old wild rabbits

Flavouring Ingredients:
250 g (9 oz) carrots
250 g (9 oz) onions
1 Bouquet garni
15 juniper berries
1 sprig of sage

Liquid:
6 litres (10½ pt or 1⅝ U.S. gal) water
1 bottle white wine

Preparation:
Cut the game into pieces and colour brown in a hot oven. Cut the carrots and onions into slices, fry brown with the flavourings and place in the bottom of a heavy pan. Add the game; deglaze the tray in which this was browned with the wine and add to the game and vegetables together with an equal amount of water. Place on the stove and reduce to a glaze. Add the rest of the water and bring to the boil. Skim carefully and allow to simmer very gently skimming carefully for 3 hours. Pass through a strainer and use as required.

6 Fish Stock

To make 10 litres (2¼ gal or 2¾ U.S. gal)

Basic Ingredients:
10 kg (22 lb) bones and trimmings of sole, whiting or brill

Flavouring Ingredients:
500 g (1 lb 2 oz) sliced onions
250 g (9 oz) mushroom trimmings
15 g (½ oz) peppercorns
100 g (3½ oz) parsley stalks
juice of 1 lemon

Liquid and Seasoning:
10 litres (2¼ gal or 2¾ U.S. gal) water
1 bottle white wine
40 g (1½ oz) salt

Preparation:
Place the onions, parsley stalks and mushroom

Note: This stock should be kept clear by continuous, even simmering and by removing the scum and fat with great care.

White stock can also be made in the same way as brown stock by placing the broken bones alone in the stockpot with the water and simmering gently for 5 hours; then straining it and adding the stock to the meat, vegetables and flavourings and proceeding as for brown stock. This method has the advantage of extracting all the gelatinous properties of the bones. It is, however, necessary to use more water to compensate for the added length of time of cooking the bones. There should still be 12 litres (2⅝ gal or 3¼ U.S. gal) of liquid left to add to the meat.

3 White Chicken Stock

This stock is prepared in the same way and with the same ingredients as basic white stock but with the addition of extra chicken giblets and carcasses and three boiling fowls.

4 Brown Veal Stock or Gravy

To make 10 litres (2¼ gal or 2¾ U.S. gal)

Nutritive Ingredients:
6 kg (13 lb) boned shin or shoulder of veal, tied
5 kg (11 lb) veal bones, chopped very small

Flavouring Ingredients:
600 g (1 lb 5 oz) carrots
400 g (14 oz) onions
2 bay leaves
2 sprigs of thyme
100 g (3½ oz) parsley stalks

Liquid:
12 litres (2⅝ gal or 3¼ U.S. gal) water or ordinary white stock
40 g (1½ oz) salt—only if using water

Preparation:
Cover the base of a thick bottomed pan or stockpot with the carrots and onions cut into slices; add the rest of the flavouring ingredients and the meat and bones which have been previously browned in the oven.

Cover the pan, place on top of the stove and sweat the ingredients for 10 minutes. Add a little of the stock or water and cook rapidly to reduce it to a glaze. Repeat this operation once or twice more then add the remainder of the stock or water; bring to the boil, skim carefully and allow to simmer gently and evenly for 6 hours. Pass through a strainer and reserve for use. This stock may be reduced before being used, according to requirements.

5 Game Stock

To make 5 litres (8¾ pt or 1⅜ U.S. gal)

Nutritive Ingredients:
3 kg (7 lb) neck, breast and trimmings of venison, old if possible but fresh
1 kg (2¼ lb) hare trimmings
2 old partridges
1 old pheasant
2 old wild rabbits

Flavouring Ingredients:
250 g (9 oz) carrots
250 g (9 oz) onions
1 Bouquet garni
15 juniper berries
1 sprig of sage

Liquid:
6 litres (10½ pt or 1⅝ U.S. gal) water
1 bottle white wine

Preparation:
Cut the game into pieces and colour brown in a hot oven. Cut the carrots and onions into slices, fry brown with the flavourings and place in the bottom of a heavy pan. Add the game; deglaze the tray in which this was browned with the wine and add to the game and vegetables together with an equal amount of water. Place on the stove and reduce to a glaze. Add the rest of the water and bring to the boil. Skim carefully and allow to simmer very gently skimming carefully for 3 hours. Pass through a strainer and use as required.

6 Fish Stock

To make 10 litres (2¼ gal or 2¾ U.S. gal)

Basic Ingredients:
10 kg (22 lb) bones and trimmings of sole, whiting or brill

Flavouring Ingredients:
500 g (1 lb 2 oz) sliced onions
250 g (9 oz) mushroom trimmings
15 g (½ oz) peppercorns
100 g (3½ oz) parsley stalks
juice of 1 lemon

Liquid and Seasoning:
10 litres (2¼ gal or 2¾ U.S. gal) water
1 bottle white wine
40 g (1½ oz) salt

Preparation:
Place the onions, parsley stalks and mushroom

Modern cookery has established this formal and logical rule so that there is accordance between the meats and their sauces. Thus a piece of game must be served with sauces made from game stock or from a neutral-flavoured stock and not with meat stock. It is true that game stock is not so strong but the fundamental and proper flavour is fully retained. The same is true as regards the preparation of fish which because of the neutral flavour of the sauces normally used with it, require the addition of *fumets* which give their particular flavour to each individual preparation.

It is recognized that the dictates of economy are frequently an obstacle to the observance of these rules but at least the diligent cook who is mindful of his reputation will adhere to them as closely as possible so that he may achieve, if not a perfect result, at least a satisfactory one.

BASIC PREPARATIONS USED IN THE MAKING OF SAUCES

STOCKS

1 Estouffade—Brown Stock
To make 10 litres ($2\frac{1}{4}$ gal or $2\frac{3}{4}$ U.S. gal)

Nutritive Ingredients:
6 kg (13 lb) shin of beef on the bone
6 kg (13 lb) knuckle of veal (or lean veal trimmings)
1 knuckle of raw ham (blanched)
650 g (1 lb 7 oz) fresh pork rind (blanched)

Flavouring Ingredients:
650 g (1 lb 7 oz) roughly chopped carrot
650 g (1 lb 7 oz) roughly chopped onion
1 Bouquet garni—comprising:
100 g ($3\frac{1}{2}$ oz) parsley stalks
10 g ($\frac{1}{3}$ oz) thyme
5 g ($\frac{1}{6}$ oz) bay leaves
1 clove garlic

Liquid:
14 litres (3 gal or $3\frac{3}{4}$ U.S. gal) water

Preparation:
Bone out the meats. Break the bones small and lightly brown them in the oven. Fry the carrot and onion brown in a little fat. Prepare the stock by placing these bones, vegetables, ham, pork rind and Bouquet garni into a stockpot, add the cold water, bring to the boil, skim and simmer very gently for at least 12 hours keeping the liquid at the same level throughout this time by adding boiling water as required. Cut the meat into very large dice, fry brown in hot fat and place in a pan. Cover with some of the prepared stock and boil until it is reduced to a glaze; repeat this process two or three times. Add the remainder of the stock, bring to the boil, skim to remove all fat and allow to simmer gently until all the flavour has been extracted from the meat. Pass through a strainer and reserve for use.

Note: When preparing brown stock which includes bones, especially those from beef, it is recommended that the procedure should be in accordance with the above recipe by first preparing a stock from the bones, simmering it gently for 12–15 hours and using it as the liquid for moistening the meat.

It is incorrect to place all the ingredients in the stockpot and fry them together in fat before adding the water as there will be a danger of overcolouring the ingredients thus spoiling the flavour of the stock. In practice the principle of diffusion is sufficient in itself to colour the stock; this is the most natural and suitable method of obtaining the required colour.

2 Ordinary White Stock
To make 10 litres ($2\frac{1}{4}$ gal or $2\frac{3}{4}$ U.S. gal)

Nutritive Ingredients:
10 kg (22 lb) shin of veal, veal trimmings and veal bones
4 raw chicken giblets or carcasses

Flavouring Ingredients:
800 g ($1\frac{3}{4}$ lb) carrots
400 g (15 oz) onions
300 g (11 oz) leek
100 g ($3\frac{1}{2}$ oz) celery
4 cloves
1 Bouquet garni—comprising:
100 g ($3\frac{1}{2}$ oz) parsley stalks
a sprig of thyme
1 bay leaf

Liquid and Seasoning:
12 litres ($2\frac{5}{8}$ gal or $3\frac{1}{4}$ U.S. gal) water
60 g (2 oz) salt

Preparation:
Bone out the shin and chop the bones very small; tie the meat. Place all the bones and meat into a stockpot, cover with the water and add the salt. Bring to the boil. Skim carefully and add the vegetables and flavouring. Allow to simmer very gently and evenly for 3 hours. Pass through a strainer and reserve for use.

trimmings into a pan, add the bones and trimmings of fish, cover with the water and add the wine and lemon juice. Bring to the boil quickly and skim carefully. Allow to simmer very gently for 20 minutes then add the peppercorns and continue cooking for another 10 minutes. Pass through a strainer and use as required.

Notes:

1) The use of inferior quality white wine will cause the stock to go a grey colour and it is far better to omit the wine altogether rather than use one of doubtful quality.
2) This stock is used mainly in the preparation of fish sauces; if it is to be used for making Lenten or fish Espagnole the ingredients should be stewed in a little butter before the liquid is added.

7 Red Wine Fish Stock

To make 5 litres (8¾ pt or 1⅜ U.S. gal)

This stock is seldom used as it is normally obtained in the natural process of cooking a specific fish dish such as a Matelote. This recipe has been included because the demand of modern practice is for fish to be served free of skin and bone, i.e. in filleted form. In principle, the bones and trimmings of the actual fish being prepared should be used for making this stock so as to give it its specific flavour. This recipe is used for whatever kind of fish is being prepared.

Basic Ingredients:
2½ kg (5½ lb) head, bones and trimmings of the fish under preparation

Flavouring Ingredients:
300 g (11 oz) sliced and blanched onions
100 g (3½ oz) mushroom trimmings
100 g (3½ oz) parsley stalks
5 cloves garlic
15 g (½ oz) salt
1 sprig thyme
2 small bay leaves

Liquid and Seasoning:
3½ litres (6 pt or 7¾ U.S. pt) water
2 litres (3½ pt or 9 U.S. cups) good quality red wine

Preparation:
Proceed in the same way as for Fish Stock.

Note: Although it is possible to make a reduction of this stock without it losing its delicate flavour, it is advisable to prepare the exact amount required rather than having to reduce it before use.

ESSENCES

As the name implies, essences are stocks made in a reduced form so as to retain a very pronounced flavour.

They are made in the same way as ordinary stocks using much less liquid than usual so as to ensure that they have a concentrated flavour of the main ingredient; however, the usefulness of essences is nullified if they are used to complete a preparation which has been made with a stock which was poor in flavour and quality.

It is much easier to prepare a rich succulent stock of irreproachable quality than to use poor quality or mediocre stock and then to complete it with the addition of a specially prepared essence. The result is far better and is more economical of time and materials. It is recommended to use essences prepared from highly flavoured products such as celery, mushroom, morels, truffles etc. Again it is worth remembering that nine times out of ten it is far better to add the product itself to the stock during its preparation rather than to prepare a special essence. For these reasons the usefulness of essences becomes meaningless where the basic stocks themselves contain the desirable qualities of strength and flavour; therefore, it is judged unnecessary to give more than one recipe.

8 Fish Essence

To make 1 litre (1¾ pt or 4½ U.S. cups)

Basic Ingredients:
2 kg (4½ lb) head, bones and trimmings of sole or whiting

Flavouring Ingredients:
125 g (4½ oz) sliced onions
50 g (2 oz) parsley stalks
300 g (11 oz) mushroom trimmings
juice of 1 lemon
100 g (3½ oz) butter

Liquid:
1½ litres (2⅝ pt or 6½ U.S. cups) clear fish stock
3 dl (½ pt or 1¼ U.S. cups) good quality white wine, pinch of salt.

Preparation:
Melt the butter, add the onions, mushroom trimmings and parsley stalks and cook without colouring. Add the fish, cover and allow to stew for 15 minutes, turning the ingredients occasionally. Add the wine and reduce it by half then add the fish stock, lemon juice and salt. Bring to the boil, skim carefully and allow to simmer gently for 15 minutes. Pass through a fine strainer and use as required.

Note: This essence is used for the shallow poaching of fillets of sole, turbot and brill etc. where after being cooked, the remaining cooking liquor is reduced and added to the sauce which is to accompany the fillets.

GLAZES

The various glazes of meat, poultry, game and fish are merely stocks reduced to a syrupy consistency and are widely used in cookery.

They are used to impart a brilliant shine and an unctuous coating to finished dishes, to reinforce the quality and tone of a sauce, to strengthen a preparation of which the stock was too weak, or they can be used in their own right as a sauce after having been correctly buttered or creamed according to the type of dish with which they are to be used.

Glazes can be distinguished from essences in the sense that the latter are only prepared with the object of extracting all of the flavour of the product under treatment, whereas glazes unite in a reduced form the principal strength and flavour of the ingredients themselves. In most cases there are advantages to be gained from using glazes rather than essences.

Nevertheless, many chefs of the old school do not allow the use of glazes and justify their opposition to their use by suggesting that each culinary operation should be prepared from its proper basic ingredients and produce its own glaze when needed.

Certainly the theory is correct when one is not limited in terms of time or expense but, unfortunately, rarely in these days does an establishment apply these theories; indeed, if the use of glazes is made judiciously and without abuse and if they are prepared with great care, one can obtain excellent results from their use and they become of real value in most cases.

9 Meat Glaze

Place sufficient brown stock into a large pan and allow it to reduce; from time to time after an appreciable degree of reduction has taken place, strain the stock into a smaller pan and continue to do this as the process of reduction progresses. It is necessary to skim the stock carefully throughout the process as the quality of the resultant glaze depends very much on this. Reduce the heat progressively as the reduction of the stock increases until the final stage when the reduction must be finished over a very moderate heat. The glaze is ready when it adheres to the back of a spoon in the form of a glossy coating.

Note: For a lighter coloured clear glaze, ordinary white stock should be used instead of brown stock.

10 Chicken Glaze

This is made in the same way as meat glaze using chicken stock instead of brown stock.

11 Game Glaze

This is made in the same way as meat glaze using game stock. If it is necessary to obtain a glaze of a specific game flavour use game stock prepared from one particular game.

12 Fish Glaze

This kind of glaze is not used as much as meat or chicken glaze. It is made in the same way as meat glaze using fish stock instead of brown stock. In practice the fish essence which is used for poaching the fish will have a more delicate flavour than fish glaze and should be reduced and added to the sauce. (See Fish Essence.)

THE ROUX

The various kinds of Roux are used as the thickening agents for basic sauces, and their preparation, which appears to be of little importance, should actually be carried out with a great deal of care and attention. Three kinds of Roux are used—brown Roux for brown sauces, blond Roux for Veloutés and cream sauces and white Roux for Béchamel and white sauces. In large kitchens brown Roux is usually made in advance; blond and white Roux are made as required. The time necessary for the cooking of Roux depends upon the intensity of the heat being applied and cannot be determined mathematically. It is advisable to cook it slowly rather than too quickly as the application of a fierce heat will cause the starch granules to harden. This will constrict the contents of the starch granules and prevent them from combining with the liquid when added to form the sauce. In this case it produces an analogy with that which takes place when cooking pulses in boiling water. It is necessary to start with a moderate heat, increasing it progressively so as to allow the outer coating of the starch granules to distend, thus allowing the starch which they contain to swell and, under the influence of the heat, to break down, transforming it into dextrin, a soluble substance which is involved in the thickening process.

The use of clarified butter is recommended for the making of Roux as the amount of casein which is present in ordinary butter is detrimental to the making of a good Roux. It should be remembered that the butter contained in a Roux gives very little flavour to the finished sauce, what little flavour there is, being removed during the skimming process.

It is also worth remembering in the study of the making of Roux that the starting point of the thickening of a sauce comes from the starch in the flour and it is on this that the balance of the sauce depends.

A Roux made from a pure starch such as arrowroot would give the same result as one made from flour, the only difference being that it is necessary to take into account the other substances contained in flour which would mean that a smaller amount of pure starch is required.

13 Brown Roux
To make 1 kg ($2\frac{1}{4}$ lb)

Ingredients:
500 g (1 lb 2 oz) clarified butter
600 g (1 lb 5 oz) sifted flour

Preparation:
Mix the butter and flour together in a heavy pan and place in a moderate oven to cook, stirring frequently until an even, light brown colour is obtained. When cooked, the Roux should have a smell resembling that of hazelnuts or baked flour and be without grains.

Note: It is advisable to use clarified butter in the preparation of brown Roux, other kinds of fat should only be used for serious reasons of economy. If the need for economy is an important factor, it should be born in mind that the butter used in the Roux can be recovered from the skimmings which are removed from the sauce, and can be re-used.

14 Blond Roux
Using the same amount of ingredients as for brown Roux, cook the Roux very slowly until it takes on a light straw colour.

15 White Roux
Using the same amount of ingredients as for brown Roux, cook the Roux for a few minutes only, just sufficient to eliminate the rawness of the flour.

BASIC SAUCES

16 Sauce Espagnole
To make 5 litres ($8\frac{3}{4}$ pt or $1\frac{3}{8}$ U.S. gal)

Ingredients:
625 g (1 lb 6 oz) brown Roux—using: 285 g (10 oz) clarified butter and 340 g (12 oz) sifted flour
12 litres ($2\frac{5}{8}$ gal or $3\frac{1}{4}$ U.S. gal) brown stock
150 g (5 oz) roughly diced salt belly of pork
250 g (9 oz) roughly diced carrots
150 g (5 oz) roughly diced onions
2 sprigs thyme
2 small bay leaves
500 g (1 lb 2 oz) tomato purée or 2 kg ($4\frac{1}{2}$ lb) fresh tomatoes
2 dl (7 fl oz or $\frac{7}{8}$ U.S. cup) white wine

Preparation:
1) Place 8 litres ($1\frac{3}{4}$ gal or $2\frac{1}{4}$ U.S. gal) of the stock in a heavy pan and bring to the boil; add the Roux, previously softened in the oven. Mix well with a wooden spoon or whisk and bring to the boil mixing continuously. Draw the pan to the side of the stove and allow to simmer slowly and evenly.
2) Meanwhile, place the salt pork in a pan and fry to extract the fat, add the vegetables and flavourings and fry until light brown in colour. Carefully drain off the fat and put the ingredients into the sauce; deglaze the pan with the wine, reduce it by half and also add to the sauce. Allow to simmer gently for 1 hour skimming frequently.
3) Pass the sauce through a conical strainer into another pan, pressing lightly. Add another 2 litres ($3\frac{1}{2}$ pt or 9 U.S. cups) stock, bring to the boil and allow to simmer gently for a further 2 hours. Pass the sauce through a fine strainer and stir occasionally until completely cold.
4) The next day, add the remainder of the stock and the tomato purée; bring the sauce to the boil stirring continuously with a wooden spatula or whisk, then allow to simmer gently and evenly for 1 hour skimming carefully.

   Pass through a fine strainer or tammy cloth and stir occasionally until the sauce is completely cold.

Notes:
1) The time required for the preparation and refining of this sauce cannot be indicated exactly as it depends to a large extent on the quality of the stock used in its making. The refining of this sauce will be quicker if the stock is of very good quality in which case an excellent Espagnole can be prepared in five hours.
2) Before adding tomato purée to this sauce it is advisable to spread the required quantity on a tray and to cook it in the oven until it turns a light brown colour. This will destroy most of the excess acidity found in tomato purées, and when prepared in this way, the purée assists in clarifying the sauce and at the same time gives it a smoother taste and a more agreeable colour.

17 Sauce Espagnole Maigre—Lenten or Fish Espagnole

To make 5 litres (8¾ pt or 1⅜ U.S. gal)

Ingredients:

500 g (1 lb 2 oz) brown Roux—using: 225 g (8 oz) clarified butter and 275 g (10 oz) sifted flour
10 litres (2¼ gal or 2¾ U.S. gal) fish stock
250 g (9 oz) roughly diced carrots
150 g (5 oz) roughly diced onions
250 g (9 oz) mushroom trimmings
150 g (5 oz) butter
2 sprigs thyme
2 bay leaves
2 dl (7 fl oz or ⅞ U.S. cup) white wine
500 g (1 lb 2 oz) tomato purée or 2 kg (4½ lb) fresh tomatoes

Preparation:

This is prepared in the same way as ordinary Espagnole, using the butter in place of the salt belly of pork and adding the mushroom trimmings at the same time as the tomato purée, and cooking for a total time of 5 hours. Pass through a fine strainer or tammy cloth and stir occasionally until the sauce is completely cold.

Note: There is a division of opinion as to whether it is correct to include this sauce with the other basic sauces, and it should be noted that the same result can be obtained by using ordinary Espagnole, which has a fairly neutral taste, and adding some fish stock during the process. If a completely meatless Espagnole is absolutely necessary in the preparation of a dish, then the above must be used.

18 Sauce Demi-glace

This sauce, commonly referred to as Demi-glace, is made with Espagnole which is brought to a final stage of perfection by further careful simmering and skimming.

It should be finished at the last moment with a little meat or other glaze.

Demi-glace can be flavoured with various wines such as sherry, port and Madeira. The addition of a particular wine naturally changes the flavour and character of the Demi-glace and will decide its ultimate use. It is advisable to add the wine being used at the last moment; by boiling the sauce the aroma of the wine will be destroyed by evaporation.

19 Jus de Veau Lié—Thickened Veal Gravy

To make 1 litre (1¾ pt or 4½ U.S. cups)

Ingredients:

4 litres (7 pt or 8¾ U.S. pt) Brown Veal Stock
30 g (1 oz) arrowroot

Preparation:

Bring the stock to the boil then allow it to reduce by three-quarters to yield 1 litre (1¾ pt or 4½ U.S. cups). Dilute the arrowroot in a little cold stock, stir into the boiling stock and cook for 1 minute. Pass through a fine strainer.

Note: This gravy, which is frequently referred to throughout this book, should have a clean taste, be transparent and have a pleasing light brown colour.

20 Velouté or Sauce Blanche Grasse—Ordinary Velouté

To make 5 litres (8¾ pt or 1⅜ U.S. gal)

Ingredients:

625 g (1 lb 6 oz) blond Roux—using: 285 g (10 oz) clarified butter and 340 g (12 oz) sifted flour
5½ litres (9½ pt or 1½ U.S. gal) very clear White Veal Stock

Preparation

Make the Roux in the usual manner and gradually mix in the hot or cold stock making sure that a smooth consistency is obtained. Bring to the boil stirring continuously and allow to simmer very gently and evenly for 1½ hours skimming carefully from time to time. Pass through a fine strainer. Stir occasionally until completely cold and use as required.

Note: The practice of adding vegetables and flavourings such as carrots, studded onions or Bouquet garni in the preparation of this Velouté is unnecessary. If the stock is made in accordance with the recipe it will already contain sufficient flavour. However, it is advisable to add approximately 30–40 g (1–1½ oz) of fresh white mushroom trimmings or preferably 2½ dl (9 fl oz or 1⅛ U.S. cup) of mushroom cooking liquor for the amount of sauce indicated.

21 Velouté de Volaille—Chicken Velouté

This is prepared in the same way and with the same proportion of ingredients as Ordinary Velouté using white chicken stock instead of veal stock.

22 Velouté de Poisson—Fish Velouté

This is made in the same way and with the same proportion of ingredients as Ordinary Velouté using fish stock instead of veal stock and cooking it quickly for 20 minutes only.

23 Sauce Allemande (*also known as Sauce Parisienne*)

To make 1 litre (1¾ pt or 4½ U.S. cups)

Ingredients:

1 litre (1¾ pt or 4½ U.S. cups) Ordinary Velouté

5 dl (18 fl oz or $2\frac{1}{4}$ U.S. cups) Ordinary White Stock
2 dl (7 fl oz or $\frac{7}{8}$ U.S. cup) mushroom cooking liquor
5 egg yolks
pinch of grated nutmeg
squeeze of lemon juice
pinch of coarsely ground pepper
100 g ($3\frac{1}{2}$ oz) butter

Preparation:
Place the stock, mushroom liquor, yolks of egg, lemon juice, pepper and nutmeg in a heavy shallow pan, mix well together with a whisk and add the Velouté. Bring to the boil and reduce by one-third stirring constantly with a metal spatula; reduce until the sauce reaches the point where it coats the spatula. Pass through a fine strainer or tammy cloth and coat the surface of the sauce with butter to prevent a skin forming. Keep in a Bain-marie until required then add 100 g ($3\frac{1}{2}$ oz) butter before using.

Notes:
1) In effect this sauce is an Ordinary Velouté thickened with egg yolks.
2) This sauce is also known as Sauce Parisienne a name which is more logical and proper than Sauce Allemande. This was pointed out in an article in '*l'Art Culinaire*' in 1883 by Mons. Tavenet, a well-known chef. The name 'Parisienne' has been adopted by several chefs but not as widely as could be wished.

24 Sauce Suprême
Sauce Suprême is Ordinary Velouté finished with cream; it should be very white in colour and delicate in flavour.
To make 1 litre ($1\frac{3}{4}$ pt or $4\frac{1}{2}$ U.S. pt)

Ingredients:
1 litre ($1\frac{3}{4}$ pt or $4\frac{1}{2}$ U.S. cups) chicken Velouté
1 litre ($1\frac{3}{4}$ pt or $4\frac{1}{2}$ U.S. cups) white chicken stock
1 dl ($3\frac{1}{2}$ fl oz or $\frac{1}{2}$ U.S. cup) mushroom cooking liquor
$3\frac{1}{2}$ dl (12 fl oz or $1\frac{1}{2}$ U.S. cups) fresh double cream
80 g (3 oz) best quality butter

Preparation:
Place the Velouté, stock and mushroom liquor in a heavy shallow pan; bring to the boil and reduce quickly adding $2\frac{1}{2}$ dl (9 fl oz or $1\frac{1}{8}$ U.S. cups) of the cream in small quantities during the process, working the sauce continuously with a metal spatula. When the sauce has been reduced by one-third, pass it through a fine strainer or tammy cloth. Finish the sauce with the remainder of the cream and the butter.

25 Sauce Béchamel
To make 5 litres ($8\frac{3}{4}$ pt or $1\frac{3}{8}$ U.S. gal)

Ingredients:
650 g (1 lb 7 oz) white Roux—using: 300 g (11 oz) clarified butter and 350 g ($12\frac{1}{2}$ oz) sifted flour
5 litres ($8\frac{3}{4}$ pt or $1\frac{3}{8}$ U.S. gal) boiling milk
300 g (11 oz) lean veal
2 finely sliced small onions
1 sprig of thyme
50 g (2 oz) butter
pinch of coarsely ground pepper
pinch of nutmeg
25 g (1 oz) salt

Preparation:
Make the Roux in the normal manner and allow to cool. Mix the milk into the Roux so as to obtain a smooth sauce and bring to boiling point. Meanwhile, cut the veal into small cubes and stew with the butter without colouring, adding the onions, seasonings and thyme; place into the sauce. Allow to simmer gently for 2 hours and pass through a fine strainer. Coat the surface of the sauce with butter to prevent the formation of a skin.

Notes:
1) If the Béchamel is to be used for meatless dishes the veal should be omitted but the flavourings, as indicated, should still be included.
2) It is possible to make the sauce more quickly in the following manner: bring the milk to the boil with the onion and seasonings, cover and allow to infuse for 10 minutes. Strain the milk on to the Roux, mix, bring to the boil and allow to simmer gently for 15–20 minutes.

26 Sauce Tomate—Tomato Sauce
To make 5 litres ($8\frac{3}{4}$ pt or $1\frac{3}{8}$ U.S. gal)

Ingredients:
100 g ($3\frac{1}{2}$ oz) butter
150 g (5 oz) salt belly of pork diced and blanched
150 g (5 oz) flour
200 g (7 oz) roughly diced carrot
150 g (5 oz) roughly diced onion
1 bay leaf
1 sprig of thyme
4 litres (7 pt or $8\frac{3}{4}$ U.S. pt) purée of tomatoes or 6 kg (13 lb) fresh tomatoes
2 litres ($3\frac{1}{2}$ pt or 9 U.S. cups) ordinary white stock
2 cloves garlic
20 g ($\frac{2}{3}$ oz) salt
30 g (1 oz) sugar
pinch of ground pepper

Preparation:
Melt the butter in a heavy pan, add the salt pork and fry lightly; add the vegetables, bay leaf and thyme and fry to a light brown colour. Sprinkle with the flour and mix in; cook until light brown then add the purée or fresh tomatoes previously squashed. Mix in the stock, add the crushed garlic, salt, sugar and pepper and bring to the boil whilst stirring.

Cover with a lid and place in a moderate oven to cook very gently for 1½–2 hours. When cooked, pass through a fine strainer into a clean pan, stir and reboil for a few minutes; pour into a basin and coat the surface with butter to prevent the formation of a skin.

Notes:
1) A purée of tomatoes can be used as a sauce in place of this recipe; it is prepared exactly as indicated above except that the flour is omitted and the sauce should be reduced after straining until it reaches the correct consistency.
2) Care should be taken when using a concentrated purée and an adjustment should be made to the amount used.

SMALL COMPOUND BROWN SAUCES

27 Sauce Bigarade

For braised duck: Pass the braising liquor from cooking the duck through a strainer and remove the fat carefully; reduce it until fairly thick. Add the juice of four oranges and one lemon to each 1 litre (1¾ pt or 4½ U.S. cups) of reduced braising liquor so as to reconstitute it to the required consistency.

For poêléed duck: Remove the duck from the pan, add a little brown veal stock to the sediment, bring to the boil, pass through a strainer and carefully remove the fat. For each 1 litre (1¾ pt or 4½ U.S. cups) add the following: 20 g (⅔ oz) of sugar caramelized and diluted with ¼ dl (1 fl oz or ⅛ U.S. cup) of vinegar, and the juice of four oranges and 1 lemon. Lightly thicken with diluted arrowroot.

In both cases this sauce is finished with 2 tbs of very fine Julienne of orange zest and 1 tbs Julienne of lemon zest, both well blanched.

28 Sauce Bordelaise

Place 3 dl (½ pt or 1¼ U.S. cups) of red wine into a small pan with 30 g (1 oz) finely chopped shallot; a little coarsely ground pepper; ½ a bayleaf; and a sprig of thyme; reduce by three-quarters. Add 5 dl (18 fl oz or 2¼ U.S. cups) of Espagnole and allow to simmer gently for 15 minutes skimming as necessary. Pass through a fine strainer and finish the sauce with 1 tbs melted meat glaze; the juice of ¼ of a lemon; and 50 g (2 oz) bone marrow cut into small dice or slices and poached.

This sauce is specially suitable for serving with grilled red meat.

Note: Originally this sauce was made with white wine but nowadays red wine is always used. (See Sauce Bonnefoy for Sauce Bordelaise made with white wine.)

29 Sauce Bourguignonne

Place 1½ litres (2⅝ pt or 6½ U.S. cups) of good red wine in a pan with 75 g (2½ oz) sliced shallots; a few parsley stalks; ½ a bayleaf; a small sprig of thyme; and 25 g (1 oz) of mushroom trimmings; reduce by half. Pass through a fine strainer and thicken by adding 80 g (3 oz) of Beurre Manié made from 45 g (1½ oz) of butter and 35 g (1¼ oz) of flour. Finish it at the last moment with 150 g (5 oz) of butter and a little Cayenne.

This sauce is specially suitable for serving with eggs and dishes designated à la Bourguignonne.

30 Sauce Bretonne

Heat 50 g (2 oz) butter in a pan, add 100 g (3½ oz) chopped onions and cook until light golden brown. Add 2½ dl (9 fl oz or 1⅛ U.S. cups) of white wine and reduce by half; add 3½ dl (12 fl oz or 1½ U.S. cups) Espagnole, 3½ dl (12 fl oz or 1½ U.S. cups) Tomato Sauce and one small clove of crushed garlic. Bring to the boil and allow to simmer gently for 7–8 minutes and finish with a pinch of coarsely chopped parsley.

This sauce is used exclusively in the preparation of Haricots à la Bretonne.

31 Sauce aux Cerises—Cherry Sauce

Place 2 dl (7fl oz or ⅞ U.S. cup) of Port Wine into a small pan with a pinch of mixed spice and ½ tbs of grated orange rind; reduce by one-third. Add 2½ dl (9 fl oz or 1⅛ U.S. cups) redcurrant jelly and the juice of one orange and when dissolved add 200 g (7 oz) of stoned cherries which have been previously poached in syrup.

This sauce is suitable as an accompaniment for venison but is more appropriate with braised and poêléed duck.

32 Sauce aux Champignons—Mushroom Sauce

Place 2½ dl (9 fl oz or 1⅛ U.S. cups) of mushroom cooking liquor in a small pan and reduce by half. Add 8 dl (1⅜ pt or 3½ U.S. cups) of Sauce Demi-glace and allow to simmer gently for a few minutes. Pass through a fine strainer, mix in 50 g (2 oz) butter and finish by adding 100 g ($3\frac{1}{2}$ oz) very small button mushrooms, cooked in a little butter.

33 Sauce Charcutière

To 1 litre ($1\frac{3}{4}$ pt or $4\frac{1}{2}$ U.S. cups) of Sauce Robert, add 100 g ($3\frac{1}{2}$ oz) of gherkins cut into thick short Julienne. The gherkins should be added at the last moment just before serving.

This sauce is specially suitable for serving with grilled pork chops and any grilled meats which require a highly seasoned sauce.

34 Sauce Chasseur

Melt 30 g (1 oz) butter in a small pan, add 150 g (5 oz) sliced buttom mushrooms and lightly fry. Add 50 g (2 oz) finely chopped shallots and cook together for a few minutes. Add 3 dl ($\frac{1}{2}$ pt or $1\frac{1}{4}$ U.S. cups) white wine, reduce by half then add 3 dl ($\frac{1}{2}$ pt or $1\frac{1}{4}$ U.S. cups) Tomato Sauce and 2 dl (7 fl oz or $\frac{7}{8}$ U.S. cup) Sauce Demi-glace. Bring to the boil, allow to simmer gently for a few minutes and finish with 150 g (5 oz) butter and $1\frac{1}{2}$ tbs of mixed chopped tarragon and chervil.

35 Sauce Chasseur (*Escoffier's method*)

Heat 15 g ($\frac{1}{2}$ oz) butter and $\frac{1}{4}$ dl (1 fl oz or $\frac{1}{8}$ U.S. cup) olive oil in a pan; add 150 g (5 oz) sliced button mushrooms and fry until lightly coloured. Add 25 g (1 oz) finely chopped shallots, cook together for a few moments and drain off half the fat. Add 2 dl (7 fl oz or $\frac{7}{8}$ U.S. cup) dry white wine and $\frac{1}{2}$ dl (2 fl oz or $\frac{1}{4}$ U.S. cup) brandy; reduce by half. Add 4 dl (14 fl oz or $1\frac{3}{4}$ U.S. cups) of Sauce Demi-glace, 2 dl (7 fl oz or $\frac{7}{8}$ U.S. cup) Tomato Sauce and 1 tbs meat glaze; simmer gently for 5 minutes and finish with a little chopped parsley.

36 Sauce Chaud-froid Brune—Brown Chaud-froid Sauce

To make 1 litre ($1\frac{3}{4}$ pt or $4\frac{1}{2}$ U.S. cups)

Ingredients:

$7\frac{1}{2}$ dl ($1\frac{1}{3}$ pt or $3\frac{1}{4}$ U.S. cups) Sauce Demi-glace
1 dl ($3\frac{1}{2}$ fl oz or $\frac{1}{2}$ U.S. cup) truffle essence
$\frac{1}{2}$ dl (2 fl oz or $\frac{1}{4}$ U.S. cup) Madeira or Port wine
7 dl ($1\frac{1}{4}$ pt or 3 U.S. cups) ordinary aspic jelly

Preparation:

Place the Demi-glace and truffle essence in a pan and reduce quickly stirring with a metal spatula and adding the jelly a little at a time until the total quantity of all the ingredients is reduced by one-third.

Correct the seasoning and check that the consistency of the Chaud-froid is correct for its uses. Finish with the wine and pass through a fine strainer then stir the Chaud-froid until it reaches the right stage for coating the items for which it is required.

37 Brown Chaud-froid Sauce for Ducks

This is prepared in the same way as ordinary brown Chaud-froid omitting the truffle essence and replacing it with $1\frac{1}{2}$ dl (5 fl oz or $\frac{5}{8}$ U.S. cup) of essence prepared from the duck carcass and trimmings. Reduce the sauce a little more than in the previous recipe and after passing it through a fine strainer add the juice of three oranges and 2 tbs of very fine Julienne of orange zest, well blanched and drained.

38 Brown Chaud-froid Sauce for Game

This is prepared in the same way as ordinary brown Chaud-froid omitting the truffle essence and replacing it with 2 dl (7 fl oz or $\frac{7}{8}$ U.S. cup) of game essence prepared from the carcass and trimmings of the game which is to be coated with the Chaud-froid.

39 Tomato-Flavoured Chaud-froid Sauce

Place 1 litre ($1\frac{3}{4}$ pt or $4\frac{1}{2}$ U.S. cups) of well-reduced purée of fresh tomatoes in a pan and reduce whilst adding approximately 7 dl ($1\frac{1}{4}$ pt or 3 U.S. cups) of ordinary aspic jelly, a little at a time. Reduce until the total quantity is approximately 1 litre ($1\frac{3}{4}$ pt or $4\frac{1}{2}$ U.S. cups). Pass through a fine strainer and stir until the Chaud-froid reaches the correct stage for coating.

40 Sauce Chevreuil

Prepare 1 litre ($1\frac{3}{4}$ pt or $4\frac{1}{2}$ U.S. cups) of ordinary Sauce Poivrade, using 50 g (2 oz) of bacon in the mirepoix if the finished sauce is to be served with marinated butcher's meat, or with the addition of game trimmings cooked with the mirepoix if the finished sauce is to be served with game. Pass the sauce firmly through a strainer. Allow to simmer gently and skim whilst adding $1\frac{1}{2}$ dl (5 fl oz or $\frac{5}{8}$ U.S. cup) of good quality red wine a little at a time. Finish the sauce with a pinch of sugar and a little Cayenne and pass through a fine strainer.

41 Sauce Colbert

Correctly speaking, Sauce Colbert is Beurre Colbert which is Beurre Maître-d'Hôtel with the addition of meat glaze. To differentiate between Beurre Colbert and Sauce Chateaubriand some people add chopped tarragon to the Beurre Maître-d'Hôtel but this is not an absolute rule. In effect the two preparations are completely differrent—Sauce Chateaubriand is a buttered light meat glaze containing chopped parsley whereas in the Sauce or Beurre Colbert the butter is the main ingredient and the meat glaze is only an additive.

42 Sauce Diable—Devilled Sauce
Place 3 dl ($\frac{1}{2}$ pt or $1\frac{1}{4}$ U.S. cups) white wine in a pan, add 20 g ($\frac{2}{3}$ oz) chopped shallot and reduce by two-thirds. Add 2 dl (7 fl oz or $\frac{7}{8}$ U.S. cup) Sauce Demi-glace and allow to simmer gently for a few minutes then season the sauce strongly with Cayenne pepper.

This sauce is specially suitable for serving with grilled chicken and pigeons.

Notes:
1) Vinegar may be used instead of wine and chopped Fines Herbes may be included in the reduction; the above recipe, however, is preferable.
2) This sauce should be prepared in a small quantity as required. The above recipe yields approximately $2\frac{1}{2}$ dl (9 fl oz or $1\frac{1}{8}$ U.S. cup).

43 Sauce Diable Escoffier—Escoffier's Devilled Sauce
This sauce is obtainable commercially under the brand name of Escoffier. It is only necessary to add an equal amount of softened butter to the sauce before use.

This sauce is suitable for serving with grilled or poached fish and for all grilled foods.

44 Sauce Diane
Lightly whip 2 dl (7 fl oz or $\frac{7}{8}$ U.S. cup) of cream and add it at the last moment to 5 dl (18 fl oz or $2\frac{1}{4}$ U.S. cups) well seasoned and reduced Sauce Poivrade. Finish with 2 tbs each of small crescent-shape pieces of truffle and hard-boiled white of egg.

This sauce is suitable for serving with cutlets, noisettes and other cuts of venison.

45 Sauce Duxelles
Place 2 dl (7 fl oz or $\frac{7}{8}$ U.S. cup) white wine and 2 dl (7 fl oz or $\frac{7}{8}$ U.S. cup) mushroom cooking liquor in a pan with 40 g ($1\frac{1}{2}$ oz) chopped shallot and reduce by two-thirds. Add 5 dl (18 fl oz or $2\frac{1}{4}$ U.S. cups) Sauce Demi-glace, $1\frac{1}{2}$ dl (5 fl oz or $\frac{5}{8}$ U.S. cup) tomato purée and 4 tbs dry Duxelles; allow to simmer gently for 5 minutes and finish the sauce with $\frac{1}{2}$ tbs chopped parsley.

This sauce is specially used in the preparation of dishes designated *au Gratin.*

Note: Sauce Duxelles is sometimes confused with Sauce Italienne which it resembles but in reality there is a difference as Sauce Duxelles does not contain chopped ham or salted ox tongue.

46 Sauce Estragon—Tarragon Sauce
To prepare $2\frac{1}{2}$ dl (9 fl oz or $1\frac{1}{8}$ U.S. cups) of sauce, place 2 dl (7 fl oz or $\frac{7}{8}$ U.S. cup) white wine in a pan and bring to the boil. Add 20 g ($\frac{2}{3}$ oz) tarragon leaves, cover with the lid, remove from the heat and allow to infuse for 10 minutes. Add $2\frac{1}{2}$ dl (9 fl oz or $1\frac{1}{8}$ U.S. cups) Sauce Demi-glace or thickened veal gravy, bring to the boil and reduce by one-third. Pass through a fine strainer and finish with 1 tsp chopped tarragon.

This sauce is specially suitable for serving with noisettes of white meat and poultry etc.

47 Sauce Financière
Place $1\frac{1}{4}$ litres ($2\frac{1}{4}$ pt or $5\frac{1}{2}$ U.S. cups) Madeira Sauce in a pan and reduce by a quarter. Remove from the heat, add 1 dl ($3\frac{1}{2}$ fl oz or $\frac{1}{2}$ U.S. cup) truffle essence and pass through a fine strainer.

This sauce is normally associated with the garnish Financière but may be served with other entrées.

48 Sauce aux Fines Herbes
Place 3 dl ($\frac{1}{2}$ pt or $1\frac{1}{4}$ U.S. cups) of white wine in a small pan and bring to the boil. Add 10 g ($\frac{1}{3}$ oz) of picked parsley and the same amount of picked chervil, tarragon and chives. Cover with a lid, remove from the heat and allow to infuse for 20 minutes. Pass through a clean cloth and add this infusion to 6 dl (1 pt or $2\frac{5}{8}$ U.S. cups) of Sauce Demi-glace or thickened veal gravy. Simmer gently for a few minutes and finish it at the last moment with $2\frac{1}{2}$ tbs of chopped Fines Herbes as used in the infusion and in equal proportions; finish with a squeeze of lemon juice.

Note: In the old classical kitchen, Sauce aux Fines Herbes was often confused with Sauce Duxelles. Sensibly, modern practice has successfully established the actual difference between the two sauces.

49 Sauce Genevoise
Heat 50 g (2 oz) of butter in a pan. Add 100 g ($3\frac{1}{2}$ oz) of carrots, 80 g (3 oz) of onion and 20 g ($\frac{2}{3}$ oz) parsley stalks, all cut in fine Mirepoix; 1 small sprig of thyme and $\frac{1}{2}$ a bayleaf. Cook together till lightly browned. Add 1 kg ($2\frac{1}{4}$ lb) salmon head and a pinch of coarsely ground pepper; cover with a lid and allow to stew for 15 minutes.

Drain off the butter, add 1 litre ($1\frac{3}{4}$ pt or $4\frac{1}{2}$ U.S. cups) of red wine and reduce by half. Add 5 dl (18 fl oz or $2\frac{1}{4}$ U.S. cups) fish Espagnole and allow to simmer gently for 1 hour. Pass firmly through a strainer into a clean pan.

Allow to rest for a few minutes and then carefully remove any fat which has risen to the surface of the sauce.

Add an extra 5 dl (18 fl oz or 2¼ U.S. cups) of red wine and the same amount of fish stock; simmer gently with careful skimming and reduce to the required consistency. Pass the sauce through a fine strainer and finish with 1 tbs of anchovy essence and 150 g (5 oz) of butter, mixed in well.

This sauce is specially suitable for serving with salmon and trout.

Note: In the old classical kitchen this sauce was entitled Genoise by Carême but Reculet first and Gouffé afterwards called it Genevoise but with less logic; Geneva is not known particularly as a wine-producing area.

However, whether called Genoise or Genevoise, all the classical authors, Carême, Reculet, Dubois and Gouffé, indicate the use of red wine in the preparation of this sauce.

50 Sauce Godard

Place 4 dl (14 fl oz or 1¾ U.S. cups) of Champagne or dry white wine in a pan with a very fine Mirepoix containing ham, and reduce by half. Add 1 litre (1¾ pt or 4½ U.S. cups) Sauce Demi-glace and 2 dl (7 fl oz or ⅞ U.S. cup) mushroom essence. Simmer gently for 10 minutes and pass through a fine strainer, then continue to simmer gently, reduce by one-third and pass again through a fine strainer.

This sauce is specially used to accompany relevés garnished 'à la Godard'.

51 Sauce Grand-Veneur

Prepare 1 litre (1¾ pt or 4½ U.S. cups) Sauce Poivrade using a game stock prepared from venison. Dilute 1 dl (3½ fl oz or ½ U.S. cup) hare's blood with 1 dl (3½ fl oz or ½ U.S. cup) marinade and add to the sauce. Keep on the side of the stove for a few minutes without boiling, so as to allow the blood to cook then pass the sauce through a fine strainer.

This sauce is specially suitable for serving with joints of venison.

52 Sauce Grand-Veneur (*Escoffier's Method*)

Prepare 1 litre (1¾ pt or 4½ U.S. cups) fairly thin Sauce Poivrade for game and finish with 2½ dl (9 fl oz or 1⅛ U.S. cup) cream and 2 tbs of redcurrant jelly. This sauce is also specially suitable for serving with joints of venison.

53 Sauce Gratin

Place 3 dl (½ pt or 1¼ U.S. cups) of white wine in a pan with 3 dl (½ pt or 1¼ U.S. cups) fish stock prepared from the bones of the fish under preparation; add 1½ tbs chopped shallot and reduce by a good half. Add 3 tbs dry Duxelles and 5 dl (18 fl oz or 2¼ U.S. cups) fish Espagnole or Demi-glace; allow to simmer gently for 5 to 6 minutes. Finish at the last moment with 1 tbs chopped parsley.

This sauce is specially suitable for the preparation of fish *au Gratin*, such as sole, whiting and fillets of brill etc.

54 Sauce Hachée

Heat 50 g (2 oz) of butter in a pan, add 100 g (3½ oz) chopped onion and 1½ tbs finely chopped shallot and cook without colour. Moisten with 3 dl (½ pt or 1¼ U.S. cups) vinegar and reduce by half then add 4 dl (14 fl oz or 1¾ U.S. cups) Espagnole and 1½ dl (5 fl oz or ⅝ U.S. cup) Tomato Sauce and simmer gently for 5–6 minutes.

Finish the sauce by adding 1½ tbs chopped lean ham, 1½ tbs small capers, 1½ tbs dry Duxelles and ½ tbs chopped parsley.

This sauce which has a similarity to Sauce Piquante is suitable for serving with the same dishes.

55 Sauce Hachée (*Lenten*)

Heat 50 g (2 oz) of butter in a pan, add 100 g (3½ oz) of finely chopped onion and 1½ tbs finely chopped shallot and cook without colour. Moisten with 3 dl (½ pt or 1¼ U.S. cups) vinegar and reduce by half.

Add 5 dl (18 fl oz or 2¼ U.S. cups) of the Court-bouillon from the fish under preparation and thicken with 45 g (1½ oz) brown Roux or 50 g (2 oz) Beurre Manié. Allow to simmer gently for 8 to 10 minutes.

Finish the sauce by adding 1 tbs chopped Fines Herbes, 1½ tbs small capers, 1½ tbs dry Duxelles and ½ tbs of anchovy essence and 60 g (2 oz) butter, or 80–100 g (3–3½ oz) ordinary anchovy butter.

This sauce is specially suitable for boiled fish of second quality, e.g. skate.

56 Sauce Hussarde

Heat 50 g (2 oz) of butter in a pan. Add 100 g (3½ oz) finely sliced onion and 50 g (2 oz) finely sliced shallot and cook to a golden colour. Moisten with 4 dl (14 fl oz or 1¾ U.S. cups) white wine, reduce by half and add 4 dl (14 fl oz or 1¾ U.S. cups) Sauce Demi-glace, 2 tbs tomato purée, 2 dl (7 fl oz or ⅞ U.S. cup) white stock, 80 g (3 oz) raw lean ham, 1 small clove of crushed garlic and 1 Bouquet garni. Bring to the boil and simmer gently for 25–30 minutes.

Remove the ham and keep on one side and pass the sauce through a fine sieve.

Reheat the sauce and finish by adding the ham cut in very small dice, a little grated horseradish and a good pinch of chopped parsley.

This sauce is specially suitable for serving with grilled or spit-roasted red meats.

57 Sauce Italienne

Prepare $7\frac{1}{2}$ dl ($1\frac{1}{3}$ pt or $3\frac{1}{4}$ U.S. cups) of tomato-flavoured Demi-glace. Add 4 tbs dry Duxelles and 125 g ($4\frac{1}{2}$ oz) lean cooked ham cut in very small dice. Allow to simmer gently for 5–6 minutes and finish at the last moment with 1 tbs of chopped mixed tarragon, chervil and parsley.

This sauce is used in the preparation of many small entrées.

Note: When this sauce is used for a fish dish, a little of the stock from the fish under preparation should be reduced and added to the sauce and the chopped ham should be omitted.

58 Jus lié à l'Estragon—Thickened Gravy, tarragon flavoured

Infuse 50 g (2 oz) tarragon in 1 litre ($1\frac{3}{4}$ pt or $4\frac{1}{2}$ U.S. cups) of brown veal or chicken stock. Pass through a fine strainer and thicken with 30 g (1 oz) arrowroot or fecula diluted with a little water.

This sauce is used to accompany noisettes of white meat, suprêmes of chicken etc.

59 Jus lié Tomaté—Thickened Gravy, tomato flavoured

Add 3 dl ($\frac{1}{2}$ pt or $1\frac{1}{4}$ U.S. cups) tomato essence to 1 litre ($1\frac{3}{4}$ pt or $4\frac{1}{2}$ U.S. cups) of brown veal stock and reduce by one-fifth. Pass through a fine strainer and thicken with 30 g (1 oz) arrowroot or cornflour diluted with a little water.

This sauce is specially suitable for use with butcher's meats.

60 Sauce Lyonnaise—Brown Onion Sauce

Heat 50 g (2 oz) butter in a pan, add 250 g (9 oz) chopped onion and cook slowly to a golden colour. Add 2 dl (7 fl oz or $\frac{7}{8}$ U.S. cup) each of white wine and vinegar, reduce by two-thirds and add $7\frac{1}{2}$ dl ($1\frac{1}{3}$ pt or $3\frac{1}{4}$ U.S. cups) Sauce Demi-glace; simmer gently, skimming as necessary for 5–6 minutes and pass through a sieve.

Note: This sauce may be served unpassed or passed through a sieve according to the requirements of the dish with which it is to be served.

61 Sauce Madère—Madeira Sauce

Reduce 1 litre ($1\frac{3}{4}$ pt or $4\frac{1}{2}$ U.S. cups) of Sauce Demi-glace until slightly thickened. Remove from the heat and add 1 dl ($3\frac{1}{2}$ fl oz or $\frac{1}{2}$ U.S. cup) Madeira wine to correct its consistency. Pass through a fine strainer and do not reboil.

62 Sauce Matelote

Place 3 dl ($\frac{1}{2}$ pt or $1\frac{1}{4}$ U.S. cups) of red wine Court-bouillon in a pan with 25 g (1 oz) mushroom trimmings. Reduce by two-thirds and then add 8 dl ($1\frac{2}{5}$ pt or $3\frac{1}{2}$ U.S. cups) of fish Espagnole. Simmer gently for a few minutes and pass through a fine strainer. Finish the sauce with 150 g (5 oz) of butter and lightly season with Cayenne pepper.

63 Sauce Moelle—Bone Marrow Sauce

This sauce is prepared in the same way as Sauce Bordelaise finishing it with 150–180 g (5–6 oz) poached, small dice of bone marrow and 1 tbs blanched chopped parsley per 1 litre ($1\frac{3}{4}$ pt or $4\frac{1}{2}$ U.S. cups) of sauce. If the sauce is to be served with a vegetable, 75 g ($2\frac{1}{2}$ oz) butter may be added.

64 Sauce Moscovite

Prepare $7\frac{1}{2}$ dl ($1\frac{1}{3}$ pt or $3\frac{1}{4}$ U.S. cups) of ordinary Sauce Poivrade made with venison stock. Finish it at the last minute with 1 dl ($3\frac{1}{2}$ fl oz or $\frac{1}{2}$ U.S. cup) Malaga wine, $\frac{3}{4}$ dl (3 fl oz or $\frac{3}{8}$ U.S. cup) of an infusion of crushed juniper berries, 40 g ($1\frac{1}{2}$ oz) of toasted pine-seed kernels or toasted shredded almonds and 40 g ($1\frac{1}{2}$ oz) currants which have been soaked in warm water till swollen and then drained.

This sauce is specially suitable for serving with joints of venison.

65 Sauce Périgueux

Prepare $7\frac{1}{2}$ dl ($1\frac{1}{3}$ pt or $3\frac{1}{4}$ U.S. cups) fairly thick and well flavoured Demi-glace. Add $1\frac{1}{2}$ dl (5 fl oz or $\frac{5}{8}$ U.S. cup) truffle essence and 100 g ($3\frac{1}{2}$ oz) chopped truffle.

This sauce is suitable for serving with small Entrées, timbales and hot pâtés.

66 Sauce Périgourdine

This sauce is a variation of Sauce Périgueux where the truffles, instead of being chopped are cut in the shape of small olives, small balls or cut into thick slices.

67 Sauce Piquante

Place 3 dl ($\frac{1}{2}$ pt or $1\frac{1}{4}$ U.S. cups) white wine, and the same amount of vinegar in a pan with 50 g (2 oz) chopped shallot; reduce by half; add 6 dl (1 pt or $2\frac{5}{8}$ U.S. cups) Sauce Espagnole, bring to the boil and simmer gently, skimming as necessary for 10 minutes. Remove from the heat and finish the sauce with 2 tbs of a mixture of chopped gherkins, tarragon, chervil and parsley.

This sauce is usually served with grilled, roast or boiled pork. It can also be served with boiled beef and Emincés of butcher's meat.

68 Sauce Poivrade

Heat ½ dl (2 fl oz or ¼ U.S. cup) oil in a pan; add a Mirepoix comprising 100 g (3½ oz) carrots, 80 g (3 oz) onion, a few parsley stalks, a pinch of thyme, and half a crushed bayleaf and cook until lightly coloured. Moisten with 1 dl (3½ fl oz or ½ U.S. cup) vinegar, 2 dl (7 fl oz or ⅞ U.S. cup) of marinade and reduce by two-thirds. Add 1 litre (1¾ pt or 4½ U.S. cups) Sauce Espagnole and allow to simmer gently for 45 minutes. Ten minutes before passing the sauce, add 8 crushed peppercorns; pass through a sieve with a little pressure then add a further 2 dl (7 fl oz or ⅞ U.S. cup) of marinade. Bring to the boil, skim and carefully simmer for approximately 35 minutes so as to reduce the sauce to the required quantity.

Pass again through a fine strainer and finish with 50 g (2 oz) butter.

This sauce is suitable for serving with butcher's meat which has been either marinated or not.

Note: If the pepper is allowed to cook for too long a time in the sauce, its dominating flavour will become detrimental to its taste.

69 Sauce Poivrade (*For Game*)

Heat 1 dl (3½ fl oz of ½ U.S. cup) oil in a pan; add a Mirepoix comprising 125 g (4½ oz) carrot, 125 g (4½ oz) onion, a pinch of thyme, half a crushed bayleaf, a few parsley stalks and 1 kg (2¼ lb) of trimmings of venison; cook until well coloured and drain off the oil. Moisten with 3 dl (½ pt or 1¼ U.S. cups) vinegar, 2 dl (7 fl oz or ⅞ U.S. cup) white wine and reduce completely.

Add 1 litre (1¾ pt or 4½ U.S. cups) Sauce Espagnole, 2 litres (3½ pt or 9 U.S. cups) brown game stock and 1 litre (1¾ pt or 4½ U.S. cups) marinade; cover with a lid and cook slowly in the oven, if possible, for 3½–4 hours. Eight minutes before passing the sauce add 12 crushed peppercorns; pass firmly through a sieve and add 2½ dl (9 fl oz or 1⅛ U.S. cups) brown game stock and 2½ dl (9 fl oz or 1⅛ U.S. cups) marinade. Simmer again gently, skimming as necessary for approximately 40 minutes so as to reduce the sauce to 1 litre (1¾ pt or 4½ U.S. cups). Pass through a fine strainer and finish with 75 g (2½ oz) butter.

Note: Although it is not the practice to butter game sauces, in this case it is advisable to do so but only lightly. The resultant sauce will be less peppery in flavour and will gain in delicacy and smoothness.

70 Sauce au Porto—Port Wine Sauce

This is prepared in the same way as Madeira Sauce replacing the Madeira wine with Port wine.

71 Sauce Portugaise

Heat ½ dl (2 fl oz or ¼ U.S. cup) oil in a pan, add 150 g (5 oz) very finely chopped onion and cook quickly to a golden colour. Add 750 g (1¾ lb) of roughly chopped flesh only of tomato, a touch of crushed garlic, salt, pepper and a pinch of sugar if the tomatoes are acid. Cover the pan with a lid and allow to cook gently. Finish with 1 dl (3½ fl oz or ½ U.S. cup) each of tomato essence and melted meat glaze, 5 dl (18 fl oz or 2¼ U.S. cups) of thin Tomato Sauce and 1 tbs fresh coarsely chopped parsley.

72 Sauce Provençale

Heat 2½ dl (9 fl oz or 1⅛ U.S. cups) oil in a pan until almost smoking hot, add 1½ kg (3 lb 6 oz) roughly chopped flesh only of tomato and season with salt, pepper and a pinch of caster sugar. Add 1 small clove of crushed garlic and 1 tsp chopped parsley; cover with a lid and allow to cook very gently for 30 minutes.

Note: Although there are several recipes for preparing this sauce, the above is an authentic one which is derived from the provincial bourgeois kitchen of Provence and is actually a *Fondue* of tomatoes.

73 Sauce Régence

Place 3 dl (½ pt or 1¼ U.S. cups) Rhine wine in a pan with 150 g (5 oz) of finely cut Mirepoix previously cooked in a little butter and 25 g (1 oz) raw truffle peelings or, if out of season, use 1 dl (3½ fl oz or ½ U.S. cup) truffle essence; reduce by half. Add 8 dl (1⅗ pt or 3½ U.S. cups) Sauce Demi-glace, simmer gently for a few minutes and skim carefully. Pass through a fine strainer.

This sauce is specially suitable for serving with relevés of butcher's meat.

74 Sauce Robert

Heat 75 g (2½ oz) butter in a pan, add 300 g (11 oz) finely chopped onion and cook without colour. Moisten with 4 dl (14 fl oz or 1¾ U.S. cups) white wine and reduce by two-thirds. Add 6 dl (1 pt or 2⅝ U.S. cups) Sauce Demi-glace and simmer gently for 10 minutes.

Pass the sauce through a fine strainer and finish away from the heat with a pinch of sugar and 2 tsp of English mustard diluted with a little water.

This sauce is usually served to accompany grilled pork.

Notes:

1) This sauce must not be boiled once the mustard has been added.
2) It may be passed or not, as required.

75 Sauce Robert Escoffier

This sauce may be obtained commercially under

the brand name of Escoffier. It can be used either hot or cold; if used hot an equal quantity of excellent quality brown veal stock should be added.

It is specially suitable for serving with grilled pork, veal or chicken and grilled fish.

76 Sauce Romaine

Place 50 g (2 oz) sugar in a pan, cook to a golden caramel colour and immediately dissolve it with $1\frac{1}{2}$ dl (5 fl oz or $\frac{5}{8}$ U.S. cup) vinegar. Add 6 dl (1 pt or $2\frac{5}{8}$ U.S. cups) Espagnole and 3 dl ($\frac{1}{2}$ pt or $1\frac{1}{4}$ U.S. cups) game stock. Reduce by a good quarter, pass through a fine strainer and finish the sauce with 20 g ($\frac{2}{3}$ oz) toasted pine-seed kernels, and 20 g ($\frac{2}{3}$ oz) each of sultanas and currants which have been cleaned, soaked in warm water until plump and then drained.

Note: This sauce is specially suitable for serving with venison but it can also be served with joints of marinated butcher's meat, in which case the game stock should be replaced by ordinary brown stock.

77 Sauce Rouennaise

Prepare 8 dl ($1\frac{2}{5}$ pt or $3\frac{1}{2}$ U.S. cups) Sauce Bordelaise taking care to use good quality red wine.

Pass 6 medium-sized raw duck livers through a fine sieve and add this purée to the hot sauce and mix well in. Heat the sauce very carefully so as to cook the liver but do not boil it, as this will have the effect of granulating the purée. Pass through a fine strainer and season well.

The characteristic of this sauce is a reduction of red wine with shallots with the addition of the purée of raw duck livers.

This sauce is the essential accompaniment for roast Rouen duck.

78 Sauce Salmis

Place 75 g ($2\frac{1}{2}$ oz) butter in a pan, add 150 g (5 oz) of finely cut Mirepoix and cook to a light brown colour. Add the skin and chopped carcasses of the game under preparation; moisten with 3 dl ($\frac{1}{2}$ pt or $1\frac{1}{4}$ U.S. cups) white wine and reduce by two-thirds. Add 8 dl ($1\frac{2}{5}$ pt or $3\frac{1}{2}$ U.S. cups) Sauce Demi-glace and allow to simmer gently for 45 minutes then pass firmly through a sieve so as to extract the maximum of flavour from the flavourings and carcasses.

Dilute the cullis obtained with 4 dl (14 fl oz or $1\frac{3}{4}$ U.S. cups) of stock in keeping with the game being prepared; simmer gently and skim carefully for 45 minutes so as to reduce the sauce by a good third.

Bring back the sauce to its correct consistency with the addition of mushroom cooking liquor and truffle essence. Pass through a fine strainer and finish with a little butter.

Notes:

1) The principle used in the making of this sauce, which closely resembles a cullis, should not be altered; it is only the moistening agent which varies according to the type of bird or game under preparation and according to whether the game is considered ordinary or Lenten. If it is required to serve the game as a Lenten dish, the liquid used should be mushroom cooking liquor.
2) The finishing of the sauce with butter using approximately 50 g (2 oz) per 1 litre ($1\frac{3}{4}$ pt or $4\frac{1}{2}$ U.S. cups) of sauce, is optional.

79 Sauce Tortue

Place $2\frac{1}{2}$ dl (9 fl oz or $1\frac{1}{8}$ U.S. cups) veal stock in a pan, bring to the boil and immediately add a small pinch each of sage, basil, sweet marjoram, rosemary and thyme, a pinch of picked parsley, $\frac{1}{2}$ a bayleaf and 25 g (1 oz) mushroom trimmings; cover, allow to infuse for 25 minutes then add 4 crushed peppercorns, allow to infuse for a further 2 minutes and pass through a muslin.

Add sufficient of this infusion to 7 dl ($1\frac{1}{4}$ pt or 3 U.S. cups) Sauce Demi-glace and 3 dl ($\frac{1}{2}$ pt or $1\frac{1}{4}$ U.S. cups) Tomato Sauce so as to obtain a definite flavour of the herbs. Reduce by a good quarter, pass through a fine strainer and finish with 1 dl ($3\frac{1}{2}$ fl oz or $\frac{1}{2}$ U.S. cup) Madeira, a little truffle essence and season fairly well with Cayenne.

Note: Although this highly seasoned sauce calls for the use of Cayenne pepper, care should be taken with the amount used so as not to allow it to become the dominant flavour.

80 Sauce Venaison—Venison Sauce

Prepare $7\frac{1}{2}$ dl ($1\frac{1}{3}$ pt or $3\frac{1}{4}$ U.S. cups) Sauce Poivrade for Game. At the last moment add away from the heat, 100 g ($3\frac{1}{2}$ oz) melted redcurrant jelly mixed with $1\frac{1}{2}$ dl (5 fl oz or $\frac{5}{8}$ U.S. cup) cream.

This sauce is specially suitable for joints of large furred game.

81 Sauce au Vin Rouge—Red Wine Sauce

Heat 50 g (2 oz) butter in a pan, add 125 g ($4\frac{1}{2}$ oz) finely cut Mirepoix and cook to a light brown colour; moisten with 5 dl (18 fl oz or $2\frac{1}{4}$ U.S. cups) good quality red wine and reduce by half. Add 1 clove of crushed garlic and $7\frac{1}{2}$ dl ($1\frac{1}{3}$ pt or $3\frac{1}{4}$ U.S. cups) Espagnole; simmer and skim carefully for 12–15 minutes.

Pass through a fine strainer and finish with 100 g ($3\frac{1}{2}$ oz) butter, 1 tsp anchovy essence and a little Cayenne pepper.

This sauce is specially suitable for serving with fish.

Note: There are two other sauces which can be loosely termed red wine sauces, the first is Sauce Bourguignonne which is basically a reduction of red wine thickened with Beurre Manié. The other is Sauce Matelote which is prepared from red wine after it has been used in the cooking of a fish; in this last case, however, the wine tends to lose its own particular character and is really nothing more than the cooking liquor for the fish and provides flavour for the sauce. These two red wine sauces each have their own special characteristics and should carry their own name which is determined by the methods of preparation. These sauces can be found under their own name in this chapter.

The above recipe is a true red wine sauce.

82 Sauce Zingara

This sauce may be made in either of the following ways:

1) Place $2\frac{1}{2}$ dl (9 fl oz or $1\frac{1}{8}$ U.S. cups) vinegar in a pan with $1\frac{1}{2}$ tbs finely chopped shallot and reduce by half. Moisten with 7 dl ($1\frac{1}{4}$ pt or 3 U.S. cups) brown stock and add 160 g ($5\frac{1}{2}$ oz) breadcrumbs fried in butter; simmer gently for 5–6 minutes and finish with 1 tbs chopped parsley and the juice of half a lemon.
2) Place $1\frac{1}{2}$ dl (5 fl oz or $\frac{5}{8}$ U.S. cup) each of white wine and mushroom cooking liquor in a pan and reduce by two-thirds. Add 4 dl (14 fl oz or $1\frac{3}{4}$ U.S. cups) Sauce Demi-glace, $2\frac{1}{2}$ dl (9 fl oz or $1\frac{1}{8}$ U.S. cups) Tomato Sauce and 1 dl ($3\frac{1}{2}$ fl oz or $\frac{1}{2}$ U.S. cup) white stock; simmer gently and skim carefully for 5–6 minutes. Season with a little Cayenne pepper and finish with a Julienne comprising 70 g ($2\frac{1}{2}$ oz) lean cooked ham and salted ox tongue, 50 g (2 oz) mushrooms and 30 g (1 oz) truffle.

These sauces are specially suitable for serving with entrées of veal and poultry.

Note: Sauce Zingara 1) has no connection with the classical garnish à la Zingara but is derived from English cookery; a number of other similar sauces may be found in this Chapter.

SMALL COMPOUND WHITE SAUCES

83 Sauce Albuféra

To 1 litre ($1\frac{3}{4}$ pt or $4\frac{1}{2}$ U.S. cups) of Sauce Suprême, add 2 dl (7 fl oz or $\frac{7}{8}$ U.S. cup) of melted light meat glaze and 50 g (2 oz) of Pimento Butter.

This sauce is used to accompany poached and braised poultry.

84 Sauce Américaine

This sauce is a constituent part of the preparation of Homard à l'Américaine (2109). As it can also be served as part of a fish dish, e.g. Fillets of Sole Américaine, the flesh of the lobster cooked in its preparation should be cut into small slices and used as a garnish for the fish.

85 Sauce Anchois—Anchovy Sauce

Take 8 dl ($1\frac{2}{5}$ pt or $3\frac{1}{2}$ U.S. cups) unbuttered Sauce Normande and add, away from the heat, 125 g ($4\frac{1}{2}$ oz) of Anchovy Butter. Finish the sauce with 50 g (2 oz) of anchovy fillets which have been well washed, dried well and cut into small dice.

This sauce is specially suitable for serving with fish.

86 Sauce Aurore

Place $7\frac{1}{2}$ dl ($1\frac{1}{3}$ pt or $3\frac{1}{4}$ U.S. cups) Ordinary Velouté in a pan, add $2\frac{1}{2}$ dl (9 fl oz or $1\frac{1}{8}$ U.S. cups) tomato purée and bring to the boil; simmer for a few minutes and finish away from the heat with 100 g ($3\frac{1}{2}$ oz) butter.

This sauce is specially suitable for eggs, white butcher's meat and poultry.

87 Sauce Aurore Maigre

This sauce is prepared in the same way as Sauce Aurore using fish Velouté instead of Ordinary Velouté and finishing with 125 g ($4\frac{1}{2}$ oz) butter per 1 litre ($1\frac{3}{4}$ pt or $4\frac{1}{2}$ U.S. cups) of sauce. This sauce is particularly used for serving with fish.

88 Sauce Bavaroise

Place 5 dl (18 fl oz or $2\frac{1}{4}$ U.S. cups) vinegar in a pan with a little broken thyme and bayleaf, 10 g ($\frac{1}{3}$ oz) chopped parsley stalks, 7 or 8 crushed peppercorns and 10 g ($\frac{1}{3}$ oz) grated horseradish; reduce by half and allow to cool. Add 6 egg yolks to the reduction, and prepare the sauce as for Sauce Hollandaise with 400 g (15 oz) butter and $1\frac{1}{2}$ tbs water added a little at the time during the making of the sauce. Pass through a fine strainer and finish with 100 g ($3\frac{1}{2}$ oz) Crayfish Butter, 2 tbs whipped cream and some diced cooked crayfish tails.

Note: Sauce Bavaroise should have a light fluffy texture and is specially suitable for serving with fish.

89 Sauce Béarnaise

Place 2 dl (7 fl oz or $\frac{7}{8}$ U.S. cup) each of white wine and tarragon vinegar in a small pan with 4 tbs chopped shallots, 20 g ($\frac{2}{3}$ oz) chopped tarragon leaves, 10 g ($\frac{1}{3}$ oz) chopped chervil, 5 g ($\frac{1}{6}$ oz) crushed peppercorns and a pinch of salt. Reduce by two-thirds and allow to cool.

Add 6 egg yolks to the reduction and prepare the sauce over a gentle heat by whisking in 500g (1 lb 2 oz) of ordinary or melted butter. The cohesion and emulsification of the sauce is effected by the progressive cooking of the egg yolks which depends to a great extent on its preparation over a slow heat.

When the butter has been completely incorporated, pass the sauce through a fine strainer; correct the seasoning, add a little Cayenne and finish by mixing in 1 tbs chopped tarragon and ½ tbs chopped chervil.

This sauce is specially suitable for serving with grilled meats.

Note: Sauce Béarnaise which is rather like a Mayonnaise but made with butter, cannot be served very hot as this will result in the sauce separating; it should be served lukewarm.

If the sauce should become too hot and separate, it can be reconstituted by whisking in a few drops of cold water.

90 Sauce Béarnaise Tomatée, also called Sauce Choron

Prepare a Sauce Béarnaise omitting the final addition of chopped tarragon and chervil and keeping it fairly thick. Add up to a quarter of its volume of tomato purée which has been well concentrated or reduced, in order that the addition will not alter the consistency of the sauce.

This sauce is an essential accompaniment for Tournedos à la Choron and is suitable for other grilled meats and poultry.

91 Sauce Béarnaise à la Glace de Viande, also called Sauce Foyot, or Sauce Valois

Prepare a Sauce Béarnaise keeping it fairly thick and finish with 1 dl (3½ fl oz or ½ U.S. cup) of melted meat glaze added a little at a time.

This sauce is specially suitable for serving with grills of butcher's meat.

92 Sauce Bercy

Heat 50 g (2 oz) butter in a pan, add 2 tbs finely chopped shallot and cook without colour. Moisten with 2½ dl (9 fl oz or 1⅛ U.S. cups) white wine and 2½ dl (9 fl oz or 1⅛ U.S. cups) of either fish stock or cooking liquor from the fish under preparation. Reduce by one-third and add 7½ dl (1⅓ pt or 3¼ U.S. cups) fish Velouté, bring to the boil and simmer for a few minutes; remove from the heat and finish with 100 g (3½ oz) butter and 1 tbs chopped parsley.

This sauce is specially suitable for serving with fish.

93 Sauce au Beurre, also called Sauce Batârde—Butter Sauce

Mix together 45 g (1½ oz) flour and 45 g (1½ oz) melted butter in a pan; moisten with 7½ dl (1⅓ pt or 3¼ U.S. cups) boiling water whisking thoroughly, then add 7 g (¼ oz) salt. Mix in a liaison consisting of 5 egg yolks; ½ dl (2 fl oz or ¼ U.S. cup) cream and a squeeze of lemon juice; reheat to thicken, pass through a fine strainer and finish away from the heat with 300 g (11 oz) very good butter.

This sauce is suitable for serving with asparagus and poached or boiled fish.

Note: It is advisable to keep this sauce in a Bain-marie after it has been thickened, and also to add the butter at the last moment.

94 Sauce Bonnefoy or Sauce Bordelaise au Vin Blanc—White Bordelaise Sauce

This sauce is prepared in the same way and with the same proportions as Sauce Bordelaise (28) using white wine—a Graves or Sauternes for preference—instead of red wine, and Ordinary Velouté instead of Espagnole. Finish the sauce with a little chopped tarragon.

This sauce is suitable for serving with grilled fish and grilled white meats.

95 Sauce Bretonne

Heat 50 g (2 oz) butter in a pan, add a fine Julienne comprised of 30 g (1 oz) each of white of leek, white of celery, onion and mushrooms; stew carefully without colouring. Add 7½ dl (1⅓ pt or 3¼ U.S. cups) fish Velouté and simmer gently together for a few minutes; skim and finish with ¾ dl (3 fl oz or ⅜ U.S. cup) cream and 50 g (2 oz) butter.

This sauce is mainly suitable for serving with fish.

96 Sauce Canotière

Reduce by two-thirds the cooking liquor obtained from the cooking of a freshwater fish in a white wine Court-bouillon which should be strongly flavoured and very lightly salted. Thicken with 80 g (2½ oz) Beurre Manié per 1 litre (1¾ pt or 4½ U.S. cups) of reduction; bring to the boil and simmer for a few minutes then remove from the heat, pass through a fine strainer and finish with 150 g (5 oz) butter and a very small pinch of Cayenne.

This sauce is served as an accompaniment with boiled or poached freshwater fish.

Note: With the addition of small glazed onions and button mushrooms this sauce can be used instead of Sauce Matelote Blanche.

97 Sauce aux Câpres—Caper Sauce

This is Butter Sauce with the addition of 120 g (4 oz) capers per 1 litre (1¾ pt or 4½ U.S. cups) sauce, added at the last moment.

This sauce is suitable for serving with all kinds of boiled fish.

98 Sauce Cardinal
Place $\frac{3}{4}$ dl (3 fl oz or $\frac{3}{8}$ U.S. cup) each of fish stock and truffle essence in a pan and reduce by a quarter. Add this reduction to $7\frac{1}{2}$ dl ($1\frac{1}{3}$ pt or $3\frac{1}{4}$ U.S. cups) Sauce Béchamel together with $1\frac{1}{2}$ dl (5 fl oz or $\frac{5}{8}$ U.S. cup) cream; bring to the boil, allow to simmer for a few moments and pass through a fine strainer. Finish, away from the heat, with 100 g ($3\frac{1}{2}$ oz) very red Lobster Butter and a pinch of Cayenne.

This sauce is suitable for serving with fish.

99 Sauce aux Champignons—White Mushroom Sauce
Place 3 dl ($\frac{1}{2}$ pt or $1\frac{1}{4}$ U.S. cups) mushroom cooking liquor in a pan and reduce by two-thirds; add $7\frac{1}{2}$ dl ($1\frac{1}{3}$ pt or $3\frac{1}{4}$ U.S. cups) Sauce Allemande and allow to simmer gently for a few minutes. Cook 250 g (9 oz) turned button mushrooms keeping them very white and add to the finished sauce.

This sauce is suitable for serving with poultry; it can also be served with fish, in which case fish Velouté which has been thickened with a liaison of yolks and cream should be used instead of Sauce Allemande.

100 Sauce Chantilly
The sauce frequently called Sauce Chantilly is none other than the one indicated under the name of Sauce Mousseline (132).

101 Sauce Chateaubriand
Place 8 dl ($1\frac{2}{5}$ pt or $3\frac{1}{2}$ U.S. cups) white wine in a pan; add 40 g ($1\frac{1}{2}$ oz) chopped shallot, a pinch of thyme, a small piece of bayleaf and 80 g (3 oz) mushroom trimmings; reduce by two-thirds.

Add 8 dl ($1\frac{2}{5}$ pt or $3\frac{1}{2}$ U.S. cups) brown veal stock and reduce again by half. Pass through a fine strainer and finish away from the heat with 250 g (9 oz) Maître d'Hôtel Butter and $\frac{1}{2}$ tbs chopped tarragon.

This sauce is specially suitable for grilled red butcher's meat.

102 White Chaud-froid Sauce
Place $7\frac{1}{2}$ dl ($1\frac{1}{3}$ pt or $3\frac{1}{4}$ U.S. cups) Ordinary Velouté in a shallow pan and reduce rapidly, stirring continuously with a spatula, whilst adding 6–7 dl (1–$1\frac{1}{4}$ pt or $2\frac{5}{8}$–3 U.S. cups) chicken aspic jelly and 1 dl ($3\frac{1}{2}$ fl oz or $\frac{1}{2}$ U.S. cup) cream, a little at a time. Reduce these ingredients by approximately a third to yield 1 litre ($1\frac{3}{4}$ pt or $4\frac{1}{2}$ U.S. cups); correct the seasoning, pass through a fine strainer and finish with 2 dl (7 fl oz or $\frac{7}{8}$ U.S. cup) cream. Stir continuously until it becomes cool and reaches coating consistency.

103 Blond Chaud-froid Sauce
This is prepared in the same way as White Chaud-froid Sauce using Sauce Allemande instead of Ordinary Velouté and a little less cream to finish the sauce.

104 Pink Chaud-froid Sauce
This is prepared in the same way as White Chaud-froid Sauce with the addition whilst reducing the sauce of $1\frac{1}{2}$ dl (5 fl oz or $\frac{5}{8}$ U.S. cup) very red tomato purée passed through a muslin, and a pinch of paprika infused in a very little quantity of Bouillon.

This sauce is used in the preparation of special poultry dishes.

Note: If a very light shade of pink is required, omit the tomato purée and colour with the infusion of paprika to the required shade.

105 Green Chaud-froid Sauce
Place 2 dl (7 fl oz or $\frac{7}{8}$ U.S. cup) white wine in a pan, bring to the boil and add a pinch each of chervil, tarragon, chopped chives and parsley; cover and allow to infuse, away from the heat, for 10 minutes then strain the infusion through a clean cloth.

Prepare a White Chaud-froid Sauce and add the infusion a little at a time during the reduction, the yield of which should be 1 litre ($1\frac{3}{4}$ pt or $4\frac{1}{2}$ U.S. cups). Finish the sauce with a little natural green colour prepared from spinach so as to give a pale green colour to the sauce, adding it a little at a time until the required tint is obtained.

This sauce is used in the preparation of Chaud-froids of Poultry in particular when designated Chaud-froids Printaniers.

106 Fish Chaud-froid Sauce
This sauce is prepared in the same way as White Chaud-froid Sauce with the following differences:

a) Replace the Ordinary Velouté with fish Velouté, and
b) Replace the Chicken Aspic Jelly with White Fish Aspic Jelly.

Note: The use of this sauce is preferable to jellied Mayonnaise for use in the glazing of fillets and medallions of fish and shellfish. Jellied Mayonnaise has one pronounced disadvantage inasmuch as the oil in the Mayonnaise is inclined to ooze out from the surface of the sauce due to the contraction of the gelatine; the noticeably clear flavour of Fish Chaud-froid Sauce is preferable to that of jellied Mayonnaise.

107 Sauce Chivry
Place 1½ dl (5 fl oz or ⅝ U.S. cup) white wine in a pan, bring to the boil and add a pinch each of chervil, parsley, tarragon, chopped shallot, chopped chives and fresh young salad burnet; cover and allow to infuse away from the heat for 10 minutes then squeeze the infusion through a clean cloth.

Add this to 7½ dl (1⅓ pt or 3¼ U.S. cups) boiling Ordinary Velouté and finish away from the heat with 100 g (3½ oz) of Beurre à la Chivry (228).

This sauce is specially suitable for poached and boiled poultry.

Note: It is essential that the salad burnet used in this sauce should be very young as this is a herb which becomes bitter as it matures.

108 Sauce Choron
See Sauce Béarnaise tomatée.

109 Sauce à la Crème—Cream Sauce
Place 1 litre (1¾ pt or 4½ U.S. cups) Sauce Béchamel in a pan and add 2 dl (7 fl oz or ⅞ U.S. cup) cream. Bring to the boil and reduce to 7½ dl (1⅓ pt or 3¼ U.S. cups) stirring continuously with a spatula. Pass through a fine strainer and adjust the consistency of the sauce by adding little by little, 1½ dl (5 fl oz or ⅝ U.S. cup) very fresh double cream and the juice of half a lemon.

This sauce is suitable for serving with boiled and poached fish, poultry, vegetables and eggs.

110 Sauce aux Crevettes—Shrimp Sauce
Place 1 litre (1¾ pt or 4½ U.S. cups) fish Velouté or Sauce Béchamel in a pan; add 1½ dl (5 fl oz or ⅝ U.S. cup) cream and 1½ dl (5 fl oz or ⅝ U.S. cup) of fish stock; bring to the boil and reduce to approximately 9 dl (1⅗ pt or 4 U.S. cups) stirring continuously with a spatula. Remove from the heat and add 100 g (3½ oz) Shrimp Butter and 25 g (1 oz) Red Colouring Butter so as to give the sauce the appropriate pale pink colour. Finish with the addition of 3 tbs shelled cooked shrimps and season lightly with Cayenne.

This sauce is specially suitable for serving with fish and certain egg dishes.

111 Sauce Currie—Curry Sauce
Heat 75 g (2½ oz) butter in a pan; add 250 g (9 oz) onions, 100 g (3½ oz) celery and 30 g (1 oz) parsley stalks, all roughly sliced, and cook to a light colour. Add a sprig of thyme, ½ a bayleaf and a little mace; sprinkle with 50 g (2 oz) flour and 1 tsp curry powder and cook for a few minutes without colour. Then moisten with 7½ dl (1⅓ pt or 3¼ U.S. cups) white Bouillon, bring to the boil and simmer gently for 45 minutes then pass firmly through a fine strainer; reheat the sauce, skim off the fat and keep the sauce in a Bain-Marie.

This sauce is suitable for serving with fish, shellfish, poultry and various egg dishes.

Note: A quarter of the volume of Bouillon may be replaced with coconut milk.

112 Sauce Currie à l'Indienne—Curry Sauce (*Indian Style*)
Heat 30 g (1 oz) butter in a pan; add 125 g (4½ oz) finely sliced onion, a Bouquet garni comprising parsley stalks, thyme, ½ a bayleaf and a small piece each of mace and cinnamon; cook gently together without colour.

Sprinkle with 1 tsp curry powder and moisten with 5 dl (18 fl oz or 2¼ U.S. cups) each of coconut milk and veal or fish Velouté according to whether the sauce is to accompany meat or fish and allow to simmer gently for 15 minutes. Pass through a fine strainer and finish with 1 dl (3½ fl oz or ½ U.S. cup) cream and a few drops of lemon juice.

Note:
1) The quantity of coconut milk indicated in this recipe can be obtained by soaking 700 g (1½ lb) grated fresh coconut in 4½ dl (16 fl oz or 2 U.S. cups) lukewarm milk, which should then be strained by squeezing firmly through a cloth. If coconut is unobtainable, the same quantity of almond milk may be used instead.
2) In India, there are innumerable variations of this sauce but the basis of its preparation always remains the same. It may be of interest to note that the authentic type of Indian curry is not suitable for European tastes, but the flavour of the above sauce is generally acceptable.

113 Sauce Diplomate
Add 75 g (2½ oz) Lobster Butter to 1 litre (1¾ pt or 4½ U.S. cups) finished Sauce Normande and garnish the sauce with 2 tbs small dice of cooked lobster and 1 tbs small dice of truffle.

This sauce is specially suitable for serving with whole large fish.

114 Sauce Ecossaise
Prepare a Brunoise of 30 g (1 oz) each of carrot, celery, onion and French beans. Heat 30 g (1 oz) butter in a pan, add the Brunoise and a little white Bouillon and stew together gently until almost dry. Add this cooked Brunoise to 9 dl (1⅗ pt or 4 U.S. cups) Sauce à la Crème.

This sauce is suitable for serving with eggs and poultry.

115 Sauce Estragon—Tarragon Sauce
Blanch quickly 30 g (1 oz) roughly chopped tarragon leaves and drain well. Place in a basin and crush with a spoon mixing in 4 tbs of the Velouté being used. Pass through a fine sieve and mix the purée obtained into 1 litre (1¾ pt or 4½ U.S. cups) of the appropriate Velouté, either fish or chicken according to the dish the sauce is to be served with. Correct the seasoning and finish the sauce with ½ tbs chopped tarragon.

This sauce is suitable for serving with eggs, chicken and fish.

116 Sauce aux Fines Herbes
Add 80 g (3 oz) Shallot Butter and 1½ tbs of mixed chopped parsley, tarragon and chervil to 1 litre (1¾ pt or 4½ U.S. cups) White Wine Sauce prepared according to any of the methods indicated under that title.

This sauce is most suitable for serving with fish.

117 Sauce Foyot
See Sauce Béarnaise à la Glace de Viande.

118 Sauce Groseilles—Gooseberry Sauce
Blanch 500 g (1 lb 2 oz) very green gooseberries in a copper bowl allowing them to boil for 5 minutes and then drain them well. Place in a pan with 3 tbs caster sugar and ¾ dl (3 fl oz or ⅜ U.S. cup) white wine and complete their cooking.

Pass through a fine sieve, add the purée obtained to 5 dl (18 fl oz or 2¼ U.S. cups) Sauce au Beurre and mix well together.

This sauce is served principally with grilled and boiled mackerel à l'Anglaise but may be used with other fish.

Note: This sauce can also be prepared using very green white currants.

119 Sauce Hollandaise
Place 4 tbs water and 2 tbs vinegar in a pan with a pinch each of coarsely ground pepper and salt. Reduce it by two-thirds and remove the pan to the side of the stove or place it in a Bain-marie.

Add 1 tbs water and 5 yolks of egg to the reduction and whisk continuously over gentle heat whilst gradually adding 500 g (1 lb 2 oz) soft or melted butter, ensuring the cohesion and emulsification of the sauce by the progressive cooking of the yolks. Add a few drops of water occasionally and as necessary during the mixing of the sauce so as to ensure its lightness.

Correct the seasoning with salt if necessary and add a few drops of lemon juice. Pass through a fine strainer and keep at a lukewarm temperature so as to prevent the sauce from separating.

This sauce is specially suitable for serving with fish and vegetables.

Note: It is advisable to increase the amount of water in the reduction if there is any doubt about the quality of the vinegar but it is essential that a reduction is made; the required amount of acidity can be obtained by the addition of more lemon juice.

120 Sauce Homard—Lobster Sauce
To 7½ dl (1⅓ pt or 3¼ U.S. cups) fish Velouté add 1½ dl (5 fl oz or ⅝ U.S. cup) cream, 80 g (3 oz) Lobster Butter and 40 g (1½ oz) Red Colouring Butter.

This sauce is most suitable for serving with fish.

Note: If used to accompany whole fish, 3 tbs diced cooked lobster should be added to the sauce.

121 Sauce Hongroise
Melt 50 g (2 oz) butter in a pan; add 120 g (4½ oz) chopped onion and cook without colouring; season with a pinch of salt and 1 tsp paprika. Add 1 litre (1¾ pt or 4¼ U.S. cups) fish or Ordinary Velouté according to the dish it is to accompany, and allow to simmer gently for a few minutes. Pass through a fine strainer and finish the sauce with 100 g (3½ oz) butter.

This sauce is an excellent accompaniment for Noisettes of lamb and veal, eggs, poultry and fish.

Note: This sauce should be of a delicate pink colour which should be obtained only from the paprika.

122 Sauce aux Huîtres—Oyster Sauce
This is Sauce Normande with the addition of poached and bearded oysters.

This sauce is specially suitable for serving with poached and boiled fish.

123 Sauce Indienne
This is the same as Sauce Currie à l'Indienne.

124 Sauce Ivoire
To 1 litre (1¾ pt or 4½ U.S. cups) Sauce Suprême add 3 tbs melted light coloured meat glaze just sufficient to give the required ivory tint to the sauce.

This sauce is most suitable for serving with poached poultry.

125 Sauce Joinville
Prepare 1 litre (1¾ pt or 4½ U.S. cups) Sauce Normande finishing it with 60 g (2 oz) each of Crayfish Butter and Shrimp Butter instead of the cream and butter.

This sauce should not contain any garnish if it is to be served with a garnished fish dish. If it is to be served with an ungarnished large boiled fish, 2 tbs Julienne of very black truffle should be added to it.

Note: It is the completion of the sauce with Crayfish Butter and Shrimp Butter which differentiates this sauce from other similar sauces.

126 Sauce Laguipierre
To 1 litre (1¾ pt or 4½ U.S. cups) Butter Sauce add the juice of 1 lemon and 4 tbs fish glaze, or its equivalent of reduced fish stock.

This sauce is used to accompany boiled fish.

Note: This sauce which was originated and named Sauce au Beurre à la Laguipierre, by Carême, has been modified in the above recipe only by the use of fish glaze instead of chicken glaze.

127 Sauce Livonienne
Prepare 100 g (3½ oz) fine Julienne comprised of carrots, celery, mushrooms and onion and stew together with 60 g (2 oz) butter; add it to 1 litre (1¾ pt or 4¼ U.S. cups) fish Velouté and finish with 25 g (1 oz) Julienne of truffle and a little coarsely chopped parsley. Correct the seasoning as necessary.

This sauce is suitable for serving with fish such as trout, salmon, sole, turbot and brill.

128 Sauce Maltaise
Prepare 5 dl (18 fl oz or 2¼ U.S. cups) Sauce Hollandaise and at the last moment add the juice of 2 blood oranges which is essential and a good pinch of grated zest of the same oranges.

This sauce is a suitable accompaniment for asparagus.

129 Sauce Marinière
Prepare 1 litre (1¾ pt or 4½ U.S. cups) Sauce Bercy (92), add 1 dl (3½ fl oz or ½ U.S. cup) reduced mussel cooking liquor and thicken with 6 egg yolks.

This sauce is particularly suitable for serving with mussels.

130 Sauce Matelote Blanche
Place 3 dl (½ pt or 1¼ U.S. cups) White Wine Court-bouillon used in the cooking of the fish under preparation, and 25 g (1 oz) fresh mushroom trimmings into a pan and reduce by two-thirds.

Add 8 dl (1⅖ pt or 3½ U.S. cups) fish Velouté and allow to simmer for a few minutes; pass through a fine strainer and finish with 150 g (5 oz) butter and a little Cayenne. Add 20 button onions glazed in butter and 20 very white cooked button mushrooms.

131 Sauce Mornay—Mornay Sauce
To 1 litre (1¾ pt or 4½ U.S. cups) Sauce Béchamel add 2 dl (7 fl oz or ⅞ U.S. cup) of the cooking liquor from the fish with which the sauce is to be served. Reduce by a good third and add 50 g (2 oz) each of grated Gruyère cheese and grated Parmesan; reheat for a few seconds, mix well to ensure that the cheese is melted and finish with 100 g (3½ oz) butter.

Note: When Mornay Sauce is required for dishes other than for fish, the preparation is the same as in this recipe except that the fish cooking liquor is replaced by cooking liquor from the dish under preparation or milk as the case may be.

132 Sauce Mousseline, also called Sauce Chantilly
Prepare Sauce Hollandaise in accordance with the recipe and at the last moment carefully mix in 4 tbs stiffly whipped cream.

This sauce is suitable as an accompaniment for boiled fish and vegetables such as asparagus, cardoons and celery etc.

133 Sauce Mousseuse
Scald a small pan by immersing it in boiling water and wipe it clean and dry. Place 500 g (1 lb 2 oz) well softened butter and 8 g (¼ oz) salt in the pan and whisk whilst adding the juice of a quarter of a lemon and 4 dl (14 fl oz or 1¾ U.S. cups) cold water, a little at a time. At the last moment mix in 4 tbs well whipped cream.

This preparation although classified as a sauce, is more a compound butter for serving with boiled fish. The heat of the fish is then sufficient to melt this sauce and its appearance and flavour are infinitely better than that of ordinary melted butter.

134 Sauce Moutarde—Mustard Sauce
To the required amount of Butter Sauce add, away from the heat, 1 tbs made English mustard per 2½ dl (9 fl oz or 1⅛ U.S. cups) of sauce.

This sauce should normally be prepared to order; if not being served immediately it should be kept in the Bain-marie making sure that it does not boil.

135 Sauce Nantua
Add 2 dl (7 fl oz or ⅞ U.S. cup) cream to 1 litre (1¾ pt or 4½ U.S. cups) Sauce Béchamel and reduce by one-third. Pass through a fine strainer and add 1½ dl (5 fl oz or ⅝ U.S. cup) cream to bring the sauce back to its normal consistency. Finish it with 125 g (4½ oz) very fine Crayfish Butter and the addition of 20 small cooked crayfish tails.

136 Sauce Newburg—Newburg Sauce (*using raw lobster*)

Take a raw lobster weighing 800–900 g ($1\frac{3}{4}$ lb–2 lb) and cut into pieces as described for Homard Américaine A; remove the creamy parts and pound them together with 30 g (1 oz) butter and place aside.

Heat 40 g ($1\frac{1}{2}$ oz) butter and $\frac{3}{4}$ dl (3 fl oz or $\frac{3}{8}$ U.S. cup) oil in a shallow pan, add the pieces of lobster, season with salt and Cayenne and fry on all sides until they turn very red. Drain off all the fat, add 2 tbs brandy and flame; add 2 dl (7 fl oz or $\frac{7}{8}$ U.S. cup) Marsala or old Madeira and reduce by two-thirds. Moisten with 2 dl (7 fl oz or $\frac{7}{8}$ U.S. cup) cream and 2 dl (7 fl oz or $\frac{7}{8}$ U.S. cup) fish stock and allow to simmer gently for 25 minutes.

Drain the liquor through a sieve, remove the flesh from the pieces of lobster and cut it into small dice. Finish the sauce by mixing the reserved creamy paste into the cooking liquid and boil gently to ensure that the creamy parts are cooked; add the diced lobster and correct the seasoning if necessary.

Note: The addition of the lobster flesh to the sauce is optional; alternatively, the flesh may be cut into neat slices and arranged on the fish for which the sauce has been prepared.

137 Sauce Newburg—Newburg Sauce (*with cooked lobster*)

Cook the lobster in Shellfish Court-bouillon (1551), remove the flesh from the tail, cut it into neat slices and arrange in a well-buttered shallow pan. Season well with salt and Cayenne and heat through on both sides so as to develop the red colour of the skin. Barely cover the lobster with Madeira and allow it to reduce almost completely. Just before serving, add a thickening of 2 dl (7 fl oz or $\frac{7}{8}$ U.S. cup) cream and 3 egg yolks; shake the pan gently away from the direct heat until the sauce thickens without it boiling.

Note: Originally the above two sauces were made in the same way as Sauce Américaine, the sauce and the lobster constituting a single preparation. In both of these two forms, the lobster is better if served for lunch because people with delicate stomachs find difficulty in digesting it at an evening meal.

To overcome this difficulty it is advisable to adopt the method of serving the lobster sauce with fillets or Mousselines of sole, using the flesh of the lobster as a garnish only. This innovation has met with public approval.

By using certain condiments such as curry powder or paprika, excellent variations of this sauce may be obtained which are particularly suitable for serving with sole and other white fish. In this case it is a good practice to serve plain boiled rice (riz à l'Indienne) as a garnish.

138 Sauce Noisette

Prepare Sauce Hollandaise in accordance with the proportions given in that recipe and finish it at the last minute with 75 g ($2\frac{1}{2}$ oz) Hazelnut Butter (Beurre de Noisette) (248), made with very good quality butter.

This sauce is specially suitable for serving with poached salmon and trout.

139 Sauce Normande

To $7\frac{1}{2}$ dl ($1\frac{1}{3}$ pt or $3\frac{1}{4}$ U.S. cups) fish Velouté add 1 dl ($3\frac{1}{2}$ fl oz or $\frac{1}{2}$ U.S. cup) each of mushroom cooking liquor and cooking liquor from mussels, 2 dl (7 fl oz or $\frac{7}{8}$ U.S. cup) fish stock made from sole bones, a few drops of lemon juice and a thickening of 5 egg yolks mixed with 2 dl (7 fl oz or $\frac{7}{8}$ U.S. cup) cream. Reduce it quickly by one-third over an open fire, using a metal spatula, to give approximately 8 dl ($1\frac{2}{5}$ pt or $3\frac{1}{2}$ U.S. cups) of sauce. Pass through a fine strainer and finish with 1 dl ($3\frac{1}{2}$ fl oz or $\frac{1}{2}$ U.S. cup) double cream and 125 g ($4\frac{1}{2}$ oz) butter.

This sauce is special for serving with Sole Normande but also has a wide range of applications as a basis for other fish sauces.

Note: Contrary to general usage it is advisable not to include cooking liquor from oysters in those preparations which appear to call for it, as this is simply a salty liquid devoid of almost all flavour. It is preferable to use cooking liquor from mussels where this is possible.

140 Sauce Orientale

Take 5 dl (18 fl oz or $2\frac{1}{4}$ U.S. cups) Sauce Américaine, flavour it with curry powder and reduce by two-thirds. After this add $1\frac{1}{2}$ dl (5 fl oz or $\frac{5}{8}$ U.S. cup) cream, away from the heat.

This sauce has the same uses as Sauce Américaine.

141 Sauce Paloise

Prepare Sauce Béarnaise in accordance with the proportions and method given in the recipe but with the following differences: 1) replace the principal flavouring of tarragon with the same quanity of mint in the reduction of white wine and vinegar, and 2) replace the chopped tarragon with chopped mint at the final stage.

This sauce has the same uses as Sauce Béarnaise.

142 Sauce Poulette

Place 2 dl (7 fl oz or $\frac{7}{8}$ U.S. cup) mushroom cooking liquor in a pan and reduce by two-thirds; add 1 litre ($1\frac{3}{4}$ pt or $4\frac{1}{2}$ U.S. cups) Sauce Allemande and allow to simmer for a few minutes. Finish, away from the heat, with a little lemon juice, 60 g (2 oz) butter and 1 tbs chopped parsley.

This sauce is suitable for serving with certain vegetables but is eminently suitable for serving with sheep's trotters.

143 Sauce Ravigote

Place $1\frac{1}{2}$ dl (5 fl oz or $\frac{5}{8}$ U.S. cup) each of white wine and vinegar in a pan and reduce by half; add 8 dl ($1\frac{2}{5}$ pt or $3\frac{1}{2}$ U.S. cups) Ordinary Velouté and allow to simmer for a few minutes. Finish the sauce away from the heat with 100 g ($3\frac{1}{2}$ oz) Shallot Butter and $\frac{1}{2}$ tbs each of chopped chervil, tarragon and chives.

This sauce is a suitable accompaniment for boiled or poached poultry and for serving with certain white offals such as calf's head.

144 Sauce Régence *(for fish and fish garnishes)*

Place 2 dl (7 fl oz or $\frac{7}{8}$ U.S. cup) each of Rhine wine and fish stock, and 20 g ($\frac{2}{3}$ oz) each of fresh mushroom trimmings and raw truffle trimmings in a pan and reduce by half. Strain this reduction through a clean cloth, add it to 8 dl ($1\frac{2}{5}$ pt or $3\frac{1}{2}$ U.S. cups) Sauce Normande and finish with 1 tbs truffle essence.

145 Sauce Régence *(for poultry garnishes)*

Place 2 dl (7 fl oz or $\frac{7}{8}$ U.S. cup) each of Rhine wine and mushroom cooking liquor in a pan with 40 g ($1\frac{1}{2}$ oz) raw truffle trimmings and reduce by half. Strain the reduction through a clean cloth, add it to 8 dl ($1\frac{2}{5}$ pt or $3\frac{1}{2}$ U.S. cups) Sauce Allemande and finish with $\frac{1}{4}$ dl (1 fl oz or $\frac{1}{8}$ U.S. cup) truffle essence.

146 Sauce Riche

Prepare a Sauce Diplomate in accordance with the proportions and method given in the recipe and finish it with 1 dl ($3\frac{1}{2}$ fl oz or $\frac{1}{2}$ U.S. cup) truffle essence and 80 g (3 oz) very black truffles cut into small dice.

This sauce is suitable for serving with large whole poached fish.

147 Sauce Rubens

Heat 50 g (2 oz) butter in a pan; add 100 g ($3\frac{1}{2}$ oz) ordinary Mirepoix cut into Brunoise and cook until lightly coloured. Moisten with 2 dl (7 fl oz or $\frac{7}{8}$ U.S. cup) white wine and 3 dl ($\frac{1}{2}$ pt or $1\frac{1}{4}$ U.S. cups) fish stock and allow to cook gently for 25 minutes.

Pass through a fine strainer, allow to stand for a few minutes and remove the fat. Reduce it to $\frac{1}{2}$ dl (2 fl oz or $\frac{1}{4}$ U.S. cup), add 1 tbs Madeira and thicken this reduction with 2 egg yolks; finish with 100 g ($3\frac{1}{2}$ oz) butter, 30 g (1 oz) Beurre Rouge and a few drops of anchovy essence.

This sauce is specially suitable for serving with boiled or poached fish.

148 Sauce Saint-Malo

Prepare 1 litre ($1\frac{3}{4}$ pt or $4\frac{1}{2}$ U.S. cups) Sauce Vin Blanc in accordance with any of the methods indicated under that recipe, and add 1 tbs finely chopped shallot cooked and reduced down in a little white wine, or preferably, 50 g (2 oz) Shallot Butter. Add also $\frac{1}{2}$ tbs made mustard and a few drops of anchovy essence.

This sauce is specially suitable for serving with grilled salt water fish.

149 Sauce Smitane

Heat 50 g (2 oz) butter in a pan, add 125 g ($4\frac{1}{2}$ oz) finely chopped onion and cook until lightly coloured. Moisten with 2 dl (7 fl oz or $\frac{7}{8}$ U.S. cup) white wine and reduce until almost completely evaporated; add 5 dl (18 fl oz or $2\frac{1}{4}$ U.S. cups) sour cream and simmer gently for 5 minutes; pass through a fine strainer and add a few drops of lemon juice to enhance the sour taste.

This sauce is suitable for serving with sautés of game and for game cooked *en Casserole.*

150 Sauce Solferino

Squeeze the liquid firmly from 1 kg ($2\frac{1}{4}$ lb) very ripe tomatoes, then pass through a clean cloth. Reduce the resultant liquid to a thick syrupy consistency and add 100 g ($3\frac{1}{2}$ oz) melted meat glaze, a touch of Cayenne and the juice of half a lemon. Work this into a sauce, away from the heat, by whisking in 100 g ($3\frac{1}{2}$ oz) Maître d'Hôtel Butter to which has been added a little chopped tarragon and 100 g ($3\frac{1}{2}$ oz) Shallot Butter.

This sauce is an excellent accompaniment for all grilled meats.

Note: As is well known, the plains of Lombardy which so often resounded to the noise of battle, was the birthplace of many culinary innovations and this sauce can be included among them. It was served at a lunch given for the general staff of the French Sardinian forces in the village of Capriana where the battle of Solferino reached its peak of ferocity and carnage. The recipe was probably brought back by an army chef and consequently accepted into the current repertoire; it is wrong to call it Sauce Saint-Cloud as nothing in its preparation or ingredients justifies the use of this name.

151 Sauce Soubise, or Coulis d'Oignons Soubise

This sauce may be prepared by either of the following recipes:

1) Slice 500 g (1 lb 2 oz) onions and blanch them well; drain thoroughly and stew in 50 g (2 oz) butter without colouring. Add 5 dl (18 fl oz or $2\frac{1}{4}$ U.S. cups) thick Sauce Béchamel, a pinch of salt, a little white pepper and a good pinch of caster sugar; cover, place in the oven and allow to cook gently.

Pass through a fine sieve, reheat and finish the sauce with 80 g (3 oz) butter and 1 dl (3½ oz or ½ U.S. cup) cream.

2) Slice 500 g (1 lb 2 oz) onions and blanch them well; drain thoroughly and place them immediately in a suitably-sized pan previously lined completely with thin slices of salt pork fat; add 120 g (4 oz) carolina rice, 7 dl (1¼ pt or 3 U.S. cups) white Bouillon, a pinch of salt, a little white pepper, a good pinch of caster sugar and 25 g (1 oz) butter. Cover with a lid, bring to the boil and allow to cook gently in the oven. When cooked, pound the rice and onions in the mortar then pass through a sieve; reheat and finish with 80 g (3 oz) butter and 1 dl (3½ fl oz or ½ U.S. cup) cream.

Note: Soubise is more of a cullis than a sauce and it should be very white in colour.

When prepared with Béchamel it is much smoother than the same sauce prepared with rice but a much thicker consistency can be obtained by using rice.

The use of either method is determined by the kind of preparation for which it is required.

152 Sauce Soubise Tomatée—Tomato-flavoured Soubise Sauce

Prepare Sauce Soubise in accordance with either of the two preceding methods and add one-third its volume of very smooth and red tomato purée.

153 Sauce Souchet

Prepare 150 g (5 oz) Julienne of mixed carrot, celery and parsley root, place in a pan with 30 g (1 oz) butter and stew it without colour. Moisten with 7½ dl (1⅓ pt or 3¼ U.S. cups) fish stock and 2 dl (7 fl oz or ⅞ U.S. cup) white wine. Finish cooking the vegetables gently and pass the liquid through a strainer reserving the Julienne. Cut the fish into pieces, moisten with the cooking liquor from the vegetables and poach. Remove the fish from the liquid, strain the cooking liquor and reduce it by three-quarters to approximately 2½ dl (9 fl oz or 1⅛ U.S. cups). Add sufficient White Wine Sauce to give the right consistency or, if necessary, thicken with a little Beurre Manié and finish by lightly buttering the sauce; add the Julienne of vegetables and use it to coat the pieces of fish.

Note: This sauce is derived from the Dutch and Flemish Waterzoïs; it was adopted by the English kitchen and slightly modified to its present method which is in accordance with modern culinary practice.

154 Sauce Tyrolienne

Prepare a reduction of white wine, vinegar and flavourings exactly in the same way as for Sauce Béarnaise; squeeze through a cloth, twisting firmly and add 100 g (3½ oz) very red, well reduced tomato purée and 6 yolks of egg. Whisk over a gentle heat and add 5 dl (18 fl oz or 2¼ U.S. cups) oil in the same way as when making Mayonnaise. Correct the seasoning and at the last minute finish with a little Cayenne.

This sauce is suitable for serving with grilled meats and fish.

155 Sauce Tyrolienne à l'Ancienne

Heat 50 g (2 oz) butter in a pan, add 250 g (9 oz) finely shredded onions and cook until lightly coloured. Add 250 g (9 oz) roughly chopped flesh only of tomato and 5 dl (18 fl oz or 2¼ U.S. cups) Sauce Poivrade and cook gently for 7–8 minutes.

156 Sauce Valois

This is Sauce Béarnaise finished with a little meat glaze.

Note: This sauce was created by Gouffé around the year 1863 and it would seem that it was at this time that it first appeared on menus. More recently the name Foyot has been substituted for Valois and it is now more widely known under its newer name. It has been thought necessary to outline the origin of this sauce if only to prevent any possible arguments.

157 Sauce Vénitienne

Place 4 dl (14 fl oz or 1¾ U.S. cups) tarragon vinegar, 2½ tbs chopped shallot and 25 g (1 oz) chervil in a pan and reduce by two-thirds; squeeze the reduction through a muslin, twisting lightly, then add to it 7½ dl (1⅓ pt or 3¼ U.S. cups) White Wine Sauce; finish with 125 g (4½ oz) Green Butter and 1 tbs mixed chopped chervil and tarragon.

This sauce is suitable for serving with various preparations of fish.

158 Sauce Véron

To 7½ dl (1⅓ pt or 3¼ U.S. cups) Sauce Normande, add 2½ dl (9 fl oz or 1⅛ U.S. cups) Sauce Tyrolienne; mix them together and finish with 2 tbs melted light coloured meat glaze and 1 tbs anchovy essence.

This sauce is suitable for serving with fish.

159 Sauce Villageoise

Add 1 dl (3½ fl oz or ½ U.S. cup) light-coloured veal gravy and 1 dl (3½ fl oz or ½ U.S. cup) mushroom cooking liquor to 7½ dl (1⅓ pt or 3¼ U.S. cups) Ordinary Velouté; reduce by a good third then pass through a fine strainer. Add 2 dl (7 fl oz or ⅞ U.S. cup) Soubise Sauce made with Sauce Béchamel and thicken with 4 egg yolks by reheating gently but without bringing to the boil. Finish away from the heat with 100 g (3½ oz) butter.

This sauce is particularly suitable for serving with white meat.

160 Sauce Villeroy

Place 1 litre (1¾ pt or 4½ U.S. cups) Sauce Allemande in a pan with 4 tbs each of ham and truffle essence.

Reduce quickly over an open fire using a metal spatula until the sauce becomes thick enough to coat the articles of food which are to be dipped into it.

Note: The only use of this sauce is to coat certain items of food which are afterwards egg and bread crumbed and deep fried. Foods prepared in this way are always designated à la Villeroy.

This sauce is one of a type which in the kitchen of earlier times were known as Sauces Perdues.

161 Sauce Villeroy Soubisée

To 6½ dl (1⅕ pt or 2⅞ U.S. cups) Sauce Allemande add 2½ dl (9 fl oz or 1⅛ U.S. cups) Sauce Soubise and reduce in exactly the same way as for Sauce Villeroy. According to the nature of the items of food and the purpose for which they are required, 80–100 g (3–3½ oz) chopped truffle may be added per 1 litre (1¾ pt or 4½ U.S. cups) of the sauce.

162 Sauce Villeroy Tomatée

Proceed in exactly the same way as for Sauce Villeroy adding to the Sauce Allemande a third its volume of very fine red tomato purée.

163 Sauce Vin Blanc—White Wine Sauce

This sauce can be prepared by any of the three following methods:

1) Place 1 litre (1¾ pt or 4½ U.S. cups) fish Velouté in a pan with 2 dl (7 fl oz or ⅞ U.S. cup) fish stock from the fish under preparation and 4 egg yolks; reduce by one-third and finish the sauce with 150 g (5 oz) butter.

Note: White Wine Sauce prepared in this way is particularly suitable for fish dishes which require glazing.

2) Place 1 dl (3½ fl oz or ½ U.S. cup) good fish stock in a pan and reduce by half; add 5 egg yolks and make the sauce by adding 500 g (1 lb 2 oz) butter in the same way as for Hollandaise Sauce.
3) Place 5 egg yolks in a pan and whisk whilst heating slightly; gradually whisk in 500 g (1 lb 2 oz) butter, cooking it over a gentle heat; during this process, add 1 dl (3½ fl oz or ½ U.S. cup) good quality fish stock a little at a time.

HOT ENGLISH SAUCES

164 Albert Sauce

Moisten 150 g (5 oz) grated horseradish with 2 dl (7 fl oz or ⅞ U.S. cup) white Bouillon and allow to simmer gently for 20 minutes.

Add 3 dl (½ pt or 1¼ U.S. cups) Butter Sauce (169), 2½ dl (9 fl oz or 1⅛ U.S. cups) cream and 40 g (1½ oz) breadcrumbs and thicken the sauce by reducing it quickly on a hot stove. Pass through a fine sieve and thicken with 2 egg yolks; season with a pinch of salt and pepper and finish with 1 tsp of diluted mustard and 1 tbs of ordinary vinegar.

This sauce is suitable for joints of braised beef, especially the fillet.

165 Apple Sauce—Sauce aux Pommes

Peel, core and slice 750 g (1 lb 10 oz) apples and place in a pan with 30 g (1 oz) sugar, a pinch of cinnamon, and 1 dl (3½ fl oz or ½ U.S. cup) water. Cover with a lid and cook gently until soft then make into a smooth sauce by beating with a whisk.

This sauce should always be served lukewarm and is suitable for serving with roast duck, goose and pork.

Note: The use of apple sauce as an accompaniment with certain roast joints is not peculiar to Great Britain as it is also served in Germany, Belgium and Holland. In these countries apple sauce or cranberry sauce, or sometimes hot or cold stewed fruits, are always served with roast game.

166 Aromatic Sauce

Place 5 dl (18 fl oz or 2¼ U.S. cups) White Bouillon in a pan with a sprig of thyme; a good pinch of basil; a pinch of savory, marjoram, sage and chopped chives; 1 tbs chopped shallots; a small pinch of grated nutmeg and 4 peppercorns; bring to the boil and allow to infuse for 10 minutes.

Pass the infusion through a fine strainer and thicken it with 50 g (2 oz) blond Roux made with butter; allow the sauce to simmer for a few minutes then finish with the juice of ½ a lemon and 1 tbs mixed chopped and blanched tarragon and chervil.

This sauce is suitable for serving with relevés of boiled or poached large fish or joints of butcher's meat.

167 Bread Sauce

To 5 dl (18 fl oz or 2¼ U.S. cups) boiling milk add 80 g (3 oz) fresh white breadcrumbs, a good pinch of salt, a small onion stuck with a clove and 30 g (1 oz) butter.

Allow to cook very gently for 15 minutes then remove the onion. Make the sauce smooth by beating it with a whisk and finish by adding 1 dl ($3\frac{1}{2}$ fl oz or $\frac{1}{2}$ U.S. cup) cream. This sauce is served with roast poultry and roast game birds.

Note: When this sauce accompanies poultry, a sauceboat of gravy should also be served; for game birds, a sauceboat of fried breadcrumbs and a dish of game chips should be served in addition to the bread sauce and gravy.

168 Brown Gravy

To 4 dl (14 fl oz or $1\frac{3}{4}$ U.S. cups) Butter Sauce (169), add 2 dl (7 fl oz or $\frac{7}{8}$ U.S. cup) good roast gravy, $\frac{1}{2}$ tbs ketchup and $\frac{1}{2}$ tbs of Harvey's Sauce.

This sauce is used as an accompaniment with roast veal.

169 Butter Sauce, English Style

This sauce is prepared in the same way as Sauce au Beurre (93) with the difference that it should be made thicker by using the following ingredients: 60 g (2 oz) butter, 60 g (2 oz) flour, $7\frac{1}{2}$ dl ($1\frac{1}{3}$ pt or $3\frac{1}{4}$ U.S. cups) boiling water, 5 g ($\frac{1}{6}$ oz) salt, 5–6 drops of lemon juice and 200 g (7 oz) butter.

This sauce should not be thickened by adding egg yolks.

170 Caper Sauce

This is Butter Sauce made as in the above recipe with the addition of 4 tbs capers per 1 litre ($1\frac{3}{4}$ pt or $4\frac{1}{2}$ U.S. cups) of sauce.

This sauce is suitable for serving with boiled fish and is an indispensable accompaniment for boiled leg of mutton.

171 Celery Sauce

Prepare and wash 6 celery hearts, place them in a shallow pan, cover with White Bouillon, add a Bouquet garni, an onion stuck with a clove and cook together gently until tender.

Drain the celery well, pound it in a mortar and pass through a fine sieve. Add an equal quantity of Cream Sauce (173) and 2–3 tbs of reduced cooking liquor from the celery. Reheat without boiling and keep in a Bain-marie.

The sauce is specially suitable for serving with roast turkey.

172 Cranberry Sauce

Place 500 g (1 lb 2 oz) cranberries in a pan with 1 litre ($1\frac{3}{4}$ pt or $4\frac{1}{2}$ U.S. cups) water, cover and cook gently until the berries are soft. Drain, reserve the cooking liquor and pass the cranberries through a fine sieve.

Add sufficient cooking liquor to this purée to give a fairly thick sauce, and add sufficient sugar to taste.

This sauce can be obtained in ready prepared form which only needs reheating with a little water.

This sauce is specially suitable for serving with roast turkey.

173 Cream Sauce

Prepare a white Roux with 100 g ($3\frac{1}{2}$ oz) butter and 60 g (2 oz) flour; add 7 dl ($1\frac{1}{4}$ pt or 3 U.S. cups) White Bouillon, 1 dl ($3\frac{1}{2}$ fl oz or $\frac{1}{2}$ U.S. cup) mushroom essence and 2 dl (7 fl oz or $\frac{7}{8}$ U.S. cup) cream. Bring to the boil, add a small onion, a bouquet of parsley and allow to simmer gently for 15 minutes.

Remove the onion and bouquet before serving.

This sauce is served with roast best end of veal.

174 Devilled Sauce

Place $1\frac{1}{2}$ dl (5 fl oz or $\frac{5}{8}$ U.S. cup) vinegar and 1 good tbs chopped shallots in a pan and reduce by half; add $2\frac{1}{2}$ dl (9 fl oz and $1\frac{1}{8}$ U.S. cups) Sauce Espagnole and 2 tbs tomato purée and simmer gently for 15 minutes. Finish with 1 tbs Derby Sauce, a good pinch of Cayenne and pass through a fine strainer.

This sauce is most suitable for serving with grilled poultry.

Note: Derby Sauce is recommended as a flavouring for various hot and cold sauces in place of Worcester Sauce; it is obtainable in ready prepared form.

175 Egg Sauce

Prepare a blond Roux with 60 g (2 oz) butter and 30 g (1 oz) flour; mix in 5 dl (18 fl oz or $2\frac{1}{4}$ U.S. cups) boiling milk and season with salt, white pepper and a little grated nutmeg. Allow to simmer gently for 5–6 minutes and add 3 hard-boiled eggs cut into dice whilst still hot.

This sauce is the usual accompaniment for poached smoked haddock or salt cod.

176 Egg and Butter Sauce

Melt 250 g (9 oz) butter, season with salt and pepper, add the juice of half a lemon, 1 tsp chopped and blanched parsley and 3 hard-boiled eggs cut into dice whilst still hot.

This sauce is suitable for serving with large whole boiled or poached fish.

177 Fennel Sauce

This is an ordinary Butter Sauce which is flavoured with blanched chopped fennel in the proportions of 1 tbs fennel per $2\frac{1}{2}$ dl (9 fl oz or $1\frac{1}{8}$ U.S. cups) of sauce.

This sauce is usually served as an accompaniment with grilled or boiled mackerel.

178 Fried Bread Sauce
Place 2 dl (7 fl oz or ⅞ U.S. cup) ordinary White Bouillon in a pan with 2 tbs lean ham cut into small dice and 30 g (1 oz) chopped shallot and bring to the boil; allow to simmer gently for 10 minutes. Meanwhile, fry 50 g (2 oz) white bread-crumbs in butter and add at the last moment; finish the sauce with a pinch of chopped parsley and a few drops of lemon juice.

This sauce is particularly suitable for serving with small roast birds.

179 Gooseberry Sauce
Place 1 kg (2¼ lb) picked and washed goose-berries into a copper bowl with 125 g (4½ oz) sugar and 1 dl (3½ fl oz or ½ U.S. cup) water. Bring to the boil, cook until tender then pass through a fine sieve.

This purée is used as an accompaniment for grilled mackerel.

180 Horseradish Sauce
This is prepared in exactly the same way as Sauce Albert.

181 Lobster Sauce, English Style
To 1 litre (1¾ pt or 2¼ U.S. cups) Sauce Béchamel add 1 tbs anchovy essence, 100 g (3½ oz) diced cooked lobster flesh and a little Cayenne.

This sauce is used to accompany fish.

182 Onion Sauce
Place 200 g (7 oz) sliced onions in a pan with 6 dl (1 pt or 2⅝ U.S. cup) milk, a pinch of salt, pepper and grated nutmeg and bring to the boil. Allow to cook gently until tender; drain well, reserve the milk, then chop the onions.

Prepare a white Roux with 40 g (1½ oz) butter and 40 g (1½ oz) flour, mix in the milk from the onions, bring to the boil and add the chopped onions, keeping the sauce very thick. Allow to simmer very gently for 7–8 minutes.

This sauce is a useful accompaniment with rabbit, poultry, tripe, boiled mutton, braised game etc. and is always poured over the meat with which it is served.

183 Oyster Sauce
Prepare a blond Roux with 20 g (⅔ oz) butter and 15 g (½ oz) flour; mix in 1 dl (3½ fl oz or ½ U.S. cup) milk and 1 dl (3½ fl oz or ½ U.S. cup) cream; season with salt, bring to the boil and simmer gently for 10 minutes.

Pass through a fine strainer, season with a little Cayenne and add 12 poached and bearded oysters cut into slices.

This sauce is specially suitable for serving with boiled or poached fish.

184 Oyster Sauce, Brown
Prepare an Oyster Sauce as indicated in the preceding recipe, replacing the milk and cream with 2 dl (7 fl oz or ⅞ U.S. cup) of brown stock.

This sauce is used to accompany grills, meat puddings and grilled cod.

185 Parsley Sauce
Add 1 dl (3½ fl oz or ½ U.S. cup) infusion of parsley to 5 dl (18 fl oz or 2¼ U.S. cups) Butter Sauce and finish with 1 good tbs chopped and blanched parsley.

This sauce is suitable for serving with calf's head, calf's feet and brains etc.

186 Parsley Sauce for Fish
Prepare 60 g (2 oz) white Roux and add 5 dl (18 fl oz or 2¼ U.S. cups) cooking liquor from the fish for which the sauce is being prepared. The cooking liquor should be well flavoured with parsley or have an infusion of parsley added to it so as to give it a pronounced flavour.

Allow the sauce to simmer for 5–6 minutes and finish with 10 g (⅓ oz) chopped and blanched parsley and a few drops of lemon juice.

187 Port Wine Sauce
Place 1½ dl (5 fl oz or ⅝ U.S. cup) Port wine into a pan with 1 tbs chopped shallot and a sprig of thyme and reduce by half. Add the juice of 2 oranges and half a lemon, 1 tsp grated orange rind, a pinch of salt and a little Cayenne; pass this through a muslin and add it to 5 dl (18 fl oz or 2¼ U.S. cups) good quality thickened veal gravy.

This sauce is specially suitable for serving with wild duck and roast game birds.

Note: This English sauce is served in many first class French restaurants.

188 Reform Sauce
To 2½ dl (9 fl oz or 1⅛ U.S. cups) each of Sauce Poivrade and Sauce Demi-glace, add a garnish of 30 g (1 oz) gherkin, the white of 1 hard-boiled egg, 20 g (⅔ oz) cooked mushrooms, 20 g (⅔ oz) truffle and 30 g (1 oz) cooked salted ox tongue—all these cut into short Julienne.

This sauce is always served with mutton and lamb cutlets à la Réforme.

189 Roebuck Sauce
Cut 60 g (2 oz) onion and 80 g (3 oz) raw ham into

fine Paysanne; place 40 g ($1\frac{1}{2}$ oz) butter in a pan, add the Paysanne and cook to a light brown colour. Moisten with $1\frac{1}{2}$ dl (5 fl oz or $\frac{5}{8}$ U.S. cup) vinegar, add a Bouquet garni and reduce almost completely.

Add 3 dl ($\frac{1}{2}$ pt or $1\frac{1}{4}$ U.S. cups) Sauce Espagnole and simmer gently for 15 minutes, skimming carefully. Remove the Bouquet garni and finish the sauce with $\frac{3}{4}$ dl (3 fl oz or $\frac{3}{8}$ U.S. cup) port and a good tbs redcurrant jelly.

This sauce is an excellent accompaniment for joints of venison.

190 Sage and Onion Sauce

Bake 2 large onions in the oven until tender, allow to cool then peel and chop them. Add and mix this onion into 150 g (5 oz) white breadcrumbs which have been soaked in milk and squeezed to remove the surplus milk plus 2 tbs chopped sage; season with salt and pepper.

This preparation can be used to stuff ducks.

Note: This preparation may be served in a sauceboat after adding approximately $1\frac{1}{2}$ dl (5 fl oz or $\frac{5}{8}$ U.S. cup) good roast gravy; sometimes 150 g (5 oz) chopped cooked beef suet is added to the mixture.

191 Scotch Egg Sauce

Prepare a Sauce Béchamel using 60 g (2 oz) butter; 30 g (1 oz) flour; and 4 dl (14 fl oz or $1\frac{3}{4}$ U.S. cups) boiling milk; season as usual. As soon as the sauce is simmering add the sliced white of 4 hard-boiled eggs and when about to serve the sauce, add the 4 yolks passed through a coarse sieve.

This sauce is an essential accompaniment with salt cod.

192 Shrimp Sauce

To 1 litre ($1\frac{3}{4}$ pt or $4\frac{1}{2}$ U.S. cups) Butter Sauce add a little Cayenne, 1 tsp anchovy essence, and 125 g ($4\frac{1}{2}$ oz) peeled cooked shrimps.

This sauce is a suitable accompaniment for fish.

193 Yorkshire Sauce

Place 2 dl (7 fl oz or $\frac{7}{8}$ U.S. cup) Port wine in a pan with 1 good tbs very fine Julienne of orange zest and cook gently until tender. Remove the Julienne; then add to the port 1 good tbs each of Sauce Espagnole and redcurrant jelly and a touch each of ground cinnamon and Cayenne. Reduce for a few minutes, pass through a fine strainer and finish with the juice of 1 orange and the cooked Julienne of orange.

This sauce is suitable for serving with roast or braised duck and with braised ham.

COLD SAUCES

194 Aïoli, or Beurre de Provence

Pound 30 g (1 oz) garlic as finely as possible in the mortar, add 1 raw egg yolk and a pinch of salt and gradually mix in $2\frac{1}{2}$ dl (9 fl oz or $1\frac{1}{8}$ U.S. cup) oil allowing it to fall drop by drop to begin with, then faster as a thread as the sauce begins to thicken. The thickening of the sauce takes place by turning the pestle vigorously whilst adding the oil.

The consistency of the sauce should be adjusted during its making by adding the juice of 1 lemon and $\frac{1}{2}$ tbs cold water little by little.

Note: Should the sauce separate it can be reconstituted by working it into 1 egg yolk as for Mayonnaise.

195 Sauce Andalouse

To $7\frac{1}{2}$ dl ($1\frac{1}{3}$ pt or $3\frac{1}{4}$ U.S. cups) fairly thick Mayonnaise add $2\frac{1}{2}$ dl (9 fl oz or $1\frac{1}{8}$ U.S. cups) very fine and red tomato purée, and finally add 75 g ($2\frac{1}{2}$ oz) red pimento cut into very small dice.

196 Sauce Bohémienne

Place $1\frac{1}{2}$ dl (5 fl oz or $\frac{5}{8}$ U.S. cup) very thick cold sauce Béchamel into a basin with 4 raw egg yolks, 10 g ($\frac{1}{3}$ oz) salt, a pinch of pepper and a few drops of vinegar.

Mix well together with a whisk and add 1 litre ($1\frac{3}{4}$ pt or $4\frac{1}{2}$ U.S. cups) oil and 2 tbs tarragon vinegar proceeding in the same way as for making Mayonnaise. Finish the sauce with 1 tbs made mustard.

197 Sauce Chantilly

Prepare $7\frac{1}{2}$ dl ($1\frac{1}{3}$ pt or $3\frac{1}{4}$ U.S. cups) Mayonnaise using lemon juice instead of vinegar and keeping the sauce very thick. Just before serving add 4 tbs stiffly whipped cream; adjust the seasoning after adding the cream.

This sauce is specially suitable for serving with cold or lukewarm asparagus.

Note: The cream must be added to the Mayonnaise at the very last moment as the sauce is liable to separate if added too soon in advance.

198 Sauce Génoise

Place 40 g ($1\frac{1}{2}$ oz) freshly skinned pistachio nuts and 25 g (1 oz) pine seed kernels or if unavailable, 25 g (1 oz) skinned sweet almonds, in a mortar and pound to a fine smooth paste adding a little less than 1 tbs of cold Sauce Béchamel; pass it through a fine sieve. Place the purée in a basin with 6 egg yolks, a pinch of salt and a little pepper and mix together with a whisk proceeding as for Mayonnaise by adding 1 litre ($1\frac{3}{4}$ pt or $4\frac{1}{2}$ U.S. cups) oil and the juice of 2 lemons.

Prepare $\frac{3}{4}$ dl (3 fl oz or $\frac{3}{8}$ U.S. cup) of a purée composed of equal quantities of parsley, chervil, tarragon, chives and fresh pimpernel, rapidly blanched for 2 minutes then drained, refreshed, squeezed thoroughly and passed through a fine sieve. Mix into the sauce.

This sauce is usually served as an accompaniment with cold fish.

199 Sauce Gribiche

Place the yolks of 6 freshly cooked hard-boiled eggs in a basin, crush them and work to a smooth paste adding 1 tsp mustard and a pinch of salt and pepper, then proceed in the same way as for Mayonnaise by adding 5 dl (18 fl oz or $2\frac{1}{4}$ U.S. cups) oil and $1\frac{1}{2}$ tbs vinegar.

Finish the sauce with 100 g ($3\frac{1}{2}$ oz) mixed chopped capers and gherkins; 1 tbs mixed chopped parsley, tarragon and chervil; and the whites of 3 hard-boiled eggs cut into short Julienne.

This sauce is usually served as an accompaniment with cold fish.

200 Sauce Groseilles au Raifort—Redcurrant and Horseradish Sauce

Place 1 dl ($3\frac{1}{2}$ fl oz or $\frac{1}{2}$ U.S. cup) Port wine in a pan with a pinch each of ground nutmeg, cinnamon, salt and pepper, and reduce by one-third; add 4 dl (14 fl oz or $1\frac{3}{4}$ U.S. cups) melted redcurrant jelly and 2 tbs finely grated horseradish.

This sauce has a number of general uses.

201 Sauce Italienne

Poach half a calf's brain or the same amount of ox or mutton brain in a well-flavoured Vinegar Court-bouillon and allow to cool. Drain and pass through a fine sieve; place the purée in a basin and whisk until smooth, and add to it a Mayonnaise made from 5 egg yolks, 1 litre ($1\frac{3}{4}$ pt or $4\frac{1}{2}$ U.S. cups) oil, the juice of 1 lemon, 10 g ($\frac{1}{3}$ oz) salt and a pinch of pepper; finish with a good tbs of chopped parsley.

This sauce is suitable for serving with any kind of cold meat.

202 Sauce Mayonnaise

Many composed cold sauces are derived from Mayonnaise and it is therefore classified as a basic sauce in the same way as Espagnole and Velouté.

Its preparation is very simple provided note is taken of the principles outlined in the following recipe:

Ingredients:

6 egg yolks (these must be unblemished)
1 litre ($1\frac{3}{4}$ pt or $4\frac{1}{2}$ U.S. cups) oil
10 g ($\frac{1}{3}$ oz) fine salt
pinch of ground white pepper
$1\frac{1}{2}$ tbs vinegar (or its equivalent in lemon juice if the sauce is required to be very white)

Method:

1) Whisk the yolks of egg in a basin with the salt, pepper and a little of the vinegar or a few drops of lemon juice.
2) Add and whisk in the oil, drop by drop to begin with, then faster in a thread as the sauce begins to thicken.
3) Adjust the consistency occasionally by adding the vinegar or lemon juice.
4) Lastly add 2 tbs boiling water which is added to ensure that the emulsification holds if the sauce is to be reserved for later use.

Notes:

1) The supposition that the separation of the sauce is brought about by adding the seasoning to the yolks is unacceptable to practising cooks—conversely it has been proved scientifically that salt in solution aids the cohesive qualities of the yolks.
2) It is erroneous to think that it is necessary to work Mayonnaise on ice; in fact coldness is deleterious to Mayonnaise and is the most frequent cause of its separating. During cold weather the oil should be warmed slightly or at least brought to kitchen temperature.
3) The reasons why Mayonnaise separates may be:
   a) the result of adding the oil too quickly to begin with,
   b) using oil which is too cold,
   c) using too much oil in proportion to the number of yolks of egg; the assimilating properties of 1 egg yolk is limited to $1\frac{3}{4}$ dl (6 fl oz or $\frac{3}{4}$ U.S. cup) oil when the sauce is to be used later on and 2 dl (7 fl oz or $\frac{7}{8}$ U.S. cup) if the sauce is for immediate use.

203 Sauce Mayonnaise Collée—Jellied Mayonnaise

This sauce is prepared in the proportions of 3 dl ($\frac{1}{2}$ pt or $1\frac{1}{4}$ U.S. cups) melted aspic jelly to 7 dl ($1\frac{1}{4}$ pt or 3 U.S. cups) Mayonnaise; it is used to bind vegetable salads and to coat Chaud-froid dishes designated à la Russe.

Note: In the note to Fish Chaud-froid Sauce, mention has already been made of the advantage of using that sauce in preference to Sauce Mayonnaise Collée because it gives better results in flavour and appearance. The explanation is also given of how the gelatine in the sauce contracts under the influence of coldness and as it sets, exerts pressure in the Mayonnaise causing small beads of oil to appear on the surface thus making the food look unsightly. To prevent this greasiness it is therefore recommended that Sauce Mayonnaise Collée be replaced by Fish Chaud-froid Sauce for all dishes which were generally made with the former.

204 Sauce Mayonnaise fouettée à la Russe—Whipped Mayonnaise, Russian Style

Place 4 dl (14 fl oz or $1\frac{3}{4}$ U.S. cups) melted aspic jelly, 3 dl ($\frac{1}{2}$ pt or $1\frac{1}{4}$ U.S. cups) Mayonnaise, 1 tsp tarragon vinegar and 1 tbs grated and very finely chopped horseradish in a china basin and mix well together with a whisk.

Place on ice and whisk until it becomes frothy and starts to set then stop whisking, remove from the ice and use whilst still sufficiently liquid for its particular purpose.

This sauce is principally used for binding vegetable salads together for moulding.

205 Various Mayonnaise Sauces

Using the eggs and creamy parts of large shellfish, crayfish or prawns, anchovies, caviare etc., it is possible to prepare several different Mayonnaise Sauces which are suitable for serving with Hors-d'oeuvre and cold Entrées. The appropriate ingredient should be pounded to a purée and mixed with a little Mayonnaise, passed and added to the required quanity of Mayonnaise.

206 Sauce Mousquetaire

To 1 litre ($1\frac{3}{4}$ pt or $4\frac{1}{2}$ U.S. cups) Mayonnaise add 80 g (3 oz) finely chopped shallot which have been cooked and completely reduced with $1\frac{1}{2}$ dl (5 fl oz or $\frac{5}{8}$ U.S. cup) white wine, 3 tbs melted meat glaze and 1 tbs chopped chives. Season the sauce with a touch of Cayenne or milled pepper.

This sauce is suitable for serving with cold meat.

Note: It is best to add the shallots in the form of a purée after they have been passed through a sieve.

207 Sauce Moutarde à la Crème—Mustard and Cream Sauce

Place 20 g ($\frac{2}{3}$ oz) mustard, a pinch of salt and pepper and a few drops of lemon juice in a basin and mix together; gradually add 2 dl (7 fl oz or $\frac{7}{8}$ U.S. cup) very fresh double cream drop by drop, as for making Mayonnaise.

This sauce is specially suitable for use in the preparation of various Hors-d'oeuvre.

208 Sauce Raifort aux Noix—Horseradish Sauce with Walnuts

Mix together in a basin, 250 g (9 oz) each of grated horseradish and skinned and chopped walnuts, 15 g ($\frac{1}{2}$ oz) sugar, 3 dl ($\frac{1}{2}$ pt or $1\frac{1}{4}$ U.S. cups) double cream and a pinch of salt

This sauce is specially served as an accompaniment with cold char.

209 Sauce Ravigote or Vinaigrette

Ingredients:

5 dl (18 fl oz or $2\frac{1}{4}$ U.S. cups) oil
2 dl (7 fl oz or $\frac{7}{8}$ U.S. cup) vinegar
2 tbs small capers
2 tbs chopped parsley
40 g ($1\frac{1}{2}$ oz) mixed chopped tarragon, chervil and chives
70 g ($2\frac{1}{2}$ oz) finely chopped onion
a good pinch of salt
a pinch of pepper

Method:

Mix all the ingredients together well.

This sauce is specially suitable for serving with calf's head, calf's feet and sheep's trotters etc.

210 Sauce Remoulade

To 1 litre ($1\frac{3}{4}$ pt or $4\frac{1}{2}$ U.S. cups) Mayonnaise add and mix in $1\frac{1}{2}$ tbs mustard, 100 g ($3\frac{1}{2}$ oz) chopped gherkins, 50 g (2 oz) capers chopped and squeezed to remove the liquid, 1 tbs mixed chopped parsley, tarragon and chervil, and $\frac{1}{2}$ tbs anchovy essence.

This sauce can be suitably served with various items of cold food.

211 Sauce Russe

Pound 100 g ($3\frac{1}{2}$ oz) creamy parts of lobster or crawfish and 100 g ($3\frac{1}{2}$ oz) caviare in a mortar, adding 2–3 tbs of Mayonnaise. Pass through a fine sieve and add this purée to $7\frac{1}{2}$ dl ($1\frac{1}{3}$ pt or $3\frac{1}{4}$ U.S. cups) Mayonnaise, finishing it with 1 tbs mustard and the same amount of Derby Sauce.

This sauce is a suitable accompaniment with cold fish and shellfish.

212 Sauce Tartare

Place 8 yolks of hard-boiled eggs in a basin; crush and work them to a smooth paste. Season with a pinch of salt and milled pepper and add 1 litre ($1\frac{3}{4}$ pt or $4\frac{1}{2}$ U.S. cups) oil and 2 tbs vinegar as for making Mayonnaise. Finish with 20 g ($\frac{2}{3}$ oz) purée of spring onions or chives made by pounding them with 2 tbs Mayonnaise then passing through a fine sieve.

This sauce is suitable for serving with cold fish and shellfish, cold meat and poultry and may also be served with poultry and meat cooked *à la Diable.*

213 Sauce Verte—Green Sauce

Blanch rapidly for 5 minutes 50 g (2 oz) each of spinach leaves and watercress leaves and 50 g (2 oz) of mixed parsley, tarragon and chervil; drain well, refresh quickly and squeeze out all the water.

Pound the leaves then squeeze them very firmly in a clean cloth so as to obtain 1 dl (3½ fl oz or ½ U.S. cup) of thick herb juice. Add this juice to 9 dl (1⅗ pt or 4 U.S. cups) well seasoned, very thick Mayonnaise.

This sauce is suitable for serving with cold fish and shellfish.

214 Sauce Vincent

This sauce can be made in either of the following ways:

1) Well blanch for 2–3 minutes, 100 g (3½ oz) sorrel, parsley, tarragon, chervil, chives and very fresh salad burnet in absolutely equal proportions, plus 60 g (2 oz) each of watercress leaves and spinach leaves. Drain well, refresh and squeeze out all the water. Place in a mortar and pound well adding and mixing in 6 freshly cooked hard-boiled egg yolks. Pass through a fine sieve and place the purée in a basin. Add a pinch of salt and pepper and 5 raw egg yolks; then proceed as for Mayonnaise by adding 8 dl (1⅗ pt or 3½ U.S. cups) oil and a little vinegar as necessary. Finish the sauce by adding 1 tbs Derby Sauce.
2) Prepare the purée in the same way and in the same proportions as for Sauce Vincent 1) adding it to 9 dl (1¾ pt or 4 U.S. cups) Mayonnaise; correct the seasoning and finish with the Derby Sauce.

This sauce is particularly suitable for serving with cold fish and shellfish.

Note: This sauce was created by Vincent Lachapelle, a master chef of the 18th Century.

215 Sauce Suédoise

Peel, core and slice 500 g (1 lb 2 oz) cooking apples and cook gently with a few tbs white wine in a tightly closed pan: the cooking of the apple should be carried out in the steam produced in the process. Pass through a fine sieve and reduce the purée to 2½ dl (9 fl oz or 1⅛ U.S. cups) and when very cold add it to 7½ dl (1⅓ pt or 3¼ U.S. cups) Mayonnaise; finish the sauce with 1½ tbs grated or finely chopped horseradish.

This sauce is particularly suitable for serving with cold pork and also with cold roast goose.

Note: If sweet apples are used, add a few drops of lemon juice to acidulate the purée. If apples are not available, a purée of whitecurrants or green gooseberries may be used instead and in the proportions of 2½ dl (9 fl oz or 1⅛ U.S. cups) purée to 1 litre (1¾ pt or 4½ U.S. cups) Mayonnaise which should be very thick. Mustard can be used to flavour this sauce.

COLD ENGLISH SAUCES

216 Cambridge Sauce

Finely pound 6 yolks of hard boiled eggs together with 4 well washed fillets of anchovy, 1 tbs of capers and 1 tbs of chopped tarragon, chervil and chives in equal proportions. Add 1 tsp mustard and proceed as for Mayonnaise by adding 1½ dl (5 fl oz or ⅝ U.S. cup) oil and 1 tbs vinegar; season with a little Cayenne and pass through a fine sieve.

Place in a basin and whisk until smooth then finish with 1 tsp chopped parsley.

This sauce is suitable for serving with any kind of cold meat.

217 Cumberland Sauce

To 4 tbs melted redcurrant jelly add 1 dl (3½ fl oz or ½ U.S. cup) Port wine, ½ tbs finely chopped shallot blanched and squeezed dry; 1 tbs each of orange zest and lemon zest cut into fine Julienne and well blanched, well drained and cooled; the juice of 1 orange and ½ a lemon; 1 tsp of mustard, a touch of Cayenne and a touch of ground ginger. Mix all the ingredients together well.

This sauce is specially suitable for serving with cold venison.

218 Gloucester Sauce

To 1 litre (1¾ pt or 4½ U.S. cups) very thick Mayonnaise add 2 dl (7 fl oz or ⅞ U.S. cup) sour cream, the juice of ½ a lemon, a pinch of chopped fennel and 2 tbs Derby Sauce.

This sauce is mainly served with cold meat.

219 Cold Horseradish Sauce

Mix together in a basin 1 tbs mustard, 50 g (2 oz) finely grated horseradish, 50 g (2 oz) caster sugar, a pinch of salt, 5 dl (18 fl oz or 2¼ U.S. cups) cream, ½ dl. (2 fl oz or ¼ U.S. cup) vinegar and 250 g (9 oz) breadcrumbs soaked in milk and squeezed out. The vinegar should be added at the last minute.

This sauce should be served very cold; it is a suitable accompaniment for joints of roast and boiled beef.

220 Mint Sauce

Chop or cut into fine Julienne 50 g (2 oz) mint leaves; place in a basin and add 25 g (1 oz) caster sugar, 1½ dl (5 fl oz or ⅝ U.S. cup) vinegar, a pinch of salt and pepper and 4 tbs water; mix all the ingredients together.

This sauce is served with hot and cold roast lamb.

221 Oxford Sauce

This sauce is prepared in the same way as Cumberland Sauce but using only half the quantity of orange and lemon zest which should be grated instead of being cut into Julienne.

This sauce has the same uses as Cumberland Sauce.

COMPOUND BUTTERS FOR GRILLS AND FOR THE FINISHING OF SAUCES AND HORS-D'OEUVRE

Notes on the preparation of Compound Butters

Many of the compound butters included in this chapter, with the exception of those made from shellfish, are little used today. However, they can play a valuable role in certain areas such as the herb butters being served with grilled foods and other butters being used for finishing soups and sauces. In these cases the butters help to accentuate and stabilize the particular flavour and properties in a very definite manner. It is therefore suggested that the foregoing observations regarding the use of compound butters be given all due consideration.

As regards the butters made from shellfish, experience has shown that when these are prepared by the method of infusion in a Bain-marie and thereafter passed through a muslin into iced water, they will have a better colour than those prepared by the cold method. On the other hand, those butters prepared by heating lose a great deal of their delicate flavour and may even acquire a disagreeable taste.

In order to counteract these drawbacks it is suggested that two separate types of shellfish butter be used. The first is made from the creamy parts debris and trimmings of the shellfish which are pounded with butter and passed through a sieve—this type gives perfect taste and flavour to sauces more especially those using sauce Béchamel as a base.

The other type of butter is prepared from the shells only, pounded with butter and infused over heat—this one provides the colouring for the final result. This method of using two types of butter gives an excellent result and is recommended.

In some instances it is advisable to replace the butter with an equivalent amount of good quality cream which absorbs the flavour and aroma much better than does butter and gives a perfect cullis of the highest quality for finishing sauces and soups.

The use of colouring butter gives a clean translucent colour to sauces which should be characteristic of them; under all circumstances it is to be preferred to the use of red colour which can provide only a rather gaudy and indeterminate colour for sauces and soups.

Compound butters are usually made as required; if prepared in advance they should be kept in the refrigerator covered with greaseproof paper.

222 Beurre d'Ail—Garlic Butter

Well blanch 200 g (7 oz) peeled cloves of garlic, drain well and pound, then add and mix in 250 g (9 oz) butter; pass through a fine sieve.

223 Beurre d'Anchois—Anchovy Butter

Finely pound 100 g ($3\frac{1}{2}$ oz) washed and dried fillets of anchovy then add and mix in 250 g (9 oz) butter and pass through a fine sieve.

224 Beurre d'Amandes—Almond Butter

Pound 150 g (5 oz) freshly shelled and washed sweet almonds to a fine paste with the addition of a few drops of water. Add and mix in 250 g (9 oz) butter and pass through a very fine sieve.

225 Beurre d'Aveline—Hazelnut Butter

Pound 150 g (5 oz) skinned and roasted hazelnuts to a fine paste with the addition of a few drops of water so as to prevent it from becoming oily. Add 250 g (9 oz) butter, mix in and pass through a fine sieve.

226 Beurre Bercy

Place 2 dl (7 fl oz or $\frac{7}{8}$ U.S. cup) white wine and 1 tbs finely chopped shallot in a pan and reduce by half. Allow to cool and mix in 200 g (7 oz) softened butter, 500 g (1 lb 2 oz) bone marrow cut into dice, poached and drained well, 1 tbs chopped parsley, 8 g ($\frac{1}{4}$ oz) salt, a good pinch of milled pepper and the juice of $\frac{1}{2}$ lemon.

227 Beurre de Caviar—Caviare Butter

Finely pound 75 g ($2\frac{1}{2}$ oz) caviare until smooth, add 250 g (9 oz) butter and mix in, then pass through a fine sieve.

228 Beurre Chivry or Beurre Ravigote

Blanch, refresh and squeeze 100 g ($3\frac{1}{2}$ oz) mixed parsley, chervil, tarragon, chives and fresh salad burnet leaves and pound them together with 25 g (1 oz) blanched chopped shallot. Add 125 g ($4\frac{1}{2}$ oz) butter, mix in and pass through a fine sieve.

229 Beurre Colbert

Add 2 tbs melted meat glaze and 2 tsb chopped tarragon to 200 g (7 oz) Maître d'Hôtel Butter.

230 Red Colouring Butter

Remove any of the remaining flesh and particles from the outside and inside of any shellfish shells; dry the shells in a slow oven then pound them until fine. Add and mix in an equal quantity of butter, place this mixture in a Bain-marie pot and allow it to melt stirring frequently. Pass through a muslin held over a basin of ice cold water and when solidified place the resultant butter in a cloth and squeeze to remove the water.

Note: If shellfish carcasses are not available to prepare this butter, paprika butter can be used instead. In any event, it is inadvisable to use artificial colourings for the final colouring of sauces.

231 Green Colouring Butter
Pound 1 kg (2¼ lb) well washed and drained raw spinach, place it in a cloth and squeeze tightly so as to extract all the juices. Place the juice in a small pan in a Bain-marie of hot water and allow the juice to coagulate.

Tip it out into a clean cloth stretched taut over a bowl and allow to drain well. Scrape the colouring substance from the cloth by means of a palette knife and mix it together with twice its amount of butter; pass through a fine sieve and keep in a cool place.

Note: This colouring butter replaces artificial green colour to advantage.

232 Beurre de Crevette—Shrimp Butter
Finely pound 150 g (5 oz) cooked shrimps to a fine paste, add and mix in an equal amount of butter and pass through a fine sieve.

233 Beurre d'Echalote—Shallot Butter
Roughly chop 125 g (4½ oz) shallot, blanch quickly, drain and squeeze well in a cloth. Pound until fine then add and mix in 125 g (4½ oz) butter and pass through a fine sieve.

234 Beurre d'Ecrevisse—Crayfish Butter
Finely pound the remains of crayfish previously cooked with a Mirepoix as for Bisque; add and mix in an equal amount of butter and pass through a fine sieve.

235 Butter for Snails
For 50 snails: mix together 350 g (13 oz) butter, 30 g (1 oz) finely chopped shallots, 1 clove garlic, crushed to a paste, 25 g (1 oz) chopped parsley, 12 g (½ oz) salt and a pinch of pepper; keep in a cool place until required.

236 Beurre d'Estragon—Tarragon Butter
Blanch 125 g (4½ oz) very fresh tarragon leaves for 2 minutes, drain, refresh and squeeze dry. Pound until fine then add and mix in 250 g (9 oz) butter and pass through a fine sieve.

237 Beurre de Hareng—Herring Butter
Scale 3 large smoked, salted herrings, remove the fillets and cut into dice; pound them finely and add and mix in 250 g (9 oz) butter. Pass through a fine sieve.

238 Beurre de Homard—Lobster Butter
Pound the creamy parts, eggs and coral of lobster; add and mix in an equal amount of butter and pass through a fine sieve.

239 Beurre de Laitance—Soft Roe Butter
Poach 125 g (4½ oz) soft roes, allow to cool then pound to a fine paste. Add 250 g (9 oz) butter and mix in together with 1 tsp of mustard then pass through a fine sieve.

240 Beurre à la Maître d'Hôtel
Mix 250 g (9 oz) butter until soft and smooth, add a good tbs chopped parsley, a little salt and pepper and the juice of ¼ lemon; mix well together.

Note: The addition of 1 tbs mustard to this butter is recommended as a variation which is particularly suitable for serving with grilled meat and fish.

241 Beurre Manié
This butter is used as a quick thickening for sauces such as that used in a Matelote; it is made by mixing butter and flour to a smooth paste in the proportions of 75 g (2½ oz) flour per 100 g (3½ oz) butter.

Sauces thickened with Beurre Manié should not boil as such if it can be avoided; there is the risk of a disagreeable taste of raw flour developing in the finished sauce.

242 Beurre Marchand de Vins
Place 2 dl (7 fl oz or ⅞ U.S. cup) red wine and 25 g (1 oz) chopped shallot in a pan and reduce by half. Add a pinch of salt, a small pinch of freshly ground or crushed pepper, 1 tbs melted meat glaze, 150 g (5 oz) softened butter, the juice of ¼ lemon and 1 tbs chopped parsley; mix all the ingredients well together.

This butter is specially suitable for serving with grilled sirloin steaks.

243 Beurre à la Meunière—Meunière Butter
This is butter which is cooked to a light golden brown colour with the addition, at the moment of service, of a few drops of lemon juice. It is principally used for fish dishes designated *à la Meunière*.

244 Beurre de Montpellier
Using a copper bowl, blanch 90 g–100 g (3–3½ oz) of mixed leaves of watercress, parsley, chervil, tarragon and chives in equal quantities and 25 g (1 oz) spinach leaves; refresh, drain and squeeze out all the moisture. Separately, blanch 40 g (1½ oz) finely chopped shallot, drain and squeeze. Pound the herbs and shallot together finely.

Add 50 g (2 oz) gherkins, 1 tbs squeezed capers, 1

small clove of garlic and 8 fillets of anchovy and pound all together to a fine paste. Add 750 g (1 lb 10 oz) butter, 3 hard-boiled egg yolks and 2 raw egg yolks; mix in, then finally add 2 dl (7 fl oz or $\frac{7}{8}$ U.S. cup) oil, drop by drop. Pass through a fine sieve, mix together with a whisk until smooth, season with salt and finish with a very small pinch of Cayenne.

This butter is used as an accompaniment for cold fish and it may be used to coat fish prepared for a cold buffet.

245 Montpellier Butter for decorating dishes
When this butter is specially prepared for the purpose of decoration, the oil, the cooked yolks and the raw yolks should be omitted. The butter is spread on a tray to an even thickness and allowed to become quite cold and firmly set but not so cold as to make it difficult for cutting into various shapes as required.

246 Beurre de Moutarde—Mustard Butter
Add $1\frac{1}{2}$ tbs French mustard to 250 g (9 oz) softened butter and mix in; keep in a cool place until required.

247 Beurre Noir, for large numbers
For 10 persons: cook 125 g ($4\frac{1}{2}$ oz) butter in a frying pan until brown in colour and pass through a fine strainer into a Bain-marie pot. When lukewarm, add 1 tsp vinegar previously reduced with a little coarsely ground pepper. When required for service, reheat this butter to the correct serving temperature; add a little coarsely chopped parsley fried in butter and 1 tbs capers to the food being prepared. Finally pour the Beurre Noir over it.

248 Beurre de Noisette—Hazelnut Butter
See Beurre d'Aveline (225).

249 Beurre de Paprika—Paprika Butter
To 250 g (9 oz) softened butter, add 2 tsp paprika previously cooked in butter with 1 tbs chopped onion; mix in and pass through a fine sieve.

250 Beurre de Pimento—Pimento Butter
Pound 100 g ($3\frac{1}{2}$ oz) braised red pimento together with 250 g (9 oz) butter and pass through a fine sieve.

251 Beurre de Pistache—Pistachio Butter
Pound 150 g (5 oz) freshly peeled pistachios until fine, moistening with a few drops of water; add 250 g (9 oz) butter, mix in and pass through a fine sieve.

252 Beurre à la Polonaise
Cook 250 g (9 oz) butter to a nut brown colour, immediately add 60 g (2 oz) very fine white breadcrumbs and cook until the crumbs are a golden brown colour.

253 Beurre de Raifort—Horseradish Butter
Pound 50 g (2 oz) grated horseradish, add 250 g (9 oz) butter and mix in, then pass through a fine sieve.

254 Beurre Ravigote or Beurre Vert—Ravigote or Green Butter
These are alternative names for Beurre à la Chivry (228).

255 Beurre de Saumon Fumé—Smoked Salmon Butter
Pound 100 g ($3\frac{1}{2}$ oz) smoked salmon with 250 g (9 oz) butter and pass through a fine sieve.

256 Beurre de Truffe—Truffle Butter
Pound 100 g ($3\frac{1}{2}$ oz) very black truffles with $\frac{1}{2}$ tbs Béchamel; add 200 g (7 oz) best quality butter and mix in, then pass through a fine sieve.

257 Beurres Printaniers—Printanier Butters
These butters are prepared using vegetables and are frequently employed in the finishing of soups and sauces.

The vegetables are first of all cooked according to their particular nature, e.g. carrots and turnips are stewed in butter and Bouillon, and green vegetables such as French beans, peas and asparagus tips are cooked in boiling salted water until just tender. The cooked vegetables are then pounded with an equal amount of butter and passed through a very fine sieve.

258 Various Cullises
Pound the shells of crayfish or the remains of prawns, or the creamy part, eggs and coral of lobsters and crawfish. Add and mix in $\frac{3}{4}$ dl (3 fl oz or $\frac{3}{8}$ U.S. cup) very fresh cream to each 100 g ($3\frac{1}{2}$ oz) of the mixture and pass through a very fine sieve. These cullises should be made only for immediate use and then used as indicated in the Notes at the beginning of this Chapter.

259 Shellfish Oil
This preparation can be used to complete a Sauce Mayonnaise which can then serve as an accompaniment for lobster and crawfish and can thus be said to create a new derivation of Mayonnaise.

Pound any available remains and shells of shellfish. Instead of butter use the same amount of oil, weight for weight, as the shellfish, i.e. 1 dl oil equals 95 g (3½ oz approximately) or 6 tbs.

Pound the shellfish remains to a fine paste and add the oil little by little, turning the pestle in the mortar to mix. Pass through a fine sieve and then through a tammy cloth. On no account should this preparation be warmed.

MARINADES AND BRINES

These are of different types although they are all used for the same purpose; that is:

1) to penetrate the items which are submitted to the action of the combined flavours of the ingredients used,
2) to tenderize the muscle fibres of certain meats,
3) in certain cases to assist in the preservation of foods, particularly during the time when there is a risk of deterioration through inadequate storage facilities or during a change in the weather. However, the composition of marinades and brines is determined by the use to which they are to be put.

MARINADES

260 Quick Marinades

These kinds of marinade are particularly suitable for small cuts of meat destined for fairly quick use such as grills of red meat, and for those meats which are to be used as ancillary ingredients in such cold preparations as galantines, terrines, pâtés etc.

1) In the case of meats for grilling, sprinkle the surface of the meat with finely chopped shallot, a few pieces of parsley stalks, thyme, bayleaf, salt and pepper in the appropriate amounts, then sprinkle with oil and lemon juice in the proportion of the juice of ½ lemon to 1 tbs of oil.
2) In the case of strips of veal, or game, or ham, pork fat for galantines etc., season them with salt and pepper and sprinkle with a marinade composed of three parts white wine, three parts brandy and one part oil.

The marinade is afterwards added to the forcemeat under preparation.

In both cases the items should be turned in the marinade frequently so as to ensure even penetration.

261 Raw Marinade for Butcher's meats and Venison

To make 2 litres (3½ pt or 9 U.S. cups)

Flavouring Ingredients:
100 g (3½ oz) carrot
100 g (3½ oz) onion
40 g (1½ oz) shallot
30 g (1 oz) celery
2 cloves of garlic
30 g (1 oz) parsley stalks
1 sprig of thyme
½ bayleaf
6 peppercorns
2 cloves

Liquid:
1¼ litre (2¼ pt or 5½ U.S. cups) white wine
5 dl (18 fl oz or 2¼ U.S. cups) vinegar
2½ dl (9 fl oz or 1⅛ U.S. cups) oil

Method:
Season the meat with salt and pepper. Slice the carrots, onions and shallots and place half of these ingredients in a suitable receptacle of a size just large enough to hold the piece of meat and the marinade. Cover with the remainder of the flavourings, the wine, vinegar and oil and keep in a cool place turning the piece of meat frequently.

262 Cooked Marinade for Butcher's meats and Venison

To make 2 litres (3½ pt or 9 U.S. cups)

Flavouring Ingredients:
100 g (3½ oz) carrot
100 g (3½ oz) onion
40 g (1½ oz) shallot
30 g (1 oz) celery
2 cloves of garlic
30 g (1 oz) parsley stalks
1 sprig of thyme
½ bayleaf
6 peppercorns
2 cloves

Liquid:
1½ litres (2⅝ pt or 6½ U.S. cups) white wine
3 dl (½ pt or 1¼ U.S. cups) vinegar
2½ dl (9 fl oz or 1⅛ U.S. cups) oil

Method:
Slice the carrots, onions and shallots finely and cook and colour them lightly in the oil with the remainder of the flavourings. Add the wine and vinegar and allow to simmer gently for 30 minutes. The marinade should not be used until it is completely cold.

263 Raw or Cooked Marinade for Large Game
To make 2 litres (3½ pt or 9 U.S. cups)

Flavouring Ingredients:
These are the same as for Marinade for Butcher's Meats and Venison with the addition of 12 g (⅓ oz) of rosemary.

Liquid:
1 litre 6 dl (2¾ pt or 7 U.S. cups) vinegar
4 dl (14 fl oz or 1¾ U.S. cups) oil

Method:
Whether cooked or raw the preparation is the same as in the preceding recipes.

264 Cooked Marinade for Mutton prepared *en Chevreuil*
To make 2 litres (3½ pt or 9 U.S. cups)

Flavouring Ingredients:
These are the same as for the Marinade for Butcher's Meats and Venison with the addition of 10 juniper berries and a pinch each of basil and rosemary.

Liquid:
This is the same as those for Marinade for Butcher's Meat and Venison.

Method:
Slice the onion, carrots and shallots and lightly colour them with the rest of the flavourings in the oil. Add the wine and vinegar and simmer gently for 30 minutes.

Use only when the marinade is cold.

265 Cooked Marinade for Mutton prepared *en Chamois*
to make 2 litres (3½ pt or 9 U.S. cups)

Flavouring Ingredients:
These are the same as the Raw Marinade for Butcher's meats and Venison, with the addition of 15 juniper berries and 15 g (½ oz) each of basil and rosemary.

Liquid:
1½ litres (2⅝ pt or 6½ U.S. cups) good quality red wine
3 dl (½ pt or 1¼ U.S. cups) vinegar
2½ dl (9 fl oz or 1⅛ U.S. cup) oil

Method:
As for the Marinade for Mutton *en Chevreuil.*

When this Marinade is made using good quality wine vinegar the proportion of liquids may be:

1 litre 2 dl (2 pt 2 fl oz or 5¼ U.S. cups) good quality red wine, 6 dl (1 pt or 2⅝ U.S. cups) wine vinegar and 2½ dl (9 fl oz or 1⅛ U.S. cups) oil.

The amount of vinegar used may be altered according to the degree of acidity of the wine.

266 Notes regarding the uses of Marinades

1) The use of cooked marinade is to speed up the penetration of the item under preparation.
2) The time required for leaving a piece of meat in a cooked or raw marinade is determined by the following factors: (*a*) the nature and size of the piece of meat, (*b*) the temperature of the surrounding area and (*c*) any atmospheric variations.
3) It is absolutely incorrect to use pure vinegar only in any particular marinade for pieces of meat in general or for joints of venison which are tender; the corrosive action of the vinegar will destroy the flavour of the meat. The use of vinegar alone is permissible only for very tough joints of furred game such as those of wild boar, stag and reindeer.

266a The Keeping of Marinades
When a marinade has to be kept for a lengthy period, especially during hot weather, it is recommended that 2–3 g of boric acid be added to the recipes given. The marinade should be boiled every day during the summer weather and every 4 to 5 days in winter: it should be replenished after each boiling with 2 dl (7 fl oz or ⅞ U.S. cup) of the appropriate wine and 1 dl (3½ fl oz or ½ U.S. cup) vinegar.

DRY SALT CURING AND PICKLING BRINES

267 Dry Salt Curing
The proportion of ingredients for dry salt curing are 40 g (1½ oz) saltpetre to 1 kg (2¼ lb) coarse salt. The total amount of salt and saltpetre required is determined by the quantity and size of the items being salted which must be covered with the salt and weighted down under pressure.

Method:
The joints of meat should be pierced right through the centre with a large needle; then rubbed with the saltpetre. The joints are then placed into a suitable receptacle with the salt, a sprig of thyme and ½ a bayleaf to each 1 kg (2¼ lb) salt.

268 Pickling Brine for Tongues

Ingredients:
5 litres (8¾ pt or 1⅜ U.S. gals) water
2¼ kg (5 lb) coarse salt
150 g (5 oz) saltpetre
300 g (11 oz) brown sugar
12 peppercorns
12 juniper berries
1 sprig of thyme
1 bayleaf

Method:
Place all the ingredients into a suitable pan and bring to the boil. Allow to cool completely and pour over the tongues which have previously been pierced in several places with a needle and rubbed well with salt and saltpetre.

The time required to pickle a medium-sized tongue is 8 days in winter and 6 days in the summer.

269 General Purpose Pickling Brine

Ingredients for 50 litres (11¼ gal or 14 U.S. gals)
50 litres (11¼ gals or 14 U.S. gals) water
25 kg (56 lb) salt
2 kg 700 g (6 lb) saltpetre
1 kg 600 g (3½ lb) brown sugar

Method:
Place all the ingredients in a well-tinned copper pan and bring to the boil quickly. When boiling place a peeled potato into it and if it floats, add sufficient water to cause it to begin to sink. On the other hand, if the potato sinks immediately it is placed into the brine, it will be necessary to reduce the liquid by boiling to the stage where the density of the brine will keep the potato just below the surface.

Remove the brine from the heat, allow to get quite cold and then pour it into the brine tank which should be constructed of stone, slate, cement or well-jointed tiles. It is necessary to have wooden slats in the bottom of the tank on which to place the joints of meat. If the meat were to rest directly on the bottom of the tank it would not absorb the pickle from all sides.

If the joints of meat for pickling are very large, the pickling brine should be injected into the centre of the joint by means of a brine syringe. Without this precaution the pickling of the joint will be irregular—the outside will be found to be too salty whilst the centre will only just be pickled. Allow 8 days for pickling all sizes of joints. Any joint of meat weighing over 4–5 kg (9–10 lb) should be injected with brine; it is this process which equalizes the time required for any size of joint.

Ox tongues for salting by this method must be as fresh as possible, trimmed of the greater part of the cartilage at the root and carefully beaten with a cutlet bat or rolling pin. They should then be pricked all over with a trussing needle before being placed into the brine and weighted down by a suitable method to prevent them from floating on the surface.

Note: Although a pickling brine does not turn sour or go bad so easily as a cooked marinade, it is advisable, especially during stormy weather, to take care to boil it from time to time. Since the boiling tends to concentrate the liquid slightly, a little water must be added each time and the density tested with a potato as previously indicated.

SAVOURY OR ASPIC JELLIES

In terms of nutritive value, savoury jellies of all types obtain their savour and quality from the particular special flavour of the stock used and it is this which determines their ultimate use.

To ensure that a jelly sets without recourse to the use of artificial setting substances it is necessary to add the requisite amount of gelatinous ingredients such as calves' feet and rinds of pork. These not only ensure that the jelly will set but also that it sets to a soft consistency.

During the summer months it is essential to try the consistency of the stock before clarifying it by placing a little on ice then, if necessary, adding a few leaves of gelatine. In this case the proportion of gelatine should not exceed 9 g (⅓ oz) or 6 leaves per 1 litre (1¾ pt or 4½ U.S. cups) of stock. The gelatine leaf used should be crisp and clear without a gluey taste; it should be soaked in cold water or washed well before being used.

It is advisable to avoid the use of artificial colouring in the making of Ordinary Aspic Jelly as it will develop sufficient colour naturally. In any case the final addition of Madeira will impart a good amber colour which is one of its characteristics.

270 Stock for Ordinary Aspic Jelly

To make 5 litres (8¾ pt or 1⅜ U.S. gal)

Nutritive Ingredients:
2 kg (4½ lbs) knuckle and shin of veal
1½ kg (3¼ lbs) veal bones, chopped small
1½ kg (3¼ lbs) round piece of shank of beef

These meats and bones must be lightly coloured in the oven.

Gelatinous Ingredients:
3 calf's feet, blanched and boned
250 g (9 oz) fresh pork rind

Flavouring Ingredients:
200 g (7 oz) carrot
200 g (7 oz) onion
50 g (2 oz) leek
50 g (2 oz) celery
1 large Bouquet garni

Liquid:
8½ litres (1 gal 7 pt or 2 U.S. gal 3 U.S. pt) water

Cooking time:
6 hours

Method:
Proceed in exactly the same way as for Brown Stock (1) but the colour should be less pronounced.

271 Stock for White Aspic Jelly
Use the same amount of ingredients and liquid as for Stock for Ordinary Aspic Jelly but use very white stock instead of water. The method and cooking time is the same as for White Stock.

272 Stock for Chicken Aspic Jelly
To make 5 litres (8¾ pt or 1⅜ U.S. gal)

Nutritive Ingredients:
1½ kg (3¼ lb) knuckle of veal
1½ kg (3¼ lb) shank of beef
1 kg (2¼ lb) veal bones, broken small
1½ kg (3¼ lb) chicken carcasses and giblets and in particular, scalded legs

Gelatinous Ingredients:
3 small boned and blanched calf's feet

Flavouring Ingredients:
150 g (5 oz) carrot
150 g (5 oz) onion
50 g (2 oz) leek
50 g (2 oz) celery
1 Bouquet garni

Liquid:
8 litres (1¾ gal or 2¼ U.S. gals) lightly flavoured white stock

Cooking time:
4½ hours

Method:
Proceed as for White Chicken Stock for sauces.

273 Stock for Game Aspic Jelly
To make 5 litres (8¾ pt or 1⅜ U.S. gal)

Nutritive Ingredients:
1 kg (2¼ lb) knuckle of veal
2 kg (4½ lb) shank of beef
750 g (1 lb 10 oz) veal bones, broken small
1¾ kg (3 lb 14 oz) trimmings and carcasses of game

All the above ingredients must be coloured in the oven.

Gelatinous Ingredients:
3 small calf's feet, boned and blanched

Flavouring Ingredients:
200 g (7 oz) carrot
200 g (7 oz) onion
50 g (2 oz) leek
75 g (2½ oz) celery
1 large Bouquet garni with additional thyme
7–8 juniper berries

Liquid:
8 litres (1¾ gal or 2¼ U.S. gal) water

Cooking time:
4 hours

Method:
Proceed in the same way as for Game Stock for sauces.

274 Stock for Ordinary Fish Aspic Jelly
To make 5 litres (8¾ pt or 1⅜ U.S. gal)

Basic Ingredients:
750 g (1 lb 10 oz) second quality fish such as whiting, gurnet, weever
750 g (1 lb 10 oz) bones and trimmings of sole

Flavouring Ingredients:
200 g (7 oz) sliced onions
30 g (1 oz) parsley stalks
100 g (3½ oz) mushroom trimmings

Liquid:
6 litres (10½ pt or 1⅝ U.S. gal) clear, lightly flavoured fish stock

Cooking time:
45 minutes

Method:
Proceed in the same way as for Fish Stock.

275 Stock for Red Wine Fish Aspic Jelly

This stock is usually the one which has been used in the cooking of a fish such as carp, trout etc. and the proportions of liquid for it are always half good red Burgundy and half gelatinous fish stock so as to ensure the setting of the prepared jelly. The additional flavour is supplied by the ingredients used in the cooking of the fish.

Notes on the use of stocks to be used in the making of jellies

Whenever possible stocks used for the making of jellies should be made the day before. When they have been prepared to the correct stage they should be skimmed of all fat, strained and allowed to cool in a china basin.

Whilst cooling, the stock congeals and the small amount of fat which is held in suspension accumulates on the surface where it solidifies in a flat piece thus allowing of its easy removal. At the same time any sediment which has passed through the cloth or strainer, sinks to the bottom because of its weight, thus permitting it to be removed without difficulty.

THE CLARIFICATION OF ASPIC JELLIES

276 Ordinary Aspic Jellies

To make 5 litres (8¾ pt or 1⅜ U.S. gal)

1) Ascertain the consistency and setting quality of the stock to be used so as to estimate the amount of gelatine required.
2) Skim and decant the stock.
3) Place 500 g (1 lb 2 oz) finely chopped lean minced beef with 3 egg whites and 10 g (⅓ oz) chervil and tarragon in a suitable thick-bottomed pot.
4) Add the cold or lukewarm stock to the meat and mix well with a whisk or spatula; bring to the boil gradually, mixing gently to ensure that the action of the albumen in the egg white which is the clarifying agent is distributed throughout the jelly.

Allow the jelly to simmer gently for 15 minutes without disturbing it then pass through a clean cloth.

Notes: If wine is to be added to a jelly this should be done when the jelly is almost cold. It is absolutely incorrect to add wine during the clarifying process as the action of boiling destroys the flavour of the wine and completely alters its taste. On the other hand when the wine is added to the cold jelly it will preserve its aroma intact.

To ensure that the addition of wine at the final stage does not interfere with the consistency of the jelly, steps should be taken to allow for this addition when judging the degree of setting of the jelly. Wines such as Madeira, Sherry and Marsala should be added in the proportion of 1 dl (3½ fl oz or ½ U.S. cup) per 1 litre (1¾ pt or 4½ U.S. cups) of jelly.

Wines such as Hock, Moselle and Champagne or other good quality white wine should be used in the proportion of 2 dl (7 fl oz or ⅞ U.S. cup) of wine per 1 litre (1¾ pt or 4½ U.S. cups) of jelly. In every case the wine used must be of the best quality; it is better not to use any wine at all than to add a poor quality one which would spoil the jelly.

277 Chicken Aspic Jelly

The principles of clarification for chicken jelly are exactly the same as for Ordinary Aspic Jelly—including the use of tarragon and chervil and the clarification of egg whites. Only half the quantity of beef is used, the other half being replaced by its equivalent of chicken necks thus, 250 g (9 oz) chopped chicken necks per 5 litres (8¾ pt or 1⅜ U.S. gal) is used.

Note: An excellent result may be obtained by the addition of roasted chicken carcasses, roughly chopped and well dried in a slow oven to extract the fat.

278 Game Aspic Jelly

The preparation of this jelly is the same as for Ordinary Aspic Jelly with the following differences: For a game jelly not having a specific flavour, the clarification is composed of 250 g (9 oz) very lean chopped beef and the same quantity of chopped flesh of ground game.

If the jelly is to have a well-determined specific flavour it is necessary to use the flesh of a particular item of game in the clarification, e.g. the flesh of partridge, grouse, ptarmigan etc.

All game jellies can be improved in flavour and aroma by the addition of 2 tbs of fine old brandy per 1 litre (1¾ pt or 4½ U.S. cups) of jelly—it is essential that the brandy be of the finest quality and it is better not to use it at all rather than to use a poor quality one. The jelly may not be perfect without the brandy but it will be passable.

279 White Fish Aspic Jelly

The clarification of fish jelly is carried out as follows:

1) Use egg whites in the proportions of 3 whites per 5 litres (8¾ pt or 1⅜ U.S. gal) of the fish stock and 250 g (9 oz) chopped fillet of whiting to compensate for the weakness of this type of clarification.
2) Fresh caviare may be used if this is possible, if not, pressed caviare in the proportion of 50 g (2 oz) per 1 litre (1¾ pt or 4½ U.S. cups) of the fish stock; proceed as explained in the clarification of Fish Consommé.

Dry Champagne or good quality white Burgundy may be used for flavouring and to give aroma to fish aspic jelly, taking note of the instructions relating to the use of wines in jelly given in the Notes appended to Ordinary Aspic Jelly.

Note: For certain uses, fish jelly can be given a special flavour and aroma by adding crayfish in the proportion of 4 small crayfish per 1 litre ($1\frac{3}{4}$ pt or $4\frac{1}{2}$ U.S. cups) of jelly. The crayfish are sautéed and cooked as for Bisque then pounded finely and added to the fish stock 10 minutes before it is strained.

280 Red Wine Fish Aspic Jelly

The clarification of this jelly is carried out using 4 egg whites per 5 litres ($8\frac{3}{4}$ pt or $1\frac{3}{8}$ U.S. gal) of the fish stock. During the clarification of this jelly it frequently happens that the wine breaks down precipitating certain colouring matter of tannic origin. It would appear that this is provoked by the contact of the wine with the gelatine suspensed in the stock and up to now there seems to be no way of preventing this.

It is therefore necessary to compensate for the absence of colouring matter by the addition of artificial or red vegetable colouring. This must be used with the greatest possible care so as to ensure that the colour of the jelly is no more than a light delicate pink.

CHAPTER 2

GARNISHES

In the work of the kitchen, garnishes have an importance and play a role which no practising cook can afford to misunderstand. Their composition should always be in direct keeping with the item or piece that they will accompany. All fanciful outlandish ideas should be rigorously avoided.

According to the need and above all to the nature of the item that they will accompany, garnishes are prepared from vegetables, farinaceous products, various moulded forcemeats, Quenelles of different sizes and shapes, cockscombs and kidneys, all types of mushrooms, olives, truffles, molluscs and crustaceans, and sometimes eggs, small fish and certain meat products.

In other cases garnishes can be the result of the flavouring of dishes that they accompany as in the Matelotes and Compotes and in preparations of dishes *à la Bourguignonne* etc.

Vegetables destined for use as a garnish are shaped and prepared according to the role assigned to them in the dish, but in some cases they are cooked in their own particular way as an ordinary vegetable; this also applies to farinaceous products, molluscs and crustaceans. This chapter indicates only the items of each garnish and their proportions leaving to each particular chapter details of their preparation.

VARIOUS FORCEMEATS

A very large number of garnishes having forcemeats or their direct derivatives such as Quenelles as a principle ingredient, and also because forcemeats are used in many preparations of whole joints, it is considered necessary to give their proportions and methods of making first, and to give their uses further on in the Chapter. There are five main categories of forcemeat:

1) forcemeat with veal and fat, or Godiveau of the classical kitchen,
2) forcemeat of which the basic ingredient is variable but which always includes a panada as a prime factor of binding,
3) forcemeat made up with cream according to modern procedures and which is used for Mousses and Mousselines,
4) special forcemeat using liver as a base, called *Gratin* which includes many types but where the method is always the same,
5) the plain forcemeats which are used principally in the preparation of cold dishes such as galantines, pâtés and terrines.

PANADAS FOR FORCEMEATS

These panadas are of many types; they are used according to the type of forcemeat and the nature of the preparation for which the forcemeat is required.

In principle the proportions of panada should not exceed half the weight of the basic ingredient of the forcemeat. If the type of panada adopted includes eggs and butter it is especially important that the amount of panada is used in exactly the right proportion.

Panadas should only be used when completely cold, except in the case of Potato Panada. When they have been prepared they should be spread flat on a buttered tray or dish so as to cool quickly, taking care to cover the surface with a buttered paper or to smooth the surface with a little butter to prevent the formation of a skin.

The proportions of the following panadas are calculated to give a net weight of 500 g (1 lb 2 oz). It is simple to multiply or divide these proportions to obtain the amount of panada required.

281 Bread Panada
Specially suitable for forcemeats of firm textured fish.

Ingredients:
3 dl (½ pt or 1¼ U.S. cups) boiling milk
250 g (9 oz) stale white breadcrumbs
5 g (⅙ oz) salt

Method:
Soak the breadcrumbs in the milk until the milk is completely absorbed, add the salt, then mix with a wooden spoon over a good heat so as to dry it out and leave the sides of the pan clean. Turn out on to a buttered tray or dish and allow to cool.

282 Flour Panada
Suitable for all fish and meat forcemeats.

Ingredients:
3 dl (½ pt or 1¼ U.S. cups) water
pinch of salt
50 g (2 oz) butter
150 g (5 oz) sifted flour

Method:
Place the water, salt and butter in a pan and bring to the boil; add and mix in the flour away from the fire, then return to a good heat and mix with a wooden spoon as for Chou Paste. Turn out on to a buttered tray or dish and allow to cool.

283 Frangipane Panada
Specially for chicken and fish forcemeats.

Ingredients
125 g (4½ oz) flour
4 egg yolks
90 g (3 oz) melted butter
pinch of salt
very small pinch of pepper
very small pinch of grated nutmeg
2½ dl (9 fl oz or 1⅛ U.S. cups) milk

Method:
Place the flour and yolks in a pan and mix together; add the melted butter, salt, pepper and nutmeg and mix in the boiling milk little by little.

Bring to the boil mixing with a whisk and allow to cook for 5–6 minutes; when it has thickened to the required texture, remove and allow to cool.

284 Rice Panada
Suitable for various forcemeats.

Ingredients:
200 g (7 oz) rice
6 dl (1 pt or 2⅝ U.S. cups) white Bouillon
20 g (⅔ oz) butter

Method:
Place the rice in a pan with the Bouillon and the butter; bring to the boil, cover and cook in the oven for 40–45 minutes without stirring. Remove from the oven and mix vigorously with a wooden spoon so as to work the rice to a paste; allow to cool.

285 Potato Panada
Suitable for large stuffed Quenelles of veal and other white meats.

Ingredients:
400 g (15 oz) freshly boiled and peeled potatoes
3 dl (½ pt or 1¼ U.S. cups) milk
pinch of salt
small pinch of pepper
small pinch of grated nutmeg
20 g (⅔ oz) butter

Method:
Reduce the milk by one-sixth, add the butter, seasoning and the potatoes cut in thick slices, allow to cook for 15 minutes then mix well to a purée.

The mixture should be used whilst still slightly warm, never completely cold as the purée will become elastic if it is worked when cold.

FORCEMEATS

The proportions of ingredients and method of preparation of these is the same for all forcemeats no matter what the basic ingredient, whether veal, poultry, game, fish or shellfish. A single recipe for each type of forcemeat will be sufficient considering that it is only the basic ingredient which changes, thus it is unnecessary to devote a whole special section to each forcemeat which is used in the kitchen.

286 Forcemeat with Panada and Butter
Suitable for ordinary Quenelles and the bordering of entrées.

Ingredients:
1 kg (2¼ lb) flesh, free from sinews
500 g (1 lb 2 oz) Flour Panada
12 g (⅓ oz) salt
pinch of pepper
small pinch of grated nutmeg
500 g (1 lb 2 oz) butter
4 whole eggs
8 egg yolks

Method:
Cut the flesh in dice and pound with the seasoning; remove the pounded flesh then pound the panada, add the butter and replace the flesh. Work the mixture vigorously with the pestle so as to ensure the complete amalgamation of the ingredients.

Add the eggs and yolks one or two at a time to the mixture, and mix well. Pass through a fine sieve, place in a basin then work the mixture well until smooth, using a wooden spatula.

Note: No matter which type of forcemeat is being prepared it is always necessary to poach a small piece so as to test the quality before proceeding to prepare the Quenelles.

287 Forcemeat with Panada and Cream

For fine Quenelles.

Ingredients:
1 kg (2¼ lb) flesh, free from sinews
400 g (15 oz) Frangipane Panada
5 egg whites
15 g (½ oz) salt
pinch of white pepper
small pinch of nutmeg
1½ litre (2⅝ pt or 6½ U.S. cups) double cream

Method:
Whichever flesh is used it should be pounded together with the whites added a little at a time with the seasoning. Add the panada and work the mixture vigorously with the pestle so as to ensure the complete amalgamation of the two main ingredients.

Pass the mixture through a fine sieve, place in a basin and work well until smooth, using a wooden spatula. Place on ice for 1 hour, then add one-third of the cream little by little, then finally add the other two-thirds which has been lightly whipped. After the addition of the cream the forcemeat should be very white, smooth and light in texture.

Note: If first quality cream is not available, it is better to prepare a Panada and Butter Forcemeat using Frangipane Panada.

288 Fine Forcemeat with Cream, known as Mousseline Forcemeat

For Mousses, Mousselines and Quenelles for soup, etc.

Ingredients:
1 kg (2¼ lb) flesh, well trimmed and free from sinew
4 egg whites
1½ litres (2⅝ pt or 6½ U.S. cups) thick fresh cream
18 g (⅔ oz) salt
pinch of white pepper

Method:
Pound the flesh finely with the seasoning adding the whites a little at a time; pass through a fine sieve.

Place the mixture in a shallow and sloping sided pan and work well until smooth, using a wooden spatula, then place on ice for 2 hours. Add the cream little by little, taking care to work well with the spatula without removing the pan from the ice.

Notes:
1) The proportions of cream given above are average because the quantity which can be absorbed varies more or less according to the albuminous content of the flesh used, be it meat, fish or shellfish.
2) In terms of delicacy this type of fine forcemeat cannot be surpassed and the method of preparation is applicable to any type of flesh such as game, poultry, fish, shellfish etc.
3) The amount of egg white used depends on the nature and the condition of the flesh used; meats rich in albumin and which are very fresh, such as poultry, veal etc., will need less whites than those meats which are obtained from older and tougher animals. It is possible to prepare a Mousseline forcemeat with the still warm flesh of a young, recently killed chicken without adding any egg white.
4) It is absolutely essential to use the best quality cream in the preparation of this type of forcemeat and above all for shellfish.

289 Godiveau Prepared with Ice

Ingredients:
1 kg (2¼ lb) cushion of veal, free from sinew
1½ kg (3 lb 6 oz) very dry beef kidney suet
8 eggs
25 g (1 oz) salt
5 g (⅙ oz) white pepper
pinch of nutmeg
700–800 g (1½–1¾ lb) clear ice or 7–8 dl (1¼–1⅗ pt or 3–3½ U.S. cups) ice cold water

Method:
Firstly chop the veal and add the seasoning; break up the suet into small pieces taking care to remove all the skin and tissue and chop; pound the veal and suet separately then place them together in the mortar. Pound again to ensure the amalgamation of the ingredients, adding the eggs one at a time whilst working continuously.

Pass through a fine sieve, spread the mixture on a tray in a thin layer and keep on ice until the next day. The next day pound the mixture again and add the ice, broken in small pieces or the ice water, a little at a time so as to ensure the complete mixing.

Always test the quality of the Godiveau before moulding by cooking a little piece; add a little more ice water if too firm or a little egg white if too loose in texture.

Note: Quenelles made from this Godiveau mixture are used principally as a garnish for *Vols-au-Vent* and for Financière garnishes accompanying joints of butcher's meat.

As in all other cases these Quenelles can be piped out using a piping bag and tube but in most cases they are moulded by hand and poached in salted water.

However, dry poaching in a very slow oven is the most suitable method of cooking these. The following method is very quick and is particularly recommended: make sure that the Godiveau mixture is not too stiff and pipe out with a plain tube in the required shape, close together on sheets of buttered paper. These in turn should be on buttered trays; place in a slow oven to cook.

After about 7–8 minutes small beads of fat will appear on the surface of the Quenelles which is an indication that they are just cooked. Remove from the oven and turn the sheet of Quenelles over on to a tray or a marble slab. As soon as they are slightly cool remove the paper by pulling from one corner; allow them to cool completely and place on a tray or for preference, a wicker mat.

290 Godiveau with Cream

Ingredients:
1 kg ($2\frac{1}{4}$ lb) very white cushion of veal, trimmed of sinew
1 kg ($2\frac{1}{4}$ lb) very dry beef kidney suet
4 eggs
3 egg yolks
7 dl ($1\frac{1}{4}$ pt or 3 U.S. cups) cream
25 g (1 oz) salt
5 g ($\frac{1}{6}$ oz) pepper
pinch of nutmeg

Method:
Chop the veal and suet separately, then pound together working vigorously in a mortar to ensure the amalgamation of the two items then adding the seasoning and the eggs and yolks one by one.

Pass through a fine sieve, spread on a tray and keep on ice until the following day. The next day, chill the mortar by filling it with ice; remove the ice then pound the mixture again and add the cream little by little working it in with the pestle. Test the quality before moulding the Quenelles and correct if necessary.

291 Pike Forcemeat with Suet, known as Godiveau Lyonnaise

Ingredients:
500 g (1 lb 2 oz) pike flesh, free from skin and bone
500 g (1 lb 2 oz) very dry beef kidney suet, free from skin and tissue and broken into pieces, or
250 g (9 oz) beef suet and 250 g (9 oz) very white beef bone marrow
500 g (1 lb 2 oz) Frangipane Panada
4 egg whites
15 g ($\frac{1}{2}$ oz) salt
good pinch of pepper
pinch of nutmeg

Method:
Pound the pike flesh and remove from the mortar, then pound the suet adding the very cold panada and the egg white little by little. Replace the pike, add the seasoning and work the mixture vigorously with the pestle then pass through a fine sieve. Place in a basin and work well until smooth using a wooden spatula; keep on ice until required for use.

It is also possible to prepare this forcemeat as follows:

Pound the pike flesh with the seasoning then add the panada and pass through a fine sieve; replace in the mortar, work it vigorously with the pestle to develop a firm consistency then incorporate the suet in very small pieces. If using suet and bone marrow, melt them first before adding little by little. Work the mixture well with the pestle then remove and place in a basin. Keep on ice until required.

292 Veal Forcemeat for the borders and bases of Entrées and for stuffed Quenelles etc.

Ingredients:
1 kg ($2\frac{1}{4}$ lb) very white cushion of veal, free from sinew
500 g (1 lb 2 oz) Potato Panada
300 g (11 oz) butter
5 eggs
8 egg yolks
2 tbs cold thick Sauce Béchamel
20 g ($\frac{2}{3}$ oz) salt
pinch of pepper
small pinch of nutmeg

Method:
Pound the veal finely with the seasoning and remove from the mortar. Place in the Potato Panada when lukewarm and work to a paste with the pestle. When cold, or nearly cold, add the pounded veal and work together with the butter, eggs and yolks added one at a time; finally add the Béchamel.

Pass the mixture through a fine sieve, place in a basin and work until smooth using a wooden spatula.

293 Gratin Forcemeat A—for Raised Pies, Bordering of Entrées etc.

To make 1 kg ($2\frac{1}{4}$ lb) forcemeat.

Ingredients:
250 g (9 oz) fat salt belly of pork, cut in dice
250 g (9 oz) veal from the leg, free from sinew and cut in dice

250 g (9 oz) very pale calf's liver, cut in dice
150 g (5 oz) butter
40 g (1½ oz) mushroom trimmings
25 g (1 oz) truffle trimmings (raw if possible)
6 egg yolks
½ bayleaf
1 sprig of thyme
50 g (2 oz) chopped shallot
20 g (⅔ oz) salt
good pinch of pepper
pinch of mixed spice
1½ dl (5 fl oz or ⅝ U.S. cup) Madeira
1½ dl (5 fl oz or ⅝ U.S. cup) cold, very well reduced Espagnole

Method:
Fry the belly of pork quickly until brown in a pan with 50 g (2 oz) butter; remove and place on one side then fry the veal in the same fat until brown; remove and place with the belly of pork. Fry the liver very quickly in the same fat until coloured, replace the veal and pork and add the mushrooms, truffles, thyme, bayleaf, shallots and seasonings. Fry together for 2 minutes then turn out on to a tray. Deglaze the pan with the Madeira. Pound the fried ingredients very finely adding the remainder of the butter, the egg yolks one at a time, the reduced sauce and the deglazed Madeira. Pass through a fine sieve, place the mixture in a basin and work together until smooth, using a wooden spatula.

Note: In the preparation of this forcemeat, the calf's liver can be replaced with chicken, duck, goose or turkey livers taking care that the gall bladder and any parts blemished by it, are first removed.

294 Gratin Forcemeat B—for Game Pies
To make 1 kg (2¼ lb) forcemeat.

Ingredients:
250 g (9 oz) fat salt belly of pork, cut in dice
250 g (9 oz) wild rabbit flesh, cut in dice
250 g (9 oz) chicken and game livers
40 g (1½ oz) mushroom trimmings
25 g (1 oz) truffle trimmings (raw if possible)
1 sprig of thyme
½ a bayleaf
50 g (2 oz) chopped shallot
20 g (⅔ oz) salt
a good pinch of pepper
pinch of mixed spice
50 g (2 oz) butter
100 g (3½ oz) raw or cooked foie gras
6 egg yolks
1½ dl (5 fl oz or ⅝ U.S. cup) Madeira
1½ dl (5 fl oz or ⅝ U.S. cup) cold, very well reduced Game Espagnole, or Sauce Salmis

Method:
Fry the pork, rabbit and liver in the butter as in Gratin Forcemeat A. Replace together in the pan with the seasonings and flavourings and fry together for a few moments. Add the Madeira and allow to cook together gently for 5 minutes. Drain well and finely pound in the mortar. When sufficiently smooth add the foie gras, the egg yolks, the cold sauce and the Madeira. Pass through a fine sieve, place in a basin and mix together until smooth using a wooden spatula.

295 Gratin Forcemeat C—for Croûtons, Canapés, Small Game Birds and Duckling
To make 1 kg (2¼ lb) forcemeat.

Ingredients:
300 g (11 oz) finely chopped fresh pork fat
600 g (1 lb 5 oz) chicken livers
75 g (2½ oz) sliced shallot
25 g (1 oz) mushroom trimmings
½ a bayleaf
sprig of thyme
18 g (⅔ oz) salt
pinch of pepper
small pinch of mixed spice

Method:
Heat the pork fat in a shallow pan and add the liver with the seasoning and flavourings; fry quickly to stiffen the outside of the livers, leaving them underdone so as to give a pink colour to the resultant forcemeat. Allow to cool, pound in a mortar until smooth, pass through a fine sieve and place in a basin; mix together until smooth and keep in a cool place covered with a buttered paper.

FORCEMEATS FOR COLD GALANTINES, PIES AND TERRINES

These forcemeats are of three different types and are completely different from the other forcemeats and gratin forcemeats which have already been given.

They are seasoned in the proportions of 25–30 g (1 oz) spiced salt and finished with 1½ dl (5 fl oz or ⅝ U.S. cup) of brandy per 1 kg (2¼ lb) forcemeat. If found necessary to bind the mixture this can be effected by adding 2 egg whites per 1 kg (2¼ lb) forcemeat.

296 Spiced Salt
This can be prepared by mixing together 100 g (3½ oz) very dry fine salt, 20 g (⅔ oz) ground white pepper and 20 g (⅔ oz) mixed spice. If this

salt is not to be used immediately it should be kept in a tightly closed container in a dry place.

297 Pork Forcemeat
This is composed of equal parts of lean pork flesh and pork fat chopped separately, pounded together and seasoned and flavoured according to the proportions indicated above. This forcemeat can be used in the preparation of ordinary pies and terrines and is basically a sausage meat.

298 Veal and Pork Forcemeat

Ingredients:
250 g (9 oz) diced leg of veal
250 g (9 oz) diced lean pork flesh
500 g (1 lb 2 oz) diced pork fat
2 eggs
seasoning and brandy as indicated above

Method:
Pound the veal, pork and fat together until fine, together with the seasoning and eggs. At the last moment add the brandy, flamed, and pass the mixture through a fine sieve.

This forcemeat is particularly suitable for galantines but equally useful for pies and terrines.

299 Chicken or Game Forcemeat
The proportions of the ingredients in this forcemeat are determined by the net weight of the flesh being used. The weight of flesh obtained from 1 eviscerated chicken weighing 1½ kg (3 lb 6 oz) minus the fillets which are usually used as a garnish, is roughly 500–600 g (1 lb 2 oz–1 lb 5 oz). Thus the proportions of the ingredients for this forcemeat can be established at 550 g (1 lb 4 oz) chicken flesh, 200 g (7 oz) veal, free from sinew, 200 g (7 oz) lean pork, 900 g (2 lb) pork fat, 4 eggs, 50–60 g (2 oz) spiced salt and 3 dl (½ pt or 1¼ U.S. cups) brandy.

Method:
Chop the meats and fat separately, then place together in the mortar with the seasoning; pound finely, adding the eggs one by one and the brandy at the last moment. Pass through a fine sieve.

Game forcemeat is prepared in the same proportions using the same method.

Note: In certain cases 125 g (4½ oz) fresh foie gras passed through a fine sieve, and 50 g (2 oz) chopped truffle can be added to the veal and pork forcemeat or the chicken forcemeat.

If a very fine game forcemeat is required a quarter of its total weight can be added of Gratin Forcemeat B together with a little very well reduced essence of the game under preparation.

300 Special Forcemeats for the Stuffing of Fish for Braising
Forcemeat A

Ingredients:
250 g (9 oz) chopped raw soft roes
180 g (6 oz) white breadcrumbs soaked in milk and squeezed
5 g (⅙ oz) salt
pinch of pepper
a very small pinch of nutmeg
10 g (⅓ oz) chopped chives
pinch of parsley
20 g (⅔ oz) chopped chervil
50 g (2 oz) butter
1 egg
3 egg yolks

Method:
Place all the ingredients in a basin and mix well together with a wooden spoon so as to ensure that they are thoroughly mixed.

Forcemeat B

Ingredients:
200 g (7 oz) white breadcrumbs soaked in milk and squeezed
50 g (2 oz) finely chopped onion, lightly cooked in butter
25 g (1 oz) finely chopped shallot, lightly cooked in butter
80 g (3 oz) very fresh raw mushrooms, chopped and squeezed
10 g (½ oz) chopped parsley
touch of crushed garlic
1 egg
3 egg yolks
8 g (¼ oz) salt
pinch of pepper
very small pinch of nutmeg

Method:
Place all the ingredients in a basin and mix well together with a wooden spoon to ensure that they are thoroughly mixed.

301 Quenelles
Quenelles may be prepared from various forcemeats such as the Mousseline (288), the Godiveau (289 or 290) and Veal Forcemeat (292) etc. and may be prepared in various shapes and sizes as follows:

1) by rolling with the hand or on a floured table in the shape of small cylinders,
2) by piping the mixture on to a buttered tray,

3) by moulding with spoons,
4) by moulding with the finger in the shape of a cockscomb.

These preparations are too well known to require fuller explanations except on how to poach them.

It is only necessary to state that Quenelles for ordinary garnishes such as Financière, Toulouse etc. should be moulded with teaspoons or piped out using a plain or star tube.

The average weight of these Quenelles would be in the region of 12–15 g ($\frac{1}{3}$–$\frac{1}{2}$ oz) each. Quenelles for large garnishes such as Godard, Régence and Chambord should be moulded with tablespoons and should be 20–22 g ($\frac{3}{4}$ oz) in weight.

Decorated Quenelles which are Quenelles featured in large garnishes should be approximately 40–50 g (1$\frac{1}{2}$–2 oz) in weight and should be moulded in round, oval or elongated oval shapes.

Truffle or red salted ox tongue is almost always used to decorate these Quenelles, often both together. These items of decoration should be fixed on with raw egg white.

Excepting Quenelles of Godiveau which should preferably be poached dry, all Quenelles should be poached in salted water using 10 g ($\frac{1}{3}$ oz) salt per 1 litre (1$\frac{3}{4}$ pt or 4$\frac{1}{2}$ U.S. cups) water. This water should be boiling and poured gently into the pans or trays containing the Quenelles and then kept at just below boiling point until they are cooked.

VARIOUS PREPARATIONS FOR HOT GARNISHES

302 Bases and Cases for Presentation and Service

Bases and cases for the presentation of food are losing their importance because of the requirements of modern methods of service. They are made from bread but more often from rice.

Bases and cases made from bread: These are cut to the required shape from stale white sandwich loaves then fried in butter and stuck to the service dish using starch paste.

Preparation of bases and cases made from rice: Wash 2 kg (4$\frac{1}{2}$ lb) Patna rice under running cold water until the water is clear and shows no traces of starch. Blanch the rice for 5 minutes in plenty of boiling water then refresh until cold. Drain well and rewash the rice in hot water; drain again, then place in a large pan lined with a clean strong cloth or with slices of pork fat. Add 10 g ($\frac{1}{3}$ oz) alum and cover the rice with another cloth or salt pork fat; cover with the lid and cook in a slow oven for 3 hours.

Remove the rice and pound vigorously in a mortar, then place it in a cloth which has been well smeared with lard and knead it well. Place the mixture into moulds which have been greased with lard, and allow to cool.

When it is very cold the rice can be cut into the required shapes. They can then be kept for a long time by keeping in fresh water with the addition of alum, changing it frequently.

303 Borders of Forcemeat

These borders should be made of a forcemeat of the same nature as the principle item of the dish which it is called upon to contain. They are poached in well buttered plain or fancy border moulds.

The plain moulds are decorated as required with nice slices of truffle, pieces of poached egg white, red salt ox tongue and pistachios etc., but it is not essential to decorate the fancy moulds.

These borders are used above all for the service of entrées of poultry and fish and for small entrées of butcher's meat with sauces.

304 Borders of Noodle Paste

These borders are made with very firm noodle paste cut into shapes as required such as oblongs 4–5 cm (1$\frac{1}{2}$–2 in) long by 6–7 mm ($\frac{1}{4}$ in) thick, which are decorated by cutting out small pieces with fancy cutters.

These shapes should be gilded with egg yolk and dried in a hot-plate or a slow oven before being stuck around the edges of the serving dish with flour paste.

305 Borders of Vegetables

These are made in well-buttered plain border moulds the bottom and sides of which are decorated in the Chartreuse style with various vegetables prepared for this purpose. The mould is then filled with fairly firm Veal Forcemeat (292) and poached *au Bain-marie* in the oven.

These borders are used principally for the service of entrées of butcher's meats garnished with vegetables.

306 Borders of White Paste

Place 2 dl (7 fl oz or $\frac{7}{8}$ U.S. cup) water in a pan with 5 g ($\frac{1}{6}$ oz) salt and 20 g ($\frac{2}{3}$ oz) lard; bring to the boil, add 100 g (3$\frac{1}{2}$ oz) sifted flour and mix over heat until the mixture is cooked and leaves the side of the pan; turn out on to a marble slab.

Work 100 g (3½ oz) of a starch such as cornflour or arrowroot into the mixture; give 10 turns as for puff paste and allow to rest. Roll out the paste to approximately 7 mm (¼ in) thick and cut out shapes with a fancy pastry cutter to choice. Dry out the pieces in a hot-plate or slow oven and stick them on to the edges of the serving dish with a little flour paste.

307 Croquette and Cromesquis Mixtures
See the Chapter on Hot Hors-d'oeuvre.

308 Croûtons
Croûtons are cut from white bread into shapes and sizes as determined by the requirements of the dish with which they are to be served. They are fried in clarified butter and should always be prepared at the last minute.

309 Dauphine, Duchesse and Marquise Potato Mixtures
See the Chapter on vegetables and potatoes.

310 Dry Duxelles
The base of Duxelles is invariably chopped mushrooms but it can be prepared with any edible fungus. Heat 30 g (1 oz) butter in a pan with an equal amount of oil, add 20 g (⅔ oz) each of chopped onion and chopped shallot and cook gently for a few minutes. Add 250 g (9 oz) finely chopped trimmings and stalks of mushrooms, which have been firmly squeezed to remove all the vegetable juices. Cook gently until the complete evaporation of all the moisture. Season with salt and pepper and finally add a pinch of chopped parsley. Place the mixture in a basin and cover with a buttered paper. This dry Duxelles is used in a number of preparations.

311 Duxelles à la Bonne Femme, for certain preparations derived from household cookery
Mix together equal amounts of dry Duxelles and well seasoned raw sausage meat.

312 Duxelles for Stuffed Vegetables (*tomatoes, mushrooms etc.*)
Take 100 g (3½ oz) dry Duxelles and add ½ dl (2 fl oz or ¼ U.S. cup) white wine and allow it to reduce almost completely. Add 1 dl (3½ fl oz or ½ U.S. cup) well-tomatoed Sauce Demi-glace, a touch of crushed garlic and 25 g (1 oz) white breadcrumbs. Allow the mixture to stew gently until it is reduced to the consistency required for its particular use.

313 Duxelles for Various Garnishes (*tartlets, onions, cucumbers etc.*)
Mix 100 g (3½ oz) dry Duxelles into 60 g (2 oz) of either Mousseline Forcemeat, a Forcemeat with Panada, or a Gratin Forcemeat—whichever is the most applicable. Vegetables stuffed with this type of Duxelles should be cooked in the oven instead of being gratinated.

314 Tomato Essence
Pass very ripe tomatoes through a fine sieve; place the juice in a pan and cook very gently until it becomes syrupy in consistency. Pass through a cloth without pressure and keep until required.

Note: This essence is very useful for giving the finishing touch to a number of small brown sauces.

315 Tomato Fondue or Fondue Portugaise
Cook 120 g (4 oz) chopped onion in a little butter or oil; add 500 g (1 lb 2 oz) roughly chopped flesh only of tomato, a touch of crushed garlic and a little salt and pepper. Allow to cook gently until the complete reduction of moisture. According to the season, that is to say the degree of ripeness of the tomatoes, a little caster sugar can be added to improve the flavour.

316 Frying Batter for Fritters of Brains, Soft Roes, Fritots etc.
Place in a basin 125 g (4½ oz) sifted flour, a pinch of salt, ⅓ dl (1½ fl oz or ⅕ U.S. cup) oil or melted butter and approximately 2 dl (7 fl oz or ⅞ U.S. cup) lukewarm water. If required for immediate use, mix together by turning over with a wooden spoon and without working the batter; this avoids the development of elasticity which in its turn prevents it sticking to the items to be dipped. If the batter is prepared in advance it can be mixed well and allowing it to rest for a while will be sufficient for it to lose its elasticity.

Add 2 stiffly beaten egg whites to the batter just before using.

317 Frying Batter for Vegetables (*salsify, celery, Japanese artichoke etc.*)
Place in a basin, 125 g (4½ oz) sifted flour, a pinch of salt and 2 tbs melted butter; mix together with sufficient cold water to obtain a light smooth batter. Where possible prepare it 1 hour in advance of use.

318 Kache of Buckwheat for Soups

For 10 persons
Add 7–8 dl (1¼–1⅔ pt or 3–3½ U.S. cups) of

lukewarm salted water to 1 kg (2¼ lb) buckwheat flour and work to a firm paste. Place the paste into a tall saucepan and press it down evenly then bake it in a hot oven for approximately 2 hours.

Remove from the oven, cut off the crust from the top and scoop out the inside without getting any of the outer crust into the mixture.

Work 100 g (3½ oz) butter into this Kache then allow it to cool under pressure in a layer of approximately 1 cm (⅖ in) thickness. Cut into 3 cm (1 in) rounds using a plain cutter, fry in clarified butter to a light brown colour and arrange in dishes or on a serviette.

Note: Kache can also be served as it comes from the oven in which case it is cooked in special moulds.

319 Kache of Semolina for Coulibiac

For 10 persons
Mix well together 200 g (7 oz) coarse semolina and 1 beaten egg; spread the mixture flat on a baking tray and place in a cool oven to dry.

Rub through a coarse sieve then poach in Bouillon for approximately 20 minutes. Drain well and use as required.

320 Maintenon Mixture (*for stuffing cutlets of this name*)

Reduce by half 4 dl (14 fl oz or 1¾ U.S. cups) Sauce Béchamel and 1 dl (3½ fl oz or ½ U.S. cup) Soubise. Thicken the mixture with 3 egg yolks and add 100 g (3½ oz) sliced mushrooms previously stewed in a little butter.

321 Matignon

Cut 125 g (4½ oz) red of carrot, 125 g (4½ oz) onion, 50 g (2 oz) celery and 100 g (3½ oz) raw ham all into thin Paysanne; add 1 bayleaf and a sprig of thyme. Stew together in a little butter and deglaze with a little white wine.

322 Mirepoix

The ingredients are the same as those for Matignon with the following differences: the vegetables are cut into large or small Brunoise according to how the Mirepoix is to be used and the raw ham is replaced by lean salt belly of pork cut in dice and blanched. Lightly brown all the ingredients in a little butter.

323 Mirepoix Fine, also called Mirepoix à la Bordelaise

The large Mirepoix used in certain preparations to give flavour and aroma are normally prepared as required but this is not the same for Mirepoix à la Bordelaise which is used particularly with crayfish and lobsters. It should be prepared in advance and as follows: cut 125 g (4½ oz) red of carrot, 125 g (4½ oz) onion and 30 g (1 oz) parsley stalks into very fine Brunoise and add a pinch of thyme and crushed bayleaf. Place all these ingredients in a small pan with 50 g (2 oz) butter and stew gently together until tender. Place in a small basin and spread level with the back of a fork; cover with a round of buttered greaseproof paper and keep until required.

Note: To obtain a smaller Mirepoix, the ingredients can be chopped, only in this case it is necessary to squeeze the chopped ingredients firmly in the corner of a cloth so as to extract the vegetable juices which would otherwise not evaporate properly during the cooking. These juices remaining in the Mirepoix encourage mouldiness or fermentation if kept for any length of time.

324 Montglas Mixture (*for cutlets etc.*)

Take 150 g (5 oz) cooked salted ox tongue, 150 g (5 oz) foie gras, 100 g (3½ oz) cooked mushrooms, and 100 g (3½ oz) truffle, and cut into short thick Julienne. Mix this Julienne together with 2½ dl (9 fl oz or 1⅛ U.S. cups) very well reduced Sauce Demi-glace with Madeira. Spread flat on a buttered tray and allow to cool before using.

325 General Purpose Chou Paste

Place 1 litre (1¾ pt or 4½ U.S. cups) water in a pan with 200 g (7 oz) butter and 10 g (⅓ oz) salt. Bring to the boil and add, away from the heat, 625 g (1 lb 6 oz) sifted flour; mix well together, replace on the heat and stir until the paste leaves the side of the pan clean.

Remove from the heat, allow to cool slightly then add 12–14 eggs according to size, mixing them in well, one or two at a time.

This Chou Paste is more frequently used in the preparation of Pommes à la Dauphine and Gnocchi etc. and should be much firmer in texture than the ordinary Chou Paste used in pastry work.

326 Pearl Barley for Stuffed Chicken and other Uses

Cook 75 g (2½ oz) chopped onion in a little butter until golden in colour and add 250 g (9 oz) washed, drained and dried pearl barley. Heat, mixing with a wooden spoon then cover with 7½ dl (1⅓ pt or 3¼ U.S. cups) boiling White Bouillon. Season with a pinch of pepper, cover with a lid and cook in a slow oven for approximately 2 hours. At the last moment mix in 50 g (2 oz) butter cooked until light brown in colour.

327 Provençale Mixture (*for stuffed cutlets*)
Reduce 5 dl (18 fl oz or $2\frac{1}{4}$ U.S. cups) Sauce Soubise until very thick; add a touch of crushed garlic and thicken with 3 egg yolks.

328 Rice for Stuffed Poultry served as a Relevé or as an Entrée
Gently fry 50 g (2 oz) chopped onion in 50 g (2 oz) butter; add 250 g (9 oz) Carolina or Patna rice and mix over the fire until the rice becomes very white.

Moisten with 5 dl (18 fl oz or $2\frac{1}{4}$ U.S. cups) White Bouillon and allow to cook for 15 minutes under cover. Then add $1\frac{1}{2}$ dl (5 fl oz or $\frac{5}{8}$ U.S. cup) cream, 125 g ($4\frac{1}{2}$ oz) foie gras fat or butter, a few tablespoons of Sauce Suprême and the garnish indicated by the name of the preparation of the poultry for which the rice is being prepared.

Note: Because the rice will be further cooked during the cooking of the poultry it should only be three-quarters cooked beforehand.

The poultry should not be filled completely with the rice as the rice will swell inside during the cooking process.

329 Various Salpicons
Under the general term Salpicon, is understood a large number of preparations.

A Salpicon can be simple or compound—it is simple when comprised of a single item such as the flesh of poultry or game, meat, sweetbreads, or again foie gras, fish or shellfish, ham or tongue. It is a compound Salpicon when composed of different items, as cited before, capable of being appropriately mixed together with the addition of mushrooms and truffles etc.

The first stage in the preparation of a Salpicon consists of cutting the items of which it is to be composed, into small even shaped $\frac{1}{2}$ cm ($\frac{1}{5}$ in) dice. The next stage in the preparation of a Salpicon is the combination of these items in accordance with the requirements of their own particular name, e.g. Salpicon à la Royale, à la Financière, à la Parisienne, à la Montglas, au Chasseur etc.

330 Twarogue for Piroguis
Take 250 g (9 oz) well drained white cream cheese, place in a serviette and squeeze it firmly to remove excess moisture. Place it in a basin, add 250 g (9 oz) well mixed softened butter and 1 egg. Mix together with a wooden spoon until very smooth then season with salt and pepper.

VARIOUS COLD MIXTURES AND PREPARATIONS FOR GARNISHING

331 Cold Mousses, Mousselines and Soufflés
The terms Mousses and Mousselines can be used to describe hot and cold preparations; that which differentiates between Mousse and Mousseline is not the composition but its moulding. A Mousse, hot or cold, is made in a large mould of which the size is generally sufficient for more than one person. The Mousselines are moulded either with spoons, a piping bag or in special moulds having the form of large Quenelles, and one only is served per person. The Soufflés are moulded in small cassolettes or soufflé moulds.

332 Composition of the Mixture for Cold Mousses and Mousselines

Ingredients:

1 litre ($1\frac{3}{4}$ pt or $4\frac{1}{2}$ U.S. cups) cooked purée of the principal ingredient such as chicken, game, foie gras, fish or shellfish
$2\frac{1}{2}$ dl (9 fl oz or $1\frac{1}{8}$ U.S. cups) melted aspic jelly
4 dl (14 fl oz or $1\frac{3}{4}$ U.S. cups) appropriate Velouté
4 dl (14 fl oz or $1\frac{3}{4}$ U.S. cups) double cream which being correctly whipped will be equal to 6 dl (1 pt or $2\frac{5}{8}$ cups)

The proportions of the above ingredients may be slightly adjusted according to the nature of the main ingredients being used and in the preparation of certain Mousses either jelly by itself or Velouté alone need be used.

Method:
Add the cool jelly and Velouté (or just one of these ingredients if called for) to the basic purée and mix together on ice.

When cold and thicker in consistency, add and fold in the cream. Seasoning is very important in cold preparations and it should always be checked and adjusted with great care.

Note: the cream should not be more than half whipped, if it is fully whipped the quality of the Mousse will be less delicate and of a dryer texture.

333 Moulding of Cold Mousses
The following method of moulding Mousses is still used today by practising cooks. They are moulded in special plain or fancy moulds which have been lined with very clear aspic jelly and decorated with items in keeping with the Mousse mixture being used. But nowadays the following procedure is to be preferred: set a layer of very clear aspic jelly in the bottom of a timbale or deep silver dish. Surround the outside with a band of greaseproof paper approximately 2 cm ($\frac{4}{5}$ in) higher than the rim of the dish so that when it is removed the Mousse has the appearance of a sort of Soufflé; the paper can be fixed in position with the help of a

little butter; alternatively it could be placed inside the timbale. It must be removed just prior to service by detaching it from the Mousse with the blade of a knife dipped in lukewarm water whilst at the same time pulling off the paper gently.

When the timbale has been filled with the mixture it should be placed in the refrigerator to set. These Mousses can also be prepared in small silver cassolettes or soufflé moulds but this method of moulding them is usually reserved for cold Soufflés so as to observe the difference between the two even though the mixture may be the same.

Mousses can also be presented, particularly those made of game or foie gras, in one of the deep silver or glass dishes used in modern service; in this case the Mousse mixture is simply poured into the bowl which has previously been lined with a layer of jelly at the bottom; the surface should be smoothed flat and the Mousse allowed to cool and set. The decoration is then applied directly to the Mousse and is finally covered with a layer of jelly.

In the presentation of a Mousse of game it is recommended that it be surrounded with glazed suprêmes of the game being used.

334 Moulding of Cold Mousselines

This can be carried out in two different ways, by either simply lining the mould with jelly or afterwards coating with a Sauce Chaud-froid. In either case they should be made in oval moulds of the type used in the making of large Quenelles or Mousseline eggs.

Method 1

Line the moulds with very clear aspic jelly and cover with a layer of the Mousseline mixture; garnish the centre with a Salpicon composed of the same basic ingredient as that in the Mousse, e.g. poultry, game, shellfish etc. and of truffle. Cover with more Mousseline mixture; smooth dome-shape and place in the refrigerator to set.

Method 2

Place a layer of the mixture in the bottom of the moulds, garnish the centre with a Salipicon, cover with more mixture and place to set. After demoulding, coat the Mousselines with Sauce Chaud-froid in keeping with the composition of the mixture; decorate with truffle and other items in keeping with the Mousseline and glaze with aspic jelly to fix the decorations.

Set a layer of very clear aspic jelly in the bottom of a silver or glass dish and arrange the Mousselines on top; coat them once more with jelly and keep in the refrigerator until required.

335 Cold Soufflés

Cold Soufflés are nothing other than Mousses; that is to say, their composition is the same but as stated previously, a Mousse is moulded sufficiently large for the service of a number of people whereas Soufflés, correctly described, are made in small cassolettes or soufflé moulds each sufficient for one person. The moulding is carried out in the same way as for Mousses; that is, the mixture is placed on a layer of set jelly at the bottom of the cassolettes and they are surrounded with a band of greaseproof paper which allows the mixture to come above the rim of the cassolette so as to give the illusion of a hot Soufflé when the paper is finally removed.

Note: The principle of these three preparations of which the basis is the same, can be clearly established as follows:

1) Although a Mousse can be served under the title of Soufflé, to avoid confusion the name Mousse should only be used when it is moulded in a size sufficient for a number of people.
2) Mousselines are large Quenelles, stuffed or not with a Salpicon and are made in a size sufficient for one person only.
3) Soufflés are small Mousses moulded in cassolettes or other utensils of this type of a size sufficient for one person only

336 Aspics

The first point that must be given serious consideration in the preparation of an Aspic of whatever type is that the jelly should be succulent, absolutely clear and not too firm in texture.

When the Aspics are moulded as in the case of the old classical kitchen, the moulds used are always those with a central funnel, either plain or fancy. Border moulds can also be utilized but should normally be used when the particular aspic requires a garnish which is placed in the centre of the dish.

The preparation of a moulded Aspic is started by decorating the bottom and sides of the mould; for this the mould must be well chilled in crushed ice; a little jelly almost at setting point, is poured in and by rolling the mould on the ice it will adhere to the sides. The items of decoration are then dipped into cool melted jelly and immediately fixed in place: the decoration is at the taste and discretion of the person doing it and cannot be defined precisely, the only thing that can be said is that it must be absolutely correct and should appear neat and clean when the Aspic is demoulded.

The items used for decoration should be in keeping with the nature of the principle ingredient of the Aspic; these are usually truffles, poached egg whites, gherkins, capers, various sprigs of herbs, thin slices of radish, lobster coral, salted ox tongue etc.

If the garnish of an Aspic comprises slices of various foods, rectangles of foie gras etc., and if the size of the mould makes it necessary to make several layers of ingredients they should be interposed with a layer of jelly between each. Each additional layer should not be started until the previous layer of jelly is sufficiently set.

The Aspic should always be finished with a fairly thick layer of jelly and where possible, the mould should be kept on ice while it is being garnished and filled. Salt should not be added to the ice as this will reduce the temperature to a point at which it may affect the clarity of the jelly.

For demoulding: Dip the mould in hot water, wipe it dry and turn the Aspic over on to either a folded serviette, a decorated rice base or a block of carved ice. Surround it with shapes of jelly in the form of diamonds, squares etc. or with chopped jelly.

Note: The moulding of Aspics requires of necessity a fairly stiff jelly which, however, is not really desirable as in this case the jelly is less fine in quality. Modern service has adopted the following more practical method of moulding: the components of the Aspic are arranged in layers on a layer of jelly set in the bottom of the dish—this can be a timbale or a deep silver, glass or porcelain dish—and finally covered with a fairly thick layer of almost setting jelly, it is then placed on ice for service. Any decoration required is applied directly on the components of the Aspic and before they are placed in the mould.

337 Chaud-froids

The items requiring to be coated with Sauce Chaud-froid are usually cut into neatly shaped portions but whole items can also be coated in the same manner; in this case, however, the whole item would be given a particular name.

If the Chaud-froid is composed of portions which have been cut from a large piece they are dipped in the sauce and laid on wire racks. When the sauce is cold the items are decorated, glazed with jelly and trimmed of any excess sauce before being arranged on the dish. When preparing a whole item it is coated in one operation with Sauce Chaud-froid which is cold but still liquid; it is then decorated and glazed with jelly. Individual portions of Chaud-froid can be arranged on a base made from bread, rice or semolina; or as a border, the centre of which is filled with a centrepiece made from bread, rice or semolina. They may also be arranged in a timbale or a deep silver, glass or porcelain dish.

According to requirements the arrangement of whole items may be done on bases or on a dish set in a block of carved ice. Poultry and game for Chaud-froids should be cut into neat even pieces and the skin removed. The drumsticks and winglets should not be utilized but reserved for other uses. The additional items used in the preparation of portioned Chaud-froids are mushrooms, cockscombs and kidneys coated with sauce, and truffles which are simply glazed with jelly.

338 Cold Fish or Meat Loaf

In the old classical kitchen cold fish or meat loaf was nothing other than a poached, moulded forcemeat which was cooled, then decorated and glazed with jelly. They were also prepared *en Belle-vue* in another mould which was coated inside with clear jelly and then decorated. Modern culinary practice has abandoned this procedure and in general has replaced these loaves with Mousses.

339 The Garnishing of Cold Dishes

According to the requirements of the dish, these garnishes comprise halves or quarters of stuffed eggs decorated and glazed with jelly; very small stuffed or garnished tomatoes, or large tomatoes stuffed according to requirements and then cut into even size quarters; small timbales or barquettes of vegetable salad; small meat or fish moulds; tartlets of tomato purée mixed with jelly; nice hearts of very light green lettuce; fillets of anchovy; olives etc.

340 GARNISHES

Notes concerning modifications in the size and shape of garnishes

The principles underlying the composition of garnishes as in all other culinary preparations, is intangible. Where in certain cases, modifications are found to be necessary they only imply a difference in arrangement and shape according to the requirements of the dish and do not indicate a change in the items of the garnish.

Also the same garnish applied on the one hand to a large joint such as Fillet of beef and on the other hand a preparation such as Tournedos should necessarily undergo a modification in its shape, size and arrangement so that the garnish is in keeping with either. These observations hold good for small cuts from the fillet and Chateaubriands where logic may indicate something else.

In consequence, the proportions of the following garnishes have been established for services of ten covers and they will require altering in terms of size and quantity according to the kind of garnish being prepared and its ultimate use—that is whether they are for a large joint or for smaller items.

At this point it is necessary to consider a matter of great importance: taking into account that this book, being a collection of traditional French culinary techniques, it necessarily includes a number of garnishes the composition of which is no longer in keeping with modern practice which requires the avoidance of complications and the need to simplify the garnishes in such a way as to ensure a rapid and consequently, perfect service. The dishes cannot be eaten in all their perfection unless they are served very hot and this cannot be done unless the garnishes are kept very simple lending themselves to a quick arrangement on the dish.

It is also advisable wherever possible, to serve the garnishes separately instead of placing them around the item which they are to accompany; in this case the item is sliced, arranged on the dish and presented to the guest, and then the garnish as well as the sauce is served immediately. This method of service is the only one which allows for a rapid arrangement of the dish and a correct and very hot service. These observations apply above all to large joints (Relevés).

For small entrées such as Noisettes and Tournedos, especially when they are being served for a lesser number of persons than in services of ten, there is not the same need to adhere to the foregoing observations. However, it is a good thing to apply the above observations and to suggest one absolute rule: where the separate arrangement of the garnish allows a rapid service one should not hesitate to adopt it whichever kind of dish is being arranged.

Important remarks concerning suitable sauces for Entrées of meat garnished with vegetables

Sauces derived from Espagnole are not suitable for small entrées of butcher's meat garnished with vegetables. Jus lié is infinitely preferable but the most highly recommended accompaniment is a light meat glaze buttered in the proportions of 125 g (4½ oz) of butter to 1 dl (3½ fl oz or ½ U.S. cup) of glaze and acidulated with a few drops of lemon juice. This buttered glaze should, however, be sufficiently light so as not to bind the vegetables together.

Vegetables such as asparagus tips, peas, French beans, Macédoines etc. may spoil the quality of the sauce owing to their natural moistness and because of their fragile texture. This results in a rather unappetizing appearance when the foods are served on the customer's plate; the problem does not arise if Sauce Chateaubriand or buttered meat glaze is used, bearing in mind that these sauces do not spoil but marry very well with vegetable garnishes whilst at the same time adding a considerable amount of smoothness.

At this stage it must be strongly stated that the sauces derived from Espagnole or Sauce Tomate should be reserved wherever possible for preparations accompanied by garnishes of items such as truffles, cockscombs and kidneys, Quenelles, mushrooms etc. (For example Financière or Godard garnishes.) For vegetable garnishes the use of Jus lié or buttered meat glaze is preferable.

LIST OF GARNISHES

(Quantities for one service of 10)

341 Garnish à l'Algérienne (*for joints or cuts of meat*)
10 croquettes of sweet potato moulded cork-shape; 10 small tomatoes emptied, seasoned and stewed in a little oil.
Accompaniment: thin Tomato Sauce with the addition of a fine Julienne of pimento which has been previously grilled and peeled.

342 Garnish à l'Alsacienne (*for joints of meat, fillets of beef and Tournedos*)
10 tartlet cases filled with braised Choucroute and each finished with a round slice of lean ham.
Accompaniment: Jus de Veau lié.

343 Garnish à l'Américaine (*specially for fish*)
This garnish is comprised of slices of lobster tails prepared à l'Américaine.
Accompaniment: lobster sauce from the cooking of the lobster.

344 Garnish à l'Andalouse (*for joints or cuts of meat and poultry*)
10 halves of grilled pimento filled with rice à la Grecque; 10 slices of eggplant 4 cm (1½ in) thick with the centre hollowed out, fried and filled with tomatoes sautéed in oil.
Accompaniment: Jus lié.

345 Garnish à l'Arlésienne (*for Tournedos and Noisettes*)
Round slices of eggplant cut 1 cm (⅖ in) thick, seasoned, floured and fried in oil; peeled tomatoes, sliced and sautéed in butter; bouquets of onion rings, floured and deep fried.
Accompaniment: tomato-flavoured Sauce Demi-glace.

346 Garnish à la Banquière (*for large chicken*)
10 larks boned, stuffed with gratin forcemeat, coloured and cooked *à la Casserole*: 10 small Quenelles of chicken forcemeat; 10 slices of truffle.
Accompaniment: Sauce Demi-glace with truffle essence.

347 Garnish à la Berrichonne (*for large joints of meat*)
10 balls of braised cabbage; 10 small slices of lean streaky bacon cooked with the cabbage; 20 small onions and 20 large chestnuts cooked in the stock from the joint under preparation.
Accompaniment: the braising liquor from the joint, thickened with arrowroot.

348 Garnish à la Berny (*for game and marinated joints of meat*)
10 croquettes of Pommes à la Berny moulded cork-shape; 10 tartlet cases filled dome-shape with buttered chestnut purée with a slice of glazed truffle on each.
Accompaniment: light Sauce Poivrade.

349 Garnish à la Bizontine (*for cuts or joints of meat and Tournedos*)
10 small croustades of Duchesse potato, eggwashed and coloured in the oven and filled with a piped purée of creamed cauliflower; 10 halves of stuffed and braised lettuce.
Accompaniment: buttered veal gravy.

350 Garnish à la Boulangère (*for mutton, lamb and poultry*)
250 g (9 oz) sliced onions lightly cooked in butter
750 g (1 lb 10 oz) potatoes, sliced or cut in quarters
15 g ($\frac{1}{2}$ oz) salt.
5 g ($\frac{1}{6}$ oz) pepper

These ingredients are mixed together and placed around the joint after it has been coloured and are then cooked together. For poultry, the garnish is modified as follows: olive-shape potatoes and small onions fried brown in butter in advance.
Accompaniment: a little good gravy.

351 Garnish à la Bouquetière (*for large joints of meat*)
250 g (9 oz) each of carrots and turnips, cut with an oval spoon-cutter and glazed; 250 g (9 oz) small Château potatoes; 150 g (5 oz) each of peas and French beans cut in dice and buttered at the last moment; 250 g (9 oz) bouquets of cauliflower.

These items are arranged in bouquets around the joint, well separated and alternating the colours. The bouquets of cauliflower are lightly coated with Sauce Hollandaise.
Accompaniment: a clear gravy made from the cooking juices, with the fat removed.

352 Garnish à la Bourgeoise (*for cuts or joints of meat*)
500 g (1 lb 2 oz) carrots trimmed to the shape of garlic cloves and glazed; 500 g (1 lb 2 oz) glazed button onions; 125 g ($4\frac{1}{2}$ oz) salt belly of pork, cut in dice, blanched and fried in butter.

This garnish is added to the joint when it is almost ready and is thus cooked in the braising liquor.

353 Garnish à la Bourguignonne (*for joints of beef*)
500 g (1 lb 2 oz) glazed button onions; 250 g (9 oz) mushrooms cut in quarters and sautéed in butter; 125 g ($4\frac{1}{2}$ oz) salt belly of pork, cut in dice and fried brown.

These items are added to the joint during the final stages of its preparation. The liquid used in the preparation of this dish should be a good quality red wine which is its special characteristic.
Accompaniment: the sauce from the braising.

354 Garnish à la Brabançonne (*for cuts or joints of meat*)
10 tartlet cases filled with a purée of Brussels sprouts, blanched and stewed in butter, coated with Mornay sauce and glazed at the last moment; 10 croquettes of Duchesse potato moulded to the shape of small discs.
Accompaniment: Jus lié.

355 Garnish Bréhan (*for joints of beef and veal*)
10 small artichoke bottoms filled dome-shape with a purée of broad beans; 10 bouquets of cauliflower lightly coated with Hollandaise Sauce; 10 small potatoes cooked in butter and sprinkled with chopped parsley.
Accompaniment: the braising liquor from the joint.

356 Garnish à la Bretonne (*for mutton*)
1 litre ($1\frac{3}{4}$ pt or $4\frac{1}{2}$ U.S. cups) cooked haricot or flageolet beans, mixed with Sauce Bretonne and sprinkled with chopped parsley.
Accompaniment: the gravy from the joint.

357 Garnish Brillat-Savarin (*for game birds*)
Very small tartlet cases filled dome-shape with a Soufflé mixture made from woodcock and truffles and cooked at the last moment; thick slices of truffle.
Accompaniment: a fine quality Sauce Demi-glace made with stock of the game under preparation.

358 Garnish Bristol (*for joints of meat*)
10 small croquettes of braised rice, moulded to the shape and size of an apricot; 5 dl (18 fl oz or $2\frac{1}{4}$ U.S. cups) cooked flageolet beans bound with a little Velouté; 20 small potatoes trimmed round to the size of a walnut, cooked in butter, then rolled in melted meat glaze.
Accompaniment: the braising liquor from the joint.

359 Garnish à la Bruxelloise (*for cuts and joints of meat*)
10 very white braised Belgian endives; 10 Château potatoes; 500 g (1 lb 2 oz) small Brussels sprouts, blanched and stewed in butter.
Accompaniment: a light Sauce Demi-glace flavoured with Madeira wine.

360 Garnish à la Cancalaise (*for fish*)
20 poached and bearded oysters; 125 g ($4\frac{1}{2}$ oz) peeled prawns. Sauce Normande.

361 Garnish à la Cardinal (*for fish*)
10 nice slices of lobster tail; 10 slices of very black truffle; 60 g (2 oz) diced lobster flesh and 50 g (2 oz) diced truffle. Sauce Cardinal.

362 Garnish à la Castillane (*for Tournedos and Noisettes*)
10 small cases made from Duchesse potato, egg-washed and coloured in the oven, filled with Tomato Fondue lightly flavoured with garlic. Surround the dish with a border of onion rings, seasoned, floured and fried in oil.
Accompaniment: the deglazed cooking juices, flavoured with tomato.

363 Garnish Chambord (*for large braised fish*)
10 Quenelles of truffled fish forcemeat moulded with spoons; 5 large decorated long oval Quenelles; 200 g (7 oz) small grooved button mushrooms; 10 thick slices of soft roes, seasoned, floured and sautéed in butter; 200 g (7 oz) truffles trimmed in the shape of olives; 10 trussed or untrussed crayfish, cooked in Court-bouillon; 10 Croûtons cut in the shape of cockscombs and fried in butter.

The sauce is prepared from the braising liquor.

364 Garnish Châtelaine (*for joints of meat and poultry*)
10 artichoke bottoms filled with thick Sauce Soubise; 30 shelled chestnuts stewed in the braising liquor from the joint; 300 g (11 oz) Noisette potatoes.
Accompaniment: the cooking liquor from the joint added to Sauce Madère.

365 Garnish à la Chipolata (*for joints of meat and poultry*)
20 button onions, glazed brown; 10 grilled chipolata sausages; 10 chestnuts cooked in a little Bouillon; 125 g ($4\frac{1}{2}$ oz) salt belly of pork, cut in dice and fried to a light brown colour; 20 pieces of carrot trimmed olive-shape and glazed (this item is optional).
Accompaniment: Sauce Demi-glace with the addition of the cooking liquor from the joint being prepared.

366 Garnish Choisy (*for Tournedos and Noisettes*)
10 halves of braised lettuce; 20 small Château potatoes
Accompaniment: Buttered meat glaze.

367 Garnish Choron (*for Tournedos and Noisettes*)
10 small to medium artichoke bottoms, garnished with buttered asparagus tips or if asparagus is unavailable, small buttered peas; 30 pieces of Noisette potatoes.
Accompaniment: Sauce Choron.

368 Garnish à la Clamart (*for cuts or joints of meat*)
10 tartlet cases filled with peas à la Française containing the finely shredded lettuce from the cooking; dress each tartlet on a small round of Macaire potatoes.
Accompaniment: Jus lié.

369 Garnish de Compote (*used particularly for pigeons and young grain-fed chickens*)
250 g (9 oz) lean salt belly of pork cut in batons, blanched and fried to a light brown colour in butter; 300 g (11 oz) button onions, glazed brown; 300 g (11 oz) button mushrooms, cut in half and sautéed in butter.

This garnish should be cooked with the pigeons or chickens and served over them.

370 Garnish Conti (*for braised joints of meat*)
750 g (1 lb 10 oz) purée of lentils; 250 g (9 oz) lean salt belly of pork cooked with the lentils then cut into rectangles.
Accompaniment: the braising liquor from the joint.

371 Garnish à la Commodore (*for whole or large cuts of fish*)
10 small cassolettes garnished with crayfish tails; 10 Quenelles made from whiting and crayfish butter; 10 nice mussels à la Villeroy. Sauce Normande finished with Crayfish Butter.

372 Garnish Cussy (*for Tournedos, Noisettes and poultry*)
10 large grilled mushrooms filled with chestnut purée; 10 small truffles trimmed round shape and cooked with Madeira; 20 large cockscombs.
Accompaniment: Sauce Madère.

373 Garnish Daumont (*for fish*)
10 large mushrooms cooked in butter, each garnished with 6 halves of crayfish tails bound with Sauce Nantua; 10 small round Quenelles made of fish and cream forcemeat and decorated with truffle; 10 thick slices of soft roe, egg and breadcrumbed and deep fried. Sauce Nantua.

374 Garnish à la Dauphine (*for joints of meat, Tournedos and Noisettes*)
20 croquettes prepared from Dauphine potato mixture in the shape of a cork for large joints or in the shape of a disc for Tournedos or Noisettes.
Accompaniment: Sauce Demi-glace flavoured with Madeira.

375 Garnish à la Dieppoise (*for fish*)
100 g (3½ oz) shelled prawns; 30 nice mussels poached in white wine and bearded. White Wine Sauce with the addition of the reduced cooking liquor from the fish being prepared.

376 Garnish Doria (*for fish*)
30 pieces cucumber, trimmed olive shape and stewed in butter; slices of peeled depipped lemon placed on the fish which should be prepared *à la Meunière*.

377 Garnish Dubarry (*for joints of meat, Noisettes and Tournedos*)
10 small balls of cauliflower coated with Sauce Mornay, sprinkled with grated cheese and gratinated; 10 pieces of Fondante potatoes.
Accompaniment: the cooking liquor from the joint or the deglazed juices from the pan.

378 Garnish à la Duchesse (*for joints of meat, Noisettes and Tournedos*)
20 small oval medallion or brioche shapes of Duchesse potato mixture, eggwashed and coloured golden brown in the oven at the last moment.
Accompaniment: Sauce Madère.

379 Garnish à la Favorite (*for Noisettes and Tournedos*)
10 small slices of foie gras, seasoned, floured and sautéed in butter with a nice slice of truffle on each; bouquets of asparagus tips.
Accompaniment: Jus lié.

380 Garnish à la Fermière (*for poultry*)
150 g (5 oz) each of red of carrot and turnip, 50 g (2 oz) onion, and 50 g (2 oz) celery all cut in Paysanne and lightly stewed in butter with a pinch of salt and a good pinch of sugar. Finish cooking the garnish with the poultry.

381 Garnish à la Financière (*for cuts of joints of meat and poultry*)
20 ordinary Quenelles made with veal or chicken forcemeat according to whether the garnish will be served with a joint of meat or poultry; 150 g (5 oz) small grooved mushrooms; 100 g (3½ oz) cockscombs and kidneys; 50 g (2 oz) slices of truffle; 12 turned and blanched olives. Sauce Financière.

382 Garnish à la Flamande (*for joints of meat*)
10 small balls of braised cabbage; 10 carrots and 10 turnips trimmed olive shape and cooked in a little stock; 10 small plain boiled potatoes; 250 g (9 oz) salt belly of pork cooked whole with the cabbage then cut into 10 small rectangles; 10 slices smoked sausage (150 g or 5 oz).
Accompaniment: the cooking liquor from the joint.

383 Garnish à la Florentine

For fish:
250 g (9 oz) spinach, blanched and stewed in butter; place the spinach in the bottom of the dish, the poached fish on top, coat with Mornay Sauce and glaze.

For joints of meat:
10 Subrics of spinach; 10 small croquettes the shape of discs made from a mixture of semolina cooked in Bouillon, bound with eggs and grated cheese.
Accompaniment: light Sauce Demi-glace strongly flavoured with tomato.

384. Garnish Florian (*for joints of lamb*)
3 nice braised lettuces cut in quarters and trimmed; 20 glazed carrots cut olive shape; 20 very small button onions glazed in butter; 10 small Fondante potatoes.
Accompaniment: gravy prepared from the cooking of the joint.

385 Garnish à la Forestière (*for cuts or joints of meat and poultry*)
300 g (11 oz) morels, sautéed in equal quantities of oil and butter; 125 g (4½ oz) very lean salt belly of pork cut in batons, blanched and fried to a light brown in butter; 300 g (11 oz) potatoes cut in large dice and sautéed in butter.
Accompaniment: Sauce Duxelles with the addition of the braising liquor or the deglazed juices from the pan.

386 Garnish Frascati (*for large joints of meat*)
10 slices of foie gras (raw if possible) seasoned, floured and sautéed in butter; 300 g (11 oz) buttered asparagus tips; 10 very white grooved button mushrooms; 10 truffles cut to the shape and size of a large olive and lightly glazed; 10 long crescent-shaped pieces made from Duchesse potato mixture containing chopped truffle, eggwashed and coloured golden brown in the oven at the last moment—these crescents are used to enclose the other items of garnish when arranged on the dish.
Accompaniment: a lightly thickened gravy prepared from the cooking of the joint.

387 Garnish à la Gastronome (*for joints of meat and poultry*)
20 nice shelled chestnuts cooked in a little Bouillon and glazed as for button onions; 10 medium-sized truffles cooked in Champagne; 20 nice cocks' kidneys coated with light-coloured meat glaze; 10 large morels cut in halves and sautéed in butter.
Accompaniment: Sauce Demi-glace with the addition of truffle essence.

388 Garnish Godard (*for large joints of meat and poultry*)
10 Quenelles made from forcemeat with butter containing chopped mushroom and truffles and moulded with spoons; 4 large oval Quenelles decorated with truffle and very red salt ox tongue; 10 small turned mushrooms; 125 g ($4\frac{1}{2}$ oz) cockscombs; 200 g (7 oz) nice glazed lambs' sweetbreads or a veal throat sweetbread glazed and cut into thick slices; 10 truffles trimmed olive shape.

389 Garnish Grand-Duc (*for fish*)
200 g (7 oz) buttered asparagus tips; 10 shelled crayfish tails; 10 nice slices of truffle. Sauce Mornay.

390 Garnish à la Grecque (*for lamb and poultry*)
250 g (9 oz) rice prepared à la Grecque (4237).
Accompaniment: Tomato Sauce.

391 Garnish Henri IV (*for Noisettes and Tournedos*)
10 medium to small artichoke bottoms, according to the item under preparation, filled with small Noisette potatoes rolled in melted meat glaze.
Accompaniment: Sauce Béarnaise.

392 Garnish à la Hongroise (*for various dishes*)
Bouquets of cauliflower moulded in small dariole moulds, turned out on to a buttered gratin dish sprinkled with grated cheese, the cauliflower then coated with Mornay Sauce containing chopped ham and flavoured with paprika, then glazed.
Accompaniment: a light sauce as required for the dish under preparation flavoured with paprika.

393 Garnish à l'Italienne (*for cuts or joints of meat and poultry*)
20 small quarters of artichokes prepared à l'Italienne; 10 croquettes of macaroni, well bound and flavoured with cheese and shaped in the form of discs.
Accompaniment: Sauce Italienne.

394 Garnish à l'Indienne (*for fish and joints of meat and poultry*)
125 g ($4\frac{1}{2}$ oz) Patna rice prepared à l'Indienne (4238).
Accompaniment: Sauce à l'Indienne.

395 Garnish à la Japonaise (*for cuts or joints of meat*)
625 g (1 lb 6 oz) Japanese artichokes bound with Velouté and placed in nicely coloured small deep fluted pastry cases; 10 croquettes of rice.
Accompaniment: a clear gravy made from the cooking of the joint.

396 Garnish à la Jardinière (*for joints of meat*)
125 g ($4\frac{1}{2}$ oz) each of carrot and turnip cut oval-shape with a plain or fancy vegetable scoop, or cut into short cylinder shapes using a column cutter, then cooked in Bouillon and glazed; 125 g ($4\frac{1}{2}$ oz) each of peas, small flageolet beans and French beans cut into small diamonds and buttered separately at the last moment; 10 bouquets of freshly cooked cauliflower.

Arrange these items in separate bouquets around the joint, alternating the colours. Coat each bouquet of cauliflower with a spoonful of Sauce Hollandaise.
Accompaniment: a clear gravy made from the cooking of the joint.

397 Garnish Joinville (*for fish*)
125 g ($4\frac{1}{2}$ oz) cooked mushrooms, 50 g (2 oz) truffle cut into small dice or short Julienne, 125 g ($4\frac{1}{2}$ oz) shelled prawns. Mix these ingredients together with a little Sauce Joinville. In addition 10 slices of truffle and one very large white cooked mushroom stuck with 8 prawns from which the shell of the tail has been removed. Sauce Joinville.

398 Garnish Judic (*for Noisettes, Tournedos and poultry*)
10 small well-trimmed halves of braised lettuce; 10 nice cocks' kidneys; 10 slices of truffle.
Accompaniment: an excellent Sauce Demi-glace.

399 Garnish à la Languedocienne (*for cuts or joints of meat and poultry*)

10 round slices of eggplant, 1 cm ($\frac{2}{5}$ in) thick, floured and fried in oil; 400 g (15 oz) sliced flap mushrooms sautéed in oil; 400 g (15 oz) flesh only of tomato, roughly chopped and sautéed in oil with the addition of a touch of crushed garlic; coarsely chopped parsley.
Accompaniment: Jus lié.

400 Garnish Lorette (*for Noisettes and Tournedos*)
10 small croquettes of chicken; buttered asparagus tips or buttered peas; slices of truffle.
Accompaniment: Jus lié.

401 Garnish Louisiane (*for poultry*)
500 g (1 lb 2 oz) creamed maize; 10 dariole moulds of rice cooked *au Gras* (4326); 20 round slices of fried banana.
Accompaniment: a reduced gravy prepared from the cooking of the poultry.

402 Garnish Lucullus (*for cuts or joints of meat and poultry*)
10 truffles of approximately 60 g (2 oz) each in weight, cooked in a Mirepoix with Madeira then hollowed out in the shape of a case, reserving the tops as covers. Fill each with 2 cocks' kidneys rolled in buttered meat glaze, cover with the lids and seal these with a little ring of chicken forcemeat. Place in the oven for a few moments to ensure the cooking of the forcemeat. Also 10 spoon-moulded Quenelles prepared from fine chicken forcemeat containing the truffle removed from the cases which must be pounded and passed through a sieve; 10 nice cockscombs.
Accompaniment: Sauce Demi-glace with the addition of truffle essence.

403 Garnish Macédoine (*for joints of meat*)
This garnish is composed of the same items as Jardinière but in this case they are mixed together and buttered.

This garnish can be served in a deep dish or timbale or in artichoke bottoms; or arranged dome-shape in the centre of the service dish, surrounded by the meat which it is to accompany.

404 Garnish Madeleine (*for cuts or joints of meat and poultry*)
10 small artichoke bottoms filled with thick Soubise; 10 dariole moulds of haricot bean purée mixed with 6 egg yolks and 1 whole egg per 1 litre ($1\frac{3}{4}$ pt or $4\frac{1}{2}$ U.S. cups) of purée, finished with 150 g (5 oz) butter then moulded and cooked.
Accompaniment: Sauce Demi-glace.

405 Garnish à la Maillot (*for joints of meat but especially for ham*)
10 carrots and 10 turnips trimmed to the shape of large olives and cooked in Bouillon; 20 glazed button onions; 10 halves of braised lettuce; 100 g ($3\frac{1}{2}$ oz) each of buttered peas and French beans.
Accompaniment: Jus lié.

406 Garnish à la Maraîchère (*for joints of meat*)
500 g (1 lb 2 oz) cooked salsify cut into 4 cm ($1\frac{3}{5}$ in) lengths, bound with a little fairly thick Velouté; 10 fairly large Château potatoes; 300 g (11 oz) small Brussels sprouts blanched and stewed in butter.
Accompaniment: the cooking liquor from the joint.

407 Garnish Maréchal

For calves sweetbreads, joints of meat and poultry:
10 Quenelles of chicken forcemeat with truffles moulded with spoons; 60 g (2 oz) sliced truffles bound with a little Sauce Italienne; 20 cockscombs.
Accompaniment: Sauce Demi-glace with Madeira.

For suprêmes of chicken, escalopes of calves sweetbreads, Noisettes and cutlets of lamb:
In this case the garnish consists of a nice slice of glazed truffle placed on the item and buttered asparagus tips, or if out of season, very small peas. The items with which this garnish is used are always egg and breadcrumbed, using 2 parts fresh breadcrumbs to 1 part of finely chopped truffles.

408 Garnish à la Marie-Louise (*for Noisettes, Tournedos and poultry*)
Artichoke bottoms of a size in keeping with the item being prepared, stewed in butter and filled dome-shape with a very thick mushroom purée mixed with a quarter its amount of Soubise.
Accompaniment: Jus lié.

409 Garnish à la Marinière (*for fish*)
$7\frac{1}{2}$ dl ($1\frac{1}{3}$ pt or $3\frac{1}{4}$ U.S. cups) small mussels—(approximately 35 in number) cooked with white wine then bearded; 100 g ($3\frac{1}{2}$ oz) peeled prawns. Sauce à la Marinière.

410 Garnish Marquise (*for Noisettes, Tournedos and poultry*)
10 small cooked fluted tartlet cases filled with a mixture consisting of 250 g (9 oz) poached spinal marrow of beef or veal (Amourettes) cut in small pieces; 125 g ($4\frac{1}{2}$ oz) asparagus tips; 50 g (2 oz) Julienne of truffle—all bound together with $1\frac{1}{2}$ dl (5 fl oz or $\frac{5}{8}$ U.S. cup) Sauce Allemande finished with Crayfish Butter also 20 small oval shapes of Duchesse potato mixture containing some well-

reduced tomato purée piped out with a plain tube and coloured in the oven for a few minutes before being required.

411 Garnish à la Marseillaise (*for cuts or joints of meat*)
10 small halves of tomatoes, emptied and lightly cooked in the oven with a little oil and just a touch of garlic; in each half tomato place a large stoned stuffed olive encircled at its base with a nice fillet of anchovy. The tomatoes should be separated on the serving dish with pieces of Pommes Frites en Copeaux (4192).
Accompaniment: Sauce Provençale.

412 Garnish Mascotte (*for Noisettes, Tournedos and poultry*)
10 raw artichoke bottoms cut in quarters and sautéed in butter; 20 small potatoes trimmed olive-shape and cooked in butter; 10 small balls of truffle.
Accompaniment: the cooking juices deglazed with white wine and veal stock.

Note: The Mascotte garnish should be placed around the items of food which should always be prepared *en Cocotte.*

413 Garnish Masséna (*for Noisettes and Tournedos*)
10 medium to small artichoke bottoms filled with thick Sauce Béarnaise; 10 thick slices of very fresh bone marrow poached in Bouillon.
Accompaniment: Tomato Sauce.

414 Garnish Matelote (*for fish and other items of food*)
300 g (11 oz) small button onions glazed in butter; 200 g (7 oz) small sautéed mushrooms; 10 small heart-shaped Croûtons of bread fried in butter. In certain cases, crayfish cooked in Court-bouillon.

415 Garnish Médicis (*for joints of meat, Noisettes and Tournedos*)
10 cooked tartlet cases filled with macaroni and truffles cut in dice and bound with a purée of foie gras; small peas tossed in butter.
Accompaniment: Jus lié.

416 Garnish à la Mexicaine (*for cuts or joints of meat and poultry*)
10 grilled mushrooms filled with some very thick Tomato Fondue; 10 grilled pimentos.
Accompaniment: well seasoned, tomato-flavoured Jus lié.

417 Garnish Mignon (*for Noisettes and Tournedos*)
10 small artichoke bottoms stewed in butter, filled with buttered peas; 10 small round Quenelles made of chicken forcemeat each decorated with a nice slice of truffle.
Accompaniment: the cooking juices deglazed then thickened and enriched with butter.

418 Garnish à la Milanaise (*for cuts and joints of meat*)
400 g (15 oz) cooked macaroni or spaghetti cut into approximately 4 cm (1⅔ in) lengths; 50 g (2 oz) each of salt ox tongue, ham and mushrooms and 40 g (1½ oz) truffles—all cut in Julienne; 50 g (2 oz) each of grated Gruyère and Parmesan; 1 dl (3½ fl oz or ½ U.S. cup) light tomato purée and 100 g (3½ oz) butter.
All the above ingredients should be mixed together carefully.
Accompaniment: thin Tomato Sauce.

419 Garnish Mirabeau (*for grills of meat*)
20 thin strips of anchovy fillet arranged trellis-fashion on the items of food; 10 nice stoned olives; a border of blanched tarragon leaves; 125 g (4½ oz) Anchovy Butter.

420 Garnish Mirette
10 individual portions of Mirette potatoes (4213) moulded in dariole moulds.
Accompaniment: Sauce Chateaubriand.

421 Garnish à la Moderne (*for joints of meat*)
10 pieces of braised cabbage moulded in hexagonal moulds with a slice of truffle at the bottom of each mould; 10 halves of braised stuffed lettuce; 10 small oval Quenelles made from veal and butter forcemeat, decorated with red salt ox tongue.
Accompaniment: Jus lié.

422 Garnish Montbazon (*for poultry*)
10 even-size lambs sweetbreads, studded with truffle and poêléed; 10 oval Quenelles made from chicken and butter forcemeat, decorated with truffle; 10 very white grooved mushrooms; 10 slices of truffle.
Accompaniment: Sauce Suprême.

423 Garnish Montmorency (*for cuts and joints of meat and poultry*)
10 artichoke bottoms stewed in butter and filled with buttered Macédoine; 10 small bouquets of asparagus tips.
Accompaniment: Sauce Madère with the addition of the cooking juices.

424 Garnish à la Moissonneuse (*for joints of meat*)
1 litre ($1\frac{3}{4}$ pt or $4\frac{1}{2}$ U.S. cups) peas cooked à la Française with the addition of shredded lettuce; 2 sliced potatoes and 125 g ($4\frac{1}{2}$ oz) lean salt belly of pork cut in dice and blanched. All these are cooked together, then lightly thickened with a little Beurre Manié.

425 Garnish Montreuil (*for fish*)
20 trimmed plain boiled potatoes arranged as a border around the prepared fish. Coat the fish with White Wine Sauce and the potatoes with Sauce Crevettes.

426 Garnish Montpensier (*for Noisettes, Tournedos and chicken*)
Bouquets of buttered asparagus tips; slices of very black truffle on the items of food.
Accompaniment: the cooking juices, deglazed then thickened and enriched with butter.

427 Garnish Nantua (*for fish*)
30 shelled crayfish tails bound with Sauce Nantua; 20 slices of truffle. Sauce Nantua.

428 Garnish à la Napolitaine (*for cuts and joints of meat and poultry*)
500 g (1 lb 2 oz) cooked spaghetti mixed with 50 g (2 oz) each of grated Gruyère and Parmesan and 1 dl ($3\frac{1}{2}$ fl oz or $\frac{1}{2}$ U.S. cup) light tomato purée; finish by mixing in 100 g ($3\frac{1}{2}$ oz) of butter.
Accompaniment: where applicable, the cooking juices from the joint.

429 Garnish aux Navets (*for mutton and duck*)
30 pieces of turnips, trimmed to the shape of large elongated olives and coloured in a frying pan with butter and a pinch of caster sugar; 20 glazed button onions. These vegetables are then cooked with the item of food being prepared.

430 Garnish à la Niçoise

For fish:

250 g (9 oz) flesh only of tomato, sautéed in butter with a touch of crushed garlic and a pinch of chopped tarragon at the last moment; 10 fillets of anchovy; 10 black olives; 1 tbs capers; 30 g (1 oz) Anchovy Butter; slices of peeled and depipped lemon.

For cuts and joints of meat and poultry:

250 g (9 oz) tomatoes prepared as above; 300 g (11 oz) buttered French beans; 400 g (15 oz) small Château potatoes. For the arrangement of the dish, place the tomatoes on the items of food and the beans and potatoes around it in alternate bouquets.
Accompaniment: Jus lié.

431 Garnish Nivernaise (*for joints of meat*)
500 g (1 lb 2 oz) carrots trimmed olive-shape. cooked in Bouillon and glazed; 300 g (11 oz) button onions, glazed in butter.
Accompaniment: the braising liquor from the joint.

432 Garnish à la Normande (*for fish*)
10 each of poached and bearded oysters and mussels; 10 small button mushrooms; 100 g ($3\frac{1}{2}$ oz) shelled prawns; 10 slices of truffle; 10 medium-sized trussed crayfish cooked in Court-bouillon; 10 gudgeons or small smelts, prepared *en Manchon* (1646); 10 small diamond-shaped Croûtons of bread fried in butter at the last moment, or small shapes of puff paste, cooked to a light colour. Sauce Normande.

Note: The use of truffle in this garnish is optional.

433 Garnish of Noodles (*for joints of meat and poultry*)
500 g (1 lb 2 oz) fresh noodles cooked and kept slightly firm, mixed with 50 g (2 oz) each of grated Gruyère and Parmesan and finished with 50 g (2 oz) butter.
Accompaniment: the braising liquor from the joint.

434 Garnish Opéra (*for Noisettes and Tournedos*)
10 cooked tartlet cases of a size in keeping with the item being prepared, filled with sautéed chicken livers mixed with Madeira Sauce; small round shapes of Duchesse potato, egg and breadcrumbed, deep fried, emptied out to form cases then filled with buttered asparagus tips.
Accompaniment: the cooking juices deglazed then thickened and enriched with butter.

435 Garnish à l'Orientale (*for poultry*)
10 small moulds of rice à la Grecque each placed on a seasoned half tomato which has been lightly stewed in oil; 10 croquettes of sweet potato prepared in the shape of corks.
Accompaniment: Tomato Sauce.

436 Garnish à l'Orléanaise (*for joints of meat*)
Chopped braised frizzy endive bound with eggs and butter; Maître d'Hôtel potatoes served separately in a dish.
Accompaniment: the cooking liquor from the joint.

437 Garnish of Haricots Panachés (*for joints of meat*)

350 g (13 oz) French beans and 350 g (13 oz) flageolet beans tossed together in butter and sprinkled with chopped parsley.
Accompaniment: clear gravy.

438 Garnish à la Parisienne (*for cuts and joints of meat and poultry*)
600 g (1 lb 5 oz) Parisienne potatoes; 10 artichoke bottoms stewed in butter and filled dome-shape with a Salpicon of tongue, mushrooms and truffle in equal quantities, bound with a thick Velouté then glazed in a very hot oven or under the salamander.
Accompaniment: Sauce Demi-glace.

439 Garnish Parmentier (*for joints of meat and poultry*)
600 g (1 lb 5 oz) potatoes cut in dice or cut with a plain oval vegetable scoop, cooked in butter as for Château potatoes and sprinkled with chopped parsley.
Accompaniment: clear gravy.

440 Garnish à la Paysanne (*for cuts and joints of meat and poultry*)
Fermière garnish with the addition of potatoes trimmed to the shape of small olives; and lean salt belly of pork cut in dice and blanched.

441 Garnish à la Péruvienne (*for Tournedos and other items of food*)
Peel some oxalis and cut the bottoms straight so that they will stand upright; hollow them out to form cases and fill with a finely chopped mixture comprised of two-thirds raw chicken, one-third raw ham and the chopped pulp removed from the oxalis; according to the type of food with which the garnish is to be served, the mixture should be bound with either Sauce Demi-glace or well-reduced Sauce Allemande. Sprinkle with a little oil and cook in the oven.
Accompaniment: thin Tomato Sauce.

442 Garnish à la Piémontaise (*for cuts and joints of meat and poultry*)
10 oval-shape Gâteau de Riz moulds filled with Risotto containing 150 g (5 oz) grated white truffle per 1 litre (1¾ pt or 4½ U.S. cups) Risotto.
Accompaniment: Tomato Sauce.

443 Garnish à la Portugaise (*for cuts and joints of meat and poultry*)
10 small whole tomatoes stuffed with Duxelles mixture; 30 Château potatoes.
Accompaniment: Sauce Portugaise.

444 Garnish à la Printanière (*for Sautés of meat and poultry*)
125 g (4½ oz) each of small new carrots and turnips, both trimmed, cooked in Bouillon and glazed; 20 small new onions glazed in butter; 125 g (4½ oz) peas; 125 g (4½ oz) blanched asparagus tips.

All these vegetables should be cooked gently with the item of food they are to accompany for 8–10 minutes before serving.

445 Garnish à la Provençale (*for joints of meat*)
10 whole small tomatoes; 10 large mushrooms stuffed with Duxelles mixture containing a little garlic.
Accompaniment: Sauce à la Provençale.

446 Garnish of Vegetable Purées
The vegetables which are suitable for preparing as purées are to be found in the chapter on vegetables.

447 Garnish Rachel (*for Noisettes and Tournedos*)
20 medium artichoke bottoms each garnished with a nice slice of poached bone marrow and with a pinch of chopped parsley on each slice.
Accompaniment: Sauce Bordelaise.

448 Garnish of Raviolis (*for cuts and joints of meat and poultry*)
30 pieces of Ravioli with a filling prepared according to the kind of food they will accompany (see Farinaceous items at the end of the chapter on Vegetables).

449 Garnish Régence

For fish:

20 Quenelles prepared from a forcemeat of whiting and Crayfish Butter moulded with spoons; 10 poached and bearded oysters; 10 very white button mushrooms; 10 truffles trimmed olive-shape; 10 thick slices of poached soft roe. Sauce Normande finished with truffle essence.

For poultry and veal sweetbreads:

10 Quenelles made from a fine chicken and truffle forcemeat moulded with spoons; 2 large round Quenelles decorated with truffles; 10 large cockscombs; 10 thick round slices of foie gras; 10 small grooved mushrooms; 10 truffles trimmed olive-shape. Sauce Allemande with truffle essence.

For game birds:

The ingredients are the same as those for poultry and sweetbreads except that the Quenelles are made smaller and from a fine forcemeat of game. Sauce Salmis with the addition of truffle essence.

450 Garnish Renaissance (*for joints of meat*)
The composition of this garnish is indicated by the derivation of the word, it being synonymous with renewal or spring-like; therefore it can include a complete range of spring vegetables prepared according to their own particular quality. To produce a desirable effect, the Renaissance garnish for large joints should be arranged in carefully separated bouquets comprised of carrots and turnips cut with a fancy oval vegetable scoop then cooked in Bouillon and glazed; bouquets of small whole French beans, or cut in half only, and buttered peas; bouquets of asparagus tips; bouquets of cauliflower lightly coated with Sauce Hollandaise; and buttered new potatoes.
Accompaniment: a gravy prepared from the cooking of the joint.

Note: Although it is current practice to coat the cauliflower in the garnish with Sauce Hollandaise it is felt that this procedure should be abandoned. The sauce adds little of value to the cauliflower and can interfere with and spoil the appearance of the brown sauce served with the joint. It is better to serve the cauliflower as a garnish after cooking it in butter keeping it white; or by cooking it in boiling salted water. However, after all is said and done, a sauceboat of Sauce Hollandaise can be served separately.

451 Garnish Richelieu (*for joints of meat*)
10 small tomatoes and 10 medium-sized mushrooms both stuffed in the usual manner with Duxelles; 10 very small whole or halves of braised lettuce; 20 potatoes trimmed to the shape and size of a large olive, cooked in butter at the last moment.
Accompaniment: a lightly thickened gravy prepared from the cooking of the joint.

452 Garnish Rohan (*for poultry*)
10 artichoke bottoms coated with meat glaze then garnished with a thick round slice of foie gras and a slice of truffle on top; 10 cooked tartlet cases filled with cocks' kidneys bound with Sauce Allemande; 20 cockscombs placed between the artichokes and the tartlets.
Accompaniment: Sauce Allemande with mushroom essence.

453 Garnish à la Romaine (*for joints of meat*)
10 cooked tartlet cases filled with small Gnocchi à la Romaine and gratinated (see Farinaceous items at the end of the chapter on vegetables); 10 small fluted brioche moulds of a mixture of spinach and diced fillets of anchovy, bound with egg yolks and cooked *au Bain-marie*, or 10 Subrics of spinach.
Accompaniment: Sauce Romaine with the addition of one-third its volume of Tomato Sauce.

454 Garnish Rossini (*for Noisettes and Tournedos*)
10 nice slices of foie gras seasoned and sautéed in butter; 100 g (3½ oz) slices of truffle.
Accompaniment: Sauce Demi-glace with the addition of truffle essence.

455 Garnish Saint-Florentin (*for cuts and joints of meat*)
10 pieces of Saint-Florentin potatoes (4226); 300 g (11 oz) medium-sized flap mushrooms sautéed à la Bordelaise.
Accompaniment: Sauce Bordelaise Bonnefoy.

456 Garnish Saint-Germain (*for joints of meat*)
10 moulds of the following items mixed together and poached in small dariole moulds: 200 g (7 oz) very green purée of cooked peas, 50 g (2 oz) butter, 1 dl (3½ fl oz or ½ U.S. cup) cream, 4 egg yolks, 1 whole egg, a pinch of caster sugar. Also 20 small Fondante potatoes; 20 pieces of carrot trimmed olive shape and glazed.
Accompaniment: a gravy prepared from the cooking of the joint and Sauce Béarnaise served separately.

457 Garnish Saint-Mandé (*for cuts and joints of meat and poultry*)
10 pieces of Macaire potatoes cut out with a 3½ cm (1⅔ in) round cutter; 200 g (7 oz) each of buttered peas and French beans.
Accompaniment: Jus lié.

458 Garnish à la Sarde (*for joints of meat*)
10 small ball-shape croquettes made from a stiff Riz au Gras (4236), flavoured and coloured with saffron; 10 small stuffed tomatoes; 10 thick slices of cucumber, peeled, hollowed out and stuffed with Duxelles then braised and gratinated.
Accompaniment: thin Tomato Sauce.

459 Garnish à la Sicilienne (*for various items*)
500 g (1 lb 2 oz) cooked lasagne mixed with 50 g (2 oz) each of grated Gruyère and Parmesan, 1 tbs Velouté, 50 g (2 oz) butter and 75 g (2½ oz) purée of chicken liver sautéed in butter.

460 Garnish à la Strasbourgeoise (*for goose and turkey*)
600 g (1 lb 5 oz) braised Choucroute; 10 oblong pieces of smoked streaky bacon cooked in with the choucroute; 10 slices of sautéed foie gras.
Accompaniment: a gravy prepared from the cooking of the joint.

461 Garnish Talleyrand (*for cuts and joints of meat and poultry*)
250 g (9 oz) cooked macaroni cut into 3 cm ($1\frac{1}{5}$ in) lengths and mixed with 50 g (2 oz) each of grated Gruyère and Parmesan and 50 g (2 oz) butter plus 100 g ($3\frac{1}{2}$ oz) each of a Julienne of truffle and large dice of foie gras.
Accompaniment: Sauce Périgueux containing a short Julienne of truffle.

462 Garnish Tortue (*especially for calf's head*)
20 small Quenelles made of veal and butter forcemeat; 10 small mushrooms; 20 stoned olives, stuffed and poached; 10 gherkins trimmed olive-shape; 5 small trussed crayfish; 5 slices of calf's tongue; 5 slices of calf's brain; 5 small French fried eggs from which half of the white has been removed beforehand; 10 slices of truffle; 10 small heart-shaped croûtons of bread fried in butter at the last moment. Sauce Tortue.

463 Garnish Toulousaine (*for poultry and Vol-au-vent*)
20 Quenelles made from chicken forcemeat; 10 slices of white braised calf's or lamb's sweetbreads; 100 g ($3\frac{1}{2}$ oz) cockscombs and kidneys; 200 g (7 oz) very white button mushrooms; 50 g (2 oz) slices of truffle. Sauce Allemande with the addition of mushroom essence.

464 Garnish à la Tourangelle (*for joints of meat*)
Equal quantities of French beans and flageolets beans cooked and mixed with an appropriate amount of Sauce Béchamel.
Accompaniment: the reduced gravy prepared from the cooking of the joint.

465 Garnish à la Trouvillaise (*for fish*)
100 g ($3\frac{1}{2}$ oz) peeled prawns; 30 mussels poached in white wine and bearded; 10 small grooved white button mushrooms. Sauce aux Crevettes.

466 Garnish à la Tyrolienne (*for grills of meat and venison*)
250 g (9 oz) onions, cut in rings, seasoned, floured and fried in oil; 250 g (9 oz) roughly chopped flesh only of tomato cooked in butter. Sauce Tyrolienne.

467 Garnish Vert-pré
For grills:

Bouquets of watercress or garden cress; bouquets of straw potatoes.
Accompaniment: Beurre Maître d'Hôtel.

For white meats and duck:

300 g (11 oz) peas, 300 g (11 oz) French beans and 200 g (7 oz) asparagus tips all mixed together and tossed in butter.
Accompaniment: clear gravy.

468 Garnish à la Vichy (*for cuts and joints of meat*)
Carottes à la Vichy (4008).

469 Garnish à la Viroflay (*for cuts and joints of meat*)
10 small balls of spinach à la Viroflay (4099); 10 artichoke bottoms cut in quarters and sautéed in butter with chopped Fines Herbes; 10 Château potatoes.
Accompaniment: Jus lié.

470 Garnish Walewska (*for fish*)
10 tails of Dublin Bay Prawns or 10 slices of crawfish; 10 nice slices of truffle.

471 Garnish Washington (*for poultry*)
600 g (1 lb 5 oz) maize of which one-third should be prepared à la Grecque for stuffing the bird; the remainder prepared à la Crème for serving separately in a deep dish.

472 Garnish à la Zingara (*for veal and poultry*)
100 g ($3\frac{1}{2}$ oz) each of lean ham and salt ox tongue, 100 g ($3\frac{1}{2}$ oz) mushrooms and 50 g (2 oz) truffle—all cut in Julienne. Sauce Demi-glace flavoured with tomato and tarragon.

CHAPTER 3

SOUPS

General Observations

The culinary preparations included in this section are of fairly recent origin in their present form, dating from only the early part of the 19th century.

Soups of the old classical kitchen were in fact complete dishes in themselves and contained, apart from the liquid content and its vegetable garnish, a wide variety of meat, poultry, game and fish. It is only the liquid part of these classical dishes which has retained the name of soup.

Examples of the old style of soup which still survive are the Flemish Hochepot, the Spanish Oilles and the French Petite Marmite. The way in which this kind of soup is served all together, gives only a vague idea of how they were made, since nowadays their preparation is much more simplified.

It was these preparations which contributed to some extent to the confusion which reigned in menus of those days. Then the balance of the menu was only regulated by the progressive satisfaction of the guest's appetite, by the pattern of the dishes served and their over-abundancy rather than their judicious selection.

On this point as on many others, culinary art owes much to Carême. Even if he was not strictly speaking the innovator of the changes which paved the way for modern principles, at least he made a great contribution to the dissemination of new ideas. Nevertheless, it took almost a hundred years before his successors were able to bring soups to the state of perfection which they have reached today. All the same, in creating a soup which is light and savoury in accordance with the ideals of taste and finesse, Carême's successors presumably failed to take sufficient account of the need to justify the names they gave to the new soups. It can be frequently seen, particularly in the case of thick soups, that the same formula is used indiscriminately for Bisque, Purées, Coulis and Veloutés as well as for Creams, whereas each term should logically designate a particular preparation of which the formula for each is totally different. In this book the confusion has, not without difficulty, been remedied; each type has been categorized and the classification of the various forms has been rationalized.

It has been accepted that the fairly recently adopted names of Veloutés and Creams as applied to soups appear to have been given as replacements for the names Bisque and Coulis which are now virtually obsolete, as is also the common and incorrect term Purée as applied to soups. It has therefore been found necessary to draw up a precise classification so as to lay down the rules and so fill this void in culinary practice. The following summary lists the characteristics of each type of soup, demonstrating the way in which the reforms have been implemented.

473 CLASSIFICATION OF SOUPS

Soups can be divided into two main categories: the clear Soups and the thick Soups. An extensive high class menu should always include at least one soup from each category; for more commonplace menus if the menu includes only one soup, the two categories should be used alternately and the appropriate one should be included in accordance with the overall pattern of the menu.

CLEAR SOUPS

Clear soups are all of one type whether they are made from meat, poultry, game, fish, shellfish or turtle. They are almost always clarified Consommés, sometimes lightly thickened with tapioca and often including a light garnish which should be in keeping with their character.

There are also a number of clear soups which are based on the Bouillon prepared from the Petite Marmite which should not be clarified in the same way as Consommés. Its clearness comes from the very careful attention paid during its cooking.

THICK SOUPS

The category of thick soups includes 5 distinct kinds:

1) Purées, Coulis and Bisques
2) Creams
3) Veloutés
4) Thickened Bouillons
5) Special blended soups of which the formula is invariably the same although there are many different types.

In order to simplify this classification, thickened Bouillons such as Germiny have been placed in the special blended groups and the reasons for this are explained at the beginning of the relevant section. The soups in the first three sections have a purée as a base and they only differ one from another by the use of the particular thickening agent. For Purées, Coulis and Bisques the thickening is effected by the nature of the ingredients used, e.g. rice, fried bread or a starchy vegetable such as potatoes, haricot beans, lentils etc. of which the proportions are strictly determined by the nature of the principal ingredients of the soup; these proportions are given in the introduction to the chapter on thick soups.

For Creams and Veloutés the thickening is always based on a white Roux and these two types of thick soup differ from each other only by the nature of the thickening and final finishing of the soup. For Veloutés the final finishing always comprises a liaison of egg yolks and cream and butter. No liaison is used for Cream Soups and the butter is replaced by the appropriate quantity of good quality cream. It is the principle of the addition of a liaison that establishes the clearly defined difference between these two kinds of soups.

It is important to note that the terms Coulis, Purée and Bisque when used to designate those soups of which the preparation is almost identical are not synonymous. On the contrary, they each have a distinct difference. The established habit of applying the word Purée to those soups having a vegetable base and the looseness with which this term is used, has led to the state where it is being used less and less.

The term Coulis, however, is applied with more jusitification to Purées of poultry, game and fish as well as to shellfish.

The term Bisque in so far as it concerns the foregoing, distinguishes and characterizes only a certain type of preparation, notwithstanding the fact that right from their origin and until the end of the 18th Century soups with a base of poultry and pigeon were called Bisque.

Many of the thick soups which have the same type of basic ingredients can by a simple alteration to the preparation, serve as soups under the form of Purées, Creams and Veloutés.

In the first edition of this book these soups were divided into three categories comprising:

1) those which could be served equally well in the form of Purées, Veloutés or Creams,
2) those which could be served only as Purées or Creams,
3) those which are more suitable served in the forms of Veloutés or Creams.

The reasoning which determined this classification made the need for a more simplified classification even more obvious. These three types of soup have therefore been united into one category and are classified alphabetically; at the end of each recipe the different methods of preparation for which they are suitable are given. As a result of this, a new classification for this section has been established as follows:

1) clear garnished Consommés and Bouillons,
2) soups which can be served in the three forms of Purées, Veloutés and Creams; or only in the two forms of Purées or Creams, or which can be served as Veloutés or Creams,
3) special blended soups where the preparation is invariably the same, and thickened Bouillons,
4) soups which are derived from simple bourgeois cookery and from different local cuisines,
5) foreign soups.

Observations concerning the serving of soup

It is not intended here to refute the arguments of certain gourmets who have for many years mounted a crusade against soups and wish this course to be abolished. The subject could be of interest but our professional standing will not allow us to lend ourselves to it.

We refer ourselves simply to the authority of Grimod de la Reynière who pronounced a veritable aphorism in speaking on this subject: 'The soup is to a meal as the doorway is to a monument or a building; that is to say that not only is it the first part of the meal but it also combines to give a true idea of the meal, rather as the overture to an opera announces the subject of the work.'

The idea of this most illustrious of gastronomes is the same as ours: the usefulness of soup is beyond argument and in the writing of a Menu there is not one professional who disagrees as to the importance and absolute necessity of this course.

Among all the items which comprise the programme of a gourmet, which is the Menu, soups are those which require the strictest attention; they should have a most delicate perfection because the good or bad impression they produce on the guest affects to a great extent the success of the rest of the meal which follows.

Soup should be served boiling hot in plates which are as hot as possible: this is a very important point especially for the service of a Consommé which has been preceded by cold Hors-d'oeuvre.

The service of an Hors-d'oeuvre in a dinner is undesirable and even though these may be oysters, they are really only admissible in the absence of a Soup. Those Hors-d'oeuvre which include various types of fish in oil, smoked fish or strongly seasoned salads have a very strong taste on the palate and the customer finds that the soup which follows is flat and insipid unless it is served absolutely boiling hot.

It follows from this that the obligation of serving soup very hot is one of the fundamental principles of service from the kitchen.

NUTRITIONAL, AROMATIC AND SEASONING INGREDIENTS FOR BOUILLONS AND PETITES MARMITES, AND THE CLARIFICATION OF VARIOUS CLEAR SOUPS

474 White Bouillon
To make 10 litres ($2\frac{1}{4}$ gal or $2\frac{3}{4}$ U.S. gal)

Nutritive Ingredients:
7 kg ($15\frac{1}{2}$ lb) shin and lean beef which should consist of 4 kg (9 lb) lean meat and 3 kg ($6\frac{1}{2}$ lb) meat on the bone

Flavouring Ingredients:
1 kg 100 g ($2\frac{1}{2}$ lb) carrots
900 g (2 lb) turnips
500 g (1 lb 2 oz) leek
200 g (7 oz) parsnips
200 g (7 oz) onions
3 cloves
20 g ($\frac{2}{3}$ oz) garlic
120 g (4 oz) celery

Liquid:
14 litres (3 gal or $3\frac{3}{4}$ U.S. gal) cold water

Seasoning:
70 g ($2\frac{1}{4}$ oz) coarse salt

Cooking time:
5 hours

Method:
Proceed in the same way as for Ordinary White Stock, simmering it for 5 hours.

Observations on the making of this Bouillon:
It is the practice to give 5 hours of cooking time for this Bouillon and this time is more than sufficient to extract the nutritive juices from the meat. On the other hand it is insufficient to bring about the disintegration of the bones so as to ensure the extraction of their main soluble ingredients. To obtain this very important result, very slow simmering of up to 12–15 hours is necessary.

Culinary practice has increasingly established the need, especially in large kitchens, for the technique of preparing a first Bouillon from the bones only which have been simmered for not less than 12 hours. This Bouillon then serves as the moistening for a second stockpot which contains the meat only: this is then simmered for approximately 4 hours, that is to say, the time strictly necessary for the cooking of the meat. It is possible to shorten the time of the second operation by chopping up the meat and vegetables instead of leaving them whole. In this case then the procedure is the same as for ordinary clarification (479).

475 Petite Marmite
For 10 persons.

Nutritive Ingredients:
1 kg ($2\frac{1}{4}$ lb) beef, half of which should be rump or chuck and the other half, well fleshed flat ribs
1 marrow bone tied in a piece of muslin
1 small boiling fowl—more tough than tender
the giblets from 4 chickens

Liquid:
3 litres ($5\frac{1}{4}$ pt or $6\frac{1}{2}$ U.S. pt) White Bouillon not too highly seasoned so that it will interfere with the final result

Flavouring Ingredients:
200 g (7 oz) carrots } both trimmed
200 g (7 oz) turnips } small barrel-shape
150 g (5 oz) leek
80 g (3 oz) celery (1 small heart)
250 g (9 oz) cabbage, blanched and cooked separately in some fatty Bouillon.

Method:
Place the White Bouillon in a special earthenware marmite together with the meat, poultry, the

marrow bone and giblets. Bring to the boil, skim and simmer very gently, taking care that the liquid remains as clear as possible. One hour before the meats are cooked add the vegetables and continue to simmer until all is cooked.

Note: The Bouillon of a Petite Marmite should not be clarified; it contains only the quality of the ingredients it is made from and should reflect the meticulous care with which it is made. It should not be skimmed completely of fat.

Its flavour should be different to that of a clarified Consommé but similar to that of a family Pot-au-Feu and to such soups as Croûte au Pot, Consommé à la Bouchère etc., which use the Bouillon from the Petite Marmite as a base. The only difference which should be noted is that these Consommés do not include poultry in their preparation whereas it is absolutely necessary for a Petite Marmite.

476 Game Bouillon
To make 10 litres (2¼ gal or 2¾ U.S. gal)

Nutritive Ingredients:
1 kg (2¼ lb) head and forequarter of hare
3 kg (6½ lb) collar and shoulder of roebuck
2 kg (4½ lb) old wild rabbit
2 partridges
1 old pheasant

All this game should be coloured in the oven in advance.

Flavouring Ingredients:
500 g (1 lb 2 oz) carrots
500 g (1 lb 2 oz) green of leek
500 g (1 lb 2 oz) onions
5 cloves
250–300 g (9–11 oz) celery
125 g (4½ oz) juniper berries, tied in a piece of muslin
100 g (3½ oz) parsley stalks
25 g (1 oz) thyme
10 g (⅓ oz) bayleaf
400 g (15 oz) mushrooms or mushroom trimmings

Liquid:
11½ litres (2½ gal or 3⅜ U.S. gal) water

Seasoning:
70 g (2¼ oz) salt

Cooking time:
3 hours

Method:
Proceed in the same way as for Game Stock.

477 Fish Bouillon
To make 10 litres (2¼ gal or 2¾ U.S. gal)

Nutritive Ingredients:
3 kg (6½ lb) pike
1 kg (2¼ lb) carp
1 kg (2¼ lb) tench
1 kg (2¼ lb) sole trimmings
2 kg (4½ lb) turbot or whiting heads

Flavouring Ingredients:
700 g (1½ lb) sliced onions
200 g (7 oz) parsley stalks or root
400 g (15 oz) leek
50 g (2 oz) celery
1 bayleaf

Liquid:
9½ litres (2⅛ gal or 2⅝ U.S. gal) water
1 litre (1¾ pt or 4½ U.S. cups) white wine

Seasoning:
80 g (2½ oz) salt

Cooking time:
40–50 minutes of gentle simmering

Method:
Proceed in the same way as for Fish Stock.

478 Beef Tea and Meat Jelly for Invalids

To make 5 dl (18 fl oz or 2¼ U.S. cups) of Beef Tea: Place in a basin, 1¼ kg (2¾ lb) very fresh beef from the leg, completely free of fat and chopped very finely; add and mix in 1½ dl (5 fl oz or ⅝ U.S. cup) filtered water a little at a time so that the meat absorbs it; add a little salt. Place in a hermetically sealable utensil such as a glazed porcelain marmite or glass jar. Place this container in a pot, cover completely with cold water and bring to the boil. Allow to simmer gently for 3 hours taking care to add more water to the pan to compensate for evaporation. Remove the pan from the heat and when the water is lukewarm, remove the utensil, tip the contents into a clean cloth and allow to drain into a container.
For Meat Jelly: proceed in the same way as for Beef Tea, adding 200 g (7 oz) boned calf's foot, blanched and cut into small pieces. When the jelly has been strained, place into small cups and allow to set.

CLARIFICATION OF CONSOMMES

479 Consommé Ordinaire—Ordinary Consommé
To make 4 litres (7 pt or 8¾ U.S. pt)

Liquid:
5 litres (8¾ pt or 1⅜ U.S. gal) White Bouillon

Nutritive Ingredients:
1½ kg (3 lb 6 oz) very lean beef, well trimmed and chopped

Flavouring Ingredients:
100 g (3½ oz) carrots
200 g (7 oz) leek
both roughly chopped into small pieces

Clarifying agent:
2 egg whites

Cooking time:
1½ hours

Method of clarification:
Place the chopped meat, vegetables and whites in a small stockpot, mix well together, add the White Bouillon, bring to the boil stirring it gently from time to time, then allow it to simmer very gently for the time indicated. When ready, pass the Consommé through a clean cloth.

480 Consommé de Volaille—Chicken Consommé
To make 4 litres (7 pt or 8¾ U.S. pt)

Liquid:
5 litres (8¾ pt or 1⅜ U.S. gal) White Bouillon

Nutritive Ingredients:
1½ kg (3 lb 6 oz) very lean beef, well trimmed and chopped
the chopped giblets of 6 chickens
2 roast carcasses of chicken
1 boiling fowl, lightly browned in the oven

Flavouring Ingredients:
100 g (3½ oz) carrot
200 g (7 oz) leek
both roughly chopped into small pieces

Clarifying agent:
2 egg whites

Cooking time:
1½ hours

Method:
As for Ordinary Consommé.

481 Consommé de Gibier—Game Consommé
To make 4 litres (7 pt or 8¾ U.S. pt)

Liquid
4¾ litres (8½ pt or 1⅛ U.S. gal) Game Bouillon

Nutritive Ingredients:
1½ kg (3 lb 6 oz) chopped lean game flesh, in keeping with the consommé being prepared
2 kg (4½ lb) roast game carcasses

Flavouring Ingredients:
200 g (7 oz) leek, roughly chopped into small pieces
100 g (3½ oz) mushrooms, or Mousserons or morels: dried for preference
1 sprig of sage
a pinch of rosemary
5–6 crushed juniper berries
a little milled pepper added to the game flesh

Clarifying agent:
3 egg whites

Cooking time:
55–60 minutes

Method:
Proceed as indicated for Ordinary Consommé.

482 Consommé Double de Poisson—Double Fish Consommé
To make 4 litres (7 pt or 8¾ U.S. pt)

Liquid:
4 litres (7 pt or 8¾ U.S. pt) Fish Bouillon

Flavouring and Clarifying Ingredients:
1½ kg (3 lb 6 oz) fish flesh (half pike half whiting) pounded with 3 egg whites
100 g (3½ oz) roughly chopped leek
100 g (3½ oz) roughly chopped parsley stalks
1 bottle dry white wine

Cooking time:
25–30 minutes

Method:
Place the pounded fish and egg white with the leek and parsley into a pan with the white wine and mix well together. Add the Fish Bouillon and clarify in the normal manner.

Observations concerning the clarification of Fish Consommé:
The clarification of Fish Consommé can also be effected by using half the amount of fish flesh but with the addition of 30 g (1 oz) of caviare per 1 litre of Fish Bouillon. It can also be made equally well using caviare only in the proportion of 60 g (2 oz) per litre of Fish Bouillon proceeding in the following manner:

Pound the pressed or fresh caviare, add the cold Fish Bouillon and bring to the boil mixing gently and continuously. Remove the pan to the side of the stove and allow to simmer very gently for 20 minutes. Pass the Consommé through a clean cloth. If not for immediate use, place in a Bain-marie and cover it so as to prevent the formation of a gelatinous skin on the surface.

VARIOUS GARNISHES FOR SOUPS

483 Chiffonade and Pluches
A chiffonade is composed of finely shredded leaves of lettuce and sorrel, stewed in butter; in some cases it comprises rounds of lettuce and sorrel leaves which are blanched in salted water for a few moments before being added to the soups.

Pluches for soups are generally of chervil and consist of the whole leaf spray without the central stalk and when used to complement the flavour of a soup, should be added at the last moment.

484 Savoury Pancakes
Mix 250 g (9 oz) sifted flour with 4 eggs and $7\frac{1}{2}$ dl ($1\frac{1}{3}$ pt or $3\frac{1}{4}$ U.S. cups) milk boiled so as to reduce it by one-third; season with 10 g ($\frac{1}{3}$ oz) salt. The milk may be replaced by White Bouillon in which case it is necessary to take account of the fact that the Bouillon is already salted and only sufficient seasoning should be added to ensure the correct taste of the mixture.

Cook in the same manner as for ordinary pancakes.

485 Croûtes and Croûtons
Croûtes are generally prepared from long thin French loaves cut in half lengthways and then into pieces 4–5 cm ($1\frac{3}{4}$–2 in) in length. Remove the soft bread from inside and trim the corners neatly. Lightly butter them, sprinkle with unclarified fat from a Bouillon and then place to dry in the oven. Allow one Croûte per person.

Soup sometimes includes Croûtes made from household bread cut into small slices; in certain cases these slices are dried in the oven, in others they are sprinkled with grated cheese and gratinated.

Croûtons are $\frac{1}{2}$ cm ($\frac{1}{5}$ in) dice of bread fried in clarified butter, where possible, just before serving. Allow approximately 40–45 g ($1\frac{1}{2}$–2 oz) Croûtons per 1 litre ($1\frac{3}{4}$ pt or $4\frac{1}{2}$ U.S. cups) soup.

486 Fine Chicken Forcemeat for Quenelles for Soups
Finely pound 100 g ($3\frac{1}{2}$ oz) raw chicken breast adding little by little one small egg white; season with a little salt and a suspicion of nutmeg. Pass through a fine sieve, place in a basin on ice and mix in 1 dl ($3\frac{1}{2}$ fl oz or $\frac{1}{2}$ U.S. cup) fresh double cream.

487 Fine Game Forcemeat for Quenelles for Soups
Proceed as for the chicken forcemeat above using the same proportions but using the breast of the game required instead of chicken.

488 Fine Fish Forcemeat for Quenelles for Soups
The preparation is the same as for the chicken forcemeat above using fillets of fish in keeping with the soup and increasing the quantities of egg white by one quarter.

489 Tomato Fondue, and Dice of Tomatoes
Tomato Fondue is widely used as a garnish but its preparation is always the same. The tomatoes used should be just ripe, carefully skinned and the pips removed. To peel tomatoes, place them in boiling water for a few seconds so that the skin can be removed easily.

The flesh is then finely sliced and stewed with 30 g (1 oz.) butter per 125 g ($4\frac{1}{2}$ oz) tomato flesh together with a pinch of salt and caster sugar, taking care that the tomato is not so overcooked that it becomes a purée.

For preparing diced tomato for use as a garnish, choose firm very red tomatoes. Peel them and remove the pips; cut the flesh into dice as evenly as possible and place in boiling hot White Bouillon or lightly salted water and poach for 7–8 minutes. Remove with a large perforated spoon, drain and place directly in the soup.

490 Juliennes and Brunoises
Juliennes and Brunoises are sometimes prepared from ordinary vegetables either as a garnish in their own right or as part of a garnish, allowing 1–2 tbs for 1 litre ($1\frac{3}{4}$ pt or $4\frac{1}{2}$ U.S. cups) of soup. In other cases they can be a Julienne or Brunoise of breast of chicken or game, fillet of fish, salt ox tongue, artichoke bottoms etc., allowing 1–$1\frac{1}{2}$ tbs per 1 litre ($1\frac{3}{4}$ pt or $4\frac{1}{2}$ U.S. cups) of soup according to whether the garnish is composed of one or more items.

491 Threads of egg for clarified Consommés
For 2 litres ($3\frac{1}{2}$ pt or 9 U.S. cups) of Consommé: well beat one egg, pass through a muslin and pour into a fine strainer held over a shallow pan containing boiling Bouillon. Move the strainer over the surface of the Bouillon until all the egg has passed through. As the coagulation of the egg is instantaneous remove it as soon as possible by skimming it off with a perforated skimmer and place immediately in the Consommé.

492 Various Pastas and Cereals for Clear Soups
Neige de Florence: this product is served separately at the same time as the soup allowing 30–40 g (1–$1\frac{1}{2}$ oz) for 10 persons. Each guest takes what is required and mixes it directly into the Consommé.

Pâtes d'Italie—Small Italian Paste Shapes: allow 55–60 g (2 oz) per 1 litre ($1\frac{3}{4}$ pt or $4\frac{1}{2}$ U.S. cups)

Consommé; according to its size and quality the cooking time is approximately 8–12 minutes.

Perles du Japon—Tapioca Pearls: allow 65–70 g (2–2½ oz) per 1 litre (1¾ pt or 4½ U.S. cups) Consommé. The cooking time is 20–25 minutes of gentle poaching.

Rice: when used as a single garnish, allow 45 g (1½ oz) raw rice per 1 litre (1¾ pt or 4½ U.S. cups) Consommé. It is cooked in White Bouillon taking care that the grains are kept separate. The cooking time is 20–25 minutes.

Salep: allow 65–70 g (2–2½ oz) per 1 litre (1¾ pt or 4½ U.S. cups) Consommé; the cooking time is 18–20 minutes.

Sago: allow the same amount and cooking time as for Salep.

Tapioca: allow the same amount and cooking time as for the two preceding products.

Vermicelli: allow 55–60 g (2 oz) per 1 litre (1¾ pt or 4½ U.S. cups) Consommé. The cooking time is 5–12 minutes according to size and quality.

Notes:

1) It is always useful to parcook Patês d'Italie and Vermicelli in boiling salted water for one minute before straining and placing it into the Consommé to complete the cooking.
2) The amount of most of these pastes and cereals for soups can be measured with a spoon; one tablespoonful equalling approximately 20 g (⅔ oz).

493 Profiteroles for Soups

In the classical kitchen Profiteroles were nothing other than small balls of ordinary bread; not without reason in modern cooking chou paste Profiteroles are infinitely more delicate.

Profiteroles are piped out the size of hazelnuts and cooked in the same way as for all chou paste items. They should be cooked until very dry and then usually stuffed with an appropriate puree filling. Allow approximately 30 pieces per service of 10 persons.

Ingredients for making 100 Profiteroles:
3½ dl (12 fl oz or 1½ U.S. cups) water
150 g (5 oz) butter
8 g (⅓ oz) salt
220 g (8 oz) sifted flour
5 medium eggs

The paste should be of a fairly firm consistency. For its preparation, see General Purpose Chou Paste (325).

494 Quenelles for Soups

These Quenelles are prepared from any of the forcemeats previously given in this section and are laid on a buttered tray and, where possible, poached at the last moment. They may be moulded with small spoons or piped into various shapes.

The size and shapes of Quenelles are indicated in each separate recipe as are the additions which are necessary in the preparation of these forcemeats, notably that of chicken. Allow at least 15 Quenelles per 1 litre (1¾ pt or 4½ U.S. cups) Consommé.

495 Royales

The proportions necessary for preparing Royales are laid down as being the amount of garnish required for 2 litres (3½ pt or 9 U.S. cups) of Consommé. It is easy to increase or reduce the total amount if necessary and to adjust the cooking times in consequence.

The following recipes are the most important ones and it is felt unnecessary to lengthen the list as the method is always the same, taking into account the type of the main ingredients used.

It is essential that a Royale should be completely cold before being cut into shapes; unless it is completely cold and set all the way through it will be impossible to cut it properly. It should be remembered that no matter what form it takes, a Royale should always be cut into regular and correct shapes. Also, to ensure the extreme delicacy of this preparation it is important that the quantity of whole eggs indicated is not increased as the proportions have been determined so as to ensure the correct texture.

496 Ordinary Royale

Infuse two pinches of chervil in 2 dl (7 fl oz or ⅞ U.S. cup) boiling Bouillon; well beat 1 whole egg and 3 yolks and add the infused Bouillon a little at a time. Remove the froth and pour the mixture into buttered moulds; poach them *au Bain-marie* taking care that no boiling takes place. Allow 12–15 minutes cooking time if using dariole moulds and 25–30 minutes for a 4 dl (14 fl oz or 1¾ U.S. cups) capacity mould.

497 Carrot Royale, also called Royale Crécy

Stew gently in a little butter, 75 g (2½ oz) sliced red of carrot until completely cooked and dry; add ½ tbs cold Sauce Béchamel and 2 tbs cream, then pass through a fine sieve. Season with a pinch of sugar and mix in 1 small egg and 2 egg yolks. Poach *au Bain-marie* as indicated above.

498 Celery Royale

Stew gently in a little butter, 100 g (3½ oz) finely sliced celery until completely cooked; add 1½ tbs

Sauce Béchamel and pass through a fine sieve. Mix in 3 egg yolks and poach *au Bain-marie* in the usual manner.

499 Cream Royale, also called Royale Deslignac
Beat together 1 medium egg and 3 yolks; mix in 2 dl (7 fl oz or $\frac{7}{8}$ U.S. cup) cream, season with a pinch of salt, a suspicion of grated nutmeg and pass through a muslin. Poach *au Bain-marie* in the usual manner.

500 Cream of Rice and Almond Milk Royale
Take 1 dl ($3\frac{1}{2}$ fl oz or $\frac{1}{2}$ U.S. cup) cooked cream of rice made by mixing 10 g ($\frac{1}{3}$ oz) rice flour into $\frac{1}{4}$ dl (1 fl oz or $\frac{1}{8}$ U.S. cup) cold Bouillon then adding and mixing this into $\frac{3}{4}$ dl (3 fl oz or $\frac{3}{8}$ U.S. cup) boiling Bouillon. Failing this, use an equal quantity of very well cooked rice passed through a fine sieve. To either of these, add 4 tbs almond milk obtained by pounding 10 freshly skinned almonds together with 3 tbs milk. Season with a little salt, mix together with 4 egg yolks then pass through a muslin and poach *au Bain-marie* in the usual manner.

501 Game Royale
Pound 50 g (2 oz) cooked game of the type indicated by the soup it is to garnish. Add $1\frac{1}{2}$ tbs cold Sauce Espagnole, $\frac{1}{2}$ dl (2 fl oz or $\frac{1}{4}$ U.S. cup) double cream, 1 small egg and 2 yolks well beaten together. Pass through a fine sieve and poach *au Bain-marie* in the usual manner.

502 Asparagus Royale
Mix together 100 g ($3\frac{1}{2}$ oz) asparagus tips half cooked in boiling salted water, $1\frac{1}{2}$ tbs cold Sauce Béchamel, 2 tbs cream, a little green spinach colour and 3 egg yolks. Pass through a fine sieve and poach *au Bain-marie* in the usual manner.

503 Leek Royale
Stew 100 g ($3\frac{1}{2}$ oz) finely sliced leek in butter without colour. Add $1\frac{1}{2}$ tbs Sauce Béchamel and 3 tbs cream, and finish cooking gently. Pass through a fine sieve and mix together with 3 egg yolks. Poach *au Bain-marie* in the usual manner.

504 Foie gras Royale
Pass 100 g ($3\frac{1}{2}$ oz) foie gras through a fine sieve and mix in 1 tbs lukewarm Sauce Béchamel. Add half an egg and 3 yolks beaten well together and mix in. Poach *au Bain-marie* in the usual manner.

505 Chestnut Royale
Mix together 100 g ($3\frac{1}{2}$ oz) very fine cooked chestnut purée and 3 tbs White Bouillon. Add and mix in a small pinch of caster sugar and 3 egg yolks. Poach *au Bain-marie* in the usual manner.

506 Green Pea Royale
Mix together 100 g ($3\frac{1}{2}$ oz) very fine purée of freshly cooked peas with 2 tbs White Bouillon. Add a very small pinch of caster sugar and enhance the colour with a little green spinach colour. Add and mix in half an egg and 3 egg yolks beaten well together and poach *au Bain-marie* in the usual manner.

507 Fish or Shellfish Royale
Pound 60 g (2 oz) fillets of sole poached with butter or the same amount of any cooked fish or shellfish according to the nature of the soup for which the Royale is intended; add 1 tbs cold Sauce Béchamel, $\frac{1}{2}$ dl (2 fl oz or $\frac{1}{4}$ U.S. cup) cream and a suspicion of nutmeg; pass through a fine sieve. Add 3 egg yolks, mix together and poach *au Bain-marie* in the usual manner.

508 Tomato Royale
Mix together 1 dl ($3\frac{1}{2}$ fl oz or $\frac{1}{2}$ U.S. cup) very red tomato purée which has been passed through a cloth, with 2 tbs White Bouillon. Season with a little salt and caster sugar; add and mix in 1 small egg and 2 egg yolks beaten well together and poach *au Bain-marie* in the usual manner.

509 Truffle Royale
Finely pound 100 g ($3\frac{1}{2}$ oz) very black truffle; add $1\frac{1}{2}$ tbs very well reduced cold Sauce Demi-glace and 3 egg yolks. Pass through a fine sieve and poach *au Bain-marie* in the usual manner.

510 Chicken Royale
Finely pound 50 g (2 oz) cooked breast of chicken; add $1\frac{1}{2}$ tbs Sauce Béchamel, $\frac{1}{2}$ dl (2 fl oz or $\frac{1}{4}$ U.S. cup) cream and a suspicion of grated nutmeg. Pass through a fine sieve and add and mix in half an egg and 2 egg yolks beaten well together. Poach *au Bain-marie* in the usual manner.

GARNISHED CONSOMMES AND CLEAR SOUPS

The thickening of soups with tapioca is often indicated for Consommés and the result gives an acceptable consistency, the procedure is, however, entirely optional. If a Consommé is thickened with tapioca it should be cooked very carefully then strained through a clean cloth. The addition of

Pluches of chervil although recommended, is also optional.

All the following proportions are for 10 persons unless otherwise stated.

511 Consommé aux Ailerons—Consommé with Chicken Winglets

2 litres (3½ pt or 9 U.S. cups) Chicken Consommé.

Garnish: 10 boned chicken winglets stuffed with forcemeat and braised; 4 tbs well separated grains of boiled rice.

512 Consommé Alexandra

2 litres (3½ pt or 9 U.S. cups) Chicken Consommé lightly thickened with 4 tbs tapioca.

Garnish: 1 tbs fine Julienne of cooked white of chicken; 2 tbs small grooved Quenelles made from chicken forcemeat; 1 tbs Chiffonade of lettuce.

513 Consommé à l'Ancienne

2 litres (3½ pt or 9 U.S. cups) Bouillon from the Petite Marmite.

Garnish: 10 emptied Croûtes cut from a large French loaf and filled with the vegetables from the Petite Marmite cut into large dice. After filling, place the Croûtes in a fairly deep earthenware dish, add a little fatty Petite Marmite Bouillon and allow to simmer very gently for 30 minutes. Lightly gratinate just before serving.

514 Consommé d'Aremburg

2 litres (3½ pt or 9 U.S. cups) Chicken Consommé.

Garnish: ½ tbs each very small balls of carrots cut with a small vegetable scoop and glazed; small balls of turnips cooked in Bouillon; small balls of very black truffle; very small peas and slightly larger balls moulded from chicken forcemeat poached at the last moment; 1 dariole mould of asparagus Royale cut into small rounds.

515 Consommé à l'Aurore

2 litres (3½ pt or 9 U.S. cups) Chicken Consommé lightly thickened with tapioca with the addition of 4 tbs very red tomato purée, then passed through a cloth.

Garnish: 4 tbs fine Julienne of cooked white of chicken.

516 Consommé Belle Fermière

2 litres (3½ pt or 9 U.S. cups) very clear and well flavoured Beef Consommé.

Garnish: 2 tbs very fine Julienne of cabbage; 1 tbs diamonds of small French beans; 1 tbs Pâtes d'Italie.

517 Consommé Bellini

2 litres (3½ pt or 9 U.S. cups) Chicken Consommé.

Garnish as an accompaniment: 20 small lightly gratinated semolina Gnocchi.

518 Consommé à la Bouchère

2 litres (3½ pt or 9 U.S. cups) Bouillon from the Petite Marmite.

Garnish: 10 very small balls of braised cabbage. Serve separately 20 slices of very fresh beef bone marrow poached in Bouillon and arranged on small rounds of toast.

519 Consommé à la Bouquetière

2 litres (3½ pt or 9 U.S. cups) Chicken Consommé lightly thickened with tapioca. The garnish should consist of 4 tbs of early spring vegetables cut into various shapes and cooked in boiling salted water. This soup is similar to Consommé Printanier (604) but with as varied a selection of vegetables as possible.

520 Consommé à la Brunoise

Quantity of vegetables for 2 litres (3½ pt or 9 U.S. cups) soup:

300 g (11 oz) red of carrot
200 g (7 oz) turnips
100 g (3½ oz) white of leek
100 g (3½ oz) celery
50 g (2 oz) onion

Cut the vegetables into 3 mm (⅛ in) dice, place in a pan, season with salt, a pinch of caster sugar and stew gently with a little butter. Finish cooking with 5 dl (18 fl oz or 2¼ U.S. cups) Consommé. At the moment of service add sufficient Consommé to make up the required quantity together with 1 tbs very small green peas, 1 tbs French beans cut into small squares and Pluches of chervil.

Note: This soup lends itself to several different variations by adding other ingredients, in which case the designation is altered accordingly. For example with the addition of small poached eggs the ordinary Brunoise becomes Consommé Brunoise à la Colbert; with the addition of small Quenelles, cooked pearl barley, rice or pastes etc., it becomes Consommé Brunoise aux Quennelles, Brunoise à l'Orge, Brunoise au Riz etc. A Brunoise soup can also be prepared based on a purée or thickened with a Velouté.

521 Consommé Carmen

The special flavouring of this Consommé requires the addition of half of a pimento and 8 tbs of tomato essence or well reduced tomato purée per 1

litre ($1\frac{3}{4}$ pt or $4\frac{1}{2}$ U.S. cups) Consommé, added during its clarification.
Garnish: 1 tbs diced flesh only of tomato poached in White Bouillon; 1 tbs cooked fine Julienne of sweet pimento; 1 tbs grains of boiled rice; Pluches of chervil.

522 Consommé Célestine
2 litres ($3\frac{1}{2}$ pt or 9 U.S. cups) Chicken Consommé lightly thickened with tapioca.
Garnish: Prepare 3 small pancakes without sugar and spread each with a thin layer of chicken and cream forcemeat. Place the pancakes on top of each other and sprinkle the top layer with very finely chopped truffle. Smooth the surface carefully with a palette knife so as to incorporate the truffle into the forcemeat, place in a moderate oven for sufficient time to cook the forcemeat then cut out with a 2 cm ($\frac{4}{5}$ in) plain round cutter and add to the Consommé.

Note: The method indicated is the author's own interpretation. Usually the pancakes are not stuffed but cut into Julienne or into 2 cm ($\frac{4}{5}$ in) rounds.

523 Consommé Cendrillon
2 litres ($3\frac{1}{2}$ pt or 9 U.S. cups) Chicken Consommé.
Garnish: 60 g (2 oz) truffle cooked with Marsala and cut into Julienne; 8 tbs rice cooked in White Bouillon.

524 Consommé Chancelière
2 litres ($3\frac{1}{2}$ pt or 9 U.S. cups) Chicken Consommé.
Garnish: 1 dariole mould of Green Pea Royale cut into small rounds; 1 tbs Julienne of cooked white of chicken; 1 tbs Julienne of truffle.

525 Consommé au Chasseur
2 litres ($3\frac{1}{2}$ pt or 9 U.S. cups) Game Bird Consommé finished at the last moment with 1 dl ($3\frac{1}{2}$ fl oz or $\frac{1}{2}$ U.S. cup) Port wine.
Garnish: 2 tbs Julienne of mushrooms; Pluches of chervil. Small stuffed Profiteroles served separately.

526 Consommé Châtelaine
2 litres ($3\frac{1}{2}$ pt or 9 U.S. cups) Consommé lightly thickened with tapioca.
Garnish: 1 dariole mould of Royale prepared from two-thirds Soubise purée, and one-third purée of artichoke bottoms and Velouté, cut into small cubes; 2 tbs of very small Quenelles prepared from chicken forcemeat moulded with spoons and stuffed with a creamed purée of chestnuts.

527 Consommé aux Cheveux d'Anges
Cheveux d'Anges is a very fine vermicelli. It is placed in the boiling Consommé just before service allowing 100–120 g ($3\frac{1}{2}$–4 oz) per 2 litres ($3\frac{1}{2}$ pt or 9 U.S. cups) of Consommé.

528 Consommé Colbert
2 litres ($3\frac{1}{2}$ pt or 9 U.S. cups) Chicken Consommé.
Garnish: 10 very small poached eggs kept fairly soft; 4 tbs cooked small Printanier of vegetables.

Note: The eggs used should be very small and absolutely fresh. See Notes on the subject of poached eggs, Page 155.

529 Consommé Colombine
2 litres ($3\frac{1}{2}$ pt or 9 U.S. cups) Chicken Consommé.
Garnish: 2 tbs vegetables from the White Bouillon, trimmed, cut into batons and simmered in a little fatty White Bouillon; 1 tbs small green peas; 1 tbs Julienne of breast of pigeon; 10 poached pigeons' eggs.

530 Consommé Croûte au Pot
2 litres ($3\frac{1}{2}$ pt or 9 U.S. cups) Petite Marmite Bouillon.
Garnish: 6 tbs vegetables from the Petite Marmite trimmed, cut into batons and simmered in the Bouillon which should be left slightly fatty; 20 Croûtes cut from long thin French bread, emptied, sprinkled with fat from the Marmite and dried in the oven.

531 Consommé Cyrano
2 litres ($3\frac{1}{2}$ pt or 9 U.S. cups) Duck-flavoured Consommé.
Garnish: 20 Quenelles made from duck forcemeat moulded with dessert spoons, placed on a buttered tray and slightly flattened. Poach them, arrange in a small earthenware dish, sprinkle with grated Parmesan and a little chicken glaze and gratinate. These Quenelles are served from the dish as an accompaniment to the Consommé.

532 Consommé Dame Blanche
2 litres ($3\frac{1}{2}$ pt or 9 U.S. cups) Chicken Consommé very lightly thickened with tapioca.
Garnish: 1 dariole mould of almond milk Royale cut into cubes; 40 star-shaped pieces cut from thin slices of chicken breast.

533 Consommé Demidoff
2 litres ($3\frac{1}{2}$ pt or 9 U.S. cups) Chicken Consommé.
Garnish: 1 tbs each of small balls of carrot and turnip, scooped out with a vegetable scoop and

glazed; $\frac{1}{2}$ tbs small balls of truffle; 1 tbs peas; 2 tbs small Quenelles made from chicken forcemeat with Fines Herbes; Pluches of chervil.

534 Consommé Deslignac
2 litres ($3\frac{1}{2}$ pt or 9 U.S. cups) Chicken Consommé lightly thickened with tapioca.
Garnish: 2 dariole moulds of cream Royale cut into cubes; a layer of chicken forcemeat sandwiched between 2 large blanched lettuce leaves, cooked and cut into small rounds; Pluches of chervil.

535 Consommé aux Diablotins
2 litres ($3\frac{1}{2}$ pt or 9 U.S. cups) Chicken Consommé lightly thickened with tapioca.
Garnish: Serve separately, 6 mm ($\frac{1}{4}$ in) thick slices of long thin French bread covered dome-shape with a mixture made of reduced Sauce Béchamel and grated cheese seasoned with Cayenne and gratinated a few moments before being required.

536 Consommé Diane
2 litres ($3\frac{1}{2}$ pt or 9 U.S. cups) Pheasant-flavoured Consommé.
Garnish: 2 tbs small Quenelles made from pheasant forcemeat; 1 tbs Brunoise of white of celery; 1 tbs pearl barley.

537 Consommé Diplomate
2 litres ($3\frac{1}{2}$ pt or 9 U.S. cups) Chicken Consommé lightly thickened with tapioca.
Garnish: Chicken forcemeat with the addition of Crayfish Butter moulded to the shape of a thin sausage, poached, then cut into thin slices and trimmed; 1 tbs fine Julienne of very black truffle.

538 Consommé Divette
2 litres ($3\frac{1}{2}$ pt or 9 U.S. cups) Chicken Consommé.
Garnish: 1 dariole mould of Royale prepared from a base of crayfish Velouté, cut into small ovals; 2 tbs small ball-shape Quenelles made from a forcemeat of smelts; 1 tbs small balls of truffle.

539 Consommé Dominicaine
2 litres ($3\frac{1}{2}$ pt or 9 U.S. cups) Chicken Consommé.
Garnish: 1 tbs Julienne of breast of chicken; 2 tbs small Pâtes d'Italie. Serve grated cheese separately.

540 Consommé Doria
2 litres ($3\frac{1}{2}$ pt or 9 U.S. cups) Chicken Consommé.
Garnish: 1 tbs small chicken Quenelles; 2 tbs balls of glazed cucumber; Pluches of chervil; 20 small balls of cheese-flavoured chou paste deep fried at the last moment and served separately.

Note: Because of the confusion that exists regarding the garnishing of recipes designated Doria, it is proposed to take the majority view and to standardize recipes where this name is used; thus the main item of garnish which characterizes this preparation is accepted as being cucumber.

541 Consommé Douglas
2 litres ($3\frac{1}{2}$ pt or 9 U.S. cups) well flavoured Ordinary Consommé.
Garnish: 100 g ($3\frac{1}{2}$ oz) braised calf's sweetbreads cooled under pressure, cut into 1 cm ($\frac{2}{5}$ in) thicknesses and then into 2 cm ($\frac{4}{5}$ in) round pieces; 1 tbs small round artichoke bottoms cut into round pieces of the same size; 1 tbs asparagus tips.

542 Consommé Dubarry
2 litres ($3\frac{1}{2}$ pt or 9 U.S. cups) Ordinary Consommé lightly thickened with tapioca.
Garnish: 2 dariole moulds of cauliflower Royale cut into small rounds; 2 tbs small fleurets of cooked cauliflower; Pluches of chervil.

543 Consommé à l'Ecossaise
2 litres ($3\frac{1}{2}$ pt or 9 U.S. cups) specially prepared mutton Bouillon kept very clear and skimmed of all fat.
Garnish: 4 tbs large dice of flesh of the breast of mutton used to make the Bouillon; 2 tbs well-cooked pearl barley; 2 tbs large Brunoise of vegetables.

544 Consommé Edouard VII
2 litres ($3\frac{1}{2}$ pt or 9 U.S. cups) Chicken Consommé flavoured with curry.
Garnish: 4 tbs large dice of flesh of the breast of mutton used to make the Bouillon; 2 tbs well-cooked pearl barley; 2 tbs large Brunoise of vegetables.

545 Consommé Flavigny
2 litres ($3\frac{1}{2}$ pt or 9 U.S. cups) Chicken Consommé.
Garnish: 10 small fresh morels stewed in butter; 2 tbs rice cooked in White Bouillon; 1 tbs Julienne of white of chicken.

546 Consommé Florial
2 litres ($3\frac{1}{2}$ pt or 9 U.S. cups) Chicken Consommé.
Garnish: 1 tbs each of carrot and turnip cut in daisy shape pieces, 3 mm ($\frac{1}{8}$ in) thick, then cooked in White Bouillon and glazed; 2 tbs asparagus tips; 1 tbs peas; 2 tbs small Quenelles prepared from fine chicken forcemeat containing a purée of pistachio nuts, piped in the shape of small

long leaves or other suitable shape; Pluches of chervil.

547 Consommé Florentine
2 litres (3½ pt or 9 U.S. cups) Chicken Consommé.
Garnish served separately: 5 small lettuce stuffed with rice à la Florentine (4244) braised in a little White Bouillon and cut into suitable shapes; nice slices of very fresh bone marrow poached in White Bouillon.

548 Consommé Florian
2 litres (3½ pt or 9 U.S. cups) Chicken Consommé.
Garnish: 4 tbs small Printanier of vegetables; 10 poached plovers' eggs.

549 Consommé à la Gauloise
2 litres (3½ pt or 9 U.S. cups) Chicken Consommé lightly flavoured with tomato.
Garnish: 20 each of freshly cooked small cockscombs and cocks' kidneys; 1 dariole mould of very pink ham Royale cut in large diamonds.

550 Consommé Georges V
2 litres (3½ pt or 9 U.S. cups) Chicken Consommé flavoured with pheasant.
Garnish: 2 tbs small Quenelles prepared from pheasant and cream forcemeat with chopped truffle; 1 tbs pearl barley; 2 tbs fine Julienne of white of celery.

551 Consommé Germinal
2 litres (3½ pt or 9 U.S. cups) Ordinary Consommé with 1 dl (3½ fl oz or ½ U.S. cup) infusion of tarragon added at the last moment.
Garnish: 2 tbs small grooved Quenelles prepared from chicken forcemeat containing chopped chervil and tarragon; 1 tbs small green peas; 1 tbs French beans cut in diamonds; 1 tbs asparagus tips.

552 Consommé Gladiateur
2 litres (3½ pt or 9 U.S. cups) of specially prepared Bouillon made from very fresh oxtail and chicken and flavoured with celery and basil. The meats should be covered with ordinary White Bouillon and the cooking should take place very very slowly for 5–6 hours so as to obtain a very clear Bouillon which does not require further clarification. Finish with ½ dl (2 fl oz or ¼ U.S. cup) Madeira.
Garnish: 2 tbs pearl barley and 1 poached egg per person. The eggs should be served separately.
This recipe originated in the Restaurant du Petit-Moulin Rouge in the summer of 1865.

553 Consommé Grimaldi
2 litres (3½ pt or 9 U.S. cups) Ordinary Consommé prepared with the addition of 6 tbs tomato purée in the clarification.
Garnish: 2 dariole moulds of Ordinary Royale cut into any suitable shape; 2 tbs Julienne of celery stewed in butter and a little White Bouillon.

554 Consommé Hélène
2 litres (3½ pt or 9 U.S. cups) Chicken Consommé flavoured with tomato.
Garnish: 2 dariole moulds of Ordinary Royale cut in small thick rounds; 30 small Profiteroles flavoured with Parmesan.

555 Consommé Henriette
2 litres (3½ pt or 9 U.S. cups) Ordinary Consommé flavoured with curry.
Garnish: 2 dariole moulds of Ordinary Royale pre-Serve separately 1 egg poached in salted water (no vinegar) per person, and freshly grated Parmesan.

556 Consommé à l'Indienne
2 litres (3½ pt or 9 U.S. cups) Ordinary Consommé flavoured with curry.
Garnish: 2 dariole moulds of Ordinary Royale prepared with coconut milk, cut into small dice. Serve a dish of plain boiled rice separately.

557 Consommé à l'Infante
2 litres (3½ pt or 9 U.S. cups) Chicken Consommé very lightly thickened with tapioca.
Garnish: 2 tbs very fine Julienne of sweet pimento; 2 tbs boiled rice; Pluches of chervil.

558 Consommé Isabelle de France
2 litres (3½ pt or 9 U.S. cups) very strongly flavoured Chicken Consommé.
Garnish: 2 tbs plain boiled peas; 20 Quenelles made of chicken and cream forcemeat, moulded with teaspoons; 2 tbs very black truffles cooked in Frontignan wine and cut in fine Julienne.

559 Consommé Ivan
2 litres (3½ pt or 9 U.S. cups) Chicken Consommé with the addition of 2 dl (7 fl oz or ⅞ U.S. cup) beetroot juice.
Garnish: 6 tbs boiled rice cooked in White Bouillon. Serve separately 20 small hot patties.

Note: This Consommé may be served in cups for suppers but without the garnish of rice. The small patties should, however, still be served.

560 Consommé Jeanne Granier
2 litres (3½ pt or 9 U.S. cups) Chicken and Pigeon Consommé.

Garnish: 5 crayfish tails cooked in Champagne and 2 tbs rice cooked in Bouillon per person.

561 Consommé Judic
2 litres ($3\frac{1}{2}$ pt or 9 U.S. cups) very strongly flavoured Chicken Consommé.
Serve separately in small china dishes, 10 very small whole or halves of braised lettuce; 20 chicken and cream forcemeat Quenelles piped with a star tube in the form of rosettes; 2 tbs truffle cut in rounds or in Julienne.

562 Consommé Julienne
2 litres ($3\frac{1}{2}$ pt or 9 U.S. cups) Ordinary Consommé.

Ingredients for the Garnish:
125 g ($4\frac{1}{2}$ oz) red of carrot; 125 g ($4\frac{1}{2}$ oz) turnip; 50 g (2 oz) white of leek; 50 g (2 oz) white of celery; 30 g (1 oz) onion; 70 g ($2\frac{1}{2}$ oz) cabbage.

Method:
Cut the carrot, turnip, leek and celery into even-size Julienne and slice the onion very finely; stew all these vegetables except the cabbage with a little butter, a pinch of salt and sugar, moisten with 5 dl (18 fl oz or $2\frac{1}{4}$ U.S. cups) Ordinary Consommé, then add the previously blanched Julienne of cabbage. Allow to cook gently then finish at the last moment with $1\frac{1}{2}$ litres ($2\frac{5}{8}$ pt or $6\frac{1}{2}$ U.S. cups) Ordinary Consommé; 1 tbs of small peas; 1 tbs Chiffonade of sorrel and lettuce, and Pluches of chervil.

563 Consommé Juliette
2 litres ($3\frac{1}{2}$ pt or 9 U.S. cups) Chicken Consommé flavoured with tarragon.
Garnish: 10 small poached eggs; 2 tbs small peas; 2 tbs small cooked Pâtes d'Italie.

564 Consommé Kléber
2 litres ($3\frac{1}{2}$ pt or 9 U.S. cups) Petite Marmite Bouillon to which is added a piece of brisket during its cooking.
Garnish: 1 tbs small balls of potato cooked in White Bouillon; 1 tbs small balls of carrots; 1 tbs small green peas; 4 tbs of the cooked brisket from the soup, cut into small cubes.

565 Consommé La Pérouse
Pour 100 g ($3\frac{1}{2}$ oz) semolina into 2 litres ($3\frac{1}{2}$ pt or 9 U.S. cups) boiling Ordinary Consommé stirring gently until cooked.
Garnish: 4 tbs green peas; 10 small poached eggs.

566 Consommé Lorette
2 litres ($3\frac{1}{2}$ pt or 9 U.S. cups) Chicken Consommé flavoured with pimento.
Garnish: 2 tbs fine Julienne of truffle; 2 tbs asparagus tips; Pluches of chervil.

567 Consommé Lucette
2 litres ($3\frac{1}{2}$ pt or 9 U.S. cups) Ordinary Consommé containing 6 tbs Pâtes d'Italie.
Garnish: 1 tbs Tomato Fondue and 1 poached egg per person.

568 Consommé Lucullus
2 litres ($3\frac{1}{2}$ pt or 9 U.S. cups) Chicken Consommé well flavoured with quail.
Garnish: 10 breasts from the roast quails of which the carcasses and legs have been used in the making of the Consommé; 20 chicken and cream forcemeat Quenelles, moulded with teaspoons and poached in White Bouillon; 2 tbs Julienne of truffle cooked with Champagne. Serve separately 20 small hot patties filled with foie gras purée.

569 Consommé à la Madrilène
2 litres ($3\frac{1}{2}$ pt or 9 U.S. cups) Chicken Consommé well flavoured with tomato, celery and a little red pimento, all added with the clarification. This soup can be served hot or cold; if hot it should be garnished with 3 tbs small dice of tomato flesh and 2 tbs small dice of pimento. If served cold no garnish should be added.

570 Consommé Maintenon
2 litres ($3\frac{1}{2}$ pt or 9 U.S. cups) excellent Veal Bouillon flavoured with partridge and fresh or dried morels.
Garnish: 10 small cockscombs braised in veal stock; 20 Quenelles made from partridge and cream forcemeat containing chopped truffle and moulded with teaspoons; 10 tbs rice cooked in White Bouillon.

571 Consommé Messaline
2 litres ($3\frac{1}{2}$ pt or 9 U.S. cups) strongly tomato-flavoured Chicken Consommé.
Garnish: 20 small cocks' kidneys; 2 tbs Julienne of pimento; 2 tbs boiled rice.

572 Consommé Midinette
2 litres ($3\frac{1}{2}$ pt or 9 U.S. cups) Chicken Consommé thickened with tapioca.
Garnish: 1 very small freshly poached egg per person.

573 Consommé Mikado
2 litres ($3\frac{1}{2}$ pt or 9 U.S. cups) Chicken Consommé clarified with the addition of 6 tbs tomato purée previously dried in the oven.

Garnish: 2 tbs diced white of chicken; 4 tbs very red tomato flesh cut in dice and poached in White Bouillon.

574 Consommé Mireille
2 litres (3½ pt or 9 U.S. cups) Chicken Consommé.
Garnish: Using tomato-flavoured chicken forcemeat prepare 40 very small oval medallion-shape Quenelles, or make a roll in the shape of a sausage of the same forcemeat which after poaching should be cut into slices and stamped out with a small plain oval cutter; 3 tbs Pilaw rice lightly flavoured with saffron.

575 Consommé Mirette
2 litres (3½ pt or 9 U.S. cups) Petite Marmite Bouillon.
Garnish: 4 tbs chicken Quenelles piped in the shape of small balls; 2 tbs Chiffonade of lettuce; Pluches of chervil. Serve cheese straws separately.

576 Consommé Mistral
2 litres (3½ pt or 9 U.S. cups) Petite Marmite Bouillon.
Garnish: 2 tbs very fine vermicelli cooked in White Bouillon; 4 tbs diced tomato flesh cooked in olive oil, seasoned and flavoured with Provence herbs; 2 tbs small green peas. Serve grated cheese separately.

577 Consommé Monsigny
2 litres (3½ pt or 9 U.S. cups) Chicken Consommé.
Garnish: 10 small cockscombs; 2 braised lettuces cut in small squares; 2 tbs rice cooked in White Bouillon.

578 Consommé Montespan
2 litres (3½ pt or 9 U.S. cups) Chicken and Pigeon Consommé.
Garnish: 10 very small dariole moulds of lightly seasoned crayfish forcemeat, poached at the last moment; 2 tbs Julienne of very black truffle cooked in Frontignan wine. Serve separately 10 puff pastry patties each enclosing a boned Ortolan which has been stuffed with Parfait of Foie gras.

579 Consommé Montmorency
2 litres (3½ pt or 9 U.S. cups) Chicken Consommé lightly thickened with tapioca.
Garnish: 4 tbs asparagus tips; 2 tbs grooved chicken Quenelles; 2 tbs boiled rice; Pluches of chervil.

580 Consommé Murat
2 litres (3½ pt or 9 U.S. cups) Petite Marmite Bouillon. Serve separately 40 ravioli arranged in layers in a deep dish with tomato-flavoured Jus lié and grated Parmesan; cover the dish and allow to heat through for a few minutes before serving.

581 Consommé Murillo
2 litres (3½ pt or 9 U.S. cups) Chicken Consommé.
Garnish: 2 dariole moulds of Royale made with pumpkin, cut into thick rounds; 2 tbs green peas; 2 tbs rice cooked in White Bouillon.

582 Consommé Nana
2 litres (3½ pt or 9 U.S. cups) Chicken Consommé.
Garnish: Arrange thin slices of French bread in layers in soup tureens, alternating with a mixture of grated Gruyère and Parmesan; cover with the boiling Consommé. Serve 1 poached egg per person separately.

583 Consommé Nantua
2 litres (3½ pt or 9 U.S. cups) well-flavoured Chicken Consommé.
Garnish: 10 each of very fresh cockscombs and kidneys; 4 tbs green asparagus tips. Serve separately 10 small tartlet shapes made of chicken forcemeat, each garnished with 4 poached and drained crayfish tails, coated with Sauce Nantua flavoured with truffle essence, sprinkled with freshly grated cheese and gratinated at the last minute.

584 Consommé à la Neige de Florence
2 litres (3½ pt or 9 U.S. cups) Ordinary or Chicken Consommé served boiling hot. Serve 30–40 g (1–1½ oz) of Neige de Florence separately. Each guest adds a little of this to his soup.

585 Consommé Nelson
2 litres (3½ pt or 9 U.S. cups) Fish Consommé thickened with 60 g (2 oz) arrowroot.
Garnish: 8 tbs boiled rice. Serve separately 30 small Profiteroles stuffed with a finely chopped mince of lobster prepared à l'Américaine.

586 Consommé Nesselrode
2 litres (3½ pt or 9 U.S. cups) Game Consommé prepared with the addition of hazel hen.
Garnish: 2 dariole moulds of Royale prepared from two-thirds purée of chestnut and one-third game Salmis sauce, cut into large fancy round slices; 2 tbs Julienne of cooked breast of hazel hen; 2 tbs Julienne of Gribouis.

Translators' Note: Gribouis are a type of mushroom frequently used in Russian cookery.

587 Consommé aux Nids d'Hirondelle—Birds Nest Soup
2 litres ($3\frac{1}{2}$ pt or 9 U.S. cups) Chicken Consommé prepared with three times the normal amount of meat.

This soup is garnished with the nests of a species of swallow which are prepared as follows:

For 2 litres of soup soak 4–6 nests in cold water for 2 hours so as to swell the mucilagenous materials of which they are composed; this will also render them transparent. When sufficiently soaked take great care to remove any pieces of feather, shell or other undesirable debris, using the point of a needle. When cleaned, blanch the nests in boiling water for 5–6 minutes, drain them then place in the boiling Consommé.

At this stage the cooking should be very slow and regular for approximately 45 minutes, this being sufficient time to effect the break up of the nests, providing they are of good quality. After this the garnish of the soup consists of nothing more than threads, the mucilagenous parts of the nests having been dissolved in the soup, so providing its characteristic viscidity.

588 Consommé Ninon
2 litres ($3\frac{1}{2}$ pt or 9 U.S. cups) Chicken Consommé.
Garnish: 2 tbs each of small balls of glazed carrot and turnip; 1 tbs small balls of truffle; Pluches of chervil; 10 tartlet-shaped moulds made as follows: butter 10 very small tartlet moulds, decorate with a star-shaped slice of truffle, line with a thin layer of chicken forcemeat then fill with finely chopped cooked chicken bound with Velouté and egg yolks. Place on a tray and cook in a fairly hot oven.

589 Consommé à l'Orge Perlé
2 litres ($3\frac{1}{2}$ pt or 9 U.S. cups) Ordinary Consommé.
Garnish: Wash 90 g (3 oz) pearl barley in lukewarm water, blanch, drain well, cover with White Bouillon, add a small piece of celery and simmer gently until cooked; time approximately $2\frac{1}{2}$ hours.
To serve: Drain the pearl barley well and add to the Consommé.

590 Consommé à l'Orientale
2 litres ($3\frac{1}{2}$ pt or 9 U.S. cups) Mutton Consommé prepared in the same way as Ordinary Consommé using mutton instead of beef plus the addition of 6 tbs tomato purée and a little saffron. Pass through a clean cloth when ready.
Garnish: 2 tbs hard-boiled egg yolks passed through a coarse sieve; 1 dariole of ordinary Royale prepared with mutton brains, poached and cut into crescent-shaped pieces; 2 tbs grains of boiled rice.

591 Consommé Olga
2 litres ($3\frac{1}{2}$ pt or 9 U.S. cups) Ordinary Consommé with the addition of 1 dl ($3\frac{1}{2}$ fl oz or $\frac{1}{2}$ U.S. cup) Port wine added at the last minute.
Garnish: 2 tbs Julienne of celeriac; 2 tbs Julienne of pickled cucumbers; 2 tbs Vesiga cooked in White Bouillon, drained and cut in dice.

592 Consommé à la d'Orléans
2 litres ($3\frac{1}{2}$ pt or 9 U.S. cups) Chicken Consommé lightly thickened with tapioca.
Garnish: 2 tbs each of three different kinds of grooved Quenelles made from chicken forcemeat as follows: 1) white Quenelles by the addition of cream, 2) red Quenelles by the addition of a little thick tomato purée and 3) light green Quenelles by the addition of a purée of pistachio nuts or spinach; Pluches of chervil.

593 Consommé Orloff
For 2 litres ($3\frac{1}{2}$ pt or 9 U.S. cups) of soup prepare a Petite Marmite (475) using 1 kg ($2\frac{1}{4}$ lb) boned and stuffed oxtail; 1 small boiling fowl; 1 old pheasant; 1 knuckle of veal; the usual vegetables; a few dried flap mushrooms and 3 litres of White Bouillon. When ready, strain through a clean cloth.
Garnish: 120 g (4 oz) of the cooked oxtail cut in small round pieces and the vegetables from the Marmite. Serve separately 30 small hot patties filled with a mince made from the chicken and pheasant from the Marmite.

594 Consommé d'Orsay
2 litres ($3\frac{1}{2}$ pt or 9 U.S. cups) Chicken Consommé.
Garnish: 10 poached egg yolks; 20 small Quenelles prepared from pigeon forcemeat moulded with teaspoons; 2 tbs fine Julienne of pigeon breasts; 2 tbs very green asparagus tips.

595 Consommé Otello
2 litres ($3\frac{1}{2}$ pt or 9 U.S. cups) Chicken Consommé flavoured with tomato; serve separately a dish of Risotto Piémontaise (4284) containing white truffle.

596 Consommé Otero
2 litres ($3\frac{1}{2}$ pt or 9 U.S. cups) Consommé Madrilène.
Garnish: 5 pairs of frogs legs poached in white wine, separated into two, trimmed then cut in half; 2 tbs grains of boiled rice; 2 tbs small green peas. Serve separately paprika-flavoured Paillettes prepared in the same way as cheese straws substituting paprika for the Parmesan.

597 Consommé Palestro
2 litres ($3\frac{1}{2}$ pt or 9 U.S. cups) Chicken Consommé.
Garnish: 3 tbs Tomato Fondue; 10 small poached eggs. Serve separately slices of dry French bread arranged in a vegetable dish, sprinkled with a little Consommé and grated cheese and allowed to heat for a few minutes.

598 Consommé with Italian Pasta or Cereals
2 litres ($3\frac{1}{2}$ pt or 9 U.S. cups) Ordinary or Chicken Consommé. These Consommés can be served with any of the Italian pastas or cereals cooked in accordance with the details given at the beginning of this Chapter (492). The particular pasta or cereal used should be included in the menu title, e.g. Consommé au Vermicelle.

599 Consommé Petite Mariée
2 litres ($3\frac{1}{2}$ pt or 9 U.S. cups) pale coloured Chicken Consommé.
Garnish: 2 dariole moulds of chicken and almond milk Royale, cut into small fancy rounds; Pluches of chervil.

600 Petite Marmite
The Petite Marmite should be made in a special earthenware pot in accordance with the recipe given at the beginning of this Chapter (475).

When the soup is finished, correct the seasoning, remove the chicken, untie it and replace it whole in the Marmite; remove the marrow bone. Clean the sides of the Marmite and place on a serviette on a dish. Serve accompanied with small toasted slices of French bread garnished with the poached bone marrow and thin slices of French bread sprinkled with the fat from the Petite Marmite and dried in the oven.

Note: This soup is frequently called Petite Marmite Henri IV, Poule-au-Pot or Pot-au-Feu. A simple Croûte-au-Pot presented in an earthenware marmite, garnished with vegetables and small pieces of trimmed boiled beef, is often served under the name of Petite Marmite. The Bouillon of the Petite Marmite with the addition of a garnish of the chicken cut into Julienne and the vegetables into Paysanne is sometimes served under the name of Consommé Béarnais.

601 Consommé Polaire
2 litres ($3\frac{1}{2}$ pt or 9 U.S. cups) Chicken Consommé lightly thickened with tapioca. This soup is served in cups with the addition of a very fresh raw egg yolk in each cup.

602 Consommé Pompadour
2 litres ($3\frac{1}{2}$ pt or 9 U.S. cups) Chicken Consommé.
Garnish: 20 chicken Quenelles moulded with teaspoons; 30 crayfish tails cooked in Champagne; 1 tbs Julienne of truffle; 1 tbs Julienne of heart of celery cooked in White Bouillon.

603 Consommé Portalis
2 litres ($3\frac{1}{2}$ pt or 9 U.S. cups) Ordinary Consommé flavoured with tomato and a little saffron.
Garnish: 50 g (2 oz) vermicelli cooked in White Bouillon. Serve grated cheese separately.

604 Consommé Printanier
2 litres ($3\frac{1}{2}$ pt or 9 U.S. cups) Chicken Consommé.
Garnish: 2 tbs each of carrot and turnip cut into small batons $2\frac{1}{2}$ cm (1 in) long by 3 mm ($\frac{1}{8}$ in) in diameter, using a column cutter and cooked in a little White Bouillon; 2 tbs very small green peas; 2 tbs diamonds of French beans; small rounds of sorrel and lettuce cooked at the last minute; Pluches of chervil.

Note: This garnish can also include small Quenelles, ordinary Royale, vegetable Royale or any other suitable Royale. In any case the additional garnish should be mentioned in the name of the Consommé, e.g. Consommé Printanier aux Quenelles, Consommé Printanier à la Royale, Consommé Printanier aux Trois Royales etc.

605 Consommé aux Quenelles à la Moelle
2 litres ($3\frac{1}{2}$ pt or 9 U.S. cups) Ordinary Consommé lightly thickened with tapioca.
Garnish: 30 bone marrow Quenelles moulded with teaspoons and poached in White Bouillon; 3 tbs diced fresh bone marrow poached in White Bouillon.
Bone marrow Quenelles: 90 g (3 oz) very fresh beef bone marrow passed through a very fine sieve, placed in a basin, and allowed to soften in a warm place. Mix well with a wooden spoon until smooth and add 3 egg yolks one at a time. Finish by mixing in 50 g (2 oz) very fine fresh white breadcrumbs, 1 tsp flour, 1 tbs finely chopped parsley, a pinch of salt and pepper and a suspicion of nutmeg.

606 Consommé Queue de Boeuf à la Française
Place 1 kg ($2\frac{1}{4}$ lb) oxtail cut into sections in a pan with 500 g (1 lb 2 oz) knuckle of veal and 3 litres ($5\frac{1}{4}$ pt or $6\frac{1}{2}$ U.S. cups) White Bouillon. Bring to the boil, skim and add 200 g (7 oz) each of carrot and turnip; 150 g (5 oz) leek; 80 g (3 oz) celery; simmer very gently for 5 hours. Clarify the resultant Bouillon in the normal manner using 400 g (15 oz) chopped lean beef and veal which has been lightly fried in a little butter and sprinkled with 20 g ($\frac{2}{3}$ oz) arrowroot.

Garnish: The sections of the cooked oxtail carefully trimmed; small trimmed carrots and turnips cooked in White Bouillon.

Note: This soup was known in the old classical kitchen as *Le Grand Hochepot* or *Potage aux Queues de Boeuf.* It was moistened with a highly concentrated Bouillon used for potting meat and was garnished with the carrots and turnips from the Marmite sliced and simmered in a little fatty Bouillon.

607 Consommé Rabelais

2 litres (3½ pt or 9 U.S. cups) Chicken Consommé flavoured with partridge.

Garnish: 30 Quenelles prepared from partridge and cream forcemeat, moulded with teaspoons and cooked at the last minute; 2 tbs fine Julienne of truffles cooked with Madeira. Serve separately, small Parmesan-flavoured Profiteroles.

608 Consommé Rachel

2 litres (3½ pt or 9 U.S. cups) Chicken Consommé.

Garnish: 1 dariole mould of green Asparagus Royale and 1 dariole mould of Chicken Royale, both cut into small rounds; 40 Parmesan-flavoured Profiteroles.

609 Consommé aux Raviolis

2 litres (3½ pt or 9 U.S. cups) Ordinary Consommé.

The garnish may be composed of raviolis made with one particular filling or with different fillings; they should be of the normal size. The cooking time is 12–18 minutes according to whether the filling is cooked or raw. See Raviolis (4299–4301).

610 Consommé Récamier

2 litres (3½ pt or 9 U.S. cups) delicately flavoured Chicken Consommé.

Garnish: 4 birds nest cooked in the Consommé; 3 tbs green asparagus tips; 2 tbs Julienne of truffles cooked in Champagne. Serve separately 20 small puff pastry patties filled with finely chopped and creamed crayfish tails.

611 Consommé à la Reine

2 litres (3½ pt or 9 U.S. cups) Chicken Consommé lightly thickened with tapioca.

Garnish: 2 dariole moulds of Chicken Royale cut into cubes; 2 tbs fine Julienne white of chicken.

612 Consommé Renaissance

2 litres (3½ pt or 9 U.S. cups) Chicken Consommé.

Garnish: 30 g (1 oz) each of carrot and turnip cut with a grooved vegetable scoop and cooked in a little White Bouillon; 30 g (1 oz) each of peas and French beans cut diamond shape; 2 dariole moulds of Royale made with a purée of early season herbs bound with a little Velouté and whole eggs cooked, then cut into the shape of small leaves when cold, using fancy cutters of different shapes and sizes; Pluches of chervil.

613 Consommé Rossini

2 litres (3½ pt or 9 U.S. cups) Chicken Consommé lightly thickened with tapioca. Serve separately and very hot, 40 Profiteroles cooked very crisp, then stuffed with a mixture of half foie gras purée and half truffle purée.

614 Consommé à la Royale

2 litres (3½ pt or 9 U.S. cups) Chicken Consommé thickened with tapioca.

Garnish: 2 dariole moulds of ordinary Royale cut into small cubes.

615 Consommé au Sagou

2 litres (3½ pt or 9 U.S. cups) Ordinary or Chicken Consommé.

Garnish: 60 g (2 oz) sago cooked in the Consommé.

616 Consommé Saint-Hubert

2 litres (3½ pt or 9 U.S. cups) Game Consommé made with hare, with the addition of 1 dl (3½ fl oz or ½ U.S. cup) of reduced Pouilly wine.

Garnish: 2 dariole moulds of Royale made from two-thirds purée of cooked roebuck and one-third purée of cooked lentils, cut in the shape of a cross which is symbolic of the Holy Ghost; 2 tbs short Julienne of cooked hare.

Note: The designation à la Saint-Hubert always denotes the use in one form or another of furred game.

617 Consommé au Salep

2 litres (3½ pt or 9 U.S. cups) Ordinary or Chicken Consommé.

Garnish: 60 g (2 oz) salep cooked in the Consommé.

618 Consommé Sapho

2 litres (3½ pt or 9 U.S. cups) Chicken Consommé flavoured with partridge.

Garnish: 20 Quenelles made from partridge and cream forcemeat; 2 tbs Julienne of truffle cooked with Marsala; 2 tbs small batons of cucumber blanched then cooked in a little White Bouillon.

619 Potage Sarah Bernhardt

Sprinkle 120 g (4 oz) seed tapioca into 2 litres (3½ pt or 9 U.S. cups) boiling Chicken Consommé and allow to cook gently for 15–18 minutes.

Garnish: 30 small grooved Quenelles made from

chicken forcemeat containing Crayfish Butter; 20 slices of very fresh beef bone marrow poached in a little Bouillon; 1 tbs short Julienne of truffle; 2 tbs cooked asparagus tips.

Note: The correct preparation of this soup has not been established and it has been thought best to adopt the above method which is the one generally used.

620 Consommé Séverine
2 litres ($3\frac{1}{2}$ pt or 9 U.S. cups) Chicken Consommé.
Garnish: 2 tbs each of small balls of potato and cucumber cooked in White Bouillon; 2 tbs peas; 2 tbs grains of lightly blanched rice cooked in White Bouillon.

621 Consommé Sévigné
2 litres ($3\frac{1}{2}$ pt or 9 U.S. cups) Chicken Consommé.
Garnish: 20 chicken Quenelles moulded with teaspoons; 5 braised lettuce cut into 10 neatly trimmed pieces; 2 tbs green peas; Pluches of chervil.

622 Consommé Solange
2 litres ($3\frac{1}{2}$ pt or 9 U.S. cups) Ordinary Consommé.
Garnish: 2 tbs pearl barley; 2 lettuces cooked in Bouillon and cut into squares; 5 tbs short Julienne of white of chicken.

623 Consommé Staël
2 litres ($3\frac{1}{2}$ pt or 9 U.S. cups) Chicken Consommé.
Garnish: 10 poached pigeons eggs; 4 tbs peas. Serve separately small Parmesan-flavoured Profiteroles.

624 Consommé Stanley
2 litres ($3\frac{1}{2}$ pt or 9 U.S. cups) Chicken Consommé.
Garnish: 20 Quenelles made with chicken forcemeat lightly flavoured with curry; 1 tbs Julienne of truffle; 2 tbs Julienne of white mushrooms; 2 tbs grains of boiled rice.

625 Consommé Suzette
2 litres ($3\frac{1}{2}$ pt or 9 U.S. cups) Petite Marmite Bouillon.
Garnish: 2 tbs Julienne of celery cooked in White Bouillon; 2 tbs Julienne of truffle cooked with Madeira; 2 dariole moulds of Cream Royale cut in small squares. Serve separately Parmesan cheese straws.

626 Consommé Talleyrand
2 litres ($3\frac{1}{2}$ pt or 9 U.S. cups) Chicken Consommé.
Garnish: 30 Quenelles made from partridge and cream forcemeat, moulded with teaspoons; 2 tbs Julienne of truffle cooked with Frontignan wine; 20 small cockscombs cooked in White Bouillon and skinned.

627 Consommé au Tapioca
2 litres ($3\frac{1}{2}$ pt or 9 U.S. cups) Ordinary or Chicken Consommé.
Garnish: 60 g (2 oz) tapioca cooked in the Consommé.

628 Consommé Théodora
2 litres ($3\frac{1}{2}$ pt or 9 U.S. cups) Chicken Consommé.
Garnish: 2 tbs Julienne of white of chicken; 1 tbs Julienne of truffle; 2 tbs asparagus tips; 1 dariole mould ordinary Royale cut into small cubes.

629 Consommé Toréador
2 litres ($3\frac{1}{2}$ pt or 9 U.S. cups) Chicken Consommé.
Garnish: 2 tbs tomato flesh cut in dice and poached in White Bouillon; 2 tbs grains of boiled rice; 20 small chipolatas poached in Bouillon and skinned; 2 tbs green peas.

630 Consommé Tosca
2 litres ($3\frac{1}{2}$ pt or 9 U.S. cups) Chicken Consommé lightly thickened with tapioca.
Garnish: 30 small Quenelles made from chicken forcemeat with the addition of finely chopped truffle and one-third its quantity of foie gras purée; 3 tbs fine short Julienne of red of carrot cooked in a little White Bouillon. Serve separately 40 small Profiteroles stuffed with a purée of chicken.

631 Consommé Toulousaine
2 litres ($3\frac{1}{2}$ pt or 9 U.S. cups) Petite Marmite Bouillon prepared in the usual manner but with the addition of some legs of geese and dried mushrooms.
Garnish: 40 small Quenelles made from goose and cream forcemeat with the addition of chopped truffle. Serve separately 30 very small puff pastry Bouchées filled with a purée of foie gras.

632 Consommé à la Trévise
Sprinkle 60 g (2 oz) seed tapioca into 2 litres ($3\frac{1}{2}$ pt or 9 U.S. cups) boiling Chicken Consommé and allow to cook gently for 15–18 minutes.
Garnish: 2 tbs Julienne of white of chicken; 2 tbs Julienne of salt ox tongue; 2 tbs Julienne of truffle.

Note: This Consommé is also known as Consommé aux Trois Filets.

633 Consommé Tyrolienne
2 litres ($3\frac{1}{2}$ pt or 9 U.S. cups) Ordinary Consommé flavoured with tomato and pheasant.
Garnish: 4 tbs fine Julienne of breasts of roast pheasant (the legs and carcase of the pheasant should be used in the flavouring of the Consommé); 50 g (2 oz) very thin fresh noodles lightly blanched and finished cooking in the Consommé. Serve grated Parmesan separately.

634 Consommé d'Uzès
2 litres ($3\frac{1}{2}$ pt or 9 U.S. cups) Ordinary Consommé flavoured with hare.
Garnish: 30 Quenelles made from hare and cream forcemeat, moulded with teaspoons; 2 tbs pearl barley; 2 tbs very small dice of red carrot cooked in White Bouillon.

635 Consommé Valromey
2 litres ($3\frac{1}{2}$ pt or 9 U.S. cups) Chicken Consommé.
Garnish: 10 medium-sized cockscombs, blanched and braised; 2 dariole moulds of Crayfish Royale cut to shape as required; 2 tbs Julienne of truffle cooked with Marsala.

636 Consommé Vendôme
2 litres ($3\frac{1}{2}$ pt or 9 U.S. cups) Petite Marmite Bouillon.
Garnish: 4 tbs fresh beef bone marrow cut in dice and poached in the Consommé just before serving. Serve separately round slices of thin French bread dried in the oven then sprinkled with grated cheese and gratinated at the last moment.

637 Consommé Verdi
2 litres ($3\frac{1}{2}$ pt or 9 U.S. cups) Ordinary Consommé.
Serve separately 30 Quenelles made from chicken and cream forcemeat containing one-fifth its amount of buttered spinach purée and moulded with dessert spoons. Cook the Quenelles, drain and arrange them neatly in a deep dish, sprinkle with Parmesan, melted butter and a little well reduced veal gravy.

638 Consommé Vermandoise
Sprinkle 60 g (2 oz) seed tapioca into 2 litres ($3\frac{1}{2}$ pt or 9 U.S. cups) boiling Chicken Consommé and allow to simmer gently for 15–18 minutes.
Garnish: 2 tbs asparagus tips; 2 tbs green peas; 2 tbs French beans cut diamond shape; 2 tbs sorrel and lettuce leaves cut into small rounds and poached; Pluches of chervil.

639 Consommé au Vermicelle
2 litres ($3\frac{1}{2}$ pt or 9 U.S. cups) Ordinary or Chicken Consommé.
Garnish: 120 g (4 oz) vermicelli blanched, drained and finished cooking in the Consommé.

640 Consommé des Viveurs
2 litres ($3\frac{1}{2}$ pt or 9 U.S. cups) Chicken Consommé flavoured and coloured with beetroot and the addition of 2 dl (7 fl oz or $\frac{7}{8}$ U.S. cup) beer reduced by half.
Garnish: 4 tbs finely sliced, braised celery. Serve separately 40 Diablotins using paprika instead of Cayenne pepper.

641 Consommé Warwick
2 litres ($3\frac{1}{2}$ pt or 9 U.S. cups) Petite Marmite Bouillon.
Garnish: 2 tbs each of small balls of carrot and turnip cooked with a little butter; 2 tbs green peas; 2 tbs lettuce leaves cut into small rounds and poached; 2 tbs chicken livers cut in dice, fried quickly in butter at the last moment and drained; Pluches of chervil.

642 Consommé Washington
2 litres ($3\frac{1}{2}$ pt or 9 U.S. cups) Petite Marmite Bouillon.
Garnish: 100 g ($3\frac{1}{2}$ oz) cooked calf's cheek cut into 2–3 cm (1 in) squares, placed in a pan with a little Madeira and veal gravy and simmered gently for 15 minutes; 2 tbs Julienne of white of celery cooked in White Bouillon; 2 tbs Julienne of truffle cooked with Madeira.

643 Consommé Wladimir
2 litres ($3\frac{1}{2}$ pt or 9 U.S. cups) Chicken Consommé.
Garnish: Cheese Quenelles prepared as follows and served separately. Place 125 g ($4\frac{1}{2}$ oz) cream cheese in a basin and mix well with a wooden spatula; add a pinch of salt, 125 g ($4\frac{1}{2}$ oz) melted butter, 2 egg yolks, 125 g ($4\frac{1}{2}$ oz) flour and 2 tbs double cream; mix well together then fold in 2 stiffly beaten egg whites. Mould into Quenelles using dessert spoons, poach, drain and arrange them neatly in a deep dish. Sprinkle with grated Parmesan and melted butter and gratinate in a hot oven in time for serving with the Consommé.

644 Consommé Yvetot
2 litres ($3\frac{1}{2}$ pt or 9 U.S. cups) Petite Marmite Bouillon.
Garnish: Pascalines prepared as follows. Place 3 Gervais cream cheeses in a basin, mix well with a wooden spatula and add 6 fresh egg yolks and a pinch of salt. Mould and poach in the usual way for Quenelles. Serve separately slices of poached bone marrow and small slices of very hot toast.

645 Consommé Zola
2 litres (3½ pt or 9 U.S. cups) Consommé Croûte au Pot.
Garnish: 6 tbs small Gnocchi made from ordinary chou paste containing grated white Piedmont truffle and grated Parmesan cheese, cooked just before serving. Serve grated Parmesan cheese separately.

646 Consommé Zorilla
2 litres (3½ pt or 9 U.S. cups) Consommé Madrilène with an additional garnish of 4 tbs chick peas cooked in the usual manner and 4 tbs rice cooked in White Bouillon.

647 SPECIAL CONSOMMES FOR SUPPERS

These special Consommés for suppers whether hot or cold, are always served in Consommé cups and should not be garnished. They should, however, be perfect in every detail, of great delicacy and absolute clarity.

They are prepared by the same method as all other Consommés, it being necessary only to slightly increase the amount of meat used in the clarification and to add to this clarification the correct amount of aromatic and flavouring ingredients which determine the character of the finished Consommé. For example, a few extra pieces of celery should be added to the clarification if the Consommé is to be designated *à l'Essence de Céleri*, some sliced morels if *à l'Essence de Morille* or some roasted partridges if *au Fumet de Perdreau* etc.

It is very important that these flavours or aromas should not dominate but merely add a discrete note which should nevertheless be clearly perceptible so as to contribute to the overall quality of the Consommé.

When the Consommé is served cold it should have the appearance of a very light jelly, soft and barely set; should it be liquid the Consommé would not produce that feeling of perfection on the palate as anticipated by the customer; too set and gelatinous, it would be frankly disagreeable. It is thus absolutely necessary to prepare these cold Consommés to the correct consistency if they are to be appreciated.

The special cold Consommés with wine should be prepared from chicken and the wine used must be beyond reproach from the point of view of quality and taste. The amount of wine used according to type, is approximately ¾ dl (3 fl oz or ⅜ U.S. cup) per 1 litre (1¾ pt or 4½ U.S. cups) of Consommé and should be added to the finished Consommé.

648 Consommé à l'Essence de Caille
Allow 4 quails per 1 litre (1¾ pt or 4½ U.S. cups) of Consommé. Roast the quails, remove the breasts for other uses and place the remainder in the Consommé during the clarification.

649 Consommé à l'Essence de Céleri
The amount of celery used to flavour this Consommé is approximately 100 g (3½ oz) celery per 1 litre (1¾ pt or 4½ U.S. cups) added to the clarification.

650 Consommé à l'Essence d'Estragon
It is necessary to use tarragon with care; a few leaves per 1 litre (1¾ pt or 4½ U.S. cups) of Consommé is sufficient to give the required flavour and aroma.

651 Consommé Ivan
This can be found in the section on hot Consommés (559).

652 Consommé à l'Essence de Morille
Allow approximately 150 g (5 oz) fresh morels or 90 g (3 oz) dried morels per 1 litre (1¾ pt or 4½ U.S. cups) Consommé. They should be finely sliced and pounded before adding to the clarification.

653 Consommé aux Piments Doux
Add 15 g (½ oz) pounded fresh or canned pimento per 1 litre (1¾ pt or 4½ U.S. cups) Consommé.

654 Consommé à l'Essence de Truffe
Add to the clarification 60 g (2 oz) pounded peelings and trimmings of truffle per 1 litre (1¾ pt or 4½ U.S. cups) Consommé. This Consommé can only be prepared with fresh truffles.

655 Consommé aux Paillettes d'Or
This is a good Chicken Consommé with the addition of approximately ½ dl (2 fl oz or ¼ U.S. cup) good quality brandy per litre (1¾ pt or 4½ U.S. cups) of Consommé. When it is poured into the Consommé cups add a few flakes of gold leaf. This Consommé is only served cold.

656 Consommé à la Portugaise
To 1 litre (1¾ pt or 4½ U.S. cups) of Consommé add 2 dl (7 fl oz or ⅞ U.S. cup) purée of very red fresh tomatoes and 1 dl (3½ fl oz or ½ U.S. cup) strained liquid of tomatoes. Cover with a lid and cook very gently for 20 minutes but without boiling then pass through a fine cloth using very little pressure. Serve the Consommé very cold.

657 Consommé au Fumet de Perdreau
Allow 1 partridge per 2 litres ($3\frac{1}{2}$ pt or 9 U.S. cups) Consommé. Roast the partridge, remove the breasts for other uses and place the remainder in the Consommé during the clarification.

658 Consommés with Wine
It will be remembered that the wine destined to perfume these Consommés should be of perfect quality; the amount used should be $\frac{3}{4}$ dl (3 fl oz or $\frac{3}{8}$ U.S. cup) per 1 litre ($1\frac{3}{4}$ pt or $4\frac{1}{2}$ U.S. cups) Chicken Consommé.

The following are examples of Consommés using wine: Consommé au Vin de Chypre; Consommé au Vin de Madère; Consommé au Vin de Malvoisie; Consommé au Vin de Marsala; Consommé au Vin de Samos; Consommé au Vin de Zucco, etc.

659 Gelée de Volaille Napolitaine
This is prepared in the same way as Consommé à la Portugaise but using very strongly flavoured chicken Consommé.

660 Gelée de Volaille aux Pommes d'Amour
This is prepared in the same way as Gelée Napolitaine but finishing it with $\frac{3}{4}$ dl (3 fl oz or $\frac{3}{8}$ U.S. cup) old Marsala per 1 litre ($1\frac{3}{4}$ pt or $4\frac{1}{2}$ U.S. cups) Consommé.

661 Cold Chicken Velouté for Suppers
The Roux for this Velouté is made with 30 g (1 oz) butter and 35 g ($1\frac{1}{4}$ oz) flour per 1 litre ($1\frac{3}{4}$ pt or $4\frac{1}{2}$ U.S. cups) Chicken Bouillon. Prepare in the same way as for Ordinary Velouté using very clear and strongly flavoured Chicken Bouillon. Allow to simmer gently for $1\frac{1}{2}$ hours adding an additional half of the original quantity of Bouillon during the process.

When the Velouté is cooked and has been well skimmed of all traces of fat, pass it through a very fine strainer and add $2\frac{1}{2}$ dl (9 fl oz or $1\frac{1}{8}$ U.S. cups) very fresh light cream per 1 litre ($1\frac{3}{4}$ pt or $4\frac{1}{2}$ U.S. cups) Velouté. Allow to cool, stirring continuously with a wooden spoon, pass once more through the strainer and finish if necessary, with a little more cold Chicken Bouillon so that the Velouté has the consistency of a lightly thickened Consommé.

Suitable additions to this soup are: essence of tomatoes or pimentoes; Crayfish, Prawn or Game Cream but care must be taken to ensure that only sufficient of these essences and creams is added so as to give a discrete flavour to the soup.

Note: The kind of cream known as Fleurette Normande is the most suitable for the preparation of this Velouté.

THICK SOUPS

Under the general heading of thick soups are classified: the Purées, the Creams, the Veloutés, the thickened Bouillons such as Germiny, and the special blended thick soups.

662 PUREE SOUPS

The ingredients and methods of thickening:
Purée Soups are composed of a basic ingredient which can be a single vegetable, a combination of vegetables or a single item of poultry, game or shellfish. Almost all forms of these soups should be supported by a thickening agent, i.e.

1) rice for Purées of poultry, shellfish and certain vegetables,
2) potatoes for Purées having a base of leaf vegetables and certain root vegetables such as pumpkin,
3) lentils for all Purées of game,
4) Croûtons of fried bread for Purées prepared in the old classical style.

In the old classical kitchen these Croûtons were the principal if not the only thickening agent used, notably for Coulis and Bisques. This procedure which merits reintroduction to modern cookery gives soups an incomparably smooth texture.

The Purées using pulses as the main ingredient such as haricot beans or lentils and those where the main ingredient is a starchy vegetable such as potatoes, have no need for an additional thickening agent, bearing in mind that these vegetables already contain the necessary thickening quality.

Proportions of liquids and thickening agents:
The liquids used in the preparation of Purée Soups are White Bouillon, Game Bouillon or Fish Bouillon according to the nature of the basic ingredient of the Purée and sometimes milk for Purées of vegetables.

The usual proportion of liquid is 2 litres ($3\frac{1}{2}$ pt or 9 U.S. cups) liquid to 1 litre ($1\frac{3}{4}$ pt or $4\frac{1}{2}$ U.S. cups) actual purée.

The proportions of thickening agents are established as follows:

1) 85–120 g (3–4 oz) rice per 500 g (1 lb 2 oz) of vegetables or 75–100 g ($2\frac{1}{2}$–$3\frac{1}{2}$ oz) rice per 500 g (1 lb 2 oz) poultry, game or shellfish flesh,
2) 190 g (7 oz) raw lentils per 500 g (1 lb 2 oz) of game flesh,
3) 250 g (9 oz) potatoes per 500 g (1 lb 2 oz) of leaf or root vegetables,

4) 270 g (10 oz) fried bread Croûtons per 500 g (1 lb 2 oz) of vegetables or shellfish flesh.

Preparation and finishing of Purée soups:
The vegetables used for making Purée soups are either sliced and stewed raw with 80–100 g (3–3½ oz) butter per 600–700 g (1 lb 5 oz–1½ lb) vegetable or sliced and blanched before being stewed in butter; this will be indicated in the following recipes.

The game for Purée soups is roasted as for Salmis and finished cooking with the lentils; the bones are carefully removed when cooked. The flesh is then pounded with the lentils, passed through a sieve and the consistency of the purée is then adjusted. Care must be taken to remove the required amount of breast meat for its garnish at the moment when the game is just cooked.

The poultry for Purées is poached or cooked in White Bouillon together with the rice for thickening it. When cooked the bones are removed carefully and the flesh is made into a purée in the same way as for game taking care to remove the required amount of white meat for its garnish at the moment when the poultry is just cooked.

When the consistency of vegetable based Purée soups has been adjusted, the soup must then be simmered very gently for 25–30 minutes and skimmed very carefully. It is advisable to occasionally add a few spoonfuls of cold Bouillon during this procedure as this will help to remove impurities which are suspended in the Purée, thus bringing them to the surface.

Purées of poultry, game or shellfish are placed in a Bain-marie to keep hot immediately after boiling, no further simmering or skimming is necessary. All Purée soups should be passed through a fine strainer at the last moment and should finally be finished away from the heat with 80–100 g (3–3½ oz) butter per 1 litre (1¾ pt or 4½ U.S. cups) soup.

Those Purée soups of which the basic thickening agent is a whitish starch such as haricot beans, rice, potatoes etc. or bread Croûtons, can be finished with a liaison of egg yolks and cream.

It must be considered as a firm principle that a soup which has been finally buttered must not be reboiled; butter gives the soup a clean fresh flavour which would be destroyed if it was reboiled.

Garnishes for Purée Soups:
Purée soups should be garnished according to their type with either of the following:

1) small diced bread Croûtons fried in butter allowing 50 g (2 oz) or 2 tbs per 1 litre (1¾ pt or 4½ U.S. cups) soup,
2) small dice of poultry or game cut from the cooked and reserved flesh, or small Quenelles made from some of the reserved raw flesh.
3) small dice of cooked flesh of the shellfish used in making the Purée.

Note: Where no garnish is indicated in the following recipes for Purée soups it should be understood that Croûtons of bread cut into dice and fried in butter at the last moment, should be served.

Changes in the preparation of certain soups
A large number of Purée soups are capable of being transformed into Velouté or Cream soups by adding to the main ingredient, a Velouté of chicken or fish, or a thin Sauce Béchamel instead of the thickening agent normally used in their preparation. However, some of these Purée soups, because of the nature of their ingredients can only be served as a Purée.

Those Purée soups suitable for preparing as Veloutés and Creams are noted in the following recipes.

663 VELOUTE SOUPS

Velouté soups are prepared from a base of

1) an ordinary Velouté made a little thinner than usual, for Veloutés of vegetables,
2) poultry, game or fish Veloutés, whichever is applicable to the main ingredient of the soup.

Veloutés for soups are made with 100 g (3½ oz) white Roux per 1 litre (1¾ pt or 4½ U.S. cups) liquid which can be White Bouillon for vegetables, Chicken Bouillon for Chicken Veloutés; Game Bouillon for Veloutés of game; and Fish Bouillon for Fish Veloutés.

Proportions for Velouté Soups:
All the thick soups made by this method have the following proportions:

1) half the finished soup should be a Velouté,
2) a quarter should be the appropriate Purée which characterizes the soup,
3) the other quarter should be the Bouillon for adjusting the consistency always taking account of the amount of cream used in the liaison.

For example, the proportions for preparing 2 litres (3½ pt or 9 U.S. cups) of Velouté à la Reine will be:

1 litre (1¾ pt or 4½ U.S. cups) Chicken Velouté
5 dl (18 fl oz or 2¼ U.S. cups) purée of chicken
3 dl (½ pt or 1¼ U.S. cups) white Chicken Bouillon for final adjustment
2 dl (7 fl oz or ⅞ U.S. cup) liaison of egg yolks and cream

General rules concerning the preparation of Veloutés:

1) Certain basic ingredients such as chicken and fish should be cooked in the Velouté after having been boned or filleted—after which the flesh should be removed, pounded, mixed with the soup and then the whole passed through a sieve. The consistency of the soup should then be adjusted with the Bouillon.
2) If preparing a Velouté of vegetables, place the appropriate vegetables to cook in the Velouté after they have been prepared according to their kind, i.e. blanched and stewed with butter, or simply stewed with butter. The vegetables should be cooked in the soup until tender and the Velouté is then finished as before.
3) In the preparation of a Velouté of shellfish, the shellfish are cooked with a Mirepoix in the usual manner, then finely pounded and added to the Velouté before passing through the sieve. In all cases the soup should be passed finally through a fine strainer before adding the liaison.

Liaison and final adjustment:
The liaison for Veloutés is made in the proportion of 3 egg yolks and 1 dl (3½ fl oz or ½ U.S. cup) cream per 1 litre (1¾ pt or 4½ U.S. cups) soup.

The liaison should be added to the reheated but not boiling soup at the last moment, taking care to mix it in quickly and thoroughly away from the heat. The final adjustment of the consistency is made by adding 80–100 g (3–3½ oz) butter at the last moment.

Garnishes for Velouté Soups:
These are furnished by the basic ingredient of the Velouté in the form of dice, Julienne, Quenelles and Royales, or if the basic ingredient is a vegetable in the form of Brunoises, fine Printaniers and Chiffonades.

In certain cases these garnishes may be supplemented with no more than 1 tablespoon of boiled rice per 1 litre (1¾ pt or 4½ U.S. cups) of soup.

The special characteristics of the Velouté Soups:
The basic principles are fixed and can be summarized as follows:

1) The composition is fixed in the proportions previously stated which are: 2 parts Velouté, 1 part basic ingredient which characterizes the soup, and 1 part White Bouillon and the liaison of cream and eggs for adjusting the consistency.
2) The finishing of the soup with the liaison of cream and yolks and the final addition of butter.

664 CREAM SOUPS

The preparation of Cream Soups is the same as Veloutés with the following differences:

1) The Velouté used as the thickening base is replaced by thin Sauce Béchamel made in the proportions of 100 g (3½ oz) white Roux per 1 litre (1¾ pt or 4½ U.S. cups) milk.
2) In a number of cases the liquid used for adjusting the consistency is milk instead of Bouillon.

Proportions for Cream Soups:
This is the same as Velouté, i.e.

1) half the finished soup should be Sauce Béchamel.
2) a quarter should be the appropriate Purée which characterizes the soup,
3) the other quarter should be the Bouillon or milk used for adjusting the consistency, always taking account of the amount of cream for finishing the soup.

General rules concerning the preparation of Cream Soups:
Whether prepared with poultry, game, vegetables or shellfish the method is always the same as for Velouté soups, it is therefore not necessary to repeat them here.

Garnishes for Cream Soups:
These are furnished by the basic ingredient which characterizes the soup, in the same manner as for Veloutés.

Final adjustment:
This is done at the last minute after passing the soup through a fine strainer, with 2 dl (7 fl oz or ⅞ U.S. cup) very fresh cream per 1 litre (1¾ pt or 4½ U.S. cups) soup.

The special characteristics of Cream Soups:
These are carefully established as follows

1) the base used for thickening is thin Sauce Béchamel,
2) Cream soups should not be finished with butter, except in certain special cases as when a compound butter is an essential part of the soup. Cream soups are never finished with a liaison of yolks and cream,
3) only cream should be added in the finishing of the soup.

Note: Velouté soups and Cream soups should not be reboiled or allowed to simmer once the final consistency has been achieved; it should only be reheated to just below boiling point then placed immediately in a Bain-marie with a little butter placed on the surface of the soup to prevent a skin from forming.

The finishing of soups using a liaison and butter for Veloutés, and cream for Cream soups should be done at the last moment.

Observations

Without actually altering the basic principles, a Velouté can be used to replace Sauce Béchamel as the thickening agent for a cream soup except where the soup is required to be completely meatless.

It is advised that moderation is exercised in the use of Sauce Béchamel and to simplify the work it is suggested that it may be replaced by:

1) a thickening of arrowroot or other suitable starch, using 75 g (2½ oz) per 1 litre (1¾ pt or 4½ U.S. cups) milk or
2) a light panada obtained by simmering 150 g (5 oz) sliced French bread in 9 dl (1⅗ pt or 4 U.S. cups) milk for 15 minutes; this gives 1 litre of panada.

The use of this panada is equally recommended for Creams and Veloutés of fish.

IMPORTANT NOTICE TO THE READER

In the preceding article concerning thick soups, the general rules, principles, formulas and recommendations which have been judged necessary for removing any hesitation or doubt in the mind of the reader have been indicated.

In the following recipes long details have been dispensed with and they have been made as succinct as possible without indicating all the details about boiling, simmering, finishing etc. which have already been explained.

PUREE SOUPS

(The following recipes are for 10 persons)

665 Bisque or Coulis d'Ecrevisses—Bisque or Cullis of Crayfish

Ingredients:
30 small crayfish, approximately 40 g (1½ oz) each

For the Mirepoix:
50 g (2 oz) carrots
50 g (2 oz) onions
50 g (2 oz) butter
1 sprig thyme
½ bayleaf
3 parsley stalks
1 small tbs flamed brandy
2 dl (7 fl oz or ⅞ U.S. cup) white wine

For the Thickening and Moistening:
120–150 g (4–5 oz) rice
1½ litres (2⅝ pt or 6½ U.S. cups) White Bouillon

For finishing:
1 dl (3½ fl oz or ½ U.S. cup) cream
150 g (5 oz) butter

Method:

1) Cut the carrots, onions and parsley stalks into very small dice and cook to a light brown in the butter together with the thyme and bayleaf. Wash the crayfish, remove the trails then cook the crayfish with the Mirepoix until they turn red.
   Season with 12 g (⅓ oz) salt and a little milled pepper, sprinkle with the brandy and the wine and allow to cook gently to reduce. Add 2½ dl (9 fl oz or 1⅛ U.S. cups) White Bouillon and allow to cook gently for 10 minutes.
2) Cook the rice in 7½ dl (1⅓ pt or 3¼ U.S. cups) of the White Bouillon.
3) Shell the crayfish and reserve all the tails and ten of the heads.
4) Finely pound the remainder of the shells, add the rice and its cooking liquid together with the cooking liquid from the crayfish.

Pass through a fine sieve and dilute this purée with 5 dl (18 fl oz or 2¼ U.S. cups) White Bouillon. Bring to the boil, pass through a fine strainer and keep in the Bain-marie.

Finish the soup before serving with 150 g (5 oz) butter and 1 dl (3½ fl oz or ½ U.S. cup) cream; correct the seasoning and add a little Cayenne.

Garnish: Cut the reserved crayfish tails in dice and add to the soup. Serve separately the ten crayfish heads which have been trimmed, cleaned and filled with a fish and cream forcemeat and cooked at the last moment.

666 Bisque or Coulis d'Ecrevisses à l'Ancienne

Sauté the crayfish with a Mirepoix as for the Bisque in the preceding recipe; add the brandy and white wine; reduce and add 1 litre (1¾ pt or 4½ U.S. cups) White Bouillon. Replace the rice for thickening with 450 g (1 lb) Croûtons of bread freshly fried in butter at the last moment. Allow to simmer with the crayfish and proceed and finish as in the preceding recipe.

667 Bisque or Cullis of Crab
Proceed in the same way as for Bisque of Crayfish replacing the crayfish with small or medium-sized crabs. The crabs should preferably be allowed to clean themselves by soaking for 2–3 hours in cold water.

668 Bisque or Cullis of Lobster
Replace the crayfish with 1 kg (2¼ lb) small live lobsters cut into sections. Sauté with the Mirepoix and proceed in exactly the same way as for Bisque of Crayfish using rice for thickening.
Garnish: Small dice of the reserved lobster meat.

669 Bisque or Cullis of Shrimps or Prawns
Replace the crayfish with 750 g (1 lb 10 oz) raw shrimps or prawns, proceeding in exactly the same way as for Bisque of Crayfish. Finish the Bisque at the last moment with 100 g (3½ oz) Shrimp Butter.
Garnish: 50 g (2 oz) small cooked shrimps or prawn tails which have been reserved from the cooking.

670 Bisque or Cullis of Dublin Bay Prawns
Replace the crayfish with 1 kg (2¼ lb) raw Dublin Bay prawns (Norway lobsters) proceeding in exactly the same way as for Bisque of Crayfish.
Garnish: 50 g (2 oz) cooked flesh of the shellfish cut in thin slices, which has been reserved from the cooking.

671 Purée Bonvalet
Heat 75 g (2½ oz) butter in a pan and add 200 g (7 oz) sliced turnips, 200 g (7 oz) sliced potatoes and 100 g (3½ oz) sliced white of leek; stew gently without colouring. Add 7½ dl (1⅓ pt or 3¼ U.S. cups) White Bouillon and 250 g (9 oz) new season's haricot beans or 200 g (7 oz) cooked old haricot beans.

Allow to simmer gently until cooked, pass through a fine sieve and adjust the consistency with 7½ dl (1⅓ pt or 3¼ U.S. cups) White Bouillon. Pass through a fine strainer and finish at the last moment with a liaison of 6 egg yolks and 2 dl (7 fl oz or ⅞ U.S. cup) cream and 150 g (5 oz) butter.
Garnish: 1 dariole of Royale prepared with a purée of turnips, cut in dice; 1 tbs small green peas; 1 tbs diamond-shaped pieces of French beans; Pluches of chervil.

672 Purée Bressane
Cut 750 g (1 lb 10 oz) pumpkin in large pieces, add 7½ dl (1⅓ pt or 3¼ U.S. cups) milk, 20 g (⅔ oz) salt, a good pinch of caster sugar and bring to the boil. Add 300 g (11 oz) Croûtons of bread fried in butter and simmer together gently until cooked. Pass through a fine sieve, adjust the consistency with 7½ dl (1⅓ pt or 3¼ U.S. cups) boiling milk, then pass through a fine strainer. Finish at the last moment with 150 g (5 oz) butter and 1 dl (3½ fl oz or ½ U.S. cup) cream.
Garnish: 60 g (2 oz) small Italian pasta cooked in milk.
This soup may also be made as a Cream or a Velouté.

673 Purée de Céleri—Celery Soup
Slice 750 g (1 lb 10 oz) celery and blanch in boiling water for a few moments; drain and stew together with 75 g (2½ oz) butter without colouring. Add 1½ litres (2⅝ pt or 6½ U.S. cups) White Bouillon and 350 g (13 oz) sliced potatoes for the thickening, bring to the boil and allow to simmer gently until cooked. Pass through a fine sieve, then through a fine strainer and finish at the last moment with 150 g (5 oz) butter.
This soup may also be made as a Cream or a Velouté.

Note: This soup can be thickened with 150 g (5 oz) rice instead of potatoes.

674 Purée Clermont
Blanch and remove the skins of 750 g (1 lb 10 oz) chestnuts; cook together with 200 g (7 oz) blanched sliced celery, 100 g (3½ oz) sliced onions stewed in butter without colour and 7½ dl (1⅓ pt or 3¼ U.S. cups) White Bouillon. Pass through a fine sieve and adjust the consistency with 5 dl (18 fl oz or 2¼ U.S. cups) boiling milk; pass through a fine strainer. Finish at the last moment with 150 g (5 oz) butter.
Garnish: Thinly sliced rings of small onions, floured and fried in butter until crisp; 60 g (2 oz) Auvergne paste cooked in White Bouillon.

675 Purée Compiègne
Cook together 375 g (14 oz) dry haricot beans, 1 litre (1¾ pt or 4½ U.S. cups) water, 12 g (⅓ oz) salt, 100 g (3½ oz) sliced onions stewed with a little butter, 1 small carrot cut in quarters and a Bouquet garni containing a clove. When tender, drain the beans, remove the carrot and Bouquet garni; pound the beans and replace in the cooking liquid. Mix together, adjust the consistency with 5 dl (18 fl oz or 2¼ U.S. cups) boiling milk, correct the seasoning, pass through a fine strainer and finish at the last moment with 150 g (5 oz) butter.
Garnish: 50 g (5 oz) finely shredded sorrel stewed with a little butter, and Pluches of chervil.
This soup can also be made as a Cream or a Velouté.

676 Purée Condé

Cover 400 g (15 oz) red beans with 1½ litres (2⅝ pt or 6½ U.S. cups) cold water and add 18 g (⅔ oz) salt; bring to the boil, skim and add 2½ dl (9 fl oz or 1⅛ U.S. cups) boiling red wine, a Bouquet garni, 1 onion stuck with a clove and 1 carrot cut in pieces. Allow to cook gently.

When the beans are tender, drain and remove the Bouquet garni, onion and carrot; pound the beans, pass through a sieve and replace in the cooking liquor; mix together, pass through a fine strainer and finish at the last moment with 150 g (5 oz) butter.

677 Purée Conti

Cook together 600 g (1 lb 5 oz) lentils, 1 litre (1¾ pt or 4½ U.S. cups) water, 125 g (4½ oz) salt belly of pork cut into dice and blanched, a Bouquet garni, 1 onion stuck with a clove and 1 carrot cut in pieces. When tender, drain the lentils and remove the carrot, onion and Bouquet garni. Pound the lentils and pork, pass through a sieve and replace in the cooking liquor. Mix together and pass through a fine strainer. Adjust the consistency with 2½ dl (9 fl oz or 1⅛ U.S. cups) White Bouillon and finish at the last moment with 150 g (5 oz) butter and Pluches of chervil.

678 Purée Conti à la Brunoise

Take 1½ litres (2⅝ pt or 6½ U.S. cups) Purée Conti prepared as in the preceding recipe and add at the last moment 5 dl (18 fl oz or 2¼ U.S. cups) thick Consommé à la Brunoise and Pluches of chervil.

679 Purée Cormeilles

Blanch 625 g (1 lb 6 oz) French beans in boiling water for 5 minutes. Drain then stew together with 75 g (2½ oz) butter and 400 g (15 oz) sliced potatoes. Add 7½ dl (1⅓ pt or 3¼ U.S. cups) White Bouillon and allow to simmer gently until cooked. Pass through a fine sieve, adjust the consistency with 3–4 dl (10–14 fl oz or 1¼–1¾ U.S. cups) boiling milk and pass through a fine strainer. Finish at the last moment with 150 g (5 oz) butter; and garnish with 60 g (2 oz) small freshly cooked French beans cut diamond-shape.

This soup may also be made as a Cream or a Velouté.

Note: The thickening of this soup can be advantageously carried out by using flageolet beans instead of potatoes.

680 Purée Crécy

Slice 600 g (1 lb 5 oz) red part of carrots or whole carrots if new seasons. Stew together with 75 g (2½ oz) butter, 100 g (3½ oz) sliced onion, a sprig of thyme, a good pinch of salt and a pinch of sugar. Add 1 litre (1¾ pt or 4½ U.S. cups) White Bouillon and 125 g (4½ oz) rice; bring to the boil and allow to simmer gently until cooked. Pass through a fine sieve, adjust the consistency with 2 dl (7 fl oz or ⅞ U.S. cup) White Bouillon, pass through a fine strainer and finish at the last moment with 150 g (5 oz) butter.

This soup may also be prepared as a Cream or a Velouté.

681 Purée Crécy à l'Ancienne

Proceed in exactly the same way as for Purée Crécy replacing the thickening of rice with 300 g (11 oz) Croûtons of bread fried in butter.

682 Purée Crécy à la Briarde

Stew the carrots in butter with the onions as for Purée Crécy but replace the thickening of rice with 250 g (9 oz) potatoes and moisten with 1 litre (1¾ pt or 4½ U.S. cups) water; season with salt. When cooked pass through a fine sieve and adjust the consistency with 2 dl (7 fl oz or ⅞ U.S. cup) very fresh cream; pass through a fine strainer at the last moment and add 150 g (5 oz) butter. This soup does not now require any further simmering or skimming. Garnish with Pluches of chervil and serve separately small Croûtons of bread fried in butter.

683 Purée Crécy au Riz, aux Perles etc.

The preparation of these soups is the same as for Purée Crécy with the substitution of the normal garnish of Croûtons by a garnish of cooked rice, Perles du Japon etc. the quantity of which should be calculated according to the total proportions of the soup. The soup represents 1½ litres (2⅝ pt or 6½ U.S. cups) when finished and the garnish 5 dl (18 fl oz or 2¼ U.S. cups) which can be obtained from 35 g (1¼ oz) of rice or pearls when cooked in 4 dl (14 fl oz or 1¾ U.S. cups) White Bouillon.

Note: The name of the garnish used, other than Croûtons, should be added to the title of the soup after Crécy.

684 Purée Cressonière

Stew 500 g (1 lb 2 oz) fresh watercress leaves with 75 g (2½ oz) butter. Moisten with 1 litre (1¾ pt or 4½ U.S. cups) White Bouillon and add 300 g (11 oz) sliced potatoes. When cooked pass through a fine sieve then through a fine strainer and adjust the consistency with 2½ dl (9 fl oz or 1⅛ U.S. cups) boiling milk added at the last moment.

Garnish: 50 g (2 oz) watercress leaves placed in the soup 5 minutes before serving.

685 Purée Dubarry

Cook 600 g (1 lb 5 oz) blanched cauliflower and 350 g (13 oz) sliced potatoes in 1 litre ($1\frac{3}{4}$ pt or $4\frac{1}{2}$ U.S. cups) milk; season with 10 g ($\frac{1}{3}$ oz) salt. Pass through a fine sieve and adjust the consistency with $2\frac{1}{2}$ dl (9 fl oz or $1\frac{1}{8}$ U.S. cups) boiling milk then pass through a fine strainer. Finish at the last moment with 150 g (5 oz) butter and Pluches of chervil.

This soup may also be prepared as a Cream or a Velouté.

Note: When prepared as a Purée the garnish for this soup should be small Croûtons of bread fried in butter. When prepared as a Cream or a Velouté the Croûtons should be replaced by small pieces of cooked cauliflower reserved for this purpose. In either case the Pluches of chervil are an essential part of the garnish.

686 Potage Esaü

Cook 40 g ($1\frac{1}{2}$ oz) rice in 4 dl (14 fl oz or $1\frac{3}{4}$ U.S. cups) White Bouillon then add to $1\frac{1}{2}$ litres ($2\frac{5}{8}$ pt or $6\frac{1}{2}$ U.S. cups) finished Purée Conti soup.

687 Purée de Fèves

Cook 800 g ($1\frac{3}{4}$ lb) skinned broad beans in 1 litre ($1\frac{3}{4}$ pt or $4\frac{1}{2}$ U.S. cups) water with 2 sprigs of savory and 18 g ($\frac{2}{3}$ oz) salt. Drain off the beans and reserve 30 small halves of the beans as garnish. Pound the remainder of the beans and mix together with the reserved cooking liquid. Pass through a fine sieve and adjust the consistency by thickening with 30 g (1 oz) arrowroot mixed into 5 dl (18 fl oz or $2\frac{1}{4}$ U.S. cups) cold milk. Bring to the boil then pass through a fine strainer. Finish at the last moment with 150 g (5 oz) butter and add the reserved garnish of broad beans.

This soup may also be prepared as a Cream or a Velouté.

688 Purée Freneuse

Stew 700 g ($1\frac{1}{2}$ lb) sliced blanched turnips with 75 g ($2\frac{1}{2}$ oz) butter. Add $2\frac{1}{2}$ dl (9 fl oz or $1\frac{1}{8}$ U.S. cups) White Bouillon and simmer gently until cooked. Cook separately 250 g (9 oz) potatoes in $2\frac{1}{2}$ dl (9 fl oz or $1\frac{1}{8}$ U.S. cups) White Bouillon. Pass both preparations through a fine sieve then mix well together. Adjust the consistency with 5 dl (18 fl oz or $2\frac{1}{4}$ U.S. cups) boiling milk; pass through a fine strainer and finish at the last moment with 150 g (5 oz) butter.

689 Purée Georgette

Blanch 8 medium-sized globe artichokes. Trim them and gently stew the white part of the leaves and the bottoms with 75 g ($2\frac{1}{2}$ oz) butter until tender. Remove three of the bottoms and reserve. To the remainder add 300 g (11 oz) small Croûtons of bread fried in butter and 1 litre ($1\frac{3}{4}$ pt or $4\frac{1}{2}$ U.S. cups) White Bouillon; finish cooking together gently. Pound, pass through a fine sieve, adjust the consistency with $2\frac{1}{2}$ dl (9 fl oz or $1\frac{1}{8}$ U.S. cups) boiling milk, then pass again through a fine strainer.

Pound the reserved atrichoke bottom with 200 g (7 oz) butter and pass through a very fine sieve. Reheat the soup and finish at the last moment with the prepared artichoke butter.

Garnish: 2 dl (7 fl oz or $\frac{7}{8}$ U.S. cup) Perles du Japon cooked in White Bouillon.

690 Purée de Gibier

1) Whichever game is used always allow 650 g (1 lb 7 oz) to 700 g ($1\frac{1}{2}$ lb) game per 2 litres ($3\frac{1}{2}$ pt or 9 U.S. cups) soup.
2) The game must first be roasted underdone as for Salmis.
3) If the garnish includes Quenelles, remove from the raw game the necessary amount of flesh before roasting it. If the garnish is to be cut into dice or if it is to be a Royale, the required amount of meat should be removed from the game after it has been roasted.
4) To the remainder of the game which should now be approximately 550 g ($1\frac{1}{4}$ lb) add 200 g (7 oz) lentils and 1 litre ($1\frac{3}{4}$ pt or $4\frac{1}{2}$ U.S. cups) Game Bouillon and allow to cook gently together.
5) When cooked, remove the bones from the game and pound the flesh with the drained lentils. Mix this purée with the cooking liquid and pass through a fine sieve, then through a fine strainer. Reheat just to boiling point but do not allow it to simmer as for other Purée soups. Finish at the last moment with 150 g (5 oz) butter.

Garnish: As mentioned above and according to requirements, this can be the cooked flesh cut into small dice or used in the preparation of game Royale, or small Quenelles made from the reserved raw flesh.

This soup may also be prepared as a Cream soup.

Note: For Crème de Gibier, replace half the lentils with an equivalent quantity of thick game Velouté; Sauce Béchamel is not suitable.

691 Purée aux Herbes

Shred 150 g (5 oz) sorrel leaves, 75 g ($2\frac{1}{2}$ oz) watercress leaves and 75 g ($2\frac{1}{2}$ oz) chervil and fresh salad burnet, and stew them gently together with 75 g ($2\frac{1}{2}$ oz) butter. Moisten with 1 litre ($1\frac{3}{4}$ pt or $4\frac{1}{2}$ U.S. cups) water, add 700 g ($1\frac{1}{2}$ lb) sliced potatoes and 12 g ($\frac{1}{3}$ oz) salt and allow to simmer until cooked. Pass through a fine sieve then through a fine strainer; reheat and finish at the last moment with 200 g (7 oz) Beurre Printanier made with fresh herbs including a few leaves of basil and chervil.

692 Purée Malakoff

Slice 200 g (7 oz) white of leek and stew with 75 g (2½ oz) butter; add 400 g (15 oz) sliced potatoes; 750 g (1 lb 10 oz) depipped and sliced tomatoes, and 1 litre (1¾ pt or 4½ U.S. cups) White Bouillon; simmer until cooked and pass through a fine sieve. Adjust the consistency with 2½ dl (9 fl oz or 1⅛ U.S. cups) White Bouillon, pass through a fine strainer, reheat and finish with 150 g (5 oz) butter at the last moment.
Garnish: 125 g (4½ oz) spinach leaves which have been finely shredded, blanched and stewed with a little butter.

693 Purée Maria, or Purée Québec

Cook 400 g (15 oz) haricot beans in 1 litre (1¾ pt or 4½ U.S. cups) water with 8 g (⅓ oz) salt and the usual vegetables and flavouring for dried vegetables; when in season, use 1 litre (1¾ pt or 4½ U.S. cups) fresh haricot beans.

Drain the beans, remove the vegetables and pound the beans. Add this purée to the cooking liquor then pass through a fine sieve. Adjust the consistency with 2½ dl (9 fl oz or 1⅛ U.S. cups) White Bouillon and the same amount of boiling milk; pass through a fine strainer and reheat without boiling.
Garnish: 3 tbs very small Printanier of vegetables and Pluches of chervil.
This soup may also be prepared as a Cream.

694 Purée Marianne

Cook 500 g (1 lb 2 oz) sliced pumpkin and 300 g (11 oz) sliced potato together with 7½ dl (1⅓ pt or 3¼ U.S. cups) White Bouillon. Pass through a fine sieve and adjust the consistency with 5 dl (18 fl oz or 2¼ U.S. cups) White Bouillon. Pass through a fine strainer, reheat and finish at the last moment with 150 g (5 oz) butter.
Garnish: 125 g (4½ oz) finely shredded lettuce and sorrel stewed with a little butter; thin rounds of French bread sprinkled with grated cheese and gratinated.

695 Purée Palestine

Slice 800 g (1¾ lb) Jerusalem artichokes and stew with 75 g (2½ oz) butter. Add 25 g (1 oz) crushed, roasted hazelnuts and 1 litre (1¾ pt or 4½ U.S. cups) White Bouillon; simmer gently until cooked. Pass through a fine sieve and adjust the consistency by thickening it with 40 g (1⅓ oz) arrowroot mixed with 2½ dl (9 fl oz or 1⅛ U.S. cups) cold milk. Bring to the boil then pass through a fine strainer; reheat and finish at the last moment with 150 g (5 oz) butter.
This soup may also be prepared as a Cream or a Velouté.

696 Purée Parmentier

Stew 300 g (11 oz) sliced white of leek with 75 g (2½ oz) butter and without colouring; add 750 g (1 lb 10 oz) sliced floury potatoes, moisten with 1 litre (1¾ pt or 4½ U.S. cups) White Bouillon and cook together quickly. As soon as the potatoes are cooked, break them up with a whisk; pass the whole through a fine sieve and then through a fine strainer. Reheat, adjust the consistency with 2½ dl (9 fl oz or 1⅛ U.S. cups) cream and finish at the last moment with 150 g (5 oz) butter.
Garnish: Small Croûtons of bread fried in butter; Pluches of chervil.
This soup may also be prepared as a Cream or a Velouté.

697 Purée Pastorelle

Stew together 400 g (15 oz) sliced white of leek, 60 g (2 oz) sliced onion and 100 g (3½ oz) sliced mushrooms with 75 g (2½ oz) butter. Moisten with 7½ dl (1⅓ pt or 3¼ U.S. cups) White Bouillon, add 600 g (1 lb 5 oz) sliced potato and cook gently. Pass through a fine sieve and adjust the consistency with 3–4 dl (10–14 fl oz or 1¼–1¾ U.S. cups) boiling milk. Pass through a fine strainer, reheat and finish at the last minute with 150 g (5 oz) butter.
Garnish: Slices of small white mushrooms well stewed in butter; small dice of potato sautéed and coloured in butter.
This soup may also be prepared as a Cream or a Velouté.

698 Purée de Pois aux Croûtons—Pea Soup with Croûtons

Cook together 400 g (15 oz) green split peas, 1 litre (1¾ pt or 4½ U.S. cups) water, a piece of knuckle of ham, 10 g (⅓ oz) salt, a Mirepoix comprised of 60 g (2 oz) streaky bacon diced and blanched, 60 g (2 oz) each of carrot, onion and green of leek, a small sprig of thyme and a small piece of bayleaf. Simmer gently and when cooked, remove the knuckle, pass the remainder through a very fine sieve and adjust the consistency with 3 dl (½ pt or 1¼ U.S. cups) White Bouillon; reheat and finish at the last minute with 150 g (5 oz) butter.
Garnish: 2 tbs small Croûtons of bread fried in butter at the last minute.

699 Purée de Pois Frais—Fresh Pea Soup
This soup may be prepared in either of the following ways:

1) Cook 1 litre (1¾ pt or 4½ U.S. cups) very fresh peas in boiling salted water, drain them well, pound and pass through a fine sieve then reheat together with 1 litre (1¾ pt or 4½ U.S. cups) White Bouillon. Prepared in this way the soup will have a perfect colour.
2) Stew gently together until cooked 1 litre (1¾ pt or 4½ U.S. cups) fresh peas, 100 g (3½ oz) butter, 100 g (3½ oz) sliced green of leek, 50 g (2 oz) shredded lettuce leaves, 8 g (⅓ oz) salt, 15 g (½ oz) sugar, a pinch of chervil and 1 dl (3½ fl oz or ½ U.S. cup) water. Pound well and pass through a fine sieve, adjust the consistency of the purée with 1 litre (1¾ pt or 4½ U.S. cups) White Bouillon and pass through a fine strainer. Prepared in this way the soup does not have such a good colour as the first method but has a much finer flavour.

In either case these soups should be finished at the last moment with 125 g (4½ oz) butter per 1 litre (1¾ pt or 4½ U.S. cups) of soup and garnished with very small cooked green peas and Pluches of chervil.
These soups may also be prepared as Creams.

700 Purée de Pois Frais à la Menthe—Fresh Pea Soup with Mint
Cook the peas in accordance with either of the two methods described above, adding a small bunch of fresh mint. The garnish remains the same except that the Pluches of chervil should be replaced with an equal quantity of chopped young tender leaves of mint.

701 Purée de Potiron à la Bourgeoise
Cook together 750 g (1 lb 10 oz) sliced pumpkin, 1 litre (1¾ pt or 4½ U.S. cups) water, 18 g (⅔ oz) salt and 25 g (1 oz) sugar. Pass through a fine sieve, adjust the consistency with 5 dl (18 fl oz or 2¼ U.S. cups) milk and pass through a fine strainer. Bring to the boil, add 75 g (2½ oz) vermicelli and cook gently in the soup; finish at the last moment with 150 g (5 oz) butter.
This soup may also be prepared as a Cream or a Velouté.

702 Purée de Potiron à la Maraîchère
Cook together 500 g (1 lb 2 oz) sliced pumpkin, 250 g (9 oz) sliced potatoes, 1 litre (1¾ pt or 4½ U.S. cups) water and 18 g (⅔ oz) salt. Pass through a fine sieve, adjust the consistency with 5 dl (18 fl oz or 2¼ U.S. cups) boiling milk and pass through a fine strainer. Finish at the last moment with 150 g (5 oz) butter.
Garnish: 100 g (3½ oz) Julienne of white of leek stewed with a little butter, 1 tbs cooked peas, 1 tbs finely shredded lettuce sorrel and spinach stewed with butter, 2 tbs cooked rice and Pluches of chervil.

703 Purée Portugaise, or Purée de Tomate—Tomato Soup
Heat 75 g (2½ oz) butter in a pan and add a Mirepoix consisting of 50 g (2 oz) diced lean bacon, 60 g (2 oz) onion, 60 g (2 oz) carrot, a sprig of thyme and a small piece of bayleaf; fry together until light brown. Add 700 g (1½ lb) tomatoes freed from pips and roughly chopped, a crushed clove of garlic, 10 g (⅓ oz) sugar, 125 g (4½ oz) rice and 1 litre (1¾ pt or 4½ U.S. cups) White Bouillon. Simmer gently until tender, pass through a fine sieve and adjust the consistency with 2½ dl (9 fl oz or 1⅛ U.S. cups) White Bouillon; pass through a fine strainer and reheat. Finish at the last minute with 200 g (7 oz) Tomato Butter.
Garnish: 2 tbs flesh only of tomato cut into small dice and very lightly cooked in butter; 2 tbs boiled rice.
This soup may also be prepared as a Cream or a Velouté.

704 Purée au Pourpier
Proceed in the same way as for Purée Cressonière replacing the watercress with very fresh purslane.

705 Purée Québec
This is another name for Purée Maria (693).

Note: This name has been included here only because it is frequently used. However, it should be understood that it really does nothing to enrich the culinary repertoire as it is more commonly and correctly known as Purée Maria. It can be found under this name in Carême's *Traité des Potages*—only latterly has the garnish been slightly modified.

706 Purée or Coulis à la Reine—Chicken Soup
Cook a 1 kg (2¼ lb) eviscerated chicken in 1½ litres (2⅝ pt or 6½ U.S. cups) White Bouillon with 125 g (4½ oz) rice. When the chicken is cooked, remove the bones which will leave 550–600 g (1¼ lb to 1 lb 5 oz) cooked meat; reserve 80 g (3 oz) of the white meat for a garnish.

Pound the remaining flesh and rice together with a little of the liquid to a fine paste; pass through a very fine sieve. Add the remaining cooking liquid, bring to the boil, and finish at the last minute with a liaison of 4 egg yolks mixed with 2 dl (7 fl oz or ⅞ U.S. cup) cream, and 200 g (7 oz) butter.

Garnish: The reserved cooked white of chicken cut in small dice.
This soup may also be prepared as a Cream or a Velouté.

707 Purée Saint-Germain
This is another name for Purée de Pois Frais and may be prepared by either of the two methods described.

708 Purée Soissonaise
Cook 400 g (15 oz) haricot beans in 1½ litres (2⅝ pt or 6½ U.S. cups) water with 10 g (⅓ oz) salt and the usual vegetables and flavourings. Drain, remove the garnish and pound the beans; mix in 5 dl (18 fl oz or 2¼ U.S. cups) of the cooking liquid and pass through a fine sieve.

Adjust the consistency with 5 dl (18 fl oz or 2¼ U.S. cups) White Bouillon and 2 dl (7 fl oz or ⅞ U.S. cup) boiling milk and finish at the last minute with 125 g (4½ oz) butter.
This soup may also be prepared as a Cream or a Velouté.

CREAM SOUPS

(The following recipes are for 10 persons)

709 Crème Agnes Sorel
Wash 500 g (1 lb 2 oz) fresh white mushrooms, peel them if necessary and pass through a fine sieve; mix this with 5 dl (18 fl oz or 2¼ U.S. cups) fairly thin Sauce Béchamel made as explained for the preparation of cream soups at the beginning of this Chapter.

Allow to cook very gently for 7–8 minutes, pass through a fine sieve and add this cream of mushrooms to 7½ dl (1⅓ pt or 3¼ U.S. cups) Crème de Volaille of the correct consistency but without the cream; pass through a fine strainer, reheat without allowing it to boil and finish with 4 dl (14 fl oz or 1¾ U.S. cups) cream at the last moment.
Garnish: 1 tbs each of Julienne of raw mushrooms cooked in butter, white of chicken and salt ox tongue.
This soup may also be prepared as a Velouté.

710 Crème Antonelli
To 1¼ litres (2⅕ pt or 5½ U.S. cups) slightly thin Sauce Béchamel add 3 dl (½ pt or 1¼ U.S. cups) very red Tomato Fondue passed through a strainer or the same amount of tomato purée if fresh tomatoes are unobtainable; and 2½ dl (9 fl oz or 1⅛ U.S. cups) White Bouillon; pass through a fine strainer.

Reheat and finish with 4 dl (14 fl oz or 1¾ U.S. cups) cream.
Garnish: 1 chicken winglet boned, stuffed and braised per person.

711 Crème Argenteuil
Blanch 750 g (1 lb 10 oz) tender part only of asparagus tips for 10 minutes. Drain them well and place in 1 litre (1¾ pt or 4½ U.S. cups) slightly thin boiling Sauce Béchamel; finish cooking together gently then pass through a fine sieve.

Adjust the consistency with a little White Bouillon, pass through a fine strainer and reheat. Finish at the last moment with 4 dl (14 fl oz or 1¾ U.S. cups) cream.
Garnish: Very green heads of cooked asparagus and Pluches of chervil.

712 Crème d'Artichauts à la Noisette
Blanch 8 medium-sized artichoke bottoms; slice 6 and leave 2 whole. Stew all of them together with 50 g (2 oz) butter taking care not to colour.

Place the 2 whole ones aside for the garnish and add the rest to 1 litre (1¾ pt or 4½ U.S. cups) fairly thin Sauce Béchamel together with 4 nice roasted and crushed hazelnuts. Allow to cook gently for 10 minutes and pass through a fine strainer. Adjust the consistency with 2½ dl (9 fl oz or 1⅛ U.S. cups) White Bouillon; pass through a fine strainer and reheat.

Finish at the last moment with 4 dl (14 fl oz or 1¾ U.S. cups) cream.
Garnish: The reserved artichokes cut into small dice.

713 Crème Cérès
Pick over 250 g (9 oz) green wheat grains and soak them in cold water for 3 hours. Cook very gently for 3 hours in 3 dl (½ pt or 1¼ U.S. cups) each of White Bouillon and water.

Add to 7½ dl (1⅓ pt or 3¼ U.S. cups) slightly thin Sauce Béchamel, pass through a fine sieve and adjust the consistency with 2 dl (7 fl oz or ⅞ U.S. cup) White Bouillon; pass through a fine strainer.

Reheat and finish at the last moment with 4 dl (14 fl oz or 1¾ U.S. cups) cream.
This soup may also be prepared as a Velouté.

714 Crème Chevreuse
To 5 dl (18 fl oz or 2¼ U.S. cups) Sauce Béchamel add 2½ dl (9 fl oz or 1⅛ U.S. cups) purée of cooked chicken, 2½ dl (9 fl oz or 1⅛ U.S. cups) purée of cooked tuberous chervil and 7½ dl (1⅓ pt or 3¼ U.S. cups) semolina cooked with White Bouillon or milk (this amount can be obtained by cooking 50 g (2 oz) fine semo-

lina in 6 dl (1 pt or $2\frac{5}{8}$ U.S. cups) Bouillon or milk.

Pass through a fine sieve then through a fine strainer. Reheat and finish at the last moment with 2 dl (7 fl oz or $\frac{7}{8}$ U.S. cup) cream.

Garnish: 1 tbs fine Julienne of cooked white of chicken and 1 tbs fine Julienne of truffle.

This soup may also be prepared as a Velouté.

715 Crème Choisy

Blanch 750 g (1 lb 10 oz) lettuce and refresh under cold running water; drain and squeeze out all the moisture. Roughly shred and stew it together with 100 g ($3\frac{1}{2}$ oz) butter, a little salt and a pinch of sugar; add 1 litre ($1\frac{3}{4}$ pt or $4\frac{1}{2}$ U.S. cups) Sauce Béchamel and cook together gently.

Pass through a fine sieve and adjust the consistency of the soup with 1 dl ($3\frac{1}{2}$ fl oz or $\frac{1}{2}$ U.S. cup) White Bouillon or milk and pass through a fine strainer. Reheat without allowing it to boil and add 4 dl (14 fl oz or $1\frac{3}{4}$ U.S. cups) cream at the moment of service.

Garnish: Small Croûtons of bread fried in butter and Pluches of chervil.

This soup may also be prepared as a Velouté.

716 Crème Comtesse

Blanch 650 g (1 lb 7 oz) large white asparagus cut into pieces for 7–8 minutes; drain well and add them to 1 litre ($1\frac{3}{4}$ pt or $4\frac{1}{2}$ U.S. cups) Sauce Béchamel. Cook together gently.

Pass the soup through a fine sieve, adjust the consistency with 1 dl ($3\frac{1}{2}$ fl oz or $\frac{1}{2}$ U.S. cup) Bouillon then pass through a fine strainer. Reheat and finish at the last moment with 4 dl (14 fl oz or $1\frac{3}{4}$ U.S. cups) cream.

Garnish: 1 tbs finely shredded sorrel and lettuce leaves stewed with butter; 2 tbs lightly cooked white asparagus heads.

This soup may also be prepared as a Velouté.

717 Crème Divette

To 1 litre ($1\frac{3}{4}$ pt or $4\frac{1}{2}$ U.S. cups) Crème d'Ecrevisses add 1 litre ($1\frac{3}{4}$ pt or $4\frac{1}{2}$ U.S. cups) Crème d'Eperlans, both soups being completely finished with cream only (see Velouté d'Ecrevisses and Velouté d'Eperlans). Stir together gently but without completely mixing them.

Garnish: 1 tbs small Quenelles made from smelt and cream forcemeat to the size of peas; 1 tbs pea-size balls of very black truffle; 1 tbs cooked crayfish tails cut in small dice.

718 Crème Hamilton

Prepare $1\frac{3}{4}$ litres (3 pt or $7\frac{1}{2}$ U.S. cups) Crème d'Orge (727) flavoured with curry. Reheat and finish at the last moment with 4 dl (14 fl oz or $1\frac{3}{4}$ U.S. cups) cream.

Garnish: 8 tbs cooked Brunoise of vegetables.

719 Crème Judic

Mix together 8 dl ($1\frac{2}{5}$ pt or $3\frac{1}{2}$ U.S. cups) Crème de Volaille and the same quantity of Crème de Laitue à la Choisy. Finish at the last moment with 4 dl (14 fl oz or $1\frac{3}{4}$ U.S. cups) cream.

Garnish: 20 small rounds of lettuce, each piped on top with a spiral or star shape of chicken and cream forcemeat plus a slice of truffle on the top of this then poached at the last moment; 20 very small, freshly cooked cockscombs.

This soup may also be prepared as a Velouté.

720 Crème La Fayette

Blanch 1 small plump, tender chicken for 2 minutes, refresh it and place in a pan to cook with $1\frac{3}{4}$ litres (3 pt or $7\frac{1}{2}$ U.S. cups) White Bouillon; 120 g (4 oz) onion; 5 dl (18 fl oz or $2\frac{1}{4}$ U.S. cups) very ripe maize grains and a Bouquet garni containing a piece of celery. Cook very gently until tender.

When cooked remove the bones from the chicken and pound the flesh together with the drained onions and maize. Add the cooking liquid and pass through a fine sieve then through a fine strainer. Reheat and finish with 4 dl (14 fl oz or $1\frac{3}{4}$ U.S. cups) cream.

Garnish: 3 poached and bearded oysters per person.

721 Crème Lafitte

To 1 litre ($1\frac{3}{4}$ pt or $4\frac{1}{2}$ U.S. cups) slightly thin Sauce Béchamel, add 400 g (15 oz) fine purée of cooked partridge and $2\frac{1}{2}$ dl (9 fl oz or $1\frac{1}{8}$ U.S. cups) White Bouillon. Pass through a fine sieve and then through a fine strainer.

Reheat and finish at the last moment with $\frac{1}{2}$ dl (2 fl oz or $\frac{1}{4}$ U.S. cup) truffle essence, $\frac{1}{2}$ dl (2 fl oz or $\frac{1}{4}$ U.S. cup) old Marsala and 4 dl (14 fl oz or $1\frac{3}{4}$ U.S. cups) cream.

Garnish: 20 small fresh cockscombs skinned and cooked in a little butter.

722 Crème de Laitue—Cream of Lettuce

Proceed in the same way as for Crème Choisy.

723 Crème La Vallière

Mix together $1\frac{1}{4}$ litres ($2\frac{1}{5}$ pt or $5\frac{1}{2}$ U.S. cups) Crème de Volaille and 5 dl (18 fl oz or $2\frac{1}{4}$ U.S. cups) Crème de Céleri; reheat and finish with $2\frac{1}{2}$ dl (9 fl oz or $1\frac{1}{8}$ U.S. cups) cream.

Garnish: 1 dariole mould of Celery Royale cut into small dice. Serve small Profiteroles separately.

724 Crème Lison

Mix together 7½ dl (1⅓ pt or 3¼ U.S. cups) Crème de Riz, (made by adding 40–50 g (1¾–2 oz) rice flour diluted with 1½ dl (5 fl oz or ⅝ U.S. cup) cold milk to 6 dl (1 pt or 2½ U.S. cups) boiling White Bouillon and cooking for 20–25 minutes), and 5 dl (18 fl oz or 2¼ U.S. cups) Crème de Céleri; then add 5 dl (18 fl oz or 2¼ U.S. cups) White Bouillon cooked with Perles du Japon (this amount can be obtained by cooking 35 g (1¼ oz) Perles du Japon in 4 dl (14 fl oz or 1¾ U.S. cups) Bouillon. Reheat and finish at the last moment with 2½ dl (9 fl oz or 1⅛ U.S. cups) cream.

725 Crème de Maïs

Cook 800 g (1¾ lb) fresh grains of maize in boiling salted water (or use an equivalent amount of tinned maize) then drain it and add to 8 dl (1⅖ pt or 3½ U.S. cups) Sauce Béchamel.

Pass through a fine sieve, then through a fine strainer, reheat and add 4 dl (14 fl oz or 1¾ U.S. cups) cream at the last moment.

Garnish: 100 g (3½ oz) cooked grains of maize.

This soup may also be prepared as a Velouté.

726 Crème Nivernaise

Stew 600 g (1 lb 5 oz) red part of carrot with 90 g (3 oz) butter; add 1 litre (1¾ pt or 4½ U.S. cups) Sauce Béchamel and cook together gently. Pass through a fine sieve and adjust the consistency with 1 dl (3½ fl oz or ½ U.S. cup) White Bouillon; reheat and finish at the last moment with 4 dl (14 fl oz or 1¾ U.S. cups) cream.

Garnish: 3 tbs fine Brunoise of red part of carrot stewed with butter and a little White Bouillon until almost dry.

This soup may also be prepared as a Velouté.

Note: Crème Nivernaise and Velouté Nivernaise are in fact Crème or Velouté Crécy under another name.

727 Crème d'Orge—Cream of Pearl Barley

Thoroughly wash 375 g (14 oz) pearl barley in several waters then cook very gently for approximately 3 hours in 1 litre (1¾ pt or 4½ U.S. cups) White Bouillon with a sliced piece of white celery, adding more liquid as required. Pound the barley, pass through a fine sieve with the cooking liquid and add 2½ dl (9 fl oz or 1⅛ U.S. cups) White Bouillon; pass through a fine strainer, reheat and finish at the last moment with 4 dl (14 fl oz or 1¾ U.S. cups) cream.

Garnish: 2 tbs small grains of pearl barley cooked separately in water, drained then rinsed in a little White Bouillon before adding to the soup.

Note: The preparation of this soup may be simplified by replacing the pearl barley with barley flour using 150–200 g (5–7 oz) diluted in 2½ dl (9 fl oz or 1⅛ U.S. cups) milk, per 2 litres (3½ pt or 9 U.S. cups) boiling liquid.

728 Crème d'Oseille à l'Avoine—Cream of Sorrel and Oatmeal

To 1 litre (1¾ pt or 4½ U.S. cups) boiling milk add 80–100 g (3–3½ oz) oatmeal flour diluted in 2½ dl (9 fl oz or 1⅛ U.S. cups) cold milk; whisk together until it boils, season with a little salt then allow to simmer very gently on the side of the stove for 1 hour.

Add 150 g (5 oz) sorrel stewed with 80 g (3 oz) butter, simmer gently for a further 15 minutes and pass through a fine sieve. Add 2 dl (7 fl oz or ⅞ U.S. cup) boiling milk, pass through a fine strainer and finish at the last moment with 4 dl (14 fl oz or 1¾ U.S. cups) cream.

729 Crème d'Oseille à l'Orge—Cream of Sorrel with Barley

Proceed in the same way as for Crème d'Oseille à l'Avoine using the same proportions and replacing the oatmeal flour with barley flour.

Note: The two above soups may also be prepared as Veloutés and can be garnished as required with a Chiffonade of sorrel and lettuce; dice of tomato flesh lightly stewed in butter; boiled rice; Italian pastas; Perles du Japon; pearl barley; fine Brunoise or Printanier of vegetables etc.

730 Crème Perette

Prepare 1¾ litres (3 pt or 7½ U.S. cups) Velouté de Homard using Crème de Riz (724) instead of Ordinary Velouté and finish at the last moment with 4 dl (14 fl oz or 1¾ U.S. cups) cream.

Garnish: 6 pieces of frogs legs cooked in White Wine Court-bouillon, per person.

731 Crème Princesse

Mix together 8 dl (1⅖ pt or 3½ U.S. cups) each of thin Crème de Riz (see the beginning of Crème Lison 724) and Crème de Volaille. Finish the soup at the last moment with 4 dl (14 fl oz or 1¾ U.S. cups) cream.

Garnish: 100 g (3½ oz) very small slices of cooked white of chicken; 2 tbs cooked white asparagus tips; Pluches of chervil.

This soup may also be prepared as a Velouté.

732 Crème Régence

Prepare 1¾ litres (3 pt or 7½ U.S. cups) Crème d'Orge, reheat without boiling and finish at the last moment with 100 g (3½ oz) Crayfish Butter and 2½ dl (9 fl oz or 1⅛ U.S. cups) cream.

Garnish: 30 small grooved Quenelles made from chicken forcemeat with the addition of some Crayfish Butter; 20 small, freshly cooked cockscombs; 3 tbs cooked pearl barley.

733 Crème Reine Margot

Prepare 1½ litres (2⅝ pt or 6½ U.S. cups) Crème de Volaille and add 2 dl (7 fl oz or ⅞ U.S. cup) almond milk; reheat and finish at the last moment with 4 dl (14 fl oz or 1¾ U.S. cups) cream.

Garnish: 60 small Quenelles made from chicken forcemeat with the addition of 25 g (1 oz) purée of pistachios per 100 g (3½ oz) forcemeat.

This soup may also be made as a Velouté.

734 Crème Sultane

Completely remove the bones from a 1 kg (2¼ lb) chicken which should give 550–600 g (1¼ lb–1 lb 5 oz) flesh. Cut this into pieces, add to 1 litre (1¾ pt or 4½ U.S. cups) Sauce Béchamel and cook gently together. When the chicken is very well cooked remove it from the Béchamel and pound very finely. Replace in the Béchamel then pass through a fine sieve.

Add 2½ dl (9 fl oz or 1⅛ U.S. cups) hazelnut milk, pass through a fine strainer, reheat without boiling and finish the soup at the last moment with 175 g (6 oz) Pistachio Butter and 2 dl (7 fl oz or ⅞ U.S. cup) cream.

Garnish: Small round slices of truffle.

Note: The colour of this soup should be a very pale green. If it is necessary to improve on the colour given by the Pistachio Butter, add a little spinach green colour.

735 Crème Suzanne

Prepare 1½ litres (2⅝ pt or 6½ U.S. cups) Crème d'Avoine (728) but omitting the sorrel and add 2½ dl (9 fl oz or 1⅛ U.S. cups) milk. Reheat and finish the soup at the last moment with 4 dl (14 fl oz or 1¾ U.S. cups) cream.

Garnish: 300 g (11 oz) very small green peas.

736 Crème Turbigo

To 1 litre (1¾ pt or 4½ U.S. cups) slightly thin Sauce Béchamel add 5 dl (18 fl oz or 2¼ U.S. cups) very red Tomato Fondue and 2½ dl (9 fl oz or 1⅛ U.S. cups) White Bouillon.

Pass through a fine strainer, reheat and finish at the last moment with 2½ dl (9 fl oz or 1⅛ U.S. cups) cream.

Garnish: 120 g (4 oz) small Italian pasta cooked in White Bouillon. Serve grated Parmesan separately.

VELOUTE SOUPS

(The following recipes are for 10 persons)

Note: It should be remembered that Veloutés always include a liaison of 3 egg yolks and 1 dl (3½ fl oz or ½ U.S. cup) cream per 1 litre (1¾ pt or 4½ U.S. cups) soup and that butter is added at the last moment in the proportion of 75–100 g (2½–3½ oz) per 1 litre (1¾ pt or 4½ U.S. cups) of soup according to type.

737 Velouté Albuféra

Prepare 1¾ litres (3 pt or 7½ U.S. cups) Velouté d'Ecrevisses made slightly thinner than usual. Reheat and finish at the last moment with a liaison of 6 egg yolks, 2 dl (7 fl oz or ⅞ U.S. cup) cream and 150 g (5 oz) butter.

Garnish: One poached pigeon's egg per person.

738 Velouté à l'Andalouse

To 1 litre (1¾ pt or 4½ U.S. cups) slightly thin Ordinary Velouté, add 3 dl (½ pt or 1¼ U.S. cups) very red tomato purée; 2 dl (7 fl oz or ⅞ U.S. cup) Soubise made with Spanish onions; and 2½ dl (9 fl oz or 1⅛ U.S. cups) White Bouillon; pass through a fine strainer.

Reheat the soup without allowing it to boil and finish at the last moment with the liaison of 6 egg yolks and 2 dl (7 fl oz or ⅞ U.S. cup) cream and 150 g (5 oz) butter.

Garnish: 1 tbs very red tomato flesh cut in dice and poached in Bouillon; 1½ tbs boiled rice; 1 tbs very fine Julienne of pimento.

This soup may also be made as a Cream.

739 Velouté de Blanchailles au Currie—Velouté of Whitebait with Curry

Lightly cook 200 g (7 oz) chopped onion in 80 g (3 oz) butter without colour, sprinkle with 10 g (⅓ oz) curry powder and continue cooking gently for 2–3 minutes. Moisten with 1¼ litres (2⅕ pt or 5⅕ U.S. cups) warm water, season with 20 g (⅔ oz) salt and add a pinch of saffron and a Bouquet garni. Bring to the boil, add 500 g (1 lb 2 oz) very fresh whitebait and boil rapidly for 10 minutes.

Pass through a fine sieve then through a fine strainer; reheat without bringing to the boil and finish at the last moment with the liaison of 6 egg yolks and 2 dl (7 fl oz or ⅞ U.S. cup) cream and 150 g (5 oz) butter.

Garnish: 2 tbs boiled rice or vermicelli. Serve separately thin slices of dried and buttered French bread.

Note: It is essential that this soup is prepared very quickly; it takes no longer than 20 minutes and should be served immediately it is ready. If allowed to stand even for a short while it is likely to separate.

740 Velouté Carmen

Prepare 1½ litres (2⅝ pt or 6½ U.S. cups) slightly thin Chicken Velouté with the addition of 150 g (5 oz) sweet red pimento. Pass through a fine sieve then through a fine strainer; reheat and finish at the last moment with the liaison of 6 egg yolks and 2 dl (7 fl oz or ⅞ U.S. cup) cream and 150 g (5 oz) butter.

Garnish: 50 g (2 oz) grains of rice cooked in White Bouillon.

741 Velouté Cardinal

Prepare a Velouté using 150 g (5 oz) white Roux and 1¾ litres (3 pt or 7½ U.S. cups) very clear Fish Bouillon; add a small bouquet of parsley stalks, some trimmings of white mushrooms and allow to cook gently for 20 minutes. Pass through a fine strainer and finish at the last moment with the liaison of 6 egg yolks and 2 dl (7 fl oz or ⅞ U.S. cup) cream, 150 g (5 oz) Lobster Butter and 50 g (2 oz) red colouring butter.
Garnish: 80 g (3 oz) cooked lobster cut in small dice.

742 Velouté Colombine

Heat a little butter in a pan, place in 2 plump pigeons and heat to stiffen the flesh taking care not to colour the exterior. Place them in 1½ litres (2⅝ pt or 6½ U.S. cups) slightly thin Chicken Velouté, add 4 grains crushed aniseed and allow to cook very gently. Remove the pigeons when they are well done and bone them out; reserve three of the breasts for use as the garnish and finely pound the remainder of the cooked flesh. Replace this purée in the Velouté and pass all through a very fine sieve. Reheat the soup and finish at the last moment with the liaison of 6 egg yolks and 2 dl (7 fl oz or ⅞ U.S. cup) cream and 150 g (5 oz) butter.
Garnish: The reserved breasts of pigeon cut into fine Julienne and 30 small Quenelles made of pigeon and cream forcemeat.

743 Velouté de Crevettes à la Normande

Cook 750 g (1 lb 10 oz) raw shrimps with a fine Mirepoix and butter as indicated for Bisque d'Ecrevisses (665) to the end of Stage 1. Reserve 20 small tails for the garnish and finely pound the remainder of the shrimps with the Mirepoix. Add this purée to 1¼ litres (2¼ pt or 5½ U.S. cups) thin Fish Velouté, pass through a fine sieve then through a fine strainer; reheat and finish at the last moment with the liaison of 6 egg yolks and 2 dl (7 fl oz or ⅞ U.S. cup) cream and 200 g (7 oz) Shrimp Butter.
Garnish: The reserved shrimps; 20 poached and bearded oysters.
This soup may also be prepared as a Cream.

744 Velouté Dame Blanche

Prepare 1½ litres (2⅝ pt or 6½ U.S. cups) Chicken Velouté using 100 g (3½ oz) white Roux per 1 litre (1¾ pt or 4½ U.S. cups) liquid; pass through a fine strainer, add 2½ dl (9 fl oz or 1⅛ U.S. cups) almond milk and reheat without boiling. Finish at the last moment with the liaison of 6 egg yolks and 2 dl (7 fl oz or ⅞ U.S. cup) cream and 150 g (5 oz) butter.
Garnish: 100 g (3½ oz) white of chicken cut into very small dice; 40 very small Quenelles made from chicken and cream forcemeat.
This soup may also be prepared as a Cream.

745 Velouté Dieppoise

Stew 60 g (2 oz) white of leek and 50 g (2 oz) white mushroom trimmings with 30 g (1 oz) butter. Add 1½ litres (2⅝ pt or 6½ U.S. cups) Fish Velouté. Pass through a fine strainer, add 2½ dl (9 fl oz or 1⅛ U.S. cups) of the cooking liquid from mussels cooked in white wine, reheat without boiling and finish with the liaison of 6 egg yolks and 2 dl (7 fl oz or ⅞ U.S. cup) cream and 150 g (5 oz) butter.
Garnish: 1 tbs small shelled shrimps; 10 small, poached, bearded mussels.
This soup may also be prepared as a Cream.

746 Velouté Doria

To 1 litre (1¾ pt or 4½ U.S. cups) Ordinary Velouté add 625 g (1 lb 6 oz) peeled, depipped and sliced cucumber which has been stewed in butter. Cook gently together, pass through a fine strainer and adjust the consistency of the Velouté with 2½ dl (9 fl oz or 1⅛ U.S. cups) White Bouillon. Reheat without boiling and finish with the liaison of 6 egg yolks and 2 dl (7 fl oz or ⅞ U.S. cup) cream and 150 g (5 oz) butter.
Garnish: 2 tbs pea-size balls of cucumber blanched and stewed with 25 g (1 oz) butter and a few tablespoons of White Bouillon; 2 tbs grains of boiled rice.

747 Velouté Doris

Prepare 1½ litres (2⅝ pt or 6½ U.S. cups) Velouté de Merlan; prepared in the same way as Velouté d'Eperlans (751) but using whiting instead of smelts; reheat without boiling and finish with the liaison of 6 egg yolks and 2 dl (7 fl oz or ⅞ U.S. cup) cream and 200 g (7 oz) Shrimp Butter.
Garnish: 3 poached and bearded oysters per person.

748 Velouté d'Ecrevisses Joinville

Cook 30 small crayfish with a fine Mirepoix and butter as indicated for Bisque d'Ecrevisses (665) to the end of Stage 1.

Reserve 10 shelled tails for the garnish and finely pound the remainder of the crayfish with the Mirepoix. Add this purée and the cooking liquor to 1 litre (1¾ pt or 4½ U.S. cups) Fish Velouté, pass through a fine sieve and then through a fine strainer.

Adjust the consistency with 2½ dl (9 fl oz or 1⅛ U.S. cups) clear fish stock made with sole bones. Reheat without boiling and finish with the liaison of 6 egg yolks and 2 dl (7 fl oz or ⅞ U.S. cup) cream and 150 g (5 oz) butter.
Garnish: The reserved crayfish tails and 1 tbs each of small dice or fine Julienne of truffle and mushroom.
This soup may also be prepared as a Cream.

749 Velouté d'Ecrevisses Princesse
This soup is prepared in the same way as for Velouté d'Ecrevisses Joinville without reserving any crayfish tails for the garnish.
Garnish: 2 tbs very green asparagus tips; 40 small Quenelles made from whiting and cream forcemeat containing Crayfish Butter.

750 Velouté d'Ecrevisses à la Normande
This soup is prepared in the same way as Velouté d'Ecrevisses Joinville without reserving any crayfish tails for the garnish but adding the cooking liquid from 20 poached oysters used as the garnish.
Garnish: 20 small poached and bearded oysters.

751 Velouté d'Eperlans
Stew together 150 g (5 oz) fillets of smelt; 350 g (13 oz) flesh of whiting, John Dory or sole; 100g (3½ oz) finely chopped onion, the juice of half a lemon and 100 g (3½ oz) butter. Add 1 litre (1¾ pt or 4½ U.S. cups) Ordinary Velouté or milk panada made by adding 150 g (5 oz) white breadcrumbs to 9 dl (1⅗ pt or 4 U.S. cups) boiling milk.

Finish cooking these ingredients together and pass them through a fine sieve. Adjust the consistency with 2½ dl (9 fl oz or 1⅛ U.S. cups) fish stock made from sole bones, pass through a fine strainer and reheat without boiling. Finish with the liaison of 6 egg yolks and 2 dl (7 fl oz or ⅞ U.S. cup) cream and 150 g (5 oz) butter; season lightly with Cayenne.

Observations concerning the preparation of Velouté d'Eperlans and other Veloutés made of fish

1) Because the flavour of smelts can be almost disagreeable, the proportions of the flesh of this fish should not exceed a third of the total required. The other two-thirds of flesh should be obtained from such fish as whiting, sole or particularly John Dory all of which have a fairly neutral flavour thus preventing the flavour of the smelts being too pronounced.
2) The use of Ordinary Velouté or milk panada as indicated in the observations concerning the theory of thick soups instead of Fish Velouté is recommended for making fish Velouté soups; this obviates a too pronounced flavour of fish. The milk panada is most suitable for all kinds of fish Velouté soups.
3) The garnish of the above Velouté should be very small Quenelles made from a mixture of half smelt and cream forcemeat and half whiting or sole and cream forcemeat.
4) All fish Velouté soups and those Veloutés moistened with fish stock should be prepared as quickly as possible and served immediately. If allowed to rest they are likely to separate and lose their flavour; it is therefore recommended that these fish-based Veloutés should not be started more than half an hour before they are required for service.

752 Velouté d'Eperlans Dieppoise
Prepare a Velouté d'Eperlans as in the preceding recipe but adjust the consistency with some well decanted mussel cooking liquid instead of fish stock, which should be added when reheating and just before finishing with the liaison and butter.
Garnish: 4 tbs cooked shrimps; 30 small poached and bearded mussels.

753 Velouté d'Eperlans Joinville
Prepare a Velouté d'Eperlans as previously indicated. Finish with the usual liaison and 200 g (7 oz) Shrimp Butter.
Garnish: 30 small whole crayfish tails; 1 tbs each of fine Julienne of truffle and mushrooms.

754 Velouté d'Eperlans Princesse
Prepare a Velouté d'Eperlans as previously indicated.
Garnish: small Quenelles made from a forcemeat as indicated in the preceding observations, with the addition of Crayfish Butter; 2 tbs very green cooked asparagus tips.

755 Velouté d'Eperlans Saint-Malo
Prepare a Velouté d'Eperlans as previously indicated. Finish with the usual liaison and 200 g (7 oz) Shrimp Butter.
Garnish: 4 tbs cooked shrimps; 40 small Quenelles made from sole and cream forcemeat.

756 Velouté Eugénie
Prepare 1¾ litres (3 pt or 7½ U.S. cups) fairly thin Velouté de Crevettes; reheat and finish with the liaison of 6 egg yolks and 2 dl (7 fl oz or ⅞ U.S. cup) cream and 150 g (5 oz) butter.
Garnish: 40 cooked prawns cut in half lengthways.

757 Velouté Excelsior
To 1¼ litres (2⅕ pt or 5½ U.S. cups) of Crème d'Orge (727) add 3 dl (½ pt or 1¼ U.S. cups)

purée of cooked green asparagus. Finish with 2½ dl (9 fl oz or 1⅛ U.S. cups) White Bouillon, pass through a fine strainer and reheat without boiling. Finish with the liaison of 6 egg yolks and 2 dl (7 fl oz or ⅞ U.S. cup) cream and 150 g (5 oz) butter at the last moment.
Garnish: 2 tbs small grains of pearl barley cooked in water then rinsed in a little White Bouillon before adding to the soup.
This soup can also be prepared as a Cream.

758 Velouté Fédora
To 1½ litres (2⅝ pt or 6½ U.S. cups) very thin Chicken Velouté add 2 dl (7 fl oz or ⅞ U.S. cup) very fine and red tomato purée and pass through a fine strainer. Finish with the liaison of 6 egg yolks and 2 dl (7 fl oz or ⅞ U.S. cup) cream and 150 g (5 oz) butter.
Garnish: 100 g (3½ oz) fine vermicelli cooked in White Bouillon.

759 Velouté de Homard à la Cleveland
Take a medium-sized lobster of 650–700 g (1 lb 7 oz–1½ lb) weight and prepare it *à l'Américaine* (2110). Reserve sufficient of the cooked flesh of the lobster for the garnish and finely pound the rest of the flesh and the shell. Add this purée and the sauce from the cooking to 7½ dl (1⅓ pt or 3¼ U.S. cups) Ordinary Velouté.

Rub through a sieve and then pass through a fine strainer. Add 2½ dl (9 fl oz or 1⅛ U.S. cups) White Bouillon, reheat without boiling and finish with the liaison of 6 egg yolks and 2 dl (7 fl oz or ⅞ U.S. cup) cream and 150 g (5 oz) butter at the last moment.
Garnish: the reserved lobster cut into small dice.

760 Velouté de Homard à l'Indienne
Proceed in the same way as for Velouté de Homard à la Cleveland seasoning the lobster with curry powder. Reserve approximately 100 g (3½ oz) of the cooked lobster for the garnish and add this cut into small dice; serve plain boiled rice separately.

761 Velouté de Homard à l'Orientale
Take a medium-sized lobster of 650–700 g (1 lb 7 oz–1½ lb) weight and prepare it *à la Newburg* (2123); reserve a quarter of the cooked flesh for the garnish. Finely pound the remainder of the flesh and the shell and add this purée, together with the sauce from the cooking, to 7½ dl (1⅓ pt or 3¼ U.S. cups) Ordinary Velouté. Rub through a sieve, then pass through a fine strainer and add 2½ dl (9 fl oz or 1⅛ U.S. cups) White Bouillon.

Reheat without boiling and finish with the liaison of 6 egg yolks and 2 dl (7 fl oz or ⅞ U.S. cup) cream and 150 g (5 oz) butter.
Garnish: the reserved lobster cut into small dice; 4 tbs grains of boiled rice.

762 Velouté de Homard au Paprika
Proceed in the same way as for Velouté de Homard à la Cleveland adding extra tomatoes, 120 g (4 oz) chopped onion and flavour with 20 g (⅔ oz) paprika. Reserve 60 g (2 oz) cooked lobster for the garnish. Finely pound the remainder of the flesh and the shell and add this and the lobster sauce to 7½ dl (1⅓ pt or 3¼ U.S. cups) Ordinary Velouté.

Rub through a sieve, pass through a fine strainer and add 2½ dl (9 fl oz or 1⅛ U.S. cups) White Bouillon. Reheat without boiling and finish with the liaison of 6 egg yolks and 2 dl (7 fl oz or ⅞ U.S. cup) cream; and 150 g (5 oz) butter.
Garnish: the reserved lobster cut into small dice; 2 tbs cooked red pimento cut into dice; 2 tbs grains of boiled rice.

763 Velouté aux Huîtres
Prepare 1¾ litres (3 pt or 7½ U.S. cups) very delicate Fish Velouté made in accordance with the recipe and observations for Velouté d'Eperlans.
Garnish: poach 40 oysters in their juices, discard the beards and add the oysters, together with the cooking liquid, to the soup.

764 Velouté Isoline
Cook 600 g (1 lb 5 oz) boneless chicken flesh in 1 litre (1¾ pt or 4½ U.S. cups) slightly thin Chicken Velouté. When cooked pound the flesh finely and replace it in the Velouté. Rub through a fine sieve and adjust the consistency with 2 dl (7 fl oz or ⅞ U.S. cup) White Bouillon.

Reheat without boiling, pass through a fine strainer and finish at the last moment with the liaison of 6 egg yolks and 2 dl (7 fl oz or ⅞ U.S. cup) cream and 200 g (7 oz) Crayfish Butter.
Garnish: 50 g (2 oz) Perles du Japon cooked in White Bouillon.
This soup can also be prepared as a Cream.

765 Velouté Jouvence
To 1¼ litres (2⅕ pt or 5½ U.S. cups) slightly thin Ordinary Velouté add 4 dl (14 fl oz or 1¾ U.S. cups) purée of frogs legs which have been cooked in chicken stock with some rice. Pass through a fine strainer, reheat without boiling and finish with the liaison of 6 egg yolks and 2 dl (7 fl oz or ⅞ U.S. cup) cream and 200 g (7 oz) Shrimp Butter added at the last moment.
Garnish: 4 tbs shrimps cut in half.

766 Velouté Marie-Louise
To 1 litre (1¾ pt or 4½ U.S. cups) boiling Chicken Bouillon, add and whisk in 100 g (3½ oz) barley

flour diluted in 2½ dl (9 fl oz or 1⅛ U.S. cups) milk; season with a little salt, bring to the boil and allow to simmer very gently on the side of the stove for 20–25 minutes.

Pass through a fine strainer, add 3 dl (½ pt or 1¼ U.S. cups) Chicken Bouillon and finish with the liaison of 6 egg yolks and 2½ dl (9 fl oz or 1⅛ U.S. cup) cream and 150 g (5 oz) butter.

Garnish: 100 g (3½ oz) cooked macaroni cut into small sections.

This soup can also be prepared as a Cream.

767 Velouté Nelusko

To 1 litre (1¾ pt or 4½ U.S. cups) Chicken Velouté add 5 dl (18 fl oz or 2¼ U.S. cups) cooked chicken purée and 2½ dl (9 fl oz or 1⅛ U.S. cups) Chicken Bouillon.

Pass through a fine strainer and reheat without boiling; finish at the last moment with a liaison of 6 egg yolks mixed with 1 dl (3½ fl oz or ½ U.S. cup) cream and 1 dl (3½ fl oz or ½ U.S. cup) Chicken Bouillon in which 50 g (2 oz) finely crushed roasted hazelnuts have been infused; and 150 g (5 oz) butter.

Garnish: 40 small Quenelles made from chicken forcemeat with the addition of 1 tbs finely ground hazelnuts per 100 g (3½ oz) forcemeat.

768 Velouté d'Orléans

Cook 600 g (1 lb 5 oz) chicken flesh in 1 litre (1¾ pt or 4½ U.S. cups) slightly thin Ordinary Velouté; when cooked, pound the flesh finely and replace it in the Velouté.

Rub through a very fine sieve, adjust the consistency with 2½ dl (9 fl oz or 1⅛ U.S. cups) Chicken Bouillon and pass through a fine strainer, reheat without boiling and finish at the last moment with the liaison of 6 egg yolks and 2 dl (7 fl oz or ⅞ U.S. cup) cream and 150 g (5 oz) butter. *Garnish:* small grooved Quenelles of chicken and cream forcemeat finished in 3 different colours, i.e. white using the forcemeat as it is; pink, made by adding Crayfish Butter to the forcemeat; and green, made by adding a fairly dry fine purée of green herbs to the forcemeat.

769 Velouté Rosemonde

To 1¼ litres (2¼ pt or 5½ U.S. cups) slightly thin Chicken Velouté add 5 dl (18 fl oz or 2¼ U.S. cups) purée of very fresh white mushrooms and cook together for a few minutes.

Pass through a fine strainer, reheat without boiling and finish at the last moment with the liaison of 6 egg yolks and 2 dl (7 fl oz or ⅞ U.S. cup) cream and 125 g (4½ oz) Crayfish Butter.

Garnish: 2 tbs fine julienne of fresh truffles cooked in Frontignan wine.

770 Velouté Thermidor

Prepare 1¾ litres (3 pt or 7½ U.S. cups) Velouté de Homard. Reheat and finish with the liaison of 6 egg yolks and 2 dl (7 fl oz or ⅞ U.S. cup) cream and 150 g (5 oz) butter.

Garnish: 40 small Quenelles made of pike forcemeat containing red pimento.

771 Velouté Yvonne

Mix together 1 litre (1¾ pt or 4½ U.S. cups) Chicken Velouté and 7½ dl (1⅓ pt or 3¼ U.S. cups) Velouté Choisy. Finish with the liaison of 6 egg yolks and 2 dl (7 fl oz or ⅞ U.S. cup) cream and 150 g (5 oz) butter.

Garnish: 50 g (2 oz) Perles du Japon cooked in White Bouillon.

SPECIAL SOUPS AND THICKENED BOUILLONS

(The following recipes are for 10 portions)

The following group of soups includes all those in which the formula is invariably the same, that is to say, they can be prepared only in the manner as given without any possibility of being transformed into a Cream or a Velouté.

In general these types of soups are prepared by mixing a thick soup, either a Purée, Cream or Velouté with other soups or preparations which are finished and ready for service, thus all that is necessary is to mix them together. These mixtures can be varied in many ways and without further work permit the extension of the range of soups which can figure on the day's menu.

For those soups which have a special composition it is indicated whether or not a liaison is necessary and the amount of butter required is given. A little Velouté is sometimes added to this type of soup particularly the Germiny and all similarly thickened Bouillons when they are produced for Table d'Hôte service. This addition of Velouté which should be as little as possible is to allow these delicate soups to be kept hot in the Bain-marie during the service period without the risk of separation.

772 Potage Ambassadeur

To 1¾ litres (3 pt or 7½ U.S. cups) finished Purée St Germain add 4 tbs Chiffonade of sorrel and lettuce stewed with butter.

Garnish: 8 tbs rice cooked in White Bouillon; Pluches of chervil.

773 Potage Américain

Prepare 1½ litres (2⅝ pt or 6½ U.S. cups) Bisque de Homard and add 2½ dl (9 fl oz or 1⅛ U.S. cups) fine

unconcentrated tomato purée and 2½ dl (9 fl oz or 1⅛ U.S. cups) Consommé au Tapioca.
Garnish: 60 g (2 oz) diced, cooked lobster.

774 Potage Bagration Gras

Cut 400 g (15 oz) leg of veal into large dice and cook quickly in butter to stiffen the meat without colouring. Add this together with 250 g (9 oz) raw chicken flesh, to 1¼ litres (2⅕ pt or 5½ U.S. cups) slightly thin Ordinary Velouté and allow to cook together very gently.

Finely pound the veal and chicken then replace it in the Velouté. Pass through a very fine sieve and then through a fine strainer. Reheat without boiling and finish at the last moment with a liaison of 4 egg yolks and 1½ dl (5 fl oz or ⅝ U.S. cup) cream and 100 g (3½ oz) butter.
Garnish: 3 tbs cooked thin macaroni cut into 2 cm (⅘ in) sections. Serve grated cheese separately.

Note: Originally this soup was made with veal only; in modern practice the total weight of meat used is comprised of two-thirds veal and one-third chicken.

775 Potage Bagration Maigre

Prepare 1½ litres (2⅝ pt or 6½ U.S. cups) slightly thin Fish Velouté, taking care that it has been quickly made. See the observations under Velouté d'Eperlans (751). Wash and peel 250 g (9 oz) very fresh mushrooms and pass through a sieve; add to the Velouté and cook together for 7–8 minutes.

Pass through a fine sieve then through a fine strainer and reheat without boiling. Finish at the last moment with a liaison of 6 egg yolks and 2 dl (7 fl oz or ⅞ U.S. cup) cream and 150 g (5 oz) butter.
Garnish: 2 small fillets of Dover sole cut into Julienne and poached with a little butter and lemon juice; 30 small Quenelles made from sole forcemeat containing Crayfish Butter; 6 cooked crayfish tails cut into slices.

776 Potage Balvet, or Potage Jubilée

Add 5 dl (18 fl oz or 2¼ U.S. cups) White Bouillon to 1¼ litres (2⅕ pt or 5½ U.S. cups) finished Purée Saint-Germain.
Garnish: 250 g (9 oz) vegetables prepared as for Consommé Croûte au Pot.

777 Potage Bohémienne

Mix together 1¼ litre (2⅕ pt or 5½ U.S. cups) Consommé Cendrillon and 7½ dl (1⅓ pt or 3¼ U.S. cups) Velouté de Volaille finished with the usual liaison and butter.

778 Potage Brunoise Lié

The various Consommés à la Brunoise indicated in the section on Consommés can furnish a series of excellent special soups by adding a liaison of 6 egg yolks and 1 dl (3½ fl oz or ½ U.S. cup) cream per 1 litre (1¾ pt or 4½ U.S. cups) of soup or by thickening with a little Velouté or light purée of potatoes.

779 Potage Chabrillan

To 1½ litres (2⅝ pt or 6½ U.S. cups) ungarnished Crème de Tomate add 5 dl (18 fl oz or 2¼ U.S. cups) well garnished Consommé au Vermicelle.

780 Potage à la Champenoise

Mix together 1½ litres (2⅝ pt or 6½ U.S. cups) Crème Parmentier and 2½ dl (9 fl oz or 1⅛ U.S. cups) Crème de Céleri-rave and finish with 2½ dl (9 fl oz or 1⅛ U.S. cups) Brunoise of carrot and white of celery cooked in White Bouillon.

781 Potage à la Chantilly

Prepare 1¾ litres (3 pt or 7½ U.S. cups) completely finished Purée Conti and add 2½ dl (9 fl oz or 1⅛ U.S. cups) cream just before serving.
Garnish: 40 small Quenelles made from chicken and cream forcemeat, cooked and added at the last moment.

782 Potage Derby

Prepare 2 litres (3½ pt or 9 U.S. cups) light Tomato Soup finished with 100 g (3½ oz) butter.
Garnish: the meat from a braised oxtail cut into fairly large dice allowing 5–6 pieces per person.

783 Potage Emilienne d'Alençon

Mix 7½ dl (1⅓ pt or 3¼ U.S. cups) garnished Consommé Edouard VII and the same amount of Velouté de Volaille. Finish with 4 dl (14 fl oz or 1¾ U.S. cups) fresh double cream.

784 Potage Fanchette

Mix 5 dl (18 fl oz or 2¼ U.S. cups) purée of white asparagus into 1½ litres (2⅝ pt or 6½ U.S. cups) Velouté de Volaille finished with the usual liaison and butter.
Garnish: lettuce leaves lightly blanched, dried, coated with chicken and Fines Herbes forcemeat, rolled up into a sausage shape, poached and cut into 1 cm (⅖ in) thick rounds; 4 tbs small peas.

785 Potage Faubonne

Mix together 1 litre (1¾ pt or 4½ U.S. cups) Purée Soissonaise and 500 g (1 lb 2 oz) Julienne of

vegetables cooked in $7\frac{1}{2}$ dl ($1\frac{1}{3}$ pt or $3\frac{1}{4}$ U.S. cups) White Bouillon.
Garnish: Pluches of chervil.

786 Potage Femina
To $1\frac{3}{4}$ litres (3 pt or $7\frac{1}{2}$ U.S. cups) Consommé Printanier, add a liaison of 8 egg yolks and 2 dl (7 fl oz or $\frac{7}{8}$ U.S. cup) cream. Finish with 2 tbs grated fresh truffles.

787 Potage Fontanges
Mix together $1\frac{1}{2}$ litres ($2\frac{5}{8}$ pt or $6\frac{1}{2}$ U.S. cups) Purée de Pois frais and 5 dl (18 fl oz or $2\frac{1}{4}$ U.S. cups) White Bouillon.
Garnish: 2 tbs Chiffonade of sorrel; Pluches of chervil.

788 Potage Gentilhomme
Prepare $1\frac{1}{2}$ litres ($2\frac{5}{8}$ pt or $6\frac{1}{2}$ U.S. cups) Purée de Perdreau aux Lentilles in accordance with the recipe for Purée de Gibier (690) and finish it with 2 tbs flamed brandy, 4 dl (14 fl oz or $1\frac{3}{4}$ U.S. cups) good quality partridge stock and a squeeze of lemon juice.
Garnish: 4 tbs small ball-shape Quenelles made from partridge forcemeat; 2 tbs small balls of truffle.

789 Potage Germiny
Stew 250 g (9 oz) shredded sorrel with 90 g (3 oz) butter, pass it through a fine sieve then add to $1\frac{1}{2}$ litres ($2\frac{5}{8}$ pt or $6\frac{1}{2}$ U.S. cups) White Bouillon. Just before serving add a liaison of 10 egg yolks and $2\frac{1}{2}$ dl (9 fl oz or $1\frac{1}{8}$ U.S. cups) cream, cook gently as for Crème Anglaise and when the soup is correctly thickened without boiling, finish away from the heat with 150 g (5 oz) butter and Pluches of chervil.

790 Potage Girondins
Prepare $1\frac{3}{4}$ litres (3 pt or $7\frac{1}{2}$ U.S. cups) Purée Condé and finish at the last moment with $2\frac{1}{2}$ dl (9 fl oz or $1\frac{1}{8}$ U.S. cups) fresh cream.
Garnish: 250 g (9 oz) Macédoine of vegetables cooked with a little White Bouillon and butter.

791 Invalid Soup
Finely pound 250 g (9 oz) white of chicken which has been cooked in Bouillon; add $2\frac{1}{2}$ dl (9 fl oz or $1\frac{1}{8}$ U.S. cups) boiling milk and pass through a fine sieve. Add a further 4 dl (14 fl oz or $1\frac{3}{4}$ U.S. cups) boiling milk then pass through a fine strainer. Reheat without boiling and finish at the last moment with a liaison of 5 egg yolks and 1 dl ($3\frac{1}{2}$ fl oz or $\frac{1}{2}$ U.S. cup) old Marsala.

792 Potage Jack
To $1\frac{3}{4}$ litres (3 pt or $7\frac{1}{2}$ U.S. cups) Consommé Julienne add at the last moment, a liaison of 8 egg yolks and 2 dl (7 fl oz or $\frac{7}{8}$ U.S. cup) cream.

793 Potage Josselin
To $1\frac{3}{4}$ litres (3 pt or $7\frac{1}{2}$ U.S. cups) Fish Bouillon add $2\frac{1}{2}$ dl (9 fl oz or $1\frac{1}{8}$ U.S. cups) well flavoured and decanted mussel cooking liquid. Pass through a clean cloth, bring to the boil and add 100 g ($3\frac{1}{2}$ oz) butter and 125 g ($4\frac{1}{2}$ oz) fine vermicelli. Finish at the last minute with a liaison of 8 egg yolks and 2 dl (7 fl oz or $\frac{7}{8}$ U.S. cup) cream.

794 Potage Jubilée
This is another name, used mainly in England, for Potage Balvet.

795 Potage Julienne Darblay
Prepare $1\frac{3}{4}$ litres (3 pt or $7\frac{1}{2}$ U.S. cups) fairly thin Potage Parmentier. Add 4 tbs Julienne of vegetables stewed in a little butter and Bouillon and finish at the last moment with a liaison of 6 egg yolks and 2 dl (7 fl oz or $\frac{7}{8}$ U.S. cup) cream and 120 g (4 oz) butter.

Note: This soup is the classical *Potage Julienne* of the Flemish cuisine and is also known as Julienne Champenoise. In most northern countries these peasant-style soups have as a base, a fairly thin Parmentier instead of Bouillon.

796 Potage Lamballe
To 1 litre ($1\frac{3}{4}$ pt or $4\frac{1}{2}$ U.S. cups) finished Purée de Pois frais add 1 litre ($1\frac{3}{4}$ pt or $4\frac{1}{2}$ U.S. cups) well garnished Consommé au Tapioca.

797 Potage Longchamps
To $1\frac{1}{2}$ litres ($2\frac{5}{8}$ pt or $6\frac{1}{2}$ U.S. cups) finished Purée de Pois frais add 5 dl (18 fl oz or $2\frac{1}{4}$ U.S. cups) Consommé au Vermicelle, 3 tbs Chiffonade of sorrel and Pluches of chervil.

Note: This soup is also known as Potage Sport.

798 Potage Madelon
To $1\frac{1}{2}$ litres ($2\frac{5}{8}$ pt or $6\frac{1}{2}$ U.S. cups) finished Purée Saint-Germain add 5 dl (18 fl oz or $2\frac{1}{4}$ U.S. cups) Tomato Soup.
Garnish: 6 tbs freshly cooked peas.

799 Potage Marigny
This is Potage Fontanges with an additional garnish of 3 tbs freshly cooked peas and 3 tbs freshly cooked small French beans cut diamond-shape.

800 Potage Marcilly
Mix $7\frac{1}{2}$ dl ($1\frac{1}{3}$ pt or $3\frac{1}{4}$ U.S. cups) Crème de Pois frais with the same amount of Crème de Volaille. Cook 30 g (1 oz) Perles du Japon in 5 dl (18 fl oz or $2\frac{1}{4}$ U.S. cups) White Bouillon and add the whole to the soup.
Garnish: 40 chicken and cream forcemeat Quenelles moulded in the shape of small balls.

801 Potage Narbonnais
To $1\frac{1}{4}$ litres ($2\frac{1}{5}$ pt or $5\frac{1}{2}$ U.S. cups) Purée Soissonaise add $7\frac{1}{2}$ dl ($1\frac{1}{3}$ pt or $3\frac{1}{4}$ U.S. cups) Consommé au Riz and 100 g ($3\frac{1}{2}$ oz) finely shredded sorrel, stewed in a little butter.

802 Potage Nicolini
Prepare $1\frac{1}{2}$ litres ($2\frac{5}{8}$ pt or $6\frac{1}{2}$ U.S. cups) Potage Garbure à l'Oignon and pass through a fine strainer. Add 5 dl (18 fl oz or $2\frac{1}{4}$ U.S. cups) fine purée of fresh tomatoes, reheat and add 120 g (4 oz) butter. Place toasted rounds of bread in the soup tureen overlapping and with thin slices of Gruyère cheese and grated Parmesan in between. Pour the soup over this garnish just before serving.

803 Potage Polignac
To $1\frac{1}{4}$ litres ($2\frac{1}{5}$ pt or $5\frac{1}{2}$ U.S. cups) Crème Crécy add 5 dl (18 fl oz or $2\frac{1}{4}$ U.S. cups) Consommé au Tapioca. Reheat without boiling and finish at the last moment with a liaison of 8 egg yolks and 2 dl (7 fl oz or $\frac{7}{8}$ U.S. cup) cream.

804 Potage Purée d'Oseille et de Vermicelle à la Crème
Stew 250 g (9 oz) shredded sorrel with 60 g (2 oz) butter and moisten with 1 litre ($1\frac{3}{4}$ pt or $4\frac{1}{2}$ U.S. cups) milk or White Bouillon according to whether the soup is to be Lenten or not. Add 300 g (11 oz) vermicelli and cook gently together. Pass through a fine sieve, adjust the consistency with 2 dl (7 fl oz or $\frac{7}{8}$ U.S. cup) milk or Bouillon and pass through a fine strainer. Reheat without boiling and finish at the last moment with a liaison of 4 egg yolks and 2 dl (7 fl oz or $\frac{7}{8}$ U.S. cup) cream.

805 Potage Purée d'Oseille et de Tapioca à la Crème
This is prepared in the same way as the preceding recipe replacing the vermicelli with 200 g (7 oz) tapioca.

Note: Soups of this type can be prepared with sago, salep or semolina as well as buckwheat flour, oatmeal and barley flour etc. They take on the special and very agreeable flavour of the particular thickening agent; it is essential, however, that the proportions of the cereal used should be calculated so as to give the soup the consistency of cream. If too thick these soups become pasty and if too thin they lack their particular flavour.

806 Potage Queue de Boeuf à la Napolitaine
Braise 1 oxtail cut into sections with white wine and Bouillon: when cooked, remove the bones and cut the flesh in large cubes. Strain the cooking liquid through a fine strainer, add the diced meat and keep hot.

Prepare $1\frac{1}{2}$ litres ($2\frac{5}{8}$ pt or $6\frac{1}{2}$ U.S. cups) Consommé à la Semoule with the addition of 5 dl (18 fl oz or $2\frac{1}{4}$ U.S. cups) fresh tomato purée and just before serving add the cooked oxtail and its cooking liquid.

807 Potage Rabagas
Mix together 1 litre ($1\frac{3}{4}$ pt or $4\frac{1}{2}$ U.S. cups) Potage Réjane and 1 litre ($1\frac{3}{4}$ pt or $4\frac{1}{2}$ U.S. cups) of Purée Saint-Germain.

808 Potage Réjane
To 1 litre ($1\frac{3}{4}$ pt or $4\frac{1}{2}$ U.S. cups) boiling White Bouillon add 150 g (5 oz) Julienne of cooked white of chicken and 100 g ($3\frac{1}{2}$ oz) Julienne of white of leek stewed in a little butter; simmer gently for 10 minutes taking care not to cloud the soup then add 100 g ($3\frac{1}{2}$ oz) large Julienne of potatoes. Simmer gently until the potatoes are cooked and serve immediately.

809 Potage Saint-Julien
Mix together 1 litre ($1\frac{3}{4}$ pt or $4\frac{1}{2}$ U.S. cups) Crème de Potiron and 1 litre ($1\frac{3}{4}$ pt or $4\frac{1}{2}$ U.S. cups) Potage Parmentier. Serve separately lightly toasted rounds of French bread and grated cheese.

810 Potage Saint-Marceaux
Stew 300 g (11 oz) fine Julienne of white of leek with 60 g (2 oz) butter; add 4 dl (14 fl oz or $1\frac{3}{4}$ U.S. cups) White Bouillon and $1\frac{3}{4}$ litres (3 pt or $7\frac{1}{2}$ U.S. cups) finished Purée de Pois frais; finish with Pluches of chervil.

811 Potage de Santé
To $1\frac{3}{4}$ litres (3 pt or $7\frac{1}{2}$ U.S. cups) fairly thin Potage Parmentier add 80 g (3 oz) shredded sorrel stewed with 60 g (2 oz) butter. Reheat without boiling and finish at the last moment with a liaison of 6 egg yolks and 2 dl (7 fl oz or $\frac{7}{8}$ U.S. cup) cream; 150 g (5 oz) butter and Pluches of chervil. Serve dry slices of French bread separately.

812 Potage Simone
To 1 litre ($1\frac{3}{4}$ pt or $4\frac{1}{2}$ U.S. cups) Consommé Solange add 5 dl (18 fl oz or $2\frac{1}{4}$ U.S. cups)

Crème Crécy and 5 dl (18 fl oz or 2¼ U.S. cups) Potage Parmentier.

813 Potage Ursuline
Blanch 200 g (7 oz) rice, refresh under cold water, drain and replace in the pan with 2 litres (3½ pt or 9 U.S. cups) boiling milk; add 40 g (2 oz) sugar and 8 g (⅓ oz) salt. Cook gently for 25–30 minutes, and finish with a little almond milk made from 12 sweet and 2 bitter almonds and 1½ dl (5 fl oz or ⅝ U.S. cup) cream.

814 Potage Valaisan
Mix together 7½ dl (1⅓ pt or 3¼ U.S. cups) each of Potage Parmentier and Purée of root vegetable soup. Finish with 2½ dl (9 fl oz or 1⅛ U.S. cups) fresh cream. Serve separately slices of French bread sprinkled with grated Gruyère and lightly browned in the oven.

815 Potage Sport
See Potage Longchamps.

816 Potage Velours
Mix 1¾ litre (3 pt or 7½ U.S. cups) Potage Crécy with 7½ dl (1⅓ pt or 3¼ U.S. cups) Consommé au Tapioca.

817 Potage Verneuil
Mix 1 litre (1¾ pt or 4½ U.S. cups) finished Crème de Pois frais with 1 litre (1¾ pt or 4½ U.S. cups) finished Crème d'Orge.
Garnish: 1 dariole mould of Ordinary Royale made with whole eggs, cut into small oval-shaped pieces; 4 tbs red of carrot cut in ovals and cooked in Bouillon; 4 tbs cooked oval-shaped pieces cut from slices of cooked very white mushrooms.

818 Potage Waldèze
To 1¾ litres (3 pt or 7½ U.S. cups) Consommé au Tapioca add either 500 g (1 lb 2 oz) very small dice of very red tomato flesh lightly poached in a little white Bouillon; or 1½ dl (5 fl oz or ⅝ U.S. cup) very red tomato purée mixed with 1 dl (3½ fl oz or ½ U.S. cup) boiling White Bouillon. Serve separately 100 g (3½ oz) grated Gruyère cheese mixed with 25 g (1 oz) grated Parmesan cheese.

819 Potage Windsor
Blanch two small boned calves' feet, refresh them and place on a Mirepoix prepared with 2½ dl (9 fl oz or 1⅛ U.S. cups) white wine; cook together gently.

At the same time make 1½ litres (2⅝ pt or 6½ U.S. cups) Crème de Riz (see the beginning of Crème Lison), add the cooking liquor from the calf's feet passed through a strainer and ¾ dl (3 fl oz or ⅜ U.S. cup) infusion of turtle herbs. Reheat without boiling, lightly season with Cayenne and finish at the last moment with a liaison of 6 egg yolks and 2 dl (7 fl oz or ⅞ U.S. cup) cream; and 150 g (5 oz) butter.
Garnish: 3 tbs cooked calf's feet cut in Julienne; 40 small grooved Quenelles prepared from a mixture of two-thirds purée of hard-boiled egg yolks and one-third chicken forcemeat.

SPECIAL VEGETABLE SOUPS

(The following recipes are for 10 persons)

The vegetables for most of the soups under this heading of which the Paysanne soup is the basic type, should first of all be stewed gently in butter. This is for two reasons: 1) to assist the release of the vegetable juices, and 2) to saturate the butter with the maximum amount of flavour from the vegetables. On the other hand some vegetables should be moistened with the required liquid without first being stewed in butter, so as to preserve their original qualities.

Except for a few of these soups the rigid proportions of the ingredients is not absolutely necessary and it is sufficient to say that the total weight of raw vegetables which are the base of the soup should be approximately 600 g (1 lb 5 oz) per 1½ litres (2⅝ pt or 6½ U.S. cups) of liquid. The weight of vegetables can be cut by 100 g (3½ oz) for those soups which have an additional garnish such as Italian pasta, vermicelli or rice etc.

820 Soupe à l'Albigeoise
Prepare a marmite with 500 g (1 lb 2 oz) silverside of beef, 500 g (1 lb 2 oz) knuckle of veal, 1 raw knuckle of ham, 300 g (11 oz) piece of raw ham, 250 (9 oz) dried pork sausage, 300 g (11 oz) Confit d'Oie and cover well with cold water. Season with salt, taking into account that the ham is salty, bring to the boil and skim.

Add 500 g (1 lb 2 oz) mixed carrots, turnips, leek and cabbage cut into Paysanne, a few shredded lettuce leaves and 600 g (1 lb 5 oz) small broad beans which should be the dominant garnish. Allow to cook very gently in the normal manner of a marmite soup.

Serve the soup accompanied with slices of Confit d'Oie and slices of French bread.

821 Soupe au Cresson Alénois
Boil rapidly in salt water, 500 g (1 lb 2 oz) potatoes cut into quarters. When cooked, drain off the water and simply crush the potatoes with a whisk. Add 1½ litres (2⅝ pt or 6½ U.S. cups) boiling milk to the potatoes with 15 g (½ oz) salt and 100

g (3½ oz) leaves of garden cress. Allow to cook for 5–6 minutes and finish away from the heat with 100 g (3½ oz) butter and Pluches of chervil.

822 Soupe à la Choucroute à l'Alsacienne
Blanch 500 g (1 lb 2 oz) fresh sauerkraut which has been well washed and the excess moisture squeezed out. Refresh, drain, squeeze to remove the excess water and roughly chop.

Stew this with 75 g (2½ oz) butter and 120 g (4 oz) chopped onion. Sprinkle with 15 g (½ oz) flour, mix in and moisten with 1½ litres (2⅝ pt or 6½ U.S. cups) White Bouillon; simmer gently for 40 minutes.

Garnish: 60 small potato Quenelles (4231).

823 Soupe à l'Ardennaise
Melt 100 g (3½ oz) butter in a pan, add 500 g (1 lb 2 oz) shredded Belgian endives, 100 g (3½ oz) shredded white of leek and 125 g (4½ oz) sliced potatoes. Moisten with 1¾ litres (3 pt or 7½ U.S. cups) boiling milk, season with 15 g (½ oz) salt and cook gently together. Finish at the last moment with 100 g (3½ oz) butter and serve thin slices of French bread separately.

824 Soupe à l'Auvergnate
Prepare a marmite with 1 boned salted pig's head covered with cold water. Bring to the boil, skim and add a garnish of 500 g (1 lb 2 oz) mixed sliced carrots, turnips and leek; 200 g (7 oz) sliced potatoes; and 300 g (11 oz) shredded cabbage hearts. Add 100 g (3½ oz) lentils and cook gently together. Serve with very thin slices of brown bread and a little of the pig's head cut into large dice.

825 Soupe à la Beaucaire
Cut in Julienne 300 g (11 oz) heart of cabbage and 150 g (5 oz) each of white of leek and white of celery and stew together with 75 g (2½ oz) butter. Moisten with 1¾ litres (3 pt or 7½ U.S. cups) White Bouillon, add a pinch of crushed basil and marjoram and 100 g (3½ oz) flesh of chickens' gizzards blanched and cut into coarse Julienne. Cook gently together.

Garnish: 100 g (3½ oz) well cooked pearl barley or rice cooked in salted water and 3 chickens' livers cut into very thin slices and sautéed in butter at the last moment. Serve grated cheese separately.

826 Soupe à la Bonne Femme
Shred 250 g (9 oz) white of leek and stew gently with 75 g (2½ oz) butter. Moisten with 1¾ litres (3 pt or 7½ U.S. cups) water or White Bouillon. Add 500 g (1 lb 2 oz) potatoes cut into thin slices from potatoes trimmed to the shape of corks and season with 15 g (½ oz) salt if using water. Cook together gently.

Finish at the last moment with 75 g (2½ oz) butter and add dried slices of French bread to the soup when serving.

Note: Milk may also be used in the preparation of this soup.

827 Soupe à la Brabançonne
Stew together 300 g (11 oz) mixed carrot, turnip, leek and onion cut in Paysanne with 75 g (2½ oz) butter in the same way as for Soupe à la Fermière. Moisten with 1½ litres (2⅝ pt or 6½ U.S. cups) boiling water and add 300 g (11 oz) Belgian endives which have been blanched, shredded and stewed in butter. Season with 15 g (½ oz) salt and cook together gently. Add a few pieces of rusk to the soup when serving.

828 Soupe à la Bûcheronne
Cut 150 g (5 oz) each of Kohlrabi, turnip and potatoes in thin Paysanne and stew together with 100 g (3½ oz) chopped fresh pork fat. Moisten with 1½ litres (2⅝ pt or 6½ U.S. cups) water, add 200 g (7 oz) very small fresh haricot beans and 15 g (½ oz) salt and cook gently together. If fresh beans are unobtainable use cooked rice placed in the soup a few moments before serving. Add small thin slices of brown bread to the soup when serving.

829 Soupe Cultivateur
Cut 400 g (15 oz) of mixed carrot, turnip, white of leek and onion into fairly large rough Brunoise and stew together gently for a fair amount of time with 75 g (2½ oz) butter but without colour. Moisten with 1½ litres (2⅝ pt or 6½ U.S. cups) White Bouillon and simmer gently. When the vegetables are half cooked, add 200 g (7 oz) sliced potatoes and 125 g (4½ oz) lean salt belly of pork free from rind, cut into dice or small batons and well blanched; the pork represents the garnish. Finish cooking together gently.

830 Soupe à la Dauphinoise
Cut into Paysanne 175 g (6 oz) each of turnip, vegetable marrow and potatoes and stew together with 60 g (2 oz) butter; moisten with 7½ dl (1⅓ pt or 3¼ U.S. cups) each of water and milk and season with 15 g (½ oz) salt. When the vegetables are half cooked, add 5–6 shredded leaves of chard or white beet and 15 minutes before the soup is completed sprinkle in 40 g (1½ oz) vermicelli. Add a few Pluches of chervil just before serving.

831 Soupe de l'Estérel, or Soupe des Maures
Stew 60 g (2 oz) shredded onion with 30 g (1 oz) butter without colouring; moisten with 5 dl (18 fl

oz or 2¼ U.S. cups) White Bouillon or cooking liquid from haricot beans; add 150 g (5 oz) pumpkin cut in dice and 225 g (8 oz) fresh undried haricot beans or 200 g (7 oz) of cooked ones. Allow to cook gently, pass through a fine sieve then add 1 litre (1¾ pt or 4½ U.S. cups) White Bouillon to this purée. Bring the soup to the boil, sprinkle in 75 g (2½ oz) vermicelli and continue cooking until ready.

832 Soupe à la Fermière
Cut into Paysanne, 125 g (4½ oz) each of carrot, turnip and white of leek; and 100 g (3½ oz) onion. Stew together with 60 g (2 oz) butter and moisten with 1½ litres (2⅝ pt or 6½ U.S. cups) White Bouillon; bring to the boil then add 125 g (4½ oz) shredded white heart of cabbage. Allow to cook gently until tender and serve with thin slices of French bread in the soup.

833 Soupe à la Franc-Comtoise
Cut 350 g (13 oz) potato and 150 g (5 oz) turnip into Paysanne and stew together with 75 g (2½ oz) butter; add 100 g (3½ oz) shredded sorrel and lettuce leaves and cook together for 5–6 minutes. Add 1¾ litres (3 pt or 7½ U.S. cups) milk and season with 15 g (½ oz) salt. Allow to cook gently and 15 minutes before service sprinkle in 60 g (2 oz) vermicelli. Add a few Pluches of chervil when serving.

834 Potage Garbure à la Béarnaise
Prepare a marmite with 500 g (1 lb 2 oz) each of salt belly of pork and Confit d'Oie; 150 g (5 oz) each of whole turnip, potato and heart of cabbage; 125 g (4½ oz) fresh new season's haricot beans or 100 g (3½ oz) dried if out of season and 125 g (4½ oz) fresh French beans when available. Cover with water, lightly season with salt and allow to simmer very gently for 3 hours.

When cooked, arrange the vegetables in a deep earthenware dish with alternate slices of the pork and Confit d'Oie, cover with slices of French bread which have been sprinkled with grated cheese and gratinated. Sprinkle with a few tablespoons of the fatty Bouillon from the cooking, cover with the lid, place in the oven and allow to heat gently for 15 minutes. Pour the remaining Bouillon into a tureen and send it together with the dish of meat and vegetables.

835 Potage Garbure-Cooper
Slice 600 g (1 lb 5 oz) onion very finely and cook with 75 g (2½ oz) butter to a light golden colour. Moisten with 1¾ litres (3 pt or 7½ U.S. cups) White Bouillon and allow to cook gently for 10 minutes.

Rub through a fine sieve and pour the whole into a shallow tureen; cover the surface with thin slices of French bread, sprinkle well with grated cheese and melted butter then gratinate quickly in a very hot oven. Serve immediately.

836 Potage Garbure Crécy
Slice 250 g (9 oz) red of carrot and stew together with 60 g (2 oz) butter, a little White Bouillon and a pinch of sugar and salt until completely cooked and reduced to a stiff consistency. Spread this on round Croûtons of bread fried in butter.

Sprinkle the surface of these Croûtons with grated cheese, gratinate and arrange them in a deep earthenware dish. Sprinkle with a few tablespoons of fatty Bouillon, cover with the lid and allow to heat in a slow oven for 15 minutes.

Serve this dish of Croûtons with the required quantity of good Bouillon.

837 Potage Garbure Dauphinoise
Cut into slices 60 g (2 oz) onion and 150 g (5 oz) each of potato and pumpkin and stew together with 75 g (2½ oz) butter. Moisten with 1 litre (1¾ pt or 4½ U.S. cups) water, add 6–8 shredded leaves of chard, 8 g (⅓ oz) salt and cook gently together.

When cooked, drain the vegetables and pound them; reduce to a thick purée then spread this thickly on dry slices of French bread. Sprinkle with grated cheese, gratinate and place in a deep earthenware dish. Sprinkle with a few tablespoons of fatty Bouillon, cover with the lid and place in a slow oven to heat for 15 minutes. To the remaining vegetable liquid add sufficient boiling milk to make the required quantity of soup; reheat it and finish at the last moment with 60 g (2 oz) butter. Serve accompanied with the dish of Croûtons.

838 Potage Garbure à la Freneuse
Slice 150 g (5 oz) each of turnip and potato and stew together with 60 g (2 oz) butter; add a little White Bouillon and allow to cook.

When tender, pound the vegetables and reduce to a thick purée. Spread this thickly on slices of French break sprinkle with grated cheese, gratinate and arrange overlapping in an earthenware dish. Sprinkle with a few tablespoons of fatty Bouillon, cover with the lid and place in a slow oven to heat for 15 minutes. Serve this dish of Croûtons with the required quantity of Bouillon.

839 Potage Garbure à l'Oignon
Finely slice 250 g (9 oz) onion and cook gently in 60 g (2 oz) butter until golden brown. Sprinkle with 25 g (1 oz) flour and complete the colouring of the onions by cooking to the stage of a blond Roux. Moisten with 2 litres (3½ pt or 9 U.S.

cups) White Bouillon and allow to simmer for 10 minutes.

For the preparation of the gratinated Croûtons either of the following methods are suitable: 1) Drain the onions and mix them together with a little very thick sauce Béchamel; spread the mixture on dry round slices of long thin French bread. 2) Drain the onions and rub them through a fine sieve; reduce to a thick purée and spread thickly on the round Croûtons of dry bread as before.

In both these cases, sprinkle with grated cheese, gratinate and finish in a deep earthenware dish as in the previous recipes. Serve the dish of Croûtons with the reserved liquid from the soup. The gratinated Croûtons may be served separately just as they are.

This soup may be made by adding milk in the proportions of 1 dl (3½ fl oz or ½ U.S. cup) per 1 litre (1¾ pt or 4½ U.S. cups) of soup and reducing the amount of Bouillon accordingly.

Note: For restaurant service this soup can be gratinated in a soup tureen in the same way as for Garbure-Cooper. In this case the Croûtons which have been covered with the onions either as a purée or not and according to the customer's wishes, are arranged on the surface of the soup, sprinkled with grated cheese and quickly gratinated.

840 Potage Garbure à la Paysanne

Cut 250 g (9 oz) mixed vegetables into Paysanne, stew together with 60 g (2 oz) butter and finish cooking with a little White Bouillon. Break up the vegetables with a whisk and reduce to a thick purée. Spread this purée thickly on rectangles of bread fried in butter, sprinkle with grated cheese, gratinate and place in a deep earthenware dish. Sprinkle with a few tablespoons of fatty Bouillon, cover with the lid and place to heat in a slow oven for 15 minutes. Serve this dish of Croûtons with the required amount of Bouillon.

841 Potage Garbure à la Savoyarde

Slice 125 g (4½ oz) celeriac and an equal amount of mixed potato, onion and leek and stew together with 60 g (2 oz) butter; finish cooking with a little White Bouillon.

Break up the vegetables with a whisk and reduce to a purée. Spread this thickly on small slices of dry rye bread, sprinkle with grated cheese and gratinate well. Place these Croûtons on the required quantity of Bouillon just before serving.

Note: By using the method stated in the preceding recipes all purées of vegetables may be used to fulfil the principle of Garbure soups either in the form of a single purée or as a purée composed of various kinds of vegetables. The Garbure soup always takes the name from the main ingredient from which the purée is made.

842 Soupe à la Grand'mère

Roughly chop 90 g (3 oz) each of white of leek, onion, celery, cabbage, potato and turnip; place in a pan with 1 litre (1¾ pt or 4½ U.S. cups) water, 10 g (⅓ oz) salt, 75 g (2½ oz) butter and cook gently together.

When half cooked add a Chiffonade of 75 g (2½ oz) mixed leaves of lettuce, sorrel and spinach allowing a greater amount of the sorrel and lettuce. About 15 minutes before service finish the soup with 5 dl (18 fl oz or 2¼ U.S. cups) boiling milk and sprinkle in 2 tbs Pâtes d'Italie, allow to cook and finish with 50 g (2 oz) butter and a few Pluches of chervil just before serving.

843 Potage Hochepot à l'Ancienne

This is another name for Consommé Queue de Boeuf à la Française (606).

844 Soupe Jeannette

Cut 150 g (5 oz) each of turnip, leek and potatoes into Paysanne, and stew together with 75 g (2½ oz) butter. Moisten with 1 litre (1¾ pt or 4½ U.S. cups) Bouillon and add during the course of the cooking, 50 g (2 oz) large fresh peas and 50 g (2 oz) French beans cut into small pieces—when they are out of season use tinned peas and beans, adding them just before serving. Add also 25 g (1 oz) finely shredded sorrel and 25 g (1 oz) very fresh picked leaves of watercress.

Finish at the last moment with 5 dl (18 fl oz or 2¾ U.S. cups) boiling milk; 50 g (2 oz) butter and Pluches of chervil. Serve slices of French bread separately.

845 Soupe Julienne à la Russe

Prepare 500 g (1 lb 2 oz) Julienne of mixed vegetables with the addition of 2 parsley roots and 60 g (2 oz) Gribouis soaked in cold water, both also cut in Julienne. Stew these ingredients together with 75 g (2½ oz) butter and finish cooking with 1 litre (1¾ pt or 4½ U.S. cups) Bouillon.

When the vegetables are cooked finish the soup with 5 dl (18 fl oz or 2¼ U.S. cups) Bouillon and finally add 2 dl (7 fl oz or ⅞ U.S. cup) sour cream and a pinch of chopped fennel.

Special garnish served separately: Small soufflé fritters containing diced ham; small Rissoles made from any ingredients to choice, the size of a walnut; very small puff pastry meat patties.

Note: The items of garnish which require cooking by deep frying should be done at the last moment. The garnish can be comprised of either a single one of the items indicated or a mixture as necessary. In all cases, whether single or mixed, they should be served on a serviette; if mixed they should be arranged in separate bouquets and not mixed together.

846 Soupe du Laboureur

Prepare a marmite with 300 g (11 oz) soaked knuckle of salt pork; 300 g (11 oz) blanched, pickled belly of pork; 150 g (5 oz) each of roughly sliced carrot, turnip and white of leek, and 60 g (2 oz) roughly chopped onion. Moisten with 2½ litres (4¼ pt or 5⅝ U.S. pt) water, bring to the boil, skim and add 100 g (3½ oz) green split peas. Allow to cook gently for 3 hours. Serve the soup with small pieces of the boned knuckle and belly of pork.

847 Soupe à la Nevers

Blanch 300 g (11 oz) very small Brussels sprouts and stew them together with 75 g (2½ oz) butter until almost cooked.

Meanwhile, slice 250 g (9 oz) red of carrot, and stew with 60 g (2 oz) butter; add a little White Bouillon and finish cooking.

About 20 minutes before service add the sprouts to the carrots along with 1½ litres (2⅝ pt or 6½ U.S. cups) boiling White Bouillon; sprinkle in 40 g (1½ oz) vermicelli and finish cooking together. Finish with Pluches of chervil just before serving.

848 Soupe à la Normande

Cut into Paysanne 200 g (7 oz) each of carrot, potatoes and white of leek; stew together with 75 g (2½ oz) butter, moisten with 1 litre (1¾ pt or 4½ U.S. cups) White Bouillon and cook gently.

During the course of cooking add 100 g (3½ oz) small fresh haricot beans or fresh flageolets (if out of season replace by very small cooked haricot beans). Finish the soup at the last moment with 5 dl (18 fl oz or 2¼ U.S. cups) boiling milk and add away from the heat, 60 g (2 oz) butter and ½ dl (2 fl oz or ¼ U.S. cup) cream.

849 Soupe à l'Oignon

See Potage Garbure à l'Oignon (839).

850 Soupe à la Paysanne

Cut into Paysanne, 200 g (7 oz) each of carrot and turnip, 100 g (3½ oz) white of leek and 50 g (2 oz) each of celery and onion; stew together slowly and gently with 75 g (2½ oz) butter. Add 1 litre (1¾ pt or 4½ U.S. cups) White Bouillon and 150 g (5 oz) potato cut into Paysanne; finish cooking together then add an additional 5 dl (18 fl oz or 2¼ U.S. cups) Bouillon.

Note: Strictly speaking, this soup can be prepared using all kinds of vegetables in season except that Chiffonade of sorrel and lettuce should not be used; this establishes the difference between this and other similar preparations.

851 Soupe Poireaux et Pommes de Terre à la Maraîchère

Prepare a Soupe à la Bonne Femme reducing the proportion of vegetables by 100 g (3½ oz) and using White Bouillon. Fifteen minutes before service add 60 g (2 oz) vermicelli; when the soup is ready add a Chiffonade of 50 g (2 oz) lettuce leaves, sorrel, spinach and, when available a few leaves of purslane. Add a few Pluches of chervil just before serving.

852 Potée Bourguignonne

Prepare a Petite Marmite with 750 g (1 lb 10 oz) salt pork, 300 g (11 oz) fresh knuckle of pork, 2¼ litres (4 pt or 5 U.S. pt) water, 1 carrot and 1 turnip cut in four lengthways, 200 g (7 oz) shredded leek and 300 g (11 oz) cabbage, bring to the boil, skim and allow to cook very gently for approximately 3 hours. Half-way through add 250 g (9 oz) potatoes cut into small quarters.

When ready, pour the soup with some of its vegetables over fairly thin slices of brown bread.

Note: In the Basse-Bourgogne the Potée always includes a few garlic Cervelas which should be added to the soup in sufficient time to be cooked for service.

853 Soupe à la Savoyarde

Slice 300 g (11 oz) celeriac and 100 g (3½ oz) each of potatoes, leeks and onions. Stew together with 120 g (4 oz) finely chopped salt pork fat; moisten with 1 litre (1¾ pt or 4½ U.S. cups) water, season with 15 g (½ oz) salt and finish cooking together.

Finish the soup with 5 dl (18 fl oz or 2¼ U.S. cups) boiling milk and finally add 50 g (2 oz) butter.

Have prepared some thin slices of rye bread sprinkled with grated chesse and gratinated and add these to the soup when serving.

854 Potage Thourins

Prepare a Potage Garbure à l'Oignon using milk instead of Bouillon and season with 25 g (1 oz) salt.

A few minutes before serving add a liaison of 4 egg yolks and 3 dl (½ pt or 1¼ U.S. cups) very fresh cream and finish at the last moment with 50 g (2 oz) butter.

Serve slices of French bread separately.

855 Potage Thourins Roumanille

Prepare this soup as in the preceding recipe; 15 minutes before service add 70 g (2½ oz) vermicelli and allow it to cook in the soup. Finish with the liaison of egg yolks, cream and butter and serve grated cheese separately.

856 Potage Villageoise
Finely shred 300 g (11 oz) white of leek and cook fairly quickly to a light golden colour with 75 g (2½ oz) butter. Moisten with 1½ litres (2⅝ pt or 6½ U.S. cups) Bouillon and add 300 g (11 oz) heart of cabbage cut in fine Julienne and well blanched in advance; allow to cook gently together. Twenty minutes before service, add 75 g (2½ oz) vermicelli and allow it to cook in the soup.

Finish with Pluches of chervil just before serving.

CLASSICAL PROVENCALE SOUPS

After the works of MM. Morard, Reboul and Caillat

(The following recipes are for 10 persons)

857 Soupe à l'Ail
Place in a pan 2 litres (3½ pt or 9 U.S. cups) water, 140 g (5 oz) crushed small cloves of garlic, 2 small sprigs of sage, 2 small cloves, 25 g (1 oz) salt and a pinch of pepper. Bring to the boil and allow to cook gently for 15 minutes.

Meanwhile, cut 20 small slices of French bread, sprinkle with grated cheese and place them in the oven for a few minutes to melt the cheese. Place these Croûtons in a soup tureen, sprinkle with a little olive oil and pass the soup over them through a fine strainer lightly pressing the ingredients. Allow the bread to soak and swell for 2 minutes before serving.

858 Soupe Aïgo–Saou
Place in a pan 1 kg (2¼ lb) cleaned white fish cut into pieces, 50 g (2 oz) sliced onions, 150 g (5 oz) chopped tomato, 450 g (1 lb) potatoes cut into small pieces, 1 bayleaf, 2 cloves of garlic, a Bouquet garni made of 3 parsley stalks and some celery, 25 g (1 oz) salt, a good pinch of pepper and 1¾ litres (3 pt or 7½ U.S. cups) water. Bring to the boil and cook rapidly for 15 minutes.

Place some slices of French bread in a soup tureen, sprinkle them with a little olive oil and pepper, reserve the fish for serving separately and pour the soup over the bread in the tureen. Serve the fish accompanied with Aïoli or Rouille.

Note: Rouille is a type of Aïoli and is prepared as follows: pound 1 clove of garlic and 1 red pimento in the mortar; add breadcrumbs which have been soaked in water and squeezed out to yield one tablespoonful and mix well in. Add a few tablespoons of olive oil a little at a time, taking care to mix continuously with the pestle to ensure its complete mixing and liaison. Finally add a few tablespoons of fish Bouillon.

For Aïoli, see the section on cold sauces (194).

859 Soupe Aïgo à la Ménagère
Cook 120 g (4 oz) shredded white of leek and 60 g (2 oz) finely sliced onion until golden brown in a little olive oil. Add 150 g (5 oz) chopped flesh only of tomato, 4 crushed cloves of garlic, a piece of fennel, a Bouquet garni, a small piece of dried orange peel, a pinch of powdered saffron, 450 g (1 lb) sliced potatoes, 18 g (⅔ oz) salt, a pinch of pepper and 1¾ litres (3 pt or 7½ U.S. cups) water. Bring to the boil and allow to cook rapidly for 15 minutes.

Poach some eggs in the soup allowing one per person. Remove the Bouquet garni and orange peel; place thick slices of French bread in a dish and soak it with some of the liquid of the soup. Place the potatoes in a separate dish and arrange the eggs on top and sprinkle with chopped parsley. Serve the remainder of the soup separately.

(This is the Provençale housewife's method.)

860 Soupe Aïgo Bouido, or Soupe à l'Eau Bouillie
Place in a pan 2 litres (3½ pt or 9 U.S. cups) water, 25 g (1 oz) sea salt, 12 crushed cloves of garlic, 1 sprig of sage, 1 dl (3½ fl oz or ½ U.S. cup) olive oil and a pinch of pepper. Bring to the boil and allow to cook for 7–8 minutes. Place slices of French bread in a soup tureen and strain the Bouillon over; sprinkle with chopped parsley.

861 Soupe Aïgo Bouido aux Oeufs Pochés
Place in a pan 2 litres (3½ pt or 9 U.S. cups) water, 3 dl (½ pt or 1¼ U.S. cup) olive oil, 20 g (⅔ oz) salt, a pinch of pepper, 8 crushed cloves of garlic and a pinch each of thyme, bayleaf, parsley leaves and sage; bring to the boil and allow to cook for 15 minutes. Poach 10 eggs in the soup, place them on slices of French bread in a dish and cover with some of the soup passed through a fine strainer.

862 Soupe de Mariage
Prepare a marmite with 1 kg (2¼ lb) thick flank of beef; 1 kg (2¼ lb) leg of mutton; 1 boiling fowl and 4½ litres (1 gallon or 1¼ U.S. gal) water. Add seasonings, vegetables and flavourings and cook as for an ordinary marmite.

To prepare the soup, pass the bouillon from the marmite into a clean pan and add 65 g (2½ oz) rice and a small pinch of powdered saffron per 1 litre (1¾ pt or 4½ U.S. cups) Bouillon. Allow to cook very gently for 35–40 minutes.

The characteristics of this soup are that it should be very thick and the rice well cooked.

863 Soupe aux Nonnats
Finely chop 150 g (5 oz) onion and cook it with 1 dl (3½ fl oz or ½ U.S. cup) olive oil without colour. Add 150 g (5 oz) chopped flesh only of tomato and allow to cook for a few minutes. Moisten with 1¾ litres (3 pt or 7½ U.S. cups) water, season with 15 g (½ oz) salt and a good pinch of pepper and add a Bouquet garni made of parsley stalks and bayleaf. Bring to the boil and allow to cook for 8 minutes, then add 200 g (7 oz) Nonnats (a small Mediterranean fish analogous to whitebait), a pinch of powdered saffron and allow to cook for a further 4 minutes. Remove the Bouquet garni and pour the soup into a tureen containing 250 g (9 oz) thin slices of French bread.

SOUPS FROM THE INTERNATIONAL REPERTOIRE

(The following recipes are for 10 persons)

864 Potage aux Abatis à l'Anglaise—Giblet Soup
Take the giblets from 3 chickens, cut the necks in three pieces, the gizzards in four and the winglets in half. Fry them in 50 g (2 oz) butter until light brown, sprinkle with 20 g (⅔ oz) flour and continue frying until all is light brown. Moisten with 1 litre (1¾ pt or 4½ U.S. cups) Bouillon and 5 dl (18 fl oz or 2¼ U.S. cups) water; add a Bouquet garni containing a little celery and cook gently for 1½ hours.

When the giblets are cooked, drain them off, trim them and replace in a pan with 4 tbs cooked rice and 2 tbs finely sliced celery which has been stewed in a little butter. Pass the cooking liquid from the giblets over this garnish and allow the soup to cook very gently for a further 15 minutes.

Season well with pepper just before serving.

865 Potage Batwinia (*Cold Russian Soup*)
Finely shred 350 g (13 oz) spinach leaves, 250 g (9 oz) each of sorrel leaves and beetroot leaves; place them in a pan with 100 g (3½ oz) butter, stew together slowly until cooked then pass through a fine sieve.

Add 1¼ litres (2⅕ pt or 5½ U.S. cups) somewhat acid white wine to the purée with 12 g (⅓ oz) salt, 10 g (⅓ oz) sugar, 150 g (5 oz) Agoursis (pickled cucumber) or fresh cucumber cut in dice, a pinch of chopped chervil and tarragon and 10 g (⅓ oz) finely chopped shallot.

Serve with small pieces of ice in the soup.

866 Bennett Soup (*U.S.A.*)
Cut 750 g (1 lb 10 oz) very lean beef into 3 cm (1 in) cubes and place in an earthenware marmite with 2½ litres (4¼ pt or 5⅜ U.S. pt) water; add a little salt, and a few peppercorns and 2 cloves tied in a piece of muslin. Bring to the boil, skim and add 200 g (7 oz) pearl barley then allow to cook gently for 2 hours.

Now add a garnish consisting of 200 g (7 oz) carrot, 150 g (5 oz) turnip, 120 g (4 oz) each of onion and celery heart and 200 g (7 oz) cabbage from which all the stalks have been removed—all of these should be cut into cubes of roughly the same size as the beef.

Allow to cook gently for another hour and serve as it is after removing the sachet of peppercorns and cloves.

Note: Potatoes, rice, lentils, dried peas or dried haricot beans are often added to this soup; if one of the dried vegetables is used it should be soaked before use. Whichever garnish is chosen it should be added to the soup at the appropriate time so that it is cooked at the same time as the beef.

Sometimes a knuckle bone of beef with the ligaments attached or a knuckle of veal are added: the gelatinous parts which become detached from either of these during cooking are cut into dice and served in the soup.

867 Potage Bortsch Koop (*Russia*)
Finely shred 350 g (13 oz) carrot, 250 g (9 oz) leek and 80 g (3 oz) each of onion and celery; stew together with 60 g (2 oz) butter and without colour. Add 1¾ litres (3 pt or 7½ U.S. cups) White Bouillon, a bouquet of fennel and marjoram, 650 g (1 lb 7 oz) raw flank of beef cut in dice and 4 chickens' necks cut in pieces; bring to the boil and allow to simmer very gently until cooked.

Pass the soup through a clean cloth and add 50 g (2 oz) grated raw beetroot to the liquid; bring it to the boil and simmer for a further 15 minutes. Finally pass the soup again and serve accompanied with small hot patties filled with Gratin Forcemeat, and small *Galettes* of Kache of Buckwheat (318).

Note: Duck is not used in the preparation of this Bortsch nor is a Julienne of vegetables served in it.

868 Potage Bortsch Polonais (*Russia*)
Cut into Julienne 300 g (11 oz) beetroot, 200 g (7 oz) each of leek and white-heart cabbage, 80 g (3 oz) onion, 50 g (2 oz) celery and 1 parsley root; stew together in a pan with 80 g (2½ oz) butter and without colour.

Add $1\frac{3}{4}$ litres (3 pt or $7\frac{1}{2}$ U.S. cups) White Bouillon, 1 dl ($3\frac{1}{2}$ fl oz or $\frac{1}{2}$ U.S. cup) juice prepared from grated beetroot, a small bouquet of fennel and marjoram, 750 g (1 lb 10 oz) blanched flank of beef and a small half roasted duck; simmer gently until cooked.
To serve: remove the beef and duck; discard the bouquet and finish the soup with 1 tbs essence of *Gribouis*, 2 tbs beetroot juice and $\frac{1}{2}$ tbs chopped blanched fennel and parsley. Cut the beef into small dice and the breast of duck into small slices and add those to the soup together with 10 grilled and skinned chipolatas. Serve a sauceboat of sour cream separately.

Note: The grilled chipolatas may be replaced by very small patties filled with duck forcemeat; these should be arranged on a serviette and sent with the soup.

869 Potage Camaro à la Brésilienne
Place a boiling fowl weighing approximately $1\frac{1}{4}$ kg (2 lb 12 oz) in a small marmite, cover with $2\frac{1}{4}$ litres (4 pt or 5 U.S. pt) water and add 15 g ($\frac{1}{2}$ oz) salt. Bring to the boil, skim and after 20 minutes add a bouquet of parsley and chervil, a small onion and 60 g (2 oz) rice. Simmer very gently for $3\frac{1}{2}$ hours and serve as it is after removing the bouquet.

870 Soupe aux Cerises
Remove the stones from 750 g (1 lb 14 oz) small plump cherries and reserve 75 g ($2\frac{1}{2}$ oz) of them as a garnish. Place the others in a copper pan with $7\frac{1}{2}$ dl ($1\frac{1}{3}$ pt or $3\frac{1}{4}$ U.S. cups) hot water, a piece of lemon rind and a small piece of cinnamon; boil together rapidly for 8 minutes.

Meanwhile, pour half a bottle of Claret or Port into another copper pan and bring to the boil; crush half the cherry stones, add to the boiling wine and allow to infuse.

Drain the cherries and rub them through a fine sieve, replace this purée in their cooking liquid and thicken it with 15 g ($\frac{1}{2}$ oz) arrowroot diluted in a little cold water. Add 1 tbs caster sugar and the reserved cherries and boil together for 4 minutes.

Finish by adding the infusion of cherry stones passed through a clean cloth; pour the soup into a tureen and complete it with some roughly broken rusks.

Note: The rusks may be replaced by Finger Biscuits (4325).

871 Potage Clam Chowder (*U.S.A.*)
Clams are a shellfish of the same family as the cockle.

Open the clams, taking care to reserve the juice which is inside and for 1 litre ($1\frac{3}{4}$ pt or $4\frac{1}{2}$ U.S. cups) of clams including the juice, chop 190 g ($6\frac{1}{2}$ oz) pork fat and melt it in a heavy pan. Add 100 g ($3\frac{1}{2}$ oz) coarsely chopped onion and 25 g (1 oz) roughly chopped parsley and cook in the fat without colouring; add 300 g (11 oz) chopped flesh only of tomato, the clams and their juices, 300 g (11 oz) potatoes cut into medium dice, 5 dl (18 fl oz or $2\frac{1}{4}$ U.S. cups) water, a little salt bearing in mind that the clam juice is already salty and a little pepper.

Bring to the boil and cook for 20 minutes; add a small spoonful of fresh leaves of thyme and sufficient crushed rusks, cream cracker biscuits or dried soup sippets to lightly thicken the soup. Cook for a further 5 minutes and serve as it is.

Note: Sometimes the clams are chopped before using but the rest of the preparation is always the same.

872 Potage Cocky-Leeky (*Scotland*)
Cook a plump chicken with a few vegetables and flavourings in $1\frac{3}{4}$ litres (3 pt or $7\frac{1}{2}$ U.S. cups) light clear veal stock. Cut 500 g (1 lb 2 oz) white of leek into fine Julienne and stew it together with 75 g ($2\frac{1}{2}$ oz) butter without colouring and finish cooking it with a little Bouillon from the chicken.

To serve the soup, remove the chicken from the Bouillon, allow this to continue to simmer gently, skimming carefully to ensure that it is very clear, then add the chicken flesh cut into small slices and the Julienne of leeks.

Note: Stewed prunes may be served separately with the soup but this is optional.

873 Potage aux Foies de Volaille à l'Anglaise—Chicken Liver Soup (*England*)
Mix $1\frac{3}{4}$ litres (3 pt or $7\frac{1}{2}$ U.S. cups) brown stock into 70 g ($2\frac{1}{2}$ oz) blond Roux and bring to the boil.

Add 250 g (9 oz) chicken livers cut into slices and quickly sautéed in 50 g (2 oz) butter to seal the outside. Allow to cook for 15 minutes then remove the livers, pound them well and replace the purée in the soup. Pass through a fine sieve, season well with pepper and finish at the last moment with 1 dl ($3\frac{1}{2}$ fl oz or $\frac{1}{2}$ U.S. cup) Madeira.
Garnish: 125 g ($4\frac{1}{2}$ oz) light coloured chicken livers, finely sliced and sautéed in a little butter added just before service.

874 Potage aux Boulettes de Foie—Leberknodeln
To prepare the liver balls or dumplings, cut 150 g (5 oz) calf's liver into very small dice, season with salt and pepper and fry quickly in a little butter and oil. Pound well, rub through a fine sieve and mix the purée until smooth. Add 60 g (2 oz) softened butter; 60 g (2 oz) finely chopped onion cooked in butter until transparent; $\frac{1}{2}$ tbs chopped

parsley; $1\frac{1}{2}$ beaten eggs; 40 g ($1\frac{1}{2}$ oz) very fresh breadcrumbs; a pinch of salt and pepper; and a very small pinch of paprika. Mix all these ingredients together well.

Mould this mixture into Quenelles with dessert spoons and poach them in White Bouillon for 15–20 minutes before needed. Drain them at the last moment and place in a tureen with $1\frac{3}{4}$ litres (3 pt or $7\frac{1}{2}$ U.S. cups) excellent Beef Bouillon.

875 Potage à la Puree de Foie—Leber-suppe
Prepare a Mirepoix of 50 g (2 oz) each of carrot and onion; 60 g (2 oz) lean salt pork; 30 g (1 oz) shallot; a small sprig of thyme; and a piece of bayleaf. Fry together in 60 g (2 oz) butter until light brown in colour, then add 200 g (7 oz) diced calf's liver and season with salt, pepper and a touch of mixed spice. Fry the liver quickly then moisten with 1 dl ($3\frac{1}{2}$ fl oz or $\frac{1}{2}$ U.S. cup) white wine, and $1\frac{1}{2}$ dl (5 fl oz or $\frac{5}{8}$ U.S. cup) Sauce Espagnole and allow to cook gently for 10 minutes.

Strain off the liver and Mirepoix and pound them finely; return this purée to the liquid and pass through a fine sieve. Dilute this with $1\frac{1}{2}$ litres ($2\frac{5}{8}$ pt or $6\frac{1}{2}$ U.S. cups) White Bouillon, bring to the boil and allow to simmer for 2 minutes.

Season well and serve with small diced bread Croûtons fried in butter.

876 Potage aux Gombos
See Potage Okra (890).

877 Potage Hochepot à la Flamande (*Belgium*)
Place in a marmite 300 g (11 oz) pig's ears, 600 g (1 lb 5 oz) pig's trotters, 125 g ($4\frac{1}{2}$ oz) pig's tails, 250 g (9 oz) salt belly of pork, 600 g (1 lb 5 oz) flank of beef, 300 g (11 oz) each of shoulder and breast of mutton.

Cover with water, season with 12 g ($\frac{1}{2}$ oz) salt, bring to the boil, skim and allow to simmer very gently.

After approximately 2 hours, add a garnish of 200 g (7 oz) each of carrot and whiteheart cabbage, 60 g (2 oz) onion, 300 g (11 oz) white of leek, 300 g (11 oz) potatoes—all roughly sliced. Allow a total cooking time of 4 hours of very gentle simmering.

For service: Serve the Bouillon in a tureen with some of the vegetables; serve the rest of the vegetables and the meats on a separate dish with 10 poached chipolatas.

Note: This preparation is the equivalent of the *Olla-Podrida Espagnole* and corresponds to the *Oille* of the old French kitchen.

878 Potage au Lièvre—Hare Soup
Cut the forepart including the shoulders and one leg of hare into small pieces; fry them until brown in a little butter together with a small Mirepoix of carrot, onion, celery, white of leek, lean ham, parsley stalks and a little thyme and bayleaf. Sprinkle with 30 g (1 oz) arrowroot and moisten with 2 litres ($3\frac{1}{2}$ pt or 9 U.S. cups) White Bouillon, bring to the boil and allow to cook very gently for $2\frac{1}{2}$ hours.

Remove the pieces of leg of hare, cut the flesh into small dice and keep warm in a little of the strained soup. Allow the soup to simmer for another 20 minutes then add the sliced liver from the hare and cook gently for a further 10 minutes until cooked. Remove the rest of the hare and liver, strain the cooking liquid and simmer gently, skimming it very carefully for 20 minutes. Meanwhile, remove all the bones from the pieces of hare, finely pound this flesh and liver then pass it through a fine sieve; place this purée into a tureen.

At the last moment finish the liquid of the soup with 3 tbs of an infusion of basil, marjoram and rosemary, a touch of Cayenne and 60 g (2 oz) butter added away from the heat. Pass this through a fine strainer over the purée and mix it well with a whisk. Finally add the reserved dice of hare and 3–4 tbs Port wine.

879 Potage Lithuanien (*Russia*)
Take $1\frac{3}{4}$ litres (3 pt or $7\frac{1}{2}$ U.S. cups) very thin Purée Parmentier which in effect would be $2\frac{1}{2}$ dl (9 fl oz or $1\frac{1}{8}$ U.S. cups) of potato purée diluted with $1\frac{1}{2}$ litres ($2\frac{5}{8}$ pt or $6\frac{1}{2}$ U.S. cups) White Bouillon.

Add 150 g (5 oz) heart of celery cut in coarse Julienne and stewed in a little butter until almost cooked; bring to the boil and finish cooking the Julienne very gently for 35–40 minutes, skimming carefully.

Finish the soup at the last moment with 2 tbs finely shredded sorrel stewed in butter and $1\frac{1}{2}$ dl (5 fl oz or $\frac{5}{8}$ U.S. cup) sour cream.

Garnish: Small rectangles of cooked lean smoked bacon, poached chipolatas and small French fried eggs from which two-thirds of their whites have been removed before frying.

880 Potage Livonien aux Kloskis (*Russia*)
Stew together 80 g (3 oz) chopped onion and 50 g (2 oz) finely shredded sorrel with 50 g (2 oz) butter. Add 500 g (1 lb 2 oz) spinach which has been blanched and squeezed to remove the water, mix together and cook for a few minutes then add 4 dl (14 fl oz or $1\frac{3}{4}$ U.S. cups) Sauce Béchamel and cook gently for 15 minutes. Pass through a fine sieve and

dilute the purée obtained with 1 litre (1¾ pt or 4½ U.S. cups) White Bouillon; allow to simmer, skimming carefully, for 20 minutes.

Finish at the last moment with 1 dl (3½ fl oz or ½ U.S. cup) cream and 60 g (2 oz) butter.

Garnish: 20 Kloskis and Pluches of chervil.

To make Kloskis: Mix 200 g (7 oz) General Purpose Chou Paste (325) together with 50 g (2 oz) finely chopped shallot, blanched and squeezed dry and 25 g (1 oz) each of chopped lean ham and very small diced bread fried in butter. Divide the mixture into pieces approximately 12 g (⅓ oz) in weight, moulding them to the shape of small round balls; drop into boiling salted water and poach for 20 minutes. They should be set to poach so as to be ready at exactly the time of service.

881 Potage Mille-fanti (*Italy*)

Mix together in a basin 100 g (3½ oz) very fine fresh white breadcrumbs, 50 g (2 oz) grated Parmesan cheese and 3 well beaten eggs added a little at a time; season with a pinch of pepper and a touch of nutmeg.

Bring 1¾ litres (3 pt or 7½ U.S. cups) White Bouillon to the boil and add the egg mixture to it little by little mixing it in well with a whisk. Cover the soup and allow to cook very gently on the side of the stove for 7–8 minutes. Just before serving, give a further mixing with the whisk.

882 Potage Mille-fanti clair

Prepare the mixture as in the previous recipe with 50 g (2 oz) breadcrumbs, 25 g (1 oz) grated Parmesan and 1½ beaten eggs; season with pepper and nutmeg.

Bring 1¾ litres (3 pt or 7½ U.S. cups) White Bouillon to the boil and add the egg mixture a little at a time, mixing it in with a whisk. Cover with a lid, cook gently for 10 minutes and lightly whisk just before service.

883 Potage Minestra—Minestrone (*Italy*)

Finely chop 60 g (2 oz) fresh belly of pork and mix with 40 g (1½ oz) scraped fat pork. Place in a thick-bottomed pan to heat and melt it; add 60 g (2 oz) chopped onion, 150 g (5 oz) shredded white of leek and cook together until lightly coloured.

Moisten with 1¾ litres (3 pt or 7½ U.S. cups) lightly flavoured White Bouillon—or water, in which case add 15 g (½ oz) salt. Add 60 g (2 oz) each of carrot and turnip, 30 g (1 oz) celery, 100 g (3½ oz) potato—all cut into Paysanne or large Brunoise; 100 g (3½ oz) shredded heart of cabbage and the roughly chopped flesh only of 2 tomatoes.

Bring to the boil, simmer gently and after approximately 25 minutes add 150 g (5 oz) fresh peas, 40 g (1½ oz) French beans cut in small pieces and 100 g (3½ oz) rice or spaghetti broken into small pieces. From now on allow the soup to cook very, very gently for 1 hour.

At the last moment add 6 g (⅕ oz) crushed garlic and a pinch each of basil and chervil chopped together with 15 g (½ oz) scraped pork fat.

Note: Minestra is the general term used for all Italian soups but it is used principally to designate a preparation which is equivalent to the Soupe à la Paysanne of the French kitchen. In principle, a Minestra can be made with any fresh vegetables.

884 Potage Miss Betsy

Well wash 125 g (4½ oz) pearl barley in plenty of cold water and place in a pan with 1¼ litres (2⅕ pt or 5½ U.S. cups) water; add a bouquet (1¾ pt or 4½ U.S. cups) water; add a bouquet of parsley, chervil and celery and allow to cook very gently for 5 hours taking care that a skin does not form on the surface so that the liquid remains clear.

When the barley is cooked, replace the soup in a clean pan and add 4 tbs very red and thick fresh tomato purée passed through a muslin. The consistency of this soup should not be too thick.

Garnish: 2 peeled and cored pippin-type apples cut into dice and cooked in a little butter.

885 Potage Fausse Tortue—Mock Turtle Soup

To most practising cooks this soup is simply a brown stock flavoured with tomato and strongly flavoured with celery and mushrooms and which is finally finished with the addition of an infusion of turtle herbs.

Carême called this soup Tortue à la Française and posed the following principles:

1) that the liquid base should be the thinned cooking liquor from a calf's head,
2) that the thickening element should be supplied by adding Espagnole in the proportion of 2½ dl (9 fl oz or 1⅛ U.S. cups) per 1 litre (1¾ pt or 4½ U.S. cups) of liquid,
3) that the flavouring should be celery, mushroom, parsley, thyme and bayleaf, and
4) that the special flavouring should be that of basil, rosemary and marjoram—these being used in very small quantities of not more than 2 g ($\frac{1}{15}$ oz) per litre (1¾ pt or 4½ U.S. Cups) of soup.

The method of Suzanne who was the popularizer of English recipes is almost the same—the only difference being that he indicates the use of Roux plus arrowroot as the thickening ingredients.

Whichever the preparation, however, the soup is always finished with 1 dl (2 fl oz or ¼ U.S. cup)

Madeira per 1 litre of soup and is fairly well seasoned with Cayenne. The garnish is composed of round pieces of cooked calf's head cut out with a 1½ cm (⅗ in) cutter and small Quenelles made from a mixture of a purée of hard-boiled egg yolks mixed with the required amount of ordinary forcemeat and then moulded with teaspoons.

886 Potage de Mouton à la Grecque (*Greece*)
Dilute 4 dl (14 fl oz or 1¾ U.S. cups) purée of fresh peas or, if out of season, a purée made with green split peas, with 1½ litres (2⅝ pt or 6½ U.S. cups) White Bouillon; simmer gently for 10 minutes and strain.

When serving, add a garnish of 375 g (14 oz) boiled breast of mutton cut in large dice and 150 g (5 oz) Brunoise of vegetables cooked in a little of the cooking liquor from the mutton.

887 Potage Mulligatawny
Cut a medium-sized chicken as for Fricassée and cook with 1¾ litres (3 pt or 7½ U.S. cups) White Bouillon, 60 g (2 oz) each of carrot and sliced onion, 25 g (1 oz) mushroom trimmings and a bouquet of parsley and celery.

Separately cook 60 g (2 oz) chopped onion in 50 g (2 oz) butter until lightly coloured; sprinkle with 20 g (⅔ oz) fecula and 10 g (⅓ oz) curry powder, moisten with the cooking liquid of the chicken and cook gently for 10 minutes. Pass through a fine strainer, place in a clean pan and simmer on the side of the stove for 15 minutes; skim carefully and finish with 1½ dl (5 fl oz or ⅝ U.S. cup) cream. Place trimmed pieces of the cooked chicken in a tureen and pass the soup through a fine strainer over them.

Serve separately in a dish, 125 g (4½ oz) plain boiled rice.

888 Mutton Broth (*England*)
Cut into large Brunoise 120 g (4 oz) each of carrot and turnip, 150 g (5 oz) white of leek and 60 g (2 oz) each of celery and onion; stew together with 60 g (2 oz) butter.

Moisten with 2 litres (3½ pt or 9 U.S. cups) lightly flavoured White Bouillon and add 300 g (11 oz) neck and breast of mutton and 100 g (3½ oz) very well blanched pearl barley. Allow to cook together very gently for 1½ hours.

Remove the meat when cooked, cut it into large dice and replace in the soup together with ½ tbs blanched chopped parsley.

889 Potage aux Noques (*Alsace*)
Prepare 1¾ litres (3 pt or 7½ U.S. cups) Ordinary Velouté or Fish Velouté, whichever is most suitable, and finish as a soup. When ready, pour it into a tureen containing some Noques prepared in the following manner.

Noques: Place 100 g (3½ oz) butter in a warm basin and mix well until soft and smooth; add 2 raw egg yolks and mix in thoroughly. Now carefully add and mix in 80 g (3 oz) flour, 1 stiffly beaten egg white, some salt, pepper and a touch of nutmeg.

Mould the mixture Quenelle-shape with dessert spoons and poach them in lightly salted water which is barely simmering on the side of the stove. When firm, drain well and place in the prepared soup.

890 Potage Okra or Potage aux Gombos (*U.S.A.*)
Cook 60 g (2 oz) chopped onion in 60 g (2 oz) butter without colour and add 125 g (4½ oz) fresh streaky bacon or lean raw ham cut in small dice. Cook together for a few minutes to lightly colour then add 500 g (1 lb 2 oz) raw chicken flesh cut in dice and cook to set and lightly colour it, stirring frequently.

Moisten with 2 litres (3½ pt or 9 U.S. cups) Chicken Bouillon, bring to the boil and allow to cook very gently for 25 minutes without covering with a lid. Complete the soup with 200 g (7 oz) okras cut in slices and 250 g (9 oz) roughly chopped flesh only of tomato; continue to cook very gently for another 25 minutes. Skim off the fat, check the seasoning and flavour according to taste, with a few drops of Worcestershire sauce. Pour into a tureen and add 2–3 tbs plain boiled rice.

891 Potage Olla-Podrida (*Spain*)
This soup is similar to the Hochepot à la Flamande but made with the following additions: 375 g (14 oz) raw ham, 1 small partridge and ½ a small chicken.

As a characteristic regional variation of this dish, add also 375 g (14 oz) chick peas (Garbanzos), 2 Chorizos (small sausages), 1 nice lettuce and an additional 1 litre (1¾ pt or 4½ U.S. cups) water; allow to cook together very gently and evenly for 6 hours. For service, arrange the meats on one dish, the vegetables on another, the Bouillon in a tureen and serve together at the same time.

892 Potage d'Orge au Céleri—Pearl Barley and Celery Soup (*U.S.A.*)
Wash 250 g (9 oz) pearl barley and drain well; place in a pan containing 100 g (3½ oz) very hot butter and mix over a hot stove for a few minutes.

Moisten with 1 litre (1¾ pt or 4½ U.S. cups) each of White Bouillon and water, season with salt and pepper, bring to the boil and cook very gently for 3 hours.

Add 350 g (13 oz) white and heart of celery cut in large dice and blanched, and continue cooking for another 30 minutes.

Just before serving, finish with a liaison of 6 egg yolks and 1 dl (3½ fl oz or ½ U.S. cup) cream and 100 g (3½ oz) butter.

893 Potage Ouka

Prepare a Fish Bouillon using 1 kg (2¼ lb) sturgeon or the same amount of tench or perch, 750 g (1 lb 10 oz) trimmings and bones of fish, 2¼ litres (4 pt or 10 U.S. cups) water, 2½ dl (9 fl oz or 1⅛ U.S. cups) white wine, 1 parsley root, 1 piece of celery, a little fennel, 25 g (1 oz) mushroom trimmings and 20 g (⅔ oz) salt. Bring to the boil and allow to cook very gently for 1 hour.

Meanwhile, prepare 1) 10 small Paupiettes of *Sigui* or *Lavaret* and 2) 350 g (13 oz) Julienne composed of equal quantities of white of celery, white of leek and parsley root, stewed together with 60 g (2 oz) butter and finish cooking with a few tablespoons of Fish Bouillon.

Pass the Fish Bouillon and clarify it with 125 g (4½ oz) pounded caviare and 500 g (1 lb 2 oz) whiting flesh, then strain it through a piece of clean cloth.

Poach the Paupiettes in a small shallow pan with the necessary quantity of Fish Bouillon.

To serve: Add the Julienne of vegetables and the Paupiettes to the clarified Bouillon and serve accompanied with a dish of Kache of Buckwheat (318) and a dish of very small Rastegaïs (1233) both arranged on a serviette.

894 Potage Oxtail-Clair—Clear Oxtail Soup

Cover the bottom of a small marmite with a layer of the usual sliced root vegetables and herbs and place on top 1½ kg (3 lb 6 oz) oxtail cut in sections. Cover with a lid and place in the oven to sweat for 15 minutes. Moisten with 2½ litres (4½ pt or 11 U.S. cups) stock made in advance from 1½ kg (3 lb 6 oz) gelatinous bones and 3¼ litres (5¾ pt or 7⅛ U.S. pt) water simmered continuously and gently for 7–8 hours.

Cook the oxtail gently for 3½–4 hours then remove the oxtail and reserve. Clarify the cooking liquor which has been skimmed and strained, with 500 g (1 lb 2 oz) finely chopped lean beef, 100 g (3½ oz) white of leek and 1 egg white; allow to cook gently for 1 hour and strain through a clean cloth.

Serve the clarified soup garnished with the cooked oxtail allowing 1 section per person and 200 g (7 oz) large Brunoise of carrot, turnip and celery cooked in butter and a little Bouillon until the liquid has evaporated.

895 Potage Oxtail Lié—Thick Oxtail Soup

Prepare the oxtail as in the preceding recipe. Strain the cooking liquid and thicken it using 50 g (2 oz) brown Roux and 100 g (3½ oz) tomato purée per 1 litre (1¾ pt or 4½ U.S. cups) stock.

In this case it is not necessary to clarify the stock but it is essential to simmer and skim it carefully for 25–30 minutes. Pass through a fine strainer and garnish with the oxtail and Brunoise of vegetables as in the previous recipe.

Note: In Belgium as in most other countries of Northern Europe, Thick Oxtail Soup is thickened in the same way as Mock Turtle soup by adding the required amount of Espagnole.

896 Oyster Soup with Okra (*U.S.A.*)

Chop 100 g (3½ oz) pork fat and place in a thick bottomed pan to heat and melt. Add 100 g (3½ oz) chopped onion and cook without colour, then add 250 g (9 oz) tomatoes cut in quarters, 6–8 sliced fresh okras, half a green pepper sliced, 1 litre (1¾ pt or 4½ U.S. cups) White Bouillon, a little salt and a little pepper or curry powder according to taste. Allow to cook for 15 minutes then add 24 raw bearded oysters with their juices and cook for a few minutes to poach the oysters. Finish the soup by thickening it lightly with arrowroot keeping the result fairly thin.

897 Potage au Pistou

Place 375 g (14 oz) French beans (the beans inside the pods to be large) cut in small pieces, in 1½ litres (2⅝ pt or 6½ U.S. cups) boiling water; add 500 g (1 lb 2 oz) potatoes cut in Paysanne, the roughly chopped flesh only of 2 tomatoes and 10 g (⅓ oz) salt.

When the vegetables are nearly cooked, add 180 g (6 oz) large vermicelli and finish cooking the soup very gently taking care that, as the soup is fairly thick, it does not stick to the bottom of the pan.

At the last moment pound together 2 small cloves of garlic, 4 g (⅐ oz) basil and the flesh only of 1 grilled tomato. Into this paste incorporate 2 tbs oil drop by drop then dilute it with 2 tbs of liquid from the soup.

Pour the soup into a tureen, add the *Aillade* prepared as above, and 75 g (2½ oz) grated fresh Gruyère cheese.

Note: The Pistou is a soup of the Italian school which is frequently used in Provence; because of its origin, however, it has been included in this section.

898 Potage de Poulet à l'Anglaise—Chicken Broth (*England*)

Place a plump medium-sized chicken and 1¾ litres (3 pt or 7½ U.S. cups) White Bouillon in a small marmite; add a Bouquet garni with celery and 1 small onion stuck with a clove. Bring to the boil, skim, add 100 g (3½ oz) long grain rice and allow to cook very gently.

To serve: Remove the onion and Bouquet garni, take off the skin and bones from the chicken, cut the flesh into large dice and replace this in the soup together with 200 g (7 oz) Brunoise of vegetables cooked in a little butter and White Bouillon.

899 Potage Puchéro (*Spain*)

This is a Spanish Pot au Feu, not so well garnished as a Potage Olla Podrida but having the same characteristic garnish of *Garbanzos* and *Chorizas*.

To serve: the meat and vegetables should be arranged on separate dishes and the Bouillon served in a tureen.

900 Potage à la Purée de Jambon (*Russia*)

Cut 500 g (1 lb 2 oz) lean cooked ham in dice, pound it until fine then add 2 dl (7 fl oz or ⅞ U.S. cup) each of Sauce Soubise and tomato purée.

Pass this mixture through a fine sieve and dilute it with 1½ litres (2⅝ pt or 6½ U.S. cups) lightly salted White Bouillon so as to take account of the salt in the ham. Reheat without boiling and finish with a touch of Cayenne, 50 g (2 oz) butter, and 1½ dl (5 fl oz or ⅝ U.S. cup) Madeira.

Serve separately some very small Croûtons of bread fried in butter at the last minute.

901 Potage au Rognon de Veau (*Russia*)

Bring 2 litres (3½ pt or 9 U.S. cups) fairly thin Chicken Velouté to the boil, add 1 tbs parsley sprigs and a pinch of chopped fennel and simmer together for a few minutes, skimming as required.

Finish with a liaison of 2 egg yolks and 1 dl (3½ fl oz or ½ U.S. cup) cream, and 2 tbs juice of Agoursis (pickled cucumbers); pass through a fine strainer.

Garnish: 1 veal kidney, finely sliced, seasoned with salt and pepper and sautéed quickly in a little butter with 30 g (1 oz) finely chopped onion previously cooked without colour in butter, 1 tbs cucumber cut in small diamonds, 1 tbs sliced Gribouis which have been pickled in vinegar, 10 small olives stuffed with forcemeat and poached at the last moment and ½ tbs chopped and blanched parsley.

902 Potage aux Rognons à l'Anglaise—Kidney Soup (*England*)

This soup is prepared in the same way as Chicken Liver Soup replacing the garnish of chicken liver with mutton or veal kidneys cut in slices and sautéed quickly in butter at the last moment.

903 Potage Rossolnick (*Russia*)

Prepare 2 litres (3½ pt or 9 U.S. cups) fairly thin Chicken Velouté and add 1 dl (3½ fl oz or ½ U.S. cup) cucumber juice.

Trim 10 pieces each of parsley root and celery root to the shape of new carrots and cut a cross on the base of each; prepare 60 g (2 oz) diamond-shaped pieces of salted cucumber. Well blanch these vegetables and add to the Velouté. Allow the soup to simmer gently for 40 minutes taking care to skim as necessary.

Finish at the last moment with a liaison of 2 egg yolks and 1 dl (3½ fl oz or ½ U.S. cup) cream and 2 tbs cucumber juice; add an additional garnish of 20 small chicken forcemeat Quenelles cooked at the last moment.

904 Potage Selianka (*Russia*)

Prepare 1¾ litres (3 pt or 7½ U.S. cups) White Bouillon flavoured with ham. Just before serving, add a garnish of 200 g (7 oz) braised Sauerkraut and 1 tbs blanched small sprigs of parsley.

905 Potage Stschy (*Russia*)

Cook 250 g (9 oz) chopped onion in 90 g (3 oz) butter without colour; sprinkle with 1 tbs flour and cook together for a few minutes. Moisten with 2½ litres (4¼ pt or 5⅜ U.S. pt) White Bouillon and bring to the boil.

Add 250 g (9 oz) flank of beet cut in dice, blanched for 10 minutes and refreshed; 250 g (9 oz) roughly chopped, blanched and refreshed sauerkraut and a bouquet of parsley stalks. Cook together very gently for 2½–3 hours.

Just before serving, remove the bouquet, correct the seasoning and finish with 1 dl (3½ fl oz or ½ U.S. cup) sour cream and ½ tbs blanched chopped parsley.

906 Potage aux Terrapines, clair ou lié—Terrapin Soup, thick or clear (*U.S.A.*)

These two luxury soups are generally based on Turtle Bouillon, either clear or thickened as required and to which is added cooked terrapin prepared as in the recipe in the Chapter on fish (2142). The cooked terrapins should be boned out and the flesh cut into medium dice before adding to the soup.

Serve accompanied with thick slices of peeled lemon, hard-boiled egg and some chopped and blanched parsley.

907 Potage à la Tortue Clair—Clear Turtle Soup

With very few exceptions turtle soup is rarely prepared in the kitchen. It is usually purchased ready prepared either fresh, tinned or bottled, from firms which specialize in its preparation and who enjoy a high reputation for their product.

Even though a considerable amount of soup may be required there is still an incontestable advantage in buying it ready made. Nevertheless, for those occasions where it is found to be absolutely necessary to make it in the kitchen, the following simple and practical recipe is given.

Details of Preparation

Slaughtering the turtle: The turtles selected for preparing the soup should be approximately 60–80 kg (135–180 lb) in weight; only fleshy and very live turtles should be selected.

To kill the turtle lay it on its back at the edge of the table with the head handing over the side. Take a double meat hook and place one hook into the upper jaw and suspend a sufficiently heavy weight in the hook at the other end so as to make the animal extend its neck. Sever the head from the body quickly, using a sharp, heavy knife.

Hang the turtle over a receptacle to collect the blood, leaving it to bleed for 1–2 hours.

Dismemberment of the turtle: For this operation thrust a heavy knife between the upper shell (carapace) and the lower shell (plastron) exactly where they meet and separate one from the other. Keeping the turtle on its back, remove all the adhering flesh from the plastron and place it on one side.

Now remove the flippers then detach and discard the intestines. The green fat which is used for making the soup must be collected carefully and placed aside. Remove any flesh adhering to the carapace and also reserve for future use.

Preparation of the carapace and plastron: These two parts which constitute the shell of the turtle, alone provide the gelatinous flesh which is used as a garnish for the soup. To prepare, saw the carapace into 6–8 pieces and the plastron into 4; blanch them in boiling water or in a steamer for a few minutes so that the shell can be removed from the flesh.

When the shell has been removed, refresh the pieces of turtle meat in cold water and place them in a pan. Well cover with water, bring to the boil, add a few vegetables as for a marmite and a small quantity of turtle herbs, and cook very gently for 5–6 hours.

Remove the pieces of turtle and discard any bones; refresh the flesh in cold water then carefully trim and cut it into 3–4 cm (1½–1¾ in) squares. These squares of gelatinous flesh and the reserved green fat, poached in salted water and cut into slices, constitute the garnish for the soup.

The cooking liquid from the gelatinous flesh should be reserved for the cooking of the soup as explained further on.

Preparation of the soup: There are two methods for preparing the soup, both giving almost identical results:

Method 1) Prepare a marmite in the usual manner for White Bouillon with the reserved meat of the turtle and vegetables and flavourings; when finished and strained, add an equal quantity of very strong gelatinous Beef Bouillon such as one would do if using tinned turtle soup. This is in effect the most practical method especially if the soup is to be reserved for any length of time.

Method 2) Prepare a bouillon using the same weight of shin of beef as the reserved turtle flesh plus half a calf's foot and 500 g (1 lb 2 oz) knuckle of veal per 1 kg (2 lb 4 oz) beef. Add the reserved turtle meat to the bouillon or keep it for clarifying the soup if necessary; however, this procedure of clarifying is not advised.

As the flavourings and seasoning are the same in both cases the preparation of the first method only will be described in detail as follows:

Cooking the soup:

Place the reserved meat from the inside of the turtle in a suitable size pan (do not confuse this meat with the flesh kept for the garnish) with the bones, and the head and the flippers which should have been blanched to remove the scales. Add the cooking liquid from the gelatinous flesh and sufficient water to give a total of 50 litres (11 gal or 14 U.S. gal) of liquid for a turtle weighing 75 kg (170 lb)—this will yield 38–40 litres (8½–9 gal or 10½–11 U.S. gal) of finished turtle soup. Add 5 g (⅙ oz) salt per 1 litre of liquid, bring to the boil, skim and add 6½ kg (14½ lb) leek, 1 kg (2¼ lb) celery, 2 kg (4½ lb) onions stuck with 10 cloves, 1 kg (2¼ lb) shallots and 125 g (4½ oz) garlic.

Simmer gently and evenly for approximately 7 hours then add the following: the zest of 4 lemons, a bunch of herbs including 8 g (¼ oz) each of basil and marjoram, 4 g (⅛ oz) each of sage, rosemary, savoury and thyme and a sachet containing 250 g (9 oz) coriander and 125 g (4½ oz) peppercorns.

Allow to simmer very gently and evenly for a further 1 hour; finally strain the bouillon through a clean cloth, add the garnish of flesh of the carapace and plastron and keep until required in special stoneware containers.

Serving the soup:

When required for service, heat the soup, adjust the seasoning and add approximately ¼ dl (1 fl oz or ⅛ U.S. cup) very old Madeira per 1 litre (1¾ pt or 4½ U.S. cups) soup.

Note: The turtle flesh used in preparing the soup has no further culinary use and only the flippers are sometimes served. In this case they are removed when three parts cooked and finished by braising with Madeira.

908 Milk Punch

A glass of milk punch is often served with Turtle Soup and is prepared as follows:

Ingredients for 1 litre (1¾ pt or 4½ U.S. cups): 3½ dl (12 fl oz or 1½ U.S. cups) syrup at 17° on the saccharometer (made from 2½ dl (9 fl oz or 1⅛ U.S. cups) water and 150 g (5 oz) sugar); the zest of 2 small oranges and 2 small lemons; 3 dl (½ pt or 1¼ U.S. cups) Rum; 1 dl (3½ fl oz or ½ U.S. cup) Kirsch; 1½ dl (5 fl oz or ⅝ U.S. cup) milk; the juice of 3 oranges and 3 lemons.

Method:

Bring the syrup to the boil, add the orange and lemon zests, cover and infuse for 10–12 minutes; add the rum, Kirsch, milk, orange and lemon juices and allow the mixture to rest for 3 hours. At the last moment pass through a very fine clean cloth and serve very cold.

909 Potage Tortue Lié—Thick Turtle Soup

This is the same clear Turtle Soup thickened with 80 g (3 oz) of blond Roux or 30 g (1 oz) arrowroot diluted in a little Bouillon, per 1 litre (1¾ pt or 4½ U.S. cups) soup.

910 Clear Turtle Soup, using the commercially prepared product

When of excellent quality this only requires the addition of an equal quantity of very strong Beef Bouillon to render it perfect: the adjustment of the seasoning and its finishing with old Madeira is carried out in the same way as for Clear Turtle Soup.

911 Turtle Soup, using dried turtle meat

To prepare this, the dried turtle meat should be soaked in cold water for at least 24 hours; it is then cooked as indicated for the carapace and plastron in the recipe for Clear Turtle Soup.

Once it is cooked it should be treated exactly as described when using fresh turtle. The cooking liquid is used to moisten the beef from which rich gelatinous Bouillon should be made and at the last moment the diced cooked flesh should be added to the soup together with the Madeira.

912 Potage à la Tortue Verte—Green Turtle Soup, using the commercially prepared product

Place 1 small chicken lightly coloured in the oven, in a suitable pan with 250 g (9 oz) knuckle of veal, 1 small onion stuck with half a clove, half a root of parsley, 15 g (½ oz) mushroom trimmings, a bouquet containing some leek, a small piece each of celery, thyme, bayleaf and mace, and a little basil and marjoram.

Moisten with 2½ litres (4¼ pt or 5⅜ U.S. pt) Ordinary Consommé, bring to the boil and allow to cook gently for 2 hours. Strain the liquid through a clean cloth and add 15 g (½ oz) arrowroot diluted with a little Bouillon; mix well with a whisk, adjust the seasoning with salt, simmer and skim carefully for 15 minutes.

Heat a 1 litre (1¾ pt or 4½ U.S. cups) tin of Green Turtle Soup in a Bain-marie; drain off the pieces of turtle meat, cut it into approximately 3 cm (1 in) squares and add together with its liquid to the prepared soup. Finish the soup with a little Cayenne and when serving, add at the last moment, a few drops of Worcestershire sauce and 1 dl (3½ fl oz or ½ U.S. cup) Sherry.

CHAPTER 4

COLD AND HOT HORS-D'OEUVRE

The name of these types of preparation clearly defines their place in the menu. They are adjuncts, and if omitted from the menu should not alter the general harmony of the meal, especially where dinner menus are concerned.

It is therefore indicated that they should be composed of light items of a delicate nature and they should not constitute a complete dish in themselves. But if these items are any less in terms of quantity they should be compensated for this by being of an excellent taste and by giving careful attention to presentation—both of these should be above reproach.

There are two types—cold Hors-d'oeuvre and hot Hors-d'oeuvre—each being entirely different from the other, both from the point of view of preparation and service.

COLD HORS-D'OEUVRE

As a general rule cold Hors-d'oeuvre are suitable only in a meal which does not include a soup—these ideas are explained in the Introduction to the Chapter on Soups. However, this rule is not always observed especially in *à la Carte* restaurants; it is a means more usually of serving de-luxe Hors-d'oeuvre such as caviare, oysters, plovers' eggs etc. which do not have an undue influence on the digestion as would be so in the case of fish, salads and marinated vegetables. It is often noted that at least most of the time when these are offered, their use as Hors-d'oeuvre is nothing more than an expedient to occupy the customer whilst waiting for the preparation of the dishes he may have ordered.

Therefore, the use of cold Hors-d'oeuvre in this case can be justified up to a certain point but it is to be regretted that their use has degenerated into a habit dictated by circumstances and where there is nothing really to justify it. The responsibility for this abuse is due largely to the infatuation in recent times for things Russian. It is well known that in Russia it is customary to arrange a buffet composed of special savoury pastries, smoked fish etc. on a sideboard adjoining the dining-room; the diners partake of these items together with strong spirits whilst standing up and waiting to take their place at table. The total of these different items which constitute this kind of prologue to a meal is given the name of *Zakouskis*.

Hosts and restaurateurs more zealous than logical, have introduced this fashion of *Zakouskis* without taking into account those differences which the influence of climate can have on different races in terms of taste, habit and temperament.

It is a fact that with very rare exceptions the items served have nothing in common with *Zakouskis* except the name; more often than not they are ordinary cold Hors-d'oeuvre served at the table in the dining-room which is already a grave breach of the principle of the service of *Zakouskis*. One comes to the conclusion therefore that it is absolutely ridiculous to cloak such a simple ordinary thing as cold Hors-d'oeuvres under such a strange almost barbarous name; happily it is now very rare to find this Russian term appearing on menus.

It is suggested that there is no good reason for the inclusion of cold Hors-d'oeuvre in a dinner menu, that their use is contrary to logic and can only result in spoiling the taste of the soup which follows. However, an exception to this statement can be made in favour of caviare which, when fresh, has a light nutty flavour and can favourably impress the palate. This observation also holds good for fine quality oysters provided that they are accompanied by a very dry Hock or white Bordeaux wine. But to repeat again, fish of all types and in all forms, salads and marinated vegetables should be rigorously excluded from dinner menus.

On the contrary, however, the use of cold Hors-d'oeuvre is traditional for luncheon menus where they are not only necessary but indispensable. The variety and composition of items combined with correct and careful presentation give a colourful appearance to the table and a favourable impression to the guests on entering the dining-room.

It is because of their importance, that they are

now prepared in a department of the kitchen whereas formerly they were prepared in the pantry or stillroom. The result of this change has produced a major improvement in the quality of Hors-d'oeuvre, as much in their preparation as in their variety and presentation; perhaps in no other area of the culinary art has there been such an improvement in recent years.

The variety of Hors-d'oeuvre is infinite and it is impossible to indicate even approximately the number of combinations which an ingenious artist can effect in this area where every single commodity employed lends itself to a variety of uses.

Also it should be stated that a good Hors-d'oeuvre cook is a most valuable member of the kitchen staff; this area, although of secondary importance, requires qualities seldom met with together—a sure and fine sense of taste, a creative ability, an artistic touch and professional knowledge. The Hors-d'oeuvre cook should be able to produce first class, well presented items from very little; it is the quality of his produce rather than the nature of the commodities he uses, which defines the value of his work.

Note: The various butters used in the following recipes can be found in the section on Composed Butters in the Chapter on Sauces.

For preference, savoury butters should be prepared as required; if made in advance they should be kept cool in a covered basin. A suitable and useful variation of composed butters for Hors-d'oeuvre is to add up to a third of its quantity of ordinary or whipped cream. Butters prepared in this way are suitable for garnishing small tartlets or Canapés, using a fancy piping tube.

They may also be used to fill small cornets of smoked salmon, ham or tongue which should then be placed in position on small shapes of toast, using a spot of butter to keep them in place.

913 Aceto-dolce (*Italy*)

This is an Italian product composed of a mixture of small fruits and vegetables; they are first of all pickled in vinegar and then preserved in a syrup of muscatel grape juice and honey with a small amount of mustard. The mixture is served as it is and is obtainable as a commercial product.

914 Achards

This is a Macédoine of vegetables preserved in vinegar and mustard and can be obtained as a commercial product.

915 Agoursis

This is a type of pickled Russian cucumber; cut them into slices and arrange in raviers.

916 Allumettes

Roll out a band of half puff paste or puff paste trimmings approximately 7 cm (3 in) wide by 7–8 mm ($\frac{1}{4}$ in) thick; spread with a thin layer of forcemeat seasoned with Cayenne, which is more often than not a fish forcemeat. Cut into rectangles $2\frac{1}{2}$ cm (1 in) wide, place on a baking tray and bake in a moderate oven for 12–14 minutes. The type of forcemeat used should be indicated in the title of the Allumette.

917 Allumettes aux Anchois—Anchovy Fingers

These are rectangles of half puff paste or puff pastry trimmings, as above, coated with a thin layer of fish forcemeat flavoured with anchovy essence. Arrange fillets of anchovy on the forcemeat either lengthways or trellis fashion and bake in a moderate oven for approximately 12 minutes.

918 Filets d'Anchois—Anchovy Fillets

Cut the fillets into thin strips, marinate in a little oil and arrange them in a ravier either trellis fashion or in straight lines. Decorate according to taste with white and yolk of hard-boiled egg, chopped parsley and capers and sprinkle lightly with oil. The fillets can also be dressed on a layer of finely shredded lettuce.

919 Anchois Frais Marinés—Marinated Fresh Anchovies

Take freshly caught anchovies, clean them well, place in salt for 2 hours then plunge into very hot fat just to stiffen them. Drain and place in a not too acidulated marinade and leave for 2–3 days. Serve in a ravier with a little of the marinade.

920 Medaillons d'Anchois—Anchovy Medallions

Take fillets of anchovy marinated in oil and wrap them around the edges of thick slices of cooked potato or baked beetroot. Fill the centre according to taste with chopped egg, caviare, purée of soft roes etc.

921 Paupiettes d'Anchois

Lightly flatten anchovy fillets and spread them with a purée of any kind of cooked fish mixed with Mayonnaise and seasoned with Cayenne. Roll up into *Paupiettes* and pipe a little Anchovy Butter on top of each.

922 Anchois aux Poivrons—Anchovies with Pimento

Arrange anchovy fillets which have been marinated in oil in a dish alternating with strips of pimento; finish with chopped hard-boiled egg, parsley and capers as for Anchovy Fillets.

923 Anchois des Tamarins
Place a thick layer of grated warm cooked potatoes along the centre of a ravier; season with a little oil and vinegar and sprinkle with chopped Fines Herbes. Around the side of the potatoes arrange Anchovy Paupiettes prepared as above with a black olive on top of each.

924 Anguille Fumée—Smoked Eel
This is served in the same way as all smoked fish; cut into sections, remove the skin and bone and arrange on a serviette.

925 Anguille au Vin Blanc et Paprika—Eel with White Wine and Paprika
Cut medium-sized eels into sections 8 cm (3 in) long and cook them as for Matelote au Vin Blanc (1565) with the addition of a little paprika.

Allow to cool in the cooking liquor, remove the pieces, discard the skin and detach the fillets along the length. Arrange these fillets in a ravier and cover with the cooking liquor which has been skimmed of fat and lightly thickened. Allow to set in a cool place.

926 Artichauts à la Grecque
Choose very small artichokes making sure that they do not have developed chokes; trim and shorten the leaves then blanch in boiling salted water and refresh them. Prepare a marinade as follows: for 15–20 artichokes place in a pan 1 litre ($1\frac{3}{4}$ pt or $4\frac{1}{2}$ U.S. cups) water; $1\frac{1}{2}$ dl (5 fl oz or $\frac{5}{8}$ U.S. cup) oil; the juice of 3 lemons and 10 g ($\frac{1}{3}$ oz) salt; add 50 g (2 oz) each of fennel and celery; 10 corianders; 10 peppercorns; a sprig of thyme and 2 bayleaves. Bring to the boil for a few minutes then add the artichokes and cook gently for 15 minutes. When ready, allow to cool in the marinade and serve very cold with a little of the marinade.

927 Small Garnished Artichoke Bottoms
Marinate small cooked artichoke bottoms in a little oil and vinegar; garnish according to taste with, for example, a purée of fish or soft roes; a small Salpicon or Macédoine of vegetables bound with Mayonnaise or any other suitable filling in keeping with the artichokes.

928 Barquettes and Tartlets
These are a type of small Croustade or case made with short paste; Barquettes are made in small boat-shape moulds and tartlets in small round moulds both cut out with a fancy cutter. They play an important part in the repertoire and represent a type of hors-d'oeuvre which is classed under the name *Frivolités*.

Paste for Barquettes and Tartlets: Mix together to a paste 500 g (1 lb 2 oz) sifted flour, a pinch of salt, 250 g (9 oz) cool melted butter, 1 egg, 2 egg yolks and a few drops of water, handling it as little as possible. Roll into a ball, cover and allow to rest in a cool place for 2 hours. Line the moulds with this paste and cook without colouring in the usual manner.

Fillings for Barquettes and Tartlets: These fillings are usually based on a composed butter or a jelly—the first type permits the use of all those garnishes used for Canapés and other similar items according to taste and inspiration; for the second type the filling is usually composed of a layer of any kind of Mousse in the bottom of the pastry case which is then covered with any suitable garnish of a different colour, decorated and coated with jelly.

Example: Garnish the bottom of the Barquette or tartlet case with a layer of Mousse of prawn, crayfish or salmon and on top place a nice white poached oyster or a round slice of hard-boiled egg cut with a fancy cutter; decorate the centre with a little lobster coral or a diamond-shaped piece of fillet sole decorated with a leaf of chervil and coat with jelly to the level of the side of the case. Obviously it is possible with taste and inventiveness to create a considerable variety of this type of Hors-d'oeuvre, many more than it is possible to indicate here.

929 Beetroot for cutting into shapes
Choose beetroots of a good colour and for preference cook them by baking in the oven; when very cold cut them into sections and fashion in the shape of small cases, Barquettes etc. They can then be filled or garnished as required.

Note: Beetroot provides a very useful item of decoration for Hors-d'oeuvre but because its colour runs easily on to any object it touches, it is advisable to use it to decorate at the last moment; when it is part of a salad it should be mixed in at the very last minute.

930 Betterave en Salade—Beetroot Salad
Bake the beetroots in the oven and when cold cut into Julienne; add one-third its volume of baked onion, kept fairly firm and also cut into Julienne; mix with oil and vinegar and season in the same way as an ordinary salad. Arrange in a ravier and sprinkle with chopped parsley and chervil.

931 Betterave en Salade à la Crème—Beetroot Salad with Cream
Prepare a Julienne of beetroot and onion as for Beetroot Salad and mix it with Mustard and Cream Sauce (207).

932 Bigarreaux Confits—Pickled White-heart Cherries
Choose very firm cherries and prepare them by leaving 2 cm (1 in) of the stalk. Place in a preserving jar with a few leaves of tarragon distributed among them. Cover with boiling vinegar containing 8 g ($\frac{1}{3}$ oz) salt per 1 litre ($1\frac{3}{4}$ pt or $4\frac{1}{2}$ U.S. cups) vinegar and allow to macerate for 15–20 days. Serve in a ravier with a few spoonfuls of the marinade.

933 Boeuf Fumé de Hambourg—Smoked Hamburg Beef
Cut this beef in very thin slices and either roll in cornets or lay flat in dishes. Serve very cold.

934 Butter for Hors-d'oeuvre
See the notes at the beginning of this Section.

935 Canapés
Canapés or Toasts which are quite different from Tartines (garnished slices of bread and butter) are made from white bread cut into various shapes and no more than $\frac{1}{2}$ cm ($\frac{1}{5}$ in) thick. These are then either fried in clarified butter or more usually toasted.

As a general rule the garnish for a Canapé should consist of only one main item. But without destroying this principle, a combination of various items is acceptable provided that the flavours and presentation are in harmony. The best sort of garnish for Canapés is fresh butter mixed with a purée of, or very finely chopped meat, poultry, shellfish, fish, cheese etc. It is recommended that the toast should be very well buttered whilst still hot so as to keep it soft and this holds good for any garnish used for Canapés even when it appears that butter does not enter logically into the composition of the garnish, e.g. when it includes marinated fish, anchovy, fillets of herring etc.

When garnishing Canapés with compound butter based on a purée it is recommended that this is done by using a piping bag and fancy tube. This method is correct, quick and gives the opportunity for individual artistry in presentation.

936 Canapés à l'Amiral (*fancy oval*)
Coat the toasts with Shrimp Butter, border with shrimps and fill the centres with the separated grains of cooked crawfish eggs.

937 Canapés d'Anchois (*diamond*)
Lightly coat the toasts with Anchovy Butter, pipe a border with the same butter and fill the centres with fillets of anchovy arranged trellis-fashion and decorate with chopped hard-boiled egg.

938 Canapés à l'Arlequine (*shape optional*)
Pipe the toasts with borders of different coloured butters and fill the centres chequer-fashion with contrasting coloured butters to justify the name.

939 Canapés au Caviar (*round*)
Coat the toasts with Caviare Butter and pipe borders around them using a small fancy tube and softened fresh butter. Place fresh caviare in the centres and serve very finely chopped onion separately.

940 Canapés aux Crevettes (*round*)
Coat the toasts with very pink Shrimp Butter and pipe borders around with the same butter; fill the centres with a rose pattern of shrimps with a caper in the middles.

941 Canapés City (*round*)
Coat the toasts with a thick layer of the following mixture: 125 g ($4\frac{1}{2}$ oz) soft fresh butter, 60 g (2 oz) each of freshly grated Gruyère and Parmesan cheese, $\frac{1}{2}$ tbs thick cream, a pinch of salt and a touch of Cayenne.

Cover the layer with 2 half circles to the same size of the Canapé, one cut from a thin slice of Saucisson de Lyons and the other from Gruyère cheese.

942 Canapés à la Danoise
Heat a slice of brown bread cut to the usual thickness; coat it with a layer of Horseradish Butter and cover this with alternate strips of smoked salmon, thin strips of herring fillets marinated in white wine and lines of caviare. Carefully cut out the garnished slice with a plain oval cutter.

943 Canapés à l'Ecarlate
Coat a toasted slice of bread with a layer of Mustard Butter half the thickness of the bread. Cover this with very thin slices of cooked salt ox tongue. Allow the butter to set firm then cut into shapes with a star-shaped cutter dipped in boiling water. Pipe a little decoration of Mustard Butter in the centre of each one.

944 Canapés d'Ecrevisses (*crescent*)
Coat the toasts with Crayfish Butter and pipe with a border of fresh butter. Fill the centres with a nice crayfish tail cut into two along the length, placing the thickest ends together.

945 Canapés au Gibier (*rectangular*)
Coat the toasts with fresh butter seasoned with a little Cayenne and garnish with any cooked game either cut in very thin slices or finely chopped, whichever is preferable.

946 Canapés de Homard (*square*)
Coat the toasts with Lobster Butter and border the edges with finely chopped hard-boiled egg mixed with Mayonnaise. Garnish the centres with a nice slice of lobster.

947 Canapés Lucile (*plain oval*)
Coat the toasts with Mustard Butter and border the edges with thin strips of chopped very red ox tongue. Fill the centres with chopped chicken.

948 Canapés au Poisson (*square*)
Coat the toasts with Soft Roe Butter and border the edges with pink butter. Fill the centres with chopped turbot or fillet of sole.

949 Canapés Printaniers (*round*)
Coat the toasts with Montpellier Butter and border the edges with chopped hard-boiled egg yolk. Fill the centres with leaves of garden cress or small leaves of watercress.

950 Canapés Rochelais (*round*)
Coat the toasts with Soft Roe Butter and pipe a border of Crayfish Butter around the edges. In the centres place a nice oyster which has been poached in white wine.

951 Carolines
These are small éclairs made from unsweetened Chou Paste and stuffed with various purées such as chicken, tongue, game, foie gras etc. They are then coated with a Sauce Chaud-froid in keeping with the filling then finally glazed with aspic jelly.

Carolines can also be used as a decorative border for certain cold dishes such as Aspics, Pains, Mousses etc.

952 Caviare
This is served from a special container surrounded in ice and accompanied by Blinis (1106) or thin slices of buttered rye bread.

Note: Caviare by which is meant that of excellent quality having large transparent grains of a light colour, is without doubt the finest of all Hors-d'oeuvre. It is sometimes accompanied by finely chopped onion and lemon which is not to be recommended at all as fresh caviare of a perfect flavour has no need of condimentation.

In place of fresh caviare, pressed or salted caviare is sometimes used in the preparation of certain Hors-d'oeuvre, but because their quality is much less than that of fresh caviare they should never be served on their own in the same way as the fresh.

953 Céleri à la Bonne Femme
Finely slice the celery across the stalks, add the same quantity of pippin apples cut in small quarters and also finely sliced. Mix together with Mustard and Cream Sauce (207).

954 Céleri à la Grecque
Select very small or medium-sized sticks of celery; cut in two or four according to size; blanch, refresh and prepare them in the same way as Artichokes à la Grecque.

955 Céleri-rave—Celeriac
Clean, peel and cut the celeriac in thick Julienne or into Paysanne and mix with either Mustard and Cream Sauce (207) or mustard-flavoured Sauce Vinaigrette.

956 Cèpes Marinés—Marinated Flap Mushrooms
Select very small fresh flap mushrooms, blanch them for 7–8 minutes in boiling water then drain and cool. Place in an earthenware terrine and cover with a boiling marinade made as follows:

Proportions for 1 kg (2¼ lb) of flap mushrooms:
5 dl (18 fl oz or 2¼ U.S. cups) vinegar; 1½ dl (5 fl oz or ⅝ U.S. cup) oil, 10 g (⅓ oz) crushed garlic, a little thyme and crushed bayleaf, 6 peppercorns, a pinch of coriander and fennel and a small root of parsley. Bring to the boil and simmer very gently for 10 minutes before passing through a strainer over the flap mushrooms.

Allow to marinate for 8 days then serve with a little of the marinade.

Note: When bottling or canning these mushrooms allow 35 minutes boiling time for a receptacle of 1 litre (1¾ pt or 4½ U.S. cups) capacity, 25 minutes for a 5 dl (18 fl oz or 2¼ U.S. cups) and 20 minutes for a 2½ dl (9 fl oz or 1⅛ U.S. cups) size.

957 Cerises au Vinaigre—Pickled Cherries
Remove the stalks from unripe Morello cherries; place the cherries in preserving jars along with 3 cloves, a small piece of cinnamon, a pinch of grated nutmeg and 10 g (⅓ oz) tarragon per 1 kg (2¼ lb) cherries. Boil 1 litre (1¾ pt or 4½ U.S. cups) vinegar with 200 g (7 oz) brown sugar, allow to cool and pour over the cherries. Leave for 15 days and serve with a little of the marinade. Cherries made in this way are obtainable as a commercial product.

958 Cerneaux au Verjus—Green Walnuts with Verjuice
This Hors-d'oeuvre can be made during the time from the beginning of August to about the 15th September, that is to say, the time when the kernel of the nut is completely formed. Open the nuts, extract the kernels without breaking them and remove the yellow skin which covers them. Place

the kernels in plenty of very cold water; remove, drain and arrange in raviers just before serving then sprinkle with well decanted verjuice. Finally sprinkle with coarse salt and, if desired, chopped chervil.

959 Various Cervelas Sausages
These should be sliced and arranged overlapping on a dish with a bouquet of picked parsley.

960 Cervelles Robert
Use lamb or mutton brains; soak them well in running cold water to extract the blood. Remove the membranes then poach the brains in a Court-bouillon. Cool, cut into small slices, trim them neatly and arrange in raviers. Cover with Mustard and Cream Sauce containing a purée of the trimmings of brain and a very fine Julienne of white of celery.

Note: The slices of brain may be dressed in tartlet cases; in this case place a border of chopped parsley around the edge and cover the centre with chopped hard-boiled egg yolk.

961 Choux-fleurs—Cauliflower
Cut the cauliflowers into small flowerets and cook in boiling salted water keeping them slightly firm. Remove, drain and marinate with oil and vinegar. Serve in a ravier coated with Mustard and Cream Sauce.

962 Choux Rouges—Red Cabbage
Finely shred the cabbage and marinate in vinegar for approximately 6 hours. Drain and add 100 g ($3\frac{1}{2}$ oz) peeled sliced pippin apples per 500 g (1 lb 2 oz) cabbage and season with salt and pepper as for an ordinary salad.

963 Paupiettes de Choux Verts
This Hors-d'oeuvre may be prepared from any kind of cabbage and may be prepared in either of the following ways:

1) Cook large green cabbage leaves in boiling salted water, keeping them slightly firm. Refresh, drain well and cut into small rectangles; cover each with a layer of boiled onion, rice salad or any other suitable savoury mixture. Season, and roll them into *Paupiettes*. Arrange in raviers and sprinkle with a little oil at the last moment.
2) Take half the cooked cabbage leaves and spread with a layer of the chosen mixture; cover each with another leaf then cut out with a $2\frac{1}{2}$ cm (1 in) round pastry cutter. Arrange these in a ravier and sprinkle with a little oil.

964 Concombres à la Danoise
Cut cucumbers into sections and trim to the shape of Barquettes or small cases; fill the centres with a mixture composed of equal quantities of purée of smoked salmon, diced fillets of herring and chopped hard-boiled egg. Sprinkle the surface of the mixture with a little grated and chopped horseradish.

965 Concombres Farcis—Stuffed Cucumbers
Cut the cucumbers into shapes as in the previous recipe. Blanch, refresh, drain and marinate them with oil and vinegar for a few minutes. Fill the centres with a suitable purée, Macédoine or salad etc.

966 Concombre en Salade—Cucumber Salad
Peel the cucumber and cut in half along the length; remove the seeds and finely slice the remainder.

Sprinkle with fine salt and leave for 25–30 minutes so as to extract some of the moisture. Drain well, arrange in a ravier and at the last minute season with vinegar, oil and pepper and sprinkle with chopped chervil.

Note: The small green cucumbers and English cucumbers do not need salting in advance but should be seasoned at the last moment.

967 Cornets d'York—Cornets of Ham
Cut very thin slices of lean ham into triangles 9 cm ($3\frac{1}{2}$ in) high × 7 cm (3 in) along the base; roll into cornets and fill the insides with chopped jelly, using a piping bag and plain tube. Arrange in a circle on a dish with sprigs of very green parsley in the centre.

968 Creams for Hors-d'oeuvre
By using caviare, smoked salmon, tunny fish, game etc. it is possible to make very fine creams which may be used to replace butters in the preparation of Hors-d'oeuvre.

Preparation:
Finely pound 125 g ($4\frac{1}{2}$ oz) of the chosen commodity and mix in 2 tbs very fresh thick cream a little at a time. Pass through a fine sieve, season accordingly and finally mix in 3 tbs stiffly whipped cream.

969 Crèmes Moulées—Moulded Creams
With the above creams it is possible to make a variety of small and delicate Hors d'oeuvres which can be highly recommended.

In this case the selected cream, prepared as in the previous recipe is mixed with a few tablespoons of melted jelly in keeping with the basic ingredient and before adding the whipped cream. This mixture is then placed in very small lightly oiled fancy moulds—the fancy moulds used for making petits fours are very suitable for this purpose. Allow to set in a cool place and demould at the last moment on to a suitable dish.

970 Duchesses
These are made from unsweetened Chou Paste as for Carolines but in the shape of small chou buns. They are filled with a suitable filling usually by means of a piping tube. However, they are different in that they are glazed with jelly only, without first being coated with Sauce Chaud-froid.

971 Duchesses Nantua
Fill the chou buns with a fine purée of crayfish, glaze with pink jelly and sprinkle with chopped pistachio nuts.

972 Duchesses à la Reine
Fill the chou buns with a fine purée of chicken and cream and glaze with white jelly.

973 Duchesses Sultane
Fill the chou buns with chicken purée flavoured with pistachio butter; glaze with jelly and place half a skinned pistachio or a pinch of chopped pistachio on each.

974 Duchesses au Caviar
Fill the chou buns with fresh or creamed caviare, glaze with jelly and serve very cold.

975 Duchesses à la Norvégienne
Fill the chou buns with a purée of Kilkis and butter and glaze with jelly.

976 Duchesses au Saumon Fumé
Fill the chou buns with a purée of smoked salmon and butter or creamed smoked salmon; glaze with jelly and serve very cold.

977 Eclairs Karoly
Prepare some very small Chou Paste éclairs and fill them with a purée of the trimmings and intestines of woodcock prepared *à la fine Champagne* then rubbed through a fine sieve and mixed with butter and well seasoned.

Coat the éclairs with brown Sauce Chaud-froid, decorate with a few shapes of truffle and glaze with jelly.

978 Eperlans Marinés—Marinated Smelts
The preparation of this fish belongs to that category of culinary preparations which are known under the general term of Escabèche. This is a corruption of the Spanish word Escabecha of which the following recipe is an example.

979 Escabèche
This term should always be followed by the name of the basic ingredient with which it is prepared: e.g. Escabèche d'Eperlans, Escabèche de Rouget etc.

Method:
Whichever fish is being used, first clean them well, dry, pass through flour and colour in very hot oil; drain well and arrange them in a deep dish or other suitable utensil.

Reheat the remainder of the oil until lightly smoking and add 8 cloves of unpeeled garlic per 5 dl (18 fl oz or 2¼ U.S. cups) of the oil, plus half a carrot and an onion cut in very thin slices. Allow to fry for a few moments, allow to cool then add 3 dl (½ pt or 1¼ U.S. cups) vinegar, 1½ dl (5 fl oz or ⅝ U.S. cup) water, 10 g (⅓ oz) coarse salt, a sprig of thyme, ½ a bayleaf, a few parsley stalks and 2 small chillies.

Bring to the boil, simmer for 12 minutes and pour the boiling liquid and ingredients over the fish. Allow to marinate for 24 hours.

Serve the fish very cold with a few spoonfuls of the marinade.

980 Pieds de Fenouils—Fennel
Cut the fennel into two or four pieces according to size and prepare them exactly as for Artichokes à la Grecque (926).

981 Figues—Figs
These are only served for Hors-d'oeuvre when fully ripe. They should be arranged on very green vine leaves surrounded with crushed ice.

982 Filet d'Anvers
Cut in very thin triangular slices and roll into cornets as for Cornets de York.

983 Foie gras
If the foie gras is obtained in a long cylindrical shape, cut it into thin slices; otherwise mould it into small shell shapes. It should always be prepared at the last minute, arranged immediately on a serviette on a dish and served very cold.

984 Frivolités
On a menu, this word describes a presentation of small Hors-d'oeuvre of which light moulded creams, Barquettes and tartlets are the best examples. The word is clear and explicit and no other can describe the delicate nature of this type of Hors-d'oeuvre which is effectively a light-hearted beginning to the meal.

985 Fruits de Mer
Under this name is included all salt water shellfish which can be served raw as a selection, with the exception of oysters. They must be very fresh and should be accompanied with very thin slices of brown bread and butter.

Note: This term is also applied to a mixture of cooked shellfish.

986 Goujons à la Russe
Poach the gudgeons very gently in a well flavoured white wine Court-bouillon and allow them to cool completely in the liquid. Drain and dry them, coat with jellied Mayonnaise; sprinkle lightly with finely chopped parsley and place in a cold room to set. Serve as they are or arranged on small Canapés of the same shape and size as the fish.

987 Harengs à la Dieppoise
Choose very fresh herrings. Clean them, arrange in a buttered shallow pan and cover with boiling marinade prepared in advance. The marinade is made with two-thirds white wine, one-third vinegar, slices of fluted carrot, onion rings, thyme, bayleaf, parsley stalks and sliced shallots. Poach the herring gently for 12 minutes and allow them to cool in the liquid.

Serve the herrings very cold with a little marinade, rings of carrot and onion, and thin slices of grooved lemon.

988 Herring Fillets
Remove the fillets from cured or salted herrings, skin them and soak in milk to remove the salt. Trim carefully, arrange them in a dish and coat with a sauce made as follows: To two parts of Mayonnaise add one part purée of cooked soft roes, dilute with a little vinegar, season with Cayenne and mix in a suitable quantity of equal parts of finely chopped onion, parsley, chives, celery, chervil and tarragon.

989 Harengs aux Haricots Verts—Herrings with French Beans
For this dish use the special herrings as prepared by Dutch fishermen from the first catch of the season which are macerated for a very short time in a specially flavoured brine which is their own particular secret.

To serve, simply remove the skins of the herrings, arrange them as they are in a dish with fresh picked parsley. Serve accompanied either with a salad of freshly cooked French beans or buttered French beans.

990 Harengs à la Livonienne
Select nice smoked herrings, fillet them and reserve the heads and tails.

Skin the fillets and cut the flesh into dice; add an equal quantity of diced cooked potatoes and russet apples, flavour with chopped parsley, chervil and fennel and mix with a little oil and vinegar.

Arrange the mixture on a dish in the shape of fish and place the heads and tails at either end to imitate whole herrings.

991 Harengs Lucas
Soak smoked herrings in lukewarm water, then skin and fillet them and place to soak in milk. Cut the fillets into strips, arrange them in a dish and cover with a sauce made in the following way: place 6 hard-boiled egg yolks in a basin and mix to a smooth paste; add 1 tbs mustard and a little vinegar and mix in 3 dl ($\frac{1}{2}$ pt or $1\frac{1}{4}$ U.S. cups) oil little by little proceeding as for Sauce Mayonnaise. Finish with a little chopped shallot and chervil and 2 tbs chopped gherkin; this sauce should be well seasoned.

992 Harengs Roulés—Roll Mops
Select firm white fleshed salted herrings with soft roes and soak them in milk to remove the salt. Fillet the fish, removing as many bones as possible, coat the inside surfaces of the fillets with a mixture of made English mustard and finely chopped onion then roll them up and tie with string.

Arrange in an earthenware dish with the roes. Boil sufficient vinegar with a Bouquet garni, onion, peppercorns and cloves to cover the fillets, then strain over the fish whilst boiling and allow to cool.

When cold, remove the fish, pass the roes through a fine sieve and mix this purée back into the vinegar with 1 dl ($3\frac{1}{2}$ fl oz or $\frac{1}{2}$ U.S. cup) oil per 5 dl (18 fl oz or $2\frac{1}{4}$ U.S. cups) vinegar.

Pour this mixture over the herrings and allow to marinate for 2–3 days. To serve, arrange the roll mops in raviers with a little of the marinade.

993 Harengs à la Russe
Cut fillets of smoked herring into thin slices and arrange in a dish, overlapping and alternating with slices of cooked potatoes. Sprinkle with oil and vinegar and a little chopped chervil, shallot, fennel and tarragon.

994 Haricot Verts—French Beans
Cook in boiling salted water keeping them fairly firm; drain and whilst still hot, mix gently with a little oil and vinegar. When cold place in raviers and sprinkle with chopped parsley, chervil and chives.

995 Huîtres—Oysters
These are the Hors-d'oeuvre *par excellence* and can be used for lunch and dinner menus.

When opened, oysters should be left in the deep

shell with the juice; they must be served very cold and therefore they are customarily served on crushed ice.

Serve accompanied with very thin slices of brown bread and butter, Sauce à la Mignonette which is vinegar well seasoned with fresh coarsely milled peppercorns, and halves of lemons.

996 Huîtres Natives au Caviar—Oysters with Caviare
This is the perfect example of the de luxe Hors-d'oeuvre.

Fill small cooked tartlet cases with caviare leaving a hollow in the centre. Place a bearded Whitstable or Burnham oyster which has been seasoned with milled pepper and a drop of lemon juice, in the centre.

997 Huîtres Marinées—Pickled Oysters
This product can be obtained commercially.

998 Anchois de Norvège—Kilkis or Norwegian Anchovies
This Hors-d'oeuvre is a commercial product; the fish is arranged in raviers with a little of their brine.

999 Macédoine
This Hors-d'oeuvre is composed of small white onions, small bouquets of lightly blanched cauliflower, small fresh gherkins, French beans, very small pimentos and slices of blanched artichoke bottoms.

Place all these ingredients in a stoneware jar and cover with boiling vinegar which has been lightly salted and well flavoured with mustard. Allow the preparation to marinate long enough for the flavours to penetrate before using.

An alternative name for this preparation is *Variantes.*

1000 Maquereaux Marinés—Marinated Mackerel
Choose very small mackerel and marinate them in the same way as Harengs à la Dieppoise.

1001 Cantaloup Melon
These should be chosen when just ripe and well perfumed. Serve on green leaves on crushed ice or surrounded with pieces of clear ice.

1002 Melon Cocktail
Cut the flesh of ripe melon into 2 cm ($\frac{3}{4}$ in) cubes or into slices and place in a timbale on ice. Sprinkle with sugar and allow to chill well.

Just before serving, sprinkle with Maraschino, Kirsch, brandy or white Port according to taste and arrange in small glass coupes in the same way as other fruit cocktails.

Note: These coupes can also be served as a sweet, in this case a spoonful of Glace à l'Orange should be placed on top of the melon.

1003 Melon Frappé au Vins—Iced Melon with various wines
Choose a Cantaloup or other similar type melon which is just ripe. Make an incision around the stalk approximately 8 cm ($3\frac{1}{4}$ in) diameter and remove this piece. Using a silver spoon remove the seeds and filament from inside then pour $2\frac{1}{2}$ dl (9 fl oz or $1\frac{1}{8}$ U.S. cups) Madeira, Port, Marsala or brandy into the melon. Add 2 tbs caster sugar and replace the top; place on crushed ice in the cold room for 2–3 hours.
To serve: send to the table whole; take out the top piece of melon and remove the inside by scooping it out with a silver spoon into shell-shaped pieces; place on iced plates with a little of the wine and serve to the guests immediately.

1004 Petits Melons Confits—Pickled Small Melons
Select very small melons picked a little while after their flowers have dropped off. Cover them with salt for 10–12 hours then wash them in a solution of two-thirds vinegar and one-third water.

Place in stoneware jars with the usual pickling spices and cover with either hot or cold vinegar—the hot should be used if the melons are required to be kept very green. They are ready for use in 7–8 days.

1005 Various Vegetable Stalks
The tender inside parts of the stems of large artichokes and the stumps of cabbage, cauliflower, cos lettuce etc. once they are trimmed of their fibrous parts, can be used as a base for delicate salads or can be prepared in the same way as Artichauts à la Grecque.

The stumps of frizzy endive or Batavian endive can also be prepared à la Grecque after simply being washed and peeled.

1006 Mortadella
This type of large Italian sausage should be thinly sliced, rolled up and arranged in dishes.

1007 Moules—Mussels
Choose medium-sized mussels and cook them in the usual way then remove from the shells and beard them. Place in a bowl and add some very finely sliced white celery and mix with Mustard and Cream Sauce well flavoured with milled pepper.

Note: The mussels can either be placed in a ravier as they are or replaced in the half shells before arranging in the dish.

1008 Mûres—Mulberries
Mulberries should be very large and very ripe; serve arranged on vine leaves.

1009 Museau et Palais de Boeuf—Ox Cheek and Muzzle
Blanch the cheek and muzzle of beef, refresh under running cold water, then scrape the insides to remove the rough surfaces. Cook in a light *Blanc* and allow to cool in the liquid.
To serve: remove from the cooking liquid, wash off and dry, cut into very thin slices then mix together with chopped onion, oil, vinegar, salt, pepper and chopped parsley. Serve arranged in raviers sprinkled with chopped parsley.

1010 Olives
All olives of whichever type are suitable for Hors-d'oeuvre and should be served as they are with a little of their brine.

1011 Olives Farcies—Stuffed Olives
Select very large olives and remove the stones either by cutting spiral fashion with a knife or using an olive stoner.

Stuff them according to taste with a composed butter such as salmon, tunny fish, sardine etc.

Note: Olives which have been stuffed with a raw force-meat and then cooked are not suitable for Hors-d'oeuvre; they are best used for garnishing.

1012 Oeufs Farcis Garnis—Stuffed Eggs
Hard-boiled eggs for Hors-d'oeuvre can be prepared in many ways and may be stuffed with all kinds of purées, Salpicons, Macédoines, salads etc. which are suitable for use in this part of the menu. The most important need for their preparation is inventiveness and artistry and even a simple but well thought out idea can be worthy of a more grandiose title.

1013 Oeufs de Vanneau—Lapwing or Plovers Eggs
Cook the eggs in boiling water for 8 minutes then cool them under running cold water. Remove the top 1 cm ($\frac{2}{5}$ in) of the shells from the pointed end and arrange the eggs, shelled ends uppermost on a bed of mustard and cress. They may also be presented arranged in an imitation nest of piped butter.

1014 Pains à la Française—Filled French Rolls
These are small oblong or oval-shaped rolls made from a dough containing butter.

Cut them open along one side, remove the soft centre and fill as required with smoked salmon; sliced meats, purées, Salpicons, salads etc. This type of roll is used only for receptions and buffets and is included here for the sake of convenience.

1015 Pains à la Varsovienne
These small rolls are the same as in the previous recipe but filled with Russian salad containing diced fillet of salted herring.

1016 Pâté d'Alouettes—Lark Pâté
Pâté or terrine of lark can be used as an Hors-d'oeuvre; serve very cold cut in thin slices, and arranged overlapping in a circle on a dish with chopped aspic jelly in the centre.

1017 Pickles and Piccalilli
These are of different kinds and are usually bought ready made.

1018 Pimentos à l'Algérienne
Grill the pimentos under a moderate heat so as to lessen the peppery taste and also to facilitate the removal of the skin. Cut them in half lengthwise and discard the seeds, then cut into Julienne and mix with oil, vinegar, salt and pepper. Arrange in raviers with very thin rings of onion around the edges.

1019 Poireaux à la Grecque
Cut whites of leek into 8 cm (3 in) lengths, blanch them well in boiling water and finish cooking in a marinade in exactly the same way as for Artichokes à la Grecque.

1020 Poireaux Farcis—Stuffed Leeks
Cut pieces of leek from the white part approximately 3–4 cm (1–1½ in) in length; cook them in boiling water keeping them fairly firm, then remove and marinate in oil, vinegar, salt and pepper. Remove the centre of the leeks so as to make small cylindrical cases with closed ends and stuff with a filling according to taste.

1021 Poitrines d'Oie Fumées—Smoked Breast of Goose
Cut in slices as thin as possible and arrange on a dish with picked parsley.

1022 Poivrons doux
This is another name for the sweet pimento.

1023 Poutargue de Mulet
This is a commercial product obtained from the Far East; it consists of the salted and pressed roes of mullet shaped in the form of a flat sausage.
To serve: cut into very thin slices, arrange in a dish and sprinkle with oil and lemon juice.

1024 Poutargue de Thon
This is a variation of the above prepared from tunny fish roes. It is served in the same way.

1025 Potted Meats and Fish
These are an English speciality and are usually commercial products made from beef, chicken, ham, tongue, salmon etc. They are prepared by pounding the selected ingredient which should be cooked and cold with one-third its weight of butter and a little of the cooked fat, if any, from the item under preparation. The purée is then seasoned, passed through a fine sieve, placed in small earthenware jars then covered with a thin layer of melted butter. They are served very cold as they are.

1026 Radis—Radishes
These are used mainly as a decoration on other Hors-d'oeuvre and are cut into shapes such as roses, or in slices. They can be served on their own as an Hors-d'oeuvre garnished with butter curls.

1027 Radis Noirs—Black Radishes
Peel and slice the radishes thinly, sprinkle with salt and allow to marinate for 15–20 minutes.
To serve: drain well and season with pepper, oil and vinegar.

1028 American Relishes
These are a type of *Aceto-dolce* which is comprised of various ingredients such as grapes, plums, apricots, small onions and gherkins pickled in vinegar and flavoured with sugar, cinnamon and Cayenne. This Hors-d'oeuvre is served accompanied by small cinnamon biscuits and it is usual to leave these on the table during the service.

1029 Rillettes de Tours
These should be served very cold from the jar.

1030 Rillons de Blois
These should be served very cold in small round porcelain dishes, or simply placed on a serviette.

1031 Rougets au Safran, or Rougets à l'Orientale —Red Mullet with Saffron
Select very small red mullets, clean them well and place in an oiled deep tray. Cover with sufficient white wine, season with 8 g (¼ oz) salt per 1 litre wine and some roughly chopped tomato flesh, a little parsley root, fennel, thyme and bayleaf, a touch of garlic, a few peppercorns and coriander seeds, and sufficient saffron to give a dominant flavour to the dish.

Bring to the boil, simmer very gently for 10–12 minutes and allow to cool in the cooking liquid.

Serve with a little of the cooking liquid and slices of peeled lemon.

1032 Royans
These can be prepared in the same way as Sardines (1056).

1033 Salades—Salads
The composition of salads for Hors-d'oeuvre is very flexible and depends on the variations that the cook can think of. They can be arranged in raviers with a border comprised of cucumber, white of hard-boiled egg or beetroot—or they may be placed in emptied halves of tomato or on large slices of tomato or cucumber. The number of mixtures that can be made is considerable—all the ingredients normally used in the kitchen may be employed.

To this large variety of salads can be added the following in which rice is the main ingredient. The rice can be cooked in any way, the essential thing being that when cooked the grains should be well separated, thus the use of a suitable rice such as Patna is absolutely necessary.

In this kind of salad the rice represents half the total quantity, the other half being composed of other ingredients as indicated and in the proportion according to their suitability and to the conception of the salad.

1034 Salade Bergerette
Cooked rice, slices of hard-boiled egg, chopped chives; lightly mix with whipped cream with the addition of salt and pepper. This salad may be additionally flavoured with grated horseradish, curry powder or mustard etc.

1035 Salade Brésilienne
Equal quantities of cooked rice and diced fresh pineapple; lightly mix with cream and lemon juice and season with salt.

1036 Salade Castelnau
Cooked rice, crayfish tails and Julienne of truffle; lightly mix with a little Vinaigrette which has been thickened slightly with Mayonnaise and flavoured with mustard and diced red pimentos.

1037 Salade Catalane
Cooked rice, Spanish onions baked in the oven and diced, peeled red peppers cut in dice and fillets of anchovy; lightly mix with Vinaigrette.

1038 Salade Dorzia
Cooked rice, slices of cucumber marinated in salt and drained and Julienne of cooked white of chicken; lightly mix with mustard-flavoured Vinaigrette.

1039 Salade Hollandaise
Cooked rice, sliced cooking apple and smoked herring fillet; lightly mix with mustard-flavoured Vinaigrette.

1040 Salade Italienne
Cooked rice, peas and diced red part of carrot cooked in a little Bouillon; lightly mix with Vinaigrette.

1041 Salade Midinette
Equal quantities of cooked rice and peas mixed with Vinaigrette containing chopped tarragon and chervil.

1042 Salade des Moines
Cooked rice, asparagus tips and Julienne of white of chicken; lightly mix with Vinaigrette containing mustard. Serve sprinkled with grated truffle.

1043 Salade Monte Carlo
Cooked rice, thin slices of Dublin Bay prawns, Julienne of celery heart, slices of truffle; mix with Vinaigrette lightly thickened with Mayonnaise and seasoned with paprika.

1044 Salade Nantaise
Cooked rice, flakes of canned tunny fish in oil and dice of tomato flesh; mix with Vinaigrette containing chopped tarragon, chervil and chives.

1045 Salade Normande
Equal quantities of cooked rice and finely sliced cooking apple; mix with cream and flavour with salt, pepper and lemon juice.

1046 Salade des Pêcheurs
Cooked rice, Spanish onion baked in the oven and cut into dice and fillets of anchovy; mix with oil, vinegar, salt, pepper, mustard and chopped parsley.

1047 Salade de Pieds de Mouton et de Pieds de Veau—Salad of Sheep's Trotters and Calf's Feet
Cook the trotters or feet in a *Blanc* in the usual way, remove the bones, cut the flesh into slices and whilst still warm mix with Vinaigrette.

1048 Salade de Pieds de Veau Clarens
Cook the calf's feet in a light *Blanc*, remove the bones and whilst still lukewarm cut the flesh in thin slices. Marinate with oil and vinegar for 20 minutes. At the last minute mix with Mayonnaise containing chopped fresh aromatic herbs such as tarragon, chives, chervil etc. Arrange in raviers and surround with halves of hard-boiled egg.

1049 Salade de Pieds de Veau à l'Hongroise
Cook the calf's feet in a *Blanc*, remove the bones and cut the flesh into thin slices whilst lukewarm. Marinate for 20 minutes with oil, vinegar and a pinch of paprika, turning over occasionally. Mix with Mayonnaise containing a light purée of fresh aromatic herbs. Arrange in raviers and surround with slices of hard-boiled egg.

1050 Salade Portugaise
Cooked rice, thin slices of peeled depipped tomatoes, Julienne of grilled and peeled red pimentos; mix with oil, vinegar, salt, pepper and a little anchovy essence.

1051 Salade Provençale
Cooked rice, small quarters of peeled tomatoes seasoned and sautéed in oil with a little crushed garlic and chopped parsley, large dice of eggplant also sautéed in oil and diced fillets of anchovy; lightly mix with Vinaigrette.

1052 Salade Réjane
Cooked rice, slices of hard-boiled egg, grated horseradish and slices of truffle; lightly mix with whipped cream and season with a little salt.

1053 Salade Vauclusienne
Cooked rice, onion baked in the oven and diced, and slices of truffle; mix with oil, salt, pepper, mustard and a little anchovy essence.

1054 Various Rice Salads
There are a number of rice salads such as Andalouse, Carmen, des Nonnes, Orientale etc. in the Chapter on Salads which are equally suitable as Hors-d'oeuvre.

1055 Salami
Cut in thin slices as for other sausages of this type and arrange on a dish overlapping, garnished with very green picked parsley.

1056 Sardines
Tinned sardines in oil should be arranged neatly in a ravier and sprinkled with a little of the oil.

Note: In his book *150 Manières d'accommoder les Sardines*, Mon. Caillat has given a number of excellent recipes for the cold preparation of this fish.

1057 Frankfurt, Strasbourg and Viennese Sausages
These should be poached in water for 10 minutes and served accompanied with grated horseradish.

1058 Lyons, Arles and Bologna Sausages
These different sausages are best cut in very thin

slices and arranged overlapping in a circle on a dish, garnished with picked parsley.

1059 Goose Liver, Pheasant and Chicken Sausages
These types of sausage should be cut in thin slices, arranged overlapping in a circle on a dish with a little chopped aspic jelly in the centre.

1060 Saumon Fumé—Smoked Salmon
Cut in very thin slices, trim, roll into cornets and arrange on a dish with a little parsley.

1061 Sigui Fumé
Cut in thin slices as for smoked eel (924).

1062 Smoked Sprats
These are similar to smoked sardines and should be selected fat and plump, as those which are dry and thin have very little flavour. Remove the heads and skins, arrange in a dish, sprinkle with a very little mixed finely chopped shallot and parsley and a little oil and vinegar. Allow to marinate for 5–6 hours turning frequently so as to allow the marinade to penetrate the flesh.

Arrange on a suitable dish for serving.

1063 Various Tartlets
See Barquettes and Tartlets (928).

1064 Tartelettes de Thon—Tunny Fish Tartlets
Fill the tartlet cases with very finely chopped tunny fish mixed with a little Mayonnaise, and cover with a nice round slice of tunny fish preferably cut with a pastry cutter. Arrange a border of alternating chopped white and yolk of hard-boiled egg on top. Finish with a little chopped parsley in the centre.

1065 Thon à l'huile—Tunny Fish in Oil
Flake the fish, arrange in a ravier, sprinkle with a little oil and garnish with picked parsley.

1066 Thon Marinette
Arrange overlapping in a ravier, slices of tunny fish and small firm tomatoes and very thin slices of spring onions. Place a border of sliced cooked potatoes around the dish and sprinkle with ordinary salad dressing.

1067 Tomates à la Génoise
Select medium-sized firm round tomatoes, cut them in slices and remove the pips; arrange in raviers alternating with small quarters of red and yellow pimentos which have been grilled to remove the skin. Sprinkle with Vinaigrette containing chopped anchovies and arrange a border of thinly sliced boiled potatoes around the dish.

1068 Tomates à la Monégasque
Cut a slice from the tops of very small tomatoes, remove the pips and sprinkle the inside with a little oil, vinegar, salt and pepper to marinate. Fill dome shape with a mixture of equal quantities of finely chopped tunny fish and hard-boiled egg flavoured with chopped onion, parsley, tarragon and chervil and mixed with a little Mayonnaise. Arrange in raviers and decorate with picked parsley.

1069 Tomates au Naturel
Peel very small tomatoes and squeeze them in a clean cloth so as to keep their shape. Marinate with a little oil, vinegar, salt and pepper. Insert a small piece of parsley stalk into each tomato and pipe a small leaf of green butter on the side. These tomatoes may be stuffed before being marinated.

1070 Tomates en Quartiers—Quarters of Tomato
Peel medium-sized, firm tomatoes, cut them in half vertically, remove the insides and allow to drain well. Fill with a purée of fish, or Macédoine of vegetables mixed with jellied Mayonnaise. Place them on ice to set the filling then cut into quarters and arrange on dishes.

Note: A good way of preparing these tomatoes is to peel them, cut each into eight quarters, remove the pips, season and fill these with any suitable butter cream using a fancy tube.

1071 Truites Marinées—Marinated Trout
Poach the trout in a very strongly flavoured White Wine Court-bouillon containing one-third its volume of vinegar; allow to cool in the cooking liquid. When cold, arrange in a ravier with a little marinade and garnish on top with slices of grooved lemon.

1072 Filets de Truites Marinés—Marinated Fillets of Trout
Carefully remove the fillets from the required number of marinated trout, skin them and coat with Mayonnaise. Sprinkle with chopped lobster coral then arrange the fillets on a bed of vegetable salad in raviers; surround with a border of slices of hard-boiled eggs, radishes and cucumber.

1073 Variantes
See Macédoine (999).

1074 Vrilles de Vignes—Vine Tendrils
This type of Hors-d'oeuvre should be prepared in July and August when the tendrils are tender; they should be gathered and used fresh.

Place the tendrils in iced water for 15 minutes, drain and place them into a pan of salted water to boil for 5 minutes. Drain well and place them immediately in a terrine with 15 g (½ oz) tarragon leaves and a bouquet of 4 blackcurrant leaves per 250 g (9 oz) of tendrils. Cover with boiling vinegar and allow to marinate in a cool place for 4–5 days. When ready, serve with a little of the marinade.

1075 Zampino

This is a speciality item of Italian pork butchery.

First soak the Zampino in cold water for a few hours then remove it and scrape the surface clean. Prick it all over with a trussing needle, tie in a cloth, place in a long deep pan and cover with cold water.

Bring to the boil and allow to poach very very gently taking care that there is hardly any visible movement of the water; allow a good 1 hour per 1 kg (2¼ lb) weight of Zampino.

When cooked, allow to cool in the cooking liquid; when cold, remove, dry and cut into very thin slices. Arrange overlapping on a dish with a border of picked parsley.

HOT HORS-D'OEUVRE

The hot Hors-d'oeuvre of our modern service are the old *Entrées Volantes* or side dishes of the French Service which have survived but with a change of name; their use, however, remains the same.

They sometimes figure on luncheon menus together with cold Hors-d'oeuvre coming after them, but their real place is on the dinner menu where they come after the soup and serve as a link between this and the main dishes.

Nowadays, there is an unfortunate tendency to exaggerate the amount and importance of hot Hors-d'oeuvre: it is too easily forgotten that the essential characteristic of these preparations is their lightness and delicacy. From the point of view of gastronomic logic they can be deemed superfluous and nothing except custom justifies their use. They should therefore be regarded as a kind of intermediate dish and should be something small and dainty which can titillate the palate of the guest without satisfying his appetite.

If Bouchées are taken as a good example of the more popular type of hot Hors-d'oeuvre, the term can clearly and definitely indicate the ideal size for all hot Hors-d'oeuvre.

In the following list of hot Hors-d'oeuvre, care has been taken to denote all those types generally used without indicating all the varieties derived from them. Actually a large number of these recipes are such that they can be slightly modified so as to lead to a new series of dishes; this depends on the ability of the cook to see their possibilities and practical application, according to his ideas and resources.

In this list the hot Russian Hors-d'oeuvre have been slotted in alphabetically as it has been considered unnecessary to give them a separate chapter of their own. They can be found in their proper order under the titles as given by Mon. Petit, who is considered to be the best guide to Russian cuisine.

1076 Allumettes aux Anchois—Anchovy Fingers

See Allumettes aux Anchois in the section on Cold Hors-d'oeuvre: prepare and serve hot. (917)

1077 Allumettes Caprice

These are prepared in the same way as Allumettes aux Anchois but coating the rectangles of puff paste with a chicken and cream forcemeat containing chopped red tongue and truffle.

1078 Allumettes aux Crevettes

These are prepared in the same way as Allumettes aux Anchois but coating the rectangles of puff paste with whiting and shrimp butter forcemeat containing sliced cooked shrimps.

1079 Various Allumettes

This type of Hors-d'oeuvre is susceptible to many variations and all types of forcemeat either simple or composed may be used. It must, however, be borne in mind that Allumettes used for Hors-d'oeuvre are an imitation of the small pastry called Allumette and should not be confused with that type of preparation called Dartois which comprises two layers of puff paste enclosing the garnish, which is then cut after being cooked.

1080 Attereaux

These Hors-d'oeuvre are derived from the old classical cuisine which in modern times has been brought back into favour. An Attereau is composed of thin slices of various ingredients and of the same size, impaled alternately on a small wooden skewer. The whole is then coated with a reduced sauce; it is this sauce which characterizes the Attereau and which is at the same time, the fundamental of its preparation.

When the sauce has set well, the Attereau is trimmed, egg and crumbed, then deep fried at the last minute before serving.

To serve: the wooden skewers are removed and replaced by silver skewers. They should be arranged on a serviette with a border of fried parsley or they can be stuck in a circle on a mould of rice or fried bread with a bouquet of fried parsley in the centre.

Previously, Attereaux were moulded in cylindrical or square moulds of the same kind as used for the jellies for garnishing the decorative skewers (*Hâtelets*).

The title of the Attereaux is always determined by the ingredients from which it is made.

1081 Attereaux à la Genevoise
Chicken livers sautéed in butter, braised lambs' sweetbreads, poached brain, mushrooms, truffles and artichoke bottoms, all cut into 2½ cm (1 in) square slices, impaled on skewers and coated with a well reduced Sauce Duxelles.

When cold, cover with a coating of forcemeat mixed with a little beaten egg; egg and crumb and fashion to a neat cylindrical shape. Deep fry at the last moment, replace the wooden skewers with decorative silver skewers and arrange as indicated above.

1082 Attereau au Parmesan, or Brochettes de Parme
Prepare a mixture of 200 g (7 oz) semolina cooked for approximately 30 minutes in 1 litre (1¾ pt or 4½ U.S. cups) White Bouillon. Remove from the heat and add 150 g (5 oz) grated Parmesan cheese and 100 g (3½ oz) butter. Spread the mixture on a buttered tray 5 mm (⅕ in) thick and allow to cool well.

Cut into rounds with a 2½ cm (1 in) plain pastry cutter and impale these on wooden skewers, alternating them with round pieces of Gruyère cheese of the same size and thickness. Egg and crumb, and deep fry at the last minute; replace the wooden skewers with silver skewers and arrange as indicated before.

Note: This kind of Attereaux is also known as *à la Royale*, *à la Princesse* and *à la Florentine* but for the majority of practising cooks the name is as stated in the title of the recipe.

1083 Attereaux Villeroy
This general name describes not only the shape of the preparation but the Attereaux themselves which can be composed of various ingredients such as braised lamb and calves' sweetbreads, brains, foie gras and cockscombs and kidneys as main ingredients, and other subsidiary ingredients according to type such as mushrooms, truffle, cooked tongue and ham—all cut the same size and shape as the main items. These Attereaux take their name from the principle ingredient, e.g. Attereaux de Ris de Veau à la Villeroy. For the preparation of the skewers and the coating of them with sauce see the first recipe for Attereaux (1080).

1084 Attereaux d'Huîtres à la Villeroy
Poach six large oysters for each skewer, remove the beards then impale the oysters on the skewers alternating with slices of cooked mushrooms.

Coat with Sauce Villeroy which has been reduced with the juices from the oysters, egg and crumb and mould cylindrical shape. Deep fry at the last minute and serve in the usual manner.

1085 Barquettes
To avoid confusion Barquettes which differ from tartlets only by their shape, should be used for fish and shellfish, and tartlets should preferably be used for preparations based on chicken, game and mixed ingredients. The result of this natural distinction makes for an appreciable simplification of them both and defines their specific uses.

As an exception to the rule of lining Barquette moulds with paste there are times where they can be lined with something else but generally the lining is either short paste or puff paste trimmings. When using these pastes the cases should be baked to a light colour.

1086 Barquettes Chevreuse
Line the bottom and sides of buttered Barquette moulds with a semolina mixture made in the following manner: pour 125 g (4½ oz) semolina into 5 dl (18 fl oz or 2¼ U.S. cups) boiling White Bouillon, mix until cooked and bind with 100 g (3½ oz) Parmesan and 4 egg yolks.

Fill the lined moulds with a mixture according to the name it will have on the menu and cover with a thin layer of the semolina. Demould by dipping in hot water, then egg and crumb with fine white breadcrumbs and deep fry at the last minute. Arrange on a serviette with a bouquet of fried parsley in the centre.

Note:
1) The mixture used as a filling for these barquettes can be a Salpicon of chicken, game, foie gras, shrimps, lobster or crayfish tails, or a purée of chicken, game or foie gras.
2) The name of the Barquette is determined by the main ingredient used in the filling and the name *à la Chevreuse* is justified by the enclosing of the mixture in semolina and is applicable to all items prepared in this manner.

1087 Barquettes de Crevettes, also called Barquettes Joinville
Fill the prepared Barquette cases with a small Salpicon of prawns mixed with Velouté containing Shrimp Butter. Cover with more sauce and place a few nice prawns on top. Finish by placing a large whole prawn with the tail peeled at each end of the Barquette.

1088 Barquettes d'Ecrevisses, also called Barquettes Nantua
Fill the barquette cases with a small Salpicon of crayfish tails mixed with Velouté finished with Crayfish Butter. Cover with Sauce Nantua and decorate each one with 2 nice crayfish tails and a small stuffed crayfish head at each end.

1089 Barquettes de Filets de Sole
Fill the Barquette cases with a small Salpicon of fillets of sole, mushrooms and truffles, mixed with Sauce Normande. Coat them lightly with the same sauce and decorate with very small slices of poached fillets of sole alternating with slices of very black truffle.

1090 Barquettes de Homard, also called Barquettes Victoria
Fill the Barquette cases dome shape with a small Salpicon of lobster, mushrooms and truffle, mixed with lobster sauce which has been finished with the addition of the creamy parts of the head pounded and passed through a fine sieve. Garnish each with a small thin slice of lobster at each end and a slice of truffle in the middle.

1091 Barquettes d'Huîtres, also called Barquettes à l'Ostendaise
Fill the Barquette cases with poached and bearded oysters mixed with creamy Sauce Béchamel containing a little fish stock. Sprinkle with a little very black chopped truffle.

1092 Barquettes de Laitances à la Florentine
Cover the bottom of the Barquette cases with a little roughly chopped leaf spinach stewed in butter. Place on top a nice slice of soft roe poached in white wine and coat with well-seasoned Mornay Sauce. Sprinkle with grated Parmesan cheese and glaze under the salamander.

1093 Barquettes de Laitances au Parmesan
Place a little Mornay Sauce in the bottom of the Barquette cases, a soft roe poached in white wine on top and, using a piping bag and tube, cover each with Parmesan soufflé mixture. Cook in a moderate oven for 7–8 minutes.

1094 Beignets—Fritters
Beignet is a general term used to designate any item or mixture of food which has been dipped in frying batter and then deep fried.

In modern practice, the word *Fritot* is often applied to this preparation; however, there is a difference—the *Fritot* is always accompanied by Tomato Sauce whereas a fritter is invariably served without an accompaniment.

Beignets must be fried in very hot fat or oil so as to prevent the batter from breaking up and thus prevent it absorbing the fat. They should be arranged on a serviette with a bouquet or border of fried parsley.

1095 Beignets d'Anchois, or Beignets à la Niçoise
Cut some tunny fish into round slices 3–4 cm (1–$1\frac{1}{2}$ in) in diameter and $1\frac{1}{2}$ cm ($\frac{3}{5}$ in) thick and completely surround each slice with thin strips of anchovy fillets marinated in oil. Dip in light frying batter at the last minute and deep fry in very hot fat. Arrange in neat piles on a serviette with a border of fried parsley.

1096 Beignets à la Bénédictine
Prepare a mixture made from two-thirds Brandade de Morue (1805) and one-third potato purée. Divide into pieces the size of a walnut and flatten to an oval shape. Dip in light frying batter at the last minute and deep fry in very hot fat. Serve as in the previous recipe.

1097 Beignets Cardinal
Poach some soft roes in White Wine Court-bouillon, remove them and cool under light pressure. Coat with very thick lobster sauce and allow to get completely cold; trim off the surplus sauce. Dip in a light frying batter at the last minute and deep fry in very hot fat quickly. Serve in the usual manner.

1098 Beignets de Cervelle—Brain Fritters
Poach the brains in Vinegar Court-bouillon, remove and cut into thick slices as evenly shaped as possible. Marinate with oil, lemon juice and chopped Fines Herbes for 20 minutes. Dip in batter and deep fry at the last minute taking care that the batter becomes very crisp. Serve in the usual manner.

1099 Beignets à l'Italienne
Prepare the following mixture: cut 250 g (9 oz) cooked white of chicken and 150 g (5 oz) lean ham into dice. Pound 125 g ($4\frac{1}{2}$ oz) fresh Parmesan cheese to a paste with a little cold cooked calf's brain and mix the diced chicken and ham into it. Divide into pieces the size of a walnut, mould into balls using a little flour, dip in frying batter at the last moment and deep fry in very hot fat. Serve as previously indicated.

1100 Beignets de Laitances—Soft Roe Fritters
Poach some fresh soft herring roes in White Wine Court-bouillon, remove and marinate with oil, lemon juice and chopped parsley for 20 minutes. Dip in frying batter and deep fry at the last minute. Serve in the usual manner.

1101 Beignets de Laitances Villeroy
Poach some soft roes in White Wine Court-bouillon, remove and cool under light pressure. Coat with very thick Sauce Villeroy containing chopped truffle and allow to get completely cold. Trim off the surplus sauce, dip in a light batter and deep fry at the last minute taking care that the batter is dry and crisp. Serve in the usual manner.

1102 Beignets à la Mathurine
Prepare Chou Paste (325) and mix in 30 g (1 oz) each of small dice of herrings in oil and sardines per 125 g (4½ oz) Chou Paste. Prepare and deep fry in the same way as for ordinary Beignets Soufflés (4919).

1103 Beignets à la Niçoise
See Beignets d'Anchois. (1095)

1104 Beignets Pignatelli
To 125 g (4½ oz) Chou Paste (325), add 2 tbs diced lean ham and 25 g (1 oz) skinned almonds cut into short Julienne and lightly grilled. Prepare and fry as for ordinary Beignets Soufflés.

1105 Beurrecks à la Turque
Cut 250 g (9 oz) fresh Gruyère cheese into very small dice and mix it together with 3 tbs well reduced and almost cold Sauce Béchamel; allow to cool completely.

Shape the mixture into pieces the size of an ordinary cigar and envelope each one in an oval piece of noodle paste rolled out as thin as paper; seal the edges with beaten egg. Egg and breadcrumb using very fine white breadcrumbs, deep fry at the last moment and serve immediately.

Note: Beurrecks can also be made using the same coatings and shapes as Rissoles but, just the same, they must always be egg and breadcrumbed before deep frying.

1106 Blinis
Prepare a light batter with 20 g (⅔ oz) yeast diluted in 5 dl (18 fl oz or 2¼ U.S. cups) lukewarm milk and 50 g (2 oz) sifted flour. Allow to prove in a warm place for 2 hours then add 250 g (9 oz) flour, 4 egg yolks, 3 dl (½ pt or 1¼ U.S. cups) lukewarm milk and a pinch of salt. Mix together but do not overmix, then mix in 4 stiffly beaten egg whites and 1 dl (3½ fl oz or ½ U.S. cup) whipped cream. Allow to prove in a warm place for 30 minutes and just before service, cook as for pancakes in the small special Blinis pans.

1107 Bouchées
Bouchées used as a hot Hors-d'oeuvre should normally be slightly smaller than usual and are sometimes described as Bouchés Mignones. Their shape varies according to the type so as to establish a clearcut difference between them. In certain cases the cover of the Bouchées are used, in others a plain or fancy round slice of truffle is used instead; in others the cover is decorated with the main item of the filling.

Bouchées should always be arranged on a serviette for service.

1108 Bouchées à la Bohémienne
Prepare small Brioches à Tête made from brioche paste without sugar and cooked in fluted moulds. Remove the soft insides of the Brioches so as to make small cases and reserve the tops for use as covers. Dry the cases carefully in a cool oven and fill with a Salpicon of foie gras and truffle mixed with light veal meat glaze thickened with a little butter and flavoured with a little Madeira. Replace the Brioche tops as covers.

1109 Bouchées Bouquetière
Prepare some very small round fancy Bouchées and fill with a Brunoise of vegetables or very small Printanier of vegetables mixed with Chicken Velouté. Use small fancy rounds of carrot as covers.

1110 Bouchées Diane
Prepare some plain round Bouchées and fill with a Salpicon of cooked flesh of game bird and truffle mixed with Salmis Sauce made from the same game. Use fancy round slices of truffle as covers.

1111 Bouchées Grand Duc
Prepare some round fancy Bouchées and fill with asparagus tips and truffles cut in fairly thick short Julienne and mixed with a little creamy Sauce Béchamel. Use slices of truffle as covers.

1112 Bouchées Isabelle
Prepare some oval fancy Bouchées and fill with a very fine Salpicon of red salt ox tongue and truffle mixed with a purée of chicken which has been mixed with a little Velouté. Use small thin oval slices of tongue as covers.

1113 Bouchées Joinville
Prepare some fancy oval Bouchées and fill with a Salpicon of shrimps, mushrooms and truffle mixed with a little Joinville sauce. Use thin diamond-shaped pieces of truffle as covers.

1114 Bouchées Marie-Rose
Prepare some plain diamond-shaped Bouchées and fill with a mixture of buttered shrimps and Julienne of truffle. For covers, use slices cut from a sausage-

shaped mould of pink coloured smelt forcemeat which has been poached just before being required.

1115 Bouchées Mogador
Prepare some fancy diamond-shaped Bouchées and fill with a Salpicon made of two-thirds salt ox tongue and one-third white of chicken mixed with Sauce Béchamel and finished with Foie gras Butter. Use diamond-shaped pieces of truffle as covers.

1116 Bouchées Montglas
Prepare some fancy square Bouchées and fill with a Salpicon of foie gras, mushrooms, salt ox tongue and truffle mixed with Madeira sauce. Use square slices of truffle as covers.

1117 Bouchées Monseigneur
Prepare some fancy oval-shaped Bouchées and fill with a purée of soft roes mixed with finely chopped truffle. Use thick diamond-shaped slices of truffle as covers.

1118 Bouchées Nantua
Prepare some fancy oval-shaped Bouchées and fill with a Salpicon of crayfish tails and truffle mixed with Nantua Sauce. Use small stuffed crayfish heads as covers.

1119 Bouchées à la Périgourdine
Prepare some fancy round-shaped Bouchées which are small but higher than usual. Fill with a purée of foie gras containing chopped truffle and mixed with a little Madeira Sauce.

1120 Bouchées à la Reine
Prepare some fancy round-shaped Bouchées; the original classical filling was creamed chicken purée but modern practice is to use a Salpicon of white of chicken, mushrooms and truffle mixed with Sauce Allemande and this is now used almost everywhere. Use the pastry tops as covers.

1121 Bouchées Petite-Princesse
Prepare some square-shaped fancy Bouchées cut with a 4–4½ cm (1½–1¾ in) cutter and thicker than usual so as to give extra height and lightness; fill with a purée of chicken mixed with Velouté and some diced very black truffle. Use thin square slices of truffle as covers.

1122 Bouchées Saint-Hubert
Prepare some very small fancy round Bouchées and fill with a purée of ground game mixed with the required amount of game Sauce Espagnole. Use thin fancy rounds of cooked mushrooms as covers.

1123 Bouchées Victoria
Prepare some fancy round Bouchées and fill with a Salpicon of lobster and truffle mixed with a little lobster sauce. Use the pastry tops as covers.

1124 Small Bouchées for Garnishing
As well as being used as hot Hors-d'oeuvre, Bouchées are often used as part of a garnish for main dishes of fish and game. In this case they are filled with a mixture which is in keeping with the fish or joint.

They may also be served with certain vegetables, notably celery and cardoons; in this special case diced poached bone marrow bound with meat glaze is used as the filling with a slice of poached bone marrow as the cover; they are arranged around the vegetables. In those circumstances where Bouchées fill the role of a garnish, they should be very small and very light.

1125 Brochettes
Brochettes are always comprised of:

1) A principle ingredient which can be, for example, calf's, pig's or lamb's liver, chicken livers, or veal or lamb's sweetbreads and
2) subsidiary items such as slices of cooked mushrooms and squares of lean bacon or ham.

When the main item is liver it should be sliced and sautéed in butter.

To prepare the brochettes, roll all the ingredients in thick Duxelles and impale them on skewers alternating the ingredients; sprinkle with breadcrumbs and place on a moderately hot grill to cook so that the items which have only been sautéed or blanched will cook through. Serve on half melted Maître d'Hôtel butter or on a light sauce which is in keeping with the main ingredient.

1126 Brochettes de Parme
See Attereaux au Parmesan (1082).

1127 Various Cases
The paper cases previously used have now been replaced advantageously by small round, fluted porcelain dishes known as *Cassolettes*, the usual fillings being large Salpicons of the same type as indicated for Bouchées and Croustades. These dishes are also used for light gratinated hot Hors-d'oeuvre and various small Soufflés etc.

1128 Cannelons
This type of hot Hors-d'oeuvre was much used in the old classical kitchen and although not so frequently used nowadays its use has not been completely abandoned. They are made in exactly the same way as the pastry kind but without sugar.

Prepare some bands of puff paste 18–20 cm (7–8 in) long by 2 cm (⅘ in) wide and wind in a spiral around cream horn moulds slightly overlapping, with the edge of one side of the strip being moistened so as to ensure that it sticks together. Brush with eggwash and bake in a moderate oven for 12–14 minutes.

These Cannelons may be filled with any kind of Salpicon, or purée of chicken, game etc. taking care that the filling used is slightly thick so as to stop it from running out when arranged on the serving dish.

The usual method of presentation is to arrange them on a dish around a base in the shape of a truncated cone—this may be of fried bread or moulded from rice.

Cannelons take their name from the filling used, e.g. Cannelons à la Reine, à la Joinville, à la Parisienne, à la Mogador or Cannelons de Volaille, de Foie Gras etc.

1129 Cannelons à l'Ancienne

Roll out a sheet of puff paste trimmings or half puff paste and cut into oblong pieces 9 cm (3½ in) by 4 cm (1½ in) wide then coat them with a layer of forcemeat with or without chopped truffle.

Roll up into *Paupiettes* taking care to keep the forcemeat in place; arrange on a baking tray and bake in a hot oven for 12 minutes. The type of forcemeat used determines the name of this kind of Cannelon of which there is a large variety.

1130 Cassolettes Aiglon

Surround the rims of small porcelain *Cassolettes* with a strip of puff paste; fill two-thirds full with a Salpicon of foie gras and truffles mixed with Sauce Demi-glace and, using a piping bag, finish filling them with a foie gras Soufflé mixture smoothing dome shape. Cook for 15 minutes in a medium oven and arrange on a serviette placed on a dish.

1131 Cassolettes Alice

Butter some small shallow porcelain *Cassolettes* and line with a thin layer of Duchesse potato mixture.

Fill the insides with small slices of white of chicken mixed with a little reduced Velouté and cover with a layer of Duchesse potato mixture cut out with a fancy cutter. Eggwash and bake for 12–14 minutes to a golden brown colour.

1132 Cassolettes Suzanne

Fill small porcelain *Cassolettes* two-thirds full with asparagus tips lightly mixed with a little Velouté; place on top of each a small fillet of chicken inset with a suitable item, e.g. a piece of salt ox tongue. These fillets should be poached at the last moment. Decorate with a slice of truffle in the middle.

1133 Ciernikis (*Russian Hors-d'oeuvre*)

Mix together the following ingredients: 250 g (9 oz) each of pressed curd cheese and flour; 50 g (2 oz) melted butter; 3 eggs and a little salt, pepper and grated nutmeg; pass through a fine sieve and mix in a further 75 g (2½ oz) flour.

Mould into small flat cakes 4–5 cm (1½–2 in) in diameter and 1 cm (⅖ in) thick, poach in boiling salted water for 15–18 minutes and drain well. Arrange the Ciernikis in a very hot deep dish and sprinkle with melted butter.

1134 Colombines

These are prepared in the same way as Barquettes à la Chevreuse but using tartlet moulds; the outside coating is the same mixture of semolina mixed with Parmesan and egg yolks.

All the fillings suitable for Bouchées, either Salpicons or Purées, are applicable making sure that the consistency is that of a Croquette mixture.

The name of the Colombine is always determined by the principal ingredient of the filling being used.

1135 Coquilles de Crevettes

See Crevettes in the Chapter on Shellfish (2085).

1136 Coquilles de Queues d'Ecrevisses

See Crayfish in the Chapter on Shellfish (2092).

1137 Various Cutlets

As a variation all mixtures for Croquettes as given further on in this chapter can be moulded in the shape of small cutlets. The bone can be simulated by a piece of macaroni or a small piece of fried bread on which a cutlet frill may be placed.

The mixture for these cutlets can be made with any of the Salpicons of poultry, game, fish and shellfish, mixed with the necessary amount of forcemeat in keeping with the main ingredient; the consistency should be adjusted with a little well-reduced sauce which should also be in keeping with the ingredients.

These cutlets should be egg and crumbed in the same way as other cutlets and they should be shallow fried and coloured in clarified butter instead of being deep fried.

1138 Crêtes de Coq Demidoff—Cockscombs Demidoff

Cook large, very white well blanched combs in a light *Blanc* keeping them slightly firm.

Cut them open and fill the interiors with a purée of foie gras containing chopped truffle then coat with Sauce Villeroy. Allow to cool and set, trim neatly then egg and breadcrumb.

Deep fry in hot fat at the last minute and arrange

in a pile on a serviette surrounded with a border of fried parsley.

1139 Cromesquis
These are made from the same mixtures as Croquettes and in the same way they take their name from the main ingredient being used whether poultry, game or fish. However, they do differ from Croquettes in the final treatment inasmuch as they are not breadcrumbed. Cromesquis may be made according to any one of the following recipes and should be served with a sauce in keeping with the composition of the mixture.

1140 Cromesquis à la Française
Whichever the mixture—divide it into equal amounts of at most 70 g (2½ oz) and mould oblong on a floured table.
To serve: dip into ordinary frying batter and deep fry in very hot fat so as to obtain a very crisp coating; arrange on a serviette and garnish with fried parsley.

1141 Cromesquis à la Polonaise
Mould the mixture into oblong shapes as previously indicated and wrap each one in a very thin unsweetened pancake. Seal the edges of the pancake together then dip the whole into frying batter and deep fry in very hot fat. Arrange on a serviette and garnish with fried parsley.

1142 Cromesquis à la Russe
Mould the mixture into oblong shapes as previously indicated and wrap each one in a very thin piece of pig's caul. Dip into light frying batter and deep fry in hot fat, taking care that the temperature of the fat allows sufficient time to cook and melt the caul.

Note: Correctly speaking, the mixtures for Cromesquis à la Polonaise and à la Russe should contain flap mushrooms or Gribouis instead of ordinary mushrooms.

1143 Croquets
The mixture is invariably composed of a farinaceous paste such as fresh noodles which should be cooked in boiling salted water and kept a little firm, then drained and mixed with a good amount of lean ham cut in fine Julienne, some reduced Sauce Béchamel and grated cheese.

Spread the mixture 1½ cm (⅗ in) thick on a buttered tray and allow to become cold.

Mould the mixture into rectangles 7–8 cm (2¾–3¼ in) long by 3 cm (1⅕ in) wide. Egg and breadcrumb twice using very fine breadcrumbs so as to give a double thickness of outside crust and deep fry at the last moment in very hot fat.

Arrange on a serviette and garnish with fried parsley.

1144 Croquettes
The proportions of the ingredients used in croquette mixtures should be carefully balanced by regulating the ratios of the subsidiary ingredients which are usually mushrooms, flap mushrooms, ham, tongue or truffle, to that of the principal ingredient which can be poultry, game, fish or shellfish.

It is the principal ingredient, of course, which determines the name of the Croquette.

The proportions are established in the following manner: half of the total mixture should be composed of the principal ingredient; a quarter should be mushrooms or flap mushrooms: one-sixth should be ham or tongue; and one-twelfth of truffle.

Thus for example, for 500 g (1 lb 2 oz) Salpicon of poultry or game, the quantity of the subsidiary ingredients would be 250 g (9 oz) mushrooms or flap mushrooms; 160–170 g (5½–6 oz) ham or tongue and 85 g (3 oz) truffle, likewise all cut in Salpicon.

These ingredients should be mixed with a well reduced sauce in keeping with the principal ingredient of the Croquette. The sauce should equal 4 dl (14 fl oz or 1¾ U.S. cups) per 500 g (1 lb 2 oz) of the total diced ingredients.

When the Salpicon has been mixed with the sauce, spread it evenly on a buttered tray and allow it to become cold.
Shapes: These vary and to some extent are optional; nevertheless, the most commonly used shapes are indicated in the actual recipes.
Method: divide the mixture into equal pieces weighing approximately 70 g (2½ oz), mould to the selected shape and flour, egg and breadcrumb, taking care that the mixture is well coated overall so as to prevent it breaking open when being deep fried.
Cooking: Always place the Croquettes into very hot deep fat so as to ensure the immediate hardening of the coating of egg and breadcrumbs; this forms a very strong crust which will prevent the mixture escaping from inside.
Presentation and Accompaniments: croquettes should always be well drained and arranged on a serviette with fried parsley.

The accompaniment should be a sauce or a light cullis in keeping with the principal ingredient.

Note: Having thus established the principles appertaining to the preparation of Croquettes it is not considered necessary to repeat them in the following recipes; only the composition of the mixture and the accompanying sauce is given.

1145 Croquettes de Morue à l'Américaine
Prepare some cooked salt cod free from skin and bone then finely flake it and mix with an equal amount of Duchesse potato and a little reduced Sauce Béchamel.

Mould into balls on a well floured table, egg and breadcrumb and fry in clarified butter. Always serve these with Tomato Sauce.

Note: These croquettes can be made with other kinds of fish and it is not essential to egg and breadcrumb them.

1146 Croquettes à la Bergère
Prepare a Salpicon of lamb, ham and mushrooms mixed with some well reduced Sauce Béchamel.

Mould to the size and shape of apricots with flour, then egg and breadcrumb, deep fry and serve in the usual manner.
Accompaniment: Sauce Fines Herbes.

1147 Croquettes à la Bohémienne
Prepare a Salpicon of two-thirds foie gras and one-third truffle mixed with some Sauce Allemande. Mould in the shape of pears with flour, then egg and breadcrumb and deep fry. Imitate the stalks with a piece of truffle and serve in the usual manner.
Accompaniment: Sauce Périgueux.

1148 Croquettes Chasseur
Prepare a Salpicon of cooked game bird, mushrooms and truffles mixed with some well reduced Sauce Demi-glace containing game essence. Mould in rectangle shapes with flour, then egg and breadcrumb, deep fry and serve in the usual manner.
Accompaniment: Sauce Demi-glace flavoured with game essence.

1149 Croquettes à la Dominicaine
Prepare a mixture of 100 poached oysters, half their weight of diced mushrooms and $2\frac{1}{2}$ dl (9 fl oz or $1\frac{1}{8}$ U.S. cups) Sauce Béchamel containing one-third its quantity of thick Soubise and finished with Lobster Butter and a little Cayenne. Mould into elongated ovals with flour, then egg and breadcrumb, deep fry and serve in the usual manner.
Accompaniment: Sauce Vin Blanc containing the reduced cooking liquor from the oysters.

1150 Croquettes, garnished
Croquettes can be served with a garnish which is in keeping with the basic mixture providing that it does not conflict with the accompanying sauce. Croquettes served with a garnish are common in England where they are very popular. For example, Chicken Croquettes are served garnished with peas, asparagus tips or a fine Macédoine of vegetables etc., those of game are served garnished with a purée of chestnuts and with a thin Poivrade or Venison Sauce served separately. It must be said that in such cases, however, the Croquettes lose much of their characteristics and should be considered more as light Entrées.

1151 Croquettes à la Gastronome
Prepare a Salpicon of three-quarters of breast of game birds and one-quarter of truffles mixed with some well reduced Sauce Suprême. Mould cork shape with flour, then egg and breadcrumb, deep fry and serve in the usual manner.
Accompaniment: a very light purée of chestnuts.

1152 Croquettes de Gibier
These may be made from any game available, and mushrooms and truffle in the usual proportions, and mixed with reduced Sauce Demi-glace. Mould cork shape with flour, then egg and breadcrumb, deep fry and serve in the usual manner.
Accompaniment: a light Poivrade Sauce or a light game cullis.

1153 Croquettes de Homard
Prepare a Salpicon of lobster, mushrooms and truffle mixed with some reduced Sauce Béchamel which has been finished with red colouring butter and seasoned with Cayenne. Mould into the shape of elongated eggs with flour, then egg and breadcrumb, deep fry and serve in the usual manner.
Accompaniment: a light Lobster Sauce.

1154 Croquettes à la Hongroise
Prepare a Salpicon of freshly cooked calf's feet cut whilst warm, mushrooms and ham mixed with well-reduced Velouté flavoured with paprika. Mould oval shape with flour, then egg and breadcrumb, deep fry and serve in the usual manner.
Accompaniment: Sauce Demi-glace flavoured with paprika.

1155 Croquettes à l'Indienne
Prepare equal quantities of rice poached in Fish Bouillon and a Salpicon of lobster, mixed with Sauce Béchamel flavoured with curry and coconut milk and well reduced. Mould cork shape with flour, then egg and breadcrumb, deep fry and serve in the usual manner.
Accompaniment: Curry Sauce.

1156 Croquettes Jean-Bart
Prepare:

1) a Salpicon of lobster mixed with reduced Sauce Béchamel seasoned with Cayenne and finished with red colouring butter, and
2) some poached drained oysters mixed with well reduced creamy Sauce Béchamel.

Mould the oyster mixture into walnut-sized pieces and envelop each one in the lobster mixture; mould into balls with flour, then egg and breadcrumb and deep fry at the last moment. Serve in the usual manner.

Accompaniment: Sauce Béchamel flavoured with Lobster Coral Butter.

1157 Croquettes à la Milanaise
Prepare a mixture of cooked macaroni cut in small pieces plus a short Julienne of chicken, ox tongue, and truffle mixed with tomato-flavoured Sauce Béchamel well flavoured with cheese and reduced. Spread on a buttered tray $2\frac{1}{2}$ cm (1 in) thick, cut into 5 cm (2 in) squares, flour, egg and breadcrumb and deep fry at the last minute. Serve in the usual manner.
Accompaniment: a light, buttered Tomato Sauce.

1158 Croquettes à la Nantaise
Prepare a Salpicon of either a single fish or of a mixture of several fish, plus one-third its weight of chopped mushrooms and mixed with some reduced fish sauce. Mould into small squares with flour, then egg and breadcrumb, deep fry and serve in the usual manner.
Accompaniment: a thin Tomato Sauce.

1159 Croquettes Savigny
Prepare a Salpicon of ham, artichoke bottoms and morels, mixed with reduced Sauce Béchamel and 4 egg yolks per 5 dl (18 fl oz or $2\frac{1}{4}$ U.S. cups) of sauce, added when making the mixture. Mould into small round flat cakes with flour, then egg and breadcrumb, deep fry and serve in the usual manner.
Accompaniment: a light, creamed Soubise.

1160 Croquettes Sully
Prepare:

1) a mixture of finely chopped chicken mixed with reduced Velouté containing mushroom essence, and
2) a purée of foie gras mixed with a fine chicken forcemeat in the proportions of 40 g ($1\frac{1}{2}$ oz) forcemeat per 125 g ($4\frac{1}{2}$ oz) purée.

Mould the foie gras mixture into 30 g (1 oz) egg-shaped pieces enclosing a small ball of truffle in each; then envelop each in a coating of the chicken mixture so as to give the shape and size of a small chicken's egg. Flour, egg and breadcrumb using very fine breadcrumbs and deep fry at the last moment.
Accompaniment: Velouté flavoured with mushroom essence.

1161 Croquettes de Volaille
Prepare a Salpicon of chicken, mushrooms and truffle in the usual proportions, mixed with Velouté reduced with mushroom essence and 3 egg yolks per 500 g (1 lb 2 oz) mixture. Mould into squares with flour, then egg and breadcrumb, deep fry and serve in the usual manner.
Accompaniment: Sauce Demi-glace or Sauce Périgueux.

1162 Croustades
These are made in several different ways according to their ultimate use.

1) *Pastry Croustades:* line buttered, round, oval or other shaped moulds with good short paste, prick the bottoms, line with greaseproof paper, fill with lentils or split peas and bake in a moderate oven. Remove the paper and filling and leave the cases in the oven, with the door open, to dry out and become crisp without further colouring.
2) *Rice or Semolina Croustades:* cook either semolina or rice in White Bouillon taking care if using rice that it is very well cooked. Drain well and bind with 6 egg yolks and 50 g (2 oz) grated cheese per 100 g ($3\frac{1}{2}$ oz) raw weight of the cereal. Spread the mixture evenly on a buttered tray 3 cm ($1\frac{1}{3}$ in) thick.
   When cold, cut out the mixture with a round 5 cm (2 in) diameter plain pastry cutter, dipping it into hot water to facilitate the cutting. Egg and breadcrumb the pieces twice and mark an impression for a lid on the top using a smaller plain cutter and deep fry.
   Carefully remove the marked centres and reserve as lids; empty the insides leaving a thickness of $\frac{1}{4}$ cm ($\frac{1}{10}$ in) all round.
3) *Duchesse Potato Croustades:* fill buttered dariole moulds with Duchesse potato mixture pressing it in firmly. Dip the moulds in hot water, turn out to demould and egg and breadcrumb them twice; mark with an impression for a lid using a plain cutter. Deep fry in a very hot fat, remove the lids and empty the insides leaving cases $\frac{1}{2}$ cm ($\frac{1}{5}$ in) thick.

1163 Croustades de Crevettes Joinville
Prepare some rice Croustades as explained above and fill with the same mixture as used for Bouchées à la Joinville (1113).

1164 Croustades Nantua
Prepare deep fried Croustades and fill with the same mixture as used for Bouchées à la Nantua (1118).

1165 Croustades de Ris de Veau Financière
Prepare some short pastry Croustades made in fluted moulds and fill with a mixture of small slices of veal sweetbreads, small Quenelles, mushrooms

cut in large dice and small cockscombs and kidneys—all mixed with Sauce Madère.

1166 Croustades de Volaille Régence

Prepare some Duchesse Potato Croustades and fill with a mixture of small slices of cooked chicken, small Quenelles made from chicken and Crayfish Butter forcemeat, small olive-shaped pieces of truffle and cockscombs and kidneys—all mixed with Sauce Allemande flavoured with mushroom essence.

1167 Croûtes à la Champenoise

Cut some round slices of bread from a sandwich loaf 4–5 cm ($1\frac{3}{4}$–2 in) in diameter and $1\frac{1}{2}$ cm ($\frac{3}{4}$ in) thick. Cut a line around the top surface of each $\frac{1}{4}$ cm ($\frac{1}{5}$ in) from the edge and fry in clarified butter. Empty the insides so as to leave small round cases.

Fill with a mixture of pig's brains cooked with butter, together with a little chopped onion which has also been cooked in butter, then seasoned with salt and pepper and flavoured with a touch of crushed garlic. Smooth the surfaces with a palette knife, arrange on a serviette on a dish and serve very hot.

1168 Croûtes aux Foies de Raie

Prepare some bread Croûtes as in the preceding recipe. Poach skate livers in a strongly flavoured Court-bouillon, drain them well and cut into dice. Fill the Croûtes with this liver and sprinkle with Brown Butter, a few drops of lemon juice and finally a little chopped parsley.

1169 Croûtes à la Moelle

Cut some slices of bread from a sandwich loaf into Croûtes 4 cm ($1\frac{3}{4}$ in) square and $1\frac{1}{2}$ cm ($\frac{3}{5}$ in) thick. Cut a line around the top surface $\frac{1}{2}$ cm ($\frac{1}{5}$ in) from the edge and fry in clarified butter. Remove the inside so as to make small square cases.

Poach some very nice slices of bone marrow in a little White Bouillon allowing one per Croûte and poach the trimmings cut in dice. Fill the Croûtes with the well drained trimmings and place a slice of bone marrow on top of each. Lightly coat with a little meat glaze and place a smaller slice of truffle in the middle of the bone marrow. Arrange on a serviette to serve.

1170 Croûtes à l'Oie Fumée

Prepare round Croûtes as indicated for Croûtes à la Champenoise using rye bread, 4 cm ($1\frac{3}{4}$ in) in diameter and 1 cm ($\frac{2}{5}$ in) thick.

Fill each with a little cooked Sauerkraut, place a thin slice of smoked breast of goose on top and lightly coat with a little Sauce Espagnole. Arrange on a serviette to serve.

1171 Dartois aux Anchois, or Sausselis

Roll out a band of puff paste 9–10 cm ($3\frac{1}{2}$–4 in) wide and $\frac{1}{2}$ cm ($\frac{1}{4}$ in) thick and of the required length; place on a damp baking tray and coat with a layer of whiting forcemeat flavoured with Anchovy Butter; leave $1\frac{1}{2}$ cm ($\frac{3}{5}$ in) clear around the outside edge so as to allow for sealing.

Arrange thin strips of fillets of anchovy lattice-fashion on top of the forcemeat. Moisten the edges all round and cover with a second band of pastry rolled out slightly thicker. Seal the edges together and trim neatly knotching the edges with the back of a knife. Eggwash and mark the divisions across the width at 3 cm ($1\frac{1}{2}$ in) intervals and score the surface three times in each division.

Bake in a hot oven for 20–25 minutes and cut into sections as soon as they are cooked. Arrange on a serviette to serve.

1172 Dartois aux Filets de Sole

Proceed as for Dartoix aux Anchois replacing the whiting forcemeat with sole and cream forcemeat and using strips of fillets of sole instead of anchovies.

1173 Dartois aux Sardines

Proceed as for Dartois aux Anchois replacing the fillets of anchovy with fillets of skinned sardines.

1174 Ecrevisses Farcies—Stuffed Crayfish

Cook the crayfish as for Ecrevisses à la Bordelaise (2090).

Remove a strip of the shells along the length of the back of the cooked crayfish using a pair of scissors; remove the flesh and cut in dice. Remove the meat from the heads and mix with a little reduced Sauce Béchamel, pass through a fine sieve and mix with the diced flesh. Fill this mixture into the empty crayfish shells, sprinkle with fine crumbs and melted butter, colour quickly and arrange on a serviette on a dish to serve.

1175 Fish Balls

This is the name used in England and America for Croquettes de Morue à l'Américaine, the recipe for which is to be found in this Chapter (1145).

1176 Fondants

This name denotes a kind of small Croquette which is always made pear shape; the mixture is made of a single purée or a purée of a basic ingredient with other purées in the appropriate proportions.

They are egg and breadcrumbed using very fine fresh white breadcrumbs and are deep fried at the last minute. Arrange on a serviette with fried parsley.

1177 Fondants de Bécasse Castellane
Prepare a mixture of three parts of purée of woodcock, one part purée of chicken livers sautéed in butter, one part of purée of chestnuts, and one of well reduced Salmis Sauce made with woodcock.

Mix all these ingredients together, spread on a buttered tray and cool quickly. Divide into 60 g (2 oz) pieces, mould elongated pear shape, egg and breadcrumb and deep fry at the last minute.

1178 Fondants de Faisan Marly
Prepare a mixture of three parts purée of pheasant, two of well reduced Salmi Sauce made with pheasant, and one of a purée of chicken livers sautéed in butter. Proceed as in the preceding recipe.

1179 Fondants de Foie Gras Monselet
Prepare a mixture of two-thirds of a purée foie gras cooked in Madeira and one-third purée of truffle and well reduced Sauce Madère. Proceed in the usual manner.

1180 Fondants de Grives à la Liégeoise
Roast the thrushes in a shallow pan keeping them underdone; deglaze the pan with a little game stock and Madeira and add 4 juniper berries per dozen birds. Remove the flesh from the birds, pound well and pass through a sieve; add one-third its quantity of equal amounts of a purée of chicken livers sautéed in butter, and firm butter.

Prepare the Fondants in the usual manner, deep fry and stick one thrushes foot in each.

1181 Fondants de Volaille Louisette
Prepare a mixture of two-thirds purée of chicken, one-third purée of foie gras and cooked ox tongue mixed, and 1 dl ($3\frac{1}{2}$ fl oz or $\frac{1}{2}$ U.S. cup) well reduced Sauce Allemande per 500 g (1 lb 2 oz) total weight of purée. Proceed in the usual manner.

1182 Fritots
In principle, Fritots differ from Beignets because they should invariably be served accompanied by Tomato Sauce. If custom causes difficulties in differentiating between these two names it is better the word Beignet be used for those preparations which come under the heading of Entremets (sweet dishes) and keeping the name Fritots for those which come under the heading of hot Hors-d'oeuvre.

Confusion really becomes marked however, when the words Fritot and Marinade are used synonymously; in reality the difference between them can be easily and clearly defined if the following observations are borne in mind.

The ingredients of Fritots are generally slices of chicken, brain, or sheep's trotters of calf's head etc. which are always cooked beforehand, marinated with lemon juice, a little oil and chopped Fines Herbes, coated with frying batter, deep fried and served accompanied with Tomato Sauce.

To designate this preparation under the name of Marinade as a hot Hors-d'oeuvre is arbitrary as there is nothing to justify it. Marinades can be distinguished from Fritots in the following ways:

1) their ingredients are always prepared raw,
2) they are marinated for a long time with the same ingredients as an ordinary raw marinade,
3) they are then dried, passed through flour and egg and breadcrumbed instead of being coated with frying batter, and
4) they are then fried in clarified butter.

Thus the absolute difference can be clearly established as follows: the ingredients for a Fritot are always already cooked whereas those for a Marinade are always raw.

1183 Harengs à l'Esthonienne
Prepare a mixture of a purée of salted herrings which have been soaked to remove the salt, with an equal amount of white breadcrumbs lightly fried in butter. To 200 g (7 oz) of this mixture add $\frac{1}{2}$ dl (2 fl oz or $\frac{1}{4}$ U.S. cup) cream and 1 egg and mix together.

Cook as for pancakes using clarified butter.

1184 Harengs en Papillote
Cook 60 g (2 oz) finely chopped onion in a little butter to a light colour; add 60 g (2 oz) rye breadcrumbs, 2 dl (7 fl oz or $\frac{7}{8}$ U.S. cup) Sauce Allemande and season with pepper and nutmeg. Mix together and cook for 5 minutes.

Soak 3 salt herrings to remove any excess salt, remove the heads and tails and keep for further use. Fillet the fish, cut into dice and add to the cooked mixture. Allow it to cool, divide into amounts the size of a herring, mould on a buttered tray to the shape of a herring and place the heads and tails back in position.

Bake in the oven to colour then finish as for *en Papillote* placing them in the oven at the last moment to swell up the paper and colour it brown.

1185 Huîtres—Oysters
Although their natural destiny is to be eaten raw, there are a number of culinary preparations from which the following recipes have been selected.

1186 Huîtres à l'Américaine
Open the oysters and poach them in their own

juices. Replace in the cleaned deep shells and coat with Sauce à l'Américaine.

1187 Huîtres à l'Anglaise
Open and remove the oysters and wrap each in a very thin rasher of bacon. Impale them on small skewers, season and grill. Arrange on slices of toast the same shape and length as the skewers, sprinkle with a few fine breadcrumbs or fried breadcrumbs and season with Cayenne.

Note: The English name for this preparation which is more usually served as a savoury, is Angels on Horseback which can be translated into French as Anges à Cheval.

1188 Huîtres Favorite
Open and remove the oysters and poach them in their own juices; remove the beards.

Place a small spoonful of Sauce Béchamel in each cleaned deep shell, place an oyster in each with a slice of truffle on top; coat with more Béchamel, sprinkle with grated Parmesan and melted butter and glaze quickly.

1189 Huîtres à la Florentine
Open and remove the oysters and poach them in their own juices; remove the beards.

Place the deep shells on a tray and fill the bottoms with some roughly chopped spinach stewed in butter. Place one oyster on top of the spinach, coat with Sauce Mornay and glaze quickly.

1190 Huîtres au Gratin
Open and remove the oysters and poach them in their own juices; beard them and replace in the cleaned deep shells. Place on a tray, squeeze some lemon juice on each one, sprinkle with a pinch of fried breadcrumbs and a little melted butter and add a small piece of butter, then gratinate them under the salamander or in the top of a hot oven.

1191 Huîtres Maréchal
Open and remove the oysters and poach them in their own juices; dry well with a piece of clean cloth. Just before serving, dip the oysters in light frying batter and deep fry in hot fat. Arrange each 3 oysters on a slice of lemon with a sprig of very green fried parsley and arrange on a serviette.

1192 Huîtres Mornay
Open and remove the oysters and poach them in their own juices; remove the beards.

Place a little Mornay Sauce in each cleaned deep shell and place 2 oysters in each. Coat with more sauce, sprinkle with grated cheese and melted butter and glaze quickly.

1193 Huîtres à la Polonaise
Open and remove the oysters, discard the beards and place 2 oysters in each cleaned deep shell on a tray. Heat the required amount of butter in a pan allowing 4 g ($\frac{1}{8}$ oz) per oyster and add 30 g (1 oz) very fine white breadcrumbs per 100 g ($3\frac{1}{2}$ oz) butter. Place a spoonful of breadcrumbs on each oyster and place to cook in a hot oven for 2 minutes.

1194 Huîtres Soufflées
Open 24 large oysters, drain them well and pound together with 2 egg whites added a little at a time. Pass through a fine sieve and work the purée on ice adding 4 dl (14 fl oz or $1\frac{3}{4}$ U.S. cups) double cream, then mix in 1 tbs of whiting Mousseline forcemeat.

Fill the bottom of cleaned deep shells with the soufflé mixture, place one poached trimmed oyster which has been coated with Sauce Villeroy on top and cover over with more soufflé mixture. Smooth dome shape and place some very fine dry breadcrumbs around the edge of each one. Place on a tray covered with hot water and cook in a hot oven for 12 minutes to cook and colour at the same time.

1195 Huîtres Villeroy
Open the oysters and poach them in their own juices; beard them and dry well with a clean cloth. Coat with Sauce Villeroy and allow to cool; flour, egg and breadcrumb with very fine breadcrumbs and deep fry at the last minute.

Arrange on a serviette, or in the cleaned deep shells and garnish with a little fried parsley.

1196 Huîtres Wladimir
Open and remove the oysters and poach them in their own juices; remove the beards and replace the oysters in the cleaned deep shells. Cover with reduced Sauce Suprême, sprinkle with fried breadcrumbs mixed with grated Parmesan, and a little melted butter and gratinate under the salamander.

1197 Mazagrans
This is a general term for all preparations which comprise a mixture enclosed in two layers of Duchesse potato mixture (4185).

Mazagrans for hot Hors-d'oeuvre are made in large tartlet moulds and all the mixtures, filings and Salpicons used for Bouchées, Croquettes and Rissoles are suitable.

Mazagrans always take the name of the main ingredient used, e.g. Mazagrans de Volaille if using chicken.

Method:
To prepare Mazagrans line buttered plain tartlet

moulds with a thin layer of Duchesse potato, fill dome shape with the selected mixture which should be cold and cover with a second layer of Duchesse potato cut out with a pastry cutter. Seal the edges, brush with eggwash and place a small fancy piece of Duchesse potato in the centre. Place in a hot oven to colour which is all that is required as all the ingredients are ready cooked. Demould as soon as ready and arrange on a serviette.

1198 Nalesnikis (*Russian Hors-d'oeuvre*)
Place 250 g (9 oz) of well drained, pressed curd cheese and 250 g (9 oz) soft butter into a basin and mix together until very smooth. Add 1 egg and a little salt and pepper and mix together.

Divide into 60–70 g (2–2½ oz) pieces, wrap each in a very small thin pancake made without sugar and shape them oblong in the same way as Cromesquis. When required for service, dip in very light frying batter, deep fry in hot fat, drain and arrange on a serviette.

1199 Oeufs de Vanneau Christiana
Hard boil the plovers' eggs and shell them. Have prepared in advance some small nests of Duchesse potato mixture, piped with a star tube, eggwashed and coloured in the oven.

Arrange the nests in a circle on a dish and place one of the prepared eggs in each; coat the eggs with Sauce Demi-glace mixed with a quarter its volume of purée of foie gras and sprinkle with chopped truffle. Care should be taken not to damage the nests whilst serving them.

1200 Paillettes au Parmesan—Cheese Straws
Cheese straws, although used in different parts of this book, are normally considered to be a savoury and have therefore been placed in that chapter (4947).

1201 Pannequets
As a variation, savoury Pannequets may be served as a hot Hors-d'oeuvre. The pancake mixture used is the ordinary one (4394a) without sugar or flavouring and the pancakes are made in the usual way. They are then coated with any suitable mixture used for Bouchées, Croquettes, Purées etc., then rolled up, the ends trimmed straight, cut into diamond-shaped pieces, at which point their correct description becomes Pannequets. Serve arranged on a serviette.

Note: Pannequets always take the name of the main ingredient used in filling the pancake, e.g. Pannequets Joinville.

1202 Pâtés à la Beauceronne (*small*)
Roll out a sheet of puff paste 3 mm (⅛ in) thick and cut into oblongs 9–10 cm (3½–4 in) long by 7–8 cm (2¾–3¼ in) wide.

Bone the required number of larks and coat with a very finely chopped and well flavoured meat and mushroom mince which has been mixed with a little well reduced Sauce Demi-glace. Place one on each piece of paste, moisten the edges and enclose the lark forming a neat shape. Decorate the top with a piece of paste in the shape of a leaf, eggwash and bake in a hot oven for approximately 20 minutes.

1203 Pâtés for Bortsch (*To make 20 small pâtés*)
Cook 30 g (1 oz) chopped onion in a little butter to a golden colour, add 125 g (4½ oz) tail end of fillet of beef cut in large dice, and a little chopped parsley, salt and pepper. Sauté quickly for a few minutes on a hot stove; pass through the fine plate of the mincer or pound and pass through a sieve. Add 1 finely chopped hard-boiled egg to the mixture and proceed as for Pâtés à la Bourgeoise but making them slightly smaller.

These are an accompaniment for Bortsch and the same mixture may also be used for Rissoles which may equally be used to accompany Bortsch.

1204 Pâtés à la Bourgeoise (*small*)
Roll out a sheet of puff paste 6–7 mm (⅕–¼ in) thick and cut as many rounds as required with a 6 cm (2½ in) round cutter. Use the trimmings to roll out a sheet thinner than the previous one and cut out a similar number of the round pieces of the same size.

Place these thin rounds on a damp baking tray, moisten the edges of the rounds and place a small ball of finely chopped cooked minced meat mixed with chopped raw mushrooms and parsley in the centre of each. Cover with the other pieces of paste, seal together by pressing with the back of a 5 cm (2 in) round pastry cutter, eggwash and bake in a hot oven for 13–15 minutes.

1205 Pâtés du Chanoine (*small*)
Roll out a sheet of puff paste 5 mm (⅕ in) thick and cut out two small oval-shaped pieces for each pâté. Place half of them on a damp baking tray, and on each place half a poached fresh herring roe or a piece of any other soft roe, previously rolled in blanched chopped Fines Herbes. Moisten the edges of the paste, cover with the tops and seal by pressing with the back of a smaller oval pastry cutter. Eggwash and bake for approximately 15 minutes in a hot oven.

1206 Pâtés Dauphine (*small*)
The characteristic of these pâtés is that they are made from an unsweetened ordinary brioche

paste kept a little firmer than usual. They are made in the usual way using any kind of stuffing, either a mince or Salpicon. The paste is rolled out as usual, cut out with a pastry cutter and, when made, the pâtés should be left in a warm place to allow for a light proving. Eggwash and cook in a hot oven as for Pâtés à la Bourgeoise.

1207 Pâtés Manon (*small*)
These are made in the same way as Pâtés à la Bourgeoise using a Godiveau mixed with some very finely chopped cooked salt ox tongue instead of mince.

1208 Pâtés Mazarin, or Petits Pâtés au Jus
Prepare the required number of small fluted Croustades from short paste and cooked to a light colour.

Roll out a sheet of puff paste trimmings $\frac{1}{2}$ cm ($\frac{1}{5}$ in) thick and cut the required number of lids the same size as the Croustades using a 6–7 cm ($2\frac{1}{2}$–$2\frac{3}{4}$ in) fancy cutter. Eggwash the lids, place a small round decorated piece of puff pastry on each; place on a moistened baking tray and bake in a moderate oven.

Fill the Croustades with a dice of Godiveau Quenelles, mushrooms, lambs' sweetbreads and truffle mixed with slightly thin Sauce Demi-glace.
To serve: arrange on serviettes and cover them with the prepared lids.

1209 Pâtés Nimoise
These are made from puff paste cut in round fancy shapes a little larger than the ordinary small pâtés. The filling is a stuffing made from the following ingredients: 250 g (9 oz) diced fillet of mutton sautéed in butter; 125 g ($4\frac{1}{2}$ oz) chicken livers; 150 g (5 oz) fresh pork fat; 1 tbs blanched Fines Herbes and 1 tbs of chopped truffle. Pound the mutton, liver and fat separately, then pound well together, pass through a fine sieve and mix with the herbs and truffle.

1210 Ordinary Pâtés
These are the same as Pâtés à la Bourgeoise using any fine mince of meat or Godiveau.

1211 Pâtés à la Parisienne
These are made in the same way as Pâtés à la Bourgeoise but filled with a Godiveau stuffing containing chopped truffle.

1212 Pâtés au Verjus
Cut some 7 cm ($2\frac{3}{4}$ in) diameter rounds of puff pastry from a sheet of paste 4 mm ($\frac{1}{6}$ in) thick. Remove the pips from unripe grapes and envelope each two in some Godiveau mixed with chopped chives. Place two of these grapes on each round of paste, cover with a second round of puff paste, and proceed in the same way as for the other Pâtés.

1213 Pellmènes Sibériens (*Russian Hors-d'oeuvre*)
These are a type of ravioli made from very thin noodle paste in the form of small pâtés being two rounds of paste enclosing a small amount of the following mixture: equal amounts of a Salpicon of roast hazel-hen flesh, and lean and fat ham. Season with salt, pepper, nutmeg and a little chopped parsley and mix together with 1 tbs reduced Sauce Demi-glace per 100 g ($3\frac{1}{2}$ oz) of Salpicon.

Poach the finished Pellmènes in boiling water for 15 minutes and drain well; place in a hot deep service dish and sprinkle with melted butter, lemon juice, chopped parsley and a little melted meat glaze.

1214 Piroguis Caucasiens (*Russian Hors-d'oeuvre*)
Prepare an ordinary Chou Paste flavoured with grated cheese and spread it flat and evenly on two trays approximately 6–8 mm ($\frac{1}{3}$ in) thick; bake in the oven. This should give two equal sized pieces of cooked paste roughly $1\frac{1}{2}$ cm ($\frac{3}{5}$ in) thick.

Spread one of the layers with a coating of reduced Sauce Béchamel flavoured with grated cheese and mixed with cooked sliced mushrooms; cover with the other layer of chou paste, press together and cut into oblongs 8 cm ($3\frac{1}{4}$ in) long by 3 cm ($1\frac{1}{4}$ in) wide.

Coat each of these pieces on all surfaces with a little of the Sauce Béchamel mixture, pass through breadcrumbs first then egg and breadcrumb. Deep fry and arrange on a serviette to serve.

1215 Piroguis en Croissants
Melt 30 g (1 oz) butter and add $\frac{3}{4}$ dl (3 fl oz or $\frac{3}{8}$ U.S. cup) well flavoured veal gravy and 250 g (9 oz) fine rye breadcrumbs; mix well together and cook until it becomes as stiff as a forcemeat panada. Spread on a buttered tray 6–8 mm ($\frac{1}{3}$ in) thick, allow to cool and cut into crescent shapes using a pastry cutter dipped in hot water so as to facilitate the ease of cutting.

Coat one side only of each crescent with Twarogue (330) and join them together in pairs. Shallow fry them in clarified butter to colour on both sides.

1216 Piroguis au Fromage
Line well buttered dariole moulds with ordinary unsweetened Brioche Paste. Fill the insides with Twarogue (330), cover with a round of Brioche Paste and seal the edges to the lightly moistened

sides of the paste. Place in a warm place for 25–30 minutes to prove, then bake in a hot oven for 20 minutes.

1217 Piroguis au Gibier
Cut out the required number of rounds of puff paste 10 cm (4 in) in diameter by ½ cm (⅕ in) thick. Place a small amount of cold mince of finely chopped game heated in butter with some chopped hard-boiled eggs and Kache of Buckwheat (318) or cooked rice. Moisten the edges of the paste and cover each with a second round of puff paste the same size and thickness as the other. Eggwash and bake in a hot oven for 15 minutes.

1218 Piroguis aux Légumes
Proceed as for Piroquis au Gibier replacing the game with the following mixture: Stew 200 g (7 oz) finely diced carrot or mixed vegetables in a little butter; add 3 chopped hard-boiled eggs, 100 g (3½ oz) Kache of Buckwheat (318) or cooked rice and mix with 3½ dl (12 fl oz or 1½ U.S. cups) reduced Sauce Béchamel. Allow to become completely cold before preparing the Piroguis.

1219 Piroguis Livoniens
Prepare a panada of rye breadcrumbs as in the recipe for Piroguis en Croissants.

When it is very cold, cut into the desired shapes and shallow fry in clarified butter until well coloured. Arrange neatly on a dish, sprinkle with Kache of Buckwheat (318) and grated Parmesan and place in a very hot oven for 5 minutes before serving.

1220 Piroguis à la Moscovite
Chop 250 g (9 oz) cooked white fish free from skin and bone, 5 hard-boiled eggs and 125 g (4½ oz) cooked Vésiga; mix together.

Roll out a sheet of ordinary unsweetened Brioche Paste ½ cm (⅕ in) thick and cut out the required number of pieces using a plain oval cutter 10 cm (4 in) in length. Place a tablespoon of the prepared mixture in the centre of each oval, lightly moisten the edges of the paste and cover the filling by bringing up the sides to the centre and seal together so as to form small pasties. Place to prove in a warm place for 25–30 minutes then bake in a hot oven for 20 minutes. Just before serving, pour a teaspoon of Sauce Colbert inside each.

1221 Piroguis au Poisson
Proceed in the same way as Piroguis au Gibier using any kind of mince of cooked fish instead of game.

1222 Piroguis Polonais
Cut 250 g (9 oz) each of calf's udder and lean veal into very small dice and cook in butter until lightly brown, together with 60 g (2 oz) chopped onion. Season well with salt and pepper and allow to cool.

Cut the required number of oval shapes from a sheet of puff paste of the same size as for the Piroguis à la Moscovite, place half a tablespoon of the prepared mixture in the centre of each, lightly moisten the edges of the paste and cover the filling by bringing up the sides together and sealing along the centre. Eggwash and bake in a hot oven for 18 minutes.

1223 Piroguis de Smolensk
Take 125 g (4½ oz) Kache of Semolina (319), 4 chopped hard-boiled eggs, 60 g (2 oz) chopped onion cooked in butter and 1½ tbs parsley; mix together and heat thoroughly in butter and allow to cool completely.

Cut out the required number of 6 cm (2¼ in) squares of puff paste 6–7 mm (⅓ in) thick and place a little of the prepared mixture in the centre of each. Moisten the edges and cover with another square piece of paste of the same size. Seal the edges together, eggwash and bake in a hot oven for 18 minutes.

1224 Piroguis aux Truffes
Cut some medium-sized cooked truffles in 1 cm (⅖ in) thick slices, coat each with well reduced Sauce Béchamel and allow to cool.

Sandwich each slice between 2 rounds of Blinis and seal the edges together with a little forcemeat; egg and breadcrumb using very fine breadcrumbs and deep fry in clarified butter making sure that they are cooked just when required.

1225 Piroguis au Vésiga
Prepare and cook 25 g (1 oz) Vésiga in White Bouillon with a piece of celery. When ready, drain and chop the Vésiga and celery and add 2 chopped roots of parsley and 2 chopped hard boiled eggs. Mix together with 3 tbs well reduced Sauce Béchamel.

Cut out the required number of 10 cm (4 in) rounds from a sheet of puff paste 7 mm (⅓ in) thick, place a little of the mixture on one side of the rounds, moisten the edges of the paste and fold over in the shape of turnovers. Seal the edges and mark with the back of a round pastry cutter; eggwash and bake in a hot oven for 20 minutes.

Note: For the preparation of Vésiga see the notes under Coulibiac (1662).

1226 Pommes à l'Ardennaise
Bake some medium-sized Dutch potatoes and

when cooked cut them in half lengthways, remove the insides and place this in a basin. Mix with a fork and add per 500 g (1 lb 2 oz) potato, 4 egg yolks, 150 g (5 oz) butter, 300 g (11 oz) finely diced lean ham, 100 g (3½ oz) chopped mushrooms, 80 g (3 oz) grated Parmesan, 10 g (⅓ oz) salt, a pinch of pepper, a pinch of grated nutmeg and 1 tbs mixed chopped parsley and chervil.

Mix all together well and refill the half sections of the potatoes; smooth the surface, sprinkle with grated cheese, place in a medium oven for 20 minutes and gratinate at the last moment.

1227 Pommes Dietrich
Bake some large-sized Dutch potatoes and when cooked cut off the tops along the length to form lids; place aside. Remove the insides of the potatoes to form empty cases and fill these with small Gnocchi au Parmesan mixed with creamy Sauce Béchamel containing sliced white Piedmont truffles.

Replace the tops of the potatoes making sure that these fit properly, place on a baking tray and reheat for 20 minutes. Arrange on a serviette to serve.

1228 Pommes Georgette
Bake some medium-sized Dutch potatoes; when cooked, open them on one side as for éclairs and remove the insides. Fill the cases with crayfish mixed with Sauce Nantua, reheat in a moderate oven and serve very hot, arranged on a serviette.

1229 Pomponettes
These are very small Rissoles made of puff paste in the shape of a small bag or sack in which is enclosed any kind of stiff purée. Pomponettes take their name from the particular filling used; they are deep fried in the same way as for Rissoles (1235).

1230 Quiche à la Lorraine (*for 10 persons*)
Line an 18–20 cm (7–8 in) plain or fluted flan case with ordinary short paste taking care that the sides are a little higher than the rim of the case. Cover the base with thin rashers of bacon which have been blanched and lightly fried in butter. These may be arranged alternatively with slices of Gruyère cheese but the addition of cheese is optional and is not correct as far as local custom is concerned.

Fill the flan with a mixture made of 4 dl (14 fl oz or 1¾ U.S. cups) cream, 3 eggs and a pinch of salt. Finish by dotting the surface with 25 g (1 oz) butter cut in small pieces; bake in a moderate oven for 30–35 minutes and cut into triangles whilst just warm.

1231 Quiches au Jambon (*small*)
Line some deep tartlet moulds with short paste or puff paste trimmings; place a thin slice of lean ham in each and fill with the same mixture as in the preceding recipe: this amount will yield 15 tartlets. Bake in a moderate oven for 15–18 minutes.

1232 Ramequins
These are a smaller version of the Gougère Bourguignonne which were once commonly served as a hot Hors-d'oeuvre. Ramequins are made in the shape of a Chou bun whereas the Gougère is made in the form of a crown.

Make unsweetened Chou Paste using milk instead of water and add 50 g (2 oz) finely grated Gruyère and another 50 g (2 oz) of the same cheese cut in very small dice per 2½ dl (9 fl oz or 1⅛ U.S. cups) Chou Paste.

Pipe the mixture into medium-sized balls as for Chou buns, egg wash, sprinkle each with a little very finely diced Gruyère and bake in a moderate oven for 12–15 minutes. Arrange on a serviette to serve.

1233 Rastegaïs (*Russian Hors-d'oeuvre*)
These are made as for Piroguis à la Moscovite replacing the cooked white fish with a Salpicon of raw salmon.

1234 Ravioles à la Sibérienne
This is a more explicit name for Pellmènes (1213).

1235 Rissoles
This is the name given to a type of hot Hors-d'oeuvre which is essentially comprised of:

1) a Salpicon bound in the same way as a croquette mixture of which the principal ingredient can be poultry, game, foie gras etc. and which determines its name, and
2) a covering or envelope of paste such as short, half puff or puff paste trimmings or unsweetened Brioche Paste. This mixture must be completely cold before being put inside the paste.

Rissoles are always finished by deep frying, then arranged on a serviette and garnished with fried parsley to serve; no accompaniment is served. Each kind of rissole is made in a different shape.

1236 Rissoles à la Bergère
Prepare a Salpicon of braised lamb's sweetbreads, mushrooms and morels mixed with some thick Béchamel Soubise (151).

Make in the shape of small fancy patties using

half puff paste; egg wash and deep fry at the last minute and serve as explained above.

1237 Rissoles Bouquetière
Prepare a mixture of two-thirds small Printanier of vegetables and one-third of asparagus tips mixed with some creamy well reduced Sauce Béchamel.

Make in the shape of pleated turnovers using puff paste trimmings. Eggwash, deep fry at the last minute and serve in the usual manner.

1238 Rissoles à la Bohémienne
Prepare a Salpicon of two-thirds foie gras and one-third diced truffle mixed with reduced Sauce Demi-glace.

Make in the shape of plain turnovers using general purpose Brioche Paste. Place in a warm place to lightly prove and deep fry at the last minute; serve in the usual manner.

1239 Rissoles à la Bressane
Prepare a Salpicon of chicken livers sautéed in butter and mixed with reduced Sauce Duxelles containing some finely sliced cooked mushrooms.

Make in the shape of small fancy turnovers using good short paste. Eggwash, deep fry at the last minute and serve in the usual manner.

1240 Rissoles à la Dauphine
These can be made from any kind of Salpicon and its name should take into account the main ingredient used; for example Rissoles de Volaille à la Dauphine or Rissoles de Crevettes à la Dauphine. Whichever mixture is used, Rissoles à la Dauphine are always enveloped in fairly firm Brioche Paste in the shape of turnovers. Deep fry at the last minute and serve in the usual manner.

1241 Rissoles à l'Indienne
Prepare a Salpicon of lobster mixed with some reduced curry-flavoured Sauce Béchamel.

Prepare also one oyster per rissole by first poaching them and coating each with Sauce Villeroy. Finally cover each prepared oyster with a little of the lobster Salpicon then enclose each in half puff paste in the shape of plain turnovers. Eggwash and sprinkle with very fine breadcrumbs before deep frying. Serve in the usual manner.

1242 Rissoles Joinville
Prepare a mixture of crayfish tails and a short Julienne of cooked mushrooms and truffles mixed with reduced Sauce Normande finished with Shrimp and Crayfish Butter.

Make in the shape of plain turnovers using puff paste trimmings. Eggwash, deep fry at the last minute and serve in the usual manner.

1243 Rissoles Marly
Prepare a Salpicon of three-quarters of cooked pheasant and one quarter of truffles mixed with Sauce Demi-glace flavoured with a little pheasant cullis.

Make in the shape of small oblong patties using puff paste trimmings. Eggwash, deep fry at the last minute and serve in the usual manner.

1244 Rissoles aux Morilles
Prepare a Salpicon of morels stewed with butter and mixed with some thick Sauce Béchamel.

Make in the shape of small round fancy patties using good short paste. Eggwash, deep fry at the last minute and serve in the usual manner.

1245 Rissoles Nantua
Prepare a Salpicon of two-thirds crayfish tails and one-third truffles mixed with reduced Sauce Béchamel finished with Crayfish Butter.

Make in the shape of fancy oval patties using puff paste trimmings. Eggwash, deep fry at the last moment and serve in the usual manner.

1246 Rissoles à la Normande
Prepare a mixture of poached oysters, very small mussels and shrimps mixed with thick Sauce Normande.

Make in the shape of plain turnovers using puff paste trimmings. Eggwash, deep fry at the last moment and serve in the usual manner.

1247 Rissoles à l'Ostendaise
Prepare a mixture of poached oysters mixed with reduced Sauce Béchamel flavoured with the oyster cooking liquid.

Make in the shape of plain turnovers using puff paste trimmings. Eggwash, deep fry at the last moment and serve in the usual manner.

1248 Rissoles Pompadour
Prepare a Salpicon of equal quantities of foie gras, salt ox tongue, mushrooms and truffle, mixed with reduced Sauce Périgueux. The garnish also includes a round slice of bone marrow poached and enclosed with the mixture in each rissole.

Make in the shape of small fancy patties using puff paste trimmings. Eggwash, deep fry at the last moment and serve in the usual manner.

1249 Rissoles à la Reine
Prepare a mixture of finely chopped chicken mixed with some well reduced creamy Sauce Béchamel.

Make in the shape of small turnovers using puff paste trimmings. Eggwash, deep fry at the last moment and serve in the usual manner.

Note: In the classical kitchen these were called Rissoles au Blanc-manger.

1250 Rissoles Victoria
Prepare a Salpicon of three-quarters of lobster and a quarter of truffle mixed with some reduced Lobster Sauce.

Make in the shape of fancy oval patties using puff paste trimmings. Eggwash, deep fry at the last moment and serve in the usual manner.

1251 Sausselis aux Anchois
The word Sausselis is the Russian name for Dartois; see Dartois aux Anchois in this Chapter.

1252 Sausselis aux Choux (*Russian Hors-d'oeuvre*)
Finely shred 500 g (1 lb 2 oz) white cabbage and stew together in butter with 125 g (4½ oz) finely chopped onion, until three-quarters cooked. Season with salt and pepper and add 3 chopped hard-boiled eggs; allow to cool.

Proceed as for Dartois aux Anchois but using this mixture. Bake in a moderate oven for approximately 30 minutes, cut into pieces immediately it is cooked and arrange on serviettes for service.

1253 Sausselis de Filets de Sole
See Dartois aux Filets de Sole (1172).

1254 Soufflés de Crustacés (*Petits*)—**Small Shellfish Soufflés**
These small Soufflés as well as those in the following recipes should be cooked in small pleated paper cases or individual porcelain soufflé moulds (cassolettes) having a capacity of approximately 1 dl (3½ fl oz or ½ U.S. cup).
For 10 small Soufflés: finely pound 250 g (9 oz) cooked flesh and trimmings of shellfish such as lobster, crayfish or prawns, pass through a fine sieve and add 1½ dl (5 fl oz or ⅝ U.S. cup) Sauce Béchamel which has been reduced with the cooking liquor from the shellfish being used. Season, mix in 3 egg yolks then fold in 3 stiffly beaten egg whites. Place in the buttered cases or moulds and bake in a moderate oven for 12 minutes.

1255 Soufflés à la Florentine (*Petits*)
For 10 small Soufflés: finely chop 100 g (3½ oz) well drained and squeezed spinach; cook with a little butter, salt, pepper and nutmeg until dry. Mix in 1½ dl (5 fl oz or ⅝ U.S. cup) Sauce Béchamel reduced with cream and 3 egg yolks, then fold in 4 stiffly beaten egg whites. Place in the buttered cases or moulds and bake in a moderate oven for 12 minutes.

1256 Soufflés de Gibier (*Petits*)—**Small Game Soufflés**
For 10 small Soufflés: finely pound 250 g (9 oz) cooked flesh of furred or feathered game and add 1½ dl (5 fl oz or ⅝ U.S. cup) Sauce Béchamel which has been reduced with a few spoonfuls of game *Fumet*. Pass through a fine sieve, season, mix in 2 egg yolks then fold in 3 stiffly beaten egg whites. Place in buttered cases or moulds and bake in a moderate oven for 12 minutes.

1257 Soufflés aux Huîtres (*Petits*)—**Small Oyster Soufflés**
For 10 small Soufflés: poach 20 small oysters and remove the beards; mix the oysters into a Parmesan soufflé mixture (1259). Place in buttered cases or moulds ensuring that there are 2 oysters in each one; cook in the usual way.

1258 Soufflés au Jambon (*Petits*)—**Small Ham Soufflés**
For 10 small Soufflés: finely pound 250 g (9 oz) lean cooked ham with 15 g (½ oz) butter. Pass through a fine sieve and mix in 1½ dl (5 fl oz or ⅝ U.S. cup) Sauce Béchamel which has been reduced with a little ham stock and well seasoned with paprika; mix in 2 egg yolks, fold in 3 stiffly beaten egg whites, place in buttered cases or moulds and bake in a moderate oven for 12 minutes.

1259 Soufflés Parmesane (*Petits*)
For 10 small Soufflés: mix 150 g (5 oz) flour with 4 dl (14 fl oz or 1¾ U.S. cups) boiled milk, season with salt, pepper and grated nutmeg and bring to the boil mixing continuously. Remove from the heat, add 60 g (2 oz) grated Parmesan, 30 g (1 oz) butter and 4 egg yolks; fold in 4 stiffly beaten egg whites and cook in the usual manner.

1260 Soufflés de Poisson (*Petits*)—**Small Fish Soufflés**
This recipe is suitable for all kinds of fish such as salmon, sole, whiting, red mullet, smelts etc. The Soufflé should take its name from the fish being used e.g. Petits Soufflés de Saumon.
For 10 small Soufflés: cut 250 g (9 oz) of the selected fish into dice, season and stew with a little butter until cooked. Pass through a fine sieve and add 1½ dl (5 fl oz or ⅝ U.S. cup) Sauce Béchamel which has been reduced with a little *Fumet* from the fish being used. Mix in 3 egg yolks, fold in 3 stiffly beaten egg whites and cook in the usual manner.

Note: It should be remembered that the taste of smelts is very pronounced and when making Soufflés d'Eperlans only a third of the weight of fish being used should be of smelts, the remainder being sole for preference.

1261 Soufflés à la Suissesse (*Petits*)
For 10 small soufflés: prepare the same mixture as for Soufflé Parmesane but using only 3 egg whites. Arrange the mixture dome shape in small buttered tartlet moulds. Place in a shallow pan with a little hot water in the bottom and cook in a moderate oven for 15 minutes taking care that the water does not boil.

Turn out the Soufflés and arrange in a buttered deep serving dish which has been sprinkled with grated Parmesan; sprinkle the Soufflés with more Parmesan and 12 minutes before service, pour in sufficient cream to come half-way up the Soufflés. Place in a moderate oven and cook until all the cream has been absorbed by the Soufflés and they have become slightly coloured.

1262 Subrics de Foie Gras
For 10 subrics: mix 100 g ($3\frac{1}{2}$ oz) flour with 1 egg, 1 egg yolk and 1 dl ($3\frac{1}{2}$ fl oz or $\frac{1}{2}$ U.S. cup) double cream. Season with a pinch of salt and pepper and carefully mix in 350 g (13 oz) of cold poached or braised foie gras cut into small dice.

Heat sufficient clarified butter to cover the bottom of a small pan, take approximately 60 g (2 oz) spoonfuls of the mixture and drop in the butter in the shape of macaroons; cook for approximately 2 minutes on each side until coloured, arrange on a serviette and serve very hot.

1263 Subrics à l'Italienne
For 10 Subrics: poach 2 calf's brains or the same amount of ox or mutton brains in Vinegar Court-bouillon; allow to get cold, drain and cut into dice.

Beat 3 eggs together with 25 g (1 oz) flour, season with salt and pepper and carefully mix in the brains and 100 g ($3\frac{1}{2}$ oz) grated Parmesan. Cook the Subrics as in the previous recipe using a mixture of very hot oil and butter; serve arranged on a serviette and garnish with quarters of lemon.

1264 Subrics Piémontais
For 10 Subrics: prepare a Risotto Italienne (4246) using 125 g ($4\frac{1}{2}$ oz) Piedmont rice, and mix in 50 g (2 oz) each of chopped lean ham and grated Parmesan, and 2 well beaten eggs. Cook the Subrics as explained for Subrics de Foie Gras.

1265 Talmouses
Line some fancy tartlet cases with thin short paste, prick the bottoms and pipe a ball of Ramequin Paste into each tartlet (see Ramequins in this Chapter). Eggwash the top of the paste and place a pinch of small diced Gruyère cheese on top.

Cook in a moderate oven then fill the inside of the Ramequin with Pastry Cream made without sugar but seasoned and flavoured with grated Parmesan. Serve arranged on a serviette.

Note: This Talmouse can be called Talmouse à la Bagration; it should not be called *à la Rohan* or *à la Royale* as is sometimes done.

1266 Talmouses à l'Ancienne
Roll out a sheet of good short paste 2 mm ($\frac{1}{12}$ in) thick and cut out rounds using a 10 cm diameter (4 in) fancy cutter. Pipe a 2 cm ($\frac{4}{5}$ in) ball of Ramequin Paste in the centre of each (see Ramequins in this Chapter), eggwash the paste and sprinkle with finely diced cheese. Moisten the edges and fold in from three sides in the shape of a three-cornered hat. Eggwash all over and cook in a moderate oven then fill the inside of the ramequin centre with Pastry Cream made without sugar but seasoned and flavoured with grated Parmesan. Arrange on a serviette to serve.

1267 Tartlets
Tartlets for hot Hors-d'oeuvre can be prepared in several ways; the moulds can be lined with a raw forcemeat or with thin short paste then filled with a raw filling; or they can be made in the same way as Croustades. For the latter, the bottom and sides of the Croustade are coated with a thin layer of the appropriate raw forcemeat, placed in the oven for a few moments to cook the forcemeat and then filled with the selected garnish and sauce.

1268 Tartelettes Châtillon
Prepare a mixture of sliced mushrooms sautéed in butter and mixed with Sauce Béchamel. Fill into lightly coloured pastry tartlet cases and cover with a thin layer of chicken and cream forcemeat. Place on a baking sheet and place in the oven for a few minutes to cook the forcemeat. Serve arranged on a serviette.

1269 Tartelettes Diane
Coat the bottom and sides of cooked fancy paste tartlet cases with a thin layer of light game forcemeat; place in the oven to cook the forcemeat. Fill the tartlets with thin slices of breast of partridge and sliced truffle mixed with Sauce Demi-glace flavoured with partridge *Fumet*. Cover with a thin layer of light game forcemeat, smooth dome shape and decorate each with a small piped crescent shape of the same forcemeat. Place in the oven for

a few minutes to cook the forcemeat and serve arranged on a serviette.

1270 Tartelettes à la Gauloise
Coat the bottom and sides of lightly coloured, fancy paste tartlet cases with a thin layer of light chicken forcemeat; place in the oven to cook the forcemeat.

Fill the tartlets with very small cooked cockscombs and kidneys mixed with a little veal meat glaze thickened with butter. Cover with some more chicken forcemeat mixed with a quarter its volume of a purée of ham and place in the oven for a few minutes to cook the forcemeat. Serve arranged on a serviette.

1271 Tartelettes aux Gnocchi
Line some large buttered tartlet moulds with very thin short paste and fill with very small Parmesan-flavoured Gnocchi prepared as for Gnocchi au Gratin (4280) and mixed with just a little Sauce Béchamel. Sprinkle with grated Parmesan, place a few pieces of butter on top and cook in a moderate oven for 20 minutes. Serve arranged on a serviette.

1272 Tartelettes Marly
Prepare some deep tartlet cases and coat the insides with a thin layer of fine game forcemeat. Place in the oven for a few minutes to cook the forcemeat.

Fill them with thin small slices of cooked breast of pheasant and truffle mixed with pheasant-flavoured Salmis Sauce. Cover with a layer of the same forcemeat and place in the oven for a few minutes to cook; serve arranged on a serviette.

1273 Tartelettes Olga
Fill some very small buttered tartlet moulds with Mousseline forcemeat made from hazel-hen. Place them in a pan containing a little boiling water and cook in a moderate oven.

Demould them when ready and place each in a slightly larger baked paste tartlet case. Lightly coat with Salmis Sauce and place a very small cooked white mushroom on top. Serve arranged on a serviette.

1274 Tartelettes à la Polonaise
Line some large plain buttered tartlet moulds with ordinary short paste, fill with well drained cooked Sauerkraut mixed with 3 tbs of Kache of Semolina (319), and 2 chopped hard-boiled eggs per 500 g (1 lb 2 oz) Sauerkraut.

Cover each with a thin round of short paste and seal together; eggwash and make a small hole in the covers to allow the steam to escape. Place on a baking tray and cook in a moderate oven for 20 minutes. Remove from the oven and pour a little Sauce Demi-glace through the holes in the tartlets. Serve arranged on a serviette.

1275 Tartelettes à la Reine
Line some baked tartlet cases with a thin layer of chicken and cream forcemeat and place in a moderate oven for a few minutes to cook the forcemeat. Fill with thin slices of chicken, mushroom and truffle mixed with a little Sauce Suprême; cover with a thin layer of the same forcemeat and place in a moderate oven to cook. Serve arranged on a serviette.

1276 Timbales Agnès Sorel (*small*)
Butter some dariole moulds and place a ring of very red ox tongue in the bottom of each with a round of truffle in the centre; line the bottom and sides with a ½ cm (⅕ in) thick layer of chicken forcemeat.

Fill with a Salpicon of tongue, white of chicken and truffle mixed with a little Velouté; cover with a layer of the same forcemeat and place in a tray with some water to cook in a moderate oven for 15–18 minutes.

Demould, arrange on a round dish and serve accompanied with Sauce Demi-glace.

1277 Timbales Dessoliers (*small*)
Well butter some deep dariole moulds and coat the bottom and sides with a sprinkling of finely chopped black truffle. Make cold to set the butter, then line the moulds with a layer of whiting forcemeat mixed with Crayfish Butter—the colour should be a nice pink.

Fill with a Salpicon of crayfish tails and lobster mixed with Sauce Normande; cover with the same forcemeat and cook as in the previous recipe for 12 minutes.

Demould, arrange on a dish and serve accompanied with a fairly thin Fish Velouté finished with Crayfish Butter.

1278 Timbales Maréchal (*small*)
Well butter some dariole moulds and place a round of truffle cut with a fancy cutter in each one. Coat the bottom and sides with a layer of chicken forcemeat mixed with a good proportion of finely chopped red tongue; fill with a purée of cooked chicken mixed with a little thick Soubise Sauce and cover with some of the same forcemeat. Cook as for Timbales Agnès Sorel allowing 12 minutes before being required.

Demould and serve accompanied with Sauce Périgueux.

1279 Timbales Médicis (*small*)
Prepare a Savarin Paste without sugar and cook it in Baba moulds. Turn them out when cooked and empty so as to leave a 7 mm (¼ in) thick case. At the last minute fill with a Salpicon of foie gras, ox tongue and truffle mixed with tomato-flavoured Sauce Allemande. Place a fancy slice of truffle on

top of each timbale and arrange on a serviette for service.

1280 Timbales Montargis (*small*)

Butter some hexagonal moulds and line with alternate thin slices of tongue and truffle. Coat with chicken forcemeat and fill with a purée of cooked mushrooms containing chopped very red ox tongue and small dice of truffle. Cover with more of the same forcemeat and cook as for Timbales Agnès Sorel allowing 12 minutes before service.

Demould and arrange on a round dish accompanied with Ordinary Velouté containing some very small dice of ox tongue.

1281 Timbales Païva (*small*)

Well butter some deep dariole moulds and place a round piece of pancake made without sugar in the bottom of each. Line the sides with strips of the same pancake cut to the height of the mould; coat with a layer of chicken and cream forcemeat and fill with a purée of cooked chicken containing some very small dice of red ox tongue. Cover with some of the same forcemeat and cook as for Timbales Agnès Sorel allowing 12 minutes before service.

Demould and arrange on a round dish and serve accompanied with Sauce Albuféra.

1282 Timbales Régine (*small*)

Butter some dariole moulds and line with a layer of fairly stiff forcemeat made from sole and mixed with 90 g (3 oz) thick purée of cooked mushrooms per 500 g (1 lb 2 oz) of forcemeat. Fill with a Salpicon of poached soft roes mixed with Fish Velouté finished with Crayfish Butter; cover with some of the same forcemeat and cook as for Timbales Agnès Sorel allowing 15 minutes before service.

Demould, place in a circle on a round dish and fill the centre with Fish Velouté finished with Crayfish Butter.

1283 Timbales Reynière (*small*)

Well butter some dariole moulds, place a slice of truffle in the bottom of each and coat the sides with a sprinkling of finely chopped firm red ox tongue (the tip of the tongue is most suitable for this purpose).

Make cold to set the butter then coat with a 5 mm ($\frac{1}{5}$ in) layer of pheasant forcemeat. Fill with a Salpicon of foie gras and truffle mixed with Sauce Demi-glace and cover with more of the same forcemeat. Cook as for Timbales Agnès Sorel allowing 25 minutes before service. Serve accompanied with Sauce Demi-glace finished with a little cullis of pheasant.

1284 Timbales Talleyrand (*small*)

Well butter some deep dariole moulds and coat the sides with alternate bands of chopped white of chicken, tongue and truffle, approximately 1 cm ($\frac{2}{5}$ in) wide.

Make cold to set the butter then coat with a layer of chicken forcemeat. Fill with a purée of truffle and cover with more of the same forcemeat. Cook as for Timbales Agnès Sorel allowing 15 minutes before service. Serve accompanied with Sauce Demi-glace finished with truffle essence.

1285 Timbales Villeneuve (*small*)

Well butter some oval moulds and coat with a sprinkling of chopped parsley which has been squeezed almost dry in a cloth; make cold to set the butter. Coat with a layer of chicken forcemeat and fill with a large Salpicon of poached spine marrow and truffle mixed with a little Sauce Allemande. Cook as for Timbales Agnès Sorel allowing 12 minutes before serving; serve accompanied with a fairly thin creamy Sauce Soubise.

1286 Varenikis Lithuaniens (*Russian Hors-d'oeuvre*)

Prepare a mixture as follows: Chop separately 250 g (9 oz) each of fillet of beef and beef suet well cleaned of connective tissue. Cook 150 g ($5\frac{1}{2}$ oz) chopped onion in a little butter, add the beef and suet and cook until the meat is lightly brown.

Season with salt, pepper and nutmeg and mix with 2 tbs of thick Sauce Béchamel; allow to cool.

Prepare some noodle paste and make into 6 cm ($2\frac{1}{2}$ in) square Raviolis using the prepared mixture and cutting them out with a fancy pastry wheel. Poach the Varenikis in boiling salted water for 15 minutes, drain well and serve in a deep dish sprinkled with melted butter.

1287 Varenikis à la Polonaise (*Russian Hors-d'oeuvre*)

Cut fancy rounds of paste as for small Pâtés (1210). Place a little Twarogue mixture (330) in the centre of half of the rounds, moisten the edges, cover with the other rounds and press them together using the top of a smaller cutter.

Poach in boiling salted water for 15 minutes, drain well and serve in a deep dish sprinkled with melted butter. Serve separately a sauceboat of sour cream, or ordinary cream which has been acidulated with lemon juice.

1288 Vatrouskis au Fromage (*Russian Hors-d'oeuvre*)

Roll out a sheet of fairly stiff ordinary Brioche Paste made without sugar, $\frac{1}{2}$ cm ($\frac{1}{5}$ in) thick and cut it into 12 cm ($4\frac{1}{2}$ in) diameter rounds using a fancy cutter.

Place a little Twarogue mixture (330) slightly to the side of each round, moisten the edges of the paste and fold over in the shape of turnovers. Place on a baking sheet, eggwash and cook for approximately 18 minutes in a moderate oven. Serve arranged on a serviette.

1289 Visnisckis (*Russian Hors-d'oeuvre*)
Finely chop any kind of cooked fish, season with salt and pepper, flavour with fennel and mix with a little thick Fish Velouté.

Roll out a sheet of fairly stiff Brioche Paste without sugar, $\frac{1}{2}$ cm ($\frac{1}{5}$ in) thick and cut out rounds as for small Pâtés (1210). Place a little of the mixture in the centre of half the rounds, moisten the edges and cover with the other rounds. Press together and seal using the top of a small cutter.

Allow to prove lightly in a warm place for 25 minutes then deep fry in hot oil for 6–7 minutes just before service. Drain well and serve arranged on a serviette.

CHAPTER 5

EGGS

'A treatise on the egg—this protean of the kitchen—is still to be written': so wrote Monselet in one of his 'Lettres Gourmandes' printed in the journal *L'Evénement* many years ago.

Since then a number of books especially devoted to this commodity which the ancients considered as a symbol of the world, have been written; however, not one of them has been able to bring together the vast number of recipes that have been created on the spur of the moment or by the inspiration of cooks.

Thus no attempt has been made in this chapter to include everything that has been written on the subject and the chapter is restricted to those recipes which are in current use, observing wherever possible the correct relationship between the name and the method of preparation which is always the guiding principle throughout this book.

1290 Oeufs sur le Plat—Eggs Cooked in the Dish

Eggs cooked by this method have the particular quality as to be found in poached eggs where the degree of cooking is all important. Their correct preparation depends on the 3 following points:

1) The cooking of the white to where it becomes milky in appearance but yet is still soft,
2) the glistening appearance of the yolk which must also be soft, and
3) careful attention to prevent the egg sticking to the bottom of the dish.

Method of Preparation:
Heat approximately 7 g (¼ oz) butter in the dish so as to cover the bottom; break in 2 eggs ensuring that they are very fresh, pour the same amount of melted butter over the yolks, season with a pinch of salt and place to cook in a fairly hot oven for a few minutes. Remove and serve as soon as the whites become milky in appearance and the yolks are glistening but still soft.

Care should be taken that they are not left too long in the oven as a few seconds more than necessary is sufficient to ruin its quality. It should also be remembered that the dishes used for this method hold the heat for a considerable time and the eggs will continue cooking for a short while after removing them from the oven.

The most important point to be remembered is that Oeufs sur le Plat should be served immediately they are ready.

1291 Oeufs Pochés and Oeufs Mollets—Poached and Soft-Boiled Eggs

As the recipes for poached eggs are equally suitable for soft-boiled eggs, they have been kept together in this section; care must be taken that in both methods the eggs used are very fresh.

Method of Preparing Poached Eggs:
Have a shallow pan of boiling water ready, containing 10 g (⅓ oz) salt and ¼ dl (1 fl oz or ⅛ U.S. cup) vinegar per 1 litre (1¾ pt or 4½ U.S. cups) of water. Break the eggs in the water at the place where it is actually boiling and allow them to cook at a poaching temperature of 95° C (203° F) for approximately 3 minutes. The white should be sufficiently solid so as to envelope the yolk and to permit it to be handled; a poached egg is therefore really only a boiled egg minus its shell.

Remove the eggs with a perforated spoon, cool in cold water, trim and reheat in hot water containing 6 g (⅕ oz) salt per 1 litre water.

Method of Preparing Soft Boiled Eggs:
Place the eggs into boiling water and allow 6 minutes from the time the water reboils; cool in cold water and immediately shell them. Reheat in hot salted water as for poached eggs.

The Dressing and Serving of Poached and Soft-Boiled Eggs:
Before being used the eggs must be well drained on a clean cloth. They are usually dressed in one of the following ways:

1) On plain or decorated Croûtons of bread fried in clarified butter—oval-shape for poached eggs and round for soft-boiled eggs,
2) on shapes of cooked puff pastry—oval for poached eggs and round for soft-boiled eggs,
3) in a border of forcemeat or other similar mixture according to the requirements of the recipe. These borders are made with a piping bag and tube or moulded on buttered dishes; these can be round or oval, and plain or decorated. According to the ingredient used they are lightly cooked or coloured in the oven,
4) in pale baked tartlet cases filled with a garnish according to the particular recipe being used. When serving poached or soft-boiled eggs on Croûtons, puff pastry bases or tartlet cases, they should be coated with the required sauce beforehand.

1292 Oeufs Moulés—Moulded Eggs
Among the many ways of cooking eggs, the moulding of eggs is certainly the most decorative; it is only because of the relatively long time needed for their preparation that poached or soft-boiled eggs which take less time to make are more often used.

They are made in well buttered moulds of different shapes, decorated according to the requirements of the recipe—the eggs being broken directly into the mould, or in the form of a mixture. They are then cooked *au Bain-marie* by placing in a shallow pan with sufficient boiling water to come halfway up. Cover with a lid leaving a little room for the steam to escape and place in a moderate oven to cook. The time needed for cooking is 10–12 minutes, the total time for preparation being at least 15 minutes.

They are almost always turned out on to small pieces of toast after having been allowed to rest for a few moments after removing from the Bain-marie—this settles the cooked egg and facilitates the demoulding.

Whatever type of mixture is used, the mould should always be well buttered.

1293 Oeufs en Cocottes and Oeufs en Caisses—Eggs in Cocottes and in Porcelain Cases
This method of cooking eggs represents again a special type of poached egg. The Cocottes are fairly thick round individual dishes made of porcelain or earthenware; the Caisses are individual white fluted porcelain dishes similar to soufflé moulds.

They are cooked *au Bain-marie* and normally require 10 minutes cooking time although there may be a variation of a few minutes either way because of the kind of dish used and the thickness through which the heat has to penetrate before acting on the egg.

For speed of service it is as well to heat up the dishes before breaking in the eggs.

Method of Preparation:
Butter the Cocottes, garnish them if required and break in the eggs. Place in a shallow pan and pour in enough boiling water to reach within $1\frac{1}{2}$ cm ($\frac{1}{2}$ in) from the rim of the Cocottes. Cover, leaving a little room for the steam to escape and place in a fairly hot oven to cook.

The eggs are done when the white is almost set and the yolks glossy. Remove and carefully wipe the Cocottes and serve arranged on a serviette or on a fancy dish paper.

1294 Oeufs Frits—French Fried Eggs
In the long list of ways of preparing eggs, that for fried eggs is relatively insignificant when compared with others. Although fried eggs are used to a great extent for breakfast in England and America, correctly speaking they are Oeufs à la Poêle or pan-cooked eggs; in both countries the true fried egg is virtually unknown.

In general the garnishes suitable for fried eggs are served separately; the eggs are arranged on serviettes or on toast with fried parsley.

Method of Preparation:
Any clarified fat is suitable for frying eggs but oil is most frequently used and gives the best results; it is well to remember that only one egg should be cooked at a time.

Heat the oil in a small deep frying pan until it begins to smoke slightly, break an egg on a plate, season and slide it into the pan. Using a wooden spoon, envelope the yolk with the white, turning it until the outside becomes light brown, yet allowing the yolk to remain soft. Drain on a clean cloth and proceed in the same way for the required number of eggs.

1295 Oeufs Durs—Hard-boiled Eggs
Although the cooking of hard-boiled eggs may seem to be an insignificant operation the correct timing of the cooking is essential. It is of no use to cook them for longer than the exact time because overcooking will toughen the white and discolour the yolk.

To ensure a uniform cooking time for a number of eggs, place them into a basket or receptacle with large holes and immerse completely in a pan of boiling water; when it reboils allow 8 minutes for medium eggs and 10 minutes for large ones. As soon as they are cooked, remove and plunge them immediately into cold water; shell the eggs without breaking them.

1296 Oeufs Brouillés—Scrambled Eggs

This method of preparing eggs is undoubtedly the best, always bearing in mind that they should not be overcooked but be kept soft and creamy.

They are usually served in a small deep silver dish but according to the recipe are also presented in small Croustades, cases made of hollowed-out Brioche or tartlet cases.

Formerly it was the custom to surround the dish of scrambled eggs with small Croûtons of various shapes or small pieces of cooked pale baked puff pastry in the form of crescents, diamonds, rounds or palm leaves etc.; this way has much to recommend it and can always be followed.

In the old classical kitchen scrambled eggs were always cooked *au Bain-marie* as this guaranteed that they were cooked perfectly; but this was a time-consuming operation. They may be cooked more quickly by using direct but gentle heat as a gradual cooking process is essential for obtaining the desired soft, smooth texture.

Method of Preparation:
Gently heat 50 g (2 oz) butter in a heavy small pan, add 6 beaten eggs seasoned with salt and pepper, place over a moderate heat and stir constantly with a wooden spoon taking care that the heat remains even; too quick cooking will cause lumps to form which is contrary to the description of the term scrambled.

When the eggs have atttained the correct smooth, creamy consistency, remove from the fire, mix in 50 g (2 oz) butter in small pieces and, if required, $\frac{1}{2}$ dl (2 fl oz or $\frac{1}{4}$ U.S. cup) cream.

A whisk should not be used unless absolutely necessary.

Note: All the recipes for scrambled eggs in this section are based on the use of six eggs, unless otherwise stated.

1297 Oeufs Froids—Cold Eggs

As with all cold preparations, cold eggs should be treated with a fine sense of taste and correct and careful attention to their presentation. Directions for this preparation will be found in the following recipes where applicable.

NOTE

In this chapter the recipes for eggs have been divided into three clearly defined sections as follows:

1) sur le Plat, poached or soft-boiled, moulded, fried, en Cocottes and en Caisses, hard-boiled, scrambled and cold.
2) The various omelettes.
3) Plovers' eggs.

EGGS *SUR LE PLAT*—POACHED OR SOFT-BOILED EGGS—MOULDED EGGS—EGGS *EN COCOTTES* AND EGGS *EN CAISSES*—FRIED EGGS—HARD-BOILED EGGS—SCRAMBLED EGGS—COLD EGGS

1298 Oeufs Alexandra

Cold: Take some cold, well drained and trimmed poached eggs; coat with white Sauce Chaud-froid and decorate each with a fancy slice of truffle in the middle. Glaze with white aspic jelly and trim the excess sauce and jelly. Have ready some lightly coloured oval tartlet cases made from puff paste trimmings and half fill each with lobster Mousse. Place a prepared egg in each one and arrange a border of caviare around the edges. Arrange on a silver dish in a circle and place some chopped jelly in the centre.

1299 Oeufs à l'Américaine

Shallow Fried: Cook 2 eggs in a frying pan with a little butter, slide on to a hot plate and garnish with 2 grilled rashers of bacon and 1 grilled tomato.

Note: There is no serious reason for calling this dish American just because it is popular with the Americans and the English; it just so happens that it is widely known by this name and it is as well to keep it.

1300 Oeufs aux Anchois

Sur le Plat: Place some diced fillet of anchovy in the bottom of buttered dishes, break in the eggs, cook and encircle the yolks with a strip of anchovy fillet.

1301 Oeufs à l'Andalouse

Cold: Take some cold, well drained and trimmed poached eggs and coat with a purée of tomato containing a third its volume of Purée Soubise and 5 dl (18 fl oz or $2\frac{1}{4}$ U.S. cups) aspic jelly per 1 litre ($1\frac{3}{4}$ pt or $4\frac{1}{2}$ U.S. cups) of purée.

Fill the required number of oval tartlet moulds with a mixture of tomato purée and aspic jelly and allow to set. Turn out, place an egg on each one and arrange on a dish in a circle; surround with an interlinked chain of white cooked small rings of onion and fill the centre of the dish with chopped white aspic jelly.

1302 Oeufs à l'Anglaise

Shallow Fried: Fry the eggs in butter in a frying pan, trim them round with a plain cutter and place each on a slice of toast of the same size. Serve accompanied with thickened veal gravy.

Poached or Soft-boiled: Place the poached or soft-boiled eggs on round or oval slices of toast, sprinkle with grated cheddar cheese mixed with a little Cayenne, pour a little Brown Butter over and glaze quickly under the salamander or in a very hot oven.

1303 Oeufs Archiduc

Poached or Soft-boiled: Sauté 3 parts chicken livers and 1 part truffle both thinly sliced, in butter and add a little brandy when cooked. Fill into tartlet cases and place the eggs on top after they have been coated with Sauce Hongroise.

1304 Oeufs Argenteuil

Poached or Soft-boiled: Fill the bottom of tartlet cases with asparagus tips which have been blanched and cooked with butter. Arrange six 4 cm ($1\frac{1}{2}$ in) sticks of asparagus on top in the form of a star, the heads sticking out from the edge. Coat the eggs with Sauce Crème containing half its quantity of a purée of green asparagus and place one on each of the prepared tartlets.

Scrambled: Scramble 6 eggs and mix with 2 tbs of asparagus tips blanched and cooked with butter. Place in a deep dish and garnish with a nice bouquet of asparagus tips.

Cold: Coat some very cold soft-boiled eggs with white Sauce Chaud-froid mixed with one-third its quantity of a purée of green asparagus.

Place a salad of asparagus tips in the centre of a round dish and surround it with thin round slices of cooked potato; arrange the eggs around the outside.

1305 Oeufs d'Aumale

Scrambled: Scramble 6 eggs, mix them with 2 tbs of very thick and very red tomato purée and place in a deep dish. Make a hollow in the centre and fill with a garnish of diced veal kidney which has been sautéed in butter then mixed with a little well flavoured Madeira Sauce.

1306 Oeufs à l'Aurore

Poached or Soft-boiled: Coat the eggs with Sauce Aurore and place them on puff pastry bases cut either oval or round according to whether the eggs are poached or boiled.

Hard-boiled: Cut the eggs lengthways, remove the yolks and pound half of them with an equal amount of butter and cold Sauce Béchamel; season with salt and pepper and add 1 teaspoon of chopped Fines Herbes per 4 yolks.

Fill the half eggs dome shape with the mixture, arrange on a dish lightly coated with Sauce Mornay, sprinkle with grated cheese and melted butter and gratinate. Sprinkle with the remaining yolks which have been passed through a sieve and surround them with a *cordon* of Sauce Aurore.

1307 Oeufs au Lard—Fried Eggs and Bacon

These may be prepared in either of the two following ways:

1) Fry some rashers of bacon in butter until light brown, place 2 slices with a little of the cooking fat in each egg dish; break 2 eggs in each dish and cook as for *sur le Plat.*
2) Grill some rashers of bacon and arrange them around shallow fried eggs. The eggs may be trimmed round with a cutter if desired.

1308 Oeufs Bagnolet

Sur le Plat: Spread 1 tbs of finely diced ham, chicken and mushroom mixed with a little reduced Tomato Sauce in the bottom of each dish; break in 2 eggs per dish and cook in the usual way. Garnish with 1 tbs of buttered asparagus tips placed between the egg yolks.

1309 Oeufs Balzac

Scrambled: Scramble 6 eggs and mix in 50 g (2 oz) each of finely diced truffle and red ox tongue. Place in a deep dish, surround with round Croûtons fried in butter, each coated with a piped rosette of very thick Soubise; pour a *cordon* of tomato flavoured Sauce Demi-glace around the eggs.

1310 Oeufs Belle Hélène

Poached or Soft-boiled: For 6 eggs prepare a croquette mixture of 500 g (1 lb 2 oz) cooked asparagus tips kept slightly firm, well drained and dried, and bound with 2 dl (7 fl oz or $\frac{7}{8}$ U.S. cup) thick Sauce Béchamel and 3 egg yolks. Mould in the form of rounds or ovals as required; egg and breadcrumb using very fine crumbs and deep fry when required. Place the eggs, which have been coated with Sauce Suprême, on the Croquettes.

1311 Oeufs Bénédictine

Poached or Soft-boiled: Cover the bottom of tartlet cases with a Brandade of salt cod (1805) mixed with a little chopped truffle. Place the eggs which have been coated with Sauce Crème, on top.

1312 Oeufs Benoîton

French Fried: For 6 eggs prepare a Gratin of salt cod as follows: cook 120 g (4 oz) finely sliced onion in butter until light brown, sprinkle with 15 g ($\frac{1}{2}$ oz) flour and cook for a few minutes; moisten with 2 dl (7 fl oz or $\frac{7}{8}$ U.S. cup) red wine and 1 dl ($3\frac{1}{2}$ fl oz or $\frac{1}{2}$ U.S. cup) fish stock.

Bring to the boil, add 200 g (7 oz) sliced hot boiled potatoes; 200 g (7 oz) flaked poached salt cod; 3 well pounded anchovy fillets; a pinch of chopped parsley, and well season with pepper.

Arrange the mixture dome shape in a buttered gratin dish, sprinkle with fine white breadcrumbs and melted butter and gratinate in a very hot oven. Arrange the well trimmed fried eggs around the gratinated mixture.

1313 Oeufs en Berceau
Poached or Soft-boiled: Bake some medium-sized potatoes; cut off a third from the tops and scoop out the inside leaving the potatoes in the shape of a crib or cradle. Half fill these with a very finely chopped mince of cooked white of chicken mixed with cream and place an egg which has been coated with Sauce Aurore, on top of each potato.

1314 Oeufs Bercy
Sur le Plat: Cook the eggs as for Oeufs sur le Plat and place one grilled sausage or 4 grilled chipolatas between the yolks. Surround with a *cordon* of Tomato Sauce.

1315 Oeufs Bergère
En Cocotte: Coat the bottom and sides of fairly large egg cocottes with a layer of a hot mince of equal parts of finely chopped cooked lamb and mushrooms mixed with Cream Sauce. Break the eggs in the centre and cook as for Oeufs en Cocotte. Surround the yolks with a little well reduced gravy or light meat glaze.
French Fried: Prepare a cooked mince of finely chopped lamb and mushrooms mixed with a little reduced Cream Sauce. Arrange this dome shape on a buttered gratin dish, lightly sprinkle with white breadcrumbs and melted butter and gratinate in a very hot oven. Arrange the fried eggs around the gratinated mixture.

1316 Oeufs au Beurre Noir
Sur le Plat: These may be prepared in either of the two following ways:

1) Break the eggs into a frying pan containing 20 g ($\frac{2}{3}$ oz) butter, heated until very brown; lightly season, cook and slide them into an egg dish. Pour a little vinegar heated in the pan over the eggs.
2) Cook the eggs as for Oeufs sur le Plat; heat 20 g ($\frac{2}{3}$ oz) butter in a frying pan until very brown, pour over the eggs then sprinkle with a little vinegar heated in the same pan.

1317 Oeufs Bignon
Poached or Soft-boiled: Prepare a fine chicken forcemeat and pipe it with a large star tube in the form of round or oval connecting compartments on the bottom of a buttered dish. Place the dish in a moderate oven to cook the forcemeat then place an egg which has been coated with tarragon-flavoured Velouté in each compartment. Decorate each egg with a small fan of blanched tarragon leaves.

1318 Oeufs Boïeldieu
Poached or Soft-boiled: Fill the bottom of tartlet cases with a Salpicon of white of chicken, foie gras, and truffles mixed with a little Chicken Velouté. Place an egg on top of each and coat with a little reduced chicken-flavoured Jus lié.

1319 Oeufs Boitelle
Moulded: Butter some deep oval moulds large enough to hold an egg and cover the bottom with sliced mushrooms cooked in butter; break 1 egg in each mould and poach as for moulded eggs.

Turn out on to oval Croûtons fried in butter of the same size as the moulded eggs, and coat with a sauce prepared in the following manner: Reduce 2 tbs of mushroom essence by half, thicken and enrich it with 50 g (2 oz) butter and finish with a few drops of lemon juice.

1320 Oeufs Bonvalet
Poached or Soft-boiled: Cut bread in the shape of round or oval Croûtons, hollow them out slightly and cut a groove around the top outer edges; fry in butter. Place one egg which has been coated with Chicken Velouté on each Croûton and pipe a cordon of thick tomato-flavoured Sauce Béarnaise in the groove using a small paper cornet. Decorate each egg with a nice slice of truffle which has been dipped in butter.

1321 Oeufs à la Bordelaise
French Fried: Cut some large tomatoes in halves, remove the pips, place a little chopped shallot in each half tomato and shallow fry in hot oil keeping them fairly firm. When cooked, fill each with finely sliced flap mushrooms sautéed *à la Bordelaise*; place a French fried egg on each filled tomato, arrange them in a circle on a round dish and garnish with fried parsley placed in the centre.

1322 Oeufs à la Boulangère
Hard-boiled: For 6 eggs, cut off the tops and remove the insides from small long oval soft rolls and fill them with the following mixture: Cut the whites of the hard-boiled eggs and half the yolks into dice and mix together with a little thick Sauce Béchamel containing 200 g (7 oz) finely shredded onion cooked in butter without colour per 5 dl (18 fl oz or $2\frac{1}{4}$ U.S. cups) of sauce.

Sprinkle the surface with the rest of the egg yolks which have been finely chopped and arrange a line of chopped parsley down the centre of the egg.

1323 Oeufs à la Bourguignonne
Poached or Soft-boiled: For 6 eggs, boil 1 litre ($1\frac{3}{4}$ pt or $4\frac{1}{2}$ U.S. cups) of red wine in a copper pan and season and flavour it well with herbs and vegetables. Pass through a clean cloth, reduce by

half and thicken with 50 g (2 oz) Beurre Manié; enrich with a little more butter away from the heat.

Place each egg on a slice of toasted and buttered French bread, arrange in a dish and coat with the sauce.

Note: In the method used in the Burgundy area, the eggs are poached directly in the flavoured wine which has been previously seasoned and strained through a cloth. The wine is then reduced, thickened with butter as explained above and the eggs are placed on slices of toasted French bread rubbed with garlic.

1324 Oeufs à la Bretonne

Hard-boiled: For 6 eggs, finely slice 50 g (2 oz) each of onion and white of leek and stew carefully together with 50 g (2 oz) butter. Finish cooking with 1 dl (3½ fl oz or ½ U.S. cup) White Bouillon then add 50 g (2 oz) mushrooms previously sliced and sautéed in butter and 3 dl (½ pt or 1¼ U.S. cups) Sauce Béchamel.

Pour one-third of the mixture in the bottom of the serving dish, arrange the eggs cut in half lengthways on top and cover with the remainder of the mixture.

1325 Oeufs à la Bruxelloise

Sur le Plat: Cover the bottom of a dish with a little chicory which has been braised, sliced and reheated in a little butter and mixed with a little Sauce Béchamel. Break the eggs on top, lightly sprinkle with finely crushed rusks and cook in the usual way.

1326 Oeufs Bûcheronne

French Fried: For 6 eggs, bake 6 medium-sized potatoes in the oven. Remove the insides and season and fry this in a little butter until light brown. Arrange dome shape on a dish and surround it with the fried eggs of which the yolks have been sprinkled with a pinch of chopped chives before being enclosed in the white during the cooking process.

1327 Oeufs en Cannelons

Scrambled: Wrap bands of puff paste trimmings around cornet moulds in the usual manner and bake in the oven. Fill the cooked cornets with scrambled eggs containing any suitable garnish and close the ends with a round slice of the same garnish, e.g. ham, tongue, mushroom, white of chicken, truffle etc.

1328 Oeufs Cardinal

Poached or Soft-boiled: Fill the bottom of tartlet cases with a Salpicon of lobster mixed with a little Sauce Béchamel. Place the eggs which have been coated with Sauce Cardinal on top of the tartlets and sprinkle each with a little chopped coral or cooked lobster eggs.

1329 Oeufs du Carême

For 6 eggs, prepare 125 g (4½ oz) artichoke bottoms, sliced and cooked with a little butter; 6 hard-boiled eggs cut in rounds; 100 g (3½ oz) sliced truffles and 5 dl (18 fl oz or 2¼ U.S. cups) Sauce Nantua. Prepare also a pale-baked shallow Timbale case (4334) large enough for 6 people. Arrange layers of the eggs, artichokes, truffle and sauce in the case, finishing with a layer of sauce; place a circle of slices of truffle on the sauce.

1330 Oeufs Carignan

Moulded: Line some madeleine moulds with a layer of chicken forcemeat mixed with Crayfish Butter. Break one egg in each mould, place in a tray containing hot water and cook in the oven very carefully. Demould the eggs onto slices of toast cut to the same size as the moulds, arrange on a dish and coat them with Sauce Chateaubriand.

1331 Oeufs Cavour

French Fried: Cut 6 large tomatoes in half horizontally, remove the pips and cook the halves carefully in a little oil. Arrange on a dish, fill each half tomato with Risotto à la Piémontaise and place a fried egg on top. Serve accompanied with a sauceboat of reduced veal gravy.

1332 Oeufs au Chambertin

En Cocotte: Prepare a red wine sauce using Chambertin wine and fill into egg cocottes one-third full. Place them on the side of the stove to bring the sauce to a boil; break in the eggs, season with a few grains of salt, place the dishes into a tray containing boiling water and cook as for Oeufs en Cocotte. Glaze under the salamander at the last moment.

1333 Oeufs Chantilly

Poached or Soft-boiled: Prepare some cooked round or oval puff pastry cases large enough to hold one egg and fill the bottoms with a purée of green peas mixed with a quarter its volume of stiffly whipped cream. Place an egg which has been coated with Sauce Mousseline in each prepared case.

1334 Oeufs à la Chartres

Poached or Soft-boiled: Place the eggs coated with tarragon-flavoured, thick veal gravy on round or oval Croûtons of fried bread and decorate each with a star of blanched tarragon leaves.

Cold: Coat some individual deep oval moulds with a layer of white aspic jelly, decorate with blanched tarragon leaves and place a poached egg in each one. Fill with more jelly, allow to set firmly then turn out at the last minute and arranged in a circle on a round dish. Fill the centre with chopped jelly and decorate the dish with cut shapes of very firm Tarragon Butter.

1335 Oeufs Chasseur
Sur le Plat: Cook the eggs in the usual way and place a tablespoon of chicken livers cut in thick slices and sautéed *à la Chasseur* at each side.
Poached or Soft-boiled: Fill some tartlet cases with chicken livers sautéed *à la Chasseur*. Coat the eggs with Sauce Chasseur and place in the prepared tartlets; set a small pinch of chopped parsley on each egg.
Scrambled: Place the scrambled eggs in a deep dish with a garnish of chicken livers prepared *à la Chasseur* in the centre. Sprinkle the centre of the garnish with a little chopped tarragon and parsley and surround the eggs with a *cordon* of Sauce Chasseur.

1336 Oeufs Châtelaine
Poached or Soft-boiled: Prepare some chestnuts cooked in White Bouillon; drain and roughly chop them and mix together with a little pale buttered meat glaze. Place a little of this mixture in the bottom of tartlet cases and set one egg coated with Sauce Soubise on top of each.

1337 Oeufs Châtillon
Scrambled: Place the scrambled eggs in a deep dish and arrange a nice bouquet of sliced mushrooms sautéed in butter in the centre. Place a pinch of chopped parsley in the centre of the mushrooms, surround the eggs with a *cordon* of meat glaze and garnish with a border of pale-coloured small crescents of puff paste.

1338 Oeufs Chimay
Hard-boiled: Cut the eggs in half lengthways and remove the yolks; pound the yolks with an equal quantity of dry Duxelles and fill the empty whites with this mixture.

Arrange them in a buttered gratin dish, coat with Sauce Mornay, sprinkle with grated cheese and melted butter and gratinate quickly.

1339 Oeufs Chivry
Poached or Soft-boiled: For 6 eggs, well blanch 100 g ($3\frac{1}{2}$ oz) spinach leaves; 50 g (2 oz) sorrel leaves and 30 g (1 oz) watercress leaves. Refresh under cold water, drain and squeeze out all the moisture. Pound these leaves together with a little Sauce Béchamel then pass through a fine sieve and reheat with a little butter.

Place a little of this purée in tartlet cases and set an egg coated with Sauce Chivry on top of each.

1340 Oeufs Clamart
Scrambled: Mix 3 tbs of Petits Pois à la Française in which the lettuce has been finely shredded, into 6 portions of scrambled eggs. Place in a deep dish and surround with a *cordon* of Cream Sauce.

1341 Oeufs Cluny
Sur le Plat: Cook the eggs in the usual way and on each side of the dish place a small round Croquette of chicken the size of an apricot. Surround with a *cordon* of Tomato Sauce.

1342 Oeufs Colbert
En Cocotte: Coat the sides and bottom of the Cocottes with a thin layer of chicken forcemeat mixed with some chopped Fines Herbes, break in the eggs and cook in the usual way. When serving, surround the eggs with a *cordon* of melted Colbert Butter.
Cold: Coat the inside of deep oval moulds large enough to hold one egg, with aspic jelly. Completely decorate with a mosaic pattern, place a very small poached egg in each mould and fill with jelly; allow to set in a cold place.

Prepare a Macédoine of vegetables bound with Mayonnaise and arrange this dome shape in the centre of the dish. Demould the eggs and arrange them around the Macédoine and surround the eggs with a border of very clear chopped aspic jelly.

1343 Oeufs Colinette
Cold: Coat the inside of deep oval moulds large enough to hold one egg, with aspic jelly; completely decorate in the pattern of a draught board using truffle and cooked white of egg. Place a very small poached egg in each mould and fill with jelly; allow to set in a cold place.

Arrange some Salade Rachel dome shape in the centre of a dish and arrange alternate slices of cooked potato and truffle around the edge. Demould the eggs and place on the dish around the salad. Finish with a border of fancy crescent-shaped pieces of very clear aspic jelly.

1344 Oeufs à la Commère
Hard-boiled: Cut the eggs in half lengthways and place them round side uppermost on a bed of well creamed mashed potato. Cover with a rice Soubise (151), sprinkle with grated Gruyère cheese mixed with one-third its volume of fine breadcrumbs, sprinkle with melted butter and gratinate.

1345 Oeufs Comtesse
Poached or Soft-boiled: Fill some tartlet cases with

a purée of white asparagus, place an egg coated with Sauce Allemande in each and sprinkle with very black chopped truffle.

1346 Oeufs à la Coque—Boiled Eggs in the Shell
The following methods for boiling eggs are based on the use of medium-sized eggs, soft-boiled for 3 minutes; for large eggs allow on average, an additional half minute:

1) Plunge the eggs in boiling water and boil gently for 3 minutes.
2) Plunge the eggs into boiling water, boil gently for 1 minute then remove the pan from the stove and leave the eggs in the water for a further 3 minutes.
3) Place the eggs in cold water, bring to boiling temperature and remove them a few seconds after it is obvious that the water is actually boiling.
4) Place the eggs in a special steamer for 3 minutes.

1347 Côtelettes d'Oeufs—Egg Cutlets
Cut some hard-boiled eggs into small dice, mix with a little well-reduced Sauce Bećhamel, and cook together with raw egg yolks to bind the mixture.

Allow to cool then divide the mixture into even-sized pieces of approximately 60 g (2 oz) each. Mould to the shape of small cutlets, egg and breadcrumb with fine white breadcrumbs, deep fry when required and arrange in a circle on a round dish. Insert a small piece of macaroni or fried bread at the point of each cutlet and place a cutlet frill on it.

Serve accompanied with Tomato Sauce.

1348 Côtelettes d'Oeufs Dauphine—Egg Cutlets Dauphine
Prepare the mixture as in the preceding recipe reserving two of the hard-boiled yolks out of every eight. When the mixture has cooled to being just warm, add and mix in 1 beaten egg.

Roll out some trimmings of puff paste thinly and with this, line some cutlet-shaped moulds. Fill with the prepared egg mixture and smooth the surfaces level; sprinkle with the finely chopped reserved yolks and a little melted butter. Cook in a moderate oven and when ready, arrange on a dish.

Serve accompanied with a dish of light creamy mashed potato.

1349 Côtelettes d'Oeufs Manon—Egg Cutlets Manon
Cut the whites of hard-boiled eggs into small dice, mix with a little thick Sauce Béchamel and allow to cool. Chop the yolks, mix them with an equal amount of finely chopped lean cooked ham and mix with a little very well reduced Soubise.

Shape into cutlets moulding the white of egg mixture around the yolk and ham mixture. Egg and breadcrumb, deep fry when required, arrange on a dish and finish as for Egg Cutlets.

Serve accompanied with a fairly thin Sauce Soubise.

1350 Oeufs Crécy
Poached or Soft-boiled: Cut some thick Croûtons to the required shape from a stale Brioche and fry in clarified butter. Remove the centres and fill with some finely sliced red of carrot stewed with butter. Arrange an egg, previously coated with Cream Sauce, on top of each and decorate with a fancy round slice of cooked carrot.
Sur le Plat: Place a tablespoon of Carottes Vichy in the bottom of the egg dishes; break in the eggs and cook in the usual way. Finish by surrounding the eggs with a *cordon* of Cream Sauce.

1351 Cromesquis d'Oeufs
Cut some hard-boiled eggs into small dice adding diced mushroom and truffle in the same proportion as for Croquette mixtures (1144). Mix with well-reduced Sauce Allemande in the proportion of 3½ dl (12 fl oz or 1½ U.S. cups) sauce per 500 g (1 lb 2 oz) of diced ingredients.

Cool the mixture, divide into 60 g (2 oz) pieces and mould into round flat shapes. Dip in light frying batter and deep fry as required. Arrange on a serviette with fried parsley in the centre and serve accompanied with Tomato Sauce.

1352 Cromesquis d'Oeufs à la Polonaise
Prepare the mixture as for Cromesquis d'Oeufs replacing the mushrooms with flap mushrooms and the Sauce Allemande with reduced Sauce Duxelles. Divide into 60 g (2 oz) pieces, mould into rectangles and enclose each in a very thin pancake. Dip in light batter and deep fry as required.

Serve accompanied with a thin Sauce Poivrade.

1353 Croquettes d'Oeufs
Prepare the mixture as for Cromesquis d'Oeufs—if required as a lenten dish replace the Sauce Allemande with Sauce Béchamel. Divide into 60 g (2 oz) pieces and mould egg shape; egg and breadcrumb with very fine breadcrumbs and deep fry as required.

Arrange on a serviette with fried parsley in the centre and serve accompanied with Cream Sauce.

1354 Oeufs à la Crème
En Cocotte: This is the basic method of prepara-

tion for this type of egg dish and which was for a long time the only one used. Heat the Cocottes in advance and place 1 tbs of boiling cream in each; break in the eggs, season and add a small piece of butter. Cover and cook *au Bain-marie* in the usual manner.

Note: It is advisable to heat the dishes and to use boiling cream; by so doing the egg will cook from the top and bottom at the same time, leaving the centre soft.

1355 Oeufs aux Crevettes

Poached or Soft-boiled: Fill some tartlet cases with prawns or shrimps mixed with Sauce Crevettes and place the eggs previously coated with Sauce Crevettes on top. Decorate the top of each with four nice shelled shrimps or prawns.

Scrambled: Prepare some scrambled eggs and place in a deep dish; in the centre place a bouquet of shrimps or prawns mixed with a little Sauce Crevettes and surround the eggs with a *cordon* of the same sauce.

1356 Oeufs Daumont

Poached or Soft-boiled: Cook some large fresh field mushrooms in butter and garnish each with a Salpicon of crayfish tails mixed with Sauce Nantua. On top of each place an egg which has been previously coated with Sauce Nantua and decorate each with a slice of truffle.

Moulded: Line some well buttered Baba moulds with thin round slices of truffle; break in the eggs and cook *au Bain-marie* in the usual way. Turn out each one onto a large mushroom which has been cooked in butter and the bottom trimmed flat to ensure that the egg stays level; arrange on a dish and surround with a border of crayfish tails coated with Sauce Nantua.

1357 Oeufs à la Diable

Shallow Fried: Break 2 eggs into a pan of very hot butter, turn them over without breaking the yolks and slide out onto a dish. Pour a little Brown Butter over the eggs and also a little vinegar reduced in the same pan.

1358 Oeufs Diane

En Cocotte: Coat the sides of Cocottes with a layer of fine mince of game bird and in the bottom, place a teaspoon of Sauce Salmis. Break in the eggs and cook *au Bain-marie* in the usual way. Finish by surrounding the yolks with a *cordon* of Sauce Salmis and decorate each yolk with a crescent of very black truffle.

1359 Oeufs Duchesse

Sur le Plat: Butter the bottom of large egg dishes and pipe out some Pommes Duchesse mixture in the shape of a figure 8 using a large star tube; eggwash and colour the potato by placing it in the oven. Break an egg in each circle, coat with a little cream and cook in the usual way. Finish by placing a slice of truffle on each yolk as soon as it is removed from the oven.

Poached or Soft-boiled: Prepare some small flat shapes of Pommes Duchesse mixture according to requirements, eggwash them and colour in the oven. Place an egg, previously coated with thickened and buttered veal gravy, on top of each.

Moulded: Place a nice slice of truffle in the bottom of well buttered Baba moulds, break in the eggs and cook *au Bain-marie* in the usual way. Turn out each egg on to a small cake of Pommes Duchesse which has been cut out with a fancy cutter, eggwashed and coloured in the oven. Coat the eggs with a little thickened and buttered veal gravy.

1360 Oeufs à l'Espagnole

Shallow fried: Prepare some well seasoned grilled halves of large tomatoes, allowing one for each egg. Shallow fry the eggs in butter and trim with a plain round cutter. Place one on each half tomato and arrange them in a circle on a round dish. In the centre place a bouquet of onions cut into thin rings, seasoned, floured and deep fried in oil.

Scrambled: (for one portion) Place the scrambled egg in 3 half-tomatoes which have been emptied, seasoned and cooked in oil. Place a ring of fried onion on each and a pinch of chopped red pimento in the centre.

1361 Oeufs à l'Estragon

Sur le Plat: Coat the bottom of the egg dishes with a spoonful of tarragon-flavoured and buttered veal gravy; break in the eggs and coat with a little more gravy. Cook in the usual way then decorate with blanched tarragon leaves on removing from the oven.

1362 Oeufs aux Fines Herbes

Scrambled: Prepare the scrambled eggs; chop together 4 tarragon leaves and a pinch each of parsley, chervil and chives and carefully mix into the eggs.

1363 Oeufs Flora

Poached or Soft-boiled: Coat each egg, half with Chicken Velouté and half with Tomato Sauce; sprinkle a little chopped parsley on the red and a little chopped truffle on the white. Place each egg on a cooked round or oval-shaped piece of puff pastry.

1364 Oeufs Florial

Poached or Soft-boiled: Coat the eggs with Velouté

containing some chopped chervil and place a nice Pluche of chervil on top of each. Set each egg on a cooked round or oval piece of cooked puff pastry cut a little larger than the egg. Pipe a scrolled border of a purée of green peas around the edge of the pastry by means of a piping bag and small star tube.

1365 Oeufs à la Florentine

Sur le Plat: Cover the bottom of each dish with some lightly cooked spinach, roughly chopped, then stewed with a little butter. Sprinkle with grated cheese and break the eggs on top. Coat with fairly thin Sauce Mornay and place in a hot oven so that the glazing and cooking of the eggs takes place at the same time.

Poached or Soft-boiled: Fill the bottom of the tartlets with spinach prepared as above and place the eggs previously coated with Sauce Mornay on top. Sprinkle with grated Parmesan cheese and glaze quickly under the salamander.

En Cocotte: Line the inside of well buttered Cocottes with leaves of spinach which have been stewed in butter. Add a ½ tbs boiling cream, break in the eggs and sprinkle with a little grated cheese. Cook in the oven *au Bain-marie* without a cover so that the top becomes glazed and the eggs cooked at the same time.

1366 Oeufs à la Forestière

Sur le Plat: Cook some sliced morels in butter with a little small dice of blanched lean bacon and a little chopped shallot. Place a little of this mixture in the bottom of each dish, break in the eggs and cook in the usual way. Place a bouquet of cooked morels on both sides of the dish and sprinkle with chopped parsley.

En Cocotte: Use large egg Cocottes and cover the bottoms with a round slice of lean bacon which has been blanched and fried in butter. Coat the sides of the Cocottes with a layer of chopped morels and shallots stewed in butter and bound with a little reduced Sauce Béchamel. Break in the eggs and cook *au Bain-marie* in the usual way. Sprinkle the yolks with a little chopped parsley before serving.

Scrambled: Scramble 6 eggs and mix with 80 g (3 oz) morels which have been quartered on the slant and sautéed in butter, and 50 g (2 oz) very small diced streaky bacon, blanched and fried in butter. Place in a deep dish and set a large cooked morel in the centre.

1367 Oeufs Frou-Frou

Cold: Prepare the required number of well trimmed small poached eggs and coat each with well creamed Sauce Chaud-froid containing one-third its volume of a purée of hard-boiled egg yolk. Decorate each egg with a fancy round slice of black truffle and surround with a neat border of chopped truffle. Glaze with clear aspic jelly and keep in a cold place.

Prepare a salad of peas, asparagus tips and small diamonds of French beans, mixed together with a little Mayonnaise Collée (203). Mould it in a lightly oiled dome-shaped mould or shape in a pyramid directly in the centre of a round dish. Surround the mould of vegetables with chopped aspic jelly and arrange the eggs around, resting on the jelly. Finish with a border of cut shapes of very clear aspic jelly.

1368 Oeufs Galli-Marié

Moulded: For 4 persons, scramble 5 eggs keeping them moist and very soft; add and mix in 3 whole beaten eggs and 1 tsp of pimento cut into small dice. Place the mixture into 4 well buttered small round flat moulds and cook *au Bain-marie* in the usual way.

Have ready 4 hot, large cooked artichoke bottoms, the edges of which have been cut tooth shape, fill them with rice à la Grecque and demould the eggs, one on each of the prepared artichoke bottoms. Arrange on a dish and coat with a well seasoned and buttered Sauce Béchamel; place in a very hot oven so as to glaze quickly and serve immediately.

1369 Oeufs Georgette

Scrambled: Bake 3 nice Dutch potatoes, cut them in half and remove the potato from inside. Prepare 6 portions of scrambled eggs, add 8–10 crayfish tails, then finish with 60 g (2 oz) Crayfish Butter. Fill the potato cases with this mixture and serve very hot arranged on a serviette.

1370 Oeufs Grand-Duc

Poached or Soft-boiled: These eggs may be prepared in either of the following ways:

1) Place the eggs on round Croûtons of fried bread and arrange them in a circle on a round dish. Place a nice crayfish tail between each egg and a slice of truffle on top of each egg. Cover with Sauce Mornay and glaze quickly in a very hot oven. After removing the dish, and before serving, place a nice bouquet of buttered asparagus tips in the centre.
2) Prepare and cook a flan case of a size in proportion to the number of eggs to be served; arrange the eggs around the inside edge of the flan, place a crayfish tail between each egg and a slice of truffle on top of each egg. Coat with Sauce Mornay and glaze quickly. Fill the centre with neatly arranged buttered asparagus tips.

1371 Oeufs Grand'Mère
Scrambled: Scramble 6 eggs and carefully mix in 30 g (1 oz) very small diced Croûtons fried in butter—they should be very hot. Arrange in a deep dish with a pinch of chopped parsley in the centre.

1372 Oeufs Jeanne Granier
Sur le Plat: Place a tablespoon of creamed asparagus tips in each dish with 4 large thin slices of truffle; break in the eggs and cook in the usual way. Finish with a small spoonful of asparagus tips between the yolks and a slice of truffle on top of each yolk.

1373 Oeufs au Gratin
Sur le Plat: Spread a spoonful of Sauce Mornay on the bottom of each dish; break in the eggs, coat with a little of the same sauce and sprinkle with a mixture of grated cheese and fine breadcrumbs and a little melted butter. Place in a hot oven to cook and gratinate at the same time.
Poached or Soft-boiled: Place the eggs on rounds of bread fried in butter, coat with Sauce Mornay, sprinkle with a mixture of grated Gruyère cheese, grated Parmesan and a little fine breadcrumbs; sprinkle with melted butter and gratinate quickly.

1374 Oeufs Grillés à la Diable
Poached: Cool the eggs as soon as they have been poached and dry them well. Dip in melted butter and roll in very fine white breadcrumbs. Place each egg on a square of buttered greaseproof paper, place on the grill and grill gently on both sides. Arrange them on thin slices of toast, sprinkle well with grated cheese mixed with a little Cayenne and gratinate them quickly.
Serve accompanied with Sauce Diable.

1375 Oeufs Halévy
Poached or Soft-boiled: Fill some tartlet cases on one side with Tomato Fondue and on the other with diced cooked white of chicken mixed with a little Velouté. Coat each egg, half with Sauce Tomate and half Sauce Allemande and pipe a line of meat glaze between the two sauces. Place one on each prepared tartlet case.

1376 Oeufs Héloise
Poached or Soft-boiled: Coat the eggs with well buttered and mushroom-flavoured Sauce Allemande containing some finely diced cooked white of chicken, red ox tongue and truffle in equal quantities. Place them on Croûtons of fried bread cut a little larger than the eggs; arrange on a dish and glaze quickly in a very hot oven. Before serving surround each egg with a *cordon* of well reduced tomato purée using a piping bag and small plain tube.

1377 Hot Eggs for Luncheon Hors-d'oeuvre
Prepare:

1) scrambled eggs which can contain any garnish to choice, and
2) a Soufflé au Parmesan mixture.

Place the eggs in large tartlet cases filling them three-quarters full, and cover slightly dome shape with the soufflé mixture. Arrange on a tray and place in a hot oven to cook and colour at the same time.

1378 Oeufs à la Huguenote
Sur le Plat: Place 2 tbs of good mutton gravy and a little butter in each dish and make it boiling hot; break in the eggs and cook in the usual way. Garnish between the yolks with a spoonful of the following mixture: cut sheep's kidneys into small dice, season them, sauté in butter and mix with a little finely chopped onion previously cooked in butter; mix with a little Sauce Demi-glace. Sprinkle a little chopped parsley on the kidneys.

1379 Oeufs à la Hussarde
Poached or Soft-boiled: Cut some large tomatoes in half, remove the pips, season and either grill or cook them in the oven. Fill each half with chopped onion sautéed in butter, mixed with diced lean ham and a little Sauce Demi-glace. On each prepared tomato place an egg previously coated with Velouté seasoned with Cayenne.

1380 Oeufs Isoline
Sur le Plat: Cook the eggs in the usual way and arrange very small half tomatoes prepared *à la Provençale* around the side. On each half tomato place a nice piece of chicken liver sautéed in butter and coated with a little Sauce Madère.

1381 Oeufs Jeannette
En Cocotte: Coat the bottom and sides of the Cocottes with a layer of chicken and cream forcemeat containing a fifth its weight of foie gras; break in the eggs and cook *au Bain-marie* in the usual way. Surround the yolks with a *cordon* of Chicken Velouté before serving.

1382 Oeufs Jockey Club
Sur le Plat: Cook the eggs as for *sur le Plat* in the usual way and trim them round with a plain cutter. Place each egg on a very thin round slice of toast spread with foie gras. Arrange in a circle on a round dish and fill the centre with a garnish of diced veal kidney sautéed in butter, mixed with

diced truffle and a little fairly thick Sauce Demi-glace.

1383 Oeufs au Jus

En Cocotte: Break the eggs in well buttered Cocottes and cook in the usual way. When about to serve, surround the yolks with a *cordon* of reduced veal gravy.

1384 Oeufs Léontine

En Cocotte: Coat the bottom and sides of Cocottes with a very fine Salpicon of crayfish tails and truffle mixed with a little fish and cream forcemeat; place in a medium oven to cook. Break in the eggs and cook *au Bain-marie* in the usual way. Just before serving surround the yolks with a *cordon* of Tomato Sauce.

1385 Oeufs Lili

Moulded: Butter some oval moulds and sprinkle the insides with chopped lobster coral or separated lobster eggs. Scramble 8 eggs and mix with 1 tbs cream, 2 tbs very fine Salpicon of prawns and truffle and 25 g (1 oz) butter. Beat 4 whole eggs, season and add and mix in the scrambled eggs; fill into the moulds and cook *au Bain-marie*. Turn out and arrange in a circle on a round dish and finish by pouring a little light Sauce Crevettes in the centre of the dish.

1386 Oeufs Lorette

Poached or Soft-boiled: Prepare oval or round Croustades made with Pommes Dauphine mixture; fill them with buttered asparagus tips and place an egg on top with a nice slice of truffle on each. Serve accompanied with Jus lié.

1387 Oeufs à la Lorraine

Sur le Plat: Place slices of lean bacon previously blanched and lightly grilled in the bottoms of egg dishes together with some thin slices of Gruyère cheese. Break in the eggs, surround the yolks with a tablespoon of cream and cook in the usual way.

1388 Oeufs Lully

Sur le Plat: Fry the eggs in butter in a frying pan and trim round with a plain pastry cutter. Place each one on a slice of raw ham sautéed in butter and of the same size as the egg, then place each on a round slice of toast of the same size. Arrange in a circle on a round dish and fill the centre with buttered macaroni mixed with Tomato Fondue.

1389 Oeufs Magda

Scrambled: Scramble 6 eggs and mix in 1 tsp chopped Fines Herbes; 1 tsp mustard and 1 tbs grated Gruyère cheese. Place in a deep dish and surround with small rectangular Croûtons of bread fried in butter at the last minute.

1390 Oeufs Maintenon

Poached or Soft-boiled: Fill some tartlet cases with a fairly thick Béchamel Soubise. Coat the eggs with Sauce Mornay, sprinkle with grated Gruyère cheese and place in the tartlets. Glaze quickly, arrange on a dish and surround with a *cordon* of meat glaze just before serving.

1391 Oeufs Malmaison

Poached or Soft-boiled: Fill some fairly large tartlet cases with a mixture of buttered peas, diamonds of French beans and asparagus tips. Place one egg in the centre of each and surround each egg with a *cordon* of Sauce Béarnaise. Place a pinch of chopped chervil and tarragon in the centre of each.

1392 Oeufs à la Maraîchère

Sur le Plat: Place a tablespoon of Chiffonade of lettuce, sorrel and chervil in the bottom of each dish; break in the eggs and cook in the usual manner. On each side of the yolks place a small slice of lean bacon, blanched and sautéed in butter.

1393 Oeufs Marinette

Scrambled: Scramble 6 eggs and mix in a teaspoon of chopped chervil; place in a deep dish and arrange a circle of rounds of red salt ox tongue on top. In the centre place a Salpicon of asparagus tips, white of chicken and truffle tossed in butter.

1394 Oeufs Marivaux

Scrambled: Scramble 6 eggs with the addition of 40 g (1½ oz) grated truffle. Place in a deep dish with a large grooved mushroom in the centre and surround the mushroom with a line of meat glaze. Finish with a border of nice slices of very white mushrooms cooked in butter.

1395 Oeufs Masséna

Poached or Soft-boiled: Prepare some large artichoke bottoms, hollowing out the base a little more than usual; reheat in butter and fill with thick Sauce Béarnaise. Coat the eggs with Tomato Sauce and place one in each of the filled artichoke bottoms. Place a poached slice of bone marrow on each and finish with a pinch of chopped parsley in the centre of the bone marrow.

1396 Oeufs Matelote

Sur le Plat: Place a tablespoon of hot Sauce Matelote Marinière (1567) in each dish, break in the eggs and cook in the usual manner. Surround with a *cordon* of buttered Sauce Matelote Marinière just before serving.

1397 Oeufs Maupassant

Cold: Use well dried and trimmed poached eggs and coat each with red wine Sauce Matelote containing some fish aspic jelly. Glaze with some of the same jelly and arrange in a circle on a dish with some chopped fish jelly in the centre. Arrange cut shapes of pink coloured fish jelly around the edge of the dish.

1398 Oeufs Maximilienne

Sur le Plat: Discard the pips from halves of large round tomatoes and fry the tomatoes gently in a little oil. Sprinkle the insides with chopped parsley mixed with a little chopped garlic and break an egg in each half. Sprinkle with grated cheese mixed with chopped parsley and breadcrumbs fried in butter. Place them in a fairly hot oven to cook and gratinate at the same time.

1399 Oeufs Mexicaine

French fried: Discard the pips from halves of large round tomatoes and fry the tomatoes gently in a little oil. Place on a dish, fill them with Riz à la Créole (4234) and place a fried egg on each.

Serve accompanied with Tomato Sauce.

1400 Oeufs Meyerbeer

Sur le Plat: Cook the eggs in the usual manner and when ready, garnish with a lamb or mutton kidney which has been opened and grilled without breadcrumbs. Surround with a cordon of Sauce Périgueux.

1401 Oeufs Mignon

Poached or Soft-boiled: Reheat some large artichoke bottoms in butter and fill each, half with buttered peas and half with buttered prawns. Coat the eggs with Sauce Crevettes, place each on a prepared artichoke and decorate with a nice slice of very black truffle.

1402 Oeufs Mirabeau

Sur le Plat: Coat each dish with 10 g ($\frac{1}{3}$ oz) Anchovy Butter, break in the eggs and cook in the usual manner. When ready, place a large olive stuffed with tarragon butter on each side of the dish, surround each yolk with thin strips of anchovy fillet and decorate with blanched leaves of tarragon.

1403 Oeufs Mireille

Poached or Soft-boiled: Well butter some tartlet moulds; fill with saffron-flavoured Riz Pilaw, press in fairly firmly and demould them on to a round dish alternating with round Croûtons of bread fried in oil. Coat the eggs with saffron-flavoured Cream Sauce and place one on each Croûton of bread. Place a little fairly thick Tomato Fondue on the centre of the rice moulds.

1404 Oeufs Mogador

Poached or Soft-boiled: Using a piping bag and large star tube, pipe circles of Pommes Marquise on a buttered dish either joined together around the edge of the dish or placed in the centre in the form of a rosette; colour quickly in a hot oven. Coat the eggs with Sauce Béchamel containing 150g (5 oz) foie gras per 5 dl (18 fl oz or $2\frac{1}{4}$ U.S. cups) of sauce. Place one egg in each circle of potato with a round piece of very red ox tongue on top and a slice of truffle in the centre of the tongue.

1405 Oeufs des Moissonneurs

French fried: Blanch the same number of rectangles of streaky bacon as there are eggs, then grill them. Arrange in a circle on a dish alternating with the fried eggs; fill the centre with large peas cooked *à la Paysanne* with shredded lettuce and thin slices of potato.

1406 Oeufs Montargis

Shallow fried: Fill some tartlet cases with a mixture of chicken liver cut in Julienne and sautéed in butter and a Julienne of tongue and mushrooms—all mixed with a little Sauce Béchamel flavoured with a little meat glaze. Coat the mixture in each tartlet with half a spoonful of Sauce Mornay, sprinkle with grated Parmesan and gratinate. Fry the eggs in a pan, trim round with a plain cutter and place one on each tartlet. Set a round slice of red ox tongue on top of each yolk.

1407 Oeufs Montmorency

Sur le Plat: Place a tablespoon of creamed asparagus tips in the dishes; break in the eggs and cook in the usual manner. When cooked, garnish each by placing 4 nice green tips of asparagus between the yolks and at the side a small bouquet of sliced artichoke bottoms sautéed in butter.

1408 Oeufs Mornay

This is another name for poached eggs au Gratin.

1409 Oeufs Mortemart

Moulded: Scramble 5 eggs, keeping them very soft and moist; add 3 seasoned and beaten eggs and mix in. Butter some small flat round moulds, place a nice slice of truffle in the bottom of each, fill with the prepared mixture and cook *au Bain-marie* in the usual manner.

Demould each one on to a tartlet case which has been filled with a cooked purée of mushrooms. Arrange in a circle on a round dish and serve a sauceboat of melted and lightly buttered meat glaze separately.

1410 Oeufs Mosaïque
Cold: Take moulds which are the shape of a half egg and coat with clear aspic jelly; line the surface with a mosaic decoration of diamonds of red tongue, white of egg, truffle and French beans. Place a poached egg in each mould, fill up with more jelly and allow to set in a cool place.

Prepare a Salade Russe moulded in a dome-shaped mould which has been equally coated with jelly and decorated in a mosaic pattern. When required for service, demould the salad on to a round dish, surround with the eggs and decorate the dish with cut shapes of aspic jelly.

1411 Oeufs à la Moscovite
Cold: Cut the tops and bottoms of hard-boiled eggs level so as to give the shape of a barrel. Surround the top and bottom of each with three strips of anchovy fillets and place a very small round of truffle in the middle to represent the bung of a barrel which the eggs are meant to resemble.

Empty the centre of the eggs by means of a column cutter and fill each one with caviare, moulding it to a point on top. Place each one on a very white artichoke bottom and surround the base of the egg with a line of chopped jelly.

1412 Oeufs Nantua
Sur le Plat: Place a tablespoon of Salpicon of cooked crayfish tails mixed with a little Sauce Nantua in each dish; break in the eggs and cook in the usual manner. When cooked, surround the yolks with 3 nice crayfish tails and place a slice of truffle on the yolks. Surround the eggs with a *cordon* of Sauce Nantua.

If desired, an additional garnish of 2 small stuffed crayfish shells per dish may be added.
Poached or Soft-boiled: Fill tartlet cases with a Salpicon of crayfish tails mixed with a little Sauce Nantua. Coat the eggs with Sauce Nantua and decorate each with 2 crayfish tails cut along the length and placed on top in the form of a cross; place the eggs on the prepared tartlets.
Cold: Prepare the eggs in the shape of a barrel as for Oeufs à la Moscovite and empty them in the same way. Fill with a Salpicon of crayfish tails mixed with Mayonnaise containing a purée made from the trimmings and remains of the crayfish which has been passed through a fine sieve. Mould the Salpicon dome-shape above the top of the eggs, decorate each with 4 halves of crayfish tails and 4 diamonds of truffle and glaze with aspic jelly. Arrange each egg on an artichoke bottom filled with a little of the same prepared Mayonnaise.

1413 Oeufs à la Napolitaine
Moulded: Scramble 5 eggs with the addition of a little grated Parmesan cheese; add 2 seasoned and beaten eggs and mix together. Place in well buttered Brioche moulds having large flutings and cook *au Bain-marie* in the usual manner.

When sufficiently solidified, demould the eggs on to a buttered gratin dish, sprinkle with grated Parmesan and coat with Sauce Demi-glace that has been well flavoured with tomato then reduced and buttered; glaze quickly in a very hot oven.

1414 Oeufs Négus
Sur le Plat: Cook the eggs in the usual way and garnish each dish with 2 small round flat-shape Croquettes of game and surround the eggs with a *cordon* of Sauce Périgueux.

1415 Oeufs à la Niçoise
Poached or Soft-boiled: Trim some potatoes to the shape of artichoke bottoms and cook in the same way as for Pommes Château, then fill them with cooked French beans, cut in dice and buttered.

Place an egg on top of each, set a little Tomato Fondue on each one and surround with a *cordon* of thickened veal gravy.
Cold: Fill some tartlet cases with French beans, boiled potatoes and tomato flesh all cut into neat dice. On each one place a poached egg previously coated with Mayonnaise mixed with a fifth its volume of a purée of fresh tomatoes.

1416 Oeufs Ninon
Poached or Soft-boiled: Place the eggs on thin oval or round-shaped Croûtons of bread fried in butter; set a slice of truffle on each and arrange in a circle on a round dish. Place 3 nice asparagus tips approximately 5 cm (2 in) long, between each egg, the heads pointing outwards. Fill the centre with green asparagus tips mixed with Sauce Béchamel containing a little chopped chervil.

1417 Oeufs à la Normande
Sur le Plat: Place 2 tbs cream seasoned with salt and pepper, 1 tbs fish essence and 6 bearded oysters with their juice in each dish. Break in the eggs and cook in the usual manner. Surround with a *cordon* of Sauce Normande.
Poached or Soft-boiled: Coat the eggs with Sauce Normande and place in tartlet cases which have been garnished with 3 bearded and poached oysters and mixed with a little Sauce Normande.
Scrambled: Scramble 6 eggs and place in a deep

dish; place 6 poached and bearded oysters mixed with a little Sauce Normande in the centre and surround the eggs with a *cordon* of the same sauce.

Note: The scrambled eggs may also be served in Barquettes, in which case the cooked oysters should be mixed in with the scrambled eggs and the Barquettes then bordered with a *cordon* of Sauce Normande.

1418 Oeufs Opéra
Sur le Plat: Cook the eggs in the usual manner and when ready, garnish the dishes on one side with a bouquet of diced, sautéed chicken liver mixed with a little Madeira Sauce, and on the other side with a bouquet of buttered asparagus tips. Surround with a *cordon* of reduced and buttered veal gravy.

1419 Oeufs à la d'Orléans
Poached or Soft-boiled: Fill some tartlet cases with a Salpicon of white of chicken mixed with Tomato Sauce. Coat the eggs with Sauce Béchamel finished with Pistachio Butter in the proportion of 150 g (5 oz) of this butter per 5 dl (18 fl oz or $2\frac{1}{4}$ U.S. cups) of sauce; place the eggs on the prepared tartlets.

1420 Oeufs Orloff
Scrambled: Beat 6 eggs together with a little cream, season them and scramble in the usual way; add 9 crayfish tails and place in individual white porcelain dishes. Place a nice slice of truffle on each portion and arrange the dishes on a serviette to serve.

1421 Oeufs d'Orsay
Poached or Soft-boiled: Place the eggs on Croûtons of bread fried in butter and coat them with Sauce Chateaubriand.

1422 Oeufs à la Parisienne
En Cocotte: Coat the inside of the Cocottes with chicken forcemeat mixed with the same quantity of equal parts of chopped tongue, mushroom and truffle. Break in the eggs, poach *au Bain-marie* in the usual manner. Surround with a *cordon* of Sauce Demi-glace.

1423 Oeufs Parmentier
Sur le Plat: Bake the required number of large Dutch potatoes. Cut them open from the top with a plain oval cutter and remove the insides; whilst this is still hot, pass it through a sieve, season and make into a soft mashed potato.

Half fill the emptied potatoes with the mashed potato, break an egg in each, coat with cream and place to cook in the oven.

When cooked, replace the cover on each potato and arrange on a serviette for service.

Scrambled: Scramble 6 eggs and place in a deep dish; place a nice bouquet of diced potatoes sautéed in butter and mixed with a little meat glaze, in the middle and sprinke this with chopped parsley.

1424 Oeufs au Parmesan
Sur le Plat: Break the eggs into well buttered dishes, sprinkle well with grated Parmesan cheese and cover each one with 10 g ($\frac{1}{3}$ oz) melted butter. Cook in the normal manner taking care that the eggs cook and become glazed at the same time.

1425 Oeufs à la Pastourelle
French fried: Blanch and grill some rectangular-shaped pieces of lean bacon. Arrange them in a circle on a round dish, place an egg on each piece of bacon and set a grilled half of lamb or mutton kidney on each egg. Fill the centre with sliced small mushrooms, sautéed in butter with a little finely chopped shallot. Sprinkle this lightly with chopped parsley.

1426 Oeufs à la Percheronne
Hard-boiled: Cut 6 hard-boiled eggs and 2 cooked medium potatoes into slices whilst still hot. Arrange the eggs and potatoes in a deep dish in alternate layers with a little buttered Sauce Béchamel between them and finishing with a layer of sauce.

1427 Oeufs à la Périgourdine
Sur le Plat: Place 10 g ($\frac{1}{3}$ oz) butter and 1 tsp of truffle essence in the bottom of the dishes, break in the eggs and cook in the usual manner. When ready, place a small bouquet of diced truffle on each side of the yolks and surround with a *cordon* of thick Sauce Demi-glace which has been thinned with a little truffle essence.

Poached and Soft-boiled: Place each egg on a large thick slice of truffle and coat with Sauce Périgueux.

Moulded: Well butter some shell-shaped Madeleine moulds and sprinkle with chopped truffle. Break one egg in each mould and cook *au Bain-marie.* Demould each on a slice of truffle of the same shape as the mould and coat the eggs with Sauce Demi-glace containing truffle essence.

En Cocotte: Line the bottom and sides of the Cocottes with a layer of chicken forcemeat mixed with the addition of a good amount of chopped truffle; break in the eggs and cook *au Bain-marie* in the usual manner. When ready, surround the yolks with a *cordon* of meat glaze and place a slice of truffle on top.

1428 Oeufs Petit-Duc
Poached or Soft-boiled: Place each egg in a large

grilled mushroom which has been slightly hollowed out; coat the eggs with Sauce Chateaubriand.

1429 Oeufs à la Piémontaise

Sur le Plat: Butter the dishes, sprinkle with grated cheese and break in the eggs. Sprinkle the surface with grated cheese and cook in the usual way. On each side of the yolks place a tablespoon of Risotto, flavoured and mixed with grated Parmesan cheese and finely chopped white Piedmont truffles.

Scrambled: Scramble 6 eggs and mix in 60 g (2 oz) each of grated Parmesan cheese and grated white Piedmont truffle. Place in a deep dish and decorate with a border of sliced white Piedmont truffles.

1430 Fried Poached Eggs, Garnished

These are prepared in exactly the same way as for Oeufs à la Villeroy but are served accompanied with a garnish of a single vegetable such as peas, French beans, asparagus tips etc.; a Macédoine of vegetables, a purée of vegetable or a cullis, artichoke bottoms, morels or mushrooms sliced and sautéed in butter, or perhaps some Tomato Fondue.

Deep fry the prepared eggs 3–4 minutes before service, drain well on a clean cloth and lightly season with salt. Arrange in a circle on a round dish and place the selected garnish in the centre. The garnish may also be served separately.

1431 Oeufs Polignac

Moulded: Well butter some Baba moulds and place a large slice of truffle in the bottom of each. Break in the eggs, season and cook *au Bain-marie* in the usual manner.

Demould each egg onto a small round of toast and arrange them in a circle on a round dish. At the last moment coat each egg with melted Maître d'Hôtel butter which has been mixed with a little melted meat glaze.

1432 Oeufs à la Portugaise

Sur le Plat: Spread a tablespoon of Tomato Fondue in the bottom of each dish, break in the eggs and cook in the usual manner. When ready, place a small bouquet of thick Tomato Fondue on each side of the yolk with a pinch of chopped parsley on top.

En Cocotte: Place half a tablespoon of Tomato Fondue in the bottom of each Cocotte, break in the eggs and cook *au Bain-marie* in the usual manner. When ready, surround each egg with a *cordon* of Tomato Sauce.

Hard-boiled: Use fairly firm and large tomatoes, cut them in half and remove the pips; lightly season and cook the tomatoes in a little oil. Place half a hot hard-boiled egg in each half tomato and coat with thick Sauce Portugaise.

Scrambled: Prepare the scrambled eggs in the usual way and arrange in a deep dish. Place in the centre a nice bouquet of roughly chopped flesh only of tomato, sautéed in butter; surround with a *cordon* of meat glaze and place a pinch of chopped parsley on top of the tomato.

1433 Oeufs Princesse

Poached or Soft-boiled: Fill each tartlet case, half with asparagus tips and half with Julienne of white of cooked chicken mixed with a little Cream Sauce. Coat the eggs with the same sauce, place a nice slice of truffle on each, then place one on each of the prepared tartlets.

Moulded: Place a slice of truffle in the bottom of well-buttered tall narrow dariole moulds. Coat the sides with a layer of chicken and cream forcemeat about 3 mm ($\frac{1}{8}$ in) thick and three-quarters fill them with a light soft scrambled egg mixture containing asparagus tips and diced truffles. Finish filling the moulds with scrambled eggs made in the proportion of 4 scrambled eggs and 1 seasoned beaten raw egg. Finally cover with a layer of chicken forcemeat and cook *au Bain-marie* for 12 minutes. Demould each on to a small round of toast, arrange on a suitable dish and surround with a little thin Chicken Velouté; the Velouté may be served separately.

1434 Oeufs Princesse Marie

Scrambled: Prepare:

1) the required number of small puff paste cases moulded in dariole moulds and
2) an equal number of lids for them using half puff paste cut out with a fancy paste cutter 5 cm (2 in) in diameter; lightly eggwash these and place a small decorated circle of the same paste in the centre of each but do not eggwash. Cook the paste cases and lids in a slow oven without colour.

Fill the paste cases with Parmesan-flavoured scrambled eggs mixed with a little Velouté which has been reduced with truffle essence and finished with a small dice of truffle. Arrange on a serviette and place one of the lids on each.

1435 Oeufs Printanière

Moulded: Line some well-buttered hexagonal moulds with vegetables in the *Chartreuse* fashion, break in the eggs and poach *au Bain-marie* in the usual manner. Demould the eggs on to suitably shaped slices of bread fried in butter and coat each one with a light Cream Sauce which has been finished with Beurre Printanier in the proportions of

100 g ($3\frac{1}{2}$ oz) butter per 5 dl (18 fl oz or $2\frac{1}{4}$ U.S. cups) of sauce.

1436 Oeufs à la Provençale

French fried: Place each egg on half a large tomato prepared *à la Provençale*, then place each egg and tomato on a large thick slice of eggplant which has been seasoned, floured and fried in oil. Arrange in a circle on a round dish with fresh parsley in the centre.

1437 Oeufs Rachel

Sur le Plat: Shallow fry the eggs and trim round with a plain cutter. Place each one on a round slice of bread fried in clarified butter and of the same size as the egg. Place in egg dishes with a nice slice of poached bone marrow on each yolk and a small slice of truffle on the marrow. Surround with a *cordon* of reduced veal gravy.

1438 Oeufs à la Ravigote

Cold: Coat some egg-shaped moulds with a layer of aspic jelly and decorate with small pieces of gherkin, tarragon and capers. Place a spoonful of Sauce Rémoulade mixed with a little jelly into each mould whilst the sauce is still liquid. Place either poached or soft-boiled eggs quickly in the moulds so that the sauce comes up and completely covers the egg. Allow the sauce to set then demould on to oval decorated shapes of aspic jelly.

1439 Oeufs Régina

Poached or Soft-boiled: Fill some tartlet cases with a Salpicon of poached fillets of sole, prawns and mushrooms mixed with a little Sauce Crevettes. Coat the eggs with Sauce Normande and sprinkle the surface with a fine short Julienne of truffle. Place an egg on each prepared tartlet and arrange on a suitable dish.

1440 Oeufs à la Reine

Poached or Soft-boiled: Fill some tartlet cases with a thick purée of chicken; coat the eggs with Sauce Suprême and place one on each tartlet case.

Moulded: Butter some hexagonal moulds and line with alternate thin slices of white of chicken and truffle. Break in the eggs and cook *au Bain-marie*; demould on to small flat cooked moulds of chicken forcemeat and surround with Sauce Suprême or serve the sauce separately.

En Cocotte: Place a little finely chopped white of chicken mixed with a little thick Velouté in the bottom of egg Cocottes. Break in the eggs, cook *au Bain-marie* and surround the yolks with a *cordon* of Sauce Suprême.

Cold: Cut off the tops of small *Brioches à Tête* at the level of the fluted sides and empty them out so as to form cases. Line the insides with very fine chopped white of chicken mixed with a little Mayonnaise and lightly flavoured with Cayenne. Place a soft-boiled egg in each case after having been coated with Mayonnaise. Decorate with a small ball of truffle and glaze with jelly.

1441 Oeufs Reine Margot

Scrambled: Prepare 6 scrambled eggs and finish with 35 g ($1\frac{1}{4}$ oz) Almond Butter. Place the eggs in pale baked tartlet cases and surround with a *cordon* of Sauce Béchamel finished with Pistachio Butter.

1442 Rissoles d'Oeufs

Prepare an egg croquette mixture and make it into Rissoles using small spoonfuls of the mixture and puff paste trimmings. Form in the shape of turnovers, deep fry in the usual way for Rissoles and arrange on a serviette with fried parsley in the centre.

1443 Oeufs Roland

Poached or Soft-boiled: Prepare some shallow cases from bread fried in butter—round for poached or oval for soft-boiled eggs. Place a little Salpicon of cooked white of chicken mixed with a little Chicken Velouté in each case. Coat the eggs with some of the same sauce containing a quarter its volume of chopped chicken and truffle. Place the eggs in the cases and quickly glaze under the salamander.

1444 Oeufs à la Romaine

French fried: Place the fried eggs on small oval-shaped spinach Subrics (4100), the mixture for which should contain a few fillets of anchovies cut into small dice.

1445 Oeufs Rossini

Sur le Plat: Shallow fry the eggs in butter and trim them round with a plain cutter. Place each egg on a round slice of foie gras which has been sautéed in butter, arrange in egg dishes and place a slice of truffle on each yolk. Surround with a *cordon* of Sauce Demi-glace finished with truffle essence.

Poached or Soft-boiled: Place some round slices of foie gras sautéed in butter, in tartlet cases. Coat the eggs with Madeira-flavoured thickened veal gravy, place the eggs on top and set a slice of truffle on each egg.

1446 Oeufs Rosita

Cold: Prepare some nicely shaped poached eggs and coat with white Sauce Chaud-froid containing lobster coral; decorate with crescent-shaped pieces of truffle of graduated sizes in an overlapping fashion and glaze with aspic jelly.

Arrange in a circle on a bed of chopped aspic jelly and surround with a circle of very small tomatoes which have been peeled, depipped, then stuffed with finely chopped tunny fish in oil.

1447 Oeufs Rothomago
Sur le Plat: Well butter the dishes and line each with a thin slice of lean ham; break in the eggs and cook in the usual manner. When ready, garnish each egg with four grilled chipolatas then surround with a *cordon* of Tomato Sauce.

1448 Oeufs à la Rouennaise
En Cocotte: Coat the bottoms and sides of the Cocottes with a layer of Gratin Forcemeat C (295); break in the eggs and cook *au Bain-marie* in the usual way. Surround the yolks with a *cordon* of Sauce Rouennaise.

1449 Oeufs Rougemont
Poached or Soft-boiled: Fill some well buttered tartlet moulds with rice à la Milanaise and demould in a circle on a round dish. Coat the eggs with Sauce Mornay and place one on top of each rice mould. Glaze quickly under the salamander and surround with a *cordon* of Tomato Sauce.

1450 Oeufs Rothschild
Scrambled: Cook 6 crayfish with a Mirepoix then pound in a mortar and add ½ dl (2 fl oz or ¼ U.S. cup) of double cream. Pass the mixture through a fine sieve and add this to 6 beaten eggs; season and scramble gently so as to obtain a smooth, soft, creamy mixture.

Place in a deep dish and place a nice bouquet of asparagus tips in the centre; around this arrange a circle of cooked crayfish tails and then around the crayfish arrange a circle of large slices of very black truffle.

1451 Oeufs Saint-Amand
French fried: Prepare the eggs by breaking into the frying pan and sprinkling the yolks with a little finely chopped ham before enclosing them in the cooking process.

Arrange the eggs in a circle each placed on a rectangular piece of blanched and grilled streaky bacon. In the centre place a garnish of sliced mushrooms sautéed in butter with a little finely chopped shallot and mixed with a little Sauce Demi-glace; finally sprinkle a little chopped parsley on top of the garnish.

1452 Oeufs Saint-Hubert
Poached or Soft-boiled: Prepare a very fine mince of roebuck and mix it with a little Sauce Civet; mould this mixture dome shape on a buttered dish and glaze quickly under the salamander. Coat the eggs with game-flavoured Sauce Poivrade, arrange them around the mince of roebuck and surround with a border of lightly baked puff pastry crescents.

Note: For individual service, the eggs may be placed directly on to the mince of game without glazing it.

1453 Oeufs Sardou
Poached or Soft-boiled: Arrange the eggs in a circle on either oval or round cooked shapes prepared from puff paste trimmings. Coat the eggs with a purée of fresh artichoke bottoms mixed with cream. Place buttered asparagus tips mixed with an equal quantity of fine Julienne of truffle in the centre.

1454 Oeufs à la Savoyarde
Sur le Plat: Place some thin slices of raw potato sautéed in butter in the dishes and sprinkle with a little grated cheese. Break in the eggs, coat with a little cream and cook in the usual manner.
Poached or Soft-boiled: Prepare the eggs au Gratin (1373) and place each one on a small base of Pommes à la Savoyarde.

1455 Oeufs Senora
Poached or Soft-boiled: Place the eggs in a circle on a bed of Riz Pilaw and serve surrounded with Tomato Sauce flavoured with tarragon.

1456 Oeufs à la Serbe
French fried: On a suitable dish, place a bed of Riz Pilaw containing a little diced eggplant sautéed in oil. Arrange the eggs on top with a small slice of grilled ham between each one.

1457 Oeufs Sévigné
Poached or Soft-boiled: Prepare some thin Croûtons of bread fried in butter and spread with a fine purée of braised lettuce. Coat the eggs with Sauce Suprême, decorate with a slice of truffle and place each on a prepared Croûton.

1458 Oeufs Soubise
Poached or Soft-boiled: Fill some tartlet cases with Soubise purée; coat the eggs with thickened veal gravy and place on the tartlets.
En Cocotte: Coat the bottom and sides of the Cocottes with a very thick Soubise, break in the eggs and cook *au Bain-marie* in the usual manner. When ready, place a *cordon* of meat glaze around the yolks.

1459 Oeufs Stanley
Poached or Soft-boiled: Fill some tartlet cases with a rice Soubise flavoured with curry, coat the eggs

with curry-flavoured Sauce Suprême and place one on each of the tartlets.

1460 Oeufs Sultane

Scrambled: Mould some Pommes Duchesse mixture into buttered deep brioche moulds. Demould, lightly egg and breadcrumb, deep fry and empty them from the top, so as to form into cases. Fill these with scrambled eggs containing Pistachio Butter in the proportion of 30 g (1 oz) butter to 6 scrambled eggs.

1461 Oeufs Toupinel

Poached: Bake the required number of large Dutch potatoes and when cooked, empty them so as to form long cases. With part of the potato removed, prepare a light creamy mashed potato and half fill the prepared cases with it. Shred sufficient spinach and stew this with a little butter until cooked; place half a spoonful of this mixture in each potato then place in an egg and cover with some more spinach. Finally coat with Sauce Mornay, sprinkle with grated Gruyère cheese and melted butter and gratinate the potatoes in a very hot oven. Arrange on a folded serviette on a dish.

1462 Oeufs Toussenel

Poached or Soft-boiled: Coat the eggs with a cullis made from game birds plus $\frac{1}{5}$ its quantity of purée of chestnuts. Sprinkle with chopped truffle and place each egg on a flat round Croquette made from any cooked game bird.

1463 Oeufs à la Tripe

Hard-boiled: Stew 100 g ($3\frac{1}{2}$ oz) finely sliced onion in a little butter taking care not to colour; when cooked, add 2 dl (7 fl oz or $\frac{7}{8}$ U.S. cup) Sauce Béchamel and allow to cook gently for a few minutes. Place some sliced hard-boiled eggs carefully in this sauce and turn out into a deep dish. Alternatively, the eggs may be cut in half lengthways, put in the dish and coated with the sauce.

1464 Oeufs Tripe à la Bourgeoise

Hard-boiled: Cook 150 g (5 oz) chopped onion in a little butter without colouring it; sprinkle with 20 g ($\frac{2}{3}$ oz) flour and moisten with $3\frac{1}{2}$ dl (12 fl oz or $1\frac{1}{2}$ U.S. cups) boiling milk. Season with salt, white pepper and nutmeg and cook gently for 20 minutes. Pass through a fine sieve, replace the purée in a pan and reheat. Cut the eggs into quarters, place in a deep dish and cover with the prepared purée.

1465 Oeufs aux Truffes

Scrambled: Prepare 6 scrambled eggs and mix in 30 g (1 oz) small dice of truffle cooked in Madeira. Arrange in a deep dish and place a circle of sliced truffle coated with meat glaze on top. An alternative method is to place the eggs in pale-baked, fluted tartlet cases made from trimmings of puff paste, and place a nice slice of truffle on each.

1466 Oeufs à la Turque

Sur le Plat: Cut some chicken livers into dice, sauté them in a little butter and mix with a little thick tomato-flavoured Sauce Demi-glace. Cook the eggs in the usual way and place a bouquet of the chicken livers on each side of the yolks; surround with a *cordon* of the tomato-flavoured Sauce Demi-glace.

1467 Oeufs Vaucourt

Sur le Plat: On a suitable buttered dish and using Pommes Duchesse mixture and a large star tube, pipe either a border around the edge, a rosette of separate compartments, or cover the dish with a number of connecting circles; eggwash and colour light brown in the oven.

Place in the bottom of the borders some very lightly cooked scrambled eggs mixed with asparagus tips and truffle. Break the eggs on top of this mixture and cook them as for *sur le Plat* by placing the dish on a suitably sized pan of cold water in a hot oven; this will prevent the scrambled eggs from cooking too much, whilst cooking the other eggs lightly to give the white transparent appearance on the yolks, termed *au miroir*. Place a round slice of truffle on each yolk.

1468 Oeufs Vauluisant

Poached: Arrange the eggs on a dish in a circle, each placed on an oval flat Croquette of chicken; coat with Cream Sauce and fill the centre with a purée of French beans.

1469 Oeufs Verdi

Moulded: Decorate the bottom of buttered dariole moulds with a nice slice of truffle. Prepare some scrambled eggs flavoured with grated Parmesan and garnished with small dice of truffle, taking care that the mixture is kept very soft. Add 2 well beaten and seasoned eggs for each 4 scrambled eggs and fill the moulds with this mixture; cook *au Bain-marie* in the oven. Demould on to small round slices of bread fried in butter and surround with a little Sauce Demi-glace flavoured with truffle essence. The sauce may also be served separately.

Note: For this type of moulded scrambled egg which can be varied, the method of lining the moulds with a thin layer of forcemeat in keeping with the nature of the dish, is to be recommended. This ensures that the scrambled eggs becomes lightly set without the addition of the raw eggs.

The advantages of this method are 1) it ensures perfect demoulding, and 2) it becomes possible to keep the scrambled eggs at the right degree of softness. It is absolutely essential that the layer of forcemeat be very thin so as to preserve the character of a moulded egg, if too thick the dish would be nothing but a *Timbale* of eggs.

1470 Oeufs Victoria

Sur le Plat: Cook the eggs in the usual manner and on each side of the yolks place a bouquet of Salpicon of lobster and truffle mixed with a little thick Lobster Sauce.

Poached or Soft-boiled: Fill some tartlet cases with a Salpicon of lobster and truffle mixed with a little Lobster Sauce. Coat the eggs with Sauce Victoria, place on the prepared tartlets and glaze quickly.

1471 Oeufs Villaret

Poached: Arrange the eggs on a bed of thinly sliced artichoke bottoms cooked with butter and mixed with a little puree Soubise; coat with Sauce Mornay and glaze.

1472 Oeufs Villeroy

Poached or Soft-boiled: Carefully dry the cooked eggs, coat with Sauce Villeroy and allow to become quite cold.

Trim carefully, then egg and breadcrumb them using very fine breadcrumbs. Deep fry in very hot fat for a few minutes just before serving; drain well, arrange on a serviette with fried parsley in the centre and serve Tomato Sauce separately.

1473 Oeufs Viroflay

Poached or Soft-boiled: Cut some thick slices of unsweetened Brioche and fry in butter as Croûtons; hollow out the top surface and fill with leaf spinach blanched and stewed with a little butter. Coat the eggs with Sauce Allemande and place one on each Croûton.

Moulded: Line some buttered Baba moulds with leaves of spinach which have been blanched and lightly stewed with butter; break in the eggs, cook *au Bain-marie* then demould on to small rounds of toast. Finish by coating the eggs with Sauce Allemande.

1474 Oeufs des Viveurs

Cold: Prepare some soft boiled eggs cooked for 7 minutes; cool, shell and trim the bottoms level so that they stand up straight. Coat with Sauce Homard à l'Américaine mixed with a little aspic jelly, and allow to set.

Place each egg on a round slice of crawfish which has been coated with Mayonnaise Collée and arrange on a dish around a shaped potato salad à la Parisienne. Surround the eggs with a circle of round slices of potato alternating with round slices of very red, marinated beetroot.

1475 Vol-au-vent d'Oeufs

Hard-boiled: Prepare a garnish of the following items: 6 sliced hard-boiled eggs, 100 g (3½ oz) mushroom cut into quarters on the slant and cooked very white, 100 g (3½ oz) sliced truffle cooked in Madeira, 3 dl (½ pt or 1¼ U.S. cups) Sauce Béchamel reduced with the cooking liquor from the truffles and 1 dl (3½ fl oz or ½ U.S. cup) cream. In a suitably sized Vol-au-vent case, arrange the eggs, mushrooms and truffle in alternate layers with the sauce, finishing with a layer of sauce and a circle of sliced truffle.

1476 Oeufs Yorkshire

French fried: Arrange the eggs in a dish alternating with thin slices of fried bread and slices of raw ham fried in butter. Place a bouquet of fried parsley in the centre and serve Tomato Sauce separately.

1477 Oeufs Yvette

Scrambled: Prepare 6 scrambled eggs and carefully mix in 2 tbs Sauce Nantua and 1 tbs each of asparagus tips and diced crayfish tails.

Place the mixture in pale baked tartlet cases made from puff paste trimmings and place a nice slice of truffle on top of each.

OMELETTES

The theory of the preparation of an omelette is both simple and at the same time very complicated, for the simple reason that people's tastes for this type of dish are very different—one likes his omelette very well cooked, another likes it to be just done, and there are others who only like their omelette when it is extremely soft and underdone. The important thing is to know and understand the preference of the guest.

It is not necessary to dwell too much on the actual method of preparation which after all, is a question of practice and manual dexterity. Suffice it to say simply that what is required is homogeneity of the egg and the softness of the whole.

In a few words, what is an omelette? It is really a special type of scrambled egg enclosed in a coating or envelope of coagulated egg and nothing else.

The following recipes are for an omelette of 3 eggs each, of which the seasoning comprises a small pinch of fine salt and a touch of pepper, and which requires 15 g (½ oz) of butter for its preparation.

The preparation of an Omelette: Heat the butter in an omelette pan until it just begins to turn brown, this will not only give an excellent flavour to the omelette, but will also provide the required amount of heat necessary to ensure the correct setting of the eggs. Pour in the eggs which have been well beaten until the yellow and whites are thoroughly blended and seasoned, shake the pan and stir briskly with a fork at the same time so as to ensure even cooking. If the omelette is to be stuffed inside with a garnish, this should be placed in the centre at this time and the omelette should be quickly folded, rolled into shape and turned over on to a suitable dish, then finished according to the requirements of its recipe. When the omelette is on the dish it is good practice to draw a piece of butter over it in order to make its surface glossy.

1478 Omelette Agnès Sorel
Stuff the omelette with 30 g (1 oz) sliced mushrooms sautéed in butter and mixed with a spoonful of purée of cooked chicken. Place 8 small rounds of overlapping red ox tongue on the omelette. Surround with a *cordon* of veal gravy.

1479 Omelette Archiduc
Stuff the omelette with 2 nice sliced chicken livers sautéed in butter and mixed with a little Sauce Demi-glace. Place 8 slices of truffle on the omelette and surround with a *cordon* of Sauce Demi-glace.

1480 Omelette Bénédictine
Stuff the omelette with 1 tbs of Brandade of salt cod (1805) containing a quarter its volume of chopped truffle. Surround the omelette with a *cordon* of Cream Sauce.

1481 Omelette à la Bouchère
Stuff the omelette with 30 g (1 oz) very fresh bone marrow cut in dice, poached, drained and mixed with a little meat glaze. Place 4 nice slices of poached bone marrow coated with a little light meat glaze on the omelette.

1482 Omelette à la Boulonnaise
Stuff the omelette with a nice soft mackerel roe which has been sautéed in butter and a small piece of Maître d'Hôtel butter. Surround the omelette with some melted Maître d'Hôtel butter.

1483 Omelette Bretonne
Add to the beaten eggs, ½ tbs each of shredded onion and white of leek both stewed in butter, and ½ tbs sliced mushrooms also cooked in butter. Prepare the omelette in the usual manner.

1484 Omelette Brillat-Savarin
Stuff the omelette with a small spoonful each of diced breast of cooked woodcock and truffle, mixed together with a little cullis of woodcock. Place 3 nice slices of truffle on top of the omelette and surround with a *cordon* of game glaze finished with truffle essence.

1485 Omelette à la Bruxelloise
Stuff the omelette with 50 g (2 oz) braised Belgian endives shredded and mixed with cream. Surround the omelette with a *cordon* of Cream Sauce.

1486 Omelette à la Chartres, or Omelette à l'Estragon
Add a pinch of chopped tarragon to the beaten eggs; prepare the omelette in the usual manner and decorate the middle of the omelette with blanched leaves of tarragon.

1487 Omelette Chasseur
Stuff the omelette with 2 nice chicken livers, sautéed à la Chasseur; cut open the omelette lengthways and place a bouquet of the same garnish in the opening. Surround the omelette with a *cordon* of Sauce Chasseur.

1488 Omelette Châtelaine
Stuff the omelette with 40 g (1½ oz) chestnuts cooked in a little White Bouillon, drained, roughly broken and mixed with a little meat glaze. Surround the omelette with a *cordon* of Chicken Velouté containing a purée of cooked onions.

1489 Omelette aux Champignons
Add 40 g (1½ oz) sliced mushrooms sautéed in butter to the beaten eggs and place 6 nice slices of sautéed mushrooms on the finished omelette.

1490 Omelette Choisy
Stuff the omelette with 1 tbs of braised lettuce, shredded and mixed with a little Cream Sauce. Surround the omelette with a *cordon* of the same sauce.

1491 Omelette Clamart
Stuff the omelette with 2 tbs of peas cooked with shredded lettuce and mixed with butter. Cut open the omelette lengthways and place a spoonful of the same peas in the opening.

1492 Omelette Crécy
Stuff the omelette with 1 tbs of sliced red of carrot cooked in butter with a little sugar, then passed through a fine sieve. On top place 4 rounds of carrot cooked in White Bouillon and glazed. Surround with a *cordon* of Cream Sauce.

1493 Omelette aux Crevettes
Stuff the omelette with 25 g (1 oz) cooked shrimps

mixed with 1 tbs Sauce Crevette. Cut open the omelette lengthways and place a bouquet of shrimps or prawns heated in a little butter in the opening. Surround with a *cordon* of Sauce Crevette.

1494 Omelette Durand
Add to the eggs 15 g (½ oz) each of sliced mushrooms and sliced artichoke bottoms both sautéed in butter. Make the omelette and stuff it with a small spoonful of Julienne of truffle and the same amount of asparagus tips mixed with 1 tbs of Velouté. Surround the omelette with a *cordon* of tomato-flavoured Sauce Demi-glace.

1495 Omelette à l'Espagnole
To the beaten eggs add ½ tbs finely sliced onions cooked in butter, 1 tbs Tomato Fondue and a pinch of chopped parsley. Prepare the omelette which should not be rolled, but left flat in the pan, turning it over to cook on both sides.

1496 Omelette à la Fermière
Add 100 g (3½ oz) lean chopped ham to the beaten eggs. Make the omelette flat, do not turn it over and keep it very soft. Slide it on to a dish and sprinkle the surface with a pinch of chopped parsley.

1497 Omelette aux Fines Herbes
Those chopped Fines Herbes which are added to the eggs are parsley, chives, chervil and tarragon in equal quantities and using 1 tbs per omelette. It is absolutely incorrect to consider an omelette made only with parsley as an Omelette aux Fines Herbes.

1498 Omelette aux Fleurs de Courges
Add to the eggs, 15 g (½ oz) freshly gathered calyxes from the flowers of vegetable marrow which have been shredded and stewed with a little butter and mixed with a pinch of chopped parsley. The omelette may be made with butter or oil, but should always be served surrounded with a *cordon* of Tomato Sauce.

1499 Omelette à la Florentine
Stuff the omelette with 1 tbs of spinach leaves which have been blanched and stewed with butter. Surround the omelette with a *cordon* of Sauce Béchamel.

1500 Omelette aux Fonds d'Artichauts
To the beaten eggs, add 50 g (2 oz) sliced raw artichoke bottoms cooked in butter. At the same time prepare 5 thicker slices, cooked in butter and placed on one side. Make the omelette and place the five thick slices on top. Surround the omelette with a *cordon* of Jus lié.

1501 Omelette à la Forestière
Sauté 50 g (2 oz) of morels in butter of which three of the best are cut in half and the rest sliced; mix the sliced ones with a little meat glaze. Sauté 40 g (1½ oz) lean bacon cut in dice and blanched; add the beaten eggs, make the omelette and stuff it with the sliced morels mixed with a pinch of chopped parsley. Place the 6 half morels in a line on top of the omelette and serve surrounded with a *cordon* of Jus lié.

1502 Omelette Grand'mère
Add to the beaten eggs a pinch of chopped parsley and whilst still hot 25 g (1 oz) small dice of bread fried in butter. Make the omelette immediately.

1503 Omelette Grandval
Stuff the omelette with 2 tbs of Tomato Fondue flavoured with garlic. Coat the omelette with a well-buttered Tomato Sauce and arrange slices of hot hard-boiled egg overlapping on top.

1504 Omelette Hongroise
Stuff the omelette with 1 tbs of finely shredded onion cooked in butter with a small pinch of paprika and mixed with 1 tbs roughly chopped flesh only of tomato, seasoned and sautéed in butter. Surround the omelette with a *cordon* of Sauce Hongroise.

1505 Omelette Jurassienne
Add a pinch each of chopped chives and chervil to the beaten eggs. Fry 25 g (1 oz) small batons of streaky bacon in the omelette pan, add the eggs and cook the omelette in the fat provided by the bacon. Stuff the omelette with 1 tbs of shredded sorrel stewed in a little butter.

1506 Omelette Lorraine
Add to the beaten eggs 30 g (1 oz) lean bacon blanched, grilled and cut into 6 small rectangles, 25 g (1 oz) fresh Gruyère cheese, cut into very small pieces, a pinch of chopped chives and 1 tbs double cream. Prepare the omelette in the usual manner.

1507 Omelette Lyonnaise
Cook 50 g (2 oz) very finely sliced onion in the omelette pan with a little butter until lightly coloured. Add the beaten eggs with a good pinch of chopped parsley and make the omelette in the usual manner.

1508 Omelette Mancelle
Stuff the omelette with 1 tbs chestnuts cooked in a little Bouillon, broken into pieces and mixed with 1 tbs short Julienne cooked partridge breast and 1 tbs game glaze. Pour a line of the same glaze along

the length of the omelette and surround with a *cordon* of game-flavoured Sauce Demi-glace.

1509 Omelette Marie-Jeanne
In the pan fry 20 g ($\frac{2}{3}$ oz) streaky bacon and 30 g (1 oz) potatoes both cut in small dice. Mix 1 tbs double cream, 1 tbs stewed sorrel and spinach, and 1 tbs chopped chervil, into the beaten eggs; pour into the pan and make the omelette in the usual manner. Butter the surface and sprinkle with chopped parsley.

1510 Omelette Masséna
Stuff the omelette with 25 g (1 oz) finely sliced artichoke bottoms sautéed in butter and mixed with 1 tbs Tomato Sauce. Place 2 nice slices of poached bone marrow coated with meat glaze on top of the omelette and surround with a *cordon* of Sauce Béarnaise.

1511 Omelette Maxim
Prepare the omelette in the usual manner and place a line of crayfish tails alternating with slices of truffle on top. Surround the omelette with a nice border of frogs legs cooked *à la Meunière*.

1512 Omelette Mexicaine
Add to the eggs 25 g (1 oz) sliced sautéed mushrooms and 10 g ($\frac{1}{3}$ oz) chopped red pimento. Make the omelette in the usual manner and stuff it with 1 tbs thick Tomato Fondue.

1513 Omelette Mireille
Stuff the omelette with 1 tbs Tomato Fondue flavoured with a little crushed garlic. Make the omelette in the usual manner using oil and serve surrounded with a *cordon* of saffron-flavoured Cream Sauce.

1514 Omelette Monselet
Stuff the omelette with 1 tbs light purée of foie gras mixed with $\frac{1}{2}$ tbs each of short Julienne of cooked mushroom and truffle, and $\frac{1}{2}$ tbs asparagus tips. Place 3 nice slices of truffle on the omelette and surround with a *cordon* of Sauce Demi-glace.

1515 Omelette Mousseline
In a basin mix 3 egg yolks with a small pinch of salt and 1 tbs very thick cream. Add the three egg whites, stiffly beaten, mix in and pour the mixture into a pan which contains 30 g (1 oz) very hot butter. Shake the pan briskly and keep tossing the egg quickly from the side to the centre. When the omelette is evenly set roll it in the usual manner and turn it over on to a dish for immediate service.

1516 Omelette Nantua
Stuff the omelette with 30 g (1 oz) crayfish tails mixed with a little Sauce Nantua and place 2 nice crayfish tails on the top with a slice of truffle between them. Surround the omelette with a *cordon* of Sauce Nantua.

1517 Omelette aux Nonnats
Just before tipping the beaten eggs into the pan, add 30 g (1 oz) Nonnats sautéed in clarified butter and make the omelette in the usual manner.

1518 Omelette à la Normande
Stuff the omelette with 6 poached and bearded oysters mixed with 1 tbs Sauce Normande. Surround the omelette with a *cordon* of the same sauce.

1519 Omelette à l'Oseille
Stuff the omelette with 1 good tbs finely shredded sorrel stewed in butter and mixed with a pinch of chopped chervil.

1520 Omelette Parmentier
Add to the beaten eggs a pinch of chopped parsley and just before pouring into the pan, add whilst still hot 2 tbs potato cut in small dice, seasoned and sautéed in butter. Make the omelette in the usual manner.

1521 Omelette à la Paysanne
Fry until light brown 50 g (2 oz) lean bacon which has been cut into small dice and blanched. To the beaten eggs, add 1 tbs thin slices of potato sautéed in butter, $\frac{1}{2}$ tbs shredded sorrel stewed with butter, and a pinch of coarsely chopped chervil. Tip this mixture on to the bacon, cook the eggs keep them soft and turn the omelette over in the pan like a pancake. Slide the omelette immediately on to a round dish.

1522 Omelette aux Pointes d'Asperges
Add to the beaten eggs $1\frac{1}{2}$ tbs asparagus tips blanched and stewed with butter. Make the omelette in the usual manner, cut open along the centre and place a nice bouquet of asparagus tips inside.

1523 Omelette à la Portugaise
Stuff the omelette with 1 good tbs Tomato Fondue and surround it with a *cordon* of well buttered Tomato Sauce.

1524 Omelettes des Prelats
Stuff the omelette with 1 good tbs large Salpicon of cooked soft herring roes, crayfish tails, prawns and short Julienne of truffle, all mixed with 1 tbs Sauce Normande finished with Crayfish Butter.

Coat the omelette with the same sauce and sprinkle well with very black chopped truffle.

1525 Omelette Princesse
Stuff the omelette with 1 tbs asparagus tips mixed with a little Cream Sauce. Place a line of overlapping slices of truffle on it and surround with a *cordon* of the same sauce.

1526 Omelette à la Provençale
Lightly rub the bottom of the pan with a piece of garlic then add 2 tbs oil; heat it until it is very hot and add 50 (2 oz) roughly chopped flesh only of tomato and a pinch of coarsely chopped parsley. Toss the tomatoes over quickly then add the eggs and make the omelette in the usual manner.

Note: The character of this omelette demands the use of oil to sauté the tomatoes, but in certain circumstances it is permissible to use clarified butter.

1527 Omelette à la Reine
Stuff the omelette with 1 tbs purée of white of chicken mixed with a little Sauce Suprême. Surround it with a *cordon* of Sauce Suprême.

1528 Omelettes aux Rognons
Stuff the omelette with $1\frac{1}{2}$ tbs veal or lamb kidneys cut in dice, seasoned, quickly sautéed in butter and mixed with a little Sauce Demi-glace. When the omelette has been turned out on to the dish, cut an opening along the middle and fill it with 1 tbs of the same garnish. Surround with a *cordon* of Sauce Demi-glace.

1529 Omelette Rossini
Add to the beaten eggs 1 tbs each of small dice of foie gras and truffle and make the omelette in the usual way. Place a small slice of foie gras heated in butter on top and a slice of truffle at each end. Surround the omelette with a *cordon* of Sauce Demi-glace flavoured with truffle essence.

1530 Omelette à la Rouennaise
Stuff the omelette with 1 good tbs duck livers sauteed in butter with a little chopped shallot, then pounded and passed through a fine sieve.

Surround the omelette with a *cordon* of Sauce Rouennaise or, more simply, a reduction of good red wine containing a little meat glaze and lightly thickened with butter.

1531 Omelette à la Savoyarde
To the beaten eggs, add 2 tbs double cream, 25 g (1 oz) finely sliced rounds of potato sautéed in butter, and 20 g ($\frac{2}{3}$ oz) coarsely grated Gruyère cheese. Make the omelette flat.

1532 Omelette à la Suissesse
Add to the beaten eggs, 50 g (2 oz) grated Emmenthal cheese and 1 tbs of cream and make the omelette in the usual manner.

1533 Omelette au Thon
Add to the beaten eggs, 30 g (1 oz) tunny fish in oil cut in dice; make the omelette in the usual manner and pour 2 tbs of melted Anchovy Butter over it when placed on the dish.

1534 Omelette aux Truffes
Add to the beaten eggs, 1 good tbs of truffles cut into thin slices; place a row of sliced truffle on the omelette and surround it with a little meat glaze.

1535 Omelette Victoria
Stuff the omelette with 1 tbs Salpicon of crayfish tails and truffle mixed with Lobster Sauce. Surround the omelette with a *cordon* of the same sauce.

PLOVER AND GREEN PLOVERS' EGGS

Although the plover and green plover may be distinguished by the difference in their plumage they both have the same habits and haunts and their eggs are almost identical in appearance.

These eggs which are roughly the same size as those of a pigeon, have a light green coloured shell touched with black spots. When cooked, the white of the eggs takes on a milky tint and is not quite so firm as the whites of other eggs.

Although all the usual preparations of eggs are applicable, plovers eggs are usually served hard-boiled and cold.

To hard-boil these eggs allow 8 minutes of cooking from the time the water reboils after placing them in. Before cooking the eggs, make sure they are fresh by placing into a bowl of cold water; any which float will be of doubtful freshness and should therefore be discarded.

1536 Oeufs de Vanneau en Aspic
Cold: Coat the inside of a Savarin mould with a layer of aspic jelly and decorate to choice, fixing the items of decoration with a little jelly. Cover with a little more jelly and allow to set firmly. Arrange the cold shelled hard-boiled plovers eggs in the mould with the points of the eggs downwards so that they will be the correct way up when demoulded.

Finish by filling the mould with jelly adding it a little at a time; allow to set in a cold place then demould on to a serviette when required.

1537 Oeufs de Vanneau Christiana
Hot: See Hot Hors-d'oeuvres (1199).

1538 Oeufs de Vanneau à la Danoise
Hot: Poach the eggs, then place them in small tartlet cases which have been filled with a purée of salmon.

1539 Oeufs de Vanneau Gabriel
Cold: Coat the inside of dariole moulds with aspic jelly and sprinkle with cooked separated lobster or crawfish eggs. In each one place a cold soft-boiled plover's egg with the point downwards, completely fill with aspic jelly and allow to set in a cold place.

Demould each egg on to a small cooked tartlet case and surround the base of the egg with a purée of creamed fillets of sole; this is best piped out with a piping bag and small star tube.

1540 Oeufs de Vanneau à la Moderne
Cold: Coat the inside of dariole moulds with aspic jelly and line with a Chartreuse decoration. Place a cold hard-boiled plover's egg in each mould the point facing downwards; finish by filling with more jelly and allow to set in a cold place.

Place a garnish of a Macédoine of vegetable bound with Mayonnaise in the centre of a round dish and mould it dome shape; demould the eggs and arrange in a circle around the Macédoine.

1541 Oeufs de Vanneau à la Moscovite
Cold: Hard-boil the eggs then refresh them and shell them. Place each egg on a tartlet case filled with caviare.

1542 Oeufs de Vanneau dans un Nid
Cold: Shape a nest out of Montpelier Butter on a round dish and fashion the outside like a nest with the same butter using a fine piping tube. Arrange cold soft-boiled plover's eggs around the inside edge of the nest, fill the centre with chopped aspic jelly and surround the nest with garden cress.

1543 Omelette d'Oeufs de Vanneau
These are made in the same way as other omelettes but it is advisable to add 1 ordinary egg to each 6 plover's eggs so as to give strength and body to the mixture.

All the ordinary recipes for omelettes are suitable.

1544 Oeufs de Vanneau Petite-Reine
Cold: Coat the inside of dariole moulds with aspic jelly and decorate the surface of this jelly with pieces of truffle and white of egg in a chessboard pattern. Place a cold hard-boiled plover's egg in each mould with the point downwards, fill up the mould with more jelly and allow to set in a cool place.

Demould when required and arrange in a circle on a round dish. Fill the centre with a salad of asparagus tips and decorate the border of the dish with fancy crescent-shaped pieces of jelly.

1545 Oeufs de Vanneau à la Royale
Hot: Prepare the required number of moulded tartlet cases made from a purée of chicken bound with raw eggs; place in a moderate oven so as to cook and set them. Demould them in a circle on a dish and remove a round piece from the centre of each one. Place a soft-boiled plover's egg in the centre of each tartlet, coat it with light purée of mushrooms and sprinkle with chopped truffle.

1546 Oeufs de Vanneau Troubadour
Hot: Select a number of large morels allowing one per egg, remove the stalks and free the openings; season and cook them in a little butter. Soft boil the plovers eggs and shell them. Fill some small tartlet cases with a light purée of foie gras, place an egg in each tartlet case and a morel on top of the egg. Arrange in a circle on a dish.

CHAPTER 6

FISH

VARIOUS COOKING LIQUORS FOR FISH

1547 Vinegar Court-bouillon (*for whole and large cuts of salmon and trout*)
To make 5 litres (8¾ pt or 1⅜ U.S. gal)

Ingredients:
5 litres (8¾ pt or 1⅜ U.S. gal) water
2½ dl (9 fl oz or 1⅛ U.S. cups) vinegar
60 g (2 oz) coarse salt
600 g (1 lb 5 oz) sliced carrots
500 g (1 lb 2 oz) sliced onions
1 sprig of thyme
2 small bayleaves
100 g (3½ oz) parsley stalks
20 g (⅔ oz) peppercorns

Method:
Place all the ingredients into a pan excepting the peppercorns; bring to the boil and simmer gently for approximately 1 hour. Ten minutes before it is completely cooked, add the peppercorns; pass through a strainer when ready.

1548 White Wine Court-bouillon (*for trout, eels, pike etc.*)
To make 5 litres (8¾ pt or 1⅜ U.S. gal)

Ingredients:
2½ litres (4¼ pt or 5⅜ U.S. pt) white wine
2½ litres (4¼ pt or 5⅜ U.S. pt) water
600 g (1 lb 5 oz) sliced onion
80 g (3 oz) parsley stalks
1 sprig thyme
½ small bayleaf
60 g (2 oz) coarse salt
15 g (½ oz) peppercorns

Method:
Place all the ingredients excepting the peppercorns into a pan, bring to the boil and simmer gently for 30 minutes. Ten minutes before it is cooked, add the peppercorns; pass through a strainer when ready.

1549 Red Wine Court-bouillon (*general use for trout, carp and Matelotes*)
The ingredients and method are the same as for White Wine Court-bouillon except that the white wine is replaced by red wine and 400 g (15 oz) sliced carrots are added.

Note: When fish is prepared with only a little White or Red Wine Court-bouillon, and when they are to be served with some of the Court-bouillon including the vegetables, these last should be very well cooked; a little fresh butter should be added to the Court-bouillon at the last moment.

1550 Plain Court-bouillon (*for large cuts of turbot and brill*)
Cover the fish with cold water containing 15 g (½ oz) salt, 1 dl (3½ fl oz or ½ U.S. cup) milk and 1 slice of peeled and depipped lemon per 1 litre (1¾ pt or 4½ U.S. cups) water.

1551 Shellfish Court-bouillon (*for crayfish and lobsters*)
Use Vinegar Court-bouillon (1547), but with salt in the proportion of 15 g (½ oz) per 1 litre (1¾ pt or 4½ U.S. cups) water.

1552 Salted Water Court-bouillon (*for sea perch, mullet and various other fish*)
Simply add 15 g (½ oz) salt per 1 litre (1¾ pt or 4½ U.S. cups) water.

Remarks regarding the use of the various cooking liquors for fish

1) Where any fish requires less than 30 minutes cooking, the Court-bouillon should be cooked in advance.
2) Where any fish requires more than 30 minutes cooking the Court-bouillon should be used cold with the flavourings and vegetables placed underneath the grill in the fish kettle.
3) Where the fish is to be cooked in a small amount of liquid it should be placed in either a White or Red Wine Court-bouillon and only at the last moment. The amount of Court-bouillon used should be sufficient to cover

one-third of the way up and the fish should be basted frequently with the liquor during the cooking process. In this method the Court-bouillon is generally served with the fish and is lightly buttered at the last moment before serving.

4) Fish which is to be served cold should be allowed to cool thoroughly in the Court-bouillon and the cooking time should therefore be reduced accordingly.

Note: Cooking times applicable to certain fish are given in the recipes where appropriate.

THE VARIOUS WAYS OF COOKING FISH

The different ways of preparing fish all come under one or other of the following methods:

1) Cooking in salted water—this can be used for whole large fish and cuts of fish equally as well as White Wine Court-bouillon.
2) The poaching of fish in very little liquid—this is applicable to fillets and small cuts of fish.
3) Braising—which is used above all, for large whole fish.
4) Cooking *au Bleu*—which is particularly suitable for trout, carp and pike.
5) Deep frying—which is applicable above all, for whole small fish and cuts of fish.
6) Cooking of fish in butter called *à la Meunière*—applicable to small whole fish and cuts of fish.
7) Grilling—for small whole fish and cuts of fish.
8) The cooking method called *au Gratin*—suitable for medium-sized fish and for cuts of fish.

1553 The Cooking of Fish in Salted Water or in White Wine Court-bouillon

If the fish is to be cooked whole, it should be laid on the grill of a suitably shaped fish kettle; in the case of turbot it should be cleared of blood and well trimmed. Cover with either cold salted water or cold Court-bouillon, according to the type of fish. Bring to the boil rapidly, skim and pull the fish kettle to the side of the stove so as to allow the fish to continue cooking by poaching.

If the fish is cut in pieces these should never be too thin; they should be placed into boiling salted water or Court-bouillon, and the pan pulled to the side of the stove so as to allow the fish to cook slowly without boiling. This method has the effect of concentrating all the juices contained in the fish, a large amount of which would be lost if the fish were to be placed to cook in cold water. On the other hand, if a whole fish is placed into boiling liquid, this would cause a sudden contraction of the flesh, resulting in some breaking up and distortion.

Fish cooked in salt water or Court-bouillon should be placed on a serviette or on a special grill, surrounded with fresh parsley and served accompanied with plain boiled potatoes and the sauce or sauces as specified on the menu. The parsley should be placed around the fish just before it is served and on no account should a dish containing parsley be covered with a lid.

1554 The Poaching of Fish in a Small Amount of Liquid

This method is mainly applicable to small turbot, brill, soles and to fillets of these fish.

Place the fish or fillets on a buttered tray or shallow pan, season lightly with salt and moisten with the required amount of fish stock or mushroom cooking liquor, or as is sometimes the case, a mixture of both. Cover, place in a moderate oven and baste the fish with the liquid from time to time, especially in the case of whole fish.

When the fish is cooked, drain it carefully and place on the service dish, surround with the garnish if called for in the recipe, and cover with the appropriate sauce. The reduced cooking liquid from the fish is almost always added to the fish sauce chosen.

Notes:

1) It is particularly recommended that only very little fish stock should be used when fish is poached in this manner and that this fish stock should be faultless and above all, have been cooked only for the time necessary.
2) It is advisable not to cover the fish with a buttered paper for this method, as it is extremely difficult to find the correct kind of paper. The use of certain chemicals in the manufacture of some papers can cause a disagreeable smell, more or less pronounced, but this is always deleterious to the fish. This observation holds good not only for fish but for every item of food for which paper may be used.

1555 The Braising of Fish

This method of cooking is mainly used for whole salmon, cuts of salmon, large trout and turbot. Sometimes the fish is larded on one side with strips of salt pork fat, truffle, gherkin, carrot etc., before braising; the usual vegetables and herbs for braising are used, omitting pork rind.

According to the manner in which the fish is to be served it is first moistened with half red or white wine and half fish stock taking care that the liquid is just sufficient to come three-quarters of the way up the fish. Unless the preparation is to be completely Lenten the fish may also be covered with thin slices of salt pork fat; it should be basted frequently during cooking.

The utensil used should be one with a lid that is not too tight fitting so that the reduction of the liquid can take place at the same time as the fish is cooking.

When the fish is almost cooked, remove the cover so as to allow it to glaze. When this has been done, drain the fish well, arrange it on the serving dish and keep it warm.

Strain the cooking liquid, allow it to settle, then skim off the fat; reduce as necessary and add to the fish sauce.

Braised fish are usually accompanied with a garnish, the composition of which is indicated in each recipe of its type.

1556 The Cooking of Fish *au Bleu*

The name *au Bleu* indicates a special method of preparation and cooking applicable only to trout, carp and pike and is based on the following principles which must be carefully observed.

1) The fish of whatever kind must be live.
2) It should be gutted with the least possible handling so as not to remove the natural slimy coating and it should then be placed in the cooking liquid without being scaled.
3) Large fish are placed on the grill of the fish kettle and basted with boiling vinegar which should be that amount required for the Court-bouillon used to cover the fish. The required amount of lukewarm Court-bouillon prepared without the vinegar should then be carefully poured over the fish so as to lessen as much as possible the risk of any damage to the flesh. The cooking of the fish should then take place in the usual manner.
4) Small trout for preparation *au Bleu* should be caught alive, quickly emptied and placed in a boiling Court-bouillon comprised only of water, vinegar and salt.
5) Fish prepared *au Bleu* can be served either hot or cold and with its accompaniment as indicated in the different recipes.

1557 The Deep Frying of Fish

In principle the deep frying of fish should not be applied to fish which are too large or to cuts of fish which are too thick, the reason being that the high temperature required to cook them will cause the outside of the fish to become dry before the middle is cooked through.

If the fish chosen for deep frying should be a little thick it should be *Ciselé*, that is to say, cuts should be made into the flesh on both sides of the fish so as to facilitate the cooking; this is not necessary for small fish. For flat fish it is advsiable to partly detach the fillets at the backbone on one side of the fish only.

Fish intended for frying, except Blanchailles and Whitebait should first be soaked in salted milk and passed through flour before being deep fried; however, if the fish is to be egg and crumbed the soaking in milk is unnecessary. In this case it should be lightly floured, dipped into beaten egg and coated with white breadcrumbs. The fish should then be patted with the flat of a knife so as to ensure the adhesion of the coating then marked trellis-fashion with the back of a knife for presentation purposes.

Fried fish should be served either on a serviette, on a grill or on a dish paper and garnished with fried parsley and correctly cut and trimmed halves of lemons.

The theory of the deep frying of fish: The *Friture*, or frying utensil used for deep frying fish should be kept only for fish because the fat being used can become too coloured and flavoured for any other use.

All kinds of fat and oil may be used for frying provided that they are clarified but the ideal media for cooking fish, especially small ones, is olive oil which can be brought to an approximate temperature of 290 °C (554 °F) without burning, whereas some ordinary fats will start to burn at approximately 180 °C (356 °F).

As an absolute principle, great care must be taken that the temperature of the frying media should be regulated according to the size of the fish being cooked—the smaller the fish the higher the temperature—so as to ensure the sealing of the outer surface of the fish. Very small fish such as Nonnats and Whitebait should be plunged into very hot lightly smoking fat.

The quantity of fat required is determined by the size and amount of fish to be fried, but there should always be sufficient to enable the fish to float freely whilst at the same time being immersed in it.

Care should be taken to strain the fat each time after use because the flour and breadcrumbs which become detached from the pieces being fried form a residue which can cause the frying media to burn, or attach themselves to any fish being fried afterwards thus spoiling its appearance.

1558 The Cooking of Fish in Butter, called *à la Meunière*

This excellent method of cooking can be applied to small whole fish and to cuts of large fish. However, it is possible with a certain amount of care and attention to apply this method to small turbot of no more than 1½ kg (3 lb 6 oz) in weight.

The method consists of cooking the whole fish, slices or fillets of fish in a frying pan in very hot butter after having been seasoned and lightly coated with flour.

For small fish, ordinary butter can be used but for larger ones the use of clarified butter is to be preferred. After the fish has been turned over in the pan and is just cooked, it is placed on a very hot serving dish; it can be served as it is with a simple accompaniment of a trimmed half of lemon. Fish served in this way is usually termed *Doré* so as to distinguish it from the exact designation *à la Meunière*.

In the case of *à la Meunière*, a little lemon juice is squeezed over the fish, it is seasoned with a little salt and pepper and the surface sprinkled with blanched, coarsely chopped parsley. Finally it is coated with some butter cooked until it is brown in colour (*à la Noisette*) and served immediately so that the bubbling produced by the contact of the hot butter on the moist parsley is still discernible when the dish is presented to the guest.

1559 The Grilling of Fish

This method of cooking can be applied to most small fish, to small turbot and to cuts of fish.

Unless very small, whole fish for grilling should have some shallow cuts made in the thickest part so that the heat can more easily penetrate and facilitate the cooking.

For fish with white flesh or of a dry texture, it is advisable to coat it with flour and then brush it with melted butter or oil before placing it on the grill. This coating of flour under the application of the heat, creates a sort of crisp coating which prevents the fish from drying out and gives it a nice golden colour which it is impossible to obtain without being floured.

Salmon, trout, red mullet, mackerel and herring have flesh which is already oily and should not be coated with flour but simply brushed with butter or olive oil.

Because of the fragile nature of the flesh of some fish, the use of a special type of double grill in which the fish is placed, is recommended. This, in turn, is placed on the grill and permits the turning of the fish without the risk of damage.

Grilled fish are placed directly on to a hot dish, surrounded with fresh parsley and slices of grooved lemon. Parsley Butter, Anchovy Butter, Beurre à la Ravigote, Sauce Diable and Sauce Robert-Escoffier are suitable accompaniments.

1560 The Cooking of Fish *au Gratin*

This method is applied particularly to small whole fish such as sole, red mullet, whiting and young turbot, etc. The theory of cooking *au Gratin* can be found in the Chapter on Relevés and Entrées (2182).

1561 The Crimping of Fish

Although the crimping of fish is exclusively an English method of cooking, it is still thought important enough to warrant an explanation in this chapter as to its preparation. This method of preparation is applied above all, to salmon, cod, haddock and skate; the first three of these may be prepared whole or in sections but skate is always cut into more or less large pieces, after having been skinned on both sides.

In order to crimp a whole fish it should be taken live as it leaves the water, laid on a flat surface and then deep lateral gashes cut in both sides from the head to tail, 4–5 cm ($1\frac{3}{4}$ in to 2 in) apart; the fish should then be placed in very cold water to soak for 1 hour.

When it is to be prepared in sections it should be cut as soon as it has been caught and these should be soaked in very cold water as for the whole fish.

But does this method which makes the flesh firmer really influence the quality of the fish as much as the connoisseurs would lead us to believe? It would be rather rash to support this view and opinions are divided on the subject; however, what is certain is that fish prepared in this manner has many fervent supporters.

Whole or in sections, crimped fish are always cooked in boiling salted water and its cooking poses a real difficulty because the fish should be removed from the cooking liquid at the precise moment when it is just cooked. Overcooking results in a loss of the special characteristics obtained by the use of this method.

Crimped fish should be served in the same way as all boiled fish and the same sauces are applicable. It is customary to send at the same time a sauceboat of the cooking liquor.

1562 Forcemeat for Mousses and Mousselines of Fish

Ingredients:

1 kg ($2\frac{1}{4}$ lb) fish—salmon, trout, whiting, sole etc., free from skin and bone
4–5 egg whites
$1\frac{1}{4}$ litres ($2\frac{1}{5}$ pt or $5\frac{1}{2}$ U.S. cups) cream
10 g ($\frac{1}{3}$ oz) salt
Pinch of ground white pepper

Method:

Pound the fish with the seasoning, adding the egg whites a little at a time, then pass through a fine sieve. Place in a flat pan, mix it smooth with a spatula and place on ice and leave for 2 hours.

Carefully mix in the cream until it is completely incorporated.

Note: This preparation may include a panada but although it becomes cheaper to make, it loses some of its quality. If using panada, the proportions of ingredients should be as follows:

1 kg (2¼ lb) flesh of fish
450 g (1 lb) Frangipane Panada
4 egg whites
15 g (½ oz) salt
Pinch of ground white pepper
1½ litres (2⅝ pt or 6½ U.S. cups) double cream

1563 Mousses and Mousselines of Fish
Mousses are made in large buttered moulds of a suitable size for a given number of people and are cooked *au Bain-marie* in the oven allowing approximately 35–40 minutes for a mould of 1 litre (1¾ pt or 4½ U.S. cups) capacity; they may also be cooked in a steamer provided that the pressure is fairly low.

Mousselines are moulded with tablespoons in the shape of large oval Quenelles and are cooked in the same way as Quenelles but they may also be cooked in a very slow oven or *Etuve*, in which a pot of boiling water is placed; this will produce sufficient moisture to facilitate their proper cooking.

Note: The cooking of Mousselines requires great care; they should be moulded and placed in a buttered shallow pan, carefully covered with boiling salted water using 10 g (⅓ oz) per 1 litre (1¾ pt or 4½ U.S. cups) water. The pan should then be covered and the Mousselines cooked carefully for 12–15 minutes, making sure that the water is just barely simmering.

1564 Mousselines of Shellfish
The method and proportions for making Mousselines of shellfish are the same as for ordinary fish Mousses but using shellfish. Mousselines are best cooked in dariole moulds slightly shallower than the usual ones because of the looser texture of this mixture; the instructions given regarding care in the cooking of Mousselines must be adhered to.

The most appropriate sauce for serving with Mousselines of shellfish is Sauce à l'Américaine; it should be made from the shells of the fish used for making the Mousselines and according to the recipe for Homard à l'Américaine.

FRESH WATER FISH

THE MATELOTES

Matelotes which are a type of fish stew are placed at the beginning of this Chapter because of the large number of fresh water fish which may be prepared in this manner, and because the method of preparation is the same for all of them.

It is only the cooking time which differs according to the species and nature of the fish. Thus it is possible in consequence to prepare a Matelote comprised of different fish, by starting to cook the firmly fleshed ones first and then adding at a predetermined time, the more delicate fish. In this way all the fish will be cooked correctly at the same time.

1565 Basic Preparation for Matelotes
For 10 persons allow 1½ kg (3 lb 6 oz) of either a single fish or a mixture.
Whatever fish is used they should be first of all cleaned, washed and cut into pieces as necessary. Arrange them in a shallow pan with 2 sliced onions; a Bouquet garni; 4 cloves of garlic; 8 g (¼ oz) salt and 4 peppercorns.

Moisten with 1 litre (1¾ pt or 4½ U.S. cups) of red or white wine according to the type of Matelote, bring to the boil, add 1 dl (3½ fl oz or ½ U.S. cup) brandy, flame, cover and finish cooking.

When the fish is just cooked, transfer them to a clean pan and strain the cooking liquid into another pan to finish it in accordance with either of the two methods applicable—*Marinière* or *Meunière*.

The difference between these two is that the Matelote Marinière is moistened with white wine and has the ordinary Matelote garnish of mushrooms, glazed button onions, crayfish and heart-shape Croûtons of bread fried in butter and the sauce is prepared by first reducing the cooking liquid and adding it to a fish Velouté. On the other hand, the Matelote à la Meunière is moistened with red wine, garnished with crayfish and Croûtons only and the cooking liquid is invariably thickened with Beurre Manié, using 100 g (3½ oz) butter and 60 g (2 oz) flour per 1 litre (1¾ pt or 4½ U.S. cups) of cooking liquid.

In the following recipes only the appropriate cooking liquids and variations of the garnish are indicated, as the basic method and proportions have been established above.

1566 Matelote à la Canotière (*This Matelote should be made with carp and eel only*)
Moisten the fish with white wine, flame it with brandy, cover and cook. Reduce the cooking liquid by two-thirds, thicken with Beurre Manié and finish with 200 g (7 oz) butter per 1 litre (1¾ pt or 4½ U.S. cups) of sauce.
Garnish: Mushrooms; glazed button onions; small gudgeons, prepared *en Manchon* (1646); and crayfish cooked in Court-bouillon.

1567 Matelote à la Marinière
Moisten the fish with white wine and flame with brandy. Reduce the cooking liquid and thicken with Fish Velouté and butter.
Garnish: Mushrooms; glazed button onions; crayfish and heart-shaped Croûtons fried in butter.

1568 Matelote à la Meunière
Moisten the fish with red wine, flame with brandy and thicken with Beurre Manié.
Garnish: Crayfish and heart-shaped Croûtons fried in butter.

1569 Matelote, known as Meurette
This is a Burgundian version of the Matelote and can include any kind of fish in its preparation.

Moisten the fish with red wine, flame with Marc. Thicken the sauce with Beurre Manié as for Matelote à la Meunière. Surround the prepared dish with small square slices of bread, which have been buttered, dried in the oven then rubbed with garlic.

1570 Matelote à la Normande
This Matelote should contain sole, gurnet and sections of small conger eel.

Moisten with dry cider and flame with Calvados. Reduce the cooking liquid and thicken with fish Velouté. Finish the sauce with $1\frac{1}{2}$ dl (5 fl oz or $\frac{5}{8}$ U.S. cup) cream per 1 litre ($1\frac{3}{4}$ pt or $4\frac{1}{2}$ U.S. cups) of sauce.
Garnish: Mushrooms; poached mussels; poached and bearded oysters; crayfish; and small heart-shaped Croûtons fried in butter.

1571 Matelote, known as Pochouse
This is a variation of the Meurette and can also be prepared using any kind of fish.

Moisten the fish with red wine, flame with brandy, then thicken with Beurre Manié as for Matelote à la Meunière.
Garnish: Fried, diced, salt belly of pork; button mushrooms; glazed button onions; and small square slices of bread which have been buttered, dried in the oven, then rubbed with garlic.

1572 Waterzoï
In Belgium and Holland this preparation is the equivalent of the Bouillabaisse.

Ingredients:
2 kg ($4\frac{1}{2}$ lb) eel, pike, carp, tench or other fresh-water fish, live or as fresh as possible, well washed and cut into sections
1 litre ($1\frac{3}{4}$ pt or $4\frac{1}{2}$ U.S. cups) water
12 g ($\frac{1}{3}$ oz) salt
Pinch of pepper
1 Bouquet garni comprising 50 g (2 oz) parsley stalks and 15 g ($\frac{1}{2}$ oz) sage
150 g (5 oz) celery
100 g ($3\frac{1}{2}$ oz) butter

Method:
Cover the fish with the water, add the rest of the ingredients, bring to the boil and cook fairly rapidly so that the cooking liquid reduces and becomes sufficiently thickened at the same time that the fish is just cooked. If, however, the cooking liquid is not sufficiently thick, this can be rectified by the addition of a few crumbs made from rusks.

For service, remove the Bouquet garni and serve the Waterzoï as it is, accompanied with a dish of bread and butter.

ALOSE—SHAD

For 10 persons allow $1\frac{1}{3}$ kg (2 lb 13 oz)–$1\frac{1}{2}$ kg (3 lb 6 oz).

1573 Alose Farcie—Stuffed Shad
Empty and clean the fish and fill the inside with Fish Forcemeat A (300). Cut a number of shallow incisions on each side of the fish, season and wrap in oiled paper. Place it in a dish and bake in the oven for 35–40 minutes. Remove the paper and serve accompanied with Sauce Bercy.

1574 Alose Grillée—Grilled Shad
For serving whole fish: Cut shallow incisions on both sides of the fish, season and marinate with oil, lemon juice, parsley stalks and pieces of thyme and bayleaf, for 1 hour. Grill gently over a moderate heat, basting frequently with melted butter; cooking time 35–40 minutes.
For serving in slices: Cut the shad into thick slices on the bone, approximately $1\frac{1}{2}$ cm ($\frac{3}{5}$ in) thick; season and marinate as for whole fish allowing 20 minutes. Grill in the usual way for 10–15 minutes according to thickness.

In both cases, place the fish on a dish surrounded with a border of slices of lemon. Serve accompanied with Parsley Butter or Anchovy Butter or any sauce suitable for grilled fish.

The sauce should be served from a sauceboat for whole fish but poured over cut fish.

1575 Alose Grillée à l'Oseille—Grilled Shad with Sorrel
Whether whole or in sections, grill it as directed in the preceding recipe. Serve accompanied with 600 g (1 lb 5 oz) of sorrel stewed in butter then braised and presented in a deep dish; and 100 g ($3\frac{1}{2}$ oz) Melted Butter served in a sauceboat.

1576 Alose à la Provençale
Empty and clean the shad and stuff it with Fish Forcemeat A (300) which has been lightly flavoured with garlic. Place in a deep tray and braise it with 300 g (11 oz) roughly chopped flesh only of tomato; 1½ dl (5 fl oz or ⅝ U.S. cup) white wine; ¾ dl (3 fl oz or ⅜ U.S. cup) oil; and a little salt and pepper.

When cooked, arrange the fish on a suitable dish and cover with the tomatoes and the reduced braising liquor enriched and thickened with 2 tbs oil and 50 g (2 oz) Anchovy Butter. Sprinkle with coarsely chopped parsley.

ANGUILLE—EEL

For 10 persons allow 1 kg 200 g (2 lb 11 oz)—1 kg 400 g (3 lb 3 oz).

1577 Anguille à la Beaucaire
Skin and remove the bone from the eel; stuff it with a whiting and butter forcemeat having an addition per 500 g (1 lb 2 oz) of forcemeat of 125 g (4½ oz) chopped mushrooms, squeezed to remove excess moisture, lightly cooked in butter and cooled.

Sew up the eel and form in the shape of an oval; cook in a little hot butter to stiffen the flesh, then braise it in a terrine with 20 g (⅔ oz) chopped shallot, 2 dl (7 fl oz or ⅞ U.S. cup) Pouilly wine, ½ dl (2 fl oz or ¼ U.S. cup) brandy, 150 g (5 oz) butter, 100 g (3½ oz) raw button mushrooms and 20 button onions coloured in butter. When cooked, serve it from the terrine as it is.

1578 Anguille Benoîton
Skin and remove the fillets from the eel; cut them into thin slices approximately 10 cm (4 in) long and twist into spirals. Season, flour and when required, deep fry in hot fat; drain and arrange in a pile on a dish with fried parsley.

As an accompaniment, prepare the following sauce: place 3 dl (½ pt or 1¼ U.S. cups) red wine in a pan with 25 g (1 oz) chopped shallots, 10 g (⅓ oz) chopped parsley stalks and the chopped trimmings of the eel. Reduce by two-thirds, pass firmly through a fine strainer and thicken and enrich the liquid with 150 g (5 oz) butter. Serve this sauce separately in a sauceboat.

1579 Coulibiac d'Anguille (A)
Skin the eel, remove the fillets and cut into even-sized slices. Proceed in all respects as for Coulibiac de Saumon (1662).

1580 Coulibiac d'Anguille (B)
This is prepared from the same ingredients as Coulibiac (A) but the pastry and the shape are different.

Roll out 700 g (1½ lb) puff paste trimmings and cut a round approximately 25 cm (10 in) in diameter keeping the edge a little thinner than the centre. Place the filling on one side of the paste, moisten the edges and fold over into the shape of a turnover. Seal and crimp the edge, make an opening in the top, brush with eggwash and decorate by scoring with the point of a knife. Allow to rest for 30 minutes, then cook it in a moderate to hot oven for 30–35 minutes. When cooked, pour some melted butter through the hole in the top.

1581 Coulibiacs d'Anguille (*small*)
Roll out 500 g (1 lb 2 oz) ordinary Brioche paste or puff paste trimmings and cut into rounds with a 12 cm (5 in) fancy cutter. Place 2 small slices of eel in the centre of each, add a little of the items of garnish as used for Coulibiac de Saumon (1662), moisten the edges and close up in the shape of a Russian pâté by bringing up the two sides to the top centre and sealing together using a little pressure. If using Brioche paste, allow to prove—if puff paste, allow to rest for 30 minutes. Brush with eggwash and cook in a moderate to hot oven for 18–20 minutes.

1582 Anguille Frite—Fried Eel
Use very small eels; skin them and incise shallow cuts on both sides. Fold each into a figure 8 and keep in shape with skewers. Deep fry in the usual way and serve on a dish garnished with fried parsley.

Note: A dish of braised sorrel is sometimes served with fried eels, but this is, of course, entirely optional.

1583 Anguille Frite à l'Anglaise—Fried Eel, English method
Skin and bone out the eels; cut the fillets into thin slices and marinate with salt, pepper, chopped parsley, oil and lemon juice for 4 hours. Egg and breadcrumb and deep fry immediately. Serve accompanied with Sauce Bâtarde finished with Anchovy Butter.

1584 Anguille en Matelote
This may be prepared by either of the two methods indicated at the beginning of this Chapter.

1585 Anguille à la Menagère
Skin and cut medium-sized eels into 7–8 cm (2¾ in) sections; incise each section neatly with some shallow cuts on both sides. Season and grill them, arrange on a dish and surround with a border of gherkins.

Serve accompanied with softened Parsley Butter mixed with a small spoonful of made mustard per 100 g ($3\frac{1}{2}$ oz) butter.

1586 Anguille à la Meunière
Skin some small eels and cut into sections; season, pass through flour and shallow fry in butter finishing with Beurre à la Noisette as indicated in the method for cooking fish *à la Meunière* at the beginning of this chapter.

1587 Pâté Chaud d'Anguille—Hot Eel Pie
Remove the bone from the eel, cut the flesh into 5–6 cm (2 in) slices, and lard each one with truffle. Season and marinate with white wine, a little brandy and a little oil for 2 hours.

Dry the slices and shallow fry quickly in butter to colour, adding a little chopped shallot and chopped parsley.

Line a long pie mould with ordinary short paste and coat the bottom and sides with pike and truffle forcemeat having 50 g (2 oz) Anchovy Butter added per 500 g (1 lb 2 oz) forcemeat. Arrange the sliced eel in layers alternating with the forcemeat, adding the marinade and finishing with a layer of forcemeat. Finally, sprinkle with 2 tbs melted butter. Cover the top with a layer of paste and decorate with overlapping leaves of paste; eggwash, allow to rest for 30 minutes and bake in a moderate oven for approximately 2 hours. Serve accompanied with a Lenten Sauce Demi-glace.

Note: This pie may also be served cold.

1588 Pâté Chaud d'Anguille à l'Anglaise—Hot Eel Pie, English Style
Fillet the eels and cut into 8 cm (3 in) thick slices; blanch these slices in salted water, refresh them and drain well. Season with a little salt, pepper, grated nutmeg and chopped parsley then arrange them in layers in a deep pie-dish alternating with layers of seasoned, sliced hard-boiled eggs.

Moisten with 2 dl (7 fl oz or $\frac{7}{8}$ U.S. cup) white wine, add 25 g (1 oz) butter and cover with a layer of puff paste. Eggwash the surface and decorate by scoring with the point of a small knife. Make an opening in the centre to allow the steam to escape and cook in a moderate oven for $1\frac{1}{2}$ hours.

Just before serving, pour 2 dl (7 fl oz or $\frac{7}{8}$ U.S. cup) Sauce Demi-glace flavoured with fish essence through the hole.

Note: This pie may also be served cold.

1589 Anguille Pompadour
Skin and cut shallow incisions into both sides of a large eel; form it into the shape of a ring and cook in White Wine Court-bouillon. When cooked, allow to cool in the cooking liquor, then drain and dry carefully.

Coat it with Sauce Villeroy flavoured with Sauce Soubise and finally egg and breadcrumb, using very fine breadcrumbs. Deep fry when required, allowing sufficient time for the eel to become hot all through and to colour a golden brown on the outside.

Arrange on a serviette with fried parsley in the middle and surround with small round Croquettes of Pommes Dauphine; serve accompanied with tomato-flavoured Sauce Béarnaise.

Note: The eel may also be prepared cut into sections.

1590 Anguille à la Rouennaise
Skin and cut shallow incisions into both sides of an eel and form it into the shape of a ring; poach in red wine having the addition of a Mirepoix for flavouring. When cooked, place the eel on a tray and glaze in the oven using the cooking liquid to baste it.

Arrange on a round dish and in the centre place a garnish consisting of mushrooms, poached and bearded oysters and thick slices of poached soft roe. Coat this garnish with the reduced cooking liquid thickened with the addition of a little Sauce Espagnole. Serve surrounded with smelts, cooked *à la Meunière*, the heads having been removed.

1591 Anguille à la Romaine
Skin and cut some small eels into sections; season and cook lightly in butter to stiffen the flesh. Add 500 g (1 lb 2 oz) small fresh peas, 100 g ($3\frac{1}{2}$ oz) butter, 1 coarsely shredded lettuce and $\frac{1}{2}$ dl (2 fl oz or $\frac{1}{4}$ U.S. cup) white wine. Cover and allow to stew very gently until cooked; lightly thicken with a little Beurre Manié and serve in a deep dish as soon as it is ready.

1592 Anguille à la Tartare
Skin and poach the eel, either whole or cut into sections, in White Wine Court-bouillon. Drain, dry carefully and egg and breadcrumb. Deep fry when required and place on a dish garnished with fried parsley and surrounded with gherkins. Serve accompanied with Sauce Tartare.

1593 Tourte d'Anguille à la Saint-Martin
Roll out a $\frac{1}{2}$ cm ($\frac{1}{5}$ in) thick layer of short paste and cut out a circle 16 cm ($6\frac{1}{2}$ in) in diameter. Spread a layer of pike forcemeat mixed with chopped Fines Herbes on this leaving a clear edge all round. Cover the forcemeat with fairly thick slices of eel which have been seasoned and lightly cooked in butter just to stiffen, along with 100 g ($3\frac{1}{2}$ oz) chopped onion and 50 g (2 oz) chopped

shallot both previously cooked in butter; and thick slices of raw mushroom.

Cover with more of the same forcemeat, moisten the edge of the paste then place a second round of short paste or puff paste trimmings on top; in either case, the top should be a little thicker than the bottom. Seal by crimping the edges together, brush with eggwash and decorate by scoring with the point of a knife. Make an opening in the centre to allow the steam to escape and allow to rest for at least 30 minutes.

Cook in a moderate oven for approximately 35 minutes; when removing the *Tourte* from the oven, add a few spoonfuls of melted butter by means of the hole.

1594 Anguille au Vert

Clean and skin some small eels and cut in 5 cm (2 in) thick sections. Place 50 g (2 oz) butter in a pan and add 100 g (3½ oz) sorrel leaves—the stalks removed, 25 g (1 oz) freshly gathered tender nettle leaves, 10 g (⅓ oz) parsley, 5 g (⅙ oz) each of salad burnet, young green sage, savoury and chervil, and a good pinch of tarragon.

Cook gently until tender then add a very small pinch of fresh green thyme and the eel. Cook until the flesh of the eels stiffens then add 5 dl (18 fl oz or 2¼ U.S. cups) white wine, season with salt and a little pepper and cook gently for 10 minutes. Thicken the liquid with 4 egg yolks, finish with a little lemon juice and place in a china terrine.

This dish is usually served cold.

1595 Anguille au Vert à la Flamande

Prepare the eels as for Anguille au Vert and cook in 50 g (2 oz) butter to stiffen the flesh. Moisten with 5 dl (18 fl oz or 2¼ U.S. cups) beer, season with salt and pepper, cook gently for 10 minutes and at the last moment add the roughly chopped cooked herbs as in the preceding recipe. Allow to boil for a few minutes, thicken with a little arrowroot if the cooking liquid appears to be too thin, and place in a china terrine.

This dish also is usually served cold.

BARBEAU ET BARBILLON—BARBEL

The small barbel weighing between 400 g (15 oz) and 1 kg (2¼ lb) is referred to in French as the Barbillon and is very often one of the ingredients used in the preparation of Matelotes which require different species of fish.

1596 Barbeau à la Bourguignonne

Place the barbel in a buttered fish kettle with a Bouquet garni and some mushroom trimmings. Add sufficient red wine to come halfway up the fish and 25 g (1 oz) butter per 1 litre (1¾ pt or 4½ U.S. cups) wine; braise gently. When cooked, pass the cooking liquid through a strainer, reduce it, lightly thicken with Beurre Manié and mix in some more butter to enrich the sauce. Serve the fish with the sauce as an accompaniment.

1597 Barbel with Various Sauces

Cook the barbel in a Vinegar Court-bouillon. The sauces most frequently used to accompany barbel cooked in this way are Sauce Blanche aux Câpres and Sauce Hollandaise; always serve plain boiled potatoes as an accompaniment.

1598 Barbillon Grillé—Grilled Small Barbel

Incise the barbel with thin shallow cuts on each side, season, brush with oil and grill them gently. The usual accompaniment is either Shallot Butter, or Parsley Butter containing 25 g (1 oz) chopped and well blanched shallot per 100 g (3½ oz) of Parsley Butter.

1599 Barbillon à la Meunière

Choose only the smallest fish and cook them *à la Meunière* as indicated at the beginning of this Chapter.

1600 Barbillon Rôti—Roast Small Barbel

Choose medium-sized fish and neatly lard them with fillets of anchovy. Season, brush with oil and roast in the oven. Serve accompanied with Anchovy Butter.

1601 BREME—BREAM

Bream is a fairly ordinary fish which is occasionally used in the preparation of Matelotes to give added variety. Large bream are usually grilled and served with Shallot Sauce or Shallot Butter.

BROCHET—PIKE

In modern cooking the pike does not hold the same pride of place which it held formerly in the old classical kitchen. Nowadays it is mainly used in the preparation of forcemeats; however, certain of the classical preparations of pike are worthy of being preserved and because of this they are included here.

Whenever possible, fish of from 2 kg (4½ lb) to 4 kg (9 lb) in weight should be selected where the fish is to be presented whole. Larger fish should be used for making forcemeat and for cutting into portions.

1602 Brochet au Bleu
For this preparation choose for preference, a medium-sized pike and follow the recipe for *au Bleu* as indicated at the beginning of this Chapter under the Cooking Methods for Fish. Serve it accompanied with melted butter if served hot, or Sauce Ravigote à l'Huile if cold.

1603 Côtelettes de Brochet Soubise
Coat the bottom and sides of well buttered cutlet-shaped moulds with a fine pike forcemeat. Fill with a Salpicon of truffle and mushroom mixed with a little thick Sauce Allemande, cover with more of the same forcemeat and cook *au Bain-marie* in the oven.

When cooked, demould the cutlets, dry them carefully, dip into melted butter, allow the butter to set then egg and breadcrumb them. Shallow fry until golden brown in clarified butter, drain and arrange in a circle on a round dish, decorating each one with a cutlet frill.

Serve accompanied with Sauce Soubise.

1604 Filets de Brochet Régence
Cut the skinned fillets of pike into fairly thick, large oval-shaped slices; remove the bones carefully and inset the pieces of fish with slices of truffle. Place in a well buttered tray, moisten with a little white wine and fish stock and poach in the oven, basting from time to time. Glaze the fillets at the last moment.

Arrange in a circle on a round dish with a Régence garnish for fish (449) in the centre and surround with small trussed crayfish which have been cooked in a Court-bouillon.

1605 Grenadins de Brochet
Cut the skinned fillets of pike into fairly thick oval-shaped slices, smaller than in the previous recipe; remove the bones carefully and lard the pieces of fish with truffle. Place on a well buttered tray, moisten with a little white wine and fish stock and poach in the oven, basting from time to time. Glaze at the last moment.

Arrange in a circle on a round dish and serve with any suitable sauce and garnish.

1606 Grenadins de Brochet à l'Oseille
Cut the Grenadins as in the previous recipe and lard with strips of gherkin and blanched red carrot, alternating the two colours. Place in a pan containing a little hot clarified butter to set the flesh quickly. Add a little fish stock made from the trimmings of the pike and poach in the oven, basting from time to time. Glaze at the last moment.

Arrange the Grenadins in a circle on a round dish and pour a sauce in the centre, prepared from the reduced cooking liquid, thickened with a little fish Velouté and enriched with 150 g (5 oz) butter.

Serve accompanied with a dish of a purée of sorrel.

1607 Brochet à la Montebello
Carefully clean a nice medium-sized pike and stuff it with a good fish forcemeat. If the fish is to be presented on its side, remove the skin from the middle two-thirds of the fish on one side. If it is going to be presented standing up on its belly, remove the skin from both sides. Coat the skinned area with a fine fish and cream forcemeat (288) and cover this with well flattened fillets of sole trimmed to the correct size and inset with slices of truffle.

Braise the pike with white wine on a bed of vegetables and herbs keeping it covered so as to preserve the whiteness of the fillets.

When cooked, place the pike on an oval base made of rice or semolina and surround it with a garnish of semi-flattened Croquettes of prawns, Barquettes of soft roes, and cooked trussed crayfish.

Serve accompanied with a fish Velouté finished with Anchovy Butter, and containing some poached and bearded oysters.

1608 Pain de Brochet à l'Ancienne
Fill a well buttered, plain round deep mould with pike forcemeat, and poach in the oven *au Bain-marie*. Demould onto a round dish and decorate the surface with very white cooked mushrooms and sliced truffle. Serve accompanied with Sauce Bâtarde.

1609 Brochet au Persil—Pike with Parsley
Cut the pike into thick slices on the bone, poach in salted water and arrange them on a serviette.

Serve accompanied with quarters of lemon and some Beurre Noisette to which is added when almost ready, 100 g ($3\frac{1}{2}$ oz) small sprigs of parsley per 250 g (9 oz) butter.

1610 Brochet, Sauce Persil—Pike with Parsley Sauce
Whether whole or cut into sections, cook the fish in Court-bouillon strongly flavoured with parsley. Place on a serviette and serve accompanied with Parsley Sauce and a dish of plain boiled potatoes.

1611 Quenelles de Brochet à la Lyonnaise
Take the required amount of Godiveau Lyonnaise (291) and mould it into Quenelles with tablespoons, placing them in a buttered shallow pan.

Poach them in the usual way, drain well, then place the Quenelles to simmer very gently for 10 minutes in the selected fish sauce so as to allow them to swell in size, which is the characteristic of this type of Quenelle.

If the Quenelles are to be served with a thick sauce to which they cannot be added except at the last minute because of the nature of the sauce, they should be placed in a closed container with sufficient excellent fish stock to simmer gently so that they swell up as required.

1612 Quenelles de Brochet Morland

Take the required amount of fairly firm pike and butter forcemeat (286) and divide into approximately 70 g ($2\frac{1}{2}$ oz) pieces. Mould them into the shape of flattish oval Quenelles enclosing in each a slice of poached soft carp roe which has been dipped in melted butter and rolled in chopped truffle.

Dip the Quenelles into beaten egg, roll in chopped truffle and remould to the correct shape; shallow fry gently in clarified butter.

Arrange them in a circle on a round dish and place a light, cooked purée of mushrooms in the centre.

1613 Pike with Various Sauces

For serving with a sauce, pike should always be poached in Court-bouillon, placed on a serviette and served accompanied with plain boiled potatoes.

Suitable sauces as accompaniments are: aux Câpres, Genevoise, Hollandaise, aux Huîtres, Ravigote, Vénitienne.

BROCHETON—SMALL PIKE

1614 Brocheton à la Martinière

Incise a small pike on both sides with shallow cuts and marinate it for 1 hour before being required with white wine, a little oil, aromatic herbs and seasonings.

Dry well and grill, basting with oil from time to time. Serve accompanied with Sauce Mayonnaise containing some finely chopped, skinned walnuts.

1615 Brocheton en Matelote à la Rémoise

Cut a small pike or 2 smaller ones depending on size, into sections and poach them in a Champagne Court-bouillon, strongly flavoured with herbs and vegetables. Strain the Court-bouillon and reduce it to prepare a sauce in accordance with the method for Matelote à la Marinière (1567).

Place the pike on a dish, coat with the sauce and garnish it with poached soft roes; mushrooms; sliced truffle and heart-shaped Croûtons of bread fried in clarified butter.

1616 Brocheton à la Normande

Stuff a small pike with Fish Forcemeat A (300). Wrap it in thin slices of salt pork fat and braise with white wine on a bed of herbs and vegetables.

When cooked, remove the skin and place the pike on a long dish; surround with Normande garnish (432) and coat with Sauce Normande containing the cooking liquid from the fish which has been strained and reduced.

1617 Brocheton à la Tartare

Prepare a small pike exactly as in the preceding recipe but serve accompanied with Sauce Tartare.

1618 Brocheton à la Valvins

Remove the skin from one side of a small pike and lard this bare area with anchovy fillets. Wrap completely in oiled paper and roast in the oven; serve accompanied with a well flavoured Sauce Ravigote, or Beurre à la Maître d'Hôtel flavoured with mustard.

CARPE—CARP

For 10 persons allow one fish of $1\frac{1}{2}$ kg (3 lb 6 oz) or several making the same weight.

1619 Carpe à l'Ancienne

This is a preparation of the old classical kitchen which borders on the realms of fantasy as far as the preparation of food is concerned. Although little used today, it has some claim to originality and the following is a resumé of the recipe.

Remove the head and tail from the carp and with the flesh prepare a forcemeat using butter and keeping the mixture rather firm. On to a suitable base or dish, mould this forcemeat into the shape of the body of the carp enclosing in it a Régence garnish for fish (449) mixed with some thick Sauce Espagnole made with fish *Fumet*. Place the head and tail in their correct positions taking care that they are joined to the forcemeat, then decorate it all over with crescents of truffle cut into graduated sizes so as to represent the scales of the fish.

Sprinkle with melted butter, cover with thin slices of salt pork fat and then with sheets of paper; cook carefully in a fairly slow oven and when ready, remove the paper and fat; serve accompanied with Sauce Genevoise.

1620 Carpe à la Bière—Carp with Beer

Cook 150 g (5 oz) sliced onions in butter without colour and place in the bottom of a fish kettle, place the carp either whole or in fillets on top and add 50 g (2 oz) sliced celery, 25 g (1 oz) diced gingerbread (Pain d'Epice), a Bouquet garni and sufficient light beer to barely cover the fish. Cover with the lid and braise gently in the oven.

Serve the fish with a garnish of the poached soft roes from the carp and coat with a sauce made from the cooking liquid, which has been reduced by a good third, passed through a fine strainer and thickened and enriched with a little butter.

1621 Carpe au Bleu
Prepare the carp *au Bleu* as indicated for the cooking of fish at the beginning of this Chapter. If it is to be served hot, send with a sauceboat of Melted Butter; if to be served cold, with a sauceboat of Sauce Ravigote à l'Huile.

1622 Carpe à la Canotière
Stuff some small carp of 400–500 g (15 oz–1 lb 2 oz) in weight with a Fish Forcemeat B (301). Incise the sides with shallow cuts then place in a dish which has been buttered and sprinkled with chopped shallots; season and surround the fish with turned raw button mushrooms.

Cook according to the method *à la Bercy* (1933) and a few minutes before it is cooked, sprinkle the fish with very fine breadcrumbs and melted butter so that the final cooking will form a light gratin.

Serve the carp on a dish surrounded with untrussed crayfish cooked in Court-bouillon and small gudgeons prepared *en Manchon* (1646). Surround the edge of the dish with a border of lightly baked shapes of puff pastry.

1623 Carpe Chambord
Select a mirror carp of approximately 2 kg (4½ lb) in weight and stuff it with a fine fish forcemeat containing 250 g (9 oz) soft roes passed through a fine sieve and 125 g (4½ oz) chopped mushrooms per 1 kg (2¼ lb) forcemeat. Sew it up, remove the skin from the middle of the fish on both sides and lard or stud the bared areas with truffle; or coat with a little of the same forcemeat, simulating the scales with crescents of truffle.

Place the carp on the grill of a fish kettle and braise it with vegetables and herbs and just sufficient red wine and fish stock to come two-thirds of the way up the fish in the proportion of two parts of wine to one of stock. At the last moment remove the lid and glaze the fish by frequent basting with the cooking liquid.

Place the fish on a prepared rice base so as to raise it for presentation and surround with Chambord garnish (363). Decorate the carp with decorative skewers on which are impaled some of the same items as in the garnish; serve accompanied with Sauce Genevoise prepared from the reduced cooking liquid.

1624 Carpe à la Juive (*Israeli Method*)
Cut a medium-sized carp into sections on the bone 1 cm (⅓ in) thick; place them in a fish kettle with 150 g (5 oz) onion and 50 g (2 oz) shallots both finely chopped and cooked in 2 dl (7 fl oz or ⅞ U.S. cup) oil, keeping them white. Cover with the lid, place on the stove and start it cooking in its own juices for a few minutes. Sprinkle with 70 g (2½ oz) flour, cook for a few more minutes without colour then moisten with 1 litre (1¾ pt or 4½ U.S. cups) white wine and the same quantity of fish stock or water.

Season with salt, add a very small pinch of Cayenne pepper, 20 g (⅔ oz) crushed garlic, a Bouquet garni and 2 dl (7 fl oz or ⅞ U.S. cup) oil. Bring to the boil, cover and allow to cook very gently for 25 minutes.

Remove the pieces of fish and place them on a long dish in such a way as to reform the fish; reduce the cooking liquid by two-thirds and shake in, away from the heat, 3 dl (½ pt or 1¼ U.S. cups) oil so as to thicken it to a sauce. Pour this over the carp and allow it to become cold and set. Sprinkle with coarsely chopped parsley before serving.

1625 Carpe à la Juive au Persil
Prepare the fish in the same way as for Carpe à la Juive but adding 100 g (3½ oz) very fresh picked parsley to the cooking liquid; also sprinkle with plenty of coarsely chopped parsley when serving.

1626 Carpe à la Juive à l'Orientale
Prepare in the same way as for Carpe à la Juive adding to the reduced and finished sauce, a pinch of saffron and 60 g (2 oz) chopped, skinned almonds before pouring it over the fish.

1627 Carpe à la Juive aux Raisins
Prepare the fish in the same way as Carpe à la Juive adding to the reduced and finished sauce, 30 g (1 oz) caster sugar; ½ dl (2 fl oz or ¼ U.S. cup) vinegar; and 80 g (2½ oz) depipped raisins and 50 g (2 oz) each of currants and sultanas all previously allowed to swell in lukewarm water.

1628 Carpe à la Polonaise
Stuff the carp with a Fish Forcemeat A (300), braise it gently in a fish kettle with 50 g (2 oz) chopped onion; 25 g (1 oz) chopped shallot; a Bouquet garni; 1½ litres (2⅝ pt or 6½ U.S. cups) red wine; 5 dl (18 fl oz or 2¼ U.S. cups) fish stock and 100 g (3½ oz) gingerbread (Pain d'Epice) cut into large dice.

Serve accompanied with a sauce prepared in the following manner: Cook 1 dl (3½ fl oz or ½ U.S. cup) vinegar and 50 g (2 oz) sugar until a light blond caramel. Pass the cooking liquid, vegetables and gingerbread through a fine sieve, add this to the caramel and reduce it to 3 dl ($\frac{1}{2}$ pt or $1\frac{1}{4}$ U.S. cups). Thicken and enrich this sauce with 100 g ($3\frac{1}{2}$ oz) butter, add a touch of Cayenne pepper and finish with 50 g (2 oz) lightly grilled, shredded almonds.

1629 Quenelles de Carpe Morland
Prepare in the same way as for Quenelles de Brochet Morland, using a Mousseline forcemeat of carp instead of a forcemeat of pike.

1630 Filets de Carpe à la Royale
Remove the fillets from a medium-sized carp and skin them; cut the fillets into long slices, place them on a buttered tray and poach carefully under cover with a few aromatic herbs and seasoning, and moistened with a mixture of two-thirds Chablis wine to one-third fish stock.

Arrange the cooked fillets on a dish in a circle placing a nice slice of truffle on each one. In the centre place a garnish of thick slices of soft carp roe poached in White Wine Court-bouillon; small turned mushrooms and small turned truffles the size of olives. Serve accompanied with Sauce Normande containing the strained, reduced cooking liquid from the fish.

LAITANCES DE CARPE—SOFT CARP ROES

1631 Soft Carp Roes
Soft roes of carp are usually poached in Court-bouillon, but they are better if cooked fairly dry in a covered, buttered shallow pan with the simple addition of a few drops of lemon juice and a little mushroom cooking liquor.

1632 Barquettes de Laitances—Barquettes of Soft Carp Roes
See Page 135—using soft roes of carp.

1633 Beignets de Laitances—Soft Carp Roe Fritters
See Page 135—using soft roes of carp.

1634 Bordure de Laitances Mornay
Cut some poached soft carp roes into fairly thick slices and place them inside a small border of Duchesse potato, piped on a round dish and coloured in the oven. Cover with Sauce Mornay and glaze in a very hot oven or under the salamander.

1635 Bouchées de Laitances Monseigneur
See Recipe No. 1117 in the Chapter on Hot Hors-d'oeuvre but use soft carp roes.

1636 Caisses de Laitances Nantua
Poach the soft carp roes in salted water, cut into thick slices and place in small white fluted porcelain cases with 2 crayfish tails on top of each. Fill them with Sauce Nantua and finish with a nice slice of truffle on top.

1637 Crème de Laitances
Cook the soft carp roes gently in butter and pass through a fine sieve; mix the purée obtained with an equal amount of uncooked ordinary cream Royale; poach the mixture in small porcelain cases.

With the addition of extra egg yolks this mixture may be cooked in dariole moulds, turned out and coated with a fine light Sauce Béchamel finished with Crayfish Butter.

1638 Coquille de Laitances à la Parisienne
Place a little Sauce Vin Blanc with the addition of some chopped truffle in the bottom of scollop shells. Arrange thick slices of poached soft carp roes on top of the sauce, alternating with large slices of cooked mushrooms. Cover with more of the same sauce and glaze in a very hot oven or under the salamander.

1639 Laitances Maréchal
Poach, drain and dry the soft carp roes. Dip in melted butter than flour, egg and breadcrumb; fry gently in clarified butter until golden brown.

Arrange on a serviette and serve accompanied with Sauce Périgueux.

1640 Laitances à la Meunière
Season and flour the raw soft carp roes and proceed in the usual way as for *à la Meunière*.

1641 Soufflés de Laitances
For 10 small soufflé moulds:

Poach 250 g (9 oz) soft carp roes and pass them through a fine sieve; add $1\frac{1}{2}$ dl (5 fl oz or $\frac{5}{8}$ U.S. cup) reduced sauce Béchamel and 3 egg yolks to the purée, then season and fold in 4 stiffly beaten egg whites.

Place the mixture in buttered individual soufflé moulds and cook for approximately 12 minutes in a moderate oven. A little chopped truffle may be added to the mixture.

ESTURGEON—STURGEON

The flesh of this fish is quite firm but it has no pronounced flavour; it is therefore more suitable for braising or preparing *en Fricandeau* or as Grenadins, etc.

1642 Fricandeau d'Esturgeon
This is prepared in the same way as Fricandeau of Veal (2603) and may be accompanied by any of the garnishes suitable for that dish. It may also be served garnished with black or stuffed green olives.

1643 Esturgeon à la Normande
This is prepared with the smaller size sturgeons as caught around the coast from January to March.

Scale and empty the fish and from the opening in the belly, cut through the vertebrae in several places so as to prevent deformation during the cooking.

Braise it with vegetables, herbs and white wine; when cooked, remove the skin, place the sturgeon on a tray and glaze the fish by frequent basting with the cooking liquid which has been strained.

Arrange the sturgeon on a dish, surround with a Normande garnish and serve accompanied with Sauce Normande.

1644 Esturgeon en Tortue
This is prepared *en Fricandeau* (2603). Lard the fish first with fillets of anchovy then braise in the usual manner with herbs and vegetable flavourings. Serve accompanied with a Tortue garnish and Sauce Tortue.

1645 FERA

This fish is found in Alpine lakes principally Lake Geneva; it is similar to the Shad and is best when filleted and prepared *à l'Anglaise, au Gratin, à l'Hôtelière, à la Meunière*, etc.

1646 GOUJON—GUDGEON

Gudgeon are usually deep fried. They may also be prepared *à la Meunière* but it is essential in this case that they are well coloured and cooked very crisp.

They are also used as a garnish, prepared *en Manchon*.

Note: The term *en Manchon* is frequently used and the preparation is as follows: When the gudgeons have been egg and breadcrumbed, the heads and tails are cut off in such a way that after having been deep fried the fish appear to have been placed in the centre of a sleeve or muff made from the crisp coating of the egg and breadcrumbs.

LAMPROIE—LAMPREY

The flesh of the lamprey is more delicate and oily than that of eel and all the preparations given for eel are suitable for lampreys. They should first be scalded in boiling water to remove the slimy coating then well soaked in cold water before using. As a matter of interest the following original recipe is given.

1647 Lamproie à la Solognote
Pound 100 g ($3\frac{1}{2}$ oz) pineseed kernels until fine and add $\frac{1}{2}$ dl (2 fl oz or $\frac{1}{4}$ U.S. cup) vinegar a little at a time.

Remove the skin from the lampreys then cut them into 15 cm (6 in) lengths. Season with salt and pepper and marinate for 6 hours with the pineseed kernels and vinegar, plus 2 bayleaves and some wild thyme; turn them over frequently.

Cook 500 g (1 lb 2 oz) small button mushrooms in butter, add the lamprey and cook for a few minutes to set the flesh then add the marinade and allow to cool.

Enclose the lamprey mixture in a pastry envelope made of flour mixed with lukewarm water then wrap the whole in greaseproof paper. Place in the fireplace or on the hearthstone, cover with hot cinders and cook for $1\frac{1}{2}$ hours renewing the cinders frequently.

To serve: brush the Pâté as clean as possible and break open the crust at the last moment.

Note: This recipe is a truly local method of cooking lamprey and it may, of course, be baked in the oven.

1648 LAVARET

This fish is caught in the lakes of French Savoy and Switzerland and may be prepared in the same ways as Féra.

1649 LOTTE—BURBOT

This fish is not considered to be of much value except for the reputation of the quality of its liver; this is prepared in the same way as soft roes bearing in mind that it takes a little longer to cook.

1650 OMBLE-CHEVALIER, AND OMBLE COMMUN—CHAR AND GRAYLING

These fish are members of the salmon family and for culinary purposes are usually treated as river trout. Both species are rarely obtainable in the markets.

The char is caught in certain localized lake dwelling areas in countries such as Scotland and Switzerland and then only for a short season of about two months. It is a variety of this fish which the lakeside dwellers on the shores of Lake Zug in Switzerland call Rothel or Ruthel about which more information is given later on.

The flesh of both fish is extremely delicate rivalling that of the finest river trout, thus it can be prepared in any of the ways applicable to it.

In England the char is used in the preparation of potted char as in the following recipe.

1651 Potted Char

Poach the fish with a Mirepoix and white wine and allow to cool completely in the cooking liquid. Drain well, discard the skin and remove the fillets, carefully eliminating all the bones.

Arrange the fillets carefully in the special deep glazed earthenware container and cover completely with clarified butter, place in a warm oven for 15 minutes, allow to cool until the following day then add more clarified butter so as to cover the fish to a depth of approximately 8 mm ($\frac{1}{3}$ in).

Keep in a very cool place.

1652 PERCHE—PERCH

Small perch are usually deep fried; the medium-sized ones are prepared *à la Meunière* and may also be used as one of the fish in a mixed Matelote; the very large ones are usually stuffed and cooked as for stuffed Shad.

1653 ROTHEL OR RUTHEL

This fish which is a variety of the Char, is similar in shape to a large smelt. The delicacy of the flesh surpasses that of all fish, even that of the mountain river trout. They are found in Lake Zug in Switzerland where they inhabit the deepest waters and are fished only during November and December when they rise to the surface. They may be prepared in any of the ways applicable to river trout.

1654 SAUMON—SALMON

For 10 persons allow 1 kg ($2\frac{1}{4}$ lb).

Whole salmon and Darnes of salmon are usually cooked in a Vinegar Court-bouillon started from cold, covered with a serviette or piece of clean cloth, brought gently to the boil, then finished cooking without boiling, on the side of the stove. This general method for cooking whole fish and large cuts of salmon has a few exceptions which are given in the Methods of Cooking Fish at the beginning of this Chapter.

It is usual to serve salmon cooked in Court-bouillon with two sauces: those which are most suitable are Sauces Anchois, Câpres, Crevette, Genevoise, Hollandaise, Homard, aux Huîtres, Mousseline, Nantua, Noisette, Ravigote and Vénitienne; these Sauces are also suitable for serving with crimped salmon.

In England salmon is always served accompanied with plain or salted sliced cucumber. When served cold, cucumber is used as an item of decoration.

Note: Correctly speaking, a Darne is a section cut from the middle of the fish on the bone, which may vary in size according to the number of people it is to be served to.

1655 Cadgery de Saumon—Kedgeree of Salmon

Prepare 600 g (1 lb 5 oz) cooked salmon, remove all of the skin and bone then break the flesh carefully into flakes; at the same time prepare 600 g (1 lb 5 oz) well cooked Riz Pilaw and mix it with 6 dl (1 pt or $2\frac{5}{8}$ U.S. cups) curry-flavoured Sauce Béchamel and 6 hard-boiled eggs cut in dice.

The fish and the rice mixture should be arranged hot in alternate layers in a deep dish and covered with a little of the same curry-flavoured Sauce Béchamel.

Note: Kedgeree may also be prepared in dry form without using the Sauce Béchamel; in this case the rice itself should be flavoured with curry.

1656 Coquilles de Saumon

These may be prepared using either Sauce Mornay or Sauce Vin Blanc.

Place a little sauce in the bottom of scollop shells, arrange some flaked cooked salmon on top, cover with more of the sauce and glaze in a very hot oven or under the salamander.

The name of the dish should be used to qualify the menu term, e.g. Coquille de Saumon Mornay.

1657 Côtelettes de Saumon—Salmon Cutlets

These may be prepared in either of the following ways:

A) *Ingredients:*

500 g (1 lb 2 oz) cooked salmon, free from skin and bone
300 g (11 oz) cooked mushrooms
150 g (5 oz) cooked prawns

50 g (2 oz) truffle
$6\frac{1}{2}$ dl ($1\frac{1}{5}$ pt or 3 U.S. cups) thick Sauce Béchamel
3 egg yolks

Method:
Cut the salmon, mushrooms, prawns and truffle into small dice, place in a shallow pan with the Béchamel and reheat to boiling point. Season, add the egg yolks and cook and mix to thicken the mixture.

Spread the mixture on a buttered tray, butter the surface and allow to get cold. Divide 'the mixture into 75 g ($2\frac{1}{2}$ oz) pieces and mould cutlet shape; egg and breadcrumb and deep fry when required. Serve arranged on a serviette garnished with fried parsley and accompanied with a suitable sauce.

B) Prepare the cutlets in the same way as Côtelettes de Brochet Soubise but using Mousseline forcemeat of salmon instead of the pike forcemeat.

1658 Côtelettes de Saumon d'Artois
Cut a fillet of salmon into fairly thin slices each weighing 100–110 g ($3\frac{1}{2}$–4 oz). Trim these slices to the shape of a cutlet, spread one side neatly with a layer of fairly stiff whiting forcemeat, brush the surface with egg white and decorate with shapes of truffle.

Heat some clarified butter in a shallow pan until very hot, place in the cutlets carefully, cook for a few minutes then place in the oven to complete the cooking of the forcemeat. Arrange carefully on a suitable dish and serve accompanied with Sauce aux Huîtres.

1659 Côtelettes de Saumon Clarence
Line some buttered cutlet moulds with thin slices of raw salmon which have been flattened with a cutlet bat and trimmed. With the trimmings of salmon and the flesh of a small lobster prepare a Mousseline forcemeat and fill the lined moulds with it. Use the rest of the forcemeat to mould a thin base on the serving dish using the required size of flan ring to keep it in shape; cook it in a moderate oven.

Near the time of serving poach the cutlets carefully in the oven *au Bain-marie*, demould on to a serviette to dry and arrange in a circle on the prepared base of forcemeat. Place a large cooked mushroom in the centre and a small one on each cutlet and between each cutlet stick a large cooked prawn with the shell removed from the tail.

Serve accompanied with Sauce Newburg prepared from the lobster shells.

1660 Côtelettes de Saumon à l'Italienne
Prepare the slices of salmon coated with forcemeat as for Côtelettes de Saumon d'Artois and coat again with a thick purée of mushrooms bound with a little Sauce Béchamel. Egg and breadcrumb twice using breadcrumbs containing one-third its volume of grated cheese. Deep fry when required in very hot fat and serve accompanied with Sauce Anchois.

1661 Côtelettes de Saumon Pojarski
Trim 500 g (1 lb 2 oz) salmon taken from the tail, roughly chop it with a knife and add 125 g ($4\frac{1}{2}$ oz) fresh butter and 125 g ($4\frac{1}{2}$ oz) breadcrumbs soaked in milk and squeezed out. Chop well together until fine, smooth and well mixed, then season with salt, pepper and nutmeg.

Divide the mixture into 10 even-sized pieces and mould cutlet shape on a floured table. Cook at the last moment in clarified butter colouring them on both sides. Arrange overlapping on a dish placing a cutlet frill on the end of each on a small piece of macaroni representing the bone.

The following garnishes and sauces are suitable for this dish:

Garnishes: prawns; oysters; mussels; mushrooms; cucumbers stewed in butter; fresh peas, etc.
Sauces: all fish sauces particularly Sauce Vin Blanc, à la Newburg, and à l'Américaine.

1662 Coulibiac de Saumon
This may be prepared in either of the following ways:

A) *Ingredients:*
1 kg ($2\frac{1}{4}$ lb) approximately of fairly firm ordinary Brioche Paste without sugar
650 g (1 lb 7 oz) salmon cut in small thick slices, cooked in butter to set and allowed to cool
75 g ($2\frac{1}{2}$ oz) mushrooms } both chopped and cooked in butter, allowed to cool and mixed with 1 tbs chopped parsley
75g ($2\frac{1}{2}$ oz) onion }
200 g (7 oz) Kache of Semolina (319), or the same amount of rice cooked in Bouillon
2 chopped hard-boiled eggs
500 g (1 lb 2 oz) cooked and roughly chopped Vésiga (90 g dried Vésiga will produce this amount when cooked—see end Note)

Method:
Roll out the paste to an oblong approximately 32–35 cm (13–14 in) long by 18–20 cm (7–8 in) wide; place the ingredients in layers one on top of the other along the centre, alternating the layers

and starting and finishing with the Kache or rice. Lightly moisten the edges of the paste and pull over from the sides and ends so as to enclose the filling. Seal and turn over on to a baking tray so that the sealed edges are underneath.

Allow the pastry to prove for 25 minutes in a warm place; completely coat the surface of the Coulibiac with melted butter using a brush and sprinkle with very fine breadcrumbs; make one or two openings in the centre to allow steam to escape whilst cooking.

Bake in a moderately hot oven preferably in the older type of back oven, for approximately 45 minutes. On removing it from the oven, pour a few tablespoons of melted fresh butter through the holes in the top.

Notes and Information on Vésiga:
Vésiga is the spinal cord of the sturgeon and is used only in the preparation of certain Russian dishes. It is obtainable commercially in the shape of a dried gelatinous ribbon, white and semi-transparent.

Experience in the handling of Vésiga gives the following relative results concerning its weight after soaking, cooking, etc.

1) Before cooking, Vésiga must be soaked in cold water; this will cause it to swell by absorption of water which makes it easier to cook; the average time for soaking is 5 hours.
2) At this time it becomes approximately a little more than five times the dry volume, if soaked longer it will still swell further, but for all purposes five hours soaking is sufficient.
3) The weight of 10 g (⅓ oz) of Vésiga after 5 hours soaking will be approximately 52–55 g (2 oz).
4) When soaked, the Vésiga should be cooked in a liquid—either White Bouillon or water and should be simmered very gently under cover; 50 g (2 oz) dried Vésiga after soaking will need 3½ litres (6 pt or 7¾ U.S. pt) of liquid for its cooking and will give a yield of 260–270 g (9 oz).
5) The cooking time for Vésiga depends to some extent on its thickness, the small to medium ones will take approximately 3½ hours, the larger ones up to 4½ hours.

B) Use the same ingredients as before but replace the Brioche paste with puff paste trimmings.

Roll out the paste into a circle 28–30 cm (11–12 in) in diameter. Place the ingredients to one side of the circle in the same alternate layers as before, leaving a 2½ cm (1 in) border around the edge, lightly moisten this and fold the other half over so as to enclose the contents. Seal the edges together by decorating it with the back of a knife. Place the Coulibiac on a baking tray. (The circle of paste may be placed on the baking tray first and then garnished.)

Eggwash, decorate by scoring with the point of a knife and make an opening in the centre for steam to escape whilst cooking.

Cook in a moderately hot oven for approximately 40 minutes. On removing from the oven pour a few spoonfuls of melted fresh butter through the hole in the top.

1663 Coulibiacs de Saumon (*small*)
Using either firm ordinary Brioche paste or puff paste trimmings, cut out round pieces with a 12 cm (8 in) fancy cutter. Garnish each one with a small round slice of salmon and the rest of the ingredients as for Coulibiac. Moisten the edges, fold over to the top and seal together down the centre in the shape of a Russian pastry.

If the Coulibiacs are being made with Brioche paste, allow them to prove in a warm place for 15 minutes then brush with butter and sprinkle with breadcrumbs; if made with puff paste simply eggwash. In both cases cook in a moderate oven for approximately 18 minutes.

1664 Darne de Saumon Chambord
Place the Darne on a bed of vegetables and herbs and moisten two-thirds of the way up with a mixture of two parts of red wine and one part of fish stock; cover and braise gently.

At the last moment remove the lid and glaze the fish by frequent basting with the cooking liquid.

Place the salmon on a dish, surround with a Chambord garnish and serve accompanied with Sauce Genevoise made from the reduced cooking liquid.

1665 Darne de Saumon à la Danoise
Poach the Darne in salted water and serve accompanied with plain boiled potatoes and Sauce Bâtarde finished with Anchovy Butter.

1666 Darne de Saumon Daumont
Poach the Darne in a White Wine Court-bouillon which has been prepared in advance. Place on a dish, surround with a Daumont garnish and serve Sauce Nantua separately.

1667 Darne de Saumon à la Dieppoise
Poach the Darne in White Wine Court-bouillon which has been prepared in advance. Place on a dish, coat with a garnish and sauce à la Dieppoise and serve plain boiled potatoes separately.

1668 Darne de Saumon à l'Ecossaise
Poach the Darne in White Wine Court-bouillon and serve accompanied with Sauce Hollandaise containing a fine *Brunoise* of vegetables stewed in butter and a little White Bouillon.

1669 Darne de Saumon Lucullus
Remove the skin from one side of the Darne, lard with truffles then braise with Champagne on a bed of vegetables and herbs.

Place on a dish and surround with a garnish of small Bouchées filled with crayfish tails; small Cassolettes of soft roes; and small Mousselines of oysters cooked in dariole moulds.

Serve accompanied with the cooking liquid, reduced and enriched and thickened with an equal quantity each of butter and Crayfish Butter.

1670 Darne de Saumon Nesselrode
Remove the bones from the Darne and stuff with a Mousseline forcemeat made of lobster and sufficient pike forcemeat to give the required firm texture.

Line a well buttered plain round pie mould with a thin layer of Hot Water paste (3775) which has been prepared well in advance and kept stiff. Cover the paste with thin slices of salt pork fat then place in the prepared Darne, standing upright. Cover with a round of the same paste, make a small opening in the top and cook in a very hot oven.

When cooked, remove from the oven, turn it upside down so that the fat and liquid can drain out but do not demould it yet. Slide it on to a dish and then remove from the mould. The cooked pastry should not be broken open until it is in front of the guest.

Serve with Sauce à l'Américaine prepared from the shells and remains of the lobster and finished with cream and the addition of small poached and bearded oysters.

1671 Darne de Saumon Régence
Braise the Darne with white wine on a bed of vegetables and herbs. Place on a dish and surround with fish Régence garnish; serve accompanied with Sauce Normande finished with truffle essence.

1672 Darne de Saumon à la Royale
Braise the Darne with Sauternes wine on a bed of vegetables and herbs. Place on a dish and surround with a bouquet of crayfish tails, small Quenelles of Mousseline forcemeat, small mushrooms, truffles cut in the shape of small olives and balls of potato cut with a large-sized vegetable scoop and plain boiled. Serve accompanied with Sauce Normande.

1673 Darne de Saumon Valois
Poach the Darne in White Wine Court-bouillon which has been prepared in advance. Place on a dish and surround with plain boiled olive-shaped pieces of potatoes; thick slices of poached soft roe; and trussed crayfish cooked in Court-bouillon.

Serve accompanied with Sauce Valois.

1674 Escalopes de Saumon—Escalopes of Salmon
This is a very practical preparation for *Table d'Hôte* service.

Remove the fillets from a medium-sized salmon, cut them in half along the length and remove the skin. Cut the fillets across on the slant into thickish slices weighing from 80–100 g (3–3½ oz); trim oval shape, place them in a buttered shallow pan, season and poach with fish stock and either white or red wine according to the way in which the dish will be finished.

These cuts of salmon can be served with the same garnish and sauces as for fillets of sole and brill; they can also be cooked and coloured on both sides in clarified butter and served with the same garnishes and sauces as for Côtelettes de Saumon Pojarski (1661). To sum up, the number of ways in which these cuts of salmon may be served is almost unlimited.

1675 Saumon Grillé—Grilled Salmon
Cut some Darnes from a medium-sized salmon thick enough to give an average weight of 200 g (7 oz) each. Season, brush with oil and grill with a fierce heat to begin with then finish cooking over a moderate heat.

Serve accompanied with Anchovy Butter or Maître d'Hôtel Butter.

1676 Saumon à la Meunière
Cut the salmon into slices either on or off the bone but not too thick; season, lightly flour and cook in very hot clarified butter in a frying pan. It is important that the salmon should be set quickly in the fat and that it be cooked quite quickly. Serve as required in either of the two ways indicated for the cooking of fish *à la Meunière*.

1677 Mousses and Mousselines of Salmon
As stated before at the beginning of this chapter, Mousses and Mousselines are both prepared from exactly the same kind of forcemeat, the only difference being that Mousses are made in plain or fancy buttered moulds of a size sufficient for a number of portions and Mousselines are moulded in individual portions using tablespoons.

Mousselines may also be moulded by piping out the mixture in the shape of a meringue the same size as an egg. In general, Mousses and Mousselines are best when decorated with truffle. For the recipe for Mousseline forcemeat and details of cooking them see Recipes (1562) and (1563).

1678 Mousselines de Saumon Alexandra
Mould the Mousselines with tablespoons placing them in a buttered shallow pan.

Press a small thin oval slice of salmon on each one and cook in the usual way. When cooked, drain on a clean cloth and arrange on a round dish in a circle. Place a slice of truffle on each piece of salmon, coat with Sauce Mornay, glaze and place a garnish of very small buttered peas or asparagus tips in the centre.

1679 Mousselines de Saumon Tosca
Mix 50 g (2 oz) creamy parts of raw crayfish which have been passed through a fine sieve into 1 kg ($2\frac{1}{4}$ lb) of Salmon Mousseline Forcemeat. Fill into small buttered dariole moulds and cook *au Bain-marie*.

Demould, drain on a clean cloth, then arrange in a circle on a round dish.

Garnish with thick slices of soft roe fried in brown butter; crayfish tails cut in half lengthways; and slices of truffle. Coat with a light creamy Sauce Mornay containing Crayfish Butter and glaze quickly.

Note: As well as the above, all the garnishes and sauces given for fillets of sole are suitable for Mousselines. The garnishes of purées of fresh vegetables are also useful and may be used to create a number of further variations.

1680 Saumon Régence (*whole*)
Stuff the salmon with whiting forcemeat and braise it in the usual manner on a bed of vegetables and herbs and moistened with Sauternes wine.

Prepare a dish by piping Pommes Marquise in a decorative border of a size and shape large enough to contain the salmon; dry it in the oven. Place the cooked salmon in the border and surround the outside with a Régence garnish for fish (449) arranged in bouquets.

Stick 3 decorative silver skewers in the salmon, each garnished with a large trussed crayfish, a large round decorated Quenelle and a glazed truffle. Serve Sauce Régence for fish separately.

Note: Hot salmon is seldom served whole and even in this recipe the salmon should not be a very large one, the reason being that it is difficult, nigh impossible, to serve it very hot for 15–20 people.

On the other hand it is preferable to cook a salmon whole when it is required cold and to allow it to become cold in the cooking liquid; in this way there is always a gain in quality.

1681 SAUMON FROID—COLD SALMON

As already noted, salmon for serving cold should, whenever possible, be cooked whole or in large pieces and allowed to cool in the Court-bouillon. Small *Darnes* or slices of salmon which are cooked separately are, of course, much easier to serve but the flesh becomes much drier than that of salmon which is cooked whole or in a large piece. It is also worth remembering that when cooked whole there is a great gain in quality which offsets any loss in ease of service, which is the case when cooked in individual portions.

For the presentation of cold salmon, the skin should be removed leaving the flesh bare so as to allow ease of decoration but the true gourmet always prefers to see cold salmon covered with its natural silver skin.

The most suitable items of decoration are cucumber, anchovy fillets, capers, slices of tomato, sprigs of chervil and parsley, leaves of tarragon and lobster coral, etc.

The use of softened butter, whether coloured or not, piped on as decoration is to be deprecated; other than the fact that there is nothing artistic in this form of decoration the taste of the butter does not marry with a cold sauce or the flesh of the salmon. The only suitable butter for salmon is Beurre de Montpellier because it is a true sauce.

Cold salmon can be served with most of the cold sauces and vegetable salads; when served in the English style, sliced cucumber is the usual accompaniment.

Among the other garnishes suitable for serving with cold salmon are small tomatoes, peeled, emptied and filled with various kinds of salad; stuffed hard-boiled eggs left whole or cut into halves or quarters; Barquettes, tartlets and Cassolettes made of beetroot or cucumber, blanched until nearly cooked and filled with a puree of tunny fish, anchovies, sardines, etc; and small aspics of prawns, crayfish tails or small slices of lobster, etc.

1682 Saumon Froid, or Darne de Saumon Froide, en Belle-vue
Remove the skin from the cooked salmon and stand it upright on its belly, decorate with truffle, cooked white of egg, leaves of tarragon and chervil, etc. fixed with a little melted aspic jelly. Glaze with a number of coats of white Fish Aspic Jelly in such a fashion as to cover the whole with a transparent veil.

Place the prepared salmon in a suitable crystal glass dish the same shape as the salmon and fill to the edge with very clear melted jelly. Place the prepared dish on a block of clear ice on the serving dish or, alternatively, place the glass dish on the service dish and surrounded with finely crushed ice.

1683 Saumon Froid, or Darne de Saumon Froide, au Beurre de Montpellier

Remove the skin from the salmon and coat it with Montpellier Butter and decorate with crescents of truffle in graded sizes to imitate the scales of the fish; coat with white Fish Aspic Jelly.

Arrange it on a flat base, surround with halves of hard-boiled eggs standing up and with the yolks outwards; decorate the edge of the dish with shapes cut from very firm Montpellier Butter.

1684 Saumon Froid, or Darne de Saumon Froide, au Chambertin

Poach the salmon in Court-bouillon made from half very clear fish stock and half Chambertin wine. Allow to cool in the cooking liquid then prepare a clear jelly from the liquid. Remove the skin from the salmon, decorate, glaze with the jelly and present in the same manner as *Saumon en Belle-vue*.

1685 Côtelettes Froides de Saumon—Cold Salmon Cutlets

These may be prepared in any of the three following ways:

A) Trim some small slices of salmon, cutlet shape; poach them carefully in a buttered dish with white wine and lemon juice and place to cool under light pressure. Coat with white fish Sauce Chaud-froid, lightly decorate and glaze with Fish Aspic Jelly.

Mould a pyramid of vegetable salad bound with Mayonnaise on a dish and arrange the cutlets around the sides.

Serve accompanied with Sauce Mayonnaise.

B) Well butter some small cutlet moulds and line each with a slice of very red salmon previously flattened thin and overlapping the edges of the mould by approximately 1½ cm (⅗ in). Fill the mould with the well seasoned trimmings of salmon and fold over the edges of the slice so as to completely enclose them. Place on a tray and cook dry in a slow oven or in a steamer.

Demould the cutlets on to a tray, allow to cool, decorate neatly and carefully with peas, chervil, lobster, coral etc. The decoration must be very neat and simple. Glaze with clear white Fish Aspic Jelly.

Mould a pyramid of vegetable salad bound with Mayonnaise on a dish, arrange the cutlets upright around it and insert a garnished decorative skewer in the centre of the vegetable mould. Alternatively, the cutlets may be arranged in a circle in a slightly deep glass or silver dish and covered with clear jelly.

These cutlets which are served mainly at ball suppers can also be presented in a large silver bowl or on a base of rice, semolina, cornflour or stearin; whichever form the presentation takes the cutlets should always be accompanied with a cold sauce.

C) Proceed in the same way as for Côtelettes de Homard Arkangel (2130) replacing the lobster flesh and Mousseline forcemeat with salmon flesh and Mousseline forcemeat.

1686 Mayonnaise de Saumon—Salmon Mayonnaise

Cover the bottom of a salad bowl with lightly seasoned shredded lettuce and cover this with flaked cold salmon taking care that there is no skin or bone. Coat with Sauce Mayonnaise and decorate with fillets of anchovy; capers; stoned olives; small quarters or slices of hard-boiled egg; small hearts of lettuce and a border of thin slices of radish etc.

1687 Medaillons de Saumon Froids—Cold Medallions of Salmon

These medallions are generally used to serve at ball suppers as are the cold salmon cutlets.

Cut some 8 mm (¼ in) thick slices from a fillet of salmon and poach them in a buttered dish in a slow oven. Allow to cool under light pressure then trim oval or round-shape using a plain pastry cutter. Coat with Sauce Mayonnaise or one of its derivatives having the addition of a little jelly or, alternatively, coat with white, pink or green Sauce Chaud-froid.

Decorate neatly to taste and glaze with jelly. Present for service in either of the ways given for Cold Salmon Cutlets A or B.

1688 Mousse de Saumon Froide—Cold Salmon Mousse

This is prepared according to the directions given under the heading of Cold Mousses, Mousselines and Soufflés in the Chapter on Garnishes.

1689 Mousselines de Saumon Froides—Cold Salmon Mousselines

These are prepared according to the directions given under the heading of Cold Mousses, Mousselines and Soufflés in the Chapter on Garnishes. These Mousselines may be presented on a layer of jelly set in the bottom of a deep glass or silver dish, then covered with the same clear jelly. Keep in a cold place for service.

1690 Saumon Froid, or Darne de Saumon Froide, à la Norvégienne

Remove the skin from the cooked salmon, decorate and glaze with white Fish Aspic Jelly as for

Saumon en Belle-vue. Set a layer of the same jelly on a serving dish and place a semolina base cut to the required shape on top.

Place the salmon on the base and stick a line of nice large prawns, the tails of which have been shelled, down the centre.

Surround with a garnish of small round cucumber cases which have been well blanched, marinated and filled dome shape with a purée of smoked salmon; halves of hard-boiled egg glazed with jelly; very small tomatoes or halves of peeled tomatoes, squeezed in the corner of a cloth to a round shape and stuck with a small piece of parsley then decorated with piped leaves of green butter; and small Barquette shapes of cooked beetroot, marinated and filled with cooked prawns mixed with a little Mayonnaise.

Serve accompanied with Sauce Russe.

1691 Saumon Froid, or Darne de Saumon Froide, à la Parisienne

Remove a rectangle of skin from the cooked salmon so that its two edges are an equal distance from both the head and tail of the salmon. If using a Darne of salmon the rectangle of skin should be equivalent to approximately two-thirds of the surface of the fish.

Coat the bared surface with Mayonnaise mixed with a little melted jelly and allow to set in a cool place.

Place the salmon on a flat base of rice or semolina the size and shape of the fish; pipe a border of Montpellier Butter around the coated rectangle using a small star tube and decorate the centre with coral, chopped white and yolk of hard-boiled egg, sprigs of chervil etc. Surround the salmon with a border of small artichoke bottoms filled dome shape with a fine Macédoine of vegetables mixed with Mayonnaise Collée.

Serve accompanied with Sauce Mayonnaise.

1692 Saumon Froid, or Darne de Saumon Froide, Riga

Prepare the salmon in the same way as for *à la Parisienne*; present it on a flat base but garnish it with small round cucumber cases, well blanched, marinated with oil and lemon juice and filled with vegetable salad mixed with Mayonnaise; tartlets filled with the same salad plus a trimmed crayfish head stuffed with cold crayfish Mousse on top; and halves of hard-boiled eggs cut fancy shape and filled with caviare. Surround the edge of the dish with shapes of very clear aspic jelly.

1693 Saumon Froid, or Darne de Saumon Froide, à la Royale

Remove the skin from one side of the cooked salmon and coat the bared surface with a layer of cold salmon Mousse moulding it to a slight swell in the centre. Coat this Mousse with Mayonnaise mixed with a little jelly and allow to set in a cool place.

Set a layer of very clear jelly on the serving dish, place the salmon on top and surround with a decorative border of Montpellier Butter piped with a medium star tube.

Decorate the centre of the salmon with a nice Fleur-de-lys cut from truffle and place a crown made from fillets of anchovy at each end.

1694 Salade de Saumon—Salmon Salad

This is prepared with the same ingredients as Salmon Mayonnaise and arranged in the same way but with salad dressing instead of Mayonnaise.

The items of garnish are placed directly on the salmon.

1695 STERLET

It is not necessary to give recipes for this fish which is little used outside of Russia, and then only when the fish are actually caught at certain times of the year when in season.

It is worth remembering that the eggs of this fish supply the finest caviare and that its spinal cord as well as that of the sturgeon supplies Vésiga, that indispensable ingredient of Coulibiac.

1696 TANCHE—TENCH

This fish is most commonly used in the preparation of Matelotes. It may also be prepared *au Gratin*; *à la Meunière*; *à la Bercy*; *au Bleu* etc.

TRUITES—TROUT

From the culinary point of view, trout may be divided into two distinct types—the large ones of which the salmon-trout is typical, and the small or river trout.

Whether for serving hot or cold, salmon-trout may be prepared in any of the ways given for salmon. Because it is usually smaller than salmon it is seldom cut into Darnes and is almost always served whole.

The following selection of recipes are particularly applicable to salmon-trout.

1697 Truite Saumonée Cambacérès

For preference, a male salmon-trout should be selected. Wash it well, remove the gills and take off the skin from one side of the fish up to $2\frac{1}{2}$ cm (1 in) from the head and 5 cm (2 in) from the tail end.

Lard the bared flesh with truffle and red of carrot; stand the trout on its belly on a clean cloth and separate the two fillets from both sides of the backbone starting from the head to where the tail begins. When the bone is freed remove it by cutting with scissors at both extremities then carefully ease it out along with all the bones adhering to it. Also remove the intestine and clean the inside.

Wash the inside of the fish, dry with a clean cloth then season the inside and fill with crayfish Mousseline Forcemeat. Close up the sides to re-form the fish into its normal shape, enclose in thin slices of salt pork fat and braise in the usual way with Sauternes wine.

When just cooked, remove the fat and glaze the fish by leaving it uncovered and basting with the cooking liquid.

Arrange the salmon-trout on a dish and surround with alternate bouquets of morels sautéed in butter, and soft roes cooked *à la Meunière*. Serve accompanied with a fine Sauce Béchamel containing the reduced and passed cooking liquid from the fish, and finished with Crayfish Butter.

1698 Coulibiac de Truite

This is prepared in exactly the same way as either Salmon Coulibiac A or B but using the flesh of a trout instead of salmon. The recipes for small Coulibiacs using Brioche Paste or puff paste trimmings are also applicable.

1699 Mousselines de Truite Alexandra

These are prepared in the same way as Mousselines of Salmon Alexandra but using trout instead of salmon.

1700 Mousselines de Truite Helvétia

Prepare the Mousselines from trout forcemeat and cook in the usual manner. Drain, arrange on a dish and place a small poached *Paupiette* made from half fillets of very small trout, at each end of the Mousselines. On top of each Mousseline place a slice of truffle and 4 cooked crayfish tails and coat all over with a fine well-seasoned Sauce Béchamel which has been finished with Crayfish Butter.

1701 Mousselines de Truite Tosca

These are prepared in the same way as Mousselines of Salmon Tosca but using trout instead of salmon.

TRUITE SAUMONEE FROIDE— COLD SALMON TROUT

1702 Truite Saumonée en Belle-vue

Poach the trout in White Wine Court-bouillon standing it upright on its belly and allow it to cool in the cooking liquid. Prepare a clear jelly from the cooking liquid.

Skin the trout and decorate with truffle, white of egg, chervil, leaves of tarragon etc. fixing them with a little jelly.

Coat the inside of a deep oval-shaped mould, large enough to hold the trout, with a thick layer of the prepared jelly; place in the trout with the back downwards, wedge it in place with lengths of carrot and surround the fish with jelly. When this jelly has set well, remove the carrot and fill up the mould with jelly. Allow to set firmly then demould on to a flat base of rice or semolina and surround with cut shapes of jelly.

Serve accompanied with Sauce Mayonnaise or Sauce Verte.

1703 Truite Saumonée Froide au Chambertin

Prepare the trout in the same way as in the preceding recipe using half fish stock and half Chambertin wine instead of white wine.

1704 Truite Saumonée Froide au Champagne

Prepare in the same way as Truite Saumonée en Belle-vue using Champagne instead of white wine.

1705 Médaillons de Truite Saumonée Froids à la Moderne

Remove the fillets from the trout, wash and remove the skin. Cut into fairly thick slices, lightly flatten and trim oval shape. Poach with white wine and lemon juice in a buttered tray and allow to cool under light pressure.

Coat the médallions with cold crayfish Mousse and pipe a decorative border of Montpellier Butter around each one, using a small star tube.

Place a pinch of chopped coral, truffle and white of hard-boiled egg in the centre; arrange and present as either Cold Médallions or Cutlets of Salmon.

1706 Truite Saumonée Froide à la Norvégienne

Poach the trout in Court-bouillon and allow to cool in the cooking liquid. Remove the skin, decorate the fish and glaze well with clear Fish Aspic Jelly.

Set a layer of the same jelly on a suitable dish, place a sculpted base of rice in the centre and arrange the trout on top. Stick a line of nice large prawns, the tails of which have been shelled, down the centre of the trout. Surround with the same garnish as for Cold Salmon à la Norvégienne (1690) and serve accompanied with Sauce Russe.

1707 Ondines aux Crevettes Roses

Line some hinged egg moulds thickly with a fine

Mousse of salmon-trout then fill both halves of the mould with trimmed cooked prawns. Close the mould and allow to set well in a cool place.

Demould these Ondines and arrange in a deep dish with a few nice whole prawns with the shell removed from the tail, between each. Cover the whole, layer by layer, with good Fish Aspic Jelly almost at setting point, adding a few sprigs of chervil between each layer and taking care that the Ondines are finally covered completely.

1708 Cold Salmon-trout on Mousse *(for lunches and suppers)*

Under this heading are included a whole list of entirely new preparations all of which are at the same time of great delicacy, of a most agreeable appearance, and which can be served easily and correctly.

Cook a trout of $1\frac{1}{4}$–$1\frac{1}{2}$ kg (2 lb 13 oz–3 lb 6 oz) in weight in White Wine Court-bouillon and allow to cool in the liquid. Drain the fish, remove the head and tail and keep on one side for further use. Remove the skin from the fish then carefully remove the two fillets from the centre bone. Decorate each fillet with leaves of tarragon, chervil, lobster coral, cooked white of egg etc.

Arrange the fillets side by side with the backs to the centre, on a tomato Mousse (4265) which has been set in a long white or coloured, porcelain or china dish, approximately 5 cm (2 in) deep.

Replace the head and tail correctly and coat the whole with good Fish Aspic Jelly almost at setting point. Allow the jelly to set then present the dish on a block of clear ice or set it in a bed of crushed ice.

Variations of the above recipe:

Fillets of salmon-trout decorated with crayfish tails and tarragon leaves presented on a Mousse of crayfish.

Fillets of salmon-trout decorated with slices of lobster, lobster coral and chervil presented on a Mousse of lobster flavoured with paprika.

Fillets of salmon-trout decorated with prawns and capers presented on a Mousse of prawns.

Fillets of salmon-trout decorated with strips of pimento trellis-fashion presented on a Mousse of pimento.

Fillets of salmon-trout decorated with leaves of tarragon and chervil presented on a Mousse of physalis and surrounded with bouquets of physalis.

Fillets of salmon-trout decorated with strips of green pimento arranged trellis-fashion, presented on a Mousse of green pimento.

Fillets of salmon-trout decorated with chopped hard-boiled eggs and parsley presented on a Mousse of new season leaf herbs.

Fillets of salmon-trout decorated with fillets of anchovy, capers and olives presented on a Mousse au Volnay.

Fillets of salmon-trout decorated with fillets of anchovy, capers and olives presented on Mousse au Chambertin.

Etc. etc.

Note: To make a Mousse of Volnay or Chambertin or of any other fine wine, the base of the mixture is provided by Fish Velouté mixed with some melted Fish Aspic Jelly and the cooking liquid from the fish which includes the particular wine reduced to 2 dl (7 fl oz or $\frac{7}{8}$ U.S. cup).

The above recipes are equally suitable for fillets of turbot and sole.

TRUITE DE RIVIERE—RIVER TROUT

1709 Truites au Bleu

For this preparation it is absolutely essential to have trout which are alive.

Have ready in a shallow pan a well vinegared, boiling Court-bouillon.

About 10 minutes before being required remove the trout from the tank, stun them with a sharp blow on the head, empty and wash quickly. Immediately place in the boiling liquid whereupon the fish will quickly curl up and the flesh split open. It will require only a few minutes to cook a trout of approximately 150 g ($5\frac{1}{2}$ oz). Drain them for service and arrange immediately on a serviette with pickled parsley.

Serve accompanied with Sauce Hollandaise and Melted Butter.

Note: If the trout are to be served cold, they should be accompanied with Sauce Ravigote à l'Huile.

1710 Truites Farcies—Stuffed Trout

Clean and remove the centre bones from some trout weighing approximately 250 g (9 oz) each. Stuff them with good fish forcemeat containing chopped truffle then wrap them in sheets of oiled greaseproof paper and either grill over a hot grill or cook in the oven basting with melted butter.

As soon as cooked, remove the paper and arrange the trout on a dish with half of a decorated lemon per trout.

Serve accompanied with Sauce Marinière.

1711 Truites Gavarnie

Clean some very small trout and coat them with a layer of Maître d'Hôtel butter. Enclose each in a piece of oiled paper cut out as for *Papillote*, place on the serving dish and cook in the oven.

Serve in the *Papillotes* accompanied with Beurre Noisette and a dish of plain boiled potatoes.

1712 Truites à l'Hôtelière

Clean the trout and flour, egg and breadcrumb them; deep fry as required and serve arranged on some slightly softened Maître d'Hôtel Butter mixed with 15 g (½ oz) dry Duxelles per 100 g (3½ oz) of butter.

Surround the dish with slices of fluted lemon.

1713 Truites à la Hussarde

Clean some medium-sized trout, remove the centre bones from the back and stuff with fish forcemeat mixed with 100 g (3½ oz) chopped onion cooked in a little butter, per 500 g (1lb 2 oz) of forcemeat.

Butter a tray and cover with a layer of finely sliced onion which has been cooked, without colour, in a little butter; arrange the trout on top and for every 8–10 fish add 100 g (3½ oz) butter, 2 dl (7 fl oz or ⅞ U.S. cup) Chablis wine and 1 Bouquet garni. Poach in a medium oven without a lid, basting frequently.

When cooked, arrange the trout on a dish, pass the cooking liquid and onion through a fine sieve, lightly thicken this with a little fish Velouté or Beurre Manié and enrich with a little butter.

Coat the fish with the sauce and glaze quickly.

1714 Truites à la Mantoue

Clean some medium-sized trout and detach the fillets from both sides of the backbone up to the head; remove the bones flush with the head and discard them. Spread the inside of each fillet with a layer of fish forcemeat containing chopped truffle and re-form the trout, keeping them in shape by tying round with thread.

Shallow poach them gently on a bed of vegetables and herbs with a little white wine and mushroom cooking liquor, basting frequently.

When ready, arrange on a dish and coat with Sauce Italienne from which the ham has been omitted but containing the strained and reduced cooking liquid from the fish.

1715 Truites à la Meunière

This is one of the most suitable preparations for river trout. Proceed as indicated in the cooking of fish *à la Meunière*.

1716 Truites Persillées

If possible obtain trout which have been caught in mountain streams; clean them, season, flour and cook *à la Meunière*. As soon as they are cooked, arrange on a hot dish, sprinkle with a little lemon juice and chopped parsley and cover with well frothing Beurre à la Polonaise (252).

1717 Truites à la Vauclusienne

These are prepared in the same way as *à la Meunière* using olive oil instead of butter.

1718 Truites au Vin Rouge

Prepare 1 litre (1¾ pt or 4½ U.S. cups) Red Wine Court-bouillon for each 10 medium-sized trout weighing 125 g (4½ oz) each.

Poach the trout in this Court-bouillon for 10 minutes, remove and arrange on a dish.

Pass the Court-bouillon through a fine strainer, reduce it by two-thirds and thicken with a Beurre Manié made from 100 g (3½ oz) butter and 25 g (1 oz) flour.

Coat the trout with the sauce and glaze under the salamander.

1719 WHITEBAIT, NONNATS AND BLANCHAILLES

The whitebait which come from the estuary of the River Thames are very similar to the Nonnats found in the Mediterranean. They are something of an enigma to the naturalist who, whilst supporting the view that whitebait are the very young of fish, unfortunately do not give the name of the species of fish which produce them.

Whitebait are, however, the ingredient of a superb fried dish which is usually served as a second fish dish in a dinner menu. As with the Nonnats they are extremely fragile and should be cooked as soon as possible after being caught. They should be served only deep fried and the frying media should always be fresh and abundant.

Whitebait should first be rolled in plenty of flour then placed in a special cane sieve or frying basket which is then shaken to remove the excess flour. They are then plunged immediately into very hot smoking oil, a small quantity at a time; they require no more than one minute for them to become crisp. Drain immediately on a clean cloth, season with fine salt mixed with a little Cayenne and arrange on a serviette with very green fried parsley.

That which is called Blanchaille in England and which is called Poutine along the Mediterranean coast, is really a mixture of the very young of all kinds of fish of which the young of the Clupae family are the most common. Blanchaille are prepared in the same way as whitebait.

1720 Nonnats aux Epinards Gratinés

Place 1 dl (3½ fl oz or ½ U.S. cup) oil in a shallow pan and heat until it is lightly smoking. Add 500 g (1 lb 2 oz) blanched and roughly chopped spinach leaves and cook quickly to dry out; place in a basin. Add 200 g (7 oz) Nonnats, poached in Court-bouillon for 1 minute, 2 beaten eggs and a little salt and pepper. Mix carefully together, place in a dish and smooth level; sprinkle with dry breadcrumbs and some olive oil and gratinate in a medium oven for 20–25 minutes.

1721 Various Methods of Preparing Nonnats
Nonnats may be sautéed in butter and served as they are, sautéed in butter as before and served with an omelette, or poached in Court-bouillon, allowed to cool and served as a salad or in a moulded aspic.

SALT WATER FISH

UNCLASSIFIED PREPARATIONS

1722 Bouillabaisse à la Marseillaise
As with the preparation and cooking of so many well-known dishes, there is still no consensus of opinion as to which is the most correct method of preparing Bouillabaisse. Taking this fact into account, it is considered that the following recipe of Monsieur Caillat is the one that should be adopted as being the most suitable.

Ingredients for 10 Persons:
2½ kg (5 lb 10 oz) fish, the following Mediterranean fish being the ones most suitable and authentic: Rascasse, Chapon, John Dory, whiting, Fielas, Boudreuil, Red Mullet, Rouquiers, crawfish or Langoustines
125 g (4½ oz) chopped onion
50 g (2 oz) chopped white of leek
250 g (9 oz) roughly chopped flesh only of tomato
30 g (1 oz) crushed garlic
15 g (½ oz) roughly chopped parsley
1 good pinch of saffron
1 dl (3½ fl oz or ½ U.S. cup) olive oil
1 bayleaf
1 sprig of savoury
1 pinch of tops of fennel leaves
French bread

Method:
Cut the large fish into pieces and leave the small ones whole; place all the ingredients in a pan except for the soft-fleshed fish such as red mullet and whiting which are added later.

Add sufficient water to just cover the ingredients, season with salt and pepper and bring to the boil. Boil rapidly for 7–8 minutes then add the soft-fleshed fish and continue to boil quickly for a further 7–8 minutes.

Pour the cooking liquid of the Bouillabaisse into a deep dish containing slices of French bread and arrange the fish in another dish surrounding them with the pieces of crawfish or the halves of Langoustine, whichever is being used.

Note: The best kind of bread for serving with Bouillabaisse is the one known in Marseilles as *Marette*. It should be used whilst still very fresh and should not be fried or toasted for a real Bouillabaisse à la Marseillaise.

Monsieur Caillat has rightly observed that the use of white fish such as whiting is absolutely necessary to ensure the thickening of the Bouillabaisse liquid.

1723 Bouillabaisse à la Parisienne
Ingredients for 10 persons:
2½ kg (5 lb 10 oz) fish, the following being the ones most suitable: red mullet, gurnard, sole, weever, whiting, small conger eel, crawfish
1½ litres (2⅝ pt or 3¼ U.S. pt) mussels
2½ dl (9 fl oz or 1⅛ U.S. cup) olive oil
150 g (5 oz) chopped onion
70 g (2½ oz) chopped white of leek
6 dl (1 pt or 2⅝ U.S. cup) white wine
1 litre (1¾ pt or 4½ U.S. cups) water
Pinch of pepper
Pinch of saffron
1 Bouquet garni
300 g (11 oz) roughly chopped flesh only of tomato, or tomato purée
30 g (1 oz) crushed garlic
15 g (½ oz) coarsely chopped parsley
40 g (1½ oz) butter } made into Beurre Manié
15 g (½ oz) flour }
French bread

Method:
Place 1½ dl (5 fl oz or ⅝ U.S. cup) of the oil in a pan, add the onion and leek and cook without colour; add the wine, water, salt, pepper, saffron, Bouquet garni, tomato and garlic, bring to the boil and cook gently for 20 minutes. The heads of the mullet, gurnard and whiting with the gills removed, may be added if liked.

Cut the fish and crawfish into sections, place in a pan and put the cleaned mussels on top. Add 1 dl (3½ fl oz or ½ U.S. cup) oil, sprinkle with the parsley and the prepared cooking liquid, bring to the boil and cook rapidly for 15 minutes. At the last moment thicken with the Beurre Manié.

Arrange the fish and shellfish in a deep dish and serve separately, slices of toasted French bread lightly rubbed with garlic and well soaked with the cooking liquid from the Bouillabaisse.

1724 Bouillabaisse de Morue

Ingredients for 10 persons:

1 kg 200 g (2 lb 11 oz) thick white salt cod which has been well soaked to remove the salt
2½ dl (9 fl oz or 1⅛ U.S. cups) olive oil
125 g (4½ oz) chopped onion
70 g (2½ oz) chopped white of leek
25 g (1 oz) chopped garlic
1¾ litres (3 pt or 7½ U.S. cups) water
15 g (½ oz) salt
Pinch of pepper
Pinch of saffron
1 large Bouquet garni
1 kg (2¼ lb) Dutch potatoes
Coarsely chopped parsley
French bread

Method:

Place the oil in a pan, add the onion, leek and garlic and cook without colour. Add the water, salt, pepper, saffron and Bouquet garni, bring to the boil then add the potatoes cut into thick slices.

Cook for 12–15 minutes then add the cod, trimmed and cut in large square pieces, and 1 dl (3½ fl oz or ½ U.S. cup) oil. Boil rapidly until the fish and potatoes are just cooked then add 2 good pinches of coarsely chopped parsley.

Serve the fish in a deep dish with some of the liquid and serve separately a dish of slices of toasted bread rubbed with garlic and soaked with the cooking liquid from the Bouillabaisse.

1725 ANCHOIS—ANCHOVIES

The anchovy is generally used as an Hors-d'oeuvre where it serves as a flavouring for many different preparations. It can, however, be deep fried when fresh and may be prepared in any of the ways given for sardines.

1726 BAR OR LOUP DE MER—SEA PERCH OR SEA WOLF

Large fish of this species can be poached whole in salted water and served accompanied with any sauce suitable for large fish. Small ones may be deep fried, shallow fried *à la Meunière* or grilled and served with any suitable compound butter.

1727 BARBUE—BRILL

Served whole, brill can be successfully served as an excellent alternative to turbot. All the recipes for whole turbot are applicable and if prepared as fillets all the recipe for fillets of sole may be followed.

1728 BLOATERS

Bloaters are lightly smoked herrings and constitute an excellent dish for breakfast or high tea. They are simply grilled over a gentle heat. Bloaters being only slightly salted and lightly smoked will not keep for any length of time.

1729 CABILLAUD OR MORUE FRAICHE—COD

Cod may be poached in salted water and all of the sauces suitable for turbot are applicable.

1730 Cabillaud Crème au Gratin

This is prepared in the same way as Turbot Crème au Gratin using cod instead of turbot.

1731 Cabillaud à la Flamande

Cut the cod into 2½ cm (1 in) thick sections on the bone, season with salt, pepper and nutmeg and arrange in a well buttered shallow pan or tray. Moisten with white wine half-way up the fish, sprinkle with chopped shallot and chopped Fines Herbes and place slices of peeled and depipped lemon on top of each piece. Bring to the boil and poach in the oven for approximately 12 minutes.

Arrange the fish on a suitable dish, thicken the cooking liquor with crushed rusks, boil gently for 5 minutes and pour over the fish.

1732 Cabillaud Bouilli—Boiled Cod

The cod may be cooked in salted water, either whole, cut in slices or in sections as thick Darnes. It is served accompanied with its liver poached in salt water and floury plain boiled potatoes cooked at the last moment.

Serve accompanied with a suitable sauce—such as Sauce Hollandaise; Sauce aux Huîtres; or Melted Butter.

1733 Cabillaud Grillé—Grilled Cod

Cut the cod into sections on the bone approximately 3 cm (1 in) thick. Season, flour and sprinkle them well with melted butter. Grill slowly on both sides and when ready, arrange on a hot dish, garnish with slices of peeled lemon and surround with bouquets of picked parsley.

Serve Maître d'Hôtel or Anchovy Butter separately or any sauce suitable for grilled fish.

1734 Cabillaud Frit—Fried Cod

Cut the cod into sections on the bone 2–3 cm (1 in)

thick; season, flour, egg and breadcrumb them and deep fry, allowing suficient time to cook through, bearing in mind the thickness of the cuts.

Arrange on a serviette and garnish with fried parsley and lemon and at the same time serve a suitable sauce, e.g. Butter Sauce, Tomato Sauce or Tartare Sauce.

1735 Cabillaud à la Hollandaise

Poach the fish in salted water and at the same time cook some floury plain boiled potatoes.

Serve the fish with the well drained and dried potatoes and accompany with a sauceboat of Melted Butter.

1736 Cabillaud à la Portugaise

Cut the cod into thick sections on the bone, approximately 250 g (9 oz) each in weight; season with salt and pepper and arrange in a shallow pan with, for every 5 pieces of fish, 100 g ($3\frac{1}{2}$ oz) butter; 1 dl ($3\frac{1}{2}$ fl oz or $\frac{1}{2}$ U.S. cup) olive oil; 100 g ($3\frac{1}{2}$ oz) chopped onion previously lightly cooked in butter; 1 small clove of crushed garlic; 2 pinches of coarsely chopped parsley; 750 g (1 lb 10 oz) roughly chopped flesh only of tomato; 100 g ($3\frac{1}{2}$ oz) three-quarters cooked rice; and 2 dl (7 fl oz or $\frac{7}{8}$ U.S. cup) white wine.

Cover the pan and cook quickly for 10 minutes then remove the lid so that the liquid can reduce and the fish become completely cooked; a further 8 minutes is usually sufficient for this. Arrange the fish in a dish and cover with the cooking liquid and garnish.

1737 CARRELET OR PLIE FRANCHE—PLAICE

This fish may be prepared in many of the ways given for turbot but it is seldom used in the classical kitchen. It is most frequently served deep fried but the following preparations are sometimes used.

1738 Carrelet Grillé—Grilled Plaice

Incise the fillets with shallow cuts in a criss-cross pattern, season, brush them well with oil and grill gently. Serve placed on a suitable compound butter or accompanied with a sauceboat of Sauce Saint-Malo.

1739 Carrelet à la Meunière

Plaice may be cooked *à la Meunière* either as fillets or whole. If whole, partly detach the fillets from each side along the backbone so as to facilitate the cooking.

1740 Carrelet Rôti—Roast Plaice

Season the plaice, sprinkle with oil, place on a grill inside a deep roasting tray and roast in a fairly hot oven. Serve with a suitable well-flavoured sauce.

Note: One very good way of serving plaice which is to be recommended is to fillet the fish, flour, egg and breadcrumb them, shallow fry in clarified butter and serve accompanied with Sauce Chateaubriand.

1741 COLIN OR MERLAN NOIR—COALFISH

This fish is considered to be of a somewhat inferior quality: the methods of preparation for cod are suitable.

1742 CONGRE OR ANGUILLE DE MER—CONGER EEL

Other than as an ingredient of Bouillabaisse this fish is little used in classical cooking.

It may, however, be cooked *au Court-bouillon* and served with a suitable sauce, or prepared as Fillets or Aiguillettes à la Orly.

1743 DORADE—DORADO

The finest of this fish is the species which has a sort of pearly transparent excrusence between the eyes. Small fish are best grilled, fried or prepared *à la Meunière*: large ones may be poached in either red or white wine and served accompanied with a sauce made from the reduced cooking liquid. Generally speaking most of the sauces and garnishes for sole are suitable.

1744 EPERLANS—SMELTS

Because of their small size smelts can be prepared in only a limited number of ways.

They are, perhaps, best prepared deep fried either on a skewer or arranged in a pile in the same way as Goujons of fish and gudgeons; whichever way they should be presented on a serviette with fried parsley and halves of lemon.

1745 Eperlans à l'Anglaise

Split open the smelts from the back and carefully remove the backbone so as not to damage the fish. Flour, egg and breadcrumb with very fine crumbs and flatten carefully with the back of a knife.

Shallow fry in clarified butter, arrange on a long dish and sprinkle with almost melted Maître d'Hôtel Butter.

1746 Escabèche d'Eperlans

See under Cold Hors-d'oeuvre (979).

1747 Eperlans au Gratin
Prepare the smelts in the same way as Merlan au Gratin taking into account that, being much smaller, they will require placing in a very hot oven to ensure the formation of the *Gratin* and completion of their cooking at the same time.

1748 Eperlans Grillés—Grilled Smelts
Open the smelts from the back and remove most of the backbone leaving a small piece next to the head and a small piece next to the tail.

Season, flour, brush with melted butter and grill quickly.

Arrange on a hot long dish and surround with slices of lemon and bouquets fried parsley. Serve separately almost melted Maître d'Hôtel Butter or any suitable sauce for grilled fish.

1749 Eperlans à la Meunière
Proceed in the manner described for the cooking of fish *à la Meunière*.

1750 Mousseline d'Eperlans
This Mousseline forcemeat is prepared as indicated in the Chapter on Garnishes under Forcemeats (288). The remarks made in the recipe for Potage Velouté d'Eperlans, that the proportions of flesh of smelts should not exceed one-third of the total quantity of fish used, should be borne in mind. The other two-thirds of fish is best supplied by using sole or John Dory; the reason for this is that the flesh of smelts has too pronounced a flavour for it to be used by itself—its strong flavour can be disagreeable.

Other than this, an addition of neutral flavoured fish to the forcemeat allows for a greater absorption of cream, making the Mousselines lighter and softer.

1751 Mousselines d'Eperlans Alexandra
This is prepared in the same way as Mousselines de Saumon Alexandra using smelt forcemeat instead of salmon.

1752 Mousselines d'Eperlans Tosca
This is prepared in the same way as Mousselines de Saumon Tosca using smelt forcemeat instead of salmon.

1753 Paupiettes d'Eperlans
Prepare in the same way as Paupiettes of whiting, arranging them in a deep dish with a suitable sauce and garnish to choice. They may also be used for garnishing or filling fish Vols-au-vent.

1754 Eperlans sur le Plat
Prepare in the same way as Sole sur le Plat taking account of the difference in size.

1755 Eperlans Richelieu
Prepare as Eperlans à l'Anglaise with the addition of a line of slices of truffle on the Maître d'Hôtel Butter.

1756 Eperlans au Vin Blanc
Prepare in the same way as Filets de Sole au Vin Blanc.

1757 SMOKED HADDOCK

This is a small haddock with the head removed, then split open from the back and smoked; it provides an excellent dish for breakfast.

If served grilled accompany it with melted butter; if to be served poached place it in a small amount of lightly salted boiling water or milk, cover, reboil, then bring to the side of the stove and allow to poach. A haddock of 750 g (1 lb 10 oz) will need approximately 15 minutes to poach.

Serve on a dish with a little of the cooking liquor and serve fresh or melted butter separately according to the guests's requirement.

When smoked haddock is served for lunch it is usual to accompany it with a sauceboat of Egg Sauce and a dish of freshly cooked plain boiled potatoes.

HARENGS—HERRINGS

1758 Harengs à la Calaisienne
Clean the herrings, open them from the back and remove the backbones. Stuff with hard or soft roes mixed with Maître d'Hôtel Butter which has been mixed with 25 g (1 oz) chopped shallots, 20 g ($\frac{2}{3}$ oz) chopped parsley and 25 g (1 oz) chopped mushrooms per 125 g ($4\frac{1}{2}$ oz) butter.

Enclose each fish in a well oiled oval *Papillote* and cook gently in the oven. Serve on a dish as they are.

1759 Harengs Farcis—Stuffed Herrings
Clean the herrings, open them from the back and remove the backbones. Stuff with an ordinary fish forcemeat containing chopped Fines Herbes and enclose each fish in a well oiled *Papillote*. Cook gently in the oven and serve on a dish as they are.

1760 Harengs Marinés—Marinated Herrings
Prepare in the same way as Harengs à la Dieppoise, see Cold Hors-d'oeuvre (987).

1761 Harengs à la Meunière
This is prepared in the same way as for fish *à la Meunière*. Serve on a dish surrounded with slices of lemon.

1762 Harengs à la Nantaise
Use herrings with soft roes and incise with shallow cuts on both sides; flour, egg and breadcrumb them and shallow fry in clarified butter.

Remove one of the roes from each fish and pass it through a fine sieve, season the purée obtained with salt and pepper and mix in a pinch of English mustard; thicken and enrich with melted butter using 125 g ($4\frac{1}{2}$ oz) butter for 6 soft roes. Serve this butter separately with the herrings.

1763 Harengs Paramé
Clean the herrings and incise shallow cuts on both sides then place them in hot butter for a few moments, turning them over, so as to set the flesh. Place each fish in an oval oiled *Papillote* with 1 tbs of dry Duxelles and cook in the oven. Serve on a dish as they are.

1764 Harengs Portière
Cook the herrings *à la Meunière*, smear with a little made mustard, sprinkle with chopped parsley then cover with Beurre Noisette and finally a little vinegar which has been heated in the pan.

MAQUEREAUX—MACKEREL

1765 Maquereau à l'Anglaise
Cut the mackerel into sections and poach in a Court-bouillon flavoured with fennel; serve accompanied with a fairly thin purée of cooked gooseberries.

1766 Maquereau à la Boulonnaise
Cut the mackerel into large sections and poach in a Court-bouillon strongly flavoured with vinegar.

When cooked, drain the fish, remove the skin and arrange on a dish surrounded with poached mussels; coat with Sauce au Beurre made partly from the strained Court-bouillon.

1767 Maquereau à la Calaisienne
Remove the fillets from the mackerel and proceed in the same way as for Harengs à la Calaisienne (1758).

1768 Maquereau Grillé—Grilled Mackerel
Cut off the end of the head, open the fish from the back and remove the backbone without separating the two halves then lay it flat. Season, brush with melted butter and grill gently.

Arrange on a hot dish taking care not to separate the two halves and coat with almost melted Maître d'Hôtel Butter.

1769 Filets de Maquereau Bonnefoy
Season the fillets then flour and cook them *à la Meunière*. Arrange on a hot dish, cover with Sauce Bordelaise Bonnefoy and serve accompanied with a dish of plain boiled potatoes.

1770 Filets de Maquereau à la Dieppoise
Shallow poach the fillets with a little mushroom cooking liquor, white wine and butter. Drain well, remove the skin, arrange on an oval dish and surround with Dieppoise garnish.

Coat the fillets and garnish with White Wine Sauce containing some mussel cooking liquor and the reduced cooking liquid from the fish.

1771 Filets de Maquereau aux Fines Herbes
Shallow poach the fillets with half white wine and half mushroom cooking liquor. When cooked, drain, remove the skin and arrange the fillets on an oval dish. Coat with Sauce Fines Herbes containing the reduced cooking liquid from the fish.

1772 Filets de Maquereau en Papillote
Season and grill the fillets and place each in an oval oiled *Papillote* with 1 tbs of dry Duxelles mixed with some cooked sliced mushrooms. Place on a tray in the oven to colour and swell up.

1773 Filets de Maquereau au Persil
Poach the fillets in Court-bouillon strongly flavoured with parsley. Drain well, remove the skin and arrange on a dish. Surround with plain boiled potatoes and serve accompanied with Parsley Sauce.

1774 Filets de Maquereau Rosalie
Season and flour the fillets and shallow fry them in oil.

Remove the fillets and arrange on an oval dish, add a little more oil to the pan, heat well and add a little chopped onion, shallot and mushroom and a touch of crushed garlic. Fry quickly and pour this over the fish; finally heat a little vinegar in the pan, pour this over as well and sprinkle with chopped parsley.

1775 Fillets of Mackerel with Various Sauces
Poach the fillets in salted water or in mushroom cooking liquor, white wine and butter, according to choice. Coat with Sauce Ravigote, Sauce Vénitienne, Sauce Vin Blanc or any other suitable sauce.

1776 Laitances de Maquereau—Soft Mackerel Roes
These may be prepared in the same way as given in the recipes for soft carp roes and have similar uses.

MERLAN—WHITING

1777 Merlans à l'Anglaise
Open the whiting along the back from head to tail, remove the backbones and allow the fillets to lie flat and unseparated. Season, flour, egg and breadcrumb using very fine white crumbs.

Shallow fry in clarified butter on both sides, arrange on an oval dish and coat with softened Maître d'Hôtel Butter.

1778 Merlans Bercy
Cut the whiting along the back to facilitate the cooking and place on a buttered tray which has been sprinkled with some very finely chopped shallot. Moisten with white wine and fish stock, add 15 g ($\frac{1}{2}$ oz) butter per 1 dl ($3\frac{1}{2}$ fl oz or $\frac{1}{2}$ U.S. cup) liquid, season and cook in the oven basting frequently.

The almost complete reduction of the liquid and the completion of the cooking of the fish should coincide; glaze the fish at the last moment by frequently basting with the cooking liquid.

Arrange on a dish and sprinkle with a few drops of lemon juice and some chopped parsley.

1779 Merlans Colbert
Open the fish along the back and remove the backbone, allowing the fillets to lie flat and unseparated; season, flour, egg and breadcrumb and deep fry as required. Arrange on an oval dish, fill the centre with Maître d'Hôtel Butter and surround with a border of slices of fluted lemon.

1780 Merlans à la Dieppoise
Cut the whiting along the back so as to facilitate the cooking; shallow poach with white wine, mushroom cooking liquor and a little butter. Well drain and arrange on a dish; surround with Dieppoise garnish, coat the fish and garnish with White Wine Sauce containing the passed and reduced cooking liquid from the fish.

Note: In some establishments it is the practice to glaze all fish prepared *à la Dieppoise.*

1781 Merlans aux Fines Herbes
Poach the whiting in white wine and mushroom cooking liquor; drain well, arrange on a dish and place in the oven for a short while to dry out slightly. Coat with Sauce aux Fines Herbes.

1782 Merlans au Gratin
Clean and incise the whiting on both sides with shallow cuts; butter a deep dish and cover the bottom with Sauce Gratin. Place in the whiting and surround with a border of overlapping slices of raw mushrooms; place 3 small cooked mushrooms on top of each whiting, add a few spoonfuls of white wine and cover the whole with Sauce Gratin.

Sprinkle with fine breadcrumbs and melted butter and place in the oven at a temperature so regulated as to produce the reduction of the sauce, the cooking of the fish and the formation of a crust (*Gratin*)—these three factors should be completed at the same time. After removing the whiting from the oven sprinkle with a little lemon juice and chopped parsley.

Note: See Chapter 7—Principles of Cookery for a more detailed explanation of the *Gratins.*

1783 Merlans à l'Hôtellière
Prepare in the same way as Truites à l'Hôtellière (1712).

1784 Merlans en Lorgnette
Carefully remove the skin and separate the fillets from both sides of the backbone starting from the tail. Remove the backbones right up to the beginning of the head leaving the fillets attached to the heads.

Season the fish, flour, lightly egg and breadcrumb and roll up each fillet into the form of a *Paupiette* each still attached to the side of the head; keep them in place by pushing a skewer through each *Paupiette* and through the heads. Deep fry as required, remove the skewers and arrange the fish on a serviette with fried parsley. Serve accompanied with Tomato Sauce.

1785 Merlans en Lorgnette au Gratin
Carefully remove the skin and separate the fillets as indicated for Merlans en Lorgnette. Spread the outside of the fillets with a layer of fish forcemeat mixed with chopped Fines Herbes and roll each fillet up into the shape of a *Paupiette* still attached to the head.

Arrange the whiting in a buttered gratin dish the bottom of which has been coated with Sauce Gratin; place the *Paupiettes* to the centre and the heads to the outside. Place a small cooked mushroom on each *Paupiette*, surround with slices of raw mushrooms overlapping and proceed and finish exactly as for Merlans au Gratin.

1786 Merlans à la Meunière
This is prepared as indicated in the Method of Cooking Fish (1558).

1787 Merlans Montreuil
If using fillets incise with shallow cuts—if whole, cut along the back to facilitate cooking. Poach with fish stock, white wine and butter, then proceed as indicated for Sole Montreuil (1906).

1788 Mousse de Merlans—Mousse of Whiting
Prepare a Mousseline forcemeat using whiting and proceed in the usual manner for Mousses.

1789 Mousselines of Whiting
See the recipes for Mousselines of Salmon (1677), using whiting flesh for the forcemeat and the decoration of the Mousselines.

1790 Merlans à la Niçoise
Prepare in the same way as for Rougets à la Niçoise (1840).

1791 Filets de Merlan Orly
Remove the fillets, season and place in a light frying batter. Remove and deep fry in very hot fat. Arrange on a serviette with fried parsley and serve accompanied with Tomato Sauce (see the note at the end of Filets de Sole Orly 1997).

1792 Pain de Merlan à l'Ancienne
This is prepared in the same way as Pain de Brochet à l'Ancienne, replacing the pike forcemeat with whiting forcemeat.

1793 Paupiettes de Merlan
Remove the fillets and coat the inside of each with fish forcemeat; roll up into the shape of a barrel and keep in shape by tying with thread. Paupiettes of whiting are poached in the same way as Paupiettes of Sole and may be served with any of the sauces and garnishes used for sole.

1794 Merlans sur le Plat
Cut the whiting along the back and proceed in the same way as for Sole sur le Plat.

1795 Quenelles de Merlan Soubise
Prepare a whiting and butter forcemeat and mould either into Quenelles with spoons, or in small Barquette moulds, approximately 75 g (2½ oz) each. Poach in salted water for 15–18 minutes then drain, dry, arrange in a circle on a round dish and place a little thin Sauce Soubise in the centre.

Note: These Quenelles may be accompanied with any suitable garnish used for fillets of sole.

1796 Quenelles de Merlan à la Morland
These are prepared in exactly the same way as Quenelles de Brochet à la Morland using whiting forcemeat instead of pike forcemeat.

1797 Merlans Richelieu
Prepare the whiting in the same way as for Merlans à l'Anglaise and finish the dish by placing a line of slices of truffle on the Maître d'Hôtel Butter.

1798 Vol-au-Vent de Quenelles de Merlan Cardinal
Half of the filling for the Vol-au-vent should be small Quenelles of whiting and cream forcemeat moulded with teaspoons and poached at the last minute; the other half should comprise small slices of cooked crawfish, small grooved mushrooms and slices of truffle.

Mix all these ingredients together with Sauce Béchamel finished with some very red Lobster Butter then fill into a large warm Vol-au-vent case. Decorate the top with a large grooved mushroom and surround the mushroom with a circle of slices of truffle.

MORUE—SALT COD

For 10 persons allow 1–1¼ kg (2¼–2¾ lb).

Morue is a special type of dry salt cod the best of which comes from Iceland and Newfoundland. Before being used it must be soaked under cold running water for at least 12 hours—if running water is not available, the water in which the cod is soaked must be changed frequently.

If the fish is to be served whole, cut off the fins before cooking.

1799 Morue à l'Anglaise
Poach the cod in unsalted water for 15 minutes, drain and place on a dish with fresh parsley.

Serve accompanied with a dish of plain boiled parsnips and Egg Sauce.

1800 Morue à la Bamboche
Cut slices, the shape and size of a fillet of sole from a large thick salt cod having very white flesh. Dip in milk then into flour, twist spiral shape and deep fry in hot fat. Place a Macédoine of vegetables mixed with butter and cream in a deep dish and arrange the fried fish neatly on top.

1801 Morue à la Bénédictine
Poach the required amount of salt cod, drain well, remove the skin and bone and flake the flesh carefully. Pound this flesh together with 600 g (1 lb 5 oz) hot plain boiled potatoes which have been well drained and dried. Work carefully into the paste which has been formed, 2 dl (7 fl oz or ⅞ U.S. cup) oil and 5 dl (18 fl oz or 2¼ U.S. cups) boiling hot milk, a little at a time. When it has all been added, the mixture should be soft rather than firm.

Place the mixture in a buttered gratin dish, smooth the surface, sprinkle with melted butter and colour in a very hot oven.

1802 Morue Benoîton
Finely slice 250 g (9 oz) onion and cook to a light

brown colour in a little butter and oil; sprinkle with 35 g ($1\frac{1}{4}$ oz) flour and cook for a few moments. Moisten with $7\frac{1}{2}$ dl ($1\frac{1}{3}$ pt or $3\frac{1}{4}$ U.S. cups) red wine and 2 dl (7 fl oz or $\frac{7}{8}$ U.S. cup) fish stock, season with 10 g ($\frac{1}{3}$ oz) salt, a good pinch of pepper and allow to cook very gently for 15 minutes.

Meanwhile, poach the required amount of fish; drain well, remove the skin and bone and flake the fish carefully, add this to the sauce together with 600 g (1 lb 5 oz) sliced, plain boiled small potatoes and a small clove of crushed garlic. Place the prepared mixture in a buttered gratin dish, smooth the surface, sprinkle with fine white breadcrumbs and melted butter and gratinate quickly in a very hot oven.

1803 Morue au Beurre Noir or Morue au Beurre Noisette—Salt Cod with Beurre Noir or Brown Butter

Poach the cod, drain well and discard the skin. Place on a suitable dish making sure that the fish is quite dry, sprinkle with coarsely chopped parsley, a few drops of lemon juice and cover with Beurre Noir or butter cooked to a light brown colour using 200 g (7 oz) of butter per 10 portions.

1804 Bouillabaisse de Morue

See the beginning of the section on Unclassified Preparations (1724).

1805 Brandade de Morue

Cut the fish into large square pieces and poach for only 8 minutes from the time it comes back to the boil so as to keep it slightly undercooked. Immediately drain and remove all skin and bones. Place $2\frac{1}{2}$ dl (9 fl oz or $1\frac{1}{8}$ U.S. cups) oil in a shallow pan and heat until just smoking; place in the fish with 1 clove of crushed garlic and using a wooden spatula, mix vigorously over the heat until the fish becomes a fairly fine paste.

Remove from the heat and add 5–6 dl (18 fl oz–1 pt or $2\frac{1}{4}$–$2\frac{5}{8}$ U.S. cups) oil, a little at a time, mixing continuously with a spatula. Adjust the consistency of the paste from time to time with 2–3 tbs boiling milk until a maximum of $2\frac{1}{2}$ dl (9 fl oz–$1\frac{1}{8}$ U.S. cups) milk has been absorbed.

When the Brandade mixture is finished it should be very white and have the consistency of mashed potato. Finally adjust the seasoning and arrange pyramid shape in a deep dish then decorate with small triangles of bread which have been freshly fried in clarified butter.

1806 Brandade de Morue à la Crème

Prepare the salt cod as in the preceding recipe replacing the oil and milk with $7\frac{1}{2}$ dl ($1\frac{1}{3}$ pt or $3\frac{1}{4}$ U.S. cups) very fresh cream which should be added a spoonful at a time.

1807 Brandade de Morue Truffée

Add 175 g (6 oz) chopped truffle to the Brandade prepared in the usual manner and dress pyramid shape in a deep dish; decorate with slices of truffle.

1808 Morue à la Crème

Poach the fish, drain, remove the skin and bones and flake the flesh. Place this into the required amount of Cream Sauce and allow to simmer very gently for 10 minutes. Serve in a deep dish.

1809 Morue à la Créole

Finely slice 200 g (7 oz) onion and cook gently without colour in a little butter. Spread this over the bottom of an oval earthenware dish and arrange 750 g (1 lb 10 oz) tomatoes prepared *à la Provençale* (4266) on top. Place the freshly cooked and flaked salt cod on top and cover completely with 5 sweet pimentoes which have been cut in half, emptied and grilled.

Sprinkle with a little lemon juice and 60 g (2 oz) brown butter; place in the oven for a few minutes and serve very hot.

1810 Morue aux Epinards

Place $1\frac{1}{2}$ dl (5 fl oz or $\frac{5}{8}$ U.S. cup) oil in a shallow pan and heat until lightly smoking, add 700 g ($1\frac{1}{2}$ lb) lightly blanched and roughly chopped spinach and mix over heat to remove excess moisture. Add half a clove of crushed garlic, 1 tbs chopped parsley, 6 fillets of anchovies cut in dice, $1\frac{1}{2}$ dl (5 fl oz or $\frac{5}{8}$ U.S. cup) Sauce Béchamel and the fish which has been freshly cooked and flaked.

Season with salt, pepper and nutmeg and mix carefully together. Place in a buttered earthenware dish and smooth dome shape; sprinkle with white breadcrumbs and a little oil and gratinate quickly under the salamander or in the top of a hot oven.

1811 Croquettes de Morue à l'Américaine—Fish Balls

See the Chapter on Hot Hors-d'oeuvre (1175).

1812 Morue à la Hollandaise

This is prepared in the same way as for Cabillaud à la Hollandaise.

1813 Morue à l'Indienne

Mix the flaked fish with 7 dl ($1\frac{1}{4}$ pt or 3 U.S. cups) Sauce Indienne; place in a deep dish and serve accompanied with plain boiled rice.

1814 Morue à la Lyonnaise
Slice 150 g (5 oz) onion and cook to a light colour in a little butter. Add 400 g (15 oz) potatoes which have been sliced and also sautéed in butter; the fish which has been freshly cooked and flaked; a little salt and pepper, and a pinch of coarsely chopped parsley. Toss over for a few minutes to reheat, adding 2 tbs vinegar at the last moment and serve in a deep dish.

1815 Morue à la Provençale
Place 1½ dl (5 fl oz or ⅝ U.S. cup) oil in a shallow pan, add 120 g (4 oz) chopped onion and 750 g (1 lb 10 oz) coarsely chopped flesh only of tomato; cook together for a few minutes then add a touch of crushed garlic, a pinch of coarsely chopped parsley, 50 g (2 oz) capers, 125 g (4½ oz) stoned black olives, the freshly poached and flaked fish and a little salt and pepper.

Allow the whole to cook gently together for 10 minutes then serve arranged in a deep dish.

1816 Soufflé de Morue
Finely pound 250 g (9 oz) freshly poached and flaked salt cod adding 1 dl (3½ fl oz or ½ U.S. cup) very thick hot Sauce Béchamel a little at a time. Work the paste very smooth with the pestle and season with salt, pepper and grated nutmeg.

Place the mixture in a pan, reheat, then remove from the heat, mix in 6 egg yolks and finally fold in 8 stiffly whipped egg whites.

Place the mixture in a soufflé mould and cook in the normal manner.

1817 Morue Valencia
Take a deep dish and place in alternate layers of rice cooked in fish stock; freshly poached and flaked salt cod; purée of tomatoes, and rings of onions, seasoned, floured and deep fried in oil. Finish the top with a layer of rice.

Cover the surface with 125 g (4½ oz) brown butter with the addition of 1 tbs fine white bread-crumbs and arrange quarters of hard-boiled eggs around the edge of the dish.

1818 Tourte or Vol-au-Vent de Morue Bénédictine
Fill a flan case or Vol-au-vent case with Brandade de Morue à la Crème, smooth dome shape and sprinkle the surface with chopped truffle.

1819 Vol-au-Vent de Morue
Finely shred 150 g (5 oz) onion and cook without colour in a little butter; add the freshly poached and flaked fish and mix with the required amount of Sauce Béchamel and 1 dl (3½ fl oz or ½ U.S. cup) cream.

Finally mix in 125 g (4½ oz) butter and 150 g (5 oz) fairly thick slices of truffle. Fill the Vol-au-vent case with the mixture and serve hot.

1820 MOSTELE

Mostele is a fish peculiar to the Mediterranean; it has a very delicate flesh and therefore cannot be transported any distance because of the risk of deterioration.

It is for this reason that it is found and eaten only in or near the area where it is caught. Suitable methods of cooking are *à la Meunière, à l'Anglaise* and *à la Richelieu.*

1821 MULET OR LOUBINE—GREY MULLET

Although this fish is not of the same quality as bass it may be used to replace it and, whether large or small, the methods of preparation are the same as for that fish.

1822 NONNATS

The true nature of this species of fish has not been defined with any degree of exactitude; some people consider it to be the fry of the Gouby, others that it is a fully grown fish. Cooks who are not always well versed in natural history, are quite content to prepare a superb deep fried dish from this species without being too concerned as to its origin. Nonnats are best prepared in the same way as Whitebait which they resemble closely.

1823 POUTINE

Poutine is a mixture of the fry of many different kinds of fish, the most common being those of sardines and anchovies.

In culinary terms Poutine is the equivalent of Nonnats, in the same way as Blanchaille is the equivalent of Whitebait.

RAIE—SKATE

For 10 persons allow 2 kg (4½ lb).

The most useful species for cooking are the common and thornback skate. In England, Belgium and Holland skate is sold already skinned and cleaned for cooking; if it has not been prepared it should be skinned, washed well and cut into portions on the bone.

1824 Raie au Beurre Noir or Raie au Beurre Noisette—Skate with Beurre Noir or Brown Butter
Poach the skate in water containing 12 g ($\frac{1}{2}$ oz) salt and 2 dl (7 fl oz or $\frac{7}{8}$ U.S. cup) vinegar per 1 litre ($1\frac{3}{4}$ pt or $4\frac{1}{2}$ U.S. cups) water. Drain well, place in a suitable dish making sure that the fish is quite dry. Sprinkle with parsley, a few drops of lemon juice, and finally coat with either Beurre Noir or with butter cooked to a light brown colour, using 200 g (7 oz) butter per 10 portions.

1825 Coquilles de Foies de Raie—Coquilles of Skate Livers
Poach the livers in Vinegar Court-bouillon, drain them, cut into small slices and fill into scollop shells which have been previously piped with a border of Pommes Duchesse mixture and coloured in the oven.

Cover the livers with a little Beurre à la Polonaise (252), add a few drops of lemon juice and sprinkle with chopped parsley.

1826 Croûtes aux Foie de Raie
See the Chapter on Hot Hors-d'oeuvre (1168).

1827 Fritot de Raie
Cut the wings of small skate into small slices and marinate for 3 hours with lemon juice, oil, thinly sliced onion rings, thyme, bayleaf, salt, pepper and parsley stalks.

When required, dip the pieces of skate into light frying batter and deep fry. Drain and arrange on a serviette on a dish with fried parsley on one side and the floured and deep fried onion rings from the marinade on the other.

1828 Raie au Gratin
If using wings from small skate, cook them from raw according to the recipe for a complete Gratin (2182). If the pieces are from a large skate they should be cooked first then finished in accordance with the formula for complete Gratin taking into account the shorter cooking time.

1829 ROUGETS—RED MULLET

For 10 persons allow 10 mullet of at least 125 g ($4\frac{1}{2}$ oz) each.

Most people like red mullet to be cooked without being gutted, apart from removing the gills; this is because there is no gall bladder in these fish. The finest are said to be those known as red rock mullet from the Mediterranean.

Whatever the final presentation, it is advisable to cook red mullets either by grilling or shallow frying them rather than by poaching.

1830 Rougets à la Bordelaise
Cut shallow incisions on both sides of the fish, season and shallow fry in clarified butter. Serve accompanied with Sauce Bordelaise or Sauce Bonnefoy.

1831 Rougets en Caisses
Grill or shallow fry the prepared red mullets in butter. Coat the bottoms of individual cartons made from oiled greaseproof paper, with 1 tbs Sauce Italienne; place a cooked red mullet in each and surround with some roughly chopped tomato flesh stewed in butter and some sliced cooked mushrooms; cover with a little more Sauce Italienne. Sprinkle with brown breadcrumbs and melted butter and place in the oven to gratinate.

1832 Rougets au Fenouil—Red Mullet with Fennel
Cut shallow incisions on both sides of the fish and marinate for 3 hours with salt, pepper, lemon juice, oil and a little chopped fennel.

Roughly chop 200 g (7 oz) raw pork fat with a good pinch of parsley and add it to the marinade; wrap each red mullet plus some of the marinating ingredients in a piece of oiled greaseproof paper and grill slowly and gently until cooked.

Serve as they are in the paper.

1833 Rougets Francillon
Cut shallow incisions on both sides of the fish and marinate with salt, pepper, lemon juice and oil for 20 minutes; grill in the usual manner.

Cut slices of bread to the size and shape of the fish, fry them in butter then spread with anchovy butter. Place a red mullet on each of these Croûtons, arrange on a dish and garnish with bouquets of fried parsley at each end and a border of straw potatoes on both sides.

Serve accompanied with 2 dl (7 fl oz or $\frac{7}{8}$ U.S. cup) Tomato Sauce finished with 100 g ($3\frac{1}{2}$ oz) butter and 40 g ($1\frac{1}{2}$ oz) Anchovy Butter.

1834 Rougets au Gratin
Place the fish in a buttered dish, surround with slices of raw mushrooms then proceed as for Merlans au Gratin.

1835 Rougets à la Livournaise
Arrange the fish in a buttered dish and cover with some roughly chopped flesh only of tomato stewed in butter, some chopped onion cooked in oil and a touch of crushed garlic.

Sprinkle with breadcrumbs and oil and gratinate in a hot oven. On removing from the oven, finish with a few drops of lemon juice and some chopped parsley.

1836 Filets de Rougets Maréchal
Remove the fillets from the fish, season, brush with melted butter then coat with white breadcrumbs mixed with some very finely chopped truffle. Carefully flatten with a palette knife and shallow fry in clarified butter.

1837 Rougets à la Marseillaise
Place 100 g (3½ oz) chopped onion cooked in 2 dl (7 fl oz or ⅞ U.S. cup) oil, in a shallow pan with 400 g (15 oz) quartered tomatoes, a touch of crushed garlic, a pinch of saffron, 10 g (⅓ oz) salt, a pinch of pepper and 4 dl (14 fl oz or 1¾ U.S. cups) fish stock.

Cut incisions on both sides of the red mullets and arrange them carefully in the pan with the prepared ingredients. Cover and cook quickly on a hot stove and when cooked, remove the fish and arrange them on slices of toasted French bread in a deep dish. Reduce the cooking liquid together with the garnish and pour it over the mullets.

1838 Mousselines de Rouget
Prepare a Mousseline forcemeat (288) using red mullet.

For the various preparations and cooking of Mousselines see (1563).

1839 Rougets à la Nantaise
Cut shallow incisions on both sides of the fish, season, brush with oil and grill in the usual manner.

Separately, reduce 1 dl (3½ fl oz or ½ U.S. cup) white wine and 20 g (⅔ oz) chopped shallots until almost dry; add 1 dl (3½ fl oz or ½ U.S. cup) Sauce Demi-glace, 125 g (4½ oz) butter, 2 tbs melted meat glaze and the crushed livers from the mullets; heat together without letting it boil. Ladle the sauce into a dish, arrange the grilled mullets on top and surround them with slices of fluted lemon.

1840 Rougets à la Niçoise
Grill the red mullets, arrange on a suitable dish and surround with a Niçoise garnish.

1841 Rougets en Papillote
Grill the red mullets in the usual way and for each fish, spread some fairly stiff Sauce Duxelles on a sheet of oiled greaseproof paper, cut as for a *Papillote*.

Place one of the fish on top, cover with a little more sauce, carefully fold the paper to close and pleat it round to seal.

Place on a flat tray in a moderate oven to swell up and colour the paper.

1842 Rougets à la Polonaise
Season the red mullets, flour them and shallow fry in clarified butter.

Separately, reduce 4 dl (14 fl oz or 1¾ U.S. cups) fish stock by three-quarters, remove from the stove and thicken at the last moment with 2 egg yolks and 4 dl (14 fl oz or 1¾ U.S. cups) double cream; season well.

Arrange the fish on a suitable dish, coat with the sauce and sprinkle the surface with white breadcrumbs fried golden brown in butter.

1843 Rougets à la Trouvillaise
Open the red mullets by cutting down the back and remove the backbones. Stuff with a good forcemeat and re-form the fish into their proper shape.

Arrange in a deep dish and poach with white wine and melted butter. When cooked, arrange on a suitable dish and surround with slices of lemon. Serve accompanied with Beurre Colbert.

1844 Filets de Rougets Villeroy
Remove and trim the fillets, place in a dish and marinate with oil, lemon juice, salt, pepper, parsley stalks, a bayleaf and a little finely chopped onion. Drain and dry the fillets, dip into Sauce Villeroy and allow to cool and set. Egg and breadcrumb and deep fry at the last moment.

Arrange on a serviette with bouquets of fried parsley and surround with slices of fluted lemon.

ROUGETS FROIDS—COLD RED MULLET

1845 Rougets à l'Orientale
See the Chapter on Cold Hors-d'oeuvre (1031).

1846 Mousse Froide de Rougets—Cold Mousse of Red Mullet
Prepare the Mousse as indicated for the Preparation of Cold Mousses (332) taking care to use the insides of the mullets in the preparation.

1847 SAINT-PIERRE—JOHN DORY

This fish is ugly and deformed in appearance but has a firm white flesh the texture of which is perfectly suited to the preparation of fish forcemeat. When they are very fresh, fillets of John Dory can equal the quality of small turbot and sole.

Nevertheless this fish is not used as frequently as it should be, possibly because its ugly appearance has an unfavourable effect upon gourmets, or perhaps its lack of use can be attributed to the fact that it is an unfashionable fish. The recipes for small turbot and for fillets of sole may be suitably applied to fillets of John Dory.

SARDINES AND ROYANS

Fresh sardines and Royans which are a type of large sardine, lend themselves to numerous preparations. Monsieur Caillat's book *150 Manières d'Accommoder les Sardines* is devoted solely to these fish and is recommended to anyone wishing to utilize them for their menus.

The following recipes have been selected from his work.

1848 Sardines à l'Antiboise
Remove the heads and tails of the sardines, flour, egg and breadcrumb and deep fry in hot oil. Arrange in a circle on a round dish with Tomates à la Provençale in the centre.

1849 Sardines à la Basque
Remove the heads and tails of the sardines, flour, egg and breadcrumb and deep fry in hot oil. Arrange in a circle on a round dish and place in the centre some Sauce Béarnaise containing a few whole capers.

1850 Sardines Bonne-Femme
Finely slice 250 g (9 oz) onion and blanch for a few minutes in boiling water. Drain well and cook gently to a golden colour in a little oil. Moisten with $1\frac{1}{2}$ dl (5 fl oz or $\frac{5}{8}$ U.S. cup) white wine and reduce by two-thirds then add 500 g (1 lb 2 oz) roughly chopped flesh only of tomato which has been sautéed in a little oil. Season well and cook together gently.

Place the finished sauce in a gratin dish and arrange 12 nice cleaned sardines on top; sprinkle with white breadcrumbs mixed with a few crushed fennel seeds and some olive oil and gratinate in a hot oven.

1851 Coulibiac de Sardines
This is prepared in the same way as Coulibiac de Saumon but using sardines, replacing the Kache of Semolina with well drained plain boiled rice and using Poutargue (1023) instead of Vésiga.

1852 Sardines à la Courtisane
Remove the heads and fins from the sardines; carefully cut open along the backs and completely remove the bones from the insides. Coat the inside of the fillets with fish forcemeat mixed with a little dry Duxelles then close up to reform the fish. Season and shallow poach with white wine.

When cooked, drain and place each sardine on a Croûton of fried bread of the same shape as the fish. Arrange on a suitable dish, coat with reduced fish Velouté mixed with a quarter its volume of spinach purée and glaze quickly under the salamander. Finally surround with small potato Croquettes.

1853 Dartois de Sardines
This is prepared in the same way as Dartois aux Filets de Sole (1172) or Dartois aux Anchois (1171).

1854 Sardines à la Havraise
Remove the heads and fins from the sardines, carefully cut open along the backs and completely remove the bones from the insides. Coat the insides of the fillets with fish forcemeat and reform the fish. Shallow poach in white wine and when cooked, drain well.

Arrange on a dish, coat with Sauce Vin Blanc and decorate with a little piped fish glaze. Finally, surround with large, breadcrumbed and deep fried mussels.

1855 Sardines à la Hyéroise
Cook 500 g (1 lb 2 oz) shredded white of leek in a little butter without colour and moisten with 2 dl (7 fl oz or $\frac{7}{8}$ U.S. cup) each of white wine and mushroom cooking liquor. Simmer gently until the leeks are cooked, then use this to poach 12 nice sardines prepared with fish forcemeat as in the preceding recipe.

When cooked, drain well and place each sardine on a Croûton of bread the same shape as the fish and fried in butter. Arrange on a suitable dish.

Reduce the cooking liquid and thicken and enrich it with 3 egg yolks and a little butter; add a touch of Cayenne, a little chopped parsley and coat the sardines with the finished sauce.

1856 Sardines à la Menagère
Prepare and stuff 12 sardines with fish forcemeat as for Sardines à la Havraise; sprinkle a little finely chopped shallot in a buttered gratin dish and arrange the sardines on top. Surround with 250 g (9 oz) sliced mushrooms, moisten with a little white wine, sprinkle with melted butter and poach in a medium oven. When cooked, add a little lemon juice, sprinkle with chopped parsley, chervil and tarragon, and serve.

1857 Sardines à la Niçoise
Carefully fillet 12 sardines and coat each with a layer of very thick cold Duxelles (312), roll up the fillets in the form of *Paupiettes* and wrap them in pairs in the flowers of vegetable marrow. Place in a buttered shallow pan, season and shallow poach with a little fish stock.

When cooked, arrange in a deep dish. Lightly thicken the cooking liquid with Beurre Manié and add a little purée of anchovy; pour this sauce over the sardines and serve.

1858 Sardines à la Pisane
Carefully fillet 12 sardines and coat each with a layer of fish forcemeat. Roll up the fillets in the form of *Paupiettes* and shallow poach with a little white wine and mushroom cooking liquor.

When cooked, drain them well and place in the centre of a suitable dish; surround with a border of cooked chopped spinach mixed with a little crushed garlic and purée of anchovy and reheated in butter. To the cooking liquid add a little roughly chopped tomato flesh cooked in butter and sufficient Sauce Béchamel to thicken it. Place a border of hard-boiled quarters of egg around the spinach and cover the whole with the prepared sauce. Sprinkle with grated Parmesan and gratinate in a very hot oven.

1859 Sardines à la Sicilienne
Prepare the sardines as for Merlans Colbert and deep fry them in very hot oil. Arrange each sardine on a slice of peeled lemon and surround with Beurre Noisette containing a few capers, chopped fillets of anchovy and chopped hard-boiled eggs.

1860 Sardines Saint-Honorat
Prepare the sardines as for Merlan Colbert and deep fry them in very hot oil. Arrange overlapping in a circle on a suitable dish, fill the centre with roughly chopped tomato flesh cooked in butter and surround the sardines with a *cordon* of Sauce Paloise.

1861 Sardines à la Toulonnaise
Remove the heads from the sardines, carefully cut open along the back and completely remove the bones from the insides. Coat the insides of the fish with whiting and cream forcemeat and re-form the fish. Shallow poach the sardines in a little fish stock and when cooked, drain them, arrange in a circle on a suitable dish and fill the centre pyramid shape with poached and bearded mussels. Coat with a well finished Fish Velouté.

1862 Sardines à la Vivandière
Fillet the sardines and coat each fillet with a layer of very thick Duxelles. Roll up in the form of *Paupiettes* and place each *Paupiette* in the centre of a section of blanched cucumber from which the seeds have been removed. The sections of cucumber should be the same height as the *Paupiettes* and the centre holes just large enough for them to be pushed in.

Arrange in a buttered shallow pan and moisten with a little mushroom cooking liquor. Cook in a moderate oven taking care to baste them frequently with the liquid.

When cooked, drain well and arrange the *Paupiettes* on a suitable dish. Coat with a thin Tomato Sauce and sprinkle with chopped tarragon and chervil.

SOLES ET FILETS DE SOLE— SOLE AND FILLETS OF SOLE

WHOLE SOLE

It is recommended that the fins of whole sole be trimmed right up to the edges of the fillets when they are required for covering with a sauce. The black skin only should be removed and the scales of the white skin carefully removed.

Although this rather severe trimming tends to spoil the appearance of the fish there is a gain in ease of service and in the amount of garnish and sauce required for presentation.

To assist in the poaching of whole sole the fillets of the skinned side should be partially detached from the bone along the centre; this allows the heat to reach the centre of the fish more quickly. The partially opened side of the sole should always be placed downwards in the dish for cooking.

The trimmings from the preparation of the sole are always used in the preparation of the fish stock.

1863 Sole Alice
This preparation of sole is usually completed at the table by the head waiter.

Have ready a good well flavoured fish stock kept as white as possible. Trim the sole and place it in a buttered fireproof dish, add a little of the fish stock and shallow poach in a moderate oven.

When cooked, send the dish to the dining-room with a plate on which is placed separately, a little finely chopped onion, a little powdered thyme, 3 finely crushed rusks and 6 raw oysters.

In the dining-room the waiter places the dish on a chafing lamp, takes out the sole, removes the fillets and places them between two plates to keep warm. The onion is added to the cooking liquid in the dish and is cooked for a few minutes; the thyme is then added with enough of the crushed rusk to thicken the liquid. At the last minute the oysters are added together with 30 g (1 oz) butter in small pieces. When the oysters have become firm the waiter replaces the fillets of sole in the dish and well bastes them with the sauce; it is then served very hot.

1864 Sole d'Antin
This is prepared in the same way as Sole Bonne Femme adding to the sauce one-fifth its volume of fresh tomatoes which have been peeled, depipped, roughly chopped and lightly cooked in butter.

1865 Sole à l'Amiral
Prepare the sole and place in a buttered dish which has been sprinkled with a little finely chopped onion. Moisten with $\frac{1}{2}$ dl (2 fl oz or $\frac{1}{4}$ U.S. cup) white wine, the same amount of mushroom cooking liquor and fish stock, and $\frac{1}{2}$ tbs butter; shallow poach in a moderate oven.

Have ready a White Wine Sauce finished with 150 g (5 oz) Crayfish Butter and finally add the well-reduced cooking liquor from the fish. Place the sole on a suitable dish and garnish with 4 cooked crayfish tails and 2 cooked mushrooms; coat the whole with the sauce and decorate with 4 slices of truffle. At each end of the dish place 4 mussels and 4 oysters prepared *à la Villeroy*.

1866 Sole à l'Arlésienne
Prepare the sole and shallow poach in a buttered dish with a little fish stock.

Separately, cook 1 tbs finely chopped onion in a little butter, add the roughly chopped flesh of 2 tomatoes, a touch of crushed garlic, and a pinch of roughly chopped parsley; cover with a lid and cook gently.

Reduce the cooking liquid from the sole and add to the tomatoes with 12 pieces of young marrow which have been trimmed to the size of olives and cooked in butter. Place the sole on a suitable dish, cover with the sauce and garnish and place a bouquet of onion rings, floured and deep fried in oil, at each end of the dish.

1867 Sole Bedfort
Prepare, season and grill the sole. Place a layer of Maître d'Hôtel Butter mixed with a little meat glaze on a dish and arrange the sole on top. Garnish round the sides with 4 round thick Croûtons of bread fried in butter and then emptied like Bouchées, two of them filled with sliced mushrooms and truffles mixed with a little thick Sauce Demi-glace and the other two with roughly chopped spinach, coated with Sauce Mornay and gratinated.

1868 Sole Bercy
This is prepared in the same way as Filets de Sole Bercy (1933).

1869 Sole Bonne-Femme
Prepare the sole; butter a dish and sprinkle the bottom with 50 g (2 oz) sliced mushrooms, 1 tbs finely chopped shallot and a pinch of chopped parsley. Place the sole on top, add 1 dl ($3\frac{1}{2}$ fl oz or $\frac{1}{2}$ U.S. cup) white wine, the same amount of thin fish Velouté and shallow poach in a moderate oven.

When the sole is cooked, drain off the cooking liquid, reduce and enrich and thicken it with 150 g (5 oz) butter. Pour the sauce over the sole and glaze quickly under the salamander.

Note: In restaurants where there is a frequent demand for a large number of à la Carte orders both for lunch and dinner service, the method is as follows: The Fish cook keeps ready for use

1) a reserve of sliced raw mushrooms cooked with butter, chopped shallot, chopped Fines Herbes, salt, pepper and lemon juice, and
2) a fish sauce already thickened with egg yolks and enriched with butter.

In this way the fish cook has only to cook the fish ordered, mix together sufficient of the cooked mushrooms and sauce and coat and glaze the fish.

This method for the preparation of Sole Bonne Femme is equally suitable for turbot, brill, whiting and Mostele etc.

1870 Sole au Chambertin
Prepare the sole and shallow poach in a well buttered dish with 2 dl (7 fl oz or $\frac{7}{8}$ U.S. cup) Chambertin wine.

When cooked, place on a suitable dish, reduce the cooking liquid by half and add a little milled pepper and a few drops of lemon juice. Lightly thicken with a little Beurre Manié and finish with 50 g (2 oz) butter.

Coat the sole with the sauce and glaze quickly. Place at each end of the dish a bouquet of thin strips of fillets of sole, seasoned and floured, then fried in clarified butter at the last moment so that they are served whilst still crisp.

1871 Sole au Champagne
Prepare the sole and shallow poach in a buttered dish with 2 dl (7 fl oz or $\frac{7}{8}$ U.S. cup) Champagne.

When cooked, place on a suitable dish, reduce the cooking liquid by half, thicken with 1 dl ($3\frac{1}{2}$ fl oz or $\frac{1}{2}$ U.S. cup) of good Fish Velouté and finish with 30 g (1 oz) butter.

Coat the sole with the sauce and quickly glaze; place a bouquet of thin strips of fillets of sole prepared as for Sole au Chambertin at both ends of the dish.

1872 Sole Cléopâtre
Bone out the sole and stuff it with a whiting and cream forcemeat mixed with chopped truffle. Reform the sole and shallow poach in a buttered dish

with 1 dl (3½ fl oz or ½ U.S. cup) white wine, the same amount of mushroom cooking liquor and 20 g (⅔ oz) butter.

When cooked, place on a suitable dish; reduce the cooking liquid and add to the required amount of Sauce Vin Blanc together with 25 g (1 oz) fine Julienne of truffle. Coat the sole with the sauce and glaze quickly.

1873 Sole Colbert

Prepare the sole in the usual manner but do not trim closer than the fins. Cutting from the skinned side, lay back the two top fillets almost to the edge of the fish and break the centre bone in two or three places so as to facilitate its removal when cooked.

Pass the sole through milk, then flour, egg and breadcrumb. Turn back the two fillets from the centre and pat and shape with the flat of a knife to ensure that the breadcrumbs adhere properly. Deep fry then remove the centre bone; place on a hot dish and fill the cavity with Maître d'Hôtel Butter.

1874 Sole Coquelin

Prepare the sole and shallow poach in a buttered dish with 1 dl (3½ fl oz or ½ U.S. cup) white wine and the same amount of fish stock; when cooked place on a suitable dish and surround with slices of freshly cooked boiled potatoes. Reduce the cooking liquid by two-thirds and thicken and enrich it with 150 g (5 oz) butter; coat the sole and glaze quickly.

1875 Sole Cubat

Prepare the sole and shallow poach in a buttered dish with 1 dl (3½ fl oz or ½ U.S. cup) mushroom cooking liquor and 15 g (½ oz) butter.

Place a bed of purée of mushrooms in the bottom of a suitable dish, lay the well-drained sole on top and arrange 6 nice slices of truffle along the centre of the fish. Coat with Sauce Mornay and glaze quickly.

1876 Sole Daumont

Bone out the sole and stuff it with a whiting and cream forcemeat finished with Crayfish Butter. Reform the sole and shallow poach in 1 dl (3½ fl oz or ½ U.S. cup) white wine, the same amount of mushroom cooking liquor and 15 g (½ oz) butter.

When cooked, drain, place on a suitable dish, surround with a Daumont garnish and coat the whole with Sauce Nantua.

1877 Sole Deauvillaise

Prepare and shallow poach the sole in a buttered dish with 100 g (3½ oz) finely sliced onion stewed without colour in butter; 1½ dl (5 fl oz or ⅝ U.S. cup) cream, and ½ tbs of butter. When cooked, drain, place in a suitable dish and keep warm.

Pass the cream and onion through a fine sieve and thicken and enrich the resultant cullis with 40 g (1½ oz) butter. Coat the sole with the sauce and surround it with small lightly baked diamonds of puff pastry.

1878 Sole à la Dieppoise

Prepare the sole and shallow poach in a buttered dish with 1 dl (3½ fl oz or ½ U.S. cup) white wine and the same amount of mussel cooking liquor. When cooked, drain and place in a suitable dish, surround with a Dieppoise garnish and coat the whole with Sauce Vin Blanc containing the reduced cooking liquid from the sole.

1879 Sole Diplomate

Prepare and shallow poach the sole in a buttered dish with a little clear fish stock. When cooked, drain, place on a suitable dish and coat with Sauce Diplomate. Finish by placing 6 nice slices of truffle, glazed with a little pale meat glaze, in a line down the centre of the sole.

1880 Sole Dorée

Prepare the sole, pass through flour and shallow fry in clarified butter. Serve as it is on a suitable dish garnished with slices of carefully peeled lemon. (See method for the cooking of fish *à la Meunière* at the beginning of this Chapter.)

1881 Sole Dugléré

Prepare the sole and place in a buttered dish which has been sprinkled with 20 g (⅔ oz) each of finely chopped onion and shallot, 120 g (4 oz) roughly chopped flesh only of tomato, a little roughly chopped parsley and a little salt and pepper. Add 1 dl (3½ fl oz or ½ U.S. cup) white wine and shallow poach in the oven.

Drain off the cooking liquid and reduce by half; thicken with ½ dl (2 fl oz or ¼ U.S. cup) Fish Velouté and finish the sauce with 30 g (1 oz) butter and a few drops of lemon juice. Coat the fish with the sauce.

1882 Sole à l'Espagnole

Prepare the sole, season, flour and shallow fry *à la Meunière* in oil. Skin, depip and roughly chop the flesh of 250 g (9 oz) tomatoes; cook in a little oil and spread on the bottom of a suitable dish. Place the cooked sole on top and garnish, with bouquets of Julienne of pimento fried in oil at each end, and rings of onion, seasoned, floured and deep fried in oil, at each side.

1883 Sole à la Fermière
Prepare in the same way as for Sole à la Menagère (1895) but before coating the sole with the sauce, surround with a garnish of sliced mushrooms sautéed in butter.

1884 Sole à la Florentine
Prepare and shallow poach the sole in a buttered dish with a little fish stock and butter.

In a suitable dish place a layer of blanched, roughly chopped leaf spinach stewed in butter. Drain the cooked sole and place it on top; coat with Sauce Mornay, sprinkle with grated cheese and gratinate quickly in a very hot oven or under the salamander.

1885 Sole au Gratin
Prepare the sole, partly detach the fillets from the bones on the skinned side and slip half a tablespoon of butter under each fillet.

Coat the bottom of a buttered gratin dish with a layer of Sauce Gratin and place the sole on top; surround with a border of overlapping slices of raw mushroom; place 3 cooked mushrooms on top of the sole, add $\frac{1}{2}$ dl (2 fl oz or $\frac{1}{4}$ U.S. cup) white wine and cover the whole with Sauce Gratin. Sprinkle with white breadcrumbs and melted butter and gratinate in the oven at a fairly moderate temperature so as to allow the sauce to reduce, the sole to cook and the formation of the gratinated crust, to take place all at the same time.

When removing the sole from the oven, sprinkle with a few drops of lemon juice and a little chopped parsley.

1886 Sole Grillée—Grilled Sole
Prepare the sole and cut shallow incisions trellis-fashion on both sides, brush with oil and grill fairly slowly.

Place on a hot dish and garnish with slices of lemon and either picked or fried parsley.

1887 Sole Grillée aux Huîtres à l'Américaine—Grilled Sole with Oysters à l'Américaine
Prepare and grill the sole. Place on a suitable hot dish and surround at the last moment with 6 oysters which have been poached in a little boiling Derby Sauce. Immediately cover the sole with some very hot butter-fried breadcrumbs mixed with a little chopped parsley.

Notes:
1) Alternatively, the sole may be poached in a very little lemon juice and butter and then finished as in the recipe. In this case the word *Grillée* should be omitted.
2) Fillets of sole may also be prepared in this manner.

1888 Sole à la Hollandaise
Prepare the sole, then break the centre bone by folding the fish firmly in several places.

Place in a deep dish and cover with lightly salted cold water; bring to the boil, pull to one side of the stove and allow to poach, covered, for 10 minutes.

When ready, drain and serve on a serviette surrounded with very green parsley. Serve separately a dish of freshly cooked plain boiled potatoes and a sauceboat of Melted Butter.

1889 Sole à l'Hôtelière
Prepare, season and shallow fry the sole *à la Meunière*.

Spread 50 g (2 oz) Maître d'Hôtel Butter containing $\frac{1}{2}$ tbs well seasoned dry Duxelles on a suitable dish, place the cooked sole on top and surround with a border of slices of lemon.

1890 Sole Jules Janin
Prepare the sole and shallow poach in a buttered dish with 2 dl (7 fl oz or $\frac{7}{8}$ U.S. cup) Rhine wine and 2 tbs of Mirepoix Bordelaise.

When cooked, drain well, turn over and fill the partly opened cavity of the sole with a little very well reduced Sauce Duxelles containing a little chopped truffle. Place the sole, filled side down on a suitable dish and surround with 8 large poached and bearded mussels. Place 4 slices of truffle at the side and 4 cooked crayfish tails at each end.

Coat the sole and the garnish with Sauce Tortue containing the reduced cooking liquid and the Mirepoix and finished with 30 g (1 oz) Beurre d'Ecrevisse.

Note: This recipe was dedicated by Urbain Dubois in 1855 to Jules Janin the celebrated critic of the journal *Debats* and the author of the superb preface which every cook knows, to the 2nd edition of Carême's *Cuisinier Parisien*. Although since that time the dish has been modified and remodified, the basic principle has been preserved in the above recipe.

1891 Sole Jouffroy
Prepare the sole and shallow poach in a buttered dish with 2 dl (7 fl oz or $\frac{7}{8}$ U.S. cup) Pouilly wine and a little butter.

When cooked, drain and place in a suitable dish, surround with slices of cooked mushrooms and cover with a Sauce Vin Blanc containing the reduced cooking liquid from the sole, enriched with butter.

Glaze quickly under the salamander or in a very hot oven, then place around the sole 4 small dainty Bouchées filled with buttered asparagus tips with a slice of truffle on top.

1892 Sole Lutèce

Prepare, season and shallow fry the sole *à la Meunière*.

Cover the bottom of a suitable dish with leaf spinach cooked and sautéed with a little brown butter and place the cooked sole on top. Place a few rings of onion mixed with slices of artichoke bottoms and sautéed in butter on the fish, and surround with a border of slices of plain boiled potatoes, fried to a golden brown in butter.

At the last moment, cover with 40 g (1½ oz) Beurre Noisette.

1893 Sole Marchand de Vins

Prepare the sole and slip ½ tbs butter under each of the partially detached fillets.

Sprinkle a buttered dish with finely chopped shallots, place the sole on top and shallow poach with 1 dl (3½ fl oz or ½ U.S. cup) good red wine and a little seasoning.

When cooked, drain and place the sole in a suitable dish, reduce the cooking liquid by one-third and add ½ tbs fish glaze, 30 g (1 oz) butter, a pinch of chopped parsley and a few drops of lemon juice.

Pour the finished sauce over the sole.

1894 Sole à la Marinière

Prepare the sole and shallow poach in a buttered dish with 1 dl (3½ fl oz or ½ U.S. cup) fish stock and the same amount of mussel cooking liquor.

When cooked, drain the sole and place in a suitable dish, reduce the cooking liquid by one-third surround with small cooked mussels and shelled prawns. Coat the sole and garnish with Sauce Marinière (129).

1895 Sole à la Menagère

Prepare the sole; butter a dish and sprinkle the bottom with a few slices of carrot, onion and celery which have been lightly cooked in butter with a pinch of pulverized thyme and bayleaf. Place the sole on top and shallow poach with 1 dl (3½ fl oz or ½ U.S. cup) red wine.

When cooked, drain and clear the fish of the flavourings and place it in the serving dish. Pass the cooking liquid through a strainer into a pan and reduce by one-third; thicken with a little Beurre Manié, add 30 g (1 oz) butter and pour this sauce over the sole.

1896 Sole à la Meunière

Prepare the sole and cook as described in the cooking of fish *à la Meunière* at the beginning of this Chapter.

1897 Sole Meunière aux Aubergines

Prepare and cook the sole *à la Meunière* and place in a suitable dish.

Surround with a border of eggplant, cut into 8 mm (¼ in) thick rings, seasoned, floured and fried in clarified butter, but cooked at the last moment so as to remain crisp; they tend to become soft if left even for a short time.

Sprinkle the sole and garnish with chopped parsley and cover with Beurre Noisette.

1898 Sole Meunière aux Cèpes

Prepare and cook the sole *à la Meunière*; place in a suitable dish and at the last moment surround with a garnish of sliced flap mushrooms (Cèpes) which have been fried in butter keeping them slightly crisp and brown. Sprinkle with chopped parsley and cover with Beurre Noisette.

1899 Sole Meunière aux Champignons

Prepare and cook the sole *à la Meunière* and place in a suitable dish.

Arrange thick slices of mushrooms sautéed in butter on top, sprinkle with chopped parsley and cover with Beurre Noisette at the last moment.

1900 Sole Meunière aux Concombres, also known as Sole à la Doria

Prepared and cook the sole *à la Meunière* and place in a suitable dish. Sprinkle with chopped parsley and cover with Beurre Noisette.

At each end of the fish place a bouquet of pieces of cucumber which have been trimmed to the shape of olives and cooked in butter with a little salt and a touch of sugar.

1901 Sole Meunière aux Morilles

Prepare and cook the sole *à la Meunière* and place in a suitable dish.

Surround with very fresh morels sautéed in butter at the last moment; sprinkle with chopped parsley and cover with Beurre Noisette.

1902 Sole Meunière à la Provençale

Prepare and cook the sole *à la Meunière* and place in a suitable dish.

Place slices of tomato sautéed in butter on top together with fillets of anchovy arranged trellis-fashion, and stoned olives. Sprinkle with chopped parsley and cover with Beurre Noisette.

1903 Sole Meunière aux Raisins

Prepare and cook the sole *à la Meunière* and place in a suitable dish.

Sprinkle with chopped parsley, cover with Beurre Noisette and surround with peeled, depipped and well chilled Muscatel grapes.

1904 Sole Meunière à l'Orange
Prepare and cook the sole *à la Meunière* and place in a suitable dish. Arrange a line of slices of peeled orange or orange segments on top and cover with Beurre Noisette.

1905 Sole Montgolfier
Prepare the sole and shallow poach in a dish with $\frac{1}{2}$ dl (2 fl oz or $\frac{1}{4}$ U.S. cup) white wine and the same amount of mushroom cooking liquor.

When cooked, drain and place the sole in a suitable dish; reduce the cooking liquid and add it to a prepared Sauce Vin Blanc together with 1 tbs each of fine Julienne of crayfish, cooked mushroom, and truffle.

Coat the sole with the sauce and surround with lightly baked palm-leaf shapes of puff pastry.

1906 Sole Montreuil
Prepare the sole and shallow poach in a well buttered dish with $\frac{1}{2}$ dl (2 fl oz or $\frac{1}{4}$ U.S. cup) white wine and the same amount of fish stock.

When cooked, drain, place the sole in a suitable dish and surround with balls of potato the size of walnuts cooked in salt water. Cover the sole with Sauce Vin Blanc to which has been added the well reduced cooking liquid from the fish and coat the garnish of potatoes with Sauce Crevettes.

1907 Sole Mornay
Prepare and shallow poach the sole in a well buttered dish with 1 dl ($3\frac{1}{2}$ fl oz or $\frac{1}{2}$ U.S. cup) fish stock and 50 g (2 oz) butter.

When cooked, drain and place the sole in a suitable dish, the bottom of which has been coated with a little Sauce Mornay. Cover with more of the same sauce, sprinkle with grated Parmesan and Gruyère cheese and gratinate under the salamander or in a very hot oven.

1908 Sole Mornay 'des Provençaux'
This dish used to be served at the famous restaurant of the 'Frères Provençaux' and was prepared in the following manner:

Proceed as for Sole Mornay but coat the sole with Sauce Vin Blanc instead of Sauce Mornay, sprinkle well with grated cheese and gratinate.

1909 Sole Murat
Shallow fry separately in butter, 100 g ($3\frac{1}{2}$ oz) diced potatoes and 2 diced raw artichoke bottoms; when cooked, drain them well and mix together.

Prepare and cook the sole *à la Meunière*, place in a suitable dish surround it with the prepared garnish and place on top 5 slices of tomato cut 1 cm ($\frac{2}{5}$ in) thick, seasoned, floured and shallow fried in very hot oil.

Sprinkle the sole with a few drops of melted pale meat glaze, a few drops of lemon juice, a pinch of roughly chopped parsley, and cover the whole with Beurre Noisette; serve immediately.

1910 Sole à la Niçoise
Prepare the sole, grill in the usual manner and place in a suitable dish. Surround with a Niçoise garnish for fish (430) arranged in bouquets; place the peeled lemon slices on the fish and serve accompanied with Beurre d'Anchois.

1911 Sole Nantua
Prepare and shallow poach the sole in a buttered dish with $\frac{1}{2}$ dl (2 fl oz or $\frac{1}{4}$ U.S. cup) fish stock and the same amount of mushroom cooking liquor.

When cooked, drain and place the sole in a suitable dish; surround it with 12 cooked, shelled crayfish tails, and coat with Sauce Nantua containing the reduced cooking liquid from the fish.

Place a line of overlapping slices of very black truffle down the centre of the sole.

1912 Sole à la Normande
Prepare and shallow poach the sole in a buttered dish with $\frac{1}{2}$ dl (2 fl oz or $\frac{1}{4}$ U.S. cup) fish stock and the same amount of mushroom cooking liquid.

When cooked, drain and place the sole in a suitable dish; surround with shelled prawns and poached and bearded mussels. In a line along the centre of the fish place 4 poached oysters alternating with 4 nice turned mushrooms. Place the dish in the oven for a few minutes to express any surplus liquid and drain this away. Coat the sole and the garnish with Sauce Normande and decorate with a garland of pale meat glaze using a paper cornet.

Complete the dish by garnishing with 6 slices of truffle, 3 on each side of the central garnish and each alternating with a small diamond-shaped Croûton of bread fried in clarified butter. Around the side of the dish place 4 gudgeons prepared *en Manchon* (1646) and 4 medium-sized crayfish, trussed and cooked in Court-bouillon.

Note: The use of truffle is optional.

1913 Sole à la Parisienne
Prepare and shallow poach the sole in $\frac{1}{2}$ dl (2 fl oz or $\frac{1}{4}$ U.S. cup) fish stock and the same amount of mushroom cooking liquor.

When cooked, drain and place the sole in a suitable dish and coat with Sauce Vin Blanc to which has been added the reduced cooking liquid from the fish.

Arrange a line of 6 slices of truffle down the

centre of the fish alternating with 5 round slices of very white cooked mushroom. Place 4 medium-sized crayfish, trussed and cooked in a Court-bouillon, around the sole.

1914 Sole sur le Plat

Prepare the sole, partially detaching the 2 fillets from the centre bone on the skinned side; slip ½ tbs butter under each fillet and turn the fish over on to a well buttered dish.

Moisten with 1 dl (3½ fl oz or ½ U.S. cup) fish stock and a few drops of lemon juice and cook in the oven. Baste frequently with the liquid so that when the sole is cooked, the cooking liquid has been reduced to a syrup and covers the surface of the sole with a translucent, glossy coating.

Note:

1) By replacing the fish stock with a good white or red wine and adding a little melted pale meat glaze, an excellent series of other dishes may be obtained. For example, Sole sur le Plat au Champagne, au Chablis, au Chambertin etc.
2) For quick service in restaurants, the sole is shallow poached, placed in a dish and coated with a previously prepared fish sauce enriched with butter and egg yolks.

1915 Sole à la Portugaise

Prepare and shallow poach the sole in a buttered dish with ½ dl (2 fl oz or ¼ U.S. cup) white wine and the same amount of fish stock.

When cooked, drain and place in a suitable dish; surround with 150 g (5 oz) roughly chopped flesh only of tomato which has been stewed in a little butter with 1 tbs finely chopped onion, 30 g (1 oz) sliced mushrooms, and a good pinch of roughly chopped parsley.

Coat the sole only with a well buttered Sauce Vin Blanc, glaze quickly in a very hot oven or under the salamander and finally sprinkle a little chopped parsley on the tomatoes.

1916 Sole à la Provençale

Prepare and shallow poach the sole in a buttered dish with 1 dl (3½ fl oz or ½ U.S. cup) fish stock, 2 tbs oil and a touch of crushed garlic.

When cooked, drain and place the sole in a suitable dish, surround with Tomatoes à la Provençale and coat with Sauce à la Provençale to which has been added the reducing cooking liquid from the fish. Finally sprinkle lightly with coarsely chopped parsley.

1917 Sole Régence

Prepare and shallow poach the sole in a buttered dish with 1 dl (3½ fl oz or ½ U.S. cup) Chablis wine and 25 g (1 oz) butter.

When cooked, drain and place in a suitable dish, surround with a Régence garnish for fish (449) and coat with Sauce Régence for fish to which has been added the reducing cooking liquid from the sole.

1918 Sole Richelieu

Prepare the sole as for Sole Colbert but shallow fry it in clarified butter. Remove the bones from the centre and place the sole in a suitable dish; fill the cavity with Maître d'Hôtel Butter and arrange a line of nice slices of truffle which have been coated with pale meat glaze, on top.

Note: This dish was created by Mons. Martin at the Restaurant Français at Nice in 1860. It was originally called *à la Colbert* but later Mons. Escoffier renamed it Sole à la Richelieu so as to establish the justified difference between the two, the designation *à la Colbert* having already been defined and in use for a long time previously.

1919 Sole à la Rochelaise

Prepare and shallow poach the sole in a well buttered dish with 1 dl (3½ fl oz or ½ U.S. cup) red wine, the same amount of fish stock and 30 g (1 oz) finely chopped onion, previously cooked in a little butter.

When cooked, drain and place the sole in a suitable dish; surround with 2 poached soft herring roes, 4 poached and bearded oysters and 4 poached and bearded mussels.

Reduce the cooking liquid by two-thirds, pass through a fine strainer and add ½ dl (2 fl oz or ¼ U.S. cup) Sauce Demi-glace and 30 g (1 oz) butter. Coat the sole and the garnish with this sauce.

1920 Sole à la Rouennaise

Prepare and shallow poach the sole in a buttered dish with 1 dl (3½ fl oz or ½ U.S. cup) red wine, 20 g (⅔ oz) finely chopped shallot and 20 g (⅔ oz) butter.

When cooked, drain and place the sole in a suitable dish; surround it with poached and bearded mussels and oysters, shelled prawns and small cooked mushrooms.

Pass the cooking liquid through a fine strainer and reduce by half; add ½ dl (2 fl oz or ¼ U.S. cup) Sauce Demi-glace and a little butter and coat the sole and garnish with the sauce.

Finish by surrounding the sole with 4 small smelts, the heads removed, then shallow fried *à la Meunière*.

1921 Sole à la Royale

Prepare and shallow poach the sole in a well buttered dish with 1 dl (3½ fl oz or ½ U.S. cup) fish stock.

When cooked, drain and place the sole in a suitable dish; arrange on top 4 small cooked mushrooms, 4 small Quenelles of fish forcemeat, 4 crayfish tails and 4 slices of truffle.

Surround the sole with medium-sized balls of plain boiled potatoes and coat the whole with Sauce Normande.

1922 Sole à la Russe

Place 8 very thin slices of grooved carrot and a small onion cut in very thin rings, with a little butter in a pan; cook gently for a few minutes then add 1 dl (3½ fl oz or ½ U.S. cup) water, a few very small sprigs of parsley, 25 g (1 oz) butter, and cook together gently.

Place this in a deep fireproof porcelain dish and place the prepared sole on top. Cook gently on the stove, basting frequently with the liquid which should be reduced by half by the time the sole is cooked. At this moment add 40 g (1½ oz) butter and a few drops of lemon juice and serve the sole in the dish as it is.

Notes:

1) If a porcelain dish is not available, use any other suitable deep dish and when cooked, transfer the fish to a service dish then cover with the sauce.
2) Sole à la Russe is really nothing more than a sole cooked and served in a Court-bouillon which has been reduced and thickened and enriched with butter.

1923 Sole Saint-Germain

Prepare the sole, season, pass through melted butter and coat with fine white breadcrumbs. Pat and shape it with the flat of a knife to make sure that the breadcrumbs adhere properly and mark it trellis-fashion with the back of the knife. Sprinkle with melted butter and place to grill gently under the salamander.

Place on a hot dish when ready and surround with potatoes trimmed olive shape and shallow fried in butter to a golden brown.

Serve accompanied with Sauce Béarnaise.

1924 Sole Saint-Malo

This is prepared in the same way as Turbotin Saint-Malo (2080).

1925 Sole au Vin Blanc

Prepare the sole and slip ½ tbs butter under each of the partially detached fillets on the skinned side.

Place skin side up on a little finely shredded onion in a buttered dish; moisten with ½ dl (2 fl oz or ¼ U.S. cup) white wine, the same amount of fish stock and a little mushroom cooking liquor, and shallow poach in the usual manner.

When cooked, drain and place the sole in a suitable dish; coat with Sauce Vin Blanc prepared in any of the three methods given in the Chapter on Sauces and containing the reduced cooking liquid. Serve unglazed or glazed, as required. If glazed it should be done very rapidly.

Note: Correctly speaking, Sole au Vin Blanc should not be glazed; however, the custom of each establishment must be taken into account and it is accepted that it is frequently done.

1926 Sole au Vin Rouge

Proceed in the same way as for Sole sur le Plat using red wine and a little meat glaze.

1926a Soles aux Grands Vins

By using wines of the great growths of Burgundy and Bordeaux and preparing the sole in the same way as for Sole au Chambertin or Sole au Champagne, a wide variety of preparations becomes possible; for example, Volnay, Pommard, Romanée, Musigny, Saint-Estèphe and Château-Margaux as red wines; Chablis-Moutonne, Meursault, Montrachet, Haut-Barsac, Haut-Sauternes and Château d'Yquem etc. as white wines. It is only necessary to name the wine for the dish, e.g. Sole au Volnay.

FILETS DE SOLE—FILLETS OF SOLE

According to the type of dish and recipe for which they are required, fillets of sole may be,

a) left flat and long as they are,
b) folded in half,
c) coated with fish forcemeat and folded in half, or
d) spread with fish forcemeat or not and rolled up as *Paupiettes*.

Whatever the final shape of fillet, it is essential to remove the thin white membrane which is left on the outside of the fillets after the skin has been pulled off. This membrane is one of the causes of shrinkage in cooking.

After the fillets have been cleaned they should be lightly flattened and trimmed as necessary, then placed in a buttered shallow pan or dish, moistened with very little liquid, covered and poached in a moderate oven so that no actual boiling takes place. This will ensure that the fillets become very white and will also prevent them from becoming tough and shrinking excessively.

Where the amount of liquid is not given in the following recipes, allow 1 dl (3½ fl oz or ½ U.S. cup) of liquid per 4 fillets of sole.

1927 Filets de Sole à l'Américaine
Fold the fillets and shallow poach with fish stock in a buttered dish. Drain and arrange them overlapping in the shape of an oval, the thick ends of the fillets over the tail-ends.

Fill the centre of the dish with slices of lobster prepared *à l'Américaine* (2109), and coat the fillets and the garnish with the sauce obtained from the lobster preparation.

1928 Filets de Sole à l'Anglaise
Prepare the fillets and flour, egg and breadcrumb with fresh white breadcrumbs; pat and shape with the flat of a knife so as to make the crumbs adhere properly and mark trellis-fashion with the back of the knife.

Shallow fry in clarified butter, arrange on a hot dish and spread the fillets with soft Maître d'Hôtel Butter.

1929 Filets de Sole à l'Andalouse
Spread the fillets with a fish forcemeat containing 50 g (2 oz) braised and chopped pimento per 1 kg ($2\frac{1}{4}$ lb) of forcemeat; roll up *Paupiette* shape (2000) and shallow poach in a buttered shallow pan with fish stock.

Drain and place each *Paupiette* standing up in a lightly cooked half tomato containing a little Risotto mixed with chopped pimento. Arrange in a circle on a dish, placing each on a round slice of eggplant, seasoned, floured and shallow fried in oil.

Finish with a little Beurre Noisette poured over each *Paupiette*.

1930 Filets de Sole à l'Armoricaine
Shallow poach the fillets flat in a buttered dish with fish stock; drain and arrange on a suitable dish.

Place a poached soft herring roe down the centre of each fillet with a poached oyster on top of the roe and on each side of the roe place a slice of lobster which has been cooked *à l'Américaine*. Add some double cream to the required amount of thick Sauce Américaine and coat the fillets with the sauce.

1931 Filets de Sole Belle-Meunière
Shallow fry the fillets flat *à la Meunière*. Place a bed of sliced mushrooms sautéed in butter on the bottom of a suitable dish, arrange the cooked fillets on top and surround with small half tomatoes *à la Provençale*. Cover with a little Beurre Noisette.

1932 Filets de Sole Bénédictine
Fold the fillets and shallow poach in a buttered dish with fish stock.

Drain and arrange overlapping round the inside of a sufficiently large deep pastry case. Fill the centre dome shape with Brandade de Morue (1805) mixed with chopped truffle, coat the fillets only with Sauce Crème and serve accompanied with a sauceboat of the same sauce.

1933 Filets de Sole Bercy
This fish may be prepared in either of the two following ways:

A) Lay the fillets in a buttered dish which has been sprinkled with very finely chopped shallot. Moisten with $\frac{1}{2}$ dl (2 fl oz or $\frac{1}{4}$ U.S. cup) white wine and the same amount of fish stock and add 10 g ($\frac{1}{3}$ oz) butter. Poach in the oven, basting the fillets frequently with the cooking liquid and glaze at the last moment.
B) Proceed as above shallow poaching the fillets without basting and reducing the liquid. Drain and place the fillets in a dish, reduce the cooking liquid by one-third and shake in a little butter, a little meat glaze and a few drops of lemon juice. Coat the fillets with the sauce and glaze under the salamander.

1934 Filets de Sole Boitelle
Fold the fillets and shallow poach in a buttered dish with 30 g (1 oz) sliced mushrooms, a little fish stock and a few drops of lemon juice.

Drain and arrange the fillets in a deep dish with the mushrooms in the centre; thicken and enrich the cooking liquid with 25 g (1 oz) butter and pour over the fillets and garnish.

1935 Filets de Sole à la Bourguignonne
Cut a small onion into very thin rings and cook without colour in a little butter; spread it over the bottom of a buttered dish and place the flat fillets on top. Surround with 30 g (1 oz) sliced mushrooms, sautéed in butter, sprinkle with a little coarsely ground pepper and add 1 dl ($3\frac{1}{2}$ fl oz or $\frac{1}{2}$ U.S. cup) red Macon wine.

Shallow poach, then drain off the cooking liquid and reduce it by two-thirds; thicken with a little Beurre Manié and finish with 25 g (1 oz) butter. Coat the fillets with the sauce and glaze quickly.

1936 Filets de Sole à la Cancalaise
Fold the fillets and shallow poach with a little butter and mushroom cooking liquor.

Arrange in a circle on a dish and fill the centre with 25 g (1 oz) shelled prawns and 6 poached and bearded oysters. Coat with Sauce Normande containing the reduced cooking liquor from the fish.

1937 Filets de Sole Caprice
Season the fillets and pass through melted butter then through fine fresh white breadcrumbs. Pat and shape with the flat of a knife and mark trellis-fashion with the back of the knife.

Sprinkle with melted butter and grill gently under the salamander to a nice golden brown colour. Arrange on a hot dish and place half a banana cut lengthways and shallow fried in a little butter on each fillet.

Serve accompanied with Sauce Robert Escoffier, finished with butter.

1938 Filets de Sole Cardinal
Spread the fillets with a layer of whiting and lobster butter forcemeat and fold in half. Place in a buttered dish and shallow poach in a little fish stock.

Drain and arrange on a dish overlapping in a circle with a thin slice of cooked lobster tail between each.

Coat with Sauce Cardinal and sprinkle with chopped lobster coral.

1939 Filets de Sole à la Catalane
Roll up the fillets *Paupiette* shape (2000) and shallow poach with fish stock.

Prepare the required number of half tomatoes, emptied, seasoned, just cooked in the oven and each filled with 1 tbs finely sliced onion cooked in oil without colour.

Place the *Paupiettes* standing up in the half tomatoes and arrange them in a circle on a suitable dish. Reduce the cooking liquid by one-third and thicken and enrich the sauce with butter; coat the fish and glaze quickly.

1940 Filets de Sole aux Champignons
Fold the fillets and shallow poach with mushroom cooking liquor.

Drain and arrange them in a circle on a suitable dish. Place 8 nice, very white cooked mushrooms in the centre and coat with Sauce aux Champignons containing the reduced cooking liquid from the fish.

1941 Filets de Sole Chauchat
Fold the fillets and shallow poach with butter and a little lemon juice. When cooked, cover the bottom of the service dish with a little Sauce Mornay, drain the fillets and arrange on top of the sauce.

Surround with fairly thick slices of freshly cooked plain boiled potatoes; coat the fillets and garnish with Sauce Mornay, and glaze.

1942 Filets de Sole à la Chevalière
Empty the carapaces of 4 large crayfish and fill with crayfish forcemeat. Fold the fillets and insert as much as possible of the tail ends into the filled carapaces; shallow poach together with white wine and butter.

Prepare a Julienne of crawfish tails, cooked mushrooms and truffle mixed with a little thick Lobster Sauce; mould it pyramid shape on a suitable round dish and place one of the fish at each side, with the fillet downwards and the crayfish at the top. Surround with a *cordon* of Sauce Vin Blanc and finish with a border of small palm-shaped pieces of pale baked puff pastry.

1943 Filets de Sole à la Chivry
Fold the fillets and shallow poach with fish stock.

Drain and arrange the fillets in a circle on a suitable dish alternating with thin heart-shaped Croûtons of bread fried in butter.

Coat with Sauce Chivry.

1944 Filets de Sole Clarence
Fold the fillets and shallow poach with fish stock.

Prepare a Duchesse potato mixture; place this in a piping bag with a large star tube and pipe a neat open design of compartments on a suitable buttered dish, each compartment large enough to hold one of the cooked fillets. Brush with beaten egg and lightly brown in the oven.

Place a little Sauce Mornay in each of the compartments and place one of cooked and drained fillets in each with a slice of truffle on top; coat with Sauce Mornay and glaze under the salamander.

Note: There appears to be no complete agreement as far as this recipe is concerned; for example in some places the Sauce Mornay is replaced by Sauce Américaine flavoured with curry and containing some lobster cut in small dice.

1945 Filets de Sole Condé
This dish is often confused with Sole Dugléré; nevertheless, in reality the difference between them is clearly defined. Current practice is to prepare Filet de Sole Condé in the following manner.

Shallow poach the fillets flat with mushroom cooking liquor and butter; drain, arrange on a suitable dish, and coat with Sauce Vin Blanc.

Using a very small plain piping tube, pipe some buttered tomato purée in the shape of a cross on each fillet and outline each fillet with the same purée.

Glaze quickly under the salamander.

1946 Filets de Sole aux Courgettes
Peel and cut 3 or 4 very small courgettes into fairly thick slices; place them in a pan with a little butter, a few drops of lemon juice, the roughly chopped

flesh only of 1 tomato, a sprig of fresh basil and a pinch of salt and pepper; cook until nearly done.

Trim and lightly flatten the fillets of sole and place in the bottom of a buttered, fairly deep earthenware dish, cover with the prepared courgettes and sprinkle with white breadcrumbs.

Place in a hot oven so as to cook the fillets and gratinate the surface at the same time. Serve in the dish as it is.

1947 Filets de Sole aux Crevettes

Fold the fillets and shallow poach with fish stock.

Drain and arrange in a circle in a suitable dish and fill the centre with 30 g (1 oz) warm shelled prawns. Coat the fillets and garnish with Sauce Crevettes.

1948 Filets de Sole Cubat

Shallow poach the fillets flat with butter and mushroom cooking liquor.

Coat the bottom of the service dish with a purée of mushrooms; drain the fillets and arrange on top. Place 2 slices of truffle on each fillet, coat with Sauce Mornay and glaze.

1949 Filets de Sole en Dartois

See Hot Hors-d'oeuvre (1172).

1950 Filets de Sole Daumont

Spread the fillets with a fish and cream forcemeat finished with Crayfish Butter. Roll them up *Paupiette* shape (2000) and shallow poach with fish stock.

When cooked, drain and place each *Paupiette* on a large, cooked cup mushroom filled with a Salpicon of crayfish tails *à la Nantua*; coat with Sauce Normande.

Arrange in a circle on a suitable round dish with 4 crayfish carapaces filled with the same forcemeat and poached, and 4 nice soft roes, egg and breadcrumbed and shallow fried in butter, placing one of each between each *Paupiette*.

1951 Filets de Sole à la Deauvillaise

This is prepared in the same way as Sole à la Deauvillaise (1877).

1952 Filets de Sole Déjazet

Breadcrumb and shallow fry the fillets in the same way as for Filets de Sole à l'Anglaise. When cooked, place in a dish on some half melted Tarragon Butter and decorate the fillets with blanched leaves of tarragon.

1953 Filets de Sole à la Dieppoise

Shallow poach the fillets flat with white wine and mussel cooking liquor and proceed from then on as for Sole à la Dieppoise.

1954 Filets de Sole Diplomate

Fold the fillets and shallow poach with fish stock.

Drain and arrange overlapping in a circle on a suitable dish, coat with Sauce Diplomate and place a slice of truffle glazed with meat glaze on each fillet.

1955 Filets de Sole Doria

These are prepared in the same way as Sole Doria.

1956 Filets de Sole Dubois

Cut the fillets into strips as for *en Goujons* (1961), flour, egg and breadcrumb and shallow fry in clarified butter to a golden brown.

Drain well and roll in just sufficient Sauce Chateaubriand to coat them.

Arrange neatly in a deep dish and sprinkle with a few drops of lemon juice and a little chopped parsley.

1957 Filets de Sole à la Duse

Coat the fillets with a layer of fish forcemeat, fold them and shallow poach with fish stock.

Drain and arrange the fillets overlapping in a suitable sized buttered Savarin mould then fill up the mould with Riz Pilaw (4239) cooked with fish stock, pressing it in all the way round.

Demould on to a round dish, coat with Sauce Mornay and glaze in a very hot oven. On removing from the oven, fill the centre of the mould with shelled prawns mixed with Sauce Vin Blanc and sprinkle this with chopped truffle.

1958 Epigrammes de Filets de Sole

Coat the fillets with a layer of fish forcemeat, fold them and shallow poach with a liquid which should be in keeping with the garnish chosen to accompany the Epigrammes.

Drain the fillets well and lightly press between two trays until completely cold; flour, egg and breadcrumb them, sprinkle with melted butter and grill to a golden brown.

Arrange in a circle, overlapping and alternating with thin heart shapes of cooked fish forcemeat which should be approximately the same size as the fillets.

Place the selected garnish in the centre of the dish.

Notes:

1) The above is the basic recipe for Epigrammes de Filets de Sole. The garnish chosen to accompany it determines the full name, e.g. if the sole is cooked with white wine and mussel cooking liquor and then garnished with a Dieppoise garnish, the full name of the dish would be Epigrammes de Filets de Sole à la Dieppoise. Most of the garnishes for Filets de Sole are suitable for Epigrammes.

2) The garnish and/or the sauce should always be placed in the centre of the circle of Epigrammes; the Epigrammes should never be covered with sauce.
3) For large servings the cooked forcemeat can be successfully prepared in cutlet moulds of the correct size. After allowing to rest for a while they can be successfully cut to the required thickness and shape.

1959 Filets de Sole Floréal
Coat the fillets with fish forcemeat and roll up *Paupiette* shape (2000); shallow poach with mushroom cooking liquor and butter.

Fill the bottom of small round porcelain Cocottes with buttered asparagus tips, place a drained *Paupiette* on top, then coat with a delicately coloured Sauce Vin Blanc finished with Beurre Printanier. Place a slice of grooved carrot cooked in a little Bouillon on top of each *Paupiette* and a small, very green sprig of chervil in the centre of the carrot.

1960 Filets de Sole à la Florentine
Shallow poach the fillets flat with fish stock and butter.

Place a bed of leaf spinach, lightly blanched and then cooked in butter, in a suitable dish; drain and arrange the fillets on top. Coat with Sauce Mornay and glaze under the salamander.

1961 Filets de Sole en Goujons or Mignonettes de Sole
Fillets of sole *en Goujons* are mainly used as a garnish in the same way as fillets of sole *en Julienne*. They do, however, make an excellent dish for lunch but care must be taken that they are served very hot.

Cut the fillets of sole across and diagonally into strips about 2 cm ($\frac{4}{5}$ in) wide. Season, pass through milk and then flour; immediately shake in a frying basket to remove the surplus flour then deep fry in very hot fresh oil. When a good golden brown, drain well and lightly season with salt; arrange on a grill or serviette, decorate with a bouquet of fried parsley and serve with quarters or halves of lemon.

Note: Filets de Sole en Goujons may also be shallow fried in clarified butter.

1962 Filets de Sole Grand-Duc
Fold the fillets and shallow poach with mushroom cooking liquor.

Drain and arrange in a circle with the points of the fillets to the centre; place 3 small shelled crayfish tails between each and place a slice of truffle on each fillet. Coat with Sauce Mornay, glaze and then place a bouquet of buttered asparagus tips in the centre.

1963 Filets de Sole au Gratin
Prepare in the same way as Sole au Gratin (1885) cooking the fillets flat.

1964 Filets de Sole Héléna
Coat the fillets with a layer of fish and cream forcemeat, roll up *Paupiette* shape (2000) and shallow poach with fish stock.

Drain and place each *Paupiette* in a tartlet case containing some very thin fresh noodles mixed with a little Cream Sauce. Arrange in a circle on a suitable dish, coat with Sauce Mornay and glaze quickly.

1965 Filets de Sole Héloïse
Place the fillets flat in a buttered dish which has been sprinkled with 60 g (2 oz) chopped mushroom. Proceed and finish as for Filets de Sole Bercy.

1966 Filets de Sole aux Huîtres
Fold the fillets and shallow poach with fish stock and butter.

Drain and arrange overlapping in a circle on a suitable dish, fill the centre with poached and bearded oysters and coat with Sauce Normande containing the reduced cooking liquid from the fish.

1967 Filets de Sole à l'Indienne
Fold the fillets and shallow poach with butter and very little fish stock.

Drain and arrange in a suitable dish; coat with Curry Sauce and serve accompanied with a dish of plain boiled rice.

1968 Filets de Sole Ismaïla
To 125 g ($4\frac{1}{2}$ oz) of cooked Riz Pilaw (4239) add 125 g ($4\frac{1}{2}$ oz) freshly cooked peas and 50 g (2 oz) pimentos cut in dice; mould this mixture as a border in a deep dish.

Fold the fillets and shallow poach with butter and a little fish stock; drain, place in the centre of the prepared border and keep warm. Reduce the cooking liquid, enrich with 50 g (2 oz) butter and coat the fish only with the sauce.

1969 Filets de Sole Jean-Bart
Prepare a Salpicon of shelled prawns, small cooked mussels and mushrooms, mixed with a thick fish-flavoured Sauce Béchamel; mould dome shape in the centre of a round dish. Arrange half-poached flat fillets of sole in the form of an arch over the dome; place in a moderate oven to finish cooking and to set the fillets in place. Coat with Sauce Normande, sprinkle with chopped truffle and surround with large poached mussels replaced in their half shells, coated with Sauce Mornay and glazed.

1970 Filets de Sole Joinville

Fold the fillets and shallow poach with mushroom cooking liquor and butter.

Drain the fillets and insert a cooked and shelled crayfish claw into the tail end of each. Arrange overlapping on a dish in a circle with the tails of the fillets upwards. Fill the centre with Joinville garnish and coat the fillets and garnish with Sauce Joinville.

Finally place a slice of truffle dipped in meat glaze on each fillet.

The old classical method: Fold the fillets and shallow poach with mushroom cooking liquor, butter and a little lemon juice, taking care that they remain very white. Drain and attach a crayfish claw to each fillet as before.

In the middle of a round dish mould a fairly stiff *Salpicon à la Joinville* (397) dome shape. Coat with Sauce Joinville and arrange the fillets around with their tail ends pointing upwards. Place a slice of very black truffle dipped in meat glaze on each fillet and surround the whole with thin slices of grooved lemon.

It will be noted that in this method of preparation, the garnish only is coated with sauce and the fillets form a white circle round the garnish.

1971 Filets de Sole en Julienne

Cut the fillets into thin strips, pass through milk, then through flour and shake in a frying basket to remove the surplus flour.

Deep fry in very hot oil, drain well, lightly season with salt and serve arranged on a serviette with fried parsley and lemon.

Note: When Julienne de Filets de Sole is to be used as a garnish or as part of a garnish such as for Filets de Sole au Chambertin, they should always be shallow fried in clarified butter.

1972 Filets de Sole Lady Egmont

Fold the fillets and shallow poach with very good fish stock. At the same time, slice 30 g (1 oz) mushrooms and cook quickly with a little butter, lemon juice, salt and pepper. Drain the fillets.

Add the cooking liquor from the mushrooms to that from the fish and reduce by half, add 30 g (1 oz) butter, 2 tbs cream, the cooked mushrooms, and 2 tbs freshly cooked and well drained asparagus tips.

Arrange the fillets in an oval gratin dish, cover with the sauce including its garnish and glaze quickly n a very hot oven or under the salamander.

1973 Filets de Sole à la Vallière

Spread the fillets with fish forcemeat and fold; make 2 or 3 incisions in the top side of each folded fillet and insert a slice of truffle in each incision. Shallow poach with fish stock.

Have prepared a Mousseline forcemeat of fish poached in a border or Savarin mould and demoulded on to a round dish; drain the fillets and arrange around the border of forcemeat. Coat the fillets and border with Sauce Normande and place a slice of truffle on each fillet.

Fill the centre with a garnish of sliced poached soft roes, poached and bearded oysters, cooked crayfish tails and small white cooked mushrooms all mixed together gently with Sauce Normande finished with Crayfish Butter.

1974 Filets de Sole Manon

Coat the fillets with fish forcemeat and roll up *Paupiette* shape (2000). Shallow poach with mushroom cooking liquor.

Drain and arrange the cooked *Paupiettes* on a round dish which has been bordered scroll-fashion with Pommes Duchesse mixture, then egg washed and coloured golden brown in a hot oven.

In the centre of the *Paupiettes*, place a garnish of asparagus tips and a Julienne of truffles and mushrooms all carefully mixed with a little butter. Lightly coat the *Paupiettes* only with Sauce aux Fines Herbes.

1975 Filets de Sole Marcelle

Fold the fillets and coat the top surface of each with a smooth layer of fish and cream forcemeat. Decorate each with a rose shape cut from truffle or a grooved slice of truffle and shallow poach with butter and a little lemon juice.

Half fill some Barquette cases of a suitable size with a purée of cooked soft roes mixed with finely chopped truffle and a little Sauce Vin Blanc to give it the consistency of a cullis.

Drain the fillets and place one on each of the prepared Barquettes; place a folded serviette on the serving dish and arrange the Barquettes in a circle on top.

1976 Filets de Sole Marguery

Shallow poach the fillets flat with fish stock; drain and arrange them on a dish and surround with poached mussels and shelled prawns.

Coat with Sauce Vin Blanc and glaze.

1977 Filets de Sole Marie Stuart

Fold the fillets and shallow poach with fish stock.

Drain and arrange the fillets overlapping in a circle on a suitable dish, coat with Sauce Newburg prepared as for Filets de Sole Newburg (1992), and on each fillet place a small round flat Quenelle of fish forcemeat decorated with a slice of truffle and poached and drained well at the last moment.

1978 Filets de Sole Marinette

Prepare and shallow poach a whole sole with fish stock and mushroom cooking liquor. When cooked, place it on a dish, carefully remove the fillets and trim them neatly.

Break 1 egg into a basin, beat it well and add sufficient equal quantities of grated Gruyère and Parmesan cheese to make a stiff paste. Mix 1 tbs cold Sauce Béchamel into the paste and season with salt and a little Cayenne pepper.

Place 2 of the fillets side by side, coat them with an even layer of the prepared mixture 2 cm ($\frac{4}{5}$ in) thick then cover with the other 2 fillets and allow to set firm in a cold place.

When ready, dip the whole re-formed fish into Sauce à la Villeroy, place on a tray and allow to cool and set. Trim carefully, flour, egg and breadcrumb and deep fry when required in very hot oil.

Drain, arrange on a serviette and surround with very green fried parsley.

1979 Filets de Sole à la Marinière

Shallow poach the fillets flat and proceed as for Sole à la Marinière.

1980 Filets de Sole Marquise

Pipe a garland-style border round the edge of a dish with Pommes Marquise, using a star-shaped piping tube; place in the oven for a few minutes to lightly dry.

Fold the fillets and shallow poach with white wine, fish stock and butter.

Drain, and arrange the fillets overlapping in a circle on the prepared dish; fill the centre with a garnish consisting of small Quenelles made from salmon forcemeat, shelled prawns, and truffles trimmed to the shape of olives.

Coat the fillets and garnish with lightly coloured Sauce aux Crevettes.

1981 Filets de Sole Mexicaine

Coat the fillets with fish forcemeat, roll up *Paupiette* shape (2000) and shallow poach with fish stock.

Grill the required number of fairly large cup mushrooms and place half a tablespoon of roughly chopped tomato flesh stewed in butter in each.

Drain the *Paupiettes* and stand each in one of the prepared mushrooms. Coat with Sauce Béchamel containing tomato purée and small dice of pimentos in the proportions of 2 dl (7 fl oz or $\frac{7}{8}$ U.S. cup) tomato purée and 50 g (2 oz) pimento per 1 litre ($1\frac{3}{4}$ pt or $4\frac{1}{2}$ U.S. cups) of sauce.

Arrange the *Paupiettes* in a circle on a round dish.

1982 Filets de Sole Mignonette

Cut the fillets into two on the slant; cook gently in a little butter and arrange in a deep dish.

Surround with very small balls of potato, cut with a small round spoon cutter and cooked in butter. Place on each fillet 8 to 10 slices of truffle heated in a little light meat glaze. Add 1 tbs butter to the meat glaze in which the truffles were heated plus a few drops of lemon juice and coat the fillets with this sauce. Serve very hot.

1983 Filets de Sole Miramar

Cut the fillets each into three pieces on the slant, season and cook in butter.

Cut 12 round slices of eggplant $\frac{1}{2}$ cm ($\frac{1}{5}$ in) thick; season, flour and shallow fry in butter keeping them very crisp.

Coat the sides of a very deep dish with Riz Pilaw, $1\frac{1}{2}$ cm ($\frac{3}{5}$ in) thick; carefully mix the sole and eggplant together and place in the prepared dish.

Just before serving, coat with a little Beurre Noisette.

1984 Filets de Sole Mogador

Fill a border mould with whiting and cream forcemeat containing chopped truffle, cook in the usual manner and demould on to a round dish. Keep covered and warm.

Cut the fillets of sole into neat rectangles, thinly coat one side of each with more of the forcemeat and decorate with a slice of grooved truffle; shallow poach with butter and a little lemon juice.

When cooked, drain well and arrange the pieces of fish overlapping around and on top of the prepared border of forcemeat. In the centre place a Nantua garnish and surround the border with crayfish carapaces filled with diced prawns mixed with a little of the fish forcemeat and cooked gently in a moderate oven.

Note: For large numbers requiring rapid service, the border of forcemeat can be piped directly on to buttered dishes using a star-shaped tube, piping a border of the required size first and then piping another layer carefully in top of the first. Cook gently in a moderate oven.

1985 Filets de Sole Montreuil

Shallow poach the fillets flat and proceed as for Sole Montreuil.

1986 Filets de Sole Montrouge

Fold the fillets and shallow poach with mushroom cooking liquor.

Drain and arrange the fillets overlapping in a circle on a suitable dish; fill the centre with cooked sliced mushrooms mixed with a little Sauce Béchamel and coat the fillets only with Sauce Béchamel enriched with butter and containing one-third its volume of a cooked purée of mushrooms.

1987 Filets de Sole aux Moules
Fold the fillets and shallow poach with white wine and mussel cooking liquor.

Drain and arrange the fillets overlapping in a circle on a suitable dish and fill the centre with mussels which have been poached in white wine and bearded. Coat the fillets and garnish with Sauce Normande containing the reduced cooking liquor from the mussels.

1988 Mousselines de Sole
Use any of the recipes as indicated for Mousselines of Salmon, using a Mousseline forcemeat of sole instead of Mousseline forcemeat of salmon.

1989 Filets de Sole Murat
Cut 100 g ($3\frac{1}{2}$ oz) potato and 2 artichoke bottoms into approximately 1 cm ($\frac{2}{5}$ in) dice; shallow fry separately in butter to a golden brown. Cut the fillets into 2 cm ($\frac{4}{5}$ in) wide strips, season, flour and shallow fry them in butter.

Mix the sole, potatoes and artichoke together and sauté together for a few moments to reheat thoroughly, then place into a deep dish. Add 6 thick slices of tomatoes, seasoned and quickly sautéed in very hot oil, sprinkle with chopped parsley, run a few threads of melted meat glaze over the top with a few drops of lemon juice and finally coat with Beurre Noisette.

1990 Filets de Sole Nelson
Fold the fillets and shallow poach with fish stock.

Drain and arrange the fillets overlapping in a circle on a suitable dish; coat with Sauce Vin Blanc and glaze quickly.

Fill the centre with a dome-shaped pile of Pommes Noisettes shallow fried to a golden brown in clarified butter; surround the fillets with soft roes prepared *à la Meunière*.

1991 Filets de Sole Nemours
Coat the fillets with a layer of fish forcemeat, fold and shallow poach with white wine and butter.

Drain and arrange the fillets overlapping in a circle on a suitable dish, in the centre place a garnish of small poached Quenelles moulded with teaspoons from a Mousseline forcemeat of whiting, small cooked mushrooms and thick slices of poached soft roes—all mixed together lightly with a little Sauce Normande.

Coat the fillets with Sauce Crevettes and place a slice of truffle on each. Surround with small deep-fried Croquettes of prawns which have been dipped in egg and coated with finely chopped truffle instead of breadcrumbs.

1992 Filets de Sole Newburg
Prepare a cooked lobster *à la Newburg* (2122), taking care to cut the tail into as many slices as there are fillets of sole; cover and keep them warm; cut the rest of the lobster flesh into small dice and add to the sauce.

Fold the fillets and shallow poach with fish stock; drain and arrange on a suitable dish with a slice of the lobster on each and coat with the prepared sauce.

1993 Filets de Sole à la Normande
Prepare as for Sole à la Normande, poaching the fillets flat.

1994 Filets de Sole Olga, also known as Filets de Sole Otéro
Bake as many good-sized well washed potatoes as there are fillets of sole. As soon as cooked, cut off the tops and empty them so as to form cases.

Fold the fillets and shallow poach with a little excellent fish stock. Cover the bottom of the potato cases with a tablespoon of shelled prawns mixed with a little Sauce Vin Blanc; drain the cooked fillets and place one in each potato then cover with sufficient Sauce Mornay to completely fill the cases. Sprinkle with grated Parmesan cheese and gratinate quickly in a very hot oven.

Arrange on a serviette on a dish and serve immediately.

1995 Filets de Sole à l'Orientale
Prepare in the same way as Filets de Sole Newburg but lightly flavour the sauce with curry. When the fillets have been arranged overlapping in a circle on the dish, fill the centre with plain boiled rice.

If deemed more suitable the rice may be served separately.

1996 Filets de Sole à la d'Orléans
Coat the fillets with whiting forcemeat mixed with chopped truffle, roll up *Paupiette* shape (2000) and shallow poach with mushroom cooking liquor.

Fill some small round porcelain Cocottes two-thirds full with a Salpicon of shelled prawns, mushrooms and truffles mixed together with a little cream; drain the *Paupiettes* and place one in each prepared Cocotte. Coat with a tablespoon of Sauce Crevettes and place a slice of truffle on top. Finish by sticking a nice prawn, from which the shell of the tail has been removed, back in the centre of the truffle.

1997 Filets de Sole Orly
Season the fillets, dip into a light frying batter and deep fry in hot oil as required; drain well and arrange on a serviette with fried parsley and serve accompanied with Tomato Sauce.

Note: It is not suggested that the above method is the only correct one for Filets de Sole Orly. In some establishments the fillets are breadcrumbed, twisted spiral shape and deep fried; in others they are passed through milk and flour, then skewered and deep fried.

The only thing that can be said with certainty is that the fillets are always deep fried and must be served with Tomato Sauce.

1998 Filets de Sole à l'Ostendaise

Coat the fillets with fish forcemeat, fold them and shallow poach with fish stock and butter.

Drain and arrange the fillets overlapping in a circle on a suitable dish; in the centre place 8 poached and bearded oysters and coat the whole with Sauce Normande containing the reduced cooking liquid from the fish. Place a slice of truffle on each fillet and surround with small Croquettes of fillets of sole moulded diamond shape.

Note: In professional restaurant service the Croquettes of sole are sometimes replaced with diamonds of sole fillets coated with a ½ cm (⅕ in) layer of fish forcemeat mixed with chopped mushrooms and truffle; these are then egg and breadcrumbed and deep fried.

1999 Filets de Sole Otéro

This is another name for Filets de Sole Olga (1994).

2000 Paupiettes de Sole

Paupiettes are simply fillets of sole rolled in a particular shape; they provide variety to the menu and are prepared in the following manner.

Carefully remove the membrane left adhering to the outside of the fillets; lightly flatten them with a moistened cutlet bat or heavy knife so as to help in preventing shrinkage during cooking, and carefully trim them.

Coat the skinned sides of the fillets with the required fish forcemeat and roll up into the shape of a small barrel, smoothing down any forcemeat which sticks out. They can be kept in shape by (1) tying carefully with fine string or thread, (2) by placing in buttered dariole moulds of a size sufficient to hold them or (3) by placing them as they are, close together and just touching in a suitable-sized buttered shallow pan. In all cases they are shallow poached.

All the garnishes and sauces used for fillets of sole are suitable for *Paupiettes*, remembering that their shape needs to be taken into account when arranging and presenting them.

2001 Filets de Sole à la Paysanne

Cut 2 small carrots, 2 small onions, 1 small stick of celery and the white of 1 small leek, into Paysanne shape. Place in a pan, with 30 g (1 oz) butter, season with salt and a little sugar and slightly stew together for a few minutes without colour. Moisten with sufficient water to just cover, add 1 tbs fresh peas and the same amount of French beans cut in small diamonds, cover and finish cooking together gently.

Season the fillets of sole and place them flat in the bottom of a buttered earthenware dish; add the vegetables and their liquid, cover and shallow poach gently.

When cooked tip out the cooking liquid from the fish into a small pan, reduce to approximately 1 dl (3½ fl oz or ½ U.S. cup) and thicken and enrich it by mixing in 100 g (3½ oz) butter. Pour this over the fillets and the garnish.

2002 Filets de Sole à la Persane

This is prepared in the same way as Filets de Sole à la Newburg but the lobster sauce is flavoured with paprika and 30 g (1 oz) of diced cooked pimento is added. Serve accompanied with a saffron-flavoured Riz Pilaw.

2003 Filets de Sole en Pilaw à la Levantine

Prepare a Riz Pilaw (4239) and mix in 30 g (1 oz) diced cooked red pimento.

Cut the fillets on the slant into fairly thick slices, season and shallow fry them quickly in butter. Separately season and shallow fry 50 g (2 oz) diced eggplant in butter, then mix together with the fillets of sole.

Arrange the Riz Pilaw in a border on a suitable dish and place the sole and eggplant mixture in the centre; coat with Sauce Currie without touching the rice.

Note: For ordinary Filets de Sole au Riz Pilaw, the rice is cooked as a plain Pilaw without any garnish of pimentos, it is then arranged as a border on a dish and the centre filled with slices of fillets of sole sautéed in butter. The fish is then coated with Sauce Currie.

2004 Filets de Sole Polignac

Fold the fillets and shallow poach in a buttered dish with white wine, mushroom cooking liquor and butter.

Drain and arrange the fillets on a suitable dish, reduce the cooking liquid by a good half, add 2 tbs fish Velouté, mix in 30 g (1 oz) butter and finally add 1 tbs finely sliced cooked mushrooms and ½ tbs Julienne of truffle.

Coat the fillets with this sauce and glaze quickly under the salamander.

2005 Filets de Sole Pompadour

Dip the fillets in melted butter, coat them with breadcrumbs then pat and shape with a knife; sprinkle with melted butter and gently grill.

Arrange the cooked fillets on a suitable dish and

pipe a line of thick Sauce Béarnaise between each. Surround with nicely browned Pommes Noisettes (4218) and place a slice of truffle glazed with melted meat glaze on each fillet.

2006 Filets de Sole à la Portugaise
Shallow poach the fillets flat and proceed as for Sole à la Portugaise (1915).

2007 Filets de Sole Princesse
Pipe out the required number of decorative compartments of Pommes Duchesse on a round buttered dish, using a star tube; brush with beaten egg and place in a hot oven to colour golden brown.

Fold the fillets and shallow poach in a buttered dish with mushroom cooking liquor and butter.

Lay 1 tbs hot buttered asparagus tips in the bottom of each compartment, place a well drained fillet on top and carefully coat with a little Sauce Béchamel finished with Asparagus Butter in the proportions of 100 g ($3\frac{1}{2}$ oz) butter per 1 litre ($1\frac{3}{4}$ pt or $4\frac{1}{2}$ U.S. cups) sauce, taking care not to spill any sauce on the potato.

2008 Filets de Sole Rachel
Spread the fillets with a layer of fish forcemeat, place 4 slices of truffle on one half and fold over. Place in a buttered dish and shallow poach with mushroom cooking liquor and butter.

Drain, arrange in a circle on a dish and coat with Sauce Vin Blanc containing freshly cooked asparagus heads and diced truffle.

2009 Filets de Sole Régence
Spread one side of the fillets with a layer of fish forcemeat mixed with chopped truffle. Fold and shallow poach in a buttered dish with Chablis wine and butter.

Drain and arrange the fillets on a dish and complete as indicated for Sole Régence.

2010 Filets de Sole Rhodésia
Spread the fillets with fish forcemeat and roll up *Paupiette* shape (2000); shallow poach with white wine and fish stock. Drain, place each *Paupiette* on a nice large slice of lobster tail cooked *à l'Américaine*, arrange in a circle on a round dish and coat with Sauce Américaine finished with cream.

2011 Filets de Sole Riche
This is another name for Filets de Sole Victoria.

2012 Filets de Sole Rochelaise
Shallow poach the fillets flat and proceed as for Sole Rochelaise.

2013 Filets de Sole Rosine
Shallow poach the fillets flat in a buttered dish with white wine and butter; drain and arrange on a suitable dish, cover and keep warm.

Take 8 very small tomatoes, skin them, cut off the tops and empty them of pips; place a little butter in each and gently cook in a moderate oven. Fill each tomato with a poached Quenelle of fish Mousseline forcemeat (1562) moulded with teaspoons; stand these upright in the tomatoes. Coat each with a little Sauce Vin Blanc.

Coat the fillets with Sauce Vin Blanc mixed with a quarter its volume of thick tomato purée and arrange the prepared tomatoes around.

2014 Filets de Sole à la Rouennaise
Shallow poach the fillets flat and proceed as for Sole à la Rouennaise.

2015 Filets de Sole Saint-Germain
Season the fillets, dip them in butter and then coat with fresh fine white breadcrumbs; flatten and shape with the back of a knife and mark trellis-fashion.

Sprinkle with butter and grill gently to a golden brown.

Arrange on a suitable dish, surround with small Pommes Noisettes and pipe a line of thick Sauce Béarnaise between each fillet.

2016 Filets de Sole Talleyrand
Prepare sufficient Spaghetti à la Crème mixed with a little Julienne of truffle and place in the form of an oval mound on a deep dish; keep warm.

Shallow poach the fillets flat in a dish with butter and when cooked, arrange on top of the prepared spaghetti; place 2 slices of truffle on each fillet and coat with Sauce Vin Blanc made without a final addition of eggs. Glaze in a moderately hot oven.

2017 Filets de Sole Tivoli
Shallow poach the fillets flat in a buttered dish with a little fish stock.

Drain and arrange on a suitable dish with 1 poached soft herring roe, 1 poached and bearded oyster and 1 cooked whole mushroom, on each fillet.

Coat with Sauce Genevoise made with Barolo or Chianti wine and surround with a garnish of noodles which have been shallow fried raw in clarified butter.

2018 Filets de Sole Trouvillaise
Shallow poach the fillets flat in a buttered dish with fish stock. Drain and arrange on a suitable

dish; surround with Dieppoise garnish and coat the fillets and garnish with Sauce Crevettes.

Note: This preparation is frequently called Filets de Sole à la Fécampoise or Filets de Sole Maurice.

2019 Filets de Sole d'Urville
Spread one side of the fillets with a layer of fish forcemeat, fold and inset the top surface with slices of truffle; shallow poach in a buttered dish with a little lemon juice.

Prepare boat-shaped moulds of Pommes Duchesse, colour in the oven and then empty them from the top to leave Barquette cases. Fill with a Salpicon of shrimps mixed with Sauce Crevettes, place a cooked fillet on top of each and arrange in a circle on a folded serviette placed on a round dish.

2020 Filets de Sole Valentino
Fold the fillets and shallow poach in a buttered dish with fish stock; drain, coat with Sauce Mornay and glaze.

Press some Pommes Duchesse mixture into Barquette moulds. Turn out, flour, egg and breadcrumb them and deep fry to a golden brown; empty them out to leave Barquette cases. Fill with Risotto containing white Piedmont truffles and place a cooked fillet on top of each.

Arrange in a circle on a folded serviette placed on a round dish.

2021 Filets de Sole Vénitienne
Fold the fillets and shallow poach in a buttered dish with fish stock.

Drain and arrange overlapping in a circle on a suitable dish alternating with thin heart-shaped Croûtons of bread fried in clarified butter; coat with Sauce Vénitienne containing the reduced cooking liquid from the fish.

2022 Filets de Sole Verdi
Shallow poach the fillets flat in a buttered dish with fish stock.

Cook sufficient macaroni, drain, cut in very short lengths and mix with a little cream and grated cheese. Add 125 g (4½ oz) diced cooked lobster and 75 g (2½ oz) diced truffle per 250 g (9 oz) cooked macaroni.

Place a bed of the prepared macaroni on a suitable dish, arrange the cooked fillets on top, coat with Sauce Mornay and glaze quickly.

2023 Filets de Sole Véronique
Remove the fillets from a nice sole, trim them, lightly flatten and fold. Place in a buttered dish which has a cover and season.

With the trimmings and bones of the sole, the usual flavourings, lemon juice, white wine and water, prepare approximately 1 dl (3½ fl oz or ½ U.S. cup) of fish stock. Strain this over the prepared fillets, cover with the lid and shallow poach gently.

Carefully drain the cooked fillets, reduce the cooking liquid to the consistency of a light syrup and mix in 50 g (2 oz) butter. Replace the fillets overlapping in a circle in the dish in which they were cooked, coat with the sauce and quickly glaze.

At the last moment place in the centre of the fillets a nice bouquet of very cold, skinned and depipped Muscatel grapes; cover the dish with the lid and serve immediately.

2024 Filets de Sole Victoria
Fold the fillets and shallow poach in a buttered dish with fish stock.

Drain and arrange overlapping in a circle on a dish. Place 100 g (3½ oz) diced crawfish and 30 g (1 oz) diced truffle in the centre and coat the fillets and garnish with Sauce Béchamel finished with Crayfish Butter.

2025 Filets de Sole Walewska
Shallow poach the fillets flat in a buttered dish with fish stock.

Drain, arrange on a suitable dish, surround with 3 nice tails of Dublin Bay prawns which have been cut in half lengthways and cooked gently under cover with a little butter and 6 nice slices of truffle. Coat with a light Mornay Sauce and glaze quickly.

Note: As a variation the Sauce Mornay may be finished with the addition of 100 g (3½ oz) butter made from the debris and shells of Dublin Bay prawns, per 1 litre (1¾ pints or 4½ U.S. cups) of sauce.

2026 Filets de Sole Wilhelmine
Prepare the required number of potato cases as explained in the recipe for Filets de Sole Olga (1994).

Fold the fillets and shallow poach in a buttered dish with fish stock. Place 1 tbs Concombres à la Crème (4082) in each potato and place a well drained fillet on top; on each fillet set a nice Dutch oyster, coat with Sauce Mornay and glaze in the oven.

Arrange on a serviette on a suitable dish.

2027 Pâté Chaud de Sole à la Dieppoise
Line an oval pie mould with good short paste; fill the interior with alternate layers of whiting and cream forcemeat; small *Paupiettes* (2000) of stuffed sole; raw oysters and shelled prawns. Finish with a layer of the same whiting forcemeat and sprinkle the surface with a little melted butter.

Cover with a layer of the same short paste taking care to seal the edges properly and decorate the edges. Egg wash the surface and if desired, place a thin shape of puff paste in the centre. Cook in a moderately hot oven and demould on to a serviette to serve.

Serve accompanied with Sauce Dieppoise.

2028 Timbale de Filets de Sole Carême

Lightly flatten and trim the fillets of 3 medium-sized soles. Well butter a suitable shallow round mould and line with the fillets; they should be placed side by side with the pointed ends to the centre of the mould and the other ends overhanging the sides of the mould. Press down well to make sure that they take the shape of the mould.

Completely coat the fillets with a good 1 cm ($\frac{2}{5}$ in) thick layer of fish forcemeat then place the prepared mould in a fairly warm oven for a few minutes to cook and set the forcemeat. By adhering to the fillets it will give the required form to the timbale.

Cut off the overhanging parts of the fillets and then fill the mould to within 1 cm ($\frac{2}{5}$ in) of the top, with shelled prawns, poached mussels and oysters, small button mushrooms and slices of truffles all mixed with well seasoned and reduced Sauce Béchamel. Cover with the trimmings of the sole which were removed during the preparation of the mould and complete with a layer of fish forcemeat.

Place the mould in a tray containing hot water and cook gently in a warm oven for approximately 30 minutes. When cooked, remove the Timbale, allow to rest for a few minutes then overturn it on to a round dish and remove the mould. Soak up any liquid which runs out on to the dish.

Around the Timbale arrange 6 small *Paupiettes* of salmon each stuffed with a crayfish tail; alternate these with crayfish carapaces which have been filled with crayfish forcemeat and cooked.

Serve accompanied with Sauce Nantua.

2029 Timbale de Filets de Sole Cardinal

Prepare in advance a Timbale case (4334), larger in diameter than height, made with short paste and decorated with a design of noodle paste.

Flatten and trim the fillets of 3 medium-sized soles, spread the inside of the fillets with a layer of whiting forcemeat finished with Crayfish Butter, roll up *Paupiette* shape (2000) and shallow poach in the usual manner some minutes before being required. Prepare also a garnish composed of 10 medium slices of cooked lobster or crawfish, 10 small grooved, cooked mushrooms, 15 slices of truffle and 4 dl (14 fl oz or $1\frac{3}{4}$ U.S. cups) Sauce Cardinal.

To serve: arrange the well drained *Paupiettes* in a circle in the Timbale case, place the lobster and mushrooms in the centre and cover the whole of the garnish with the Sauce Cardinal.

In the centre of the sauce place a large grooved cooked, white mushroom, surround it with the slices of truffle, place the cover on the Timbale and present it on a folded serviette on a suitable dish. Serve immediately.

2030 Timbale de Filets de Sole Carmelite

Prepare in advance:

1) A decorated Timbale case (4334);
2) 1 raw lobster cooked *à la Newburg* (2122);
3) 12 *Paupiettes* (2000) of sole stuffed with fish forcemeat finished with Lobster Butter; and
4) 100 g ($3\frac{1}{2}$ oz) truffle cut in slices.

Shallow poach the *Paupiettes* in the usual manner; cut the lobster tail in slices and place together with the *Paupiettes* and sliced truffle in the Lobster Sauce.

Reheat well without boiling and pour the sauce and garnish into the Timbale case; decorate the surface with 12 slices of truffle reserved for this and place the cover on the timbale.

Present on a folded serviette on a suitable dish and serve immediately.

2031 Timbale de Filets de Sole Grimaldi

1) Prepare a fairly deep decorated Timbale case (4334);
2) Prepare 24 small Dublin Bay prawns cooked as for Bisque; remove the tails, cut in half lengthways and keep them warm in a little butter;
3) Finely pound the shells of the Dublin Bay prawns, adding 2 dl (7 fl oz or $\frac{7}{8}$ U.S. cup) of good Sauce Béchamel a little at a time. Pass first through a fine sieve, then through a fine strainer, place the resultant cullis in a pan and reheat without boiling. Adjust the seasoning and finish with a few tablespoons of cream. Add the Dublin Bay prawns and keep warm in a Bainmarie;
4) Cut 125 g ($4\frac{1}{2}$ oz) cooked but fairly firm macaroni into short lengths; whilst still hot add 1 dl ($3\frac{1}{2}$ fl oz or $\frac{1}{2}$ U.S. cup) cream and 100 g ($3\frac{1}{2}$ oz) sliced truffle. Simmer together gently until the cream is almost completely absorbed. Add 1 dl ($3\frac{1}{2}$ fl oz or $\frac{1}{2}$ U.S. cup) Sauce Béchamel finished with fish stock and 50 g (2 oz) butter cut in small pieces. Keep warm.
5) Spread 15 fillets of sole with a layer of truffled fish forcemeat, roll them up *Paupiette* (2000) shape and shallow poach them in the usual manner ready for garnishing the Timbale case when required.

To garnish the Timbale: Spread a layer of the macaroni in the bottom of the timbale, place half the *Paupiettes* on top, then cover these with half the Dublin Bay prawns and the cullis. Repeat in the same order with the remaining ingredients so that the Timbale is finished with a layer of Dublin Bay prawns and cullis.

Place the cover on top of the Timbale and present on a folded serviette on a suitable dish. Serve immediately.

2032 Timbale de Filets de Sole Marquise

For a timbale sufficient for 10 persons prepare:

1) a Timbale case moulded in a fluted mould (4334);
2) a garnish composed of 12 *Paupiettes* (2000) or folded fillets of sole shallow poached in the usual way, 12 cooked and bearded oysters, 25 small Quenelles of salmon and 20 slices of truffle. Heat this garnish with a little fish stock and thicken with the addition of 3 dl ($\frac{1}{2}$ pt or $1\frac{1}{4}$ U.S. cups) paprika-flavoured Sauce Vin Blanc.

Pour the garnish and sauce into the Timbale case, place the cover on top and present on a folded serviette on a suitable dish. Serve immediately.

2033 Timbale de Filets de Sole Richepin

Prepare:

1) a Timbale case made in a shallow mould (4334);
2) 40 raviolis of spinach prepared *à la Niçoise*;
3) 12 *Paupiettes* (2000) of sole stuffed with truffled fish forcemeat;
4) 24 crayfish tails cooked with white wine.

Cook the raviolis in salted water, drain well, mix with a little grated cheese, a little meat or fish glaze and some butter, then add 15 slices of truffle.

Shallow poach the *Paupiettes* with white wine and fish stock.

Garnish and finish the Timbale by placing the raviolis at the bottom; arrange the *Paupiettes* on top in a circle with the crayfish tails in the centre. Cover the whole with Sauce Crème finished with Crayfish Butter.

Note: For large numbers, porcelain or silver timbales may be used; in this case, however, the menu title should be Paupiette de Sole Richepin, not Timbale de Sole Richepin.

2034 Turban de Filets de Sole Villaret

Lightly flatten the fillets from 3 nice soles and trim them straight on both sides. Well butter a medium-sized Savarin mould, lay in the fillets slantwise and slightly overlapping each other, with the tail ends overlapping the inner edge of the mould and the other ends overlapping the outside edge. Fill the lined mould with a Mousseline forcemeat of lobster then gently tap the mould on a folded cloth so as to settle the forcemeat. Fold over the ends of the fillets on top of the forcemeat, cover and cook *au Bain-marie* in a moderate oven.

When cooked, remove the mould from the oven and allow to rest for a few minutes. Turn it upside down on the service dish, sponge up any liquid which runs out on to the dish then remove the mould. Brush the surface of the fillets carefully with a little melted butter so as to glaze the surface and, at the same time, remove any coagulated particles from the cooking.

In the centre of the Turban place a garnish consisting of shelled prawns, mushrooms, poached soft roes and slices of truffles all mixed together with Sauce Béchamel finished with Lobster Butter.

Serve separately a sauceboat of the same sauce.

2035 Turban de Filets de Sole et de Saumon Villaret

Proceed in the same way as in the preceding recipe but alternating the fillets of sole with slices of very red salmon cut to exactly the same size as the fillets.

This combination of fish gives an excellent result and the alternating lines of red and white arranged on top of the Turban gives a very pleasing appearance.

Note: The designation *à la Villaret* refers only to the Turban and does not affect the ingredients of the garnish which may be the same as for the Turban de Filets de Sole. Other ingredients deemed suitable may be used, but in all cases Sauce Béchamel finished with Lobster Butter should be used.

2036 Vol-au-Vent de Sole à la Marinière

Prepare a garnish composed of Quenelles of whiting forcemeat moulded with medium-sized spoons and poached at the last moment, small poached *Paupiettes* (2000) of stuffed sole, poached and bearded oysters and mussels and shelled prawns, all carefully mixed with Sauce Marinière.

Place the mixture in a Vol-au-Vent case and surround with medium-sized trussed crayfish.

2037 Vol-au-Vent de Filets de Sole Presidence

1) Cut 10 nice fillets of sole slantwise each into 2 lozenge shapes and shallow fry them *à la Meunière*;
2) Prepare and poach 10 Quenelles of whiting or sole, moulded with medium-sized spoons;
3) Prepare 10 cooked tails of crayfish.

Mix all these ingredients together carefully with a proportionate amount of creamy Sauce Béchamel mixed with one-third its quantity of grated truffle, which should be fresh if possible and cooked with a fine Mirepoix and Sauternes wine.

Place the mixture in a Vol-au-vent case and present on a folded serviette on a suitable dish.

Note: This mixture may be served and presented in a shallow Timbale case (4334).

FILETS DE SOLE FROID—COLD FILLETS OF SOLE

2038 Aspic de Filets de Sole—Aspic of Fillets of Sole
This may be prepared in either of the following ways:

A) Fold 12 fillets of sole and shallow poach with butter and lemon juice so as to keep them white. Allow to cool under pressure and trim carefully to an even shape.

Coat a plain or fancy deep mould with a layer of very clear Fish Aspic Jelly, decorate and fill with the fillets of sole in the usual manner for Aspics (336).

B) Coat 10 nice fillets of sole with a thin layer of truffled fish forcemeat and roll them up *Paupiette* shape (2000), enclosing a 1 cm (⅖ in) diameter cork-shaped piece of truffle in the centre.

Shallow poach the prepared *Paupiettes* with fish stock then cool them. Coat a plain deep mould with very clear Fish Aspic Jelly and decorate the bottom of the mould only. Trim both ends of the *Paupiettes*, cut into 1 cm (⅖ in) thick slices and line the sides of the moulds with these slices fixing them with a little melted jelly; then fill the rest of the mould with layers of the same slices, covering each layer with jelly. Demould when required.

2039 Bordure de Filets de Sole à l'Italienne
Poach 10 fillets of sole, cool them under light pressure and cut into thin strips; cut 30 g (1 oz) very black truffle and 15 g (½ oz) of red pimento into neat Julienne.

Well coat a plain border mould with very clear Fish Aspic Jelly, fill with a mixture of the above ingredients and complete with jelly added little by little, allowing it to set between each addition.

To serve, turn out the *Bordure* on to a flat semolina base placed on the service dish. Fill the centre with Salade à l'Italienne and serve accompanied with Sauce Mayonnaise.

2040 Filets de Sole Calypso
Flatten the fillets of sole and roll *Paupiette* fashion (2000) around buttered wooden cylinders of approximately 2 cm (⅘ in) diameter. Place in a buttered shallow pan and shallow poach with very clear fish stock and a little lemon juice to ensure that they keep white.

When cooked, allow to cool and remove the wooden cylinders; the *Paupiettes* should now look like short tubes.

Peel as many nice even-shaped tomatoes as there are *Paupiettes* using ones that are slightly larger than a *Paupiette*; cut off the top third and empty them. Place a *Paupiette* standing up in each and fill the hole in the centre with crayfish Mousse containing some finely diced cooked crayfish.

On top of the Mousse place a round piece of cold poached soft roe cut with a round cutter and on top of this place a shelled cooked crayfish tail.

Arrange in a circle on a round dish and fill the centre with chopped white Fish Aspic Jelly. Surround the dish with rectangles of the same jelly.

2041 Filets de Sole Charlotte
Lightly flatten the fillets of sole and shallow poach with fish stock; when cooked allow them to cool under light pressure.

Trim the fillets and coat with pink-coloured Sauce Chaud-froid; decorate each fillet with a rose design using chervil leaves and place a touch of lobster coral in the centre; glaze with Fish Aspic Jelly.

At the same time prepare a Mousse of soft roes flavoured with horseradish and mould in a fairly high narrow dome-shaped mould which has been coated with a layer of fish jelly and sprinkled with chopped lobster coral.

To serve, turn out the Mousse on to the middle of a very cold round dish, arrange the fillets against the Mousse with the tails uppermost. Surround with chopped Fish Aspic Jelly and decorate the edge of the dish with shapes of the same jelly.

2042 Filets de Sole à la Moscovite
Prepare:

1) The required number of fillets of sole in the same manner as for Filets de Sole Calypso, and
2) the same number of round grooved and emptied cases cut from cucumber; these should be well blanched, drained and marinated inside.

Place a *Paupiette* standing up in each cucumber case and fill the centre with caviare; arrange in a circle on a round dish and place chopped fish jelly in the middle.

Serve accompanied with Sauce Mayonnaise à la Russe.

2043 Cold Fillets of Sole on Mousse
In the recipe for Cold Salmon-trout on Mousse it is mentioned that fillets of sole can be prepared in the same way. When fillets of sole are prepared in this way they can be seen quite clearly through the jelly, thus it is necessary to ensure that they are cooked and remain very white.

Shallow poach the fillets as indicated and allow to cool under light pressure; trim neatly and decorate with items in keeping with the Mousse on which they will be arranged. Set the selected Mousse in a deep oval porcelain dish, arrange the decorated fillets neatly on top and cover the whole with well flavoured and very clear Fish Aspic Jelly.

Note: See the section on Cold Salmon-trout (1708) for suitable Mousses.

2044 Timbale de Filets de Sole Escoffier
Prepare 12 medium fillets of sole in the form of *Paupiettes* (2000), 6 of them with a smooth fish forcemeat finished with lobster and red colouring butter, the others with the same forcemeat finished with a purée of very black truffle. Poach the *Paupiettes* in good fish stock and allow to cool in the liquid.

When cold, drain, trim both ends neatly and cut each *Paupiette* horizontally into 4 even-sized rounds.

Take a suitable dome-shaped mould with a funnel in the centre, coat the inside with a thin layer of clear Fish Aspic Jelly and immerse it in crushed ice; cover the coating of jelly with the slices of *Paupiette* dipped in almost setting jelly and arranged in layers of the same colour or alternate colours, whichever is considered to give the best contrast.

Finish by filling the mould with crayfish Mousse and leave to set for at least 2 hours. Turn out when required and place on a block of clear ice sculpted in the shape of a shallow vase or font.

Note: This recipe with a drawing to illustrate its presentation was published in 1895 by *Mons*. Morin in the journal *L'Art Culinaire* and was later prepared and artistically presented by Madame Turtaut, a lady chef, at the Exposition Culinaire of Paris in 1900.

2045 Paupiettes de Sole en Timbale
This is a variation of Timbale de Filets de Sole Escoffier also having some relationship with Cold Fillets of Sole on Mousse but much easier to prepare.

Prepare the *Paupiettes* of sole as in the previous recipe and cut into round slices. Place a deep silver dish in crushed ice and set a thin layer of Fish Aspic Jelly in the bottom; fill two-thirds full with a Mousse of crayfish and when set, arrange the slices of *Paupiettes* on top alternating the colours. Place a small whole very black truffle in the centre and cover with almost setting jelly.

STOCKFISH OR MORUE DE NORVEGE SECHEE—STOCKFISH OR DRIED NORWEGIAN SALT COD

In Belgium, Holland and Germany, this dried cod is first soaked in limewash and then prepared in the same way as ordinary cod.

In the Midi of France it is always bought dry and then soaked in water; it is cooked in several different ways, the following recipe being chosen as representative.

2046 Stockfish à la Mode des Pêcheurs Niçois
Soak the fish in running water for at least 3 days. Remove the scales and fins and cut the fish into pieces. For 1 kg ($2\frac{1}{4}$ lb) of fish chop 300 g (11 oz) onion and cook gently in oil without colouring; add 500 g (1 lb 2 oz) roughly chopped flesh only of tomato, 2 cloves of crushed garlic, a pinch of basil and a Bouquet garni, season with salt and pepper and allow to stew very gently for 20 minutes.

Add the fish, cover with boiling water and simmer very gently for $1\frac{1}{2}$ hours. Half an hour before it is ready add 750 g (1 lb 10 oz) potatoes cut in thick rounds and 250 g (9 oz) stoned black olives.

THON—TUNNYFISH

For 10 persons allow $1\frac{1}{4}$ kg (2 lb 13 oz).

2047 Thon à la Chartreuse
Butter a braising pan and line with slices of vegetable flavourings and herbs; cut the piece of tunny into round slices, season, place on top of the vegetables and cook gently in its own juices for a few minutes. Moisten with 2 dl (7 fl oz or $\frac{7}{8}$ U.S. cup) White Bouillon and reduce to a glaze. Barely cover with liquid in the proportion of one part white wine to three parts White Bouillon, cover with a lid and place in the oven to braise for approximately $1\frac{1}{2}$ hours.

Remove the slices of tunny, arrange on a dish, surround with bouquets of glazed turnips and carrots and buttered French beans and peas. Strain the cooking liquid, reduce it then thicken and enrich it with a little butter before pouring over the tunny fish.

2048 Thon à l'Indienne
Lard the piece of tunny fish with fillets of anchovy and place to marinate for 1 hour with white wine, herbs, sliced vegetables and seasoning.

Cook a Mirepoix of vegetables in butter to a light brown colour, add a small spoonful of curry powder and a pinch of saffron. Moisten with the strained wine from the marinade and 2 dl (7 fl oz or $\frac{7}{8}$ U.S. cup) fish stock; add the tunny fish, cover with a lid and braise gently in the oven for approximately $1\frac{1}{2}$ hours.

When cooked, remove the fish and place on a dish; strain the cooking liquid, skim off the fat, thicken with a little Fish Velouté and finish with a little lemon juice.

Pour the sauce over the fish and serve accompanied with a dish of plain boiled rice.

2049 Thon à l'Italienne
Marinate the piece of tunny fish for 1 hour with oil, lemon juice, herbs, vegetable flavourings and seasoning.

Remove the fish, dry with a cloth and colour in hot oil; place in a braising pan and add 125 g ($4\frac{1}{2}$ oz) each of chopped onion, shallot and mushrooms. Cover with a lid, cook gently for 20 minutes in the oven then moisten two-thirds of the way up with equal quantities of white wine and fish stock. Replace in the oven to braise gently for approximately $1\frac{1}{2}$ hours, basting frequently.

When cooked, place the tunny on a dish and coat with the cooking liquid which has been lightly thickened with Beurre Manié.

2050 Aiguillettes de Thon Orly
Cut the tunny fish into small thin slices, lightly flatten them and season. Either flour, egg and breadcrumb or dip in frying batter and deep fry in hot oil.

Serve garnished with fried parsley and accompanied with Tomato Sauce.

2051 Thon à la Provençale
Lard the piece of tunny fish with fillets of anchovy and marinate as for Thon à l'Italienne.

Remove the fish, drain well and colour in hot oil; place in a braising pan, add 125 g ($4\frac{1}{2}$ oz) chopped onion, 750 g (1 lb 10 oz) roughly chopped flesh only of tomato, 3 cloves of crushed garlic, a pinch of basil and a Bouquet garni. Cover with a lid and cook gently in the oven for 20 minutes. Almost cover with one-third white wine and two-thirds White Bouillon, replace the lid and braise gently in the oven for approximately 1 hour.

When cooked, remove the fish and place on a dish; strain the cooking liquid, skim off the fat and reduce and thicken with a little Sauce Espagnole. Finish with 50 g (2 oz) capers and a little roughly chopped parsley and pour over the fish.

2052 Tunny Fish with various Garnishes
Braised tunny fish when prepared as for Thon à la Chartreuse may be served accompanied with various garnishes as described, such as purée of sorrel, purée of spinach, Macédoine of vegetables, Fondue of Tomatoes, braised lettuce, etc.

TURBOT

For 10 persons: allow 1 kg 800 g (4 lb) gross weight.

2053 Turbot Bouilli—Boiled Turbot
Whole Turbot: These are usually cooked in Plain Court-bouillon and presented on a serviette, garnished with bouquets of very green parsley. It is recommended that a little butter is rubbed over the surface of the cooked fish so as to give it a shiny appearance.

Before commencing to cook a whole turbot especially if it is very fresh, it is advisable to partially detach the two fillets from the centre bone on the black skin side to a depth of 4–5 cm ($1\frac{3}{4}$–2 in). Fold the fish over on itself and press hard to break the spine in two or three places; as well as facilitating the cooking, these measures also help to prevent the fish losing its shape.

Whole turbot should always be covered with a cold liquid and brought to the boil slowly; as soon as it boils, the pan should be brought to the side of the stove and left to finish cooking with a barely discernible movement of the liquid. Allow 12 minutes per 1 kg ($2\frac{1}{4}$ lb) from the time the liquid commences to boil.

Note: To keep the head of a whole turbot in shape, carefully tie it round with string before cooking.

Small Cuts of Turbot: Cut the fish into half down the centre of the spine and then across into pieces of the required size. These cuts should be cooked in Plain Court-bouillon in accordance with the principles laid down in the beginning of this section. It should, however, be noted that the time for poaching is not exactly proportional to the weight of the piece of turbot; e.g. a piece of turbot weighing 350–400 g (13–15 oz) requires approximately 30 minutes cooking time whereas a piece weighing 700–800 g ($1\frac{1}{2}$–$1\frac{3}{4}$ lb) will require only an extra 10 minutes.
Accompaniments for Boiled Turbot, whole or in

small cuts: Boiled turbot should always be accompanied with a service of plain boiled potatoes and a suitable sauce such as Sauce Câpres, Hollandaise, Crevettes, Homard, Noisette, Vénitienne, etc.

2054 Turbot Braisé—Braised Turbot

It is only in special circumstances that a whole turbot is braised and garnished and in this case it is advisable to select a medium-sized fish.

The procedure for braising is the same as that for the braising of white meats (2176).

Place the prepared vegetables and herbs on the bottom of the fish kettle, cover with the grill which should be well buttered on top, and place the prepared turbot on the grill, white skin uppermost so that when cooked it will slide off straight on to the serving dish; moisten with the cold cooking liquid. Bring to the boil, cover and cook gently in the oven, basting frequently.

Except when deemed absolutely necessary for presentation, the turbot should not be surrounded with its garnish, it is advisable that this be served separately along with the sauce. In this way the fish can be served quickly and which is more important, served very hot.

The sight of a dish containing a finely garnished and tastefully presented turbot can be flattering to the host, but this should not be at the expense of quality. Mere appearance does not compensate for the deterioration in quality of food served half cold. However, if it is necessary to serve the turbot garnished and sauced, care should be taken to do this as quickly as possible, garnishing it at the very last moment.

Note: Turbot for boiling or braising should be plump with a very white lightly grained skin.

2055 Turbot à l'Amiral

Barely cover the fish with a previously cooked White Wine Court-bouillon made with Sauternes wine; bring to the boil, cover with a lid and cook gently in the oven allowing approximately 12 minutes per 1 kg ($2\frac{1}{4}$ lb).

When cooked, drain well, place the fish on a suitable dish and brush over a few times with Red Colouring Butter (230). Surround with bouquets of large mussels and oysters prepared *à la Villeroy*; small Bouchées of crayfish tails; large mushroom heads grooved and cooked; and slices of truffle.

Serve accompanied with a dish of small round plain boiled potatoes and a sauceboat of Sauce Normande to which has been added a little of the reduced cooking liquid and finished with Crayfish Butter and a little Cayenne pepper.

2056 Cadgery de Turbot—Kedgeree of Turbot

Proceed in the same way as Cadgery de Saumon using freshly cooked turbot instead of salmon.

2057 Turbot Crème au Gratin

Decorate an oval dish with a piped border of Pommes Duchesse mixture approximately $1\frac{1}{2}$ cm ($\frac{3}{5}$ in) wide at the bottom, narrowing to the top and 3 cm ($1\frac{1}{5}$ in) high—the size of the border should, of course, be proportionate to the number of guests.

Coat the bottom of the dish with a little Sauce Mornay, fill two-thirds full with thick slices of warm, well drained cooked turbot, cover with more sauce, sprinkle with grated cheese and brush the border with beaten egg.

Place in the oven to gratinate the fish and colour the border at the same time.

2058 Coquilles de Turbot

Place a little Sauce Mornay in the bottom of scollop shells or silver shell dishes; place a few small slices of warm, well drained cooked turbot on top, cover with more sauce, sprinkle with grated cheese and gratinate quickly.

Note: When using shells it is recommended that a scrolled border of Duchesse potato is piped around the edges using a star tube in a piping bag. Not only does this prevent the sauce from spreading over the edges of the shell but it makes for a nicer presentation.

2059 Turbot Daumont

Cook the fish as for Turbot à l'Amiral but using a Court-bouillon made with Chablis wine, prepared in advance.

Arrange on a serving dish, brush the surface with butter and surround with a Daumont garnish arranged in bouquets.

Serve accompanied with a dish of small plain boiled potatoes and a sauceboat of Sauce Nantua.

2060 Turbot à la Parisienne

Cook the fish as for Turbot Daumont, arrange it on a serving dish and brush the surface with a little butter. On top of the turbot place a cooked lobster of which the flesh of the tail has been removed, cut into slices and arranged overlapping on top of its shell. Surround the turbot with Mousselines of whiting and thick slices of soft herring roe.

Serve accompanied with a dish of small plain boiled potatoes and a sauceboat of Sauce Normande, finished with Crayfish Butter and containing sliced truffles and mushrooms.

2061 Turbot Régence

Braise the turbot using White Wine Court-bouillon

made with either Graves or Sauternes wine and prepared in advance.

Decorate the service dish with a garland-shaped border of piped Marquise potato and place in the oven for a few minutes to dry. Place the cooked fish in the centre, brush its surface with a little butter and surround it with a Régence garnish for fish, arranged in bouquets. Prepare a suitable number of decorative skewers garnished with truffles, decorated oval Quenelles of fish and trussed crayfish, and insert them down the centre of the turbot.

Serve accompanied with Sauce Normande finished with truffle essence.

2062 Turbot Froid—Cold Turbot

Whether whole or in small cuts, cold turbot makes an excellent dish providing that care is taken not to cook it too long in advance. It will be found that turbot, especially in small cuts tends to harden and become insipid whilst cooling; hence the reason for cooking as late as possible for use. It is therefore essential that the fish should have just cooled down after cooking and that the cooking liquid should not have had sufficient time to set as a jelly. If these points are not adhered to, undesirable results as previously noted, will occur. The gelatinous quality of the flesh of turbot underlines the importance of these observations.

When served just cool as recommended, with a suitable cold sauce, turbot can rival the delicacy even of such fish as salmon or trout.

2063 TURBOTIN—YOUNG TURBOT

Young or chicken turbot may be classed among the most delicate and finest of fish. The varying sizes make the fish suitable for serving to 3 or 4 persons as well as up to 10 to 12 people; moreover the flesh is always white and tender. Young turbot lend themselves to a wide range of culinary preparations—they may be boiled in the same way as other turbot, grilled, prepared *à la Meunière*, *Doré*, *au Gratin* or braised in the same way as salmon or trout.

More usually they are served whole coated with a sauce but for ease of service they may be filleted, then skinned, poached and served with a selected garnish and sauce.

Note: Whether boiled, poached or braised, young turbot should always be prepared before cooking in the same way as turbot so as to facilitate cooking and prevent deformation of its flesh, i.e. cut along the back on the black skin side, partially detach the two fillets from the bone and break the spine in two or three places.

2064 Turbotin à l'Amiral

Prepare in the same way as for Turbot à l'Amiral taking into account the difference in size.

2065 Turbotin à l'Andalouse

For a young turbot of approximately 1 kg ($2\frac{1}{4}$ lb), well butter a suitable-sized earthenware dish, place in the prepared fish and moisten with 2 dl (7 fl oz or $\frac{7}{8}$ U.S. cup) white wine and 1 dl ($3\frac{1}{2}$ fl oz or $\frac{1}{2}$ U.S. cup) fish stock.

Prepare 125 g ($4\frac{1}{2}$ oz) finely sliced onion cooked in a little butter to a golden colour, 400 g (15 oz) peeled, depipped and sliced tomatoes, 200 g (7 oz) finely sliced mushrooms and 2 pimentos, skinned, cooked and cut in thin strips. Spread the onions over the fish, sprinkle the tomatoes and mushrooms on top and finally arrange the strips of pimento trellis-fashion over the whole. Sprinkle lightly with white breadcrumbs and dot the surface with 30 g (1 oz) butter.

Place in a moderate oven for approximately 30 minutes to cook and lightly gratinate; the cooking liquid will develop a slightly thick consistency by its reduction during the cooking and by the absorption of the gelatinous properties of the fish.

2066 Turbotin Bonne Femme

This is prepared in the same way as Sole Bonne Femme.

2067 Turbotin au Chambertin, or au Champagne

Proceed in the same way as for Sole au Chambertin or Sole au Champagne adjusting the amount of garnish as necessary.

2068 Turbotin Chauchat

Proceed in the same way as for Sole Chauchat.

2069 Turbotin Commodore

Poach the young turbot in salt water and for each person prepare the following garnish: 3 large Pommes Noisettes, 1 Quenelle of fish moulded with teaspoons, 1 small Croquette of lobster, 1 oyster Villeroy and 1 medium-sized crayfish, trussed and cooked in Court-bouillon.

Drain the fish when cooked, place it on a serving dish, surround with the garnish alternating the items and serve accompanied with Sauce Normande finished with Anchovy Butter.

2070 Turbotin Daumont

Proceed in the same way as for Sole Daumont.

2071 Turbotin Dugléré

Trim and split the young turbot in half lengthways through the backbone; cut each half into 5 to 6 pieces.

Prepare 400 g (15 oz) roughly chopped flesh only of tomato, 100 g ($3\frac{1}{2}$ oz) chopped onion, 20 g ($\frac{2}{3}$ oz) chopped shallot, a touch of crushed garlic and 1 tbs roughly chopped parsley.

Sprinkle half of these ingredients over the bottom of a well buttered dish, place the pieces of fish on top arranging them in the original shape of the fish; season with salt and pepper and cover with the rest of the ingredients. Add a small sprig of thyme and a bayleaf, 30 g (1 oz) butter in small pieces and 2 dl (7 fl oz or $\frac{7}{8}$ U.S. cup) white wine.

Bring to the boil and place to cook in a moderate oven. When cooked, drain off the cooking liquid into a small saucepan, reduce it by half and add $1\frac{1}{2}$ dl (5 fl oz or $\frac{5}{8}$ U.S. cup) Fish Velouté, 125 g ($4\frac{1}{2}$ oz) butter, a few drops of lemon juice and a touch of Cayenne pepper. Pour this sauce over the fish.

2072 Turbotin Fermière

Sprinkle a well buttered tray with 60 g (2 oz) sliced shallot and 30 g (1 oz) each of rings of carrot and onion, parsley stalks, a little thyme and bayleaf. Place the turbot on top, and for a fish weighing approximately 1 kg ($2\frac{1}{4}$ lb), moisten with 4 dl (14 fl oz or $1\frac{3}{4}$ U.S. cups) red wine and add 30 g (1 oz) butter in small pieces.

Poach gently in the oven basting frequently.

Cook 100 g ($3\frac{1}{2}$ oz) sliced mushrooms in a little butter. When the fish is cooked, drain it well, place on a dish, surround it with the mushrooms and keep hot. Pass the cooking liquid through a fine strainer, reduce by half, thicken with 1 tbs of Beurre Manié and finish and enrich the sauce with 100 g ($3\frac{1}{2}$ oz) butter.

Pour this sauce over the fish and the garnish and glaze quickly under the salamander.

2073 Turbotin à la Feuillantine

Cut down the centre of the turbot from the beginning of the head to the tail on the black skinned side; detach both fillets from the bones almost to the beginning of the fins; cut carefully through the spine at both ends then separate and remove the bones from the underlying flesh.

Season the inside of the fish, stuff it with sufficient Mousseline forcemeat of lobster to give it a rounded appearance when the two fillets are folded back to enclose it. Turn the fish over and lay it in a well buttered deep oval dish of a suitable size; add a little fish stock and mushroom cooking liquor using approximately two-thirds fish stock and one-third liquor; cover with a lid and shallow poach gently in the oven.

When cooked, drain the turbot well, place it on a suitable dish and coat its surface with very red Lobster Butter. Lay a line of slices of truffle overlapping along the centre of the fish from head to tail and frame these with very white poached oysters arranged in an oval.

Serve accompanied with Sauce Béchamel seasoned with Cayenne pepper.

2074 Turbotin au Gratin

Proceed in the same manner as for Sole au Gratin taking account of the size of the fish so as to obtain at the same time, the cooking of the fish, the reduction of the sauce and the formation of the Gratin. See the theory of complete Gratin (2182).

2075 Turbotin à la Mode de Hollande

Poach the turbot in salted water, drain it well and place on a suitable dish.

Place a freshly cooked lobster on top, the flesh from the tail having been removed, cut quickly into slices and replaced on top of its shell.

Serve accompanied by a dish of plain boiled floury potatoes and Sauce aux Oeufs finished with melted butter.

2076 Turbotin aux Huîtres

Proceed in the same way as Sole aux Huîtres.

2077 Turbotin à la Parisienne

Poach the turbot in a Court-bouillon prepared with Sauternes wine; or simply poach it with white wine, mushroom cooking liquor and butter. Drain it well, place on a suitable dish and surround with a border of alternate large slices of cooked mushrooms and truffles; coat with Sauce Vin Blanc and surround with trussed crayfish cooked in Court-bouillon.

Note: The garnish of mushrooms and truffles may be coated with the sauce or placed on the fish after it has been coated. This observation holds good for any fish prepared à la Parisienne.

2078 Turbotin Régence

Prepare in the same way as for Turbot à la Régence.

2079 Turbotin Soufflé Reynière

Prepare the young turbot in the same way as for Turbotin à la Feuillantine, using a Mousseline forcemeat of whiting instead of lobster forcemeat; poach in the same way, drain well and place on a suitable dish.

Arrange a row of cooked grooved, white mushroom heads along the centre of the fish from head to tail and frame the mushrooms with poached soft roes alternating with anchovy fillets, arranged in an oval.

Serve accompanied with a sauce made from two-thirds Sauce Vin Blanc, one-third Coulis Soubise (151) and the reduced cooking liquid from the fish.

2080 Turbotin à la Saint-Malo
Cut shallow incisions in the flesh of the turbot on both sides, season, sprinkle with oil and grill gently.

Place on a suitable dish and surround it with a border of small freshly boiled potatoes, skinned, cut in thick slices and fried golden brown in butter.

Serve accompanied with Sauce Saint-Malo.

2081 Turbotin Froid—Cold Young Turbot
The remarks concerning cold turbot are equally applicable to cold young turbot. The fish should not, however, be too small, approximately $1\frac{1}{2}$ kg (3 lb 6 oz) being the ideal weight.

It should be added that cold chicken turbot is suitable for all kinds of presentation and decoration.

Note: White fish such as sole, turbot, young turbot, brill, bass, mullet etc. for cold should not be cooked too far in advance. A few hours is permissible but they should never be cooked the day before as the flesh becomes too gelatinous.

2082 VIVE—WEEVER

The Weever is a fish of inferior quality but is used quite commonly in the preparation of Bouillabaisse. Nevertheless it may be fried, prepared *à la Meunière*, or in most of the ways applicable to whiting.

SHELLFISH, FROGS AND TURTLE

CRABE—CRAB

2083 Crabe à l'Anglaise—Dressed Crab
Wash the crab, place it in boiling salted water and simmer for 30–35 minutes for a crab weighing $1\frac{1}{2}$ kg (3 lb 6 oz). Allow to cool in the cooking liquid.

Detach the claws and small legs; break the claws, remove the flesh and reserve. Pull the breast away from the carapace and remove any white flesh, adding it to that already reserved from the claws.

Extract the creamy parts and place this in a basin after passing it through a fine sieve; add a little mustard and a touch of Cayenne to this purée and mix in a little vinegar and oil so as to thicken it like a Mayonnaise. Break up the reserved flesh and add to the prepared creamy parts.

Clean and dry the shell and fill it with the prepared mixture; smooth the surface and decorate to choice with chopped parsley, lobster coral and chopped hard-boiled white and yolk of egg.

Place on a folded serviette on a suitable dish and set it in place with the small legs which were removed at the beginning.

CREVETTES—PRAWNS

As well as being used as a garnish and for Hors-d'oeuvre, prawns can be prepared in a number of ways of which the following are examples.

2084 Coquilles de Crevettes Glacées
Pipe a border of Duchesse potato mixture around the edges of scollop shells, fill dome shape with a Salpicon of prawns mixed with hot Sauce Béchamel; coat with Sauce Vin Blanc containing a little chopped truffle and glaze quickly under the salamander.

2085 Coquilles de Crevettes Garnies
Pipe a border of Duchesse potato mixture round the edges of scollop shells, cover the bottoms with buttered asparagus tips mixed with a fine Julienne of truffles and fill with warmed prawns. Coat with Sauce Mornay and glaze quickly under the salamander.

Note: This type of preparation is usually considered to be a hot Hors-d'oeuvre and as such the scollop shells should not be too large; the special silver shells are most suitable for this type of service.

2086 Crevettes au Currie—Curried Prawns
Cook 120 g (4 oz) finely chopped onion together with 50 g (2 oz) butter and 1 tsp of curry powder; add 500 g (1 lb 2 oz) shelled prawns and mix together with 3 dl ($\frac{1}{2}$ pt or $1\frac{1}{4}$ U.S. cups) Fish Veloute.

Place in a deep dish and serve accompanied with a dish of plain boiled rice.

2087 Crevettes Frites—Fried Prawns
Sauté the raw prawns in hot oil or clarified butter; drain them well, season lightly with salt and Cayenne pepper and arrange on a serviette placed on a suitable dish.

Note: Fried prawns are sometimes served as a luncheon fish.

CREVETTES FROIDS—COLD PRAWNS

2088 Aspic de Crevettes—Prawns in Aspic
Coat a border mould with a layer of white Fish

Aspic Jelly then fill it with alternate layers of nice shelled prawns and fish jelly.

Allow to set in a refrigerator and demould on to a suitable dish. Decorate and garnish in the usual manner for Aspics.

2089 Mousse Froide de Crevettes—Cold Prawn Mousse

Use raw prawns and cook them as for Bisque. When cooked, shell sufficient of the prawns for lining the mould and pound the rest finely including the shells and the Mirepoix used in the cooking, plus a little butter. Pass through a fine sieve and to each 500 g (1 lb 2 oz) of the purée, add 1 dl ($3\frac{1}{2}$ fl oz or $\frac{1}{2}$ U.S. cup) Fish Velouté and 2 dl (7 fl oz or $\frac{7}{8}$ U.S. cup) Fish Aspic Jelly. Simmer together gently and allow to cool. When near setting point, half whip $2\frac{1}{2}$ dl (9 fl oz or $1\frac{1}{8}$ U.S. cup) cream and fold in.

Have already prepared a deep mould coated with a layer of Fish Aspic Jelly and lined with the reserved prawn tails which have first been dipped in a little nearly setting jelly; fill the prepared mould with the Mousse and allow to set in a cool place. Turn out when required on to a folded serviette placed on a suitable dish.

Note: This Mousse may be prepared in a deep silver, porcelain or glass dish, the prawn tails in this case being arranged on top of the Mousse when set and then finally covered with a layer of Fish Aspic Jelly.

ECREVISSES—CRAYFISH

For 10 persons allow 30 crayfish.

Whatever their method of preparation, crayfish should first be well washed and have the gut removed; the extreme end of the gut is found under the middle of the tail and can be removed by holding the middle tail segment between the point of a small knife and the thumb and then pulling so as to remove it whole without breaking. If left in the crayfish, especially during the breeding season, there is risk of a bitter taste being imparted to the fish.

It is essential that the operation of removing the gut is carried out immediately prior to cooking. If left for any length of time before cooking, the juices of the crayfish tend to leak out from the wound and finally leave the shell almost empty.

Note: For culinary purposes, crayfish are usually graded according to weight as follows:

1) Between 30–40 g (1–$1\frac{1}{2}$ oz) for Bisques.
2) Between 50–60 g (approximately 2 oz) for garnishes.
3) Between 80–100 g (3–$3\frac{1}{2}$ oz) for dishes in their own right.

It may be of some interest to study the following table of the relative age and weights of crayfish as researched by Professor Zipcy.

TABLE OF THE WEIGHTS OF CRAYFISH FROM 1 MONTH TO 20 YEARS OF AGE

AGE	WEIGHT
1 month	0·20 g
1 year	1·05 g
2 years	5–6 g ($\frac{1}{5}$ oz)
3 years	10–13 g ($\frac{1}{3}$ oz)
4 years	17–18 g ($\frac{1}{2}$ oz)
5 years	22–25 g ($\frac{3}{4}$ oz)
6 years	27–32 g (1 oz)
7 years	32–35 g ($1\frac{1}{4}$ oz)
8 years	35–40 g ($1\frac{1}{2}$ oz)
9 years	45–50 g ($1\frac{3}{4}$ oz)
10 years	52–60 g (2 oz)
15–20 years	80–120 g (3–4 oz)

2090 Ecrevisses à la Bordelaise

Prepare a very fine Mirepoix consisting of 50 g (2 oz) each of red of carrot and onion; 30 g (1 oz) shallot; 5 g ($\frac{1}{6}$ oz) parsley stalks; a pinch of thyme; and half a bayleaf. Gently stew these ingredients together with a little butter under cover and until completely cooked—or simply use a Mirepoix Bordelaise cooked in advance.

Add 50 g (2 oz) butter, 30 washed and gutted crayfish, a pinch of salt and a touch of Cayenne. Heat and mix together over a good heat until the shells become a nice red colour. Add 1 dl ($3\frac{1}{2}$ fl oz or $\frac{1}{2}$ U.S. cup) flamed brandy and 3 dl ($\frac{1}{2}$ pt or $1\frac{1}{4}$ U.S. cups) white wine; cook and reduce the liquid by one-third. Add 1 dl ($3\frac{1}{2}$ fl oz or $\frac{1}{2}$ U.S. cup) each of Fish Velouté and fish stock, cover with a lid and cook gently for 10 minutes.

Remove the crayfish and place in a deep dish, reduce the sauce by a quarter and finish with 1 tbs meat glaze, 100 g ($3\frac{1}{2}$ oz) butter and a pinch of roughly chopped parsley. Season the sauce well and pour it over the crayfish.

2091 Ecrevisses en Buisson

Cook the crayfish in a Court-bouillon as described for Ecrevisses à la Nage. Hang the prepared crayfish by their tails on the special utensil for this type of presentation or simply pile them neatly on a folded serviette and serve garnished with bouquets of fresh green parsley.

2092 Coquilles de Queues d'Ecrevisses Cardinal
Pipe a narrow border of Duchesse potato mixture around the edges of small silver scollop shells using a small star tube, brush with eggwash and colour in the oven.

Place a little Sauce Normande finished with Crayfish Butter in the bottom of the shells and garnish each with 6 cooked crayfish tails. Cover with a little of the same sauce, place a slice of truffle in the centre and surround with a border of chopped truffle.

2093 Ecrevisses à la Liégeoise
Cook the crayfish in a Court-bouillon as described for Ecrevisses à la Nage.

As soon as cooked, remove the crayfish and place them in a dish to keep warm; pass the cooking liquid through a fine strainer and reduce by three-quarters. Shake in 100 g (3½ oz) butter to thicken, pour over the crayfish and sprinkle with a little roughly chopped parsley.

2094 Ecrevisses à la Magenta
Colour the crayfish in 1½ dl (5 fl oz or ⅝ U.S. cup) oil and with the same amount of Mirepoix as for Ecrevisses à la Bordelaise; the Mirepoix need not, however, be cut small.

Lightly season, add 300 g (11 oz) roughly chopped flesh only of tomato, a pinch of roughly chopped parsley and moisten with 3 dl (½ pt or 1¼ U.S. cups) white wine; cover with a lid and cook gently for 10 minutes occasionally tossing the fish over.

Remove the crayfish to a deep dish and keep warm; finish the sauce with 50 g (2 oz) butter and a pinch of basil and pour this sauce over the crayfish.

2095 Ecrevisses à la Marinière
Heat the crayfish in 60 g (2 oz) butter over a good heat, tossing them over until the shells are completely coloured.

Season, add 60 g (2 oz) finely sliced shallots and a very small pinch of powdered thyme and bayleaf. Moisten with 6 dl (1 pt or 2⅝ U.S. cup) white wine, cover with a lid and cook gently for 12 minutes.

Remove the crayfish, place in a deep dish and keep warm. Reduce the cooking liquor by half and thicken it with 2 dl (7 fl oz or ⅞ U.S. cup) Fish Velouté. Finish away from the heat with 80 g (3 oz) butter, pour over the crayfish and sprinkle with a little roughly chopped parsley.

2096 Mousselines d'Ecrevisses Alexandra
Prepare some Mousseline forcemeat of crayfish in accordance with the recipe for shellfish forcemeat (1564).

Butter the required number of shallow dariole moulds and place a slice of truffle in the bottom of each, flanked by 2 halves of crayfish tail cut lengthways. Fill with forcemeat and proceed as for Mousselines de Saumon Alexandra (1678).

2097 Mousselines d'Ecrevisses Tosca
Prepare the Mousselines as in the preceding recipe and finish as for Mousselines de Saumon Tosca (1679).

2098 Ecrevisses à la Nage
Prepare and cook a Court-bouillon with the following ingredients: 50 g (2 oz) each of thin rings of grooved carrot and button onions, 30 g (1 oz) finely sliced shallot, 5 g (⅙ oz) parsley stalks, a pinch of powdered thyme and bayleaf, 3 dl (½ pt or 1¼ U.S. cups) white wine, 2 dl (7 fl oz or ⅞ U.S. cup) fish stock and 10 g (⅓ oz) salt. When the vegetables are cooked, place the washed and gutted crayfish in the boiling Court-bouillon, cover and cook gently for 10 minutes, occasionally turning them over. Season with a little Cayenne and place the crayfish with the Court-bouillon and its garnish in a deep dish for service.

2099 Soufflé d'Ecrevisses à la Florentine
Prepare a Parmesan Soufflé mixture adding 4 tbs Crayfish Cream (see Page 33 Notes on the preparation of Compound Butters) per 1 litre (1¾ pt or 4½ U.S. cups) of the mixture at the same time as the egg whites. Fill a buttered soufflé mould with alternating layers of the soufflé mixture, sliced truffle and cooked crayfish tails, finishing with soufflé mixture. Cook in the same way as for ordinary soufflés.

2100 Soufflé d'Ecrevisses Léopold de Rothschild
Prepare as in the preceding recipe adding a small spoonful of freshly cooked asparagus tips to the truffles and crayfish tails placed between the layers of soufflé mixture.

2101 Soufflé d'Ecrevisses à la Piémontaise
Proceed in the same way as for Soufflé d'Ecrevisses à la Florentine using shavings of raw white Piedmont truffles instead of the usual black ones.

2102 Timbale de Queues d'Ecrevisses Nantua
For a timbale for 10 persons:

1) Prepare a shallow Timbale case (4334) with a cover decorated with a design of leaves, or some other decoration.
2) Shallow fry 60 medium-sized crayfish in butter with 2 tbs previously cooked finely cut Mirepoix; toss them over and over and when they have turned red, moisten with 2 dl (7 fl

oz or $\frac{7}{8}$ U.S. cup) white wine, $\frac{1}{2}$ dl (2 fl oz or $\frac{1}{4}$ U.S. cup) flamed brandy, and season with a little salt and Cayenne. Cover with a lid and cook gently for 10 minutes, turning occasionally.

3) Remove the shells from the crayfish and place the tails in a saucepan with 20 small Quenelles made from whiting forcemeat finished with Crayfish Butter, 15 small grooved very white, cooked mushrooms and 100 g ($3\frac{1}{2}$ oz) slices of truffle. Add a little of the mushroom cooking liquor to keep it all moist, and keep warm.
4) Finely pound the shells and remains of the crayfish together with the well reduced cooking liquid; pass through a fine sieve and to this purée add 4 dl (14 fl oz or $1\frac{3}{4}$ U.S. cups) Cream Sauce. Pass through a fine strainer, bring to the boil and finish away from the heat with 100 g ($3\frac{1}{2}$ oz) butter; pour it over the crayfish tails and garnish.
5) When required for service, turn the garnish and sauce into the prepared Timbale which should have been kept warm; decorate the surface with a circle of slices of very black truffle and close the timbale with its cover. Serve presented on a folded serviette on a round dish.

2103 Timbale de Queues d'Ecrevisses à la Parisienne
Prepare a Timbale case (4334) in a round pie mould, keeping the sides fairly high and not overcolouring it.

Fill with alternate layers of short lengths of well seasoned Macaroni à la Crème finished with Crayfish Butter; crayfish tails cooked *à la Bordelaise* mixed with Sauce Béchamel and finished with Crayfish Butter; and slices of truffle and sautéed mushrooms.

Finish with a layer of crayfish tails and a border of slices of truffle placed on top.

ECREVISSES FROIDES—COLD CRAYFISH

2104 Aspic de Queues d'Ecrevisses à la Moderne
Cook 36 nice Crayfish à la Bordelaise (2090) using Champagne instead of white wine.

Remove and shell the tails; cut each in half lengthways, trim them neatly and keep in a cool place until required.

Remove the creamy parts which are found in the heads and pound until fine together with the trimmings of the tails, the flesh from the claws and the drained Mirepoix from the cooking. Pass through a fine sieve into a basin; add 4 dl (14 fl oz or $1\frac{3}{4}$ U.S. cups) cool melted Fish Aspic Jelly and fold in 2 dl (7 fl oz or $\frac{7}{8}$ U.S. cup) half whipped cream; allow to lightly set. Trim the carapaces of the crayfish, fill with a little of the prepared Mousse and place a small round slice of truffle on the top of each.

Place the rest of the Mousse in a glass bowl and mould cone-shape, narrow at the bottom and as high as possible. Arrange the prepared carapaces around the cone with their backs to the Mousse. Cover the rest of the cone with the halves of crayfish stuck on by dipping them in nearly setting jelly and arranging them in neat rows. Place a small round slice of truffle on the top of the cone to complete the decoration and finish the dish by coating the whole again and again with almost setting, very clear and succulent Fish Aspic Jelly, using a spoon for this purpose.

To serve: set the bowl on a block of clear ice or present it on a dish surrounded by crushed ice.

2105 Mousse Froide d'Ecrevisses—Cold Crayfish Mousse
Cook 36 medium-sized crayfish as for Bisque; when cooked, remove and shell the tails and reserve 12 of the best carapaces for further use.

Finely pound all the remainder with the Mirepoix from the cooking of the crayfish. Add 15 g ($\frac{1}{2}$ oz) butter, 30 g (1 oz) Red Colouring Butter, $1\frac{1}{2}$ dl (5 fl oz or $\frac{5}{8}$ U.S. cup) cold Fish Velouté and 1 dl ($3\frac{1}{2}$ fl oz or $\frac{1}{2}$ U.S. cup) cold melted fish jelly.

Pass this mixture through a fine sieve and place in a saucepan; place on ice and mix well, then fold in 4 dl (14 fl oz or $1\frac{3}{4}$ U.S. cups) half whipped cream and the crayfish tails cut in small dice or thin slices.

Pour this mixture into a Charlotte mould which has been lined on the bottom and sides with greaseproof paper, reserving sufficient to fill the reserved carapaces. Fill the trimmed carapaces with this Mousse and decorate each with a round slice of truffle. Place the mould and crayfish in a refrigerator to set.

To serve, turn out the Mousse on to a low base made of rice or semolina (302) set on a suitable dish. Carefully remove the paper from the Mousse and decorate the top with a border of round slices of truffle dipped in nearly setting Fish Aspic Jelly; surround the dish with a border of chopped jelly and place the prepared crayfish carapaces on it, standing almost upright.

Note: The most frequently used method of moulding this type of Mousse today is to pour the mixture into the inner container of a double timbale to within 1 cm ($\frac{2}{5}$ in) of the rim. When set, decorate the surface with crayfish tails and slices of truffle and cover with almost setting, clear Fish Aspic Jelly.

To serve: place crushed ice in the outer container of the double timbale, replace the prepared inner container and present on a folded serviette on a round dish.

2106 Mousse d'Ecrevisses Cardinal

Cook 40 medium-sized crayfish as for Bisque. When cooked, remove the shells, trim the tails and cut them in half lengthways.

Coat a Charlotte or dome-shaped mould with a fairly thick layer of clear Fish Aspic Jelly, embed it in crushed ice and decorate the sides with the halves of crayfish tails first dipped in nearly setting jelly. Arrange these in superimposed rows, one row with the tails inclined to the left, the next inclined to the right and so on until the mould is lined.

Prepare the Mousse as indicated in the previous recipe but using double the quantity of Red Colouring Butter. Fill 12 carapaces of crayfish with the Mousse, decorating each with a slice of truffle; add 20 slices of truffle to the remainder of the Mousse and pour this into the prepared mould.

Allow to set in the refrigerator, turn out and present according to one of the methods indicated in the previous recipe.

2107 Petits Soufflés Froids d'Ecrevisses

Prepare the Mousse as for Mousse froide d'Ecrevisses using cold Sauce Béchamel instead of Fish Velouté; the addition of this sauce is not, however, absolutely necessary as the base of the preparation may even be the crayfish cullis with the addition of extra fish jelly. The addition of the sauce, however, gives a more delicate result.

Set a thin layer of Fish Aspic Jelly in the bottoms of small porcelain *Cassolettes* or small silver timbales, surround with bands of greaseproof paper projecting about 2 cm (4/5 in) above the rims, sticking the ends together with a little jelly.

Fill them with the Mousse mixture almost to the tops of the papers and place to set in the refrigerator.

To serve: remove the bands of paper, which now gives them the appearance of small soufflés; serve arranged on a serviette on a suitable dish.

2108 Suprême d'Ecrevisses au Champagne

Cook 40 crayfish quickly in a well seasoned Mirepoix and moistened with ½ bottle of dry Champagne. When ready, remove, shell and trim the tails and keep them in a cool place.

Finely pound the shells with 150 g (5 oz) butter and place in a saucepan with 7½ dl (1⅓ pt or 3¼ U.S. cups) boiling Fish Velouté, 4 or 5 soaked leaves of gelatine and the cooking liquid from the crayfish passed through a fine strainer. Boil gently for a few minutes so that the flavour of the crayfish may permeate the sauce.

Pass through a fine strainer into a basin placed on ice, whisk gently whilst cooling and when nearly at setting point, fold in 5 dl (18 fl oz or 2¼ U.S. cups) half whipped cream.

Pour quickly into a silver or porcelain timbale taking care that it is not more than two-thirds full and place in a refrigerator to set.

When the Mousse is firm, decorate the surface with the reserved crayfish tails, some leaves of chervil and shapes of truffle. Finally, cover with a thin layer of near setting, amber-coloured Fish Aspic Jelly and keep on ice until required.

To serve: present the dish set in a block of carved ice or placed in a deep dish surrounded by crushed ice.

HOMARD—LOBSTER

2109 Homard à l'Américaine

For 1 lobster of 800–900 g (1¾–2 lbs).

The first requirement for this dish is that the lobster must be a live one.

Cut the tail into sections; remove the claws and crack them so as to facilitate the removal of the flesh after cooking; split the carapace in half lengthways and remove the sac which is found near the top of the head (this usuallly contains a little gravel). Place the creamy parts and coral from the head on one side and reserve for use. Season the pieces of lobster with salt and pepper.

Heat 4 tbs oil and 30 g (1 oz) butter in a shallow pan until very hot, place in the pieces of lobster and fry quickly on all sides until the flesh is well set and the shells have turned a good red colour.

Drain off the fat by tilting the pan on one side with its lid on, then sprinkle the lobster with 2 finely chopped shallots and 1 small clove of crushed garlic. Add ¼ dl (1 fl oz or ⅛ U.S. cup) flamed brandy, 2 dl (7 fl oz or ⅞ U.S. cup) white wine, 1½ dl (5 fl oz or ⅝ U.S. cup) fish stock, 1 tbs melted meat glaze, 150 g (5½ oz) roughly chopped flesh only of tomato or 1½ tbs tomato purée, ½ dl (2 fl oz or ¼ U.S. cup) Sauce Demi-glace, a pinch of roughly chopped parsley and a touch of Cayenne pepper. Cover with the lid and cook gently for 15–20 minutes.

When cooked, transfer the pieces of lobster to a dish, remove the flesh from the sections and claws and place them in a timbale or deep dish with the two halves of the carapace on top standing up against each other; keep warm.

Reduce the cooking liquid to 2 dl (7 fl oz or ⅞

U.S. cup) and add the reserved creamy parts and coral chopped together with approximately 15 g (½ oz) butter. Reheat and pass through a fine strainer. Reheat again for a few minutes without allowing it to boil, then add away from the heat, 100 g (3½ oz) butter in small pieces. Pour this sauce over the lobster and sprinkle with a little roughly chopped parsley.

Note: In modern English and American service the two halves of the carapace are not served, these usually being reserved for the preparation of red colouring butter.

2110 Homard à la Bordelaise

Cut up the live lobster as described in the preceding recipe and season the pieces with salt and pepper.

Place the pieces of lobster in a pan containing 50 g (2 oz) hot clarified butter and fry gently on all sides until the flesh is well set and the shells are coloured red. Drain off half of the butter and add 2 tbs chopped shallot, a pea-sized piece of crushed garlic, ¼ dl (1 fl oz or ⅛ U.S. cup) flamed brandy and 1 dl (3½ fl oz or ½ U.S. cup) white wine; reduce by half.

Now add 2½ dl (9 fl oz or 1⅛ U.S. cups) fish stock, 2 dl (7 fl oz or ⅞ U.S. cup) Lenten Sauce Espagnole, 1½ dl (5 fl oz or ⅝ U.S. cup) Sauce Tomate, a small Bouquet garni, a pinch of salt and a touch of Cayenne. Cover with a lid and cook gently for 15 minutes. Remove the pieces of lobster and then extract the flesh from the shells; place these in a small pan, cover and keep warm.

Add the chopped creamy parts and coral to the sauce, cook for a few moments and then reduce it to 2 dl (7 fl oz or ⅞ U.S. cup). Pass through a fine strainer over the lobster and reheat without boiling. Finish the sauce with a few drops of lemon juice; 75 g (2½ oz) butter added in small pieces and ½ tbs chopped tarragon and chervil. Shake the pan to ensure the complete mixing of the ingredients, tip into a timbale or deep dish and sprinkle with a little roughly chopped parsley.

2111 Homard à la Broche

Select a large very live lobster, kill it and fix it on the spit.

Place in the dripping pan 125 g (4½ oz) butter, ⅓ bottle dry Champagne, a pinch of salt and 6 peppercorns and whilst the lobster is cooking baste it almost continuously with this mixture—a perfect result is obtainable only in this way. Allow approximately 40 minutes cooking time for a lobster weighing 1 kg (2¼ lb).

When cooked, place the lobster on a suitable dish and serve accompanied by either of the following sauces: 1) Cold Sauce Ravigote mixed with the strained cooking liquid from the lobster, from which the fat has been removed. 2) Pass the cooking liquid through a fine strainer, remove all the fat and reduce by three-quarters; add 2 tbs meat glaze, 1½ tbs Derby Sauce, a pinch of chopped parsley and finish with 75 g (2½ oz) butter and a few drops of lemon juice.

2112 Homard Cardinal

Plunge the live lobster into boiling Vinegar Court-bouillon and simmer, allowing 25 minutes for a lobster weighing 800 g (1¾ lb).

As soon as it is cooked, remove and split it completely in half lengthways; remove the flesh from the tail, cut into thick slices on the slant and place in a pan to keep warm with a little Sauce Cardinal.

Discard the sac from the head, remove the claws and make a large opening in each, cutting with a knife or strong pair of scissors. Take out the flesh carefully without breaking the shells of the claws and cut it into small dice, along with any to be found in the head. Add the creamy parts from the head, an equal quantity of cooked small diced mushrooms and half the quantity of truffle also cut in small dice. Mix this Salpicon with a little Lobster Sauce.

Fill the empty claws with some of the Salpicon and spread the rest along the bottom of the two empty half shells; lay the reserved slices of lobster on top of the half shells, alternating with nice slices of truffle.

Place the two half shells on the dish and to keep them level place the filled claws on either side. Coat the half shells and claws with Sauce Cardinal, sprinkle with grated cheese and melted butter and glaze quickly in a very hot oven or under the salamander.

2113 Homard Clarence

Cook the lobster in a Vinegar Court-bouillon and remove it as soon as it is cooked.

When no more than lukewarm, split it in half lengthways, remove the flesh from the tail and claws and cut into thick slices on the slant; keep warm in a pan with a few drops of fish stock or mushroom cooking liquid.

Remove any flesh from the head along with the creamy parts and coral and finely pound together with 2 tbs cream. Pass through a fine sieve, add 2½ dl (9 fl oz or 1⅛ U.S. cups) curry flavoured Sauce Béchamel and mix together.

Fill the half shells two-thirds full with plain boiled rice and then cover this with the slices of lobster alternating with slices of truffle. Coat lightly with the prepared sauce, reheat and place on a hot oval silver dish.

Serve accompanied with the remaining sauce.

2114 Coquilles de Homard Mornay

Pipe a border of Duchesse potato mixture around the edges of small scollop or silver shells using a small star tube.

Fill with a Salpicon of cooked lobster mixed with Sauce Mornay, place a nice slice of lobster in the centre and on top of this a slice of truffle. Coat with either plain Sauce Mornay or Sauce Mornay containing chopped truffle and glaze quickly under the salamander.

Note: These Coquilles can also be coated with Sauce Vin Blanc, Sauce Allemande or Sauce Cardinal. The Salpicon should also be mixed with the same sauce.

2115 Homard à la Crème

Proceed in the same way as for Homard à la Newburg using raw lobster (2122) but deglaze with brandy only and immediately add 125 g (4½ oz) peeled thickly sliced raw truffles. Almost cover with very fresh, single cream, season with salt and a touch of Cayenne and finish cooking.

When cooked, remove the meat from the shells and place in a timbale with the truffles. Reduce the cream to 2 dl (7 fl oz or ⅞ U.S. cup), add 3 tbs melted light meat glaze and a few drops of lemon juice and pass the sauce through a fine muslin or strainer over the lobster.

2116 Croquettes de Homard—Lobster Croquettes

Prepare a Salpicon of lobster, mushrooms and truffles and mix together with a little Sauce Béchamel finished with Lobster Butter. The proportions and method should be in accordance with the instructions given in the article on Croquettes (1144).

Divide the prepared mixture into pieces of approximately 75 g (2½ oz) each, mould oval-shape and flour, egg and breadcrumb.

Deep fry when required and serve on a serviette garnished with fried parsley and accompanied with Sauce Homard.

2117 Homard à la Française

Cut the live lobster into sections and place in a shallow pan containing 50 g (2 oz) very hot butter; season with salt, pepper and a touch of Cayenne and fry on all sides until the flesh is well set and the shells coloured red.

Moisten with 2 dl (7 fl oz or ⅞ U.S. cup) white wine and ½ dl (2 fl oz or ¼ U.S. cup) brandy; add 2 tbs Julienne of onion and carrot which have been stewed in a little butter, a pinch of roughly chopped parsley and 1 dl (3½ fl oz or ½ U.S. cup) fish stock. Cover with a lid and cook gently for 15 minutes.

Remove the lobster and place in a deep dish or timbale and keep warm; thicken the cooking liquid with 2 tbs Fish Velouté and finish by shaking in 100 g (3½ oz) best butter. Pour this sauce over the lobster.

2118 Homard Grillé—Grilled Lobster

Usually the lobster is taken live, split through the centre lengthways, seasoned, sprinkled with butter and grilled over a moderate heat allowing approximately 30 minutes for a lobster weighing between 900 g–1 kg (2 lb–2¼ lb); it is preferable, however, to three-quarters cook the lobster in Court-bouillon first as in this way the flesh does not become quite so tough as when grilled from the raw state.

When removed from the Court-bouillon it is only necessary to split it in half, sprinkle with butter and grill for sufficient time to complete the cooking.

When ready, crack the claws to facilitate the removal of the flesh and place the two halves on a serviette or a special grill; surround with picked parsley and serve accompanied with Sauce Diable or any other well seasoned sauce suitable for grilled fish.

2119 Homard Bouilli à la Hollandaise

Cook the lobster in Vinegar Court-bouillon and as soon as it is cooked, drain it and cut in half lengthways without completely separating the two halves.

Arrange on a serviette, surround with picked parsley and serve accompanied with a dish of freshly cooked, floury potatoes and a sauceboat of melted butter.

2120 Homard à la Mornay, or Homard au Gratin

Proceed in the same way as for Homard Cardinal (2112) but using Sauce Mornay instead of Sauce Cardinal.

2121 Mousselines de Homard

When applied to shellfish, the term Mousse invariably indicates a cold preparation, whereas the term Mousseline denotes a hot dish.

Mousselines of lobster are made from a Mousseline forcemeat prepared with the raw flesh of lobster but as with all other crustaceans the flesh produces a forcemeat which is too soft for moulding easily with spoons. It is recommended in these cases to use the specially manufactured Quenelle moulds taking care that they are well buttered before use.

Cook in the same way as all other Mousselines; all the garnishes and sauces for Mousselines de Saumon are suitable to serve with them.

2122 Homard à la Newburg

Homard à la Newburg may be prepared in two different ways, the first using raw lobster is more suitable for large establishments although the second method using cooked lobster is the correct one.

Using raw lobster: Cut up the live lobster and fry quickly in oil and butter as for Homard à l'Américaine.

When the flesh is well set and the shells coloured, completely drain off the fat, deglaze with $\frac{1}{2}$ dl (2 fl oz or $\frac{1}{4}$ U.S. cup) flamed brandy and 2 dl (7 fl oz or $\frac{7}{8}$ U.S. cup) Marsala wine and reduce by two-thirds. Season, add 4 dl (14 fl oz or $1\frac{3}{4}$ U.S. cups) cream and 1 dl ($3\frac{1}{2}$ fl oz or $\frac{1}{2}$ U.S. cup) fish stock, cover with a lid and cook gently for 15 minutes.

When cooked, remove the lobster, extract the flesh from the shells, place in a timbale, cover and keep warm. Thicken the sauce with the reserved creamy parts and coral chopped with 30 g (1 oz) butter. Boil gently for a few minutes then pass through a fine strainer over the lobster.

Using cooked lobster: Cook the lobster in Vinegar Court-bouillon, remove the flesh from the shell and cut into even-sized, fairly thick slices.

Place the slices in a well buttered shallow pan, season well and heat on both sides so as to develop a good red colour on the outside membrane. Moisten with sufficient Madeira wine to almost cover and reduce almost completely.

When required for service, pour a liaison composed of $1\frac{1}{2}$ dl (5 fl oz or $\frac{5}{8}$ U.S. cup) cream mixed with 2 egg yolks over the slices, shake the pan gently on the side of the stove so that the sauce thickens by the slow cooking of the egg yolks but do not allow it to boil.

Place as quickly as possible into a warmed timbale to serve.

Notes:

1) It is necessary to point out that this dish when made with cooked lobster cannot be successfully cooked in advance as the sauce will carry on cooking and it will then separate and break down.
2) The lobster and sauce may be presented inside a border of Pommes Duchesse mixture piped on to a suitable dish and coloured in the oven beforehand.

2123 Homard à la Palestine

Cut the live lobster into sections and colour in butter with a Mirepoix in the same way as for Bisque (668).

Moisten with 4 dl (14 fl oz or $1\frac{3}{4}$ U.S. cups) white wine, 5 dl (18 fl oz or $2\frac{1}{4}$ U.S. cups) fish stock and $\frac{1}{2}$ dl (2 fl oz or $\frac{1}{4}$ U.S. cup) flamed brandy. Cover with a lid and cook gently for 15 minutes. When cooked, remove the pieces of lobster, take out the flesh from the shells and place in a pan with a little butter; cover and keep warm.

Finely pound the shells and remains of the lobster and fry together with 1 dl ($3\frac{1}{2}$ fl oz or $\frac{1}{2}$ U.S. cup) oil and a little finely cut Mirepoix; moisten with the cooking liquid from the lobster and cook gently for 15 minutes.

Pass through a fine strainer and allow to rest for 5 minutes to allow the oil to rise to the surface; skim off the oil completely then reduce the liquid to $1\frac{1}{2}$ dl (5 fl oz or $\frac{5}{8}$ U.S. cup). Add the creamy parts and coral of the lobster, previously passed through a fine strainer, and 2 tbs Fish Velouté. Allow to boil for a few minutes and finish away from the heat with 75 g ($2\frac{1}{2}$ oz) butter and a pinch of curry powder.

Arrange a nice border of Riz Pilaw (4239) on the serving dish, place the warm lobster in the centre and coat with a little of the prepared sauce; serve the remainder of the sauce separately.

2124 Homard Thermidor

Split the lobster in half lengthways, season and gently grill, then remove the flesh from the shell and cut into fairly thick slices on the slant.

Place some Sauce Crème finished with a little English mustard in the bottom of the two half shells, replace the slices of lobster neatly on top and coat with the sauce. Glaze lightly in a hot oven or under the salamander.

2125 Risotto de Homard Tourville

Cook the lobster in a White Wine Court-bouillon; remove the flesh from the shell and cut into fairly thick slices.

Place in shallow pan with 125 g ($4\frac{1}{2}$ oz) sliced mushrooms, cooked in a little butter without colour; 20 poached and bearded mussels; 20 poached and bearded oysters and 60 g (2 oz) slices of truffle. Add $1\frac{1}{2}$ dl (5 fl oz or $\frac{5}{8}$ U.S. cup) Fish Velouté, a little of the reduced cooking liquid from the mussels and mix all the ingredients carefully together.

Arrange a border of Risotto on the service dish, place the fish in the centre and coat the border and lobster with Sauce Mornay. Glaze quickly under the salamander.

2126 Soufflé de Homard—Lobster Soufflé

Split the live lobster in half lengthways, remove the flesh and prepare a Mousseline forcemeat in the prescribed manner (1564).

Cook the two half shells carefully so as not to deform them and to obtain a nice red colour; drain them, wipe clean and dry and fill with the prepared forcemeat. Surround each shell with a strip of buttered greaseproof paper, holding it in place with string so that it comes 2 cm (¾in) above the edge of the shells. This is necessary to stop the mixture running over the sides of the shells during the initial stages of cooking. Place the filled shells on a tray which has been covered with a little water and cook gently in a warm oven for 15 to 20 minutes.

As soon as ready, remove the string and paper and arrange the two halves of lobster on a serviette on a silver dish and surround with sprigs of very green parsley.

Serve accompanied with a sauce in keeping with the dish such as Sauce Homard, Diplomate, Normande, Vin Blanc etc.

Note: This recipe is the basic one for Lobster Soufflé but it may be altered in innumerable ways according to taste or fancy; for example, diced truffle, slices of lobster, soft roes or poached oysters may be added to the forcemeat or alternately these garnishes may be arranged on top of the soufflé when cooked.

HOMARD FROID—COLD LOBSTER

2127 Aspic de Homard—Aspic of Lobster

Coat the inside of a deep plain or fancy mould with a thin layer of Fish Aspic Jelly and decorate according to taste. Fill with alternate layers of sliced lobster, sliced truffle and very clear Fish Aspic Jelly.

Allow to set in a cool place and turn out in the usual manner when required.

2128 Aspic de Homard à la Russe

Prepare some fairly thick slices of cooked lobster cut from the tail and coat one side of each with Sauce Mayonnaise mixed with a little almost setting aspic jelly; decorate with truffle, coral etc.

Coat a suitable-sized border mould with a fairly thick layer of Fish Aspic Jelly, arrange the prepared slices of lobster decorated side downwards so that this will be apparent when demoulded; fill with the same jelly and allow to set in the refrigerator.

When required, turn out on to a round dish and fill the centre of the mould with Salade Russe.

2129 Homard Carnot

Decorate some slices of cooked lobster each with a nice slice of truffle and coat with Fish Aspic Jelly.

Prepare a moulded border using a Pain de Homard mixture (2134) and allow to set in the refrigerator. When required turn out on to a round dish and place the decorated slices of lobster in a circle on top of the mould.

Serve accompanied with Sauce Mayonnaise à la Russe.

2130 Côtelettes de Homard Arkangel—Lobster Cutlets Archangel

Carefully mix together equal quantities of caviare and cooked lobster cut in small dice and mix with an equal amount of Mousse de Homard (2133).

Immediately fill into lightly oiled cutlet moulds and place in a cold room to set. When set, turn out the cutlets and coat the surface of each with Fish Chaud-froid. Finally coat each cutlet with clear Fish Aspic Jelly and keep in a cool place until required.

To Serve: arrange the cutlets in a circle on a round dish and fill the centre with chopped fish jelly.

Serve accompanied with Salade Russe.

2131 Homard Grammont

Cut a cold cooked lobster in half lengthways; remove the claws and the flesh from the tail. Trim the flesh from the tail, cut it into even-sized fairly thick slices, coat with a thick layer of Fish Aspic Jelly and decorate each with a slice of grooved truffle. Finally, glaze the slices with a final coating of jelly.

Also glaze as many poached and dried oysters as there are slices of lobster, using the same jelly.

Pound together the creamy parts of the lobster and the flesh of the claws with a tablespoon of cold Sauce Béchamel. Pass through a fine sieve and with some melted Fish Aspic Jelly and cream, prepare a Mousse de Homard (2133) using a little paprika to give a nice pink colour. Fill the two half lobster shells with the Mousse and allow to set in the refrigerator.

When required, arrange the slices of lobster alternating with the oysters on top of the filled halves of lobster; place the halves back to back on a serviette on a dish with a heart of lettuce in the middle and sprigs of parsley at each end.

Serve accompanied with Sauce Mayonnaise or any other suitable cold sauce.

2132 Mayonnaise de Homard

Proceed in the same way as for Mayonnaise de Saumon (1686).

2133 Mousse de Homard—Lobster Mousse

Cook the lobster with a few tablespoons of Mirepoix à la Bordelaise, 5 dl (18 fl oz or 2¼ U.S. cups) white wine and ½ dl (2 fl oz or ¼ U.S. cup) flamed brandy; allow to cool in the cooking liquid.

When cold, remove the lobster, open it and extract all the flesh; pound this well while adding little by little, 2 dl (7 fl oz or ⅞ U.S. cup) cold Fish Velouté per 500 g (1 lb 2 oz) of flesh. Pass through a fine sieve, place in a pan on ice and mix well together with a wooden spoon for a few minutes. Add 1 dl ($3\frac{1}{2}$ fl oz or $\frac{1}{2}$ U.S. cup) cool melted Fish Aspic Jelly and fold in 2 dl (7 fl oz or $\frac{7}{8}$ U.S. cup) half whipped cream. Adjust the seasoning and finish with a little Cayenne.

For moulding and presentation see the recipes for Cold Crayfish Mousses.

2134 Pain de Homard
Prepare the mixture as explained for Cold Fish or Meat Loaf (338) adding a purée of the trimmings and creamy parts of the lobster cooked as for Mousse de Homard, plus the flesh and truffles cut in small dice. Mould and cook as indicated.

2135 Cold Lobster with Various Sauces
Cook the lobster in Vinegar Court-bouillon, allow to cool in the cooking liquid and when cold, remove, drain well and detach the claws. Split the lobster in half lengthways, discard the sac from the head and carefully crack the claws so that the flesh can be easily removed. Place the two halves on a folded serviette on a dish; arrange the claws at the sides and surround with parsley or hearts of lettuce.

Serve accompanied with Sauce Mayonnaise or one of its derivatives, e.g. Rémoulade, Tartare, etc.

2136 Salade de Homard—Lobster Salad
Proceed in the same way as Salade de Saumon using trimmings and dice of lobster instead of salmon.

2137 Petits Soufflés Froids de Homard—Small Cold Lobster Soufflés
Proceed in the same way as small cold Soufflés of crayfish using lobster Mousse instead of crayfish Mousse.

LANGOUSTE—CRAWFISH OR SPINY LOBSTER

2138 Langouste Froide—Cold Crawfish
Most of the recipes for cold lobster are suitable in most cases for cold crawfish, providing that they are not too large. This includes the Aspics, Côtelettes à la Arkangel, Mousses and Pains.

The following recipes for Langouste à la Parisienne and Langouste à la Russe should not be confused. They are different from each other in that the slices of crawfish are simply decorated and coated with Fish Aspic Jelly for *à la Parisienne*; and coated with jellied Mayonnaise then decorated and glazed for *à la Russe*. In modern practice, Fish Chaud-froid Sauce is commonly used instead of jellied Mayonnaise.

2139 Langouste à la Parisienne
Carefully tie a live crawfish to a board with its tail stretched out flat. Place into boiling Vinegar Court-bouillon and cook; allow to cool in its cooking liquid and when quite cold remove the flesh from the tail by either of the following ways:

1) Remove the membrane from underneath the tail, cutting close to the shell on either side.
2) Use scissors to cut 2 parallel lines about 4 cm ($1\frac{3}{5}$ in) apart down the tail and remove the strip of shell.

Take out the tail carefully keeping it in one piece; cut into even-shaped fairly thick slices and trim. Decorate each with a slice of truffle and coat well with cold Fish Aspic Jelly.

Remove the creamy parts and any flesh from the carapace; cut this flesh and the trimmings from the prepared slices into small dice and add to a vegetable salad; pass the creamy parts through a fine sieve and add to a Sauce Mayonnaise to which a little cold melted aspic jelly has been added; mix the vegetable salad with the Mayonnaise.

Fill the required number of medium-sized artichoke bottoms, dome shape with the salad; place a small round of truffle on top of each and when set because of the jelly in the Mayonnaise, coat with Fish Aspic Jelly.

Fill the empty shell of the crawfish with a coarse Julienne of lettuce and then place it with its head upwards on a wedge-shaped base made of bread or carved rice set on the serving dish; it should be poised at an angle of about 45 degrees. Place the prepared slices of crawfish overlapping along the back of the filled shell, starting with the largest at the head and graduating them according to size. Surround the base with the artichoke bottoms, alternating with quarters or halves of hard-boiled eggs set upright with the yolks showing, or with hard-boiled eggs prepared as barrels and filled with the same salad as used for the artichokes.

Surround the dish with fancy shapes of clear Fish Aspic Jelly.

2140 Langouste à la Russe
Proceed as in the previous recipe by cooking the crawfish, removing the flesh from the tail and cutting it into neatly trimmed, fairly thick slices.

Coat these slices with Sauce Mayonnaise mixed with a little cold melted aspic jelly, or preferably with white Fish Chaud-froid Sauce to which has been added a fine purée of the creamy parts from the crawfish.

Decorate each slice of crawfish with a touch of coral and 2 leaves of chervil; glaze with Fish Aspic Jelly and keep cold.

Prepare a Salade Russe without ham and tongue, add the trimmings of the crawfish cut in small dice and mix together with a little jellied Sauce Mayonnaise.

Line 10 dariole moulds with Fish Aspic Jelly, place a slice of truffle in each and fill with the prepared Salade Russe. (Instead of jellying the moulds they can be brushed with oil.)

Prepare 10 hard-boiled eggs by cutting off the top third, removing the yolks and refilling dome-shape with caviare; the top of the eggs may be cut tooth shape to give a more artistic appearance.

Arrange the crawfish on a base on the serving dish as in the preceding recipe and arrange the slices on top. Surround the base with the salads and eggs alternately and garnish with round fancy shapes of clear Fish Aspic Jelly, each with a small round slice of truffle placed on top.

Note: Lobster as well as crawfish may also be prepared à la Néva, à la Moscovite, or à la Sibérienne etc. but these are only minor variations of à la Russe. These names are only justified by slight alterations in detail or garnish which may take the form of placing the salad in Barquettes of cucumber or beetroot and placing the caviare in small pleated cases instead of in hard-boiled eggs. Since these names represent creations for special occasions and because their preparation is not based on sound or classical rules, it has not been thought necessary to give full recipes for them.

LANGOUSTINES—DUBLIN BAY PRAWNS OR NORWAY LOBSTERS

These shellfish although smaller than lobster may with relative care be prepared in the same way as any of the recipes for lobster.

2141 Langoustines au Paprika

Cut the Dublin Bay prawns in half lengthways and prepare them in exactly the same way as Lobster Newburg prepared with raw lobster. The flavouring and seasoning of the dish should include a proportionate amount of chopped onion and paprika.

Serve arranged in a deep round dish.

TERRAPENE—DIAMOND-BACK TERRAPIN

This small turtle originating from North America is so called because of the diamond shapes in relief on its back. It is prepared in a number of ways and is highly esteemed by American gourmets.

It is rarely obtained live in Europe and is usually obtained as a prepared item, either bottled or canned. Nevertheless it is thought useful to give the methods of cooking as expounded in that important book *The Epicurean* by Chas. Ranhoffer, who directed the kitchens of the famous Delmonico Restaurant in New York for so many years.

2142 The preparation and cooking of Terrapin

Place the live terrapin in a bowl of water sufficiently large for it to swim about with ease. Leave it for approximately 30 minutes then renew the water. Repeat this operation a number of times and then finally wash the terrapin well and plunge it into a pot of boiling water until the fine white skin which covers the head and flippers can be easily rubbed off with a clean cloth.

Place the terrapin to cook in unsalted boiling water or by steaming, the time required for this naturally varies according to the size and quality of the terrapin but in any case it should not exceed 45 minutes. It is possible to judge whether it is cooked by squeezing the legs between the fingers; the flesh should give under pressure.

Terrapins requiring more than 45 minutes of cooking time are usually of inferior quality and any requiring more than an hour unless they are very large should be discarded as being of no culinary value; although the meat in this case may eventually become tender, it will be stringy and not have the required delicate flavour.

When cooked, allow to cool, cut off the nails from the legs and break the flat shell on both sides near the top shell. Detach the meat from the shells and empty the insides; carefully remove and discard the gall bladder from the liver and any parts of the liver with which the gall bladder has been in contact. Reserve the liver and throw away the entrails, lights, head, tail and the white muscles from inside the shell. Remove the legs at the joints and cut into pieces of approximately 4 cm (1½ in) square; remove any eggs carefully.

Place the pieces of leg in a pan with the eggs, the liver cut in slices and the flesh from the shells cut in approximately 4 cm (1½ in) squares; season with salt, black pepper, a little Cayenne and just cover with water.

Bring to the boil, cover with a lid and cook in a moderate oven for 20 to 30 minutes and reserve for use. It can be kept for some time by dividing it into small porcelain pots or moulds using 5 or 6 eggs, 1 slice of liver and approximately 180 g (6 oz) meat for each pot. Cover with the cooking liquid making a total weight of approximately 200–210 g (7–7½ oz). Each of these moulds would thus contain sufficient for 2–3 persons.

2143 Terrapène à la Baltimore—Terrapin Baltimore

Reheat 5 moulds, i.e. approximately 1 kg (2¼ lb)

of prepared terrapin, in a Bain-marie; drain and reserve the cooking liquid.

Cook 60 g (2 oz) butter until brown, add the pieces of terrapin, season with salt and ground pepper and fry, tossing over and over, for 2 minutes. Add the cooking liquid, bring to the boil and thicken by mixing in 1 tbs cornflour or arrowroot diluted with a little water, moving the pan round and round to mix; finish with ½ dl (2 fl oz or ¼ U.S. cup) of sherry.

To serve: place the terrapin in small silver dishes covered with lids or in terrapin-shaped porcelain dishes.

2144 Terrapène à la Maryland—Terrapin Maryland

Pound 8 hard-boiled egg yolks with 125 g (4¼ oz) butter and pass through a fine sieve.

Reheat 5 moulds of terrapin in a Bain-marie and drain; place the pieces in a suitable pan and add 5 dl (18 fl oz or 2¼ U.S. cups) cream. Simmer gently for 5–6 minutes then thicken by adding the purée of egg yolks and butter. Simmer gently for a further 10 minutes, finish with a little good Madeira and adjust the seasoning with salt, pepper and a little Cayenne.

TORTUE—TURTLE

If the flesh and flippers of turtle in the preparation of turtle soup are to be used as a dish they should be removed from the soup when two-thirds cooked and finished by braising with Madeira. A suitable accompaniment would then be a brown garnish such as Financière or Tortue.

2145 Nageoires de Tortue à l'Américaine—Turtle Flippers à l'Américaine

Cook the turtle flippers as described above and when ready, carefully remove all the bones. Place them in the serving dish and cover with Sauce à l'Américaine (84).

2146 Nageoires de Tortue au Madère—Turtle Flippers with Madeira

Prepare the turtle flippers by cooking them as above, remove the bones and place in a suitable dish. Reduce the braising liquid, thicken with a little arrowroot and finish with a little old Madeira. Pour this sauce over the flippers.

HUITRES—OYSTERS

2147 Quenelles d'Huîtres à la Reine

Prepare a Mousseline forcemeat from 125 g (4½ oz) raw chicken breast and 6 oysters; mould into large Quenelles using soup spoons, enclosing 2 cold poached oysters in each. Cook in the usual manner.

As soon as they are cooked, drain them well on a clean cloth, arrange in a circle on a round dish and coat with well flavoured Sauce Suprême. Place a slice of truffle on each Quenelle and fill the centre of the dish with buttered asparagus tips.

2148 Other Recipes for Oysters

See the section on Hot Hors-d'oeuvre for the following: Huîtres à l'Anglaise, à l'Américaine, various Barquettes, à la Favorite, à la Florentine, au Gratin, à la Maréchale, à la Mornay, à la Polonaise, Soufflés, Petits Soufflés, à la Villeroy and à la Vladimir.

2149 OURSINS—SEA URCHINS

Sea Urchins are usually served raw as an Hors-d'oeuvre.

To prepare, first remove the spines, then open them on the flat side using a pair of scissors; discard the water contained inside as well as the digestive tract. The edible part of the shellfish are the ovaries or coral which is usually of a reddish purple colour and is eaten with fingers of bread as one would eat the yolk of a lightly boiled egg. These ovaries or coral provide a purée which is excellent for finishing certain fish sauces particularly those derived from Sauce Béchamel.

2150 Crème d'Oursins Chaude (*for fish*)

Prepare 5 dl (18 fl oz or 2¼ U.S. cups) Sauce Béchamel keeping it a little thick. Open 20 sea urchins as explained above, remove the edible part, pass through a fine sieve and add to the boiling sauce.

2151 Sauce à la Purée d'Oursins (*for shellfish*)

Clean and wash 20 sea urchins and cook them in boiling salted water with a few herbs and vegetable flavourings for 15–20 minutes. Drain well, allow to become cold and extract the reddish ovaries or coral; pass these through a fine sieve and add to 4 dl (14 fl oz or 1¾ U.S. cups) of well-flavoured Sauce Mayonnaise.

MOULES—MUSSELS

For 5 persons allow 1½ litres (2⅝ pt or 6½ U.S. cups) large or 2 litres (3½ pt or 9 U.S. cups) medium-sized mussels.

2152 Moules à la Catalane

Select very large mussels, scrape and wash them. Cook them, covered in a deep pan with sliced onions, parsley stalks, a little coarsely ground pepper, and a little water; they are cooked some little time after they have opened. Strain off the cooking liquid and allow it to settle, then pass it through a fine cloth taking care not to disturb any sand which may have settled at the bottom.

Reduce this cooking liquid and make it into a lightly thickened fish sauce; add 50 g (2 oz) finely chopped onion cooked in a little butter, 50 g (2 oz) butter and a few drops of lemon juice. Remove the mussels from their shells and mix carefully into the sauce. Replace the mussels together with a little sauce into the larger shells, arrange them on a tray and glaze very quickly under the salamander.

2153 Moules Frites—Fried Mussels
Select large mussels, cook as above and remove the beards. Place in a dish to marinate for 15 minutes with a little lemon juice, olive oil, and chopped parsley and when required, dip in a thin frying batter and deep fry in hot fat.

Drain well, arrange on a serviette on a dish and garnish with fried parsley.

2154 Moules à la Marinière
Cook the mussels in the usual manner, drain them and remove one of the shells from each mussel.

Reduce 2 dl (7 fl oz or $\frac{7}{8}$ U.S. cup) white wine and 1 large tbs chopped shallot by two-thirds; add 2 dl (7 fl oz or $\frac{7}{8}$ U.S. cup) of the cooking liquid from the mussels, 1 dl ($3\frac{1}{2}$ fl oz or $\frac{1}{2}$ U.S. cup) Fish Velouté and 50 g (2 oz) butter.

Place the mussels in the sauce and mix in gently; add a few drops of lemon juice and place into a timbale or deep dish; sprinkle with chopped parsley.

2155 Moules à la Poulette
Cook the mussels in the usual manner, drain them and remove one of the shells from each. Add 1 dl ($3\frac{1}{2}$ fl oz or $\frac{1}{2}$ U.S. cup) reduced cooking liquid from the mussels to 3 dl ($\frac{1}{2}$ pt or $1\frac{1}{4}$ U.S. cups) Sauce Poulette and flavour with a few drops of lemon juice, add the mussels and mix gently into the sauce.

Pour into a timbale or deep dish and sprinkle with chopped parsley.

2156 Rizot de Moules Toulonnaise
Cook the mussels in the usual manner, drain them and remove from the shells. Thicken 2 dl (7 fl oz or $\frac{7}{8}$ U.S. cup) of the cooking liquid with 2 egg yolks and a little butter; place the mussels in this sauce and mix together carefully.

Mould a border of Risotto cooked with fish stock on the serving dish and fill the centre with the prepared mussels and sauce.

2157 Moules Villeroy
Select large mussels and cook in the usual manner, drain them, take from the shells and remove the beards.

Place the mussels into Sauce à la Villeroy and remove them one by one, making sure that they are well coated; place on a tray. When cold, egg and breadcrumb and deep fry in hot oil when required.

Note: Mussels prepared *à la Villeroy* are used mainly as a garnish rather than as a dish in their own right.

COQUILLES SAINT-JACQUES, OR PELERINES—SCOLLOPS

2158 To Cook Scollops
Place the scollops round side down on top of a hot stove until the shells open. Remove the top shell and detach the fish by cutting underneath it with a pliable knife. Wash the scollops very well in plenty of water then poach them gently for 8–10 minutes in a White Wine Court-bouillon. When cooked, cut the round white part into thick slices, the red tongue or coral into slices and the beard into a Salpicon.

2159 Coquilles Saint-Jacques au Gratin
Scrub the deep scollop shells well, dry them and coat the bottom of each with Sauce Duxelles plus $\frac{1}{2}$ tbs white wine. Place the slices of white flesh, coral and beard on top, surround with slices of raw mushrooms and cover with Sauce Duxelles.

Sprinkle with white breadcrumbs and melted butter and gratinate in the usual manner for a Complete Gratin (2182).

2160 Coquilles Saint-Jacques à la Nantaise
Prepare and cook the scollops in the usual manner then gently braise the slices of white flesh and coral with a little white wine and mushroom cooking liquor.

Scrub and dry the deep shells from the scollops; coat the bottom of each with a little Sauce au Vin Blanc, arrange the slices of white flesh and coral on top with a small cooked mushroom and 2 slices of truffle per shell. Surround with a line of small poached mussels, coat with more sauce and glaze quickly under the salamander.

2161 Coquilles Saint-Jacques à la Parisienne
Prepare and cook the scollops in the usual manner, then gently braise the slices of white flesh and coral with a little white wine and mushroom cooking liquor.

Scrub and dry the deep shells, pipe a scrolled

border of Pommes Duchesse mixture round the edges, brush carefully with a little beaten egg and colour in the oven.

Coat the bottom of each with a spoonful of Sauce au Vin Blanc containing a little chopped truffle, arrange the slices of white flesh and coral on top, alternating with slices of cooked mushroom. Coat with more sauce and glaze under the salamander.

ESCARGOTS—SNAILS

2162 To Prepare Snails

Select snails which are closed and with a knife remove the calcareous membrane covering the opening of the shell. Wash the snails well in a few changes of water and then place them in a container with coarse salt, some vinegar and a pinch of flour. Allow them to disgorge and cleanse themselves for approximately 2 hours then rewash well in plenty of cold water so as to remove all traces of mucous. Cover with water, bring to the boil and simmer for 5–6 minutes.

Refresh the snails in cold water and drain well; extract the snails from their shells and discard the black part (Cloaca) from the tail end. Place the snails in a pan and well cover with half white wine and half water; add a little sliced carrot, onion and shallot, a large Bouquet garni and 8 g (⅓ oz) salt per 1 litre (1¾ pt or 4½ U.S. cups) of liquid. Bring to the boil and simmer very gently for at least 3 hours. Allow the snails to cool in the cooking liquid.

Place the empty shells in a pot, cover with water, add a little soda and boil for 30 minutes. Drain off the dirty water and wash the shells well in clean water. Drain, dry well and use as required.

2163 Escargots à la Mode de l'Abbaye

For 40 snails: Cook together 1 large tbs finely chopped onion with a little butter until a golden colour. Add 40 well drained snails, cooked as in the previous recipe, and ½ tbs flour.

Mix well together, then add 2 dl (7 fl oz or ⅞ U.S. cup) boiling fresh cream and simmer gently for 12 to 15 minutes. Finish at the last moment with 4 egg yolks mixed with a little cream and 50 g (2 oz) butter.

Pour into a timbale or deep dish to serve.

2164 Escargots à la Bourguignonne—Snails Bourguignonne

Push into the inside of each empty snail shell, a small piece of Snail Butter (235) and follow this with a cooked snail. Close off the entrance to the shell with more of the butter, packing in as much as possible.

Arrange on a dish or special snail dish with the stuffed ends upwards, pour a little water over the bottom of the dish, sprinkle the buttered ends with a few fine white breadcrumbs and heat in a hot oven for 7–8 minutes.

2165 Escargots à la Chablisienne

For 60 snails: Place 4 dl (14 fl oz or 1¾ U.S. cups) good white wine in a pan with 30 g (1 oz) chopped shallot and reduce to 1½ dl (5 fl oz or ⅝ U.S. cup). Pass through a clean cloth using light pressure, then mix together with 1 tbs melted meat glaze.

Pour a little of this sauce into each shell then carefully push in a cooked snail and close with Snail Butter (235).

Arrange on a dish or special snail dish and finish as for Escargots à la Bourguignonne.

2166 Escargots à la Dijonnaise

Prepare a white wine and shallot reduction as in the preceding recipe.

Mix together 250 g (9 oz) each of butter and very fresh white bone marrow, passed first through a fine sieve; add a good pinch of pepper, a touch of mixed spice, 30 g (1 oz) finely chopped shallot, 2 cloves of crushed garlic and 20 g (⅔ oz) chopped truffle and mix in. Pour a little of the reduction into the shell, carefully push in a cooked snail and fill with the prepared butter.

Finish in the same way as for Escargots à la Chablisienne.

2167 Beignets d'Escargots à la Vigneronne

Cook the snails in the usual manner. Whilst still hot, drain them and dry well. Shallow fry them tossing over and over in butter with a little finely chopped shallot, crushed garlic and salt and pepper. Allow to cool a little, then drop the snails into a light frying batter containing plenty of chopped chives.

Deep fry in very hot oil, drain well, arrange on a serviette on a dish and garnish with fried parsley.

Note: Although ordinary fats may be used for the frying of snails in the above recipe, oil, especially nut oil, suits the characteristics of the dish better.

GRENOUILLES—FROGS

2168 Grenouilles Sautées aux Fines Herbes

Trim the frog's legs, season with salt and pepper and shallow fry on all sides in butter. Place in a deep dish and sprinkle with a few drops of lemon juice and chopped parsley.

2169 Grenouilles Frites—Fried Frogs' Legs
Trim the frogs' legs and marinate for one hour with a little lemon juice, oil, salt and pepper, and a touch of crushed garlic and chopped parsley.

When required, dip the legs in a light frying batter and deep fry in hot fat; drain well and serve on a serviette garnished with fried parsley.

2170 Grenouilles au Gratin
Well butter a suitable dish and in it arrange a border of thin slices of large raw mushrooms. Cover the bottom of the dish with a layer of Sauce Gratin and place on top the well trimmed frogs' legs; add a few cooked mushrooms and then cover with fairly thick Sauce Gratin. Sprinkle with fine white breadcrumbs and melted butter and gratinate in a hot oven.

Note: Alternatively, the dish may be bordered with slices of plain boiled potatoes or piped with Pommes Duchesse mixture.

2171 Grenouilles à la Meunière
Trim the frogs' legs well, season them and cook *à la Meunière*.

2172 Mousselines de Grenouilles
As the method of preparation of Mousseline forcemeat is always the same, it is only necessary in this case to use the flesh of frogs' legs as the basic material and to proceed in the same way as indicated.

When the forcemeat is ready, proceed as indicated in the recipes for Mousselines de Saumon (1677) taking account of the need to modify the size of the Mousselines in keeping with the material used making them a little smaller than usual.

2173 Grenouilles à la Poulette
Trim the frogs' legs well and poach in either a very light *Blanc* or in white wine and mushroom cooking liquor with a little sliced onion and a Bouquet garni.

When cooked, drain and dry well and mix gently into sufficient Sauce à la Poulette.

Serve in a timbale or deep dish, and sprinkle lightly with chopped parsley.

GRENOUILLES FROIDES—COLD FROGS' LEGS

2174 Nymphes à l'Aurore
Trim the frogs' legs well, poach them in white wine and allow to cool in the cooking liquid.

When cold, drain and dry them carefully with a clean cloth. Coat each with white Fish Chaud-froid Sauce which has been coloured by the addition of a little paprika.

Set a layer of very clear Champagne-flavoured Fish Aspic Jelly in the bottom of a deep square silver dish or glass bowl; place the prepared frogs' legs on top and intersperse them with tarragon leaves and chervil *Pluches* so as to imitate water plants. Cover the legs completely with the same jelly and allow to set in a cool place.

To serve: present the dish of frogs' legs set in a suitably sculpted block of clear ice.

CHAPTER 7

RELEVES AND ENTREES OF BUTCHERS' MEAT

THE GENERAL PRINCIPLES UNDERLYING METHODS OF COOKING—BRAISING; POÊLING; THE SAUTÉS; POACHING; BLANCHINGS: THE THEORY OF GRATINS; GRILLING; DEEP FRYING

These principles of cooking together with those used by the roast cook which are dealt with separately, and the Sauces, constitute the main culinary operations. Together, they embrace the main procedures, the basic principles of cookery and the formal rules on which are based correct working methods; a sound understanding of these is the only true professional knowledge. It can also be said that a proper understanding of the causes and effects of cooking constitute a high level of culinary scientific knowledge.

Every cook with an ambition to reach the top of his profession will have a deep interest in gaining an understanding of these theoretical explanations which will complement his own personal experience and observations.

The explanations given are of such importance that they must be properly understood; it is on a sound knowledge of them all that the quality of the final results depend.

2175 The Braising of Red Meats

Of all the various methods of preparation, braisings are the most costly and difficult to produce. Only by long experience and careful attention to detail can a cook expect to become familiar with its problems. In addition to the care required in preparation and the quality of the meat, which are of equal importance in braising as in any other method of cooking, it is essential to have first quality liquids and properly prepared vegetables and herbs.

Suitable meats for braising: Whilst joints of beef and mutton can be braised by the basic method, veal, lamb and poultry require a different method as indicated later on in this Chapter.

Red meats intended for braising, in contrast to those for roasting, do not need to be from young animals, in fact the best results are obtained from joints of older beasts; meat from very old animals, however, is unsuitable as the cooking time would need to be greatly extended and the result would be of a dry and stringy nature. Strictly speaking, the meat from very old animals is suitable only for the making of stocks and bouillons.

To lard the joints of meat: Joints for braising which are cut from the sirloin or ribs of beef are usually marbled or mottled with small flecks of fat—a sure sign of quality and tenderness—which is not apparent in joints cut from a leg of beef or a leg of mutton. These last joints do not contain sufficient fat to prevent them drying out in the long cooking process. This is remedied by larding, which is the insertion of long strips of salt pork fat (*Lardons*) approximately 1 cm (⅖ in) square, completely through the joint and along the grain of the meat. These *Lardons* should first of all be seasoned with pepper, nutmeg and other spices, sprinkled with chopped parsley and allowed to marinate in a little brandy for 2 hours. They are then inserted evenly spaced in the meat using a special larding pin allowing approximately 175 g (6 oz) of *Lardons* per 1 kg (2¼ lb) of meat.

To marinate the joints for braising: Whether larded, or not, joints of meat for braising gain in flavour by being marinated for several hours in wine with vegetables, herbs and spices before being cooked. To this effect they are first of all seasoned with salt, pepper and spices, being rolled in them so that their flavours penetrate the meat. They should then be placed into a suitable container just large enough to hold the joints, between two layers of vegetables and herbs, then just covered with ordinary red or white wine in the proportion of 3 dl (½ pt or 1¼ U.S. cups) per 1 kg (2¼ lb) meat.

Allow the meat to marinate for 5–6 hours turning it from time to time in the marinade.

The braising base: This is composed of thick slices of carrots and onions lightly fried in butter or fat, allowing 60 g (2 oz) of each, plus a Bouquet garni containing a clove of garlic, and 50 g (2 oz) blanched fresh pork rind per 1 kg (2¼ lb) of meat.

The first stage of braising: When the meat is sufficiently marinated, remove it from the marinade and allow it to drain on a sieve for half an hour, then dry it all over with a clean cloth.

Heat some clarified fat obtained from White Bouillon, in a thick-bottomed pan and fry the meat on all sides to colour it well and at the same time form a hard crust. This will serve to prevent the meat juices from escaping too soon which would result in more of a boiled than a braised piece of meat.

The length of time taken to brown the joint should be in keeping with its size and the crust should be thicker for a large piece of meat than that for a small one.

Once it is browned, the joint should be covered with thin slices of salt pork fat and tied up—this is not necessary for joints such as rib and sirloin as they already have an outer covering of fat.

Fry the vegetables from the marinade in the same fat and place in a pan just large enough to hold the piece of meat; place the prepared meat on top, add the wine of the marinade and the Bouquet garni and place the pan on the stove to boil until the liquid is reduced to a syrup. Then cover the meat with good brown stock, bring to the boil, cover with the lid and place in a medium oven so that the cooking is slow and uninterrupted.

Allow to cook until such time as when the meat is pierced with a trussing needle no blood appears; it is at this point that the first stage of the braising process ends, the second being explained later on. According to the kind of sauce desired, one or other of the following procedures should be adopted:

1) *For a clear gravy:* Strain the cooking liquid over the joint which has been removed to a clean pan and continue braising; baste the meat from time to time then finally thicken the gravy with diluted arrowroot to the consistency of ordinary Jus lié.
2) *For an accompanying sauce:* Reduce the braising liquor by half and bring it back to its original quantity by adding a mixture of two-thirds of Sauce Espagnole and one-third of tomato purée, or its equivalent of fresh tomatoes. Pour this sauce over the joint in a clean pan and resume the braising whilst basting the joint frequently.

   The joint is cooked when the point of a knife meets no resistance when inserted into it.

   When cooked, carefully remove the joint. Strain the sauce and allow it to settle for about 10 minutes so that all the fat rises to the surface and can be completely removed, then correct its consistency by adding more stock if too thick or by reducing if it is too thin.

The second stage of braising: As already stated, it is necessary to start the process by setting and browning the outside of the meat sufficiently, in keeping with its size; the reason for this being to drive the juices to the centre of the joint to prevent them from escaping and to build up a coating on the outside. This concentration of juices increases from the outside to the centre in keeping with the progression of the cooking.

Under the influence of the heat of the surrounding liquid the fibres of the meat contract, so forcing the juices they contain towards the centre of the joint. When the full force of the heat reaches the middle of the joint the juices are fully concentrated and drive out the water content which is vaporized; it expands causing the breakdown of the fibres of the meat.

So during the first stage, it is obvious that the concentration of the juices is towards the centre of the joint.

During the second stage, this process is reversed; in effect, the breakdown of the tough fibres begins at the centre of the joint because once the maximum internal temperature is reached, it is high enough to cause the concentrated meat juices to vaporize and produce a considerable pressure on the muscle fibre but this time from the other direction, that is from the middle to the outside. Thus the muscular fibres break down as the degree of cooking and its consequent pressure builds up, and little by little the thick brown outside of the joint has to give way to the returning juices; they escape through the crust and mingle with the liquid which surrounds the meat and at the same time the sauce penetrates back into the meat.

It is at this stage that careful attention is necessary. The braising liquid will be considerably reduced and therefore insufficient to cover the joint; the meat being uncovered will obviously dry out quickly unless it is basted frequently and turned over and over. In this way it is constantly moistened and saturated with the sauce thus acquiring the succulence and tenderness which characterizes a good braised joint and which distinguishes it from other methods of cooking.

The glazing of braised meats: If the braised meat is to be presented whole it is essential that it be glazed, but this is not necessary if the joint is going to be cut. The joint for glazing should be removed when just cooked, placed on a tray in a warm oven and basted again and again with a little of its braising liquor; because of the gelatinous nature of this liquid it sticks to the meat and is then reduced by the heat of the oven to a thin shiny glaze. When ready, the joint should be placed on the serving dish and kept covered until served.

General observations concerning the braising of meats.

1) When a braised joint is to be served with a vegetable accompaniment such as for Boeuf à la Mode, the vegetables may be cooked in with the meat during the second stage of the braising process having been coloured previously in butter. Alternatively, they can be cooked separately in some of the braising liquid.

   The best method is the first, but as this does not make for a very neat presentation it is up to the cook to decide which of these two methods to adopt.
2) There are at least two different malpractices, both to be deplored, but which are, unfortunately, frequently used.

The first is a method of frying the braising base, referred to in French as *Pinçage*. In this case, instead of placing the fried joint on the previously fried vegetables from the marinade, the meat is put in the braising pan often without being fried, on a bed of raw vegetables, adding a little fat and allowing it to fry until it sticks to the pan. If this is carried out carefully, the procedure can be accepted, but as well as the vegetables being coloured on only one side thus not giving as much flavour as those fried on both sides, nine times out of ten the colouring process is allowed to go on for so long that it ends up by being burnt, thus imparting a bitter flavour which completely spoils the taste of the sauce.

Frying the meat and vegetables in this way is really making a mockery of the method used in days gone by when there was no prior preparation of stocks and all the ingredients for making the stock were put in with the braise itself.

This old-fashioned method was good, but very extravagant, since thick slices of raw ham and veal were used as the base for the joint. Economic considerations caused this method to be discontinued a long time ago, but force of habit has kept the method in use and the fault has even been aggravated by including various bones in place of the ham and veal previously used.

It is this use of bones which is the other malpractice previously referred to.

It is well known that bones, including the most commonly used, veal bones, need at least 10–12 hours of cooking to extract their complete properties. As proof of this, the resultant liquid from bones which have been moistened again and cooked for a second time for 6 hours, produce more meat glaze than that taken from the first moistening of bones cooked for only 5–6 hours. It is true to say that meat glaze made from the second moistening has less taste than the first, but it is more gelatinous and it is this that is equally as useful in a braise as the taste.

It is this that gives the smoothness of consistency which nothing else can replace, and provides the correct quality of the sauce produced.

If raw bones are added to a braise and the maximum cooking time for it does not exceed 4–5 hours, it is obvious that the bones will be only partially cooked by the time the meat is completely cooked and the bones will only have been able to give up a small part of their properties, therefore their addition will have been of little value.

This malpractice produces yet another problem—that of causing an excessive moistening of the piece of meat. It is known and understood that a braise is perfect only if its sauce is of a minimum, well concentrated amount, and so the greater the amount of liquid used the less the flavour of the sauce—in short the joint is merely washed over. It is this fact which confirms the need to use a braising pan which is just big enough to hold the piece of meat; the more appropriate the size of the pan the better the meat is bathed in its liquid whilst keeping it to a minimum quantity and ensuring that it becomes strengthened by the flavour extracted from the meat.

2176 The Braising of White Meats

The modern way of carrying out the braising of white meats is not strictly braising at all. In the method used the process stops at the end of the first stage of the two, which together characterize a brown braise. Cooks in days gone by did not fully understand the process and so it was that large joints particularly those of veal, were frequently cooked for such a long time that they could be cut with a spoon. This practice is no longer carried out, but its description has remained.

The items which can be braised by the white method include best ends, saddles, loins and cushions of veal, calves sweetbreads, turkeys and large chickens and occasionally, legs, saddles and barons of lamb. The method is the same for all these, the only difference being the amount of time each requires.

The braising base is the same as for brown braises but the vegetables should be lightly cooked in butter without colour. The cooking liquid is always white stock.

Method of braising white meats: With the exception of calves sweetbreads which must always be blanched before braising, all meat and poultry for white braising is usually stiffened and lightly coloured on all sides in butter so as to prevent it from getting too dry, but it is not essential to do this.

The meat is placed on the prepared vegetable

base in a braising pan just large enough to hold the joint but without it touching the lid. It is then moistened with a little veal stock, covered with the lid, placed over a moderate heat and cooked until the stock is reduced to a glaze. This is repeated, then the joint is moistened half-way up with more stock, brought to the boil and placed to cook in a moderate oven just sufficiently hot to maintain a slow uninterrupted cooking.

It is necessary to frequently baste the joint from time to time in order to prevent it drying out; the gelatinous nature of the stock forms a coating on the surface above the level of the stock which helps to prevent loss of the meat juices. These tend to vaporize under the application of heat and are not contained within the meat because of the very light amount of frying that it has received.

This explains why it is necessary to reduce some of the stock to a glaze before the full amount is added. If the full amount of stock was put in with the joint at the beginning it would not be sufficiently dense to form a coating and the joint would become dry.

To test if the meat is cooked, prick it deeply with a trussing needle; the juices which exude should be absolutely colourless. This denotes that the item is cooked right through and the blood which it contained has been converted under the influence of heat.

It is here that the big difference between the brown and the white methods of braising is so noticeable. The white braises are almost roasts, they can only be carried out with young well fleshed meat and poultry and they should not be overcooked or as with roasts, they will lose all their qualities.

White braises are usually glazed especially those joints which have been larded with salt pork fat—a procedure which although less common these days, still has its adherents.

2177 Poaching

The most appropriate phrase to describe this process is boiling without actually boiling, if such an expression really makes sense.

The term to poach is used to indicate all the procedures of slow cooking which takes place in a liquid, no matter how small the amount. Thus it is that the term is applicable to the cooking of large cuts of turbot and salmon in a Court-bouillon, equally as well as for fillets of sole poached in a small quantity of fish stock, and to hot Mousses and Mousselines, Quenelles, Creams and Royales.

It is plain to see that among such a variety of items there is a vast difference in the cooking times but all conform to the overriding principle that the liquid in which they are being cooked must never actually boil though staying as close as possible to boiling point.

Another principle which applies is that whole fish and poultry should be placed to poach in cold liquid which is brought rapidly to the desired temperature. The same applies to fillets of sole and *Suprêmes* of chicken which are poached in hardly any liquid. On the other hand some items for poaching are best plunged into a liquid already at the desired cooking temperature.

Preparation of poultry for poaching: Clean the bird, fill with a stuffing if applicable and truss after folding back the legs and entering them inside the body.

If it needs studding or larding with truffle, ham or tongue, rub the breast and legs where the studding is to be done with a half lemon then immerse the chicken in boiling white stock for a few minutes. This assists the process of studding by stiffening the surface of the bird.

The poaching of poultry: Having been stuffed and studded, or larded in accordance with its particular recipe, but always after enveloping it in thin slices of salt pork fat, place the bird in a pan just large enough to hold it and add sufficient good quality white stock to cover.

Bring to the boil, skim, cover with a lid and allow to cook gently with only a barely discernible movement of the liquid taking place which is sufficient to ensure that the cooking process takes place by a gradual penetration of the heat. The results of cooking at too high a temperature would be, firstly, too much evaporation of the cooking liquid and its consequent clouding, and secondly, the danger of causing the skin to break, especially if the bird is stuffed.

The way to tell when the bird is just cooked is to pierce the thick part of the leg just above the drumstick with a needle; the juice which exudes from the opening should be perfectly clear and white.

Other points to be observed are,

1) the need to use the right size of saucepan for the particular bird; this is obvious, inasmuch as:
   a) the bird must be kept covered with the cooking liquid throughout the process, and
   b) since the cooking liquid is invariably used to make the accompanying sauce the less there is of it, the more concentrated will be its flavour; the sauce therefore benefits by the amount of cooking liquid being just right.
2) *a*) the white stock used for poaching the bird must always be made in advance and should be very clear, and

b) if the bird was to be put to cook with the ingredients necessary for making the stock, even were these abundant, the result would be unsatisfactory. This is because the normal time necessary to poach a chicken is 1 to 1½ hours at most, whereas it needs at least 6 hours to extract all the goodness from the ingredients used in making stock. The bird would therefore be cooking in a liquid little better than hot water and the accompanying sauce would be without flavour.

2178 Poêling

Poêling is, practically speaking, roasting although of a special kind. The degree of cooking is the same as for roasting but the process of arriving at this stage is somewhat different. This difference involves cooking entirely or almost entirely with butter and in some instances the use of herbs and vegetable flavourings but always by cooking in a closed container. Poêling is a simplification of a procedure much used in the old kitchen which consisted of covering the item to be cooked with a thick layer of *Matignon*—the meat having previously been browned all over by frying—wrapping it in thin slices of salt pork fat and then enclosing it in a sheet of buttered paper. It was cooked in the oven or on a spit and basted with melted butter.

As soon as cooked it was unwrapped and the fat allowed to drain off; the *Matignon* was put back in the roasting pan or into another saucepan with some Madeira and strong stock. As soon as the liquid had absorbed the flavour from the *Matignon* it was strained and the fat removed.

This fine way of cooking deserves to be retained for certain large items of poultry.

Method for Poêling: Place a layer of *Matignon* in a deep heavy pan just large enough to hold the piece of meat or poultry; well season, place the item on top of the vegetables and coat well with melted butter. Cover with the lid, place in a not too hot oven and allow to cook gently, basting frequently with the butter.

When cooked, remove the lid and allow the meat or poultry to become well coloured then remove it to a dish and keep covered until required.

Add sufficient clear well flavoured brown veal stock to the vegetables which should not have been allowed to burn, bring to the boil and allow to simmer very gently for 10 minutes. Strain, remove the fat carefully and send the gravy in a sauceboat with the meat which would normally be surrounded with a garnish.

General observations concerning Poêling.

1) It is most important not to add any liquid to the item whilst it is cooking because this will give it the same quality as that of braised white meats; Poêling is carried out with butter only. The exception to this rule is that for some game birds such as pheasant, partridge, quail, etc., it is permissible to add a little flamed brandy when they are nearly cooked.
2) It is equally important not to remove the fat from the vegetables before adding the stock. The reason for this is that the butter used in the cooking absorbs a lot of the flavour of the meat and the vegetables; this flavour must be recovered, so it is necessary for the stock to be added whilst the fat is still present and be allowed to simmer for at least 10 minutes. After this time, the butter can be skimmed off without weakening the flavour of the gravy.

Special Poêling known as en Casserole or en Cocotte: These preparations of meat, poultry and game known as and called *en Casserole* and *en Cocotte* are authentic Poêlings being cooked in and served from special fireproof earthenware dishes.

Generally speaking, items prepared *en Casserole* are cooked in butter only without the addition of a garnish. When cooked, the item is removed for a while and some good veal stock is added and allowed to boil for a few minutes; it is then skimmed of excess butter and the item put back in to be kept hot without boiling, until required.

The method for cooking *en Cocotte* is the same except that the item is garnished with various vegetables trimmed according to which kind they are, such as mushrooms, artichoke bottoms, button onions, carrots, turnips etc.; they should be partly cooked in butter before being added to the meats. Whenever possible, only young spring vegetables should be used and each kind should be placed around the item according to the time each takes to cook, so as to be ready at the same time as the meat.

These earthenware dishes improve with use and are much better after having been used several times but care must be taken to wash them in clean water without soap or soda. Before new ones are put into use it is advisable to soak them in water for at least 12 hours, then to fill them with water and place on the stove to boil out for a while. After this they should be wiped out thoroughly, and placed to soak once more in clean cold water before being used.

2179 The Sautés

The main characteristic of this method of cooking is that it is a dry cooking method, that is to say only a fat of some kind such as butter, oil or other clean fat is used.

Sautés are made with poultry and game cut into sections or with meat cut into small pieces.

All foods cooked in this manner must be *seized* which means they must be set to cook in very hot fat so that a coating is quickly formed on the outside which is capable of preventing the juices from escaping; this is particularly necessary for red meats such as beef and mutton.

After the pieces have been browned, the cooking of Sautés of poultry and game must be finished on top of the stove with a lid on the pan, or without a lid in the oven, basting the pieces from time to time with the fat in the same way as roasting.

When they are cooked, the pieces of poultry or game are removed from the pan which is then deglazed; if they are then to be put back in the resultant sauce with its garnish, it must only be for a short while, just long enough for them to become impregnated with the flavour of the sauce.

Sautés of meat such as Tournedos, Noisettes, cutlets, fillet steaks and sirloin steaks must be *seized* and cooked in a small amount of clarified butter in a pan on top of the stove.

The smaller and thinner the pieces are, the quicker they should be *seized.* When blood appears on the uncooked surface the pieces should be turned over and when pink beads of juice arise on the browned surface they are cooked to the correct degree. Remove the meat from the pan, drain off the fat and moisten with the necessary liquid to make the sauce, boiling it so as to dissolve the meat juices which will have solidified on the bottom of the pan. It is this operation which constitutes *deglazing* and to which is added the sauce; in other cases the deglazed juices are added to the sauce or to the accompanying garnish for the Sauté.

It must be remembered that the process of *deglazing* is a strictly necessary process for all Sautés.

The size of the pan used to cook a Sauté should be just large enough to hold the total amount; if too large, that part of the pan where there is no food will burn, thus making it impossible for a good *deglazing*. This would result in a lesser quality sauce because of the lack of one of its most important parts—that of the juices of the meat.

Sautés of white meats such as veal and lamb also need to be *seized* at the beginning of the process but thereafter cooked slowly; these meats should be cooked right through and should not be left underdone.

Also included under the heading of Sautés are certain preparations of a mixture of two cooking processes which are part Sauté and part braising: perhaps the most suitable term for these is *Ragoût*. They are stews made from beef, veal, lamb, game etc., and the recipes may be found in the appropriate section under the names of Estouffade, Goulash, Sautés of veal and lamb, Carbonnade, Navarin, Civet etc.

The first part of the preparation consists of cutting the meat into small pieces, quickly frying them until brown in exactly the same way as for Sauté, and in the second stage, cooking them slowly in a sauce or with a garnish in a similar way to braising.

2180 Blanchings

The term Blanching although basically an unsuitable one, applies to three types of culinary operation each different from the other with regard to its final use. They are:

1) the blanching of meats, more particularly offals of butchers meat,
2) the blanching of some vegetables which is in effect par-cooking,
3) the blanching of other kinds of vegetables which in reality amounts to a method of cooking, that of boiling.

The blanching of meat applies mainly to calf's head, calf's feet, veal and lamb sweetbreads, and sheep's trotters. They are first of all disgorged, that is to say, placed under cold running water until all traces of blood have disappeared, then put into a pan, well covered with cold water and brought slowly to the boil. The scum is then removed and the item is boiled for a time according to type: that is 15–20 minutes for calf's head and feet and 10–15 minutes for sheep's and lambs' trotters; they are then drained and placed in plenty of cold water before being put to cook in a *Blanc*.

Calf's sweetbreads need only to be boiled for 3 minutes, just long enough to harden the outside so as to make it easy to insert any items for larding or studding; lambs' sweetbreads should be drained and made cool in running water immediately after they first come to the boil. Both kinds of sweetbreads are usually cooked by the method of White Braising.

The blanching of cockscombs differs from ordinary blanching in that after having been disgorged they are placed in a pan of cold water and brought to a temperature of 40–45 °C (104–113 °F). At this point they should be removed and each one rubbed with a piece of cloth dipped in salt to remove the skin; after being washed in cold water they should then be cooked in a light *Blanc*.

Many people blanch meat and poultry when it is to be prepared as Blanquette and Fricassée; this is as great an error as that of soaking meat in cold water. If the meat or poultry being used is of good quality (and only good quality should be used) it is only necessary to place them in cold water or cold stock and to bring slowly to the boil, stirring occasionally. If care is taken to remove the scum as it rises, both the meat and the stock will be perfectly clean and both will retain all their flavours.

In so far as poor quality meat and poultry is concerned, no amount of soaking and blanching will make them any better; whatever method is adopted, they will remain grey, dry and flavourless—it is thus more sensible to use good quality items.

A valid proof of the futility of soaking and blanching meat for a Blanquette or Fricassée is that the same meats, if of good quality, are always perfectly white whether braised, Poêléed or roasted and yet these methods of cooking are much less conducive to retaining their whiteness than that of boiling. Good sense thus disproves bad practice.

Under the term Blanching, is included the system of par-cooking certain kinds of vegetables in plenty of water to rid them of their bitter or strong flavour.

The time needed to boil them varies according to how old the vegetables are; they need only be briefly dipped into the boiling water if they are new season and tender.

The green vegetables which are usually blanched are lettuce, chicory, celery, artichokes and cabbage. Carrots, turnips and button onions need blanching when they are old and for marrows, cucumbers and chow-chow the blanching process is carried on until they are practically cooked which is almost the same as the plain boiling of vegetables in salted water.

It is under this heading of boiling and not under that of blanching that the cooking in boiling salted water of such green vegetables as peas, French beans, Brussels sprouts and spinach should be carried out.

Those vegetables named above which are only blanched should always be refreshed and drained on a cloth before proceeding to the next stage of cooking which is nearly always braising.

2181 Blanc for Meat and Certain Vegetables

This preparation has no culinary value in itself, being solely a means of cooking things to keep them white.

Whatever is being cooked, the *Blanc* should be brought to the boil before adding the food then covered with a layer of suet which acts as a barrier thus keeping the food from coming into contact with the air and discolouring.

Method:

Mix together flour and water in the proportions of 1 large tbs of flour per 1 litre ($1\frac{3}{4}$ pt or $4\frac{1}{2}$ U.S. cups) cold water, plus 6 g ($\frac{1}{5}$ oz) salt and 2 tbs of vinegar. Bring to the boil, add 1 onion studded with a clove, a Bouquet garni, the food to be cooked, and finally the layer of fat which can be either beef or veal kidney suet chopped finely and if necessary, previously soaked in cold water to remove any blood.

Note: For cooking vegetables, it is advantageous to use lemon juice instead of vinegar.

2182 The Gratins

This operation holds a sufficiently important place in culinary practice for an explanation to be given and if not the complete theory of it, at least the broad outlines.

The various kinds of gratins which come under this heading are: 1) the Complete Gratin, 2) the Quick Gratin, 3) the Light Gratin and 4) Glazings; which are a form of the Quick Gratin.

The Complete Gratin: This is the original form of the method and the one that takes the longest. It is the most painstaking because firstly, the main ingredient whatever it is, is always raw and has to undergo a complete process of cooking. Secondly, the process of cooking has to keep in step with the reduction of the sauce which is the agent of the gratin and thirdly, the cooking and reduction of the sauce has to keep in step with the formation of the crust on the surface which is the actual gratin; this is brought about by the combination of the sauce, breadcrumbs and butter under the direct action of the heat.

To obtain this triple result, the item under preparation has to be submitted to a degree of heat in keeping with its nature and size.

The basis of a Complete Gratin is Sauce Duxelles—either meat or meatless according to circumstances. The food to be gratinated is laid in a dish which has been buttered and coated with a few tablespoons of the sauce then surrounded with slices of raw mushroom and a few whole cooked mushrooms placed on top. A little white wine is added, the whole is coated with more of the same sauce, then sprinkled with dry white breadcrumbs and melted butter. It should then be placed in the oven at the required temperature, and in accordance with the following observations:

1) The larger the item being cooked, the more sauce must be used and inversely, less sauce the smaller the item of food.
2) When preparing Complete Gratins remember that if more sauce is used than necessary the food will be cooked and the gratin formed before the sauce has reached the right degree of reduction; it will then be necessary to continue reduction on top of the stove thus creating steam which will soften the crust of the gratin.

3) If insufficient sauce is used it will have reduced too much before the food is cooked; more sauce will then have to be added thus destroying the evenness of the gratin.
4) Finally, remember that the larger the item of food, the more moderate the temperature of the oven; on the other hand, the smaller it is, the hotter the oven.

   When the dish is brought from the oven a few drops of lemon juice should be squeezed on top and a little chopped parsley sprinkled over.

The Quick Gratin: This is the same as the *Complete Gratin* except that the main ingredient, be it meat, fish or vegetable is always cooked and reheated in advance so that all that is necessary is to bring about the formation of the gratin in the shortest space of time.

The food only needs therefore to be covered with just sufficient sauce to completely cover it, sprinkled with dry white breadcrumbs and melted butter and placed in a very hot oven to finish like a *Complete Gratin.*

The Light Gratin: This is applicable mainly to farinaceous foods such as macaroni, lasagnes, noodles and gnocchi and is formed by a combination of grated cheese, dry white breadcrumbs and butter. Here again the ultimate objective is the formation of a gratinated coating, uniform in colour and resulting from the melting of the cheese; for this a moderate heat is sufficient.

In this category of gratins can be included those which finalize the preparation of stuffed vegetables such as tomatoes, mushrooms, eggplant and cucumber. In this case the gratin consists of the dry white breadcrumbs sprinkled with butter or oil; the item of food is then placed under either a fairly hot or moderate heat according to whether the vegetables are fully cooked, partly cooked or if they are absolutely raw.

Glazings: There are two kinds of glazings—one produced by a sauce which has been well buttered, the other results from cheese sprinkled on top of a sauce covering the food.

In the first kind it is essential to put the dish holding the food into another receptacle containing a little water which prevents the breakdown of the sauce by stopping it from boiling. The more plentifully buttered the sauce is, the greater the heat it must be placed under so that the glazing is almost instantaneous thus giving a light brown coating.

In the second kind, Sauce Mornay is used; the item of food is coated with the sauce, then sprinkled with grated cheese and melted butter. Finally, the dish is placed in a very hot oven or under the salamander so that a light brown crust is quickly formed from a combination of the cheese and butter.

2183 Grilling

The culinary preparations carried out under this title are classified as concentrated cooking, in fact the main objective being attempted in grilling is to keep the juices inside the pieces of meat being grilled.

Grilling which is actually roasting over an open fire is the most primitive form of cooking and the basis of departure for more advanced culinary methods. It was the first idea to be born in the mind of prehistoric man as progress brought forth an instinctive desire to eat better cooked foodstuffs. A little later on in time was born the logical sequence of this first experiment of grilling, the spit, and already in bringing it into being, man's innate intelligence took over from primitive instinct. Reason deduced the consequences and experience brought the conclusions and cookery advanced along the road which since then it has continuously followed.

Fuels for Grilling: The kind of fuel most often used and also the best, is charcoal. The main point about the choice of fuel for grilling is that it should not contain anything likely to give off smoke even though there may be a strong ventilation system attached to the grill which extracts it efficiently.

It is necessary to introduce an artificial draught into the grill if it is lit in the open although this is a rare occurrence; the reason is obvious because if the smoke produced by any foreign material in the fire or by fat dropping on the flaming charcoal were not extracted by artificial ventilation or a strong natural draught, it would inevitably impart a bad taste to the food being grilled.

A grill may be fired by fuels other than charcoal and alternative fuels can be just as good if they are used carefully.

The Bed of Fuel: The arrangement of a bed of fuel under a grill is of some importance. It should not only be regulated according to the nature and size of the item to be grilled but also in such a manner as to allow the production of more or less heat according to circumstances. Thus the bed should be arranged in an even layer in the centre but varying in thickness according to whether the fire should be more or less fierce. It should also be raised at those sides which are in contact with the draught of air in order that the entire burning surface may present an equal degree of heat.

The actual metal grill itself should always be placed over the glowing fuel in advance and thus should be very hot when the items for grilling are placed on it. If this is not done the food will stick to the bars and will probably be spoiled when turned over.

Classification of items of food for grilling: Grilled foods call for particular methods; these may be divided into four main classes each of which calls for its own particular care. These are: 1) grills of red meats (beef, mutton and game), 2) grills of white meats (veal, lamb and chicken), 3) grilled fish, 4) those foods which have been simply coated with dry breadcrumbs or have been egg and breadcrumbed.

Grilled Red Meats: When grilling a food the first thing to be considered is an estimate of the degree of heat most suitable to be applied to it. The bigger the item of food and the more protein it contains, the quicker and harsher the initial browning of the exterior should be. The section on braising included an explanation of the reason for browning the meat and the results this gave but it is necessary to refer to this in connection with the subject of grilling.

When grilling large cuts of beef or mutton the better the quality and the juicier the meat, the more the exterior should be cooked hard and brown. The pressure of the juices against the outside crust will be more intense the more there is of it and the pressure will gradually increase as the juices become hotter. If the fire is regulated correctly so as to assist in the steady penetration of heat into the food being grilled, the following will happen: the heat striking directly on to that part of the meat exposed to the blazing fire causes the fibres to contract and then penetrates into the flesh, spreading layer by layer and driving back the juices which finish up on the opposite side and appear as pearls of moisture on the raw surface. The piece of meat must now be turned over on the grill so that the same process begins from the other side until the juices driven up against the hardened grilled surface, manage to break through forming small droplets of blood which indicates that the meat is just cooked.

This shows that if the piece being grilled is very large, the intensity of the heat should be diminished as soon as the outside has become brown so as to ensure that there is a gradual penetration of heat into the interior. If the heat was to be kept at the same degree of intensity the exterior would become carbonized and the burnt crust would resist any further penetration of heat. The end result would be a piece of meat that is completely burnt on the outside and absolutely raw inside.

When grilling meat of medium thickness, a quick *seizing* over a fierce heat followed by a few more minutes of cooking, suffices to cook them to the right degree and in such a case there is no need to moderate the intensity of the fire. For example, to cook a rump steak or a Châteaubriand to the degree of being just cooked it must first of all be *seized* so as to form a brown crust to act as a barrier against the loss of the meat juices. Then it must be drawn to the side of the grill where the intensity of the heat is less and can penetrate gradually and ensure that the interior is cooked. Small cuts such as Tournedos, small fillet steaks, Noisettes and cutlets after the necessary rigorous browning of the exterior can be kept over the same intense heat because the thickness of the meat through which it has to penetrate is so much the less.

The care to be given to grills whilst they are cooking: Before being placed on the grill, the meat should be brushed all over with clarified butter and brushed from time to time during the grilling process so as to prevent drying out. Grilled steaks should be turned over with a palette knife or better still, grill tongs; they should not be pierced as this will destroy all the previous precautions taken, by opening an easy passage for the juices to escape.

To ascertain when cooked: The degree of cooking of grilled red meats is ascertained as follows: if the crust resists when touched with the finger the interior has been reached by the heat and the steak is just cooked through. If, on the other hand, it contracts without offering any resistance, this indicates that the inside is underdone. The surest way to ascertain the correct degree of being cooked is the appearance of pinkish coloured drops of blood on the browned surface of the meat.

Grilled White Meats; Whilst red meats must be *seized* quickly, the opposite is true of white meats; in this case there is no need to worry about ensuring the concentration of juices since these exist only in an albuminous form, that is to say it is in a less complex form as to be expected from the calf or lamb. For these grills the heat must be moderate so as to ensure that the meat is cooked through and the exterior coloured at the same time; they must be brushed with butter frequently to prevent the exterior from drying out. To tell when they are cooked, the juices which escape should be completely white.

Grilled Fish; Fish, whether large or small, are grilled over a moderate heat; they should first be well brushed with butter or oil and brushed frequently whilst cooking. To tell when it is cooked the flesh should come away easily from the bone. Except for fatty fish such as mackerel, red mullet, herrings etc. all fish should be coated with flour then brushed with melted butter before being placed on the grill; the object of this is the formation of a golden coating which helps to prevent drying out as well as making them more agreeable in appearance.

The grilling of coated items of food: Items of food which are coated with dry breadcrumbs, butter and breadcrumbs or with egg and breadcrumbs are usually small in size. They must be grilled over a very moderate heat in order to cook through and at the same time colour the coating.

They should be basted frequently with clarified butter and turned very carefully so as not to damage the coating. The aim is to retain the juices inside.

2184 Deep Frying

There are such a large number of items capable of being cooked by deep frying that it has become one of the most frequently used methods of cookery. The process is subject to strict regulations which it is wiser not to infringe because of the danger of accidents.

Some of these can be easily avoided by experience in deep frying and by taking the necessary care; others can be avoided by prudent operation.

The equipment used: The choice of utensils for deep frying is not of such minor importance as some seem to think, and the bad accidents which arise are often caused by careless choice. Careless and hurried handling by the cook are often the cause but accidents are more frequently caused by defective equipment which is difficult to use.

Utensils for deep frying can be made of copper or any other strong metal cast in one piece. They can be oval or round and must be of a size sufficiently large and deep that when only half full of fat there is still sufficient room to cook in it. If the frying utensil was too full of fat even a slight sharp movement might cause some to spill over on to the stove where it might ignite and burn the person using it.

Frying utensils with straight sides are better than those with sloping sides especially in the professional kitchen where there will be a good deal of deep frying to do, so calling for large-sized pans.

The selection and preparation of the fat for deep frying: Most animal fats and vegetable oils are suitable for this type of cooking provided that they are pure and resistant to high temperatures without burning.

The use of clarified fat from the skimmings of the stockpot or roasting trays is not recommended; only fresh raw fat, properly clarified, is suitable for ensuring good results and prolonged use.

Butter is not suitable for deep frying because even if perfectly pure it reaches only a moderate degree of heat before burning; it is, however, quite suitable for occasional special use. Beef kidney fat is the most commonly used fat for deep frying. As a by-product of the butchery section it is the most preferable because of its price and the fact that it lasts longer than others, provided that it is given proper care and attention both when being made and being used. The fat from veal is good but soon loses its strength. Mutton fat should not be used, as coming from an old animal it has a taste and smell of tallow; even if from a younger animal it should not be used as it gives off a great deal of frothiness and there is the risk that it will overflow the utensil causing an accident. Pork fat or lard used on its own or in conjunction with another fat makes a good frying medium but because of its higher price, lard is mainly used as an ingredient in certain preparations. So to sum up, clarified beef fat is the best for large-scale deep frying although for home use where there is less chance of the fat being used continuously, half beef and half veal fat or a mixture of two parts beef fat, one part veal fat and one part of pork fat, can be used.

When clarifying fat for deep frying it is not enough to simply melt it; only its complete cooking will provide pure fat. Fat which is not cooked sufficiently will froth when first put to use thus requiring careful attention until after being used for a number of times, it settles down. Again, if the fat has not been properly clarified it easily penetrates foods placed in to cook and makes them indigestible.

To render fat for frying, cut it into very small pieces or mince it and place in a heavy pan with 1 litre (1¾ pt or 4½ U.S. cups) cold water per 5 kg (11 lb) of fat. The water helps in melting the fat because as it vaporizes it penetrates into the tissues of the fat and helps to break it down. Until all the water has evaporated the fat suffers only a disintegration caused by the breakdown of the tissues and it is only when no more water is left that it starts to cook properly and to become completely pure fat.

It is ready when the membrane around the fat is left as small crisp brown pieces floating in the liquid fat and when a white haze that can also be smelt, arises. At this stage the fat is very hot indeed and is best removed from the heat and left for 10 minutes before being strained; pressure can be applied to extract all the fat from the residue.

Temperatures of the frying media and their application: The highest temperature which a fat can attain without burning is governed by the type of fat and its purity; in practice, there are three broad degrees of heat known as moderately hot, hot and very hot.

The term boiling fat is a misnomer and should not be used to describe the high temperature of a fat.

Butter, because of the composition of its fat, cannot be heated to more than 120 °C without burning although if completely pure, it can reach 132 °C to 135 °C, but this temperature is not high enough for general use.

Animal fats used for deep frying reach 135 °C to 140 °C when moderately hot, and 155 °C to

160°C when hot. When very hot, giving off a faint haze at 180 °C, pork fat or lard used on its own can reach 200 °C before it burns and goose fat 220 °C or more. Vegetable oils can go higher without burning—coconut oil 250 °C, ordinary vegetable oil 270 °C and olive oil 290 °C.

The temperature of a fat can be judged as follows: When a sprig of parsley or crust of bread is placed in and it immediately starts to sizzle, the fat is moderately hot; when a moist piece of food is placed in and it crackles the fat is hot and if it gives off a pronounced smell it is very hot.

The fat should be moderately hot at the first stage, for frying foods which contain a certain amount of moisture which needs to be driven off and for fish which because of its thickness needs to be cooked through gradually before it becomes crisp on the outside. Under this description of its use the frying process really acts as a complete phase of cooking.

The fat should be hot at the second stage, for foods which have already undergone some degree of cooking by evaporation or penetration, needing only to be finished cooking or to be covered by a crisp brown coating.

It is also used for frying food where the heat must have the immediate effect of forming a coating to keep the fat from penetrating and to prevent the escape of any of the substances from inside. The kind of foods which are cooked at this temperature include all those that are egg and breadcrumbed or dipped into frying batter such as Croquettes, Cromesquis, items prepared *à la Villeroy* and all kinds of fritters.

At this temperature the process acts by sealing the outside which in many cases is of vital importance. Firstly, items of food which are egg and breadcrumbed require abrupt immersion in the hot fat to set the coating of egg and breadcrumbs; this crust gets progressively harder as the frying proceeds and stops any of the inside from escaping.

If the fat is not hot enough when the food is put in, not only would the coating of egg and breadcrumbs become saturated with fat but there is the danger that it will break up, letting loose the contents it is supposed to contain.

Secondly, the same thing applies to foods cooked in frying batter where it is absolutely necessary for the coating of batter around the food to solidify immediately it enters the fat. If the food is already cooked it follows that reheating the food and colouring the coating take place at one and the same time, quite quickly.

Finally, the temperature described as very hot is used for all items which need to be sealed instantly on immersion and for very small items such as Whitebait for which instant sealing is the most important need, the cooking being completed in only a few seconds.

The deep frying of fish: Instructions for the deep frying of fish are dealt with in its rightful place in the Fish chapter (1557).

The amount of fat to use: This should be in direct proportion to the number of items being fried at any one time and to their size and in all cases the foods must be totally submerged and covered by the fat.

The size of the frying utensil and the correct proportionate amount of fat which it contains should be larger than would appear necessary but, of course, without taking it to extreme limits. The reason for this is that the greater the quantity of fat and its accumulated temperature, the less fear there is of it dropping too low in temperature when the food is placed in to cook. The overcooling of the fat can only be prevented if the heat source is sufficiently fierce to bring the fat back to its original working temperature within a few seconds.

It is equally important to limit the items of food being fried at one time and, for preference, to fry the food in several small batches so as not to overload the frying utensil.

Care of the frying media: It is advisable to strain the fat at the end of each service period to remove the residue of the foods which have been fried as these would spoil those being fried subsequently. What happens is that foods which have been egg and breadcrumbed always lose some of the coating in the fat and this becomes a black powder; similarly when floured foods are fried, some of the flour comes off, accumulating at the bottom of the friture in the form of a muddy residue.

With some foods it is not just the residue which causes trouble even to the extent of burning the fat but the flavour escapes and contaminates other foods when they are fried later on.

It is for these reasons that fats must be strained regularly; good results and the working life of the fat depend on this.

RELEVES AND ENTREES
BEEF

2185 ALOYAU—
SIRLOIN, INCLUDING THE FILLET

The *Aloyau* is that part of the carcase of beef between the rump and fore-ribs, in effect the sirloin of beef; correctly speaking and to justify the name *Aloyau*, it should always comprise the sirloin of beef proper and the fillet, together in one piece.

If the *Aloyau* is to be cooked whole the trimming of the piece should be confined to removing most of the flank, carefully cutting away the ligament found running along the sirloin next to the chine bone and trimming only a little of the fat from the fillet.

The fat covering the sirloin should not be trimmed at all. In current practice the *Aloyau* is cut across the whole joint into pieces of not less than 3 kg (6¾ lb) in weight when required for braising. For roasting it is best left whole.

The *Aloyau* when served as a Relevé should be either braised or roasted; if roasted it can be kept underdone if required. When braised, however, unless of first quality, the joint can often be dry.

All garnishes suitable for fillet of beef are applicable to the *Aloyau*, but the more generally used are: Bourgeoise, Céleris, Flamande, Richelieu, Provençale etc. The accompanying gravy should always be that indicated by each garnish.

2186 ALOYAU FROID—COLD SIRLOIN, INCLUDING THE FILLET

Carefully trim the cold joint and coat with a fairly thick layer of aspic jelly. Place on a suitable dish to serve surrounded by large neatly cut shapes of the same jelly.

2187 AMOURETTES ET CERVELLES—SPINE MARROW AND BRAINS

The term *Amourettes* refers to the spine marrow of veal and beef. It is usually sold with the brains from these animals and is often served with them. However, in certain cases they are cooked separately as special dishes in their own right or as an item for certain garnishes.

Because of their delicacy and easy digestibility, spine marrow and brains are of great nutritional value for children and old people.

For the finest preparation the spine marrow and brains of veal are preferable to those of beef; however, the methods of preparation are identical.

Preparation:
Place the spine marrow and brains under gently running cold water so as to extract as much of the blood as possible, then carefully remove all of the membrane and connective tissue which surrounds them. When this is done, place them again under gently running water to soak out any remaining blood.

For cooking, place into a boiling Vinegar Court-bouillon which may either be cooked in advance or prepared fresh; allow to poach gently for approximately 25–30 minutes. It is important to remember that they be placed into a boiling Court-bouillon as this is the only way to ensure that they become firm.

AMOURETTES—SPINE MARROW

2188 Cromesquis d'Amourettes à la Française
Prepare a Salpicon of cooked spine marrow, mushrooms, and truffles mixed with reduced Sauce Allemande and in the proportions as indicated in the article on Croquettes (1144). Allow the mixture to cool, divide into pieces of approximately 75 g (2½ oz) and mould rectangle shape.

When required, dip in a light frying batter and deep fry in hot fat, drain well and serve arranged on a serviette garnished with fried parsley.

Serve accompanied with Sauce Périgueux, Sauce aux Fines Herbes or other suitable sauce.

2189 Cromesquis d'Amourettes à la Polonaise
Prepare a Salpicon of cooked spine marrow, flap mushrooms and truffles mixed with reduced Sauce Espagnole and in the proportions as indicated for Croquettes (1144).

When cold, mould into rectangles of equal size and envelope each in a very thin unsweetened pancake. Dip in a light frying batter and deep fry in hot fat.

Drain well and serve arranged on a serviette with bouquets of fried parsley. Serve accompanied with Sauce aux Fines Herbes or Sauce Duxelles.

2190 Cromesquis d'Amourettes à la Russe
Prepare a mixture as in the preceding recipe and mould into rectangles.

Envelop each in fresh pig's caul, dip in frying batter made with beer and deep fry in hot fat.

Drain well and serve arranged on a serviette with bouquets of fried parsley.

Serve accompanied with Sauce aux Fines Herbes or Sauce Duxelles.

2191 Cromesquis d'Amourettes
Prepare a mixture as for Cromesquis à la Française (2188) and mould into round flat shapes.

Flour, egg and breadcrumb and when required, deep fry in hot fat. Drain well, arrange on a serviette with bouquets of fried parsley and serve accompanied with Sauce Périgueux or buttered Sauce Demi-glace.

2192 Fritot d'Amourettes
Cut freshly poached spine marrow into 7 cm (3 in)

lengths and marinate for 20 minutes with a little lemon juice, oil, salt, pepper and chopped parsley.

When required, dip in a light frying batter and deep fry in hot fat; drain well and arrange on a serviette with bouquets of fried parsley.

Serve accompanied with Sauce Tomate.

2193 Timbales d'Amourettes à l'Ecossaise
Line some buttered hexagonal-shaped moulds with thin slices of cooked red ox tongue and cover with a 3–4 mm (⅛ in) thick layer of veal forcemeat. Fill the centre with a Salpicon of cooked spine marrow and red ox tongue mixed with a little Sauce Allemande, then cover with a layer of the same forcemeat.

Place the moulds in a deep tray containing hot water and cook in the oven for approximately 12 minutes. When cooked, demould the Timbales on to a round dish and arrange in a circle.

Serve accompanied with Sauce Ecossaise.

2194 Timbales d'Amourettes à la Napolitaine
Line some well buttered dariole moulds with lengths of cooked macaroni which have been kept a little firm in cooking then well drained and dried before being placed slantwise in the moulds. Seal the insides with a thin layer of forcemeat, fill the centre with a Salpicon of spine marrow and mushrooms mixed with reduced tomato-flavoured Sauce Demi-glace, then cover with the same forcemeat.

Cook and present as in the preceding recipe and serve accompanied with Sauce Demi-glace, well flavoured with tomato and lightly buttered.

2195 Timbales d'Amourettes Villeneuve
See in the Chapter on Hot Hors-d'oeuvre (1285).

CERVELLES—BRAINS

2196 Cervelle au Beurre Noir
Cut the cooked brains into thick slices, arrange overlapping in a circle on a round dish and fill the centre with the spine marrow cut in short lengths.

Season with salt and pepper and cover with 150 g (5 oz) butter cooked dark brown with 25 g (1 oz) small leaves of parsley added to it at the last moment. Swill out the pan with a little vinegar and add to the brains.

2197 Cervelle au Beurre Noisette
Prepare and arrange the brains and spine marrow as in the preceding recipe; season with salt and pepper. Cover with 150 g (5 oz) butter cooked nut brown and sprinkle with a few drops of lemon juice and a little chopped parsley.

2198 Cervelle à la Bourguignonne
Cut the cooked brains into thick slices and add a proportionate amount as a garnish, of cooked mushrooms and glazed button onions. Cover with Sauce Bourguignonne and simmer gently for 7–8 minutes.

Arrange in a timbale or deep dish and surround with heart-shaped Croûtons of bread fried in clarified butter.

2199 Coquille de Cervelle au Gratin
Pipe a scrolled border of Pommes Duchesse mixture around the edges of scollop shells; cover the bottom of each with a little Sauce Duxelles and place slices of cooked brains on top with a few slices of large cooked mushrooms and a small cooked mushroom in the centre. Cover with fairly thick Sauce Duxelles and sprinkle with fine white dry breadcrumbs and melted butter.

Gratinate in a hot oven then sprinkle with a few drops of lemon juice.

2200 Coquilles de Cervelle à la Parisienne
Pipe a scrolled border of Pommes Duchesse mixture around the edges of scollop shells; brush with a little beaten egg and colour in the oven.

Coat the bottom of each shell with a little Sauce Allemande, fill with thin slices of cooked brains and arrange a circle of slices of mushroom and truffle on top with a small cooked mushroom in the centre.

Cover with nicely buttered Sauce Allemande and glaze quickly under the salamander.

2201 Cromesquis and Croquettes de Cervelle
Proceed as indicated in the recipes for Amourettes.

2202 Fritot de Cervelle
Cut the cooked brains into fairly thick slices, marinate and deep fry as indicated for Fritot d'Amourettes.

2203 Cervelle à l'Italienne
Cut some raw brains into large but fairly thin slices, season with salt and pepper, flour and shallow fry in a mixture of half butter and half oil.

Arrange in a circle on a hot round dish and fill the centre with Sauce Italienne.

2204 Marinade de Cervelle
Cut the raw brains into slices and marinate as for Fritot d'Amourettes (2192); egg and breadcrumb and deep fry in hot fat when required.

Drain well and serve arranged on a serviette garnished with fried parsley and accompanied with Sauce Tomate.

2205 Matelote de Cervelle

Use well soaked and cleaned brains, free of all blood. Cook them in Red Wine Court-bouillon well flavoured with herbs and vegetables and prepared in advance.

Cut the cooked brains into thick slices, place in a timbale and add a garnish of small cooked mushrooms and glazed button onions. Pass the Court-bouillon through a fine strainer into a pan, reduce it, thicken with a little Beurre Manié and pour over the brains.

Serve surrounded with small heart-shaped Croûtons of bread fried in clarified butter.

Note: Apart from the method of cooking, this Matelote is really nothing more than Cervelle à la Bourguignonne.

2206 Mazagran de Cervelle

Well butter an oval or round dish and decorate with a piped border of Pommes Duchesse mixture as for Turbot Crème au Gratin keeping it a little narrower but higher.

Fill the centre with a mixture of sliced poached brains and slices of cooked mushrooms and truffle mixed with Sauce Allemande containing reduced mushroom cooking liquor.

Cover the ingredients with a thin layer of Pommes Duchesse mixture taking care to close it carefully to the border; lightly brush with beaten egg and decorate with small shapes of Pommes Duchesse prepared in advance, or simply mark with the back of a fork. Colour in a hot oven.

When removed from the oven surround with a *cordon* of Sauce Tomate and a circle of grilled Chipolata sausages.

2207 Mousseline de Cervelle

Carefully cook a nice white brain together with a little butter, pass through a fine sieve and with the purée obtained, prepare a Royale using the proportions as indicated for Royales for soups.

Pour the mixture into a well buttered mould and cook *au Bain-marie*; allow to rest for 7–8 minutes then turn out on to a suitable dish.

Serve accompanied with Sauce Crème containing finely sliced very white cooked mushrooms.

2208 Pain de Cervelle à la Bourgeoise

Carefully cook 400 g (15 oz) brains with a little butter; pound finely in a mortar adding 100 g (3½ oz) butter; 200 g (7 oz) Frangipane Panada (283); a little salt, pepper and nutmeg and 3 eggs added one by one.

Pass through a fine sieve, mix well together with a wooden spoon and place into a plain buttered mould; cook *au Bain-marie* for 30–35 minutes.

Allow to rest for 7–8 minutes to allow the mixture to settle, turn out on to a suitable dish and serve accompanied with Sauce Velouté containing sliced very white cooked mushrooms.

Note: The cooking time indicated above is for a mould of 1 litre (1¾ pt or 4½ U.S. cups) capacity; for individual portions the mixture may be cooked in dariole or any other suitable mould of the same capacity, allowing 12–14 minutes cooking time.

2209 Cervelle à la Poulette

Slice some freshly cooked brains and mix very carefully together with Sauce Poulette.

Serve in a timbale or deep dish.

2210 Cervelle à la Ravigote

Pipe a border of Pommes Duchesse mixture on a round or oval dish and colour it lightly in the oven. Place slices of freshly cooked brains in the centre and cover with Sauce Ravigote.

2211 Soufflés de Cervelle en Caisses

For 20 small soufflé moulds prepare the following: Pass 500 g (1 lb 2 oz) brains, sliced and cooked in butter, through a fine sieve; mix with 2½ dl (9 fl oz or 1⅛ U.S. cup) well reduced Sauce Béchamel, 5 egg yolks and seasoning as necessary; then fold in 5 stiffly beaten egg whites.

Divide the mixture equally into the moulds and cook in a moderate oven for 12 minutes.

Arrange quickly on a folded serviette on a dish and serve immediately.

2212 Subrics de Cervelle

Cut 500 g (1 lb 2 oz) cooked brains into large dice and mix together with 1 dl (3½ fl oz or ½ U.S. cup) Sauce Allemande and 3 eggs; allow to cool.

Heat some clarified butter in a frying pan until very hot and using a large spoon drop some of the mixture into the pan in the shape of a macaroon; repeat this operation to fill the pan. When the Subrics are nicely coloured turn them over carefully with a palette knife and colour on that side as well.

Arrange neatly on a hot round dish and serve Sauce Tomate separately.

2213 Cervelle Villeroy

Cut the raw brains into thick slices, cook them gently in butter, then dip in Sauce Villeroy to coat them. Allow to become quite cold then egg and breadcrumb and deep fry in hot fat when required. Drain well, arrange on a serviette on a dish and garnish with bouquets of fried parsley.

Serve a light Sauce Périgueux separately.

2214 CONTREFILET—SIRLOIN, WITHOUT THE FILLET

The *Contrefilet* is the same part of the carcase of

beef as the *Aloyau* except that the fillet is removed; all the recipes for fillet of beef are applicable to the *Contrefilet*.

When required for braising, the *Contrefilet* is generally boned; for roasting it may be boned but it is preferable to leave it on the bone in keeping with the English style of roasting. In this case the large sinew near the chine bone should be removed and the bones of the chine broken close to where they join the bones uncovered by the removal of the fillet. This will allow them to be easily discarded when cooked thus facilitating the carving of the joint.

When of excellent quality the *Contrefilet* is best when roasted.

2215 Contrefilet froid—Cold Sirloin
If required as a whole cold joint it should be first trimmed, coated with jelly and presented on a suitable dish surrounded by chopped jelly. The edges of the dish can be bordered with cut shapes of jelly.

2216 ENTRECOTES—SIRLOIN STEAKS

For 10 persons allow 3 large thick sirloin steaks of approximately 650 g (1 lb 7 oz) each or 10 single steaks weighing approximately 200 g (7 oz) each. Although the French term *Entrecôte* suggests that it should be a steak cut from between 2 rib-bones, the general practice is to cut the steaks from a boned-out sirloin of beef. The *Entrecôte* or sirloin steak is considered here as a derivative of the sirloin.

2217 Entrecôte à la Béarnaise
Season and grill the sirloin steaks; place on a long oval hot dish. At each end of the dish place a bouquet of small Pommes Château, brush the steaks lightly with some light meat glaze and finally border each steak with thick Sauce Béarnaise.

Note: The Sauce Béarnaise may be served separately from a sauceboat.

2218 Entrecôte à la Bercy
Season and grill the sirloin steaks; arrange neatly on 150 g (5 oz) of Bercy Butter spread on the serving dish. Lightly brush each steak with some light meat glaze.

Note: In some establishments the butter is placed on the steaks after having been softened; in others the half melted butter is served separately from a sauceboat but there is no absolute rule for deciding this matter.

2219 Entrecôte à la Bordelaise
Season and shallow fry the sirloin steaks in butter; arrange them on a long oval hot dish.

Place an overlapping line of poached slices of beef bone marrow along the centre of each steak and serve Sauce Bordelaise separately.

Note: Although contemporary practice permits Sauce Bordelaise to be made with red wine, it is worth stating again that this is wrong. The true Sauce Bordelaise is made with white wine and was previously known as Sauce Bordelaise Bonnefoy.

2220 Entrecôte aux Champignons
Season and shallow fry the sirloin steaks in butter; arrange on a suitable dish. Deglaze the pan with 1 dl ($3\frac{1}{2}$ fl oz or $\frac{1}{2}$ U.S. cup) mushroom cooking liquor and reheat 40 small cooked mushrooms in it; remove them and place on the steaks.

Add $1\frac{1}{2}$ dl (5 fl oz or $\frac{5}{8}$ U.S. cup) Sauce Demi-glace to the remaining liquid, reduce by half and pass through a fine strainer. Enrich and thicken this by shaking in 50–60 g (2 oz) butter; coat the steaks lightly with a little of the sauce and serve the rest separately in a sauceboat.

2221 Entrecôte à la Forestière
Season and shallow fry the sirloin steaks in butter; arrange them on a suitable dish.

Cook separately in butter, 300 g (11 oz) each of morels and large dice of potatoes, and arrange around the steaks in bouquets alternating with short slices of shallow fried lean bacon. Sprinkle the morels and potatoes with chopped parsley.

Deglaze the pan with a few tablespoons of white wine, add $1\frac{1}{2}$ dl (5 fl oz or $\frac{5}{8}$ U.S. cup) good veal gravy, pass through a fine strainer and serve separately.

2222 Entrecôte à la Hongroise
Season and shallow fry the sirloin steaks in butter.

At the same time fry separately in butter, 125 g ($4\frac{1}{2}$ oz) blanched diced streaky bacon; add 150 g (5 oz) chopped onion and fry together till well coloured then add $\frac{1}{2}$ tbs paprika and 1 dl ($3\frac{1}{2}$ fl oz or $\frac{1}{2}$ U.S. cup) white wine. Reduce by two-thirds, add $2\frac{1}{2}$ dl (9 fl oz or $1\frac{1}{8}$ U.S. cups) Chicken Velouté and allow to cook gently for 7–8 minutes.

Arrange the cooked steaks on a suitable dish, cover with the prepared sauce and surround with small round plain boiled potatoes.

Note: The sauce may be served separately.

2223 Entrecôte à la Hôtelière
Season and shallow fry the sirloin steaks in butter; arrange on a suitable dish.

Cover with 150 g (5 oz) Maître d'Hôtel Butter mixed together with 1 tbs dry Duxelles which has been well flavoured with onion and shallot.

Deglaze the pan with 1½ dl (5 fl oz or ⅝ U.S. cup) white wine and reduce by two-thirds. Add 1 tbs melted meat glaze and pour over the prepared steaks.

2224 Entrecôte à la Lyonnaise
Shallow fry the sirloin steaks in butter and arrange on a suitable dish. Garnish along the sides with 300 g (11 oz) finely sliced onions fried in butter and mixed with 1 tbs melted pale meat glaze; sprinkle with chopped parsley.

Deglaze the pan with 1½ dl (5 fl oz or ⅝ U.S. cup) white wine and a few drops of vinegar; reduce by two-thirds and add 1 dl (3½ fl oz or ½ U.S. cup) Sauce Demi-glace. Pass through a fine strainer, shake in 50 g (2 oz) butter and pour over the prepared steaks.

2225 Entrecôte Marchand de Vins
Season and grill the sirloin steaks; arrange on a suitable dish. Cover with 150 g (5 oz) softened Beurre Marchand de Vins, or serve it separately in a sauceboat.

2226 Entrecôte à la Marseillaise
Season and grill the sirloin steaks; arrange on a suitable dish.

Cover with 150 g (5 oz) Maître d'Hôtel Butter which has been mixed with a quarter its volume of Tomato Butter and a touch of crushed garlic.

Surround with Pommes en Copeaux (4192) and small halves of tomatoes prepared as for garnish à la Marseillaise (411).

2227 Entrecôte Mexicaine
Season and grill the sirloin steaks; arrange on a suitable dish. Surround with mushrooms and pimentos prepared as for garnish à la Mexicaine (416).

Serve with well seasoned veal gravy, flavoured with tomato.

2228 Entrecôte Mirabeau
Season and grill the sirloin steaks; arrange on a suitable dish.

Decorate with thin anchovy fillets arranged trellis-fashion and stoned olives; border the steaks with blanched tarragon leaves.

Serve accompanied with Anchovy Butter.

2229 Entrecôte Tyrolienne
Season and grill the sirloin steaks; arrange on a suitable dish. Cover with 250 g (9 oz) finely sliced onion, fried in butter and mixed together with a little Sauce Poivrade. Surround the steaks with a *cordon* of Tomato Fondue.

2230 Entrecôte au Vert-pré
Season and grill the sirloin steaks; arrange on a suitable dish. Cover with 150 g (5 oz) Maître d'Hôtel Butter and surround with bouquets of straw potatoes and watercress.

2231 COTE DE BOEUF, OR TRAIN DE COTES—RIBS OF BEEF

This part of the carcase is one of the finest joints for presentation and carving in the dining-room. For this it is always roasted, placed on a carving trolley with a Bain-marie for the roast gravy as well as containers for any garnishes. The trolley is wheeled before the guest and carved to order by a specially trained carver.

Ribs of beef may also be braised but in both cases the joint should be trimmed and the bones of the chine removed along with the sinew running along the top. The cooking time for roasting naturally varies according to the size and quality of the joint, but the following approximate times are useful as a guide. If roasted on a spit allow 30–35 minutes per 1 kg (2¼ lb) or 25–30 minutes if roasted in the oven.

This joint should not be roasted until it has been well hung; this is the only way of ensuring that the meat will be tender when cooked.

2232 Small cuts from Ribs of Beef
Single ribs of beef cut from the large joint, or steaks (*Entrecôtes*) cut from between two ribs, may be grilled. Care should be taken to cut these steaks to a suitable thickness for ease of grilling. These small cuts may also be braised and garnished as for fillet of beef.

The weight of these steaks which are in effect the true *Entrecôte* should not exceed 1 kg to 1 kg 200 g (2 lb 4 oz to 2 lb 11 oz); all the methods of preparation for sirloin steaks are suitable.

2233 HAMPES OR ONGLEES

These parts are the muscles of the *Pleura* and are usually found to be both tender and juicy. They are excellent when prepared as *Carbonades* and *Paupiettes*. They may be cut into small squares, shallow fried in clarified butter then rolled in a mixture of half Beurre Bercy and half meat glaze. Over and above these uses, it should be added that they are frequently used for meat juice by lightly grilling and then pressing out the juices. Whichever way they are used it is important that the skin and sinew which covers them should first be removed.

2234 FILET DE BOEUF—FILLET OF BEEF

The fillet is the best part of the whole carcase of beef and logically it should thus be named the *Filet Mignon*; the boned sirloin could then be known as the upper fillet (*Contrefilet*) as frequently is the case.

The whole fillet when used as a Relevé, is generally larded with strips of salt pork fat and sometimes when called for it is larded with truffle or red tongue. In other cases it may be coated with dry Duxelles or Matignon and finally wrapped in thin slices of salt pork fat, instead of being larded.

Even though a recipe may call for the insertion of other ingredients into the fillet, it is recommended that they be mixed with salt pork fat, e.g. strips of fat and truffle or strips of fat and tongue. The fat is always advantageous as adding flavour and succulence to the meat whilst it is cooking.

Whatever the case, the fillet when required for use as a Relevé, should be either roasted or, for preference Poêléed, as this method of cooking gives added flavour to the fillet and also to the accompanying sauce which should utilize the pan juices, vegetables and herbs from the cooking.

Unless otherwise required the fillet should always be kept slightly underdone and pink in the centre.

For 10 persons, 1½ kg (3 lb 6 oz) raw weight of trimmed fillet will be sufficient. On average there is an approximate wastage of one-third occasioned by trimming the fat and sinew from the fillet.

Note:

1) Except where some special garnishes are called for, there will only be brief details of garnishes in the following recipes. More specific descriptions of the garnishes will be found in the Chapter on Garnishes.
2) Where there is no specific indication concerning the larding of the fillet it should be taken that it is done with strips of salt pork fat.

2235 Filet de Boeuf à l'Andalouse

Lard the fillet and either roast or Poêlé it.

Place it on a long dish and surround with pimentos à la Grecque; shallow fried rounds of eggplant garnished with cooked roughly chopped tomato flesh, and grilled chipolatas.

Serve thickened gravy finished with sherry separately.

2236 Filet de Boeuf à l'Arlésienne

Lard the fillet and either roast or Poêlé it.

Place it on a long dish and surround with bouquets of sliced fried eggplant; peeled, sliced and sautéed tomatoes; and rings of deep-fried onions.

Serve tomato-flavoured Sauce Demi-glace separately.

2237 Filet de Boeuf à la Berrichonne

Lard the fillet and roast it.

Place it on a long dish and surround with small balls of braised cabbage, slices of streaky bacon cooked with the cabbage, small glazed onions and large braised chestnuts.

Serve separately a lightly thickened gravy prepared from the juices in the roasting tray.

2238 Filet de Boeuf à la Bisontine

Lard the fillet and Poêlé it.

Place it on a long dish and surround with Croustades made from Pommes Duchesse filled with creamed purée of cauliflower, and halves of lettuce stuffed with an ordinary meat forcemeat mixed with Fines Herbes and braised.

Serve separately a gravy prepared from the juices of the cooking after first removing the fat and passing through a fine strainer.

2239 Filet de Boeuf Bouquetière

Lard the fillet and either roast or Poêlé it.

Place it on a long dish and surround with bouquets of glazed carrots, glazed turnips, buttered peas, diamond-shaped beans, cauliflower coated with a little Sauce Hollandaise and small Pommes Château; alternate the colours of the bouquets.

Serve separately if roast, a lightly thickened veal gravy, or if poêléed a gravy prepared from the juices from the cooking, after first removing all fat and passing through a fine strainer.

2240 Filet de Boeuf Bréhan

Lard the fillet and either roast or Poêlé it.

Place it on a long dish and surround with artichoke bottoms filled with a purée of broad beans and bouquets of cauliflower coated with Sauce Hollandaise; place a bouquet of parsley potatoes at each end of the dish.

Serve separately, if roast, a lightly thickened veal gravy or, if Poêléed, a gravy prepared from the juices from the cooking after first removing all fat and passing through a fine strainer.

2241 Filet de Boeuf Bristol

Lard the fillet and Poêlé it.

Place it on a long dish and garnish with small round potatoes cooked in butter, rolled in light meat glaze and placed at each side of the fillet, and small Croquettes of Risotto placed at each end.

Serve accompanied with a dish of buttered flageolets and a gravy prepared from the juices from the cooking after first removing all fat and passing through a fine strainer.

2242 Filet de Boeuf Châtelaine
Lard the fillet and Poêlé it.

Place it on a long dish and garnish with artichoke bottoms filled with Soubise placed along the sides and braised chestnuts and Pommes Noisettes placed at each end.

Serve separately a Sauce Madère to which has been added the reduced juices from the cooking after removing all fat and passing through a fine strainer.

2243 Filet de Boeuf Clamart
Lard the fillet and roast it.

Place it on a long dish and surround with small tartlet cases filled with peas à la Française containing shredded lettuce and alternating with small round shapes of Pommes Macaire.

Serve separately a lightly thickened gravy prepared from the juices from the cooking.

Note: The tartlets filled with peas may be placed on top of the Pommes Macaire.

2244 Filet de Boeuf Dauphine
Lard the fillet and Poêlé it.

Place it on a long dish and surround with Pommes Dauphine moulded cork shape arranged either in a line or in bouquets.

Serve Sauce Madère separately.

Note: It has become the rule to serve a green vegetable with this dish and also with Filet de Boeuf Duchesse.

2245 Filet de Boeuf Dubarry
Lard the fillet and roast it.

Place it on a long dish and surround with moulded balls of cauliflower coated with Sauce Mornay and gratinated; and Pommes Fondantes.

Serve separately an unthickened gravy prepared from the juices from the cooking.

2246 Filet de Boeuf Duchesse
Lard the fillet and Poêlé it.

Place it on a long dish and surround with Pommes Duchesse, brushed with eggwash and coloured in the oven at the last moment.

Serve fairly thin Sauce Madère separately.

2247 Filet de Boeuf Financière
Lard the fillet and Poêlé it.

Place it on a long dish and surround with bouquets of the ingredients used for Financière garnish, lightly coating them with the sauce.

Serve Sauce Financière separately.

2248 Filet de Boeuf Frascati
Lard the fillet and Poêlé it.

Place it on a long dish and surround with squares of foie gras lightly fried in butter, grooved cooked mushrooms and small truffles. Place a bouquet of asparagus tips at each end of the dish and arrange a line of glazed crescent-shaped pieces of Duchesse potato containing a little chopped truffle around the edge of the dish.

Serve separately a thickened gravy made from the juices from the cooking after first removing all the fat and passing through a fine strainer.

2249 Filet de Boeuf des Gastronomes
Lard the fillet with truffle and place it to marinate with Madeira for 4–5 hours. Drain well, wrap in slices of salt pork fat and tie carefully with string. Braise with the Madeira wine from the marinade and glaze at the last moment after removing the string and fat.

Place on a long dish and surround with large chestnuts cooked in Bouillon and glazed, nice cockscombs cooked and rolled in pale meat glaze and morels sautéed in butter. These items should be arranged in bouquets alternating with large thick slices of truffle cooked in a Mirepoix with Champagne.

Serve with reduced Sauce Demi-glace to which has been added the cooking liquor from the truffles.

2250 Filet de Boeuf Godard
Lard the fillet with salt pork fat and tongue and Poêlé it.

Place it on a long dish and surround with the items of a Godard garnish arranged in separate bouquets and lightly sauced. Place the well decorated Quenelles of the garnish at the sides and ends of the dish.

Serve separately a Sauce Godard to which has been added the juices from the cooking after first removing the fat and passing through a fine strainer.

2251 Filet de Boeuf à la Hongroise
Lard the fillet and roast it.

Place it on a long dish and surround with small balls of cauliflower, coated with paprika-flavoured Sauce Mornay containing chopped ham; and button onions cooked in Bouillon and glazed.

Serve separately a fairly thin Sauce Soubise flavoured with paprika.

2252 Filet de Boeuf Hussarde
Lard the fillet and roast it.

Place it on a long dish and surround with small Pommes Duchesse piped with a star tube and coloured at the last minute; and large grilled mushrooms filled with thick Sauce Soubise.

Serve a fairly thin Sauce Hussarde separately.

2253 Filet de Beouf à l'Italienne
Lard the fillet and Poêlé it.

Place it on a long dish and surround with quarters of artichoke bottoms à l'Italienne; set a small pyramid of Croquettes of macaroni at each end.

Serve a fairly thin Sauce Italienne separately.

2254 Filet de Boeuf Japonaise
Lard the fillet, Poêlé it and glaze at the last moment.

Place it on a dish and surround with small Croustades filled with Japanese artichokes mixed with a little Ordinary Velouté, alternating with Croquette Potatoes.

Serve with an unthickened gravy made from the juices from the cooking after first removing the fat and passing through a fine strainer.

2255 Filet de Boeuf Jardinière
Lard the fillet and roast it.

Place it on a long dish and surround with well-separated bouquets of Jardinière garnish.

Serve separately a gravy made from the juices from the cooking after first removing the fat and passing through a fine strainer.

2256 Filet de Boeuf London-House
Trim the fillet and remove the chain from the thick side; open the fillet lengthwise along the thick side, stopping short of each end and not cutting completely through. Fill it with thick slices of seasoned raw foie gras, alternating with slices of raw truffle; close it up and stud the top surface with pieces of raw truffle.

Tie fairly tightly with string and place the fillet in a suitable pan lined with slices of raw ham and spread with a cooked Mirepoix. Moisten with sufficient Madeira wine and veal gravy to come halfway up the fillet and braise it, carefully glazing it at the last minute after removing the string.

Place on a long dish and surround with truffles cooked in Madeira and nice mushroom heads cooked in a little butter, arranging them alternately.

Serve separately a Sauce Demi-glace containing the braising liquid after first removing any fat, passing through a fine strainer and reducing it by two-thirds.

Note: In the first edition of this book the creation of Filet de Boeuf London-House was attributed to a chef by the name of Baron.

It has been pointed out subsequently by one of our collaborators that this dish, sometimes known under other names, should really be designated Filet de Boeuf à la Bec, as being created by a chef named Drouhin around about the year 1849 and dedicated by him to a rich Marseilles businessman by the name of Bec.

The foregoing has also been stated in Monsieur Morard's book *Les secrets de la cuisine dévoilés.* This information is included and accepted without comment to the contrary.

2257 Filet de Boeuf Lorette
Lard the fillet, Poêlé it and glaze at the last moment.

Place it on a long dish and surround with bouquets of buttered asparagus tips, and place a pile of Pommes Lorette at each end of the dish.

Serve a fairly thin tomato-flavoured Sauce Demi-glace separately.

2258 Filet de Boeuf Macédoine
Lard the fillet and roast it.

Place it on a long dish and surround with a Macédoine of vegetables and small Pommes Château arranged in alternate bouquets.

Serve separately an unthickened gravy made from the juices from the cooking.

2259 Filet de Boeuf Madeleine
Lard the fillet and roast it.

Place it on a long dish and surround with artichoke bottoms filled with thick Sauce Soubise, and small moulded timbales of a purée of French beans, arranging them alternately.

Serve a fairly thin Sauce Demi-glace separately.

2260 Filet de Boeuf au Madère et Champignons
Lard the fillet, Poêlé it and glaze at the last moment.

Place it on a long dish and surround with large grooved mushrooms cooked in butter. Serve accompanied with a Sauce aux Champignons containing the juices from the cooking after removing the fat and passing through a strainer, and either some very small cooked whole mushrooms or quarters of large cooked mushrooms.

2261 Filet de Boeuf Mexicaine
Lard the fillet and roast it.

Place it on a long dish and surround with alternate bouquets of grilled mushrooms and pimentos, both filled with Riz à la Créole.

Serve separately a lightly thickened veal gravy well flavoured with tomato.

2262 Filet de Boeuf à la Moderne
Lard the fillet with salt pork fat and tongue, Poêlé it and glaze at the last moment.

Place it on a long dish and surround with the following garnish: 1) On either side of the fillet place a line of small *Chartreuses* made in small hexagonal moulds as follows: butter the moulds and place a slice of truffle in the bottom of each;

line the sides with various vegetables such as carrots, turnips, peas and beans, all plain boiled in salted water, cutting them to a suitable size and arranging them so as to vary the colours. Carefully spread a thin layer of light textured forcemeat over the vegetables then fill with well squeezed braised cabbage. Cook *au Bain-marie* for 10 minutes before being required. 2) At either end of the fillet place halves of braised lettuce in a fan shape so as to frame the ends in semi-circles. 3) Place poached round Quenelles decorated with salt ox tongue between the *Chartreuses*.

Serve separately a lightly thickened gravy prepared from the juices from the cooking after first removing the fat and passing through a fine strainer.

2263 Filet de Boeuf Montmorency

Lard the fillet; Poêlé it and glaze at the last moment.

Place it on a long dish and surround with artichoke bottoms filled with a Macédoine of vegetables and bouquets of asparagus tips, arranged alternately.

Serve separately a Sauce Madère containing the juices from the cooking after first removing the fat, passing through a fine strainer and reducing by two-thirds.

2264 Filet de Boeuf Nivernaise

Lard the fillet; Poêlé it and glaze at the last moment.

Place it on a long dish and surround with alternate bouquets of small glazed carrots and small glazed onions.

Serve separately the juices from the cooking after first removing the fat and passing through a fine strainer.

2265 Filet de Boeuf à l'Orientale

Roast the fillet without larding it or wrapping it in salt pork fat.

Place it on a long dish and surround with small timbales of Riz à la Grecque set on halves of cooked tomatoes, and Croquettes of sweet potatoes, arranged alternately.

Serve a well flavoured Tomato Sauce separately.

2266 Filet de Boeuf à la Parisienne

Lard the fillet and roast it.

Place it on a long dish and surround with artichoke bottoms filled with a Salpicon of tongue, mushrooms and truffle mixed with Velouté and place bouquets of Pommes à la Parisienne at each end of the dish.

Serve Sauce Madère separately.

2267 Filet de Boeuf à la Périgourdine

Lard the fillet; Poêlé it and glaze at the last moment.

Place it on a long dish and surround with medium-sized truffles cooked with a fine Mirepoix and Madeira wine and then glazed.

Serve Sauce Périgueux separately.

2268 Filet de Boeuf Petit-Duc

Lard the fillet, Poêlé it and glaze at the last moment.

Place it on a long dish and surround with small *Bouchées* filled with creamed asparagus tips and medium-sized artichoke bottoms cooked in butter, each garnished with a nice slice of truffle.

Serve separately a very light meat glaze finished with old Madeira wine and thickened with 25 g (1 oz) butter per 1 dl (3½ fl oz or ½ U.S. cup) of glaze.

2269 Filet de Boeuf à la Portugaise

Lard the fillet and roast it.

Place it on a long dish and surround with a row of stuffed tomatoes along each side; place a nice bouquet of small Pommes Château at each end.

Serve a fairly thin Tomato Sauce separately.

2270 Filet de Boeuf à la Provençale

Lard the fillet; Poêlé and glaze it at the last moment.

Place it on a long dish and surround with stuffed tomatoes and stuffed mushrooms, arranged alternately.

Serve a Sauce Provençale separately.

2271 Filet de Boeuf Régence

Marinade the fillet with Madeira for 2–3 hours; drain well, coat it with Matignon (321) and envelop it completely with thin slices of salt pork fat.

Tie carefully with string and braise it in the marinade together with some Rhine wine. A few minutes before being required for service, untie the string, remove the fat and Matignon and glaze the fillet.

Place it on a long dish and surround with separated bouquets of small Quenelles of veal and butter forcemeat containing chopped red tongue, moulded with teaspoons; thick slices of foie gras cooked in butter; fine cockscombs; very white button mushrooms; and large olive-shaped truffles. Place 1 large decorated Quenelle of the same forcemeat on each side of the fillet.

Remove all the fat from the braising liquid, pass firmly through a fine strainer, reduce by two-thirds and add some Sauce Demi-glace.

Coat the bouquets of garnish excepting the two large Quenelles, with some of the sauce and serve the rest separately.

2272 Filet de Boeuf Renaissance
Lard the fillet, Poêlé it and glaze at the last moment.

Place it on a long dish and surround with bouquets of Renaissance garnish.

Serve separately an unthickened gravy prepared from the juices from the cooking after first removing the fat and passing through a fine strainer.

2273 Filet de Boeuf Richelieu
Lard the fillet and either Poêlé or roast it; if Poêlé, glaze it at the last moment.

Surround with distinct bouquets, placed in such a way as to contrast the colours, of stuffed tomatoes; stuffed mushrooms; small Pommes Château; and whole or halves of neatly trimmed braised lettuce.

Prepare a lightly thickened gravy from the juices from the cooking after first removing all fat and passing through a fine strainer.

2274 Filet de Boeuf Saint-Florentin
Lard the fillet and roast it.

Place it on a long dish and surround with bouquets of Pommes Saint-Florentin and Cèpes à la Bordelaise.

Serve Sauce Bordelaise au Vin Blanc separately.

2275 Filet de Boeuf Saint-Germain
Lard the fillet and roast it.

Place it on a long dish and surround with small *Timbales* of green pea purée, and small turned glazed carrots. Place some small Pommes Fondantes at the sides of the fillet.

Serve Sauce Béarnaise separately.

2276 Filet de Boeuf Saint-Mandé
Lard the fillet and roast it.

Place it on a long dish and surround with bouquets of small Pommes Macaire, buttered asparagus tips and buttered peas, arranged alternately.

Serve separately a lightly thickened gravy prepared from the juices from the cooking.

2277 Filet de Boeuf à la Sarde
Lard the fillet and roast it.

Place it on a long dish and surround with stuffed tomatoes on one side; braised cucumbers on the other side, and Croquettes of rice arranged pyramid fashion at the ends.

Serve a light Tomato Sauce separately.

2278 Filet de Boeuf Talleyrand
Trim the fillet and stud the top with pointed pieces of truffle approximately $2\frac{1}{2}$ cm (1 in) long by 7 mm ($\frac{1}{4}$ in) wide, using 200 g (7 oz) truffle per 1 kg ($2\frac{1}{4}$ lb) of fillet; make small incisions in the flesh so as to insert the truffle easily.

Place it to marinate in Madeira wine for 2–3 hours; drain it well then wrap in slices of salt pork fat. Tie carefully with string and braise it with the marinade.

When cooked, untie the string, remove the fat and glaze the fillet just before being required. Place on a long dish and serve accompanied with a dish of Macaroni à la Talleyrand and a well-flavoured Sauce Périgueux containing a finely cut Julienne of truffle instead of chopped truffle.

2279 Filet de Boeuf à la Viroflay
Lard the fillet and either Poêlé or roast it; if Poêlé, glaze it at the last moment.

Place on a long dish and surround with alternate bouquets of small balls of spinach à la Viroflay, quarters of artichoke bottoms and small Pommes Château.

Serve separately a lightly thickened gravy prepared from the juices from the cooking after first removing the fat and passing through a fine strainer.

2280 FILET DE BOEUF FROID—COLD FILLET OF BEEF

Fillet of beef for serving cold may be either Poêléed or roast, keeping it pink towards the centre. Allow to become completely cold, trim carefully underneath and along the sides, then coat with almost setting aspic jelly.

If to be served simply *à la Gelée* it can be placed directly on a suitable dish which has first had a layer of jelly set on it. If the fillet is going to be accompanied by a vegetable garnish it is preferable to present it on a decorative base of bread or rice. This throws the fillet into relief when a garnish is placed around it and enhances the presentation of the dish as a whole.

Vegetables used as a garnish for cold fillet of beef or for other cold Entrées or Relevés should not be cooled in cold water but drained as soon as they are cooked and allowed to cool naturally. The cold vegetables should be set in neat piles, coated with near setting jelly then arranged around the fillet, alternating the colours. Finish the presentation by placing a little chopped jelly between each bouquet and surround the edge of the dish with large neatly cut shapes of jelly. This, of course, is only a suggestion for presenting the vegetables; other methods including moulding are equally suitable.

2281 Filet de Boeuf Chevet
Take a long deep mould with a rounded bottom (*Berceau* or cradle mould) and coat the inside with a layer of very clear aspic jelly. Decorate it *en*

Chartreuse, that is to say with a layer of vegetables arranged either lengthways in the mould or across it, taking care to alternate the colours in an artistic fashion. Fix the vegetables with a little almost setting jelly.

Trim the cooked fillet carefully then place it upside-down in the mould so that it will be the right side up when demoulded. Fill the mould with almost setting jelly, just to cover the fillet then place in a refrigerator to set firm.

Set a layer of jelly on a long dish; when required for service dip the prepared mould of beef quickly in hot water then turn it out on to the prepared dish.

2282 Filet de Boeuf Coquelin

Lard the fillet and Poêlé it, keeping it slightly underdone; allow to become completely cold.

Remove the fat completely from the juices from the cooking, pass through a fine strainer, add a little excellent veal stock and a fine, cooked Julienne of vegetables and truffles.

Trim the fillet and cut it into slices; place these overlapping in a fairly deep oval china dish and cover with the prepared gravy and the Julienne. Allow to cool in a refrigerator.

Serve from the dish as prepared.

2283 Filet de Boeuf Montlhéry

Trim the fillet and Poêlé it keeping it slightly underdone. When completely cold, trim it and coat with aspic jelly.

Place it on a long dish which has been previously coated with a layer of jelly and surround with 1) small *Timbales* made by decorating jelly-lined dariole moulds with French beans, placing a slice of truffle at the bottom then filling them with a small Macédoine of vegetables mixed with jellied Mayonnaise; and 2) small artichoke bottoms filled with asparagus tips and glazed with jelly.

Place a border of neatly cut shapes of jelly around the edge of the dish and serve a thin Sauce Mayonnaise separately.

2284 Filet de Boeuf Mistral

Poêlé the fillet and when cold coat it with aspic jelly.

Place it on a long dish which has been coated with a layer of jelly and surround with cold tomatoes à la Provençale. Surround with a border of neatly cut shapes of jelly set on the edges of the dish.

2285 Filet de Boeuf à la Russe

Poêlé the fillet, allow it to cool thoroughly then trim it and cut into even slices.

Remove the fat from the juices from the cooking, pass the juices through a fine strainer, reduce till thick and gelatinous and add some chopped truffle. Coat the slices of fillet with this sauce and place to cool thoroughly in a refrigerator.

Set a layer of aspic jelly on a long dish, arrange the prepared slices overlapping in a line down the centre and surround with chopped jelly. Surround with a border of neatly cut shapes of jelly set on the edges of the dish.

2286 DERIVATIVES OF FILLET OF BEEF

Beefsteak — Bitokes — Chateaubriand — Fillet Steak—Filets Mignons—Filets en Chevreuil—Tournedos and Medaillons.

It is the usual practice in commercial establishments to cut a fillet of beef into pieces as follows:

1) the head of the fillet into beefsteaks,
2) the middle of the fillet into Chateaubriands and fillet steaks,
3) the last third of the fillet into Tournedos at the thickest part and the tail end into Filets Mignons.

The average weight of these cuts should be approximately:

Beefsteak 200 g (7 oz)
Fillet Steak 200 g (7 oz)
Single Chateaubriand 300 g (11 oz)
Tournedos 120 g (4 oz)
Filets Mignons 150 g (5 oz)

Using a fillet of beef in this manner is recommended as being rational thus permitting optimum usage and maximum returns.

2287 BEEFSTEAKS

Strictly speaking, a beefsteak should be cut from the head or thick end of the trimmed fillet, it may also be cut from the sirloin without offending against this rule since the name being English does not define exactly from which part of the carcase it should come. It should be cut about 2 cm ($\frac{4}{5}$ in) thick.

Beefsteaks may be prepared according to any of the recipes for *Entrecôte* in addition to the following.

2288 Beefsteak à l'Américaine

Cut off a piece of the head of the fillet, remove any fat or sinew and finely chop the flesh, seasoning it with salt and pepper.

Mould to the shape of a round cake, make a small indentation in the top and place an egg yolk in it.

Place the steak on a small dish and serve accompanied with capers, chopped onion and chopped parsley.

2289 Beefsteak à Cheval
Cut the steak from the head of the fillet, trim it, season and shallow fry in butter. Place in a suitable dish and place two lightly fried and trimmed eggs on top.

Serve accompanied with a little lightly thickened gravy.

Note: The name of this dish is most incorrect from the point of view of taste as well as logic. It has only been included in this book because of its general use.

2290 Beefsteak à la Hambourgeoise—Hamburg Steak
Remove any sinew from the required amount of fillet and chop the flesh very finely. For each 200 g (7 oz) of flesh mix in 1 egg yolk, ½ tbs chopped onion cooked in a little butter and season with salt, pepper and a touch of grated nutmeg.

Mould into round flat-shaped cakes using flour and shallow fry them in clarified butter. They are cooked when little beads of blood show on the surface after being turned over.

Arrange the steaks on a dish and place approximately 30 g (1 oz) sliced and shallow fried onions on top of each.

2291 Beefsteak à la Russe
Prepare the steak as for Beefsteak à la Hambourgeoise replacing the fried onions with 2 fried eggs cut to a nice shape with a round pastry cutter.

Serve surrounded with a little lightly thickened gravy.

2292 Beefsteak à la Tartare
Prepare the steak as for Beefsteak à l'Américaine but without the egg yolk on top.

Serve Sauce Tartare separately.

BITOKES

2293 Bitokes à la Russe
Finely chop 800 g (1¾ lb) fillet of beef from which all fat and sinew has been removed; pound well in a mortar with 300 g (11 oz) butter, 15 g (½ oz) salt, a pinch of pepper and a touch of grated nutmeg.

Divide into 10 equal pieces of approximately 110 g (4 oz) each, mould into fairly thick oval shapes using flour then egg and breadcrumb them. Shallow fry in clarified butter and arrange in a circle on a round dish.

Deglaze the pan with 1 dl (3½ fl oz or ½ U.S. cup) cream, add ½ dl (2 fl oz or ¼ U.S. cup) Sauce Demi-glace and pass through a fine strainer.

Place 120 g (4 oz) finely sliced onions, shallow fried in butter, in the centre of the Bitokes; serve accompanied with a sauceboat of the prepared sauce and a dish of Pommes Sautées.

2294 CHATEAUBRIAND

Chateaubriands are obtained from the centre of the trimmed fillet of beef, cut two or three times the thickness of an ordinary fillet steak. However, when it is to be cooked by grilling the *Chateaubriand* should not be more than 500 g (1 lb 2 oz) in weight as, if larger than this, the outside tends to become too dry and hard before the inside is properly cooked.

Many strange ideas have been put forward concerning the proper accompaniments for *Chateaubriand*; correctly speaking it should be Sauce Colbert or a similar sauce and small potatoes cooked in butter. In modern practice though, *Chateaubriands* are served with any of the sauces and garnishes suitable for *Tournedos* and fillet steaks.

2295 GRILLED OR SHALLOW FRIED FILLET STEAKS

Fillet steaks are obtained from the centre of the trimmed fillet of beef and are cut about 3½ cm (1½ in) thick across the fillet. They should weigh approximately 200 g (7 oz) each.

Any of the recipes for Tournedos and sirloin steaks are suitable.

2296 FILETS MIGNONS

Filets Mignons of beef are usually obtained from the tail end of the trimmed fillet of beef where it is too thin for cutting into *Tournedos*.

They are cut in the shape of fairly thin triangles, seasoned, dipped in melted butter and then into breadcrumbs. Pat the breadcrumbs in gently with the flat of a knife and mark the surface trellis-fashion with the back of the knife. Sprinkle with melted butter and grill gently.

All vegetable garnishes are suitable as an accompaniment. Sauce Béarnaise, Choron, Valois, etc., are also excellent accompaniments. Any sauce or gravy, however, should be served from a sauceboat.

2297 FILETS EN CHEVREUIL

These are cut in the same way as the *Filets Mignons* as above. They are then larded in the centre with strips of salt pork fat and placed in a small quantity of marinade which is only lightly acidulated but contains plenty of oil. The time for marinating is determined above all by the temperature; this is roughly two days in summer and four days in winter.

To cook, drain the fillets well, dry them and shallow fry in very hot oil. They are usually presented by placing on heart-shaped Croûtons of bread fried in butter or arranged in a circle overlapping alternately with the Croûtons.

Serve garnished or accompanied with brown or white Soubise, or a purée of chestnuts, lentils, etc. Any well flavoured sauce such as Sauce Chevreuil à la Française, Poivrade, Romaine or Chasseur is suitable.

2298 TOURNEDOS AND MEDAILLONS

Too much has been said concerning the origin of the name *Tournedos* without any firm conclusions being drawn and thus it is not the intention of this work to attempt to resolve the argument.

The name *Médaillon* is another term for *Tournedos*.

They should be cut from the thinner part of the trimmed fillet, about 3½ cm (1½ in) thick and weighing approximately 120 g (4 oz). A nice round shape is desirable and this may be obtained by tying them round with string.

To serve: Tournedos are usually placed on a round Croûton of bread fried in clarified butter or on a flat Croquette prepared from one or more of the items of its garnish. When serving them on Croûtons it is useful to coat the Croûton with a little meat glaze first as this will prevent it from soaking up the juices which are inclined to escape from the *Tournedos*.

Whenever *Tournedos* are cooked by shallow frying (Sauté), the pan used should be deglazed with a liquid or gravy which should be in keeping with the sauce required, e.g. red wine, white wine, Madeira, mushroom cooking liquor, truffle essence, etc.

In the Chapter on Garnishes much importance is given to the types of sauce suitable and applicable to small Entrées of butcher's meat. It is not really necessary to repeat these details again except to stress two very important points:

1) Sauces derived from Espagnole or Sauce Tomate should be used exclusively where the preparation includes a garnish comprised of Quenelles, mushrooms, truffles, cockscombs and kidneys, such as Financière garnish, or just a single one of these items.
2) As a general rule a buttered meat glaze or Sauce Chateaubriand should be used where the preparation includes a vegetable garnish.

This being the case only certain sauces will be indicated in the following recipes. The details for the preparation of the items of garnish for *Tournedos* will be found in the Chapter on Garnishes.

2299 Tournedos à l'Andalouse

Season the Tournedos and shallow fry in clarified butter. Arrange each on a round Croûton of bread fried in clarified butter and surround with stuffed pimentos and grilled chipolatas. Place a round slice of fried eggplant on top of each Tournedos.

2300 Tournedos à l'Arlésienne

Season the Tournedos and shallow fry in a mixture of butter and oil.

Arrange each on a round Croûton of bread fried in clarified butter and serve surrounded with alternate bouquets of fried eggplant and sautéed tomatoes. Place a few rings of fried onion on top of each Tournedos.

2301 Tournedos Armenonville

Season the Tournedos and shallow fry in butter.

Place each on a small round mould of Pommes Anna of the same dimensions as the Tournedos; arrange on a dish and surround with alternate bouquets of creamed noodles, cockscombs and kidneys.

Deglaze the pan with Madeira, add the necessary amount of Jus de Veau Lié, pass through a fine strainer and serve separately.

2302 Tournedos Baltimore

Season the Tournedos and shallow fry in butter.

Arrange each on a tartlet case half filled with creamed maize, place a slice of seasoned and fried tomato on top of each and a slightly smaller round of fried green pimento in the centre of the tomato.

Serve Sauce Chateaubriand separately.

2303 Tournedos Béarnaise

Season the Tournedos and grill them.

Place each on a thin Croûton of bread fried in clarified butter, surround with bouquets of small Pommes Château and lightly coat the Tournedos with a little light meat glaze.

Pipe a narrow border of Sauce Béarnaise on top of each Tournedos, or serve the sauce separately decorated with a thin line of meat glaze.

2304 Tournedos Belle-Hélène
Season the Tournedos and shallow fry in butter.

Place a small round flat Croquette made from asparagus tips on each and on this place a nice slice of truffle.

Deglaze the pan with a little white wine, thicken with a little butter and serve separately.

2305 Tournedos Benjamin
Season the Tournedos and shallow fry in butter.

Arrange each on a thin Croûton of bread fried in clarified butter, surround with bouquets of small round Croquettes made from a truffled Pommes Dauphine mixture allowing 3 per person; place a small stuffed mushroom on top of each Tournedos.

Deglaze the pan with Madeira, add the necessary amount of Sauce Demi-glace and pass through a fine strainer. Serve separately with the Tournedos.

2306 Tournedos Berny
Marinate the Tournedos in advance, well drain and dry them, then shallow fry in very hot oil.

Arrange each on a small round flat cake of Pommes Berny with a slice of truffle on top of each Tournedos.

Serve a light Sauce Poivrade separately.

2307 Tournedos à la Bordelaise
Season the Tournedos and grill them.

Arrange directly on the serving dish with a nice thick slice of poached beef bone marrow on top of each and a pinch of chopped parsley in the centre of the bone marrow.

Serve a Sauce Bordelaise separately.

2308 Tournedos Bouquetière
Season the Tournedos and grill them.

Arrange neatly on a dish and surround with neatly separated bouquets of Bouquetière garnish.

2309 Tournedos Bréhan
Season the Tournedos and shallow fry in butter.

Place an artichoke bottom filled with a smooth purée of broad beans, on top of each. Arrange on a dish and surround with bouquets of cauliflower and small Pommes Persillées.

2310 Tournedos Castillane
Season the Tournedos and shallow fry in butter.

Arrange each on a round Croûton of bread fried in clarified butter, place a small tartlet case filled with Tomato Fondue on top of each Tournedos and surround with nice crisp rings of deep fried onions.

2311 Tournedos à la Catalane
Season the Tournedos, shallow fry them in butter and arrange on a dish.

Have prepared a mixture of roughly chopped tomato flesh cooked with a little oil and finely chopped onion and add to this some fine Julienne of red pimento, a little chopped parsley and just a little very thick Sauce Demi-glace.

Place half a tablespoon of this mixture in the centre of each Tournedos.

2312 Tournedos Cendrillon
Fill the required number of large artichoke bottoms with a well buttered Soubise purée mixed with chopped truffles; glaze them quickly when needed for service.

Season the Tournedos and shallow fry in butter. Place each on one of the prepared artichoke bottoms and arrange in a circle on a round dish.

Serve a lightly buttered veal gravy separately.

2313 Tournedos aux Champignons
Season the Tournedos and shallow fry in butter.

Arrange in a circle on a round dish and place a garnish of small mushrooms cooked in butter in the centre; set a nice cooked grooved mushroom on each Tournedos.

Deglaze the pan with mushroom cooking liquor, add the required amount of Sauce Demi-glace, pass through a fine strainer and pour over the mushrooms in the middle of the dish.

2314 Tournedos Chasseur
Season the Tournedos, shallow fry in butter and arrange on a suitable dish.

Deglaze the pan with white wine, add the required amount of Sauce Chasseur, boil for 2 minutes and pour over the Tournedos.

2315 Tournedos en Chevreuil
Marinate the Tournedos in advance; well drain and dry them and shallow fry in very hot oil.

Arrange each on a round Croûton of bread fried in clarified butter, place on a suitable dish and coat with Sauce Chevreuil à la Française.

Serve accompanied with a dish of chestnut purée.

2316 Tournedos Chevreuse
Season the Tournedos and shallow fry in butter.

Arrange each on a flat round Croquette of semolina containing some finely chopped mushroom.

Place a nice glazed slice of truffle on top of each

Tournedos and serve separately a fairly light Sauce Bordelaise au Vin Blanc (Sauce Bonnefoy).

2317 Tournedos Choisy
Season the Tournedos and shallow fry in butter.
Arrange each on a round Croûton of bread fried in clarified butter and coated with a little meat glaze. Surround with small halves of braised lettuce and bouquets of small Pommes Château.

2318 Tournedos Choron
Season the Tournedos and shallow fry in butter.
Arrange each on a round Croûton of bread fried in clarified butter. Place an artichoke bottom filled with buttered peas or buttered asparagus tips on top of each Tournedos and surround with Pommes Noisettes.
Serve Sauce Choron separately.

2319 Tournedos Clamart
Season the Tournedos and shallow fry in butter.
Arrange each on a round flat shape of Pommes Macaire and serve accompanied with a dish of Petits Pois à la Française containing the lettuce from its cooking which has been shredded.

2320 Tournedos Colbert
Season the Tournedos and shallow fry in butter.
Arrange each on a small round flat Croquette of chicken. Coat the Tournedos with melted Beurre Colbert and place a fried egg yolk or a small whole fried egg on top. Place a nice slice of glazed truffle on the egg.

2321 Tournedos Coligny
1) Prepare a mixture made of sweet potatoes and in the same manner as Pommes Duchesse; make as many small round flat shapes as there will be Tournedos and of the same size. Place on a tray, brush with beaten egg and colour them in a very hot oven as required. 2) Cut some chow-chow into thick Paysanne shape, allowing one chow-chow for each 4 tournedos. Parboil, drain and stew them with a little butter then add an equal quantity of Sauce Provençale.
Season the Tournedos and shallow fry in butter.
Arrange each on one of the prepared potato shapes and cover with the chow-chow mixture.

2322 Tournedos Dubarry
Season the Tournedos and shallow fry in butter.
Arrange each on a round Croûton of bread fried in clarified butter and coat each tournedos with a little light meat glaze; surround with small balls of cauliflower coated with Sauce Mornay and gratinated.
Serve a lightly buttered veal gravy separately.

2323 Tournedos à l'Estragon, or Tournedos à la Chartres
Season the Tournedos and shallow fry in butter.
Arrange them directly on the serving dish and place a spray of blanched tarragon leaves on each.
Serve separately a Jus lié which has been well flavoured with tarragon.

2324 Tournedos Favorite
Season the Tournedos and shallow fry in butter.
Arrange each on a Croûton of bread cut out with a fancy round cutter and fried in clarified butter. Place on each Tournedos a slice of foie gras which has been seasoned, floured and lightly fried in butter and on top of this place a slice of truffle. Arrange on a dish.
Place a bouquet of buttered asparagus tips on each side of the Tournedos or if the Tournedos are arranged in a circle, place the asparagus in the centre of the dish.
Serve accompanied with a dish of Pommes Noisettes rolled in a little meat glaze and sprinkled with chopped parsley.

2325 Tournedos à la Fermière
Season the Tournedos and shallow fry in butter.
Deglaze the pan with a little veal gravy, reduce and shake in a little butter. Add a Fermière garnish, mix it in and turn into a suitable dish; arrange the Tournedos neatly on top.

2326 Tournedos à la Florentine
Season the Tournedos and grill them.
Arrange each on a fried flat round Croquette of semolina the same size as the Tournedos and place a Subric of spinach on top of the Tournedos. The position of these two garnishes may be transposed.
Serve Sauce Chateaubriand separately.

2327 Tournedos à la Forestière
Season the Tournedos and shallow fry in butter.
Arrange each on a round Croûton of bread fried in butter. Surround with bouquets of morels and large dice of potatoes both fried in butter, and lardons of streaky bacon, blanched and then fried brown in butter.
Deglaze the pan with a little good veal stock, pass through a fine strainer, shake in a little butter to thicken and enrich it and serve separately with the Tournedos.

2328 Tournedos Gabrielle
Cut equal quantities of white of cooked chicken and truffles into small dice and mix together with double its quantity of Pommes Duchesse mixture. Make this mixture into round flat Croquettes and deep fry to a golden brown when required.

Season the Tournedos, shallow fry them and place each on a prepared Croquette; arrange a circle of overlapping slices of beef bone marrow and truffle on each Tournedos and coat with well buttered Sauce Madère. Surround the Tournedos with small halves of stuffed braised lettuce.

2329 Tournedos Helder
Season the Tournedos and shallow fry in butter.

Arrange each on a round Croûton of bread fried in clarified butter, encircle the top of the Tournedos with a border of thick Sauce Béarnaise and in the centre of this place half a tablespoon of Tomato Fondue.

Deglaze the pan with Madeira, add the required amount of veal gravy, pass through a fine strainer and serve separately with the Tournedos.

2330 Tournedos Henri IV
Season the Tournedos, grill them and arrange each on a round Croûton of bread fried in clarified butter.

Encircle the top of each Tournedos with a border of thick Sauce Béarnaise and place a small artichoke bottom filled with very small Pommes Noisettes in the centre.

Note: The Sauce Beárnaise may be served separately instead of being placed on the Tournedos.

2331 Tournedos à l'Italienne
Season the Tournedos and shallow fry in butter.

Arrange each on a round flat Croquette of macaroni. Surround with quarters of artichoke bottoms à l'Italienne and serve a thin Sauce Italienne separately.

2332 Tournedos Japonaise
Season the Tournedos and shallow fry in butter.

Arrange each on a flat round Croquette of potato and place a small decorated pastry case filled with Japanese artichokes mixed with Ordinary Velouté on top.

Deglaze the pan with a little good veal stock, reduce and add the required amount of Jus lié. Pass through a fine strainer and serve separately with the Tournedos.

2333 Tournedos Judic
Season the Tournedos and shallow fry in butter.

Place each on a round Croûton of bread fried in clarified butter, arrange an overlapping circle of truffle slices on the Tournedos and place a nice, very white cock's kidney in the centre.

Surround with small halves of braised lettuce.

2334 Tournedos Lakmé
Season the Tournedos and shallow fry in butter.

Arrange on a suitable dish, place a nice grilled mushroom on top of each and serve accompanied with a purée of broad beans.

2335 Tournedos La Vallière
Season the Tournedos and shallow fry in butter.

Place each on a round Croûton of bread fried in clarified butter and cover with Sauce Chasseur containing a Julienne of truffle.

2336 Tournedos Lesdiguières
Select onions of a size large enough to place a Tournedos on each; peel them, trim off the top third and place in boiling salted water to cook, keeping them firm. Remove the insides so as to give them the shape of a case; fill two-thirds full with creamed spinach, coat with Sauce Mornay then glaze in a very hot oven at the last moment.

Season the Tournedos, grill them and place each on one of the prepared onions. Arrange neatly on a suitable dish.

2337 Tournedos Lili
Season the Tournedos and shallow fry in butter.

Arrange each on a small round cake of Pommes Anna containing slices of artichoke bottoms then place a slice of foie gras lightly fried in butter and a nice slice of truffle on top.

Serve well buttered Sauce Demi-glace separately.

2338 Tournedos Lorette
Season the Tournedos and shallow fry in butter.

Arrange each on a round Croûton of bread fried in clarified butter. Surround with small Croquettes of chicken, and tartlet cases filled with buttered asparagus tips with a slice of truffle on top.

2339 Tournedos Madeleine
Season the Tournedos, shallow fry in butter and arrange directly on the serving dish.

Place a small artichoke bottom filled with thick Soubise on each Tournedos and surround the Tournedos with small moulded shapes of haricot bean purée. Alternatively, the artichokes and moulds may both be arranged around the Tournedos.

Serve separately, a buttered fairly thin meat glaze.

2340 Tournedos Maréchal
Season the Tournedos and shallow fry in butter.

Arrange each on a round Croûton of bread fried in clarified butter with a large slice of truffle coated with meat glaze on top.

Surround with bouquets of buttered asparagus tips and Pommes Noisettes.

2341 Tournedos Marguery
Season the Tournedos and shallow fry in butter.

Arrange each on a round Croûton of bread fried in clarified butter and coat the tops of the Tournedos with a little meat glaze.

Serve accompanied with a dish of creamed noodles containing slices of truffle.

2342 Tournedos Marie-Louise, or Tournedos Marion-Delorme
Season the Tournedos and shallow fry in butter.

Arrange each on a thin round Croûton of bread fried in clarified butter and coated with a little meat glaze. Place on top a small artichoke bottom filled dome shape with a purée of mushrooms mixed with a little very well reduced Soubise.

2343 Tournedos Marigny
Season the Tournedos and shallow fry in butter.

Arrange in a circle on a round dish, surround with tartlet cases filled with a mixture of buttered peas and diamonds of French beans and place a neat pile of small Pommes Fondantes in the centre of the Tournedos.

2344 Tournedos Marquise
Season the Tournedos and shallow fry in butter.

Arrange each on a round Croûton of bread fried in clarified butter, place a small tartlet case containing a mixture as indicated for Marquise garnish (410) on each and surround with small round shapes of Pommes Marquise mixture piped with a star tube and lightly coloured in the oven at the last moment.

2345 Tournedos à la Marseillaise
Season the Tournedos and shallow fry in butter.

Arrange each on a round Croûton of bread fried in clarified butter; place a nice large stoned olive surrounded at its base with an anchovy fillet, on each Tournedos and garnish the dish with Tomates à la Provençale, and Pommes en Copeaux (4192).

Serve accompanied with Sauce Provençale.

2346 Tournedos Mascotte
Season the Tournedos and shallow fry in butter.

Place in a Cocotte or deep dish with quarters of raw artichoke bottoms sautéed in butter; olive-shaped potatoes cooked in butter; and olive-shaped truffles.

Deglaze the pan with white wine, add a little veal gravy, reduce and pass through a fine strainer over the Tournedos and garnish.

Cover the dish with the lid and place in a moderate oven for a few minutes.

2347 Tournedos Masséna
Season the Tournedos and shallow fry in butter.

Arrange each on a round Croûton of bread fried in butter. Place a nice slice of poached beef bone marrow on each and surround with very small artichoke bottoms filled with Sauce Béarnaise.

Serve accompanied with a light Sauce Périgueux.

2348 Tournedos Massilia
Season the Tournedos and shallow fry in butter.

Arrange neatly on a suitable dish and garnish as for Tournedos à la Catalane replacing the Julienne of pimentos with slices of eggplant fried in oil.

2349 Tournedos à la Matignon
Season the Tournedos, shallow fry in butter and arrange each on a round Croûton of bread fried in clarified butter.

Deglaze the pan with white wine, add the necessary amount of meat glaze and mix in a little butter; add a finely cut Paysanne of carrot, celery, mushroom and truffle stewed together with a little butter in advance.

Cover the Tournedos with this garnish and surround with a border of straw potatoes.

2350 Tournedos Menagère
Place into an earthenware Cocotte in proportion to the number of Tournedos, equal quantities of fresh butter beans, or Princess beans cut in small pieces, finely sliced new carrots, very small new season's onions and very fresh peas. Add a little salt, some butter and a very little water; cover with the lid and place in the oven to cook. The vegetables should be cooked by the concentrated steam and thus the lid must fit the dish tightly.

Season the Tournedos and shallow fry in butter. Place on the vegetables in the Cocotte and cover with the lid, but only at the very last minute before serving.

2351 Tournedos Mexicaine
Season the Tournedos and shallow fry in butter.

Arrange each on a large grilled mushroom filled with a little thick Tomato Fondue. Surround with halves of grilled or fried pimentos allowing half a pimento for each Tournedos and serve separately a well seasoned, tomato-flavoured Jus lié.

2352 Tournedos Mignon
Season the Tournedos and shallow fry in butter.

Arrange each on a round Croûton of bread fried in clarified butter and coated with a little meat glaze.

Place a round Quenelle of chicken forcemeat decorated with a slice of truffle on each Tournedos and surround with small artichoke bottoms filled with buttered peas.

2353 Tournedos Mikado
Select nice firm tomatoes, cut them in half horizontally, remove the centres, season and grill them.

Season the Tournedos and shallow fry in butter, place each on a half grilled tomato and arrange in a circle on a round dish. Fill the centre of the dish with Japanese artichokes cooked in butter and surround the Tournedos with a *cordon* of Sauce Provençale.

Note: The variety of tomato known as Mikado is the most suitable for this dish.

2354 Tournedos Mirabeau
Season the Tournedos, grill them and complete as for Entrecôte Mirabeau.

2355 Tournedos Mireille
Season the Tournedos and shallow fry in butter.

Arrange in a circle on a round dish and coat each with a little meat glaze. Fill the centre of the dish with slices of new potatoes and artichoke bottoms shallow fried together with butter then mixed with a little grated truffle and melted meat glaze.

2356 Tournedos Mirette
Prepare as many small Timbales of Pommes Mirette (4213) as there will be Tournedos. When ready, turn them out on to a dish, sprinkle with grated Parmesan and melted butter and gratinate them when the Tournedos are almost ready.

Season the Tournedos and shallow fry in butter.

Arrange neatly on a suitable dish and place one of the prepared *Timbales* on each.

Serve Sauce Chateaubriand separately.

2357 Tournedos à la Moelle
Season the Tournedos and grill them.

Arrange in a circle on a suitable dish, place a nice large slice of poached beef bone marrow on each and either surround with buttered Sauce Bordelaise or serve the sauce separately.

2358 Tournedos Montmorency
Season the Tournedos and shallow fry in butter.

Arrange each on a round Croûton of bread fried in clarified butter and coated with meat glaze. Place an artichoke bottom filled with buttered Macédoine of vegetable on each Tournedos and surround with bouquets of asparagus tips.

2359 Tournedos Montmort
Season the Tournedos and shallow fry in butter.

Place each on a round Croûton of Brioche which has been fried in clarified butter, partly emptied from the top and filled with a mixture of foie gras purée and diced truffle. Lightly coat the Tournedos with a little pale meat glaze and place a nice thick slice of truffle on each.

Serve Sauce Chateaubriand separately.

Note: Although optional, it is recommended that a green vegetable such as peas, French beans, asparagus tips or at least a few Pommes Parisienne be served with this dish.

2360 Tournedos Montpensier
Season the Tournedos and shallow fry in butter.

Arrange each on a round Croûton of bread fried in clarified butter, place a small tartlet case filled with buttered asparagus tips on each Tournedos and set a nice slice of truffle on the asparagus.

2361 Tournedos aux Morilles
Season and either grill or shallow fry the Tournedos.

Arrange in a circle on a round dish and place a nice bouquet of morels sautéed in butter and sprinkled with chopped parsley, in the centre.

2362 Tournedos Narbonnaise
Season the Tournedos and shallow fry in butter.

Cover the bottom of a deep earthenware dish with a purée of haricot beans as cooked for Cassoulet; arrange the Tournedos on top and place a round slice of fried eggplant with a little Tomato Fondue in its centre on each.

2363 Tournedos à la Niçoise
Season the Tournedos and shallow fry in butter.

Arrange on a suitable dish and on each Tournedos place a small heap of roughly chopped tomato flesh stewed together with a little crushed garlic and chopped tarragon. Surround with alternate bouquets of buttered French beans and small Pommes Château.

2364 Tournedos Ninon
Season the Tournedos and shallow fry in butter.

Arrange each on a mould of Pommes Ninon (4217) or on a round of Pommes Anna cut out with a plain pastry cutter of the same size as the Tournedos. On each Tournedos place a very small Bouchée filled with buttered asparagus heads mixed with a little Julienne of very black truffle.

Deglaze the pan with Madeira, add a little veal gravy and reduce; pass through a fine strainer, mix in a little butter to thicken and enrich and pour around the Tournedos.

2365 Tournedos à l'Orientale
Season the Tournedos and shallow fry in butter.

Arrange each on a round Croûton of bread fried in clarified butter; place a small round flat Croquette of sweet potatoes on each Tournedos and surround with small *Timbales* of Riz à la Grecque and halves of tomato cooked in butter.

Serve a thin Tomato Sauce separately.

2366 Tournedos Opéra
Season the Tournedos and shallow fry in butter.

Arrange each on a tartlet case filled with chicken livers fried in butter and deglazed with a little Madeira. Surround with small Duchesse potato Croustades (1162) filled with buttered asparagus tips.

2367 Tournedos Parisienne
Season the Tournedos and shallow fry in butter.

Place each on a round Croûton of bread fried in clarified butter and arrange in a circle on a round dish. Place an artichoke bottom filled with garnish à la Parisienne on each Tournedos and place a nice bouquet of Pommes Parisienne in the centre of the dish.

Serve a thin Sauce Demi-glace separately.

2368 Tournedos Parmentier
Season the Tournedos and shallow fry in butter.

Arrange in a circle on a round dish with a nice bouquet of Pommes Parmentier in the centre, sprinkled with chopped parsley.

2369 Tournedoes à la Périgourdine
Season the Tournedos and shallow fry in butter.

Place each on a round Croûton of bread fried in clarified butter and arrange a circle of overlapping slices of truffle on each Tournedos.

Serve Sauce Périgueux separately.

2370 Tournedos à la Persane
Prepare as many small green pimentos stuffed with rice and braised, and halves of grilled tomatoes as there are Tournedos; allow also 3 slices of fried banana per Tournedos.

Season the Tournedos and shallow fry in butter, place each on a half tomato and arrange in a circle on a round dish. Surround with the stuffed pimentos and place the sliced bananas in the centre of the dish.

Serve separately, Sauce Chateaubriand containing some of the reduced cooking liquid from the pimentos.

2371 Tournedos Petit-Duc
Season the Tournedos and shallow fry in butter.

Place each on a tartlet case filled with a purée of chicken mixed with a little Velouté; set a slice of truffle on top of each Tournedos and surround with small Bouchées filled with buttered asparagus heads.

2372 Tournedos à la Piémontaise
Season the Tournedos and shallow fry in butter.

Arrange neatly on a suitable dish and surround with small shapes of Risotto containing sliced white truffle, moulded in tartlet cases.

2373 Tournedos Polignac
Season the Tournedos and shallow fry in butter.

Arrange on a suitable dish and coat with Sauce Chateaubriand; place a small slice of veal sweetbread, egg and breadcrumbed and shallow fried in butter, on each Tournedos.

Serve separately a Sauce Demi-glace flavoured with Marsala and containing a Julienne of truffles.

2374 Tournedos à la Portugaise
Season the Tournedos and shallow fry in butter.

Arrange in a circle on a round dish; place a small stuffed tomato on each Tournedos and surround with Pommes Château.

Serve a Sauce Portugaise separately.

2375 Tournedos à la Provençale
Season the Tournedos and shallow fry in a mixture of butter and oil.

Place each on a round Croûton of bread fried in clarified butter and arrange them neatly on a dish; place half a tomato prepared à la Provençale on each Tournedos and surround with stuffed mushrooms.

Serve Sauce Provençale separately.

2376 Tournedos Rachel
Season the Tournedos and shallow fry in butter.

Arrange each on a thin round Croûton of bread fried in clarified butter and coated with a little meat glaze. Place an artichoke bottom containing a nice slice of poached beef bone marrow on top of each Tournedos.

Serve Sauce Bordelaise separately.

2377 Tournedos Régence
Season the Tournedos and shallow fry in butter.

Arrange each on a round Croûton of bread fried in clarified butter and surround with the items of a Régence garnish for poultry (449) in proportion to the number of Tournedos.

2378 Tournedos Richemond
Season the Tournedos and shallow fry in butter.

Arrange neatly on a suitable dish and surround

with noodles cut in short lengths and tossed in butter with slices of truffle.

Deglaze the pan with Madeira, add sufficient lightly thickened veal gravy, pass through a fine strainer and serve separately in a sauceboat.

2379 Tournedos Rivoli

Season the Tournedos and shallow fry in butter.

Place each on a round shape of Pommes Anna and coat with Sauce Périgueux.

2380 Tournedos Rossini

Season the Tournedos and shallow fry in butter.

Arrange each on a round Croûton of bread fried in clarified butter and coated with a little melted meat glaze. Place a nice slice of foie gras lightly fried in butter on each Tournedos and on this place a nice slice of truffle.

Deglaze the pan with Madeira, add sufficient Sauce Demi-glace finished with truffle essence, pass through a fine strainer and pour over the prepared Tournedos.

2381 Tournedos Roumanille

Cut the Tournedos a little smaller than usual, season and shallow fry them in oil.

Place each on half a grilled tomato, coat with Sauce Mornay containing a little tomato purée and glaze them quickly.

Arrange the prepared Tournedos on a dish with a large stoned olive surrounded at its base with an anchovy fillet on each, surround with crisply fried round slices of eggplant.

Note: It is better to place the eggplant in the centre of the dish if the number of Tournedos will allow them to be arranged in a circle.

2382 Tournedos Saint-Florentin

Season the Tournedos and shallow fry in butter.

Arrange in a circle on a round dish, surround with small Pommes Saint-Florentin and fill the centre of the dish with small flap mushrooms sautéed à la Bordelaise.

Serve Sauce Bordelaise au Vin Blanc (Sauce Bonnefoy) separately.

2383 Tournedos Saint-Germain

Season the Tournedos and shallow fry in butter.

Place each on a tartlet case filled with a nice green purée of peas and arrange them in a circle on a round dish. Surround with small Pommes Fondantes and fill the centre of the dish with small glazed carrots.

Serve Sauce Béarnaise separately.

2384 Tournedos Saint-Mandé

Season the Tournedos and shallow fry in butter.

Arrange each on a small shape of Pommes Macaire made in tartlet moulds and surround with bouquets of buttered peas and asparagus tips.

2385 Tournedos à la Sarde

Season the Tournedos and shallow fry in butter.

Arrange in a circle on a round dish, surround with stuffed tomatoes and stuffed cucumbers and fill the centre of the dish with small Croquettes of saffron-flavoured rice.

Serve a thin Tomato Sauce separately.

2386 Tournedos Senateur

Finely chop the tail ends of fillet of beef, season with salt and pepper, divide into 80 g (3 oz) pieces and mould into the shape of Tournedos.

Shallow fry gently in butter and arrange in a circle on a round dish; coat with Sauce Madère containing a Julienne of mushrooms and truffle and serve accompanied with a dish of chestnut purée.

2387 Tournedos Tivoli

Season the Tournedos and shallow fry in butter.

Arrange each on a round Croûton of bread fried in clarified butter and coat the Tournedos with a little reduced veal gravy. Surround with large grilled mushrooms garnished with small cockscombs and kidneys mixed with a little Sauce Allemande; bouquets of buttered asparagus tips, and bouquets of Pommes Noisettes.

Serve buttered Jus lié separately.

2388 Tournedos Tyrolienne

Season the Tournedos, grill them and complete as for Entrecôte Tyrolienne.

2389 Tournedos Valençay

Season the Tournedos and shallow fry in butter.

Arrange in a circle on a round dish; place a small round flat Croquette of noodles and ham on each Tournedos and fill the centre of the dish with a small quantity of Financière garnish.

2390 Tournedos Ventadour

Season the Tournedos and shallow fry in butter.

Arrange each on a tartlet case filled with a purée of artichoke bottoms; place a slice of poached beef bone marrow and a slice of truffle on each and surround with Pommes Noisettes.

Serve Sauce Chateaubriand separately.

2391 Tournedos Vert-pré

Season the Tournedos and grill them.

Arrange neatly on a suitable dish, place a little softened Maître d'Hôtel Butter on top of each and surround with bouquets of watercress and straw potatoes.

2392 Tournedos Victoria
Season the Tournedos and shallow fry in butter.

Arrange each on a round flat Croquette of chicken and place half a tomato cooked in butter on top.

Deglaze the pan with white wine, add sufficient Jus lié, reduce a little, pass through a fine strainer and serve separately with the Tournedos.

2393 Tournedos Villaret
Season the Tournedos and grill them.

Arrange each on a tartlet case filled with a very fine purée of flageolet beans and place a grilled mushroom on top of each Tournedos.

Serve Sauce Chateaubriand separately.

2394 LANGUE DE BOEUF—OX TONGUE

Ox tongue may be used either salted or fresh but even if used fresh it gains somewhat in quality if just lightly salted for a few days in advance. Fully salted ox tongues are cooked in gently boiling water; if fresh or just lightly salted they are best if braised in the usual manner. Salted tongues should always be soaked for a few hours in cold running water before being cooked.

When boiled the skin should be immediately removed, the root trimmed and the small bones near the root removed. The tongue should then be replaced in the cooking liquor until required; this will prevent the outside of the tongue from drying and becoming tough.

When required for braising the tongue should first be boiled in water for approximately 30 minutes then trimmed and the skin removed.

2395 Langue de Boeuf à l'Alsacienne
Using a lightly salted tongue, braise it in the usual manner.

Serve whole or sliced with a garnish of Choucroute à l'Alsacienne.

Remove the fat from the braising liquid, lightly thicken with arrowroot and pass through a fine strainer.

Serve this sauce separately.

Note: A dish of mashed potato may also be served at the same time.

2396 Langue de Boeuf à la Bigarade
Using a lightly salted tongue, braise it in the usual manner.

Serve whole or sliced with Sauce Bigarade prepared from the braising liquor.

2397 Langue de Boeuf à la Bourgeoise
Using a fresh tongue, braise it in the usual manner. When approximately two-thirds cooked, add a half-cooked garnish of carrots trimmed to the shape of olives and button onions fried to a light brown in butter.

Complete the cooking gently and finish as indicated in the recipe for Pièce de Boeuf à la Mode (2418).

Note: In this preparation the tongue may be blanched and skinned before being braised.

2398 Langue de Boeuf aux Fèves Fraîches—Ox Tongue with Broad Beans
Using a lightly salted tongue, braise it in the usual manner.

Serve whole or sliced, accompanied with a dish of buttered, freshly cooked and skinned broad beans and a sauceboat of Sauce Demi-glace containing the reduced braising liquid.

2399 Langue de Boeuf à la Flamande
Using a lightly salted tongue, braise it in the usual manner.

Serve whole or sliced, surrounded with a Flamande garnish and accompanied with the reduced braising liquid, after first removing all fat and straining it.

2400 Langue de Boeuf Saint-Flour
Using a salted tongue, boil it in the usual way.

Serve whole or sliced, surrounded with a garnish of large fresh noodles mixed with butter and grated Gruyère cheese, and small Croquettes of chestnuts.

Serve lightly thickened Jus lié separately.

2401 Ox Tongue with Various Garnishes and Sauces
The following garnishes are suitable for serving with fresh or lightly salted, braised ox tongue: aux Epinards, Italienne, Jardinière, Milanaise, Nivernaise, aux Nouilles Fraîches, à la Sarde, etc., and purées of vegetables, such as celery, cauliflower, chestnuts, lentils, sorrel, fresh or dried peas and potatoes.

Suitable sauces would be: aux Champignons, Hachée, Madère, Piquante, Romaine, Soubise brune, Tomate, etc.

2402 LANGUE DE BOEUF FROIDE—COLD OX TONGUE

Ox tongue for serving cold should first be soaked in brine for approximately 8–10 days, then before being cooked it should be soaked for some hours in cold running water.

Gently boil in water for 2½–3 hours according

to size, remove the skin, replace in the cooking liquor and allow to cool. When cool remove, wrap in a buttered paper to prevent the surface becoming dark and place in a refrigerator to become quite cold.

Trim the tongue carefully and coat with a glaze made from 500 g (1 lb 2 oz) gelatine dissolved in 1 litre (1¾ pt or 4½ U.S. cups) water and coloured a deep red colour with carmine and brown colourings.

Note: This gelatine glaze will be found a great improvement on the use of a reddened gold beater's skin.

2403 MUSEAU DE BOEUF—OX CHEEK

Ox cheek may be prepared as for ox tongue but is seldom used other than as a salad for Hors-d'oeuvre. It should be cooked by gently simmering in lightly salted and acidulated water for at least 6 hours.

2404 PALAIS DE BOEUF—OX PALATE

Ox palate was frequently used in the kitchens of olden times but is completely ignored in the modern kitchen except perhaps for a few out-of-the-way places in France.

To prepare, firstly soak the palate well in cold running water, then blanch it for a few minutes in boiling water. Place under cold running water to become cold then carefully remove the white skin.

Place in a light *Blanc* and simmer gently for approximately 4 hours until tender.

2405 Attereaux de Palais de Boeuf
Proceed as indicated for Attereaux de Ris de Veau (2635) using ox palate instead of sweetbreads.

2406 Palais de Boeuf Dunoise
Cut the cooked ox palate into rectangles, dip in melted butter and then in breadcrumbs. Grill gently, arrange on a suitable dish and serve accompanied with a well flavoured Sauce Remoulade.

2407 Croquettes and Cromesquis de Palais de Boeuf
Proceed as indicated for the preparations and proportions for Croquettes (1144) and Cromesquis d'Amourettes de Boeuf (2191) using cooked ox palate as the main ingredient.

2408 Palais de Boeuf au Gratin
Cut the cooked ox palate into thin strips and place in a dish surrounded by overlapping slices of boiled potato or a piped border of Pommes Duchesse mixture.

Cover the palate with Sauce Duxelles and gratinate in the oven.

2409 Palais de Boeuf à l'Italienne
Cut the cooked ox palate into rectangles and shallow fry until light brown in butter. Arrange overlapping in a circle on a round dish and fill the centre with Sauce Italienne containing diced raw ham fried in a little butter.

2410 Palais de Boeuf en Paupiettes
These are prepared in the same way as Paupiettes de Boeuf (2483) and any of the recipes are suitable.

2411 Palais de Boeuf Sauce Poulette à la Paysanne
Cut the cooked ox palate into medium-sized strips and reheat in lightly salted hot water.

Drain well and mix carefully into some hot Sauce Poulette, tip into a deep dish and surround with a border of quarters of hot hard-boiled eggs.

2412 PALERON—CHUCK

The chuck is the fleshy part of beef lying under the shoulder and on top of the chuck ribs. It may be boiled or braised or used for Daube de Boeuf.

2413 PIECES DE BOEUF

This name is in effect a menu term for a piece of beef cut, correctly speaking, from the aitchbone or topside of the carcass. These are the best joints for boiling and particularly for braising.

If boiled or braised whole, the joint should be no more than 3–4 kg (6¾–9 lb) in weight; if required smaller than this it should be cut along its length rather than across its thickness.

If boiled, the joint should be served accompanied with the vegetables used in its cooking or with a purée of green or dried vegetables, or one of the farinaceous products such as noodles.

If braised, any of the garnishes for the whole sirloin are suitable.

2414 Pièce de Boeuf à la Bourguignonne
Lard the piece of beef along the fibres with large strips of salt pork fat which have been marinated in a little brandy, then marinate the whole piece in red wine with the usual vegetables and herbs for 2 to 3 hours.

Drain and dry the beef well, fry to colour on all sides in butter and place in a braising pan with the fried vegetables. Just cover with the liquid from the marinade plus some veal gravy and 2 dl (7 fl oz or $\frac{7}{8}$ U.S. cup) Sauce Espagnole per 1 litre ($1\frac{3}{4}$ pt or $4\frac{1}{2}$ U.S. cups) of total liquid. Add a Bouquet garni and some mushroom trimmings, bring to the boil, cover and braise in the oven in the usual manner.

When the meat is two-thirds cooked transfer it to another pan and surround with some button mushrooms cooked in a little butter, button onions browned in butter and batons of streaky bacon, blanched and fried a light brown in butter. Pass the cooking liquid through a fine strainer over the beef and garnish and complete the cooking in the oven.

When ready, remove the beef, glaze it in the oven and serve whole or in slices with its garnish, covered with the sauce which has been reduced if necessary.

2415 Pièce de Boeuf à la Cuiller à l'Ancienne
This dish is rarely produced today although it was quite common in days gone by. The recipe is given here more for the sake of interest than anything else.

Choose a square or oval piece of beef, bearing in mind that when it is cooked it will have to be fashioned into the shape of a case. Tie it carefully and braise it in the usual manner taking care that it is almost covered with the braising liquid. Do not overcook it but keep it just a little firm.

When ready, allow it to become cold under slight pressure; trim carefully and remove the meat from the inside leaving a case about $1\frac{1}{2}$ cm ($\frac{3}{5}$ in) thick at the bottom and sides.

Coat the outside of the case with a mixture of beaten egg, fine breadcrumbs and a little grated Parmesan. Sprinkle with melted butter and place it in an oven, sufficiently hot so as to cook the outside and form a well coloured brown crust.

Thinly slice the meat removed from the case and mix with slices of tongue; braised calf's or lamb's sweetbreads, rabbit fillets, mushrooms or other items considered suitable. Cover with a sauce in keeping with the ingredients, e.g. Sauce Demi-glace, Italienne, Périgueux, and reheat it before filling into the prepared case. Place on a suitable dish to serve.

2416 Pièce de Boeuf à l'Ecarlate
The piece of beef should be placed in brine for a length of time determined by its size which can be 8–10 days for a joint weighing approximately 4 kg (9 lb).

When ready for use, soak the joint in running cold water for a few hours then simply simmer gently in boiling water with an onion stuck with cloves and a Bouquet garni.

To serve: the beef may be accompanied with a suitable vegetable garnish.

2417 Pièce de Boeuf à la Flamande
Lard the beef, braise in the usual manner and glaze it at the last moment.

Meanwhile, prepare the following garnish:

1) Cut a nice firm cabbage into four and discard the centre stalk. Boil for 7 to 8 minutes in water, drain and allow to cool. Separate the leaves and cut away any of the hard stalks. Season with salt and pepper and mould into balls by squeezing in the corner of a clean cloth, approximately 90 g (3 oz) each.
   Place the prepared cabbage into a shallow pan with one carrot cut in four, one onion stuck with a clove, a Bouquet garni, a 250 g (9 oz) piece of blanched streaky bacon and a 150 g (5 oz) piece of raw garlic sausage. Add sufficient White Bouillon to just cover the cabbage and a little good stock fat, bring to the boil and cook gently in the oven for $1\frac{1}{2}$ hours.
2) Trim the required quantity of carrots and turnips into the shape of olives, cook them in White Bouillon and reduce this so as to glaze them.
3) Prepare and cook some small plain boiled potatoes.

Place the beef on a suitable dish and garnish with alternate bouquets of carrot, turnips, cabbage and potatoes. Surround with overlapping slices of the sausage and the bacon cut into slices; serve accompanied with the braising liquor, after first removing the fat, reducing it and passing through a fine strainer.

2418 Pièce de Boeuf à la Mode, also called Pièce de Boeuf à la Bourgeoise
Where possible use a piece of beef of between $2\frac{1}{2}$ kg (5 lb 10 oz) and 3 kg ($6\frac{3}{4}$ lb) in weight. This would be sufficient for 20 persons.

Lard the beef with 350 g (13 oz) strips of salt pork fat which have been marinated 20 minutes in advance in a little brandy, seasoned with pepper and a pinch of mixed spice and sprinkled with chopped parsley just before using.

Rub the piece of beef with salt, pepper and a little grated nutmeg and place in a basin to marinate for 5 to 6 hours, with 5 dl (18 fl oz or $2\frac{1}{4}$ U.S. cups) of red wine and 1 dl ($3\frac{1}{2}$ fl oz or $\frac{1}{2}$ U.S. cup) brandy, turning it over from time to time.

Braise the beef in the usual manner adding the marinade to the liquid used and 3 small or 2 medium-sized boned and blanched calf's feet, tied together.

When three-quarters cooked, remove the piece of

beef and place in a smaller pan and add 1) the calf's feet cut into small squares, 2) 400 g (15 oz) button onions coloured brown in butter and 3) 600 g (1 lb 5 oz) carrots trimmed to the shape of olives and two-thirds cooked.

Cover with the braising liquid after first removing all fat and passing through a fine strainer; complete the cooking gently. When ready place on a suitable dish, surround with the garnish arranged in bouquets and coat with the cooking liquid which has been suitably reduced.

2419 Pièce de Boeuf à la Mode (Cold)
Boeuf à la Mode is seldom prepared specially for serving cold, it is usually what is left of a fine piece prepared for serving hot.

First trim the piece of beef neatly and separate the garnish from the sauce, slightly warm the sauce and add one-third its volume of aspic jelly if the amount appears to be insufficient.

Decorate the bottom of a terrine or mould, large enough to contain the beef, with the carrots and onions of the garnish; place the beef on top, surround with the rest of the garnish and add the sauce after passing it through a fine strainer. Allow to cool and set thoroughly in a refrigerator, then demould on to a suitable dish and surround with chopped jelly.

2420 Pièce de Boeuf à la Noailles
Lard the piece of beef and marinate it in advance with red wine and brandy.

This done, drain and dry it thoroughly then fry brown on all sides in butter. Moisten with the marinade and an equal quantity of veal gravy and braise gently in the usual manner.

When half cooked add 1 kg ($2\frac{1}{4}$ lb) sliced onions sautéed in a little butter, and 100 g ($3\frac{1}{2}$ oz) rice and complete the cooking of the beef with the onions and rice.

When ready, remove the beef, then pass the onions and rice through a fine sieve. Neatly trim the beef and cut into even slices. Re-form the beef into its original shape on a dish, first spreading each slice with a spoonful of the purée of onions and rice.

Cover the piece with the rest of the purée, sprinkle with breadcrumbs fried in butter, and with melted butter and gratinate in a hot oven.

2421 Pièce de Boeuf Soubise
Lard the piece of beef and marinate it for 5 to 6 hours with white wine.

Braise it in the usual manner using the wine from the marinade and some veal gravy and when cooked glaze the piece of beef at the last moment.

Place on a suitable serving dish and serve accompanied with 1) a fairly thick Sauce Soubise and 2) the well reduced braising liquid, after first removing all fat and passing through a fine strainer.

2422 PLAT-DE-COTE—PLATE OR FLAT RIBS

The plate, or flat ribs of beef is that part of the carcase between the ribs of beef proper and the brisket.

This joint is usually used in the preparation of Bouillons or Petite Marmite but may be boiled, or salted and boiled with vegetables and herbs.

Suitable garnishes for boiled flat ribs are Choucroute, braised cabbage, red cabbage, Brussels sprouts and most vegetable purées.

Suitable sauces would be any well flavoured sauce such as Piquante, Chasseur, Hachée and Horseradish.

2423 POITRINE DE BOEUF—BRISKET OF BEEF

This joint is really the breast of the carcase and may be prepared and served in the same way as the plate or flat ribs of beef. It makes an excellent dish if salted and boiled and served either hot, or pressed for cold and is one of the finest dishes of the Cuisine Bourgeoise.

QUEUE DE BOEUF—OXTAIL

Other than being used for the making of Oxtail Soup, there are also a number of oxtail dishes serving as excellent Entrées. The following are good examples.

2424 Queue de Boeuf à l'Auvergnate
Cut the oxtail into sections and braise in the usual manner with white wine.

Place the pieces of oxtail in a deep Cocotte with rectangles of boiled lean streaky bacon, large chestnuts cooked in Bouillon and glazed, and button onions cooked gently in butter. Cover with the reduced braising liquid after first removing the fat and passing through a fine strainer.

2425 Queue de Boeuf Cavour
Butter a braising pan and cover the bottom with a layer of sliced vegetables, herbs and pieces of blanched pork rind. Place the cut oxtail on top, cover with a lid and place in a very hot oven for 15 minutes.

Moisten with a little good brown stock and

reduce this to a glaze, then almost cover with two-thirds brown stock and one-third white wine.

Cover with a lid and braise gently in the oven for approximately 3½ to 4 hours until the meat is tender.

Place the sections of oxtail in a clean pan and cover with the reduced cooking liquid, after first removing the fat, thickening it with a little arrowroot and passing through a fine strainer. Add some cooked button mushrooms and simmer very gently together for another 15 minutes.

Take a suitable dish and pipe a decorative border of chestnut purée mixed with egg yolks around the edge; place in the oven for a few minutes to cook and set fairly firm; place the oxtail with its garnish and sauce in the centre and serve.

Note: The oxtail and its garnish may be served in a deep dish accompanied with a dish of chestnut purée.

2426 Queue de Boeuf à la Charolaise
Cut the oxtail into sections and braise as explained at the beginning of the recipe for Queue de Boeuf Cavour.

When cooked, place the oxtail sections in a clean pan with a garnish of carrots and turnips trimmed to the shape of large olives and cooked in White Bouillon, and Quenelles made from a fine forcemeat of pork mixed with eggs, a little chopped parsley and a touch of garlic and poached in advance.

Remove the fat from the braising liquid, pass through a fine strainer and reduce, add some Sauce Espagnole to thicken and pour over the oxtail and garnish. Allow to simmer gently for 20 minutes.

Meanwhile, prepare a moulded border of Pommes Duchesse mixture on the serving dish and place in a hot oven to colour.

Arrange the sections of oxtail around the inside of the border and place the garnish in the centre; cover with the sauce and surround the border of potato with overlapping rectangles of boiled lean streaky bacon cooked separately.

Note: For small servings the border of Pommes Duchesse may be piped using a star tube.

2427 Queue de Boeuf Chipolata
Cut the oxtail into sections and braise as explained at the beginning of the recipe for Queue de Boeuf Cavour.

When cooked, place the oxtail sections in a clean pan with the items of a Chipolata garnish. Remove the fat from the braising liquid, pass through a fine strainer and reduce; add some Sauce Espagnole to thicken and pour over the oxtail and garnish. Allow to simmer gently for 20 minutes then place into a deep dish to serve.

2428 Queue de Boeuf Farcie—Stuffed Oxtail
Select a large oxtail and bone it out, taking care not to pierce the outside surfaces.

Place opened out on a clean cloth, season and fill with a stuffing made with the following ingredients, mixed together well: 400 g (15 oz) very lean beef and 200 g (7 oz) fat pork, both finely chopped; 150 g (5 oz) white breadcrumbs soaked in a little milk and squeezed out; 2 eggs; 100 g (3½ oz) chopped truffle trimmings; 15 g (½ oz) salt; a small pinch of pepper, and a touch of mixed spice.

Re-form the tail and sew it up carefully with string. Wrap round with a cloth and tie as for a galantine; simmer very gently for 3 hours in white stock garnished with vegetables.

Remove the cloth and place the tail in a flat pan, the bottom of which has been covered with a layer of vegetables and herbs for braising; add a little of the stock used in the cooking, cover and place in the oven to gently braise and finish cooking. Baste frequently so as to have it nicely glazed by the time it is cooked.

Pass the cooking liquid through a fine strainer, reduce it and thicken with a little arrowroot; place a little on the serving dish with the oxtail on top making sure that all string is first removed.

Serve accompanied with the prepared sauce and any of the vegetables garnishes or purées suitable for large pieces of beef. Other suitable sauces may be served instead of that prepared from the cooking liquid.

2429 Queue de Boeuf Grillée—Grilled Oxtail
Cut the oxtail into double length sections and cook in Beef Bouillon with vegetables and herbs, for approximately 5 hours.

Drain the sections and dry them well; dip in melted butter and then into breadcrumbs. Sprinkle with melted butter and grill gently.

Grilled oxtail may be served with any vegetable purée or a fairly thick Soubise, together with a sauce such as Diable, Hachée, Piquante, Robert or Tomate.

Note: If the sauce being served with the tail is a highly seasoned one, it is advisable to coat the oxtail with made mustard mixed with a little Cayenne before passing through butter and breadcrumbs.

2430 Queue de Boeuf en Hochepot
Cut the oxtail in sections and place in a pan with 2 pig's trotters, each cut into 5 pieces and 1 pig's ear. Cover with cold water and add 10 g (⅓ oz) salt per 1 litre (1¾ pt or 4½ U.S. cups) of water. Bring to the boil, skim and simmer gently for 2 hours, skimming frequently.

Now add a small cabbage cut in quarters and

blanched, 10 small onions and 150 g (5 oz) each of carrots and turnips cut and trimmed to the shape of large olives. Allow to cook together gently for a further 2 hours until the oxtail is cooked.

Arrange the oxtail and trotters in a circle in a deep round dish, place the vegetable garnish in the centre and surround with 10 grilled chipolata sausages and the pig's ear cut in strips.

Serve accompanied with a dish of plain boiled potatoes.

2431 Queue de Boeuf à la Nohant
Cut the oxtail into sections and braise as explained in the beginning of the recipe for Queue de Boeuf Cavour; when ready, glaze it with the reduced cooking liquid.

Arrange the sections of oxtail in a circle in a deep round dish and place a garnish of buttered large cut Macédoine of vegetables in the centre. Surround with overlapping, alternating slices of braised and glazed lambs' sweetbreads and rounds of red salt ox tongue.

Serve accompanied with the reduced cooking liquid.

2432 ROGNON DE BOEUF—OX KIDNEY

Ox kidney is usually sautéed although there are a few exceptions, notably their use in the various preparations of steak and kidney pies and puddings. Recipes for these dishes are given in the section 'Various other preparations of Beef'.

2433 Rognon de Boeuf Sauté—Sautéed Ox Kidney
Remove the fat, skin and gristle and cut the kidney into thickish, small slices. If it appears that the kidney has come from an old animal it is advisable to plunge the slices into boiling water for a few moments, then drain and dry them well.

Sauté the slices quickly in very hot butter keeping them underdone, then tip into a strainer so as to allow the blood to drain away. This blood has a very strong alkaline smell and should be discarded.

Deglaze the pan with a liquid in keeping with its preparation such as red or white wine, Madeira, mushroom cooking liquor, etc. then add $1\frac{1}{2}$ dl (5 fl oz or $\frac{5}{8}$ U.S. cup) of the sauce to be used; boil for a few moments and pass through a fine strainer.

Place the cooked kidneys into this sauce with the garnish required by the recipe, shake the pan to mix the ingredients into the sauce and finish by shaking in 50 g (2 oz) butter away from the heat.

Note: On no account whatsoever should the kidneys be boiled in the sauce as if this is allowed to happen, they will become unpleasantly tough.

2434 Rognon de Boeuf Bercy
Sauté the kidneys and drain them. Place 1 tbs chopped shallot in the pan used and very lightly cook with a little butter; deglaze with $1\frac{1}{2}$ dl (5 fl oz or $\frac{5}{8}$ U.S. cup) white wine, reduce by half and add, away from the heat, 3 tbs melted meat glaze, a squeeze of lemon juice, a pinch of chopped parsley and 50 g (2 oz) butter.

Add the kidney to this sauce, shake to mix in and serve in a deep dish or timbale.

2435 Rognon de Boeuf aux Champignons
Sauté the kidneys and drain them. Deglaze the pan with $1\frac{1}{2}$ dl (5 fl oz or $\frac{5}{8}$ U.S. cup) white wine, reduce well and add to some Sauce aux Champignons.

Add the kidneys, shake to mix in and serve in a deep dish or timbale, sprinkled with chopped parsley.

2436 Rognon de Boeuf Chipolata
Sauté the kidneys and drain them. Place into sufficient tomato-flavoured Sauce Demi-glace to mix then add a small amount of Chipolata garnish.

Mix in and serve in a deep dish or timbale.

2437 Rognon de Boeuf au Madère
Sauté the kidneys, drain them and add to a well buttered Sauce Madère.

Serve in a deep dish or timbale.

2438 Rognon de Boeuf Marchand de Vins
This is prepared in the same way as Rognon de Boeuf Bercy but using red wine instead of white wine.

2439 Rognon de Boeuf au Vin Blanc
Sauté the kidneys and drain them. Deglaze the pan with $1\frac{1}{2}$ dl (5 fl oz or $\frac{5}{8}$ U.S. cup) white wine, reduce and add the necessary amount of Sauce Demi-glace. Shake in 50 g (2 oz) butter away from the heat and add the kidneys.

Mix in and serve in a deep dish or timbale.

2440 RUMP

The rump is that part of the carcase of beef between the end of the sirloin and the top of the haunch. It may be braised or boiled whole but more often than not it is used for cutting into steaks. In this case it is cut into thick slices and either grilled or shallow fried as rump steaks. These steaks may be cut in individual portions or left large enough for 2 or more portions. They are served plain but all the recipes for fillet steaks, sirloin steaks and Tournedos are suitable.

In France a thick sirloin steak is generally served under the name of rump steak. This is an error—the rump steak in English means literally a slice from the rump. The rump steak is peculiar to England where it is almost always served either grilled or shallow fried.

2441 Grilled Rump Steak
Grill the steak in the same way as for other steaks. When ready place a thick slice of grilled beef kidney fat on top, and serve accompanied with a sauceboat of grated horseradish.

2442 Shallow Fried Rump Steak
Season the steak and shallow fry in butter. Place on a dish and garnish with sliced onions shallow fried in butter or deep fried onion rings.

2443 Rump Steak Grand'mere
Season the steak and colour quickly on both sides in butter. Add a few half-cooked potatoes, trimmed to the size of olives, some glazed button onions and batons of streaky bacon. Finish cooking together.

Place the steak in a dish surrounded with the garnish. Deglaze the pan with a little good Bouillon, add a few drops of lemon juice and pour over the steak. Sprinkle with chopped parsley.

2444 Rump Steak Mirabeau
This is prepared in the same way as Entrecôte Mirabeau taking account of the difference in thickness and weight of the steak.

2445 TRIPE

The term tripe includes the tripe proper and the *Gras Double* which is provided by the rumen or paunch of the ox. Tripe is usually obtained already cooked but if purchased in the raw state it simply needs cooking in salted water for approximately 5 hours. In the following recipes ordinary tripe may be used in place of *Gras Double*.

2446 Gras Double en Blanquette à la Provençale
Fry together 100 g (3½ oz) finely chopped pork fat with 250 g (9 oz) chopped onion until light brown; sprinkle with 30 g (1 oz) flour and cook gently together for a few minutes. Mix in 7½ dl (1⅓ pt or 3¼ U.S. cups) of good White Bouillon and add 1 kg (2¼ lb) of cooked Gras Double or ordinary tripe cut into 5 cm (2 in) squares, a pinch of salt and pepper and a Bouquet garni; cover and cook gently for 1 hour.

When ready, thicken the sauce with 4 egg yolks and finish by mixing in a mixture made by pounding a small pinch of basil with 25 g (1 oz) pork fat, a squeeze of lemon juice and a pinch of chopped parsley.

Serve in a deep dish or timbale.

2447 Gras Double à la Bourgeoise
Heat 80 g (3 oz) butter in a pan, add 100 g (3½ oz) sliced onion and 80 g (3 oz) carrots cut in thin rounds and cook to a light brown; add 30 g (1 oz) flour and cook together as for a brown Roux. Mix in 1 litre (1¾ pint or 4½ U.S. cups) White Bouillon and stir until it boils.

Add 1 kg (2¼ lb) cooked Gras Double or ordinary tripe cut in 3 cm (1⅕ in) squares; a pinch of salt and pepper and a Bouquet garni; cover and cook gently for 1 hour.

Ten minutes before it is finally cooked add a touch of crushed garlic and 100 g (3½ oz) sliced mushrooms, fried in a little butter.

Serve in a deep dish or timbale sprinkled with chopped parsley.

2448 Gras Double Frit—Fried Tripe
Cut the cooked Gras Double or ordinary tripe into rectangles, season with salt and pepper and dip into melted butter. Sprinkle with chopped parsley then pass through flour, beaten egg and fine white breadcrumbs.

Deep fry in very hot fat until crisp and brown.

Serve arranged on a serviette and accompanied with a suitable sauce, e.g. Diable, Hachée, Piquante, Remoulade, Tartare, Tomate etc.

2449 Gras Double Frit à la Bourguignonne
Prepare the cooked Gras Double or ordinary tripe as above and deep fry in very hot nut oil.

Arrange on a suitable dish and sprinkle with 100 g (3½ oz) melted Snail Butter (235) flavoured with a few drops of Absinthe and serve very hot.

2450 Gras Double Frit à la Troyenne
Cut the cooked Gras Double or ordinary tripe into rectangles, coat with made mustard then pass through flour, beaten egg and fine white breadcrumbs. Deep fry in very hot oil until crisp and brown.

Serve accompanied with Sauce Vinaigrette or Sauce Gribiche.

2451 Gras Double à la Lyonnaise
Cut the cooked Gras Double or ordinary tripe into large strips and shallow fry to a light brown colour in very hot lard. Season with salt and pepper and to each 1 kg (2¼ lb) tripe add 250 g (9 oz) sliced onion cooked to a light brown in butter. Mix together well and continue to fry together, tossing over and over until a nice brown colour.

Place into a deep dish or timbale; deglaze the pan with a little vinegar and sprinkle over the tripe. Finally, sprinkle with a little chopped parsley.

2452 Gras Double à la Poulette
Cut some very well cooked Gras Double or ordinary tripe into strips and reheat in sufficient Sauce Poulette.

Serve in a deep dish or timbale sprinkled with chopped parsley.

2453 Tripes à la Mode de Caen
In the preparation of this culinary speciality of Normandy the very common mistake is often made of using calf's feet instead of ox feet. This results firstly in the cooking liquid becoming less gelatinous and thus not so thick, and secondly, the calf's feet being more tender become overcooked long before the tripe has reached the state of being perfectly cooked. As a so-called improvement the use of calf's feet thus runs contrary to the requirements of this special dish.

Another mistake frequently met with, consists of presenting the finished tripe in silver dishes; this is just as bad and illogical as presenting a fine Chaud-froid on an ordinary china dish. Because of its simplicity Tripes à la Mode de Caen should be served in special stoneware or earthenware dishes which allow the heat to be retained better. Attention should thus be directed more to the serving of this tripe very hot than to an over-elegant presentation.

Preparation of the Tripe:
The items used in this dish include 1) the feet of the ox and 2) the tripes, consisting of *a*) the Rumen or Paunch, *b*) the Honeycomb bag, *c*) the Manyplies and *d*) the Reed.

All of these items should be subjected to a prolonged soaking in cold running water. They should then be lightly blanched so as to clean them thoroughly and to make it easier to cut them as required, usually into 5 cm (2 in.) squares.

Ingredients for the complete tripes of one animal:
2 kg (4½ lb) onions stuck with 4 cloves
1½ kg (3 lb 6 oz) carrot
1 Bouquet garni consisting of 1 kg (2¼ lb) leek, 150 g (5 oz) parsley stalks, 1 sprig of thyme and a bayleaf
8 g (¼ oz) salt and a pinch of pepper—per 1 kg (2¼ lb) of the tripes
2 litres (3½ pt or 9 U.S. cups) good cider which should not turn black during the cooking. If this is likely, use water
3 dl (½ pt or 1¼ U.S. cups) Calvados or brandy

The proportions of the liquid used will, of course, vary with the utensil being used but in any case the tripe should be just completely covered with liquid.

Method:
Take a stew pan or braising pan just large enough to hold the tripe and garnish; place in the carrots, onions, the ox feet boned out and cut in medium-sized pieces and the seasoning. Place the tripe on top with the Bouquet garni in the middle and the bones from the ox feet, split lengthways, on top of the tripe. Cover with 3 cm (1⅕ in) thick slices of beef fat well soaked in water and finally add the cider and Calvados or brandy.

Cover the whole with a thick layer of stiff paste made with flour and hot water sealing it well to the rim of the utensil. Place in a moderate oven and when the covering of paste is well cooked after about 2 hours, cover the utensil with its lid. Continue cooking gently in the oven at a low and unvarying temperature for approximately another 10 hours.

When ready, remove from the oven and discard the paste, fat, bones, carrots, onions and Bouquet garni. Remove the tripe carefully and place according to requirements in special earthenware dishes; normally this should consist of a selection of the different parts of the tripe. Remove any fat from the cooking liquid, pass through a fine strainer and divide equally between the dishes.

Cover the dishes, reheat if necessary and serve very hot.

Notes:
1) The double covering of beef fat and paste is to prevent a too-rapid evaporation when cooked in an ordinary kitchen oven the heat of which could possibly be uneven; it also helps to keep the tripe white.
2) Correctly speaking, Tripes à la Mode de Caen should be placed in special earthenware utensils, covered and cooked in a baker's or pastry cook's oven. These ovens have the advantage, once heating has been stopped, of cooking very slowly and regularly over a long period of hours, conditions that are ideally suited to the cooking of this dish and consequently there is absolutely no need to use the covering of fat and paste.

3) The foregoing recipe has been specially prepared thus for those who have neither the special pots nor the baker's or pastry cook's oven available.

OTHER PREPARATIONS OF BEEF

PIES AND PUDDINGS

There is nothing more simple and yet more difficult for those without experience than the making of English steak pies, puddings and their derivatives. The reason for this is that once the dish has been made up and cooked there is very little that can be done to correct any mistakes made with the seasoning, the quantity of liquid used or the cooking time.

2454 Steak Pie

Cut 1½ kg (3 lb 6 oz) lean beef into 1 cm (⅖ in) thick small slices and mix together with 60 g (2 oz) chopped onion, 10 g (⅓ oz) salt, a pinch of pepper, a touch of grated nutmeg and a little chopped parsley.

Arrange the beef around the sides of a suitably sized pie dish and place 400 g (15 oz) trimmed olive-shaped potatoes in the centre; just cover with water.

Moisten the lip of the pie dish and cover with a band of ordinary short paste, moisten this and cover the whole dish with a layer of short or puff paste. Seal the edges and decorate the surface with items of the same paste used; brush carefully with beaten egg and decorate if necessary by cutting a shallow pattern with the point of a knife.

Allow to rest for at least 1 hour then bake in a moderate oven for 1¾ to 2 hours if fillet of beef has been used, or 2½ to 3 hours for other cuts of beef.

2455 Steak and Kidney Pie

Proceed in the same way as for steak pie replacing the potatoes with the same weight of ox, veal or mutton kidney cut into small thick slices, and adding a few sliced mushrooms fried in a little butter; mix these ingredients together with the onions, seasoning and parsley.

2456 Steak Pudding

Suet Paste: Mix together 1 kg (2¼ lb) flour with 600 g (1 lb 5 oz) chopped beef suet from which all membrane and connective tissue has been first removed, and a good pinch of salt. Add approximately 2 dl (7 fl oz or ⅞ U.S. cup) cold water and mix to form a fairly stiff paste.

Preparation for the Pudding: Reserve approximately one-third of the paste for covering the pudding, roll out the remainder ½ cm (⅕ in) thick and line a suitably sized buttered pudding basin. This type of basin has no base and has a projecting lip at the top which facilitates the attaching of a cloth.

Cut 1½ kg (3 lb 6 oz) lean beef into 1 cm (⅖ in) thick small slices and mix with 10 g (⅓ oz) salt, a pinch of pepper, a touch of grated nutmeg, 60 g (2 oz) chopped onion and a little chopped parsley. Fill the prepared basin, arranging it in layers and barely cover with cold water.

Moisten the top edge of the paste in the basin and cover with the remainder of the paste rolled out as before. Seal the two edges together, cover with a buttered and floured pudding cloth and tie firmly with string under the projecting edge of the basin; bring over the corners of cloth and tie together.

Cook the pudding in a covered pot of boiling water or in a steamer for 3 hours if fillet of beef has been used, or 4 hours if other cuts of beef.

When cooked, remove, take off the pudding cloth and serve the pudding on a round silver dish with a folded serviette wrapped around it.

2457 Steak and Kidney Pudding

Proceed in the same way as for Steak Pudding replacing half the beef with ox kidney cut into large thick slices.

2458 Steak and Oyster Pudding

Proceed in the same manner as for Steak Pudding replacing 500 g (1 lb 2 oz) beef with 40 raw oysters.

CARBONADES

2459 Carbonades de Boeuf à la Flamande

Cut 1 kg 200 g (2 lb 10 oz) chuck steak or topside of beef into small thinnish slices; season with salt and pepper and quickly fry brown on both sides in a little clarified stock fat. At the same time shallow fry 600 g (1 lb 5 oz) finely sliced onions in butter until light brown.

Place the beef and onions in alternate layers in a shallow pan and add a Bouquet garni. Deglaze the pan in which the beef was fried with 1 litre (1¾ pt or 4½ U.S. cups) beer using stout or Old Lambic for preference and the same amount of brown stock; thicken with 100 g. (3½ oz) brown Roux, add 50 g (2 oz) brown or caster sugar and bring to the boil whilst stirring. Pass this sauce through a fine strainer over the beef and onions, cover with a lid and cook gently in the oven for 2½ to 3 hours.

Note: Carbonades are usually served as they are with the onions. They may, however, be served in a deep dish and covered with the sauce and onions first passed through a fine sieve.

CHOESEL—PANCREAS

2460 Choesels à la Bruxelloise
Heat 150 g (5 oz) dripping in a pan and add 1 oxtail cut in sections and 2 heifer's sweetbreads; allow to cook gently for 45 minutes then add 1 kg (2¼ lb) breast of veal cut in pieces and 150 g (5 oz) finely sliced onions. Cook altogether for another 30 minutes, add 1 ox kidney trimmed of membrane and connective tissue and cut in fairly large pieces, and continue cooking together, turning over frequently until all the ingredients are nicely coloured. Add 3 dl (½ pt or 1¼ U.S. cups) beer, using stout or Old Lambic for preference, and season with 12 g (⅓ oz) salt and a touch of Cayenne pepper. Add a Bouquet garni and cook gently together for a further 30 minutes.

Now add the Choesels (Pancreas) and 1 calf's sweetbread trimmed and cut into thick slices; 1 litre (1¾ pt or 4½ U.S. cups) of the same beer, and 5 dl (18 fl oz or 2¼ U.S. cups) mushroom cooking liquor. Continue to cook gently for another 1½ hours.

A quarter of an hour before serving, add 6 cooked sheeps' trotters cut in two; 10 Fricadelles (2469) each approximately 60 g (2 oz) in weight and 500 g (1 lb 2 oz) cooked mushrooms.

Finally, lightly thicken the cooking liquid with a little arrowroot and add 1 dl (3½ fl oz or ½ U.S. cup) Madeira. Serve in a deep dish.

Note: That which is called *Choesel* in Belgium is nothing more than the Pancreas gland of the ox. This is found in the abdomen of the animal between the liver and the spleen.

DAUBE

2461 Basic Preparation of Daube
Cut 1½ kg (3 lb 6 oz) lean chuck steak or topside of beef into fairly thick slices and lard each slice along its length with thin strips of salt pork fat rolled in chopped parsley mixed with a little crushed garlic. Season the pieces with salt and pepper, sprinkle with chopped shallot and marinate for 2 hours with 1 litre (1¾ pt or 4½ U.S. cups) red wine with a Bouquet garni.

When ready, drain and dry the slices of beef with a clean cloth and quickly colour on both sides in a little good dripping. Cover the bottom of a suitably sized pan or special earthenware utensil (Daubière) with slices of salt pork fat, add the prepared beef with the marinade and Bouquet garni and cover with the lid. Seal the lid well to the utensil with a band of stiff paste made from flour and water, leaving a very small aperture for the steam to escape.

Cook gently in the oven for approximately 4 hours. Remove the Bouquet garni and present and serve as it is.

2462 Daube à la Provençale
Cut 1½ kg (3 lb 6 oz) chuck steak, topside and silverside into large cubes and lard each piece along the grain of the meat with a strip of salt pork fat rolled in chopped parsley mixed with a little crushed garlic. Season with salt and pepper and marinate with 1 litre (1¾ pt or 4½ U.S. cups) white wine; 1 dl (3½ fl oz or ½ U.S. cup) brandy and 2 tbs oil.

Take an earthenware utensil of a suitable size and place inside in layers 1) the marinated beef, 2) 150 g (5 oz) salt pork rind, blanched and cut in 1½ cm (½ in) squares, 3) 200 g (7 oz) small cubes of blanched salt belly of pork, 4) 150 g (5 oz) thin round slices of carrots, 5) 120 g (4 oz) each of chopped raw mushrooms and onions, 6) 400 g (15 oz) chopped tomato flesh, 7) 2 cloves of crushed garlic, 8) a pinch of powdered thyme and bayleaf, 9) 30 stoned black olives.

Place a Bouquet of parsley stalks together with a strip of dried orange peel, in the centre, add the marinade and 3 dl (½ pt or 1¼ U.S. cups) veal gravy, and cover with a lid, sealing with paste as in the previous recipe. Place in a moderate oven and cook very gently for 6 to 7 hours.

When ready, remove the Bouquet and any fat on the surface of the liquid; present and serve the dish as it is.

2463 EMINCES

Emincés are in effect slices of cold meat reheated in a suitable sauce and sometimes garnished. The following points should be noted and adhered to if good results are required:

1) For preference, Emincés should be prepared from cold roast or braised sirloin or fillet of beef.
2) The meat being used should be cut into very thin slices then placed on a dish and covered with the boiling sauce selected.
3) The dish may be reheated on the side of the stove but under no circumstances should it be

allowed to boil if the meat has been roasted, as this will result in it becoming tough.

4) If the sauce selected to accompany the Emincé is prepared from a reduction of vinegar, it is useful to surround the dish with a border of sliced gherkins.

Suitable sauces for Emincés are Bordelaise, Duxelles, Hachée, Champignons, Italienne, Fines Herbes, Piquante, Poivrade, Tomate.

2464 Emincé à l'Ecarlate
Arrange the slices of meat in a circle overlapping and alternating with slices of cooked salt ox tongue, taking care not to crowd them too much together.

Cover with boiling Sauce Demi-glace containing some finely chopped tongue.

2465 Emincé à la Clermont
Finely slice some onions and cook in butter; add just sufficient thick Sauce Demi-glace to bind then mould dome shape in the middle of a buttered round dish. Sprinkle with dry white breadcrumbs and melted butter and gratinate under the salamander.

Arrange the slices of meat overlapping around the onions and cover with a thin boiling Sauce Duxelles, taking care not to cover the onions.

2466 Emincé Marianne
Bake some nice floury potatoes, remove the insides and mash well with salt, pepper and chopped chives. Fry this mixture in a pan with butter, turning over and over frequently until it becomes a nice brown colour.

Mould this mixture dome shape in the centre of a dish, surround with the overlapping slices of meat and cover the meat only with boiling Sauce aux Fines Herbes.

ESTOUFFADE

2467 Basic Preparation of Estouffade
Cut 600 g (1 lb 6 oz) each of chuck and plate of beef into approximately 100 g (3½ oz) cubes.

Fry 250 g (9 oz) diced lean salt belly of pork in butter till brown, remove, then fry 250 g (9 oz) quartered onions and the beef in the same pan, seasoning with salt and pepper and frying till brown on all sides. Drain off any surplus fat.

Replace the pork, sprinkle with 50 g (2 oz) flour, add 1 clove of crushed garlic and carry on cooking and browning all the ingredients for a few minutes. Moisten with 1 litre (1¾ pt or 4½ U.S. cups) each of red wine and brown stock, add a Bouquet garni, bring to the boil, cover and cook gently in the oven for 2½ to 3 hours.

Place a sieve over a large basin and tip out the stew on to it; allow to drain for a few moments then place the beef and pork into a clean pan together with 250 g (9 oz) button mushrooms cooked in a little butter.

Allow the sauce to rest for 15 minutes so as to let the fat rise to the surface, skim this off well then adjust the consistency of the sauce—reduce if too thin or add a little brown stock if too thick. Pass through a fine strainer over the meat and allow to simmer very gently for 15 minutes before serving.

2468 Estouffade à la Provençale
Proceed in exactly the same way as the preceding recipe with the following modifications:

1) Add 500 g (1 lb 2 oz) tomatoes to the Estouffade before placing in the oven.
2) Use white wine instead of red wine.
3) Add 250 g (9 oz) stoned black olives as a final garnish.

FRICADELLES

2469 Fricadelles Made with Raw Meat
Finely chop 800 g (1¾ lb) lean beef free from sinew and fat, together with 500 g (1 lb 2 oz) butter, 350 g (13 oz) white breadcrumbs soaked in milk and well squeezed out, 4 eggs, 25 g (1 oz) salt, a pinch of pepper and a touch of grated nutmeg. Add 125 g (4½ oz) chopped onions cooked in a little butter without colour and mix well together.

Divide the mixture into pieces weighing 100 g (3½ oz) each and mould into round flat cakes on a floured table.

Heat some butter or good clean fat in a pan, place in the Fricadelles and colour brown on both sides; complete the cooking in the oven.

Arrange them on a suitable dish and serve accompanied with a vegetable purée or a well flavoured sauce such as Sauce Piquante or Sauce Robert.

2470 Fricadelles Made with Cooked Meat
Finely chop 400 g (15 oz) cooked beef and mix together with 400 g (15 oz) dry purée of potatoes, 200 g (7 oz) chopped onion cooked in butter without colour, 10 g (⅓ oz) chopped parsley, 2 eggs and seasoning as required.

Divide the mixture, mould and cook as in the preceding recipe.

Arrange on a suitable dish and serve accompanied with a vegetable purée or a sauce suited to Fricadelles made with raw meat.

GOULASH AND SAUTES OF BOEUF

The principles laid down for the preparation of Hungarian Goulash are as vague as for those of the French *Navarin* of which it is the equivalent in Hungarian cookery. The pressures of the requirements of professional catering have resulted in the modification of the original recipes for Goulash and thus have increased the confusion surrounding what is believed to be the authentic method of preparation. Because of this it has been felt useful to include two recipes, one of which has been demonstrated by Madame Katinka, the celebrated Hungarian artiste and the other which follows the usual method used in professional kitchens.

The quality of this dish depends essentially on the quality of the paprika used in its preparation. It may be worth observing that 9 out of 10 brands of this special commodity are of poor quality, thus the following points should be noted: good paprika is sweet to the taste, very strongly perfumed and has a nice deep reddish pink colour.

2471 Goulash à la Hongroise (*Authentic Recipe*)
Cut 1 kg 200 g (2 lb 10 oz) chuck steak into 100 g (3½ oz) cubes; heat 125 g (4½ oz) lard in a suitable pan and add the beef and 200 g (7 oz) onions cut in large dice. Cook together over a moderate heat until the onions have become lightly coloured, then mix in 10 g (⅓ oz) salt and 1 tsp paprika. Cook together for a few more minutes and add 500 g (1 lb 2 oz) tomatoes, peeled, depipped and cut in quarters and 1 dl (3½ fl oz or ½ U.S. cup) water.

Cover with a lid and cook gently in the oven for 1½ hours. At this time add 600 g (1 lb 5 oz) potatoes cut in quarters and 2 dl (7 fl oz or ⅞ U.S. cup) water. Continue cooking in the oven, basting frequently until the liquid is almost completely reduced.

Serve the goulash in a deep dish or timbale.

2472 Goulash à la Hongroise
This is the modified recipe as used in professional catering establishments.

Cut 1 kg 200 g (2 lb 10 oz) chuck steak into large cubes. Heat 125 g (4½ oz) lard in a suitable pan, add the beef and 250 g (9 oz) chopped onion and cook together till lightly coloured. Add 10 g (⅓ oz) salt and 1 tsp paprika and cook together for a few moments; add 50 g (2 oz) flour and cook for a few further moments.

Moisten with 1½ litres (2⅝ pt or 6½ U.S. cups) brown stock; add 2 dl (7 fl oz or ⅞ U.S. cup) tomato purée, raw if possible, a Bouquet garni and a touch of crushed garlic. Cover with a lid and cook gently in the oven for approximately 2½ hours.

Serve the goulash in a deep dish or timbale accompanied with a dish of plain boiled potatoes.

2473 Sauté de Boeuf Tolstoi
Cut 1 kg 200 g (2 lb 10 oz) head and tail of fillet of beef into approximately 50 g (2 oz) pieces. Heat some butter in a shallow pan, place in the beef and fry quickly till brown on all sides. Season with 10 g (⅓ oz) salt and a little paprika and cook together for a few moments; add 300 g (11 oz) roughly chopped tomato flesh, 1½ dl (5 fl oz or ⅝ U.S. cup) tomato purée, 100 g (3½ oz) chopped onions, 2 dl (7 fl oz or ⅞ U.S. cup) white stock and 8 small pickled cucumbers cut diamond shape.

Bring to the boil, cover with a lid and cook in the oven for approximately 45 minutes.

Serve in a deep dish or timbale accompanied with a dish of small plain boiled potatoes.

2474 HACHIS

In culinary terms the word Hachis should not be taken in its literal sense as denoting finely chopped meat. Rather this dish should consist of a fine Salpicon or small dice of meat prepared in accordance with the same principles as the Emincés and for the same reasons.

When roast meat is used it should not be boiled in the sauce which is usually Sauce Demi-glace. It is used to effect the binding of the Hachis in the proportions of 2½ dl (9 fl oz or 1⅛ U.S. cups) per 1 kg (2¼ lb) of the diced meat being used.

2475 Hachis à l'Américaine
Sauté an equal amount of small diced potatoes as there is meat, in butter until golden brown; add half to the meat and mix together with a little tomato purée and reduced veal gravy; reheat without boiling.

Place the mixture in a deep dish, sprinkle with the remaining potatoes which must be nice and crisp and finish with a little freshly chopped parsley.

2476 Hachis en Bordure au Gratin
Prepare a Hachis mixture with roast or braised meat mixed with Sauce Demi-glace as explained in the introduction to this section. Mould a border of Pommes Duchesse mixture on a suitable dish and brush with beaten egg.

Place the prepared Hachis in the centre, sprinkle with dry white breadcrumbs and melted butter and place in a hot oven to gratinate the surface and colour the border of potatoes at the same time.

2477 Hachis en Coquilles au Gratin
Prepare a Hachis mixture as in the preceding recipe.

Using Pommes Duchesse mixture and a piping bag fitted with a large star tube, pipe out borders round the edges of deep scollop shells and brush with beaten egg.

Fill the Hachis into the prepared shells, smooth dome shape, sprinkle with dry white breadcrumbs and melted butter and gratinate in a hot oven.

Note: It is recommended that the surface of the Hachis be coated with a little Sauce Duxelles before sprinkling with the breadcrumbs and butter.

2478 Hachis à la Fermière
Arrange a compact border of overlapping large slices of freshly boiled potatoes on a round dish; place some Hachis mixture in the centre, smooth dome shape, sprinkle with dry white breadcrumbs and melted butter and gratinate in a hot oven.

On removing from the oven surround with very small French fried eggs.

2479 Hachis Grand'mère
Mix the finely diced meat with a third its volume of light mashed potato instead of Sauce Demi-glace; place into a buttered earthenware dish and smooth the surface flat. Cover with a thin layer of mashed potato, sprinkle well with grated cheese mixed with dry white breadcrumbs and sprinkle this with melted butter. Gratinate in a very hot oven.

On removing from the oven, surround the Hachis with quarters of hot, freshly hard-boiled eggs.

2480 Hachis Parmentier
Bake some nicely shaped floury potatoes in the oven. As soon as cooked, cut off the top quarter of the potatoes and remove the insides with a spoon taking care to leave the empty shells whole.

Mash the potato pulp with a fork, then shallow fry it in butter, turning over and over frequently until the mixture becomes lightly browned. Add an equal amount of meat cut in small dice, 100 g (3½ oz) chopped onion cooked in a little butter per 1 kg (2¼ lb) of the total mixture, a good pinch of chopped parsley and a few drops of vinegar. Carry on cooking the mixture for a few more minutes as before then fill into the empty potato shells.

Coat the surface again and again with a little Sauce Lyonnaise which has been rubbed through a fine sieve, allowing the mixture to absorb as much of the sauce as it can. Replace the tops of the potatoes, place on a tray and reheat in the oven for 10 minutes. As soon as they are removed from the oven, arrange on a suitable dish on a serviette.

2481 Hachis à la Portugaise
Mix the finely diced meat with sufficient Tomato Fondue prepared in advance; reheat without boiling and serve in a deep dish surrounded with very small stuffed tomatoes.

2482 Sweet-Meat
Correctly speaking, Sweet-Meat is a Hachis consisting of a mixture of various meats but it may be prepared using only one kind, such as roast fillet or sirloin of beef.

To 1 kg (2¼ lb) of finely diced meat, add 125 g (4½ oz) mixed currants and sultanas, 2 eggs, 2 tbs redcurrant jelly, a little salt and pepper and a very small pinch of ground ginger. Mix together well.

Roll out an oblong layer of puff paste trimmings and place the prepared mixture on top; cover with a layer of the same paste, pinch the edges to seal, decorate and trim to a neat shape. Brush with beaten egg and decorate with the prongs of a fork; allow to rest for one hour then bake in a moderate oven for approximately 35 minutes.

Serve accompanied with a sauce made from 1½ dl (5 fl oz or ⅝ U.S. cup) good veal gravy containing 3 tbs melted redcurrant jelly.

2483 PAUPIETTES DE BOEUF—BEEF OLIVES

Paupiettes are prepared from slices of beef, cut for preference from the thick end of the sirloin, approximately 100–110 g (3½–4 oz) in weight. They are then flattened to a size of about 10 cm (4 in) long by 5 cm (2 in) wide.

Season one side, spread with a layer of ordinary pork forcemeat mixed with a little chopped parsley and roll up cork shape.

Enclose each in a thin slice of salt pork fat and tie with thin string to keep it in shape.

Paupiettes should be braised gently in the usual manner on a layer of vegetables and herbs, then glazed at the last moment, basting with the cooking liquid after first removing the covering of fat. The use of the fat is to prevent the drying of the *Paupiettes* during cooking.

2484 Paupiettes de Boeuf Fontanges
Braise the Paupiettes and glaze them at the last moment.

Arrange in a circle on a round dish with a small round flat Croquette of potato on each; place a purée of haricot beans in the centre and surround with the braising liquid, passed through a fine strainer and reduced.

2485 Paupiettes de Boeuf à la Milanaise
Braise the Paupiettes and glaze them at the last moment.

Arrange in a circle on a round dish with a round slice of red salt ox tongue and a small grooved cooked mushroom on top of each. Place sufficient Milanaise garnish in the centre and surround with thin Tomato Sauce.

2486 Paupiettes de Boeuf à la Piémontaise
Braise the Paupiettes and glaze them at the last moment.

Arrange a border of Risotto à la Piémontaise on a round dish, place the Paupiettes in the centre and coat with the braising liquid passed through a fine strainer and reduced.

2487 Paupiettes de Boeuf Savary
Braise the Paupiettes and glaze them at the last moment.

Meanwhile prepare a small decorative border of Pommes Duchesse mixture in the middle of a round dish; fill with a mixture of chopped braised celery mixed with a little well reduced Sauce Demi-glace, sprinkle with dry white breadcrumbs and melted butter and gratinate in the oven.

Arrange the Paupiettes round this prepared *Gratin* and coat with the braising liquid, passed through a fine strainer and reduced.

2488 Loose-Vinken, or Oiseau sans Tête
The name Loose-Vinken is given in Belgium to Paupiettes of beef filled in the centre with a large strip of streaky bacon as well as the forcemeat of pork. They are then cooked in exactly the same way as Carbonades de Boeuf Flamande (2459).

Note: The foregoing recipes are only a small selection of the many methods of preparing and serving Paupiettes; suffice it then to say that all of the garnishes, purées and sauces suitable for braised meats are also suitable for Paupiettes.

2489 BOEUF FUME—SMOKED BEEF

Smoked beef should always be well soaked in running cold water well in advance of use and should then be simmered gently in plenty of boiling water.

All of the garnishes served with boiled beef are suitable but especially Choucroute, red cabbage and braised cabbage or braised, stuffed cabbage.

2490 BOEUF SALE—SALT BEEF

The usual joints of beef selected for salting are silverside, brisket and the round.

Salt beef should always be well soaked in cold running water well in advance of use then simmered gently in plenty of boiling water; the cooking time will depend on the quality of the beef and the size and shape of the joint.

All the garnishes for boiled beef are suitable but especially Choucroute, red cabbage, braised cabbage or braised stuffed cabbage.

2491 PRESSED BEEF

Salt beef is also used in the preparation of pressed beef but for this, salted brisket of beef is generally used.

After cooking the beef in the same way as indicated for salt beef, cut it into large pieces of the same size as the moulds used for pressing it; lay them on top of each other to fill the moulds, which are usually square or rectangular.

Place the cover or a thick board of the same inside dimensions as the mould on top and apply pressure with the mould's attachments or by placing heavy weights on top. Leave the beef to cool as it is then place in a refrigerator to become quite cold and set.

When ready, turn out of the mould, trim carefully and coat it completely with clear jelly, coloured a deep reddish-brown as indicated in the recipe for Cold Ox Tongue (2402).

VEAL

2492 AMOURETTES ET CERVELLES—SPINE MARROW AND BRAINS

The spine marrow and brains of the calf have been classified together because of their similarity and the recipes are suitable for either.

The preliminary treatment and cooking is exactly the same as for the spine marrow and brains of beef as well as the recipes being suitable. The following recipes, however, are special for the spine marrow and brains of veal.

2493 Amourettes Tosca
Cut 500 g (1 lb 2 oz) cooked spine marrow into 3 cm ($1\frac{1}{5}$ in) lengths.

Mix 400 g (15 oz) cooked macaroni cut in short lengths, with some butter and grated Parmesan. Add 3 dl ($\frac{1}{2}$ pt or $1\frac{1}{4}$ U.S. cups) cullis of crayfish (258), 30 cooked crayfish tails and two-thirds of the spine marrow and mix all together gently. Heat carefully.

Place the mixture in a suitable deep dish or timbale, sprinkle the surface with the remaining Amourettes and cover the whole with Coulis d'Écrevisses.

2494 Cervelle Beaumont

Cut a nice cooked calf's brain into thick slices, coat one side of each slice with a layer of Gratin forcemeat made by softening foie gras with a little cold brown sauce. Place a slice of truffle on top of each then put the slices together so as to re-form into the original shape of the brain.

Roll out some puff paste trimmings into a circle approximately 3 mm ($\frac{1}{8}$ in) thick and of a size proportionate to the brain; place the brain on the pastry to one side and coat with a little of the same forcemeat and sprinkle with a little chopped truffle. Moisten the edge of the paste and fold over the brain in the shape of a turnover; seal the edges together well and make a small opening in the top for steam to escape. Brush with beaten egg, allow to rest for 30 minutes then bake in a fairly hot oven for 15 minutes.

On removing from the oven, pour a few tablespoons of Sauce Périgueux into the opening in the top and serve on a folded serviette on a suitable dish.

2495 Cervelle au Beurre Noir, or Cervelle au Beurre Noisette

Proceed as indicated for Cervelle de Boeuf of the same names.

2496 Cervelle en Caisses

Cut the cooked brains into slices and place into small buttered porcelain cases alternating each slice with a large slice of cooked mushroom. Cover with Sauce Allemande and decorate with a few threads of melted meat glaze.

2497 Cervelle Maréchal

Cut the cooked brains into thick slices and flour, egg and breadcrumb them. Shallow fry in clarified butter to a golden brown on both sides and arrange overlapping in a circle on a round dish with a nice slice of truffle on each. Fill the centre with buttered asparagus tips.

2498 Cervelle Montrouge

Cut the cooked brains into thick slices and re-form, coating each slice with a little cooked purée of mushrooms.

Have prepared a cooked flan case of a size proportionate to the brains, coat the bottom of it with a mixture of sliced cooked mushrooms mixed with Sauce Béchamel and arrange the brains on top.

Coat with Sauce Mornay and gratinate quickly. Serve on a serviette on a suitable dish.

2499 Cervelle Sainte-Menehould

Cut the cooked brains into thick slices and dip into Sauce Villeroy containing a third its quantity of chopped and well squeezed raw mushrooms; place the slices on a tray and allow to become cold.

Envelop each slice in a very thin pliant piece of caul, sprinkle with breadcrumbs and melted butter and grill gently.

2500 Vol-au-Vent de Cervelle

Place 4 dl (14 fl oz or $1\frac{3}{4}$ U.S. cups) Sauce Allemande in a pan and carefully mix in 500 g (1 lb 2 oz) cooked brains cut in smallish pieces; 12 Quenelles of ordinary Godiveau poached and swollen in mushroom cooking liquor; 125 g ($4\frac{1}{2}$ oz) very small, white cooked mushrooms and 15 slices of truffle.

Heat very carefully and pour into a sufficiently large Vol-au-vent case, decorate the top with a circle of slices of truffle and present on a serviette on a round dish.

2501 Cervelle Zingara

Blanch the brains, cut into thick slices, season, pass through flour and shallow fry to a golden brown in clarified butter.

Arrange in a circle on a round dish alternating each slice with an oval slice of raw ham which has been shallow fried in a little butter. Fill the centre with a Zingara garnish (472) and serve a tomato and tarragon-flavoured Sauce Demi-glace separately.

2502 Various Other Preparations for Calf's Brains

The following preparations are suitable for calf's brains and can be found fully described in the section under Cervelles de Boeuf—Beef Brains.

Bourguignonne, Coquilles à la Parisienne and au Gratin, Cromesquis, Croquettes, Fritot, Italienne, Matelote, Mousseline, Mazagran, Pain, à la Poulette, Soufflés, Subrics, Timbales, Villeroy.

2503 CARRE DE VEAU—BEST END OF VEAL

A best end of veal is seldom served whole but when

it is the rib bones should be shortened and the chine bone removed to facilitate carving. It should then be completely covered with slices of bacon fat and either roasted, Poêléed or braised. In certain cases it may be larded along its length after first carefully removing any sinew.

Serve accompanied with any of the garnishes indicated for Cushion of Veal.

2504 Cold Best End of Veal

Trim the cooked best end which has been braised for preference and coat it well with good clear aspic jelly.

As for other cold joints of veal the garnish may be a Macédoine of vegetables bound with jelly or Mayonnaise arranged in a border around the meat, or moulded in dariole or other suitable moulds. Alternatively, the Macédoine may be placed in artichoke bottoms.

The joint may be garnished to choice but it is absolutely necessary to serve the braising liquid with it after removing all fat and passing through a fine strainer before it becomes cold.

The dish on which the best end is presented should always be surrounded with a border of neatly cut shapes of jelly.

COEUR DE VEAU—CALF'S HEART

2505 Coeur de Veau à la Bourgeoise

Carefully trim the heart and fry all over in clean dripping to a good brown colour, then treat in the same way as Pièce de Boeuf à la Bourgeoise taking account of the proportions and any differences in quantities.

2506 Coeur de Veau Farci—Stuffed Calf's Heart

Open the heart and remove the coagulated blood leaving a pocket. Fill with a Fricadelle forcemeat of veal (2729), sew it up with thin string and envelop in thin slices of salt pork fat. Braise very gently in the usual way for approximately 2 hours.

When ready remove the strings and serve accompanied with a suitable vegetable purée and the braising liquid after removing all of the fat, passing through a fine strainer and reducing by two-thirds.

2507 Coeur de Veau Sauté

Trim the heart and cut into very thin slices along its length; season and shallow fry quickly in hot butter tossing over frequently to obtain an even colour. Drain and add the slices to a suitable sauce with or without a garnish as the case may be.

In the same way as for kidneys, take care that the slices of heart do not boil in the sauce as this will only render them tough.

2508 COTES DE VEAU—VEAL CUTLETS

Veal cutlets may be either grilled or shallow fried but in most cases they are preferable when cooked by the latter method.

The addition of a liquid to the pan in which the cutlets have been shallow fried (Deglaçage) is absolutely necessary as has been explained before, but in this case without removing the butter used in the cooking. The deglazing should be made with a liquid in keeping with the accompanying sauce and added to the sauce which more often than not, is buttered Sauce Demi-glace.

However, the most suitable sauce to accompany veal cutlets is a lightly buttered pale veal meat glaze containing the reduced deglazing.

The general observations at the beginning of the section on Tournedos of beef are applicable to the preparation of veal cutlets and all the garnishes are suitable always bearing in mind that they should not be placed on Croûtons of fried bread.

The various garnishes indicated for cushion of veal are also suitable.

The following recipes are particular for preparations of veal cutlets and are for one cutlet only.

2509 Côte de Veau au Basilic

Season and shallow fry the cutlet in butter. Deglaze with white wine, add 1 tbs meat glaze and shake in 25 g (1 oz) Beurre de Basilic away from the fire.

Place the cutlet on a dish and coat with the sauce.

2510 Côte de Veau Bouchère

This term does not refer to a special dish but indicates the manner in which a veal cutlet is trimmed, i.e. without trimming the end part of the bone as usual. It is usually grilled and served accompanied with any suitable garnish for veal cutlets.

2511 Côte de Veau Bonne-Femme

Season the cutlet and colour it brown with butter on both sides in an earthenware casserole.

Surround with 6 button onions glazed brown and 100 g (3½ oz) small potatoes cut in fairly thick rounds. Cover with the lid and finish cooking together in the oven.

Just before serving, carefully add 2 tbs of liquid, either water, stock or gravy and serve the cutlet as it is in the casserole.

2512 Côte de Veau en Casserole

Season the cutlet and cook it very gently in an earthenware casserole with 50 g (2 oz) butter. Add just 1 tbs good veal gravy at the last moment and serve the cutlet as it is in the casserole.

2513 Côte de Veau en Cocotte
Season the cutlet and colour it brown with butter on both sides, in a Cocotte. Add 6 button onions coloured brown in butter, 100 g ($3\frac{1}{2}$ oz) potatoes trimmed to the shape of olives and 2 or 3 mushrooms cut in quarters.

Cover with the lid and complete the cooking in the oven.

Add a little good veal gravy at the last moment and serve the cutlet as it is in the Cocotte.

2514 Côte de Veau en Cocotte à la Paysanne
Season the cutlet and colour it brown on both sides in a Cocotte, with butter and 60 g (2 oz) streaky bacon cut in batons. Add 4 button onions coloured brown in butter and 100 g ($3\frac{1}{2}$ oz) small potatoes cut in round slices.

Cover with the lid and complete the cooking in the oven. Serve the cutlet as it is in the Cocotte.

2515 Côte de Veau à la Dreux
Stud the flesh of the cutlet with small pieces of tongue, ham and truffle. Season and cook the cutlet gently in butter. Trim the surface clean of any studding and place in a dish. Surround with a Financière garnish containing the deglazed juices from the pan.

2516 Côte de Veau à la Fermière
Season the cutlet and colour it brown with butter on both sides, in a Cocotte. Add a Fermière garnish prepared in advance, cover with the lid and finish cooking together in the oven.

Add a little good veal gravy at the last moment and serve the cutlet as it is in the Cocotte.

2517 Côte de Veau Financière
Season the cutlet and shallow fry it gently in butter. Place in a dish and surround with a Financière garnish containing the juices from the pan deglazed with Madeira.

2518 Côte de Veau aux Fines Herbes
Season the cutlet and shallow fry it gently in butter.

Place in a dish, deglaze the pan with white wine, reduce and add to a little Sauce Fines Herbes. Pour this sauce around the cutlet and serve.

2519 Côte de Veau au Jus
Season the cutlet and shallow fry it gently in butter.

Place in a dish, deglaze the pan with a little excellent veal gravy and pour around the cutlet.

2520 Côte de Veau Maintenon
Proceed in exactly the same way as for Côtelettes de Mouton Maintenon (2766).

2521 Côte de Veau Maraîchère
Season the cutlet and shallow fry it gently in butter.

Place in a dish and surround with a few short lengths of salsify lightly browned in butter, a few buttered Brussels sprouts or if unavailable, a few short lengths of buttered French beans, and 2 small Pommes Château.

Deglaze the pan with a little good veal gravy and pour around the cutlet.

2522 Côte de Veau Marigny
Season the cutlet and shallow fry it gently in butter.

Place in a dish and garnish with 2 small tartlet cases filled with a mixture of buttered peas and diamonds of French beans.

Deglaze the pan with a little veal stock, reduce it, add to a little lightly thickened good veal gravy and pour this around the cutlet.

2523 Côte de Veau Maréchal
Prepare the cutlet, flour, egg and breadcrumb it then shallow fry gently in clarified butter.

Place in a dish, set a nice slice of truffle on top of the cutlet and place a bouquet of buttered asparagus tips at its side.

2524 Côte de Veau Milanaise
Lightly flatten the cutlet and coat with flour, egg and breadcrumbs mixed with half as much grated Parmesan.

Shallow fry it gently in clarified butter.

Place in a dish with a Milanaise garnish (418) at its side. Surround with a *cordon* of thin Sauce Tomate.

2525 Côte de Veau Montholon
Season the cutlet and shallow fry it gently in butter.

Place in a dish and garnish the top of the cutlet with an oval of red ox tongue, 2 cooked grooved mushrooms and a slice of truffle. Surround with a *cordon* of Sauce Suprême.

2526 Côte de Veau Napolitaine
Season the cutlet and shallow fry it gently in butter.

Dry the surface of the cutlet with a piece of clean cloth, then coat each side with a layer of thick Sauce Béchamel mixed with egg yolks and well flavoured with grated Parmesan.

Egg and breadcrumb and quickly colour a golden brown on both sides in clarified butter.

Place in a dish with a Napolitaine garnish (428) at its side.

2527 Côte de Veau Orléanaise
Season the cutlet and shallow fry it gently in butter.

Place in a dish and garnish on one side of the dish with a small dariole mould of braised endive, chopped, then mixed with a little beaten egg and poached.

Deglaze the pan with a little good veal gravy and pour this around the cutlet. Serve separately a dish of Pommes Maître d'Hôtel.

2528 Côte de Veau Orloff
Season the cutlet and shallow fry it gently in butter.

With a sharp knife cut open the meat of the cutlet horizontally towards the bone. Place a little very thick Soubise and 2 slices of truffle in the opening then close together.

Place a little more of the same Soubise on top of the cutlet; smooth dome shape, coat with a little Sauce Mornay and glaze quickly under the salamander.

2529 Côte de Veau en Papillote
Season the cutlet and either shallow fry it in butter or grill it.

Have prepared a sheet of strong greaseproof paper cut to the shape of a large heart and big enough to hold the cutlet; brush the paper with either butter or oil. On one side of the paper lay a heart-shaped or triangular slice of lean cooked ham about the size of the cutlet; coat this with a spoonful of thick Sauce Duxelles. Place the cutlet on top, cover with a little more of the same sauce, then place on this another slice of ham cut as before.

Fold over the paper to enclose the cutlet then carefully pleat the edges to seal completely. Place the Papillote on a dish then into a moderate oven to swell up the paper and to colour it brown. Serve immediately.

Note: It is the custom in some establishments to add some finely sliced cooked mushrooms to the Sauce Duxelles.

2530 Côte de Veau Périgourdine
Season the cutlet and shallow fry it gently in butter. Drain well and coat each side with a thin layer of fine pork forcemeat mixed with a third as much of a purée of foie gras and chopped truffle.

Completely enclose the cutlet in a piece of caul, sprinkle with melted butter and grill it gently on both sides.

Place in a dish and surround with a little Sauce Périgueux.

2531 Côte de Veau Pojarski
Remove the meat completely from the cutlet and trim it free of all skin and gristle.

Finely chop this meat together with a quarter of its weight of butter and the same amount of breadcrumbs soaked in milk and squeezed. Season then press and mould this mixture to the cutlet bone to give it its original shape.

Shallow fry gently in clarified butter taking great care when turning it over.

Place in a dish and garnish to choice.

Note: The term Pojarski does not signify the use of any specific garnish which can thus be to choice and this can equally be replaced by a suitable sauce.

2532 Côte de Veau Printanière
Season the cutlet and colour it quickly in butter on both sides. Complete its cooking by braising gently in the usual manner.

Place in a dish with a Printanière garnish (444) to one side and serve accompanied with the braising liquid after first removing all fat, passing through a fine strainer and reducing it.

2533 Côte de Veau Provençale
Season the cutlet and colour it on one side only in butter. Remove from the pan.

Place a little Provençale mixture (445) on the coloured side and smooth it dome shape; sprinkle with grated cheese.

Return the cutlet to the pan, uncoloured side down and place it in the oven so as to ensure that the cooking and gratinating of the surface are complete together.

When ready, place the cutlet in a dish and either surround it with a little Sauce Provençale or serve it separately.

2534 Côte de Veau Talleyrand
Season the cutlet and shallow fry it gently in butter.

Place in a dish with a Talleyrand garnish (461) to one side.

Surround with a *cordon* of Sauce Périgueux containing a short fine Julienne of truffle instead of chopped truffle.

2535 Côte de Veau Vert-pré
Season the cutlet and grill it gently.

Place in a dish; cover the cutlet with a spoonful of soft Maître d'Hôtel Butter and garnish with a bouquet of straw potatoes and a bouquet of watercress.

2536 Côte de Veau à la Vichy
Season the cutlet and shallow fry it gently in butter.

Place in a dish and garnish with a nice bouquet a of Carottes à la Vichy (4008). Deglaze the pan with a little good veal gravy and pour this around the cutlet.

2537 Côte de Veau à la Viennoise
Carefully flatten the meat of the cutlet until it is very thin, using a moistened cutlet bat.

Season, flour, egg and breadcrumb the cutlet and shallow fry it quickly in butter to a golden brown on both sides.

Spread 20 g ($\frac{2}{3}$ oz) Anchovy Butter on the centre of a suitable dish and place the cutlet on top of this. Place in the centre of the cutlet a slice of peeled and depipped lemon and in the centre of this a stoned olive surrounded with a strip of anchovy fillet.

Surround the cutlet with a bouquet of capers, a bouquet of chopped hard-boiled egg yolk and the same of the white of the egg. This garnish may also be arranged in lines to one side of the cutlet.

Note: Although the use of Anchovy Butter is in complete accord with the preparation of this dish, some establishments prefer to replace it with Beurre Noisette. It is right that this deviation should be noted, but in all fairness it cannot be advised as correct practice.

2538 Côte de Veau Zingara
Season the cutlet and shallow fry it gently in butter.

Shallow fry an oval slice of raw ham and place in the serving dish with the cutlet on top. Surround the cutlet with a *cordon* of Sauce Zingara.

COTES DE VEAU FROIDES—COLD VEAL CUTLETS

2539 Côte de Veau en Belle-Vue
To present a veal cutlet en Belle-vue it is necessary to braise it first, allow it to become quite cold and then to dry the surface well with a clean cloth. It may then be prepared according to either of the two following methods.

1) Trim the cutlet and decorate the top surface with shapes of vegetables fixing them with a little almost setting jelly.

   Set a layer of jelly in the bottom of a mould which can comfortably hold the cutlet. Place the decorated cutlet on top of this, decorated side downwards. Fill with sufficient jelly to cover the cutlet and place in a refrigerator to set well.

   For service, heat the point of a small knife in hot water and trim round the cutlet to its shape and to separate off any excessive amount of jelly. Place the mould on a folded cloth dipped in hot water for a few moments and carefully turn it over to demould on to a cold dish.

   Surround with a little chopped jelly.

2) Take an oval or long dish of similar dimensions to the trimmed cutlet. Set a thinnish layer of jelly in the bottom and decorate the surface of this with shapes of vegetables. Fix this decoration with a little almost setting jelly. Place the cutlet on top, cover with jelly and allow it to set in a refrigerator.

   To serve: dip the utensil in hot water for a few moments and turn it over to demould on to a cold dish.

   Surround with a little chopped jelly.

EPAULE DE VEAU—SHOULDER OF VEAL

2540 Epaule de Veau Farcie—Stuffed Shoulder of Veal
Carefully bone out the shoulder, lay it flat on the table boned side upwards and beat with a cutlet bat to flatten it a little. Season the surface with salt and pepper and coat with a layer of pork forcemeat mixed with a quarter as much of Farce Gratin, dry Duxelles and a little chopped parsley.

Roll it up and tie with string carefully, then braise in the usual manner. Remove the string and serve the shoulder with a purée of vegetables or a farinaceous garnish such as noodles and a sauceboat of the braising liquid after first removing all fat and passing through a fine strainer.

2541 Epaule de Veau Farcie à l'Anglaise—Stuffed Shoulder of Veal, English Style
Bone and flatten the shoulder as in the preceding recipe. Season and stuff it with a mixture composed of one-third chopped veal kidney, one-third chopped veal kidney fat or fat belly of veal, one-third white breadcrumbs soaked in milk and squeezed, 2 eggs per 1 kg ($2\frac{1}{4}$ lb) of mixture and seasoning.

Roll the shoulder up and tie it fairly tightly and either roast or braise it in the usual manner.

When ready, remove the string and serve the shoulder accompanied with boiled ham and, according to the way in which it was cooked, either roast gravy or the braising liquid.

2542 Epaule de Veau Farcie à la Boulangère
Prepare and stuff the shoulder as indicated above and three-quarters roast it.

Place it on a large earthenware dish. Deglaze the roasting pan with a little veal stock and add to the dish with a Boulangère garnish (350).

Place in the oven to complete the cooking together.

Remove the string and present the shoulder as it is.

2543 Epaule de Veau Farcie à la Bourgeoise
Prepare and stuff the shoulder as previously indicated and two-thirds braise it.

Remove the shoulder and place in a clean pan and surround with a Bourgeoise garnish (352). Remove all the fat from the braising liquid, thicken with a little Sauce Espagnole and pass through a fine strainer over the shoulder and the garnish. Cover and complete the cooking together in the oven.

When ready, remove the string and serve accompanied with the garnish and sauce.

2544 FILET DE VEAU—FILLET OF VEAL

The term Filet de Veau is sometimes incorrectly used on menus as a name for *Longe de Veau* (loin of veal). The true fillet is found underneath the saddle, one on each side of the central spine and thus corresponds exactly to the fillet of beef. The *Longe* is the equivalent of the sirloin of beef.

2545 Filet de Veau Agnès Sorel
Trim the fillet and remove any sinew. Lard it finely with truffle and tongue, braise in the usual manner and glaze it at the last moment.

Place the fillet on a dish and surround with tartlet cases filled with a purée of mushrooms and decorated with a round of red tongue with a slice of truffle in its centre.

Serve accompanied with the braising liquid after first removing all fat and passing through a fine strainer.

2546 Filet de Veau Chasseur
Trim the fillet and remove any sinew. Lard it well with fine strips of salt pork fat and roast it, basting frequently with melted butter.

Serve accompanied with Sauce Chasseur.

2547 Filet de Veau à la Dreux
Trim the fillet and remove any sinew.

Lard it across the thickness of the meat with ham, tongue and truffle. Completely enclose the fillet in thin slices of salt pork fat and tie together with string. Braise it in the usual manner and glaze at the last moment after removing the fat.

Place in a dish and surround with a Financière garnish (381).

2548 Filet de Veau Orloff
Trim the fillet and remove any sinew.

Completely enclose it in thin slices of salt pork fat, tie with string and braise in the usual manner.

Allowing sufficient time before being required, first remove the string and fat, then cut a thin slice from the bottom of the fillet and along its entire length. Place this slice on a dish, then cut the fillet into fairly thick even slices. Coat each slice with a little thick Soubise and replace together on the long slice of fillet, with a slice of truffle between each, so as to re-form it to its original shape.

Coat the prepared fillet with a thin layer of Soubise then cover it with Sauce Mornay. Glaze quickly in a very hot oven and serve.

2549 Filet de Veau au Paprika
Trim the fillet and remove any sinew.

Lard it finely with strips of salt pork fat and sprinkle well with paprika. Shallow fry quickly in hot lard until brown on all sides.

Cover the bottom of a suitable pan with a layer of sliced blanched onions, place the fillet on top and Poêlé it in the usual manner.

When cooked, place the fillet on a dish and surround with a Hongroise garnish (392) in keeping with the size of the joint. Deglaze the pan with 2 dl (7 fl oz or $\frac{7}{8}$ U.S. cup) cream, pass through a fine strainer and serve it separately.

2550 Filet de Veau Sicilienne
Trim the fillet and remove any sinew.

Lard it finely with strips of salt pork fat and Poêlé in the usual manner.

As soon as it is cooked, envelop it completely with caul. Arrange a layer of Lasagnes à la Sicilienne in a dish, place the fillet on top and cover with a further layer of the same Lasagnes. Sprinkle with white breadcrumbs and melted butter and place in a hot oven to gratinate.

Remove any fat from the pan and deglaze with a little good veal stock; pass through a fine strainer and serve separately with the fillet.

2551 Filet de Veau Talleyrand
Trim the fillet and remove any sinew.

Stud it with pieces of raw truffle and Poêlé in the usual manner with the addition of a little Madeira; glaze it at the last moment.

Place the cooked fillet on a dish and surround with a garnish of Macaroni à la Talleyrand (461).

Serve accompanied with Sauce Périgueux containing very fine short Julienne of truffle instead of chopped truffle.

FOIE DE VEAU—CALF'S LIVER

2552 Foie de Veau à l'Anglaise—Calf's Liver and Bacon
Cut the liver into fairly thick slices of approximately 110 g (3½ oz) in weight. Season, pass through flour and either shallow fry in butter or grill them.

Arrange the slices on a dish alternating with slices of shallow fried or grilled back bacon. Coat with a little of the butter in which the liver was cooked if shallow fried, or a little Beurre Noisette if grilled.

2553 Foie de Veau Bercy
Cut the liver into fairly thick slices. Season, dip each into melted butter, dredge lightly with flour and grill gently.

Place the liver in a dish and coat with softened Beurre Bercy.

2554 Foie de Veau à la Bordelaise
Lard the whole liver with strips of salt pork fat and marinate for 1 hour in advance with white wine.

Remove and dry the liver with a clean cloth, season it and fry quickly in butter to a brown colour; completely enclose the liver in caul and place it in a deep pan.

Cook a little chopped onion and shallot in butter and then add a few chopped flap mushrooms. Add a little white wine, reduce and add with sufficient very thin tomato-flavoured Sauce Demi-glace to come half-way up the liver.

Cover with a lid and cook very gently in the oven and at the last moment add a garnish of thickly sliced flap mushrooms fried to a nice brown colour in butter.

Serve the liver in a dish with the sauce and garnish.

2555 Foie de Veau à la Bourgeoise
Lard the whole liver with strips of salt pork fat. Season and fry quickly in butter to a brown colour on all sides. Braise as indicated for Pièce de Boeuf à la Bourgeoise.

When two-thirds cooked place the liver into a clean pan and surround with a Bourgeoise garnish (352). Remove the fat from the sauce then pass the sauce through a fine strainer over the liver and garnish. Finish cooking together then serve in a suitable dish, the liver surrounded by the garnish and with the sauce.

2556 Brochettes de Foie de Veau
Cut the liver into pieces approximately 2½ cm (1 in) square and about 1¼ cm (½ in) thick. Season and fry quickly in very hot butter just sufficient to colour and set the surfaces of the liver.

Impale these pieces on to special skewers alternating them equally with squares of blanched streaky bacon and thick slices of mushroom cooked in butter.

Coat the whole thinly with very thick Sauce Duxelles and allow to become cold. Egg and breadcrumb, sprinkle with melted butter and grill gently.

For service, arrange the brochettes on a dish, the bottom of which is covered with one of the following sauces: Duxelles, Fines Herbes, Italienne, or Beurre Maître d'Hôtel.

These sauces or butter may be served separately.

2557 Foie de Veau à l'Espagnole
Cut the liver into slices; season, pass through flour, sprinkle with oil and grill gently.

Arrange the cooked slices overlapping along the centre of a dish. Place half a grilled tomato on each slice and surround the whole with rings of deep fried onion and bouquets of fried parsley.

2558 Foie de Veau aux Fines Herbes
Cut the liver into slices, season, pass through flour and shallow fry in butter.

Place a sufficient amount of Sauce Fines Herbes in the bottom of a dish and arrange the slices of liver on top, or serve plain with the sauce separate.

2559 Foie de Veau Frit—Fried Calf's Liver
Cut the liver into pieces approximately 5 cm (2 in) square by 1 cm (⅖ in) thick. Season, flour, egg and breadcrumb.

Deep fry in hot oil when required and arrange on a serviette on a dish, garnished with fried parsley.

2560 Foie de Veau à l'Italienne
Cut the liver into slices, season, pass through flour and shallow fry in a mixture of butter and oil.

Place a sufficient amount of Sauce Italienne in the bottom of a dish and arrange the slices of liver on top, or serve plain with the sauce separate.

2561 Foie de Veau à la Lyonnaise
Cut the liver into slices, season, pass through flour and shallow fry in a mixture of butter and oil.

Arrange the cooked slices overlapping in a circle on a round dish. Fill the centre with a garnish of sliced onions cooked in butter and mixed with a little meat glaze. Deglaze the pan with a little vinegar and pour this over the onions.

2562 Pain de Foie de Veau
Cut 1 kg (2 lb 4 oz) calf's liver into large dice and pound well together with 400 g (15 oz) fat belly of pork, 300 g (11 oz) breadcrumbs moistened with a little cream, 60 g (2 oz) chopped onion cooked in a little butter, 4 eggs, 25 g (1 oz) salt, a pinch of pepper and a pinch of grated nutmeg.

Pass the mixture through a fine sieve, then place in a basin set in crushed ice. Mix in well, 3 egg whites and 3 dl ($\frac{1}{2}$ pt or $1\frac{1}{4}$ U.S. cups) cream. Pour into a buttered Charlotte mould and knock the bottom gently on a folded cloth to settle the contents.

Place in a tray of hot water and cook gently in a moderate oven. Allow to rest for a few minutes before demoulding on to a round dish.

Serve accompanied with a suitable brown sauce.

2563 Pain de Foie de Veau (*light*)
Pound well together 500 g (1 lb 2 oz) pale coloured calf's liver with 125 g ($4\frac{1}{2}$ oz) white breadcrumbs soaked in cream and squeezed.

Pass the mixture through a fine sieve, then place in a basin. Season with salt, pepper and a little grated nutmeg, and mix in 4 eggs, 4 egg yolks and 5 dl (18 fl oz or $2\frac{1}{4}$ U.S. cups) milk in which has been infused 120 g (4 oz) sliced onions cooked without colouring them. This infusion should be prepared in advance, passed through a fine strainer and allowed to become cold before using.

Pour the preparation into a buttered Charlotte mould, place in a tray of hot water and cook in a moderate oven.

Allow to rest for a few minutes before demoulding on to a round dish. Coat with a few spoonfuls of well buttered meat glaze and serve accompanied with a sauceboat of the same glaze.

2564 Foie de Veau Provençale
Cut the liver into slices, season, pass through flour and shallow fry in oil.

Place a sufficient amount of Sauce Provençale in the bottom of a dish and arrange the slices of liver on top, or serve plain with the sauce separate.

2565 Quenelles de Foie de Veau
Prepare a forcemeat of calf's liver in accordance with the method and proportions as indicated for Mousseline Forcemeat (288).

Mould the Quenelles with tablespoons and poach them in the usual manner. Drain and dry them well, arrange in a circle on a round dish and place in the centre a suitable brown sauce such as Demi-glace, Champignons, Fines Herbes or other sauce of the same type.

2566 Quenelles de Foie de Veau à la Viennoise
Chop 500 g (1 lb 2 oz) calf's liver and pass through a fine sieve. Place in a basin and add 250 g (9 oz) very fine breadcrumbs, 50 g (2 oz) flour, 30 g (1 oz) finely chopped onion cooked in butter without colour, 1 tbs chopped parsley, 3 whole eggs, 5 egg yolks, 12 g ($\frac{1}{3}$ oz) salt and a pinch of pepper and grated nutmeg. Mix well together.

Mould the Quenelles with tablespoons and poach them in the usual manner.

Drain and dry them well and arrange in a circle on a round dish. Coat with Beurre Noisette and sprinkle with a few drops of lemon juice.

2567 Foie de Veau aux Raisins
Pick over and wash 10 g ($\frac{1}{3}$ oz) each of sultanas and currants for each portion of liver; soak them well in advance in warm water to allow them to swell. Cut the liver into slices, season, shallow fry in butter and arrange in a circle on a round dish.

Deglaze the pan with a little vinegar, add a pinch of brown sugar and the necessary amount of Sauce Demi-glace, reduce to the correct consistency and pass through a fine strainer. Add the well drained sultanas and currants to this sauce, simmer together for a few minutes and pour over the liver.

2568 Foie de Veau au Rizot
Cut the liver into large cubes, season and shallow fry quickly in butter.

Have prepared a border of Risotto moulded on a suitable dish and place the liver in the centre. Coat with Sauce Mornay and glaze quickly under the salamander.

2569 Soufflé de Foie de Veau
Finely pound 1 kg ($2\frac{1}{4}$ lb) freshly cooked liver with 125 g ($4\frac{1}{2}$ oz) butter; add 4 dl (14 fl oz or $1\frac{3}{4}$ U.S. cups) well reduced Sauce Béchamel and pass through a fine sieve.

Mix in 6 egg yolks and 1 dl ($3\frac{1}{2}$ fl oz or $\frac{1}{2}$ U.S. cup) fresh cream, season with salt and pepper and finally fold in 6 stiffly beaten egg whites.

Pour this mixture into well buttered soufflé moulds and cook in the usual manner.

2570 Foie de Veau sous Croûte
Lard the whole liver in the same manner as for Boeuf à la Mode (2418). Season with salt, pepper and a little mixed spice then fry quickly in butter to a brown colour on all sides.

Allow to become cold, cover with a layer of cold Duxelles then envelop in thin slices of salt pork fat. Now completely enclose the whole in a layer of hot water paste (3775). Seal the edges well, make a hole in the top for steam to escape and place on a baking tray.

Bake in a medium oven for approximately 2 hours occasionally pouring in a little thin Sauce Demi-glace through the opening in the top.

On removing from the oven, add a little more of the same sauce through the opening and send to the table accompanied with a sauceboat of Sauce Demi-glace finished with butter and Madeira.

Note: The baked crust enclosing the liver should be broken for service at the table.

FOIE DE VEAU FROID—COLD CALF'S LIVER

2571 Foie de Veau Poché à la Flamande

Plunge the whole liver into boiling water containing 8 g ($\frac{1}{3}$ oz) salt per 1 litre ($1\frac{3}{4}$ pt or $4\frac{1}{2}$ U.S. cups) of water. Cover with a lid and poach very gently allowing 30 minutes per 1 kg ($2\frac{1}{4}$ lb).

When ready, place the cooked liver into a basin of cold water and allow to become quite cold. This liver is very soft and should be cut only when required into thin slices and arranged on a suitable cold dish.

It is usual to accompany this dish with Sauce Ravigote.

2572 FRAISE DE VEAU

This is the membrane which encloses the intestines of the calf and is referred to in English as the 'crow' of veal.

It should be well soaked in running water to extract the blood, then blanched and made cold in running water. After this it is cooked in a *Blanc* in the same way as calf's head (2712) before being utilised for the following recipes.

Fraise de Veau should always be served very hot accompanied with a well flavoured sauce.

2573 Fraise de Veau Frite

Drain the cooked crow of veal, and dry well with a clean cloth; cut into pieces and season well.

Flour, egg and breadcrumb and deep fry in hot oil when required. Arrange on a serviette on a dish, garnished with fried parsley and serve accompanied with Sauce Diable.

2574 Fraise de Veau à la Lyonnaise

If required especially for serving à la Lyonnaise, the crow of veal should be cooked in the usual way but kept a little firm.

Drain and dry well with a clean cloth and cut into slices. Season and toss over in very hot oil; add a proportionate amount of sliced onions previously cooked in butter and toss over together for a few moments to mix well together and to heat properly.

Place into a deep dish and sprinkle with chopped parsley; deglaze the hot pan with a little vinegar and sprinkle over.

2575 Fraise de Veau à la Poulette

Well drain the hot cooked crow of veal, slice quickly and add to a Sauce Poulette. Pour into a deep dish and sprinkle with chopped parsley.

2576 Fraise de Veau à la Ravigote

Place the cooked, boiling hot crow of veal into a dish with a little of its cooking liquid and serve accompanied with a Sauce Ravigote or Vinaigrette.

Note: A Sauce Gribiche would be equally suitable but in this case the designation of the dish should be Fraise de Veau à la Gribiche.

JARRETS DE VEAU—KNUCKLE OF VEAL

2577 Jarrets de Veau à la Printanière

Cut the knuckles of veal across the bone into round sections approximately 5–6 cm (2–$2\frac{1}{2}$ in) thick. Season and colour on both sides in butter using a shallow pan; moisten with just a little white veal stock, add a Bouquet garni, cover and cook slowly in the oven for approximately $1\frac{1}{2}$ hours. Baste frequently with the liquid, adding a little more stock if too much reduction should occur.

After about 1 hour add a proportionate amount of raw Printanière garnish (444) and continue cooking together for another 30 minutes.

Serve the knuckles of veal in a deep dish with its garnish and cooking liquid.

2578 Ossi-Buchi

Cut the knuckles of veal across the bone into round sections approximately 5–6 cm (2–$2\frac{1}{2}$ in) thick. Season, pass through flour and colour on both sides in hot lard, using a shallow pan. For 10 sections of knuckle add 150 g (5 oz) chopped onion and cook together for a few minutes with the knuckles, then add 1 kg ($2\frac{1}{4}$ lb) roughly chopped flesh only of tomato and 5 dl (18 fl oz or $2\frac{1}{4}$ U.S. cups) white wine. Reduce by two-thirds, moisten half-way up the ingredients with sufficient white veal stock and add a Bouquet garni. Cover with a lid and cook slowly in the oven for $1\frac{1}{2}$ hours, by which time the cooking liquor should be reduced by approximately half.

Arrange the sections of knuckle in a deep dish with its garnish and cooking liquid. Sprinkle with a little lemon juice and chopped parsley.

2579 LANGUES DE VEAU—CALVES' TONGUES

Calves' tongues should be first trimmed, blanched then braised in the usual manner.
To serve: remove the skins and arrange the tongues in a circle on a round dish, the points of the tongues to the centre and resting on a suitable cut shape of fried bread. They may also be cut in half lengthways. If a garnish is used, this should be placed between the tongues or it may be served separately. The tongues should then be coated with the reduced braising liquid.

2580 Langues de Veau Grillées—Grilled Calves' Tongues
Braise the tongues but only three-quarters cook them. Remove the skins, cut them open with a knife from the top, lengthways, but do not separate the two halves. Open flat and keep them in this shape by piercing crossways with skewers.

Season and coat with a little made mustard, then pass through melted butter and breadcrumbs. Grill gently on both sides.

Serve accompanied with a well flavoured sauce such as Sauce Diable, Piquante or Robert.

2581 Langues de Veau Orloff
Braise the tongues and prepare in the same way as Filet de Veau Orloff.

2582 Langues de Veau en Papillote
Braise the tongues and remove the skins; cut into three lengthways then proceed in the same way as for Côte de Veau en Papillote (2529) using three pieces of tongue laid side by side for each Papillote.

2583 Langues de Veau Braisées—Braised Calves' Tongues
Suitable garnishes for serving with braised calves' tongues: Bouquetière, Jardinière; Milanaise; Portugaise etc. and purée of vegetables such as Celery, Conti, Flamande, chestnuts, turnips, fresh or dried peas, potatoes etc.
Suitable sauces: Chasseur, Duxelles, Hachée, Italienne, Périgueux, Piquante, Romaine, Soubise, Tomate etc.

2584 LONGE DE VEAU—LOIN OF VEAL

The loin of veal is the equivalent of the sirloin of beef, that is to say it is that part of the carcase lying between the top of the leg and the first ribs.

The loin of veal may be roasted or braised; for braising it is more usually completely boned out leaving the flank a little longer; it is then rolled on to the flank, enclosing the lightly defatted kidney.

If the loin is not required boned, the kidney should be left attached but not trimmed of its fat and the chine bone should be trimmed to facilitate carving when cooked.

The following are a selection of various methods suitable for the loin of veal.
Braised whole or boned and rolled: à l'Alsacienne, à la Berrichonne, à la Financière, à la Jardinière, à l'Oseille, à la Nivernaise, à la Piémontaise, à la Portugaise, à la Vichy, à la Viroflay.
Braised whole on the bone: à la Bouquetière, à la Chartreuse, à la Flamande.
Boned and braised: à la Bourgeoise.
Roasted or braised in the English style: In this case it is stuffed without being boned out. When cooked it is served with boiled ham.

MOU DE VEAU—CALF'S LIGHTS

2585 Mou de Veau en Civet
Take 1¼ kg (3 lb 6 oz) of calf's lights and well beat with a cutlet bat to expel as much of the air as possible. Cut it into pieces of approximately 50 g (2 oz) in weight, season and fry to colour quickly in butter.

Sprinkle with 50 g (2 oz) flour, place in the oven and cook for a few minutes. Moisten with 1 litre (1¾ pt or 4½ U.S. cups) red wine and 4 dl (14 fl oz or 1¾ U.S. cups) brown stock and mix in. Bring to the boil, add a touch of crushed garlic and a Bouquet garni, cover and cook in the oven for approximately 1½ hours.

When ready remove the pieces of lights, place them in a clean pan and add 15 button onions coloured in butter; 250 g (9 oz) streaky bacon cut in cubes, blanched and fried in butter and 250 g (9 oz) raw mushrooms cut in quarters. Pass the sauce through a fine strainer over the ingredients, cover with a lid and cook very gently in the oven for a further 25 minutes.

Serve in a deep dish or timbale.

2586 Mou de Veau à la Tripière
Take 1¼ kg (3 lb 6 oz) calf's lights and beat with a cutlet bat to expel as much of the air as possible. Cut it into pieces of approximately 50 g (2 oz) in weight, season and fry to colour in butter.

Moisten with 1 litre (1¾ pt or 4½ U.S. cups) stock or water; if water is used, season it proportionately. Add 450 g (1 lb) onions cut in quarters; 1 kg (2¼ lb) potatoes cut in quarters; a touch of crushed garlic and a Bouquet garni. Cover with a lid and cook gently in the oven for approximately 1½ hours.

Serve in a deep dish.

2587 NOIX DE VEAU—CUSHION OF VEAL

The cushion of veal is usually larded but only on the cut part where it is separated from the rest of the leg.

The method of cooking most suitable for the cushion of veal is braising but where it is necessary to cut the joint before presentation it is best if roasted or Poêléed. If braised to the correct point of tenderness, cutting becomes quite difficult; however, if braised to the point where it is still fairly firm, the meat is inclined to be dry and with little flavour. These remarks are also valid for the cooking of the best end and loin of veal.

2588 Noix de Veau à la Briarde

Lard the cushion of veal with strips of salt pork fat, braise it in the manner for white meats (2176) and glaze at the last moment.

When ready, place it on a suitable dish and surround with halves or quarters of lettuce stuffed with Godiveau mixed with a little chopped Fines Herbes and braised.

Serve accompanied with a dish of Carottes à la Crème and the braising liquid after first removing all fat and passing through a fine strainer.

2589 Noix de Veau Chatham

Lard the cushion of veal with strips of salt pork fat, braise it in the manner for white meats (2176) and glaze at the last moment.

Place on a suitable dish and serve accompanied with 1) a timbale of buttered noodles decorated on top with a circle of small ovals of red salt ox-tongue and 2) a thin Sauce Soubise containing some finely sliced cooked mushrooms.

2590 Noix de Veau Lison

Braise the cushion of veal in the manner for white meats without larding it and glaze at the last moment.

Place on a suitable dish and surround with 1) brioche shapes of Pommes Duchesse mixture containing some finely chopped red salt ox tongue, brushed with beaten egg and coloured in a very hot oven and 2) small dariole-sized moulds of chopped braised lettuce mixed with Sauce Béchamel and eggs, cooked *au Bain-marie*.

Serve separately the braising liquid after first removing all fat and passing through a fine strainer.

2591 Noix de Veau Nemours

Lard the cushion of veal with strips of salt pork fat, braise it in the usual manner for white meats and glaze at the last moment.

Place on a suitable dish and surround with alternate bouquets of Carottes à la Vichy, buttered peas and small balls of potatoes cooked gently in butter without colour.

Serve accompanied with the braising liquid after first removing all fat and passing through a fine strainer.

2592 Noix de Veau Renaissance

Braise the unlarded cushion of veal in the usual manner for white meats. Cut a fairly thick slice from the largest area of the meat and place it on a suitable dish. Cut the remaining veal into small even shaped slices and arrange them overlapping in a circle around the edge of the thick slice. Fill the centre with a Financière garnish (381) and on top of this, place a nice bouquet of cooked cauliflower lightly coated with Sauce Hollandaise.

Serve accompanied with the braising liquid after first removing all fat, passing through a fine strainer and reducing it.

2593 Noix de Veau en Surprise

The following recipe has been included here chiefly because of its interest and originality yet at the same time it is suggested that its preparation in this manner should not be too frequently used for inclusion on the menu. It is really the equivalent of Pièce de Boeuf à la Cuiller of the old classical kitchen.

Braise the cushion of veal in the usual manner for white meats but keeping it somewhat firm; allow it to become almost cool.

Cut off the top third of the cushion horizontally then cut round both pieces on their cut sides to within 1½ cm (⅗ in) of the edges. Remove the meat leaving an equal thickness on the bottoms and sides so that the two pieces can then be seen as a hollowed out case and its cover. The meat removed should be kept in as large pieces as possible if required for garnishing the dish.

Fill the prepared case with any suitable garnish; cover with its lid and place in the oven to reheat for service.

Serve the braising liquid separately after first removing all fat and passing through a fine strainer.

2594 Noix de Veau en Surprise à la Macédoine

Braise the cushion of veal and then fashion it into a case and cover as in the preceding recipe; cut the meat removed into neat even-shaped thin slices.

Place a layer of buttered Macédoine of vegetables in the case, cover with an overlapping layer of the slices of meat and repeat this operation until the case is filled, finishing with a layer of Macédoine. Cover with the lid of meat and place in the oven for a few minutes to reheat.

Serve the braising liquid separately.

2595 Garnishes for Braised Cushion of Veal

Suitable garnishes for braised cushion of veal are: Alsacienne, Bouquetière, Bourgeoise, Chartreuse, Choisy, Chicorée, Clamart, Champignons, Epinards, Financière, Italienne, Japonaise, Jardinière, Macédoine, Marigny, Milanaise, Orléanaise, Oseille, Petits Pois, Piémontaise, Portugaise, Romaine, Saint-Mandé, Trianon, Vichy, Viroflay.

NOIX DE VEAU FROIDE—COLD CUSHION OF VEAL

2596 Noix de Veau à la Caucasienne

Cut a cold braised cushion of veal into slices approximately 9 cm (3½ in) long, 4 cm (1⅗ in) wide and 3 mm (⅛) thick. On one side of each slice spread a little seasoned butter mixed with finely chopped chives and anchovy fillets cut in small dice; sandwich them together in pairs, trim the corners and keep under light pressure until required.

Prepare a well reduced purée of fresh tomatoes and mix together with a relative quantity of almost setting aspic jelly. Pour this into a lightly oiled dome shape or Bombe mould and allow it to set firmly on ice.

When quite firm, demould on to the centre of a round dish and surround with the prepared slices of veal arranged overlapping each other.

Border the dish with neat shapes of very clear aspic jelly.

2597 Noix de Veau à la Suédoise

From the top of a very cold cushion of veal cut a horizontal slice approximately 3 cm (1⅕ in) thick, and trim into a neat round shape.

Set a layer of aspic jelly on the bottom of a round dish and place the prepared slice of veal on top.

Cut the rest of the veal into slices approximately 5 cm (2 in) long, 3½ cm (1⅖ in) wide and 6 mm (¼ in) thick; coat one side of each slice with Horseradish Butter (253). Place a very thin slice of ox tongue cut to the same size on top of each buttered slice of veal; firm together and trim the corners. Pipe a very thin decorative border of softened butter round the edges of these veal and tongue sandwiches, using a piping bag and small star tube.

Have prepared a dome-shaped mould of vegetable salad bound with Mayonnaise Collée. When required, demould this on to the centre of a round dish and place on its top a small heart of lettuce, nicely opened. Surround with the prepared slices of veal and tongue and serve accompanied with any derivative of Sauce Mayonnaise.

DERIVATIVES OF CUSHION OF VEAL

2598 ESCALOPES DE VEAU—ESCALOPES OF VEAL

Escalopes of veal should be cut for preference from either the fillet or loin but more usually they are cut from the cushion and should weigh between 100 g (3½ oz) and 110 g (4 oz).

After removing any fat or connective tissue, they are generally flattened very thin by beating with a moistened cutlet bat, then trimmed oval or into curve-sided triangles. Because of their thinness they are then usually flour, egg and breadcrumbed then quickly shallow fried on both sides in clarified butter.

Accompanying sauces and garnishes are best served separately when the escalopes have been breadcrumbed except in the case of purées of green vegetables—this prevents them becoming soft by contact with moisture.

The following are suitable for serving with escalopes of veal.

Garnishes: Chicorée au Jus or à la Crème, Crosnes, Spinach, Jardinière or Macédoine of vegetables, Sorrel, Peas, Asparagus tips, etc.

Purées of Vegetables: Carrots, Celery, Peas, Potatoes.

Sauces: Bordelaise au Vin Blanc, Chasseur, Demi-glace, Fines Herbes, Provençale, Soubise, Tomato.

2599 Escalopes de Veau à l'Anglaise

Season the escalopes, flour, egg and breadcrumb then shallow fry quickly in clarified butter.

Arrange overlapping on a dish, alternating with slices of ham fried in butter. Coat with Beurre Noisette.

2600 Escalopes de Veau aux Champignons

Season the escalopes, flour, egg and breadcrumb them and shallow fry quickly in clarified butter.

Arrange on a suitable dish and serve accompanied with a Sauce Champignons.

2601 Escalopes de Veau Milanaise

Season the escalopes, flour, egg and breadcrumb them using fine breadcrumbs mixed with grated Parmesan cheese. Shallow fry quickly in clarified butter.

Arrange overlapping in a circle on a round dish and fill the centre with a Milanaise garnish (418).

2602 Escalopes de Veau à la Viennoise

Proceed in the same manner as for Côte de Veau à la Viennoise (2537).

2603 FRICANDEAU

The Fricandeau is a slice of veal cut from the cushion along the fibres of the meat and should not be thicker than 4 cm ($1\frac{3}{5}$ in)

After beating with a cutlet bat to break the fibres it is finely larded with thin strips of salt pork fat; this larding is absolutely essential otherwise it becomes just another piece of veal.

The Fricandeau is always braised and this should be taken to its utmost possible limits, inasmuch as it should be possible to serve it in portions when ready, with a spoon.

However, if required in individual portions it should be kept a little firmer. All the garnishes for Noix de Veau are suitable for Fricandeau of veal with the exception of those for Noix de Veau en Surprise.

2604 Cold Fricandeau
A cold Fricandeau makes an excellent luncheon dish.

When almost cold, place it on a dish and surround it with its braising liquid after first removing all fat and passing through a fine strainer. This will set in a jelly and is the finest possible accompaniment for a cold Fricandeau.

Allow to become quite cold and just before serving brush the surface of the meat with a little almost setting jelly so as to give a nice glossy appearance.

2605 GRENADINS

A Grenadin is nothing more than a small Fricandeau. They are cut like escalopes of veal but thicker and not so large, and are then finely larded with thin strips of salt pork fat. They should then be carefully braised, basting frequently then glazed at the last minute.

All of the garnishes for Côte de Veau except those which include a forcemeat, are suitable for Grenadins as are also those for Noix de Veau such as Briarde, Chartreuse, Chatham, Champignons, Epinards, Financière, Japonaise, Jardinière, Milanaise, Orléanaise, Nemours, Sorrel, Peas, Asparagus tips, Vichy.

2606 Cold Grenadins
Cold Grenadins make an excellent Entrée for lunch when prepared *en Belle-vue*. See the two methods indicated for Côte de Veau en Belle-vue (2539).

2607 MEDAILLONS AND NOISETTES

As their names suggest, *Médaillons* and *Noisettes* are round shaped and are cut for preference from the fillet of veal. It is usual to cut them approximately $1\frac{1}{4}$ cm ($\frac{1}{2}$ in) thick and to serve 2 per portion. Both names are interchangeable and there is no difference in their shape.

They should always be shallow fried in clarified butter; braising only tends to make them dry and tough.

All of the methods and garnishes indicated for Côtes de Veau are suitable.

2608 OREILLES DE VEAU—CALVES' EARS

No matter what their final preparation may be, calf's ears should first be well washed, well cleaned, the inside of the ears scraped to remove the thin skin then well blanched and cooled under cold running water.

2609 Oreilles de Veau Farcies—Stuffed Calf's Ears
Fill the opening of each ear with Panada and Butter forcemeat (286); cover the forcemeat with a round slice of carrot; envelop each ear in a piece of muslin and tie carefully.

Poach very slowly in good brown stock for at least 2 hours.

When ready, remove the string and muslin, place the ears in a dish and simply surround with a little of the reduced cooking liquid.

2610 Oreilles de Veau Frites—Fried Calf's Ears
Braise the calf's ears with Madeira wine and allow to become cold. Cut them into strips, pass through frying batter and deep fry as required in hot fat.

Drain well and arrange on a folded serviette placed on a dish; garnish with fried parsley and serve accompanied with Tomato Sauce.

2611 Oreilles de Veau Grillées à la Diable—Grilled Devilled Calf's Ears
Braise the calf's ears and cut each in two along its length. Coat with made mustard, dip into melted butter then coat with breadcrumbs; sprinkle with melted butter and grill gently.

Serve acccompanied with Sauce Diable.

2612 Oreilles de Veau à l'Italienne
Braise the calf's ears and cut them into sections.

Cover the bottom of a dish with thick Sauce Italienne and arrange the prepared ears on top.

2613 Oreilles de Veau en Tortue
Braise the calf's ears with Madeira wine. Nick the thin edges of the ears and turn them over to make a fan shape. Arrange in a suitable dish and surround with a Tortue garnish (462).

2614 Oreilles de Veau à la Toulousaine
Cook the calf's ears in a fairly thin *Blanc*. Drain well, nick the thin edges of the ears and turn them over to make a fan shape. Place a small truffle in the cavity of each ear, arrange on a suitable dish and surround with a Toulousaine garnish (463).

2615 PIEDS DE VEAU—CALF'S FEET

The calf's feet should be well cleaned, blanched and made cold by placing under cold running water. They should then be split in two lengthways, the bones removed then either cooked in a *Blanc* or braised, as required.

2616 Pieds de Veau Custine
Braise the prepared calf's feet, cut them into small square pieces and mix into a thick well reduced Sauce Duxelles containing sliced cooked mushrooms.

Allow the mixture to cool then divide into equal pieces approximately 80 g (3 oz) in weight. Envelop each piece in caul and lightly flatten. Place on a buttered tray, sprinkle with melted butter and place in a very hot oven to colour.

Serve accompanied with Sauce Demi-glace.

2617 Pieds de Veau Frits—Fried Calf's Feet
Braise the prepared calf's feet and cut each half into two pieces. Coat each piece with made mustard, dip into melted butter then into fine breadcrumbs; then pass through beaten egg and then again through breadcrumbs.

Deep fry in hot oil when required and arrange on a serviette placed on a dish. Garnish with fried parsley and serve accompanied with Tomato Sauce.

2618 Pieds de Veau Grillés—Grilled Calf's Feet
Braise the prepared calf's feet and cut each half into two pieces. Coat with made mustard, dip into melted butter, coat with breadcrumbs then sprinkle with melted butter and grill gently.

Serve accompanied with Sauce Diable.

2619 Pieds de Veau à la Poulette
Cook the prepared calf's feet in a *Blanc* then cut each half into three pieces. Place into a suitable quantity of Sauce Poulette, mix in gently then place in a deep dish or timbale. Sprinkle with a little chopped parsley.

2620 Pieds de Veau à la Rouennaise
Prepare in exactly the same way as for Pieds de Mouton à la Rouennaise (2803).

2621 Pieds de Veau à la Tartare
These may be either grilled or fried. Serve accompanied with Sauce Tartare.

2622 Pieds de Veau en Tortue
Braise the prepared calf's feet, cut each half in two, place in a suitable dish and surround with a Tortue garnish (462).

2623 Pieds de Veau à la Vinaigrette
Cook the prepared calf's feet in a *Blanc*. Arrange on a serviette placed on a dish and garnish with picked parsley. Serve accompanied with Sauce Vinaigrette.

2624 POITRINE DE VEAU—BREAST OF VEAL

If the breast of veal is to be used whole it is usually boned out carefully then cut open along its length to form a pocket; this is filled with a stuffing then sewn up with coarse thread.

The following stuffing is the one most commonly used.

1 kg (2¼ lb) very fine pork sausage meat, 125 g (4½ oz) dry Duxelles, 125 g (4½ oz) butter, 1 tbs chopped parsley and tarragon, 1 egg, salt, pepper and a touch of mixed spice. Mix all these ingredients well together.

Braise the prepared breast very slowly and gently and with a minimum of liquid, basting frequently and glaze it at the end of the process in the usual manner.

A whole stuffed breast weighing 5 kg (11¼ lb) will take approximately 3½–4 hours of cooking time.

This dish is more suited to service as a luncheon dish and may suitably be garnished with any of the pastas, purées or green vegetables.

2625 Poitrine de Veau à l'Alsacienne
Stuff the breast of veal as explained above and braise it in the usual manner. When half cooked, remove the breast and place it in a clean pan; surround with well blanched sauerkraut containing trimmings of foie gras and finish cooking together gently.

When ready, place the sauerkraut in a suitable dish, discard the thread from the breast, slice the breast and arrange it overlapping on top of the sauerkraut.

Serve the well reduced braising liquid separately.

2626 Poitrine de Veau à l'Anglaise
Stuff the breast of veal with the mixture as indicated for Epaule de Veau à l'Anglaise and cook

very gently in white stock or more simply in salted water.

Serve accompanied with a piece of boiled ham or bacon.

2627 Poitrine de Veau aux Céleris

Stuff the breast of veal and braise it. When two-thirds cooked, remove it and place in a clean pan. Surround with trimmed and blanched heads of celery, cover with the braising liquid passed through a fine strainer and complete the cooking of the breast and celery together; glaze the veal at the last moment.

Arrange the breast on a suitable dish surrounded by the celery and accompanied with the reduced braising liquid after first removing all fat.

2628 TENDRONS DE VEAU—VEAL TENDONS

The tendons of veal are obtained from the breast of veal and are in fact the ends of the ribs up to and including the *Sternum*. They should be cut to include the whole width of the breast to be correctly termed tendons; if cut across the breast into smaller square pieces they become just other useful pieces of the breast, suitable for stews and sautés.

If to be served braised the tendons should first be coloured in hot fat then braised in the usual manner. It is preferable, however, to cook them as one would a piece of veal *en Casserole*, that is to say, quickly set the tendons in hot butter, add just a little excellent veal stock, then cook gently in the oven, covered and with frequent basting so as to glaze the pieces nicely. A little more liquid should be added as and when necessary.

Suitable garnishes for Tendons of Veal: Bourgeoise, Catalane, Champignons, Chasseur, Hongroise, Jardinière, Milanaise, Montmorency, Petits Pois, Printanière, Provençale, Vichy.

2629 Tendron de Veau à l'Estragon

Prepare the tendons of veal as explained above adding a Bouquet of tarragon stalks during the cooking process.

When cooked, place the tendons of veal on a suitable dish and decorate each with leaves of blanched tarragon.

Lightly thicken the braising liquid with arrowroot, add a little chopped blanched tarragon and serve separately.

2630 Tendron de Veau à la Turque

Prepare and braise the tendons in the usual manner for white meats (2176). Cut the required number of eggplants into halves, deep fry in oil and empty them of their flesh. Chop this flesh fairly finely and mix together with a suitable amount of Riz à la Grecque. Fill the empty halves with this mixture and place one tendon on top of each. Coat with Sauce Mornay and glaze quickly in a hot oven.

2631 Tendron de Veau en Blanquette—au Currie—Marengo—à la Paysanne—à la Printanière

These dishes may be prepared by following the various directions to be found under these names in the section 'Other Preparations of Veal'.

2632 Tendron de Veau en Chaud-froid

Prepare the tendons of veal as Fricassée (2730) and allow to become cold.

Set a thin layer of aspic jelly on a suitable dish, arrange the tendons on this jelly separate from each other and garnish each with the onions and mushrooms. Coat with the sauce to which has been added sufficient aspic jelly and allow to set in a cold place.

When required, cut round each tendon with the point of a small knife, place the dish for a few seconds on a piece of cloth dipped in hot water so they can be detached from the bottom of the dish.

Remove the tendons and arrange on a very cold dish for service.

2633 QUASI AND ROUELLE DE VEAU

The *Quasi* or *Cul de Veau* is the equivalent in English to the aitchbone of veal and is that part of the carcase found between the end of the saddle and the leg proper. It is best cooked slowly *en Casserole* with butter and very little liquid and should be turned and basted frequently during the cooking process.

The *Rouelle* of Veal is a fairly thick slice cut across the leg of veal. It may be cut as thick as required and is best cooked in the same manner as the *Quasi*.

All the garnishes indicated for the cushion of veal are suitable.

2634 RIS DE VEAU—VEAL SWEETBREADS

Veal sweetbreads are one of the finest delicacies provided by the butcher and may be served for any meal, no matter how rich or sumptuous.

They should be selected very white, free from blood and should then be soaked in cold running water for as long as possible or at least in frequent changes of water.

The sweetbreads are then blanched, that is, placed in cold water, brought to the boil, simmered for a few minutes to firm the outside surfaces and then plunged into cold water.

When cold, trim them of all gristle and connective tissue, place between two clean cloths and lightly press them under weight for approximately 2 hours.

Now lard them with fine strips of salt pork fat, tongue or truffle according to the requirements of the way in which they are to be served. They may also be studded with tongue or truffle or simply braised as they are without larding or studding.

Veal sweetbreads are of two kinds, unequal in shape as in quality. They are the *Noix* (heart sweetbread) which is round and plump in shape and of superb quality and the *Gorge* (throat sweetbread) which is longer in shape and inferior in quality to the former.

As far as possible, for any special dinner of quality, only the *Noix* sweetbread should be served. According to requirements they may be braised, poached in white stock or grilled. For these methods of cooking see the braising of white meats and poaching and grilling at the beginning of this Chapter.

2635 Attereaux de Ris de Veau Villeroy

Prepare some sweetbreads and braise them in the usual manner for white meats. Allow them to become cold then cut into round slices approximately 1 cm ($\frac{2}{5}$ in) thick and trim them with a round cutter approximately $3\frac{1}{2}$ cm ($1\frac{2}{5}$ in) in diameter. Prepare also an equal number of mushrooms and truffles cut to the same shape but a little thinner.

Impale these items alternately on to small thin wooden skewers, then dip each into Sauce Villeroy. Place them on a dish, allow to become cold, then pass through flour, beaten egg and fine white breadcrumbs. Roll them gently on a board so as to mould them in the shape of a cylinder.

When required, deep fry the Attereaux in hot fat, drain them well, remove the wooden skewers carefully and replace these with the special silver skewers.

Present the Attereaux on a folded serviette on a dish and garnish with fried parsley. Alternatively, stick them upright into a mould of rice or semolina placed in the centre of a dish and garnish with fried parsley.

Serve Sauce Périgueux separately.

Note: For other considerations concerning Attereaux see the section on Hot Hors-d'oeuvre.

2636 Ris de Veau Bonne Maman

Cut the vegetables for braising the sweetbreads into a short fairly thick Julienne and add to it an equal quantity of celery cut in the same manner.

Braise the sweetbreads on this Julienne with a little excellent veal stock, taking care that the vegetables do not colour on the bottom of the pan; glaze the sweetbreads at the last moment.

Arrange them in a deep dish or cocotte with the vegetables and the reduced cooking liquid, cover with a lid and present the dish on a folded serviette for service.

2637 Ris de Veau à la Broche

Lard the prepared sweetbreads with fine strips of salt pork fat. Enclose each in buttered paper then impale them on the roasting spit. Spit roast them for approximately 45 minutes, remove the paper and continue cooking for another 10 minutes basting frequently with a little good veal gravy so as to glaze them.

Serve on a suitable dish accompanied with a suitable sauce or garnish.

2638 Ris de Veau en Caisses

Braise the sweetbreads white and cut them into slices. Arrange the slices in small buttered paper cases, or in one large case, with an equal amount of sliced truffle and mushrooms. Coat with Sauce Allemande and decorate the surface with a few slices of glazed truffle.

2639 Ris de Veau à la Cévenole

Braise the prepared sweetbreads and glaze them at the last moment.

Arrange on a suitable dish surrounded by bouquets of glazed button onions and braised and glazed chestnuts; separate these bouquets with Croûtons of brown bread cut to the shape of cockscombs and fried in clarified butter.

Serve accompanied with the lightly thickened braising liquid.

Note: The glazed chestnuts are sometimes replaced by a purée of chestnuts which should be served separately.

2640 Ris de Veau Chambellane

Lard the sweetbreads with truffle, braise them and glaze at the last moment.

Arrange on a suitable dish and surround with tartlet-shape moulds of Mousseline forcemeat filled with a Salpicon of truffle mixed with a little Sauce Demi-glace. These moulds should be prepared in small fluted petit fours moulds which have first been well buttered and a slice of truffle placed at the bottom.

Serve accompanied with a light purée of mushrooms mixed with a fine Julienne of truffle.

2641 Chartreuse de Ris de Veau

Prepare 1) thin round batons of carrots and turnips

cut with a column cutter, cooked in a little Bouillon, then well drained and allowed to become cold; 2) some cooked peas and French beans likewise drained and cold.

Line a well buttered Charlotte mould with these vegetables according to taste but taking care that the colours are arranged alternately. Spread a layer of panada and cream forcemeat (287) over the lining of vegetables so as to keep them in place. Place the mould in a tray of hot water and place in a moderate oven to cook the forcemeat.

Now fill the mould with layers of sliced braised sweetbreads, sliced cooked mushrooms and slices of truffle and interposed with layers of Sauce Allemande.

Finish with a layer of the same forcemeat and cover this with a round piece of buttered paper.

Place the prepared Chartreuse in a tray of hot water and place in a moderate oven to cook, allowing 45 minutes for a 1 litre (1¾ pt or 4½ U.S. cups) mould.

When ready, remove the Chartreuse and allow it to rest for 7–8 minutes so as to allow the contents to settle.

Demould when required on to a round dish; place a large white, grooved mushroom on top and surround this with neat, well trimmed halves of braised lettuce.

Serve accompanied with Sauce Allemande finished with mushroom essence.

2642 Ris de Veau Comtesse

Stud the prepared sweetbreads with truffle, braise them and glaze at the last moment.

Arrange on a suitable dish and surround with halves of braised lettuce, alternating with small oval decorated Quenelles of forcemeat cooked as required.

Serve accompanied with Jus lié.

2643 Crépinettes de Ris de Veau

For this dish use, for preference, blanched or unblanched throat sweetbreads and any trimmings left over from other preparations.

Chop the sweetbreads together with half their weight of raw calf's udder. To 1 kg (2¼ lb) of this mixture add and mix in well 150 g (5 oz) chopped truffle, 2 eggs, salt, pepper and a little grated nutmeg.

Divide the mixture into pieces of 100 g (3½ oz) and envelop each in a piece of pig's caul. Sprinkle with melted butter and breadcrumbs and grill gently.

Serve accompanied with Sauce Périgueux.

2644 Coquilles de Ris de Veau au Gratin

Proceed in the same manner as indicated for Coquilles de Cervelle, using slices of braised or poached sweetbreads.

2645 Coquilles de Ris de Veau à la Parisienne

Proceed in the same manner as indicated for Coquilles de Cervelle à la Parisienne using slices of poached sweetbreads.

2646 Cromesquis de Ris de Veau

Proceed in the same manner as indicated for Cromesquis d'Amourettes using braised throat sweetbreads instead of Amourettes.

2647 Croquettes de Ris de Veau

Proceed in the same manner as indicated for any of the Croquettes de Volaille.

2648 Croustades de Ris de Veau Financière

See Hot Hors-d'oeuvre (1165).

2649 Ris de Veau Demidoff

Lard the sweetbreads with strips of salt pork fat and truffle. Braise them brown but only half cook.

Place them in a shallow earthenware cocotte and surround with a proportionate garnish of carrots and turnips cut crescent shape, rings of small onions and some celery cut Paysanne fashion, all lightly stewed in butter. Add 30 g (1 oz) sliced truffle for each sweetbread and the braising liquid passed through a fine strainer.

Cover the dish with its lid and complete the cooking in a moderate oven.

When ready, remove any fat and serve as it is in the cocotte.

2650 Escalopes de Ris de Veau Favorite

Blanch the sweetbreads, cool them under light pressure and cut into slices.

Season and flour these slices and shallow fry on both sides in clarified butter.

Prepare at the same time an equal number of slices of foie gras of the same size and likewise, season, flour and shallow fry them in clarified butter.

Arrange the slices of sweetbreads and foie gras overlapping and alternating in a circle on a round dish and decorate each with a slice of truffle. In the centre, place a garnish of buttered asparagus tips and serve accompanied with a Sauce Madère flavoured with truffle essence.

2651 Escalopes de Ris de Veau Grand-Duc

Blanch the sweetbreads well; cool them and cut into slices.

Season the slices and shallow fry in clarified butter without colouring them.

Arrange overlapping in a circle on a round dish, placing a slice of truffle between each. Coat with Sauce Mornay and glaze quickly in a hot oven.

On removing the dish from the oven, place a garnish of buttered asparagus tips in the centre of the circle of sweetbreads.

2652 Escalopes de Ris de Veau Judic

Blanch the sweetbreads well; cool them and cut into slices.

Prepare and poach a roll of chicken forcemeat large enough so that slices cut from it can be of the same size as the sweetbreads.

Season, flour and shallow fry the slices of sweetbread in clarified butter.

Arrange these in a circle on a round dish, each placed on a slice of the poached chicken forcemeat. Place on top of each escalope a small, well trimmed half of braised lettuce, a slice of truffle and a cock's kidney.

Serve accompanied with Jus lié.

2653 Escalopes de Ris de Veau Maréchal

Braise the sweetbreads keeping them a little firm, then cut them into slices.

Flour, egg and breadcrumb them, shallow fry in clarified butter and arrange in a circle on a round dish with a slice of truffle on top of each. In the centre of the dish place a garnish of buttered asparagus tips.

2654 Escalopes de Ris de Veau Rossini

Proceed in the same manner as indicated for Escalopes de Ris de Veau Favorite omitting the garnish of asparagus tips.

2655 Escalopes de Ris de Veau Villeroy

Braise the sweetbreads keeping them a little firm. Cut them into slices, dip into Sauce Villeroy then place on a tray to cool thoroughly.

When cold, flour, egg and breadcrumb them and deep fry in hot fat when required. Arrange on a folded serviette and garnish with fried parsley.

Serve accompanied with a Sauce Périgueux.

Note: In former times and even not so long ago, dishes prepared *à la Villeroy* being, of course, deep fried, were served without any accompanying sauce.

Modern practice has established the custom of serving either Sauce Périgueux or Sauce Tomate according to the dictates of the menu. In some establishments Sauce Tomate only is served. Sauce Périgueux is, however, to be preferred as an accompaniment for items prepared *à la Villeroy* especially when some degree of precision is required.

2656 Ris de Veau Excelsior

Lard the sweetbreads with truffle and poach them in excellent white stock.

Prepare at the same time some small Quenelles of Mousseline forcemeat of chicken moulded with teaspoons, one-third of them containing finely chopped truffle, one-third containing finely chopped red tongue and the remaining third left plain. Cook these Quenelles in the usual manner so that they are ready at the same time as the sweetbreads.

Arrange the sweetbreads on a suitable dish surrounded with bouquets of the three types of Quenelles and serve accompanied with a creamed Sauce Soubise containing a fine Julienne of truffle, mushrooms and tongue.

2657 Ris de Veau Financière

Lard the sweetbreads with strips of salt pork fat, braise them and glaze at the last moment.

Arrange on a suitable dish surrounded by the items of a Financière garnish (381) arranged in bouquets.

Serve accompanied with a Sauce Financière.

2658 Ris de Veau au Gratin

Braise the sweetbreads in the usual manner. Cut into slices and reform to its original shape, spreading a spoonful of reduced Sauce Duxelles between each slice.

Place on a buttered gratin dish and surround with small cooked mushrooms; cover with Sauce Duxelles, sprinkle with breadcrumbs and melted butter and gratinate quickly in a hot oven.

When ready, sprinkle with a few drops of lemon juice and chopped parsley.

2659 Ris de Veau Grillé—Grilled Calf's Sweetbread

Blanch the sweetbread, cool, trim and allow it to become quite cold under light pressure.

Cut the sweetbread in half horizontally along its length, season, dip into butter and grill it gently—the sweetbread may be grilled whole although the first method is to be preferred.

Serve accompanied with a suitable sauce such as Italienne, Tomate, Périgueux etc. or a partly melted Maître d'Hôtel Butter. It may be garnished to choice.

2660 Ris de Veau Grillé Châtelaine

Prepare and cook an unsweetened Brioche in a fluted mould the opening of which should be somewhat larger than the sweetbread.

Cut off the top of the Brioche, then remove the interior following the shape of the fluting. Fill the resulting case two-thirds full with a mixture of large dice of mushrooms, truffle and foie gras mixed with Sauce Allemande.

Have ready the sweetbread, grilled whole then place it on top of the prepared Brioche case.

2661 Ris de Veau Grillé Gismonda
Prepare a lightly baked oval flan case of the same length as the sweetbread; grill the sweetbread whole.

Garnish the bottom of the flan case with equal quantities of sliced artichoke bottoms and mushrooms, cooked in butter and mixed with a little Cream Sauce.

Place the sweetbread on top of this garnish and arrange on a folded serviette to serve.

Serve accompanied with a lightly buttered meat glaze.

2662 Ris de Veau Grillé Jocelyn
Cut 3 cm ($1\frac{1}{5}$ in) thick slices from a large potato of the same width as the sweetbread. Trim them neatly then using a round plain pastry cutter, stamp the slices near to the edges but not right through to the bottoms; cook in butter. Grill the sweetbread at the same time.

Scoop out the insides of the cooked slices of potato so as to give them the appearance of cases; fill these with curry-flavoured Sauce Soubise. Arrange them on a suitable dish and place the grilled sweetbread on top. On the sweetbread lay half a grilled tomato and half a grilled green pimento.

2663 Ris de Veau Grillé Saint-Germain
Blanch, prepare and grill the sweetbread in the usual manner.

Place on a suitable dish and surround with a bouquet of small potatoes cooked in butter to a golden brown and a bouquet of carrots trimmed olive shape, cooked in a little Bouillon and glazed.

Serve accompanied with a sauceboat of Sauce Beárnaise and a dish of a purée of fresh peas.

2664 Ris de Veau des Gourmets
Braise the sweetbreads and as soon as they are ready, place them in a round shallow cocotte just large enough to hold them.

Cover with thick slices of raw truffle and add the braising liquid passed through a fine strainer. Cover with the lid and seal this to the edges of the dish with a band of paste simply made from flour and water.

Place in a very hot oven for 10 minutes and serve as it is. The cover should only be removed when the dish is at the table.

2665 Ris de Veau Montauban
Lard the sweetbreads with truffle and salt pork fat; braise them and glaze at the last moment.

Arrange on a suitable dish and surround with small Croquettes of rice and red tongue; thick slices cut from a large poached sausage shape of chicken and cream forcemeat mixed with chopped truffle, and small grooved mushrooms.

Serve separately a Velouté of veal flavoured with mushroom essence.

2666 Ris de Veau en Papillote
Braise the sweetbread and cut it into slices along its length then proceed in the same manner as indicated for Côte de Veau en Papillote (2529).

2667 Ris de Veau à la Parisienne
Lard the sweetbreads with truffle and tongue, braise them and glaze at the last moment.

Arrange on a suitable dish and surround with artichoke bottoms and potatoes prepared in accordance with garnish à la Parisienne (438).

Serve accompanied with the braising liquid after first passing through a fine strainer and reducing it.

2668 Pâté Chaud de Ris de Veau
Line a buttered Charlotte or ordinary round raised pie mould with short paste, then cover this lining with a 1 cm ($\frac{2}{5}$ in) thick layer of chicken forcemeat.

Almost fill the prepared mould with a mixture of slices of sweetbread cooked in butter and lightly coloured, sliced and cooked mushrooms and sliced truffle, all mixed together with a reduced and fairly thick Sauce Allemande flavoured with mushroom essence.

Cover this mixture with a layer of the same forcemeat and then close the pie with a thin layer of short paste. Seal the edges of the paste well by pinching all round the edges of the mould. Cover with a layer of imitated leaves cut from short paste, brush with beaten eggs and make a hole in the centre for the escape of steam. Allow to rest for a while then bake in a hot oven for 45–50 minutes.

On removing from the oven, demould carefully and present on a serviette laid on a suitable dish.

2669 Ris de Veau Princesse
Stud the sweetbreads with truffle, braise them and glaze at the last moment.

Cover the bottom of a deep dish with a layer of buttered asparagus tips, place the sweetbreads on top of this and surround with a border of overlapping slices of truffle.

Serve accompanied with a Sauce Allemande flavoured with mushroom essence.

2670 Ris de Veau aux Queues d'Ecrevisses
Stud the sweetbreads with truffle and braise them without colour.

Arrange on a suitable dish and surround with

bouquets of crayfish tails mixed with a little Cream Sauce allowing 4 tails per person.

At either end of the dish place some crayfish carapaces filled with chicken forcemeat mixed with Crayfish Butter and poached. Allow two of these for each sweetbread.

2671 Ris de Veau Rachel
Lard the sweetbreads with salt pork fat, braise them and glaze at the last moment.

Arrange on a suitable dish and surround with small artichoke bottoms filled with thick Sauce Bordelaise; on top of this, place a slice of poached beef bone marrow with a pinch of chopped parsley in its centre.

Either serve the strained braising liquid separately or pour it around the bottom of the dish.

2672 Ris de Veau Régence
Stud the sweetbreads with truffle and either braise or Poêlé them.

Arrange on a suitable dish and surround with the reduced and strained braising liquid and the items of a Régence garnish for poultry (449).

Serve accompanied with Sauce Allemande flavoured with truffle essence.

2673 Ris de Veau sous Croûte
Stud the sweetbreads with truffle and tongue and three parts braise them.

Cut an equal number of slices of salt ox tongue of the same size as the sweetbreads and place each of these in the centre of a layer of paste with a sweetbread on top. Moisten the edges of the paste, then fold over so as to completely enclose the sweetbreads and seal the edges carefully.

Place on a tray, brush with beaten egg and make an opening in the top of each for the steam to escape. Bake in a hot oven for 45 minutes and on removing from the oven, fill them through the holes in the top with Sauce Demi-glace.

Present on a folded serviette. The covering paste is broken at the table for service.

2674 Ris de Veau à la Toulousaine
Stud the sweetbreads with truffle and braise them.

Arrange on a suitable dish and surround with bouquets of the items comprising a garnish à la Toulousaine (463).

Serve accompanied with a Sauce Allemande flavoured with mushroom essence.

Note: The dish may be surrounded with a border of small triangular Croûtons of bread, hollowed out slightly on one side, and fried in butter. The hollows should then be filled with a little purée of foie gras.

2675 Timbale de Ris de Veau à la Bâloise
Prepare in advance a Timbale case (4334) moulded in a round mould the sides of which should be flared out at the top. Cook without colour.

Fill the case two-thirds full with Nouilles au Jambon, on top arrange a circle of overlapping slices of braised sweetbread and in the centre of this place a Financière garnish (381).

Present on a serviette on a round dish.

2676 Timbale de Ris de Veau Condé
Prepare a Timbale case (4334) made in a mould which is narrow at the bottom and wider at the top. Cook without colour.

Cover the bottom of the Timbale with sliced mushrooms cooked in butter; cover the sides with slices of braised sweetbread which have been coated dome-shape on one side with chicken forcemeat containing chopped mushrooms and truffle then cooked in a warm oven; these slices should be arranged in superimposed lines.

Fill the centre with slices of truffle mixed with a thick Sauce Madère. Present on a folded serviette on a dish.

Serve accompanied with Sauce Madère.

2677 Vol-au-Vent de Ris de Veau à la Nesles
Prepare a garnish consisting of one braised sweetbread cut in small slices, Quenelles of Godiveau, poached and swollen in advance in a little mushroom cooking liquor and truffle gravy, cooked cockscombs, grooved mushrooms and slices of truffle, all carefully mixed together with a proportionate amount of Sauce Allemande.

Spoon this mixture into a suitable size Vol-au-vent case and in place of the paste cover, arrange a circle of small slices of glazed sweetbread, each decorated with a round slice of truffle.

Present on a serviette on a round dish.

2678 Vol-au-Vent de Ris de Veau Régence
Prepare a garnish comprised of equal quantities of small slices of braised sweetbreads and a Régence garnish for poultry. Carefully mix together with a proportionate amount of Sauce Allemande flavoured with truffle essence.

Spoon this mixture into a suitable size Vol-au-vent case and cover the top with a circle of small slices of glazed sweetbread, each with a small decorated Mousseline of chicken on top.

Present on a serviette on a round dish.

2679 Other Suitable Garnishes for Braised Veal Sweetbreads:
Clamart, Champignons, Jardinière, Milanaise, Oseille, Petits Pois, Pointes d'Asperges, Portugaise etc.

RIS DE VEAU FROIDS— COLD VEAL SWEETBREADS

2680 Ris de Veau Richelieu
Braise the sweetbreads in accordance with the recipe for Ris de Veau Bonne-Maman (2636) using sufficient braising liquid to cover the sweetbreads when placed in a cocotte for service.

When ready, place the sweetbreads in the cocotte with a Julienne of vegetables; surround with a proportionate amount of truffle cut in Julienne and cover with the well strained braising liquid. Allow to become quite cold.

When the braising liquid is well set in a jelly, remove any fat which is on the surface and to serve, present the cocotte on a serviette.

2681 Ris de Veau à la Suédoise
Prepare and poach the sweetbreads. Allow them to become quite cold and cut into thin slices; trim these round with a pastry cutter.

Coat each slice on one side with a little Beurre de Raifort and cover with a slice of cooked ox tongue cut to the same shape.

Have ready a lightly baked flan case of a size proportionate to the number of slices of sweetbread. Garnish this with a layer of vegetable salad mixed with Sauce Mayonnaise then cover it with the prepared slices of sweetbread arranged overlapping in a circle. In the centre place a slightly opened heart of lettuce.

Serve accompanied with Sauce Mayonnaise.

2682 Palets de Ris de Veau à l'Ecarlate
Prepare and poach the sweetbreads and allow them to become quite cold. Cut them into slices approximately 1½ cm (⅗ in) thick and trim round with a pastry cutter. With the same cutter trim twice their number of 3 mm (⅛ in) thick slices of cooked salt ox tongue.

Coat each slice of sweetbread on both sides with a little butter flavoured with mustard, then sandwich each between two slices of the tongue.

Arrange them on a tray and cool thoroughly to set the butter. Glaze with clear aspic jelly and decorate each in the centre with a round slice of truffle.

Arrange them in a circle on a round dish, fill the centre with chopped jelly and decorate the edges of the dish with a border of neat shapes of very clear jelly.

Serve accompanied with a cold Sauce Raifort and a Salade Sicilienne.

2683 ROGNON DE VEAU—VEAL KIDNEY

Veal kidney when required for sauté should have all its fat removed together with any connective tissue and should then be cut into fairly thin slices but not too thin, so as to prevent toughening during the cooking process.

For grilling, the kidney should be trimmed in such a way as to leave it covered with a thin layer of its suet. It should then be cut in half lengthways and impaled on a skewer before grilling.

2684 Rognon de Veau Bercy
Cut the kidney into slices, season and sauté by quickly tossing over in hot butter; drain well.

Heat in the pan ½ tbs chopped shallot, moisten with 1 dl (3½ fl oz or ½ U.S. cup) white wine, reduce by half and add 2 tbs meat glaze and a few drops of lemon juice.

Add the kidney to this sauce and add 60 g (2 oz) butter away from the heat. Pour into a timbale or deep dish and sprinkle with chopped parsley.

2685 Rognon de Veau à la Bordelaise
Cut the kidney into slices, season and sauté by quickly tossing over in hot butter; drain well. Add the kidney immediately to 2 dl (7 fl oz or ⅞ U.S. cup) Sauce Bordelaise with the addition of 100 g (3½ oz) diced poached beef bone marrow, 125 g (4½ oz) sliced flap mushrooms cooked in butter and well drained and a pinch of chopped parsley.

Mix together well and pour into a timbale or deep dish for service.

2686 Rognon de Veau à la Berrichonne
Sauté and colour in butter 125 g (4½ oz) streaky bacon cut in dice and blanched and the same amount of sliced raw mushrooms. Drain both well. In the same butter sauté the sliced and seasoned kidney tossing over quickly and likewise drain.

Deglaze the pan with a little red wine, reduce and add 1½ dl (5 fl oz or ⅝ U.S. cup) Sauce Bordelaise without bone marrow but well buttered.

In this sauce place the kidney, bacon and mushrooms and shake the pan to ensure the complete mixing together of the ingredients.

Pour into a timbale or deep dish and sprinkle with a little chopped parsley.

2687 Rognon de Veau en Casserole
Trim the kidney leaving it covered with a thin layer of suet.

Season it and place in an earthenware casserole with 30 g (1 oz) butter, cover with a lid and place in a medium oven to cook gently for approximately 30 minutes. Turn the kidney frequently whilst cooking.

When ready, sprinkle with a spoonful of good veal gravy and serve it in the dish as it is.

2688 Rognon de Veau Sauté aux Champignons
Proceed in the same manner as indicated for Rognon de Boeuf aux Champignons (2435).

2689 Rognon de Veau en Cocotte
Trim the kidney leaving it covered with a thin layer of its suet. Place a little butter in a china cocotte, heat it, add the seasoned kidney and fry brown on all sides.

Surround with 50 g (2 oz) each of diced streaky bacon, blanched and fried brown in butter, quartered raw mushrooms cooked in butter and potatoes trimmed to the shape of garlic cloves and blanched.

Cover the dish with its lid and complete the cooking in the oven. When ready, add a tablespoon of good veal gravy and serve in the cocotte as it is.

2690 Croûtes aux Rognons
Cut slices of bread from a fancy-shaped loaf about 2½ cm (1 in) thick. Cut around near the edges of each slice and remove the bread from the inside leaving a thin layer at the bottom. Butter the insides and dry out in a medium oven.

Fill these Croûtes with, for example, Rognons de Veau sautés aux Champignons, au Chablis or au Madère etc.

Note: These Croûtes may be cut from an ordinary sandwich loaf in a square or rectangular shape; in this case they should be fried in clarified butter.

2691 Rognon de Veau au Currie à l'Indienne
Cook 60 g (2 oz) chopped onion in a little butter to a light golden brown; add a pinch of curry powder and cook together gently for a few minutes. Add 1 dl (3½ fl oz or ½ U.S. cup) Ordinary Velouté, boil for a few minutes then pass through a fine strainer.

Sauté the sliced and seasoned kidney in butter, tossing over quickly; drain, and add and mix into the prepared sauce.

Serve in a timbale or deep dish accompanied with a dish of plain boiled rice.

2692 Rognon de Veau Grillé—Grilled Veal Kidney
Trim the kidney leaving it covered with a thin layer of its suet. Cut it almost in half lengthways without actually separating the two pieces; push two skewers through and across the opened kidney so as to keep it flat.

Season and grill gently, basting frequently with butter.

Serve accompanied with Beurre Maître d'Hôtel, Beurre Bercy or any other butter suitable for grills.

2693 Rognon de Veau à la Liégeoise
Prepare the kidney as for en Casserole (2687), and one minute before serving add ¼ dl (1 fl oz or ⅛ U.S. cup) flamed gin, 2 crushed juniper berries and 1 tbs of good veal gravy.

When ready, serve the kidney as it is in the casserole.

2694 Rognon de Veau Montpensier
Trim the kidney leaving it covered with a thin layer of its own fat. Cut it across its width into 5 or 6 round slices; season these and shallow fry them quickly on both sides in hot butter. Remove and place on a plate.

Deglaze the pan with 1 tbs Madeira and add ½ dl (2 fl oz or ¼ U.S. cup) melted meat glaze, 50 g (2 oz) butter, a few drops of lemon juice and a pinch of chopped parsley.

Arrange the slices of kidney in a circle in a timbale or on a dish and coat with the prepared sauce. Place a nice bouquet of buttered asparagus tips in the centre with a dozen slices of truffle on top.

2695 Rognon de Veau à la Portugaise
Prepare the kidney and shallow fry in the same way as for Montpensier (2694).

Arrange the slices in a circle on a round dish with a stuffed half tomato on each. Garnish the centre of the dish with a well reduced Tomato Fondue and surround the kidney with the sauce prepared as for Montpensier.

2696 Rognon de Veau au Rizot
Cut the kidney into slices, season and sauté quickly by tossing over in hot butter. Drain well and place in the centre of a border of Risotto. Cover with a thin layer of the same rice then coat with Sauce Mornay and gratinate quickly in a hot oven.

2697 Rognon de Veau Robert
Trim the kidney leaving it covered with a thin layer of its suet. Season and colour it quickly on all sides in a small cocotte with a little butter; cover and place in the oven to cook for 15 minutes. Serve as it is in its cocotte.

The kidney is completed at the table in the following manner: transfer the kidney to a hot plate, place the cocotte on a spirit lamp, deglaze with ½ dl (2 fl oz or ¼ U.S. cup) excellent brandy and reduce by half. Meanwhile, cut the kidney into very thin slices and cover these with an overturned plate.

To the reduced brandy add 1 tsp mustard, 30 g (1 oz) butter in small pieces, the juice of a quarter of lemon and a pinch of chopped parsley. Mix these ingredients well together with a fork then add the prepared slices of kidney along with any of the juices which have drained from it. Reheat together without boiling and serve on hot plates.

2698 Veal Kidney with Various Wines
Prepare the kidney in the manner as described for Rognon de Boeuf au Madère (2437) replacing the Madeira with Chablis, Corton, Lafitte, Port, Saint-Julien, Sherry, Volnay etc. The title of the dish should include the name of the wine, e.g. Rognon de Veau au Chablis.

2699 SELLE DE VEAU—SADDLE OF VEAL

When the saddle of veal is required for serving as a whole joint (Relevé) it should be either braised or roasted. Braising, however, is preferable because it lessens the risk of the saddle becoming dry during the cooking process and in addition it provides an excellent cooking liquid of great value as an accompanying sauce.

Whichever method of cooking is adopted, the saddle should be obtained by cutting across the carcase, first at the front of the bones in the rump and then just before the cutlet bones. Remove the kidneys leaving a sufficiently thick layer of fat to cover the fillets, then trim the thin flanks so that when folded under they just cover the fillets. Finally, cover the saddle with slices of salt pork fat and tie up firmly with string.

If braised, very little liquid should be used and the saddle should be basted frequently whilst cooking. The time required for braising a medium-sized saddle of about 7 kg ($15\frac{1}{2}$ lb) weight would be approximately 3 hours.

Note: For a small number of persons it is permissible to use a half saddle, i.e. the saddle cut in half lengthways through the spinal column.

2700 Selle de Veau à la Chartreuse
Braise the saddle then remove the slices of salt pork fat and glaze it at the last moment.

Place it on a long dish and at each end of the saddle place a Chartreuse of vegetables of about the same height as the saddle. The Chartreuse of vegetables should be prepared in the same way as for Chartreuse de Ris de Veau (2641) but filling them with a Macédoine of vegetables bound with some thick Sauce Béchamel and a little cream.

Surround with a little of the reduced braising liquid after first removing all fat and passing through a fine strainer. Serve what remains in a sauceboat.

2701 Selle de Veau Matignon
Braise the saddle but only half cook it. Remove the fat then cover the saddle with a fairly thick layer of Matignon (321) and again with slices of salt pork fat or thin slices of raw ham. Envelop the whole saddle in thick caul or in a double thickness of caul if necessary. Re-tie with string and braise for a further two hours in a moderate oven.

When cooked, remove the string and present the saddle as it is accompanied with the braising liquid after first removing the fat, passing through a fine strainer and reducing it.

2702 Selle de Veau Metternich
Prepare and braise the saddle.

When ready, trace a line with the point of a knife along the outside edges of the saddle at both sides and ends, cutting just above the inside bones. Cut along the chine bone on either side then carefully separate the two loins from the saddle.

Cut these into slices across the grain slantwise.

In the empty areas on both sides of the saddle left by removing the two loins spread a layer of Sauce Béchamel flavoured with paprika. Replace the slices in their correct order in the saddle so as to re-form it to its original shape, placing between each slice a little of the same sauce and two slices of truffle.

Finally, coat the whole surface of the re-formed saddle with the same sauce and glaze it rapidly under the salamander. Now remove it carefully with a large square metal spatula and transfer it to a suitable dish.

Serve accompanied with 1) a dish of Riz Pilaw and 2) the braising liquid after first removing all fat, passing through a fine strainer and reducing it.

2703 Selle de Veau Nelson
Braise the saddle, remove the meat from both sides exactly as described for Selle de Veau Metternich and cut into slices.

Coat the area left empty by the removal of the two pieces of meat, with a few tablespoons of Sauce Soubise, replace the slices in their correct order, placing between each a thin slice of ham of the same size and a little Sauce Soubise.

Finally, coat the whole surface of the re-formed saddle with a layer about $2\frac{1}{2}$ cm (1 in) thick of Soufflé au Parmesan mixture containing a quarter its volume of truffle purée. Surround the saddle with a strong band of buttered greaseproof paper to keep the soufflé in place and place in a moderate oven for 15 minutes to cook.

On removing the saddle from the oven, remove the paper and send to the table for service without changing the dish.

Serve accompanied with the braising liquor after first removing all fat, passing through a fine strainer and reducing it.

2704 Selle de Veau à l'Orientale
Braise the saddle, remove the meat from both sides exactly as described for Selle de Veau Metternich and cut into slices.

Coat the area left empty with a little curry-flavoured Sauce Béchamel and replace the slices with a little of the same sauce between each so as to reform the saddle.

Finally, cover the whole surface of the saddle with Sauce Béchamel, well flavoured with tomato and glaze it quickly under the salamander. Place on a suitable dish and surround with halves of braised celery cooked with some of the braising liquor of the saddle.

Serve accompanied with the braising liquor and a dish of Riz Pilaw.

2705 Selle de Veau à la Piémontaise
Braise the saddle, remove the meat from both sides exactly as described for Selle de Veau Metternich and cut into slices.

Re-form the saddle as described before using Sauce Béchamel containing 125 g ($4\frac{1}{2}$ oz) each of grated Parmesan and grated white truffle per 1 litre ($1\frac{3}{4}$ pt or $4\frac{1}{2}$ U.S. cups) sauce.

Finally, coat the saddle with more of the same sauce and glaze it quickly under the salamander.

Place on a suitable dish and serve accompanied with 1) the braising liquid after first removing all fat and passing through a fine strainer and 2) a dish of Risotto à la Piémontaise.

2706 Selle de Veau Prince Orloff
Braise the saddle, remove the meat from both sides exactly as described for Selle de Veau Metternich and cut into slices.

Re-form the saddle as described before using Sauce Soubise and a slice of truffle between each slice of meat.

Finally, coat the saddle with Sauce Mornay containing a quarter its volume of Soubise purée and glaze quickly under the salamander.

Place on a suitable dish and serve with the braising liquid after first removing all fat, passing through a fine strainer and reducing it.

Note: The saddle may be accompanied with a dish of asparagus tips or Concombres à la Crème.

2707 Selle de Veau Renaissance
Braise the saddle and glaze it at the last moment.

Place it on a suitable dish with a large bouquet of cauliflower at each end and with the remaining Renaissance garnish (450) arranged on either side in alternate bouquets.

Serve accompanied with 1) Sauce Hollandaise for the cauliflower and 2) the braising liquid after first removing all fat, passing through a fine strainer and reducing it.

2708 Selle de Veau Romanoff
Braise the saddle, remove the meat from both sides exactly as described for Selle de Veau Metternich and cut into slices.

Re-form the saddle as described before placing between each slice a little finely sliced *Gribouis* or flap mushrooms mixed with Sauce Crème.

Coat the surface of the saddle with a well seasoned Sauce Béchamel finished with Crayfish Butter and surround with halves of fennel braised with white wine.

Serve accompanied with the braising liquid after first removing all fat passing through a fine strainer and reducing it.

2709 Selle de Veau Talleyrand
Stud the top of the saddle on both sides symmetrically with large pieces of truffle; wrap it in slices of salt pork fat, then braise and glaze it at the last moment.

Place the saddle on a suitable dish and simply surround it with a little of the braising liquid after first removing all fat, passing through a fine strainer and reducing it.

Serve accompanied with 1) the rest of the braising liquid, and 2) a dish of Macaroni à la Talleyrand (461).

2710 Selle de Veau Tosca
Braise the saddle, remove the meat from both sides exactly as described for Selle de Veau Metternich and cut into slices.

Almost fill the two empty sides of the saddle with short lengths of macaroni, mixed with cream and a good amount of truffle cut in Julienne.

Replace the slices of veal overlapping on top of the macaroni, coating each slice with a little Sauce Soubise and place a slice of truffle between each. The slices of veal will thus be raised above the chine bone.

Coat the surface of the saddle with the same sauce and glaze quickly.

Serve accompanied with the braising liquid after first removing all fat, passing through a fine strainer and reducing it.

2711 Selle de Veau froide—Cold Saddle of Veal
A cold saddle of veal can be a magnificent dish for presentation on the cold buffet

All of the garnishes for cold dishes are suitable such as Macédoine of vegetables bound with Sauce Mayonnaise or jelly, small moulded vegetable salads, artichoke bottoms or tomatoes garnished in various styles etc.

Decorate the saddle with nicely cut shapes of jelly but its essential accompaniment should be its braising liquid, skimmed of all fat, passed through a fine strainer, made cold, then served exactly as it is in a sauceboat. This cooking liquid should not be thickened or clarified.

2712 TETE DE VEAU—CALF'S HEAD

If the calf's head is to be cut in pieces, it should be first carefully boned before soaking in cold water. Then blanch it, make cold in running water, rub with lemon and finally cook in boiling *Blanc*. If to be cooked whole the head should be blanched for at least 30 minutes then cooked likewise in a *Blanc* taking care to wrap it first in a clean cloth so as to facilitate its removal when cooked.

In either case take the necessary steps as indicated in the recipe for Blanc (2181), to prevent the air from coming into contact with the head which, of course, would result in it becoming discoloured.

Whichever way the head is prepared it should always be accompanied with slices of its tongue and brain.

2713 Tête de Veau à l'Anglaise—Boiled Calf's Head, English Style
Cook the head in a light *Blanc* either whole or cut in half; it should not be boned.

Place on a serviette on a dish and serve accompanied with 1) a piece of boiled bacon, and 2) a sauceboat of Parsley Sauce.

2714 Tête de Veau Financière
Cook the head in a *Blanc* then cut it into small 3–4 cm (1¼–1½ in) squares or cut into round pieces with a pastry cutter. Remove most of the meat from the pieces so as to leave only the gelatinous skin.

Place these pieces into a deep dish or timbale along with slices of tongue and brain and cover with a Financière garnish (381).

2715 Tête de Veau Frite—Fried Calf's Head
Cook the head in a *Blanc*, cut it into pieces and trim off all meat just leaving the gelatinous skin. Marinate these pieces for 1 hour with lemon juice, a little oil, chopped parsley and seasoning. Dip each piece into a light frying batter and deep fry when required.

Drain well and arrange on a serviette or grill with fried parsley.

Serve accompanied with Sauce Tomate or Sauce Madère.

2716 Tête de Veau Godard
Calf's head à la Godard was one of the large joints or Relevés of the old classical kitchen. It was always served whole surrounded with its garnish. Today it is served cut into pieces as for Tête de Veau Financière then arranged in a timbale with a Godard garnish (388).

2717 Tête de Veau à la Poulette
Cook the head in a *Blanc* and whilst still hot, cut into small thick slices.

Place these slices into a Sauce Poulette and toss over to mix. Pour into a timbale and sprinkle with chopped parsley.

2718 Tête de Veau à la Ravigote
Prepare in the same way as for à la Poulette replacing the Sauce Poulette with hot well seasoned Sauce Ravigote.

2719 Tête de Veau Tarentaise
Place in a shallow pan 10 pieces of calf's head prepared as for Tête de Veau Financière and 150 g (5 oz) each of slices of red ox tongue and cooked mushroom cut in short thick Julienne. Add 3 dl (½ pt or 1¼ U.S. cups) Sauce Madère and allow to simmer very gently together for 30 minutes. Just before serving add 1 tbs well blanched, fine Julienne of lemon zest.

Place in a deep dish or timbale and surround with 10 halves of hot hard-boiled egg.

2720 Tête de Veau, Sauce Tomate—Calf's Head with Tomato Sauce
Cook the head in a *Blanc* and arrange very hot on a serviette with slices of tongue and brains and surround with a border of picked parsley.

Serve accompanied with Tomato Sauce.

2721 Tête de Veau en Tortue
Cook the head in a *Blanc* then cut into round 4 cm (1¾ in) pieces with a pastry cutter. Remove any flesh from the pieces leaving just the gelatinous skin.

Arrange these in a deep dish or timbale with a Tortue garnish (462) and Sauce Tortue (79).

2722 Tête de Veau à la Toulousaine
Proceed as in the previous recipe replacing the Tortue garnish with a Toulousaine garnish (463).

2723 Tête de Veau à la Vinaigrette, or Tête de Veau à l'Huile
Cook the head in a *Blanc* either whole or in pieces. Arrange on a serviette with slices of tongue and brain and surround with a border of picked parsley.

Send to the table separately, small capers, chopped onion and chopped parsley arranged in bouquets in an Hors-d'oeuvre dish; these ingredients will then be mixed together with oil, vinegar and seasoning. Alternatively a sauceboat of prepared Sauce Vinaigrette may be sent.

2724 Tête de Veau Froide à la Flamande
Bone the head and cut it into two pieces. Cut the tongue in half lengthways, remove the ears and also cut in half lengthways.

Place the two halves of the head face downwards and arrange half a tongue and two pieces of ear on each. Roll up each half of head starting at the muzzle, then tie tightly and closely with string. Cook in a *Blanc* and allow to cool in the cooking liquor.

The two halves of head may be cooked first, then prepared with the ear and tongue, rolled and tied in a serviette and then replaced in the cooking liquor to cool.

When cold, the head should be cut in very thin slices like a galantine and served with slices of brains and a Sauce Remoulade or Sauce Tartare.

2725 TETINE DE VEAU—CALF'S UDDER

Calf's udder is used frequently in Jewish cookery where it takes the place of salt pork.

It may also be braised after first soaking in water, blanching, lightly pressing and larding. Glaze at the last moment and serve accompanied with a garnish of spinach or sorrel.

OTHER PREPARATIONS OF VEAL

BLANQUETTE DE VEAU

For 10 persons allow 1½ kg (3 lb 6 oz)

2726 Blanquette de Veau à l'Ancienne
The parts of veal used in the preparation of Blanquette are the tendons, the shoulder and the neck end.

Cut the veal into small pieces, cover with white stock and add just a little salt. Bring to the boil slowly, stirring the meat frequently and skim with the greatest possible care.

Add a small carrot, one onion stuck with a clove and a Bouquet garni consisting of a leek, parsley stalks and a little thyme and bayleaf. Simmer gently for 1½ hours.

Prepare a Velouté using 100 g (3½ oz) white Roux and 1¾ litres (3 pt or 7½ U.S. cups) of the cooking liquid from the veal; add 100 g (3½ oz) trimmings of fresh mushrooms and allow to cook gently for 15 minutes, skimming the sauce as necessary.

Drain the pieces of veal and trim them as required, place in a clean pan with 20 button onions cooked white and the same number of button mushrooms.

At the last moment finish the sauce with a liaison consisting of 5 egg yolks, 1 dl (3½ fl oz or ½ U.S. cup) cream, and a few drops of lemon juice; adjust the seasoning and add a little grated nutmeg. Pass this sauce through a fine strainer over the veal and the garnish, reheat without boiling, place into a deep dish or timbale and sprinkle with chopped parsley.

2727 Blanquette de Veau aux Céleris, aux Cardons, aux Endives etc.
Prepare the Blanquette as in the preceding recipe and set it to cook. If prepared for the home, the vegetables selected should be simply added at the half-way stage and the cooking of the meat and vegetables would thus take place together. Celery, cardoons or salsify should be cleaned and well blanched and cut into 5–6 cm (2 in) lengths before adding to the Blanquette. If using chicory, it should be three-quarters cooked in the usual manner, cut into portions and then added.

For service in restaurants and hotels it is always better to cook the vegetables separately in some of the cooking liquid from the veal. They should then be well drained and the liquid returned back to the remaining cooking liquid of the veal.

For presentation the vegetables are best arranged on top or around the veal either before or after covering with the sauce.

2728 Blanquette de Veau aux Nouilles, aux Lasagnes, aux Spaghetti etc.
Prepare the Blanquette as in the preceding recipe, lightly blanching the selected pasta and finishing its cooking in the Blanquette, or cooking it separately in some of the cooking liquid. To serve though, the pasta is generally mixed with the pieces of veal before covering with the sauce.

Very often the pastas are completely cooked in salted water, then drained, tossed in butter and flavoured with a touch of grated nutmeg. When ready they are then sent in a separate dish along with the Blanquette. If noodles are used, take care to sprinkle them at the last moment with a few fresh uncooked noodles which have been sautéed in butter at the last moment.

2729 FRICADELLES

Proceed as indicated in the section on beef using either raw or cooked veal in place of beef.

FRICASSEE DE VEAU

2730 Fricassée de Veau
The Fricassée differs from the Blanquette inasmuch as the meat and garnish are cooked directly in its sauce.

Heat the pieces of veal in butter to stiffen and set the outer surfaces without colour. Sprinkle with 40–50 g ($1\frac{1}{2}$–2 oz) of flour per 1 kg ($2\frac{1}{4}$ lb) of veal, cook together for a few minutes then moisten with 1 litre ($1\frac{3}{4}$ pt or $4\frac{1}{2}$ U.S. cups) white stock stirring it in carefully so as to avoid any lumps. Season, add a Bouquet garni and bring to the boil. Finish as indicated for the Blanquette of Veal.

All of the garnishes as indicated for Blanquette are suitable and the sauce is also finished with a liaison of egg yolks and cream.

PAIN DE VEAU

2731 Pain de Veau—Veal Loaf
Veal loaf is made from a veal forcemeat mixture with panada and cream and cooked in a plain mould which has first been buttered and decorated with slices of truffle.

The mixture may also be prepared as indicated for Pain de Foie de Veau (2562) replacing the liver with very white veal.

In certain cases veal loaf may be accompanied with brown sauces or with garnishes comprising a brown sauce. The most usual accompaniment, however, and the most logical is a white sauce such as Velouté à l'Essence de Champignons, Sauce Suprême, Soubise à la Crème etc.

2732 PAUPIETTES DE VEAU

Paupiettes of veal are made from thin slices of veal approximately 12 cm (5 in) long by 5 cm (2 in) wide cut from either the cushion or under cushion. After having lightly flattened and trimmed the slices, cover them with a layer of forcemeat in keeping with their preparation, roll up into the shape of a cork, wrap in a thin layer of salt pork fat and tie them round with thread so that they keep their shape while cooking.

When their garnish comprises tartlet cases, half tomatoes or sections of cucumber or aubergine, the *Paupiettes* should, for preference, be arranged on these items for service.

2733 Paupiettes de Veau à l'Algérienne
Prepare the Paupiettes after first coating the slices of veal with Godiveau containing 100 g ($3\frac{1}{2}$ oz) chopped pimento per 1 kg ($2\frac{1}{4}$ lb) of Godiveau (290).

Braise them and when ready, arrange in a circle placed on small cooked tomatoes. In the centre of the dish place a mound of small Croquettes of sweet potato. Surround the Paupiettes with a *cordon* of thin Tomato Sauce containing a very fine Julienne of pimentos.

2734 Paupiettes de Veau Belle-Hélène
Prepare the Paupiettes, first coating the slices of veal with Godiveau (290).

Braise them and when ready, arrange in a circle with a slice of truffle on each. Place in the centre of the dish a mound of Croquettes of asparagus tips and surround the Paupiettes with a *cordon* of Jus lié.

2735 Paupiettes de Veau à la Brabançonne
Prepare the Paupiettes, first coating the slices of veal with Godiveau (290).

Braise them and when ready, arrange in a circle each placed on a tartlet case filled with small Brussels sprouts gratinated à la Mornay. Place in the centre of the dish a mound of small potato croquettes. Surround with a *cordon* of Jus lié.

2736 Paupiettes de Veau aux Champignons
Prepare the Paupiettes, first coating the slices of veal with a Panada and Cream forcemeat (287) mixed with chopped and squeezed raw mushrooms.

Braise them and when ready, arrange in a circle on a round dish with a very white grooved cooked mushroom on each Paupiette. Pour in the centre of the dish a Sauce aux Champignons well garnished with small button mushrooms.

2737 Paupiettes de Veau Fontanges
Prepare the Paupiettes, first coating the slices of veal with a Panada and Butter forcemeat (286).

Braise them and when ready, arrange in a circle each placed on a small flat, round potato croquette. Place in the centre of the dish a mound of creamed purée of haricot beans and surround the Paupiettes with a *cordon* of the reduced braising liquor.

2738 Paupiettes de Veau à la Hussarde
Prepare the Paupiettes, first coating the slices of veal with Godiveau (290).

Braise them and when ready, arrange in a circle

with small piped shape of Pommes Duchesse coloured in the oven, on each Paupiette.

Surround with very small stuffed tomatoes à la Hussarde (4260).

2739 Paupiettes de Veau Madeleine
Prepare the Paupiettes, first coating the slices of veal with a Panada and Cream forcemeat (287).

Braise them and when ready, arrange in a circle placing each Paupiette on top of an artichoke bottom filled with thick Soubise. Surround with small moulds of purée of haricot beans moulded in dariole moulds.

Serve accompanied with a Sauce Demi-glace containing the well reduced cooking liquid from the Paupiettes.

2740 Paupiettes de Veau Marie-Louise
Prepare the Paupiettes, first coating the slices of veal with a Panada and Cream forcemeat (287).

Braise them and when ready, arrange in a circle on a round dish. Place a small artichoke bottom garnished à la Marie-Louise on top of each Paupiette and surround with the reduced and lightly thickened braising liquid.

2741 Paupiettes de Veau à la Portugaise
Prepare the Paupiettes, first coating the slices of veal with Panada and Cream forcemeat (287).

Braise them and when ready, arrange in a circle each placed on a small stuffed tomato. Fill the centre of the dish with a mound of Pommes Château and surround the Paupiettes with a *cordon* of Sauce Portugaise.

2742 Paupiettes of Veal with Various Garnishes
The Paupiettes are prepared after first coating the slices of veal with a forcemeat in keeping with the selected garnish. After rolling, colouring and braising them, they are arranged in the most suitable manner with the garnish. The following garnishes are suitable: Briarde (2588), Bizontine, Fermière, Milanaise, Noodles, Sorrel, Savary (2487).

Note: In addition to their use as a dish in their own right, Paupiettes of veal may be used as an item for garnishing *Timbales* and may also be used as an extra item for such garnishes as Financière, Milanaise, Napolitaine, fresh Noodles, Lasagnes etc. When prepared for this purpose they should be made only half the usual size or in some cases may be made even smaller.

SAUTES DE VEAU—SAUTES OF VEAL

Sautés of veal are made with the same parts of veal as used for Blanquette and in the same proportions.

2743 Sauté de Veau aux Aubergines
Cut the veal into pieces of approximately 80 g (2½ oz) in weight, season and shallow fry in oil and butter until well coloured on all sides.

Drain off the excess fat, add 120 g (4 oz) chopped onion and a touch of crushed garlic. Cook together for a few minutes, moisten with 1 dl (3½ fl oz or ½ U.S. cup) white wine and reduce almost completely.

Add 1 litre (1¾ pt or 4½ U.S. cups) brown stock, 5 dl (18 fl oz or 2¼ U.S. cups) Tomato Sauce, a Bouquet garni and cook gently in the oven for 1½ hours.

Remove the pieces of veal and place them in a clean pan; pass the sauce through a fine strainer, reduce it by half and pour over the veal.

Reheat, then place into a deep dish or timbale and surround with thick slices of peeled eggplant, seasoned, floured and shallow fried in butter or oil in time to serve.

2744 Sauté de Veau Catalane
Prepare the Sauté of veal as in the preceding recipe.

Remove the pieces of veal, place in a clean pan and add a garnish of peeled, depipped tomatoes cut in quarters and sautéed in butter, chestnuts cooked in a little Bouillon, glazed button onions, chipolata sausages and stoned and blanched olives.

Pass the sauce through a fine strainer over all the ingredients and simmer gently together for 15 minutes. Place in a deep dish or timbale for service.

2745 Sauté de Veau aux Champignons
Season and shallow fry the pieces of veal in oil and butter until well coloured on all sides. Drain off the fat, moisten with 1 litre (1¾ pt or 4½ U.S. cups) brown stock and add 5 dl (18 fl oz or 2¼ U.S. cups) Sauce Demi-glace, and a Bouquet garni. Cook together gently for 1½ hours in the oven.

Remove the pieces of veal and place in a clean pan along with 500 g (1 lb 2 oz) mushrooms cooked in butter.

Pass the sauce through a fine strainer and reduce to ⅓ litre (12 fl oz or 1½ U.S. cups) adding 1½ dl (5 fl oz or ⅝ U.S. cup) mushroom cooking liquor during the reduction. Pour this sauce over the veal and mushrooms and simmer gently for 15 minutes.

Place in a deep dish or timbale for service.

2746 Sauté de Veau Chasseur
Season and shallow fry the pieces of veal in oil and butter until well coloured on all sides. Drain off the fat, moisten with 1¼ litres (2⅕ pt or 5½ U.S. cups) brown stock and add 2 dl (7 fl oz or ⅞ U.S. cup) good tomato purée and a Bouquet garni. Cook together gently for 1½ hours in the oven.

Remove the pieces of veal and place in a clean pan. Pass the cooking liquid through a fine strainer and reduce it almost completely. Add this to $\frac{1}{3}$ litre (12 fl oz or $1\frac{1}{2}$ U.S. cups) of Sauce Chasseur and pour over the veal. Simmer gently for 15 minutes.

Place in a deep dish or timbale and sprinkle with a little roughly chopped and blanched parsley.

2747 Sauté de Veau aux Fines Herbes
Season and shallow fry the pieces of veal in oil and butter until well coloured on all sides. Drain off the fat, moisten with $1\frac{1}{2}$ litres ($2\frac{5}{8}$ pt or $6\frac{1}{2}$ U.S. cups) brown stock, add a Bouquet garni and cook gently for $1\frac{1}{2}$ hours in the oven.

At this stage proceed as for Sauté de Veau Chasseur replacing the Sauce Chasseur with Sauce Fines Herbes.

2748 Sauté de Veau à l'Indienne
Season and shallow fry the pieces of veal in oil until well coloured on all sides; add 180 g (6 oz) chopped onion and a good pinch of curry powder. When all the ingredients are well coloured, drain off the oil and add 50 g (2 oz) flour; mix in and cook for a few minutes. Moisten with $1\frac{1}{2}$ litres ($2\frac{5}{8}$ pt or $6\frac{1}{2}$ U.S. cups) white stock, season, add a Bouquet garni and cook gently for $1\frac{1}{2}$ hours in the oven.

Arrange the pieces of veal in a deep dish or timbale, and pass the sauce through a fine strainer over the meat. Serve accompanied with a dish of plain boiled rice.

2749 Sauté de Veau Marengo
Season and shallow fry the pieces of veal in very hot oil until well coloured on all sides; add 120 g (4 oz) chopped onion and a small clove of crushed garlic. When well coloured together, drain off the oil and add 2 dl (7 fl oz or $\frac{7}{8}$ U.S. cup) white wine and reduce. Moisten with 1 litre ($1\frac{3}{4}$ pt or $4\frac{1}{2}$ U.S. cups) brown stock; add 1 kg ($2\frac{1}{4}$ lb) of peeled, depipped and roughly chopped tomatoes or $7\frac{1}{2}$ dl ($1\frac{1}{3}$ pt or $3\frac{1}{4}$ U.S. cups) Tomato Sauce, and a Bouquet garni. Cook gently for $1\frac{1}{2}$ hours in the oven.

Remove the pieces of veal and place in a clean pan with 20 button onions cooked in butter, 20 button mushrooms and 2 pinches of roughly chopped parsley. Reduce the sauce by one-third and pass it through a fine strainer over the veal and garnish and simmer together for 15 minutes. Remove any oil at the last moment and place in a deep dish or timbale for service; surround with small heart-shaped Croûtons of bread fried in oil or clarified butter.

2750 Sauté de Veau aux Nouilles, aux Spaghetti, aux Lasagnes etc.
Proceed in the same way as for Sauté de Veau aux Champignons replacing the mushrooms with one or other of the pastas as indicated. These should be half cooked and thus will finish cooking in the sauce during the final 15 minutes of simmering.

Place in a deep dish or timbale for service; the selected pasta may be cooked separately and arranged in bouquets around the sides.

2751 Sauté de Veau à l'Oranaise
Proceed for the first stage in the same way as for Sauté de Veau Marengo.

When the pieces of veal have been placed in a clean pan, add 500 g (1 lb 2 oz) peeled, depipped and roughly chopped tomatoes, and 500 g (1 lb 2 oz) chow-chow trimmed to the shape of olives, blanched and shallow fried in butter. Pass the sauce through a strainer over the veal and garnish and simmer gently for a further 15–20 minutes.

Place in a deep dish or timbale and surround with 100 g ($3\frac{1}{2}$ oz) thin rings of onion, seasoned, floured and deep fried in oil.

2752 Sauté de Veau Printanier
Proceed for the first stage as for Sauté de Veau aux Champignons. After one hour's cooking, remove the pieces of veal to a clean pan and add a garnish of small new carrots, turnips, onions and potatoes. Pass the sauce over the veal and garnish and cook for a further 1 hour.

Place in a deep dish or timbale and sprinkle with a few plain boiled peas and diamonds of French beans.

2753 Sauté de Veau à la Portugaise
Proceed in the same way as for Sauté de Veau Marengo.

When the pieces of veal are transferred to a clean pan add, in place of the onions and mushrooms, 1 kg ($2\frac{1}{4}$ lb) peeled, depipped and roughly chopped tomatoes and 2 pinches of roughly chopped parsley.

Pass the sauce through a fine strainer over the whole and simmer gently for a further 20 minutes.

Place in a deep dish or timbale to serve.

MUTTON AND LAMB

From a culinary standpoint there are three kinds of meat provided by the sheep. These are:

1) Mutton—which, correctly speaking, comes from the adult animal.
2) Lamb—which comes from the young weaned animal and is more highly esteemed the younger it is.
3) House or Young Lamb—this is the young unweaned animal which has not commenced

grazing. The Pauillac lamb is the most perfect example of this type.

Ordinary, or as it is sometimes called, grass lamb, is scarcely distinguishable in taste from mutton, excepting the flesh is more tender and delicate; thus the same recipes are suitable for either, taking into account the need to adjust the cooking times in keeping with the quality of the meat.

The flesh of baby or house lamb is white and absolutely different from all others and only a few of the recipes for mutton are suitable. The following recipes are for mutton and lamb and the recipes for baby or house lamb will be found in a separate section in the latter part of this Chapter.

2754 ANIMELLES DE MOUTON

In the cooking of olden times, *Animelles* held a fairly important place; today they are almost completely ignored as an item of food except for a few local cuisines. However, it is thought worthwhile mentioning them.

The *Animelles* should be first scalded and skinned, then soaked for a long time in cold running water. When required they are then dried well and cut into slices.

They may be marinated and deep fried; prepared en Fricassée; cooked in a *Blanc* as a garnish for Tourte or Vol-au-vent; sautéed in the same way as Rognon de Boeuf or cooked in a *Blanc* and served accompanied with Sauce Vinaigrette etc.

2755 BARON AND DOUBLE

The Baron is a whole joint consisting of the saddle and the two legs. It is one of the most excellent of all the large joints or Relevés.

The Double comprises the two legs unseparated.

Both of these large joints are almost always provided by ordinary or grass lamb and should only be served roast as a Relevé (large joint).

The best accompaniment for these pieces is either unthickened or very lightly thickened roast gravy. Garnishes which require a sauce should be kept very light.

Suitable Garnishes are: Bretonne, Dauphine, Duchesse, Bouquetière, Bristol, Frascati, Hussarde, Jardinière, Japonaise, Macédoine, Milanaise, Portugaise, Provençale, Renaissance, Richelieu, Sarde, Saint-Florentin.

2756 CARRE—BEST END

When required for serving whole, first shorten the best end of lamb or mutton as if for cutting into cutlets, then remove the skin and the chine bone. Uncover the ends of the cutlet bones as one would for trimmed cutlets then cover the ends of the meat with slices of salt pork fat and tie in place with string.

The best end should consist of no more than 9 or 10 cutlet bones and, for preference, it should be less than this number counting from the first and best ones.

All of the garnishes indicated for the Baron and Double are suitable.

CARRE FROID—COLD BEST END

2757 Cold Best End

Trim the cooked best end of lamb or mutton, coat with a layer of aspic jelly and surround with chopped jelly on the dish. It is usual to offer Mint Sauce as an accompaniment.

2758 CERVELLES—BRAINS

All of the recipes indicated for Cervelles and Amourettes of Beef or Veal are suitable.

2759 COTELETTES—CUTLETS

Mutton or lamb cutlets are sometimes shallow fried although grilling is the most suitable method of cooking.

When the recipe calls for the cutlets to be breadcrumbed they should be shallow fried in clarified butter or a mixture of oil and butter. The term *Côtelette Bouchère* refers to a cutlet of which the end of the cutlet bone has not been trimmed and bared.

2760 Côtelettes à la Bretonne

Season and shallow fry the cutlets in butter. Arrange in a circle on a round dish, fill the centre with Flageolets à la Bretonne and surround the cutlets with a *cordon* of Jus lié.

2761 Côtelettes Buloz

Season and grill the cutlets on one side only.

Coat the grilled sides with well reduced Sauce Béchamel flavoured with grated Parmesan; flour, egg and breadcrumb the cutlets using white breadcrumbs containing one-third its volume of grated Parmesan; shallow fry in butter.

Arrange in a circle on a base of Risotto aux Truffes.

2762 Côtelettes Carignan
Flour, egg and breadcrumb the cutlets using breadcrumbs containing one-third its volume of grated Parmesan then shallow fry them in butter and oil.

Arrange closely overlapping in a circle on a round dish and fill the centre with a pile of cockscombs and kidneys dipped in a light frying batter and fried at the last moment.

Serve accompanied with a well flavoured Tomato Sauce.

2763 Côtelettes Champvallon
Take 10 cutlets from that part of the best end uncovered by the removal of the shoulder. Trim them but do not trim and bare the ends of the cutlet bones. Season and colour them quickly on both sides in butter.

Arrange them in a deep earthenware dish with 250 g (9 oz) sliced onions lightly cooked in butter without colour. Moisten with enough white stock to almost cover the cutlets and onions; add a small clove of crushed garlic and a Bouquet garni. Bring to the boil and place in a moderate oven.

After 20 minutes, cover neatly with 600 g (1 lb 5 oz) potatoes trimmed cylinder-shape and cut in slices. Season and complete the cooking in the oven basting frequently with its cooking liquid.

When the cutlets are cooked the liquid should be almost completely reduced.

2764 Côtelettes Financière
Cut open the meaty part of the cutlets along their thick part so as to form a pocket but keeping the part where the knife enters as small as possible. Using a small piping tube and bag fill these pockets with a creamed forcemeat mixed with finely chopped truffle. Close the openings of the cutlets carefully and well.

Season and shallow fry the cutlets in butter colouring both sides, then finish their cooking by braising them with a little good stock. Glaze at the last moment.

Arrange in a circle on a round dish with a slice of truffle on each cutlet. Fill the centre with a Financière garnish (381), or serve the garnish separately.

2765 Côtelettes Laura
Season and grill the cutlets. Sandwich each between two layers of small sections of cooked macaroni mixed with cream and a quarter its weight of roughly chopped flesh only of tomato cooked in butter. Envelop each prepared cutlet in a triangle of pig's caul.

Arrange the cutlets on a tray, sprinkle with fine white breadcrumbs and melted butter and cook and colour under the salamander or in a hot oven for 7–8 minutes.

Arrange in a circle on a round dish surrounded with a *cordon* of thin tomato-flavoured Sauce Demi-glace.

Note: As a variation, the tomatoes used in the preparation of the macaroni may be replaced by a Julienne of truffle.

2766 Côtelettes Maintenon
Season and shallow fry the cutlets in butter on one side only. Drain them well, coat the cooked sides with a spoonful of Maintenon mixture (320) and smooth it dome shape. Sprinkle with fine breadcrumbs and melted butter and place them uncooked sides down, on a buttered tray. Place in a hot oven for 7–8 minutes to finish cooking the cutlets and to lightly gratinate the mixture at the same time.

Arrange in a circle on a round dish and serve accompanied with Sauce Périgueux containing slices of truffle.

2767 Côtelettes Montglas
Season and shallow fry the cutlets in butter on one side only. Drain them well and coat the cooked sides with a spoonful of Montglas mixture (324).

Smooth dome shape, sprinkle with fine white breadcrumbs and melted butter and place them uncooked sides down, on a buttered tray. Place in a hot oven for 7–8 minutes to finish cooking the cutlets and to lightly gratinate the mixture at the same time.

Arrange in a circle on a round dish and surround with a *cordon* of Sauce Demi-glace.

2768 Côtelettes Mousquetaire
Place the cutlets to marinate 1 hour in advance with lemon juice, a little oil and the usual flavourings.

When ready, shallow fry them quickly in very hot oil but on one side only. Drain well and coat the cooked sides dome shape with ordinary Godiveau (290) mixed with dry Duxelles and chopped Fines Herbes.

Arrange the cutlets uncooked sides down, on a tray containing very hot butter, brush the tops with melted butter then place in a medium oven to finish cooking the cutlets and the Godiveau.

Arrange in a circle on a round dish and fill the centre with a garnish composed of sliced artichoke bottoms and mushrooms cooked in butter and mixed together with Sauce Duxelles.

2769 Côtelettes Murillo
Season and shallow fry the cutlets in butter on one side only making sure that they are two-thirds cooked. Drain well and coat the cooked sides dome

shape with a mixture of finely sliced cooked mushrooms mixed with reduced Sauce Béchamel.

Arrange the cutlets uncooked sides down on a buttered tray. Sprinkle with grated Parmesan and melted butter and place in a hot oven to complete the cooking of the cutlets and lightly gratinate the mixture.

Arrange in a circle on a round dish and surround with a *cordon* of buttered fresh tomato purée.

Note: In place of the tomato purée the cutlets may be surrounded with roughly chopped flesh only of tomato cooked in butter, and grilled pimentos.

2770 Mutton Chop

The mutton chop is cut on the bone from the loin and should be at least 3 cm (1⅓ in) thick. The flank is rolled towards the inside of the chop and fixed in place with a skewer.

Mutton chops are almost always grilled and although generally served plain, they may be very well accompanied with some of the more usual garnishes for cutlets.

2771 Côtelettes Panées—Breadcrumbed Cutlets

For this preparation it is usual to use the cutlets from that part of the best end from where the shoulder has been removed.

After lightly flattening they should be passed simply through melted butter and breadcrumbs if required for grilling; if for shallow frying they should be floured, egg and breadcrumbed. Either way they may be garnished to choice.

2772 Côtelettes à la Parisienne

Season, grill and arrange the cutlets in a circle on a round dish.

Place in the centre of the dish a garnish of Pommes Parisienne. Surround the cutlets with artichoke bottoms filled with a Parisienne garnish (438) and serve accompanied with a light gravy.

2773 Côtelettes Pompadour

Season, shallow fry the cutlets in butter and arrange in a circle on a round dish. Place in the centre of the dish a mound of small potato croquettes about the size of a walnut. Surround with small artichoke bottoms filled with a thick buttered purée of lentils with a slice of truffle on top. Surround with a *cordon* of thin Sauce Périgueux.

2774 Côtelettes à la Provençale

Season and shallow fry the cutlets in oil on one side only, drain well and coat the cooked sides with a layer of Provençale mixture (327).

Arrange the cutlets uncooked sides down on a buttered tray and sprinkle the tops with a little melted butter. Place in a hot oven to finish cooking the cutlets and to glaze the mixture.

Arrange in a circle on a round dish and place on each cutlet a grilled mushroom dark side upwards, with a stuffed olive in the centre. Surround with a *cordon* of Sauce Provençale.

2775 Côtelettes à la Réforme

Lightly flatten the cutlets, season, flour, dip in melted butter then in white breadcrumbs containing a third its volume of very finely chopped lean ham. Flatten carefully with the flat of a knife to ensure the cohesion of the crumbs and shallow fry in clarified butter.

Arrange in a circle on a round dish and serve accompanied with Sauce Réforme.

2776 Côtelettes Sévigné

Season and shallow fry the cutlets in butter on one side only.

Well coat the cooked sides with a Salpicon of artichoke bottoms and mushrooms mixed with Sauce Allemande. Smooth dome shape.

Flour, egg and breadcrumb, then place them uncooked sides down on a tray containing very hot butter; sprinkle with melted butter. Place in a hot oven to finish cooking and to colour the coating of breadcrumbs.

Arrange in a circle on a round dish and surround with a *cordon* of buttered meat glaze.

2777 Côtelettes Valois

Season and grill the cutlets on one side only.

Coat the cooked sides with a mixture of a short Julienne of salt ox tongue, mushrooms and truffle bound with a little veal or chicken forcemeat. Smooth dome shape. Arrange the cutlets uncooked sides down on a buttered tray, sprinkle with melted butter and place in a moderate oven to finish cooking the cutlets and the mixture at the same time.

Arrange in a circle on a round dish and place in the centre a garnish of large olives stuffed with veal or chicken forcemeat and poached at the last moment.

Serve accompanied with Sauce Valois.

2778 Côtelettes Villeroy

This preparation is particular for lamb cutlets.

Season and grill the cutlets, allow to become cold under light pressure then dip in Sauce Villeroy. Place on a tray, allow to cool, then flour, egg and breadcrumb.

Shallow fry them gently in clarified butter.

Arrange in a circle on a round dish and serve accompanied with Sauce Périgueux.

COTELETTES FROIDES—COLD CUTLETS

2779 Côtelettes en Belle-Vue

Lamb cutlets are generally used in the preparation of this cold dish.

Cook the cutlets and when cold trim them neatly. Decorate with items of truffle and hard-boiled egg white and coat with aspic jelly to keep the decoration in place.

Now proceed as indicated for Côtes de Veau en Belle-Vue (2539).

2780 Côtelettes Bergeret

Prepare and trim a best end of lamb or a small one of mutton to the correct size.

Trim the ends of the cutlet bones, then braise it white using an excellent veal stock. Allow to cool in its cooking liquid.

Drain and well dry the best end, cut it into cutlets and trim these to an even shape. Dip each into a white Sauce Chaud-froid containing one-third its quantity of a purée of cooked mushrooms. Arrange each cutlet laying on its same side on a tray.

When the sauce has set, decorate the wide parts of the cutlets with a rose-shaped decoration cut from very red ox tongue and border this with very small dots of truffle. Coat with very clear aspic jelly.

To serve: remove the cutlets from the tray carefully, trim with a small knife and arrange in a circle on a round dish. Fill the centre with chopped jelly mixed with chopped truffle.

2781 Côtelettes en Chaud-froid

Prepare the best end as above and braise in the usual manner. Allow to cool in its cooking liquid, drain, well dry, cut into cutlets and trim them to an even shape.

Remove all the fat from the cooking liquid then pass it through a fine strainer and reduce; add to a brown Sauce Chaud-froid. Dip the cutlets into this sauce when almost setting and arrange each laying on its same side on a tray.

Decorate the wide parts of the cutlets with a nice slice of truffle and coat with aspic jelly.

To serve: remove the cutlets from the tray carefully, trim with a small knife and arrange lying on a dish around a mould of vegetable salad. Alternatively, arrange in a circle standing up against a pyramid-shaped mould of vegetable salad placed in the centre of the dish.

EPAULE—SHOULDER

2782 Epaule Bonne-Femme

Bone out the shoulder and stuff it with a fine forcemeat. Roll and tie carefully with string, season and shallow fry till brown on all sides in lard.

Either cook in the oven or *en Casserole* until half cooked, then place in an earthenware dish with, for a medium-sized shoulder, 500 g (1 lb 2 oz) two-thirds cooked haricot beans, 100 g ($3\frac{1}{2}$ oz) sliced carrots cooked with the beans, 100 g ($3\frac{1}{2}$ oz) sliced onions, cooked in butter and a touch of crushed garlic. Sprinkle this garnish with the fat from the cooking of the shoulder and finish cooking together in the oven, basting frequently.

When ready, remove the string and serve as it is.

2783 Epaule à la Boulangère

Bone out the shoulder, season the inside, then roll and tie carefully with string. Place in a hot oven to colour and partly cook it.

Remove the shoulder, place in an earthenware dish and surround with 1 kg ($2\frac{1}{4}$ lb) potatoes cut in pieces or slices and 250 g (9 oz) onions sliced and lightly shallow fried in butter. Sprinkle with the fat from the roasting of the shoulder and finish cooking together in the oven, basting frequently.

When ready, remove the string, sprinkle the garnish with a pinch of chopped parsley, and serve as it is.

2784 Epaule Braisée—Braised Shoulder

Bone out the shoulder and either stuff it or not, whichever is required. Roll and tie carefully with string in a long or round shape.

Braise in the usual manner making sure that it is fairly well cooked.

When ready, remove the string, place the shoulder in a suitable dish and surround with the braising liquid after first removing all fat, passing through a fine strainer and reducing.

Serve accompanied with a suitable plain vegetable or vegetable purée.

2785 Epaule aux Navets—Shoulder with Turnips

Bone out the shoulder, stuff with a suitable forcemeat, roll and tie carefully with string. Braise in the usual manner.

When three-quarters cooked remove the shoulder and place in a shallow pan. Surround with 1 kg ($2\frac{1}{4}$ lb) turnips trimmed to the shape of large long olives and coloured in butter with a pinch of caster sugar, and 20 button onions coloured in butter.

Remove the fat from the braising liquid and pass through a fine strainer over the whole. Cover and complete the cooking in the oven.

When ready, remove the string and serve the shoulder in a suitable dish surrounded by the sauce and garnish.

2786 Epaule aux Racines—Shoulder with Root Vegetables

Braise the shoulder as for Epaule Braisée.

Place on a suitable dish and surround with bouquets of carrots, turnips and celeriac trimmed to the shape of large long olives, cooked in Bouillon and glazed, and brown glazed button onions.

Serve accompanied with the braising liquid after removing all fat, reducing and passing it through a fine strainer.

2787 Epaule au Riz—Shoulder with Rice

Bone out the shoulder, season the inside, roll and tie carefully with string. Braise in the usual manner, using 50 per cent more liquid than usual and until three-quarters cooked.

Remove the shoulder, place in a clean small braising pan with 300 g (11 oz) blanched rice and strain the braising liquid without removing the fat, over the whole. Cover and cook gently in the oven until the rice has completely absorbed the cooking liquor.

When ready, remove the string, place the shoulder on a suitable dish and surround with the rice. Serve accompanied with a sauceboat of lightly thickened gravy.

GIGOT—LEG

2788 Gigot à l'Anglaise—Boiled Leg

Shorten the knuckle end of the leg and trim and bare the last 5 cm (2 in).

Place into a pan of boiling water salted in the proportion of 8 g (¼ oz) salt to 1 litre (1¾ pt or 4½ U.S. cups) water.

For a medium-sized leg add 3 medium carrots, 2 medium onions, each stuck with 1 clove, a Bouquet garni and 2 cloves of garlic. Simmer gently allowing 30 minutes per 500 g (1 lb 2 oz) weight of the leg.

When cooked, place on a suitable dish with the vegetables and serve accompanied with an English Butter Sauce (169) containing 100 g (3½ oz) capers per 1 litre (1¾ pt or 4½ U.S. cups) of sauce.

Note: Boiled leg of mutton or lamb can be served with a purée of turnips or celery which have been cooked with the leg. A purée of potatoes or haricot beans may also be served at the same time.

2789 Gigot Braisé—Braised Leg

Remove the aitch bone from the leg, shorten the knuckle end and trim and bare the last 5 cm (2 in). Place in a hot oven to colour well, then braise in the usual manner, using white stock to almost cover it. Cook very gently allowing 40 minutes per 500 g (1 lb 2 oz) weight of the leg. For small joints cut from the leg, the times should naturally be lessened.

When cooked, remove the leg, drain well and place it on a tray. Remove the fat from the braising liquid, pass through a fine strainer and reduce to about 3 dl (½ pt or 1¼ U.S. cups). Baste the leg with a few spoonfuls of this gravy and glaze in the oven.

Place the leg on a dish and serve accompanied with 1) a purée of either potatoes, turnips, celery, haricot beans or cauliflower and 2) the rest of the gravy.

2790 Gigot à la Bordelaise

Remove the centre bone from inside the leg separating it from the knuckle. Do not remove the knuckle bone and do not cut open the leg whilst boning it out.

Lard the leg along the grain of the meat with large strips of ham and fill the empty space made by the removal of the bone with a very fatty uncooked Fricadelles de Veau forcemeat (2729).

Sew up the leg, place in a braising pan which will just contain it and colour in the oven. Almost cover with a good stock, cover with a lid and cook gently in the oven allowing 40–50 minutes per 500 g (1 lb 2 oz) weight of leg.

When two-thirds cooked, add a 750 g (1 lb 10 oz) well blanched piece of streaky bacon, 1 kg (2¼ lb) carrots and 500 g (1 lb 2 oz) turnips both cut in quarters, 2 cloves of garlic and a Bouquet garni. Finish cooking together.

When ready, place the leg on a dish, surround with the vegetables and border these with the bacon cut in rectangles.

Serve accompanied with Sauce Tomate containing some of the cooking liquid passed through a fine strainer and reduced.

2791 Gigot à la Boulangère

Remove the aitch bone from the leg, shorten the knuckle end and trim and bare the last 5 cm (2 in); or for preference, completely bone out the leg, season the inside and tie up with string.

Place in an earthenware dish and two-thirds cook in the oven, then surround with a garnish of sliced onions lightly coloured in butter and potatoes either cut in quarters or slices. The amount of this garnish should be proportionate to the size of the leg.

Complete and finish as for Epaule Boulangère (2783).

2792 Gigot Bonne-Femme

Proceed as indicated for Epaule Bonne-Femme (2782), taking account of the difference in size when calculating the cooking time and the amounts of the garnish.

2793 Gigot à la Bretonne
Roast the leg and serve accompanied with 1) its roast gravy left a little fatty, and 2) a dish of Flageolets à la Bretonne or a purée of haricot beans cooked à la Bretonne.

2794 Gigot Mariné en Chevreuil
Remove the aitch bone from the leg, shorten the knuckle and completely skin the leg. Lard with fine strips of salt pork fat, and place in the marinade (264). The time for marinating should be determined by reference to the tenderness of the meat and the temperature. On average, allow 2 days in summer and 4 days in winter.

When ready for cooking, remove the leg from the marinade and dry it thoroughly. Place it on a trivet in a roasting tray so as to raise it and prevent it coming into contact with the fat and juices whilst cooking. Place in a very hot oven to set the surfaces of the leg quickly, thus preventing the moisture absorbed during the marinating from producing steam and rendering its colouring more difficult.

Reduce the heat as required and when almost cooked, ensure that the larding fat becomes well coloured.

Place the leg on a dish and serve accompanied with a Sauce Chevreuil à la Française.

2795 Gigot Rôti, Sauce Menthe—Roast Leg of Mutton or Lamb with Mint Sauce
Mint Sauce as an accompaniment for roast lamb and mutton is little used in France; in England, however, it is not only an acceptable accompaniment but an absolute necessity; all roast joints of mutton and lamb, either hot or cold are always served accompanied with Mint Sauce. Its use is to be recommended.

2796 Gigot Soubise
Prepare and braise the leg as for Gigot Braisé (2789).

When two-thirds cooked, place the leg in a clean pan and surround with 1½ kg (3 lb 6 oz) of blanched sliced onions, or a little less if not new seasons and 300 g (11 oz) rice. Strain the braising liquid over the whole and finish cooking gently in the oven.

At the last moment glaze the leg and place on a suitable dish.

Serve accompanied with a Purée Soubise obtained by passing the onions and rice through a sieve then reheating and lightly buttering at the last moment.

Note: The Soubise accompaniment may be prepared separately but it is infinitely preferable to cook the ingredients in the braising liquid; by this method it gains considerably in flavour.

2797 Gigot froid—Cold Leg
As for all large cold joints the leg should be presented and garnished in as simple a manner as possible after being trimmed and coated with aspic jelly.

2798 LANGUES DE MOUTON—SHEEP'S TONGUES

Sheep's tongues can be successfully used to help in providing the necessary variety for menus. Their preparation and methods of cooking are the same as for calf's tongues and thus it is felt unnecessary to repeat here those details concerning them. See the section of Calf's Tongues.

2799 PIEDS DE MOUTON—SHEEP'S TROTTERS

Sheep's trotters should first be singed then rubbed with a piece of clean cloth. The small tuft of hair in the cleft of the hoof is next removed and then the covering of the hoof itself. Now split the trotters open lengthways and bone them out.

They are generally cooked in a *Blanc*.

2800 Pieds de Mouton en Blanquette
Cook the trotters in a *Blanc*. Drain them well and place in a shallow pan with 10 button onions cooked in White Bouillon and 25 cooked button mushrooms. Add 5 dl (18 fl oz or 2¼ U.S. cups) Sauce Allemande, mix together and simmer very gently for five minutes.

Tip into a deep dish or timbale and sprinkle with chopped parsley.

2801 Fritots de Pieds de Mouton
Cook the trotters in a *Blanc*. Drain them well and whilst still warm, marinate for 20 minutes in a dish with lemon juice, a little oil, chopped parsley and a little salt and pepper. Toss over occasionally.

For serving, dip the half trotters in frying batter and deep fry in hot oil.

Drain well and arrange on a serviette; decorate with fried parsley and serve accompanied with Sauce Tomate.

2802 Pieds de Mouton à la Poulette
The preparation à la Poulette is the most common method of presenting sheep's trotters.

Cook the trotters in a *Blanc*, drain well and add to 4 dl (14 fl oz or 1¾ U.S. cups) Sauce Poulette containing mushrooms.

Tip into a deep dish or timbale and sprinkle with chopped parsley.

2803 Pieds de Mouton à la Rouennaise
Prepare and blanch the trotters then braise them, adding a little Madeira to the braising liquid; make sure that they are well cooked. When ready, cut them in two lengthways and carefully remove all the bones.

Pass the cooking liquid through a fine strainer and well reduce together with 1 dl ($3\frac{1}{2}$ fl oz or $\frac{1}{2}$ U.S. cup) brandy for each 10 half trotters. Add this reduction to a forcemeat prepared from 1 kg ($2\frac{1}{4}$ lb) fine sausage meat, 125 g ($4\frac{1}{2}$ oz) chopped onion cooked in butter and a good pinch of chopped parsley; mix all together well.

Place 2 halves of trotter together, spread top and bottom with the prepared forcemeat and completely wrap and close up in a rectangle of pig's caul. Sprinkle with melted butter and white breadcrumbs, grill gently and serve.

2804 Pieds de Mouton à la Tyrolienne
Cook 120 g (4 oz) chopped onion in a little butter; add 450 g (1 lb) roughly chopped flesh only of tomato, a pinch of chopped parsley, a touch of crushed garlic and season with salt and pepper. Cook together gently for a few minutes then add 2 dl (7 fl oz or $\frac{7}{8}$ U.S. cup) Sauce Poivrade.

To this sauce add 10 freshly cooked and well drained sheep's trotters and simmer gently for 10 minutes. Serve in a deep dish or timbale.

2805 Other Preparations Suitable for Sheep's Trotters
The recipes for Calf's feet such as à la Custine, Grillés, Vinaigrette etc. are also suitable for sheep's trotters.

2806 POITRINE—BREAST

The breast of mutton is generally used in the preparation of stews such as Navarin, Irish Stew, Cassoulet etc. and sometimes also for Epigrammes, although the breast of lamb is usually more suitable for this dish. However, breast of mutton may be served as dishes in their own right in accordance with the following recipes.

2807 Poitrine à la Bergère
Braise the breast, remove all bones and allow to become cold pressed between weighted trays. Cut into diamond shapes of approximately 80 g (3 oz) in weight and flour, egg and breadcrumb using white breadcrumbs mixed with half their quantity of finely chopped mushrooms squeezed until almost dry. Sprinkle with butter and gently grill them.

Arrange overlapping in a circle on a round dish and fill the centre with a mound of long-cut straw potatoes. Serve accompanied with Sauce Duxelles made with *Mousserons* or morels.

2808 Poitrine à la Diable
Braise the breast, remove the bones and allow to become cold pressed between weighted trays. Cut into rectangles, coat well with made mustard flavoured with Cayenne then flour, egg and breadcrumb. Sprinkle with melted butter and grill gently.

Arrange in a circle on a round dish and serve accompanied with a well flavoured Sauce Diable.

2809 Breast of Mutton with Various Purées
Prepare the breast as in the previous recipes and cut as required, either heart shape or into rectangles or triangles. Flour, egg and breadcrumb, grill them gently and arrange in a circle on a round dish.

Serve accompanied with a vegetable purée to choice.

2810 Poitrine Vert-Pré
Prepare and grill the breast as in the preceding recipe. Arrange in a circle on a round dish, fill the centre with straw potatoes and surround the dish with bouquets of watercress.

Serve accompanied with a sauceboat of very soft Maître d'Hôtel Butter.

ROGNONS—KIDNEYS

2811 Rognons Sautés à la Berrichonne
Remove the skin which covers the kidneys, cut them in half then into fairly thick slices. Season and sauté quickly in hot butter tossing them over and over. Drain and add to a Sauce Bordelaise containing diced streaky bacon, blanched and fried, and mushrooms, as for Rognon de Veau à la Berrichonne.

2812 Rognons Brochette—Grilled Kidneys
Remove the skin which covers the kidneys, open them by cutting almost through from the convex side but not separating the two halves. Impale them crossways on a skewer to keep them open, then season and grill.

For service, arrange the grilled kidneys on a dish with a small knob of Maître d'Hôtel Butter in the centre of each.

Note: In certain establishments, lamb or mutton kidneys are first dipped in melted butter and then in breadcrumbs before grilling. Although breadcrumbed kidneys have a better appearance when cooked, this method of preparation is completely optional. It may appear that the foregoing observations seem to justify the breadcrumbing of kidneys before grilling but there is no serious gastronomic reason for doing so.

2813 Rognons Brochette à l'Espagnole

Prepare and grill the kidneys as in the preceding recipe.

Fill the centre of each with a small knob of Maître d'Hôtel Butter containing 25 g (1 oz) chopped pimento per 100 g (3½ oz) of butter.

Place each kidney on a grilled half of tomato then arrange them in a circle in the centre of a dish. Surround with a nice border of onion rings, seasoned, floured and deep fried in oil at the last moment.

2814 Brochettes de Rognons

Remove the skin from the kidneys then cut them into round slices approximately 7–8 mm (¼ in) thick. Season with salt and pepper and quickly sauté in very hot butter just sufficient to stiffen the outside surfaces.

Impale these slices on small skewers alternating with squares of blanched streaky bacon and thick slices of mushrooms sautéed in butter. Dip into melted butter, sprinkle with fine breadcrumbs and grill them.

These Brochettes are usually served as they are without a sauce.

2815 Rognons Sautés Carvalho

Remove the skin from the kidneys, cut them in half lengthways, season and sauté quickly in hot butter, tossing over frequently. Drain them well then arrange in a circle, each half placed on a Croûton of bread cut to the shape of a cockscomb and fried in butter. Place 2 slices of truffle and a small grooved mushroom on top of each.

Deglaze the pan with Madeira, add the necessary amount of Sauce Demi-glace, remove from the heat and shake in a little butter. Strain this sauce over the kidneys and garnish.

2816 Rognons Sautés au Champagne

Remove the skin from the kidneys, cut in half lengthways, season and sauté quickly in hot butter, tossing them over frequently. Drain them well and arrange in a deep dish or timbale.

Deglaze the pan with 1 dl (3½ fl oz or ½ U.S. cup) Champagne per 4 kidneys, reduce, then add 1 tbs meat glaze, a few drops of lemon juice and finish with a little butter. Strain this sauce over the kidneys.

2817 Rognons au Gratin

Remove the skin from the kidneys, cut them in half lengthways, season and simply stiffen the cut surfaces only by placing in hot butter for a few moments. Using 30 g (1 oz) ordinary forcemeat mixed with a good third its quantity of dry Duxelles per 2 kidneys, fashion a small dome in the centre of a buttered dish. Surround the base of this with slices of raw mushroom and press the half kidneys into the forcemeat, stiffened sides inwards and in pairs; place a nice grooved mushroom on top of the dome. Coat the whole with a fairly thick Sauce Duxelles, sprinkle with fine breadcrumbs and melted butter and place in the oven to gratinate.

On removing the dish from the oven surround the base of the mould with Sauce Demi-glace and sprinkle the gratinated surface with a few drops of lemon juice and chopped parsley.

2818 Rognons à la Hussarde

For 6 kidneys: Cook 125 g (4½ oz) chopped onion in butter until lightly coloured and mix into 125 g (4½ oz) Pommes Duchesse mixture finished with a little beaten egg. Using this mixture, pipe a border around the edge of a buttered dish, sprinkle with fine white breadcrumbs and melted butter and gratinate in the oven.

Remove the skin from the kidneys, cut in half lengthways and sauté quickly in hot butter, tossing them over frequently. Drain well and arrange neatly inside the border.

Deglaze the pan with 1 dl (3½ fl oz or ½ U.S. cup) white wine, almost completely reduce, then add 1 dl (3½ fl oz or ½ U.S. cup) Sauce Demi-glace, the same amount of Sauce Tomate and 1 tsp grated horseradish. Pour this sauce over the kidneys.

2819 Rognons Michel

For 6 kidneys: Cut 200 g (7 oz) foie gras into large dice, season, pass through flour and sauté quickly in butter, tossing over frequently. Add the foie gras and its fat to approximately 750 g (1 lb 10 oz) braised Sauerkraut and mix together carefully. Arrange this mixture slightly dome-shaped in a lightly baked flan case and surround with the 12 halves of kidney, sautéed in butter, drained and rolled in some melted pale meat glaze.

2820 Turban de Rognons à la Piémontaise

Take a buttered Savarin mould, of a size proportionate to the number of kidneys, and fill it with Risotto à la Piémontaise.

Remove the skin from the kidneys, cut in half lengthways, season and sauté quickly in hot butter, tossing them over frequently. Drain well.

Demould the border of Risotto on to a round dish and arrange the halves of kidney on top alternating with slices of white truffle. Fill the centre of the rice with Sauce Demi-glace flavoured with tomato and truffle essence.

2821 Rognons Turbigo
Remove the skin from the kidneys, cut in half lengthways, season and sauté quickly in hot butter, tossing them over frequently. Drain well then arrange in a circle in a deep dish. Place in the centre a garnish of small cooked mushrooms and grilled chipolata sausages.

Deglaze the pan with white wine, reduce and add the necessary amount of tomato-flavoured Sauce Demi-glace. Season with a touch of Cayenne and strain over the kidneys and garnish.

2822 Rognons Vert-Pré
Prepare and grill the kidneys as for Rognons Brochette (2812) and arrange on an oval dish with bouquets of straw potatoes at the sides and bouquets of watercress at both ends.

2823 Rognons Viéville
Remove the skin from the kidneys, cut in half lengthways and sauté quickly in hot butter tossing them over quickly. Drain well.

Arrange in a circle each on a Croûton of bread cut to the shape of a cockscomb and fried in clarified butter. Fill the centre with glazed button onions, chipolata sausages fried in butter and small cooked mushrooms.

Deglaze the pan with Madeira, reduce, add the necessary amount of Sauce Demi-glace and shake in a little butter. Strain this sauce over the kidneys and garnish.

2824 Various other Preparations suitable for Lamb and Mutton Kidneys
Bercy, Bordelaise, Champignons, Chasseur, Currie à l'Indienne, Liégeoise, Montpensier, Portugaise, with various wines. (See Veal Kidney with Various Wines (2698).)

2825 SELLE—SADDLE

Although occasionally braised, the saddle of mutton or lamb is most frequently served roasted. The widely prevalent practice of larding the saddle with strips of fat is completely wrong; it is preferable to leave it in its natural state.

Suitable garnishes for braised or roast saddle are: Boulangère, Dauphine, Duchesse, Bouquetière, Bristol, Frascati, Gnocchis à la Romaine, Jardinière, Japonaise, Provençale, Renaissance, Richelieu, Sarde, Saint-Florentin, Saint-Germain.

2826 FILET AND FILETS MIGNONS—LOIN AND FILLETS

The loin (Fr. *Filet*) of mutton or lamb is the half of a saddle cut lengthways through the vertebrae. It is then boned out, rolled, tied with string and either braised or roasted like the shoulder or leg; it may be served with the same garnishes.

The two fillets (Fr. *Filets Mignons*) of mutton or lamb are to be found lying along and underneath the saddle; they may be shallow fried or grilled and accompanied with the various garnishes as indicated for Tournedos. They may also be marinated and prepared in accordance with the directions for *Filets en Chevreuil* of Beef (2297).

2827 NOISETTES

Noisettes of mutton and especially those of lamb may be classed among the finest and most delicate of the Entrées.

They are cut either from the loin or best end but if using the best end, only the meat from the first 5 or 6 ribs should be used.

Noisettes may be either shallow fried or grilled and all the recipes for Tournedos and cutlets of lamb and mutton are suitable.

OTHER PREPARATIONS OF MUTTON AND GRASS LAMB

2828 Cassoulet

1) Place 1 kg ($2\frac{1}{4}$ lb) haricot beans in a pan with 3 litres ($5\frac{1}{4}$ pt or $6\frac{1}{2}$ U.S. pt) water, 10 g ($\frac{1}{3}$ oz) salt, 1 carrot, 1 onion stuck with a clove, 1 Bouquet garni, 3 cloves of garlic, add 300 g (11 oz) fresh pork rind, blanched and tied together. Bring to the boil, skim, cover and cook gently for 1 hour. At this time add 300 g (11 oz) blanched belly of pork and a garlic sausage of the same weight. Complete the cooking together gently keeping the beans firm and whole.
2) Fry together in lard until coloured, 400 g (15 oz) of boned shoulder of mutton and the same amount of breast of mutton, both cut into pieces approximately 45 g ($1\frac{1}{2}$ oz) in weight. Drain off half the fat, add 250 g (9 oz) chopped onion and 2 cloves of crushed garlic and continue cooking until the onions are lightly coloured. Now add sufficient of the cooking liquid from the beans to cover the meat plus $1\frac{1}{2}$ dl (5 fl oz or $\frac{5}{8}$ U.S. cup) tomato purée and a Bouquet garni. Cover and

place in the oven to cook very gently for $1\frac{1}{2}$ hours at least.

3) Cover the bottom and sides of deep or special earthenware dishes with the pork rind then fill them with alternate layers of mutton and sauce, beans, the belly of pork cut in large cubes and slices of the sausage. Sprinkle with breadcrumbs and gratinate in a moderate oven for 1 hour basting from time to time with a little of the remaining cooking liquid from the beans.

Note: For restaurant service, the following method may be used: 1) make sure that all the components of the dish are completely cooked, 2) cut the pork rind into small squares and add to the mutton, 3) place the ingredients in the dishes and 4) sprinkle with breadcrumbs and a little of the cooking liquid from the beans and gratinate quickly in a hot oven. Obviously this method is quicker and thus more expedient but the final result is less satisfying.

The Cassoulet may also be made with goose or chicken. If using chicken care should be taken to adjust the cooking time in proportion to the tenderness of the chicken.

2829 Currie à l'Indienne

Cut 1 kg ($2\frac{1}{4}$ lb) lean mutton into 3 cm ($1\frac{1}{3}$ in) cubes; season with salt and fry in 90 g (3 oz) lard until well coloured. Add 120 g (4 oz) chopped onion, a good pinch of curry powder and continue frying together until the onions start colouring. Add 40 g ($1\frac{1}{2}$ oz) flour, cook for a few moments then add $7\frac{1}{2}$ dl ($1\frac{1}{3}$ pt or $3\frac{1}{4}$ U.S. cups) coconut milk. Stir to the boil, then cover and cook gently in the oven for approximately $1\frac{1}{2}$ hours. Ten minutes before it is ready add 250 g (9 oz) cooking apples, peeled, cored and cut in small dice.

To serve: remove any fat from the sauce, place the whole in a deep dish and serve accompanied with a dish of plain boiled rice.

Preparation of Coconut Milk: Remove the flesh from a coconut and either grate or pound it. Moisten with the necessary amount of water and allow it to steep for 1 hour. Tip everything into a piece of strong cloth then press and twist firmly so as to extract the maximum of liquid. If fresh coconut is unobtainable use desiccated coconut which should be steeped for 1 hour in hot water.

2830 Daube à l'Avignonnaise

Bone out a leg of mutton and cut it into cubes 90 g (3 oz) in weight. Lard each of these pieces along the grain of the meat with a strip of salt pork fat seasoned with spiced salt, then marinate them for 2 hours in a basin with 1 bottle red wine, 1 dl ($3\frac{1}{2}$ fl oz or $\frac{1}{2}$ U.S. cup) oil, 1 sliced carrot, 1 sliced onion, 4 cloves of garlic, a sprig of thyme, 1 bayleaf and a few parsley stalks.

Prepare: 1) 200 g (7 oz) chopped onion mixed with 2 cloves of crushed garlic, 2) 250 g (9 oz) salt belly of pork cut in dice and blanched, 3) 250 g (9 oz) fresh pork rind blanched and cut in $2\frac{1}{2}$ cm (1 in) squares, 4) a large Bouquet of parsley stalks enclosing a small piece of dried orange peel.

Cover the bottom and sides of an earthenware casserole or terrine with thin slices of salt pork fat. Inside arrange the mutton, onions, belly of pork and pork rind in alternate layers, lightly seasoning each layer of mutton and sprinkling with a pinch of powdered thyme and bayleaf. Place the Bouquet in the middle.

Add the marinade passed through a fine strainer and sufficient brown stock to just cover the ingredients. Cover with slices of salt pork fat, place on the lid and seal down with a strip of paste simply made from flour and water. This is to ensure the concentration of the steam inside the utensil whilst cooking.

Bring to the boil on top of the stove then place in a slow to moderate oven and at an even temperature for 5 hours.

To serve: remove the lid from the casserole, discard the slices of fat and the Bouquet and skim off any fat from the surface of the cooking liquid. The Daube is then served as it is in its casserole.

For individual service, the Daube may be transferred to small individual earthenware terrines so as to preserve its rustic character.

2831 Emincés and Hachis of Mutton

These preparations should follow the same rules and observations as laid down for Emincés and Hachis of Beef. The recipes for these are all suitable for Emincés and Hachis of Mutton.

2832 Epigrammes

The Epigramme consists of one cutlet, and one piece of breast, braised, boned out, cooled under pressure and cut heart-shape. Both the cutlet and piece of breast are then floured, egg and crumbed, and either grilled or shallow fried.

As this preparation is usually applied to lamb, suitable preparations will be found in the section House or Young Lamb.

2833 Haricot de Mouton

Heat 90 g (3 oz) lard in a shallow pan and add 250 g (9 oz) salt belly of pork cut in dice and blanched and 20 button onions. Fry until coloured brown then remove and keep on one side. In the same fat fry 2 kg ($4\frac{1}{2}$ lb) breast, neck and shoulder of mutton cut for stew and likewise colour brown.

Drain off half the fat and add 3 small cloves of crushed garlic and 40 g (1½ oz) flour and cook together for a few minutes. Add 1 litre (1¾ pt or 4½ U.S. cups) water, a Bouquet garni and season with salt and pepper. Bring to the boil whilst stirring, cover with a lid and cook in the oven for 30 minutes.

Now transfer the pieces of mutton to a clean pan, add the pork and onions, 1 kg (2¼ lb) half cooked haricot beans and strain the sauce over the whole. Cover and finish cooking gently in the oven.

When ready, serve in small earthenware terrines.

2834 Irish Stew

Cut 1 kg 250 g (3 lb 7 oz) breast and boned shoulder of mutton as for stew and slice 1 kg (2¼ lb) potatoes and 250 g (9 oz) onion.

Take a suitable-sized pan and place inside the pieces of meat in layers alternating with the potatoes and onions. Season each layer of meat with salt and pepper. Add a large Bouquet garni, 7½ dl (1⅓ pt or 3¼ U.S. cups) water and cover with a tight fitting lid. Cook gently in the oven for 1½ hours.

The potatoes in this preparation answer the twofold purpose of providing a garnish and thickening the liquid.

Place in a deep dish or timbale for service.

2835 Moussaka

1) Cut 6 nice eggplants into half lengthways, incise the flesh deeply with a number of cuts then deep fry in hot oil until soft.
2) Peel 2 more eggplants and cut into round slices approximately 7–8 mm (⅓ in) thick. Season, flour and likewise deep fry in hot oil.
3) Remove the pulp from the cooked halves of eggplant with a spoon, chop it and place in a basin. Add 750 g (1 lb 10 oz) of cooked lean mutton, either chopped or cut in small dice; 60 g (2 oz) very finely chopped onion lightly cooked in butter; 125 g (4½ oz) raw mushrooms, roughly chopped and cooked in butter; 2 eggs; a pinch of chopped parsley; half a clove of crushed garlic; 1 dl (3½ fl oz or ½ U.S. cup) reduced tomato-flavoured Sauce Espaghole, and season with salt and pepper. Mix all these ingredients together well.
4) Completely line a well buttered shallow Charlotte mould with the skins from the eggplants, dark sides to the mould. Fill with layers of the mixture alternating with the slices of fried eggplant and finally cover with the remaining skins. Place in a deep tray and cook *au Bain-marie* in the oven for 1 hour. On removing the mould from the oven, allow it to stand for a few minutes to allow the ingredients to settle.

To serve: demould on to a round dish and sprinkle the surface with chopped parsley.

2836 Mutton Pie and Mutton Pudding

Proceed in the same manner as indicated for Beefsteak Pie (2454) and Beefsteak Pudding (2456) replacing the beef with mutton.

2837 Navarin

Heat 100 g (3½ oz) clarified fat in a shallow pan, add 2½ kg (4 lb 10 oz) breast, uncovered cutlets, neck and shoulder of mutton all cut in pieces of approximately 90 g (3 oz) in weight. Fry quickly until well coloured, having added 12 g (⅓ oz) salt, milled pepper and 5 g (⅙ oz) caster sugar. The sugar will settle slowly to the bottom of the pan where it will caramelize, then dissolve when the liquid is added thus giving the required colour to the sauce. When well coloured, drain off almost all the fat, sprinkle with 60 g (2 oz) flour and cook together for a few minutes. Moisten with 1½ litres (2⅝ pt or 6½ U.S. cups) water or stock and add 500 g (1 lb 2 oz) chopped fresh tomatoes or 1½ dl (5 fl oz or ⅝ U.S. cup) tomato purée, 1 clove of crushed garlic and a large Bouquet garni.

Bring to the boil whilst stirring, cover with a lid and cook in the oven for 1 hour.

Transfer the pieces of meat to a clean pan, add 20 button onions coloured in butter and 30 potatoes trimmed to the size and shape of Pommes à l'Anglaise. Skim off the fat from the sauce and strain over the ingredients, cover with a tight fitting lid and place in the oven to continue cooking for a further 1 hour.

To serve: skim off any remaining fat and place the Navarin in a deep dish or timbale.

2838 Navarin Printanier

Proceed as for the first part of the preceding recipe.

When the pieces of mutton are transferred to a clean pan, add 20 button onions, 300 g (11 oz) each of small trimmed carrots and turnips, both coloured and glazed in butter, 500 g (1 lb 2 oz) small even-sized potatoes, 150 g (5 oz) fresh peas and the same amount of fresh French beans cut diamond shape.

Skim off the fat from the sauce and strain over the ingredients, cover with a lid and place in the oven to continue cooking for a further 1 hour. Baste the overlying vegetables frequently with the sauce.

To serve: remove any remaining fat, place the Navarin in a deep dish or timbale and serve very hot.

Note: The vegetables take longer to cook when placed in the sauce than if they were to be simply cooked in boiling water. In a Navarin the vegetables are cooked by the progressive penetration of heat thus necessitating very slow cooking.

2839 Pilaw Caissi

Cut 750 g (1 lb 10 oz) lean loin or leg of mutton into dice and fry in butter until well coloured. Add 15 small dried apricots previously soaked in water for 2 hours, and 125 g (4½ oz) caster sugar. Barely cover these ingredients with tepid water and cook gently for 1¼ hours.

Meanwhile, heat 150 g (5 oz) butter in a thick-bottomed pan and add 500 g (1 lb 2 oz) picked Patna rice; stir over heat until the rice becomes milky in appearance then moisten with 3 times its volume of mutton Bouillon (1½ litres (2⅝ pt or 6½ U.S. cups)), or failing this, White Bouillon to which has been added 1 dl (3½ fl oz or ½ U.S. cup) tomato purée and 500 g (1 lb 2 oz) melted butter. Season with a touch of Cayenne.

Bring to the boil, cover with a lid and cook gently in the oven for 35 minutes. When ready, carefully move the rice with a fork to separate the grains and place in a timbale or deep dish.

Serve accompanied with the *Ragoût* of mutton and apricots.

Note: This dish originates from the Turkish cuisine and always figured on the menu of the banquet of the Turkish Colony in Paris. In days gone by this banquet took place at the Restaurant Bonvalet.

2840 Pilaw de Mouton à la Turque

Pilaw de Mouton is nothing more or less than a Navarin dominantly flavoured with tomato, additionally flavoured and seasoned with ginger or saffron and where rice takes the place of the vegetables.

Prepared in this manner it is not ideally suited to the requirements of a restaurant. Thus it is most commonly prepared like a curry of mutton but instead of serving it with plain boiled rice, it is placed in the centre of a border of Riz Pilaw. Sometimes the Riz Pilaw is served separately.

2841 Ragoût de Mouton au Riz—Mutton Stew with Rice

Proceed in exactly the same way for the first part of Navarin. Place the meat in a clean pan with the strained sauce after first removing the fat; cover and continue cooking in the oven.

About half an hour before it is cooked add 300 g (11 oz) Carolina rice. When ready, the rice should have almost completely absorbed the sauce.

Place in a timbale or deep dish to serve.

2842 Haggis

Take a sheep's stomach, wash it well, soak for 24 hours in cold salted water then well scrape it and replace in cold water.

Meanwhile place the liver and lights of a sheep in a pan, cover with water, season with salt and crushed peppercorns, bring to the boil, skim and cook gently for 1½ hours.

Drain the liver and lights well, then pass them through the fairly coarse plate of a mincer. To this mince add 200 g (7 oz) each of finely chopped onion and finely chopped beef kidney suet, 250 g (9 oz) oatmeal, a little grated nutmeg, the juice of 1 lemon and a few tablespoons of the cooking liquid from the liver and lights. Mix these ingredients together well and make sure that it is well seasoned with pepper.

Wash and dry the stomach and fill with the above mixture taking care that there is sufficient space left to counteract the swelling of the mixture and the shrinkage of the stomach during its cooking, thus preventing it bursting; sew it up carefully with thread. As a precaution it may also be wrapped in a clean cloth when ready.

Place the Haggis in a pan with the cooking liquid from the liver and lights plus sufficient water to well cover it. Bring to the boil and gently simmer for 3 hours.

Note: When paying homage to their national poet Robert Burns, the Scots have the Haggis presented and served with due pomp and ceremony. It is carried into the room by a servant who is preceded by a piper and it is customary to drink whisky whilst eating.

2843 AGNEAU DE LAIT—HOUSE OR YOUNG LAMB

As has already been explained, there are two types of lamb used in cookery, grass lamb and house or young lamb. The preceding recipes for mutton are suitable for and can be applied to grass lamb. The following recipes are especially suited to the second kind, that is, house or young lamb.

The large joints of house lamb are the same as those for mutton, that is to say:

- the Baron which comprises the 2 legs plus the saddle,
- the Double which comprises the 2 legs not separated,
- the Quarter (*Quartier*) which comprises one leg plus the loin.

Large joints of house lamb should either be Poêléed or roasted and their most suitable accompaniment is either their own cooking juices or a lightly thickened, well seasoned clear gravy.

They are chiefly garnished with young or early season vegetables but may also be accompanied with any of the garnishes as indicated for mutton, provided that account is taken of the difference in size.

Suitable garnishes for large joints of house lamb are: Boulangère, Bouquetière, Brabançonne, Favorite, Frascati, à la Greque, Jardinière, Montmorency, Renaissance, Richelieu etc.

2844 CERVELLES D'AGNEAU— LAMB'S BRAINS

All of the recipes as indicated for Calf's Brains are suitable.

2845 CARRE D'AGNEAU— BEST END OF LAMB

The best end of house lamb should be Poêléed or roasted in preference to any other method of treatment. Whichever method is decided upon, the side of the best end adjoining the breast should be shortened and the cutlet bones bared and trimmed.

2846 Carré d'Agneau en Cocotte à la Bonnefemme
Season the prepared best end and fry it quickly in butter to a nice brown colour. Transfer it to an oval cocotte with 10 button onions coloured in butter, 50 g (2 oz) streaky bacon cut in dice, blanched and fried in butter, and two medium potatoes, trimmed into olive-shaped pieces and blanched. Sprinkle with butter, cover with the lid and cook gently in the oven.

Place the cocotte on a folded serviette on a dish and serve as it is.

2847 Carré d'Agneau à la Boulangère
Season the prepared best end and fry it quickly in hot butter to a nice brown colour. Transfer to an earthenware dish and surround with sliced onions lightly fried in butter, and sliced potatoes. The proportions of these vegetables should take account of the size of the best end. The procedure for cooking is the same as indicated as for Epaule à la Boulangère (2783). making allowances for the size and tenderness of the joint.

2848 Carré d'Agneau Grillé
Season the prepared best end, sprinkle with butter and grill it gently. When almost ready sprinkle it well with fine breadcrumbs and colour these whilst completing the cooking.

Serve accompanied with a suitable vegetable or Mint Sauce.

2849 Carré d'Agneau Limousine
Poêlé the prepared best end in a cocotte with 20 chestnuts previously cooked in Bouillon and 10 glazed button onions.

Serve as it is in the cocotte.

Note: The chestnuts are sometimes replaced with a purée of chestnuts which should be served separately.

2850 Carré d'Agneau Louisiane
Poêlé the prepared best end in a cocotte with a few slices of sweet potato.

When ready, place the best end on a suitable dish and surround with small moulds of rice and bouquets of fried sliced bananas. See Louisiane garnish (401). It is optional to serve this dish accompanied with a dish of Maïs à la Crème.

2851 Carré d'Agneau Marly
Season the prepared best end and fry it quickly in butter to a nice brown colour. Transfer it to an earthenware terrine or casserole and add 500 g (1 lb 2 oz) Mange-tout peas broken in small pieces, a pinch of caster sugar, salt and 1 tbs water.

Cover with the lid and seal down with a band of paste simply made with flour and water. Cook in a moderate oven for 45 minutes.

Serve as it is.

2852 Carré d'Agneau Mireille
In an oval earthenware dish large enough to contain the best end, prepare a layer of Pommes Anna containing one-third its amount of sliced raw artichoke bottoms.

Place in the oven and when the potatoes are three-quarters cooked, place on top the best end of lamb which has been seasoned and coloured quickly in butter. Replace in the oven to complete the cooking of the potatoes and lamb together, basting frequently with melted butter.

Serve as it is in the dish.

2853 Carré d'Agneau Printanière
Season the prepared best end and fry it quickly in butter to a nice brown colour. Transfer it to an oval earthenware terrine or casserole and add 8 button onions, half cooked in butter, 10 pieces each of carrot and turnip, trimmed to the shape of olives, cooked in Bouillon and glazed, 2 tbs of peas and the same of raw French beans cut in diamonds and 2–3 tbs of good clear stock.

Cover with the lid and cook in the oven.

Serve as it is in the dish.

2854 Carré d'Agneau Saint-Laud, also called Carré d'Agneau Beaucaire
Season the prepared best end and fry it quickly in butter to a nice brown colour. Transfer it to an earthenware casserole with 8 small Provence artichokes cut in halves and a little butter. Cover with the lid and cook in the oven, basting frequently.

Meanwhile roughly chop 500 g (1 lb 2 oz) peeled and depipped tomatoes, cook them with a little butter, season and when ready, add a good pinch of chopped tarragon.

Spread this tomato mixture in the centre of an oval dish, place the best end on top and surround with the half artichokes.

2855 Carré d'Agneau Soubise
Season the prepared best end and fry it quickly in butter to a nice brown colour. Transfer it to a casserole and surround with 300 g (11 oz) finely sliced onions, well blanched and lightly cooked in butter without colour. Cover with the lid and place in the oven to cook.

When ready, remove the best end and keep warm. Add 1½ dl (5 fl oz or ⅝ U.S. cup) boiling Sauce Béchamel to the onions, mix together then quickly pass the whole through a fine sieve. Reheat this Soubise and finish it with 50 g (2 oz) butter.

Place the best end in the centre of a suitable dish, surround with a *cordon* of light meat glaze and serve accompanied with the Soubise in a sauceboat.

2856 Carré d'Agneau à la Toscane
Season the prepared best end and fry it quickly in butter to a nice brown colour.

Arrange a layer of Pommes Anna in the bottom of a deep oval earthenware dish, place the best end on top and then cover it with a further layer of Pommes Anna in such a manner that the best end is sandwiched between two layers of potatoes. Sprinkle with grated Parmesan and melted butter and cook in the oven as for Pommes Anna. Take care that the underlying layer of potatoes is quickly set so that the juices from the meat do not soak through to the dish and form a deposit there.

When cooked, carefully demould on to a suitable dish.

Note: There are specially manufactured earthenware dishes in which this dish can be prepared and then served as it is in the dish; this is, of course, both better and more practical than having to demould it on to another dish.

2857 COTELETTES D'AGNEAU— LAMB CUTLETS

It is customary to serve two lamb cutlets per person.

Excepting any indication to the contrary, lamb cutlets should be dipped in melted butter and sprinkled with fine breadcrumbs before grilling. If they are to be shallow fried they should be floured, egg and breadcrumbed excepting where the preparation requires them to be stuffed or served with a sauced garnish.

2858 Côtelettes d'Agneau à la Bergère
Season and shallow fry the cutlets in butter on both sides but only half cook them. Arrange them in a circle in a cocotte alternating with slices of lean ham or rectangles of streaky bacon, blanched and fried in butter. Surround with a proportionate quantity of glazed button onions and morels or mushrooms cut in quarters and cooked in butter. Cover with the lid and complete the cooking in the oven.

Just before service, place a nice bouquet of straw potatoes in the centre of the cutlets.

2859 Côtelettes d'Agneau à la Bretonne
Season and shallow fry the cutlets in butter and arrange them in a circle on a suitable dish.

Serve accompanied with a dish of a purée of Flageolets à la Bretonne and a sauceboat of Jus lié.

2860 Côtelettes d'Agneau Buloz
Season and grill the cutlets keeping them a little underdone.

Proceed in the same manner as for Côtelettes de Mouton Buloz (2761).

2861 Côtelettes d'Agneau Carignan
Lightly flatten the cutlets and flour, egg and breadcrumb them using white breadcrumbs containing one-third its volume of grated Parmesan. Shallow fry in butter and oil.

Arrange in a circle on a suitable dish and fill the centre with a mound of cockscombs and kidneys, dipped in frying batter and deep fried at the last moment.

Serve accompanied with a well flavoured Tomato Sauce.

2862 Côtelettes d'Agneau Charleroi
Season and shallow fry the cutlets on one side only and allow to become cold under light pressure. Coat the cooked sides with a little well reduced Purée Soubise and smooth dome shape; sprinkle with grated Parmesan then flour, egg and breadcrumb them.

Finally, shallow fry the prepared cutlets in clarified butter.

Arrange in a circle on a dish and serve accompanied with a sauceboat of Jus lié.

2863 Côtelettes d'Agneau Châtillon
Lightly flatten the cutlets, season them and shallow fry in butter on one side only. Drain them well then coat the cooked sides dome shape with a little finely chopped raw mushrooms cooked with butter and mixed with a little thick Sauce Béchamel.

Arrange the cutlets uncooked sides downward on a tray, sprinkle with grated Parmesan and melted butter then place in a hot oven to complete the cooking and glaze the surface of the cutlets at the same time.

Arrange in a circle on a dish, fill the centre with a thick purée of French beans and surround the cutlets with a *cordon* of lightly buttered thin meat glaze.

2864 Côtelettes d'Agneau Choiseul
Season the cutlets and shallow fry them in butter on one side only. Drain them well then coat the cooked sides dome shape with a little veal and cream forcemeat containing chopped salt ox tongue and truffle. Decorate each cutlet with a grooved round slice of very red, salt ox tongue and place a small slice of truffle in the middle of this.

Place the prepared cutlets on a tray uncooked sides downwards, sprinkle with butter and place in a moderate oven to cook the forcemeat and complete the cooking of the cutlets.

Arrange in a circle on a dish and fill the centre with a garnish composed of: braised lamb's sweetbreads, small cooked, grooved mushrooms and quarters of very white, small artichoke bottoms all mixed together with a little Sauce Allemande finished with mushroom essence.

Serve accompanied with a sauceboat of the same sauce.

2865 Côtelettes d'Agneau en Crepinettes
Flatten the cutlets very thinly, season and shallow fry quickly in butter, keeping them very underdone.

Sandwich each cutlet between two thin layers of very fine pork sausage meat containing chopped truffle, then completely wrap each in a sufficiently large triangle of pig's caul. Sprinkle with melted butter and grill gently.

When ready, arrange the cutlets in a circle on a dish and serve accompanied with a Sauce Périgueux.

2866 Côtelettes d'Agneau Cyrano
Season the cutlets and shallow fry them in butter. Arrange in a circle on a dish alternating with very thin heart-shaped Croûtons of bread fried in clarified butter.

Surround with very small artichoke bottoms filled dome-shaped with a purée of foie gras mixed with one-third its quantity of reduced Sauce Allemande. Decorate each of the filled artichoke bottoms with 4 small fluted olive shapes of truffle cut with a special vegetable scoop. These should be pushed half-way into the purée.

Serve accompanied with a Sauce Chateaubriand.

2867 Côtelettes d'Agneau Farcies Périgueux
Season the cutlets and shallow fry them on one side only; allow to become cold under light pressure. When cold, coat the cooked sides dome shape with some good pork sausage meat passed through a fine sieve and mixed with a good amount of chopped truffle.

Place them on a buttered tray, uncooked side downward then place in a moderate oven to cook the sausage meat and complete the cooking of the cutlets.

Arrange in a circle on a dish and pour some Sauce Périgueux in the middle.

2868 Côtelettes d'Agneau Henriot
Season the cutlets, grill them and allow to become cold under light pressure. Dip them into a Sauce Villeroy made with lamb stock, place on a tray and when they are cold, flour, egg and breadcrumb them.

Shallow fry the prepared cutlets then arrange them in a circle on a dish. Place in the centre a garnish of small button mushrooms cooked in butter and a little lemon juice, then mixed with a little Sauce Crème.

2869 Côtelettes d'Agneau à l'Italienne
Flour, egg and breadcrumb the cutlets using white breadcrumbs mixed with one-third its volume of grated Parmesan. Shallow fry in clarified butter.

Arrange in a circle on a dish and place in the centre a garnish of quarters of small artichokes à l'Italienne.

Serve accompanied with a thin Sauce Italienne.

2870 Côtelettes d'Agneau Malmaison
Flour, egg and breadcrumb the cutlets and shallow fry them gently in clarified butter. Have prepared a dish containing a base of Pommes Duchesse mixture, smoothed, brushed with beaten egg and coloured in the oven. Arrange the cooked cutlets in a circle on this base.

Surround with small tartlet cases, half of them filled with a purée of lentils, the other half with a purée of fresh peas; alternate these tartlets with small stuffed tomatoes.

Serve accompanied with a thin Sauce Demi-glace or Jus lié.

2871 Côtelettes d'Agneau Maréchal
Flour, egg and breadcrumb the cutlets and shallow

fry them in clarified butter. Arrange in a circle on a dish with a large slice of truffle on each. Place in the centre of the dish a nice bouquet of buttered asparagus tips.

2872 Côtelettes d'Agneau Marie-Louise
Flour, egg and breadcrumb the cutlets and shallow fry them in clarified butter. Arrange in a circle on a dish and surround with very small artichoke bottoms cooked in butter then filled dome shape with a purée of mushrooms mixed with a quarter its volume of thick Purée Soubise.

Serve accompanied with a sauceboat of Jus lié.

2873 Côtelettes d'Agneau à la Minute
Cut the cutlets very thin, season them and shallow fry very quickly in very hot clarified butter. Arrange them in a circle on a dish, sprinkle with a little lemon juice and the cooking butter after adding a pinch of chopped parsley. Serve immediately.

2874 Côtelettes d'Agneau Mirecourt
Season and shallow fry the cutlets in butter on one side only. Drain them well then coat the cooked sides dome shape with a Panada and Cream forcemeat. Place uncooked sides downward on a deep buttered tray, cover and place in the oven to cook the forcemeat and complete the cooking of the cutlets.

When ready, arrange the cutlets in a circle on a dish and place a dome of creamed purée of artichoke bottoms in the centre.

Serve accompanied with a fairly thin Velouté finished with mushroom essence.

2875 Côtelettes d'Agneau Morland
Lightly flatten the cutlets, dip them into seasoned beaten egg then roll in chopped truffle. Pat them firmly with the flat of a knife so that the chopped truffle adheres well, then shallow fry in clarified butter.

Arrange them in a circle on a dish, fill the centre with a purée of mushrooms and surround the cutlets with a *cordon* of lightly buttered meat glaze.

2876 Côtelettes d'Agneau à la Navarraise
Season and grill the cutlets on one side only. Coat the cooked sides dome shape with a mixture prepared to the following proportions: 150 g (5 oz) chopped lean ham; 150 g (5 oz) chopped cooked mushrooms, and 15 g ($\frac{1}{2}$ oz) chopped red pimentos. All these ingredients should be mixed together with $1\frac{1}{2}$ dl (5 fl oz or $\frac{5}{8}$ U.S. cup) reduced Sauce Béchamel flavoured with mushroom essence.

Place the cutlets on a buttered tray uncooked sides downward and sprinkle them with grated Parmesan and melted butter. Place in the oven to gratinate the surface of the cutlets and to complete their cooking.

When ready, arrange in a circle on a dish, each cutlet placed on a half tomato, seasoned and shallow fried in oil. Surround the cutlets with a *cordon* of Tomato Sauce.

2877 Côtelettes d'Agneau Nelson
Season and grill the cutlets on one side only. Allow to become cold under light pressure and when cold, coat the cooked sides dome shape with a Panada and Cream forcemeat containing a quarter its volume of reduced Purée Soubise.

Arrange the prepared cutlets on a buttered tray uncooked sides downward; sprinkle the forcemeat with very fine breadcrumbs and melted butter and place in the oven for 6–7 minutes to cook the forcemeat and complete the cooking of the cutlets.

Arrange them in a circle on a dish and surround with a *cordon* of fairly thin Sauce Madère.

2878 Côtelettes d'Agneau d'Orsay
Season and shallow fry the cutlets in clarified butter. Arrange them in a circle on a dish, and place in the centre a garnish composed of a short thick Julienne of salt ox tongue, cooked mushrooms and truffle, bound together with a little Velouté flavoured with truffle essence and mushroom cooking liquor.

2879 Other Preparations Suitable for Cutlets of House or Young Lamb
Maintenon, Milanaise, en Papillote, Pompadour, Soubise, à la Fondue de Tomates, Valois, Villeroy.

EPAULE D'AGNEAU—SHOULDER OF LAMB

Shoulder of grass lamb may be prepared in the same manner as shoulders of mutton. Shoulders of house lamb, however, should not be boned out.

2880 Epaule d'Agneau Boulangère
Season and colour the shoulder in butter and then Proceed exactly as for Epaule de Mouton Boulangère (2783), taking account of the difference in size and tenderness when calculating the cooking time.

2881 Epaule d'Agneau Florian
Season the shoulder, sprinkle with butter and roast in the oven placed on a trivet in the roasting tray so as to prevent it coming into contact with the fat and juices.

Baste well and turn it over from time to time, allowing approx 30 minutes cooking time. Just before it is ready, sprinkle with breadcrumbs and melted butter and replace in the oven to colour the crumbs a golden brown.

Place the finished shoulder on a dish and surround with quarters of braised lettuce, small glazed carrots trimmed to the size of olives, button onions cooked in butter and round balls of potato cut with a vegetable scoop and cooked as for Pommes Fondantes.

Serve accompanied with a clear gravy.

2882 Epaule d'Agneau de Pauillac Grillée—Grilled Shoulder of Pauillac Lamb
Season the shoulder, make a few light incisions on the skin side, sprinkle with butter and grill gently for about 25 minutes. At this time sprinkle with fine breadcrumbs and melted butter and place in the oven to colour golden brown.

Serve accompanied with a clear gravy.

2883 Epaule d'Agneau Windsor
Bone out a shoulder of lamb, season the inside and stuff with 200 g (7 oz) Panada and Butter forcemeat (286) mixed with 2 tbs dry Duxelle and ½ tbs chopped parsley. Roll it up, tie carefully and braise in the usual manner, glazing it at the last moment.

When the shoulder is ready, remove the string, cut into fairly thick slices and arrange on a dish alternating with slices of salt ox tongue so arranged as to re-form the joint.

Serve accompanied with the braising liquid after first removing all fat and passing through a fine strainer.

GIGOT D'AGNEAU—LEG OF LAMB

All of the garnishes and preparations indicated for the Baron, Double and Quarter of House Lamb plus the following recipes, are suitable for the leg of House Lamb.

2884 Gigot d'Agneau Chivry
Season the leg, flour it and tie up carefully in a clean piece of cloth. Place into lightly salted boiling water and poach gently allowing 15 minutes per 500 g (1 lb 2 oz) weight of leg.

Remove from the cooking liquid when required for service, place on a dish and serve accompanied with a Sauce Chivry.

2885 Gigot d'Agneau à l'Estragon
Prepare the leg in exactly the same way as for Gigoy à la Menthe (2887) replacing the mint with tarragon.

2886 Gigot d'Agneau à la Liégeoise
Poêlé the leg in a Cocotte or casserole. A few minutes before serving add to the prepared gravy 5 crushed and finely chopped juniper berries and ½ dl (2 fl oz or ¼ U.S. cup) of flamed gin. Pour this gravy over the leg in the Cocotte and serve as it is.

2887 Gigot d'Agneau à la Menthe
Braise the leg in the usual manner adding a bouquet of mint to the braising liquid; glaze it at the last moment. Remove the fat from the braising liquid, pass through a fine strainer, reduce and add some chopped blanched fresh mint. Place the leg on a suitable dish and serve accompanied with the prepared sauce.

2888 Gigot d'Agneau Sous Croûte
Season the leg and colour it quickly in a hot oven. Cover with a layer of forcemeat made from 500 g (1 lb 2 oz) very fine white pork sausage meat mixed with 1 medium truffle pounded together with 50 g (2 oz) pork fat and passed through a fine sieve. Envelop the whole with pig's caul then place on a sheet of firm pastry, either short paste made with lard or hot water paste (3775). Close up and seal the edges well; turn over on to a tray and make a small hole in the top to allow the steam to escape. Bake in a moderate oven for approximately 1½ hours.

When ready, place on a dish and pour 1½ dl (5 fl oz or ⅝ U.S. cup) of Sauce Périgueux through the hole at the top and so into the interior of the pastry. Serve as it is; the pastry should be broken at the table.

2889 LANGUES ET PIEDS D'AGNEAU—LAMB'S TONGUES AND TROTTERS

These may be prepared according to the recipes for the trotters and tongues of mutton. See Page 336.

2890 POITRINE D'AGNEAU—BREAST OF LAMB

The breast of lamb is utilized principally in the preparation of Epigrammes (2903) but any of the recipes for breast of mutton are suitable. See Page 337.

RIS D'AGNEAU—LAMB'S SWEETBREADS

2891 Ris d'Agneau—Lamb's Sweetbreads
Lamb's sweetbreads are used either as a principal component of various dishes or simply as part of a special garnish. In either case they should be pre-

pared initially in the same manner as for veal sweetbreads and cooked as required, due care being taken of the difference in size.

In addition to the special recipes further on, the following preparations for Veal Sweetbreads are suitable: Attereaux, Brochettes, Coquilles au Gratin, Coquilles à la Parisienne, Cromesquis, Croquettes, Croustades, etc.

2892 Pâté Chaud de Ris d'Agneau à la Chevrière

Line the bottom and sides of a well buttered dome-shaped mould, or a Charlotte mould if unobtainable, with long even rolls of short paste, about the thickness of a pencil. These should be laid spiral fashion. Now coat the inside of the prepared mould with a layer of Godiveau (290) containing chopped chives. Place in a moderate oven for a few moments to set the Godiveau then fill the interior with a mixture of braised lamb's sweetbreads and mushrooms mixed with some thick Sauce Allemande. Cover with a layer of Godiveau, then close the mould with a layer of short paste. Seal the edges together well, brush with beaten egg and cook in a moderate oven for approximately 45 minutes.

To serve: demould the Pâté on to a round dish and surround the base with a circle of nice braised and glazed lamb's sweetbreads.

2893 Timbale de Ris d'Agneau

Prepare a lightly baked Timbale case (4334) in a shallow Charlotte mould, i.e. the height of the sides should be less than its diameter. Line the bottom and sides of the case with a 2 cm ($\frac{4}{5}$ in) thick layer of Godiveau (290) containing finely chopped truffle. Place in a slow oven to cook the Godiveau.

To serve: fill the Timbale with a mixture of half the total quantity of lamb's sweetbreads braised white and the other half consisting of small cooked mushrooms, small round slices of salt ox tongue and slices of truffle, all bound with a thick Velouté finished with mushroom essence.

In the centre of the filling place a circle of veal and cream forcemeat Quenelles moulded with teaspoons, cooked at the last moment and coated with Velouté.

Place the Timbale on a serviette on a dish and serve accompanied with a sauceboat of Velouté finished with mushroom essence.

2894 Vol-au-Vent de Ris d'Agneau Soubise

Blanch and refresh 10 nice lamb's sweetbreads.

On the bottom of a thick well buttered shallow pan, place 1 kg (2 lb 4 oz) sliced and blanched Spanish onions; season with salt and pepper; arrange the sweetbreads on top and add a very little white stock. Cover with slices of salt pork fat and a lid and cook gently in the oven.

When ready, transfer the sweetbreads to a clean pan along with 10 small cooked mushrooms and 2 medium-sized truffles cut in slices.

Pass the onions through a fine sieve and mix the resultant purée together with a few tablespoons of well creamed Sauce Béchamel. Pour this over the sweetbreads and the garnish; reheat without boiling and add a little butter away from the heat.

Pour the whole into a large Vol-au-vent case and place on a serviette on a dish to serve.

Note: To vary the character of this preparation a little paprika or curry powder may be added to the onions.

2895 SELLE D'AGNEAU—SADDLE OF LAMB

The saddle of grass lamb can be prepared according to any of the recipes for saddle of mutton.

The saddle of house lamb may be suitable prepared to any of the recipes for saddle of veal, taking account, naturally, of the difference in size between the two.

Other than this they may be prepared to the following recipes which are particularly suitable.

2896 Selle d'Agneau à la Grecque

Prepare and trim the saddle keeping the breast flaps a little long. At each end of the saddle, arrange and sew on carefully, a thin piece of breast of lamb, of the same size as the flaps on the saddle so that the whole forms a perfect square.

Turn the prepared saddle on to its back and fill the inside with 500 g (1 lb 2 oz) of two-thirds cooked Riz à la Grecque. Turn in the flaps of breast to the centre and sew up carefully.

Braise the saddle in the usual manner and glaze it at the last minute. Remove the thread and place the lamb on a suitable dish. Surround with the braising liquid after first removing the fat, passing through a fine strainer and reducing it.

2897 Selle d'Agneau Washington

Proceed in exactly the same way as for the previous recipe using maize instead of rice.

Note: In either case the saddle may be accompanied with new season's vegetables, or a green vegetable which should be served separately.

2898 Selle d'Agneau de Lait Edouard VII (*cold*)

Completely bone out the saddle from underneath in such a manner as to leave the skin intact. Season the inside and place in the centre a nice raw foie gras which has been studded with truffle and marinated in Marsala. Re-form the saddle to its original shape and wrap it tightly in a piece of muslin. Place in a pan just large enough to hold it and the bottom of which is covered with a layer of de-fatted, blanched pork rinds. Moisten just to cover, with the braising liquid from a cushion of veal and add the Marsala used for marinating the foie gras. Poach very carefully for approximately 45 minutes.

Before removing the saddle make sure that the foie gras is cooked. When ready, remove the muslin, place the saddle in an earthenware terrine just large enough to hold it and strain the cooking liquid over it without removing any fat. Allow to cool.

When quite cold and set firm, carefully remove the fat, first with a spoon and then with a little boiling water.

Serve the saddle very cold as it is in the terrine.

2899 NOISETTES D'AGNEAU

As for mutton and grass lamb, Noisettes of house lamb are cut from the saddle or the first part of the best end, allowing two per person.

Their preparation is the same and all the recipes for Tournedos are suitable.

OTHER PREPARATIONS OF LAMB

2900 Blanquette d'Agneau
Proceed in exactly the same way as indicated for Blanquette de Veau (2726) observing the same instructions for both parts of the operation but reducing the cooking time by 45 minutes.

According to the recipes in the same section, Blanquette d'Agneau may also be prepared, aux Céleris, aux Cardons, aux Endives, aux Mousserons, aux Nouilles, etc.

2901 Crépinettes d'Agneau à la Liégeoise
Finely chop 800 g ($1\frac{3}{4}$ lb) lean lamb free from skin and sinew, and add 300 g (11 oz) white breadcrumbs soaked in milk and well squeezed, 150 g (5 oz) finely chopped onion, partly cooked in butter and finished cooking with a little Bouillon, 2 crushed and chopped juniper berries and 10 g ($\frac{1}{3}$ oz) salt and a little pepper. Mix all these ingredients together well.

Divide the mixture into pieces of 100 g ($3\frac{1}{2}$ oz) and wrap each in a rectangle of very soft pig's caul. Shallow fry these Crépinettes very slowly in clarified butter.

Arrange them in a circle on a dish and sprinkle with the butter in which they were cooked.

Serve accompanied with a dish of mashed potato.

2902 Currie d'Agneau—Curry of Lamb
Proceed as indicated for Currie a l'Indienne (2829) taking account of the difference in the tenderness of the meat and adjusting the cooking time accordingly.

2903 Epigrammes d'Agneau
The Epigramme of lamb consists of a cutlet of lamb and a piece of braised breast of lamb, boned out, cooled under light pressure then cut to the shape of a cutlet or a long heart shape. Both these pieces of lamb are then floured, egg and breadcrumbed, and they may be either grilled or shallow fried in butter.
To serve: arrange the cooked Epigrammes in a circle, alternating the pieces, with the garnish in the centre or served separately.
Suitable Garnishes for Epigrammes are: Chicorée, Macédoine, Maréchal, Petits Pois, Pointes d'Asperges, purées of vegetables, Vert-Pré, etc.

2904 Pilaw d'Agneau
Proceed in the same manner as indicated for Pilaw de Mouton (2840).

2905 SAUTES D'AGNEAU—SAUTES OF LAMB

Two important points need to be stressed in the preparation of Sautés of lamb.

1) It is preferable that the lamb should be treated literally as a Sauté of chicken, that is, the pieces of lamb should be completely cooked when shallow frying them in the clarified butter before adding the sauce and they should not then be boiled in the sauce.
2) The quantity of sauce should be kept to a minimum. If the sauté includes a vegetable garnish, the items of this garnish should be cooked separately and only added to the sauté some 10 minutes before serving.

2906 Sauté d'Agneau Chasseur
Season the pieces of lamb and shallow fry them in butter and oil until completely cooked.

Remove the pieces and keep on a dish; drain off the fat completely, deglaze the pan with white wine, reduce and add the required amount of Sauce Chasseur. Replace the lamb in this sauce and keep hot without boiling for 5 minutes.
To serve: place in a timbale or deep dish and sprinkle with chopped parsley.

2907 Sauté d'Agneau à la Forestière
Proceed in exactly the same way as for Poulet Sauté Forestière (3213).

2908 Sauté d'Agneau Printanier

Have prepared the following garnish: 20 small carrots cooked in Bouillon and glazed, 20 pieces of turnip trimmed to the shape of long olives, likewise cooked in Bouillon and glazed, 15 small onions cooked in butter, 20 potatoes the size of a walnut, cooked in butter without colour and 3 tbs each of peas and French beans both plain boiled in salted water.

Cut 500 g (1 lb 2 oz) shoulder and the same amount of breast of lamb into pieces of approximately 60 g (2 oz) in weight. Season them and shallow fry in butter until completely cooked and brown in colour.

Transfer the pieces to a dish, drain off all the fat and deglaze the pan with ½ dl (2 fl oz or ¼ U.S. cup) of water. Add 1 dl (3½ fl oz or ½ U.S. cup) pale meat glaze and reheat without boiling. Finish with 50 g (2 oz) butter then add the pieces of lamb and the garnish to this sauce. Shake the pan carefully on the side of the stove so as to cover the ingredients with the sauce.

Place in a timbale or deep dish and serve hot.

PORK

2909 Joints of Pork

Large joints (Relevés) of fresh pork are used more frequently in household or Bourgeois cookery than in the professional kitchen. They are always roasted and may be accompanied with any garnish of fresh or dried vegetables, purées of vegetables, or any of the pastas such as macaroni, noodles, Polenta, Gnocchi, etc.

CARRE DE PORC—BEST END OF PORK

2910 Carré de Porc à la Choucroute—Roast Best End of Pork with Sauerkraut

Roast the best end of pork but only three-quarters cook it then place in an *Etuve* to finish cooking slowly. If an *Etuve* is not available complete the cooking in a slow oven.

Prepare a garnish of braised sauerkraut and during the last hour of its cooking, frequently sprinkle with fat from the roasting pork.

When ready, arrange the pork on a suitable dish; drain off the excess fat from the sauerkraut and arrange the sauerkraut around the pork.

2911 Carré de Porc aux Choux Rouges—Roast Best End of Pork with Red Cabbage

Roast the best end as in the preceding recipe and present it on a dish surrounded by a garnish of Choux Rouges à la Limousine (4056) or à la Flamande (4055).

2912 Carré de Porc aux Choux de Bruxelles—Roast Best End of Pork with Brussels Sprouts

Roast the best end in an earthenware dish. Blanch the sprouts and arrange them around the pork 20 minutes before it is finally cooked. Finish cooking together, frequently basting the sprouts with the fat and juices from the pork.

Serve as it is in the dish.

2913 Carré de Porc à la Marmelade de Pommes—Roast Best End of Pork with Apple Sauce

Roast the best end in the usual manner.

Peel and core 750 g (1 lb 10 oz) apples and cut into slices. Place in a pan with 1 dl (3½ fl oz or ½ U.S. cup) water and 30 g (1 oz) caster sugar; cover tightly with a lid to concentrate the steam and cook quickly. Whisk firmly to make the sauce smooth.

Place the best end of pork on a dish and surround with its gravy from which three-quarters of the fat has been removed. Serve the apple sauce separately.

2914 Carré de Porc à la Paysanne

Roast the best end in an earthenware dish. When it is half cooked surround it with 1 kg (2¼ lb) potatoes cut in quarters and 250 g (9 oz) sliced onions cooked in butter. Complete the cooking together, basting the garnish frequently with the fat from the roasting of the pork.

On removing from the oven, sprinkle a little roughly chopped parsley on the garnish and serve the dish as it is.

2915 Carré de Porc à la Soissonaise

Roast the best end in an earthenware dish. When it is three-quarters cooked, surround with 1½ kg (3 lb 6 oz) cooked and well drained haricot beans. Finish cooking together, frequently basting the beans with the fat from the pork.

Serve as it is in the dish.

2916 Roast Best End of Pork with Various Purées

Roast the best end in the usual manner. Place on a suitable dish and surround with its roast gravy after removing three-quarters of the fat.

Serve accompanied and to choice with a purée of either celery, lentils, onions, split peas or potatoes.

2917 Roast Best End of Pork with Various Sauces

Roast the best end in the usual manner. Place on a

suitable dish and serve accompanied with a suitable sauce such as Charcutière, Piquante, Robert, Tomate, etc.

Note: If the selected sauce includes a reduction of vinegar, surround the edges of the dish with gherkins.

CARRE DE PORC FROID—COLD BEST END OF PORK

2918 Carré de Porc, Salade de Choux Rouges
Trim the cooked best end then cut it into very thin slices. Arrange these slices overlapping on a dish and surround with a border of gherkins.

Serve accompanied with 1) a salad of pickled red cabbage containing some finely sliced sweet apples and 2) a sauceboat of Sauce Suédoise.

2919 CERVELLES DE PORC—PIG'S BRAINS

The preparation of pig's brains is the same as for any other brains. All of the recipes for ox and calf's brains are suitable.

COTES DE PORC—PORK CUTLETS

2920 Côtes de Porc Charcutière
Flatten the cutlets, season, pass through melted butter and breadcrumbs and grill them gently.

Arrange in a circle on a dish and place in the centre a mound of mashed potatoes; serve accompanied with a Sauce Charcutière.

2921 Côtes de Porc à la Flamande
Season the cutlets and colour them brown quickly in butter. Arrange them in an earthenware dish and surround with thick slices of peeled, cored sweet apples, allowing 100 g (3½ oz) per cutlet. Finish cooking gently together in the oven and serve as it is in the dish.

2922 Côtes de Porc Grand'mère
Remove the meat from the cutlet bones, chop it finely and add per 500 g (1 lb 2 oz) of meat, 100 g (3½ oz) butter, 50 g (2 oz) chopped onion, cooked in butter without colour, 1 egg, salt, pepper and a touch of grated nutmeg. Mix these ingredients well together.

Mould the mixture to the shape of cutlets and attach one of the cutlet bones to the side of each. Wrap in a piece of pig's caul, sprinkle with butter and grill them gently.

Arrange in a circle on a dish and serve accompanied with a dish of mashed potatoes.

2923 Côtes de Porc à la Milanaise
Flatten the cutlets well, season, then flour, egg and breadcrumb with white breadcrumbs containing one-third its quantity of grated Parmesan. Shallow fry gently in butter.

Arrange in a circle on a dish, place a Milanaise garnish (418) in the centre and serve accompanied with Tomato Sauce.

2924 Côtes de Porc, Sauce Piquante or Sauce Robert
Pork cutlets accompanied with a sauce are either grilled or shallow fried in butter, then arranged in a circle on a dish with the sauce in the middle.

They may also be passed through melted butter and crumbed for grilling, or floured, egg and breadcrumbed for shallow frying; in this case they should be fairly well flattened first. In either case the sauce should be served separately.

Note: The various garnishes indicated for best end of pork are also suitable for pork cutlets.

2925 ECHINEE DE PORC—SPARE RIB OF PORK

The spare rib of pork is a joint taken from the back of the carcase above the shoulder proper. The French term Echinée can also refer to a joint when it is removed from the neck, best end or loin of the carcase but as a joint without bones.

The spare rib may be prepared as Carbonades à la Flamande (2459) or roasted and accompanied with the same garnishes as for the best end of pork as well as with braised, stuffed or gratinated cabbage. Half salted, then roasted and served cold, the spare rib of pork becomes one of the great dishes of the *Charcuteries* of central France. In this area it is often referred to as *Epinée*.

2926 EPAULE DE PORC SHOULDER OF PORK

The shoulder of pork when boned out, salted, rolled and smoked is prepared in the same way as ham. Salted, it is frequently used as an ingredient for the preparation of special local soups in France, these being referred to as *Potées*.

The fresh shoulder of pork can be roasted and served with any of the garnishes applicable to the best end and spare ribs of pork as well as pork cutlets. However, the joint is really too ordinary for anything other than the family table.

2927 FILET DE PORC—LOIN OF PORK

The loin of pork is commonly used as a luncheon Entrée. It is that part of the carcase lying between the leg and the best end and may be prepared in the same manner as the best end. It also provides chops, Noisettes and fillets (Fr. *Filets Mignons*) which can be prepared in the same manner as pork cutlets.

2928 FOIE DE PORC—PIG'S LIVER

Pig's liver is not very popular and is most frequently used in the preparation of forcemeats.

The methods of preparation specially suitable for pig's liver are: à la Bourgeoise, à l'Italienne, Sauté au Vin Rouge, etc.

2929 JAMBE FARCIE, OR ZAMPINO

The Zampino or stuffed shank of pork is a speciality product of the Italian pork butchers. It is cooked in the same way as ham, taking care first to prick it well all over with a trussing needle then to wrap it in a piece of clean cloth and tie up. This prevents the skin splitting whilst cooking. When served hot it can be accompanied with a Tomato or Madeira Sauce, or with a garnish of sauerkraut, boiled, braised or gratinated cabbage, French beans, purée of peas, mashed potatoes etc.

2930 Cold Zampino
Cold Zampino is served as often cold as hot and either by itself or mixed with other cold meats, but above all it is used for Hors-d'oeuvre. It should be cut as thinly as possible.

2931 JAMBON—HAM

In spite of Monselet's eulogistic poem and the title *Animal Encylopedique* bestowed upon it by Grimod de la Reynière, it is certain that without the culinary value of its hams, pork would not hold the place it does in the repertoire of the classical kitchen.

In effect, the ham provides a valuable resource and whether it be Bayonne, York, Prague or Westphalian it is hardly necessary to say that no other joint enjoys such favour when served as a Relevé.

The question as to which ham should be used is very difficult to decide. Nevertheless the preference must go to the sweet ham of Bohemia—the Prague ham—for serving hot and to the York ham for cold. This last ham is also excellent when served hot but even so is inferior to the Prague, the delicacy of which is incomparable. However, the York ham holds one of the first places in the esteem of gourmets and it is the most used and most highly recommended ham after the Prague.

The Cooking of Ham: Soak the ham in cold water for 6 hours, brush it well then remove the aitch bone. Place it in a large pot with plenty of cold water and with no seasoning or flavouring whatsoever. Bring to the boil, then allow to simmer very, very gently indeed, sufficient only to cook the ham by poaching.

If required for cold, where possible leave the ham to cool in the cooking liquid.

The cooking time for a ham varies, naturally, according to its weight and quality. Allow approximately 20 minutes per 500 g (1 lb 2 oz) for a York ham and likewise for Hamburg and Westphalian hams. Bohemian and Spanish hams require only 15 minutes per 500 g (1 lb 2 oz).

The Braising of Ham: When required for serving hot, remove the ham from the liquid 30 minutes before the completion of cooking. Remove the skin, trim off the excess fat, i.e. just remove the surface leaving the fat approximately $1\frac{1}{2}$ cm ($\frac{3}{5}$ in) thick. It is always better to leave it too thick than to remove too much.

Place the trimmed ham in a braising pan just large enough to hold it and add about 4 dl (14 fl oz or $1\frac{3}{4}$ U.S. cups) of a fortified wine such as Port, Madeira, Sherry or Chypre. The wine used would be chosen as designated by its name on the menu.

Cover with a tight-fitting lid, seal with a flour and water paste and place in a warm oven for 1 hour so as to complete the cooking and to allow the ham to become completely impregnated with the aroma of the wine.

If the ham is to be presented whole it should first be glazed.

The usual accompaniment is a light Sauce Demi-glace with the addition of the braising liquid, skimmed of all fat and pass through a fine strainer.

The Glazing of Ham: The ham may be glazed if necessary in the same manner as other braised joints but this is not very practical, neither does it add anything to the quality of the joint. The most widely used method and the one to be recommended is to well cover the surface of the cooked ham with icing sugar, using a sugar sifter. When covered with an even coating, place it in a very hot oven or under the salamander. The sugar will caramelize instantly, enveloping the ham in a golden and appetizing coating which adds an excellent flavour to that of the ham.

Note: Having indicated the principal methods used in the

preparation of ham it is felt unnecessary to repeat these in the following recipes. Only the additions for braising and other items are given.

2932 Jambon à la Bayonnaise
Braise the ham with Madeira and glaze it. Prepare a Riz Pilaw with 500 g (1 lb 2 oz) rice, 150 g (5 oz) chopped onion and $1\frac{1}{2}$ litres ($2\frac{5}{8}$ pt or $6\frac{1}{2}$ U.S. cups) White Bouillon. When the rice is half cooked add 250 g (9 oz) roughly chopped flesh only of tomato, 20 small, cooked button mushrooms and 20 small chipolata sausages coloured in butter. Complete the braising and 10 minutes before service add 125 g ($4\frac{1}{2}$ oz) Beurre Noisette.

Place the ham on a suitable dish and serve accompanied with 1) the rice in a timbale or deep dish, and 2) a Sauce Madère prepared from the cooking liquid of the ham.

2933 Jambon à la Bourguignonne
Braise the ham with a Mirepoix Bordelaise (323) plus half its quantity of mushroom trimmings and some Pouilly wine.

Place the ham on a suitable dish and serve accompanied with 1) a Sauce Madère containing *Mousserons* or ordinary mushrooms cut in fairly thick slices and cooked in butter, and 2) the braising liquid from the ham passed firmly through a fine strainer to extract the essential flavours of the Mirepoix.

2934 Jambon à la Chanoinesse
Braise the ham with white wine using Chablis or Graves and adding 100 g ($3\frac{1}{2}$ oz) mushroom trimmings.

Place on a suitable dish and surround with a garnish of fresh noodles mixed with butter and Purée Soubise and completed with a Julienne of truffle.

Serve accompanied with a well buttered meat glaze to which has been added the braising liquid, passed through a fine strainer, skimmed of fat and reduced.

2935 Jambon à la Choucroûte
Completely cook the ham by poaching, remove the skin and trim off the excess fat.

If to be served whole, surround the ham with braised sauerkraut and freshly cooked boiled potatoes.

If to be served cut in slices, arrange them overlapping in a circle and place the braised sauerkraut and boiled potatoes in the centre.

In either case, serve accompanied with a Sauce Demi-glace finished with Rhine wine.

2936 Jambon aux Epinards
Braise the ham with Madeira.

Serve accompanied with a dish of leaf spinach cooked à l'Anglaise (4095) and a Sauce Demi-glace containing the reduced cooking liquid from the ham after removing all fat, passing through a fine strainer and reducing it.

2937 Jambon Financière, or Jambon Godard
The garnishing of hams with other than vegetables or farinaceous items is not generally favoured by modern culinary practice whereas Financière and Godard garnishes were commonly used for ham in the old classical cuisine. However, these types of garnish are quite suitable and can be used when needed.

When the ham is served with one of these garnishes, it is braised with Madeira and the garnish served separately. The reduced wine from the braising of the ham is added to the sauce used for the garnish.

2938 Jambon Fitz-James
Braise the ham with Madeira and glaze it.

Place on a suitable dish and surround with alternate small moulds of tomato-flavoured Risotto and stuffed mushrooms.

Serve accompanied with a Sauce Madère containing cockscombs and kidneys and the reduced wine from the braising of the ham.

2939 Jambon aux Fèves de Marais—Braised Ham with Broad Beans
Braise the ham with a suitable wine and glaze it.

Place on a suitable dish and serve accompanied with 1) a dish of buttered very fresh, broad beans, their skins removed and finally mixed with a little chopped savory, and 2) the braising liquid from the ham.

2940 Jambon Frais Braisé, or Rôti—Braised or Roast Leg of Pork
The fresh leg of pork may be prepared in the same manner as the cushion of veal.

If braised, allow at least 40 minutes per 1 kg ($2\frac{1}{4}$ lb) cooking time.

If roasted in the oven, allow at least 45 minutes per 1 kg ($2\frac{1}{4}$ lb) cooking time.

Suitable garnishes for braised or roasted leg of fresh pork are: vegetable purées, green vegetables, Chicorée, endives or pastas such as noodles etc.

Serve accompanied with a lightly thickened gravy.

2941 Jambon aux Laitues—Braised Ham with Lettuce
Braise the ham with Madeira and glaze it.

Place on a suitable dish and surround it with halves of braised lettuce. If served cut in slices, place the halves of lettuce between the slices.

Serve accompanied with a light Sauce Demi-glace.

2942 Jambon à la Maillot

Braise the ham with Madeira and glaze it.

Place on a suitable dish and surround with a garnish à la Maillot (405) arranged in well separated bouquets.

Serve accompanied with Jus lié containing some of the wine from the braising of the ham.

2943 Jambon à la Milanaise

Braise the ham with Marsala and glaze it.

Place on a suitable dish and serve accompanied with 1) a Milanaise garnish (418), and 2) a light Sauce Demi-glace, strongly flavoured with tomato.

2944 Jambon Monselet

Braise the ham with Sherry and glaze it.

Place on a suitable dish and surround with bouquets of Rissoles of spinach (1235) containing chopped salt ox tongue. These Rissoles may be moulded to different shapes as required.

Serve accompanied with a Sauce Financière containing slices of truffle and the reduced wine from the braising of the ham.

2945 Jambon de Prague Sous Croûte

Poach the ham in water, drain it well and allow it to half cool. Remove the skin, trim it all over and glaze it.

Prepare a large sheet of Pie Paste or Hot Water Paste (3775) and place the ham in the centre glazed side down. Draw the edges of the paste over the ham so as to completely enclose it and seal the edges together carefully. Turn the ham over so that the joins are underneath and place on a baking tray. Brush with beaten egg, decorate by lightly scoring the surface with a small knife and make a hole in the centre to allow the steam to escape.

Place in a hot oven and bake carefully until the pastry becomes very dry and well coloured.

On removing the ham from the oven, pour 2 dl (7 fl oz or $\frac{7}{8}$ U.S. cup) of Port or Sherry into the interior through the hole in the pastry, then close up the hole with a small piece of paste.

Place on a suitable dish and serve accompanied with a light Port Wine flavoured meat glaze, well buttered at the last moment.

Note: If using Hot Water Paste instead of short paste, it is not brushed with egg or decorated but is just moistened with water; it is then placed in a very hot oven. When the pastry is set, the selected wine is introduced through a hole in the middle which is then closed up. The pastry should then be cooked and coloured until burnt and quite black all over.

2946 Prague Ham with Pastas or Fresh Vegetables

In addition to the garnishes and methods of preparation already indicated, Prague ham and for that matter, any ham served hot, may be garnished with any pasta such as Noodles, Gnocchi, Lasagnes, Spaghetti etc. These should be lightly buttered or mixed with cream, then finished with grated cheese.

All green and fresh season vegetables such as French beans, peas, kidney beans, hop shoots, nettles, spinach, lettuce etc., provide equally excellent garnishes. Care should be taken, however, to see that they are cooked at the last possible moment then very lightly buttered.

In all cases where these garnishes are used they should be served separately as well as the sauce.

2947 Jambon de Prague Metternich

Prepare the ham as for Sous Croûte (2945).

Serve at the same time 1) some nice thick slices of foie gras, shallow fried in butter then each covered with a large slice of truffle, 2) a dish of buttered asparagus tips and 3) a Sauce Demi-glace finished with truffle essence.

For the actual service, on each plate place a slice of ham, a slice of foie gras, a spoonful of asparagus tips and a little of the sauce.

2948 Jambon de Prague Norfolk

Prepare the ham as for Sous Croûte (2945).

Serve at the same time 1) some nice slices of braised veal sweetbreads, 2) a dish of Petits Pois à la Paysanne (4166), and 3) the braising liquid from the sweetbreads.

For service, each slice of ham should be accompanied with a slice of sweetbread, a spoonful of peas and a little of the braising liquid.

2949 Jambon Ordinaire Sous Croûte

Poach the ham but only half cook it. Drain it well, remove the skin and trim. Cover with a thick layer of Matignon well cooked in butter, then enclose the whole in a sheet of Hot Water Paste (3775). Draw the edges of the paste over the ham and seal the edges together carefully. Turn over on to a baking tray, make a hole in the centre and place in a hot oven.

After about $1\frac{1}{2}$ hours pour as much Madeira into the hole as will fill the interior. Close up the hole with a piece of paste and continue cooking gently for another 30 minutes.

Place on a suitable dish and serve accompanied with a Sauce Madère.

2950 HOT MOUSSE AND MOUSSELINES OF HAM

Mousses and Mousselines of ham are made from the same basic preparation which is a Mousseline forcemeat of ham.

The need to use two different names has already been explained. A Mousse is cooked in a mould and is usually for a number of persons whereas Mousselines are moulded with spoons in the form of egg-shaped Quenelles and are usually used for individual portions.

Composition of the Forcemeat: The preparation of a Mousseline forcemeat is always the same no matter which basic item of flesh is used; see the section of forcemeats, (288). However, in the preparation of Mousseline forcemeat of ham, account should be taken of the degree of salt, more or less, in the ham being used and to adjust the amount in consequence.

If the ham is not very red, the colour of the forcemeat may be made a little deeper by adding a few drops of red vegetable colour, but only sufficient to give it a nice clean pale pink tone.

The cooking of Hot Mousse of Ham: Place the forcemeat in a well buttered deep Charlotte-type mould and poach it under cover in a Bain-marie keeping the water at a constant temperature of 98 °C.

For a mould of 1 litre (1¾ pt or 4½ U.S. cups) capacity, allow a cooking time of 40 minutes. The mousse is cooked when it starts rising in the mould and begins to swell.

When the mousse is removed from the Bain-marie, allow it to rest for 5 minutes so as to settle in the mould, then turn it over on to a dish leaving it for 2 minutes before removing the mould. This should not be done until all the liquid which has drained into the dish has been sponged up.

Accompaniments for Hot Mousse of Ham: The most suitable accompaniments are 1) well flavoured, smooth textured brown sauces, such as, au Madère, au Porto, au Marsala etc., or Sauce Suprême, Velouté au Currie or au Paprika, and 2) garnishes of young vegetables or a Financière garnish.

2951 Mousselines Chaudes de Jambon—Hot Mousselines of Ham

As has already been stated, Mousselines are moulded with spoons like Quenelles. They may also be piped out with a piping bag and tube to a plain or grooved meringue shape on to the bottom of a buttered shallow pan. This method of moulding is highly recommended as being both practical and quick.

In either case the Mousselines should be decorated with small shapes of ham and truffle then covered with lightly salted boiling water and poached for 18–20 minutes.

They may also be cooked dry in a very slow oven or in a steamer.

2952 Mousselines de Jambon Alexandra

Decorate the Mousselines with a thin diamond of ham and two diamonds of truffle.

Poach them, drain well and arrange in a circle on a suitable dish. Coat with Sauce Suprême flavoured with ham essence and containing 100 g (3½ oz) grated Parmesan per 1 litre (1¾ pt or 4½ U.S. cups) of sauce. Glaze quickly in a very hot oven.

On removing from the oven, place a bouquet of buttered asparagus tips in the centre of the Mousselines.

2953 Mousselines de Jambon à la Florentine

Place a layer of coarsely chopped, cooked and buttered spinach leaves in a suitable dish. Arrange the poached and well drained Mousselines on top, coat with the same sauce as for Mousselines Alexandra and glaze quickly.

2954 Mousselines de Jambon à la Hongroise

When preparing the forcemeat, flavour it with paprika. Mould the Mousselines, poach them, drain well and arrange in a circle on a suitable dish. Coat with Sauce Hongroise and glaze quickly in a hot oven.

On removing from the oven, place a bouquet of Cauliflower au Gratin in the centre of the Mousselines.

Note: The cauliflower can also be placed in the centre of the Mousselines, then coated with sauce and gratinated at the same time as the Mousselines.

2955 Mousselines de Jambon aux Petits Pois

Proceed in exactly the same way as for Mousselines Alexandra but replacing the buttered asparagus tips with buttered peas.

SOUFFLES CHAUDS DE JAMBON—
HOT HAM SOUFFLÉS

Soufflés of ham are made from a mixture using either cooked or raw ham. The mixture using raw ham is in effect a type of Mousseline forcemeat and being less fragile it has the advantage of keeping its quality for some time if prepared in advance. Thus it is more suitable for serving large numbers of people.

2956 The preparation of Soufflé Mixture with Cooked Ham

Finely pound 500 g (1 lb 2 oz) very lean cooked

ham, adding little by little 3 tbs cold Sauce Béchamel; pass through a fine sieve.

Place the resultant purée in a pan, mix in 2 dl (7 fl oz or $\frac{7}{8}$ U.S. cup) Sauce Béchamel flavoured with ham essence and 5 egg yolks. Finally fold in 7 stiffly beaten egg whites.

Note: 100 g ($3\frac{1}{2}$ oz) grated Parmesan may be added to this mixture; the two flavours blend very well together. Prepared in this way the mixture is especially suitable for the preparation of Ham Soufflé (2958).

2957 The Preparation of Soufflé Mixture with Raw Ham

Prepare a Mousseline forcemeat of ham (288) replacing one-quarter of the cream normally used with the same quantity of very cold Sauce Béchamel.

Keep the mixture fairly stiff and finish it with 4 stiffly beaten egg whites per 500 g (1 lb 2 oz) of ham.

2958 Jambon Soufflé—Ham Soufflé

Remove the central bone from the ham starting at the thick end and without cutting it open. Leave the end bone (Tibia) untouched. Poach the ham and allow to become quite cold.

Remove the skin and trim neatly all round. Cut horizontally from the thick end to the head of the tibia bone, then cut across and down to meet the first incision. This should leave a flat platform of ham about $2\frac{1}{2}$ cm (1 in) thick attached to the end bone. The removed cushion of ham is put on one side for some other use.

Trim the platform of ham neatly, surround with a band of strong buttered paper and secure this in place by tying round with string. The purpose of this is to hold in the actual soufflé. Place the whole on the serving dish.

This done, place inside a quantity of either cooked ham soufflé mixture (2956) or raw ham soufflé mixture (2957) sufficient to mould it to the original shape of the ham.

Smooth the surface with a palette knife dipped in cold water so as to give it a correct ham shape and decorate the surface with thin shapes of lean cooked ham and truffle.

Place the dish containing the ham on a flat pan of boiling water which has been put in the oven in advance. This is to obtain the maximum amount of steam in the oven which will facilitate the cooking by poaching of the soufflé mixture.

When properly cooked, remove the band of paper, clean the dish and present and serve accompanied with any of the sauces and garnishes indicated for braised ham.

2959 Soufflé de Jambon Alexandra

Prepare a cooked ham soufflé mixture (2956) or a raw ham soufflé mixture (2957).

Spread it in layers in a buttered soufflé mould alternating with layers of buttered asparagus tips. Smooth the surface dome shape, decorate with slices of truffle, cook in a moderate oven and serve immediately.

Note: If the soufflé is small, use only one layer of asparagus tips between two of the mixture; if large, two or three layers of asparagus finishing with the mixture, would be necessary.

2960 Soufflé de Jambon Carmen

Prepare a cooked ham soufflé mixture (2956) or a raw ham soufflé mixture (2957).

Spread it in layers in a buttered soufflé mould alternating with layers of a mixture prepared from 500 g (1 lb 2 oz) tomato flesh cooked together with 1 sweet pimento then passed through a fine sieve and well reduced.

Smooth the final layer of soufflé mixture dome shape, sprinkle with a little very fine Julienne of red pimento and cook in a moderate oven. Serve immediately.

Note: Instead of interposing layers of the two mixtures, the prepared purée of tomato and pimento may be mixed directly into the soufflé mixture before placing in the dish.

2961 Soufflé de Jambon des Gastronomes

Prepare a cooked ham soufflé mixture (2956) or a raw ham soufflé mixture (2957). Spread it in layers in a buttered soufflé mould alternating with layers of sliced Morels sautéed in butter. Smooth the final layer of soufflé mixture dome shape, sprinkle with a little chopped truffle and place a small ball of truffle in the centre. Cook in a moderate oven and serve immediately.

2962 Soufflé de Jambon à la Milanaise

Prepare a cooked ham soufflé mixture (2956) or a raw ham soufflé mixture (2957).

Spread it in layers in a buttered soufflé mould alternating with layers of a thinly cut Milanaise garnish (418). Smooth the final layer of soufflé mixture dome shape and decorate the surface with small pieces of buttered macaroni which should be slightly set into the mixture. Cook in a moderate oven and serve immediately.

2963 Soufflé de Jambon à la Périgourdine

Prepare a cooked ham soufflé mixture (2956) or a raw ham soufflé mixture (2957).

Spread it in layers in a buttered soufflé mould alternating with layers of thick slices of truffle.

Smooth the final layer of mixture dome shape and sprinkle with chopped truffle. Cook in a moderate oven and serve immediately.

JAMBON FROID—COLD HAM

2964 Jambon à la Gelée
When a ham is required for cold it should, where possible, be allowed to cool in its cooking liquid, excepting where it has to be boned. In this case remove it as soon as it is cooked, then cut it underneath following the edges of the cushion; detach the bones and remove them. Then roll up the ham, bind tightly in a piece of clean cloth and allow it to cool under pressure.

Whether boned or not, remove the skin when it is cold and trim it carefully of any excess fat. Coat evenly with a fairly thick layer of aspic jelly and place on a dish. Fix a ham frill on the bared bone at the end of the ham and surround with nice cut shapes of jelly.

2965 Jambon de Prague en Surprise
Braise the ham with Champagne and allow it to cool.

When quite cold remove the skin and trim off the excess fat. Cut out a hollow from the top in the centre of the ham so as to form a sort of case or well and fill this with a Parfait of foie gras. Smooth the surface, decorate with slices of truffle then coat the whole ham with a layer of aspic jelly.

Place the prepared ham on a dish and surround with thin slices of the ham which was removed from the centre.

Serve a slice of ham with a spoonful of foie gras per person.

2966 Jambon Soufflé Froid—Cold Ham Soufflé
Proceed as indicated for Jambon Soufflé (2958) replacing the soufflé mixture with a cold ham Mousse mixture as in the following recipe.

Coat with aspic jelly, place on a suitable dish and surround with nice cut shapes of jelly.

2967 Mousse Froide de Jambon—Cold Ham Mousse
Finely pound 500 g (1 lb 2 oz) very lean cooked ham, adding 2 dl (7 fl oz or $\frac{7}{8}$ U.S. cup) cold Velouté, then pass the whole through a fine sieve.

Place the resultant purée in a basin, adjust the seasoning and mix on ice for a few minutes. Add and mix in little by little, $1\frac{1}{2}$ dl (5 fl oz or $\frac{5}{8}$ U.S. cup) cool melted aspic jelly and finally fold in 4 dl (14 fl oz or $1\frac{3}{4}$ U.S. cups) half whipped cream.

For the moulding of this Mousse see (333).

2968 Mousse Froide de Jambon à l'Alsacienne
Prepare the Mousse as in the previous recipe adding to the ham, one-third its amount of cooked foie gras before passing through the sieve. Lastly, after adding the half whipped cream, carefully mix in a garnish of foie gras and truffle both cut in small dice.

Demould the Mousse on to a dish at the last moment if it has been moulded, and surround with small Mousselines of Parfait of foie gras, fashioned with dessert spoons and set in the refrigerator before using. If the Mousse is set in a glass bowl the Mousselines should be arranged neatly on top.

2969 Mousse Froide de Jambon au Foie Gras—Cold Ham Mousse with Foie Gras
Half fill a deep square dish with a fine ham Mousse. Smooth the surface carefully and when set, arrange on top a garnish of small shell shapes of foie gras obtained by using a spoon dipped in hot water.

As soon as this is done cover the foie gras shells with an excellent, almost setting Chicken Aspic Jelly and then allow this to set.
To serve: present the Mousse set in a block of ice.

2970 Mousse de Jambon au Blanc de Volaille—Cold Ham Mousse with White of Chicken
Two-thirds fill a deep square dish with a fine ham Mousse. When this is set, arrange on the surface a garnish of neatly shaped thick slices of very white poached breast of chicken coated with white Sauce Chaud-froid. Cover with almost setting Chicken Aspic Jelly and then allow this to set.
To serve: present the dish set in a block of ice.

Note: If required, the chicken need not be coated with Chaud-froid but it should still be well covered with jelly.

2971 Mousselines Froides de Jambon—Cold Ham Mousselines
For this preparation see (332).

2972 Petits Soufflés Froids de Jambon—Small Cold Ham Soufflés
These may be prepared according to the recipe for Cold Soufflés (335) using small moulds.

2973 Pâté de Jambon—Cold Ham Pie
See Pâté de Jambon (3781).

2974 LANGUES DE PORC—PIG'S TONGUES

Pigs' tongues are prepared in the same way as calf's tongues and all the recipes for these are suitable.

2975 OREILLES DE PORC—PIG'S EARS

Carefully singe the ears and clean out the insides. If to be served plain or with a sauce, cook them gently in water allowing 8 g ($\frac{1}{3}$ oz) salt per 1 litre ($1\frac{3}{4}$ pt or $4\frac{1}{2}$ U.S. cups) of water with the addition of 1 carrot, 1 onion studded with a clove and a Bouquet garni.

If the ears are to be served with a garnish of sauerkraut, Choux à la Flamande or lentils, they should be cooked with the garnish. If to be accompanied with a garnish à la Flamande, the bacon should be omitted. If served with lentils, these should be made into a purée after the ears are cooked.

2976 Oreilles de Porc à la Rouennaise
Cook the pig's ears as described above. When ready, cut each ear in half keeping the thick parts separate from the flat parts. Chop the thick parts, cut the flat parts into pieces. Place all together in a pan with $1\frac{1}{2}$ dl (5 fl oz or $\frac{5}{8}$ U.S. cup) Sauce Madère and stew together very gently for 30 minutes. Allow to cool.

Remove the pieces of ear only and place on one side. Add 350 g (13 oz) of pork sausage meat for each ear to the remaining chopped ear and Madeira plus a pinch of chopped parsley and mix together well. Divide this into pieces of 100 g ($3\frac{1}{2}$ oz) each then roll them into balls. Push one of the reserved pieces of ear into the centre of each ball; wrap in a piece of pig's caul, sprinkle with butter and grill gently.

When three-quarters cooked, sprinkle with white breadcrumbs and finish cooking to a golden brown.

Serve accompanied with Sauce Madère.

2977 Oreilles de Porc Sainte-Menehould
Cook the ears as before and cut in half lengthways. Coat them lightly with made mustard, dip in melted butter and then into white breadcrumbs. Finally, sprinkle with melted butter and grill them gently.

Serve the ears as they are or accompanied with a dish of mashed potatoes.

2978 PIEDS DE PORC—PIG'S TROTTERS

Pig's trotters should be prepared and cooked plain the same way as pig's ears. They may be served plain as they are but more usually they are breadcrumbed and grilled, or truffled.

2979 Pieds de Porc Panés—Breadcrumbed and Grilled Pig's Trotters
Cook the trotters as described and cut in half lengthways. Flour, egg and breadcrumb them, sprinkle with melted lard or butter and grill gently as for all breadcrumbed items.

Serve the trotters as they are or accompanied with a dish of mashed potatoes.

2980 Pieds de Porc Truffés—Truffled Pig's Trotters
These are usually bought already prepared; they are rarely made up in the kitchen, excepting perhaps in large establishments. Their preparation, however, is not particularly complicated as may be seen from the following recipe.

Cook the trotters plain as described for pig's ears; completely remove all bones and allow to become cold. This done, cut them into large dice and mix well together with 200 g (7 oz) pork sausage meat per trotter then add 150 g (5 oz) chopped truffle, raw where possible, per 500 g (1 lb 2 oz) of mixture.

Divide this into pieces of 100 g ($3\frac{1}{2}$ oz) each and mould into rectangular shapes. Fashion slightly pointed at one end. Place 3 slices of truffle, one at each corner then wrap each in a piece of very supple pig's caul.

Sprinkle with melted butter and grill gently and slowly to ensure that the heat has sufficient time to penetrate the complete thickness of the mixture.

Arrange overlapping in a circle on a dish and serve accompanied with a Sauce Périgueux. A dish of very fine mashed potato may also be served.

2981 QUEUES DE PORC—PIG'S TAILS

These are cooked plain in the same way as pig's ears; when cold dip them in melted butter, roll in breadcrumbs and grill gently.

The usual accompaniment is a dish of mashed potatoes.

2982 ROGNONS DE PORC—PIG'S KIDNEYS

These may be prepared and cooked in accordance with any of the recipes for veal kidneys.

2983 TETE DE PORC—PIG'S HEAD

The pig's head is usually utilized for the preparation of Fromage de Tête or pig's brawn. However, it may be served hot in accordance with the methods indicated for pig's ears.

OTHER PREPARATIONS OF PORK

2984 ANDOUILLES AND ANDOUILLETTES

Andouilles are usually prepared raw and then cooked in lightly salted water for the length of time indicated by their size. After this they are grilled.

Andouillettes, on the other hand, are bought already cooked. They only require a few shallow incisions to be made on each side, then to be wrapped in paper, buttered or greased with lard and finally gently grilled.

For either the Andouille or Andouillette, the usual garnish is mashed potato.

2985 Andouillettes à la Bourguignonne
Cut 1 kg (2¼ lb) Andouillettes into 1 cm (⅖ in) thick slices. Place into a frying pan containing very hot butter and lard and toss over and over until nicely browned. Drain off the fat and replace it with 100 g (3½ oz) well seasoned Snail Butter (235). Toss over away from the heat until the butter is melted then tip into a timbale or deep dish to serve.

2986 Andouillettes à la Lyonnaise
Cut the Andouillettes as above. Place into a frying pan containing a mixture of very hot butter and oil and toss over and over until nicely browned. Add 250 g (9 oz) sliced onion, cooked and lightly coloured in butter, adjust the seasoning and toss over to completely mix the ingredients. Finish with a pinch of chopped parsley, a few drops of vinegar, then tip into a timbale or deep dish to serve.

BOUDINS—BLACK OR WHITE PUDDINGS

Although black puddings and white puddings are generally bought as a commercially prepared product, it is thought useful to include a few recipes.

2987 Boudins Blancs Ordinaire—Ordinary White Puddings
Chop together 250 g (9 oz) lean pork and 400 g (15 oz) pork fat.

Pound well together with 50 g (2 oz) fresh foie gras and pass it through a fine sieve. Place this mixture in a basin and add 2 eggs, 50 g (2 oz) finely chopped onion cooked in butter without colour, 1 dl (3½ fl oz or ½ U.S. cup) cream, 15 g (½ oz) salt, a pinch of white pepper and a little grated nutmeg. Mix well together then put it into the prepared gut without overfilling it; the mixture swells during the cooking process and if too full the puddings are likely to burst. Tie off with string at the required lengths then arrange on a grill or lattice wicker frame.

Plunge the whole into a pot three-quarters full of boiling water, reheat the water to 95 °C but no hotter, and poach the puddings at this temperature for 12 minutes.

When cooked, remove from the water and allow to cool.

To serve: do not make any incisions in them but prick them all over with a thin trussing needle; wrap each in buttered paper and grill gently.

Serve accompanied with a dish of creamed mashed potato.

2988 Boudins Blanc de Volaille—White Chicken Puddings
Pound separately 500 g (1 lb 2 oz) raw white breast of chicken and 400 g (15 oz) fresh pork fat cut in dice, then pound them together to completely mix adding 100 g (3½ oz) chopped onion cooked in butter without colour, a little thyme and bayleaf, 15 g (½ oz) salt, a pinch of white pepper, a little grated nutmeg and 4 egg whites added one by one. The whole mixture should be worked vigorously with the pestle during the adding of these ingredients.

Pass through a fine sieve, replace in the mortar and work in little by little 5 dl (18 fl oz or 2¼ U.S. cups) very cold, boiled milk. Put this forcemeat into the prepared gut and poach as in the preceding recipe. Allow to cool.

For grilling the puddings, observe the same precautions as before and serve accompanied with a dish of creamed mashed potato.

2989 Boudins Noirs—Black Puddings
Place in a basin 500 g (1 lb 2 oz) pork kidney fat cut in large dice and half melted, 4 dl (14 fl oz or 1¾ U.S. cups) pig's blood, 1 dl (3½ fl oz or ½ U.S. cup) cream, 200 g (7 oz) chopped onion cooked in lard without colour, 20 g (⅔ oz) salt, a good pinch of pepper and a pinch of mixed spice. Mix these ingredients well together, then place into the prepared gut without overfilling it; this mixture tends to swell during the cooking process and this will prevent the puddings bursting. Tie off with string at the required lengths and arrange them on a grill or lattice wicker frame.

Plunge the whole into a pot of boiling water, reheat to 95 °C but no hotter and poach the puddings at this temperature for 20 minutes. Prick any which float to the surface with a pin so as to release the air which they contain; this will prevent them from bursting.

When cooked, remove from the water and allow them to cool on the frame.

To serve: make shallow incisions on both sides of the puddings and grill very gently. Serve accompanied with a dish of creamed mashed potato.

2990 Boudins Noirs à l'Anglaise—Black Puddings, English Method
Prepare the puddings as in the preceding recipe adding to the mixture 250 g (9 oz) rice cooked in Bouillon and kept a little firm. Poach in the same way and allow to cool.

Make shallow incisions on both sides of the puddings, grill them gently and serve accompanied with a dish of mashed potato.

2991 Boudins Noirs à la Flamande—Black Puddings, Flemish Method
Prepare the same mixture as for Black Puddings. Add to this 100 g ($3\frac{1}{2}$ oz) brown sugar and 60 g (2 oz) each of currants and sultanas, picked over, soaked in warm water to make them swell, then well drained and dried.

Fill the prepared gut with this preparation and poach as before.

To serve: make shallow incisions on both sides of the puddings and grill them gently. Serve accompanied with Apple Sauce.

2992 Boudins Noirs à la Lyonnaise
Proceed in the same manner as for Andouillettes à la Lyonnaise (2986) using Black Puddings.

2993 Boudins Noirs à la Normande
Cut cold black puddings into slices and sauté them in butter, tossing over and over.

Prepare separately in the same manner, slices of peeled, depipped sweet apple using 500 g (1 lb 2 oz) apple per 1 kg ($2\frac{1}{4}$ lb) of black pudding.

Place both ingredients together in the frying pan and toss over to mix well together then tip into a deep earthenware dish for service.

2994 CARBONADES DE PORC

These Carbonades are thin slices of pork cut from the neck of the carcase. They are usually shallow fried and garnished in the same way as pork cutlets and chops.

Their most suitable preparation, however, is à la Flamande. See Carbonades de Boeuf à la Flamande (2459).

CREPINETTES

2995 Ordinary Crépinettes
Mix well together 1 kg ($2\frac{1}{4}$ lb) excellent pork sausage meat, 1 tbs chopped parsley and $\frac{1}{4}$ dl (1 fl oz or $\frac{1}{8}$ U.S. cup) brandy. Divide into pieces of 100 g ($3\frac{1}{2}$ oz); mould each into a rectangular shape and wrap in pig's caul.

Sprinkle with melted butter and grill them gently.

2996 Crépinettes Truffées—Truffled Crépinettes
Mix well together, 1 kg ($2\frac{1}{4}$ lb) excellent pork sausage meat, 125 g ($4\frac{1}{2}$ oz) chopped truffle and 2 tbs truffle cooking liquor. Divide into pieces of 100 g ($3\frac{1}{2}$ oz), mould each into a rectangular shape and wrap in pig's caul.

Sprinkle the Crépinettes with melted butter and grill them gently.

Arrange in a circle on a dish, pour some Sauce Périgueux in the centre and serve accompanied with a dish of creamed mashed potato.

2997 Crépinettes Cendrillon
Method used in earlier days: Wrap each Truffled Crépinette in a double sheet of very strong thick, buttered paper. Arrange them in the hearth of a fireplace and cover with glowing embers. Renew these embers as required for an approximate cooking time of 20 minutes.

To serve: remove the outside papers and leave the Crépinettes in the second one.

Modern method: Enclose each Truffled Crépinette in an oval layer of ordinary Pie Paste (3775). Place on a baking tray, brush the tops with beaten egg and decorate by scoring with the point of a knife.

Bake in a moderate oven for 20 minutes and arrange on a serviette to serve.

2998 EMINCES AND HACHIS

The recipes for Emincés and Hachis of beef are all suitable and the same directions and rules should be followed using pork.

2999 FRICADELLES

Proceed in the same manner and in the same proportions as for Fricadelles de Boeuf (2469) using pork instead of beef.

GAYETTES

3000 Gayettes
Cut 500 g (1 lb 2 oz) each of pig's liver and pork fat into small dice. Place in a basin, add 3 cloves of crushed and finely chopped garlic, 20 g ($\frac{2}{3}$ oz) salt, a pinch of pepper and a little mixed spice. Mix together well then divide the mixture into pieces of

100 g ($3\frac{1}{2}$ oz) each. Mould rectangular shape as for Crépinettes and wrap each in a piece of pig's caul previously soaked in warm water and dried.

Tie round carefully with thread, arrange them on a buttered tray, sprinkle with melted lard and cook in a moderate oven for approximately 30 minutes. Remove the thread when cooked.

Gayettes are generally served cold.

HOT PORK PIE

3001 Hot Pork Pie, English Style

Completely cover the bottom and sides of a pie dish with thin slices of raw ham and prepare, for a medium-sized dish, 1) 600 g (1 lb 5 oz) small thickish slices of fresh pork, seasoned with salt and pepper and sprinkled with 50 g (2 oz) dry Duxelles and a pinch of chopped parsley and sage, 2) 600 g (1 lb 2 oz) raw, sliced potatoes and 3) 200 g (7 oz) chopped onion.

Fill the prepared pie dish with alternate layers of the pork, potatoes and chopped onion finishing with pork. Add $1\frac{1}{2}$ dl (5 fl oz or $\frac{5}{8}$ U.S. cup) water, cover with a layer of short paste or puff paste trimmings and seal well to the edges of the dish. Brush with beaten egg, decorate by lightly scoring with a fork and bake in a moderate oven for approximately 2 hours.

3002 PETIT SALE—SALT NECK OF PORK

The neck of pork should be only lightly salted then gently simmered until tender in unsalted water. It is served accompanied with a garnish of boiled or braised cabbage or with a dish of mashed potatoes and with a little of its cooking liquid.

It may be cooked together with cabbage but in this case the salt pork should be very well blanched first so as to remove much of the taste of the brine.

PORC SALE BOUILLI—BOILED SALT PORK

3003 Porc Salé bouilli à l'Anglaise—Boiled Salt Pork, English Style

Cook 1 kg ($2\frac{1}{4}$ lb) salt shoulder or belly of pork in plain boiling water adding a garnish of vegetables as for Boiled Beef (2422) plus 6 parsnips.

Serve the meat on a dish surrounded with the vegetables and accompanied with pease pudding prepared as in the following recipe:

Pease Pudding: Place 500 g (1 lb 2 oz) purée of split peas, yellow for preference, in a basin and mix together with 3 eggs, 100 g ($3\frac{1}{2}$ oz) butter, and a little salt, pepper and grated nutmeg. Pour this mixture into a buttered pudding basin and poach in a steamer or *au Bain-marie*.

This mixture may also be put into a buttered and floured pudding cloth, securely tied with string then cooked together in the same pan with the pork. This procedure is much simpler and the results equally as good.

Note: In place of the pudding prepared as above, an ordinary purée of yellow split peas is very often served.

SAUCISSES—SAUSAGES

3004 Saucisses Anglaises—English Sausages

The finest and best known of English sausages are those of Cambridge.

They are cooked in the same way as the French kind, being either grilled or cooked in the oven and are often served for breakfast with bacon and sometimes as a garnish for roast poultry such as turkey or chicken.

They are frequently very highly seasoned, sometimes to excess.

3005 Saucisses aux Choux—Sausages with Cabbage

Grill or poach the sausages. If poached, any of the fat from their cooking should be added to the cabbage, which is usually green cabbage. They may also be served with braised cabbage or red cabbage à la Flamande (4055).

3006 Saucisses de Francfort et de Strasbourg—Frankfurter and Strasbourg Sausages

Poach these sausages gently in boiling water covered with a lid for not much more than 10 minutes. Prolonged cooking only results in loss of quality.

They may be served plain accompanied with grated horseradish and a dish of mashed potato but are more usually served with braised sauerkraut.

3007 Saucisses à la Marmelade de Pommes—Sausages with Apple Sauce

Cook the sausages in the oven with butter and a little white wine. Arrange them on a dish and sprinkle with their cooking liquor.

Serve accompanied with a sauceboat of lightly sweetened apple sauce.

3008 Pouding de Saucisses à l'Anglaise—Sausage Pudding, English style

Line a pudding basin with Suet Paste and almost fill with layers of small English sausages which have been well blanched and cooled under running cold water. Cover with brown onion sauce then close up with a layer of the same paste. Seal the edges then cover with a buttered and floured cloth; tie up and place in boiling water to cook for approximately 2½ hours.

Remove the cloth and serve the pudding on a dish, as it is, surrounded with a folded serviette.

3009 Saucisses au Risotto

Colour the sausages quickly in butter, remove them, cut into 5 cm 2 (in) lengths then finish cooking them in the same pan with 100 g (3½ oz) sliced white truffles per 500 g (1 lb 2 oz) of sausages. Place the sausages and truffles in the centre of a border of Risotto moulded on the serving dish.

Note: In Italy where this dish is very popular, chopped cabbage is added to the Risotto during its cooking.

3010 Saucisses au Vin Blanc

This dish may be prepared in two different ways:

A) Cook the sausages in the oven with a little butter and arrange them on Croûtons of bread fried in butter. Drain off the fat and deglaze the pan with white wine. Reduce by half, add the required amount of Sauce Demi-glace then finish with a little butter and pour over the sausages.

B) Colour the sausages quickly in butter then poach them in 2 dl (7 fl oz or ⅞ U.S. cup) white wine per 20 sausages. Arrange the sausages on Croûtons of bread fried in butter; then reduce the wine by two-thirds then add 1 egg yolk, a few drops of lemon juice, 2 tbs meat glaze and 100 g (3½ oz) butter. Mix in and pour over the sausages.

3011 COCHON DE LAIT—SUCKING PIG

Whether stuffed or not the sucking pig is always roasted whole; the important thing to remember is to arrange the procedure of cooking so that when just cooked, the skin should be crisp and brown.

The cooking time for a small sucking pig varies from 1½ to 2 hours; if stuffed the time should be increased by 15 minutes for each 500 g (1 lb 2 oz) of stuffing.

It should be basted for preference with oil whilst cooking; this allows the skin to become more crisp in comparison with the results obtained by the use of other fats.

Serve accompanied with a good roast gravy.

3012 Stuffing for Sucking Pig

Prepare a Gratin forcemeat (295) using the liver from the pig which should be simply stiffened and lightly coloured in butter on the outside and kept very underdone inside.

Add to this forcemeat the same weight of pork sausage meat, 200 g (7 oz) white breadcrumbs soaked in milk and squeezed, 2 eggs, 1 dl (3½ fl oz or ½ U.S. cup) brandy and a small pinch of powdered wild or ordinary thyme. Mix well together.

Fill the pig's belly with this stuffing and sew up with fine string. Arrange in its proper shape on a roasting tray or skewer on a roasting spit and roast as indicated.

3013 English Stuffing for Sucking Pig

Bake in the oven 1 kg 200 g (2 lb 11 oz) very large unpeeled onions and allow them to cool.

Peel and then chop them very finely, place in a basin with 500 g (1 lb 2 oz) white breadcrumbs soaked in milk and squeezed, 500 g (1 lb 2 oz) chopped beef kidney suet, 30 g (1 oz) salt, a pinch of ground pepper, a little ground nutmeg, 125 g (4½ oz) blanched and finely chopped sage and 2 eggs.

Mix all these ingredients well together.

Note: This stuffing is equally suitable for ducks and geese etc.

3014 Cochon de Lait Farci et Rôti à l'Anglaise—Roast Stuffed Sucking Pig, English Style

Fill the belly of the pig with English stuffing as in the preceding recipe, sew up with fine string and skewer on the pit. Sprinkle with oil and roast in the usual manner.

Serve accompanied with a dish of mashed potato and a lightly sweetened apple sauce containing an equal amount of washed selected currants, swollen in lukewarm water.

3015 Cochon de Lait Saint-Fortunat

Select a small, very white sucking pig, lightly salt the inside of the belly and sprinkle with a few tablespoons of brandy.

Meanwhile prepare 150 g (5 oz) pearl barley as a Pilaw (4239) and mix into this the liver of the pig cut in large dice and sautéed in butter, 2 tbs chopped Fines Herbes, 200 g (7 oz) cooked pork chipolatas and 50 braised chestnuts. Stuff the pig with this mixture, sew up with fine string and truss the pig into its natural position of repose. Place in a large braising pan and roast in the oven frequently basting with butter so as to obtain a crisp and golden brown crackling.

Serve accompanied with 1) the roasting juices deglazed with veal stock, 2) Sauce Groseilles au Raifort (200) and 3) a thick Apple Sauce made from cooking apples.

CHAPTER 8

RELEVES AND ENTREES OF POULTRY

General Observations

It is generally accepted that the term Volaille (poultry) includes not only chickens but also turkeys, geese, ducks and pigeons—yet in culinary terms when the word Volaille is used on the menu it indicates chicken only.

Four categories of chickens are used in cookery, each having its own attributes and definite usages; they are: 1) Fattened Pullets (Fr. *Poulardes*) and Capons (Fr. *Chapons*) which are usually served whole as Relevés and roasts, 2) Queen chickens (Fr. *Poulets à la Reine*) which are mainly used for Sautés and for roast, 3) Spring chickens (Fr. *Poulets de Grains*) which are most suitable for cooking *en Cocotte* and for grilling, 4) Poussins or baby chicks which are served only *en Cocotte* or grilled.

Chicken *Suprêmes* and chicken wings are classed as some of the finest Entrées and are cut from the 2nd and 3rd categories according to the size required.

The offals of chicken such as winglets, necks, gizzards, livers, cockscombs and kidneys are utilized in a number of dishes which are brought together further on in a special section entitled Other Preparations of Chicken.

3016 The Preparation of Fattened Pullets and Capons

Under the heading General Principles at the beginning of the chapter on Relevés and Entrées of butchers meat, the methods of braising, poaching and Poêling were given, so it is only necessary here to briefly refer to this in so far as it concerns fattened pullets and capons. These are poached or Poêléed and sometimes, although rarely, braised. For poaching, the birds are trussed with the lower part of the legs turned back; they should be rubbed with lemon over the breast and legs to keep them white then covered with slices of salt pork fat.

Chickens which have to be studded or larded should be dipped in boiling stock so as to stiffen the flesh over the breast and legs thus making it easier to stud them or insert the larding needle. The items for studding are, according to circumstances, salted ox tongue, ham or truffle; for larding they are red of carrot, mushroom and truffle; in both cases they are then covered with salt pork fat. The cooking of these birds should then take place in very white stock. To tell when cooked, a needle should be inserted into the thickest part of the leg and if the juice which runs out is white or a very pale pink the bird is ready.

To Poêlé a chicken it should be trussed as for poaching, covered with slices of salt pork fat to protect the breast during the first stage of its cooking, then cooked with butter on a layer of root vegetables and herbs in a deep pan having a thick base and covered with a lid.

When the chicken is nearly cooked it should be moistened with either a little rich chicken stock, truffle or mushroom liquor, or Madeira or red or white wine; the liquid is used to baste the bird and should be replenished if it reduces too quickly. The fat is skimmed off and the remainder of the cooking liquid added to the sauce which is to be served with the chicken.

It is not necessary to rub lemon over poultry which is to be braised but the breast should be covered with slices of salt pork fat to protect it as otherwise the breast will become dry by the time the legs are cooked. In other respects the normal braising method should be followed.

Note: Whatever way that fattened pullets and capons are cooked it is advisable first of all to remove the wishbone so as to facilitate carving.

3017 Rice and Pearl Barley for Stuffed Poultry

The method for preparing these items is given in the Chapter on garnishes; it is only necessary to add the garnish or the ingredients at the last minute in accordance with the name of the dish.

It is advisable to stuff the chicken loosely bearing in mind that the rice will swell; apart from this there is no need for further details as the uses of stuffings are given in the recipes which follow.

3018 To Serve Relevés of Poultry Quickly and Hot

It is felt necessary to call attention here to a very important point regarding the serving of large items of poultry, as it is rarely carried out correctly. This could be because cutting up a chicken and arranging it with its garnish on plates calls for skill and application not normally within the capabilities of the person in charge or because of the lack of facilities or for some other reason.

What is certain is that more often than not, the guest finds himself faced with pieces of chicken which are not very hot and are poorly presented; all the care given by the cook to its preparation being undone.

To remedy this state of things and produce a method of service which is both quick and easy and does not detract from the presentation, the following method has much to recommend it.

The breasts of the cooked bird are removed in the kitchen and kept hot in a little cooking liquid until the moment of service. All the breast bones are removed and the item of poultry re-formed with the aid of a mixture in keeping with the name of the dish, either light chicken forcemeat, braised rice with added cream, truffled foie gras, creamed spaghetti or noodles; this mixture is moulded dome shape. It then suffices only to place the chicken at one end of an oval dish or to place it on a low base of fried bread on which it can sit upright; it can then be coated with Sauce Mornay, sprinkled with grated cheese and quickly glazed. The bird being thus prepared and in place, it is then surrounded with nice tartlet cases containing the indicated garnish; the breasts are then quickly cut into thickish slices and one of these placed on each tartlet. The chicken is served like this with the sauce separate.

In this way the dish reaches the room hot where it can be served quickly and correctly. Each guest gets a nice slice of chicken and not just some of the garnish as is frequently the case in the older method of serving.

Instead of tartlet cases, thin Croûtons of bread fried in fresh butter, the shape and size of the slices of poultry may be used. This is typified by Poularde à la Derby in which the bird being stuffed with rice, can be built into a suitable shape after the breasts have been removed and the breast bones cut off; the bird is then placed on a base for presentation.

A slice of foie gras per person is quickly sautéed in butter, each placed on a Croûton and these are then arranged around the prepared pullet. The breasts are quickly sliced and one slice is placed on each foie gras with a slice of truffle on top. The whole dish is then placed in the oven to reheat and sent to the room with the sauce separately.

There, the Maître d'Hôtel places each Croûton with its foie gras, chicken and truffle on a very hot plate together with a spoonful of the rice stuffing and one of sauce; less than two minutes after it is taken into the room, a portion of chicken is served correctly and hot to each guest.

The foregoing is for when the dish is to be presented to the customer; when this is not necessary it is enough to dress the rice taken from the chicken in the middle of a deep Entrée dish and to arrange the slices of chicken, foie gras and truffle around alternately; covered with a lid this can be kept hot without difficulty. The sauce is served separately.

The legs, which are not usually served at a very high class dinner, and the carcase remain in the kitchen.

This method of service cannot be too highly recommended for each occasion when it is possible; it is the only way to ensure perfection of service and give complete satisfaction.

POULARDES—FATTENED PULLETS

3019 Poularde Albuféra

Stuff the fattened pullet with rice containing large diced foie gras and truffle and poach it.

Arrange on a dish and coat with Sauce Albuféra.

Surround with a garnish of: small balls of truffles cut with a round spoon cutter, small round Quenelles made from chicken forcemeat, button mushrooms and cocks' kidneys—all mixed with a little Sauce Albuféra; border the dish with shapes of ox tongue cut in the shape of cockscombs.

3020 Poularde Alexandra

Lard the fattened pullet with ox tongue and truffle and poach it.

When cooked, remove the breasts and re-form the bird with chicken Mousseline forcemeat making it smooth. Place in a warm oven to cook the forcemeat then coat with Sauce Mornay and glaze it quickly.

Arrange on a dish, surround with tartlet cases filled with buttered asparagus tips and place a slice of the reserved breasts on each; surround with a thin line of light meat glaze.

3021 Poularde à l'Ambassadrice

Stud the fattened pullet with truffle, cover with Matignon, wrap in a piece of muslin and tie at both ends.

Braise it and when cooked, unwrap it and arrange on a dish.

Coat with fairly thick Sauce Suprême, and surround with lamb's sweetbreads previously studded with truffles, braised and glazed; alternate these with bouquets of asparagus tips.

3022 Poularde à l'Andalouse
Poach the fattened pullet.

Arrange on a dish and coat with Sauce Suprême which has been finished with 150 g (5 oz) pimento butter per 1 litre ($1\frac{3}{4}$ pt or $4\frac{1}{2}$ U.S. cups) of sauce. Surround with braised, stuffed pimentos filled with rice and shallow fried round slices of eggplant.

Note: Another way in which this dish is sometimes prepared is that the chicken is Poêléed instead of being poached, then coated with tomato-flavoured Sauce Demi-glace finished with pimento butter. The same garnish is used.

3023 Poularde Pochée à l'Anglaise—Poached Fattened Pullet, English Style
This dish is sometimes confused with Poularde Printanière but this is quite wrong; the correct recipe is as follows.

Poach the fattened pullet in very white stock, arrange on a dish and coat with chicken-flavoured Sauce Béchamel. Surround with overlapping slices of salt ox tongue at the sides and bouquets of small balls of carrot and turnip, peas and celery at each end of the dish. These vegetables should be plain boiled.

3024 Poularde Bouillie à l'Anglaise—Boiled Fattened Pullet, English Style
Cook the fattened pullet in water with the usual vegetables and herbs and a 500 g (1 lb 2 oz) piece of blanched streaky bacon. Serve the chicken on a dish surrounded with sliced squares of bacon.

Serve accompanied with: 1) a sauceboat of Parsley Sauce and 2) a sauceboat of the cooking liquid.

3025 Poularde d'Aumale
Stud the fattened pullet with truffle, stuff with 250 g (9 oz) chicken Mousseline forcemeat containing 100 g ($3\frac{1}{2}$ oz) truffle and braise it.

When cooked, arrange on a dish surrounded with braised celery hearts; coat with Sauce Demi-glace containing poached slices of bone marrow and the reduced braising liquid.

Serve the rest of the sauce separately.

3026 Poularde à l'Aurore
Stuff the fattened pullet with 250 g (9 oz) fairly firm Godiveau with cream (290) containing 3 tbs very red reduced tomato purée, and poach it.

When cooked, arrange on a dish and coat with Sauce Aurore. The stuffing is removed and diced when serving the chicken and constitutes the garnish.

3027 Poularde Banquière
Stuff the fattened pullet with 200 g (7 oz) Mousseline forcemeat containing 100 g ($3\frac{1}{2}$ oz) diced foie gras and Poêlé it.

Deglaze the pan with truffle essence. Arrange the pullet on a dish and surround with a Banquière garnish (346). Serve accompanied with the cooking liquid mixed with an equal quantity of chicken glaze and enriched with 100 g ($3\frac{1}{2}$ oz) butter.

3028 Poularde Boïeldieu
Stuff the fattened pullet with 250 g (9 oz) chicken Mousseline forcemeat containing 150 g (5 oz) foie gras purée; stud with truffles and Poêlé it.

When cooked, arrange on a dish and surround with 10 small balls of truffle and the diced stuffing cut when the chicken is carved.

Make the sauce by deglazing the pan in which the chicken was cooked with Sauternes wine. Reduce, flavour with strong chicken stock, strain and lightly thicken with arrowroot.

Serve this sauce separately.

3029 Poularde Bouquetière
This is the same as Poularde Renaissance.

3030 Poularde Cardinalisée
Prepare the fattened pullet as for Poularde Soufflé.

Arrange on a dish and surround with small Bouchées filled with crayfish tails, alternating with small Croûtons of bread fried in butter each having a slice of the breast of chicken on top surmounted with a nice slice of truffle.

Serve accompanied with Sauce Suprême finished with Crayfish Butter.

3031 Poularde aux Céleris
Poêlé the fattened pullet basting it with a little good veal stock towards the end of the cooking time; meanwhile braise sufficient celery for the garnish.

When cooked, arrange the chicken on a dish; surround it with the celery and coat them both with the deglazed and strained cooking liquid.

3032 Poularde aux Champignons (*brown*)
Poêlé the fattened pullet then deglaze the pan with mushroom essence and add 2 dl (7 fl oz or $\frac{7}{8}$ U.S. cup) Sauce Demi-glace.

Arrange the chicken on a dish and surround with 20 nice cooked grooved mushrooms.

Serve the lightly buttered sauce separately.

3033 Poularde aux Champignons (*white*)
Poach the fattened pullet.

Arrange it on a dish, coat with Sauce Allemande

flavoured with mushroom essence and surround with 20 very white cooked grooved mushrooms.

3034 Poularde Châtelaine
Poêlé the fattened pullet but without allowing it to become too coloured.

Arrange on a dish and surround alternately with artichoke bottoms cooked in butter then filled with fairly stiff Soubise, and bouquets of chestnuts cooked in Bouillon. Surround with a little of the thickened cooking liquid and serve the remainder separately.

3035 Poularde à la Chevalière
Remove the breasts of a fattened pullet and separate the two small fillets from them. Lard the breasts with two lines each of truffle and ox tongue; make incisions in the fillets, insert small slices of truffle into them and shape into rings. Place the breasts and fillets into separate buttered pans just large enough to hold them and cover with the lids.

Remove the legs of the chicken and bone out the thighs to the joints with the drumsticks; lard them with a ring of strips of salt pork fat. Braise the legs and glaze them so that they are ready at the moment of service. Ten minutes before service time, cook the breasts and a little later the fillets, both with mushroom cooking liquor.

For service: stick to the dish a pyramid-shaped Croûton of fried bread, approx 12 cm (5 in) high with the sides of the base 5 cm (2 in) wide.

Arrange the legs and breasts upright against the Croûton alternating them and each placed on a decorated Quenelle of chicken so as to raise them higher. Place the fillets on the legs and fill in between each portion of chicken with bouquets of cockscombs, kidneys and white button mushrooms.

Insert a decorative skewer garnished with a glazed truffle, a cockscomb and a large grooved mushroom in the centre of the Croûton.

Serve accompanied with Sauce Suprême.

Note: A border of pale baked noodle pastry or short paste is usually placed around the chicken. It may also be presented on a special silver dish having a raised decorative border.

3036 Poularde Chimay
Stuff a fattened pullet with 250 g (9 oz) cooked noodles tossed in butter and mixed with 100 g (3½ oz) diced foie gras and a few tablespoons of cream. Poêlé it slowly.

Arrange on a dish and lightly coat with some of the cooking liquid lightly thickened with arrowroot.

Finally, cover the chicken with raw noodles sautéed in clarified butter. Serve the remainder of the sauce separately.

3037 Poularde Chipolata
Poêlé the fattened pullet then place it into an earthenware terrine with sufficient Chipolata garnish (365).

Add the deglazed cooking juices from the pan, allow to heat gently in the oven for 10 minutes and serve as it is.

3038 Poularde Chivry
Poach the fattened pullet; arrange on a dish and coat with Sauce Chivry.

Serve accompanied with a dish of Macédoine of new season's vegetables mixed with either a little butter or cream.

3039 Poularde Cussy
Braise the fattened pullet. When cooked, arrange on a dish and surround with alternate bouquets of medium-sized truffles cooked with a Mirepoix and Madeira, and large grilled mushrooms filled with a purée of globe artichokes. Place a sautéed cock's kidney between each bouquet of truffle and mushrooms.

Serve accompanied with Sauce Madère to which the reduced braising liquid has been added.

Note: Another way of presenting this dish is to arrange the truffles in bouquets at each side with the sautéed cock's kidneys in a silver shell dish in front and the mushrooms at the back of the chicken.

3040 Poularde Demi-deuil
Slide several slices of very black truffle under the skin on the breast of the fattened pullet; stuff it with 200 g (7 oz) Mousseline forcemeat containing 100 g (3½ oz) grated or finely diced truffle then poach it.

When cooked, pass the cooking liquid through a fine strainer, reduce it and add to some Sauce Suprême together with some slices of truffle.

Arrange the chicken on a dish and coat with some of the sauce. The garnish consists of the stuffing from the bird removed and cut into large dice.

Serve the remainder of the sauce separately.

3041 Poularde Demidoff
Poêlé the fattened pullet; when three-quarters cooked, remove and place it in an earthenware Cocotte with a garnish consisting of 200 g (7 oz) carrots and 150 g (5 oz) turnips cut crescent shape with a 2½ cm (1 in) fancy cutter; 10 thinly sliced button onions; and 150 g (5 oz) diced celery—all previously cooked together with butter.

Finish to cook together and at the last moment

add 100 g ($3\frac{1}{2}$ oz) crescent-shaped slices of truffle and 1 dl ($3\frac{1}{2}$ fl oz or $\frac{1}{2}$ U.S. cup) reduced chicken stock.

Serve in the dish as it is.

3042 Poularde Derby

Stuff the fattened pullet with 200 g (7 oz) Riz Pilaw mixed with 100 g ($3\frac{1}{2}$ oz) each of foie gras and truffle cut into large dice.

Poêlé the bird then place it on a dish and surround with alternate large truffles cooked in Champagne, and slices of sautéed foie gras each placed on a small Croûton of bread fried in butter.

Serve separately the cooking liquid from the pan to which 1 dl ($3\frac{1}{2}$ fl oz or $\frac{1}{2}$ U.S. cup) veal gravy and the cooking liquor of the truffles has been added, then reduce it to 2 dl (7 fl oz or $\frac{7}{8}$ U.S. cup) and lightly thicken with arrowroot.

3043 Poularde Devonshire

Bone out the breast of a fattened pullet from the inside, season and fill with a stuffing made of equal amounts of chicken and cream forcemeat and good quality pork sausage meat.

Insert a well-trimmed cooked salt calf's tongue into the middle of the stuffing with the thick end towards the neck end of the bird.

Sew up the opening loosely using thin string and allowing room for the stuffing to expand during the cooking; truss, cover with thin slices of salt pork fat and poach it.

Drain the pullet when required; cut around the breast with the point of a knife and remove the breast, stuffing and tongue in one piece, by cutting horizontally underneath the stuffing next to the spine.

Place a Croûton of bread fried in butter on the serving dish and set the bottom part of the pullet with its legs attached on top.

Cut the breast and stuffing of the chicken in half down the middle so that the tongue is evenly divided in two; cut each half into slices and replace on the carcase so as to re-form the pullet to its original shape.

Lightly coat with Sauce Allemande containing some very small dice of cooked salt ox tongue and surround with small moulds of a purée of green peas each set on an artichoke bottom.

Serve the remainder of the sauce separately.

3044 Poularde Diva

Stuff the fattened pullet with 200 g (7 oz) of Riz Pilaw mixed with 100 g ($3\frac{1}{2}$ oz) each of diced foie gras and truffles, and poach it.

Arrange on a dish, coat with Sauce Suprême, coloured and flavoured with paprika, and serve accompanied with a dish of creamed flap mushrooms.

3045 Poularde à la Dreux

Stud a fattened pullet with pieces of salt ox tongue and truffle, and poach it.

Arrange on a dish, coat with Sauce Allemande, decorate the breast with a circle of slices of truffle and surround the bird with 4 medium-sized decorated Quenelles and 2 bouquets each of cockscombs and kidneys.

3046 Poularde Duroc

Stuff the fattened pullet with 200 g (7 oz) Gratin forcemeat made with foie gras and containing 150 g (5 oz) each of a coarse Julienne of salt ox tongue and truffle; Poêlé it.

Arrange on a dish and decorate the breast with a circle of large slices of truffle.

Serve accompanied with a sauceboat of well-flavoured Sauce Madère.

3047 Poularde à l'Ecossaise

Stuff the fattened pullet with 200 g (7 oz) Godiveau with cream (290) containing 100 g ($3\frac{1}{2}$ oz) Brunoise of mixed vegetables cooked in butter and 125 g ($4\frac{1}{2}$ oz) pearl barley which has been cooked as for Riz Pilaw; poach the pullet in the usual manner.

Arrange on a dish, coat with Sauce Ecossaise and serve accompanied with a dish of French beans mixed with cream.

3048 Poularde Edouard VII

Stuff the fattened pullet with 200 g (7 oz) Riz Pilaw mixed with 100 g ($3\frac{1}{2}$ oz) each of large dice of foie gras and truffle and poach it in the usual manner.

Arrange on a dish and coat with curry-flavoured Sauce Suprême containing 100 g ($3\frac{1}{2}$ oz) diced red pimento per 1 litre ($1\frac{3}{4}$ pt or $4\frac{1}{2}$ U.S. cups) sauce.

Serve accompanied with a dish of Concombres à la Crème.

3049 Poularde à l'Elysée

Stuff the fattened pullet with 200 g (7 oz) Mousseline forcemeat containing 125 g ($4\frac{1}{2}$ oz) each of diced foie gras and truffle; stud the breast with pieces of truffle and poach the pullet in the usual manner.

Arrange on a dish and surround with 5 whole truffles on each side and a bouquet of chicken Quenelles, mushrooms, cockscombs and kidneys mixed with Sauce Suprême, at both ends.

Serve accompanied with a sauceboat of Sauce Suprême.

3050 Poularde en Estouffade
Cook the fattened pullet *en Casserole* until half cooked then transfer it to an earthenware terrine just large enough to hold it and previously lined with thin slices of raw ham.

Add 500 g (1 lb 2 oz) of mixed carrot, onion and celery cut into Paysanne, seasoned with salt and sugar and lightly cooked in butter. Deglaze the pan in which the pullet was cooked with 2 dl (7 fl oz or $\frac{7}{8}$ U.S. cup) strong veal stock, reduce by half and pour over the chicken in the terrine. Cover with the lid and seal down with a strip of flour and water paste.

Complete the cooking for a further 45 minutes in a fairly hot oven then serve as it is in the terrine.

3051 Poularde à l'Estragon
Poach the fattened pullet in white stock with the usual vegetables and herbs plus a bouquet of tarragon stalks.

When cooked, arrange on a dish and decorate the breast with a wreath of blanched tarragon leaves.

Serve accompanied with some of the cooking liquid which has been reduced, thickened with arrowroot then passed through a fine strainer and finished with a little chopped fresh tarragon.

3052 Poularde Favorite
Stuff the fattened pullet with 200 g (7 oz) Mousseline forcemeat containing 100 g ($3\frac{1}{2}$ oz) each of large dice of foie gras and truffle and poach it in the usual manner.

Arrange on a dish, coat with Sauce Suprême and surround with bouquets of cockscombs and kidneys and slices of truffle.

3053 Poularde à la Fermière
This is prepared in the same way as Poularde en Estouffade except that the ham is cut Paysanne shape and added to the vegetables instead of being used to line the dish, and the garnish is increased by the addition of 125 g ($4\frac{1}{2}$ oz) each of raw peas and diamonds of French beans.

3054 Poularde Financière
Braise the fattened pullet in the usual manner and glaze it.

Arrange on a dish and surround with a Financière garnish (381) arranged in bouquets.

Serve accompanied with Sauce Financière.

3055 Poularde des Gastronomes
Stuff a fattened pullet with 250 g (9 oz) morels which have been slightly sautéed in butter and mixed with 100 g ($3\frac{1}{2}$ oz) diced raw truffle; Poêlé it in the usual manner.

Deglaze the pan with $1\frac{1}{2}$ dl (5 fl oz or $\frac{5}{8}$ U.S. cup) Champagne.

Arrange the pullet on a dish and surround it with alternate bouquets of medium-sized truffles and glazed chestnuts cooked in Bouillon. Place a cock's kidney between the truffles and chestnuts.

Serve accompanied with Sauce Demi-glace flavoured with truffle essence and the reduced cooking liquid from the chicken.

3056 Poularde Godard
Braise the fattened pullet.

When cooked, place on a dish and surround with a Godard garnish (388) arranged in bouquets. Lightly coat with Sauce Godard containing the reduced and strained braising liquid. Serve the remainder of the sauce separately.

3057 Poularde Grammont
Poach the fattened pullet and allow to become half cold.

Remove the breasts, cut off the breast bones and fill the carcase with a garnish composed of lark's breasts cooked in butter at the last moment, cooked button mushrooms, cockscombs and cocks' kidneys, all mixed together with a little Sauce Béchamel containing truffle essence.

Cut the breasts into slices, replace in position on the carcase and coat with fairly thick Sauce Suprême. Sprinkle with grated Parmesan and melted butter and glaze quickly. Serve immediately.

3058 Poularde Grand Hôtel
Cut a fattened pullet as for Sauté then cook with butter in a pan covered with a lid.

Arrange the pieces of chicken in a very hot terrine and cover with thick slices of raw truffle lightly seasoned with salt and pepper.

Deglaze the pan with $1\frac{1}{2}$ dl (5 fl oz or $\frac{5}{8}$ U.S. cup) white wine, add a little chicken stock and strain over the chicken. Cover tightly with the lid and place in a very hot oven for 8–10 minutes so as to cook the truffle.

Serve in the terrine as it is.

3059 Poularde au Gros sel
Poach a fattened pullet in white stock with the addition of 10 pieces of trimmed carrot and 10 button onions.

When cooked, arrange on a dish and surround with the carrots and onions in bouquets.

Serve accompanied with a sauceboat of the cooking liquid and a silver shell dish of coarse salt.

3060 Poularde à la Grecque
Stuff a fattened pullet with 400 g (14 oz) Riz à la Grecque and Poêlé it in the usual manner.

Arrange on a dish and coat with some of the reduced cooking liquid thickened with arrowroot.

3061 Poularde Héloïse

Poach a fattened pullet keeping it undercooked. Remove the breasts, cut them into slices and cut off the breast bones from the chicken.

Prepare a mixture of 200 g (7 oz) Mousseline forcemeat and 150 g (5 oz) grated or very finely diced raw truffle. Fill the carcase with this mixture in alternate layers with the slices of breast. Smooth dome shape to the original form of the bird, decorate with small pieces of cooked egg white and cover with a sheet of buttered paper. Place in a medium oven to cook.

On removing from the oven, coat with Sauce Allemande of such a consistency that the decoration will show through clearly against the background of the forcemeat.

Serve accompanied with a sauceboat of Sauce Allemande.

3062 Poularde à la Hongroise

Poêlé the fattened pullet in the usual manner.

Arrange on a dish, coat with Sauce Hongroise and surround with small moulds of Riz Pilaw containing diced tomato flesh.

Serve accompanied with a sauceboat of Sauce Hongroise.

3063 Poularde aux Huîtres

Poach the fattened pullet in light chicken stock, letting it cook slowly until well cooked.

Make the cooking liquid into a Sauce Suprême and add 24 poached and bearded oysters.

Arrange the chicken on a dish and coat with the sauce.

3064 Poularde à l'Impératrice

Poach the fattened pullet in the usual manner.

Place on a dish and arrange a bouquet of white braised lamb's sweetbreads at each end. Place two bouquets of poached calf's brain kept very white and cut into dice, at each side together with bouquets of button onions cooked in a little thin Velouté.

Coat with Sauce Suprême finished with cream.

3065 Poularde à l'Indienne

Poach the fattened pullet in the usual manner.

Arrange on a dish, coat with Sauce Indienne and serve accompanied with a dish of plain boiled rice.

3066 Poularde Isabelle de France

Stuff a fattened pullet with a Risotto made with 60 g (2 oz) sliced truffle and 18 crayfish tails which have been cooked *à la Bordelaise*. Poach it in half white stock and half Chablis wine.

When the chicken is cooked, make the cooking liquid into a Sauce Suprême and season it well.

Arrange the pullet on a small base of bread fried in butter, coat it with some of the sauce and surround with large black truffles cooked with Champagne, each placed on a small round, slightly hollowed out Croûton of bread fried in butter.

Serve the remainder of the sauce separately.

3067 Poularde à l'Ivoire

Poach the fattened pullet keeping it very white.

Arrange on a dish and serve as it is, accompanied with 1) a sauceboat of Sauce Ivoire, 2) a sauceboat of the cooking liquid and 3) a garnish such as macaroni or noodles à la Crème, flap mushrooms, cucumber etc.

3068 Poularde Lady Curzon

Stuff the fattened pullet with rice as indicated for Poularde à la Diva and poach it in the usual manner.

Arrange on a dish and coat with Sauce Suprême flavoured with curry powder.

Serve accompanied with a dish of creamed cucumber or flap mushrooms.

3069 Poularde à la Languedocienne

Poêlé the fattened pullet in the usual manner.

Arrange on a dish and place a bouquet of sautéed flesh only of tomatoes at each corner and bouquets of fried round slices of eggplant and flap mushrooms at the sides.

Coat the chicken with chicken-flavoured Jus lié finished with Madeira.

3070 Poularde Louis d'Orléans

Stud a whole foie gras with truffle and cook it in a little good veal stock with 1 dl (3½ fl oz or ½ U.S. cup) old Madeira for 15 minutes; allow to cool then place it inside a fattened pullet and truss it.

Place the chicken to set and colour with butter in a hot oven for 20 minutes, basting occasionally.

On removing from the oven, cover the bird completely with thick slices of truffle, then with thin slices of salt pork fat and finally enclose it in Hot Water Paste (3775). Seal the edges well, place on a baking tray and make a hole in the top to allow the steam to escape. Cook in a moderate oven for 1½ hours.

Serve as it is either hot or cold.

3071 Poularde Louisiane
Stuff the fattened pullet with 400 g (15 oz) creamed maize mixed with 50 g (2 oz) diced pimento and Poêlé it in the usual manner.

Arrange on a dish and surround with alternate moulds of Riz Pilaw and fried bananas.

Deglaze the pan with a little brown veal stock, skim off the fat, pass through a fine strainer and serve it separately with the pullet.

3072 Poularde Lucullus
Stuff the fattened pullet with 250 g (9 oz) Mousseline forcemeat containing 150 g (5 oz) grated raw truffle and braise it in the usual manner.

When cooked, place on a dish, surround with truffles cooked with Champagne and place some cockscombs at each end of the dish.

Serve accompanied with Sauce Demi-glace flavoured with truffle essence and containing the reduced and strained braising liquid after removing the fat.

3073 Poularde Maintenon
Lard the fattened pullet with thin strips of truffle and salt ox tongue and braise it.

Arrange on a dish and coat with Sauce Ivoire. Surround with Quenelles, grooved mushrooms and small fresh artichoke bottoms filled with a Salpicon of white of cooked chicken and truffle, coated with Sauce Mornay and glazed under the salamander.

Serve accompanied with a sauceboat of Sauce Ivoire and a dish of Riz à la Créole.

3074 Poularde Mancini
Poach the fattened pullet in the usual manner.

Remove the breasts and cut off the breast bones leaving the legs and winglets in place. Place on a flat base of either fried bread or rice fixed to the dish with a little flour and water paste.

Fill the carcase with macaroni mixed with cream and grated cheese to which has been added 100 g ($3\frac{1}{2}$ oz) diced cooked foie gras and 50 g (2 oz) truffle cut in Julienne.

Cut the breasts into slices and replace on the carcase with a slice of truffle between each.

Coat the pullet with reduced Sauce Tomate containing a little pale meat glaze and finished with butter and cream.

3075 Poularde Maréchal
Stuff the fattened pullet with 6 halves of lamb's sweetbreads, 20 button mushrooms and a poached and sliced calf's brain—all mixed with a little reduced Velouté.

Cover the pullet with thin slices of salt pork fat and poach it in the usual manner.

When cooked, arrange it on a dish, coat with Sauce Suprême and surround with alternate bouquets of Quenelles, truffles cut to the shape and size of olives, and cockscombs and kidneys.

3076 Poularde Marguerite de Savoie
Quickly fry 10 blackbirds in hot butter until coloured on all sides.

Add a nice white truffle cut into shavings, cover tightly with a lid and remove from the fire. Whilst still hot insert them into a nice pullet and braise it in half veal stock and half white Savoy wine.

Meanwhile, prepare a Polenta (4284) using milk; spread it 2 cm ($\frac{4}{5}$ in) thick on a buttered tray and allow to cool. When cold, cut it into 4 cm ($1\frac{1}{2}$ in) diameter rounds with a pastry cutter.

When required, flour the rounds of Polenta and shallow fry to a golden brown on both sides in clarified butter; sprinkle them with grated Parmesan and glaze quickly under the salamander.

Arrange the pullet on a flat base of bread fried in butter and set on a dish; surround with the prepared pieces of Polenta, coat the bottom of the dish with a little of the thickened braising liquid and serve the remainder in a sauceboat.

Serve accompanied with a dish of sliced white Piedmont truffles sautéed in butter and sprinkled with a few drops of melted meat glaze.

3077 Poularde Marie-Louise
Stuff the fattened pullet with a mixture of 150 g (5 oz) Riz Pilaw, 300 g (11 oz) sliced and sautéed mushrooms and 100 g ($3\frac{1}{2}$ oz) slices of truffle—all mixed together with $1\frac{1}{2}$ dl (5 fl oz or $\frac{5}{8}$ U.S. cup) of thick Sauce Soubise.

Poach the pullet and, when ready, arrange on a dish and coat with Sauce Allemande.

Surround with small artichoke bottoms filled with a purée of mushrooms mixed with a little Soubise, and halves of braised lettuce.

3078 Poularde Menagère
Poach the fattened pullet in a fairly gelatinous chicken stock.

Cut 6 carrots, 6 new potatoes and 6 spring onions into slices and cook them slowly and without a lid in a little of the chicken stock. When the vegetables are cooked and the liquid has been reduced, place the pullet in a terrine and cover it with the vegetables and their liquid.

Serve as it is in the terrine.

3079 Poularde Montbazon
Stud the fattened pullet with pieces of truffle and poach it in the usual manner.

When cooked, place it on a dish, coat with Sauce Suprême and surround with alternate bouquets of chicken Quenelles, lambs' sweetbreads and mushrooms.

Serve accompanied with Sauce Suprême.

3080 Poularde Montmorency

Lard the fattened pullet with thin strips of truffle and braise it with Madeira.

When cooked, arrange on a dish and place a nice decorated Quenelle at each end. Around the sides place a line of artichoke bottoms filled with buttered asparagus tips and truffle cut in short Julienne.

Serve accompanied with Sauce Madère.

3081 Poularde Nantua

Poach the fattened pullet in the usual manner.

Arrange on a dish and coat with Sauce Suprême finished with Crayfish Butter.

Surround with bouquets of Quenelles made from chicken forcemeat and Crayfish Butter, crayfish tails cooked with a Mirepoix, and slices of truffle.

3082 Poularde à la Niçoise

Poêlé the fattened pullet in the usual manner.

Arrange on a dish with a nice bouquet of buttered French beans at each end and along each side place alternate bouquets of diced flesh only of tomato cooked with butter and stoned black olives. The olives are to replace the potatoes which are normally part of the Niçoise garnish.

Serve accompanied with the cooking liquid lightly thickened with arrowroot.

3083 Poularde aux Nouilles

Stuff the fattened pullet with 200 g (7 oz) of half-cooked noodles mixed with cream and grated cheese, and 100 g ($3\frac{1}{2}$ oz) each of diced foie gras and truffle.

Poach the pullet, place on a dish, coat with Sauce Mornay and glaze quickly.

3084 Poularde à l'Orientale

Stuff the fattened pullet with 400 g (15 oz) Riz Pilaw lightly flavoured with saffron and poach it in the usual manner.

When cooked, remove the breasts and cut off the breast bones with scissors and without disturbing the rice inside. Coat the rice with Sauce Béchamel flavoured and coloured with tomato purée and saffron.

Arrange the pullet on a dish, cut the breasts into slices and replace on the chicken, coat them with some of the same sauce and surround with quarters of chow-chow which have been gently cooked in butter.

3085 Poularde Paramé

Cover the fattened pullet with a thick coating of Matignon then with thin slices of salt pork fat; tie it in a piece of muslin and Poêlé in the usual manner.

When cooked, place the pullet on a dish and surround with alternate bouquets of trimmed carrots and turnips cooked in Bouillon and glazed, and halves of braised lettuce.

Serve accompanied with Jus lié.

3086 Poularde à la Parisienne

Poach the fattened pullet in the usual manner.

Place on a dish, coat with Sauce Allemande and decorate the breasts with crescent-shaped pieces of salt ox tongue and truffle.

Surround the pullet with equal quantities of two kinds of small chicken Quenelles, one containing chopped truffle and the other chopped ham.

Finish by bordering the dish with a line of light chicken glaze.

3087 Poularde or Coq, en Pâte

The above name was given by the old classical kitchen to a chicken which was stuffed with either truffles, foie gras, morels etc. or even not stuffed then trussed with the lower part of the legs turned back; it was then coloured in butter, covered with a Matignon, then with some caul and finally with Pie Paste. This covering of paste was sealed well together, brushed with egg-wash and a hole made for the steam to escape; it was then cooked in the oven.

When this dish is prepared nowadays the covering of Matignon and caul is omitted. The well-coloured chicken is placed in a terrine just large enough to hold it; a piece of fresh butter is added and the dish is covered with paste. It is then cooked in the oven so that the chicken and pastry are cooked and coloured at the same time.

3088 Poularde Adelina Patti

Stuff the fattened pullet with rice as for Poularde à la Diva and poach it in white chicken stock.

When cooked, place on a dish on a low base of bread fried in clarified butter, coat with Sauce Suprême flavoured with paprika and surround it with medium-sized artichoke bottoms each containing a whole truffle glazed with light meat glaze.

Serve accompanied with a sauceboat of Sauce Suprême flavoured with paprika.

3089 Poularde à la Paysanne

Poach the fattened pullet in the usual manner.

Meanwhile, cut 125 g ($4\frac{1}{2}$ oz) red of carrot, 100 g ($3\frac{1}{2}$ oz) onion and 50 g (2 oz) celery into

Paysanne, cook together with butter until soft then add it to 2 dl (7 fl oz or $\frac{7}{8}$ U.S. cup) Sauce Allemande together with 2 tablespoons each of freshly cooked peas and diamonds of French beans.

Arrange the pullet on a dish and coat with the sauce.

Another way of preparing this dish is to colour the pullet in butter then place it in an earthenware terrine.

Surround with the same sliced and cooked vegetable as indicated above and finish cooking together basting frequently with a little good veal stock. Add the peas and beans at the last moment and serve as it is.

3090 Poularde à la Périgord

Stuff the fattened pullet with 200 g (7 oz) truffles trimmed to the shape of large olives, cooked together with 50 g (2 oz) fresh pork fat, then mixed whilst still hot with 400 g (14 oz) fresh pork fat pounded and passed through a sieve.

Truss the bird, closing all the apertures and Poêlé it slowly in the usual manner.

When cooked, place it on a dish and coat with Sauce Demi-glace containing the reduced cooking liquid and finished with truffle essence.

3091 Poularde à la Périgourdine

Slide some slices of raw truffle under the skin of the breast of the fattened pullet and stuff it with the same mixture as in the preceding recipe. Cover with thin slices of salt pork fat and Poêlé it.

Arrange on a dish and coat with Sauce Suprême containing truffle essence.

3092 Poularde Petite Mariée

Poach the fattened pullet in a small quantity of very white stock with the addition of 6 button onions, 6 small carrots, 6 small new potatoes and 150 g (5 oz) freshly shelled peas.

When cooked, place in a terrine together with the garnish and coat with the cooking liquid after reducing it and adding a little Sauce Suprême.

3093 Poularde à la Piémontaise

Stuff the fattened pullet with 300 g (11 oz) Risotto mixed with 200 g (7 oz) of sliced white truffles and Poêlé it in the usual manner.

When cooked, arrange on a dish and serve accompanied with chicken Jus lié containing the cooking liquid which has been skimmed, reduced and passed through a strainer.

3094 Poularde Polignac

Poach the fattened pullet in the usual manner.

Remove the breasts, cut off the breast bones and fill the carcase with 400 g (14 oz) Mousseline forcemeat mixed with 100 g ($3\frac{1}{2}$ oz) each of mushrooms and truffle cut in Julienne.

Cut the breasts into slices and replace on the carcase with alternate slices of truffle, cover with a buttered paper and place in a moderate oven to cook the forcemeat. Take care not to dry the slices of breast.

Arrange the pullet on a dish and coat with Sauce Suprême containing a quarter its quantity of a purée of mushrooms and 2 tbs each of a thin Julienne of truffle and mushrooms.

3095 Poularde à la Portugaise

Stuff the fattened pullet with 350 g ($12\frac{1}{2}$ oz) Riz Pilaw containing 150 g (5 oz) Tomato Fondue; Poêlé it in the usual manner.

Arrange on a dish, coat with Sauce Portugaise containing the reduced cooking liquid and surround with 10 halves of stuffed tomatoes à la Portugaise.

3096 Poularde Princesse

Poach the fattened pullet in the usual manner.

When cooked, place on a dish and coat with Sauce Allemande finished with 100 g ($3\frac{1}{2}$ oz) Asparagus Butter per 1 litre ($1\frac{3}{4}$ pt or $4\frac{1}{2}$ U.S. cups) of sauce.

Surround the chicken with alternate Croûstades of Pommes Duchesse (1162) filled with buttered asparagus tips with a slice of truffle on top, and bouquets of asparagus tips. Surround with a line of small round Quenelles made from chicken and cream forcemeat.

3097 Poularde Princesse Hélène

Stuff the fattened pullet with rice as for Poularde à la Diva, and poach it in the usual manner.

When cooked, arrange on a dish, coat with Sauce Suprême and surround with Subrics d'Epinards (4100) cooked at the last moment. Place a silver shell dish containing shavings of white truffle lightly warmed in butter, at the back of the chicken.

3098 Poularde Printanière

Place 100 g ($3\frac{1}{2}$ oz) Beurre Printanier flavoured with herbs inside the fattened pullet; truss it closing all the apertures and Poêlé until half cooked.

Transfer the pullet to an earthenware terrine, surround with Printanière garnish (444), sprinkle with a few tablespoons of stock and finish to cook in the oven.

Serve in the dish as it is.

3099 Poularde Régence

Stuff the fattened pullet with 400 g (14 oz) Mousseline forcemeat mixed with 100 g ($3\frac{1}{2}$ oz) purée of crayfish and poach it in the usual manner.

When cooked, place on a dish, coat with Sauce Suprême flavoured with truffle essence and surround with bouquets of a Régence garnish for poultry (449).

3100 Poularde à la Reine

Poach the fattened pullet in the usual manner.

When cooked, arrange on a dish and surround with small moulds of chicken purée mixed with egg yolks and cooked in dariole moulds which have been decorated with a slice of truffle on the bottom.

Serve accompanied with Sauce Suprême.

3101 Poularde Reine-Anne

Poêlé the fattened pullet in the usual manner.

When cooked, remove the breasts, cut off the breast bones and fill the carcase with macaroni mixed with cream and diced foie gras and truffle.

Coat the macaroni with Sauce Mornay, glaze it quickly then place the pullet on a low base of bread fried in clarified butter.

Surround with tartlet cases filled with cockscombs and kidneys mixed with Sauce Allemande and arrange a slice of the breast on each one; place a silver shell dish of truffles piled in a pyramid at the back of the chicken.

Serve accompanied with Sauce Allemande flavoured with truffle essence.

3102 Poularde Reine-Blanche

Stuff the fattened pullet with 300 g (11 oz) Mousseline forcemeat containing 100 g ($3\frac{1}{2}$ oz) each of diced salt ox tongue and truffle and poach it in the usual manner.

Arrange on a dish and surround with 100 g ($3\frac{1}{2}$ oz) cockscombs and kidneys, 60 g (2 oz) slices of truffle and 10 button mushrooms.

Coat with Sauce Allemande.

3103 Poularde Reine-Margot

Stuff the fattened pullet with 300 g (11 oz) Mousseline forcemeat containing 50 g (2 oz) purée of freshly skinned almonds and Poêlé it in the usual manner.

When cooked, arrange on a dish and coat with Sauce Suprême finished with a little almond milk; surround with Quenelles of chicken forcemeat flavoured and coloured with Pistachio Butter and Quenelles of chicken forcemeat flavoured and coloured with Crayfish Butter. These should be arranged in alternate bouquets.

3104 Poularde Reine-Marguerite

Poach the fattened pullet in the usual manner. Remove the breasts and cut off the breast bones leaving the legs and winglets in place.

Place the trimmed carcase on a low base of rice or bread fried in clarified butter.

Cut the breasts into thin small slices, add the same number of slices of truffles and mix both into a fairly firm cheese soufflé mixture.

Use this mixture to reform the fattened pullet, smooth the surface and surround with a band of buttered paper.

Cover with very thin slices of Gruyère cheese, place on the serving dish and cook as a soufflé in a moderately hot oven.

Serve accompanied with Sauce Suprême containing slices of white truffle.

3105 Poularde Renaissance

Poach the fattened pullet in the usual manner.

When cooked, arrange on a dish, coat with Sauce Allemande finished with mushroom essence and surround with a Renaissance garnish (450) arranged in well separated bouquets.

3106 Poularde au Riz

Poach the fattened pullet in the usual manner.

When cooked, place on a dish, coat with Sauce Allemande flavoured with chicken essence and surround with small moulds of rice cooked with some of the cooking liquid from the chicken.

3107 Poularde Rossini

Poêlé the fattened pullet in the usual manner.

When cooked, remove the breasts, cut into slices and arrange in a circle on a round dish with alternate slices of foie gras which have been shallow-fried in butter. Add a little well flavoured chicken stock to the pan, remove the fat, pass through a strainer and add a little truffle essence; pour this gravy into the centre of the dish.

Serve accompanied with a dish of buttered noodles covering them at the last moment with some raw noodles sautéed in butter.

Note: It is recommended to use a shallow oval earthenware dish with a lid for serving Poularde Rossini and to place it on a serviette on a silver dish.

3108 Poularde Saint-Alliance

Heat 12 nice truffles in butter, season with salt and pepper, sprinkle with $\frac{1}{2}$ dl (2 fl oz or $\frac{1}{4}$ U.S. cup) very good Madeira, cover tightly and allow them to cool as they are.

When cold place the truffles inside a fattened pullet and Poêlé it so as to be ready at exactly the time required to serve.

When it is cooked, shallow fry as many slices of foie gras in butter and cook as many Buntings as there are guests; send these to the room together with the pullet and a sauceboat of the deglazed and strained cooking liquid.

In the room, the head waiter with three assistants and a very hot chafing lamp on the service table should be awaiting the arrival of the dishes. He quickly removes the breasts from the pullet and cuts them into slices.

Each slice is placed on a slice of the foie gras which the first assistant has already placed on a hot plate together with one of the truffles from inside the bird.

The second assistant to whom the plate is immediately passed adds a Bunting and some of the gravy.

The third assistant immediately places the plate in front of the guest, and so on.

In this way the pullet is served very quickly and under conditions which make it a dish of high gastronomic value.

Note: The name adopted as the title of this dish of chicken and which Brillat-Savarin in his *Physiologie du Goût* used to designate a famous toast, appears to be very suitable for a dish in which are to be found united in a most admirable fashion the four veritable gems of cookery—the breast of a fine fattened pullet, the foie gras, the Bunting and the truffle.

3109 Poularde Santa-Lucia

Fill the fattened pullet with truffles prepared as in the preceding recipe and braise it with Marsala.

When cooked, set it on a low base of bread fried in clarified butter placed on a dish and surround with small tartlet shapes of Gnocchi à la Romaine and slices of foie gras shallow fried in butter, arranged alternately.

Serve accompanied with buttered Sauce Demi-glace flavoured with tomato.

3110 Poularde à la Sicilienne

Poach the fattened pullet in the usual manner.

When cooked, remove the breasts leaving the winglets attached to the carcase and remove the breast bones. Fill the carcase with a mixture of macaroni, diced foie gras and truffle, cockscombs and kidneys—all mixed with a little well-flavoured gravy from some braised beef à la Napolitaine.

Wrap the pullet in a piece of pig's caul re-forming it to its original shape, sprinkle with dry white breadcrumbs and melted butter and place in the oven to cook and colour the caul.

When ready, place it on a low base of rice or bread fried in butter, and coat with buttered meat glaze; surround with tartlet cases, each filled with a slice of the chicken breast, then a slice of foie gras shallow fried in butter and with a slice of truffle on top.

Serve accompanied with a sauceboat of buttered Sauce Demi-glace flavoured with tomato.

3111 Poularde Soufflé

Poach a fattened pullet in the usual manner.

When cooked, remove the breasts and cut them into thin slices. Cut off the breast bones with scissors and fill the carcase with 500 g (1 lb 2 oz) Mousseline forcemeat containing 150 g (5 oz) foie gras purée, spreading it in layers alternating with slices of the breast and slices of truffle.

Smooth dome shape to give the appearance of the bird and decorate with pieces of truffle, salt ox tongue and cooked egg white. Place on a dish and put this in a deep tray containing a little boiling water, the steam from which will assist in the cooking of the forecemeat, and place in a moderate oven to cook.

Serve accompanied with Sauce Allemande flavoured with truffle essence.

Another way of preparing this dish is to fill the carcase of the pullet with Mousseline forcemeat containing the foie gras purée and then to cook it in a moderate oven.

When cooked, surround with the slices of chicken each placed on a cooked tartlet shape of the same Mousseline forcemeat.

Serve accompanied with the same sauce as above.

Note: The use of this type of Bain-marie consisting of a tray of boiling water in which the dish holding the pullet is placed is highly recommended; the ideal method of cooking this type of preparation, however, is by steaming it.

3112 Poularde Souvaroff

Stuff a fattened pullet with a mixture of 250 g (9 oz) foie gras and 150 g (5 oz) truffle both cut in large dice and Poêlé it until three-quarters cooked.

Place the pullet in an earthenware terrine with 10 medium-sized truffles which have been cooked for a few minutes with a little Madeira in the same pan used for the chicken.

Add 1 dl ($3\frac{1}{2}$ fl oz or $\frac{1}{2}$ U.S. cup) well flavoured chicken stock, cover with the lid and seal with a band of flour and water paste. Place in a moderate oven for 30 minutes to complete the cooking and serve as it is.

3113 Poularde Stanley

Stuff the fattened pullet with 250 g (9 oz) Riz Pilaw mixed with 100 g ($3\frac{1}{2}$ oz) each of mushroom and truffle cut in Julienne.

Poach in a little white stock together with 500 g (1 lb 2 oz) well blanched sliced onion and a little curry powder.

When cooked, pass the onions and stock through a sieve and add to it 2 dl (7 fl oz or $\frac{7}{8}$ U.S. cup) each of Velouté and cream. Reduce until fairly stiff, pass through the sieve once more and add another 1 dl ($3\frac{1}{2}$ fl oz or $\frac{1}{2}$ U.S. cup) of cream.

Arrange the pullet on a dish and coat with this sauce.

3114 Poularde Sylvana

Stuff the fattened pullet with mushrooms sautéed in Beurre Noisette then roast it in the oven until nicely coloured but only half cooked.

Place 250 g (9 oz) peas in a pan together with 10 small new onions, 1 small shredded lettuce, a Bouquet garni comprised of parsley, chervil and thyme and a pinch of salt and sugar. Mix in 50 g (2 oz) butter, add 2 tbs water, cover with a lid and half cook tossing them over from time to time.

Place the half-cooked pullet in an earthenware terrine, surround with the garnish, cover with the lid and seal with flour and water paste. Place in the oven to finish cooking for 45 minutes.

Serve the chicken in the dish as it is. If required it may be accompanied with a sauceboat of good chicken gravy.

3115 Poularde Talleyrand

Poêlé the fattened pullet and when cooked, remove the breasts and cut them into large dice.

Add the diced chicken to an equal amount of cooked macaroni cut in short pieces and mixed with Sauce Crème and grated Parmesan; then add and mix in 150 g (5 oz) foie gras and 50 g (2 oz) truffle both cut in large dice.

Cut off the breast bones from the chicken and fill the carcase with the macaroni mixture; cover this with a layer of Mousseline forcemeat smoothing it to the original shape of the bird.

Decorate the top with a circle of slices of truffle, cover with a sheet of buttered paper and place in a moderate oven to cook the forcemeat and at the same time reheat the filling.

Arrange on a dish; pour around the bird a little Sauce Demi-glace flavoured with truffle essence and containing a Julienne of truffle; serve the remainder of this sauce in a sauceboat.

3116 Poularde Tivoli

Poêlé the fattened pullet in the usual manner.

When cooked, arrange on a dish and surround with grilled mushrooms filled with cockscombs and kidneys mixed with a little Sauce Allemande, and bouquets of asparagus tips, arranging them alternately.

Add a little veal stock to the pan, reduce to 1 dl ($3\frac{1}{2}$ fl oz or $\frac{1}{2}$ U.S. cup) skim and add a few drops of lemon juice; pass through a fine strainer and finish with 100 g ($3\frac{1}{2}$ oz) butter and a Julienne of truffle. Coat the pullet with this sauce.

3117 Poularde Tosca

Stuff the fattened pullet with Riz Pilaw and Poêlé it with very little liquid.

Arrange on a dish on a low base of bread fried in butter and surround with braised fennel.

Serve accompanied with the reduced cooking liquid from the chicken enriched with butter.

3118 Poularde à la Toulousaine

Poach the fattened pullet in the usual manner.

When cooked, arrange on a dish, coat with Sauce Allemande and surround with bouquets of Toulousaine garnish (463).

Serve accompanied with Sauce Allemande flavoured with mushroom essence.

3119 Poularde Trianon

Poach the fattened pullet in the usual manner.

Meanwhile, prepare 24 small chicken Quenelles moulded with teaspoons, one-third of them containing chopped truffle, one-third containing chopped salt ox tongue and the remainder containing chopped Fines Herbes. In the moulding of these Quenelles a small amount of foie gras purée should be enclosed in each.

Arrange the pullet on a dish, place the three kinds of Quenelles around in separate bouquets with a whole truffle between each bouquet. Insert into the pullet a decorative skewer garnished with a large grooved mushroom, a glazed truffle and a Quenelle decorated with shapes of salt ox tongue.

Serve accompanied with Sauce Suprême finished with a little Foie gras butter.

3120 Poularde à la Valenciennes

Poêlé the fattened pullet in the usual manner.

When cooked, arrange on a dish and surround with Risotto containing some diced ham.

Arrange slices of grilled ham overlapping on top of the Risotto and serve accompanied with a well-seasoned Sauce Suprême flavoured with tomato.

3121 Poularde à la Vénitienne

Poach the fattened pullet in the usual manner.

When cooked, arrange on a dish, coat with Sauce Suprême finished with Beurre Ravigote (254) and surround with grooved mushrooms, slices of freshly poached calf's brains and cockscombs.

3122 Poularde Vert-Pré

Poach the fattened pullet in the usual manner.

When cooked, arrange on a dish and coat with Sauce Suprême finished with 100 g ($3\frac{1}{2}$ oz) Beurre Printanier (257) per 1 litre ($1\frac{3}{4}$ pt or $4\frac{1}{2}$ U.S. cups) of sauce. Surround with bouquets of buttered peas, French beans and asparagus tips.

3123 Poularde à la Vichy
Poach the fattened pullet in the usual manner.

When cooked, arrange on a dish and coat with 2 dl (7 fl oz or $\frac{7}{8}$ U.S. cup) Sauce Suprême to which has been added 100 g ($3\frac{1}{2}$ oz) red of carrot, stewed in butter and passed through a sieve, and $\frac{1}{2}$ dl (2 fl oz or $\frac{1}{4}$ U.S. cup) cream.

Surround with tartlet cases filled with Carottes à la Vichy.

3124 Poularde Victoria
Stuff the fattened pullet with foie gras and truffle as for Poularde Souvaroff and Poêlé it until three-quarters cooked.

Place in an earthenware terrine, add 400 g (15 oz) potatoes cut in large dice and coloured in butter, cover with the lid and finish cooking together in the oven.

Serve in the dish as it is.

3125 Poularde à la Vierge
Poach the fattened pullet in the usual manner.

When cooked, arrange on a dish, coat with Sauce Béchamel finished with cream and chicken essence and surround with alternate slices of poached calf's brains and slices of poached veal sweetbreads, separated with very white cockscombs.

3126 Poularde Villars
Poach the fattened pullet in the usual manner.

Place on a dish, coat with Sauce Allemande finished with mushroom essence and surround with bouquets of lambs' sweetbreads, cockscombs and mushrooms, placing a slice of salt ox tongue cut in the shape of a cockscomb between each.

3127 Poularde Washington
Stuff a fattened pullet with 300 g (11 oz) green sweetcorn cooked in the same way as Riz à la Grecque and braise it in the usual manner.

Glaze it at the last moment; arrange on a dish and serve accompanied with a dish of creamed sweetcorn and a sauceboat of the cooking liquid after removing the fat, passing through a fine strainer and reducing it.

3128 Other Preparations of Fattened Pullets
A very good way of preparing chickens is to either stuff with rice or leave empty, cook in very little but very good chicken stock and then to make a Sauce Suprême from this liquid.

They can be served accompanied with cucumber, celery, new carrots, cardoons or artichoke bottoms stewed in butter without colour, with slices of truffle added and then lightly covered with some of the prepared sauce.

There are at least a dozen cxcellent recipes here for fattened pullets as can be seen from the above indications but it is left to the inspiration of the cook to decide on the most suitable and appropriate name.

3129 Poularde or Chapon aux Perles du Périgord
Stuff the bird with nice truffles, cover with very thin slices of veal cut from the cushion and braise it with brandy.

Arrange on a dish and serve accompanied with the prepared braising liquid and a dish of Cardons au Jus.

3130 FILLETS, SUPREMES AND CUTLETS OF CHICKEN

The terms *FILET* and *SUPRÊME* are synonymous and both may be used on the menu so as to avoid awkward repetition. They are names given to the breast of the chicken divided along the breast bone, removed from the carcase and the skin completely removed. They consist of the breast proper and the minion fillet (Fr. *Filet Mignon*) on its underside.

With Suprêmes of chicken the small fillet is usually left attached to the breast, it being too small to be used on its own; the small fillets from Suprêmes cut from large chickens are often used on their own; in this case the sinew is removed, a few small incisions are made in it at regular intervals and small slices of truffle are half inset in the cuts. They are then formed into crescents or rings.

Cutlet is the name given to a Suprême cut from a queen or spring chicken but with the end of the wing bone (Humerus) left attached. Suprêmes are also cut from the same kind of chicken, although they are sometimes cut from larger ones in which case they have to be cut into three or four even-sized pieces then lightly flattened and trimmed oval- or heart-shape, excepting when they are to be stuffed.

For stuffing they are cut through the thick part to form a pocket and filled with sufficient stuffing to fill it out, using a piping bag and tube.

Suprêmes and cutlets are cooked without liquid, or at least almost so because the least chance of boiling liquid coming into contact will cause them to toughen. When a recipe calls for Suprêmes to be poached it is advisable to cook the whole chicken first then to remove the two Suprêmes. According to whether they are prepared brown or white the method is as follows, although it should be remembered that the brown method is more applicable to cutlets of chicken.

Cutlets or Suprêmes cooked brown: Season with salt, dip in flour, place in a shallow pan containing very hot clarified butter and cook quickly to colour on both sides; being so tender the colouring and the cooking of the cutlets or Suprêmes takes place at one and the same time.

Cutlets or Suprêmes cooked white or poached: Season the cutlets or Suprêmes and place them in a shallow pan in melted but not clarified butter; turn them in the butter, add a few drops of lemon juice, cover tightly with the lid and place in a very hot oven. They will be cooked in a few minutes being ready when they feel elastic to the pressure of the finger.

Cutlets and Suprêmes of chicken may be floured, egg and breadcrumbed for shallow frying and deep frying, or dipped in melted butter and breadcrumbed for grilling.

Important remark: It is important to remember that cutlets and Suprêmes will become hard if they are not served immediately; they should be cooked rapidly at the last moment, arranged quickly and simply on the dish and served very hot whilst still soft—this is the most important thing.

The following recipes are suitable for both Suprêmes and Cutlets of chicken.

Note: In those recipes which follow where a Jus lié is mentioned, it is advisable to proceed as follows: deglaze the pan in which the Suprêmes were cooked with a little white stock without removing the butter and add a few spoonfuls of meat glaze. The gravy will thicken by the liaison of the butter and the glaze, and the addition of the liquid which should not be allowed to reduce completely. By this means a good gravy with an exquisite nutty flavour can be obtained.

3131 Suprême de Volaille Agnès Sorel
Coat some buttered oval tartlet moulds with a layer of Mousseline forcemeat, half fill with sliced mushrooms sautéed in butter and cover with more of the forcemeat; cook in the oven *au Bain-marie.*

Turn out and arrange in a circle on a round dish. Place a poached suprême on each, coat with Sauce Suprême and decorate with a round slice of ox tongue with a slice of truffle in its centre. Surround each suprême with a thin line of melted chicken glaze.

3132 Suprême de Volaille Albuféra
Cut the suprêmes heart shape, stuff them with Mousseline forcemeat, season and cook under cover with butter, keeping them white.

Place each on a tartlet case filled with small balls of truffles, very small chicken quenelles, button mushrooms, and cocks' kidneys—all mixed with Sauce Albuféra. Arrange on a dish, lightly coat the suprêmes with the same sauce and serve some separately in a sauceboat.

3133 Suprême de Volaille Alexandra
Season and cook the suprêmes under cover with butter, keeping them slightly underdone.

Arrange on a dish with a slice of truffle on each, coat with chicken-flavoured Sauce Mornay, glaze then surround with bouquets of buttered asparagus tips.

3134 Suprême de Volaille à l'Ambassadrice
Season and cook the suprêmes under cover with butter, keeping them white.

Arrange on a dish, coat with Sauce Suprême and surround with white cooked lamb's sweetbreads studded with truffle, and bouquets of buttered asparagus tips.

3135 Suprême de Volaille à l'Arlesienne
Season, flour and shallow fry the suprêmes in clarified butter.

Arrange on a circle of slices of eggplant fried in oil, fill the centre with diced tomato flesh cooked in oil, and surround with deep fried onion rings.

Serve tomato-flavoured Sauce Demi-glace separately.

3136 Suprême de Volaille Belle-Hélène
Cut the suprêmes heart shape, season and shallow fry in clarified butter.

Arrange in a circle on a dish each placed on a Croquette of asparagus tips of the same shape; place a slice of truffle on each suprême and coat with a little Beurre Noisette.

Serve separately a sauceboat of Jus lié finished with some of the butter from the cooking of the suprêmes.

3137 Suprême de Volaille Boitelle
Cut the suprêmes heart shape, place in a buttered shallow pan with 300 g (11 oz) sliced mushrooms, season with salt and pepper and sprinkle with a few drops of lemon juice; cover and cook slowly in a moderate oven.

Arrange in a circle in a deep dish, with the mushrooms in the centre.

Add to the cooking liquor, which has come from the mushrooms, 80 g ($2\frac{1}{2}$ oz) butter and a few drops of lemon juice. Pour this sauce over the suprêmes and sprinkle with chopped parsley.

3138 Suprême de Volaille aux Champignons (*White*)
Season and cook the suprêmes under cover with a little mushroom cooking liquor keeping them white.

Arrange in a circle on a dish with very white grooved mushrooms in the centre and coat with

Sauce Allemande containing some of the cooking liquor.

Serve the rest of the sauce separately.

3139 Suprême de Volaille aux Champignons (*Brown*)

Season, flour and shallow fry the suprêmes in clarified butter.

Arrange in a circle on a dish, surround with sautéed sliced mushrooms and coat with thin Sauce Champignons.

3140 Suprême de Volaille Chimay

Season, flour and shallow fry the suprêmes in clarified butter.

Arrange on a dish and garnish with bouquets of sautéed morels and buttered asparagus tips, surrounded with a *cordon* of Jus lié.

3141 Suprême de Volaille Cussy

Cut the suprêmes into fairly thick slices, flatten them slightly and trim. Season, flour and shallow fry in butter.

Place each on an artichoke bottom of the same size, decorate with a thick slice of truffle and place a very white cock's kidney on the truffle.

Arrange on a dish and serve accompanied with a lightly thickened and buttered chicken gravy.

3142 Suprême de Volaille Doria

Season the suprêmes, flour, egg and breadcrumb and shallow fry them quickly in clarified butter.

Arrange on a dish and surround with pieces of cucumber, trimmed to the shape of garlic cloves and stewed in butter, or simply floured and deep fried.

Just before serving, coat with a little Beurre Noisette and sprinkle with a few drops of lemon juice.

3143 Suprême de Volaille à la Dreux

Make some incisions at short intervals in the suprêmes and half insert into these, small round slices of truffle and cooked salt ox tongue. Season and cook under cover with butter in a moderate oven keeping them white.

Arrange on a dish and surround with a garnish of cockscombs and kidneys and slices of truffle. Coat the garnish lightly with Sauce Allemande.

3144 Suprême de Volaille à l'Ecarlate

Inset the suprêmes with round slices only of salt ox tongue as in the preceding recipe. Season and cook under cover with butter in a moderate oven, keeping them white.

Place each on a Croûton of bread fried in butter and between them place an oval Quenelle made from a Mousseline forcemeat of chicken and sprinkled with chopped salt ox tongue before being cooked. Coat with clear Sauce Suprême so that the red colour of the tongue can be seen.

3145 Suprême de Volaille à l'Ecossaise

Season and cook the suprêmes under cover with butter, keeping them white.

Arrange on a dish, coat with Sauce Ecossaise and serve accompanied with a dish of buttered French beans.

Another way is to cut the suprêmes heart shape, stuff them with Godiveau (290) containing a cooked Brunoise of vegetables, cook them in the same way as before and serve coated with the same sauce and garnished with bouquets of buttered French beans.

3146 Suprême de Volaille Elizabeth

Remove the suprêmes from two small chickens and cook them in Beurre Noisette. Place them in a square dish, coat with Sauce Suprême and place on each a few slices of truffle.

Place in the centre 12 nice oysters which have been kept on ice for at least 2 hours in advance.

Note: This recipe was prepared at the request of a customer and is included in this book as an oddity.

3147 Suprême de Volaille Favorite

Season and shallow fry the suprêmes in clarified butter.

Arrange in a circle on a dish, each placed on a slice of foie gras, shallow fried in butter; place a bouquet of buttered asparagus tips in the centre.

Serve separately a sauceboat of buttered light meat glaze.

3148 Suprême de Volaille Financière

Cut the suprêmes heart shape, stuff with chicken forcemeat containing chopped truffle and cook under cover with butter, keeping them white.

Arrange on a dish, each placed on a heart-shaped Croûton of bread fried in butter and fill the centre with a Financière garnish.

Coat the suprêmes and garnish with Sauce Financière.

3149 Suprême de Volaille à la Florentine

Season and cook the suprêmes under cover with butter, keeping them white.

Arrange on a bed of roughly chopped buttered spinach placed on a dish; coat with chicken-flavoured Sauce Mornay and glaze quickly under the salamander.

3150 Suprême de Volaille aux Fonds d'Artichaut

Season and shallow fry the suprêmes in clarified butter.

Arrange on a dish surrounded with sliced fried artichoke bottoms sprinkled with chopped parsley and pour a little Beurre Noisette over the suprêmes.

Serve Jus lié separately.

3151 Suprême de Volaille Henri IV
Cut the suprêmes into round slices, flatten them slightly and trim; season, flour and shallow fry in clarified butter. Arrange on a dish, each on an artichoke bottom containing a little buttered meat glaze, and decorate with a slice of truffle.

Serve Sauce Béarnaise separately.

3152 Suprême de Volaille à l'Hongroise
Season the suprêmes with paprika, shallow fry in clarified butter and arrange on a bed of Pilaff rice cooked with diced tomato flesh.

Deglaze the pan with a little cream, add the necessary amount of Sauce Hongroise and coat the suprêmes with it.

3153 Suprême de Volaille à l'Indienne
Season and shallow fry the suprêmes in butter; place them into some Sauce Currie à l'Indienne for a few minutes without letting it boil.

Arrange the suprêmes in a deep dish with the sauce and serve accompanied with a dish of plain boiled rice.

Another way of preparing this dish is to poach a chicken keeping it white, then remove the breasts and cut each in half. Place each piece on a chicken Quenelle, decorate with a slice of truffle and coat with Sauce Suprême lightly flavoured with curry.

Serve accompanied with a dish of Riz Pilaff containing some plain boiled peas.

3154 Suprême de Volaille Jardinière
Season and shallow fry the suprêmes in butter.

Arrange on a dish surrounded with well separated bouquets of Jardinière garnish (396). Coat the suprêmes with a little Beurre Noisette when about to serve.

3155 Suprême de Volaille Judic
Cut the suprêmes heart shape, season and cook them under cover with butter, keeping them white.

Arrange on a dish each placed on a half of braised lettuce; decorate each with a slice of truffle and a cock's kidney and coat lightly with Jus lié.

3156 Suprême de Volaille Maréchal
Prepare the suprêmes, flour, egg and breadcrumb and shallow fry them in clarified butter.

Arrange in a circle on a dish with a nice slice of truffle on each and place a nice garnish of buttered asparagus tips in the centre.

Note: Strictly speaking, most articles prepared à la Maréchal should be coated with finely chopped truffle but during cooking the truffle gets dry and loses its flavour and aroma. It is therefore advisable to coat the items with a mixture of two-thirds white crumbs and one-third chopped truffle, or with breadcrumbs alone.

3157 Suprême de Volaille Marie-Louise
Cut the suprêmes into round pieces, flatten them, trim, then flour, egg and breadcrumb them; shallow fry in clarified butter.

Arrange on a dish each placed on a small artichoke bottom filled with a fairly stiff mushroom purée mixed with a little Sauce Soubise. Coat with a little Beurre Noisette.

3158 Suprême de Volaille Marie-Thérèse
Prepare a Riz Pilaw made with chicken stock and when cooked, mix in a little butter together with 200 g (7 oz) chopped cooked white of chicken per 500 g (1 lb 2 oz) of cooked rice. Fill a well buttered dome-shaped mould with this rice pressing it in fairly firmly.

Season and cook the suprêmes under cover with a little butter and a few drops of lemon juice, keeping them white.

Demould the rice on to the centre of a round dish and arrange the suprêmes around it. Coat with Sauce Suprême and place a slice of salt ox tongue cut to the shape of a cockscomb between each suprême.

Serve Sauce Suprême separately.

3159 Suprême de Volaille Maryland
Season the suprêmes, flour, egg and breadcrumb and shallow fry them in clarified butter.

Arrange on a dish, each placed on rashers of grilled bacon; surround with small fried *Galettes* of maize flour and fried slices of banana.

Serve creamed Horseradish Sauce separately.

3160 Suprême de Volaille Mireille
Cut the suprêmes from well fleshed chicken, season them and shallow fry in clarified butter.

Arrange on a dish of Pommes Mireille (4212).

Deglaze the pan with white wine, add a few tablespoonfuls of meat glaze and sprinkle it over the suprêmes.

3161 Suprême de Volaille Montpensier
Season the suprêmes, flour, egg and breadcrumb and shallow fry them in clarified butter.

Arrange in a circle on a dish with a slice of truffle on each; surround with bouquets of buttered asparagus tips.

Coat with a little Beurre Noisette.

3162 Suprême de Volaille Orly
Marinate the suprêmes with a little oil, lemon juice, finely chopped onion and parsley stalks for 1 hour. Dry on a cloth, dip into light frying butter and deep fry quickly.

Arrange on a serviette with fried parsley and serve a sauceboat of Tomato Sauce separately.

3163 Suprême de Volaille à l'Orientale
Season and shallow fry the suprêmes in clarified butter.

Arrange on a dish, each placed on thick slices of chow-chow cut the shape of the suprêmes, blanched and cooked in butter. Coat with Sauce Suprême to which a quarter its volume of tomato purée and a touch of saffron has been added; serve accompanied with a dish of Riz Pilaw containing diced red pimento.

3164 Suprême de Volaille en Papillote
Season and quickly colour the suprêmes in butter; enclose each in an oiled or buttered sheet of paper cut heart shape, placing it between 2 slices of ham and layers of thick Sauce Italienne.

Seal the edges by pleating and place on a tray in a fairly hot oven to finish cooking the suprêmes and to blow up the paper.

3165 Suprême de Volaille Parisienne
Cut the suprêmes into heart-shaped pieces, season them and cook under cover with butter, keeping them white.

Arrange in a circle on a dish, coat with Sauce Allemande and fill the centre with small chicken Quenelles containing chopped truffle and ox tongue; then decorate each suprême with two crescent shapes of ox tongue enclosing one of truffle. Coat these with a little melted meat glaze.

3166 Suprême de Volaille au Parmesan
Dip the suprêmes into seasoned beaten egg then coat them with a mixture of grated Parmesan and breadcrumbs.

Shallow fry in butter and arrange on a dish, each placed on a piece of Polenta cut the size and shape of the suprême and shallow fried in butter. When about to serve, coat the suprêmes with a little Beurre Noisette.

3167 Suprême de Volaille à la Périgueux
Cut the suprêmes heart shape and stuff them with truffled Mousseline forcemeat; cook under cover with butter, keeping them white.

Arrange in a circle on a dish and pour some Sauce Périgueux in the middle.

3168 Suprême de Volaille Polignac
Season and cook the suprêmes under cover with butter, keeping them white.

Arrange in a circle on a dish and coat them with Sauce Suprême containing a thin Julienne of mushroom and truffle.

3169 Suprême de Volaille Pojarski
Finely chop the flesh of the suprêmes adding 125 g ($4\frac{1}{2}$ oz) breadcrumbs soaked in milk and squeezed, 125 g ($4\frac{1}{2}$ oz) butter and 1 dl ($3\frac{1}{2}$ fl oz or $\frac{1}{2}$ U.S. cup) double cream, per 500 g (1 lb 2 oz) of chicken flesh. Season with salt, pepper and nutmeg and form into the shape of suprêmes, using flour. Shallow fry in clarified butter and serve immediately.

Note: The garnish for Pojarski in any of its forms is entirely optional and at one's discretion.

3170 Suprême de Volaille Régence
Cut the suprêmes heart shape and lightly flatten them; season and cook under cover with butter, keeping them white.

Arrange on a dish, each placed on a Quenelle of the same shape made from chicken forcemeat and Crayfish Butter. Coat with truffle-flavoured Sauce Suprême. On each suprême place a piece of truffle cut to the shape of an olive and a cock's kidney; place a cockscomb between each of these two items.

3171 Suprême de Volaille Richelieu
Season the suprêmes, flour, egg and breadcrumb and shallow fry in clarified butter.

Arrange on a dish, coat with half melted Maître d'Hôtel Butter and decorate each suprême with 4 slices of truffle.

3172 Suprême de Volaille Rimini
Lard the suprêmes with thin strips of very black truffle; season and cook under cover with butter, keeping them white.

Arrange on a dish, each suprême placed on a cooked puff pastry Barquette case filled with mushroom purée.

Serve Sauce Allemande separately.

3173 Suprême de Volaille Rossini
Season and shallow fry the suprêmes in butter.

Arrange on a dish, each placed on a shallow fried slice of foie gras and coat with strongly flavoured Sauce Madère containing sliced truffle.

3174 Suprême de Volaille Saint-Germain
Season the suprêmes, dip in melted butter and

grill slowly on a sheet of oiled paper, brushing occasionally with clarified butter.

Serve accompanied with a sauceboat of Sauce Béarnaise and a dish of creamed fresh peas.

3175 Suprême de Volaille Talleyrand

Prepare 1) a pale baked deep flan case using good short paste and of a size proportionate to the number of suprêmes and the garnish; 2) a garnish of Macaroni à la Crème containing 100 g ($3\frac{1}{2}$ oz) each of diced foie gras and truffle per 250 g (9 oz) of macaroni; and 3) heart-shaped suprêmes seasoned and cooked under cover with butter, and kept white.

Arrange the macaroni in the case, moulding it dome shape; coat the suprêmes with Sauce Allemande then arrange them in the case around the macaroni.

Place the finished case on a serviette on a dish and serve accompanied with a Sauce Madère containing a Julienne of truffle.

3176 Suprême de Volaille Valencay

Stuff the suprêmes with finely diced truffle mixed with a little well reduced Sauce Allemande, flour, egg and breadcrumb and shallow fry them in clarified butter.

For each suprême prepare two Croûtons of bread cut cockscomb shape and fried in butter; cover them dome-shape with chicken forcemeat containing chopped truffles and place in a warm oven to cook the forcemeat.

Arrange the suprêmes in a circle on a dish and surround with the prepared Croûtons.

Serve accompanied with a dish of a purée of mushrooms.

3177 Suprême de Volaille Valois

Season the suprêmes, flour, egg and breadcrumb and shallow fry in clarified butter; arrange in a circle on a round dish and fill the centre with small poached stuffed olives.

Serve Sauce Valois separately.

3178 Suprême de Volaille Verneuil

Marinate the suprêmes with oil, lemon juice, finely chopped onion and parsley stalks for 1 hour.

Flour, egg and breadcrumb and shallow fry them in clarified butter.

Arrange on a dish, coat with Sauce Colbert and serve accompanied with a dish of a purée of artichokes.

3179 Suprême de Volaille Villeroy

Season and cook the suprêmes under cover with butter keeping them slightly undercooked. Allow to cool then coat each with Sauce Villeroy. Flour, egg and breadcrumb, deep fry at the last moment and serve accompanied with Sauce Périgueux.

3180 Suprême de Volaille Wolseley

Cut the suprêmes heart shape and stuff them with Mousseline forcemeat. Season and cook under cover with butter, keeping them white.

Coat with Sauce Suprême, arrange on a dish and place a small bouquet of buttered asparagus tips between each suprême.

3181 POULETS SAUTES—SAUTES OF CHICKEN

As stated at the beginning of this chapter, the best chickens to use for Sauté are the Queen chickens (Poulet à la Reine); these should be medium-sized birds which are well fleshed and tender.

In an extreme case, fattened pullets or large spring chickens could be used but neither of these is so well suited for the preparation of Sautés as the Queen chicken.

The dissection of a chicken for Sauté is carried out in the following manner: clean and singe the chicken; cut the skin round each leg, turn each leg back and cut through the joint where it meets the carcase and remove them. Cut through the joints between the thighs and drumsticks; separate the lower part of the legs from the drumstick above the joint.

Remove the bone (Femur) from the thighs just above the lower joint; trim the lower part of the leg below the joint and cut off the claws.

Cut off the winglets and remove the pinions; cut along the sides of the breast and remove the wing portions cutting through the joint of the carcase; remove the centre part of the breast from the carcase and divide it in half along the centre if a large bird or leave whole if smaller.

Lastly, cut the carcase into two pieces and trim neatly along both sides.

Whatever the recipe being followed, the method for cooking all Sautés of chicken is always carried out as follows: melt 50 g (2 oz) clarified butter, or half butter and half oil, in a shallow pan just big enough to hold all the pieces of chicken. When it is very hot, put in the pieces of chicken previously lightly seasoned with salt and pepper, and colour them quickly, turning on all sides to ensure even colouring. Now put the lid on the pan and place it to cook in a fairly hot oven until completely cooked.

The tenderest pieces such as the wings and breast will be cooked quite quickly and should be taken out after a few minutes and kept warm and covered. The legs being thicker and firmer should be cooked for a further 7–8 minutes and when cooked, should be removed and kept with the rest of the already cooked chicken.

Drain off some of the fat and deglaze the pan with the liquid as indicated by the recipe; this could be an appropriate wine, mushroom cooking liquor, chicken stock etc.—the idea of deglazing the pan is to dissolve the caramelized juices in the bottom of the pan. Reduce the deglazing liquid by half then add the sauce in accordance with the recipe.

Replace the pieces of carcase, lower legs, legs and winglets in the sauce and allow to reheat very gently for a few minutes then add the wing portions and the breast but only when the sauce has been correctly finished. It should not boil any further.

It is not necessary to boil the pieces of chicken in the sauce as they are already cooked—boiling will only toughen them.

A few minutes before service, arrange the pieces of chicken in the following order in a deep Entrée dish having a cover; the pieces of carcase and the lower legs and winglets in the bottom of the dish; the pieces of leg on top of these finishing with the wing portions and breast.

The sauce thus being ready according to its recipe is then poured over the chicken.

For white preparations of Sautés of chicken, the pieces are simply stiffened in hot butter without colouring then placed in the oven to cook as indicated for brown Sautés. The liquid used for deglazing is nearly always a white one as would be the sauce, these being finished with cream.

3182 Poulet Sauté Algérienne

Season the pieces of chicken and sauté them in butter.

Deglaze the pan with 1 dl ($3\frac{1}{2}$ fl oz or $\frac{1}{2}$ U.S. cup) white wine; add a touch of crushed garlic and the roughly chopped flesh of 1 tomato.

When cooked, arrange the chicken in a deep dish, coat with the sauce and surround with bouquets of sweet potato and chow-chow both trimmed to the shape of large olives and cooked in butter.

3183 Poulet Sauté Anversoise

Season the pieces of chicken and cook them in butter without colour.

Deglaze the pan with cream, add 1 dl ($3\frac{1}{2}$ fl oz or $\frac{1}{2}$ U.S. cup) Sauce Suprême and reduce by one-third. Add 250 g (9 oz) hop shoots cooked in water keeping them slightly firm and 125 g (4 oz) Julienne of very red salt ox tongue.

Arrange the pieces of chicken in a deep dish and coat with the sauce.

3184 Poulet Sauté Archiduc

Season the pieces of chicken and stiffen them in butter; add 100 g ($3\frac{1}{2}$ oz) sliced onions previously cooked in butter and cook together without colour.

Remove the pieces of chicken, arrange in a deep dish and keep warm.

Add $\frac{1}{4}$ dl (1 fl oz or $\frac{1}{8}$ U.S. cup) brandy to the pan and reduce; add 1 dl ($3\frac{1}{2}$ fl oz or $\frac{1}{2}$ U.S. cup) each of cream and Velouté then pass all through a sieve.

Reduce this sauce until fairly thick and finish away from the heat with 50 g (2 oz) butter, the juice of $\frac{1}{4}$ lemon and 1 tbs of Madeira. Pour over the chicken and garnish with 10 slices of truffle.

3185 Poulet Sauté Arlésienne

Season the pieces of chicken and sauté them in oil; remove, cover and keep warm.

Deglaze the pan with white wine, add a small crushed clove of garlic and 1 dl ($3\frac{1}{2}$ fl oz or $\frac{1}{2}$ U.S. cup) tomato-flavoured Sauce Demi-glace and reduce by one-third.

Arrange the chicken in a deep dish and surround with alternate bouquets of onion rings and slices of eggplant both seasoned, floured and deep fried in oil, and roughly chopped flesh only of tomato cooked in a little butter.

3186 Poulet Sauté à l'Armagnac

Season the pieces of chicken and cook them in butter without colour together with 100 g ($3\frac{1}{2}$ oz) sliced raw truffle.

Arrange the chicken and truffles in a terrine; deglaze the pan with $\frac{1}{4}$ dl (1 fl oz or $\frac{1}{8}$ U.S. cup) old Armagnac, add a little lemon juice and 1 dl ($3\frac{1}{2}$ fl oz or $\frac{1}{4}$ U.S. cup) of cream. Heat through and finish away from the heat with 50 g (2 oz) Crayfish Butter.

Pour this sauce over the chicken and serve in the terrine.

3187 Poulet Sauté d'Artois

Season the pieces of chicken and sauté them in butter; when cooked, remove and arrange in a dish.

Deglaze the pan with $\frac{1}{2}$ dl (2 fl oz or $\frac{1}{4}$ U.S. cup) Madeira, add the same amount of pale meat glaze, 5 small cooked and quartered artichoke bottoms sautéed in butter, 10 pieces of carrot trimmed to the shape of small olives, cooked in Bouillon and glazed, and 10 button onions cooked in butter. Finish with 50 g (2 oz) butter and a pinch of chopped chives and pour the sauce and garnish over the chicken.

3188 Poulet Sauté Beaulieu

Season the pieces of chicken and sauté them in butter; add 150 g (5 oz) very small new potatoes or potatoes cut and trimmed small, and the same amount of quarters of small globe artichokes both previously cooked in butter together. Cook in the oven covered with a lid for 10 minutes.

Arrange the chicken and garnish in an earthenware casserole together with 10 black olives.

Deglaze the pan with a few tablespoons of white wine and a few drops of lemon juice; finish with a little veal gravy then pour over the chicken and garnish.

Cover with the lid, allow to heat for a further 5 minutes then serve as it is in the casserole.

3189 Poulet Sauté Bercy

Season the pieces of chicken and sauté them in butter; when cooked, arrange in a deep dish, cover and keep warm.

Add 1 tbs chopped shallots to the pan and cook for a few seconds then deglaze with 1 dl (3½ fl oz or ½ U.S. cup) white wine and reduce by half. Add ½ dl (2 fl oz or ¼ U.S. cup) meat glaze, the juice of ½ a lemon, 50 g (2 oz) butter, 5 poached chipolatas cut in slices and 100 g (3½ oz) sliced mushrooms sautéed in butter.

Pour the whole over the chicken and sprinkle with chopped parsley.

3190 Poulet Sauté Boivin

Season the pieces of chicken and colour them quickly in butter. Add 12 button onions coloured in butter, 12 quarters of blanched tender globe artichokes and 24 pieces of potato the size of hazelnuts; cover with a lid and cook together in the oven.

When cooked, arrange the chicken in a deep dish with the onions and potatoes and surround with the artichokes.

Deglaze the pan with a little White Bouillon, a few drops of lemon juice, ½ dl (2 fl oz or ¼ U.S. cup) pale meat glaze and 50 g (2 oz) butter.

Pour the sauce over the chicken and garnish, and sprinkle with a little coarsely chopped parsley.

3191 Poulet Sauté à la Bordelaise

Season the pieces of chicken and sauté them in butter. When cooked, arrange in a deep dish.

Surround the chicken with bouquets of small quarters of globe artichokes cooked in butter, slices of potato sautéed in butter and deep fried onion rings. Place a small sprig of very green fried parsley between each bouquet.

Deglaze the pan with a few tablespoons of chicken gravy and pour over the chicken.

3192 Poulet Sauté à la Bourguignonne

Fry 125 g (4½ oz) blanched diced streaky bacon in butter until brown together with 8 button onions and 100 g (3½ oz) mushrooms cut in quarters.

Remove the bacon, mushrooms and onions and keep warm. Sauté the seasoned pieces of chicken in the same pan until nicely coloured, add the prepared garnish, cover with a lid and finish cooking in the oven.

Arrange the chicken and garnish in a deep dish; drain off the fat from the pan then add a touch of crushed garlic and 2 dl (7 fl oz or ⅞ U.S. cup) good quality red wine and reduce by half. Thicken it with 30 g (1 oz) butter mixed with a good pinch of flour and pour over the chicken and garnish.

3193 Poulet Sauté à la Bressane

Season the pieces of chicken and sauté them in butter without colouring too much and without letting the butter burn. When nearly cooked, add 50 g (2 oz) finely chopped onion and 24 very fresh cocks' kidneys.

When the onion is lightly coloured add 1½ dl (5 fl oz or ⅝ U.S. cup) white wine, reduce, then add 3 dl (½ pt or 1¼ U.S. cups) cream and allow to simmer for 10–12 minutes.

Finally add 36 crayfish tails cooked in Court-bouillon; arrange in a timbale or deep dish and serve.

3194 Poulet Sauté à la Bretonne

Season the pieces of chicken and stiffen them in butter without colour. Add 100 g (3½ oz) sliced white of leek and 50 g (2 oz) sliced onion both previously cooked in butter. Cover with a lid and finish cooking in the oven.

About 5 minutes before the chicken is cooked, add 100 g (3½ oz) sliced mushrooms sautéed in butter and complete the cooking.

When cooked, arrange the chicken in a deep dish. Add 1 dl (3½ fl oz or ½ U.S. cup) each of cream and Velouté to the vegetables in the pan, reduce by half then pour this sauce and the vegetables over the chicken.

3195 Poulet Sauté à la Catalane

Season the pieces of chicken and sauté them in hot oil. When ready, remove them and keep warm.

Drain off the oil and deglaze the pan with white wine, add 1 dl (3½ fl oz or ½ U.S. cup) Sauce Espagnole, 100 g (3½ oz) quartered mushrooms sautéed in butter, 6 glazed button onions, 6 small chestnuts cooked in Bouillon, 3 poached chipolatas cut in half and 1 tbs of Tomato Fondue.

Replace the chicken in the pan and allow to reheat gently for 5 minutes.

Arrange the chicken in a deep dish and cover with the sauce and garnish.

3196 Poulet Sauté aux Cèpes
Season the pieces of chicken and sauté them in oil. Remove and arrange in a deep dish.

Drain off the oil from the pan, add 1 tbs of chopped shallot and just heat. Deglaze with 1 dl (3½ fl oz or ½ U.S. cup) white wine and reduce by half.

Finish this sauce with 50 g (2 oz) of butter, pour over the chicken and surround with 250 g (9 oz) flap mushrooms à la Bordelaise (4017); sprinkle with chopped parsley.

3197 Poulet Sauté Champeaux
Season the pieces of chicken and sauté them in butter. When cooked, arrange in a deep dish and add a garnish of button onions and Pommes Noisette both cooked separately in butter.

Deglaze the pan with a little white wine; add 1 dl (3½ fl oz or ½ U.S. cup) veal gravy and 1 tbs meat glace; reduce by half and finish with 50 g (2 oz) butter. Pour over the chicken and serve.

3198 Poulet Sauté Chasseur
Season the pieces of chicken and sauté them in butter and oil. Arrange in a deep dish, cover and keep warm.

In the same pan quickly cook 125 g (4½ oz) sliced mushrooms then add 3 finely chopped shallots; moisten with 1 dl (3½ fl oz or ½ U.S. cup) white wine and ¼ dl (1 fl oz or ⅛ U.S. cup) brandy and reduce by half. Add 1 dl (3½ fl oz or ½ U.S. cup) tomato-flavoured Sauce Demi-glace and a pinch of chopped tarragon and chervil. Pour this sauce over the chicken and sprinkle with a little coarsely chopped parsley.

3199 Poulet au Currie
Cut the chicken into small pieces, season and sauté them in oil together with some finely sliced onion and a good pinch of curry powder.

Remove the pieces of chicken, cover them and keep warm. Deglaze the pan with 1 dl (3½ fl oz or ½ U.S. cup) coconut milk or almond milk; add 2 dl (7 fl oz or ⅞ U.S. cup) Velouté, replace the chicken and finish cooking it whilst the sauce reduces.

Arrange in a deep dish and serve accompanied with a dish of plain boiled rice.

Note: Strictly speaking, there is no definitive recipe for the various curries and even Indian cooks themselves prepare them in different ways. It is therefore impossible to try to lay down an original typical recipe since they are all so different.

The above recipe is entirely suited to European tastes which is the important thing.

3200 Poulet Sauté Cynthia
Season the pieces of chicken and sauté them in butter; arrange in a deep dish.

Deglaze the pan with 1½ dl (5 fl oz or ⅝ U.S. cup) dry Champagne; reduce by half and add 1 tbs pale chicken glaze. Finish with 50 g (2 oz) butter, the juice of ½ a lemon and 1 tbs Curaçao.

Pour this sauce over the chicken and surround with 20 peeled and depipped grapes and 10 segments of orange, free of skin and pith.

3201 Poulet Sauté Demidoff
Season the pieces of chicken and colour them in butter. Add half the amount of Demidoff garnish as indicated for Poularde Demidoff (3041); cover and finish cooking together in the oven.

Ten minutes before the chicken is cooked, add 50 g (2 oz) sliced truffle and 3 tbs good veal stock.

Arrange the chicken in a deep dish and cover with the garnish.

3202 Poulet Sauté Doria
Season the pieces of chicken and colour them in butter and oil. Add 250 g (9 oz) cucumber trimmed to the shape of small elongated olives, cover and finish cooking together in the oven.

When cooked, arrange the chicken and cucumber in a deep dish. Deglaze the pan with a little veal stock and a few drops of lemon juice, and pour over the chicken.

Finally sprinkle with a little Beurre Noisette.

3203 Poulet Sauté d'Orsay
Season the pieces of chicken and sauté them in butter with some quarters of raw globe artichoke, raw mushrooms cut in quarters and slices of truffle.

When cooked, arrange the chicken and garnish in a deep dish, cover and keep warm.

Deglaze the pan with 1 dl (3½ fl oz or ½ U.S. cup) white wine; reduce by half and add a few tbs Sauce Allemande, a touch of paprika and finish with 50 g (2 oz) butter. Pour this sauce over the chicken and the garnish.

3204 Poulet Sauté Durand
Season the pieces of chicken, flour them and sauté in oil.

When cooked, arrange the pieces in a circle on a dish and place a bouquet of deep fried onion rings in the centre. In the centre of the onions place a large cornet of ham filled with some roughly chopped flesh only of tomatoes cooked in butter.

3205 Poulet Sauté Egyptienne

Season the pieces of chicken and colour them in oil. Remove and fry in the same oil 100 g ($3\frac{1}{2}$ oz) chopped onion, 50 g (2 oz) sliced mushrooms and 200 g (7 oz) fairly large dice of raw ham.

Place the chicken in layers in a terrine with the well drained garnish and cover with thick slices of tomatoes.

Cover with the lid and finish cooking in the oven for 20 minutes.

At the last moment add 1 tbs veal stock; serve as it is in the terrine.

3206 Poulet Sauté Escurial

Colour 100 g ($3\frac{1}{2}$ oz) diced raw ham and 150 g (5 oz) quartered mushrooms in butter. Remove and sauté the seasoned pieces of chicken in the same butter until coloured and cooked; remove and keep warm.

Deglaze the pan with 1 dl ($3\frac{1}{2}$ fl oz or $\frac{1}{2}$ U.S. cup) white wine, add the same quantity of Sauce Demi-glace; replace the ham and mushrooms together with 20 poached stuffed olives and 100 g ($3\frac{1}{2}$ oz) diced truffle. Allow to simmer together for 7–8 minutes.

Mould a border of well-drained and dried plain boiled rice on a dish; place the chicken, garnish and sauce in the centre and surround the border with very small French fried eggs; or egg yolks simply coated with a thin layer of white, fried in the same manner.

3207 Poulet Sauté à l'Espagnole

Season the pieces of chicken and sauté them in oil. Drain off the oil and add to the chicken 250 g (9 oz) Riz Pilaw containing 50 g (2 oz) diced pimento, 100 g ($3\frac{1}{2}$ oz) cooked peas and 2 sliced poached sausages. Cover with the lid and cook gently in the oven for 10 minutes.

Arrange the chicken in a deep dish, cover with the rice and surround with 6 small grilled tomatoes.

3208 Poulet Sauté à l'Estragon

Season the pieces of chicken and sauté them in butter; arrange in a deep dish.

Deglaze the pan with 1 dl ($3\frac{1}{2}$ fl oz or $\frac{1}{2}$ U.S. cup) white wine; reduce by half and add 1 dl ($3\frac{1}{2}$ fl oz or $\frac{1}{2}$ U.S. cup) Sauce Demi-glace flavoured with tarragon.

Pour this sauce over the chicken and place a few blanched leaves of tarragon on the pieces of breast.

3209 Poulet Sauté Fédora

Season the pieces of chicken and cook in butter without colour together with 125 g ($4\frac{1}{2}$ oz) sliced raw truffle. When cooked, arrange in a deep dish.

Deglaze the pan with 1 dl ($3\frac{1}{2}$ fl oz or $\frac{1}{2}$ U.S. cup) cream, add 3 tbs Sauce Béchamel and reduce by half.

Finish away from the heat with 50 g (2 oz) Crayfish Butter; a little lemon juice and a touch of Cayenne.

Pour over the chicken and surround with bouquets of buttered asparagus tips.

3210 Poulet Sauté au Fenouil

Season the pieces of chicken and stiffen them well in butter without colour; add some cream to the pan to deglaze it.

Cut 2 tuberous fennel into quarters, trim into large olive shapes and blanch them well in boiling salted water until nearly cooked; drain and add to the chicken. Cover with the lid and finish cooking together in the oven.

Arrange the pieces of fennel in a circle in an oval earthenware dish, place the pieces of chicken in the centre and coat the whole with Sauce Mornay flavoured with chicken glaze and the cream from the cooking. Glaze quickly under the salamander.

3211 Poulet Sauté Fermière

Season the pieces of chicken and colour them in butter. Place in a terrine and add a Fermière garnish half cooked in butter and 80 g (3 oz) diced ham. Cover with the lid and finish cooking together in the oven.

At the last moment sprinkle with 4–5 tbs veal stock and serve as it is in the terrine.

3212 Poulet Sauté aux Fines Herbes

Season the pieces of chicken, sauté them in butter and 2 minutes before they are cooked, sprinkle with 1 tbs chopped shallot.

Arrange the chicken in a dish, cover and keep warm.

Deglaze the pan with 1 dl ($3\frac{1}{2}$ fl oz or $\frac{1}{2}$ U.S. cup) white wine, reduce by half and add 3 tbs each of well flavoured veal stock and Sauce Demi-glace. Finish with 50 g (2 oz) butter and 1 tbs chopped mixed parsley, chervil and tarragon.

Pour over the chicken and serve.

3213 Poulet Sauté à la Forestière

Season the pieces of chicken and colour them well in butter. Sprinkle with 1 tbs chopped shallot and add 150 g (5 oz) morels cut in quarters. Cover with the lid and cook in the oven for 10 minutes.

When cooked, arrange in a deep dish, cover and keep warm.

Deglaze the pan with a little white wine, add 1 dl ($3\frac{1}{2}$ fl oz or $\frac{1}{2}$ U.S. cup) veal gravy and reduce by one-third. Pour this sauce with the morels over the chicken and sprinkle with chopped parsley.

Surround the chicken with 4 bouquets of potatoes cut in small cubes and sautéed in butter and place a rectangle of fried streaky bacon between each bouquet.

3214 Poulet Sauté Gabrielle
Season the pieces of chicken and cook them in butter without colour. Arrange in a deep dish and keep warm.

Deglaze the pan with 1 dl (3½ fl oz or ½ U.S. cup) mushroom cooking liquor, add 1 dl (3½ fl oz or ½ U.S. cup) each of Sauce Béchamel and cream, and reduce by half.

Remove from the heat and finish the sauce with 50 g (2 oz) butter; pour over the chicken. Sprinkle with a Julienne of very black truffle and surround with some pale baked leaf-shapes of puff pastry.

3215 Poulet Sauté Georgina
Season the pieces of chicken and stiffen them in butter without colour. Add 12 button onions and a Bouquet garni containing a piece of fennel. Cover and finish cooking together in the oven.

When cooked, arrange the chicken in a dish and keep warm.

Deglaze the pan with a little mushroom cooking liquor and Rhine wine. Add 2 dl (7 fl oz or ⅞ U.S. cup) cream, 12 very white button mushrooms cooked and cut in slices and a pinch of chopped tarragon and chervil.

Pour the sauce over the chicken and serve.

3216 Poulet Sauté à la Hongroise
Season the pieces of chicken and stiffen them in butter without colour. Add 30 g (1 oz) chopped onion and a pinch of paprika. When the onion begins to lightly colour, add the roughly chopped flesh only of 3 tomatoes; cover and finish cooking together in the oven.

Arrange the pieces of chicken in the centre of a border of Riz Pilaw containing some diced tomato flesh. Finish the sauce by adding 1 dl (3½ fl oz or ½ U.S. cup) cream, reduce it by half then pass through a fine strainer and pour over the chicken.

3217 Poulet Sauté aux Huîtres
Season the pieces of chicken and sauté them in oil together with 30 g (1 oz) chopped onion, and 2 medium mushrooms, a stick of white celery and a few parsley stalks—all cut in Brunoise. Cover and finish cooking together in the oven.

When cooked, arrange the chicken in a dish together with 12 large poached and bearded oysters.

Deglaze the pan with a little white stock and reduce by half; add 1 dl (3½ fl oz or ½ U.S. cup) Velouté and 2 tbs pale meat glaze and reduce by one-third. Pass the sauce and vegetables through a fine sieve and pour over the chicken.

3218 Poulet Sauté à l'Indienne
See Poulet au Currie.

3219 Poulet Sauté à l'Italienne
Season the pieces of chicken and sauté them in butter. Arrange in a deep dish, cover and keep warm.

Deglaze the pan with 1½ dl (5 fl oz or ⅝ U.S. cup) of Sauce Italienne and pour over the chicken.

Surround with a border of small globe artichokes à l'Italienne.

3220 Poulet Sauté Japonaise
Season the pieces of chicken and colour them in butter. Add 500 g (1 lb 2 oz) lightly blanched, drained and dried Japanese artichokes; cover and finish cooking together in the oven.

When cooked, arrange the chicken and artichokes in a deep dish.

Deglaze the pan with 1 dl (3½ fl oz or ½ U.S. cup) lightly thickened veal gravy and finish away from the heat with 50 g (2 oz) butter; pour over the chicken and serve.

3221 Poulet Sauté Joséphine
Season the pieces of chicken and sauté them in butter and oil. When half cooked, drain off nearly all the fat and add 1 tbs Mirepoix Bordelaise, 2 tbs chopped lean cooked ham and 50 g (2 oz) roughly chopped mushrooms. Finish cooking together then arrange the chicken in a deep dish with the garnish.

Deglaze the pan with 1 dl (3½ fl oz or ½ U.S. cup) each of brandy and mushroom cooking liquor. Reduce by two-thirds then add 1 dl (3½ fl oz or ½ U.S. cup) thickened veal gravy. Remove from the heat and finish with 50 g (2 oz) butter.

Pour the sauce over the chicken and surround with a border of medium-sized flap mushrooms which have been sautéed to a brown colour in oil at the last moment.

3222 Poulet Sauté Jurassienne
Season the pieces of chicken and sauté them in butter until two-thirds cooked. Add 250 g (9 oz) blanched and fried fairly large batons of salt belly of pork and finish cooking together.

When the chicken is cooked, pour off three-quarters of the butter, deglaze the pan with 1½ dl (5 fl oz or ⅝ U.S. cup) thin Sauce Demi-glace then place the pieces of chicken and the bacon in a deep dish.

Add a pinch of chopped chives to the sauce and pour over the chicken.

3223 Poulet Sauté Lathuile

Heat 100 g ($3\frac{1}{2}$ oz) butter until very hot in a pan just large enough to hold the chicken and its garnish. Season the pieces of chicken and arrange them in this butter together with 250 g (9 oz) potatoes and 150 g (5 oz) raw artichoke bottoms, both cut in medium-sized dice.

When the underside is set and well coloured, turn the whole over in one piece and complete the cooking of the other side. Sprinkle with 3 tbs pale meat glaze, a pinch of chopped parsley and a touch of crushed garlic. Turn out on to a dish in the same way as for Pommes Anna.

Pour a little Beurre Noisette over and surround with alternate bouquets of onion rings fried in oil, and very green fried parsley.

3224 Poulet Sauté Madras

Season the pieces of chicken and cook as for Poulet Sauté Stanley omitting the truffle. At the same time cook 125 g (5 oz) rice as for Riz à l'Indienne.

Select a medium-sized cantaloup melon, cut around the stalk end and remove a circular piece 10 cm (4 in) in diameter. Remove the seeds and water, line the inside with the rice and at the last moment fill with the pieces of chicken.

Serve the chicken and rice with pieces of the melon cut with a spoon.

3225 Poulet Sauté Marengo

Season the pieces of chicken and sauté them in oil. Drain off the oil and deglaze the pan with $1\frac{1}{2}$ dl (5 fl oz or $\frac{5}{8}$ U.S. cup) white wine and reduce by half. Add the roughly chopped flesh only of 2 tomatoes, or $1\frac{1}{2}$ tbs tomato purée, a touch of crushed garlic, 10 cooked small buttom mushrooms, 10 slices of truffle and $1\frac{1}{2}$ dl (5 fl oz or $\frac{5}{8}$ U.S. cup) Jus lié.

Finish cooking together then arrange the pieces of chicken in a deep dish and coat with the sauce and garnish. Surround with 4 heart-shaped Croûtons of bread fried in butter, 4 trussed crayfish cooked in Court-bouillon and 4 small French fried eggs. Sprinkle with coarsely chopped parsley.

3226 Poulet Sauté Marigny

Season the pieces of chicken and colour them in butter; add 125 g ($4\frac{1}{2}$ oz) each of fresh peas and French beans cut diamond shape. Cover with the lid and cook together in the oven.

Deglaze in the pan at the last moment with a few tablespoons of Jus lié, arrange the chicken and vegetables in a deep dish with the sauce and surround with Pommes Fondantes.

3227 Poulet Sauté Maryland

This is prepared in exactly the same way as Suprême de Volaille Maryland using pieces of chicken instead of *suprêmes*.

3228 Poulet Sauté à la Marseillaise

Season the pieces of chicken and sauté them in oil; when half cooked, add a clove of crushed garlic, and 60 g (2 oz) finely sliced green pimento and 3 small tomatoes cut in quarters—both previously sautéed in oil.

When the chicken is cooked, drain off the oil and deglaze the pan with 1 dl ($3\frac{1}{2}$ fl oz or $\frac{1}{2}$ U.S. cup) white wine and a squeeze of lemon juice. Reduce until almost dry.

Arrange the chicken in a deep dish with the garnish on top and sprinkle with coarsely chopped parsley.

3229 Poulet Sauté Mathilde

Season the pieces of chicken and colour them in butter; add 30 g (1 oz) chopped onion and 250 g (9 oz) pieces of cucumber trimmed to the shape of elongated olives. Cover and finish cooking together.

Deglaze the pan with $\frac{1}{4}$ dl (1 fl oz or $\frac{1}{8}$ U.S. cup) brandy and finish with 1 dl ($3\frac{1}{2}$ fl oz or $\frac{1}{2}$ U.S. cup) Sauce Suprême.

Arrange the pieces of chicken in a deep dish and cover with the sauce and garnish.

Note: The cucumber may be cooked in butter separately and added to the chicken when it is arranged in the dish.

3230 Poulet Sauté à la Mexicaine

Season the pieces of chicken and sauté them in oil.

When cooked, drain off the oil, deglaze the pan with a little white wine and reduce entirely, then add 1 dl ($3\frac{1}{2}$ fl oz or $\frac{1}{2}$ U.S. cup) tomato-flavoured Jus lié.

Arrange the pieces of chicken in a deep dish, coat with the sauce and surround with grilled pimentoes and grilled medium-sized mushrooms filled with Tomato Fondue.

3231 Poulet Sauté aux Morilles

Season the pieces of chicken and sauté them in butter. When two-thirds cooked, add 300 g (11 oz) morels previously cooked in butter, cover and finish cooking together in the oven.

When cooked, arrange the pieces of chicken in a deep dish, cover with the morels and keep warm.

Deglaze the pan with 1 tbs brandy, add the cooking liquor from the morels and 2 tbs meat glaze. Reduce to 1 dl ($3\frac{1}{2}$ fl oz or $\frac{1}{2}$ U.S. cup) then thicken away from the heat with 50 g (2 oz) butter. Pour over the chicken and sprinkle with chopped parsley.

3232 Poulet Sauté à la Normande
Season the pieces of chicken and sauté them in butter.

When half cooked, arrange in a terrine and add 400 g (15 oz) peeled sliced pippin apples.

Deglaze the pan with a little Calvados, pour over the chicken, cover with the lid and finish cooking in the oven.

Serve in the terrine as it is.

3233 Poulet Sauté à l'Orléanaise
Season the pieces of chicken and sauté them in butter. Arrange in a deep dish, cover and keep warm.

Deglaze the pan with 1 dl ($3\frac{1}{2}$ fl oz or $\frac{1}{2}$ U.S. cup) red wine, add the same amount of veal stock and reduce by half. Thicken away from the heat with 40 g ($1\frac{1}{2}$ oz) butter and pour over the chicken.

Surround with alternate bouquets of glazed button onions and grooved mushrooms.

3234 Poulet Sauté au Paprika
This is the same as Poulet Sauté à la Hongroise.

3235 Poulet Sauté Parmentier
Season the pieces of chicken and colour them in butter. Add 400 g (15 oz) potatoes cut in cubes or cut with a medium-sized oval spoon cutter, and lightly coloured in butter.

Cover with the lid and finish cooking in the oven. When cooked, arrange the chicken in a deep dish and surround with the potatoes arranged in bouquets.

Deglaze the pan with a little white wine, add 1 tbs of veal stock and pour over the chicken. Sprinkle with chopped parsley.

3236 Poulet Sauté à la Périgord
Season the pieces of chicken and colour them in butter. Add 200 g (7 oz) raw truffles trimmed olive shape, cover with the lid and cook together gently in the oven.

When cooked, arrange the chicken and truffles in a deep dish. Deglaze the pan with Madeira, reduce and add 1 dl ($3\frac{1}{2}$ fl oz or $\frac{1}{2}$ U.S. cup) Sauce Demi-glace; finish away from the heat with 40 g ($1\frac{1}{2}$ oz) butter and pour over the chicken.

3237 Poulet Sauté à la Piémontaise
Season the pieces of chicken and sauté them in butter together with 100 g ($3\frac{1}{2}$ oz) sliced white truffles. When cooked, arrange in the centre of a border of Risotto moulded on a dish.

Deglaze the pan with 1 dl ($3\frac{1}{2}$ fl oz or $\frac{1}{2}$ U.S. cup) white wine, add 1 tbs pale meat glaze and pour over the chicken. Sprinkle with chopped parsley.

Note: The chicken may be arranged directly on the dish and served accompanied with a dish of Risotto.

3238 Poulet Sauté à la Portugaise
Season the pieces of chicken and sauté them in oil and butter. When two-thirds cooked, drain off some of the fat and add 30 g (1 oz) chopped onion and a touch of crushed garlic.

When the onion is slightly coloured, add 100 g ($3\frac{1}{2}$ oz) roughly chopped flesh only of tomatoes, 50 g (2 oz) sliced cooked mushroom, a little white wine and a pinch of chopped parsley.

Finish cooking together until almost all of the moisture has been evaporated.

Arrange the chicken in a dish with the garnish on top and surround with whole small stuffed tomatoes or stuffed halves of tomatoes.

3239 Poulet Sauté à la Provençale
Season the pieces of chicken and sauté them in oil. When cooked, arrange in a deep dish, cover and keep warm.

Deglaze the pan with a little white wine, add a clove of crushed garlic, 200 g (7 oz) roughly chopped flesh only of tomato, 4 chopped anchovy fillets, 12 blanched stoned black olives and a pinch of chopped basil.

Allow to simmer for a few minutes then pour over the chicken.

3240 Poulet Sauté au Samos
Season the pieces of chicken and sauté them in oil. When half cooked, drain off the oil and deglaze the pan with 1 dl ($3\frac{1}{2}$ fl oz or $\frac{1}{2}$ U.S. cup) Samos wine; add 50 g (2 oz) roughly chopped flesh only of tomato, cover and allow to cook together for 7–8 minutes.

Arrange the pieces of chicken in a deep dish, cover with the cooking liquor and garnish with large peeled and depipped white grapes, or muscatel grapes for preference.

3241 Poulet Sauté Saint-Mandé
Season the pieces of chicken and sauté them in butter. At the last moment add 125 g ($4\frac{1}{2}$ oz) each of peas and asparagus tips which have been quickly plain boiled and drained but not refreshed.

When cooked, arrange the chicken on a round base of Pommes Macaire set on a dish. Deglaze the pan with a little Jus lié and pour the sauce and the garnish over the chicken.

3242 Poulet Sauté Saint-Lambert
Finely chop some carrot, turnip, onion, mushrooms, lean bacon, parsley stalks and celery and cook gently together with a little butter; add a little Bouillon to complete the cooking then pass through a fine sieve. There should be approximately 1 dl ($3\frac{1}{2}$ fl oz or $\frac{1}{2}$ U.S. cup) of this purée.

Season the pieces of chicken and sauté them in butter. When cooked, arrange in a deep dish, cover and keep warm. Deglaze the pan with 1 dl ($3\frac{1}{2}$ fl oz or $\frac{1}{2}$ U.S. cup) each of white wine and mushroom cooking liquor. Reduce by half, add the prepared vegetable purée and allow to boil for a moment.

Thicken the sauce with a little butter, pour over the chicken then sprinkle with 2 small spoonfuls each of glazed small balls of carrot and very green peas. Finish with a pinch of coarsely chopped parsley.

3243 Poulet Sauté Stanley
Season the pieces of chicken and stiffen them in butter, without colour. Add 250 g (9 oz) finely sliced onion, cover with the lid and finish cooking together gently in the oven.

When cooked, arrange the chicken in a shallow dish and place a bouquet of cooked mushrooms at each side. Cover and keep warm.

Add 2 dl (7 fl oz or $\frac{7}{8}$ U.S. cup) cream to the onions in the pan and allow to simmer for 10 minutes; pass through a sieve and reduce this Soubise by a quarter; finish with 30 g (1 oz) butter and a touch each of Cayenne and curry powder.

Coat the chicken with this sauce and decorate with 10 slices of truffle.

3244 Poulet Sauté aux Truffes
Season the pieces of chicken and sauté them in butter. When almost cooked, add 200 g (7 oz) sliced raw truffle. Cover with a lid, allow to cook for a few minutes then add $\frac{1}{2}$ dl (2 fl oz or $\frac{1}{4}$ U.S. cup) Madeira and 1 dl ($3\frac{1}{2}$ fl oz or $\frac{1}{2}$ U.S. cup) Sauce Demi-glace; allow to reduce for about a minute.

Arrange the chicken in a deep dish, place the truffle on top and coat with the sauce.

3245 Poulet Sauté à la Vichy
Season the pieces of chicken and colour them in butter. Add 200 g (7 oz) half-cooked Carottes Vichy, cover with the lid and finish cooking together in the oven.

Deglaze with a little veal stock. Arrange the chicken in a dish and cover with the carrots.

3246 Poulet Sauté Verdi
Season the pieces of chicken and sauté them in butter. When cooked, arrange them in the centre of a border of Risotto Piémontaise. On top of this border arrange a circle of alternate slices of foie gras shallow fried in butter, and slices of truffle, resting against the chicken.

Deglaze the pan with Asti wine, reduce and add either 3 tbs brown veal stock or meat glaze. Pour over the pieces of chicken.

POULETS DE GRAINS—SPRING CHICKENS

Spring chickens are the most suitable ones for grilling and for cooking *en Casserole* and *en Cocotte* in accordance with the following recipes.

3247 Poulet de Grains à la Belle-Meunière
Stuff the chicken with 4 sliced chicken livers and 100 g ($3\frac{1}{2}$ oz) roughly chopped mushrooms, lightly cooked in butter; slide 5 or 6 slices of truffle under the skin on the breast and truss *en Entrée.*

Colour the chicken in butter then place it in a Cocotte with 4 rectangular slices of blanched streaky bacon, 100 g ($3\frac{1}{2}$ oz) quartered mushrooms previously tossed in butter, and 50 g (2 oz) butter.

Cover with the lid and cook in the oven; add 2 tbs of veal gravy at the last moment and serve as it is.

3248 Poulet de Grains à la Bergère
Stuff the chicken with 30 g (1 oz) chopped onions and 100 g ($3\frac{1}{2}$ oz) chopped Mousserons cooked in butter and mixed when cold with 100 g ($3\frac{1}{2}$ oz) butter, 1 tsp chopped parsley and a little salt and pepper; truss *en Entrée.*

Fry in butter 125 g ($4\frac{1}{2}$ oz) diced and blanched salt belly of pork and 250 g (9 oz) small whole Mousserons; remove when lightly coloured.

Colour the prepared chicken in the same fat and surround with the pork and mushrooms; deglaze the pan with 1 dl ($3\frac{1}{2}$ fl oz or $\frac{1}{2}$ U.S. cup) white wine, reduce by two-thirds and add 4 tbs veal gravy, cover and finish cooking in the oven.

Place the chicken on a round dish, thicken the cooking liquid with a little arrowroot or a hazelnut-sized piece of *Beurre Manié* then pour the sauce and garnish round the chicken. Surround with a border of freshly prepared straw potatoes.

3249 Poulet de Grains en Casserole
Poêlé the chicken with butter in an earthenware casserole and baste it frequently whilst cooking.

When ready, drain off half the butter and add a tablespoon of veal gravy.

Serve as it is without any garnish.

3250 Poulet de Grains en Cocotte
Colour the chicken in a covered Cocotte with butter.

When half cooked, add 50 g (2 oz) blanched and fried batons of salt belly of pork, 12 button onions cooked in butter and 20 olive-shaped potatoes. Finish cooking together and sprinkle with a little veal gravy just before serving.

3251 Poulet de Grains en Cocotte Bonne Femme
Fry and colour in butter 125 g (4½ oz) salt belly of pork cut in small rectangular slices and blanched.

Remove the pork, colour the chicken in the same fat and place it in an oval Cocotte together with the slices of pork and 400 g (15 oz) potatoes, trimmed cork shape, sliced and sautéed in the butter from the chicken.

Cover with the lid and cook in the oven; sprinkle with a few tablespoons of veal gravy just before serving.

3252 Poulet de Grains en Compote
Colour the chicken with butter in a casserole then drain off the fat. Deglaze with 1 dl (3½ fl oz or ½ U.S. cup) each of white wine and mushroom cooking liquor, reduce by two-thirds then add 2 dl (7 fl oz or ⅞ U.S. cup) Sauce Demi-glace and pass it through a fine strainer. Replace the chicken in the casserole with batons of salt belly of pork, button onions and mushrooms previously cooked as for Compote garnish (369); add the sauce, cover and cook in the oven glazing the chicken towards the end.

Place the chicken on a round dish and surround with the garnish and sauce.

3253 Poulet de Grains à la Crapaudine
Cut the chicken horizontally from the point of the breast along the tops of the legs and right up to the joints of the wings, but without cutting right through; open it out and flatten lightly then remove all the small bones as carefully as possible.

Fix a skewer through the 2 wings, season with salt and pepper, brush with butter and place in the oven until half cooked. Sprinkle with breadcrumbs and more butter and finish cooking gently on the grill.

Serve with a highly seasoned sauce such as Sauce Diable.

3254 Poulet de Grains grillé à l'Anglaise—Grilled Chicken, English style
This is prepared in the same way as Poulet à la Crapaudine but without the breadcrumbs.

3255 Poulet de Grains grillé Diable
Prepare the chicken for trussing *en Entrée* but do not string it; cut along the backbone of the chicken, open it out and cut off the backbone. Flatten it lightly, season, brush with butter and place in the oven until half cooked.

Coat it with made mustard flavoured with Cayenne, sprinkle well with breadcrumbs and with melted butter and finish cooking on the grill.

Place on a round dish bordered with thin slices of lemon and serve accompanied with a sauceboat of Sauce Diable.

3256 Poulet de Grains à la Fermière
Colour the chicken in butter, place it in a Cocotte and proceed as for Poularde Fermière adjusting the items of garnish in keeping with its size.

3257 Poulet de Grains aux Fonds d'Artichaut
Colour the chicken in butter and place in a Cocotte with 5 raw artichoke bottoms cut in quarters and sautéed in butter.

Cover and cook in the oven adding a tablespoonful of veal gravy and a squeeze of lemon juice at the last moment.

3258 Poulet de Grains à la Grand'Mère
Cook in a frying pan 25 g (1 oz) each of finely chopped bacon and onion; add 4 sliced chicken livers, season with salt, pepper and a little mixed spice and sauté together quickly. Add 50 g (2 oz) breadcrumbs and a little chopped Fines Herbes then pass the whole through a fine sieve.

Stuff the chicken with this mixture and cook it as for Poulet de Grains en Cocotte.

3259 Poulet de Grains à l'Hôtelière
Bone out the breast of the chicken from inside then stuff it with 250 g (9 oz) very fine sausage meat containing 50 g (2 oz) dry Duxelles; truss it *en Entrée*.

Colour it in butter in an earthenware casserole, cover and cook in the oven. When two-thirds cooked, surround it with 125 g (4½ oz) sautéed sliced mushrooms and when finished, add 3 tbs of veal gravy.

3260 Poulet de Grains grillé Katoff
Cut the chicken open along the back as for Poulet de Grains grillé Diable. Flatten lightly, season and brush with butter; half cook in the oven and finish cooking on the grill. Place it on a flat cake of Pommes Duchesse mixture moulded on the service dish and coloured in the oven. Surround with a *cordon* of Jus lié.

Serve accompanied with a sauceboat of the Jus lié.

Note: Instead of Jus lié, a lightly buttered meat glaze may be served.

3261 Poulet de Grains à la Limousine
Stuff the chicken with 250 g (9 oz) sausage meat containing 50 g (2 oz) sautéed chopped mushrooms; truss *en Entrée.*

Colour the chicken in butter in an earthenware Cocotte; surround with 6 blanched rectangles of streaky bacon and 15 chestnuts partly cooked in Bouillon. Cover and cook in the oven.

Add 2–3 tbs veal gravy at the last moment and serve as it is.

3262 Poulet de Grains Mascotte
Colour the chicken in butter in a pan and surround with 100 g ($3\frac{1}{2}$ oz) each of olive-shaped pieces of potato and quartered or diced artichoke bottoms, both sautéed in butter. Cover and place in the oven.

When almost cooked, remove the chicken and place in a hot terrine with its garnish plus 10 slices of truffle and 2 tbs veal gravy. Cover with the lid, place in a warm oven for 10 minutes and serve as it is.

3263 Poulet de Grains Mireille
Arrange a layer of Pommes Anna containing one-third its amount of sliced raw artichoke bottoms, in an earthenware dish of a suitable size to hold the chicken; place to cook.

Meanwhile, cut the chicken for grilling, flatten it and remove as many bones as possible; season and place it in the oven until half cooked. When the potatoes are three parts cooked, place the chicken on top, return to the oven to complete the cooking of both together, basting frequently with butter.

Serve as it is in the dish.

3264 Poulet de Grains aux Morilles
Prepare the chicken as for en Casserole (3249) and when half cooked, add 250 g (9 oz) morels lightly sautéed in butter. Cover and finish cooking and add a tablespoon of veal gravy just before serving.

3265 Poulet de Grains Printanière
This is prepared in the same way as Poularde Printanière using only a third of the quantity of ingredients of the garnish.

3266 Poulet de Grains à la Russe
Truss the chicken, immerse the breast in boiling water for 5 minutes to stiffen it then lard the breast with thin strips of salt pork fat and anchovy fillets. Stuff with truffled pork sausage meat then roast on a spit.

When cooked, baste with very hot pork fat poured over the breast through a special metal funnel so as to make the skin crisp.

Serve accompanied with Sauce Remoulade.

3267 Poulet de Grains Souvaroff
Proceed as indicated for Poularde Souvaroff reducing the quantities of the items of the garnish proportionately.

3268 Poulet de Grains à la Tartare
This is prepared in the same way as Poulet grillé Diable (3255). Arrange on a dish bordered with gherkins and serve accompanied with a sauceboat of Sauce Tartare.

POUSSINS

The most perfect type of poussin would be the Hamburg one were it not for the fact that it is kept in confinement and fed on a diet of fishmeal, thus giving it a disagreeable taste. When properly kept and fed they can, however, be very good. Good progress has been made in the production of poussins in England which are now superior in quality to those of Hamburg.

3269 Poussins Cendrillon
Cut the poussins open along the back and open them out; flatten lightly, then remove as many bones as possible.

Trim them and colour in hot butter; season with salt and Cayenne and cover both sides with finely chopped truffle. Wrap each in a piece of pig's caul, dip in melted butter, coat with breadcrumbs and grill them gently for 20–25 minutes.

Serve accompanied with Sauce Périgueux.

3270 Poussins Hermitage
Cut the poussins open along the back, bone out completely and lightly flatten them. Season, flour, egg and breadcrumb them and shallow fry in clarified butter.

Arrange on a dish and surround with small balls of potato fried in butter mixed with a spoonful of melted meat glaze. Coat the poussins with Sauce Château containing sliced truffle and serve accompanied with a dish of Petits Pois à l'Anglaise.

Note: This recipe can also be used for small spring chickens.

3271 Poussins à la Piémontaise
Stuff each poussin with 40 g ($1\frac{1}{2}$ oz) white

Piedmont truffle pounded together with an equal amount of pork kidney fat; truss *en Entrée* and colour quickly in hot butter.

After 10 minutes of cooking, place them in a Cocotte, cover with half-cooked Risotto à la Piémontaise and finish cooking uncovered in the oven.

A few minutes before serving, sprinkle with grated Parmesan, allow to glaze and sprinkle with Beurre Noisette at the last moment.

3272 Poussins à la Polonaise
Stuff each poussin with a stuffing made of 50 g (2 oz) Gratin forcemeat C (295), 20 g ($\frac{3}{4}$ oz) soaked and squeezed breadcrumbs, 10 g ($\frac{1}{3}$ oz) butter and a pinch of chopped parsley. Truss *en Entrée*, brown in butter in a hot oven then transfer them to an earthenware dish; cover and finish cooking in the oven.

Sprinkle with a few drops of lemon juice and coat with Beurre Noisette containing 30 g (1 oz) fine white breadcrumbs per 150 g (5 oz) butter.

3273 Poussins à la Tartare
Prepare the poussins as indicated for Poulet de Grains à la Tartare.

3274 Tourte de Poussins à la Paysanne
Prepare: 10 halves of poussin, lightly coloured and stiffened in butter, 500 g (1 lb 2 oz) sausage meat mixed with 250 g (9 oz) dry Duxelles, 300 g (11 oz) sliced mushrooms sautéed in butter and a round layer of short paste 25 cm (10 in) in diameter.

Place the layer of paste on a baking tray, spread half the sausage meat mixture on top leaving a margin of bare paste all round. Arrange the poussins on the sausage meat, sprinkle with the mushrooms then cover with the rest of the sausage meat and cover this with a round slice of salt pork fat. Moisten the edges of the paste then cover with another round of paste a little larger than the first. Seal the edges well and pleat them to decorate. Brush with beaten egg, score with the point of a knife and make a hole in the centre for the steam to escape. Bake in a moderate oven for approximately 40 minutes.

When removing the Tourte from the oven, pour a few tablespoons of Sauce Demi-glace into it through the hole on top.

3275 Poussins Valentinois
Completely bone out 2 poussins, lightly flatten them, season and coat the insides with a thin layer of Mousseline forcemeat. On one of the poussins arrange 6 slices of truffle, cover with thin slices of Parfait of foie gras and place a few more slices of truffle on top. Cover with the other poussin, sew around the edges with thread, dip in flour and shallow fry gently in butter.

Discard the thread from the poussins and place on a dish; deglaze the pan with white wine and Jus lié and add a few tablespoons of meat glaze. Pour this sauce over the poussins.

Serve accompanied with a dish of buttered asparagus tips.

3276 Poussins à la Viennoise
Cut the poussins into four; season, flour, egg and breadcrumb and shallow fry in clarified butter or lard, or deep fry in oil.

Arrange on a dish on a serviette and surround with fried parsley and quarters of lemon.

OTHER PREPARATIONS OF CHICKEN

ABATTIS—GIBLETS

These recipes are applicable to all kinds of giblets of poultry; the larger ones like those of a turkey should, of course, be cut into more pieces than those of chicken and duck.

3277 Abattis à la Bourguignonne
Fry 250 g (9 oz) blanched diced streaky bacon in butter and remove; add $1\frac{1}{2}$ kg (3 lb 6 oz) giblets (without the livers which should be added 10–15 minutes towards the end of the cooking time) and 100 g ($3\frac{1}{2}$ oz) onion cut in large dice; fry together until lightly coloured.

Sprinkle with 3 tbs flour, cook in the oven, then moisten with 5 dl (18 fl oz or $2\frac{1}{4}$ U.S. cups) red wine and 1 litre ($1\frac{3}{4}$ pt or $4\frac{1}{2}$ U.S. cups) white stock or water. Season, add a clove of crushed garlic and a Bouquet garni and allow to cook slowly.

A quarter of an hour before it is cooked, drain on a sieve; place the giblets in a clean pan, add the bacon, 20 cooked button onions and the raw sliced livers. Remove the fat from the sauce, reduce, pass through a fine strainer over the whole and finish cooking together.

Arrange in a deep dish to serve.

3278 Abattis Chipolata
This is prepared in the same way as the preceding recipe, using white wine instead of red wine and adding a Chipolata garnish (365) when adding the reduced sauce. Allow to cook together for a further 15–20 minutes.

3279 Abattis aux Navets
This is prepared in the same way as Abattis à la

Bourguignonne using only white stock. When half cooked, place the giblets into a clean pan, add the bacon, 24 button onions sautéed in butter and 500 g (1 lb 2 oz) turnips trimmed to the shape of olives then sautéed in butter and glazed.

Pass the sauce through a fine strainer over the whole and complete the cooking gently.

3280 Pâté d'Abattis—Giblet Pie

Fry the pieces of giblets in butter until coloured; lightly sprinkle with flour, cook in the oven and moisten with sufficient Bouillon to barely cover. Cook until three-quarters ready then allow to cool.

Place in a pie dish, cover with puff pastry in the usual manner, brush with eggwash, score with the point of a knife and bake in a moderately hot oven for 25–30 minutes.

3281 Abattis Printanier

Prepare the giblets in the same way as Abattis à la Bourguignonne.

When half cooked, add a Printanière garnish (444) after changing the giblets to a clean pan. Pass the reduced sauce through a fine strainer and allow to finish cooking gently together.

AILERONS—WINGLETS

Winglets are prepared in the same way as giblets and are suitable as a luncheon dish; they are more often served boned and stuffed, especially turkey winglets which are stuffed with a fairly fatty sausage meat.

3282 Ailerons Dorés à la Purée de Marrons

Take large chicken or turkey winglets and fry them in butter in a shallow pan just large enough to hold them. When coloured, remove them and colour 1 sliced carrot and 1 sliced onion per 10 winglets in the same butter; add a few parsley stalks, thyme and a bayleaf and replace the winglets on top.

Season with salt and pepper, place in a warm oven basting frequently with the butter and cook slowly without liquid; a few drops of water may be added, however, to prevent the butter from clarifying if the oven should be too hot.

When cooked, arrange in rows on a dish, cover and keep warm. Add a little white stock or water to the pan and simmer gently for 10 minutes. When the liquid is reduced to a quantity sufficient to half cover the winglets, pass through a fine strainer, remove the fat and pour over the winglets.

Serve accompanied with a dish of chestnut purée.

3283 Terrine d'Ailerons Farcis à la Boulangère

Cut off the small ends of 12 turkey winglets, bone them out then stuff with a fine sausage meat and colour them in butter.

Place in a hot earthenware terrine with 125 g (4½ oz) sliced onion and 600 g (1 lb 5 oz) sliced small potatoes, both sautéed separately in butter.

Sprinkle with butter, cover with the lid and seal with flour and water paste. Cook in a moderate oven for 45 minutes and serve as it is from the terrine.

3284 Ailerons Farcis Chipolata

Bone out the winglets, stuff with sausage meat and braise them in the usual manner. Fifteen minutes before they are cooked, add a Chipolata garnish (365) and finish cooking together slowly.

Arrange the winglets in a circle on a dish and place the garnish in the centre.

3285 Ailerons Farcis Grillés

Bone out the winglets, stuff them and braise in the usual manner.

Allow to cool, drain and dry them, then enclose each in 60–70 g (2–2½ oz) of truffled sausage meat; wrap in a piece of caul and dip in melted butter and white breadcrumbs. Grill them gently, arrange in a circle on a dish and pour some Sauce Périgueux in the centre; a dish of some sort of vegetable purée may be served separately.

3286 Risotto d'Ailerons

Bone out the winglets and stuff them with sausage meat containing 80 g (3 oz) chopped white truffle per 500 g (1 lb 2 oz) sausage meat; braise them with white wine.

Just before serving cut them into slices and mix with the reduced braising liquid after removing the fat and passing through a fine strainer.

Place the prepared winglets in the centre of a border of Risotto moulded on the serving dish.

3287 BALLOTTINES AND JAMBONNEAUX

These two preparations are ways of using the legs of chickens after the *Suprêmes* have been removed for other uses. The legs are boned out and stuffed with a forcemeat; the skin should be left fairly long and turned over to give the leg its shape as either a small round ball or a small ham. They are then braised and may be served with any of the garnishes suitable for chicken.

Note: If to be served cold, Ballottines should be glazed with aspic jelly or coated with white or brown Sauce Chaud-froid and garnished to choice.

3288 BOUDINS AND QUENELLES OF CHICKEN

(Mignonettes, Nonettes, Pascalines etc.)

Boudins of chicken are products of the kitchen of bygone days being altogether different from the dishes of the same name as given in the Chapter on Pork and which are the true Boudins of chicken.

The ones being dealt with here are those which are moulded in the shape of small cylinders the size of a sausage, or else moulded in rectangular moulds made of white metal. It is even possible to use small oval Quenelle moulds which is recommended because it saves time.

In the first case the forcemeat being used is divided into 80 g (3 oz) pieces and formed into small sausage shapes, they are then cut open and filled with a suitable Salpicon in keeping with the preparation and sealed up to enclose it. The moulds selected for use in the second example are buttered and spread with a layer of forcemeat 7–8 mm ($\frac{1}{3}$ in) thick then filled with a Salpicon and finally covered with another layer of forcemeat and smoothed dome shape.

In all cases they are poached prior to being egg and breadcrumbed, and they are then shallow fried in clarified butter.

Quenelles are different to Boudins in so far as they do not have a garnish inside and they are usually only poached. There are certain recipes where they are breadcrumbed or coated with chopped truffle and these form an intermediate type half-way between a Boudin and a Quenelle proper but they are still referred to as Quenelles.

3289 Boudins de Volaille Carignan

Line some small well buttered rectangular moulds with fine chicken forcemeat; fill with a layer of diced cooked mushrooms mixed with reduced Sauce Allemande then cover with more of the forcemeat. Smooth the surface then poach them in salted water.

Drain and dry the Boudins well and flour, egg and breadcrumb them; shallow fry in clarified butter, arrange in a close circle on a dish and fill the centre with a mound of cockscombs dipped in frying batter and deep fried at the last moment.

Serve Tomato Sauce separately.

Note: To poach the Boudins, place the moulds in a shallow pan and cover with boiling salted water; after a few seconds of poaching the Boudins will come out of the moulds and rise to the surface. The pan should be covered during the cooking process.

3290 Boudins de Volaille Ecossaise

Take the required amount of chicken forcemeat prepared with panada and butter and mould oval pointed shape. Stuff them with a Salpicon of salt ox tongue mixed with a little cold well reduced Sauce Demi-glace.

Poach these Boudins in the usual manner, drain and dry them well then flour, egg and breadcrumb them; shallow fry to a golden brown in clarified butter and arrange in a circle on a dish alternating with slices of salt ox tongue cut to the same size.

Serve accompanied with Sauce Ecossaise.

3291 Boudins de Volaille Richelieu

Take the required amount of chicken forcemeat prepared with panada and cream and prepare the Boudins in moulds as explained in the beginning of this section, filling them with a Salpicon of white of chicken, mushroom and truffle mixed with a little thick Sauce Allemande.

Poach them in the usual manner, drain and dry them well then flour, egg and breadcrumb them. Shallow fry to a golden brown in clarified butter, arrange in a circle on a dish and place a bouquet of fried parsley in the centre.

Serve accompanied with Sauce Périgueux.

3292 Boudins de Volaille Soubise

Prepare these Boudins in the same way as for Boudins Richelieu but filling them with a thick Soubise purée containing chopped truffle.

Serve accompanied with a thin lightly buttered Sauce Soubise.

3293 Mignonettes de Poulet

Take the required number of minion fillets of chicken and inset them with small slices of ox tongue and truffle. Arrange in a buttered tray forming them in the shape of circles.

Take the same number of cooked artichoke bottoms, trim them and cut tooth shape around the edges; heat them in butter and fill with a fairly stiff purée of white of chicken mixed with a little Sauce Suprême; smooth dome shape.

Poach the minion fillets with butter and mushroom cooking liquor and when ready, place one on each of the prepared artichoke bottoms; arrange in a circle on a dish and serve accompanied with Sauce Suprême.

3294 Pascaline de Poulet

Take equal parts of Parmesan-flavoured Chou Paste made with milk and chicken Mousseline forcemeat.

Mix the two items together very well then pipe out on a buttered tray in the shape of meringues; poach them in the usual manner. When ready, arrange on a buttered dish, cover with slices of truffle and coat the whole with Sauce

Béchamel; sprinkle with grated Parmesan and melted butter and glaze in a hot oven or under the salamander.

3295 Nonettes de Poulet Agnès Sorel
Truss 12 buntings *en Entrée* and brown them quickly in butter.

Take the Suprêmes from 12 spring chickens, remove any sinew and lightly flatten them. Place each 2 Suprêmes side by side so as to obtain a largish flat surface. In the middle of each of these place one of the prepared buntings, wrap around and tie up as for *Paupiettes*.

Place these *Paupiettes* in a buttered shallow pan and when required for service, coat with 125 g ($4\frac{1}{2}$ oz) very hot melted butter; season lightly and cook in a hot oven.

When cooked, remove the string and place each Nonette on a square Croûton of bread, hollowed out, fried in butter and filled with foie gras purée. Coat lightly with buttered chicken glaze and squeeze a drop of lemon juice on each Nonette.

3296 Quenelles de Volaille à l'Ecarlate
Mix 100 g ($3\frac{1}{2}$ oz) each of chopped truffle and chopped and squeezed raw mushrooms together with 1 kg ($2\frac{1}{4}$ lb) chicken Mousseline forcemeat.

Mould into flat round pieces 5 cm (2 in) in diameter and 1 cm ($\frac{2}{5}$ in) thick. Poach, drain, dry the Quenelles and allow them to cool slightly; coat both sides with thick Velouté and stick on each one a thin round of salt ox tongue of the same size.

Flour, egg and breadcrumb and deep fry in clarified butter; arrange on a serviette garnished with fried parsley and serve accompanied with a Velouté containing a Julienne of very red ox tongue.

3297 Quenelles de Volaille à l'Estragon
Mix 50 g (2 oz) chopped tarragon into 1 kg ($2\frac{1}{4}$ lb) chicken forcemeat with panada and cream.

Decorate the bottoms of well buttered, fluted Barquette moulds with a rose shape of blanched tarragon leaves then fill with the prepared forcemeat. Poach, drain and dry them and arrange in a circle on a dish; cover the bottoms of the dish with thin tarragon-flavoured Velouté and serve the rest of the sauce separately.

3298 Quenelles de Volaille Morland
Take a fairly stiff chicken forcemeat with panada and cream; divide it into pieces of approximately 90 g (3 oz) in weight and mould into oval-shaped Quenelles.

Roll them in finely chopped truffle, flatten slightly then cook them slowly on both sides in clarified butter. Arrange in a circle on a dish and fill the centre with a purée of mushrooms.

3299 Quenelles de Volaille à la Périgueux
Take some truffled chicken forcemeat with panada and butter.

Decorate the bottoms of large well buttered oval Barquette moulds with a star-shape of truffle or a slice of truffle, and fill with the forcemeat.

Poach, drain and dry these Quenelles and arrange in a circle on a dish; cover the bottom of the dish with Sauce Périgueux and serve separately a sauceboat of the same sauce.

3300 Quenelles de Volaille d'Uzès
Take some chicken forcemeat with panada and cream and mix with a suitable amount of finely chopped white of cooked chicken.

Mould into the shape of oval Quenelles then poach, drain and dry them. Arrange in a circle on a dish and cover the bottom of the dish with a little Sauce Aurore containing a fine Julienne of truffle; serve the rest of the sauce separately.

3301 BLANQUETTE DE VOLAILLE

A Blanquette of chicken is made in the same way as a Blanquette of Veal taking account of the difference in texture of the two kinds of meat and adjusting the cooking time accordingly.

3302 CAPILOTADE DE VOLAILLE

A Capilotade of chicken is made from the boned-out left-overs of roast, boiled or braised chickens.

Cut the chicken into thin slices and reheat without actually boiling, in Sauce Italienne containing some cooked sliced mushrooms. Arrange in a deep dish, lightly sprinkle with chopped parsley and surround with small heart-shaped Croûtons of bread fried in butter.

3303 COQUILLES DE VOLAILLE

It should be remembered that, although not completely indispensable, it is nevertheless very useful to pipe a scrolled border of Duchesse potato mixture using a star tube, around the edge of the shells. If the shells are simply filled with the chicken and sauce or if the filling is to be glazed rapidly, the border of potato should be brushed with beaten egg and coloured prior to filling.

Normally, only left-over chicken is used for these preparations.

3304 Coquilles de Volaille à l'Ecarlate
Cover the bottom of the shells with Sauce Allemande and fill them with alternate slices of well reheated chicken and ox tongue. Coat with more of the same sauce and sprinkle with some chopped ox tongue—this is best obtained from the tip of the tongue which is usually the reddest part.

3305 Coquilles de Volaille au Gratin
Cover the bottom of shells with Sauce Duxelles and fill with alternate slices of chicken and cooked mushrooms. Place a button mushroom on the top of each and cover with some fairly thick Sauce Duxelles. Sprinkle with dry white breadcrumbs and melted butter and gratinate quickly.

3306 Coquilles de Volaille Joffrette
Cover the bottom of the shells with buttered asparagus tips, arrange the sliced chicken on top and coat with Sauce Allemande flavoured with mushroom essence. Decorate with a circle of slices of truffle.

3307 Coquilles de Volaille Mornay
Coat the bottom of the shells with Sauce Mornay and fill with reheated slices of chicken. Coat with more of the same sauce, sprinkle with grated Parmesan and glaze quickly.

3308 Coquilles de Volaille Parisienne
Cover the bottom of the shells with buttered Sauce Allemande, and fill with reheated slices of chicken, mushroom and truffle. Coat with more of the same sauce and glaze quickly.

3309 COTELETTES DE VOLAILLE—CHICKEN CUTLETS

There are two distinct kinds of chicken cutlet—the first being the breasts or fillets cut from a chicken with the winglet bone left attached; these cutlets are described in the beginning of the section devoted to Fillets, Suprêmes and Cutlets of Chicken. The terms Cutlet and Suprême in this case are synonymous.

In the second, a chicken cutlet is simply a variation of a chicken Croquette but in this case moulded cutlet-shape. See Croquettes de Volaille in the section on Hot Hors-d'oeuvre.

CREPINETTES DE VOLAILLE

3310 Crépinettes de Volaille
Finely chop 500 g (1 lb 2 oz) raw chicken flesh, 100 g ($3\frac{1}{2}$ oz) lean pork and 400 g (14 oz) fresh pork fat and mix together with 150 g (5 oz) foie gras trimmings passed through a sieve, 100 g ($3\frac{1}{2}$ oz) chopped truffle, 12 g ($\frac{1}{2}$ oz) salt, a little pepper and nutmeg and $\frac{1}{2}$ dl (2 fl oz or $\frac{1}{4}$ U.S. cup) brandy.

Divide this mixture into 80–90 g (3 oz) pieces; mould oval shape, place a nice slice of truffle in the middle of each and wrap each in a piece of soft thin caul.

Dip the Crépinettes into melted butter then breadcrumbs and either grill them gently or cook in the oven.

Arrange in a circle on a dish and serve accompanied with a sauceboat of a thin brown or white sauce and a dish of vegetable purée.

3311 CRETES ET ROGNONS DE COQ—COCKSCOMBS AND KIDNEYS

As explained in the section on blanching the skins of the cockscombs must first be removed and then placed to soak in water to remove all blood before being cooked in very light *Blanc*. The aim is to get them as white as possible.

Cocks' kidneys are soaked in cold water and added to the same *Blanc* a few minutes before the combs are completely cooked. The main use of these two items is as a garnish although it is possible to use them as the principal ingredient in certain recipes as follows.

3312 Crêtes de Coq Demidoff
For this recipe see Hot Hors-d'oeuvre (1138).

3313 Crêtes de Coq Villeroy
This is made in the same way as all items à la Villeroy. Deep fry them at the last moment, arrange on a serviette and serve accompanied with a sauceboat of Sauce Périgueux.

3314 Crêtes et Rognons de Coq à la Grecque
Cook 250 g (9 oz) Riz Pilaw with 50 g (2 oz) diced pimento and a touch of saffron. Carefully mix into this rice 24 fresh cocks' kidneys fried in butter and 12 large cockscombs blanched and braised in the same way as lamb's sweetbreads.

Arrange in a silver casserole and place on top a circle of slices of eggplant, seasoned, floured and deep fried in oil at the last moment.

3315 Brochettes de Rognons de Coq
Select some very nice large cocks' kidneys; poach, drain, season and impale them on small silver skewers—7 or 8 on each. Sprinkle them with

melted butter and very fine dry white breadcrumbs and grill gently.

Serve accompanied with Sauce Béarnaise.

3316 Désirs de Mascotte

Place 100 g ($3\frac{1}{2}$ oz) butter in a frying pan and cook until it begins to turn brown; immediately add 24 very fresh cocks' kidneys, season them with salt, pepper and a touch of Cayenne and cook for 5–6 minutes.

Cut 12 small rounds of bread with a plain cutter 2 cm ($\frac{4}{5}$ in) in diameter and 8 mm ($\frac{1}{3}$ in) thick and fry them in butter at the last moment.

Add 4 very black truffles cut in fairly thick slices to the required amount of reduced Sauce Demi-glace; add in the drained kidneys, the Croûtons, 50 g (2 oz) good butter and a few drops of lemon juice. Shake the pan to ensure the complete mixing of the ingredients.

Place in a very hot silver timbale and serve immediately.

3317 Stuffed Cocks' Kidneys for Cold Entrées and Garnishing etc.

Select some nice large poached cocks' kidneys and cut them open lengthways; trim them slightly underneath so that they can remain level.

Using a small piping bag and tube, stuff them with a well seasoned purée of either foie gras, ham, white of chicken or truffle, mixed with an equal amount of butter.

Coat the prepared kidneys with a white or pink Sauce Chaud-froid according to requirements then arrange them in a small shallow timbale and cover with a light aspic jelly.

These kidneys may be placed in Petits-fours moulds, covered with jelly then used to provide a garnished border for cold poultry dishes.

CROQUETTES AND CROMESQUIS OF CHICKEN

(See under these names in the section on Hot Hors-d'oeuvre.)

EMINCES DE VOLAILLE

3318 Emincé de Volaille Bonne-Femme

Arrange on a buttered dish a border of overlapping slices of boiled potato shallow fried in butter.

Cover the bottom of the dish with a little Velouté and some freshly cooked sliced mushrooms; on top of this arrange some reheated thin slices of chicken. Coat with buttered Velouté and glaze quickly.

3319 Emincé de Volaille Maintenon

Arrange on a dish a border of very small, flat, round or rectangular Croquettes of chicken. Fill the centre of this border with slices of reheated white of chicken, thin slices of white mushrooms and slices of truffle all mixed with some Sauce Allemande containing a little Soubise.

3320 Emincé de Volaille Valentino

Prepare a Salpicon as for chicken Croquettes and mix it together with some Pommes Duchesse mixture. Arrange this as a narrow border around a buttered dish. Brush with beaten egg and colour it in the oven.

Fill the centre of this border with slices of chicken, small oval slices of tongue and slices of mushroom and truffle, all mixed and reheated with Velouté.

FOIES DE VOLAILLE—CHICKENS' LIVERS

As chickens' livers may be used in the same way as mutton kidneys, the following suitable preparations are thus only indicated; En Brochettes, Sautés Chasseur, Sautés aux Fines Herbes, au Gratin, en Coquilles, en Pilaw, etc.

3321 Foies de Volailles et Rognons Sautés au Vin Rouge

This is prepared in the same way as Rognons de Boeuf Sautés au Madère (2437), using equal quantities of kidney and chickens' livers and substituting red wine for Madeira.

FRICASSEE DE POULET—CHICKEN FRICASSEE

The preparation of a *Fricassée* of chicken is exactly the same as for a *Fricassée* of veal taking account of the difference in texture of the meat and adjusting the cooking time in consequence. It is also necessary to remember that the main difference between a *Fricassée* and a *Blanquette* is that in a *Fricassée* the meat is cooked directly in the sauce.

For this preparation the legs should always be cut in two pieces.

3322 Fricassée de Poulet à l'Ancienne

Prepare the Fricassée in the usual manner as for veal, adding 15 cooked button onions and 15 grooved cooked white button mushrooms about 10 minutes before it is cooked.

At the last moment thicken the sauce with a liaison of 2 egg yolks, 4 tbs cream and 30 g (1 oz) of butter and finish with a pinch of chopped parsley and chives.

Arrange in a deep dish and surround with small, pale baked crescents of puff pastry.

3323 Fricassée de Poulet aux Ecrevisses
About 10 minutes before the Fricassée is cooked, add 15 button mushrooms and 18 crayfish cooked as for Bisque and shelled.

Finish the sauce with 50 g (2 oz) Crayfish Butter made from their shells and also the cooking liquor from the crayfish passed through a muslin.

3324 Fricassée de Poulet Demidoff
Prepare the Fricassée in the usual manner. When half cooked, add a vegetable garnish as indicated for Poularde Demidoff, adjusting the proportions accordingly.

Arrange in a deep dish and decorate with crescent-shaped slices of truffle.

3325 Fricassée de Poulet Printanière
When the Fricassée is half cooked, add 20 small olive-shaped pieces each of carrot and turnip, both cooked in White Bouillon, and 12 new season button onions two-thirds cooked in White Bouillon.

At the last moment, complete the garnish with 50 g (2 oz) each of plain boiled peas and diamonds of French beans.

FRITOT OR MARINADE DE VOLAILLE

3326 Fritot, or Marinade de Volaille
Marinate thin slices of cooked chicken with oil, lemon juice and chopped Fines Herbes.

To serve: dip the slices into thin frying batter and deep fry in very hot fat. Serve arranged on a serviette and surround with a border of picked parsley.

Serve accompanied with Tomato Sauce.

Note:

1) The flesh of boiled chicken is more suitable than roast chicken for this dish as it is more porous and soaks up the marinade better.

2) In these days, the two preparations, Fritot and Marinade are often confused; previously the difference between them was clearly defined inasmuch as the Fritot was made with cooked chicken and the Marinade with raw chicken.

MAZAGRAN DE VOLAILLE

The preparation of a Mazagran is always the same—it is only the main ingredient of the preparation which changes. See Mazagran de Cervelle (2206).

MOUSSE ET MOUSSELINES DE VOLAILLE

Both these dishes are made with Mousseline forcemeat—the difference between them being that a Mousse is made for a number of portions whereas Mousselines are small and only one or two are served per portion.

There are several references to the making of these items in this book so there is no need to repeat them here.

3327 Mousselines de Volaille Alexandra
Mould the Mousselines and poach them; drain and arrange in a circle on a round dish. Place a thin slice of chicken and a slice of truffle on each, coat with Sauce Mornay and glaze quickly in the oven.

On removing from the oven place a bouquet of buttered asparagus tips or peas in the centre of the Mousselines.

3328 Mousselines de Volaille Florentine
This is prepared in the same way as Sylphides de Volaille but filling the bottom of the Barquettes with buttered leaf spinach instead of coating with Sauce Mornay.

3329 Mousselines de Volaille à l'Indienne
Mould the Mousselines and poach them; drain and arrange in a circle on a round dish. Coat with Sauce Indienne and serve accompanied with a dish of plain boiled rice.

3330 Mousselines de Volaille au Paprika
When the Mousselines are cooked and drained, arrange them on a dish; place a thin slice of white of chicken on each and coat with paprika-flavoured Sauce Suprême. Surround with small moulds of Riz Pilaw stuffed with Tomato Fondue.

3331 Mousselines de Volaille Patti
Poach, drain and arrange the Mousselines in a circle on a round dish. Coat them with Sauce Suprême finished with Crayfish Butter and fill the centre with buttered asparagus tips. Decorate these with a few slices of truffle coated with meat glaze.

3332 Mousselines de Volaille à la Sicilienne
Poach the Mousselines, drain them and place each on an oval tartlet case filled with Macaroni à la Napolitaine.

Coat with Sauce Suprême, sprinkle with grated Parmesan and glaze quickly.

3333 Sylphides de Volaille

Mould and poach the Mousselines in the usual manner; place a little Sauce Mornay in the bottom of Barquette cases and place a Mousseline in each. Place a slice of white of chicken on top and lightly coat with some of the same sauce. Cover the surface of the coated Mousselines with a fairly stiff Soufflé au Parmesan mixture. This should be applied in a decorative fashion using a piping bag and plain tube.

Place the Sylphides in the oven to cook the Soufflé and serve them immediately when ready.

3334 Ursulines de Nancy

Mould the Mousselines in the shape of large round Quenelles and poach them in White Bouillon to be ready for exactly when required.

Drain them well and place each in the centre of a Barquette case filled with foie gras purée which has been softened with a little port—or sherry-flavoured Sauce Demi-glace; decorate with a large thin slice of truffle, place a small bouquet of buttered asparagus tips on each side of the Mousseline and coat with buttered chicken glaze.

Serve separately a sauceboat of the same buttered chicken glaze.

PATES CHAUDS DE POULET—HOT CHICKEN PIES

3335 Pâté de Poulet à l'Anglaise—Chicken Pie, English style

Cut a chicken as for sauté; season the pieces and sprinkle them with 30 g (1 oz) finely chopped shallot, 60 g (2 oz) finely chopped onion, 50 g (2 oz) sliced mushrooms lightly cooked in butter and a pinch of chopped parsley.

Line a pie dish with thin slices of veal and fill with the prepared chicken, placing the leg pieces at the bottom. Add 150 g (5 oz) thin streaky bacon rashers, 4 hard-boiled yolks of egg cut in half and moisten three-quarters of the way up the dish with Chicken Bouillon.

Stick a band of puff paste around the rim of the dish, moisten and cover the pie with a layer of the same paste sealing it firmly to the band of paste around the edge.

Decorate the edge, brush with eggwash, score a pattern with the point of a knife and make a hole in the centre.

Bake in a moderate oven for 1½ hours. On removing from the oven pour a few spoonfuls of well flavoured gravy into the pie.

3336 Pâté Chaud de Poulet à la Challonaise

Line a Charlotte mould with good short paste and cover this with a thick layer of chicken forcemeat containing chopped raw mushrooms.

Fill with a chicken cut and cooked as a Fricassée and containing 100 g (3½ oz) each of cockscombs and cocks' kidneys—this must be cold. Cover with a layer of the same forcemeat and close up the pie with a round of paste sealing it well to the sides; bake in a moderate oven for 1 hour. Turn out on to a suitable dish and serve accompanied with Velouté finished with mushroom essence.

3337 Pâté Chaud Financière

Line a round fluted pie mould with good short paste and cover this with a 2 cm (⅘ in) thick layer of truffled Godiveau. Fill with a cold Financière garnish containing extra cockscombs and kidneys, and mixed with thick Sauce Madère.

Cover with a layer of Godiveau on top, close up the pie with a round of paste sealing it well and bake in a fairly hot oven for approximately 50 minutes.

3338 Pâté Chaud de Poulet Vallauris

Cut 2 medium-sized chickens into portions and colour on all sides in olive oil; add 50 g (2 oz) chopped onion, 1½ dl (5 fl oz or ⅝ U.S. cup) white wine, ½ dl (2 fl oz or ¼ U.S. cup) brandy and a pinch of powdered thyme and bayleaf. Reduce almost completely then add 5 dl (18 fl oz or 2¼ U.S. cups) veal gravy; simmer for 5 minutes and add 48 stoned black olives.

Take an oval or round Vallauris earthenware dish and line it with very thin slices of veal, place inside the pieces of chicken, pour in the sauce and garnish, then cover with more very thin slices of veal seasoned with salt and pepper. Close up the pie with a layer of Pie Paste (3775) sealing it well to the edges of the dish.

Cook in a moderate oven for approximately one hour. This pie may be served hot or cold as required.

TIMBALES OF CHICKEN

3339 Timbale à l'Ambassadrice

Line the bottom and sides of a buttered Charlotte mould with alternate rows of rings of ox tongue each with a round of truffle placed in its centre, and rings of truffle each with a round of ox tongue placed in its centre.

Coat these carefully with a layer of chicken forcemeat then three-quarters fill with the following garnish in which the noodles should alternate in layers with a mixture of the other items: 200 g (7 oz) noodles mixed with Jus lié, 200 g (7 oz) sliced chicken livers, 150 g (5 oz) sliced raw mushrooms, 100 g (3½ oz) lambs' sweetbreads and 100 g (3½ oz) sliced truffle.

The chicken livers, mushrooms and sweetbreads should be sautéed in butter and mixed together with the truffle, some tomato-flavoured Sauce Madère and the deglazed juices from the pan.

Finish the timbale with a layer of the same forcemeat and cook *au Bain-marie* in the usual manner.

When cooked, allow it to rest for a few minutes then demould on to a round dish and surround with a *cordon* of Sauce Madère.

Serve accompanied with a sauceboat of the same sauce.

3340 Timbale Bontoux

Prepare a Timbale case (4334) decorated with noodle paste and bake it keeping it pale in colour. Fill with alternate layers of 1) cooked macaroni tossed in butter, flavoured with grated Parmesan and a liberal amount of tomato purée, and 2) a mixture of thick slices of cooked Boudin de Volaille containing chopped truffle, cockscombs, cocks' kidneys, and sliced truffle, all mixed with tomato-flavoured Sauce Demi-glace.

3341 Timbale Bourbonnaise

Line a buttered Charlotte mould with a 2 cm (⅘ in) thick layer of chicken forcemeat containing chopped salt ox tongue; place in the oven for a few minutes to cook the surface of the forcemeat.

Fill the mould with a mixture of slices of breast of chicken, cooked in butter (main ingredient), cockscombs, cocks' kidneys, mushrooms and slices of truffle—all mixed with fairly thick Sauce Allemande. Cover with more forcemeat and cook *au Bain-marie* in the usual manner.

Demould when ready on to a round dish and surround with a *cordon* of Velouté flavoured with mushroom essence.

3342 Timbale Maréchal Foch

1) Cut 500 g (1 lb 2 oz) peeled truffle into slices, lightly season with salt, place in a pan with 1 dl (3½ fl oz or ½ U.S. cup) old Marsala, cover and reserve for later use.

2) Pound together 250 g (9 oz) fresh pork fat with 80–100 g (2½–3½ oz) raw truffle peelings and season with a little salt and mixed spice.

3) Take 2 very nice Mons capons, season their insides lightly with salt and stuff each with half of the pork and truffle mixture. Truss them *en Entrée* and cover with thin slices of salt pork fat.

Method of Preparation:

1) Place the capons in a casserole with 60 g (2 oz) butter, cover and cook in a moderate oven taking care not to burn the butter.

2) Half an hour before the dish is to be served, boil 500 g (1 lb 2 oz) good quality medium size macaroni for 12–14 minutes, drain well, toss in 60 g (2 oz) butter and add 2½ dl (9 fl oz or 1⅛ U.S. cups) Sauce Demi-glace made from veal stock and very well flavoured with tomato.

Allow to simmer gently until the sauce is completely absorbed by the macaroni then add 250 g (9 oz) of truffled foie gras crushed with a fork and 60 g (2 oz) grated Parmesan; mix together very well so as to ensure the perfect cohesion of the whole.

3) Cook the prepared truffles with the Marsala adding 5 dl (18 fl oz or 2¼ U.S. cups) of the same sauce as used for the macaroni; allow to simmer gently.

All the above items should be ready for when the truffles are finally cooked.

To serve: place two-thirds of the macaroni into a Timbale or deep silver dish; sprinkle with grated Parmesan and spread a layer of a few tablespoons of the sliced truffle and sauce on top.

Quickly remove the breasts of the capons and cut into fairly thick slices, arrange on top of the truffles and cover with two-thirds of the remaining truffle and sauce.

Sprinkle with 1 tbs grated Parmesan then fill the Timbale with the rest of the macaroni. Sprinkle with more Parmesan cheese and complete the dish by covering with the rest of the truffles and sauce.

Cover with the lid and place in a moderate oven for a few minutes to allow the aroma of the truffles to develop.

Note: Only the breasts of the capons are used in this dish; the legs being used for other purposes.

3343 Timbale Milanaise

Prepare a Timbale case (4334) as for Timbale Bontoux.

Cover the bottom and sides with a layer of cooked spaghetti, tossed in butter, mixed with grated Parmesan and Gruyère cheese and finished with tomato purée. Fill the centre with a Financière garnish strongly flavoured with tomato and meat glaze. Cover with more of the spaghetti and place on top of this a circle of nice slices of truffle.

Replace the lid and present the Timbale on a serviette on a dish.

3344 Timbale Milanaise à l'Ancienne

Decorate a buttered Charlotte mould with noodle paste then line it with short paste. Cover the bottom and sides with tomato and cheese-flavoured spaghetti prepared as above and fill with the Financière garnish; cover with more of the

spaghetti then close up the mould with a round of paste, sealing it well to the edge; bake in a hot oven for 45–50 minutes.
To serve: demould the Timbale on to a dish, remove the top which was previously the bottom and cut it into small triangles; arrange these around the Timbale.

Coat the bared filling with a few spoonsful of tomato sauce and decorate the surface with mushrooms, cockscombs and slices of truffle.

VOL-AU-VENT

3345 Vol-au-Vent à la Financière
Prepare a garnish Financière (381) and fill into a Vol-au-vent case. Place on a serviette on a dish and surround with trussed crayfish.

3346 Vol-au-Vent Frascati
Fill the Vol-au-vent case with a buttered garnish of asparagus tips, thin slices of white of chicken, sliced mushrooms and slices of truffle.

3347 Vol-au-Vent à la Toulousaine
The filling of this Vol-au-vent is composed of half a Toulousaine garnish (463) and half of either sliced white of chicken, brain, or veal or lambs' sweetbreads mixed together with Sauce Allemande. Fill into the Vol-au-vent case and serve surrounded with trussed crayfish.

PILAW DE VOLAILLE

Pilaw which is the national dish of several Eastern countries is prepared in accordance with an endless number of recipes.

The various curries of veal, lamb and chicken are all Pilaws and all of them excepting the following recipe for Pilaw à la Parisienne are similar in preparation to a curry, except that the flavourings are different and the rice is cooked in a different way to Riz à l'Indienne.

3348 Pilaw de Volaille à la Grecque
Cut the chicken into small pieces and colour them in mutton fat together with 100 g ($3\frac{1}{2}$ oz) chopped onion. Sprinkle with 30 g (1 oz) flour, moisten with 5 dl (18 fl oz or $2\frac{1}{4}$ U.S. cups) White Bouillon, add 50 g (2 oz) sultanas and currants and a small diced pimento; cook gently together. Place in a timbale or deep dish and serve accompanied with a dish of Riz Pilaw.

3349 Pilaw de Volaille à l'Orientale
Prepare the chicken as in the preceding recipe flavouring it only with a little ground ginger, and adding 2 grilled, skinned and sliced green pimentos.

Place in a timbale or deep dish and serve accompanied with a dish of Riz Pilaw.

3350 Pilaw de Volaille Parisienne
Cut the chicken into pieces as for Fricassée, season them and colour in butter; add 100 g ($3\frac{1}{2}$ oz) rice which has been lightly coloured in butter together with a chopped onion, 1 bayleaf, the roughly chopped flesh only of 2 tomatoes and sufficient White Bouillon to more than just cover. Cover with a lid and cook in the oven for 25 minutes by which time the chicken and rice should be cooked and the rice completely dry.

Sprinkle with 1 dl ($3\frac{1}{2}$ fl oz or $\frac{1}{2}$ U.S. cup) veal stock and carefully mix this into the Pilaw using a fork.

Place in a timbale or deep dish and serve accompanied with Tomato Sauce.

3351 Pilaw de Volaille à la Turque
Proceed as indicated for Pilaw à la Parisienne, flavouring it with a touch each of Cayenne and saffron.

3352 Pilaw using Cooked Chicken
Cut the cooked chicken into small slices and reheat them in butter.

Line the bottom and sides of a buttered mould with a thick layer of tomato-flavoured pilaw rice, place the chicken in the centre and cover with more of the rice packing it fairly firmly. Place in the oven for a few minutes.

Demould on to a dish and surround with a *cordon* of Tomato Sauce.

SOUFFLES DE VOLAILLE— CHICKEN SOUFFLES

When preparing chicken soufflés for a large number it is always preferable to use raw chicken flesh; for small numbers the mixture may be made with cooked chicken.

Note: The cooking time for Soufflés of chicken is relatively long and it is better that they should be well cooked. Allow between 25–30 minutes of cooking in a moderate oven for a soufflé mould of 1 litre ($1\frac{3}{4}$ pt or $4\frac{1}{2}$ U.S. cups) capacity.

3353 Soufflé Mixture made with Raw Chicken
Mix 5 stiffly beaten egg whites into 1 kg ($2\frac{1}{4}$ lb) chicken Mousseline forcemeat; fill into buttered soufflé moulds and cook in a moderate oven.

3354 Soufflé Mixture made with Cooked Chicken
Finely pound 500 g (1 lb 2 oz) white of chicken, adding 6 tbs cold Sauce Béchamel; pass through a sieve.

Place the purée obtained in a pan and reheat it without boiling; add 50 g (2 oz) butter and 5 egg yolks, then fold in 6 stiffly beaten egg whites.

Fill into buttered soufflé moulds and cook in a moderate oven.

3355 Soufflé de Volaille à la Périgord
This soufflé may be prepared using either of the above mixtures. Fill the selected mixture into a buttered soufflé mould with alternate layers of slices of truffle, finishing with the soufflé mixture. Cook in a moderate oven.

COLD FATTENED PULLETS AND CHICKENS

3356 Poularde Carmelite
Remove the breasts from a cold poached pullet; discard the skin and cut the breasts into slices; coat them with white Sauce Chaud-froid and decorate neatly with truffle.

Trim the carcase and coat the outside with some of the same Chaud-froid then build up the carcase to the original shape of the bird with crayfish Mousse; allow to set firm in the refrigerator then replace the prepared slices of chicken on top, arranged in two rows and correctly positioned.

Place a line of trimmed crayfish tails between the two rows.

Coat the whole with aspic jelly, arrange in a deep dish and fill the dish half-way up the chicken with some very good aspic jelly.

3357 Poularde au Champagne
Stuff a pullet two days in advance with a whole foie gras studded with truffle and which has been cooked very gently for 20 minutes in butter to stiffen and lightly colour it.

Poêlé the prepared pullet with Champagne then place in an earthenware terrine just large enough to hold it and pour in the strained cooking liquid containing sufficient jelly to set it; allow to become cold in the refrigerator.

The following day remove the fat set on top of the jelly with a spoon, then pass a little boiling water two or three times over the surface to remove the last traces of fat.

Serve this pullet very cold from the terrine.

3358 Poularde Dampierre
Bone out the inside of the pullet completely and fill it with good chicken forcemeat; truss it *en Entrée*, poach in chicken stock and allow it to cool in the cooking liquid.

When cold, drain and trim it, then coat with white Sauce Chaud-froid flavoured with a little almond milk. Glaze with aspic jelly without having decorated the bird and arrange on a low base set on an oval dish.

Surround with 6 small Mousses of red ox tongue and 6 of foie gras, all of them moulded in fairly deep dariole moulds—arrange these alternately.

Border the edge of the dish with neat shapes of jelly.

3359 Poularde à l'Ecarlate
Prepare the pullet and poach it in the same way as above but adding some finely diced red ox tongue to the chicken forcemeat. When the pullet is cold, coat it with white Sauce Chaud-froid, decorate with very red ox tongue and glaze it with aspic jelly.

Arrange the prepared pullet on a low base set on an oval dish and surround with halves of veal tongues, glazed with red aspic jelly; border the dish with neat shapes of jelly.

3360 Poularde Lambertye
Poach the pullet, allow it to cool thoroughly then remove the two breasts.

Cut off the breast bone and fill the carcase with cold chicken Mousse containing a quarter its volume of foie gras purée; mould to the original shape of the pullet.

Cut the breasts into long thin slices, coat them with white Sauce Chaud-froid, then lay them overlapping back on the prepared bird. Decorate with shapes of truffle, glaze with jelly, allow to set, then place it in a deep rectangular dish and surround with cool melted jelly.
To serve: place the dish on a block of sculpted ice.

3361 Poularde Néva
Stuff the pullet with good chicken forcemeat containing raw foie gras and diced truffle; poach it in chicken stock and allow to cool in the cooking liquid.

When very cold, coat it with white Sauce Chaud-froid, decorate with truffle, glaze with aspic jelly and allow to set.

Place the prepared pullet on a rice base set on an oval dish. Behind the bird place a vegetable salad arranged in either a carved rice or silver shell.

Border the dish with neat shapes of jelly.

3362 Poularde Parisienne
Bone out the inside of the pullet then stuff it with chicken forcemeat; truss *en Entrée*, poach it in chicken stock and allow to cool in the cooking liquid.

When very cold, remove the breasts. Take out the forcemeat, cut in dice and add to a chicken Mousse mixture. Use this Mousse to fill the carcase and re-form the bird to its original shape, then coat it with white Sauce Chaud-froid.

Cut the breasts into slices and also coat with Chaud-froid; decorate these as well as the legs on the bird with truffle. Place the slices back on the bird and glaze the whole with aspic jelly.

Place the finished pullet on a low base set on a dish and surround with small timbales of Macédoine of vegetables bound with jelly and moulded in dariole moulds.

Border the dish with neat shapes of jelly.

3363 Poularde Rose de Mai

Poach the pullet and allow it to cool in the cooking liquid; when very cold, remove the breasts and cut off the breast bone.

Coat the carcase with white Sauce Chaud-froid and re-form the bird to its original shape with tomato Mousse; decorate this with shapes of truffle and egg white and finally glaze with aspic jelly.

Cut the breasts in slices, coat with white Sauce Chaud-froid, decorate with truffle and glaze with jelly.

Fill the required number of small, pale baked Barquette cases with the same Mousse as used for the chicken and allow them to set.

Place the chicken on a low base of rice set on an oval dish and surround with the Barquettes of Mousse each having one of the prepared slices of chicken breast placed on top.

Border the dish with neat shapes of aspic jelly.

3364 Poularde Rose-Marie

Poach the pullet and allow it to cool; when very cold, remove the breasts and after discarding the skin, cut them into thick slices and coat with white Sauce Chaud-froid. Place a slice of truffle on each and glaze with aspic jelly.

Trim the carcase leaving the wings attached and re-form it to its original shape with some very smooth and very pink ham Mousse; allow to set firmly in the refrigerator.

Fill as many Barquette moulds, as there are slices of chicken, with some of the same ham Mousse.

When the Mousse in the bird has set, coat it with a nice delicate pink, paprika-flavoured Sauce Chaud-froid; decorate to choice and glaze with aspic jelly.

Place the pullet on a low base set on a long dish and surround with the demoulded Barquettes of ham Mousse, each having one of the prepared slices of chicken placed on top.

Border the dish with neat shapes of aspic jelly.

Note: The method of presenting Poularde Rose de Mai and Rose-Marie can be adapted to all types of poultry.

3365 Poularde Saint-Cyr

Poêlé the pullet with white wine and allow it to cool in the cooking liquid. Remove the breasts, discard the skin and cut them into even shape slices; coat with white Sauce Chaud-froid and decorate with truffle.

Meanwhile, sauté 15 larks together with a Mirepoix, then remove the breasts from the 6 best ones; coat these with brown Sauce Chaud-froid, decorate with cooked egg white and glaze with jelly.

Use the other larks and 150 g (5 oz) of foie gras to make a cold Mousse and use it to reshape the chicken as explained in the previous recipe. Coat with brown Sauce Chaud-froid and when set, arrange the prepared slices of chicken on either side of the mousse; place the larks breasts slightly overlapping down the centre.

Place the pullet thus prepared in a deep rectangular dish and surround with cool melted aspic jelly. When set, present the dish on a block of sculpted ice.

3366 Poularde en Terrine à la Gelée

Bone out the pullet leaving the legs intact and stuff it with a forcemeat made from 100 g ($3\frac{1}{2}$ oz) veal, 100 g ($3\frac{1}{2}$ oz) fresh pork fat, 100 g ($3\frac{1}{2}$ oz) Gratin Forcemeat made with chicken livers, 2 tbs brandy, 2 tbs truffle essence and 1 egg yolk.

In the middle of the stuffing insert $\frac{1}{2}$ a raw foie gras together with 1 raw truffle cut in quarters on each side. Reshape the bird, truss *en Entrée*, cover with thin slices of salt pork fat and Poêlé it with Madeira for $1\frac{1}{2}$ hours.

Leave to half-cool in the cooking liquid, then remove it, discard the fat and place the chicken in a terrine just large enough to hold it.

Add a little chicken jelly to the cooking liquid without first removing the fat; pass through a fine cloth and pour over the bird in the terrine.

Do not serve until it has been kept for 24 hours, then remove the fat from the surface of the jelly as indicated for Poularde au Champagne.

Present the terrine on a block of ice or on a dish surrounded by crushed ice.

3367 Terrine de Poularde en Conserve

Prepare the chicken as in the preceding recipe. Place it in a can just large enough to hold it; seal on the lid and finish the top with a bit of tin. Place in a pan, cover completely with water and boil gently for $1\frac{1}{4}$ hours.

Remove from the water, turn upside down so that the fat is at the bottom and the jelly covers the breast of the pullet; allow to cool thoroughly.

OTHER COLD PREPARATIONS OF CHICKEN

3368 Ailerons de Poulet Carmelite

Remove the breasts from a cold poached chicken leaving the winglet bones attached; trim these clear of any flesh. Discard the skin and coat the breasts with a little aspic jelly.

Half fill a silver timbale, just large enough for the breasts, with crayfish Mousse; place the breasts on top side by side and arrange between them a line of shelled and trimmed crayfish tails cooked as for Bisque.

Cover the whole with an excellent almost setting Chicken Aspic Jelly, and place in the refrigerator for 2 hours before serving.

3369 Ailerons de Poulet Lady Wilmer

Poach 3 nice plump spring chickens for just sufficient time to cook the breasts. Allow to cool, remove the breasts leaving the winglet bones attached; trim these clear of any flesh. Discard the skins and coat the breasts with a little aspic jelly.

Prepare a Mousse with 3 of the legs from the chickens and mould it in a dome-shaped mould. When this Mousse is set, demould it on to a dish and surround with the prepared breasts, fixing them with a little almost setting jelly to the Mousse, with their points upwards.

Cover the Mousse on top and the gaps between the breasts with chopped truffle and red ox tongue, arranged alternately. In the centre of the Mousse stick a small decorative silver skewer garnished with a nice glazed truffle.

3370 Aspic de Volaille à l'Italienne

Line a plain border mould with aspic jelly, decorate it with large slices of truffle and coat with another layer of jelly. Fill the mould with alternate layers of a large Julienne of white of chicken, red ox tongue and truffle, sprinkling each layer with cool melted jelly; finish filling the mould with jelly and allow to set.

Turn out when required on to a very cold dish and fill the centre with a mould of Salade Italienne. Serve accompanied with Sauce Remoulade.

3371 Aspic de Volaille Gauloise

Line a fancy mould with jelly and decorate with grooved slices of truffle, then fill with alternate layers of thin slices of chicken, cockscombs coated with brown Sauce Chaud-froid, cocks' kidneys coated with white Sauce Chaud-froid and oval slices of ox tongue; each layer should be separated with jelly.

When set, turn out on to a cold dish and surround with neat shapes of jelly.

3372 Chaud-froid de Volaille

Poach the chicken and allow it to become cold in the cooking liquid; remove the skin completely then cut the chicken into even-sized pieces. Dip these into a Sauce Chaud-froid prepared when possible with the stock from the cooking of the chicken. Arrange them on a tray, decorate each with a nice slice of truffle, glaze with aspic jelly and allow them to set. Trim the edges of the pieces before arranging them for service.

Notes on presentation: In former times the Chaud-froid de Volaille used to be arranged and presented on a base of bread or rice set in the middle of a border of jelly, and cockscombs and mushrooms coated with Chaud-froid or jelly were arranged between the pieces of chicken.

It was also sometimes arranged in special decorative bowls moulded in stearine but these methods of the old classical kitchen are not to be preferred to the following presentation created at the Savoy Hotel in London and which is being used more and more.

Set a layer of excellent aspic jelly in the bottom of a deep rectangular dish. Arrange the pieces of chicken, which have been coated with Chaud-froid and decorated, on the layer of jelly then cover them completely with some of the same jelly and allow to set.

For service, set the dish in a block of sculptured ice or surround with crushed ice.

This procedure allows less gelatine to be used in the preparation of the jelly which thus becomes much more delicate, smooth and soft.

3373 Chaud-froid de Volaille à l'Ecossaise

Remove the breasts from a cold poached chicken and cut each into 4 or 5 pieces after removing the skin. Cover these slices dome shape with a Salpicon of the trimmings of the chicken plus an equal quantity of ox tongue and truffle all mixed with reduced aspic jelly.

Coat with white Sauce Chaud-froid and immediately sprinkle with a mixture of chopped red ox tongue, truffle, gherkin and cooked egg yolk. Glaze with jelly and allow to set.

Arrange the prepared breasts in a deep silver rectangular dish alternating with oval slices of red ox tongue. Fill the centre with French beans cut diamond-shape and bound with jelly.

3374 Chaud-froid de Volaille Gounod

Remove the breasts from a cold poached chicken and cut into thin rectangular-shaped slices after removing the skin.

Prepare a Mousse from the legs and trimmings and spread it smoothly on a tray twice the thickness of the slices of chicken; place in the refrigerator to set firmly.

When ready, cut the Mousse into rectangles of the same size as the slices of chicken. Stick a slice of the chicken on each piece of Mousse, using a little jelly. Coat with white Sauce Chaud-froid and decorate each with some notes of music cut from truffle. Arrange in a deep silver rectangular dish cover with some excellent almost setting aspic jelly and allow to set.

To serve: present the dish set on a block of sculpted ice.

3375 Chaud-froid de Volaille Rossini

Prepare the pieces of chicken as for an ordinary Chaud-froid de Volaille and coat them with white Sauce Chaud-froid to which a quarter its volume of very smooth foie gras purée has been added. Decorate each piece with a lyre cut from truffle, arrange them in a deep dish and cover with jelly as in the preceding recipe.

3376 Mayonnaise de Volaille—Mayonnaise of Chicken

Cover the bottom of a salad bowl with some shredded lettuce arranged dome shape and season it with a little salt and a few drops of vinegar. On this lettuce arrange slices of cooked chicken completely free of skin and cover the whole with Sauce Mayonnaise; smooth the surface and decorate with capers, stoned olives, quarters of hard-boiled egg and small hearts of lettuce etc.

These items which act as both garnish and decoration should be arranged according to taste. Just before serving, mix together as for a salad.

3377 Medaillons de Volaille Rachel

Remove the breasts from a cold poached chicken and cut them into slices after removing the skin; trim round with a plain pastry cutter.

Make a Mousse with the legs and spread it 1 cm ($\frac{2}{5}$ in) thick on a tray. When firmly set cut into rounds with a cutter slightly larger than the one used for the slices of chicken and dipped in hot water. Glaze the slices of chicken with jelly and place one on each of the rounds of Mousse fixing them with some almost setting jelly.

Arrange the Medaillons thus prepared in a deep rectangular dish; place a nice bouquet of asparagus tips in the middle and garnish between the Medaillons with a salad of creamed asparagus tips.

3378 Cold Mousses and Mousselines of Chicken

Cold poached chicken may be used for making this Mousse but a freshly roasted, and just cold chicken is to be preferred; the flavour of the flesh is finer and more pronounced.

The recipes and details of preparation for Mousses and Mousselines can be found in the Chapter on Garnishes.

3379 Breast of Chicken on Various Mousses

With the exception of certain shellfish, all of the Mousses listed for fillets of salmon-trout on Mousse (1708) are suitable for serving with breasts of cold chicken; other suitable Mousses are listed below.

The preparation and presentation of these Mousses is exactly the same as for Mousse de Tomates (4265).

The breasts of chicken may be coated with Sauce Chaud-froid or aspic jelly and neatly and simply decorated; when served with these Mousses they constitute excellent dishes for supper.

The following are a few of these preparations:

Breast of chicken on Mousse of ham
Breast of chicken on Mousse of crayfish
Breast of chicken on Mousse of cranberries
Breast of chicken on Mousse of foie gras
Breast of chicken on Mousse of tongue
Breast of chicken on Mousse of tomatoes
Breast of chicken on Mousse of Cape gooseberries

3380 Salade de Volaille—Chicken Salad

This is prepared with the same ingredients as Mayonnaise de Volaille but without the Sauce Mayonnaise; this should be replaced with ordinary salad dressing added when the salad is being mixed just before serving.

3381 Suprêmes de Volaille Jeannette

Remove the breasts from a cold poached chicken and cut each into 4 slices after removing the skin. Trim the slices oval shape, coat with white Sauce Chaud-froid and decorate with very green leaves of blanched tarragon.

Set a 1 cm ($\frac{2}{5}$ in) thick layer of excellent Chicken Aspic Jelly in the bottom of a Timbale or deep rectangular dish and arrange on top of this some slices of Parfait of foie gras of the same size as the slices of chicken; place one of the prepared slices of the chicken on each of the foie gras and cover the whole with some of the same almost setting jelly. Allow to set.

To serve: set the dish on a block of sculpted ice.

DINDONNEAU—YOUNG TURKEY

3382 Ailerons de Dindonneau Dorés à la Purée de Marrons

Proceed as indicated for chicken winglets of the same name, taking account of the longer time necessary for cooking.

3383 Dindonneau à l'Anglaise—Poached Young Turkey, English style

Poach the turkey, keeping it very white, and proceed in the same manner as indicated for Poularde Pochée à l'Anglaise.

3384 Dindonneau à la Bourgeoise
Braise the young turkey until it is three-quarters cooked, change it into a clean pan and surround it with a Bourgeoise garnish (352) which is almost cooked. Remove the fat from the cooking liquid then pass through a strainer over the turkey and garnish; replace in the oven to finish cooking.

Glaze the turkey at the last moment. Place on a suitable dish and surround with a little of the reduced braising liquid.

Serve the garnish separately.

3385 Dindonneau à la Catalane
Cut the young turkey as for Fricassée and well colour in hot butter. Deglaze the pan with 1 bottle of white wine, season with salt and pepper, add a touch of crushed garlic and reduce until almost dry.

Moisten with Sauce Espagnole, brown stock and tomato purée in equal quantities and sufficient to cover the pieces of turkey. Cook in the oven for 40 minutes.

Remove the pieces of turkey to a clean pan and add a Catalane garnish the tomatoes for which should be cut into quarters.

Pass the sauce through a fine strainer over the turkey and replace in the oven to finish cooking gently for a further 25 minutes. See Sauté de Veau à la Catalane (2744).

Arrange in a timbale or deep dish for service.

3386 Dindonneau aux Céleris Braisés—Young Turkey with Braised Celery
Poêlé the young turkey then proceed as indicated for Poularde aux Céleris.

3387 Dindonneau aux Cèpes—Young Turkey with Flap Mushrooms
Stuff the young turkey with a forcemeat prepared from 400 g (15 oz) each of veal and fresh pork fat, 150 g (5 oz) soaked and squeezed breadcrumbs, 500 g (1 lb 2 oz) stalks of flap mushrooms prepared as a dry Duxelles, 15 g (½ oz) salt and a little pepper and grated nutmeg.

Poêlé the turkey until three-quarters cooked, remove it to a clean pan and surround with 600 g (1 lb 5 oz) salt belly of pork, cut in large dice, blanched and sautéed in butter and 1 kg (2¼ lb) small unopened flap mushrooms, quickly sautéed in butter. Pass the deglazed juices from the cooking over the turkey and garnish, cover very tightly with a lid and complete the cooking gently in the oven.

Present the turkey on a dish surrounded with its garnish or serve this separately.

3388 Dindonneau aux Champignons—Young Turkey with Mushrooms
This can be prepared in either of the two following ways:

1) Cut the young turkey into pieces and cook as for a Sauté adding 600 g (1 lb 5 oz) mushrooms, cut in quarters and sautéed in butter. See Sauté de Veau aux Champignons (2745).
2) Braise the young turkey whole in the usual manner and serve it accompanied with Sauce aux Champignons made with the braising liquid.

The first preparation is suitable as a luncheon dish whilst the second being a large joint (Relevé) is more suitable for dinner.

3389 Dindonneau Chipolata
The young turkey may be prepared in either of the ways as indicated in the preceding recipe.

If it is prepared as a Sauté, remove the pieces to a clean pan after 40 minutes of cooking time and add 20 glazed button onions, 20 chestnuts, cooked in Bouillon, 150 g (5 oz) salt belly of pork, cut in large dice and sautéed in butter and 20 olive-shaped pieces of carrot, cooked in Bouillon and glazed. Pass the sauce through a fine strainer over the whole, cover and complete the cooking in the oven.

If the turkey is braised, glaze it at the last moment then place on a suitable dish and surround with a Chipolata garnish (365) combined with the reduced braising liquid.

3390 Dindonneau à l'Estragon
Poêlé the young turkey on a bed of sliced vegetables and herbs plus the addition of some blanched tarragon stalks.

When cooked, place the turkey on a dish, decorate the breast with blanched tarragon leaves and surround with a gravy prepared in the following manner: add some brown stock to the juices, vegetables and herbs in the pan, simmer for a few minutes, pass through a fine strainer, remove the fat, then reduce it and flavour with a few tablespoons of an infusion of tarragon.

3391 Dindonneau Financière
Braise the young turkey and proceed as indicated for Poularde Financière (3054).

3392 Dindonneau Godard
Braise the young turkey in the usual manner and present it on a dish surrounded with bouquets of Godard garnish (388). In the breast insert 3 decorative silver skewers each garnished with a white

truffle, a trussed crayfish and a decorated Quenelle.

Serve accompanied with Sauce Godard.

3393 Dindonneau à la Jardinière

Cover the young turkey with a layer of Matignon, wrap it in thin slices of salt pork fat and finally in a sheet of buttered greaseproof paper, then Poêlé it slowly. Place on a dish and surround with a Jardinière garnish (396) arranged in bouquets.

Add the Matignon to the juices and vegetables in the pan together with 5 dl (18 fl oz or 2¼ U.S. cups) brown gravy; reduce by a good half, remove the fat, pass through a fine strainer and pour a little of this gravy over the turkey.

Serve the remainder of the gravy separately.

3394 Dindonneau Farci aux Marrons—Roast Young Turkey with Chestnut Stuffing

For a medium-sized young turkey of about 3 kg (6 lb 12 oz) in weight.

Slit the shells of 1 kg (2¼ lb) chestnuts and dip them for a few seconds in very hot fat; remove the shells and inner skins then two-thirds cook them in Bouillon and allow to become cold. Drain the chestnuts well and mix together with 800 g (1 lb 12 oz) smooth well seasoned pork sausage meat.

Remove the breast bones from inside the turkey then stuff it with the prepared forcemeat; truss it carefully to a good shape and roast it on the spit or in the oven at not too high a temperature and basting it frequently.

When cooked, place on a dish and serve accompanied with a gravy prepared from the cooking juices kept a little fatty.

3395 Blanc de Dindonneau à la Toulousaine

This can be prepared in either of the two following ways:

A) Remove the breasts from the young turkey and cut them into thin slices after removing the skin. Lightly flatten them and lard with thin strips of truffle; place in a buttered shallow pan.

A little while before being required, add a little lemon juice and mushroom liquor, cover and cook gently without colour in the oven. Arrange overlapping in a circle on a round dish, place a Toulousaine garnish (463) in the centre and surround with a *cordon* of Sauce Allemande.

B) Poêlé the young turkey, and just before being required remove the breasts, skin them and cut into thickish slices.

Arrange these slices overlapping in a circle on a dish, alternating with slices of foie gras shallow fried in butter. Place the Toulousaine garnish in the centre and surround the slices of turkey and foie gras with a *cordon* of thin meat glaze.

Note: The turkey may also be prepared and served whole as indicated for Poularde à la Toulousaine.

DINDONNEAU FROID—COLD YOUNG TURKEY

3396 Cold Young Turkey

For cold turkey it is better to Poêlé the bird rather than to poach it; the juices from the cooking should be added to the jelly being used.

All the recipes for cold fattened pullet are equally suitable for turkey.

3397 Dindonneau en Daube

Bone out the young turkey proceeding as for a galantine and stuff it with very good sausage meat mixed with ¼ dl (1 fl oz or ⅛ U.S. cup) brandy per 1 kg (2¼ lb) of sausage meat plus some large dice of ham or bacon and dice of raw truffle. Place a very small and very red ox tongue, wrapped in slices of salt pork fat in the centre of the stuffing.

Re-form the turkey, truss it carefully and place it in a terrine just large enough to hold it together with the stock for moistening it—this stock should be prepared in advance from the trimmings and bones from the turkey, 2 knuckles of veal, 2 calf's feet, 1 kg (2¼ lb) beef coloured brown in fat, 1 bottle white wine, 2 litres (3½ pt or 9 U.S. cups) water and the usual vegetables and herbs; after cooking, pass it through a fine strainer and reduce to 1½ litres (2⅝ pt or 6½ U.S. cups).

Add this stock to the turkey, cover the terrine with its lid and seal it hermetically with a band of flour and water paste; cook in a hot oven for 2½ hours.

When cooked, allow to cool in the terrine and for service slightly heat the latter so as to demould the Daube.

PIGEONNEAUX—YOUNG PIGEONS

It is important that only young pigeons which have just reached full maturity should be used in cookery. Those older than one year should be viewed as being old and should be completely excluded from use except for the preparation of forcemeat. For this reason the term Pigeonneaux which is the diminutive of pigeon is used exclusively in this section.

3398 Pigeonneaux à la Bordelaise

Cut the young pigeons in half and flatten them slightly; season and shallow fry in butter. Arrange in a circle on a dish and surround with the same garnish as indicated for Poulet Sauté à la Bordelaise (3191).

3399 Pigeonneaux en Casserole à la Paysanne

Cook the young pigeons with butter in an earthenware casserole and in the oven; when two-thirds cooked surround them with 50 g (2 oz) salt belly of pork cut in dice and blanched and 75 g (2½ oz) potatoes sliced and sautéed in butter, for each pigeon.

Complete the cooking in the oven and add a little good gravy just before serving.

3400 Pigeonneaux en Chartreuse

Decorate a buttered Charlotte mould in the same way as for Chartreuse de Ris de Veau (2641), then cover the bottom and sides with a thick layer of braised cabbage, previously drained and squeezed.

Fill the centre with the pigeons cooked *en Casserole* and cut in quarters and interspacing these pieces with small rectangles of blanched salt belly of pork and slices of smoked sausage. Cover with more cabbage then cook *au Bain-marie* in the oven for 30 minutes. Turn the Chartreuse over on to a dish, allow to stand for 5 minutes then remove the mould. Sponge up any liquid which has escaped and surround with a few spoonfuls of Sauce Demi-glace.

3401 Pigeonneaux Chipolata

Colour the young pigeons in butter; deglaze the pan with white wine, reduce and add equal quantities of Sauce Demi-glace and brown stock to barely cover the pigeons; complete the cooking of the pigeons in the sauce and a few minutes before serving add a Chipolata garnish (365).

Arrange the pigeons in a deep dish with the sauce and surround with the garnish.

3402 Pigeonneaux en Compote

Proceed as indicated for Poulet de Grains en Compote.

3403 Côtelettes de Pigeonneaux à la Nesles

Cut the young pigeons in half, leaving the lower legs attached to represent the cutlet bone. Flatten them slightly, season, shallow fry them on the inside only and allow to cool under light pressure. When cold, coat the fried sides dome shape with Godiveau made with cream and containing one-third its quantity of Gratin forcemeat C (295) and chopped truffle.

Arrange the halves of pigeon thus prepared on a tray and place in a moderate oven to complete the cooking of both the pigeons and forcemeat.

Arrange in a circle alternating with slices of calf's sweetbreads which have been floured, egg and breadcrumbed and shallow fried in clarified butter. Fill the centre with mushrooms and sliced chickens liver, sautéed in butter and mixed with a few tablespoons of Sauce Madère.

3404 Côtelettes de Pigeonneaux en Papillotes

Cut the young pigeons into two leaving the lower legs on; season and shallow fry them in butter. Enclose each half in a heart-shaped piece of oiled greaseproof paper between two slices of very lean ham and two layers of reduced Sauce Duxelles and proceed as indicated for Côte de Veau en Papillote (2529).

3405 Côtelettes de Pigeonneaux Sévigné

Cut the young pigeons in half, seal the outsides by frying in hot butter and place them under pressure until cold. Coat the inside part dome shape with a mixture of finely chopped cooked white of chicken, mushrooms and truffle mixed with reduced Sauce Allemande.

Flour, egg and breadcrumb and shallow fry them in clarified butter. Arrange overlapping in a circle, fill the centre with buttered asparagus tips and serve accompanied with a fairly thin Sauce Madère.

3406 Pigeonneaux Crapaudine

Cut the young pigeons horizontally from the point of the breast along the top of the legs and right up to the joints of the wings but without cutting right through. Open them out, lightly flatten, season, dip in butter and grill gently.

Arrange them when ready on a suitable dish, surround with a border of gherkins and serve accompanied with Sauce Diable.

3407 Pigeonneaux à l'Estouffade

Colour the young pigeons in butter and place them in an earthenware dish lined with lightly fried slices of streaky bacon. Surround with quarters of mushrooms sautéed in butter and browned button onions; add a few tablespoonfuls of veal stock and the juices of the pan deglazed with a little brandy.

Cover tightly with the lid and cook in a moderate oven for 45 minutes.

3408 Pigeonneaux Financière

Poêlé the young pigeons, cut them in half, arrange in a circle on a dish and place a Financière garnish in the centre.

3409 Pigeonneaux Gauthier au Beurre d'Ecrevisse

The word *Gauthier* does not indicate a particular species of pigeon but is the word once used to denote baby pigeons as taken from their nest.

Cut the young pigeons in half and place them in a shallow pan containing sufficient melted butter, lightly acidulated with lemon juice to nearly cover; cook them very slowly in this butter over a gentle heat. When cooked, drain and dry them, arrange in a circle on a dish and coat with Sauce Allemande, well flavoured with Crayfish Butter.

3410 Pigeonneaux à la Minute

Cut the young pigeons in quarters, flatten them lightly and season and shallow fry in butter. A few minutes before they are cooked, add a little finely chopped onion and parsley; continue cooking until the onions are also cooked then arrange the pieces of pigeon in a circle on a dish.

Deglaze the pan with a little brandy and lemon juice; add a few tablespoonfuls of meat glaze and a little butter then pour over the pieces of pigeon. Fill the centre with sliced mushrooms which have been sautéed in butter.

3411 Mousselines de Pigeonneaux à l'Epicurienne

Bone out the young pigeons reserving a few of the breasts for the garnishing of the Mousselines.

With the rest of the flesh prepare a Mousseline forcemeat. Mould into Mousselines about half the usual size of chicken ones and poach them in the usual manner.

At the last moment season and shallow fry the reserved breasts of pigeons in butter keeping them very slightly underdone.

Drain the Mousselines, arrange in a circle on a dish and place a nice slice of prepared breast on each. Coat with a sauce made from a *fumet* of the bones and trimmings of the birds thickened with a little Velouté; fill the centre with Petits Pois aux Laitue.

Note: The Mousseline forcemeat can be made with the breasts of old birds, the remainder being used for the making of the sauce. In this case the breasts required for garnishing the Mousselines could come from young Poêléed pigeons.

3412 Pigeonneaux aux Olives

Poêlé the young pigeons and when two-thirds cooked add the required amount of Sauce Demi-glace; allow the pigeons to simmer in this sauce for 10 minutes, then remove them.

Pass the sauce through a fine strainer, remove any fat, then replace the pigeons and sauce in a clean pan together with 10 small stoned and blanched olives per pigeon. Allow to cook gently together for a further 7–8 minutes.

Arrange the pigeons whole or cut in half on a dish and either surround with the olives or place them in the centre.

3413 Pigeonneaux aux Olives Noires

Cook 4 young pigeons *en Cocotte* basting them well with butter. A few minutes before they are cooked, add 3 tbs white wine, 1 tbs brandy and 60 stoned black olives. Finish at the last moment with a few tablespoonsful of reduced veal gravy and a little light chicken glaze.

Arrange for serving as in the preceding recipe.

3414 Pâté de Pigeonneaux à l'Anglaise—Pigeon Pie, English style

Line the inside of a pie dish with slices of smoked streaky bacon, sprinkled with chopped shallot; arrange inside, the pigeons cut in quarters, seasoned and sprinkled with chopped parsley and add two halves of hard-boiled egg yolk per pigeon. Moisten with sufficient good gravy to come halfway up, cover with a layer of puff paste, brush with eggwash and score with the point of a small knife to decorate. Make an opening in the top and bake in a fairly hot oven for approximately $1\frac{1}{2}$ hours.

3415 Pâté chaud de Pigeonneaux à l'Ancienne

Roast 4 young pigeons keeping them a little underdone; cut each into four pieces and remove the skin.

Line a buttered Timbale or Charlotte mould with good short pastry and fill with alternate layers of Gratin forcemeat A (286), mixed with a little well reduced Sauce Madère, the pieces of pigeon, cooked sliced mushrooms and slices of truffle. Finish with a layer of forcemeat, sprinkle the surface of this with a pinch of powdered thyme and bayleaf and close up the pie with a thin layer of short paste, sealing the edges well.

Bake in a moderate oven for approximately 50 minutes.

To serve: turn out the pie on to a dish, remove what is now the top, cut it into triangles and arrange these around the pie. Lightly coat the bared surface of the pie with a little thin Sauce Demi-glace and serve accompanied with a sauceboat of the same sauce.

3416 Pâté chaud de Pigeonneaux Périgord

Remove the breasts from 4 young pigeons and keep them on one side for later use.

Prepare a very fine smooth forcemeat with the rest of the flesh plus that from another whole pigeon, and 50 g (2 oz) fresh pork fat per 100 g ($3\frac{1}{2}$ oz) of pigeon flesh.

Remove the skins from the reserved breasts, flatten them fairly thin, coat with a layer of the forcemeat and roll them up as *Paupiettes* with an olive-shaped piece of truffle in the middle.

Line a round pie mould with good short paste and fill it with layers of the remaining forcemeat and the prepared *Paupiettes*.

Finish with a layer of forcemeat; close up the pie with a thin layer of the same paste and bake in a moderate oven for $1\frac{1}{4}$ hours.

On removing from the oven, turn out the pie on to a dish, remove what is now the top and cut into triangles as explained for Pâté chaud à l'Ancienne. Place these round the pie, coat the bared surface of forcemeat with a little Sauce Périgueux and serve accompanied with a sauceboat of the same sauce.

3417 Pigeonneaux aux Petits Pois
For each young pigeon, colour in butter 60 g (2 oz) salt belly of pork, cut in dice and blanched and 6 button onions. Remove and colour the pigeons in the same pan. Pour off the fat, deglaze the pan with a little stock and add sufficient Sauce Demi-glace plus $1\frac{1}{2}$ dl (5 fl oz or $\frac{5}{8}$ U.S. cup) peas, the bacon and onions, and a Bouquet garni. Cook very gently together until tender and serve as required in a deep dish.

3418 Pigeonneaux à la Polonaise
Stuff the young pigeons with Gratin-Forcemeat C (295) and cook them with butter in a pan and in the oven.

When ready, place in an earthenware terrine and lightly coat with good veal gravy; add a few drops of lemon juice and at the last moment sprinkle with some Beurre à la Polonaise.

3419 Pigeonneaux à la Printanière
Colour the young pigeons in butter, deglaze the pan with little veal gravy and add sufficient thin Sauce Demi-glace, a Bouquet garni and a variety of new season's vegetables. Finish cooking slowly together and serve the pigeons surrounded with the garnish of vegetables.

3420 Pigeonneaux Saint-Charles
Lard the breasts of the young pigeons with thin strips of ox tongue and braise them in the usual manner.

When ready, arrange in a dish and surround with small stuffed flap mushrooms; coat the pigeons with the braising liquid reduced to the consistency of a Demi-glace after removing the fat and finish with a few drops of lemon juice.

3421 Pigeons Ramiers en Salmis
Roast the pigeons until three-quarters cooked, remove the legs and breasts, trim them and remove the skin. Place the legs and breasts in a shallow pan with a little mushroom cooking liquor, 4 button mushrooms and 4 slices of truffle per pigeon; keep warm without boiling.

Prepare a Sauce Salmis from the chopped bones and skin, pass through a fine strainer over the pigeons and heat together without boiling.

Place the Salmis thus prepared in a deep dish and surround with small heart-shaped Croûtons of bread fried in clarified butter.

3422 Pigeonneaux au Sauternes
Poêlé the young pigeons.

Deglaze the pan with Sauternes wine allowing 1 dl ($3\frac{1}{2}$ fl oz or $\frac{1}{2}$ U.S. cup) per pigeon; reduce it by two-thirds, add a tablespoonful of light meat glaze per pigeon and pass through a fine strainer. Arrange the pigeons in a hot earthenware terrine, cover with the prepared sauce and serve as it is.

3423 Suprêmes de Pigeonneaux Diplomate
Remove the breasts of the pigeons, flatten them slightly and stiffen and lightly colour them in butter before placing under light pressure.

When cold, dip into Sauce Villeroy containing chopped Fines Herbes and chopped mushrooms; flour, egg and breadcrumb them and shallow fry when required.

Arrange in a circle on a dish and fill the centre with small Quenelles made from pigeon forcemeat and mushrooms and truffles trimmed olive shape; coat this garnish with a Sauce Demi-glace flavoured with pigeon essence.

3424 Suprêmes de Pigeonneaux Marigny
Remove the legs from the young pigeons.

Cover the breasts still attached to the carcase with slices of salt pork fat and Poêlé them taking care to keep them underdone. Remove the breasts from the carcase and discard the skin.

Mould a pyramid shape of a purée of fresh peas in the centre of a dish and surround with the Suprêmes. Coat these with Velouté containing an essence prepared from the remains of the pigeon and the cooking juices of the breasts.

3425 Suprêmes de Pigeonneaux Saint-Clair
Prepare a Mousseline forcemeat from the legs of the young pigeons; mould into Quenelles the size of small olives and poach them.

Place the breasts of the pigeons still attached to the carcase on a bed of finely sliced and blanched onions spread on the bottom of a shallow pan; add some butter, cover with the lid and Poêlé them keeping them underdone. Remove the breasts then add a little thin Velouté to the onions; pass this through a sieve and add the prepared Quenelles to this Soubise. Remove the breasts from the carcase and trim them after discarding the skin.

Place a pyramid of flap mushrooms sautéed in butter in the centre of a baked flan case; arrange the Suprêmes on this pyramid, coat them with the Soubise and surround with the Quenelles. Border the inside edge of the flan case with a *cordon* of meat glaze.

3426 Suprêmes de Pigeonneaux Verneuil
Cook 10 small young pigeons in butter; remove the breasts and after discarding the skins place the breasts in a pan with 200 g (7 oz) slices of peeled truffle; keep warm with a suitable amount of Sauce Demi-glace containing the cooking juices deglazed with a little Madeira.

Cook 1 tbs chopped onion in butter until golden in colour, add 250 g (9 oz) finely sliced, fresh white mushrooms, season with salt and pepper and cook rapidly until completely dry then add and mix in 2 dl (7 fl oz or $\frac{7}{8}$ U.S. cup) Sauce Béchamel.

Line 10 Barquette or oval-shaped moulds with puff paste, fill with the above mixture, smooth the surfaces level and bake them in a hot oven.

When cooked, arrange them on a suitable dish and place two of the prepared Suprêmes of pigeon on each; on top of these arrange a few of the slices of truffle lightly coated with its sauce.

Serve the rest of the sauce and slices of truffle separately.

Notes:
1) The Barquettes can be arranged around a hot Mousse of pigeon.
2) The Suprêmes may be accompanied with fresh buttered noodles.
3) This recipe can also be used for Suprêmes of partridge, woodcock, snipe, plover etc. remembering that 1 Suprême of partridge or woodcock per person is sufficient.

3427 Sauté de Pigeonneaux des Sylvains
Cut the young pigeons into 4 pieces, season them and cook in butter in an earthenware dish.

For each pigeon add 100 g ($3\frac{1}{2}$ oz) sautéed wild mushrooms such as *Cèpes, Chanterelles* or *Mousserons*, 1 leaf of sage and a sprig of wild thyme. Cover and allow to cook for 7–8 minutes. At the last moment, if the juices appear to be excessive, add a few breadcrumbs to partly absorb them.

Serve in the earthenware dish as it is.

3428 Timbale de Pigeonneaux La Fayette
1) Prepare a Timbale case (4334) in a mould which is wider than deep.

2) Cook 60 small crayfish together with a Mirepoix cooked in butter plus 3 dl ($\frac{1}{2}$ pt or $1\frac{1}{4}$ U.S. cups) white wine, 1 dl ($3\frac{1}{2}$ fl oz or $\frac{1}{2}$ U.S. cup) brandy, salt, pepper and a little red pepper. When cooked, shell the tails and keep them warm in the cooking liquid passed through a fine strainer together with 100 g ($3\frac{1}{2}$ oz) slices of truffle.

Finely pound the shells and trimmings of the crayfish together with 50 g (2 oz) butter; mix the resultant paste into 5 dl (18 fl oz or $2\frac{1}{4}$ U.S. cups) creamed Sauce Béchamel. Bring to the boil, pass through a fine strainer and keep warm.

3) At the same time, cook *en Casserole*, 10 small young pigeons which have been wrapped in thin slices of salt pork fat. When cooked, remove the fat, cut off the breasts, discard the skin and keep the breasts warm in the juices of the pan which have been deglazed with white wine and a few tablespoons of melted meat glaze; add a further 100 g ($3\frac{1}{2}$ oz) slices of truffle.

4) Cook 400 g (15 oz) short lengths of medium size macaroni in salted water, keeping it slightly firm; drain well and mix together with 100 g ($3\frac{1}{2}$ oz) butter, 150 g (5 oz) freshly grated Parmesan, a pinch of freshly milled pepper and one-third of the Sauce Béchamel flavoured with the Crayfish purée.

Add the second third of this sauce to the crayfish tails and the rest to the breasts of the pigeons.

Presentation and Service: Place two-thirds of the macaroni in the Timbale case and arrange half the crayfish on top. Cover them with more of the macaroni and on top of this arrange the breasts of pigeon in a circle, place in the centre of these the other half of the crayfish tails, cover with the remaining macaroni and decorate the surface with nice slices of truffle.

Note: This Timbale was created by the author for a dinner given by his friends on the occasion of his first voyage to New York.

3429 Pigeonneaux Valenciennes
Stuff the young pigeons with Gratin Forcemeat C (295) mixed with sliced sautéed chicken livers and mushrooms; truss them *en Entrée* and colour in butter.

Deglaze the pan with white wine, reduce by two-thirds and add sufficient good Bouillon to cover the birds and add a Bouquet garni; cook slowly until tender then glaze them at the last moment.

Arrange the pigeons, either whole or cut in half against the sides of a pyramid of Riz à la Valenciennes (4243) placed in the centre of a round dish. Place a heart-shaped slice of lean ham between each pigeon and surround with Tomato Sauce flavoured with the reduced cooking liquid.

3430 Pigeonneaux Villeroy
Cut the pigeons in half, flatten them slightly and remove as many of the bones as possible. Season and shallow fry them in butter, then allow to cool under slight pressure. When cold, dip into Sauce Villeroy, flour, egg and breadcrumb them and deep fry when required.

Arrange on a serviette on a dish, garnish with fried parsley and serve accompanied with Sauce Périgueux.

3431 Vol-au-Vent de Pigeonneaux
Remove the feet and winglets of the young pigeons, truss them and Poêlé until just cooked.

Cut each into four pieces and add to a Financière garnish (381) together with the deglazed juices from the pan. Fill into a large Vol-au-vent case and place on a serviette on a dish.

PIGEONNEAUX FROIDS—COLD YOUNG PIGEONS

3432 Côtelettes de Pigeonneaux en Chaud-froid
Bone out the young pigeons without removing the lower part of the legs. Stuff them with Gratin Forcemeat A (293) inserting a piece of foie gras and a few small quarters of truffles into the middle of the stuffing. Reshape to their original form, tie each in a piece of muslin and poach them in a good stock; allow to cool in the stock.

Drain and dry the pigeons, cut in half, straighten out the legs and coat them with brown Sauce Chaud-froid containing some of the reduced cooking liquid. Decorate with shapes of truffle and cooked egg white and arrange the cutlets of pigeon on a layer of jelly, set in a deep rectangular dish. Cover with cool melted jelly and allow to set.

Serve the dish presented on a block of sculpted ice, or surrounded with crushed ice.

3433 Pigeonneaux à la Gelée
Bone out the breasts of the young pigeons from inside and stuff them with a galantine forcemeat (298) containing chopped truffle. Truss them, wrap in slices of salt pork fat, and poach them; leave to cool in the stock. When cold arrange in a glass bowl or deep dish.

Add sufficient jelly to the stock, clarify it and when almost setting, pour it around the pigeons. Allow to set and serve on a block of sculpted ice.

3434 Medaillons de Pigeonneaux Laurette
Bone out the young pigeons and fill them with nice smooth Gratin Forcemeat A (293) containing diced red ox tongue, truffle and freshly skinned pistachio nuts. Roll up in the shape of nice round galantines of equal thickness; wrap and tie each in a piece of muslin and poach them in stock; allow to cool.

When cold, cut into $1\frac{1}{2}$ cm ($\frac{3}{5}$ in) thick rounds and coat with a fairly thin brown Sauce Chaud-froid; decorate each of these Medaillons with a rose-shape of halves of pistachio nuts with a small point of cooked eggwhite in its centre. Glaze with aspic jelly.

Arrange some chopped aspic jelly dome shape in the centre of a round dish and surround with the prepared Medaillons.

3435 Mousse de Pigeonneaux
Poêlé 4 young pigeons, allow them to cool and remove the breasts of 3 of them; discard the skin. Cut each breast in half, coat with brown Sauce Chaud-froid, decorate with small neat shapes of truffle and cooked egg white, and glaze with aspic jelly.

Make a cold Mousse from the remaining pigeon and any trimmings from the others, and place it to set in a silver timbale or deep dish. Arrange the pieces of pigeon on top and cover with very clear lightly setting aspic jelly.

To serve: present the dish set on a block of sculpted ice.

3436 PINTADE—GUINEA FOWL

Guinea fowl are far from having the gastronomic value of pheasants, nevertheless they are frequently used to replace pheasant as a roast when the close season deprives the table of this excellent member of the chicken family.

Nearly all the recipes for pheasant are suitable for guinea fowl but those which are particularly applicable are: à la Bohémienne, à la Choucroute and en Salmis; see the appropriate recipes in the section on pheasants.

3437 Pintade en Chartreuse
Lard the guinea fowl with strips of salt pork fat, brown it in butter then braise it with cabbage, salt belly of pork and smoked sausage.

Cut the bird into even-sized pieces and build up the Chartreuse in the same way as for Chartreuse de Pigeonneaux.

OIE—GOOSE

The goose's main merit from a culinary standpoint is that it provides the most delicate, the most firm and the most perfect foie gras of all. Apart from this the goose is really only used in ordinary household or bourgeois cookery and even then, it must be a young bird at the gosling stage or just coming to the age of maturity.

3438 Oie à l'Alsacienne
Stuff the goose with good sausage meat, brown it in butter then Poêlé in the usual way.

Present on a dish surrounded with braised sauerkraut cooked with the fat from the goose, and slices of lean streaky bacon that has been cooked in with the sauerkraut.

3439 Oie à l'Anglaise—Roast Goose, English Style
Prepare the following stuffing: bake 1 kg ($2\frac{1}{4}$ lb) unpeeled onions until soft, peel them when cold, then chop them and add to the same amount of soaked and squeezed breadcrumbs together with 50 g (2 oz) fresh or dried chopped sage, 10 g ($\frac{1}{3}$ oz) salt and a pinch of pepper and nutmeg.

Stuff the goose, truss it and roast in the oven or on a spit. Arrange the goose on a dish and surround with a gravy made from the roasting juices and left slightly fatty.

Serve accompanied with a sauceboat of slightly sweetened apple sauce.

3440 Oie à la Bordelaise
Prepare a stuffing from 1 kg ($2\frac{1}{4}$ lb) sliced flap mushrooms à la Bordelaise, 125 g ($4\frac{1}{2}$ oz) soaked and squeezed breadcrumbs, 125 g ($4\frac{1}{2}$ oz) small stoned olives, 100 g ($3\frac{1}{2}$ oz) Anchovy Butter, the chopped liver from the goose, $\frac{1}{2}$ tbs chopped parsley, a touch of crushed garlic, 1 egg and salt and pepper. Stuff the goose, wrap it in thin slices of salt pork fat and either roast on a spit or in the oven.

Place on a dish and serve accompanied with a gravy made from the roasting juices.

3441 Oie Chipolata
The goose may be cooked either whole or cut into portions in exactly the same way as for Dindonneau Chipolata (3389).

3442 Oie en Civet
Keep the blood of the goose when it is killed; immediately add the juice of a lemon and whisk it gently until cold so as to prevent it from coagulating.

Cut the goose into pieces and continue in exactly the same way as for Civet de Lièvre (3556).

3443 Oie en Confit or Confit d'Oie
Since this preparation has been mentioned in several recipes elsewhere in this book, it is felt necessary to give details of its preparation.

Select very fat geese so as to expect at least $1\frac{1}{4}$ kg (3 lb 6 oz) of fat from each. Clean them and cut each into 6 pieces being the 2 legs, 2 pieces of breast and 2 of carcase.

Rub the pieces with coarse salt mixed with a touch of mixed spice and a little powdered thyme and bayleaf; place in deep dishes, cover with more salt and leave for 24 hours.

The next day, melt in a suitable pan all of the fat removed from the pieces of the geese and the intestines. Wash off the pieces of geese, dry them well and place to slowly cook in the fat for approximately $2\frac{1}{2}$ hours keeping them slightly firm in keeping with their ultimate uses.

Place each 6 pieces of geese into a glazed earthenware pot which has been sterilized in boiling water, and cover with the cooking fat. Leave to set, then cover the goosefat with a 1 cm ($\frac{2}{5}$ in) thick layer of melted lard. When this is set, cover with a round of strong paper and tie down firmly.

3444 Oie à la Flamande
Braise the goose and at the same time prepare a Flamande garnish (382).

Place the goose on a dish, surround with the garnish and coat with the reduced braising liquid.

3445 Oie Farcie aux Marrons—Roast Goose with Chestnut Stuffing
This is prepared in the same way as Dindonneau Farci aux Marrons (3394).

3446 Oie braisée aux Navets—Braised Goose with Turnips
Proceed as indicated for Canard aux Navets (3458).

3447 Oie au Raifort
Braise the goose, arrange on a dish surrounded with buttered noodles or Riz au Gras (4236) and sprinkle this garnish with the reduced braising liquid.

Serve accompanied with a sauceboat of creamed Horseradish Sauce.

3448 Oie à la Mode de Vise
Select a goose which has not yet begun to lay eggs and poach it in White Bouillon together with its giblets and 2 heads of garlic.

When cooked, cut it into portions, arrange in a shallow pan, sprinkle well with goose fat and leave to steep until required for service.

Make a thick Velouté with the cooking liquid from the goose and equal amounts of goose fat and flour; allow to simmer gently, skimming as necessary for 1 hour then thicken it with 4 egg yolks; pass through a fine strainer and bring back to its normal consistency with cream. Finish the sauce with a heaped spoonful of garlic cooked in milk and made into a purée.

Add the drained and dried pieces of goose to the sauce and serve arranged in a timbale or deep dish.

3449 Oie en Daube (*Cold*)
Proceed as indicated in the recipe for Dindonneau en Daube (3397) taking account of the size of the bird in calculating the cooking time.

3450 CANARDS AND CANETONS—DUCKS AND DUCKLINGS

There are three types of ducks used in cookery: the Nantes, the Rouen and the various kinds of wild duck, the last being used mainly for roasting and for Salmis.

Rouen ducks are also roasted rather than being used as Entrées, the main feature of their preparation being that they should be cooked underdone so that only rarely would they be braised. As is well known, the Rouen duck is not bled like other poultry but is killed by being suffocated.

A Nantes duck which is similar to the Aylesbury, being less plump than a Rouen is usually braised, Poêléed or roasted.

NANTES DUCKLINGS

3451 Ballottines de Caneton
Bone out the duckling and remove the skin reserving it for later use; remove any sinew from the flesh. Finely chop the flesh together with the same weight of fresh pork fat, half its weight of leg of veal and one-third its weight of panada. Pound the whole together with 15 g ($\frac{1}{2}$ oz) salt, a pinch of pepper and a little grated nutmeg. Add 4 egg yolks, pass through a fine sieve and mix this together with 100 g ($3\frac{1}{2}$ oz) each of Gratin Forcemeat C (295) made with foie gras, and chopped mushrooms sautéed in butter.

Divide this mixture into 60 g (2 oz) pieces and wrap each first in a piece of the skin from the duck then tie up in a piece of muslin. Place them in a shallow pan, cover with stock made from the duck bones and poach gently. When cooked, remove the muslin and glaze the Ballottines.

Arrange the Ballottines in a circle on a dish and place a suitable garnish in the centre such as turnips, peas, olives, sauerkraut etc.

3452 Caneton farci à la Bordelaise
This is prepared in the same way as Oie à la Bordelaise taking into account the difference in size of the bird when calculating the quantity of ingredients.

3453 Caneton Chipolata
Braise the ducklings; add the necessary quantity of Sauce Demi-glace to the reduced braising liquid together with a Chipolata garnish (365). Allow to cook gently together for several minutes then arrange the duckling on a dish surrounded with the garnish.

3454 Caneton à la Choucroute
Prepare an egg-sized piece of butter mixed with some chopped shallots and parsley; insert this inside the duckling.

Brown the duckling in the oven and then place it in a braising pan on a bed of sliced vegetables and herbs; moisten with 2 parts veal stock and 1 part white wine to just cover and braise it until tender.

At the same time, braise 1 kg ($2\frac{1}{4}$ lb) sauerkraut with a 250 g (9 oz) piece of streaky bacon; when three-quarters cooked, drain it and finish its cooking with 2 dl (7 fl oz or $\frac{7}{8}$ U.S. cup) veal gravy and 1 dl ($3\frac{1}{2}$ fl oz or $\frac{1}{2}$ U.S. cup) white wine. Cook until all the liquid is completely reduced.

Place the duckling on a dish, surround with the sauerkraut and on top of this arrange a border of the bacon cut into rectangles.

Serve separately the reduced cooking liquid from the duck thickened with Sauce Demi-glace.

As an alternative the duckling may be presented as follows: Arrange the sauerkraut as a border on a dish and surround with the bacon cut in rectangles; cut the duck in portions, place in the centre of the sauerkraut and coat with the reduced braising liquid thickened with Sauce Demi-glace.

3455 Caneton à la Lyonnaise
Braise the duckling and make the braising liquid into Sauce Demi-glace. Arrange the duckling on a dish and surround with alternate bouquets of glazed button onions and chestnuts which have been cooked in Bouillon.

3456 Caneton Poêlé à la Menthe
Insert 30 g (1 oz) of butter mixed with a pinch of chopped mint inside the duckling and Poêlé it.

Deglaze the pan with 1 dl ($3\frac{1}{2}$ fl oz or $\frac{1}{2}$ U.S. cup) clear veal gravy and a little lemon juice, pass through a fine strainer and add a pinch of chopped mint. Place the duckling on a dish and pour the sauce over.

3457 Caneton Molière

Bone out the duckling and stuff it with 400 g (15 oz) Gratin Forcemeat C (295) made with foie gras and mixed with 300 g (11 oz) very fine sausage meat; arrange two lines of small truffles in the middle of the thickest part of the stuffing. Reshape the duckling, sew it up and tie in a cloth as for a galantine; cook in a stock made from the bones of the duckling.

Pass the rest of the stock through a fine strainer, remove the fat and reduce; glaze the duckling with this at the last moment.

After removing the thread from the bird, place it on a dish and coat with the prepared sauce.

3458 Caneton braisé aux Navets—Braised Duckling with Turnips

Colour the duckling in butter and remove it from the pan; drain off the butter and deglaze the pan with white wine. Reduce well then add 3 dl (½ pt or 1¼ U.S. cups) each of Sauce Espagnole and Brown Bouillon and a Bouquet garni; replace the duckling and braise gently.

Use the same butter to colour 400 g (15 oz) elongated olive-shaped pieces of turnip, adding a good pinch of sugar to glaze them. Also half cook 20 button onions in butter.

When the duckling is half cooked, transfer it to a clean pan, surround with the turnips and onions and pass the cooking liquid through a fine strainer over the whole; complete the cooking in the oven.

Present the duckling on a dish surrounded by the turnips and onions.

3459 Caneton aux Olives—Braised Duckling with Olives

Braise the duckling in the same way as Caneton braisé aux Navets keeping the sauce succulent and to a minimum. A few minutes before serving, add 250 g (9 oz) blanched stoned olives.

Glaze the duckling at the last moment and arrange on a dish surrounded with the olives and sauce.

3460 Caneton braisé à l'Orange—Braised Duckling with Orange

This recipe should not be mistaken for the one for roast duckling served with orange, as the two are totally different. Instead of ordinary oranges, Bigarade or bitter oranges may be used but in this case the segments should not be used as a garnish because of their bitterness; only their juice should be used for the sauce.

Brown the duckling in butter and braise it slowly in 4 dl (14 fl oz or 1¾ U.S. cups) Sauce Espagnole and 2 dl (7 fl oz or ⅞ U.S. cup) brown stock until it is tender enough to cut with a spoon.

Remove the duckling from the cooking liquid when ready; remove all fat and reduce until very thick. Pass through a fine strainer and add the juice of 2 oranges and half a lemon to bring the sauce back to its original consistency.

Complete this sauce with the zest of half an orange and half a lemon, both cut in fine Julienne and well blanched and drained. Take care not to boil the sauce after adding the juice and the Julienne of zest.

Glaze the duckling at the last moment, place it on a dish, surround with a little of the sauce and border with segments of orange completely free of skin and pith. Serve the rest of the sauce separately.

3461 Pâté chaud de Caneton—Hot Duck Pie

Roast the duckling, keeping it very underdone; after removing the skin, cut the breasts into very thin slices.

Line a buttered Charlotte mould with short paste and coat this with a layer of Gratin Forcemeat A (293) mixed with 2 dl (7 fl oz or ⅞ U.S. cup) very well reduced Sauce Demi-glace per 1 kg (2¼ lb) forcemeat.

Now fill the mould with alternate layers of first the sliced duckling, then sliced cooked mushrooms, slices of truffle and forcemeat; finish with a layer of forcemeat.

Sprinkle this last layer with a pinch of powdered thyme and bayleaf and close up the pie with a thin layer of paste sealing well to the edges; make an opening in the middle for the steam to escape during cooking. Bake in a moderate oven for 1 hour.

On removing the pie from the oven, turn it out on to a dish, remove what is now the top and cut this into triangles; arrange these around the base of the pie. Coat the exposed forcemeat on top with a little Sauce Madère and place a large grooved mushroom in the centre surrounded with overlapping slices of truffle.

Serve accompanied with Sauce Madère.

3462 Caneton aux Petits Pois—Duckling with Green Peas

Fry and brown in butter 15 button onions and 200 g (7 oz) salt belly of pork cut in large dice and blanched. Remove these, colour the duckling in the same fat then drain off the fat.

Deglaze the pan with a little white stock then add 3 dl (½ pt or 1¼ U.S. cups) thin Sauce Demi-glace, 450 g (1 lb) fresh peas, 1 Bouquet garni and the pork and onions. Cook gently together.

When ready, place the duckling in a dish and cover with the peas. Reduce the sauce as necessary and serve it separately.

3463 Suprême de Caneton

Suprêmes of duckling are prepared and cooked in the same way as Suprêmes of chicken. However, because of the difference between them and the recipes adopted, the sauce should be changed; only brown sauces made from duck stock or sauces finished with duck *Fumet* are suitable.

The following recipes, which can be found in the section on Suprêmes of Chicken are the most suitable: Agnès Sorel, Chimay, Ecossaise, Maréchal, Périgueux, Vert-pré.

3464 Timbale de Caneton Mirabeau

Stone sufficient olives to line a Charlotte mould and stuff them with chicken forcemeat; poach them, drain and allow to cool.

Use these olives to line a thickly buttered Charlotte mould arranging them in concentric circles on the bottom and in superimposed lines on the sides.

Cover them carefully with a thickish layer of duck forcemeat then fill the inside with a mixture of thin slices of underdone roast duckling, mushrooms and truffles, bound with fairly thick cold Sauce Salmis. Finish with a layer of forcemeat and cook the Timbale *au Bain-marie*. When cooked, allow to rest for a few minutes to settle.

Turn out on to a dish and surround it with a *cordon* of Sauce Salmis.

Note: The name of this Timbale is derived from the lining of olives and is not used exclusively for duck; it may be filled with pigeons or lamb or calf's sweetbreads etc. but altering naturally, the forcemeat and garnish in keeping with the main ingredient being used.

3465 ROUEN DUCKLING

Except where it is to be served cold *à la Cuiller* (3483), Rouen ducklings are not braised; they should be Poêléed or roasted and always kept underdone.

If a stuffing is required this may be prepared as in the following recipe.

3466 Stuffing for Rouen Duckling

Fry together until lightly coloured 125 g (4½ oz) fresh fat pork and 60 g (2 oz) chopped onion, then add 250 g (9 oz) sliced duck livers, a pinch of chopped parsley and season with a little salt, pepper, and mixed spice. Keep the liver underdone by simply sealing the outside, then allow the whole to cool. Pound in a mortar and pass through a fine sieve.

3467 Aiguillettes de Rouennais à la Bigarade

Poêlé the duckling keeping it very underdone allowing only 20 minutes for a medium size one of 2–2¼ kg (4½–4¾ lb) in weight; remove the breasts, cut each lengthways into 10 thin slices and place them on a warm dish.

Add a little veal gravy to the cooking pan, bring to the boil, pass through a fine strainer and remove all the fat; finish as for a clear Sauce Bigarade (27).

Coat the slices of duck with a little of this sauce and serve the rest separately.

Note: Aiguillettes de Rouennais à l'Orange is prepared in the same way as in this recipe except that the duck is served surrounded with segments of orange completely free of skin and pith.

3468 Aiguillettes de Rouennais aux Truffes

Poêlé the duckling keeping it very underdone.

Add 1 dl (3½ fl oz or ½ U.S. cup) Chambertin wine to the pan and in this cook 5 medium-sized peeled truffles; remove the truffles when cooked. Reduce the cooking liquid, remove all of the fat, pass through a fine strainer and add to a fairly light Sauce Rouennaise.

Cut the breasts of the duckling into long thin slices and arrange them on a warm dish alternating with slices of the truffles. Lightly coat with the prepared sauce and serve the rest separately.

3469 Caneton Rouennais aux Cerises

Poêlé or braise the duckling.

Prepare a sauce from the cooking liquid plus some good Sauce Demi-glace.

Cut the breasts of the duckling in long thin slices, arrange them on a warm dish and coat with the sauce.

Serve accompanied with a dish of cherries prepared in the following manner: Place ½ dl (2 fl oz or ¼ U.S. cup) Port wine in a pan together with the juice of 1 orange, 1 tsp of English mixed spice and ½ tsp grated orange zest; reduce by half.

Add 3 tbs redcurrant jelly and when this is melted add 200 g (7 oz) stoned cherries poached in a light syrup.

Note: If English mixed spice is unobtainable use ground cinnamon mixed with a little ground cloves.

3470 Caneton Rouennais au Champagne

Poêlé the duck keeping it underdone.

Add 3 dl (½ pt or 1¼ U.S. cups) dry Champagne to the pan. Reduce, remove the fat, add 1 dl (3½ fl oz or ½ U.S. cup) Jus lié and pass through a fine strainer.

Place the duckling on a dish and serve accompanied with the prepared sauce.

3471 Caneton Rouennais en Chemise

Bone out the breast of the duckling from inside

and stuff it with a stuffing for Rouen duckling (3466); truss *en Entrée*.

Wrap the bird in a piece of clean cloth and tie up as for a galantine. Poach very gently for approximately 45 minutes in a very well flavoured brown stock.

For service, remove the cloth in which the duckling was poached and replace it with a clean fringed serviette to give it the appearance of being clothed in a shirt.

Place the duckling thus prepared on a dish and surround with segments of peeled orange free from skin and pith and serve accompanied with Sauce Rouennaise.

3472 Caneton Rouennais à la Dodine au Chambertin

Roast the duckling keeping it very underdone. Remove the two breasts and keep covered for later use.

Remove the legs (these are not served but should be utilized for something else); discard the parson's nose then pound the carcase.

In a pan place 3 dl ($\frac{1}{2}$ pt or $1\frac{1}{4}$ U.S. cups) Chambertin wine, $\frac{1}{2}$ dl (2 fl oz or $\frac{1}{4}$ U.S. cup) brandy, 30 g (1 oz) chopped shallots, a pinch of coarsely ground pepper; a touch of grated nutmeg and 1 bayleaf. Reduce quickly by two-thirds on a very hot stove.

Now add the pounded carcase and 3 dl ($\frac{1}{2}$ pt or $1\frac{1}{4}$ U.S. cups) Sauce Demi-glace made with veal stock and allow to simmer gently for 15 minutes.

Pass firmly with pressure through a fine strainer, reboil for a few minutes and finish away from the heat with 60 g (2 oz) butter.

For service cut the reserved breasts into 3 or 4 pieces and place them in a timbale or deep dish; add a garnish of fresh mushrooms sautéed in butter and slices of truffle both carefully mixed together with a few spoonfuls of meat glaze and a spoonful of butter.

Cover the whole with the prepared sauce and serve accompanied with a dish of fresh noodles tossed in brown butter.

3473 Escalopes, Fillets and Suprêmes of Rouen Duckling

Remove the Suprêmes in the same way as for chicken and cut each into 2 or 3 slices according to the size of the bird. Flatten them slightly, trim them then arrange in a well buttered shallow pan, cover with buttered paper and cook them dry in the oven keeping underdone.

Note: Although Aiguillettes are more suitable, the main reason for the existence of these escalopes is the need to vary menus; the garnishes used for the Aiguillettes are all suitable.

3474 Mousses and Mousselines of Rouen Duckling

These are made in the same way and in the same proportions as Mousses and Mousselines of chicken; however, the only suitable sauces to serve with them are Sauce Rouennaise and Sauce Bigarade and the only suitable garnishes are orange segments, cherries and purées or creams of vegetables.

3475 Caneton Rouennais au Porto

Roast the duckling *en Casserole* keeping it underdone.

Deglaze the pan with $1\frac{1}{2}$ dl (5 fl oz or $\frac{5}{8}$ U.S. cup) Port wine, reduce by half, remove the fat, pass through a fine strainer then add to $2\frac{1}{2}$ dl (9 fl oz or $1\frac{1}{8}$ U.S. cups) duck gravy thickened with arrowroot.

Serve the duckling accompanied with the sauce.

3476 Caneton Rouennais à la Presse

Roast the duckling for 20 minutes and send it to the table immediately, where it is finished as follows:

Remove the legs and keep for another use, cut the breasts into thin slices and arrange them overlapping on a warm dish; season them.

Chop up the carcase and press it, sprinkling with some good red wine. Add a little brandy to this juice and sprinkle it over the sliced duck; reheat the dish thoroughly over the chafing lamp without allowing it to boil and serve immediately.

3477 Caneton farci à la Rouennaise

Stuff the duckling with stuffing for Rouen duckling (3466) and roast it in a hot oven for 25–30 minutes according to size. Serve accompanied with Sauce Rouennaise.

If serving the duckling cut into portions, remove the legs and cut slits on the inside parts, season with salt and pepper and grill them.

Cut off the breast in thin slices and arrange on both sides of a long dish, place the stuffing in the centre and a grilled leg at each end of the dish. Chop the carcase roughly and press it adding a little brandy and a squeeze of lemon juice; add these juices to some Sauce Rouennaise and lightly coat the pieces of duck with it. Serve the remainder of the sauce separately.

3478 Salmis de Caneton à la Rouennaise

Remove the wishbone from the duckling and truss it. Roast in a red hot oven for only 8 minutes allowing four minutes on each side.

If possible, allow to cool for a few minutes so as

to make it easier to carve; wipe carefully with a cloth in case it has been blackened by the cooking.

Remove the legs, incise the inside part with a few shallow cuts and grill them. Sprinkle a buttered long dish with chopped shallot, crushed coarse salt, coarsely ground pepper, grated nutmeg and a little mixed spice. Arrange the breasts of the duck each cut into approximately 15 very thin slices on top and sprinkle with more of the same mixture but without the shallot.

Cut off the stumps of the wings and the skin at the end of the breast, season and grill these; chop the remainder of the carcase and press it together with half a glass of red wine. Pour this juice over the sliced duckling.

When ready to serve, dot the surface with butter and heat the dish on top of the stove before placing it in a very hot oven or under a salamander so that it glazes instantaneously.

When the slices start to curl at the edges, remove from the heat, arrange the grilled legs and other pieces of duck around the slices and serve immediately.

3479 Soufflé de Caneton Rouennais

Poêlé the duckling keeping it underdone.

Remove the breasts and keep them warm. Cut off the top of the carcase with a pair of scissors leaving the bottom in the form of a container.

Make a Mousseline forcemeat with the liver of the duck plus the flesh of another half duck, 100 g (3½ oz) raw foie gras and 1 egg white. Fill the empty cascase with this forcemeat shaping it to its original form. Tie a strip of buttered greaseproof paper around to keep it in shape, place in a small pan, cover with a lid and cook in a warm oven for 20 minutes. With some of the same forcemeat mixed with an equal amount of foie gras purée, fill sufficient tartlet cases and cook them at the same time as the soufflé.

Place the duckling at the last moment on a dish, surround with the tartlets each with a slice of the reserved breasts on top. Serve accompanied with Sauce Rouennaise.

CANETONS FROIDS—COLD DUCKLING

3480 Aiguillettes de Caneton à l'Ecarlate

Poêlé a duckling until it is just cooked and allow to cool in the pan.

Remove the breasts and skin them, then cut into thin slices. Coat with brown Sauce Chaud-froid, decorate with truffle and glaze with aspic jelly.

Cut the same number of slices of ox tongue of the same size and shape of the slices of duckling; glaze these also with jelly.

Make a Mousse with the legs and trimmings and mould it in a deep rectangular dish. When set, cover it with alternate slices of duck and tongue and cover the whole with clear aspic jelly.

3481 Aiguillettes de Caneton Saint-Albin

Poêlé a duckling, remove the breasts and skin them, then cut into thin slices.

Coat each with Gratin Forcemeat C (295) mixed with an equal quantity of foie gras, sufficient jelly to set it and a small glassful of flamed brandy. When set, coat them with brown Sauce Chaud-froid and decorate with a mosaic pattern using cooked egg white, very red ox tongue and blanched orange zest.

Line a dome-shaped mould with aspic jelly, decorate the bottom with truffle and arrange the slices of duckling around the side standing them up with the pointed end downwards. Fill the centre with duck Mousse made from the legs and trimmings of the duckling and allow to set. Turn out on to a round base set on a dish and surround with cut shapes of jelly. Insert a decorative silver skewer garnished with glazed truffles in graduated sizes, in the top of the Mousse.

3482 Caneton glacé aux Cerises, also called Caneton Montmorency—Cold Duckling with Cherries

Roast the duckling keeping it underdone.

When completely cold, remove the breasts and cut off the bones on top so as to form a container of the carcase. Cut each breast into 8 thin slices, coat with brown Sauce Chaud-froid and decorate them with truffle.

Fill the carcase with a Mousse made from the trimmings of the duckling, some foie gras and the ducks' liver, moulding it to the former shape of the duckling. Glaze with aspic jelly and allow to set.

When quite firm, arrange the prepared slices of duckling on top.

Place the bird thus prepared, in a deep rectangular dish, surround with cold stoned cherries previously cooked in red wine, and coat with duck-flavoured aspic jelly.

3483 Caneton à la Cuiller

Braise the duckling in a Madeira-flavoured stock making sure that it is well cooked.

Place it in a terrine just large enough to hold it and well cover with the braising liquid, passed through a clean cloth and to which a sufficient quantity of aspic jelly has been added. Allow to cool.

To serve: remove all of the fat from the surface as indicated for Terrine de Poularde, and present the terrine on a serviette on a dish.

3484 Caneton Lambertye
This is prepared in the same way as Poularde Lambertye using duck Mousse instead of chicken Mousse and coating the slices of duckling with brown Sauce Chaud-froid.

3485 Caneton glacé aux Mandarines, also known as Caneton à la Japonaise—Cold Duckling with Tangerines
Poêlé a Rouen duckling and allow it to become cold in the pan.

When cold, trim the underside of the duckling flat then glaze it with jelly; place on a low base of bread or rice set on an oval dish.

Surround with emptied tangerines filled with a Mousse made from the duck's liver and foie gras, alternating them with small moulds of aspic jelly, combined with the juices from the cooking and the juice from the flesh of the emptied tangerines. The last are best moulded in small dariole moulds.

3486 Mousse de Caneton Rouennais
This is made and moulded in the same way as Mousse of chicken but using duck as the main ingredient.

3487 Caneton à la Sevillane
Bone out the inside of the duckling and stuff it with a forcemeat made with 100 g (3½ oz) each of Gratin Forcemeat C (295), diced raw foie gras and Mousseline forcemeat all mixed together with 1 dl (3½ fl oz or ½ U.S. cup) reduced tomato purée. Truss the duckling, wrap it in a piece of cloth and poach in a good stock for 1 hour; when cooked, tighten the string and allow to become cold in the liquid.

Unwrap the duckling, remove the breasts, cut them into long thin slices and arrange them back on the forcemeat. Glaze with sherry-flavoured aspic jelly and place it in an oval bowl or deep rectangular dish the bottom of which is coated with a layer of set jelly. Surround the bird with large stoned Spanish olives filled with foie gras purée and half cover these with more jelly.

3488 Soufflé froid de Caneton à l'Orange
This is made in the same way as Caneton glacé aux Cerises (3482) except that the breasts are used for making the Mousse instead of being coated with Sauce Chaud-froid.

Place the duckling in a square dish on a layer of jelly, surround with orange segments free of skin and pith, and glaze with aspic jelly flavoured with Bigarade orange juice and ½ dl (2 fl oz or ¼ U.S. cup) Curaçao per 1 litre (1¾ pt or 4½ U.S. cups) of jelly.

3489 Terrine de Caneton à la Gelée
Prepare a stuffing as follows: In a pan melt 100 g (3½ oz) finely chopped pork fat then add 50 g (2 oz) butter and allow to become very hot. Place in this fat, 250 g (9 oz) duck livers seasoned with salt and pepper and sprinkled with a little chopped onion and a pinch of powdered thyme and bayleaf. Sauté them very quickly and just sufficiently to seal their outside surfaces. Allow to become cool then pass through a fine sieve.

Bone out completely the inside of a Rouen duckling; remove the parson's nose but leave the legs untouched.

Stuff it with the prepared stuffing and place in a terrine just large enough to hold it. Sprinkle with ½ dl (2 fl oz or ¼ U.S. cup) brandy, cover with a thin slice of salt pork fat, cover with the lid and cook *au Bain-marie* in the oven for 40 minutes.

Meanwhile, prepare 4 dl (14 fl oz or 1¾ U.S. cups) excellent aspic jelly from the bones of the duckling and some strong veal stock.

On removing the duckling from the oven cover it in the terrine with the prepared jelly and allow to become cold and set.

To serve: remove the fat from the surface with boiling water as explained for Terrine de Poularde and present the terrine on a serviette placed on an oval dish.

3490 Timbale de Caneton Voisin
Roast the duckling keeping it underdone and when cold remove the breasts.

Prepare a Sauce Salmis with the carcase and add sufficient jelly to allow it to set like a Sauce Chaud-froid.

Cut the breasts into slices, coat with the Sauce Salmis and allow to set.

Set a layer of the same sauce in the bottom of a Timbale case (4334), fill with alternate layers of the coated slices of duckling and slices of truffle, covering each layer with a thin layer of jelly until the Timbale is full; finish with a slightly thicker layer of jelly.

Keep cold in the refrigerator until required for service.

Note: This is an old recipe which makes an excellent cold Entrée; it is actually a cold Salmis and the method of preparation can be applied to all kinds of game birds which are suitable for preparing as a Salmis.

It is the most simple and certainly the best way of serving them cold.

FOIE GRAS

HOT PREPARATIONS OF FOIE GRAS

3491 To Cook and Present Foie gras
For serving as a hot dish the goose liver should

firstly be well trimmed and the nerves removed; it is then studded with quarters of small raw peeled truffles which have been seasoned with salt and pepper, quickly set and stiffened over heat with a little brandy together with a bay-leaf. Before using the truffles leave them to cool in a tightly closed terrine.

After the foie gras has been studded, wrap it completely in thin slices of salt pork fat or pig's caul, and place in a tightly closed terrine for a few hours.

The best method for preparing a hot whole foie gras is to cook it as follows, using a pastry that will absorb the excess fat as and when it melts.

Cut out two oval layers of Pie Paste (3775) slightly larger than the foie gras; place the foie gras on one of the ovals and surround it with medium-sized peeled truffles. Place half a bayleaf on top, moisten the edges of this paste, cover with the other oval of paste and seal the edges well together decorating the edges. Brush with eggwash, decorate by scoring with the point of a small knife and make a hole in the top for the steam to escape whilst cooking.

Bake in a fairly hot oven for 40–45 minutes for a liver weighing from 750–800 g (1 lb 10 oz).

Serve as it is accompanied with the selected garnish.

To serve: in restaurants the head waiter cuts around the top of the pie crust and removes it. He then cuts portions of the foie gras with a spoon and places each portion on a plate with some of the garnish as indicated on the menu.

Notes:

1) The method of cooking foie gras in an earthenware terrine for serving hot is not necessarily the best; the above recipe is deemed to be preferable, whichever garnish is going to be served with the foie gras.

2) A garnish of noodles, lasagne, macaroni or rice cannot be too highly recommended for serving with hot foie gras; these should be cooked in boiling salted water in the usual way then finished with cream. This kind of accompaniment makes the liver taste better and facilitates digestion.

Apart from the pastas indicated above, the best garnishes are whole or sliced truffles or a Financière garnish.

As regards the brown sauces, Sauce Madère is most suitable providing it is very delicate and not too strongly flavoured with Madeira; a light veal or chicken glaze finished with butter and some sherry or old port, is even better.

Sauce Hongroise with paprika or a very good Sauce Suprême may also be served, provided the sauce is in keeping with the garnish.

Generally speaking, goose liver is best for use in hot preparations whereas duck livers are used for preserved liver and for cold dishes.

3492 Foie Gras en Caisses

Cut equal amounts of foie gras and truffle into large dice; mix together with some well flavoured Sauce Madère and fill two-thirds of the way up into buttered or oiled paper cases which have been previously dried out in the oven. At the last moment, shallow fry some slices of raw foie gras of the same size as the case, place one in each with a slice of truffle on top and lightly coat with a little well reduced Sauce Demi-glace.

3493 Foie gras en Cocotte

Stud a firm foie gras with truffles and leave for 12 hours.

Set and seal the surfaces in hot butter and place immediately into a very hot earthenware cocotte. Deglaze the pan with truffle essence and white wine, add sufficient veal gravy to produce 1 dl ($3\frac{1}{2}$ fl oz or $\frac{1}{2}$ U.S. cup) and pass this through a fine strainer over the foie gras. Place the lid on the cocotte, seal it with a strip of flour and water paste and cook in a slow oven for approximately 1 hour.

Serve the dish as it is accompanied with a Sauce Madère flavoured with truffle essence.

3494 Côtelettes, Croquettes and Cromesquis of Foie gras

The mixture for these is prepared in the same way as for chicken Croquettes but using foie gras as the main ingredient; they are cooked in the same way as chicken cutlets and Croquettes.

3495 Foie gras cooked in a Brioche known as Foie gras à la Strasbourgeoise

Stud the liver with truffles and place it in a tightly closed terrine for several hours, as stated in the introduction to this section on foie gras. Wrap it in thin slices of salt pork fat and cook in a moderate oven for 20 minutes. Allow to cool.

Line a buttered straight-sided mould large enough to contain the foie gras, with a thick lining of unsweetened Ordinary Brioche Paste.

Place in the foie gras which should almost fill the mould; cover with a layer of the same paste and make a hole in the centre. Tie a band of buttered paper around the top part of the mould so as to keep the pie in shape when it begins to prove and leave in a warm place. When it has proved, bake it in a moderately hot oven; remove it when a trussing needle inserted in the centre comes out clean.

Serve it as it comes from the oven with any of the garnishes suitable for foie gras, but usually this preparation is served cold.

A variation of this recipe is to trim the partly cooked foie gras to the shape of a ball, place it in the centre of a sheet of unsweetened Brioche Paste with the trimmings of foie gras around it. Close and seal it up like a purse then place in a fluted Brioche mould; inset a round ball of the same paste in the top to give the appearance of a normal Brioche with a head and leave to prove for 15 minutes in a warm place. Brush with eggwash and bake in a hot oven.

3496 Escalopes de Foie gras Périgueux
From a raw foie gras cut slices, each of approximately 70 g (2½ oz) in weight; season with salt and pepper then coat with beaten egg and finely chopped raw truffle, patting this on with the blade of a knife. Shallow fry in butter at the last moment.

Arrange the escalopes in a circle on a dish and pour in the middle some Sauce Madère flavoured with truffle essence.

3497 Escalopes de Foie gras Ravignan
Roll out a sheet of unsweetened Brioche Paste 7–8 mm (⅓ in) thick and cut out 20 rounds with a 7 cm (3 in) diameter plain pastry cutter.

Arrange 10 of these rounds on a tray and fill the centre of them with a layer of chicken forcemeat leaving a space around the edges of the paste.

On the forcemeat place a slice of truffle then a round of foie gras, another slice of truffle and finally, another layer of the forcemeat. Cover with the other rounds of paste. Seal the edges together using the back of a pastry cutter, brush with eggwash and bake in a hot oven.

Serve accompanied with Sauce Périgueux.

3498 Escalopes de Foie gras Talleyrand
Prepare: 1) a lightly baked 16 cm (7½ in) diameter flan case, 2) sufficient macaroni prepared as for Talleyrand garnish (461) and 3) 10 oval slices of foie gras, seasoned, floured and shallow fried in butter.

Arrange the slices of foie gras in a circle in the flan case alternating with large slices of truffle and place the macaroni dome shape in the middle; sprinkle with grated cheese and gratinate quickly in the oven.

When ready, arrange on a serviette on a dish and serve with Jus lié or buttered light chicken glaze which has been flavoured with truffle essence.

3499 Foie gras Financière
Stud a firm foie gras with truffles, season and wrap it in thin slices of salt pork fat. Place on a bed of vegetables and herbs in a pan just large enough to hold it and moisten with Madeira. Cover with the lid and cook in a moderate oven for 45 minutes basting it frequently.

When ready to serve, remove the pieces of fat, place the foie gras on a dish and surround it with a Financière garnish to which has been added the reduced braising liquid after first removing the fat and passing through a fine strainer.

3500 Mignonettes de Foie gras
Mix well together two parts of cooked truffled foie gras crushed with a fork and one part of chicken Mousseline forcemeat; mould into small round flat cakes and flour, egg and breadcrumb using fine white breadcrumbs; shallow fry gently in clarified butter, arrange in a circle on a dish and garnish to choice with asparagus tips, peas, noodles, spaghetti, or a Toulousaine garnish.

3501 Foie gras au Paprika
Well season a foie gras with paprika and wrap it in thin slices of salt pork fat.

Braise with Madeira and when cooked, place it in a hot oval dish. Pass the braising liquid through a fine strainer, remove the fat, reduce well and add to a little Sauce Hongroise.

Coat the foie gras with a little of this sauce and serve the rest separately.

3502 Foie gras Périgord
Stud a very firm foie gras with truffles, season and place it in a terrine with 1 bayleaf, 12 medium-sized peeled truffles and ½ dl (2 fl oz or ¼ U.S. cup) brandy. Allow to marinate for 6 hours then wrap the foie gras in thin slices of salt pork fat.

Braise the foie gras with Madeira until it is three-quarters cooked then remove the slices of fat; place the liver into an oval dish and arrange the marinated truffles around it. Moisten with 1 dl (3½ fl oz or ½ U.S. cup) good Jus lié and the strained, skimmed and reduced braising liquid. Cover with the lid, seal with a band of flour and water paste and finish cooking in a moderate oven for 20 minutes.

3503 Foie gras à la Sainte-Alliance
Place a nice foie gras in an earthenware terrine, season and surround it with large peeled truffles. Moisten with dry Champagne, cover and cook gently until tender.

Serve as it is from the terrine.

3504 Soufflé de Foie gras
Pass through a fine sieve 300 g (10 oz) raw foie gras, 100 g (3½ oz) raw truffle and 300 g (10 oz) raw chicken flesh which has been finely pounded and mixed with 3 egg whites.

Mix these ingredients together in a shallow pan on ice adding 3 dl (½ [illegible] or 1¼ U.S. cups) fresh double cream a little at a time, then fold in 4 stiffly beaten egg whites.

Pour into a buttered soufflé mould and cook covered, *au Bain-marie* in the oven for 30–35 minutes.

Serve accompanied with Sauce Madère flavoured with truffle essence.

Another way of preparing this soufflé is to pass 300 g (10 oz) of parfait of foie gras through a sieve, add 1 dl (3½ fl oz or ½ U.S. cup) creamy Sauce Béchamel and 100 g (3½ oz) sliced truffle.

Season well and fold in 5 stiffly beaten egg whites, pour into a buttered soufflé mould and cook *au Bain-marie* in a moderate oven.

Serve accompanied with the same sauce as before.

3505 Subrics de Foie gras
See Hot Hors-d'oeuvre (1262).

3506 Timbale de Foie gras à l'Alsacienne
Prepare a pale-baked Timbale case (4334) moulded in a deep round fancy pie mould.

Cover the bottom and sides with a layer of Gratin Forcemeat C (295) containing a quarter its volume of foie gras purée; keep warm in the entrance to the oven.

For service, fill the Timbale with small slices of foie gras poached in Madeira, slices of truffle and slices of cooked mushroom, all mixed together carefully with Sauce Madère. Decorate the top with a large grooved mushroom surrounded by a circle of overlapping slices of truffle.

The Timbale de Foie gras à l'Alsacienne may also be prepared in the following manner: Fill the case with alternate layers of creamed noodles, slices of foie gras, shallow fried in butter, slices of truffle and slices of cooked mushroom. Finish with a layer of noodles and at the last moment sprinkle these with raw noodles which have been sautéed in butter.

3507 Timbale de Foie gras Cambacérès
Line a well buttered dome-shaped mould with rings of large cooked macaroni kept a little firm. These rings should be ½ cm (⅕ in) thick and filled with a purée of truffle bound with a little chicken forcemeat. When the mould has been lined cover the lining with a layer of chicken forcemeat mixed with truffle purée; place in a warm oven for a few minutes to cook the forcemeat.

To 2 dl (7 fl oz or ⅞ U.S. cup) Sauce Béchamel, add 3 tbs each of chicken essence and truffle essence. Reduce by half and mix in 250 g (9 oz) of cooked macaroni cut in 3 cm (1⅕ in) lengths, and about 4 tbs mixed purée of truffle trimmings and foie gras.

Fill the mould with alternate layers of the macaroni, slices of foie gras cooked in Madeira and slices of truffle. Finish with a layer of the chicken and truffle forcemeat. Cook *au Bain-marie* in the oven allowing 45 minutes for a 1 litre (1¾ pt or 4½ U.S. cups) capacity mould.

When cooked, allow the mould to rest for a few minutes then turn it as a Timbale on to a round dish; surround with a *cordon* of Sauce Périgueux.

Serve accompanied with a sauceboat of the same sauce.

3508 Timbale de Foie gras Cussy
Prepare a lightly baked pastry case moulded in a shallow round mould with sloping sides.

Coat the bottom and sides with a layer of chicken forcemeat and place in a warm oven to cook the forcemeat.

Arrange alternate round slices of foie gras sautéed in butter and ox tongue around the inside and fill the centre dome shape with a mixture of cooked mushrooms, cocks' kidneys and small turned truffles all mixed together with Sauce Madère. Place a circle of nice cockscombs between the slices of foie gras and the filling.

Serve accompanied with Sauce Madère.

3509 Tourte de Foie gras à l'Ancienne
Cut a raw foie gras into even-sized slices, season them and marinate in brandy together with an equal number of slices of truffle.

Pass the trimmings of the foie gras through a sieve then mix it together with 100 g (3½ oz) chopped truffle and 600 g (1 lb 5 oz) good quality sausage meat.

Place half of this forcemeat mixture on a round sheet of Pie Paste leaving a 4 cm (1⅗ in) wide space around the edge. Arrange the slices of foie gras and truffle on top, cover with the rest of the forcemeat and smooth the surface. Cover with a second sheet of the same paste.

Seal the edges together, moisten the top edge of the covering paste and surround with a band of puff paste. Knotch the edge of the paste to form a decoration, brush with beaten egg and bake for 45 minutes in a moderate oven.

On removing from the oven, detach the top layer of pie pastry by cutting round the inside edge of the puff pastry; coat the exposed filling of the Tourte with a little fairly thick Sauce Madère.

3510 Foie gras Truffé au Madère
Make 12 incisions in a nice firm foie gras and in each one, insert a piece of truffle cut on the slant; make sure that they are pushed well into the foie gras.

Wrap the foie gras in very thin slices of salt pork fat then place it in a pan on a layer of sliced carrots, onions and shallots plus some mushroom trimmings and a Bouquet garni; the pan should be just large enough to hold the liver.

Moisten just to cover with 2 parts veal stock and 1 part Madeira. Cover and cook gently in the oven for 40 minutes.

When ready, remove and drain the liver, discard the slices of fat then place the liver on a dish, cover it and keep warm. Pass the cooking liquid through a fine strainer, remove the fat and reduce by two-thirds. Add 2 dl (7 fl oz or $\frac{7}{8}$ U.S. cup) Sauce Demi-glace and reduce again until the sauce becomes quite thick. Bring back the sauce to its normal consistency by adding the required amount of Madeira away from the heat.

Replace the foie gras in this sauce and keep on the side of the stove for 7–8 minutes but without allowing it to boil.

Place the foie gras in a dish, coat with a little of the sauce and serve the rest separately.

PREPARATIONS OF COLD FOIE GRAS

3511 Aspic de Foie gras

Line a plain or fancy funnel mould with aspic jelly and decorate it with truffle and cooked eggwhite.

Fill with alternate layers of well trimmed rectangular slices of cooked foie gras arranged in rows or slightly overlapping, and aspic jelly. Finish with a layer of jelly, allow to set and demould in the usual manner to serve.

Instead of being cut in slices, the foie gras may be neatly cut out with a spoon in the shape of shells.

3512 Foie gras du Gastronome

Cut a Parfait of foie gras into small, rectangular slices; coat half of them with white Sauce Chaud-froid and decorate the others with neat shapes of truffle fixing them with a little cool melted jelly.

Line a large egg-shaped mould with jelly then cover this with the two kinds of slices of foie gras, alternating them. Finish filling the mould with a Mousse of foie gras and place in the refrigerator for 2 hours.

Demould on to a slightly hollowed out base placed on a dish and fashioned to the form of a nest with piped butter, using a small plain piping tube.

Surround with neat cut shapes of aspic jelly.

A variation of this preparation is as follows: Trim a Parfait of foie gras into the shape of an egg, completely coat it with a pink paprika-flavoured Sauce Chaud-froid, decorate to choice and glaze with aspic jelly.

Prepare a cushion-shaped Croûton of fried bread of a size proportionate to that of the simulated egg and coat this with a Sauce Chaud-froid of a different colour. Imitate the cords of the cushion using softened butter in a piping bag fitted with a small plain tube.

Place on a dish and set the decorated egg of foie gras on top; surround with nice truffles, which have been cooked with Madeira and then glazed with jelly.

3513 Foie gras au Paprika

Trim a nice raw foie gras, season it with salt and sprinkle with a teaspoon of paprika; sprinkle the bottom of a pan with 1 sliced large Spanish onion and a bayleaf and place the foie gras on top; cover and cook in a moderate oven for 30 minutes.

Place the foie gras in an oval terrine, after carefully removing all of the onion and bayleaf, then strain the fat over it. Fill the terrine with melted jelly and allow to set.

Note:
In Vienna where this dish is served as an Hors-d'oeuvre with baked potatoes, the onion is not discarded; the liver is left to cool in the same dish in which it was cooked, together with the fat. This information has been provided by Madame Katinka.

3514 Escalopes de Foie gras Maréchal

From a terrine of very firm foie gras cut the required number of slices and trim them oval shape. Make a Mousse with the trimmings and use this to cover the slices, smoothing the surface dome shape. Coat them with Sauce Chaud-froid, decorate with a slice of truffle and glaze with aspic jelly.

Mould some purée of foie gras into small balls the size of a cherry and press a piece of truffle into the centre of each to represent the stone; coat with reddish-brown Sauce Chaud-froid and glaze with aspic jelly.

Arrange the slices of foie gras around a circular base set on a cold dish and arrange the cherry-shaped balls of foie gras in a pyramid on top of the base. Border the dish with cut shapes of aspic jelly.

3515 Mousse de Foie gras

For the preparation and moulding of this Mousse see in the Chapter on Garnishes (332).

3516 Mousselines de Foie gras

These are prepared from the same mixture as that for Mousses. They are moulded in egg shape or Quenelle moulds or others of the same type. According to requirements they are then simply glazed with jelly or coated with Sauce Chaud-froid (332).

3517 Pain de Foie gras
Line a Charlotte mould with jelly, decorate with truffle and fill with alternate layers of Mousse of foie gras and slices of foie gras braised with Madeira; finish with a layer of Mousse. Keep in the refrigerator until required then demould on to a dish and surround with neat cut shapes of jelly.

3518 Pain de Foie gras en Belle-vue
Line a Charlotte mould with paper and fill it with a Mousse of foie gras.

Line a larger Charlotte mould with jelly and decorate with truffle and cooked egg white. Turn out the Mousse, remove the paper and very carefully place it into the second mould without disturbing the decoration. Fill with jelly and allow to set.

Turn out when required on to a small base or a dish and surround with cut shapes of jelly.

3519 Parfait de Foie gras
This is best bought from one of the firms specializing in its production. No matter how much care is given, it is difficult to produce the same result in the kitchen.

3520 Pavé de Foie gras Lucullus
Set a 1 cm ($\frac{2}{5}$ in) thick layer of aspic jelly in the bottom of a deep square timbale. On this jelly spread a $1\frac{1}{2}$ cm ($\frac{3}{5}$ in) thick layer of foie gras purée mixed with a quarter its amount of jelly.

When this purée is set, arrange on top slices of foie gras and 5–6 slices of truffle; cover with a layer of foie gras purée and continue to fill the mould with alternate layers of foie gras, slices of truffle and purée; finish with a layer of jelly.

Place in the refrigerator until required then set the timbale on a block of ice sculpted to the shape of a flagstone.

3521 Timbale de Foie gras et de Cailles Tzarine
Line a fairly deep pie mould with ordinary short paste and cover this completely with thin slices of salt pork fat.

Season a nice raw foie gras and place it standing up in the centre of the prepared mould; surround with quails each stuffed with a piece of truffle, arranging them so that they are also standing up and their breasts are outwards towards the sides of the mould.

Finish filling the mould with whole raw peeled truffles, then cover with a round slice of salt pork fat. Close up the mould with a layer of the same paste, seal the edges well, make a hole in the top for the steam to escape and bake in a moderate oven for $1\frac{1}{4}$ hours.

On removing from the oven, fill the Timbale with a Madeira-flavoured veal stock which should be sufficiently gelatinous to set as a jelly. Keep in the refrigerator for 1–2 days before serving.

CHAPTER 9

RELEVES AND ENTREES OF GAME

FURRED GAME

The Red deer, Fallow deer, Isard and Chamois together with the Roebuck, form that class of venison popularly esteemed and used in France.

As all the recipes are equally suitable for the above mentioned class of venison it is deemed unnecessary to give details for each of them. Thus the following recipes will refer to the Roebuck (Fr. *Chevreuil*) only.

The marinating of venison is optional but it is better to dispense with it altogether if the flesh is from a young animal and thus tender in consequence. The preparation of suitable marinades will be found in the section on Marinades and Brines. Bear in mind the calculation of time necessary for marinading and above all the tenderness of the flesh, especially that of the Roebuck.

CHEVREUIL—ROEBUCK

3522 Civet de Chevreuil
For this preparation the shoulder, neck, middle neck and breast of the animal are used.

Cut the meat into pieces and marinate for at least 6 hours in advance with the red wine to be used for the Civet and the vegetables and flavourings of an ordinary marinade.

When about to prepare the Civet, drain and dry the pieces, and colour them quickly in butter over a very hot stove. Then proceed in exactly the same way as for Civet de Lièvre (3556) not omitting the final thickening with blood without which this Civet would just be a stew. Taking into account the almost impossible task of obtaining the blood from the roebuck, it is permissible to thicken the Civet with hare's blood or failing that, with rabbit's blood.

3523 CUTLETS AND NOISETTES

The cutlets and Noisettes are prepared and trimmed in the same way as those of lamb and the following recipes are applicable to both. Allow usually two pieces per person.

Shallow fry them quickly in very hot oil, drain them then arrange in a circle on a dish alternating with thin heart-shaped or round Croûtons of bread fried in clarified butter, unless of course, the recipe requires some other particular type of preparation.

3524 Côtelettes de Chevreuil Beauval
Season and shallow fry the cutlets in very hot oil and arrange in a circle, each on a small flat round shape of Pommes Berny (4177) which has been floured, egg and breadcrumbed and deep fried. On each cutlet place a grilled mushroom filled with a rosette of thick Sauce Soubise piped with a star tube.

Serve accompanied with a Sauce Crème flavoured with juniper berries.

3525 Côtelettes de Chevreuil aux Cerises
Season and shallow fry the cutlets quickly in very hot oil, keeping them underdone. Arrange in a circle alternating with heart-shaped Croûtons of stale gingerbread (Pain d'Epices), lightly coloured in butter. Fill the centre with poached cherries and coat with a light Sauce Venaison.

3526 Côtelettes de Chevreuil Conti
Season and shallow fry the cutlets quickly in very hot oil. Drain them and arrange on a dish alternating with slices of cooked ox tongue cut in long heart-shapes.

Deglaze the pan with a little white wine and add this to some thin Sauce Poivrade. Coat the cutlets with this sauce and serve accompanied with a dish of buttered purée of lentils.

3527 Côtelettes de Chevreuil Diane
Spread an even layer of game forcemeat on a buttered tray approximately 1 cm ($\frac{2}{5}$ in) thick and cook in a slow oven. When cooked, cut into triangles of roughly the same size as the cutlets.

Season and shallow fry the cutlets quickly in

very hot oil and arrange them in a circle alternating with the prepared triangles of forcemeat.

Coat the whole with Sauce Diane and serve accompanied with a dish of chestnut purée.

3528 Côtelettes de Chevreuil au Genièvre
Season and shallow fry the cutlets in very hot oil and arrange them over-lapping in a circle alternating with heart-shaped Croûtons of bread fried in clarified butter. Deglaze the pan with $\frac{1}{4}$ dl (1 fl oz or $\frac{1}{4}$ U.S. cup) flamed gin, add 1 powdered juniper berry and 1 dl ($3\frac{1}{2}$ fl oz or $\frac{1}{2}$ U.S. cup) double cream and reduce by half.

Finish with a few drops of lemon juice and a few tablespoons of thick Sauce Poivrade, then pour this sauce over the cutlets.

Serve accompanied with a sauceboat of hot, lightly sweetened Apple Sauce.

3529 Côtelettes de Chevreuil à la Minute
Season and sprinkle the cutlets with a little very finely chopped onion and shallow fry them quickly in very little hot oil; arrange in a circle on a dish. Deglaze the pan with a little brandy, add $\frac{1}{2}$ dl (2 fl oz or $\frac{1}{4}$ U.S. cup) Sauce Poivrade and finish with a few drops of lemon juice and 50 g (2 oz) butter.

Coat the cutlets with this sauce and fill the centre of the dish with sliced mushrooms sautéed in butter.

3530 Côtelettes de Chevreuil, Sauce Poivrade
Season and shallow fry the cutlets quickly in very hot oil. Drain them and arrange overlapping in a circle, alternating with thin heart-shaped Croûtons of bread fried in clarified butter.

Coat the whole with Sauce Poivrade and serve accompanied with a dish of chestnut purée or celeriac purée.

Note: The chestnut purée indicated in certain of the recipes may be replaced with a purée of sweet potatoes.

3531 Côtelettes de Chevreuil aux Truffes
Season and shallow fry the cutlets in clarified butter and arrange them overlapping in a circle. Deglaze the pan with truffle essence, add the required amount of Sauce Madère, coat the cutlets with this sauce and place 4 slices of truffle on each cutlet.

3532 Côtelettes de Chevreuil Villeneuve
Season and shallow fry the cutlets quickly in butter just sufficient to colour and set the surfaces. Allow to cool under light pressure.

Coat the cutlets on one side with a cold Salpicon of game and smooth dome shape. Wrap each in a triangle of pig's caul and place on a tray. Sprinkle with melted butter and cook in a hot oven for 7–8 minutes.

Arrange overlapping in a circle and serve accompanied with a well-reduced cullis of game containing a fine Julienne of truffle.

3533 Noisettes de Chevreuil Romanoff
Cut as many thick slices of cucumber as there are noisettes. Hollow them out on one side and stew gently with a little butter. When cooked, fill them with a stiff purée of mushrooms.

Season and shallow fry the noisettes quickly in very hot oil and arrange them in a circle each on one of the prepared pieces of cucumber.

Fill the centre of the dish with a garnish of Cèpes à la Crème and serve accompanied with a Sauce Poivrade.

3534 Noisettes de Chevreuil Valencia
Season and shallow fry the noisettes quickly in very hot oil and arrange in a circle, each on a round Croûton of Brioche fried in clarified butter. Lightly coat with Sauce Bigarade and surround with small segments of orange free from all pith and skin.

Serve accompanied with a Sauce Bigarade.

3535 CUISSOT—LEG

The leg should be carefully trimmed and cleared of all sinew then finely larded with strips of salt pork fat. Either marinate or not according to the quality of the flesh then roast in the usual manner.

All of the sauces and garnishes as indicated further on for the saddle or haunch of roebuck are suitable.

FILETS MIGNONS—FILLET

3536 Filets Mignons de Chevreuil au Genièvre
Trim the fillets, lard them and roast quickly. Place on a long dish, coat with the same sauce as for the cutlets of the same name (3528) and serve accompanied with a dish of hot, lightly sweetened Apple Sauce.

3537 Timbale de Filets de Chevreuil à la Napolitaine

Note: The term *Filet* in this recipe refers to the strips of flesh lying along and on top of both sides of the saddle i.e. the loins.

Trim the loins then cut them into fairly thick slices. Finely lard these with salt pork fat and marinate in cooked White Wine Marinade for a few hours.

When ready, braise them with a little veal stock and the marinade and glaze them at the last moment with some of the reduced cooking liquid.

Blanch some macaroni in water then finish cooking it in White Bouillon. Drain well and mix with some grated Parmesan, fresh butter, tomato purée, game glaze and a little of the reduced braising liquid from the slices of fillet.

Have prepared a lightly baked shallow Timbale case (4334) and almost fill it with the prepared macaroni. Arrange the glazed slices of fillets overlapping in a circle on top.

3538 Filets Mignons de Chevreuil, Sauce Venaison

Trim the fillets and finely lard them with salt pork fat. Season and shallow fry in butter, arrange them on a dish and coat with Sauce Venaison.

Serve accompanied with a dish of chestnut purée or purée of celery.

3539 SELLE—SADDLE

The saddle is that part of the carcase lying between the legs and the ribs; in short the two unseparated loins. Sometimes it is made larger by leaving the two best ends attached but in this case making sure that the ends of these rib bones are cut short so as to allow the whole joint to sit nicely for cooking and presentation.

In either case, the joint should be cut to a point following a diagonal line on either side from the end of the loin where it joins the leg, to the root of the tail.

The saddle should be trimmed of all sinew and larded with salt pork fat.

3540 Selle de Chevreuil Briand

Prepare and marinate the saddle for 12 hours.

When required, remove from the marinade, dry the surfaces well and roast in a hot oven, placed on the vegetables from the marinade scattered over the bottom of the roasting tray.

When cooked, place the saddle on a dish and arrange at each end, a garnish of pears cooked in red wine flavoured with cinnamon, zest of lemon and a little sugar.

Add 2 dl (7 fl oz or $\frac{7}{8}$ U.S. cup) game stock to the roasting tray, simmer very gently for 10 minutes then pass through a fine strainer, remove the fat and thicken lightly with arrowroot.

Serve the saddle accompanied with the thickened gravy and redcurrant jelly.

3541 Selle de Chevreuil aux Cerises

Prepare the saddle and place in a marinade made with verjuice instead of vinegar, for 12 hours.

Roast it on the spit, basting with the marinade and keeping it pink and underdone.

Place on a dish and serve accompanied with either Sauce Poivrade, Sauce Venaison or Sauce aux Cerises. See Caneton Rouennais aux Cerises (3469).

3542 Selle de Chevreuil Cherville

Prepare the saddle without marinating and spit roast it. Hollow out the required number of pippin apples so as to form cases. Slice the removed apple, cook it in the oven, mash to a pulp and refill the apple cases with it.

When the saddle is cooked, place it on a dish and surround with the apples.

Serve accompanied with a Sauce Groseilles flavoured with grated horseradish.

3543 Selle de Chevreuil à la Crème

Prepare and marinate the saddle for 2 to 3 days in a raw marinade.

When ready, remove from the marinade, dry the surfaces well and roast in a hot oven, placed on the vegetables from the marinade scattered over the bottom of the roasting tray. Remove the saddle as soon as it is cooked and deglaze the tray with a little of the liquid from the marinade. Almost completely reduce this, remove any fat, then add 3 dl ($\frac{1}{2}$ pt or $1\frac{1}{4}$ U.S. cups) cream and 1 finely crushed juniper berry; reduce again by one-third. Finish with a little melted meat glaze and pass through a fine strainer.

Serve the saddle accompanied with this sauce.

3544 Selle de Chevreuil à la Créole

Marinate the saddle for a few hours only and roast it on the spit, basting frequently with the marinade.

When the saddle is cooked, place it on a long dish and surround with bananas sautéed in butter.

Serve accompanied with a Sauce Robert Escoffier containing one-third its volume of lightly buttered Sauce Poivrade.

3545 Selle de Chevreuil au Genièvre

Lard the saddle and roast it in the usual manner. Prepare the sauce as indicated for the preparation of Côtelettes de Chevreuil au Genièvre.

Serve the saddle accompanied with this sauce and also a dish of Apple Sauce.

3546 Selle de Chevreuil Grand-Veneur (*Scottish method*)

Marinate the saddle for two hours with white wine and flavourings of vegetables and herbs. When ready, dry it well, cover with slices of bacon fat and roast it in the usual manner.

Cover the bottom of the service dish with Sauce Poivrade, place the saddle on top and surround it with Croquette potatoes moulded ball shape.

Serve accompanied with 1) a Sauce Venaison, 2) a dish of chestnut purée and 3) a dish of freshly cooked French beans.

3547 Saddle of Roebuck with Various Sauces
The saddle, being larded, marinated or not, and roasted, may be accompanied with any of the following sauces: Diane, Grand-Veneur, Moscovite, Poivrade, Venaison, etc.

3548 SANGLIER AND MARCASSIN—WILD BOAR

In France the young boar of up to the age of 6 months is referred to as a Marcassin and its flesh is highly esteemed, whereas the term Sanglier is reserved in general for the wild boar when it has become fully mature. In this case its flesh is little used in the kitchen except perhaps for the legs, which in any case should be subjected to the action of a very strong marinade before cooking.

Noisettes, cutlets, loins and quarters of young wild boar may be prepared in any of the ways applicable to roebuck; the best-end and saddle may be roasted whole.

3549 Côtelettes de Marcassin à la Flamande
These are prepared in the same way as for Côtes de Porc à la Flamande.

3550 Côtelettes de Marcassin Saint-Hubert
Season and shallow fry the cutlets on one side only and allow them to cool under light pressure.

Coat the cooked sides with a layer of fine forcemeat prepared from 800 g ($1\frac{3}{4}$ lb) fat flesh of young boar, 200 g (7 oz) Mousserons lightly fried in butter, 2 finely powdered juniper berries and the usual seasonings for forcemeats. Wrap the prepared cutlets in pig's caul, place them on a tray, sprinkle with melted butter and dry white breadcrumbs and complete their cooking in the oven.

Arrange the cooked cutlets on a dish and serve accompanied with 1) a Sauce Venaison and 2) an unsweetened Apple Sauce.

3551 Côtelettes de Marcassin à la Romaine
Season and shallow fry the cutlets. Arrange overlapping in a circle on a dish and coat with Sauce Romaine.

Serve accompanied with a purée of either chestnuts, celery or lentils.

3552 Côtelettes de Marcassin Saint-Marc
Lard the cutlets with fine strips of salt ox tongue and braise them.

Arrange them in a circle on a dish and in the middle, place a mound of small Croquettes of chestnuts, moulded ball shape.

Serve accompanied with 1) the reduced braising liquid after first removing all the fat and passing through a fine strainer and 2) a sauceboat of Cranberry Sauce.

3553 Cuissot de Marcassin à la Mode de Tours
Keep the leg for 5 to 6 days in a cooked marinade in which the ordinary white wine has been replaced by a white Touraine wine.

When ready, well dry the leg and place it in a braising pan with 250 g (9 oz) salt belly of pork cut in cubes. Place in a hot oven and when the meat has stiffened and become firm, season with salt and add 6 chopped tomatoes and the marinade. Cover and complete the cooking gently.

When cooked, place the leg on the service dish. Remove the fat from the cooking liquid, reduce if necessary, then pass through a fine strainer. Pour a little of this over the leg. To the remaining cooking liquid add a garnish of stoned prunes which have been cooked in lightly sweetened red wine and flavoured with a little orange and lemon zest. Serve this separately with the leg.

3554 Jambon de Marcassin—Ham of Wild Boar
This is salted and smoked in the same way as ordinary ham and is generally braised. It is served with a purée of peas, turnips, celery, chestnuts or some other garnish and is accompanied with the braising liquid made into a light but well flavoured Sauce Poivrade.

In northern countries it is frequently served with a sauce called *à l'Aigre-doux* which is also used for hare and rabbit. The recipe for this follows.

3555 Jambon de Marcassin à l'Aigre-Doux
Braise the ham in the usual manner.

With the braising liquid, prepare a Sauce Romaine (76) and to this sauce add some pickled cherries, some cooked and stoned prunes and a little chocolate dissolved with water, added at the last moment.

This type of garnished sauce is also popularly used in the central regions of Italy where it has, however, an extra addition of chopped pine kernels and chopped, candied orange and citron peel.

LIEVRE AND LEVRAUT—
HARE AND LEVERETS

Excepting for its use in the preparation of terrines, pâtés and various forcemeats, the flesh of old hares is not very highly esteemed. The leveret or young hare of up to 1 year old is the most suitable for all purposes; its weight rarely exceeds 3 kilos ($6\frac{3}{4}$ lb). The ears of the young hare are very fragile and the ease with which they can be torn can be a good guide to its age.

3556 Civet de Lièvre

Skin and empty the hare taking care to collect all of its blood in so doing. Place the liver on one side after immediately removing the gall bladder and any parts of the liver with which it has been in contact.

Cut up the hare and place the pieces in a basin with a few tablespoons of brandy and olive oil, a little salt and pepper and 1 onion cut in thin rings. Allow to marinate for 2 to 3 hours.

Fry in butter, 200 g (7 oz) salt belly of pork cut in large dice and blanched; remove from the butter as soon as it is coloured. In the same butter, fry and brown 2 medium-sized onions cut in quarters, add 2 tbs flour and cook gently as a Roux to a light brown colour. Place the pieces of hare in with the Roux after having dried them well and move continuously with a wooden spoon until they have stiffened.

Moisten with sufficient good red wine to just cover, add a Bouquet garni containing 1 clove of garlic and cover and cook gently on the side of the stove.

Some little while before serving, mix a little of the sauce from the hare with the reserved blood then add it to the civet along with the liver cut in small slices. Reheat gradually then transfer the pieces of hare and the liver to a clean pan along with the fried pieces of salt pork, 20 small glazed onions and 20 small cooked mushrooms.

Pass the sauce through a fine strainer over the whole. For service, place into a hot timbale or deep dish and surround with heart-shaped Croûtons of bread fried in clarified butter.

3557 Civet de Lièvre à la Flamande

Prepare and cut the hare as for the ordinary Civet, season and fry the pieces in butter until stiffened and coloured. Sprinkle with 30 g (1 oz) flour and cook together for a few minutes. Moisten with 1 litre ($1\frac{3}{4}$ pt or $4\frac{1}{2}$ U.S. cups) red wine and the liver which has been pounded, passed through a fine sieve and mixed with 2 dl (7 fl oz or $\frac{7}{8}$ U.S. cup) vinegar.

Season with salt and pepper and add 30 g (1 oz) brown sugar, a Bouquet garni and a little later, 500 g (1 lb 2 oz) sliced onion, cooked in butter. Cook gently on the side of the stove.

As soon as the hare is just cooked, tip the whole on to a sieve. Transfer the pieces of hare to a clean pan then pass the sauce and onions through the sieve. Pour this sauce over the pieces of hare and reheat thoroughly.

To serve: place into a timbale or deep dish and surround with heart-shaped Croûtons of bread fried in clarified butter and coated on one side with redcurrant jelly.

Note: This Civet should have a distinct sweet-sour taste.

3558 Civet de Lièvre de la Mère Jean

Prepare a young hare and cut it into pieces as for the ordinary Civet.

Place the pieces into a basin with a little salt and freshly milled pepper, a few tablespoons of Armagnac and a bottle of good red wine. Allow to marinate for 24 hours. Reserve the blood and liver for later use taking care that it does not coagulate.

Fry and colour in olive oil, 150 g (5 oz) salt belly of pork cut in large cubes, sprinkle with 3 tbs flour and cook together till lightly coloured. Add the pieces of hare after well drying them and stir together until the pieces have stiffened. Now add the marinade, a Bouquet garni containing 1 clove of garlic and 750 g (1 lb 10 oz) sliced onion cooked in butter.

Cover and cook gently on the side of the stove and when cooked transfer the pieces of hare to a clean pan. Add the blood and the liver cut in thick slices to the sauce and when the liver is cooked add it to the pieces of hare.

Pass the sauce through a fine strainer and pour it over the hare and liver. Reheat without boiling and finish with 1 dl ($3\frac{1}{2}$ fl oz or $\frac{1}{2}$ U.S. cup) fresh cream.

Place the civet into an earthenware casserole and serve accompanied with a dish of Cèpes à la Provençale (4019) mixed with some small Croûtons of bread fried in clarified butter.

3559 Civet de Lièvre à la Lyonnaise

Proceed in exactly the same way as for the ordinary Civet replacing the garnish of mushrooms with nice braised and glazed chestnuts.

3560 Côtelettes de Lièvre

These cutlets may be prepared in three ways:

A) by using a Croquette mixture bound with a brown sauce, of which the principal ingredient is finely diced cooked hare. The procedure is exactly the same as for ordinary Croquettes.

B) according to the method *à la Pojarski* (2531).
C) by using a forcemeat of hare with panada and butter (286).

Although the last two preparations can be moulded cutlet-shape by hand, it is preferable that they be moulded in small tinned cutlet moulds. They should be stuffed inside with a Salpicon of the loin of hare mixed with a little Civet sauce if possible and then cooked. Allow to cool, flour, egg and breadcrumb them, then shallow fry to a golden brown in clarified butter.

For all three methods the cutlets should be served accompanied with a sauce and garnish in keeping with the ingredients.

3561 Côtelettes de Lièvre aux Champignons
Season and shallow fry the cutlets to a golden brown in butter. Arrange them overlapping in a circle on a dish and place a garnish of sautéed mushrooms in the centre. Coat the cutlets with Sauce Champignons.

3562 Côtelettes de Lièvre Diane
Shallow fry the cutlets to a golden brown in butter. Arrange them overlapping in a circle on a dish and fill the centre with a purée of chestnuts. Serve accompanied with Sauce Diane.

3563 Côtelettes de Lièvre Morland
For this preparation use a raw forcemeat which should be kept a little firm; divide it into 60 g (2 oz) pieces and mould cutlet shape by hand but without stuffing them with a Salpicon.

Dip the cutlets in melted butter, then roll them in finely chopped truffle. Pat them carefully with the flat of a knife then shallow fry in clarified butter.

Arrange in a circle on a dish and serve accompanied with 1) a dish of purée of mushrooms, and 2) a light Sauce Poivrade.

3564 Côtelettes de Lièvre Pojarski
Proceed according to the method and proportions indicated for Côte de Veau Pojarski (2531). Use the flesh from the legs of hare after carefully removing all sinew.

The garnish for these cutlets is optional but, naturally, it should be in keeping with the preparation.

3565 Cuisses de Lièvre
Carefully remove all sinew from the legs, finely lard them with salt pork fat and roast them.

Serve accompanied with one or the other of the sauces and garnishes indicated for cutlets or saddle of hare.

3566 Filets de Lièvre
The fillets of hare are represented by those pieces of meat lying along and on top of both sides of the backbone. They should be removed from the carcase of the hare along its complete length from the point of the haunch to the beginning of the neck.

Carefully remove all sinew and lard them with fine strips of salt pork fat or truffle, or cut shallow incisions and inset these with slices of truffle according to requirements. They are generally formed into the shape of crescents, each being sufficient for two or sometimes three people if fairly large.

3567 Filets de Lièvre Dampierre
Take 5 fillets (3566) of leveret and inset them with slices of truffle. Form them in the shape of crescents and place on a buttered tray. Lard the same number of minion fillets with a rosette of fine strips of very red salt ox tongue and also place them in the shape of crescents on a buttered tray.

With what remains of the flesh from the leverets prepare a Mousseline forcemeat adding some finely chopped truffle and a little truffle essence. Place this mixture in a buttered shallow round mould and cook it in a slow oven.

A few minutes before being required, sprinkle the fillets and the minion fillets with melted butter and a few drops of brandy. Cover them and cook them in a moderate oven.

As soon as ready, demould the Mousse on to the service dish and arrange the fillets and minion fillets on top of it, alternating one with the other. Surround the base of the Mousse with alternate bouquets of glazed button onions and braised and glazed chestnuts.

Serve accompanied with Sauce Poivrade containing the cooking liquid from the hare.

3568 Filets de Levraut Mornay (*Recipe from the Frères Provençaux*)
Trim two fillets (3566) of leveret and cut them into fairly thick slices on the slant about $2\frac{1}{2}$ cm (1 in) long and 1 cm ($\frac{2}{5}$ in) thick.

Have ready 1) the same number of bread Croûtons as the slices of fillet, of the same size but only half as thick, and 2) an equal number of thick slices of truffle cooked at the last minute in a little Madeira.

Some few minutes before service, season and sauté the slices of fillet quickly in clarified butter and shallow fry the Croûtons likewise. Mix the slices of hare, Croûtons and slices of truffle together in a pan.

Deglaze the cooking pan with the Madeira used for cooking the truffles, add a little light meat glaze, reduce as necessary then pass through a fine strainer. Enrich and thicken this sauce with a

liberal amount of butter then pour it over the prepared slices of hare and other ingredients.
To serve: transfer the whole to a very hot timbale or deep dish.

Note: This recipe was given personally by the Comte de Mornay to the proprietors of the famous Restaurant des Frères Provençaux in Paris, and for a long while it was one of the specialities of this establishment which unfortunately, no longer exists.

3569 Filets de Levraut Montemart
Trim the fillets (3566) of leveret and cut them slantwise into fairly thick slices. Lightly flatten them and trim round in shape.

Sauté in butter, 200 g (7 oz) each of sliced Mousserons, sliced orange agaric, and sliced flap mushrooms. Allow them to cool then add to 500 g (1 lb 2 oz) Mousseline forcemeat of hare and mix together well. Place this into a shallow round mould of 12 cm (5 in) in diameter and cook it in a warm oven.

Demould the cooked forcemeat on to a dish and arrange the slices of leveret on top after being sautéed in butter at the last moment. Place a nice slice of truffle on top of each slice.

Lightly coat the whole and surround the base of the mould with a fairly thick well flavoured Sauce Demi-glace au Marsala.

Serve some of the same sauce separately.

3570 Filets de Levraut Sully
Remove and prepare the fillets (3566) and minion fillets of leveret. Lard them finely and form into the shape of crescents. Place them on a buttered tray with a little melted butter and a few drops of brandy; cover and cook in a moderate oven.

Arrange the fillets in fours, the points of the crescents inwards so as to form a rosette. Coat with a fairly thick Sauce Poivrade and fill the centres of the crescent-shaped fillets with a purée of celery, smoothed dome shape. Place one of the minion fillets, well glazed and with a slice of truffle in its middle, between the domes of purée.

3571 Filets de Levraut Vendôme
Prepare a Mousse of leveret cooked in an oval mould. Remove the fillets (3566) from the hare, lightly flatten them and inset them with slices of truffle. Place in a buttered tray with a little *Fumet* of wild rabbit, season, cover and cook in the oven.

Cut the minion fillets on the slant into fairly thick slices and season and sauté them quickly in butter together with 150 g (5 oz) sliced mushrooms and the same amount of sliced raw truffles. Deglaze the pan with a little brandy and cooking liquid from the fillets, add a little Sauce Poivrade and enrich the sauce with butter. Return the minion fillets, mushrooms and truffle to this sauce and mix in.

Demould the Mousse on to an oval dish, lightly coat with Sauce Poivrade and surround with the fillets each placed on a Barquette case of puff pastry filled with chestnut purée.

Serve accompanied with 1) a dish containing the mixture of minion fillets, mushrooms and truffle, and 2) a dish of fine chestnut purée.

3572 Mousses and Mousselines of Hare
The method and proportions for these are exactly the same as for all other Mousses and Mousselines, of course, using the flesh of hare as the principal ingredient.

Mousses of hare are almost always accompanied with a game sauce. Mousselines are moulded and cooked in the same manner as Mousselines de Volaille and are also accompanied with a game sauce. A fine purée of mushrooms, celery or lentils may also be served at the same time.

3573 Noisettes de Lièvre Mirza
Season and shallow fry the noisettes quickly in butter. Place each on half a Pippin apple, its core removed, cooked in the oven and the cavity filled with redcurrant jelly.

Arrange on a dish and serve accompanied with a light Sauce Poivrade.

3574 Pâté chaud de Lièvre Saint-Estèphe
Cover the bottom and sides of a buttered Charlotte mould with a layer of ordinary short paste, then cover this with a thick layer of forcemeat of hare with panada and butter (286). Cut fillets from along the back of the hare into fairly long thickish slices, lightly flatten them, quickly stiffen in hot butter then roll them in a little melted game glaze.

Allow the slices to cool then press them, standing upright, against the lining of forcemeat in the mould. Completely cover the forcemeat with these slices then fill with more of the slices. Cover with a few spoonfuls of Sauce Salmis au Vin Rouge made with a stock prepared from the hare carcase. Cover the pâté with a layer of the same forcemeat then close it up with a layer of short paste. Seal the edges well, make a small opening in the centre and cook for $1\frac{1}{4}$ hours in a moderate oven.

Demould the pâté on to a dish as soon as it is removed from the oven and serve accompanied with the remaining Sauce Salmis.

3575 Lièvre farci Périgourdine
Prepare and empty the hare taking care to collect all of the blood. Break the bones in the lower part of the legs so that it will be possible to truss them

easily. Remove any sinew from the legs and along the back and lard these parts finely with strips of salt pork fat.

Chop the liver, heart, lungs and 4 chickens' livers together with 150 g (5 oz) fresh pork fat. Add to this mixture, 150 g (5 oz) white breadcrumbs soaked in milk and squeezed, 60 g (2 oz) chopped onion, cooked in butter and cooled, the blood from the hare, a pinch of chopped parsley, a touch of crushed garlic and 100 g (3½ oz) trimmings of raw truffle. Mix together well and fill the hare with this stuffing. Sew up the skin of the belly, truss it, then braise it with white wine for approximately 2½ hours. Baste the hare frequently with the cooking liquid, glaze it at the last moment and when ready place on a long dish.

Add 4 dl (14 fl oz or 1¾ U.S. cups) Sauce Demi-glace made with game stock to the braising liquid. Reduce it, remove the fat and pass through a fine strainer. Add 100 g (3½ oz) chopped truffle to this sauce, pour a little of it around the hare and serve the rest separately.

3576 Râble de Lièvre—Saddle of Hare

The saddle of hare comprises the whole of the back of the hare from the beginning of the neck to the tail, the bones of the ribs being cut very short. Sometimes, however, that part of the carcase which corresponds to the saddle in butchers' meat, i.e. from the tail to the first ribs, is used.

Whatever the particular cut, the saddle should have all the sinews removed, be well trimmed and finely larded with salt pork fat. It is completely unnecessary to marinate the saddle if it has been obtained from a young animal, but this may be done if it becomes at all necessary to keep the saddle for some length of time. Nevertheless, certain recipes do call for marinating and in these cases the time for this should be kept very short.

3577 Râble de Lièvre à l'Allemande

Marinate the saddle in a raw marinade (261).

Spread the vegetables from the marinade on the bottom of a suitable-sized roasting pan, place the well dried saddle on top and roast it in a very hot oven. When it is nearly cooked, remove the vegetables and add 1 dl (3½ fl oz or ½ U.S. cup) cream to the pan; complete the cooking of the saddle, basting with the cream.

Place the saddle on a dish, add a few drops of lemon juice to the cream and pass it through a fine strainer. Pour this sauce around the saddle.

3578 Râble de Lièvre au Genièvre

Marinate the saddle and roast it as in the preceding recipe. When cooked place on a suitable dish.

Deglaze the pan with ½ dl (2 fl oz or ¼ U.S. cup) gin and 2 or 3 tbs of the marinade and reduce by half. Add 2 tbs Sauce Poivrade and 4 crushed juniper berries; simmer for a few seconds then pass through a fine strainer.

Serve the saddle accompanied with the prepared sauce.

Note: The saddle of hare prepared *à l'Allemande* or *au Genièvre*, except when instructed to the contrary, is served with redcurrant jelly or unsweetened Apple Sauce as an adjunct.

3579 Râble de Lièvre à la Navarraise

Finely lard the saddle and marinate for a few hours in red wine marinade.

Drain and well dry the saddle and roast it in a very hot oven on the vegetables from the marinade.

Meanwhile, lightly colour in butter 250 g (9 oz) sliced onions and 50 g (2 oz) crushed sweet garlic. Sprinkle with 20 g (⅔ oz) flour, cook gently for a few minutes, then moisten with 2 dl (7 fl oz or ⅞ U.S. cup) good veal stock. Add a little thyme and bayleaf and cook gently.

Pass the whole through a fine sieve and reduce to a thick purée; fill 10 grilled mushrooms with this purée.

Arrange the cooked saddle on a dish surrounded by the prepared mushrooms. Quickly deglaze the tray with the liquid from the marinade, pass it through a fine strainer, reduce to approximately 1 dl (3½ fl oz or ½ U.S. cup) and thicken and enrich it with a little butter.

Serve the saddle accompanied with the sauce.

3580 Râble de Lièvre, Sauce aux Cerises—Saddle of Hare with Cherry Sauce

Roast a finely larded saddle of hare, either unmarinated or very lightly marinated.

Served it accompanied with Sauce aux Cerises. See Caneton Rouennais aux Cerises (3482) for the sauce.

3581 Râble de Lièvre, Sauce Groseilles au Raifort—Saddle of Hare with Redcurrant and Horseradish Sauce

Roast a finely larded saddle of hare in a very hot oven.

Serve it accompanied with Sauce Groseilles au Raifort (200).

3582 Soufflé de Lièvre

Prepare a light Mousseline forcemeat using 400 g (15 oz) flesh of hare; place this mixture in either a buttered Charlotte or soufflé mould, decorated on the bottom and sides with slices of truffle; cook *au Bain-marie* in a moderate oven.

Meanwhile, cut the minion fillets of the hare into slices and sauté them quickly in butter.

Demould the soufflé on to a round dish, coat it lightly with Sauce Demi-glace flavoured with game *Fumet*, and surround the base with alternate overlapping slices of truffle and the sautéed minion fillets.

If the soufflé has been cooked in a soufflé mould and is served as it is in the dish, the slices of truffle and minion fillets should be added to the sauce, this being served separately as an accompaniment.

Details of a young hare weighing 2 kg 800 g (6½ lb)

Skin	210 g	equal to	7·500 %
Paws	140 g	equal to	5·0000 %
Entrails	465 g	equal to	16·6000 %
Blood	120 g	equal to	4·2847 %
Liver	55 g	equal to	1·9640 %
Lungs and Heart	50 g	equal to	1·7850 %
Flesh with Bones	1 kg 760 g	equal to	62·8653 %
TOTAL:	2 kg 800 g	TOTAL:	100·0000 %
Net Weight of Flesh	979·30 g	equal to	34·98 %
Weight of Bones and Trimmings	780·70 g	equal to	27·88 %
TOTAL:	1 kg 760 g	TOTAL:	62·86 %

Details of the same hare, skinned and eviscerated

The Hind Part of the Hare cut off at the first rib	700 g	equal to	25·00 %
The Trimmed Saddle (420 g)	gross 520 g	equal to	18·58 %
Legs	540 g	equal to	19·28 %
TOTAL:	1 kg 760 g	TOTAL:	62·86 %

LIEVRE FROID—COLD HARE

3583 Lièvre Farci Beauval

Select a very fresh hare and bone it out from the back before emptying it so that the skin of the belly may be kept intact. Remove the legs and shoulders but leave the head attached. Sprinkle the legs and shoulders with a few spoonfuls of brandy and season with salt and pepper. Leave to marinate for 1 hour.

Prepare a Gratin Forcemeat C (295) with the hare's liver, some salt pork fat and trimmings of raw truffle. Prepare another forcemeat with the flesh from the legs and shoulders, the same weight of fresh pork fat, 1 egg, a pinch of wild thyme, salt, pepper, mixed spice and the brandy of the marinade. Pass this forcemeat through a fine sieve and mix well together with the prepared gratin forcemeat plus 200 g (7 oz) salt pork fat cut in large dice and 150 g (5 oz) truffle cut in large dice.

Fill the boned hare with this mixture, sew it up carefully and tie back the head to give it the appearance of the animal at rest. Wrap the stuffed hare in slices of salt pork fat; line a correctly sized terrine with layers of the same fat and place the prepared hare inside. Sprinkle with ½ dl (2 fl oz or ¼ U.S. cup) brandy and place in the oven, without the lid for 30 minutes.

Now pour into the terrine a *Fumet* prepared from red wine and the bones left from the hare. Cover the hare and cook gently in a moderate oven for approximately 3 hours.

Allow to half cool, drain off the cooking liquid and completely remove all the slices of fat. Pass the cooking liquid through a fine strainer, return it to the terrine and then completely fill up with good savoury aspic jelly. Keep in a refrigerator for 2 days before serving.

3584 Mousse Froide de Lièvre—Cold Hare Mousse

This is prepared in the usual way for cold Mousses using for preference the fillets removed from along the back of the hare, which are sautéed in butter, cooled, then pounded together with the juices of the pan, deglazed with a little brandy.

The jelly used to finish the Mousse should be flavoured with a Fumet prepared from the trimmings and bones of the hare.

3585 Mousselines de Lièvre

These are moulded in the same way as for other cold Mousselines and using the same mixture as in the preceding recipe.

When they have become well set in the refrigerator, coat them with a light brown Sauce Chaud-froid flavoured with hare *Fumet*. Decorate with neat shapes of truffle, arrange in a deep dish and cover with jelly.

3586 Pain de Lièvre

Using cooked flesh of hare, follow the directions as indicated for Pain de Foie gras (3517).

3587 Pain de Lièvre en Belle-vue

Proceed in the same way as for Pain de Foie gras en Belle-vue (3518).

LAPEREAU DE GARENNE AND LAPEREAU DE CHOUX—YOUNG WILD AND DOMESTICATED RABBIT

3588 Lapereau à l'Aigre-doux

Prepare this dish in the same way as Lapereau aux

Pruneaux (3595) and complete the sauce as for Jambon de Marcassin à l'Aigre-doux (3555).

Note: The recipes for rabbit *à l'Aigre-doux* and *aux Pruneaux* are specialities of the Belgian kitchen.

3589 Lapereau en Blanquette
Take a rabbit which has been killed the day before and of which the flesh is very white. Proceed in the same way as for Blanquette de Veau.

3590 Lapereau Bouilli à l'Anglaise—Boiled Rabbit, English Style
Fill the rabbit with a stuffing as indicated in the recipe for Epaule de Veau à l'Anglaise (2541).

Sew up the belly of the rabbit, truss, and poach it in salted water for approximately 1 hour.

Serve accompanied with Caper Sauce.

Another way of serving: Drain the cooked rabbit well, place it on a long dish and coat with Sauce Béchamel containing finely sliced onions cooked without colour in butter.

3591 Lapereau de Garenne Sauté aux Champignons
Cut the wild rabbit into pieces, season and fry quickly on all sides in butter to a nice brown colour. Add some white wine, reduce by two-thirds; add sufficient thin Sauce Demi-glace to just cover the rabbit, and a Bouquet garni; cover and place in a moderate oven to cook.

When two-thirds cooked, remove the pieces of rabbit to a clean pan and add 250 g (9 oz) mushrooms cut in quarters and cooked in butter. Pass the sauce through a fine strainer over the rabbit and mushrooms and complete the cooking together.

3592 Lapereau en Gibelotte
The preparation of the Gibelotte is the same as that for the Civet de Lièvre except that the liquid used should be half red wine and half white stock.

For Gibelotte à la Menagère, the preparation is again the same, but includes an extra garnish of quarters of potatoes.

3593 Lapereau Grillé à la Bergère
Remove the fore-part of a rabbit leaving the saddle and legs in one piece. Split the two legs at the pelvic girdle so that they lay flat; half roast in the oven.

When ready, flour, egg and breadcrumb, sprinkle with melted butter and grill gently.

Arrange on a dish, surround with slices of blanched and grilled bacon and place a bouquet of straw potatoes at each end.

Serve accompanied with a Sauce Duxelles made with Mousserons.

3594 Pâté de Lapereau de Garenne au Chasseur
Line a well buttered, round raised pie mould with Ordinary Short Paste. Coat the bottom and sides with a layer of forcemeat made from the flesh of the legs and shoulders of the rabbit.

Bone out the trunk of the rabbit into long fillets, cut into thickish slices and fry quickly in hot butter to lightly set them; arrange in the prepared mould to completely cover the forcemeat.

Fill up the centre of the mould with sliced mushrooms cooked in butter and mixed with well reduced Sauce Chasseur containing an essence prepared from the bones and trimmings of the rabbit.

Cover with more of the same forcemeat then close up the pie with a layer of short paste, seal the edges well and finish in the usual manner.

Cook in a moderate oven for 1 hour and demould as soon as ready. Serve accompanied with Sauce Chasseur.

3595 Lapin aux Pruneaux
For this dish, wild or domesticated rabbit are equally suitable.

Cut the rabbit into pieces and marinate for 24 hours in a marinade well flavoured with vinegar.

Drain the pieces, dry them well and season and fry to colour on all sides in butter. Place in a pan and moisten with the strained marinade reduced by half and a little water. Season and add 500 g (1 lb 2 oz) soaked prunes, cover and cook gently in the oven.

When ready, add a few tablespoons of redcurrant jelly then place in a deep dish to serve.

3596 Other Suitable Preparations for Rabbit
The following types of preparation are suitable for rabbit; it is only necessary to proceed in the same manner using the same proportions and, of course, using rabbit in place of that in the recipe.

Cutlets: see Côtelettes de Lièvre
Crepinettes: see Crepinettes de Volaille
Croquettes: see Croquettes
Mousse and Mousselines: see Mousse and Mousselines of Hare
Pâté de Lapin: see Pâté d'Abattis
Quenelles: see Quenelles de Volaille
Sauté Chasseur: see Sauté de Veau Chasseur
Sauté Marengo: see Sauté de Veau Marengo
Sauté Portugaise: see Sauté de Veau Portugaise
Tourte de Lapereau: see Tourte de Poussins à la Paysanne

Details of a wild rabbit weighing 1 kg 100 g (2 lb 7 oz)

Skin and Paws	132·00 g	equal to	12·00 %
Entrails	148·50 g	equal to	13·50 %
Heart, Liver, Lungs	66·00 g	equal to	6·00 %
Flesh and Bone	753·50 g	equal to	68·50 %
TOTAL:	1 kg 100 g	TOTAL:	100·00 %

3597 FEATHERED GAME

If it was necessary to list each and every edible wild bird the list would be far too long so only those in general use are given. There are 10 main categories of game birds:

1) The various species of Pheasant; grey, red, rock and American Partridge.
2) Hazel Grouse, Capercaillie, Sand Grouse, Grouse, Pintailed Grouse, Bustards.
3) The various species of wild duck; Teals, Pintails.
4) Snipe and Woodcook.
5) Various species of Plover; Lapwings, Sandpipers, Water Rails, Moorhens, Scoters.
6) Quails, Corncrakes.
7) Thrushes and Blackbirds.
8) Larks.
9) Warblers, Jacksnipes.
10) Buntings.

The birds in categories 1 and 4 improve by being allowed to go slightly gamey which means that they should be hung unplucked for a few days in an airy place so that they start to decompose; this enhances the special aroma of the flesh and brings about an added distinction to their culinary value.

Whatever opinions people may have on the subject of 'gameyness' there can be no doubting that the taste of a fresh pheasant or woodcock and that of the well hung ones, differ widely, that of the unhung being dry and flavourless whereas after proper hanging they are tender, full of flavour and of an incomparable aroma.

It was usual in days gone by to lard birds of the first category, especially if they were to be roasted but this practice should not be continued; it does nothing but harm to the quality of the flesh of a young bird and fails to improve that of an old bird from which the tenderness has long since vanished. Covering the breast with a slice of salt pork fat is much more effective than larding as a means of protecting it from the heat of the oven and does not alter its flavour. Old tough birds should not be served, as they are fit only for use in the preparation of forcemeats and for making stock.

Birds in all the remaining categories are normally used fresh but if it is considered necessary to hang them for a few days they should not be allowed to become too high. This is especially true of water fowl where too long a period of hanging can result in a rather unpleasant taste developing.

FAISAN—PHEASANT

When a pheasant is young it has grey legs and the beak and the end of the breast bone are flexible and tender. The surest sign of tenderness in both the partridge and the pheasant can be discerned by noting the end of the last large feather of the wings; these are pointed in the young bird and rounded in the old one.

3598 Faisan à l'Alcantara

Empty the pheasant by the front end and bone out the breast from inside; stuff it with nice ducks' foie gras mixed with truffles which have been cut into quarters and cooked with Port. Place to marinate in port for three days making sure that it is kept fully covered, then cook it *en Casserole* (originally the recipe said that the bird should be spit roasted but cooking it in a casserole is more suitable). Reduce the Port used as the marinade, add 12 medium truffles, place the pheasant on these and cook for a further 10 minutes.

Note: The last part of this recipe could be altered with advantage to the method for *à la Souvaroff*, that is to say, place the pheasant and truffles in the earthenware terrine and moisten with reduced port to which a little buttered game glaze has been added. Cover with the lid, seal it hermetically with paste and place to finish cooking in the oven.

Historical Note: The recipe for Pheasant Alcantara comes from the famous convent of the same name.

It is known that in 1807 at the beginning of the campaign in Portugal, the library of the convent was pillaged by Junot's soldiers and many of its precious documents were used to make cartridge cases.

But it chanced that an officer of the Commissariat who was assisting with the operation, found among a collection of recipes written by the nuns, this recipe but appertaining to partridge. It looked interesting so having tried it out on his return to France during the following year he passed it on to the Duchess of Abrantes who mentioned it in her memoirs. It is probably the only thing of any value gained by the French during the course of that unhappy campaign and helped to establish the fact that foie gras and truffles long known in Languedoc and Gascony were also to be found in Estramadure where, even today, good quality truffles are to be found.

3599 Faisan à l'Angoumoise
Stuff the pheasant with a mixture of 300 g (11 oz) very fresh pork kidney fat passed through a fine sieve, 125 g (4½ oz) truffles cut in quarters, 12 chestnuts cooked in White Bouillon and cooled, and salt, pepper and a touch of grated nutmeg.

Wrap the stuffed bird in slices of salt pork fat then roast it gently for 45 minutes. Remove the slices of fat 7–8 minutes before being completely cooked so as to allow it to colour.

Serve accompanied with Sauce Périgueux.

3600 Faisan Bohémienne
Season a small foie gras with salt and paprika then stud it with quarters of raw truffle. Poach the prepared foie gras for 20 minutes in Madeira and allow it to cool.

When cold, carefully insert it into a nice fresh pheasant. Truss it then cook *en Casserole* with butter for 45 minutes.

To serve: remove most of the butter, sprinkle with ½ dl (2 fl oz or ¼ U.S. cup) flamed brandy and a few tablespoons of reduced game gravy.

Serve as it is from the casserole.

3601 Faisan en Casserole
Truss the pheasant *en Entrée* and cook it *en Casserole* with a little butter.

When cooked, deglaze with a little brandy and a spoonful of game gravy.

Replace the lid and serve in the casserole.

3602 Faisan en Chartreuse
Take a nice cabbage, cut it in quarters and remove the stalks. Blanch it, then braise it together with an old pheasant previously browned in the oven. This pheasant is only used to impart its flavour to the cabbage.

Select a very tender pheasant for the preparation of the Chartreuse and either roast or Poêlé it.

If to be served whole, prepare the Chartreuse in an oval mould of a size proportionate to that of the pheasant. If to be cut in portions proceed in exactly the same way as for Pigeonneaux en Chartreuse (3400).

Serve accompanied with a Sauce Demi-glace flavoured with good pheasant *Fumet*.

3603 Faisan à la Choucroute
Poêlé the pheasant keeping it just cooked.

Place on an oval dish on a layer of well drained sauerkraut braised with goose fat. Surround with a border of rectangles of bacon which has been cooked with the sauerkraut.

Serve accompanied with a gravy prepared from the juices of the cooking of the pheasant and a little game stock. Strain carefully but do not remove all of the fat.

3604 Faisan en Cocotte
Prepare and cook the pheasant as indicated for Faisan en Casserole (3601); when two-thirds cooked, surround with a garnish of button onions cooked in butter, small cooked mushrooms and olive-shaped truffles. These last replace the potatoes which are usually part of the garnish for other items when prepared *en Cocotte*.

3605 Côtelettes de Faisan—Cutlets of Pheasant
These are the breasts (Suprêmes) of pheasant with the ends of the winglet bone left attached.

All of the preparations for Suprêmes de Volaille are applicable.

Note: Instead of removing the breasts of the pheasant and then cooking them in the same way as *Suprêmes* of chicken, they can be removed at the last moment after the pheasant has been roasted or Poêléed but kept underdone. In this way after their further preparation they tend to become less dry and of a better flavour.

3606 Faisan à la Crème
Prepare and cook the pheasant *en Casserole* with butter and a medium-sized onion cut in quarters.

When three-quarters cooked, baste the bird with 1½ dl (5 fl oz or ⅝ U.S. cup) sour cream or if unobtainable, fresh cream acidulated with a few drops of lemon juice and a few tablespoonfuls of meat glaze.

Complete the cooking, basting the pheasant frequently. Serve as it is in the casserole.

3607 Faisan Demidoff
Proceed as indicated for Poularde Demidoff (3041).

3608 Faisan Grillé à la Diable—Grilled Devilled Pheasant
Young pheasants are best suited to this preparation; the older birds should only be used if one is absolutely sure of their tenderness.

Proceed in the same way as for Poulet Grillé à la Diable (3255).

3609 Faisan Galitzin
Select two nice plump snipe, remove their intestines and liver and sauté these quickly in a little butter. Place on a plate and crush with a fork.

Remove the flesh from the birds and chop together finely with half its quantity of cream and the same of butter. Season with salt and pepper and add the prepared intestines and liver together with 125 g (4½ oz) truffle cut in dice.

Stuff a nice pheasant with this mixture and roast it in a covered casserole or terrine; sprinkle it at the last moment with a little excellent *Fumet* prepared from the bones of the snipe.

3610 Faisan à la Géorgienne
Truss the pheasant *en Entrée* and place in an earthenware casserole or terrine with 30 fresh, well peeled walnuts cut in half, the juice of 1 kg ($2\frac{1}{4}$ lb) white grapes, the juice of 4 oranges, $\frac{1}{2}$ dl (2 fl oz or $\frac{1}{4}$ U.S. cup) Malmsey wine, $\frac{1}{2}$ dl (2 fl oz or $\frac{1}{4}$ U.S. cup) strong green tea, 50 g (2 oz) butter and seasoning as necessary.

Cover with the lid and place in the oven to cook for approximately 40 minutes. Remove the lid and colour the pheasant when it is almost cooked.

When ready, place on a suitable dish and surround with the nuts from the cooking. Pass the cooking liquid through a fine strainer, add 2 dl (7 fl oz or $\frac{7}{8}$ U.S. cup) game Sauce Espagnole and reduce by half.

Lightly coat the pheasant and nuts with this sauce and serve the remainder separately in a sauceboat.

3611 Faisan Kotschoubey
Slide some slices of truffle under the skin on the breast of the pheasant then stuff it with truffles as described for Dindonneau Truffé (3914); cook *en Casserole* with a little butter.

When ready, remove the fat from the casserole and surround the bird with Brussels sprouts sautéed in a little brown butter and mixed with diced salt belly of pork fried in butter.

Cover the whole with a little Sauce Demi-glace flavoured with truffle essence, replace the lid and place in a warm oven for 5–6 minutes.

3612 Mousse and Mousselines of Pheasant
These are prepared according to the methods and recipes described in the preceding chapters.

The trimmings and carcase of the pheasant should be utilized in the preparation of good stocks to be used in the preparation of the accompanying sauces.

3613 Faisan à la Normande
Place the pheasant in hot butter and colour it brown on all sides.

Meanwhile, peel 6 medium-sized dessert apples, cut them into quarters then slice and sauté them quickly in butter. Place some of these as a layer on the bottom of a terrine, place the pheasant on top and surround with the rest of the apples. Sprinkle with a few tablespoons of cream, cover with the lid and place in the oven to cook for 20 to 25 minutes.

Serve as it is in the dish.

3614 Pâté chaud de Faisan—Hot Pheasant Pie
Proceed in the same way as for Pâté Chaud de Caneton taking note of the following modifications:

1) Use a Gratin Forcemeat made with the flesh and livers of pheasant.
2) Roast the pheasant keeping it very underdone, cut it into slices and mix with the mushrooms and truffles when filling the mould.
3) Serve the Pâté accompanied with a Sauce Salmis prepared from the carcase and trimmings of the pheasant.

3615 Pâté chaud de Faisan à la Vosgienne
Line a buttered deep mould with a layer of fine short paste. Coat the bottom and sides of the paste with a thick layer of buttered fresh noodles and fill the centre with the finely chopped flesh of a roast pheasant mixed with chopped mushroom and truffle and some thick Sauce Salmis.

Cover with more of the noodles then close up the Pâté with a thin layer of the same short paste. Seal the edges and bake in a moderate oven for 50 minutes.

Demould on to a round dish when required and surround with medium-sized cup mushrooms filled with very thick Sauce Salmis.

3616 Faisan à la Périgueux
Prepare and stuff the pheasant with truffles proceeding as described for Dindonneau Truffé (3914) and Poêlé it with a little Madeira.

When ready, place in a dish and surround with a border of Quenelles made from game forcemeat containing chopped truffle and moulded with teaspoons. They should be cooked at the last moment.

Serve accompanied with a Sauce Périgueux containing the cooking liquid from the pheasant after first removing all the fat, passing through a fine strainer and reducing it.

3617 Faisan Régence
Poêlé the pheasant and when ready, place on a low Croûton of bread cut from a sandwich loaf and fried in clarified butter.

Surround with a Régence garnish for game birds (449) and serve accompanied with Sauce Salmis flavoured with truffle essence and containing the deglazed juices from the pan after removing the fat, passing through a fine strainer and reducing it.

3618 Faisan à la Sainte-Alliance
This is the *Faisan Etoffé* of Brillat-Savarin which, under the name of Sainte-Alliance designates the

specially prepared fried Croûton of bread on which the pheasant completes its roasting.

Bone out two nice woodcocks and reserve the liver and intestines for further use.

Chop the flesh of the woodcock together with a quarter its weight of cold poached beef bone marrow, the same amount of fresh pork fat and a little salt, pepper and Fines Herbes. Add to this mixture, 200 g (7 oz) raw peeled truffles cut in quarters and lightly cooked in butter.

Stuff the pheasant with this preparation; truss it, wrap in thin slices of salt pork fat and keep in a cool place for 24 hours.

Roast the pheasant thus prepared on a spit—if roasted in the oven take care to place it on a trivet.

Cut a very large Croûton from a sandwich loaf and fry it in clarified butter.

Finely pound the woodcock's livers and intestines together with an equal amount of grated fresh pork fat, the well washed fillets of an anchovy, 30 g (1 oz) butter and 50 g (2 oz) raw truffle. When smooth and well mixed, spread the mixture on the Croûton.

When the pheasant is two-thirds cooked, place the prepared Croûton underneath it in such a way as to catch the juices from the completion of the pheasant's cooking.

When ready, place the pheasant on the Croûton, surround with slices of bitter oranges and serve the roast gravy separately.

When serving, each piece of the pheasant should be accompanied with a slice of orange and a small piece of the Croûton.

Note: This preparation should be designated on the menu as Faisan étoffé, sur Toast à la Sainte-Alliance.

3619 Salmis de Faisan

The Salmis is perhaps the most delicate and perfect preparation of game bequeathed to us by the old classical kitchen. If not so well esteemed today it is because its method of preparation has been ruined without discernment by applying it to game already cooked and then reheated for this purpose; reasons of economy may also be a contributory factor.

But if a Salmis is prepared in accordance with the following recipe, it may be figured on the finest and most sumptuous of menus especially when applied to game birds of categories 1 and 4.

Roast the pheasant keeping it underdone but not excessively so; cut it quickly into 6 pieces, that is: 2 legs, 2 wings (the winglets removed) and the breast cut in two lengthways.

Remove the skin from all the pieces, trim them neatly and place in a small pan with a little flamed brandy and melted meat glaze; cover and keep warm.

Pound the carcase and the trimmings and place in a pan with 2½ dl (9 fl oz or 1⅛ U.S. cups) white wine, 30 g (1 oz) chopped shallot and a little coarsely ground pepper; allow to almost completely reduce, then add 1½ dl (5 fl oz or ⅝ U.S. cup) each of game Sauce Espagnole and game stock and allow to cook for 10 minutes.

Pass through a fine sieve first, pressing and rubbing firmly, then pass through a fine strainer. Reduce this sauce by one-third skimming as necessary, then pass again through the fine strainer and add a little butter.

Add 10 small cooked mushrooms and 20 slices of truffle to the prepared pheasant and cover with the sauce. Place in a deep dish and serve hot.

Notes:

1) It will be noted in the above recipe that the Salmis is not arranged on a Croûton neither is it surrounded with Croûtons coated with Gratin Forcemeat; the use of Croûtons is more than arguable and it it strongly advised to discard this practice.

   The only absolute requirements of this dish are that it should be quickly prepared and simply arranged in the dish so that it can be served quickly and eaten hot. Moreover, the excellence of the dish is sufficient in itself and does not require any frills or fancies in presentation.

2) Although the principles involved in the preparation of a Salmis of game suggest the use of white wine, a Salmis of pheasant can be made very well with red wine.

3620 Faisan Souvaroff

Cook 6 medium-sized truffles for 5 minutes in 1 dl (3½ fl oz or ½ U.S. cup) Madeira and an equal quantity of light meat glaze. Remove the truffles and place in a terrine in which the pheasant will complete its cooking.

Cut 200 g (7 oz) raw foie gras into large dice and stiffen these in the cooking liquor from the truffles. Stuff the pheasant with this foie gras, truss it, cover with slices of salt pork fat and two-thirds Poêlé it.

This done, place it in the terrine with the truffles, add the juices from the cooking plus ½ dl (2 fl oz or ¼ U.S. cup) each of Madeira and game stock; cover very tightly and place in the oven for 15 minutes to complete the cooking.

Serve in the dish as it is.

3621 Faisan Titania

Prepare and Poêlé the pheasant keeping it moist and not too well coloured.

Place in a terrine and surround with 125 g (4½

oz) skinned and depipped black grapes and 8 to 10 segments of peeled and depipped orange.

Add a tablespoon of game stock to the juices from the cooking of the pheasant together with an equal amount of pomegranate juice. Skim off the fat and pour the gravy over the pheasant. Cover with the lid and serve immediately.

3622 Sauté de Faisan

Unless a great amount of care is taken, a Sauté of pheasant tends to be dry and should not figure on the menu without a certain amount of reservation. Nevertheless, if necessary, young plump pheasant should be selected and cut in the same way as for a Sauté of chicken—the drumsticks of the legs, however, should not be used.

Season the pieces of pheasant and sauté in butter keeping them just cooked. Arrange in a deep dish and keep covered.

Deglaze the pan and prepare the sauce as required by the chosen recipe; its quantity should be kept to a minimum and poured over the pheasant at the last moment.

3623 Sauté de Faisan aux Champignons

Season and sauté the pheasant as in the preceding recipe and when two-thirds cooked, add 10 button mushrooms cooked in butter. Complete the cooking in the usual manner and arrange the pheasant and mushrooms in a deep dish.

Deglaze the pan with a little mushroom essence, add a few drops of lemon juice and a little game stock; reduce and thicken and enrich it with 50 g (2 oz) butter. Pour this sauce over the pheasant and mushrooms.

3624 Sauté de Faisan au Suc d'Ananas

Season and sauté the pheasant in butter and arrange in a deep dish.

Deglaze the pan with $\frac{1}{2}$ dl (2 fl oz or $\frac{1}{4}$ U.S. cup) flamed brandy, add a few drops of lemon juice and at the last moment add 2 or 3 tbs fresh pineapple juice. Pour this over the pheasant, cover and serve immediately.

3625 Sauté de Faisan au Suc de Mandarine

Proceed in the same way as the preceding recipe using mandarine juice and the juice of a quarter of a lemon.

3626 Sauté de Faisan an Suc d'Orange Amère

Prepare the sauté as for au Suc d'Ananas using the juice of bitter oranges only and in the same proportions as the pineapple juice.

Note: The above preparations using the juice of certain fruits, although perhaps a little fanciful, are nevertheless much appreciated by some people.

3627 Sauté de Faisan aux Truffes

Proceed in the same manner as for Sauté de Faisan aux Champignons substituting 100 g ($3\frac{1}{2}$ oz) sliced raw truffle for the mushrooms.

3628 Soufflé de Faisan

Prepare a light Mousseline forcemeat of pheasant. Place in a buttered soufflé mould and cook *au Bain-marie* in a moderate oven.

Serve accompanied with an excellent Sauce Demi-glace flavoured with pheasant essence.

3629 Suprêmes de Faisan

Suprêmes of pheasant are prepared in the same way as Suprêmes of chicken and all of their recipes are suitable excepting those which use Sauce Mornay.

3630 Suprêmes de Faisan Berchoux

Cut open the suprêmes along the thick side and stuff with a forcemeat prepared from the minion fillets and the liver of the pheasant mixed with an equivalent amount of Gratin Forcemeat C (295) and chopped trimmings of truffle.

Prepare a Mousseline forcemeat from the flesh of the pheasant's legs and mix with an equal quantity of mushroom purée. Have ready the required number of lightly baked Barquette cases, fill them with this forcemeat and place in a moderate oven to cook.

Place the prepared and seasoned suprêmes in a well buttered shallow pan, sprinkle with a little brandy and a few drops of lemon juice, cover and cook in the oven without colour. Place one suprême on each Barquette and arrange on a suitable dish.

Serve accompanied with a Sauce Demi-glace containing a reduced *Fumet* made from the bones and trimmings of the pheasant.

3631 Suprêmes de Faisan Louisette

Season the suprêmes and shallow fry them quickly in hot butter keeping them underdone; allow to cool then dip them into Sauce Villeroy flavoured with reduced pheasant *Fumet*. Allow them to cool then flour, egg and breadcrumb them.

Prepare a Mousseline forcemeat from the flesh of the pheasant's legs. Butter a dome-shaped mould, decorate the bottom and sides with slices of truffle and fill with the forcemeat. Cook *au Bain-marie*, demould on to a round dish and surround with the suprêmes, shallow fried in clarified butter.

Serve accompanied with a Sauce Périgueux flavoured with pheasant *Fumet*.

FAISAN FROID—COLD PHEASANT

3632 Faisan à la Bohémienne

Prepare the pheasant as indicated in the beginning of the preceding section on pheasant (3600). Allow to become cold and arrange in a deep oval dish surrounded with Madeira-flavoured aspic jelly.

As a variation for presenting this dish proceed in the following manner: When the pheasant has been cooked add sufficient aspic jelly along with the brandy, to fill the terrine completely.

Keep cold for 2 days then carefully remove all traces of fat as explained for Poularde en Terrine (3366).

Present for serving set on a block of ice.

3633 Chaud-froid de Faisan

The preparation for this is the same as for Chaud-froid de Volaille using a brown Sauce Chaud-froid flavoured with pheasant *Fumet*. Decorate and glaze with jelly in the same manner.

3634 Chaud-froid de Faisan Buloz

Poêlé the pheasant keeping it very slightly underdone. Remove the breasts, cut into fairly thin slices and trim them.

Prepare a brown Sauce Chaud-froid with a *Fumet* made from the carcase of the pheasant and the Poêling liquor. Coat the slices of pheasant with this sauce.

Prepare also 10 nice cooked grooved mushrooms and coat these with white Sauce Chaud-froid.

Line the inside of a dome-shaped mould with a layer of clear jelly and decorate it with truffle. Fill with the slices of prepared pheasant and mushrooms arranged in alternate layers and separated by layers of jelly. Complete the mould by filling with jelly.

Allow to set on ice and when required, demould on to a low base of semolina or rice set on a round dish. Surround the dish with a border of cut shapes of aspic jelly.

3635 Faisan à la Croix-de-Berny

Roast the pheasant keeping it underdone. Allow to cool and when very cold, remove the breasts leaving the winglets and legs attached to the carcase. Cut away the bones of the breast and fill the empty cavity with a truffled Parfait de foie gras and cover this with a thin layer of Mousse of foie gras.

Cut the breasts of pheasant into neat slices and place them overlapping in their correct order on the Mousse; fill any gaps with some more of the Mousse and smooth and shape the whole to the original form of the bird. Allow the Mousse to set thoroughly then coat the breast only with brown Sauce Chaud-froid. Decorate and glaze the whole with aspic jelly.

Meanwhile, bone out 8 larks, stuff them with a suitable forcemeat, poach and allow to become quite cold. At this stage decorate them with shapes of truffle and ox tongue and glaze with jelly.

Place the pheasant on a low base of semolina or rice, surround with the larks and fill the space between them with chopped jelly.

3636 Faisan en Daube

Proceed in the same way as for Poularde en Terrine (3366) taking account of the size of the bird and regulating its cooking time accordingly.

3637 Mousses and Mousselines of Pheasant

For these preparations refer to cold Mousses and Mousselines of Chicken and cold Mousses and Mousselines of Foie gras.

3638 Suprêmes de Faisan à la Châtelaine

Remove the breasts from the cooked pheasant; cut and trim them into round slices. Coat one half of these with chicken Mousse and the other half with pheasant Mousse. Allow to set firm in the refrigerator.

When ready, coat those with the pheasant Mousse with white Sauce Chaud-froid and the others with brown Sauce Chaud-froid. Decorate each with small shapes of truffle.

Arrange the prepared Suprêmes overlapping and in alternate colours in a deep square dish. Cover the whole with very clear succulent aspic jelly and allow to set.

To serve: set the dish on a block of ice.

3639 Suprêmes de Faisan des Gastronomes (*Simplified Recipe*)

Poêlé the pheasant with a little Madeira and allow to become cold.

Remove the breasts, cut them into thin even-shaped slices, coat with brown Sauce Chaud-froid and decorate each to choice.

Prepare a Mousse from the trimmings and legs of the pheasant and mould it slightly dome-shape in the bottom of a deep square dish.

Arrange the prepared slices of pheasant in a line down the centre of the Mousse and surround with nice even-shaped truffles cooked with Champagne and allowed to get very cold. Cover the whole with a very clear and succulent aspic jelly.

To serve: set the dish on a block of ice.

PERDREAUX—PARTRIDGE

The grey-legged partridge found mostly in flat open country is to be preferred to the red-legged species which are more common to hilly and wooded areas. They should be young and thus tender; older birds (Perdrix) should only be used in the preparation of forcemeats and *Fumets*.

Almost all of the recipes for pheasant are suitable for partridge and these will just be noted among the following recipes.

3640 Perdreau à la Mode d'Alcantara
See Faisan à l'Alcantara.

3641 Perdreau Alexis
Poêlé the partridge and when ready, arrange on a dish surrounded with peeled and depipped Muscatel grapes.

Serve accompanied with the deglazed juices from the cooking of the partridge.

3642 Perdreau Bonne-Maman
Chop the partridge liver together with double its quantity of foie gras, a little chopped truffle and parsley and a tablespoon of fried breadcrumbs. Mix well together and stuff the partridge with it.

Truss it *en Entrée* and cook *en Casserole* with 6 cloves of well blanched garlic. When three-quarters cooked, sprinkle with a little Armagnac, add 6 slices of raw truffle, replace the lid and complete its cooking.

Serve the dish as it is.

3643 Perdreau à la Bourguignonne
Truss the partridge *en Entrée*; Poêlé it, keeping it only three-quarters cooked, then place in a terrine together with 6 glazed button onions and 6 cooked button mushrooms. Deglaze the pan with 2 dl (7 fl oz or $\frac{7}{8}$ U.S. cup) red wine, reduce by two-thirds and add 1 tbs game-flavoured Sauce Demi-glace. Pass through a fine strainer and remove any fat.

Pour this sauce over the partridge, cover with the lid and finish cooking in the oven.

Serve the dish as it is.

3644 Perdreau en Casserole
Proceed as indicated for Faisan en Casserole.

3645 Perdreau en Chartreuse
Braise the cabbage together with an old partridge which has been previously coloured in butter.

Prepare a mould lined in the Chartreuse style and fill this with the braised cabbage and young roast partridge prepared expressly for the dish. Finish cooking *au Bain-marie* as explained for Chartreuse de Pigeonneaux, and serve accompanied with Sauce Demi-glace flavoured with partridge *Fumet*.

3646 Perdrix aux Choux
Truss an old partridge *en Entrée* and colour it in the oven. Braise it together with a suitable amount of blanched cabbage, a piece of blanched streaky bacon, a small smoked pork sausage and two carrots.

Remove the bacon and sausage when cooked, leaving the cabbage and partridge to finish their cooking.

Line a buttered deep round mould with rings of the carrot and sausage and thin squares of the bacon, then cover these with a layer of the cabbage. Place the partridge in the centre after removing the string, then cover and fill with the remaining cabbage. Heat in a moderate oven for 5 minutes.

Turn over on to a round dish for service, soak up any liquid before removing the mould. Surround with a little game-flavoured Sauce Demi-glace and some grilled sausages.

Note: Where economy is not of first importance it can be useful to use the old partridge only for flavouring the cabbage and to replace it with young freshly roasted or Poêléed partridge for the completion of the dish.

3647 Perdreau à la Diable, or Perdreau à la Crapaudine
For these preparations use young partridge; in either case follow the recipe for Pigeonneaux Crapaudine (3406).

3648 Perdreau à la Crème
Proceed in the same way as indicated for Faisan à la Crème.

3649 Crépinettes de Perdreau
Replace the flesh of chicken with that of partridge and proceed in the same way and in the same proportions as for Crépinettes de Volaille (3310).

They should be made a little smaller than chicken Crépinettes and should be served accompanied with a dish of a light purée of chestnuts or lentils.

3650 Perdreau en Demi-deuil
Bone out the inside of the partridge then stuff it with a partridge forcemeat with panada and butter (286) containing chopped truffle.

Slip a few slices of very black truffle between the skin and the breast and truss *en Entrée*. Wrap in a piece of muslin and poach for 35 to 40 minutes in game stock.

When ready, remove the muslin and string and place the partridge in a suitable dish. Reduce the cooking liquid, add 3 tbs Sauce Demi-glace, pass through a fine strainer and add $\frac{1}{2}$ dl (1 fl oz or $\frac{1}{8}$ U.S. cup) flamed brandy.

Serve the partridge accompanied with the sauce and a suitable garnish such as flap mushrooms sautéed in butter, or a purée of chestnuts.

3651 Epigrammes de Perdreau
Remove the breasts of the partridge leaving a small piece of the winglet attached.

Prepare a Mousseline forcemeat with the legs and the minion fillets, fill into buttered cutlet moulds and cook *au Bain-marie* in the usual manner.

Allow to cool then flour, egg and breadcrumb them; shallow fry golden brown in clarified butter and at the same time grill the breasts of partridge.

Arrange the cutlets and breasts alternately in a circle on a dish and serve accompanied with 1) a Sauce Demi-glace prepared with the carcase and trimmings of the partridge, and 2) a dish of light chestnut purée.

3652 Perdreau en Estouffade
Colour the partridge in the oven.

Have prepared a little Matignon containing 1 crushed juniper berry. Place 1 tbs of this in a terrine of the right size, place the partridge on top and cover with another spoonful of the Matignon. Add 30 g (1 oz) butter, $\frac{1}{4}$ dl (1 fl oz or $\frac{1}{8}$ U.S. cup) flamed brandy, and $\frac{1}{2}$ dl (2 fl oz or $\frac{1}{4}$ U.S. cup) game stock.

Cover with the lid and seal the edges with a band of stiff flour and water paste.

Place in a hot oven for 25 minutes and serve the dish as it is.

3653 Perdreau à la Fermière
Truss the partridge *en Entrée*. Colour it in butter and place in a terrine with a Fermière garnish (380) prepared in advance. Add 1 tbs game stock, cover with the lid and place in the oven to complete the cooking of the partridge and vegetables.

Serve the dish as it is.

3654 Perdreau Kotschoubey
Proceed as indicated for Faisan Kotschoubey using a proportionate amount of Brussels sprouts and bacon.

3655 Perdreau Lady Clifford
Cook the partridge *en Casserole* with butter. When three-quarters cooked, surround with 50 g (2 oz) slices of raw truffle, add $\frac{1}{4}$ dl (1 fl oz or $\frac{1}{8}$ U.S. cup) flamed brandy and 1 tbs thin meat glaze.

Complete the cooking and serve accompanied with Sauce Soubise.

3656 Perdreau Lautrec
Select a young partridge, split it open along the back, open out and flatten it lightly. Push a skewer through and across so as to keep it flat, season, sprinkle with melted butter and grill it gently.

Place on a dish, surround with small cooked mushrooms each containing a little Maître d'Hôtel Butter and border the dish with a *cordon* of melted meat glaze. Sprinkle a few drops of lemon juice on the partridge.

3657 Perdreau Marly
Truss the partridge *en Entrée* and colour it in butter; place in a terrine and surround with small fresh Mousserons sautéed in butter. Close the lid tightly and cook in the oven.

Serve the dish as it is.

3658 Mousse and Mousselines of Partridge
These are prepared in accordance with the recipes and methods described in the foregoing chapters.

The carcase and trimmings of the partridge should be utilized in the preparation of stock which in its turn should act as a base for the accompanying sauce.

3659 Perdreau à la Normande
Truss the partridge *en Entrée* and colour it in butter.

At the same time peel and slice 3 pippin apples and lightly sauté these in butter. Place a layer of these apples in the bottom of a terrine, place the partridge on top and cover with the remaining apples; sprinkle with a few spoonfuls of cream, cover with the lid and complete the cooking in the oven.

Serve the dish as it is.

3660 Perdreau aux Olives
Proceed in the same way as for Pigeonneaux aux Olives.

3661 Pâté chaud de Perdreau—Hot Partridge Pie
Use 3 partridges for an ordinary size hot pie. Roast them underdone and prepare as indicated for any of the recipes for Pâté chaud de Pigeonneaux.

3662 Perdreau à la Périgueux
Prepare in the same way as for Faisan à la Périgueux.

3663 Perdreau à la Polonaise
Stuff the partridge with Gratin Forcemeat C (295) then proceed as for Pigeonneaux à la Polonaise.

3664 Salmis de Perdreau
Proceed as indicated for Salmis de Faisan.

3665 Perdreau Soubise aux Truffes
Poêlé the partridge as indicated for Faisan à la

Crème but adding 3 tbs shredded and blanched onions.

When cooked, place the partridge in a terrine; rub the onions and cream through a fine sieve then add a nice truffle cut in slices; correct the seasoning and pour over the partridge.

Cover with the lid, reheat for a few minutes and serve the dish as it is.

3666 Soufflé de Perdreau

Prepare a Mousseline forcemeat of partridge and proceed as indicated for Soufflé de Faisan.

3667 Perdreau Souvaroff

Proceed in the same way as for Faisan Souvaroff.

3668 Suprêmes de Perdreau Véron

Remove the breasts of the partridge and trim them.

Poach the legs and livers in game stock; when cooked remove all the bones and finely pound the flesh and the liver with half its quantity of truffle. Pass through a fine sieve, mix the resultant purée with a few spoonfuls of game Velouté then add an equal quantity of chestnut purée and mix together with a little butter. Keep warm.

A few minutes before serving, season and shallow fry the Suprêmes in butter.

Place the purée in the centre of a round dish, mould dome-shape and surround with the Suprêmes alternating with Croûtons of bread cut in the shape of cockscombs and fried in butter. Surround with a *cordon* of game-flavoured Sauce Demi-glace and serve some of the sauce separately.

3669 Perdreaux Froids—Cold Partridge

All of the preparations and recipes for cold pheasant are suitable; it is only necessary to substitute the word partridge for pheasant.

3670 CAILLES—QUAILS

Quails should be selected very plump and with firm white fat.

Other than spit-roasting which is to be preferred to oven roasting, quails admit to two other excellent methods of cooking—they may be cooked *en Casserole* with butter or poached in a good, well flavoured gelatinous veal stock.

This last method is admirably suited to quails and is frequently used.

3671 Cailles en Caisses

Bone out the quails from the back and stuff with a Gratin Forcemeat C (295) made from their livers, some chicken livers and containing chopped truffle.

Re-form them and wrap each in a thin slice of salt pork fat. Place in a buttered pan close together so that they will not lose their shape whilst cooking; sprinkle well with melted butter and cook in a hot oven for 12 minutes.

Place a little thick Sauce Duxelles in the bottom of buttered, oval pleated paper or porcelain cases; place one quail in each. Replace in the oven to finish cooking then glaze with a little Sauce Demi-glace flavoured with quail *Fumet*.

Place a nice slice of truffle on the top of each quail just before serving.

3672 Cailles en Casserole

Cook the quails *en Casserole* with butter. Deglaze with a little brandy and a little game stock and serve very hot as they are in the casserole.

3673 Cailles aux Cerises

For 4 Quails: Truss the quails *en Entrée* and cook them *en Casserole* with butter.

Deglaze the casserole with a little brandy and $\frac{1}{2}$ dl (2 fl oz or $\frac{1}{4}$ U.S. cup) Port wine in which a piece of orange peel has been soaked. Add 3 tbs good veal stock, 1 tbs redcurrant jelly and 40 stoned Morello cherries, poached in a syrup of about 18° on the saccharometer and cooled in the syrup. Drain these cherries before adding to the quails.

If the sauce is too sweet, acidulate it with a few drops of lemon juice.

3674 Côtelettes de Cailles d'Aumale

Remove the breasts from the quails, place them in hot butter and cook just to stiffen the surface of the flesh.

Prepare a Mousseline forcemeat with the rest of the quails. Butter the required number of small cutlet moulds and place a slice of truffle in the bottom of each, then line with a layer of the prepared forcemeat. Place one prepared Suprême of quail in each mould and cover with more of the same forcemeat. Place on a tray with a little water and cook in a medium oven.

Demould and arrange in a circle on a round dish and stick each cutlet with a blanched quail's foot. Fill the centre of the dish with a Julienne of mushrooms and truffle mixed with Sauce Demi-glace flavoured with quail *Fumet*.

3675 Cailles aux Coings

Two days before being required, enclose the quails in an earthenware terrine with a little brandy and a few peelings of very ripe and yellow quince. Keep in a cool place.

When required for cooking, remove the peelings of quince and add a nice piece of butter; seal the terrine as tightly as possible and place in a hot oven for 20 minutes.

Serve the quails as they are in the terrine accompanied with a sauceboat of quince jelly.

3676 Cailles à la Dauphinoise

Wrap each quail in a buttered vine leaf then in a thin slice of salt pork fat. Roast for 10 minutes in a very hot oven.

Have prepared a purée of fresh peas well seasoned and cooked with lettuce and reduced to a fairly stiff consistency.

Cover the bottom of a deep earthenware dish with very thin slices of cooked ham, place the purée of peas on top and smooth the surface.

Arrange the quails on top of the purée pressing them half-way into it. Place in the oven for a further 10 minutes and serve as they are.

3677 Cailles Figaro

Place a piece of truffle inside each quail then enclose each quail in a piece of gut together with a piece of light veal glaze the size of a small walnut. Sew up carefully with thread leaving a space of 2 cm ($\frac{4}{5}$ in) at each end. This will prevent the gut from bursting during cooking as it tends to shrink under the application of heat.

Poach the prepared quails in good veal stock and drain well.

Serve as they are in the gut.

3678 Cailles à la Grecque

Place the quails in a covered casserole with a little butter and cook in a hot oven.

Half fill a deep dish with Riz à la Grecque and place the quails on top. Deglaze the casserole with a few spoonfuls of good game stock, remove any fat and pour the gravy over the quails.

3679 Cailles Judic

Poêlé the quails and arrange them in a deep square dish, each one placed on a small freshly braised lettuce.

Prepare a mixture of cocks' kidneys and truffles mixed together with Sauce Demi-glace flavoured with game essence and pour this over the quails.

3680 Cailles Grillées Julie

Cut open the quails from the back without separating the two halves. Lightly flatten them, season and sprinkle with butter and finely chopped truffle.

Wrap each in a piece of caul, sprinkle with melted butter and fine white breadcrumbs and grill gently on both sides.

When ready, arrange on a dish and sprinkle with a few drops of verjuice.

3681 Cailles Lucullus

Take large truffles which have been cooked with Madeira or Champagne and cut them in half. Cut the bottom of each half level then empty them with a vegetable scoop leaving them in the shape of cases.

Bone out the quails and fill with a fine Gratin Forcemeat C (295) made with game and mixed with egg yolks, the chopped reserved insides of the truffles and a little flamed brandy.

Form the quails into the shape of balls and wrap each lightly in a square of muslin. Sew up well so as to give a nice round shape, then poach them in an excellent stock for 20 minutes.

When ready, remove, tighten up the muslin again and leave to cool for 10 minutes.

Remove the muslins and place one quail in each half truffle case; place on a tray, coat with Sauce Demi-glace containing some quail *Fumet* and place in the oven for a few minutes to heat and set a nice glossy coating on the quails.

Place a little of the same sauce on the bottom of a suitable dish, arrange the prepared quails on top and serve accompanied with a sauceboat of the same sauce.

Note: This recipe which derives from the old classical kitchen is both complicated and expensive to produce. It is little used in modern practice but has been included here as worthy of being preserved for its historical interest.

3682 Mignonettes de Cailles

Cut 6 nice plump quails in half, bone them out and reserve the ends of the feet.

Place the half quails in hot butter to set and firm the surfaces of the flesh, drain them well and allow to become cold. Cover the inside surfaces with a 1 cm ($\frac{2}{5}$ in) thick layer of a mixture consisting of two-thirds Parfait of foie gras crushed with a fork and one-third chicken forcemeat.

Flour, egg and breadcrumb them using fresh white breadcrumbs and shallow fry in clarified butter to a golden brown on both sides. Place each half quail on a shape of cooked puff pastry and arrange on a suitable dish.

Serve accompanied with a dish of buttered asparagus tips or buttered peas and a sauceboat of Sauce Chateaubriand.

Note: The halves of quails when shallow fried and cooked may be placed on Barquettes of raw puff paste filled with sliced mushrooms and truffle mixed with Sauce Béchamel then cooked at the last moment.

3683 Cailles à la Minute

Split the quails open from the back without separating the two halves; open them up, lightly flatten and prepare as indicated for Pigeonneaux à la minute (3410).

3684 Cailles au Nid
Bone out the quails, stuff them, form into round balls and poach them as for Cailles Lucullus.

When ready, place each quail in a large artichoke bottom cooked in butter; coat with a little Sauce Demi-glace finished with quail essence, and glaze them in the oven.

This done, surround the quails with small Quenelles of game forcemeat the size of very small eggs; decorate the sides of the artichoke bottoms with a very fine piping of chestnut purée about the size of vermicelli so as to imitate nests. This is best done using a small cornet and a very small plain piping tube.

Place a quail's head on top of each quail.

3685 Cailles à la Normande
Select nice even-shaped pippin apples; cut off the top third horizontally and empty them out to form cases; hollow out the tops of the apples as well.

Place 15 g ($\frac{1}{2}$ oz) butter in each quail then colour them in butter; place one quail in each of the apples, sprinkle with a little Calvados and cover with the tops of the apples.

Enclose each apple with its quail in a layer of short paste as one would a Rabotte de Pomme (4561). Place on a baking tray, brush with beaten egg and place in a hot oven for approximately 30 minutes.
To serve: arrange on a serviette.

Note: The quails may also be prepared as indicated for Pheasant or Partridge à la Normande.

3686 Cailles aux Petits Pois à la Romaine
Cook the quails *en Casserole* with a little butter.

Meanwhile, lightly colour in butter, 1 small chopped onion and 25 g (1 oz) chopped ham for each quail. Add some fresh peas, cover very tightly with a lid and cook together without any liquid. The peas should be ready at the same time as the quails.

Serve the quails and the peas in separate deep dishes or timbales covered with lids. The guest selects and mixes the two items.

3687 Cailles aux Raisins
Cook the quails *en Casserole* with a little butter; when ready, place them in a very hot terrine along with 8 to 10 peeled and depipped grapes per quail.

Deglaze the pan with a little dry white wine and a few drops of verjuice, add $\frac{1}{2}$ tbs strongly flavoured game *Fumet* per quail and pour this over the quails.

3688 Cailles Richelieu
Select very fresh, plump quails; remove the gizzards, season the inside with a few grains of salt and a few drops of brandy, insert a piece of raw truffle into each and truss them *en Entrée*.

Arrange in a shallow pan, close to each other and season with a little salt. Cover with a fairly coarse Julienne of carrot, onion and celery cooked in butter and prepared if possible from new season vegetables.

Moisten to just cover with sufficient excellent, gelatinous, amber-coloured veal stock; cover, bring to the boil and allow to poach gently for 12 minutes.

This done, add a Julienne of truffle (raw if possible) of about one-third the quantity of the vegetables and allow to cook for a further 2 minutes.

Arrange the quails in a timbale or deep dish and cover with the cooking liquid and Julienne after first removing all fat.

Note: A Pilaw of rice is often served with quails when prepared in the above fashion.

3689 Risotto de Cailles
Pound together equal quantites of fresh pork fat and white truffle; insert a hazelnut-sized piece of this mixture into each quail then cook them *en Casserole* with a little butter.

Have a Risotto prepared in advance and add to this the fat from the cooking of the quails.

Place the Risotto in a deep dish and fashion a hollow in its centre; arrange the quails in this hollow.

At the last moment deglaze the pan with game *Fumet* and sprinkle over the quails; serve immediately.

3690 Cailles sous la Cendre (*Old Method*)
Stuff the quails with a little fine game forcemeat containing chopped truffle; wrap each in a buttered vine leaf, then in a slice of salt pork fat and finally wrap in 2 sheets of strong buttered paper.

Place on the hearthstone of a fire or bed of a grill, cover with very hot cinders and allow to cook for approximately 30 minutes, replacing the cinders with fresh ones from time to time.
To serve: remove the outside charred paper and serve the quails as they are, still covered with the second sheet of paper.
Modern Method: stuff the quails with the forcemeat as before and wrap each in a slice of salt pork fat; place each on an oval of ordinary short paste. Moisten the edges and fold over the pastry to give the shape of a turnover; seal the edges well, brush with beaten egg and bake in a fairly hot oven for 25 to 30 minutes.

3691 Cailles Souvaroff
Prepare the quails in the same way as for pheasant

of the same name (3620) taking account of the difference in size, for garnishing and cooking.

3692 Cailles à la Turque

Truss the quails *en Entrée*, colour them in butter and complete their cooking in a Riz Pilaw containing a quarter its weight of cooked and chopped eggplant.

Mould the rice pyramid shape on a round dish and arrange the quails around its base standing upright against the rice. Surround with a *cordon* of well reduced quail stock.

3693 Timbale de Cailles Alexandra

Line a well buttered Timbale mould with ordinary pie paste and completely cover this paste with slices of salt pork fat. The slices of fat are to prevent any liquid from the filling of the Timbale reaching the pastry and making it soggy.

Insert a piece of foie gras in each quail then set and colour them in hot butter; arrange them against the sides of the timbale in superimposed tiers.

Fill the centre with small peeled raw truffles and add, per 6 quails, $1\frac{1}{2}$ dl (5 fl oz or $\frac{5}{8}$ U.S. cup) excellent veal stock flavoured with Madeira plus a few pieces of bayleaf. Close up the timbale with a layer of the same paste, seal the edges well and cook in a moderately hot oven for $1\frac{1}{4}$ hours.

On removing from the oven, demould the timbale on to a round dish and serve as it is.

Notes:

1) The pastry covering the timbale should not be served to the guest; its only purpose is to contain the quails and garnish.
2) The same preparation and presentation is suitable for buntings (Ortolons) but in this case only 45 minutes cooking time is needed.

CAILLES FROIDES—COLD QUAILS

3694 Chaud-froid de Cailles en Belle-vue

Bone out the quails and stuff each with a piece of Gratin Forcemeat C (295) made with game, each containing a small baton of foie gras and the same of truffle, set in its centre. Reshape the quails to their original form, wrap each in a square of muslin and poach them for 20 minutes in an excellent veal stock; allow to cool in the cooking liquor.

When quite cold, drain well, dry them and dip into a good brown Sauce Chaud-froid made with quail *Fumet*. Place on a tray and decorate the breasts of the quails neatly with fine shapes of truffle and cooked egg white. Glaze carefully with aspic jelly so as to fix the decoration then allow to set.

Carefully trim off any excess sauce from around the quails and arrange them in a deep square dish. Cover them entirely with an excellent clear aspic jelly and place in a refrigerator until required for serving.

3695 Cailles Froides en Caisses

Prepare the quails *en Chaud-froid* as in the preceding recipe. Place each in an oval, pleated fine porcelain dish or paper case and surround with a border of chopped jelly.

On each quail set a blanched quail's head, the eyes of which are imitated by a small round of cooked egg white with a spot of truffle in the centre.

3696 Cailles Cecilia

Roast the quails keeping them juicy and allow to become cold. Remove the breasts and discard the skins. With the remainder of the flesh and an equal amount of foie gras, prepare a fine smooth purée.

Place each breast of quail on a slice of foie gras of the same shape, sealing together with a little of the prepared purée; coat with brown Sauce Chaud-froid.

When the sauce has set well, arrange the breasts in a plain border mould which has been coated with jelly and decorated with truffle; the foie gras sides should be upwards in the mould. Fill the mould completely with jelly and place in the refrigerator to set.

When required, demould on to a serviette placed on a dish.

3697 Cailles au Château-Yquem

Prepare the quails as for Cailles Richelieu (3688). Add the Julienne of vegetables and moisten with two-third Château-Yquem and one-third veal stock. Cover and cook together as indicated in the recipe.

After 12 minutes of cooking, remove the quails to a clean pan, pass the cooking liquid through a fine strainer over the quails and discard the Julienne. Add 10 slices of truffle per quail and cook together for a further 2 minutes.

Arrange the quails in a timbale with the slices of truffle and cover with the cooking liquid after first removing all fat. Allow to cool and place in the refrigerator to set.

To serve: set the dish on a block of ice.

3698 Cailles Glacées Carmen

Poach the quails for 12 minutes in a strong well flavoured and gelatinous veal stock containing a suitable amount of white Port. Allow to cool in the liquid; drain well and make very cold.

Remove all fat from the liquid which should be sufficiently gelatinous to set, pass through a fine strainer and use it to glaze the quails.

Arrange the glazed quails in a circle in a timbale set in crushed ice and place a pyramid of lightly sweetened pomegranate Granité (4913) in the centre. The Granité may be placed in the centre of a very cold flat dish and surrounded with the quails.

Note: For this type of preparation, the cooked quails may be placed each in an oval mould which is then filled up with the cooking liquid, after first removing the fat and passing through a fine strainer. They are then allowed to set on ice, demoulded and arranged around the pyramid of Granité on a dish. It is felt that this is the best way of presenting quails and it is recommended for this series of recipes.

The following few recipes of this type of glazed quail which are of Eastern origin, are included here mainly for the sake of interest. It is as well to remember that they do not particularly suit French tastes.

3699 Cailles Glacées Cerisette
Poach the quails in a strong, well flavoured and gelatinous veal stock containing a suitable amount of Champagne. When cooked and cold, mould them in oval moulds as explained in the preceding note.

Demould and arrange on a very cold dish around a pyramid of Granité (4913) made with cherry juice. Between each quail place a bouquet of very cold, stoned cherries which have poached in a lightly sweetened syrup.

3700 Cailles Glacées Maryland
Poach the quails and mould them as in the preceding recipe.

Demould and arrange them around a pyramid of Granité (4913) made with pineapple juice set on a very cold dish.

3701 Cailles Glacées Reine Amélie
Poach the quails and mould them as previously indicated.

Demould and arrange them on a rock-shape layer of Granité (4913) made with tomato set on a very cold dish.

3702 Cailles Glacées au Romanée
Poach the quails in a veal stock containing Romanée wine and mould them as previously indicated.

Demould and arrange them around a pyramid of Granité (4913) made with verjuice.

3703 Filets de Cailles aux Pommes d'Or
Poach the quails in veal stock and allow to cool. Remove the breasts.

Prepare cases of orange or tangerine skins by cutting round the top third of the fruit with a knife, then removing the insides carefully. Place one or two of the quails breasts in each case, fill with a Port wine jelly and allow to set.

To serve: pipe on top of each, a small decoration of Granité prepared from the juice of the fruit used.

3704 Mandarines de Cailles
Lightly cut the tangerines around the top third and remove the segments carefully. Dry the segments, remove their skin and glaze with aspic jelly.

Fill the skins of the tangerines three-quarters full with quail Mousse containing some very small dice of foie gras.

Coat the cooked quails breasts with brown Sauce Chaud-froid and place one on top of each Mousse. Surround each breast with a few of the glazed quarters of fruit.

Keep in the refrigerator until required and arrange on a serviette on a dish to serve.

3705 Cailles Nillson
Prepare the quails as for Cailles au Château-Yquem and place each one in a small silver *Cassolette*. Cover with the cooking liquid after removing the fat and passing through a fine strainer. Allow to set.

Surround each quail with 4 nice, very white cocks' kidneys and set the *Cassolettes* on a block of ice for service.

3706 Cailles Froides Richelieu
Prepare the quails à la Richelieu (3688) and allow them to become cold in the cooking liquid.

Place in a deep square dish and cover them with the Julienne and the cooking liquid. Allow to set and place on a block of ice to serve.

3707 Timbale de Cailles Tzarine
See Timbale de Foie gras et de Cailles (3521) in the section on Cold Foie gras.

3708 Cailles à la Vendangeuse
Roast the quails, allow them to cool then place each in a small cooked basket made of light short pastry. Set a base of rice or semolina in the centre of a round dish and surround with the prepared quails in baskets; on top of the base plant a leafy vineshoot bearing grapes.

Surround the quails with peeled and depipped black and white grapes, coated with a little light setting Champagne-flavoured aspic jelly.

3709 RALE DE GENET OR ROI DE CAILLES—CORNCRAKES

The corncrake is an excellent game bird which, so far as the gourmet is concerned, should only be roasted. However, it may be prepared *en Cocotte* with a light garnish of truffle.

GRIVES AND MERLES—THRUSHES AND BLACKBIRDS

3710 Grives or Merles Bonne-Femme
Cook the birds in a covered pan with a little butter and 30 g (1 oz) small dice of salt belly of pork for each bird.

When ready, place them in a hot terrine with the dice of pork; add 25 g (1 oz) butter and 10 g ($\frac{1}{3}$ oz) small diced Croûtons of bread fried in butter for each bird. Deglaze the pan with a little brandy, sprinkle over the birds and serve very hot.

3711 Grives en Caisses
Proceed as indicated for Cailles en Caisses.

3712 Croûte aux Grives
Bone out the thrushes, season and fill the inside of each with a walnut-sized piece of Gratin Forcemeat C (295), a small cube of foie gras and the same of truffle. Re-form to their correct shape and wrap each in a sheet of buttered paper.

Arrange in a buttered shallow pan fairly close together and sprinkle with a little good roast dripping; roast in the oven for 10–12 minutes. When cooked, remove the paper and place each thrush on an oval Croûton of bread slightly hollowed out, fried in butter and coated with Gratin Forcemeat. Arrange on a tray, place in the oven and glaze the birds with a little Sauce Demi-glace flavoured with thrush *Fumet*.

Serve accompanied with a sauceboat of the same sauce.

3713 Grives or Merles au Gratin
Stuff each bird with a walnut-sized piece of Gratin Forcemeat C (295) plus one juniper berry; colour them well on all sides in butter.

Spread a 1 cm ($\frac{2}{5}$ in) layer of the same forcemeat on a dish and arrange the birds on top, pushing them into it; cover with fairly thick Sauce Duxelles, sprinkle with fine dry white breadcrumbs and melted butter and gratinate in a hot oven.

3714 Grives or Merles à la Liégeoise
Cook the birds in an earthenware casserole with a little butter, on the stove and uncovered. When almost cooked, sprinkle with 2 finely chopped juniper berries for each bird, add some small round Croûtons of bread fried in butter, cover with the lid and serve very hot.

Note: This preparation is particularly suitable for thrushes, especially those from the Ardennes.

3715 Grives or Merles au Nid
Proceed in the same way as for Cailles au Nid.

3716 Pâté chaud de Grives à la Liégeoise
Line a buttered oval fluted pie mould with fine short paste. Proceed in the same way as for Pâté chaud de Mauviettes à la Beauceronne but adding 4 finely chopped juniper berries per 500 g (1 lb 2 oz) of the Gratin Forcemeat.

Serve separately a Sauce Salmis prepared from the carcase and trimmings of the bird.

3717 Grives or Merles sous la Cendre
Proceed in either of the ways indicated for Cailles sous la Cendre.

GRIVES FROIDES—COLD THRUSHES

3718 Chaud-froid de Grives en Belle-vue
Bone out the thrushes and stuff them with Gratin Forcemeat C (295) containing 4 finely chopped juniper berries per 500 g (1 lb 2 oz) of forcemeat. Re-form them to their original shape and poach for 25 minutes in a good stock; allow to cool in the liquid.

Drain and dry them when very cold and coat with brown Sauce Chaud-froid flavoured with thrush *Fumet*; decorate with neat shapes of truffle and cooked egg white and glaze with aspic jelly. Allow to set.

Set a conical base of rice or semolina in the centre of a dish, arrange the prepared thrushes around it and place a little chopped jelly between each.

Blanch the heads of the birds, imitate the eyes with a round of egg white and a dot of truffle, coat with jelly and place one on each thrush. Border the dish with cut shapes of jelly.

Another method of presentation is to place the decorated thrushes in a deep square dish containing a layer of jelly in the bottom then cover them with clear, light setting aspic jelly.
To serve: set the dish on a block of ice.

3719 Chaud-froid de Grives en Caisses
Proceed as indicated for Chaud-froid de Cailles en Caisses.

3720 Filets de Grives Cherville
Cook the thrushes with butter in a pan on the

stove. Deglaze with a little brandy, allow them to cool, then remove the breasts.

Trim the breasts and coat with brown Sauce Chaud-froid flavoured with thrush *Fumet* and decorate each with a fancy round slice of truffle.

Prepare a Mousse from the remaining flesh of the birds and spread it in an even layer on the bottom of a deep square dish; when set arrange the prepared breasts on top and cover with a clear lightly setting jelly. Keep cold until required for service.

Preparation of the Mousse: After the breasts have been removed, finely pound the legs and carcasses of the birds and place in a pan with, for 12 thrushes, 3 dl (½ pt or 1¼ U.S. cups) excellent Sauce Demi-glace and 2 leaves of gelatine.

Simmer gently for 10–12 minutes, pass through a fine sieve and when the purée obtained is cold and almost setting, fold in approximately a third its volume of lightly whipped cream.

3721 Medaillons de Grives à la Moderne

Prepare and cook 12 thrushes as in the preceding recipe. Coat 12 of the breasts only with brown Sauce Chaud-froid.

Prepare a Mousse with the remaining flesh of the birds and the trimmings.

Coat 12 oval tartlet moulds with a layer of aspic jelly, place in each, one of the prepared breasts, chaud-froid side downwards and fill with some of the Mousse.

Coat a fairly deep dome-shaped mould with a layer of jelly, decorate with truffle and fill with the rest of the Mousse.

To serve: place a flat low base of rice or semolina in the centre of a dish, demould the Mousse on top of it and surround with the Medaillons after demoulding them. Border the dish with neat shapes of cut jelly.

ALOUETTES OR MAUVIETTES—LARKS

The French name Alouette refers to the live bird. In the autumn, when the bird has become fat and plump and is in perfect condition for culinary preparation, it is then designated as Mauviette and as such should always be described on the menu.

3722 Mauviettes à la Bonne Femme

Proceed as indicated for thrushes of the same name.

3723 Mauviettes en Caisses

Proceed as indicated for quails of the same name.

3724 Mauviettes au Gratin

Proceed as indicated for thrushes of the same name.

3725 Mauviettes Mère Marianne

Slice some peeled and cored pippin apples and three-quarters cook them in butter without sugar.

Spread these apples in a thick layer on the bottom of a buttered dish. Season and quickly fry the larks in brown butter just to set the outside surfaces and arrange them on the apples pushing them in slightly. Sprinkle with breadcrumbs and melted butter and place in a hot oven or under the salamander, for sufficient time to complete the cooking.

3726 Mauviettes à la Minute

Split the larks open from the back without separating them into halves. Lightly flatten them and proceed as indicated for Pigeonneaux à la Minute (3410).

3727 Mauviettes à la Normande

Proceed as indicated for quails of the same name (3685), placing 2 larks in each apple case.

3728 Pâté chaud de Mauviettes à la Beauceronne

Bone out the larks and stuff them with Gratin Forcemeat C (295) containing chopped truffle. Place in a buttered pan and cook in a very hot oven.

Line a buttered fluted pie mould with good short paste; place in the larks alternating with layers of gratin forcemeat, beginning and finishing with a layer of forcemeat. Sprinkle the top layer with a little powdered thyme and bayleaf and close up the mould with a layer of paste, sealing the edges well. Bake for 45 minutes in a moderately hot oven.

On removing from the oven, demould the pie on to a dish, cut off the crust on the top and cut it into triangles. Arrange these around the base of the pie.

Coat the bared layer of forcemeat with a few spoonfuls of Sauce Salmis made from the bones and trimmings of the larks.

Serve the rest of the sauce separately.

3729 Mauviettes à la Paysanne

Colour in butter and at the same time, 12 larks and 125 g (4½ oz) salt belly of pork cut in dice and blanched; add 1 bayleaf and sprinkle with a good pinch of flour. Cook together for a few minutes, moisten with 1½ dl (5 fl oz or ⅝ U.S. cup) white wine and reduce by half, then add sufficient warm water to come three-quarters of the way up the birds; season with salt and pepper.

For each lark, complete the garnish by adding

2 button onions cooked in butter and 6 pieces of potato trimmed to the shape of olives and coloured in butter.

Complete the cooking rapidly and reduce the sauce. Place into an earthenware terrine and allow to simmer gently for a few more minutes.

Serve in the dish as it is.

3730 Alouettes du Père Philippe

Select as many nice even-shaped Dutch potatoes as there are larks. Clean them well and cut off a slice from the tops about $\frac{1}{2}$ cm ($\frac{1}{5}$ in) thick; hollow these out to be used as covers; also hollow out the potatoes to a shape large enough to hold one lark and place these into the oven to just half cook.

Colour the larks quickly in hot butter together with, for each bird, 10–15 g ($\frac{1}{3}$–$\frac{1}{2}$ oz) salt belly of pork cut in dice and blanched. Place one of the larks in each potato case along with a few pieces of the salt pork and a little of the fat from the pan. Replace the potato lids, secure these by tying with thread, then wrap each potato thus prepared in a sheet of strong oiled paper.

Place on the hearthstone, cover with a thick layer of hot cinders and cook for 20 minutes renewing the cinders from time to time.

The larks may also be prepared in the following manner: bone out the insides of the larks and stuff with a Gratin Forcemeat made with foie gras and truffles. Cook under cover with butter in the oven. Bake the potatoes under hot cinders and when cooked, remove the top of each. Empty the potatoes and shallow fry the pulp with butter turning over and over until lightly coloured. Refill the potatoes with this then place a lark on top and coat with a little Sauce Chateaubriand.

3731 Mauviettes à la Piémontaise

Prepare 1) a deep round mould filled with Polenta and allow it to become quite cold, 2) some fairly stiff Risotto and 3) larks sautéed in butter with 4 white truffles cut in thick slices.

Turn out the mould of Polenta and empty it so as to form an empty case; butter the outside surface, sprinkle with fine dry breadcrumbs and replace in its mould. Fill with alternate layers of Risotto, larks and truffle; close up the mould with a round shape of Polenta and seal the edges with a band of raw forcemeat. Place in a warm oven for 30 minutes.

For service, demould on to a round dish and surround with a little Sauce Espagnole flavoured with game *Fumet*.

3732 Mauviettes Froides—Cold Larks

The recipes for cold thrushes are all suitable for larks.

ORTOLANS—BUNTINGS

The bunting as an item of food is sufficient in itself and should only be roasted—this is a gastronomic verity accepted for many years.

Those items which are sometimes added in the preparation of buntings, such as truffle and foie gras can be somewhat detrimental inasmuch as they tend to mask the subtle flavour and aroma of the bird which are much more delicate than the pronounced aromas of truffle and foie gras.

Buntings can be classed along with other luxury dishes because they are very expensive but they do not provide a dish of true gastronomic excellence. Nevertheless, a number of recipes are given here with the caution that buntings should never be boned out.

3733 Ortolans en Caisses

Stuff the buntings with a hazelnut-sized piece of foie gras; wrap each in a square of muslin and poach them for 5–6 minutes in a good strong stock.

When cooked, drain well, remove the muslin and place each bird in a porcelain or paper case half filled with a fine Salpicon of foie gras and truffle. Coat the buntings with a little very well-reduced game *Fumet*.

3734 Ortolans aux Questches

After roasting, this is the best of the preparations for buntings.

Cut some very large questche plums in half and remove the stones. Place on a tray, fill the cavities with a small piece of butter and place in the oven.

When almost cooked, place on each half plum, a bunting which has been moistened and wrapped in a vine leaf. Place in a very hot oven for 4 minutes.

On removing from the oven, lightly season with salt and brush with verjuice.

Arrange on a dish and serve as they are; the plums are not eaten but serve only as a support for the birds; they do, however, add flavour to the birds.

3735 Ortolans au Suc d'Ananas

See the Chapter on Roasts (3948).

3736 Sylphides d'Ortolans

Half fill some very small, buttered silver or porcelain *Cassolettes* with a Mousseline forcemeat of bunting flavoured with truffle essence. Place in a warm oven to cook the forcemeat.

Cook in butter for 3 minutes only as many buntings as there are *Cassolettes* and to be ready at the same time as the forcemeat is cooked.

Place one bunting in each *Cassolette* and sprinkle with a little brown butter combined with a little melted meat glaze and pineapple juice.

Serve immediately.

ORTOLANS FROIDS—COLD BUNTINGS

3737 Aspic d'Ortolans
Roast the buntings and allow them to become cold.

Place breast sides downward in a border mould previously coated with jelly; fill with excellent very clear jelly and allow to set.

Demould on to a round dish and surround with cut shapes of jelly.

3738 Mandarines d'Ortolans
The end of the season for buntings coincides with the arrival of the first tangerines which at this time are still a little sour and thus very suitable for this preparation.

Cut off the tops of the tangerines and remove the flesh, leaving empty cases and lids. Place one cold roast bunting in each empty tangerine case and fill up with an excellent lightly acidulated aspic jelly. Allow to set.

Arrange on a serviette on a dish and replace the tops of the tangerines which should have their stalks and a few leaves attached if possible.

Note: Arrange each bunting in the tangerine's case in such a way as to allow its head to keep the top open at one side.

3739 Timbale d'Ortolans Rothschild
Prepare 1) a Timbale case (4334), 2) a truffled foie gras kept a little pink, 3) 24 buntings roasted for 2 minutes only and 4) 12 small truffles cooked with Madeira.

Everything being ready, place the foie gras standing up in the middle of the Timbale case and surround it with the buntings and truffles arranged in two layers. Cover the Timbale with its lid and seal to the sides with a band of raw paste. Place the Timbale thus prepared in a medium hot oven for approximately 15 minutes.

On removing from the oven fill with a well flavoured, gelatinous veal stock containing the cooking liquor from the truffles.

Keep in the refrigerator for 2–3 days before serving.

3740 Timbale d'Ortolans Tzarine
Proceed as indicated for Timbale de Foie gras et de Cailles à la Tzarine (3521).

3741 Ortolans à la Vendangeuse
Proceed as indicated for Cailles à la Vendangeuse (3708).

BECS-FIGUES AND BEGUINETTES—FIG-PECKERS AND WARBLERS

Although these birds are of two different species, the same methods of preparation are suitable for either.

The fig-peckers are to be found more commonly in southern countries whereas the Warblers originate in the north; they are very popular in Belgium.

The following recipes may be applied to either bird.

3742 Béguinettes à la Bonne-Femme
Allow 3–4 birds per person and proceed as indicated for Grives à la Bonne-Femme (3710).

3743 Béguinettes à la Liégeoise
Proceed as indicated for Grives à la Liégeoise (3714).

3744 Béguinettes à la Polenta
Prepare a Polenta (4284) keeping it to the consistency of mashed potato, season and mix in some grated Parmesan and butter and spread it over the bottom of a deep dish.

Quickly cook the birds in butter and arrange them on the Polenta. Deglaze the pan with a little brandy and water and sprinkle over the birds and Polenta.

BECASSES AND BECASSINES—WOODCOCKS AND SNIPES

If the grouse did not exist the woodcock would hold pride of place among the game birds; but it has an advantage over grouse which can only be appreciated to the full in its country of origin, this is because the flavour and aroma of the woodcock is less fleeting than that of grouse and can be kept for a longer time before being cooked. The particular qualities of the flavour and aroma of the woodcock can only be realized if the birds are hung for sufficient time.

The snipe is a smaller version of the woodcock and is distinguished from it by the fact that it lives almost completely in marshy areas whereas the woodcock inhabits the tidal waters of rivers.

There are a number of varieties of snipe—the common snipe, the great snipe which is very rare and the jacksnipe which is perhaps the finest of all.

3745 Bécasse à la Mode d'Alcantara
See the recipe and notes concerning pheasant of the same name (3598).

3746 Bécasse de Carême
Sprinkle the woodcock with a little oil and roast it underdone. As soon as ready, remove the legs and breasts and cut each breast into two thick slices.

Place ½ tbs French mustard in a pan and mix with a few drops of lemon juice; place in the slices of breast together with the legs and turn over to coat all surfaces; heat and keep warm.

Chop the carcase and the intestines of the bird, place in a pan; pour over ½ dl (2 fl oz or ¼ U.S. cup) flamed brandy and reduce; add 1 tbs of game *Fumet* and cook gently for 5 minutes.

Pass firmly through a fine strainer over the pieces of woodcock and shake the pan to coat them with this cullis. Arrange in a deep dish and place the head of the bird on top.

3747 Bécasse à la Fine Champagne
Cook the woodcock *en Casserole* and cut into 6 pieces, that is, the two breasts each cut in half and the two legs. Place them in a round terrine with the head on top, cover and keep warm.

Deglaze the casserole with a little flamed *Fine Champagne* brandy and add the chopped intestines, the juices pressed from the carcase, 1 tbs game *Fumet*, a few drops of lemon juice and a touch of Cayenne. Strain this cullis over the woodcock and reheat without boiling.

Serve as it is in the terrine.

Note: Although the above recipe indicates the cutting of the woodcock into 6 pieces, in reality it is preferable to just cut it into two and serve one half per person.

3748 Bécasse Favart
Proceed as indicated for Soufflé de Caneton Rouennais (3479) taking care to add the intestines of the woodcock to the Mousseline forcemeat.

When the carcase has been prepared with the forcemeat, arrange the breasts of the bird cut in slices on top with a line of slices of truffle along the centre. Allow 20 minutes for cooking the forcemeat.

Serve separately a Sauce Demi-glace flavoured with woodcock *Fumet*.

3749 Mousse and Mousselines of Woodcock
The preparation of the Mousseline forcemeat is made in accordance with the recipe in the section on forcemeats to be found in the Chapter on Garnishes; the liver and intestines of the bird should be sautéed in butter, passed through a fine sieve together with the same amount of foie gras and added to the forcemeat.

The moulding and finishing of these Mousse and Mousselines is the same as indicated before.

3750 Pâté chaud de Bécasse—Hot Woodcock Pie
Proceed as indicated for Hot Pheasant Pie (3614) taking account of the main ingredient to be used.

Do not forget to add the intestines of the woodcock to the Gratin Forcemeat. These should be sautéed in butter and passed through a fine sieve together with 100 g (3½ oz) foie gras per 500 g (1 lb 2 oz) of forcemeat.

3751 Bécasse à la Riche
Proceed in the same manner as for Bécasse à la Fine Champagne with the following modifications.

1) Arrange the pieces of woodcock on a Croûton of bread fried in butter and coated with Gratin Forcemeat C (295).
2) Thicken the sauce with a little purée of foie gras, finish with 30 g (1 oz) butter and pass firmly through a coarse strainer over the pieces of woodcock.

3752 Salmis de Bécasse
Proceed in exactly the same way as for Salmis de Faisan taking care to 1) roast the woodcock keeping it very underdone, and 2) add the chopped intestines to the sauce.

3753 Bécasse Sautée au Champagne
Cut the woodcock in half and remove the intestines; trim and season the two halves and colour them quickly in hot butter. Cover and allow to cook gently for 5 minutes keeping the flesh very soft. Place the two halves in a deep dish, cover and keep warm.

Fry the chopped intestines and trimmings in the same pan, deglaze with 1½ dl (5 fl oz or ⅝ U.S. cup) Champagne without pouring off the fat and reduce by three-quarters. Pound the whole finely, adding an equal quantity of butter then pass through a fine sieve. Finish the purée obtained with a few drops of lemon juice and a touch of Cayenne.

Reheat without boiling and pour over the woodcock.

3754 Bécasse Sautée aux Truffes
Proceed as in the preceding recipe adding 50 g (2 oz) sliced truffle to the pieces of woodcock.

Deglaze the pan with Madeira and truffle essence.

3755 Soufflé de Bécasse
Proceed as indicated for Bécasse à la Favart.

3756 Bécasse Souvaroff
Proceed as indicated for Faisan Souvaroff (3620) taking account of the size of the woodcock and the quantity and proportions of truffle and foie gras.

3757 Suprêmes de Bécasse
The various recipes as indicated for Suprêmes de Perdreau are all suitable for woodcock.

3758 Timbale de Bécasse Nesselrode
Poêlé the woodcocks keeping them underdone. Remove the breasts and reserve for further use. Remove the bones from the remainder and finely pound the flesh obtained together with a quarter its weight of raw foie gras; pass through a fine sieve and mix together with an equal quantity of a game Forcemeat with Panada and Butter (286).

Chop the carcase and trimmings and add to the pan in which the bird was cooked, together with 1 dl ($3\frac{1}{2}$ fl oz or $\frac{1}{2}$ U.S. cup) brandy; allow to cook for a few minutes then pass through a fine strainer. Cook in this liquid 150 g (5 oz) olive-shaped pieces of truffle; this should be sufficient for an ordinary size Timbale.

Line a buttered Charlotte mould with a layer of good short paste then coat the paste with a layer of the prepared forcemeat. Cut the breasts of the woodcock into slices and arrange them around the inside of the mould. Fill the centre with the truffles and cover them with a few tablespoons of Sauce Espagnole reduced with a little of the cooking liquor from the truffles.

Cover with some of the same forcemeat and close up the Timbale with a layer of paste. Seal the edges and bake in a moderate oven for 45 minutes.

To serve: demould the Timbale on to a round dish and surround with a little Sauce Demi-glace containing the rest of the cooking liquor from the truffles.

Serve the rest of the sauce separately.

Note: By following the same procedure a Timbale Nesselrode may be prepared with pheasant, partridge, snipe or hazel-grouse; the name of the bird, however, should be mentioned in the menu title.

3759 Timbale de Bécasse Saint-Martin
Prepare a decorated Timbale case (4334) more wide than high.

Roast the woodcocks keeping them underdone; remove the breasts and arrange them in the Timbale case alternating with slices of fresh foie gras shallow fried in butter; cover with a coarsely cut Julienne of truffle and mushroom.

Pound the carcasses and trimmings of the birds, add a few tablespoons of truffle essence, pass firmly through a fine sieve then through a fine strainer.

Heat the cullis obtained without boiling and finish it with a few drops of lemon juice, a little brandy and butter. Pour this over the woodcock, foie gras and Julienne in the Timbale.

BECASSES FROIDES—COLD WOODCOCKS

3760 Aspic de Bécasses
Roast the woodcocks keeping them juicy, allow to become cold then remove the breasts; cut each of these into two slices.

Remove the flesh from the legs and pound together with the intestines, then pass through a fine sieve; add a few drops of brandy and a little aspic jelly to this purée. Cover the slices of woodcock dome shape with the purée, allow to set, then coat with brown Sauce Chaud-froid.

Arrange in a border mould previously lined with jelly, placing the sides coated with chaud-froid downwards. Fill with good aspic jelly, allow to set then demould on to a round dish to serve. Surround with cut shapes of jelly.

3761 Bécasses en Belle-vue
Bone out the woodcocks from inside leaving the legs and feet intact. Stuff with a mixture of half Gratin Forcemeat C (295) and half raw game forcemeat, placing in the centre of the stuffing a few small pieces of raw foie gras and small quarters of truffle.

Wrap each bird in a piece of muslin making sure that they have been reshaped, then poach them for 30 minutes in a good game stock; allow to become cold in the cooking liquid.

Drain them, dry well and coat with brown Sauce Chaud-froid flavoured with woodcock *Fumet*. Decorate the breasts with neat shapes of truffle and cooked egg white and glaze well with aspic jelly.

Set a base of rice or semolina in the centre of a dish; arrange the prepared woodcocks standing up around the base. Place the heads back on the woodcocks and imitate the eyes with cooked egg white and truffle.

3762 Bengalines de Bécasses
Roast the woodcocks and allow them to become cold; remove the breasts and cut each into three slices.

With the flesh from the legs and any trimmings prepare a Mousse in the usual manner.

Coat the required number of egg-shaped Quenelle

moulds with a layer of the Mousse, place a spoonful of cold very well reduced woodcock *Fumet* in the centre of each, cover with a slice of the woodcock and set a slice of truffle on top. Cover with more of the Mousse, smooth the surface and allow to set in the refrigerator.

When nicely set, demould the Bengalines, coat with brown Sauce Chaud-froid and decorate with truffle.

Arrange them in a timbale or deep rectangular dish previously lined with jelly annd cover with excellent light setting aspic jelly; allow to set.
To serve: set the dish on a block of ice.

3763 Chaud-froid de Bécasse
Proceed in the usual manner using brown Sauce Chaud-froid flavoured with woodcock essence.

3764 Bécasse Cecilia
Proceed as indicated for Cailles Cecilia (3696).

3765 Côtelettes de Bécasse Sarah Bernhardt
Roast three woodcocks and bone them out when cold.

Cut four of the breasts into dice and mix half of this with an equal quantity of salt ox tongue likewise cut in dice. Mix the rest of the diced breasts with double its quantity of foie gras cut in dice. Mix each of these preparations separately with a few tablespoons of brown Sauce Chaud-froid.

Take 10 medium-sized round truffles, empty them with a spoon and fill with the prepared mixture of breasts and foie gras.

Pound the rest of the flesh of the woodcocks with an equal amount of foie gras and the insides removed from the truffles. Pass through a fine sieve, place in a pan, set on ice and mix thoroughly together with 70 g (2½ oz) good butter, 1½ dl (5 fl oz or ⅝ U.S. cup) just melted brown Sauce Chaud-froid and ½ dl (2 fl oz or ¼ U.S. cup) game glaze.

Have prepared the required number of small cutlet moulds lined with aspic jelly and coat the inside of these with a layer of the prepared purée. Fill the centres with a teaspoon of the diced mixture of breast and tongue. Cover with more of the purée and allow to set in the refrigerator.

Set a layer of jelly on a round dish and place a base of rice or semolina in the centre. Demould the cutlets, arrange them around the base and place the prepared truffles on top of the base.

3766 Bécasse Esclarmonde
Remove the breasts from cold roast woodcocks and cut each into two slices.

Prepare a Mousse with the flesh from the legs and any trimmings.

Place each slice of breast on a slice of foie gras of the same shape sticking them together with a little of the Mousse. Coat with brown Sauce Chaud-froid, decorate with truffle and glaze with aspic jelly.

Place the rest of the Mousse into a small dome-shaped mould lined with jelly and allow to set.

Set a flat base of rice in the centre of a dish, demould the Mousse and place on top; arrange the prepared breasts of woodcock around the base and surround with chopped jelly.

3767 Bécasse Marivaux
Remove the breasts from a nice, cold roast woodcock and cut them into slices.

Cut off the breast bones and fill the carcase with a Mousse of woodcock and foie gras; smooth carefully to give it the original shape of the bird. Coat the legs and the end of the bird with brown Sauce Chaud-froid.

Set a layer of jelly on a dish and place the prepared woodcock on top. Arrange the slices of breast across the Mousse alternating each with a smaller slice of foie gras. Place an overlapping layer of truffle slices along the centre and fill any spaces by piping in some chopped jelly using a cornet.

Surround the woodcock with a layer of near-setting jelly and allow to set in the refrigerator before serving.

3768 Cold Mousse and Mousselines of Woodcock
See Mousse and Mousselines in the Chapter on Garnishes (332).

3769 Pain de Bécasse
See the basic recipe in the section on Cold preparations in the Chapter on Garnishes; or proceed as indicated for Pain de Foie gras.

3770 Salmis Froid de Bécasse
Prepare the Salmis in the usual way but without using mushrooms and doubling the amount of truffle.

Arrange the pieces of woodcock in a deep flat earthenware dish with the sauce and truffles and allow to become cold and set. Finally cover with a layer of aspic jelly flavoured with woodcock *Fumet* and serve very cold.

3771 OTHER GAME BIRDS

Grand Coq de Bruyère—Capercaillie: This is the largest of the birds belonging to the order *Gallinaceae* and although fairly common in northern countries, is rarely to be found in France. It is best when roasted on the spit.

Petit Coq de Bruyère—Black Grouse: This bird is

about the same size as the pheasant and there is a variety of it which is usually featured on the menu under the name of Black-Cock. Suitable preparations are, *à la Broche*, *en Salmis* and *en Chaud-froid.*

Grouse: This bird is one of the finest of the game birds and is to be found only in Scotland and England. They should be used fresh; they do not travel well especially during the beginning of the season in August. Suitable preparations are the same as those for Hazel Grouse.

Gelinotte—Hazel Grouse: This bird named by Toussenel 'Tetras huppé des myrtilles' (the myrtle-crested grouse) is from a culinary standpoint, considered to be of great value and with justification. Suitable preparations: *à la Broche, en Salmis, en Chaud-froid, en Soufflé, Mousselines, à la Crème.*

Note: The legs of the above four birds have a very pronounced flavour of pine and for this reason should not be served if the bird is roasted; they should be removed beforehand in any other preparation.

Ganga—Pin-tailed Grouse: This is a fairly rare bird, indigenous to the south of France and Algeria. It is about the same size as the partridge and its flesh is similar to that of the bustard. It should only be spit-roasted.

Prairie Grouse: This is an American bird seldom seen in France and thus of little importance, but it may be prepared in any of the ways suitable for hazel grouse.

Colin—American Partridge: This bird originates from California and is exported frozen to Europe where it is frequently used as an item of food.

In size it is half-way between that of the quail and the partridge and may be prepared in any of the ways suitable for partridge.

Francolin—Black Partridge: This bird may be prepared in accordance with any of the recipes for partridge.

Canopetière—Bustard: This bird comes principally from Tunis and Algeria and is sometimes found in France during the start of the game season. Its most suitable preparations are *à la Broche* and *en Salmis.*

Pluvier Guignard—Dotterel: This is a bird of the plains about the size of a blackbird. It was previously used as the basic ingredient in the preparation of the *Pâté de Chartres* but, unfortunately, it has become very rare. Suitable preparations: *à la Broche*, *en Salmis*, *en Chaud-froid* and *Pâté.*

3772 WATER FOWL

Note: The following birds are considered as acceptable for serving as Lenten dishes.

Canard Sauvage—Wild Duck (Mallard): This is the largest of the birds grouped under the heading of water fowl. Suitable preparations: *à la Broche*, *à la Bigarade*, *à l'Orange*, *en Salmis* and most of the preparations for Rouen Duckling.

Sarcelle—Teal: This bird is a smaller species of the Mallard. The common teal can be distinguished by its eyes which are framed in white; one of its varieties the Garganey has only a fleck of white under the eyes shaped something like a comma. Suitable preparations: *à la Broche*, *à l'Orange*, *en Salmis*, *en Chaud-froid.*

Pilet—Pintail: This bird is a little smaller than the Mallard. Some gourmets consider it to be the finest of all the water fowl. Suitable preparations: the same as those for teal.

Souchet—Shoveller: This bird can be recognized, other than by its plumage, by its flat large beak shaped something like a spoon. It may be prepared in any of the ways suitable for teal.

Pluvier Doré—Golden Plover, and Vanneau—Lapwing: Although these birds may be distinguished by their plumage, their habits and habitats are almost identical. They migrate twice each year, in the autumn when they are referred to in France as Pluviers or Vanneaux gras de la Toussaint, and in February and March. Suitable preparations: *à la Broche*, *en Salmis* and *Pâté aux Champignons.*

Chevalier—Sandpiper: The spotted sandpiper is the variety most preferred by the gourmet. They are best when spit-roasted and served on Croûtons of bread fried in butter and coated with a Gratin forcemeat.

Scoter, Crake, Coot, Moorhen and other water fowl of this type are only mentioned here as being of minor interest; in culinary terms they are of inferior quality and should only be roasted.

Note: Without exception, if prepared *en Salmis*, the skin of water fowl should not be used in the making of the sauce.

CHAPTER 10

COMPOSITE ENTRÉES

Under the heading of Composite Entrées are included the various *Croustades,* Hot Pies, *Timbales, Tourtes* and *Vols-au-vent.* In the old classical kitchen, *Casseroles au Riz* were also included under this heading but they were nothing more than a kind of *Timbale* and have been completely eliminated from modern cookery.

Croustades have also fallen into disuse but are worth mentioning as a resource that may occasionally be used to give variety to the menu. They are cut from a sandwich loaf into various shapes—round, oval or square and decorated to taste making sure that the centre is hollowed out for the garnish. After deep frying, the cavity is covered with a thin coating of forcemeat which is cooked by placing it in a slow oven. This is done to act as a barrier between the fried bread and the garnish and its sauce.

The usual fillings for this kind of preparation are *Emincés* of chicken and game or various kinds of *Salmis.*

The characteristic of a hot pie is that the cooking of the filling takes place at the same time as that of the pastry, also that it is served with a small quantity of sauce made from an essence of the main ingredient; sometimes it is additionally garnished with mushrooms and truffles.

The definition of a *Timbale* differs widely and therein lie some of the mistakes now sanctified by usage, of calling so many different dishes by the same name. Thus it is that under this general title are to be found a *Croustade* with the garnish placed straight into it; or a case of forcemeat which holds the filling and which is then covered with a lid of the same forcemeat, the whole being cooked *au Bain-marie.* In other examples, the *Timbale* is made by lining a buttered mould spiral fashion with partly cooked macaroni or with cooked stuffed olives or even with flat pieces of cooked forcemeat cut to shape.

In all these examples the lining is covered with a layer of raw forcemeat so as to keep the items in place and to ensure the solidity of the *Timbale.* The filling is then placed inside and after covering the top with another layer of forcemeat, the *Timbale* is cooked *au Bain-marie.*

Under this general heading are also included dishes in silver, porcelain and earthenware which are similar in shape and size to the *Timbale* cases.

The preparation of *Tourtes* and *Vols-au-vent* which is the responsibility of the pastry department is too well known to need any lengthy description. The same garnishes may be used in both but *Tourtes* have been almost entirely replaced by *Vols-au-vent.*

Also included under the name of *Tourtes* are various dishes, mainly of local origin, which generally consist of two layers of paste enclosing either a cooked mixture, or at least a half cooked mixture, in order that the filling and the paste are both cooked at the same time. The outer edge of the *Tourte* is frequently encircled with a band of puff pastry.

Although the foregoing types of preparation have been gathered together and retained here under the general heading of Composite Entrées, it has nevertheless been thought more suitable to place their actual recipes in those chapters and sections of the book dealing with the main ingredient of which they are composed.

To find any of these recipes it is thus only necessary to consult the Index.

CHAPTER 11

COLD PREPARATIONS

GALANTINES, PIES AND TERRINES

3773 Forcemeats for Galantines, Pâtés and Terrines
The various forcemeats for these can be found in the section on Various Forcemeats in Chapter 2—Garnishes.

3774 Fumets for Pies and Terrines
These fumets are made from the bones and trimmings of poultry and game and with the addition of a relative quantity of jelly. They should always be very delicate but at the same time, well flavoured.

3775 Pastes for Moulded Pies
There are two types of paste which are suitable for moulded pies:

A) Ordinary Pie Paste:
Ingredients:
1 kg ($2\frac{1}{4}$ lb) sifted flour
250 g (9 oz) butter
30 g (1 oz) salt
2 eggs
4 dl (14 fl oz or $1\frac{3}{4}$ U.S. cup) water
(The quantity of water can vary slightly according to the type of flour used; best quality flour tends to absorb more water.)
Method:
Make a bay with the flour and place in the centre the salt, water, eggs and butter and make into a paste in the usual manner. Knead the paste twice to ensure its complete and smooth amalgamation. Roll into a ball, wrap in a cloth and keep in a cool place until required.

B) Hot Water Paste:
Ingredients:
1 kg ($2\frac{1}{4}$ lb) sifted flour
250 g (9 oz) warm melted lard
2 eggs
30 g (1 oz) salt
4 dl (14 fl oz or $1\frac{3}{4}$ U.S. cup) warm water
Method:
Mix and prepare the paste as in the preceding recipe.

Note: These pastes should be made 24 hours in advance whenever possible so as to obviate all signs of elasticity. The handling of a paste which has been allowed to rest is much easier than that of freshly made paste and in addition its colour when cooked is better.

3776 Galantine (*Standard Recipe*)
Poultry and game selected for the preparation of galantine may be less tender than for other uses.

Bone out the selected poultry or game by starting with an incision along the back cutting off the wings and legs to the first joints; remove all the flesh carefully. Spread the skin on a clean cloth.

Cut the breasts and small fillets into long strips 8 mm ($\frac{1}{3}$ in) square, season with spiced salt, and place to marinate with brandy, together with 100 g ($3\frac{1}{2}$ oz) fresh pork fat, 60 g (2 oz) each of cooked lean ham and salt ox tongue, all cut into long thick strips, and 100 g ($3\frac{1}{2}$ oz) truffle cut into quarters; these amounts are for a medium-sized bird.

Remove any sinews from the legs and with the meat and trimmings make a forcemeat in accordance with the ingredients and proportions as given in the recipe for chicken or game Forcemeat (299) with an optional addition of 50 g (2 oz) chopped truffle.

Place a layer of forcemeat down the length of the skin, arrange the strips of garnish on this alternating the colours; on this place another layer of forcemeat then more garnish and so on until it is all used, finishing with forcemeat; fold over the skin to envelop the whole.

Wrap the galantine in slices of salt pork fat and roll it up in a cloth; tie it round with string and tie each end tightly.

An alternative way is to cut the chicken, ham, tongue, pork fat and truffles into large dice and mix them into the forcemeat together with 150 g (5 oz) freshly peeled pistachio nuts; arrange it all on the skin and finish and roll up the galantine as before. This is an easier way of making a galantine and the result when cooked and sliced is almost the same as that when using long strips arranged to form a mosaic pattern.

The Cooking of the Galantine: To cook the galantine immerse it in White Bouillon made from blanched veal bones, chicken carcasses, the usual herbs and vegetables and seasoned with 6 g ($\frac{1}{5}$ oz) salt per 1 litre ($1\frac{3}{4}$ pt or $4\frac{1}{2}$ U.S. cups) liquid; simmer gently allowing approximately 35 minutes per 1 kg ($2\frac{1}{4}$ lb) of galantine.

The Pressing of the Galantine: When the galantine is cooked, remove it from the liquid, untie it and retie firmly in the same serviette or in another clean one; place on a long tray, set a board on top with a few light weights but not that it is too heavy. Leave to become cold. The reason for pressing a galantine is simply to ensure that the ingredients which may have become separated during the cooking process are pressed back together to form a whole. If it is pressed too hard though, the juices will be squeezed out and the galantine will become dry and flavourless.

When the galantine has become quite cold, remove the cloth, wipe it dry and coat with sufficient cool melted jelly so that it becomes covered with a fairly thick layer. Place it on a very cold long dish, surround with chopped jelly and border the dish with cut shapes of jelly using an excellent Chicken Aspic Jelly.

Details of a chicken for galantine of 1 kg 100 g (2 lb 8 oz) gross weight

Intestines and Giblets	225 g	equal to	23·18 %
Skin	140 g	equal to	12·73 %
Carcase	240 g	equal to	21·82 %
Flesh (net)	465 g	equal to	42·27 %
TOTAL:	1 kg 100 g	TOTAL:	100·00 %

Following a series of tests done on chickens of various weights the results established that the actual net weight of flesh obtained from undrawn chickens is from 42–45 % of the total weight.

PATES DE POISSONS—FISH PIES

3777 Fish Forcemeat

Ingredients:
1 kg ($2\frac{1}{4}$ lb) pike, free from skin and bones
400 g (15 oz) Rice or Frangipane panada
500 g (1 lb 2 oz) butter
4 egg whites
30 g (1 oz) salt
5 g ($\frac{1}{6}$ oz) pepper
a touch of Cayenne
grated nutmeg

Method:
Prepare in the same way as for Forcemeat with Panada and Butter (286).

3778 Pâté d'Anguille—Eel Pie

Skin the eel, fillet it and cut into thin slices. Stiffen in butter with chopped shallot, chopped raw mushrooms and chopped parsley; allow to cool.

Line a buttered oblong mould with short paste, coat this with a layer of fish forcemeat then fill the mould with alternate layers of the prepared eel and forcemeat.

Cover with a sheet of the same paste, sealing it well to the moistened edges; pinch the edges to decorate and cover with leaves of paste arranged overlapping from the edges to the centre. Add one or two round fancy shapes of paste and make a hole in the centre of them to allow the steam to escape; brush with eggwash and bake in a hot oven allowing 30 minutes per 1 kg ($2\frac{1}{4}$ lb) of pie.

3779 Pâté de Saumon or Pâté de Truite—Salmon or Trout Pie

Trim 4 fillets of salmon or salmon trout cut from the tail end and season them.

Line a buttered oblong mould with short paste and coat the bottom and sides of this with pike forcemeat containing 150 g (5 oz) chopped truffle per 1 kg ($2\frac{1}{4}$ lb) forcemeat.

Place two of the fillets of salmon on the bottom layer of forcemeat, cover with more of the same forcemeat and place some medium-sized truffles in the centre of the forcemeat. Add another layer of forcemeat, then the other two pieces of salmon in the reverse order to those on the bottom layer and finish by filling with another layer of forcemeat. Close up the pie with a layer of short paste, finish and decorate as for eel pie. Brush with eggwash and bake in a hot oven allowing 30 minutes per 1 kg ($2\frac{1}{4}$ lb) of pie.

When the pie is cold, fill it with Fish Aspic Jelly.

3780 Pâté de Soles—Sole Pie

Place 24 fillets of sole in cold water for 1 hour to whiten them; drain, dry and flatten them slightly.

Place 6 of the fillets next to each other and coat them with a layer of pike forcemeat. Moisten the surface with egg white and place a small cylinder-shaped piece of truffle 1 cm ($\frac{2}{5}$ in) in diameter at the tail end of each fillet touching one another. Roll up the 6 fillets in one single piece the shape of a long sausage. Repeat this operation with the rest of the fillets.

Line a buttered oblong mould with short paste, coat the bottom and sides with pike forcemeat containing raw lobster coral; lay two of the rolled lengths of sole on top; cover with forcemeat, add some medium-sized truffles, another layer of forcemeat, then the other two rolls of sole and finish with more of the forcemeat. The arrangement should be such that when the pie is cut the truffles will be in the centre surrounded by the fillets of sole. Cover the pie with short paste, decorate as for Eel Pie, eggwash and bake in a hot oven allowing 30 minutes per 1 kg ($2\frac{1}{4}$ lb) of pie.

When the pie is cold, fill it with Fish Aspic Jelly.

PATES DE VIANDE—MEAT PIES

3781 Pâté de Jambon—Ham Pie

Line an oval pie mould with ordinary short paste, cover this with thin slices of salt pork fat and then with pork forcemeat (297) passed through a sieve and containing 150 g (5 oz) chopped lean ham and 125 g ($4\frac{1}{2}$ oz) large dice of ham per 1 kg ($2\frac{1}{4}$ lb) of forcemeat. Attention should be paid to the seasoning of the forcemeat to take account of the saltiness of the ham.

Cover with an oval piece of salt pork fat, add a few pieces of bayleaf, then cover with a layer of paste. Decorate and finish with leaves of paste or cover with a layer of puff paste; brush with eggwash and bake in a moderate oven allowing 35 minutes per 1 kg ($2\frac{1}{4}$ lb) of pie.

When cold, fill with Madeira-flavoured aspic jelly.

3782 Pâté de Veau et Jambon—Veal and Ham Pie

Line a pie mould with ordinary short paste then cover this with thin slices of salt pork fat. Fill with alternate layers of veal and pork forcemeat (298), thin strips of raw ham and fresh belly of pork, and thin slices of cushion of veal, seasoned and marinated with brandy beforehand.

Cover with paste and finish as for Ham Pie.

PATES DE VOLAILLE—PIES OF POULTRY

3783 Pâté de Poulet—Chicken Pie

Bone out 2 medium-sized chickens; remove the breasts and stiffen them by dipping in boiling water for a moment then finely lard them with very thin pieces of salt ox tongue and truffle. Use the remainder of the chicken flesh to make a forcemeat in accordance with recipe (299).

Line a round pie mould with ordinary short paste then cover this with thin slices of salt pork fat. Fill with alternate layers of the forcemeat, the larded breasts, slices of salt ox tongue and thick slices of truffle and finish with a layer of forcemeat.

Cover with a round of salt pork fat, add half a bayleaf then close it up with a round of the same paste. Pinch the edges to seal and decorate with leaves of short paste or cover with a thin layer of puff paste. Brush with eggwash and bake in a fairly hot oven.

When the pie is cold, fill it with Chicken Aspic Jelly.

3784 Pâté de Caneton—Duck Pie

Prepare a forcemeat of duck (299) and mix together with a quarter its volume of pork forcemeat. Bone out a duck and cut the breasts into thin slices.

Spread out the skin of the duck, cover with alternate layers of forcemeat and sliced duck and garnish it with long strips of foie gras and quarters of truffle; roll up into an oval shape.

Line an oval mould with short paste then coat this with thin slices of salt pork fat; place in the prepared duck.

Close up with a layer of the same paste or with a layer of puff paste, brush with eggwash and bake in a moderately hot oven.

When the pie is cold fill it with duck-flavoured jelly.

3785 Pâté de Pigeons—Pigeon Pie

Bone out the pigeons, stuff them as for galantine, reshape them and proceed as indicated for Duck Pie.

3786 Pâté de Pintade—Guinea Fowl Pie

Proceed as indicated for Chicken Pie using guinea fowl.

Details of a duck for pie or terrine weighing 1 kg 800 g gross (4 lb)

Intestines and Giblets	600 g	equal to	33·33 %
Skin only	540 g	equal to	30·00 %
Carcase	240 g	equal to	13·34 %
Flesh (net)	420 g	equal to	23·33 %
TOTAL:	1 kg 800 g	TOTAL:	100·00 %

The results of a series of tests using ducks of from 1 kg 700 g to 2 kg shows that the yield of flesh is from 23 % to 28 % of the total weight.

PATES DE GIBIER—GAME PIES

3787 Pâté d'Alouettes known as Pantin—Lark Pie

Bone out the larks and fill with Gratin Forcemeat

B (294), reshape them and wrap each in a thin slice of salt pork fat.

Roll out a piece of short paste to an oval shape allowing 35–40 g (1¼–1½ oz) paste per bird. In the centre of each piece of paste place an oblong piece of salt pork fat and cover this with a layer of pork forcemeat made with extra fat and passed through a sieve. Place one lark on top of each then cover with more forcemeat and another slice of salt pork fat.

Roll the edges of the paste thinner, moisten and bring to the centre covering the filling. Seal well, turn over on to a baking sheet and make one or two holes to allow the steam to escape. Pinch around the edges and on top to decorate, brush with eggwash and bake in a fairly hot oven.

3788 Pâté de Bécasses—Woodcock Pie
Bone out the woodcocks and fill with pork forcemeat containing a quarter its volume of Gratin Forcemeat C (295) and the chopped intestines of the woodcocks; alternate the forcemeat with some strips of foie gras and quarters of truffle. Reshape the birds, place in an oval pie mould lined with ordinary short paste and cover with thin slices of salt pork fat.

Close up the pie with a layer of paste. Cover with leaves of paste or a layer of puff paste. Brush with eggwash and bake in a moderately hot oven.

When the pie is cold, fill it with woodcock-flavoured jelly.

3789 Pâté de Faisan—Pheasant Pie
Bone out the pheasant, remove the breasts and lard them with thin strips of salt ox tongue and truffle; make the rest of the pheasant into a forcemeat (299) adding one third its volume of Gratin Forcemeat B (294).

Proceed as indicated for Chicken Pie.

When the pie is cold, fill it with pheasant-flavoured jelly.

3790 Pâté de Grives—Thrush Pie
Bone out the thrushes and fill with Gratin Forcemeat B (294) flavoured with 6 chopped juniper berries per 1 kg (2¼ lb) forcemeat. Reshape the thrushes.

Line an oval fluted pie mould with short paste and cover this with thin slices of salt pork fat. Place in the thrushes alternating them with layers of pork forcemeat made with extra fat and containing a quarter its weight of Gratin Forcemeat B (294). Cover and finish the pie as previously indicated.

When the pie is cold, fill it with thrush-flavoured jelly.

3791 Pâté de Lièvre—Hare Pie
Bone out the saddle and legs of a hare, remove the tendons and lard the fillets from the back, the minion fillets and the best parts of the legs with very thin strips of salt pork fat. Season with spiced salt and place to marinate with brandy together with an equal amount of strips of lean ham and fresh pork fat. Make the remainder of the hare into a game forcemeat (299).

Line a buttered fluted oval pie mould with short paste, cover this with thin slices of salt pork fat and fill with alternate layers of the forcemeat and the marinated hare and strips of ham and fat. Finish with a layer of forcemeat. Cover with an oval layer of salt pork fat and add a pinch of powdered thyme and bayleaf. Cover, decorate and cook in the usual manner.

When the pie is cold, fill it with hare-flavoured aspic jelly.

3792 Pâté de Perdreau—Partridge Pie
Proceed as indicated for Pheasant Pie.

PATE DE FOIE GRAS

3793 Pâté de Foie gras (*for 20–25 persons*)
Preparation of the forcemeat:

Ingredients:
750 g (1 lb 10 oz) pork fillet
950 g (2 lb 2 oz) fresh pork fat
250 g (9 oz) trimmings of raw truffle
50 g (2 oz) spiced salt

Method: Pound all of the ingredients finely, pass through a sieve and mix in the marinade from the foie gras.

Preparation of the foie gras: Take 2 medium-sized and very firm goose livers of 700–750 g (1½ lb–1 lb 10 oz) each; stud them with quarters of raw truffle which have been seasoned with spiced salt and marinated with 1 dl (3½ fl oz or ½ U.S. cup) each of brandy and Madeira for 3 hours in advance.

To make the pie: Line a suitable size round fancy mould with 1 kg 400 (3 lb 2 oz) very firm and well rested Hot Water Paste (3775).

Coat this with some of the forcemeat, place in the prepared livers and cover with the remainder of the forcemeat. On top of this place a slice of salt pork fat, a touch of mixed spice and 1 bayleaf; close up with a layer of the same paste. Cover the top with overlapping leaves of paste arranged so as to build up the surface into a dome shape. In the centre place 3 or 4 graduated fancy rounds of paste, one on top of each other and lightly moistened to make them stick. Make a hole right through them so as to allow steam to escape during the cooking. Brush with eggwash then bake in a moderately hot oven, allowing 30 minutes per 1 kg ($2\frac{1}{4}$ lb) of pie.

When the pie is nearly cold, fill it with melted lard or Madeira-flavoured jelly.

To serve the pie: There are 2 ways of cutting and serving this pie; 1) Run the point of a knife around the top edge and remove the cover of pastry in one piece; discard the fat and remove the required amount of filling by means of a spoon dipped in hot water, cutting it out in the shape of hollow shells. Replace the lid on the pie but upside down; fill this with chopped jelly and arrange the shells of foie gras on top, pyramid fashion. 2) Remove the cover of pastry in one piece; insert a thin bladed knife between the pie crust and the filling, cut round to separate then remove the required amount of the foie gras by inserting a knife through from the side and cut from side to side until it is released with as little damage as possible. Remove the piece, place on a serviette and divide it into small even square pieces.

Fill the emptied part of the pie with chopped jelly, place the cover on upside down, arrange the pieces of foie gras in a circle on top of the lid and fill the centre with more chopped jelly.

TERRINES

3794 Terrine (Standard Recipe)

Terrines are really only pies made without a pastry crust and apart from a few minor details of preparation all the pies in this section can be made in the form of Terrines.

Preparation of the Terrine: Whatever kind, the Terrine is first lined with thin slices of salt pork fat then filled with alternate layers of the forcemeat, thin strips of the flesh of the main ingredient, strips of salt pork fat and truffles.

For Terrines of chicken and game birds, the filling may be enclosed in the skin of the bird as indicated for Duck Pie.

When filled, the Terrine should be covered with a layer of salt pork fat plus a pinch of spice and a piece of bayleaf and covered with the lid.

The Cooking of the Terrine: Place the Terrine in a shallow tray, pour in some hot water and cook in a moderately hot oven; more water should be added during the cooking if necessary.

The time needed to cook a Terrine depends upon its size and the nature of the ingredients used. The fat that rises to the surface gives a reliable indication as to whether it is cooked; when it is cloudy and contains some of the raw juices it is not cooked but if completely clear it is fairly certain that it is cooked.

A trussing needle may be used to ascertain if the Terrine is cooked; it should come out hot all through when withdrawn after being inserted through the centre.

The Pressing and Serving of the Terrine: If the Terrine is to be eaten fairly soon, it should be filled with jelly a few minutes after being taken from the oven, then covered with a piece of board with a weight on top to press it down slightly whilst it is cooling and for the same reason as indicated for a galantine.

The fat is removed when cold, the top trimmed, the dish cleaned and it is cut in the dish for serving.

If to be presented whole, the Terrine should be more tightly pressed and turned out when cold; it should then be trimmed all over, replaced in the terrine on a bed of set jelly then surrounded with more melted jelly.

For service, the Terrine is turned out on a dish and surrounded with cut shapes of jelly.

If the Terrine is to be kept for any length of time it should be turned out and trimmed as above, replaced in the dish and covered with melted lard which in solidifying will prevent any contact with the air. It must be kept covered in a refrigerator.

3795 Household Terrines and Pies

These dishes of the old Bourgeois kitchen deserve to be placed on record rather than being forgotten. They are made with all kinds of butchers' meat, poultry or game and a typical basic recipe is as follows:

Cut the required amount of fillet or cushion of veal into long thin strips; season with salt, pepper and nutmeg and stiffen them quickly in hot butter. Place in a basin with strips of ham and salt pork fat in the proportions of 4 parts of veal to 1 of ham and fat. Deglaze the pan with a little brandy and Madeira and pour this over the meats; allow to cool.

Line a terrine with thin slices of salt pork fat or line a mould with short paste; fill with alternate layers of the veal and the other ingredients, cover with either salt pork fat or short paste then bake in a hot oven.

Allow to cool then fill with either ordinary jelly or a jelly flavoured with the main ingredient used.

SIMPLE, COMPOSED AND MAYONNAISE SALADS

There are two main types of salad—simple salads and composed or made-up salads.

Simple salads are raw green salads such as are served with a hot roast joint; composed salads are those made with several kinds of cooked vegetables which are usually served with Relevés, Entrées and cold roast dishes.

Mayonnaise salads are only a variation of the composed salads but because of the ingredients they contain they are accepted as being cold entrées.

In this book the recipes for the various kinds of Mayonnaise salads such as Mayonnaise of fish and poultry are included at the end of the sections dealing with the principal ingredient from which they are made.

SALAD DRESSING

Sauce Mayonnaise must be used with discretion to dress salads as it can be indigestible; some people cannot bear it particularly late at night at the end of a dinner.

Equally, raw onion should be used sparingly as many people do not like it and in any case it must be very finely sliced, washed under cold water and firmly squeezed in the corner of a clean cloth to remove the acrid juices.

3796 Oil and Vinegar Dressing
This is suitable for all salads and is made in the proportions of three parts oil to one of vinegar plus the addition of salt and pepper.

3797 Cream Dressing
This is used mainly on cabbage, lettuce and young cos lettuce; it is made with three parts fresh but not too thick cream to one of vinegar or, better still, lemon juice, then seasoned with salt and pepper.

3798 Egg Dressing
This is made by mixing oil into sieved yolks of hard-boiled eggs together with mustard, vinegar, salt and pepper. It is usual to garnish a salad seasoned with egg dressing with a fine Julienne of white of hard-boiled egg. A very thin Sauce Mayonnaise may also be used as an egg dressing.

3799 Bacon Dressing
This is used only for salads of dandelion, corn salad and red cabbage. Here the oil is replaced by the fat expressed from very small dice of fatty bacon when it is fried brown in a pan. It is poured hot together with the pieces of bacon, over the salad which has been placed in a warm bowl; it is finished with a little vinegar, already seasoned with salt and pepper and heated in the hot frying pan at the last moment.

3800 Mustard and Cream Dressing
This is used mainly for salads of beetroot, celeriac and for green salads where beetroot is the main ingredient.

It is made in the proportion of 1 dsp of mustard mixed into 2 dl (7 fl oz or $\frac{7}{8}$ U.S. cup) of light fresh cream plus the juice of a small lemon and salt and pepper.

3801 Mayonnaise Dressing
This is made and seasoned exactly according to the recipe given for Sauce Mayonnaise in the Chapter on Sauces.

SIMPLE SALADS

3802 Green Salads
The following are the most commonly used green salads: Lettuce, cos lettuce, Endive, Batavian endive, chicory, celery, corn salad, dandelion leaves, purslane, garden cress, watercress, rampion, salsify leaves and wild chicory.

3803 Salade de Betterave—Beetroot Salad
Beetroot is an adjunct rather than the main ingredient of any kind of salad whether simple or composed. It is preferable to bake the beetroots rather than boil them.

If it is to be prepared especially as a salad, cut them into thin slices or fine Julienne, flavour with chopped baked onion and mix with oil and vinegar dressing or mustard dressing to taste; a little chopped Fines Herbes may be added.

3804 Salade de Céleri—Celery Salad
For a simple salad only white celery without developed fibres should be used. Cut the stalks into short lengths and shred very finely without cutting right through. Leave in ice water to curl up, drain well then mix with a mustard and cream dressing.

3805 Salade de Céleri-rave—Celeriac Salad
Cut the celeriac into Julienne or very thin Paysanne and mix with thin Sauce Mayonnaise strongly flavoured with mustard.

3806 Salade de Choux-fleurs—Cauliflower Salad
Boil the cauliflower keeping them underdone, drain well but do not refresh them. Cut into small well trimmed flowerets and mix with oil and vinegar dressing plus a little chopped chervil.

3807 Salade de Choux Rouges—Red Cabbage Salad
Select young and tender red cabbage, remove the stumps and stalks and shred the leaves finely. Mix

with oil and vinegar dressing at least 6 hours before serving.

3808 Salade de Concombres—Cucumber Salad
Peel the cucumbers, slice them thinly and sprinkle with salt so as to express the vegetable juices.

When about to serve, drain and sprinkle with oil and vinegar dressing and plenty of chopped chervil.

Note: English cucumbers do not require salting beforehand.

3809 Vegetable Salad (*made with dried haricot beans etc*)
Drain the cooked vegetables well and mix with oil and vinegar dressing plus chopped parsley.

Serve accompanied with a dish of finely chopped, washed and squeezed onion.

Note: Dried vegetable for a salad should be seasoned whilst still warm so as to ensure penetration of the dressing.

3810 Salade de Pommes de Terre—Potato Salad
Boil the potatoes in salted water, trim cylindrical shape and cut into slices whilst still warm. Mix with oil and vinegar dressing and chopped Fines Herbes.

3811 Salade de Pommes de Terre à la Parisienne
Select firm textured potatoes such as the Vitelotte type. Boil them in salted water and cut into thin slices whilst still warm; place in a basin and marinate with 3 dl (10 fl oz or $1\frac{1}{4}$ U.S. cups) dry white wine per 1 kg ($2\frac{1}{4}$ lb) of potato. When ready to serve, mix very carefully with oil and vinegar dressing and some chopped chervil and parsley.

3812 Salade de Tomates—Tomato Salad
Skin some firm tomatoes, cut them in half horizontally and remove the seeds. Cut into very thin strips, sprinkle with oil and vinegar dressing and surround with small rings of onion.

COMPOSED SALADS

Unless they are being completely finished in the kitchen, composed salads are presented without mixing the ingredients. The various items which go to make the salad should be seasoned separately and arranged in separate bouquets.

The arrangement of a composed salad may be completed with a border of either beetroot, hard-boiled egg, gherkins, truffle, etc. There is no set pattern and the arrangement is inspired by the ideas and good taste of the cook. The practice of moulding composed salads is not recommended because if the appearance is not enhanced, neither is the taste, which in fact may lose a lot.

The most simple yet the quickest way of arranging a salad is to be preferred; building a salad pyramid fashion is only permissible if a border of cut shapes of jelly surrounds it, but even this should not be done too often.

Note: By increasing the quantities according to the requirements of the service, most of the rice salads in the section on Cold Hors-d'oeuvre can take their place among these composed salads; they can be found listed here in their alphabetic order.

3813 Salade Aïda
Take sufficient very white frizzy endive to constitute half the required amount of finished salad; the other half is made up of equal quantities of sliced peeled tomatoes, sliced raw artichoke bottoms, skinned green pimentos cut into short Julienne and sliced cooked egg white. Sprinkle well with sieved hard-boiled egg yolks.
Dressing: oil and vinegar, fairly well flavoured with mustard.

3814 Salade Alice
Choose nice medium-sized rosy apples, cut off a slice from the stalk ends and keep them to act as the lids. Remove the centres by means of a spoon cutter leaving only a thin layer of apple next to the skin. Rub the insides with lemon juice to keep them white.

Prepare sufficient of the following ingredients to fill the emptied apples: equal quantities of small balls of apples cut with a spoon cutter the size of a pea, picked redcurrants and finely shredded fresh almonds or pieces of fresh walnuts when in season. Just before serving, mix these together with some lightly salted cream, acidulated with lemon juice; fill the apples with this mixture and replace the lids.

Arrange in a circle on a bed of crushed ice and place a quartered heart of lettuce between each apple.

3815 Salade à l'Américaine
Take fairly firm skinned tomatoes cut into thin slices, potatoes cut into thin round slices, celery cut into Julienne, thin rings of onion and sliced hard-boiled eggs. Arrange in bouquets.
Dressing: oil and vinegar.

3816 Salade à l'Andalouse
Half the total quantity of this salad is composed of quarters of peeled tomato and a Julienne of sweet pimentos; and the other half of separated grains of plain boiled rice flavoured with a touch of crushed garlic, chopped onion and chopped parsley.
Dressing: oil and vinegar.

3817 Salade Aurore
Take two peeled and sliced dessert apples and 24 halves of skinned fresh walnuts, arrange them in a salad bowl and surround with leaves of lettuce.
Dressing: 6 tbs cream; 2 tbs of fresh tomato purée; 1 tsp English mustard; the juice of 2 lemons; salt and sugar.

3818 Salade Beaucaire
Take equal quantities of Julienne of celery, Julienne of celeriac, and Julienne of Belgian endive—add oil, vinegar and mustard and leave for 1 hour. Then add half its quantity of a mixed Julienne of lean ham, cooking apples and raw mushrooms.

Mix all together with a few tablespoons of Mayonnaise, arrange in a salad bowl, sprinkle with chopped parsley, chervil and tarragon and surround with a border of alternate round slices of beetroot and potato.

3819 Salade Bagration
Take equal quantities of Julienne of celery, Julienne of cooked white of chicken and thin slices of artichoke bottoms. Take twice as much thin macaroni cooked a little firm and cut into 5 cm (2 in) lengths whilst still warm. Marinate the celery and artichoke for 20 minutes with oil and vinegar then add the chicken, the macaroni and some Mayonnaise which has been lightly flavoured with tomato purée.

Mix all together, arrange dome shape in a salad bowl and smooth the surface. Decorate with a star, the points of which are made with truffle, salt ox tongue, hard-boiled egg white, hard-boiled egg yolk and chopped parsley.

3820 Salade Belle de Nuit
Take equal quantities of crayfish tails and slices of black truffle.
Dressing: oil and wine vinegar, well seasoned with freshly milled black pepper.

3821 Salade Bergerette
See Cold Hors-d'oeuvre (1034).

3822 Salade Brésilienne
See Cold Hors-d'oeuvre (1035).

3823 Salade Carmen
Take equal quantities of peeled red pimentos and cooked white of chicken—both cut into Paysanne; plain boiled peas, and well drained plain boiled rice.
Dressing: oil and vinegar with the addition of mustard and chopped tarragon.

3824 Salade Castelnau
See Cold Hors-d'oeuvre (1036).

3825 Salade Catalane
See Cold Hors-d'oeuvre (1037).

3826 Salade Crémone
Prepare equal quantities of Japanese artichokes cooked *à la Grecque* and thinly sliced flesh only of tomato. Add a quarter of this quantity of anchovy fillets.
Dressing: oil and vinegar, flavoured with mustard and chopped Fines Herbes.

3827 Salade Créole
Select small almost ripe melons; cut out a circular piece at the stem ends and reserve them for future use. Remove the melon seeds then scoop out the insides with a spoon and cut this into large dice. Season with salt and a pinch of ginger and add an equal amount of well drained plain boiled rice.

At the last moment mix in a little cream, lemon juice and salt; refill the melons with this mixture and replace the reserved tops. Serve set in a bed of finely crushed ice.

3828 Salade Cressonière
This consists of equal quantities of Salade de Pommes de Terre à la Parisienne and leaves of watercress.

Arrange dome shape and sprinkle with chopped hard-boiled egg mixed with chopped parsley.

3829 Salade Danicheff
Take equal quantities of 1) asparagus tips cooked fairly firm, boiled celeriac and potatoes and 2) raw artichoke bottoms and raw mushrooms—all these ingredients should be thinly sliced. Arrange all these ingredients in bouquets and decorate with crayfish tails, hard-boiled eggs and slices of truffle.
Dressing: thin Sauce Mayonnaise.

3830 Salade Demi-Deuil
This salad is composed of equal quantities of potatoes and truffles both cut in Julienne. Surround with a border of alternate rings of potato with a round of truffle placed in the centre and rings of truffle with a round of potato placed in the centre.

3831 Salade d'Estrées
Take equal quantities of crisp white celery and raw truffles, both cut into large Julienne.
Dressing: Sauce Mayonnaise flavoured with mustard and Cayenne.

3832 Salade Dorzia
See Cold Hors-d'oeuvre (1038).

3833 Salade Eve
Prepare medium-sized apples as for Salade Alice and cut the removed flesh into dice. Take equal quantities of the diced apple, bananas, pineapple and skinned green walnuts; mix with cream flavoured with lemon juice and salt and refill the apple cases with this mixture.

Serve arranged on a bed of crushed ice and place a quartered heart of lettuce between each apple.

3834 Salade Favourite
This is composed of equal quantities of crayfish tails, slices of white truffle and asparagus tips.
Dressing: very good olive oil, lemon juice, salt, pepper, chopped celery and chopped Fines Herbes.

3835 Salade à la Flamande
This is composed of: 1) half the total amount of Belgian endives, 2) a quarter of potatoes cut into Julienne and 3) a quarter of a mixture of peeled and chopped baked onions and diced herring fillet.
Dressing: oil and vinegar with chopped parsley and chervil.

3836 Salade Francillon
This is composed of: 1) half the total amount of boiled potatoes sliced whilst still warm and marinated with Chablis wine, 2) a quarter of bearded mussels which have been cooked with a little celery and 3) a quarter of slices of truffle.
Additional Dressing: good quality oil and vinegar.

3837 Salade des Gobelins
Take equal quantities of 1) fairly firm cooked celeriac, and 2) potatoes—both cut into shavings, 3) raw artichoke bottoms and 4) raw mushrooms—both cut into slices, 5) slices of truffle and 6) asparagus tips.
Dressing: Sauce Mayonnaise flavoured with a little lemon juice and chopped tarragon.

3838 Salade Hollandaise
See Cold Hors-d'oeuvre (1039).

3839 Salade Irma
Mix together equal quantities of diced cucumber, diamond-shaped pieces of French beans, asparagus tips and cauliflower flowerets. Mix with Sauce Mayonnaise containing a little cream and chopped tarragon and chervil.

Arrange dome shape in a salad bowl and cover with finely shredded lettuce mixed with garden cress.

Decorate with Nasturtium flowers and round slices of radish.

3840 Salade Isabelle
Take equal quantities of 1) finely sliced truffle, white of celery and raw mushrooms and 2) finely sliced cooked artichoke bottoms and potatoes.
Dressing: oil and vinegar with the addition of chopped chervil.

3841 Salade Italienne
See Cold Hors-d'oeuvre (1040).

3842 Salade Japonaise
This is another name for Salade Francillon.

3843 Salade aux Fruits à la Japonaise
This salad is composed of pineapple, orange, tomato, hearts of cabbage lettuce or cos lettuce and fresh cream. If being served on a heart of ordinary lettuce, the fruit should be cut into small squares; if on half a heart of cos lettuce, the fruit should be cut in small thin slices.

The salad is prepared as follows: sprinkle the pineapple with lemon juice; season the tomato with a pinch of sugar, very little salt and a little lemon juice.

Do not season the oranges.

Keep the fruit very cold until required for service then arrange the fruits on hearts of lettuce or half hearts of cos lettuce; sprinkle each with a tablespoon of cream acidulated with lemon juice and seasoned with a pinch of salt. Serve the remainder of the sauce separately.

If nice hearts of lettuce are not available, the fruits can be arranged in a salad bowl and surrounded with the tender inside leaves of lettuce.

Note: This salad is of American origin. It was perfected by M. Escoffier and was always served at the Carlton Hotel under the name of Salade Japonaise. As there already existed a salad of this name which is a classical one, the new presentation given above was entitled Salade aux Fruits à la Japonaise so as to avoid confusion between the two.

3844 Salade Jockey Club
Take equal quantities of asparagus tips and sliced raw truffles; dress separately with oil and vinegar then mix at the last moment with a little well seasoned Mayonnaise.

3845 Salade Lakmé
Take equal quantities of skinned and diced red pimentos, diced flesh only of tomatoes and plain boiled very white rice.

Dressing: oil and vinegar flavoured with curry and chopped onion.

3846 Salade de Légumes—Vegetable Salad
Take equal quantities of carrots and turnips cut out with a spoon cutter, diced potato, French beans cut diamond shape, peas and asparagus tips. Arrange in bouquets with a bouquet of cauliflower in the centre.
Dressing: oil and vinegar with the addition of chopped parsley and chervil.

Note: Vegetables for use in a salad should not be refreshed after cooking. They should be well drained and allowed to cool naturally.

3847 Salade Lorette
Take equal quantities of celery, corn salad and beetroot all cut into Julienne.
Dressing: oil and vinegar.

3848 Salade Maraîchère
The composition of this salad varies according to the time of the year. During the winter months it includes mainly rampion, tender white shoots of salsify and finely shredded celeriac with potato and beetroot for decoration.
Dressing: Sauce Moutarde à la Crème (207) containing grated horseradish.

3849 Salade Mascotte
Take equal quantities of green asparagus tips, hard-boiled gull's eggs, small cocks' kidneys, slices of truffle and crayfish tails. Decorate the salad to choice using some of the ingredients.
Dressing: Sauce Moutarde à la Crème (207).

3850 Salade Mignon
Take equal quantities of prawns and artichoke bottoms both cut into dice and surround with a border of thin slices of truffle.
Dressing: Sauce Mayonnaise with cream and flavoured with a little Cayenne.

3851 Salade Midinette
See Cold Hors-d'oeuvre (1041).

3852 Salade Mikado
Take equal quantities of lightly poached and bearded oysters, well drained plain boiled rice and skinned red and green pimentos cut into dice.
Dressing: Oil and vinegar flavoured with mustard.

3853 Salade des Moines
See Cold Hors-d'oeuvre (1042).

3854 Salade Monte Carlo
See Cold Hors-d'oeuvre (1043).

3855 Salade Montfermeil
Take equal quantities of freshly cooked salsify cut into small batons whilst still warm, sliced artichoke bottoms and potatoes and Julienne of cooked egg white.

Arrange dome shape in a salad bowl and cover completely with sieved hard-boiled egg yolks; sprinkle with chopped Fines Herbes.
Dressing: oil and vinegar.

3856 Salade Muguette
Take equal quantities of the white part of frizzy endive, sliced green pippin apples, celery heart cut in fine Julienne and thinly sliced flesh only of tomato. Add a third part of green walnuts which have been pickled in verjuice. Mix together with a little light Mayonnaise made with hard-boiled egg yolks.

Decorate with round slices of pink radishes and sprigs of chervil.

3857 Salade Nantaise
See Cold Hors-d'oeuvre (1044).

3858 Salade Niçoise
Take equal quantities of diced French beans, diced potato and quarters of tomatoes.

Decorate with capers, olives and anchovy fillets.
Dressing: oil and vinegar.

3859 Salade Noémi
This is composed of a roast poussin cut into pieces whilst still warm leaving the skin and bone on, 12 crayfish tails cooked in Court-bouillon and still warm and 2 hearts of lettuce.

Pound the crayfish shells with 1 dl ($3\frac{1}{2}$ fl oz or $\frac{1}{2}$ U.S. cup) cream and a little lemon juice, pass through a sieve with pressure, season with salt and milled pepper and pour over the salad when about to serve. Sprinkle with chopped chervil.

3860 Salade des Nonnes
Take equal quantities of well drained plain boiled rice and Julienne of white of chicken; mix together; pile dome shape in a salad bowl and sprinkle with grated black truffle.
Dressing: oil and vinegar flavoured with mustard.

3861 Salade Normande
See Cold Hors-d'oeuvre (1045).

3862 Salade Opéra
Take equal quantities of cooked white of chicken, salt ox tongue, celery and truffles, all cut into Julienne; arrange in a dish with a bouquet of asparagus tips in the centre.

Surround with a border of alternate slices of cocks' kidneys and gherkins.
Dressing: light Sauce Mayonnaise.

3863 Salade d'Oranges (*for roast duck, wild duck and teal etc*)
Peel ripe oranges, cut them in half vertically, remove the seeds then cut the flesh into thin even-sized slices.
Dressing: a little Kirsch.

3864 Salade Orientale
Take equal quantities of halves of small tomatoes with the seeds removed and cooked in olive oil with a clove of garlic per 6 tomatoes; diced, skinned, red and green pimentos; plain boiled French beans cut into small batons; and well drained, plain boiled rice.
Dressing: oil and vinegar with the addition of diced anchovy fillets.

3865 Salades de Poissons—Fish Salads
These may be found in the Chapter on Fish, classified under the name of the particular kind of fish.

3866 Salade Polonaise
Take equal quantities of carrots, turnips, cucumber, gherkins, potatoes, hard-boiled eggs and herring fillets—all cut into dice.

Arrange in bouquets with a quarter of hard-boiled egg filled with jellied Mayonnaise between each bouquet.
Dressing: oil and vinegar with chopped parsley and tarragon.

3867 Salade Portugaise
See Cold Hors-d'oeuvre (1050).

3868 Salade Rachel
Take equal quantities of celery, truffle, artichoke bottoms and potatoes—all cut into Julienne, and asparagus tips. Lightly mix with thin Sauce Mayonnaise.

3869 Salade Régence
Take equal quantities of thin shavings of raw truffle, sliced cocks' kidneys, very thin long strips of celery and asparagus tips.
Dressing: well seasoned oil and lemon juice.

3870 Salade Réjane
See Cold Hors-d'oeuvre (1052).

3871 Salade Russe—Russian Salad
Take equal quantities of carrot, turnips, potato, truffle, French beans, cooked mushrooms, salt ox tongue or lean ham, lobster, gherkins, smoked sausage and anchovy fillets—all cut into dice or Julienne, peas and capers.

Mix with Sauce Mayonnaise, arrange in a salad bowl and decorate with any suitable items from the salad plus beetroot and caviare.

3872 Salade Saint-Jean
Take equal quantities of 1) asparagus tips, French beans cut into diamond-shapes and peas; and 2) thinly sliced raw artichoke bottoms, sliced, salted and drained cucumber and chervil.

Mix with thin acidulated Sauce Mayonnaise, place in a salad bowl and decorate with a border of slices of hard-boiled egg, slices of gherkin and leaves of tarragon.

3873 Salade Saint-Sylvestre
Half the total amount of this salad is composed of celeriac cut into coarse Julienne and half cooked and the other half is a mixture of equal amounts of cooked artichoke bottoms and mushrooms both sliced, and truffle and hard-boiled egg white both cut into Julienne.

Decorate with slices of potato having a small round of truffle in the centre and Pluches of chervil.
Dressing: thin Sauce Mayonnaise made with hard-boiled egg yolks, and containing chopped walnuts.

3874 Salade Tourangelle
Take equal quantities of French beans cut diamond shape, flageolet beans and potatoes cut into Julienne.
Dressing: thin Sauce Mayonnaise mixed with a little cream and chopped tarragon.

3875 Salade Tosca
This is composed of equal quantities of cooked white of chicken, white truffle, and white of celery together with a slightly lesser amount of Parmesan cheese, all cut in dice.
Dressing: oil and vinegar combined with a little Sauce Mayonnaise and well flavoured with mustard and anchovy essence.

3876 Salade Trédern
Take 24 crayfish tails cut in half lengthways, 24 oysters cooked with a little lemon juice and bearded and 3 tbs of asparagus tips—all of these should still be lukewarm. Add medium-sized truffles cut into thin shavings.
Dressing: Sauce Mayonnaise with the addition of cullis made from the crayfish shells pounded with 2 tbs thin very fresh cream.

3877 Salade aux Truffes
This is composed of peeled raw truffles cut into very thin shavings.

Dressing: cooked egg yolks pounded and seasoned with salt, milled pepper and mustard and made into a sauce with oil and vinegar.

3878 Salade aux Truffes Blanches
This is made with raw white truffles cut into very thin shavings.
Dressing: hard-boiled egg yolks pounded and seasoned with salt, pepper and mustard and made into a sauce with oil and vinegar.

3879 Salade Victoria
Take equal quantities of trimmings of crawfish, truffle and cucumber, all cut into dice, and asparagus tips.
Dressing: Sauce Mayonnaise with the addition of the creamy parts from the crawfish and a purée of the coral.

3880 Salade Waldorf
Take equal quantities of pippin apples and celeriac, both cut into dice, and peeled halves of fresh walnuts when in season.
Dressing: thin Sauce Mayonnaise.

3881 Salade Windsor
Take equal quantities of celery, raw truffles, cooked white of chicken, salt ox tongue, piccalilli and raw mushrooms—all cut into Julienne.

Mix with Sauce Mayonnaise mixed with a little Sauce Derby and arrange dome shape in a bowl. Surround with a border of rampion inserted halfway into the salad.

CHAPTER 12

ROASTS

In any comparison between the two normal methods of roasting, that on a spit will be found superior to that done in an oven; this is because of the big differences between the two methods and has nothing to do with the kind of fuel that is used.

This fact is easily explained, for regardless of all the care taken with roasting in a closed oven it is not possible to avoid producing steam when carrying out the process. The effect of this steam is so much the worse the more delicate the flavour of the item being roasted and the more easy it is to ruin its quality.

As against this, spit roasting is carried out in a dry open atmosphere which enables the joint to retain its own particular flavour. This shows the superiority of spit roasting over oven roasting—more especially so when concerning small game birds.

In some establishments and under certain conditions, no choice of method is possible and for better or worse roasting has to be carried out in the oven but at least every effort should be made to avoid the effects of the steam referred to above.

3882 The Barding of Items for Roasting

In general, poultry and game for roasting should be partly covered with thin slices of salt pork (*barder*), the exception to this being those game birds which are larded with thin strips of salt pork fat.

The purpose of this covering is not just to protect the breast from the heat of the oven but to avoid it from getting dry whilst the legs are being cooked, as these require more time for the heat to penetrate than do the breasts. The slices of fat should therefore cover the breast entirely and be kept in place by tying lightly with string.

In certain circumstances joints of meat for roasting are covered with fairly thick slices of beef or veal suet for the same reasons.

3883 Spit Roasting

The theory of spit roasting can be summarized in this statement: 'regulate the degree of intensity of heat according to the kind of meat, its size, its inherent qualities and how long it has been hung'. Experience is the surest guide in all matters concerning spit roasting for no matter how detailed the theory of roasting may have been given it cannot do more than outline the basic principles—it cannot replace the telling glance and the know-how which come only from long practice.

Brillat-Savarin's saying that a man is born a roast cook is not necessarily true but the fact remains that it is impossible to become one without a lot of experience and a certain amount of dedication.

The rules governing the theory of spit roasting are:

1) Succulent red meat must be quickly sealed on the outside and then submitted to the action of a sufficient degree of heat so that it penetrates to the centre of the joint of whatever size with very little or no flames present,
2) the heat of the fire for white meats, which must be well done, should be such that the cooking and the colouring of the joint take place at one and the same time,
3) the best form of fuel to use for the roasting of small game birds is wood but whatever fuel is used the bed of the fire should be so regulated that it gives more flames than glowing heat.

Note: Avoid using woods which are resinous.

3884 Oven Roasting

The degree of heat of the oven for roasting must be regulated according to the kind of meat and its size in exactly the same way as is necessary for spit roasting.

When roasting in the oven the elementary precaution must always be taken of placing the item on a trivet with sufficient space between it and the bottom of the tray thus preventing the item from coming in contact with the fat and juice which falls to the bottom. If a trivet is not available the item should be lifted by means of a skewer with its ends resting on the edges of the roasting tray.

It is useless to add any kind of liquid to the roasting tray either gravy or water; this is harmful in the sense that as it evaporates the steam will surround the roast and destroy the brown crust so changing it from a roast to a stewed one. Nevertheless, whether cooked on a spit or in the oven, a roast must be basted frequently with fat and not with a liquid.

3885 Roast Gravies

Real roast gravy is made by deglazing the roasting tray or the dripping tray; the most natural of all is that made with water because the essential part of gravy comes from the juices which fall from the meat into the tray during the cooking process. Nevertheless, in order to obtain the right result neither the tray nor the juices must be allowed to burn; these should only be allowed to caramelize on the bottom of the tray or pan and this is why, if a roast is being cooked in a very hot oven, it must be placed in a tray just large enough to hold it and thus preventing the fat from burning.

The deglazing of the roasting tray will in any case yield only a small quantity of gravy and for this reason when much more is required, the solution is to prepare some stock in advance using bones and trimmings of the same meat, in the following way: place the bones and trimmings in a tray with a little fat and roast them until brown; place in a pan, cover with lukewarm lightly salted water and add the deglazed juices from the tray. Bring to the boil, skim and allow to simmer for 2–4 hours according to the type of bones being used then skim off any fat, pass through a fine strainer and use for deglazing.

To deglaze a roasting tray: remove the roast and pour off some of the fat from the tray; add the required quantity of prepared stock, reduce by half, pass through a fine strainer and remove almost all of the remaining fat.

It is incorrect to remove all the fat and to clarify a roast gravy; although such a gravy may appear more clear and pleasing in appearance, it will have lost a considerable amount of flavour. It should not be forgotten that a roast gravy is not a clear Consommé.

To make gravy for game birds the pan is deglazed with water and a little brandy which are just right to give the gravy a pure game flavour. It may be made with veal stock since this has a neutral flavour which will not alter the particular taste of the caramelized juice in the roasting tray. Alternatively, stock previously made from the bones and trimmings of the same kind of game bird can be used for deglazing the pan.

3886 The Presentation and Accompaniments of Roasts

As a principle a roast should not be kept waiting and it should only leave the oven or be taken off the spit to be served immediately.

All roasts should be placed on a very hot dish lightly greased with fat from the roasting pan. It may be then garnished with bunches of watercress but this should only be done at the very last moment.

If the dish is going to be covered with a lid and kept waiting for a few minutes it should not be garnished. The roast gravy should always be served separately.

Roasts of meat and poultry should be arranged and served simply.

Small game birds are placed on Canapés of bread, fried in butter and coated with the special Gratin Forcemeat C (295).

If lemons are to be served with a roast they must be sent separately; pieces of lemon used as decoration should not be served as they are nearly always spoiled by the fat.

The Medieval way of decorating roast game birds with their feathers has fallen into disuse.

Game birds served in the English style are accompanied with game chips either arranged around the bird or served separately, and with roast gravy, fried breadcrumbs and bread sauce.

Note: In northern countries roasts are always served accompanied with either lightly sweetened apple sauce or stewed cherries or apricots.

SAUCES AND ACCOMPANIMENTS FOR ROASTS PREPARED IN THE ENGLISH STYLE

The various sauces included under this heading are: Apple Sauce, Bread Sauce, Horseradish Sauce, Fried Bread Sauce and Cranberry Sauce; recipes for these will be found in the section on Hot English Sauces.

Note: Cranberry sauce which is served especially with roast turkey, roast wild duck and roast pork is a slightly sweetened purée of cranberries.

3887 Sage and Onion Stuffing (*for duck, geese and turkey*)

Bake 4 large unpeeled onions and when soft, peel and chop them finely. Melt some butter in a pan, add the onion, a pinch of chopped fresh or rubbed dry sage and cook gently for a few minutes.

Add the same weight of white breadcrumbs soaked in milk and squeezed, and half the weight of the onions of chopped veal suet.

3888 Veal Stuffing (*for veal and pork*)

This stuffing is made from equal amounts of

chopped beef suet, white breadcrumbs and chopped parsley; season with salt and pepper, flavour with grated nutmeg and mix together with 2 eggs per 1 kg ($2\frac{1}{4}$ lb) of the mixture.

3889 Yorkshire Pudding *(for roast beef)*
Sift 500 g (1 lb 2 oz) plain flour, a little salt, pepper and grated nutmeg into a bowl, add 4 eggs and gradually whisk in $1\frac{1}{4}$ litres ($2\frac{1}{5}$ pt or $5\frac{1}{2}$ U.S. cups) milk; allow to stand for 1 hour. Pour this mixture into a deep baking pan containing very hot dripping and cook in a hot oven.

If the joint is roasted on the spit, place the pan with the cooked Yorkshire under the joint so that it will become saturated with the fat and juices that drop on to it.

Cut the pudding into triangles or squares and arrange either around the meat or serve on a dish separately.

ROASTS OF BEEF

3890 Baron of Beef
The baron of beef is above all a Christmas dish for large English gatherings; it comprises the two sirloins together with some of the ribs, in one whole large joint.

It is wrapped in a layer of Hot Water Paste containing a quarter its weight of chopped beef suet, and seasoned with salt. Roast in a moderate oven allowing approximately 10–12 minutes per 1 kg ($2\frac{1}{4}$ lb). When it is judged to be nearly cooked, the covering of pastry should be removed so as to allow the joint to colour.

3891 Ribs of Beef
Ribs of beef are roasted on the bone; the ends of the rib bones are just simply shortened. If it is to be oven roasted it is advisable to cook it in a large braising pan without the lid; allow 25–30 minutes per 1 kg ($2\frac{1}{4}$ lb). The cooking time for a spit roasted rib is also 20 minutes per 1 kg ($2\frac{1}{4}$ lb) but after removing from the spit it must be kept in the hotplate or a warm oven for from $\frac{1}{2}$–1 hour according to size, so as to allow the interior concentration of juices to finish the cooking.

Note: A recommended way of roasting ribs of beef in the oven is to cover the top and sides with a 2–3 cm (1 in) thick layer of coarse salt moistened with water. As the water evaporates it leaves the crust of salt to act as a protection to the joint and all that remains is to remove it when the joint is cooked.

3892 Sirloin of Beef
It to be roasted on the bone, break the projecting bones of the vertebra and cut the yellow ligament in several places. The temperature should be higher than for ribs of beef as less time is needed for cooking. If boned out, the sirloin should be covered with thin slices of salt pork fat and roasted for 15–18 minutes per 1 kg ($2\frac{1}{4}$ lb). Allow an extra 5 minutes per 1 kg ($2\frac{1}{4}$ lb) if on the bone.

3893 Fillet of Beef
Carefully remove the two outer membranes from the fillet and either finely lard it with strips of salt pork fat or wrap in thin slices of salt pork fat. In certain cases the fillet may be wrapped around with very thin slices of flattened beef fat which are held in place with string.

It should be roasted at a high temperature allowing 12–15 minutes per 1 kg ($2\frac{1}{4}$ lb) if roasting in the oven, keeping it pink and underdone in the middle; for spit roasting allow 18 minutes per 1 kg ($2\frac{1}{4}$ lb).

3894 Roast Joints of Beef in the English Style
These are cooked rather well done and are always served accompanied with Yorkshire pudding.

ROASTS OF VEAL

3895 Best End of Veal
This is roasted in a moderate oven basting frequently with melted butter and allowing approximately 30–35 minutes per 1 kg ($2\frac{1}{4}$ lb).

3896 Loin of Veal
This joint is cooked in a covered braising pan, basting frequently with melted butter and allowing approximately 35 minutes per 1 kg ($2\frac{1}{4}$ lb).

3897 Roast Loin of Veal in the English Style
The loin and the shoulder of veal when roasted in the English style are first boned and stuffed with Veal Stuffing. They are served with boiled ham or bacon the outside of which has been covered with brown crumbs.

3898 Cushion of Veal
This is roasted in the same way as the loin and for the same length of time.

Note: Spit roasting is not a suitable method for veal no matter how delicate the flesh may be; cooking in the oven in a covered pan in the form of Poêling is infinitely better in so far as the juices, vegetables and herbs produce a better gravy than that obtainable from spit roasted veal.

ROASTS OF LAMB AND MUTTON

3899 Best End of Lamb or Mutton
Remove the chine bone then roast the best end in a

hot oven allowing approximately 30–35 minutes per 1 kg (2¼ lb). The gravy for this should be left a little fatty and served very hot.

3900 Baron of Lamb or Mutton
This comprises the 2 legs and the saddle in one joint and is roasted in a hot oven for approximately 15–18 minutes per 1 kg (2¼ lb).

3901 Saddle of Lamb or Mutton
The saddle should not be boned out or larded; its covering of fat should be simply scored with the point of a small knife and the saddle then tied up with string. Roast in a hot oven allowing approximately 15–18 minutes per 1 kg. (2¼ lb).

3902 Leg of Lamb or Mutton
Allow approximately 25–30 minutes per 1 kg (2¼ lb).

3903 Shoulder of Lamb of Mutton
Shoulders of mutton can be boned out then rolled and tied; shoulders of lamb should not be boned out and should be roasted in a very hot oven. Allow approximately 25–30 minutes per 1 kg (2¼ lb).

Note: Cooking times are basically the same for lamb and mutton bearing in mind that lamb should be well cooked.

ROASTS OF PORK

3904 Best End of Loin of Pork
The best end should be chined and the ends of the cutlet bones shortened. Pork should be roasted in a fairly hot oven until it is well cooked; average time 30–35 minutes per 1 kg (2¼ lb).

3905 Roast Pork, English Style
The leg, best end and loin are all suitable for roasting if from a very young animal; the rind is left on and should be scored as should the fat just underneath. Allow from 18–20 minutes per 500 g (1 lb 2 oz) and serve accompanied with Sage and Onion Sauce and either Apple Sauce or Cranberry Sauce.

ROAST POULTRY

3906 Fattened Pullets
Season the bird inside and out, cover the breast with thin slices of salt pork fat and roast in a fairly hot oven or on the spit; remove the fat in time to allow the breast to colour.

The time for a fattened pullet weight 1½ kg (3 lb 6 oz) is approximately 45 minutes in the oven and about 50 minutes on the spit. To test if cooked, allow a few drops of juice to drain from inside the chicken on to a plate—it is cooked when the drops are absolutely clear. Sprinkle the chicken with little of the cooking fat and serve accompanied with watercress and roast gravy.

3907 Poularde Rôtie à l'Anglaise—Roast Fattened Pullet, English Style
Roast the fattened pullet and serve surrounded with either grilled sausages or grilled rashers of bacon. Serve accompanied with Bread Sauce.

3908 Poularde Truffée—Truffled Fattened Pullet
This is prepared in the same way as Dindonneau Truffé allowing 500 g (1 lb 2 oz) each of fresh pork fat pounded and passed through a fine sieve, and truffle. Cover the breast with slices of salt pork fat and roast for 1½ hours in a moderate oven or on a moderately hot spit for 1¾ hours.

3909 Queen Chicken
Allow approximately 35 minutes in the oven or 40 minutes on the spit.

3910 Spring Chicken
Allow approximately 25–30 minutes in the oven or 35–40 minutes on the spit.

3911 Poussin
Allow approximately 12–15 minutes for roasting *en Cocotte*.

3912 Turkey
Proceed in the same way as for the roast fattened pullet.

Note: Before trussing the turkey it is essential to remove the tendons from the legs. This is done by making incisions above and below the joint of the leg proper and the drumstick. The tendons are pulled out one at a time using a trussing needle; this is pushed under each tendon then twisted round carefully until the tendon is detached from the flesh. It can then be easily removed.

3913 Roast Turkey, English Style
Stuff the bird with Sage and Onion Stuffing (3887) and roast it slowly. Place on a dish and surround with either grilled sausages or grilled rashers of bacon.

3914 Dindonneau Truffé—Truffled Young Turkey
Ingredients: 1 kg (2¼ lb) very fresh pork fat, 250 g (9 oz) raw foie gras, 800 g (1 lb 9 oz) truffles, salt, pepper and grated nutmeg.
Method:
1) Cut the pork fat and foie gras into dice,

pound finely together then add the peelings of the truffles. Soften over a gentle heat then pass through a fine sieve.

2) Melt 500 g (1 lb 2 oz) of this mixture in a pan and add the peeled truffles cut in small quarters (reserve 12 nice slices of truffle for later use); season with salt and pepper and add a bayleaf. Allow to cook gently for 10 minutes, cover with a lid and allow to become cold. When quite cold, mix in the remainder of the truffled pork fat and foie gras mixture.
3) Empty the turkey carefully from a hole in its side then remove the bones of the breast; leave the skin of the neck very long. Stuff it with the prepared truffled forcemeat; slide the reserved slices of truffle under the skin of the breast. Keep in a refrigerator for 24–48 hours.
4) Truss the turkey and sew up the hole on its side. Cover the breast with slices of salt pork fat then wrap it completely in a sheet of strong buttered paper.

Roast the prepared turkey on the spit before a concentrated fire which should be kept at the same heat during the whole of the roasting process.

If the turkey is to be oven roasted, this is best carried out in an uncovered braising pan.

Allow approximately 35 minutes per 1 kg ($2\frac{1}{4}$ lb) when spit roasting and 28 minutes per 1 kg ($2\frac{1}{4}$ lb) for oven roasting.

Serve the turkey accompanied with the roasting juices well skimmed of fat or optionally, with a thin Sauce Périgueux.

3915 Young Pigeons

Roast the young pigeons *en Casserole* in a very hot oven or spit roast them until just cooked; allow 20 minutes for *en Casserole* and 25 minutes on the spit.

3916 Guinea Fowl

Only young and very tender guinea fowl should be roasted. Lard the breast with strips of salt pork fat or cover with thin slices of the same fat. Roast in a very hot oven, basting frequently. Allow approximately 30–35 minutes cooking time.

3917 Nantes Duckling

For a duckling weighing 1 kg 200 g (2 lb 11 oz) allow approximately 35–40 minutes cooking time.

3918 Rouen Duckling

Whether in the oven or on the spit, Rouen duckling should be roasted at a very high temperature; for a duckling of 2 kg 400 g (5 lb 6 oz) gross weight or 1 kg 450 g (3 lb 4 oz) prepared weight, allow approximately 25 minutes cooking time.

3919 Caneton Rouennais au Porto

This is prepared in the same manner as Canard Sauvage au Porto (3934); it may be presented in an earthenware terrine.

3920 Caneton d'Aylesbury Rôti à l'Anglaise—Roast Aylesbury Duckling, English Style

The Aylesbury duckling is the equivalent of the Nantes duckling. It is generally stuffed with sage and onion stuffing before roasting and the most usual accompaniment is apple sauce; this can be replaced with melted redcurrant jelly or cranberry sauce.

3921 Oie Rôtie à l'Anglaise—Roast Goose, English Style

The goose should be stuffed with sage and onion stuffing before roasting and served with the same accompaniments as Roast Aylesbury Duckling.

3922 Gosling

A young goose not fully grown is best for roasting; it can be roasted in the oven or on the spit but should be kept slightly underdone.

ROASTS OF VENISON

3923 Roebuck

The leg and saddle are the joints mainly used for roasting; they can be marinated in advance if desired but are almost always larded with strips of salt pork fat. The saddle often has the two best ends left attached. Average cooking time in the oven is 15–18 minutes per 1 kg ($2\frac{1}{4}$ lb).

3924 Roast Venison, English Style

Both the fallow and red deer are used and the most suitable joint for roasting is the haunch which is the leg and loin in one piece. It is not usual to marinade the joint but it should be well hung.

Monsieur Suzanne in his book *La Cuisine Anglaise* recommends rubbing all over the joint with flour containing a small amount of pepper as a means of preserving it whilst it is hanging. This prevents the action of humidity and wards off the flies.

To roast the haunch, trim it and wrap it in Hot Water Paste with suet and salt as indicated for Baron of Beef then wrap it in paper and tie it up.

Allow approximately 4 hours for a medium-sized joint basting it frequently. When nearly cooked, remove the paper and pastry, sprinkle with flour and salt, baste with melted butter and replace it in the oven to colour.

All roasts of venison are served accompanied with redcurrant jelly.

3925 Young Wild Boar
For preference use only the best end or saddle for roasting and cook it in the same way as pork.

Roasts of young wild boar are served accompanied with well flavoured gravy and wherever possible also flavoured with rosemary.

ROASTS OF FURRED AND FEATHERED GAME

3926 Woodcock
Woodcock should be hung for several days with the feathers still on and only plucked when they are going to be cooked. After plucking, remove the gizzard only and truss the bird by pushing its beak through the thick part of its legs, the ends of which are then entwined together. Cover the breasts with a thin slice of salt pork fat and roast in a very hot oven for 15–18 minutes. Place on a Canapé of bread fried in butter; serve accompanied with gravy made by deglazing the pan with a little brandy.

3927 Snipe
Snipe are treated in exactly the same way as for woodcock but roasting them for 9 minutes only in a very hot oven. Present and serve as for woodcock.

3928 Figpeckers and Warblers
These birds are usually impaled 6 at a time on skewers and roasted at a very high temperature allowing 8 minutes of cooking time.

3929 Quails
Choose white plump birds with firm fat; wrap each in a buttered vine leaf then in a thin slice of salt pork fat and roast at a very high temperature for 10–12 minutes.

Arrange each on a Canapé of bread fried in butter and spread with Gratin Forcemeat C (295). Surround with halves of lemon and bunches of watercress and serve accompanied with a small quantity of gravy made from the juices in the pan.

3930 Wild Ducks
Wild ducks should not be covered with salt pork fat. They should be roasted at a very high temperature for 20 minutes keeping them very underdone.

Serve surrounded with halves of lemon and watercress.

3931 Roast Wild Duck, English Style
Roast as above and serve accompanied with Apple Sauce.

3932 Canard Sauvage à la Bigarade
Roast the wild duck as 3930 and serve garnished with segments of peeled orange free of skin and pith. Serve a clear Sauce Bigarade separately.

3933 Roast Wild Duck with Cranberry Sauce
Roast the wild duck as 3930 and serve accompanied with Cranberry Sauce.

3934 Canard Sauvage au Porto
Roast the wild duck as 3930 and serve accompanied with a very fine gravy thickened with arrowroot and flavoured with Port wine.

3935 Pintail
Roast the pintail as usual allowing 15–17 minutes cooking time.

3936 Teal
Roast in the same way as wild duck allowing 12–14 minutes cooking time.

3937 Sandpiper
The various species of this bird are completely emptied before cooking then roasted in the same way as plovers.

3938 Capercaillie
This bird is not held in high regard and is usually cooked in a covered pan; only young birds should be used.

3939 Hazel Grouse
This bird must be very fresh; cover with slices of salt pork fat and roast at a high temperature for 15–18 minutes.

3940 Grouse
This bird must be very fresh; the time for roasting varies from 12–15 minutes according to size.

Note: These last three birds should be cooked underdone and it is usual to serve only the breasts. If roasted in the English style they should be served accompanied with bread sauce, fried breadcrumbs and game chips.

3941 Pheasant
A pheasant for roasting should be covered with thin slices of salt pork fat but should not be larded. It is a good idea to pound a piece of fresh pork fat with some truffle peelings and place this inside the bird—or pork fat alone may be used. The fat will penetrate into the flesh helping it to cook better without drying out. This method is also suitable for partridges.

Roast at a high temperature for 25–30 minutes according to size and serve surrounded with halves of lemon and bunches of watercress; the gravy should be left slightly fatty and served separately.

3942 Faisan Truffé—Truffled Pheasant
Proceed as for Truffled Young Turkey (3914) allowing 400 g (14 oz) fresh pork fat and 200 g (7 oz) truffle. Cover with thin slices of salt pork fat and roast in a moderate oven for 50 minutes to 1 hour.

3943 Thrushes
Cover the breast with thin slices of salt pork fat, place 1 juniper berry inside each and roast in a very hot oven for 10–12 minutes. Place on Canapés of bread fried in butter but without the usual Gratin Forcemeat.

Serve accompanied with a little good gravy.

3944 Hare
The only part of the hare suitable for roasting is the saddle which comprises the whole of the back from the beginning of the rib cage to the tail, which can be left on.

Remove the sinews, lard with strips of salt pork fat, then roast at a fairly high temperature for 20 minutes.

The usual accompaniment for roast hare is a thin Sauce Poivrade.

In northern countries the accompaniment is either slightly sweet apple purée or redcurrant jelly.

3945 Larks
Wrap each bird in a thin slice of salt pork fat and impale on a skewer, or impale the birds on a skewer alternating with squares of blanched streaky bacon. Roast at a high temperature for 10 minutes.

Place the larks on Croûtons of bread fried in butter and surround with halves of lemon and bouquets of watercress.

3946 Blackbirds
These are roasted in the same way as thrushes.

3947 Buntings
Wrap each bird in a strip of vine leaf, place in a tray moistened with a very little salt water and roast in a very hot oven for 4–5 minutes; the evaporation of the water prevents the birds from loosing their fat. Thus the use of slices of pork fat, butter or gravy becomes unnecessary.

The buntings may be presented, each placed in a half lemon fashioned in the shape of a basket.

3948 Ortolans au Suc d'Ananas
For 6 birds melt some butter in a shallow earthenware dish just large enough to hold the birds, allowing 30 g (1 oz) per 6 buntings. Season them with salt, roll them in the butter, then place in a very hot oven for 3 minutes.

On removing from the oven sprinkle them with pineapple juice, cover with the lid and serve immediately.

3949 Partridge
Wrap each partridge in a buttered vine leaf then in a thin slice of salt pork fat and roast in a hot oven for 20 minutes or on a spit for 25 minutes.

Place on a Croûton of bread fried in butter and coated with Gratin Forcemeat C (295), and garnish with half a lemon and a bouquet of watercress.

3950 Perdreau Truffé—Truffled Partridge
Stuff the bird in the same way as for Dindonneau Truffé (3914) allowing 100 g (3½ oz) fresh pork fat and 80 g (2 oz) truffles; cover with thin slices of salt pork fat and roast in a moderate oven for 25 minutes.

3951 Plovers and Lapwings
It is not necessary to cover these birds with salt pork fat. They should be emptied then roasted at a very high temperature for 12–14 minutes keeping them slightly underdone. They must be served immediately they are cooked as waiting tends to spoil them.

Serve accompanied with a small quantity of good gravy.

CHAPTER 13

VEGETABLES AND FARINACEOUS PRODUCTS

VEGETABLES

THE TREATMENT, COOKING AND FINISHING OF VEGETABLES

3952 Blanching
Blanching is carried out for two different purposes. In the first of these, for example, in the treatment of spinach, peas, French beans and green vegetables in general, this blanching is really a complete cooking carried out quickly in plenty of boiling water. This is to keep them green by preserving as much as possible of the Chlorophyll they contain. The other purpose of the blanching is to remove the natural bitterness contained in some vegetables such as cabbage, celery and chicory by boiling them in water for a length of time determined by the type and quality of the vegetable. Generally speaking, new season's vegetables do not need blanching.

For those vegetables which are completely cooked by this method, 7 g (¼ oz) of salt should be added to each 1 litre (1¾ pt or 4½ U.S. cups) of the water.

3953 Refreshing
This refers to the rapid cooling of vegetables after they have been blanched. They should be placed under running cold water immediately they are ready and left to get cold; they should then be well drained. Only vegetables which are going to be further cooked by braising should be refreshed after blanching, but if because of the exigencies of the service it is necessary to cook green vegetables in advance, they must be refreshed.

A vegetable which is to have butter or cream mixed into it will lose a lot of its flavour if refreshed.

3954 The Cooking of Vegetables *à l'Anglaise*
This is simply the cooking of vegetables in boiling water. They are drained, dried and served in a deep dish accompanied by pats of butter. The guest should season and butter the vegetables for himself.

All green vegetables may be prepared and served by this method.

3955 The Cooking of Dried Vegetables
It is a bad procedure to soak dried vegetables in advance. If they have been processed during the previous 12 months and are of good quality it should be sufficient to cover them with cold water, bring them very slowly to the boil, skim, add the usual vegetables and flavourings and simmer very slowly with the lid on until cooked.

Should the dried vegetables be old ones or of poor quality they may be soaked but only for the time strictly necessary to swell them which would be for 1½–2 hours.

Prolonged soaking for several hours causes dried vegetables to start fermenting thereby altering their chemical structure and thus losing much of their goodness; this can even give rise to discomfort in the person eating them.

3956 The Braising of Vegetables
The vegetables should first be blanched then refreshed and trimmed before arranging them on a layer of sliced vegetables and flavourings in a braising pan previously lined with thin slices of salt pork fat. Cover with slices of the same fat and place on top of the stove with a lid on to stew slightly in their own juices. Barely cover with White Bouillon, replace the lid and place to cook gently in a moderate oven.

When cooked, remove the vegetables and drain them, cut or trim to an appropriate shape then keep them warm in a shallow pan with a little of the reduced braising liquid after removing the fat. If for immediate use, place the vegetables in earthenware dishes and cover with the strained but not skimmed boiling braising liquid; keep covered with greaseproof paper for future use.

3957 The Sauce for Braised Vegetables
This is prepared from the reduced braising liquid after it has been skimmed of all fat, and completed for some vegetables with the addition of meat glaze and for others, with Sauce Demi-glace. In both

cases the sauce should be made smooth by adding sufficient butter in small pieces and flavoured as needed with a few drops of lemon juice.

3958 The Finishing of Vegetables with Butter
Drain the cooked vegetables well, add the necessary seasoning and the butter and mix by tossing over and over. The butter should be added away from the stove so as to preserve its natural flavour.

3959 The Finishing of Vegetables with Cream
Vegetables which are to be finished in this way should be cooked but kept a little firmer than usual. Drain them very well and place in a pan with sufficient boiling cream to well coat but not to cover them entirely. Finish cooking together, shaking the pan from time to time.

When the cream is almost entirely reduced, finish with a little butter and a few drops of lemon juice. If a slightly thicker result is required, a little Cream Sauce may be added.

3960 Vegetables Creams and Purées
Purées of dried and floury vegetables are made by passing the cooked vegetables through a sieve; place the purée in a pan, dry it on the stove and add some butter and milk or cream to give it the correct consistency.

Purées of watery vegetables such as French beans and cauliflower etc. require the addition of a certain amount of a purée of a starchy vegetable in keeping with the flavour of the main ingredient, so as to ensure its proper cohesion.

Creams of vegetables are made by replacing the addition of a starchy purée with thick well flavoured Sauce Béchamel.

ARTICHAUTS—GLOBE ARTICHOKES

3961 Artichauts à la Barigoule
Choose some very fresh and tender artichokes; trim the tops level, cut the surrounding leaves straight, blanch them, then remove the chokes.

Season the insides of the artichokes and fill with a stuffing made from equal amounts of grated fresh pork fat and butter added to twice their amount of Duxelles. Wrap each artichoke in a thin slice of salt pork fat, tie up and place on a layer of sliced vegetables and herbs in a braising pan. Moisten with brown stock and braise gently until the artichokes are well cooked.

When required for serving, untie the artichokes, discard the fat and arrange them in a dish. Remove the fat from the braising liquid, pass through a fine strainer then add the necessary quantity of good Sauce Demi-glace and reduce sufficiently to obtain just a small quantity of sauce; pour this over the artichokes.

3962 Artichauts Cavour
Trim some small and tender Provence artichokes to the shape and size of an egg.

Cook them in White Bouillon then drain and squeeze out all the moisture. Dip them in melted butter, then in grated mixed Parmesan and Gruyère cheese. Arrange in a circle in a dish and place in a hot oven to colour.

For each 6 artichokes fry 1 chopped hard-boiled egg in butter and whilst it is still foaming, add a little anchovy essence and some chopped parsley. Pour this over the artichokes.

3963 Coeurs d'Artichauts Clamart
Choose some medium-sized tender globe artichokes, trim and cut each into six pieces.

Arrange them in a buttered Cocotte with a small raw carrot cut in quarters and 3 tbs freshly shelled peas per artichoke. Add a large Bouquet garni, a little water, and a pinch of salt; cover and cook slowly in the oven.

When cooked, remove the Bouquet garni, thicken the liquid with a little Beurre Manié and serve in the same dish.

3964 Coeurs d'Artichauts Grand-Duc
Choose some medium-sized globe artichokes of equal size; trim them and cook in salted water. When cooked, drain them well and arrange in a circle on a dish previously coated lightly with some Cream Sauce; cover with more sauce, sprinkle with grated Parmesan and melted butter and glaze under the salamander.

Place a bouquet of buttered asparagus tips in the centre of the dish; on each artichoke place a slice of truffle warmed in butter mixed with a little melted meat glaze.

3965 Globe Artichokes with Various Sauce
Cut the tops of the artichokes level, trim them, tie up and place into boiling salted water. Cook fairly rapidly then drain them and remove the strings.

Arrange on a serviette on a dish and serve accompanied with either Sauce au Beurre, Sauce Hollandaise or Sauce Mousseline.

If the artichokes are being served cold, the choke should be removed. Arrange on a serviette and serve accompanied with Sauce Vinaigrette.

3966 Artichauts à la Provençale
Select some very small Provence artichokes, trim them and place in a flat earthenware pan containing some very hot oil. Season them with salt and

pepper, cover with the lid and allow to cook for approximately 10 minutes. Now add 5 dl (18 fl oz or 2¼ U.S. cups) freshly shelled peas and 1 coarsely shredded lettuce.

Cover with the lid and allow to cook slowly without any liquid; the moisture from the vegetables will be sufficient, provided that the pan is tightly covered to prevent too much evaporation and that it is cooked on a low heat.

3967 Artichauts Stanley

Trim 20 small tender artichokes or the same number of artichoke bottoms. Place them in a well buttered shallow pan on a layer of 2 large sliced and blanched onions and 150 g (5 oz) sliced raw ham. Cover the pan and allow the artichokes to cook in their own juices for a short while; moisten with 1½ dl (5 fl oz or ⅝ U.S. cup) white wine, allow to reduce then barely cover with very thin Sauce Béchamel.

Cook until tender then arrange the artichokes in a vegetable dish.

Reduce the sauce, add 2½ dl (9 fl oz or 1⅛ U.S. cups) cream, pass firmly through a sieve and finish with plenty of butter. Pour this over the artichokes and sprinkle with very lean ham cut in small dice.

3968 Cromesquis and Croquettes of Globe Artichokes

Only the bottoms of artichokes are used in these preparations. They are prepared in the same way as other Cromesquis and Croquettes (see the Chapter on Hot Hors-d'oeuvre).

3969 Croûte aux Fonds d'Artichauts

Cut some raw artichoke bottoms into slices and half cook them in a *Blanc*. Drain them and place in a well buttered shallow pan, season with salt, pepper and grated nutmeg and finish cooking with cream.

When cooked, remove the artichokes, reduce the cream and enrich and thicken it with butter; serve in the same way as for Croûte aux Champignons (4022).

3970 Fonds d'Artichauts Cussy

Cook 12 small trimmed artichoke bottoms in the usual manner. Drain them, then fill dome shape with a fairly stiff purée of foie gras and truffle; dip into Sauce Villeroy and allow to get cold. Trim off any excess sauce, flour, egg and breadcrumb them and deep fry in hot fat.

Arrange on a serviette, garnish with fried parsley and serve accompanied with a tomato-flavoured Sauce Demi-glace.

3971 Fonds d'Artichauts Farcis—Stuffed Artichoke Bottoms

Choose some medium-sized globe artichokes, remove the leaves and chokes and trim the bottoms. Cook in salted water keeping them slightly firm. Drain well and fill with a fairly stiff Duxelles. Arrange on a buttered tray, sprinkle with fine dry breadcrumbs and a little melted butter and gratinate in a hot oven.

Serve accompanied with a tomato-flavoured Sauce Demi-glace.

3972 Fonds d'Artichauts aux Pointes d'Asperges—Artichoke Bottoms with Asparagus Tips

Prepare the artichoke bottoms in the usual manner and cook them in butter. Fill them pyramid fashion with creamed asparagus tips, arrange on a buttered tray, coat with Sauce Mornay and glaze quickly.

3973 Fonds d'Artichauts Sautés—Sautéed Artichoke Bottoms

Remove the leaves and chokes from the artichokes, trim the bottoms and cut in slices.

Season with salt and pepper, sauté in butter until cooked then place in a vegetable dish and sprinkle with chopped Fines Herbes.

3974 Quartiers d'Artichauts Dietrich

Trim and cut 12 Provence artichokes into quarters. Cook quickly in butter with a little chopped onion, then then add sufficient thin Velouté and mushroom cooking liquor to barely cover. Allow to cook gently.

When cooked, place the artichokes in the centre of a border of Risotto containing some white Piedmont truffle. Reduce the cooking liquor, finish with a little cream and pour over the artichokes.

3975 Quartiers d'Artichauts à l'Italienne

Trim some medium-sized globe artichokes and cut them into quarters. Trim the quarters, removing the chokes, then rub with a piece of lemon to prevent them discolouring and place in cold water as each is finished.

Blanch them, drain and arrange on a layer of vegetables and herbs in a braising pan; cover and stew them in their own juices for 7–8 minutes. Moisten with white wine, reduce it, then moisten half-way up with brown stock. Cover and cook in the oven gently until the artichokes are tender.

To serve: arrange the quarters of artichoke in a vegetable dish; remove the fat and pass the cooking liquid through a fine strainer. Reduce it, then add it to some Sauce Italienne; pour this over the artichokes and sprinkle with chopped parsley.

3976 Quartiers d'Artichauts Lyonnaise
Cut some trimmed globe artichokes into quarters, blanch them, then place in a shallow pan on a layer of sliced onions previously cooked in butter. Proceed in the same way as for Quartiers d'Artichauts à l'Italienne.

When cooked, arrange the artichokes in a deep dish. Reduce the cooking liquid and finish with butter away from the heat; pour over the artichokes and sprinkle with chopped parsley.

3977 Purée or Cream of Globe Artichokes
Choose some very tender artichokes and trim well into artichoke bottoms. Half cook them in salted water keeping them very white, then finish cooking in butter. Pass the bottoms through a fine sieve together with the butter from the cooking, replace in the pan, then add half its amount of smooth mashed potato.

Finish the purée with a little fresh butter and a little brown butter which is added to bring out the flavour of the artichokes.

3978 ASPERGES—ASPARAGUS

There are four main varieties of asparagus:

1) the Argenteuil which is a typical French variety,
2) the green variety,
3) the violet asparagus of Genoa typical of the Italian asparagus, of good quality but inclined to be slightly acrid,
4) the white Belgian variety which is of good quality but does not travel well.

Asparagus must be used whilst it is as fresh as possible; it should be scraped carefully, washed quickly, tied in bundles and cooked in plenty of boiling salted water.

Some varieties of which the flavour is slightly acrid should be transferred to another pan of hot water as soon as they are cooked, so as to remove or at least diminish this acridity.

Asparagus is presented on a special silver asparagus grill or on a serviette.

3979 Asperges à la Flamande
As served in the Flemish style, asparagus is accompanied with half of a hot hard-boiled egg and 30 g (1 oz) melted butter per guest. The yolk of the egg is crushed and seasoned and the butter mixed with it by each guest himself.

This accompaniment can also be prepared in advance and served in a sauceboat.

3980 Asperges au Gratin
Arrange the cooked asparagus in rows on a dish and coat the heads of each row with Sauce Mornay. Cover two-thirds of the unsauced part with a band of buttered paper and coat the rest with more sauce. Sprinkle with grated Parmesan and glaze quickly under the salamander. Remove the paper and serve immediately.

3981 Asperges à la Milanaise
Cook the asparagus in the usual manner, drain and arrange in overlapping rows on a buttered oval dish which has been sprinkled with grated Parmesan cheese. Sprinkle the head of each row with grated Parmesan cheese.

When about to serve, coat the heads well with brown butter and glaze lightly under the salamander.

3982 Asperges Mornay
Proceed as indicated for Asperges au Gratin.

3983 Asperges à la Polonaise
Cook the asparagus in the usual manner, drain them well and arrange in rows on an oval dish. Sprinkle the heads of each row with mixed chopped yolk of hard-boiled egg and parsley.

When about to serve, coat the heads with brown butter in which 30 g (1 oz) fine white breadcrumbs per 125 g ($4\frac{1}{2}$ oz) of butter have been fried a golden brown.

3984 Asparagus with Various Sauces
The most suitable sauces for serving with plain boiled hot asparagus are Sauce au Beurre, Sauce Hollandaise, Sauce Mousseline and Sauce Maltaise. Sauce Béarnaise made without the herbs is sometimes served as is Beurre Fondue.

Cold asparagus is served accompanied with an oil and vinegar dressing or more particularly Sauce Mayonnaise containing whipped cream, called Mayonnaise Chantilly.

3985 Pointes d'Asperges au Beurre—Buttered Asparagus Tips
The main use for asparagus tips is as a garnish or as part of a garnish, but they can be served as a vegetable in their own right. Cut off the tips into approximately 5 cm (2 in) long pieces and tie them in bundles; cut the remaining tender parts into pieces the size of a pea. Wash them all well and cook quickly in boiled salted water so as to keep them very green.

As soon as they are cooked, drain them but do not refresh. Place in a pan on the stove and toss over to evaporate the rest of the mixture; remove from the heat, add a little butter and toss over to mix. Place the small pieces in a deep dish and arrange the tips on top.

Asparagus tips are often served in Bouchée cases or tartlet cases placing the small pieces inside and a few tips on top.

3986 Pointes d'Asperges à la Crème
Prepare and cook the asparagus tips as in the preceding recipe. Finish with cream in the same way as for other vegetables prepared in this manner and serve as described for buttered asparagus tips.

AUBERGINES—EGGPLANT

3987 Aubergines à la Bordelaise
Cut the eggplant into round slices; season and flour them and proceed as for Cèpes à la Bordelaise.

3988 Aubergines à la Crème
Choose some very firm eggplants and cut them into ½ cm (⅕ in) thick slices; sprinkle with salt and allow to stand for 1 hour to disgorge.

Dry the slices well, cook them gently in butter and when cooked, mix in a little cream sauce.

3989 Aubergines à l'Egyptienne
Cut the eggplants in half lengthways; cut around the edges inside the skin and slash the centre crisscross to facilitate the cooking. Deep fry, then drain and scoop out the flesh from the skins; arrange the skins in a buttered earthenware dish. Chop the flesh of the eggplants and add a little chopped onion cooked in oil.

Fill the skin with this mixture, sprinkle with oil and cook in the oven for 15 minutes. On removing from the oven, place several slices of tomato sautéed in oil on each half eggplant, then sprinkle with chopped parsley.

3990 Aubergines Frites—Fried Eggplant
Cut the eggplants into thin round slices, season, flour and deep fry in very hot oil. Drain well.

Arrange on a serviette and serve immediately so that they may be eaten whilst still crisp. If kept waiting they will become soft and lose their particular quality.

Note: Alternatively, the slices can be dipped into frying batter or coated with egg and breadcrumbs before frying them.

3991 Aubergines au Gratin
Prepare and cook the eggplants as for Aubergines à l'Egyptienne; empty them, chop the flesh, add it to an equal amount of dry Duxelles and mix together.

Fill the skins with this mixture and arrange them in a buttered earthenware dish; sprinkle with fine dry white breadcrumbs and a little oil and gratinate in a hot oven. On removing from the oven surround them with a *cordon* of Tomato Sauce.

3992 Aubergines à la Napolitaine
Peel some medium-sized eggplants and cut each into six slices through the length.

Season, flour and deep fry them in oil.

Re-form the eggplants to their original shape after spreading the slices with a little reduced tomato purée flavoured with grated Parmesan. Arrange them in a gratin dish, coat with Tomato Sauce, sprinkle with grated Parmesan, a little oil and melted butter and gratinate in a hot oven.

3993 Aubergines à l'Orientale
Peel a medium-sized eggplant and cut into six slices through the length. Season, flour and deep fry them. Sandwich the slices together two by two with the following mixture: chop the flesh of a small fried eggplant, add the coarsely chopped flesh of 3 tomatoes which has been cooked in oil; a little salt, pepper and chopped parsley; a touch of crushed garlic and ½ tbs fresh white breadcrumbs. Mix together and cook to the required consistency.

Arrange the sandwiched slices in an oiled earthenware dish just large enough to hold them, sprinkle with oil and cook in a moderate oven for 30 minutes.

Serve as they are on the same dish, either hot or cold.

3994 Aubergines à la Provençale
Cut the eggplants in half and cook them in the usual manner. Remove the flesh, chop it, them cook it together with a proportionate amount of chopped onion cooked in oil. Add an equal amount of coarsely chopped tomato flesh cooked in oil, some fresh breadcrumbs, a touch of crushed garlic, a little chopped parsley and season with salt and pepper.

Fill the skins with this mixture and gratinate them. On removing from the oven, surround with a *cordon* of Tomato Sauce.

3995 Aubergines à la Serbe
Cut the eggplants in half lengthways and cook them as for Aubergines à l'Egyptienne. Remove the flesh from the skins and fill with the following mixture: the chopped flesh of the eggplant, chopped cooked mutton, coarsely chopped tomato flesh cooked in butter, chopped onion cooked in butter and plain boiled rice.

Arrange in a buttered dish, sprinkle with dry white breadcrumbs and gratinate in a hot oven. On removing from the oven surround with a *cordon* of Tomato Sauce and sprinkle with chopped parsley.

3996 Aubergines Soufflées

Cut 2 large eggplants in half, slash the flesh criss-cross and deep fry them in the usual way. Remove the flesh and lay the skins in a buttered gratin dish.

Chop the flesh finely and mix it with an equal quantity of reduced Sauce Béchamel flavoured with grated Parmesan cheese and thickened with 2 egg yolks. Fold in 3 stiffly beaten egg whites and fill the skins with this mixture.

Cook in a moderate oven as for an ordinary soufflé and serve immediately they come from the oven.

CARDONS—CARDOONS

3997 The Preparation and Cooking of Cardoons

Remove any blemished leaves from the outside, separate the white stalks and cut them into pieces 7–8 cm (3¼ in) long. Peel them and rub with lemon to prevent them discolouring and place into a basin of acidulated cold water. Discard the fibrous parts from the heart and cut and trim the hearts in the same way as the stalks.

Cook the prepared pieces of cardoon in a *Blanc*, covered with 500 g (1 lb 2 oz) chopped veal suet, spread over the surface to prevent the air from coming into contact and so discolouring them.

Allow to cook very slowly for approximately 1½ hours.

3998 Cardons au Jus

Arrange the cooked cardoons in a deep dish and coat with some very good Jus lié.

3999 Cardons à la Milanaise

This is prepared in the same way as Asperges à la Milanaise.

4000 Cardons à la Moelle

Arrange the cooked cardoons in the form of a pyramid on a round dish. Coat with Sauce Moelle and surround with very small Bouchées filled with poached diced bone marrow.

Alternatively, arrange the cardoons in a deep dish with the heart cut in slices in a circle on top, and a poached slice of bone marrow on each slice of the heart.

Cover completely with Sauce Moelle.

4001 Cardons Mornay

This is prepared in the same way as Cardons au Parmesan replacing the Sauce Demi-glace with Sauce Mornay.

Glaze quickly and serve immediately.

4002 Cardons au Parmesan

Drain the cooked pieces of cardoon and arrange them in layers in the form of a pyramid, sprinkling each layer with a few tablespoons of very good Sauce Demi-glace and some grated Parmesan cheese.

Cover with more of the same sauce, sprinkle with Parmesan and glaze quickly.

4003 Coeur de Cardon aux Fines Herbes

Trim the cooked heart of the cardoon to the shape of a cylinder and cut it into round slices 1 cm (⅖ in) thick. Roll them in very pale meat glaze containing butter and chopped Fines Ferbes and serve in a deep dish.

Notes: Cardoon hearts prepared in this manner make a very good garnish for Tournedos and Sautés of chicken.

4004 Cardoons with Various Sauces

Cardoons can be served with any of the following sauces: Demi-glace, Crème, Hollandaise, Mousseline, Italienne, Bordelaise etc.

The sauce can either be poured over the cardoons or served separately. If they are sauced over they should be served in a deep dish; if the sauce is to be served separately the cardoons should be served on a special silver grill in the same way as asparagus.

CAROTTES—CARROTS

4005 Glazed Carrots for Garnishing

It is not necessary to blanch young carrots, they can be left whole or cut into two or four pieces according to size, then trimmed. If the carrots are old ones they are trimmed to the shape of an elongated olive then blanched well before being cooked.

Place the prepared carrots in a pan with sufficient water to barely cover them, add 6 g (¼ oz) salt, 30 g (1 oz) sugar and 60 g (2 oz) butter per 5 dl (18 fl oz or 2¼ U.S. cups) water. Cook until almost all of the moisture has evaporated leaving a syrupy reduction; toss the carrots over in this to coat them with a brilliant gloss.

Note: This is the basic method for cooking carrots whatever their eventual use.

4006 Carottes à la Crème—Creamed Carrots

Prepare and cook the carrots as in the preceding recipe and when the liquid has reduced to a syrup, cover the carrots with boiling cream. Cook until sufficiently reduced and serve in a deep dish.

4007 Carottes Marianne
Cut some new carrots into coarse Julienne and cook in butter with the lid on, adding half its weight of small button mushrooms previously sautéed in butter.

When about to serve, shake in some Maître d'Hôtel Butter and a little meat glaze. Serve in a deep dish.

4008 Carottes à la Vichy
Cut the carrots into slices; if they are old ones blanch them well.

Cook in the same way as for Glazed Carrots and serve in a deep dish sprinkled with chopped parsley.

4009 Flan aux Carottes—Carrot Flan
This can be served as a vegetable or as a sweet dish.

Line a flan with puff paste; fill with a slightly sweetened purée of carrots and cover this with crescent-shaped slices of carrot cooked as for Glazed Carrots and taking care to prevent them from breaking. Bake as for an ordinary flan.

Note: This flan can be filled with new carrots cooked à la Vichy with the addition of an equal amount of rice cooked in Bouillon for 18 minutes.

CELERI—CELERY, CELERI-RAVE—CELERIAC

4010 Céleri Braisé—Braised Celery
Choose celery which is white but not fibrous or stringy.

Cut off the top leaving the celery approximately 20 cm (8 in) in length from the root, discard any green stalks and trim the root to a point. Wash well and blanch for 15 minutes then refresh and drain them.

Braise in the usual manner for vegetables. When cooked, cut each celery into two, fold the top ends over and arrange them in a dish.

4011 Other Preparations of Celery
All of the recipes given for cardoons are suitable for celery and the same methods should be followed. With reference to these recipes, celery can also be prepared au Parmesan, Mornay and à la Milanaise.

The sauces which are suitable for serving with celery are: Demi-glace, Moelle, Crème, Fines Herbes, Italienne, Hollandaise, au Jus etc.

4012 Céleri-Rave à l'Italienne
Well peel the celeriac, cut in $1\frac{1}{2}$ cm ($\frac{3}{5}$ in) slices and trim them evenly. Three-quarters cook in lightly salted water, drain well, add to some Sauce Italienne and finish cooking slowly in the sauce.

Place the celeriac with the sauce in a timbale or deep dish and sprinkle with chopped parsley.

4013 Céleri-Rave au Jus
Prepare in the same way as Céleri-Rave à l'Italienne completing the cooking in a thickened veal gravy instead of the Sauce Italienne.

4014 Purée de Céleri—Purée of Celery
Cut the celery into slices then blanch and drain them. Cook with a little very fatty White Bouillon until tender.

Drain well as soon as cooked then pass through a sieve together with some of the cooking liquid well-skimmed of fat. Add about one-third its quantity of fairly stiff and very white mashed potato; mix together, reheat and finish with butter at the last moment.

Serve in a deep dish.

4015 Purée de Céleri-Rave—Purée of Celeriac
Peel the celeriac, cut them into slices and cook in salted water. Drain well, pass through a sieve adding one-third its quantity of plain boiled floury potatoes.

Place the purée in a shallow pan, add 50 g (2 oz) butter per 500 g (1 lb 2 oz) purée, dry out on a hot stove then bring it to the correct consistency with hot milk. Finish with more butter at the last moment and serve in a deep dish.

CEPES—FLAP MUSHROOMS

4016 Cèpes (*flap mushrooms*)
Cèpes which are still unopened or barely open should not require washing. Those which are completely opened, however, must be washed and dried. They can then be grilled or cooked in butter.

4017 Cèpes à la Bordelaise
Cut the flap mushrooms into fairly thick slices on the slant; season with salt and pepper, place into a pan with hot oil and sauté until well coloured and slightly crisp.

Almost at the last moment, add 30 g (1 oz) of reserved stalks which have been chopped, 1 tbs chopped shallot and 1 tbs white breadcrumbs to absorb the excess oil for when the flap mushrooms are served—these quantities are 250 g (9 oz) of flap mushrooms.

Toss over to cook together for a few minutes then arrange in a deep dish and finish with a squeeze of lemon juice and a pinch of chopped parsley.

4018 Cèpes à la Crème
Slice the flap mushrooms and cook in butter with 1 tbs chopped onion cooked in butter without colour per 250 g (9 oz) of flap mushrooms.

When they are cooked, drain them and cover with boiling cream. Allow to cook slowly until the complete reduction of the cream.

At the last moment, add a little thin cream and serve in a deep dish.

Note: The best way of preparing this dish when using canned *Cèpes* is to wipe them well then to sauté them in butter without colour. Place in a pan together with 1 tbs cooked chopped onion, cover with boiling cream and cook until this is reduced by two-thirds. If cream is not available, use some Sauce Béchamel.

4019 Cèpes à la Provençale
This is prepared in the same way as Cèpes à la Bordelaise, replacing the shallot with onion and adding a touch of crushed garlic.

Arrange in a deep dish and finish with a squeeze of lemon juice and a pinch of chopped parsley.

4020 Cèpes Rossini
This is prepared in the same way as Cèpes à la Crème adding a third of their weight of thick slices of raw truffle; allow to cook together.

When about to serve, finish with a little pale meat glaze then serve in a deep dish.

CHAMPIGNONS—MUSHROOMS

Under this one heading is included only those generally used in cooking, that is the white cultivated mushroom and the field mushroom.

The other species of edible fungus are given under their correct names.

4021 Champignons à la Crème—Creamed Mushrooms
Proceed as indicated for Cèpes à la Crème.

4022 Croûtes aux Champignons
Prepare: 1) a filling of button mushrooms cooked in butter with a little lemon juice, then mixed with some Sauce Allemande to which the cooking liquor from the mushrooms has been added, 2) some bread cases cut from a fancy loaf, half emptied, spread with butter inside and dried in the oven, see Croûtes aux Rognons (2690).

Fill the Croûtes with the prepared mushroom filling.

For a large number, the filling can be placed in a lightly-baked flan case and surrounded on top with a border of small crescent shapes of puff paste, baked without being eggwashed.

4023 Champignons Grillés—Grilled Mushrooms
Choose some large mushrooms and wash and dry them well. Season, brush with oil and grill them slowly. Arrange on a round dish and fill the cavity of each mushroom with well-softened Maître d'Hôtel Butter.

4024 Champignons Grillés à la Bourguignonne
Prepare the mushrooms as in the preceding recipe and grill them until three-quarters cooked. Arrange on a dish, fill each with a little Snail Butter (235) and reheat in the oven for 5 minutes.

4025 Champignons Farcis—Stuffed Mushrooms
Choose some nice medium-sized mushrooms, remove the stalks and wash and dry them well.

Arrange them in a gratin dish, season and sprinkle with oil. Place in the oven for 5 minutes so as to extract some of their moisture then fill the cavities dome shape with thick Sauce Duxelles, which can be stiffened if necessary with some white breadcrumbs.

Sprinkle the mushrooms with dry white breadcrumbs and a few drops of oil or melted butter and gratinate in a hot oven.

4026 Champignons aux Fines Herbes
Wash, slice, season and sauté the mushrooms in butter using a frying pan on a very hot stove. Place in a suitable dish and sprinkle with chopped parsley at the last moment.

4027 Flan Grillé aux Champignons
Line a buttered flan ring with fine short paste. Fill it with very fresh barely opened mushrooms which have been sautéed in butter with a little chopped onion, then mixed together with Sauce Béchamel and cream and allowed to get cold.

Moisten the edges of the flan and cover with thin strips of paste arranged trellis-fashion.

Brush the trellis of paste with eggwash, bake in a hot oven and serve as soon as it is cooked.

4028 Tartelettes Grillés aux Champignons
These tartlets make an excellent and pleasing garnish especially for Tournedos and Noisettes.

They are prepared in the same way as for Flan Grillé aux Champignons using tartlets moulds of a size in keeping with the item which they are to accompany as a garnish.

4029 Turned and Grooved Mushrooms for Garnishing
Select very fresh mushrooms, wash them quickly and drain. Cut off the stalks level with the mushroom and with the point of a small knife, turn or groove the heads placing each as it is finished, into the following cooking liquor which should be boiling.

For 1 kg ($2\frac{1}{4}$ lb) mushrooms, place 1 dl ($3\frac{1}{2}$ fl oz or $\frac{1}{2}$ U.S. cup) water in a pan together with 10 g ($\frac{1}{3}$ oz) salt, 60 g (2 oz) butter and the juice of $1\frac{1}{2}$ lemons.

Cook the mushrooms in this liquor for 5 minutes and when cooked, place in a basin and cover with a buttered paper.

4030 Purée de Champignons—Mushroom Purée
Wash and dry 1 kg ($2\frac{1}{4}$ lb) mushrooms, peel them if necessary then pass through a coarse sieve.

Melt 60 g (2 oz) butter in a shallow pan, add the mushroom purée and cook quickly until all the moisture has been evaporated.

Add 3 dl ($\frac{1}{2}$ pt or $1\frac{1}{4}$ U.S. cups) Sauce Béchamel which has previously been reduced with 1 dl ($3\frac{1}{2}$ fl oz or $\frac{1}{2}$ U.S. cup) cream; season with salt, pepper and a little grated nutmeg and reduce on a hot stove.

Remove from the heat and finish with 100 g ($3\frac{1}{2}$ oz) good butter.

4031 MORILLES—MORELS

The Morel or Spring Mushroom is considered by connoisseurs of the mushroom family to be the best of all the edible fungi. There are two kinds of morels—the white and the brown; both are very good and whilst some people may express their preference for the white ones there are those who maintain that the brown are the best.

Despite those lovers of morels who say that it is wrong to wash them, it is advisable to do so carefully and to open them slightly so that the water can get in to wash away any grains of sand that might be inside.

4032 The Cooking of Morels
Wash and drain the morels; leave the small ones whole and cut the large ones in two or three pieces. Drain them well, then place in a pan with 50 g (2 oz) butter, the juice of 1 lemon and a pinch of salt and pepper per 500 g (1 lb 2 oz) morels.

Bring to the boil and cook for 10–12 minutes. It should not be overlooked that the cooking liquor from the morels should always be reduced and added to the sauce which is to accompany them.

4033 Morilles à la Crème
This is prepared in the same way as Cèpes à la Crème.

4034 Croûte aux Morilles
This is prepared in the same way as Croûte aux Champignons.

4035 Morilles Farcies à la Forestière
Select some large morels, wash them well and remove the stalks. Chop the stalks and make into a Duxelles then add half its quantity of very fine sausage meat.

Cut the morels through on one side to form a pocket and fill with the prepared stuffing. Place in a buttered earthenware dish cut side down, sprinkle with very fine dry white breadcrumbs and melted butter and cook in a moderate oven.

Serve in the dish as they are.

4036 Morilles à la Poulette
Cook the morels in the usual manner then place in a Sauce Poulette together with the reduced cooking liquor.

Serve in a deep dish sprinkled with chopped parsley.

4037 Morilles Sautées
Wash the morels well, dry them in a cloth and cut into either two or four pieces according to size.

Season them with salt and pepper then sauté quickly in butter in a frying pan over a good heat, so as to prevent the moisture from the morels being exuded.

Place in a deep dish and sprinkle with a few drops of lemon juice and chopped parsley.

4038 Timbale de Morilles Châtelaine
Take 1 kg ($2\frac{1}{4}$ lb) morels, place 8 large ones aside and make 100 g ($3\frac{1}{2}$ oz) of the stalks into a Duxelles.

Cook the remainder in the usual manner, drain them well and add to 4 dl (14 fl oz or $1\frac{3}{4}$ U.S. cups) reduced Sauce Béchamel.

Butter a shallow round mould, decorate with shapes of truffle then coat the bottom and sides with a fairly thick layer of Godiveau (290) containing chopped raw truffle and mushrooms.

Fill the mould with the morels and sauce, cover with a layer of Godiveau and cook in the oven *au Bain-marie* for 50–55 minutes.

Meanwhile cut the 8 large morels in half, stuff them with the prepared Duxelles to which has been added a little chopped parsley and 2 chopped hard-boiled egg yolks. Sprinkle them with dry white breadcrumbs and butter and gratinate.

When the mould is cooked, turn out on to a round dish and surround with the stuffed morels.

4039 Tourte de Morilles Villeneuve
Cook the morels in the usual manner and drain them. Reduce the cooking liquor by three-quarters, add a few tablespoons of Sauce Béchamel and 30 g (1 oz) butter per 500 g (1 lb 2 oz) morels; reheat without boiling, add the cooked morels and shake the pan to mix well with the sauce.

Fill this mixture into a Croûte de Tourte (4335) or simply place in the centre of a cooked circular band of puff pastry placed on a round dish.

This preparation of morels may also be served in a large Vol-au-vent case.

4040 MOUSSERONS, ORONGE AGARIC AND CHANTERELLES

These are different kinds of edible fungus which are available fresh during their brief seasons thus they are seldom used. When available the best way to cook them is to sauté them quickly in butter with a little finely chopped onion or shallot.

4041 BRIONNE OR CHAYOTTE—CHOW-CHOW

This excellent vegetable of the gourd family is only now becoming known and appreciated by gourmets.

It is in season from the end of October to the end of January at a time when cucumbers and courgettes which it resembles in flavour although much finer, are out of season.

It may be prepared in any of the ways given for these two vegetables and any of the recipes for cardoons and globe artichokes are also applicable.

CHICOREE—ENDIVE

There are three varieties of endives or chicory used in cookery. They are: 1) The frizzy or curled endive, 2) the Flemish chicory, which is the true endive when grown naturally in the open air, and which is very similar to the Batavian endive, 3) the Brussels endive which is usually called the Belgian or white endive. It is obtained by cultivating the root of Flemish chicory in the dark.

The last variety is completely different from the first two both as regards its quality and the methods of cookery; it is therefore dealt with separately under its own title.

4042 Chicorée à la Crème
Blanch the endives in plenty of boiling water for 10 minutes, refresh, squeeze out all the water then chop them.

Mix 1 litre (1¾ pt or 4½ U.S. cups) White Bouillon on to 150 g (5 oz) brown Roux made with butter, season with salt and a pinch of sugar, cook for a few minutes, then add for this amount 1 kg (2¼ lb) of the prepared endive. Cover with a lid and braise in the oven for 1½ hours.

When cooked, remove to a clean pan, mix in 3 dl (½ pt or 1¼ U.S. cups) cream and 150 g (5 oz) butter. Serve in a deep dish.

4043 Chicorée à la Flamande
Cut the endives into 5 cm (2 in) lengths; blanch them, refresh and squeeze out all the water then proceed as for Chicorée à la Crème.

The only difference between these two recipes is that here the chicory is not chopped.

4044 Pain de Chicorée
Braise the endives as for Chicorée à la Crème but instead of finishing with cream and butter, mix in 5 beaten eggs per 1 kg (2¼ lb) of chicory. Now fill it into a buttered plain mould and cook in the oven *au Bain-marie.*

When cooked, allow to rest for a few minutes to allow the contents to settle, then demould on to a dish and coat with Sauce Crème.

Serve immediately.

4045 Purée de Chicorée
Braise the endives as indicated in the recipe for Chicorée à la Crème; pass through a sieve and mix together with one-third its volume of good creamed mashed potatoes.

Reheat, then remove from the stove and add a little butter. Serve in a deep dish.

4046 Soufflé de Chicorée
Pass 250 g (9 oz) fairly stiff braised endive through a sieve; add 3 egg yolks and 60 g (2 oz) grated Parmesan then fold in 3 stiffly beaten egg whites.

Fill into a buttered soufflé mould, sprinkle with grated Parmesan then cook in the same way as for other soufflés.

Note: This soufflé may be cooked in small soufflé moulds for use as a garnish with large joints of veal or ham.

ENDIVE OR CHICOREE DE BRUXELLES—BELGIAN OR WHITE ENDIVE

4047 To Cook Belgian Endives

Whatever way they are to be ultimately finished, Belgian endives should always be cooked in the following manner.

Clean, wash and drain the Belgian endives, then lay them without being blanched, in a well tinned pan. Moisten with a cooking liquor made from 2 dl (7 fl oz or $\frac{7}{8}$ U.S. cup) cold water, the juice of 1 lemon and 50 g (2 oz) butter per 1 kg ($2\frac{1}{4}$ lb) endives.

Cover with a buttered paper and a lid, bring to the boil and cook on the side of the stove or in the oven for 30–35 minutes.

Belgian endives can be served as a much appreciated vegetable or as a garnish, especially with a Relevé of meat.

Some of the recipes for cardoons, in particular those for à la Crème and à la Milanaise are suitable for Belgian endives.

4048 Endives à l'Ardennaise

Cook the Belgian endives as described above omitting the lemon juice and adding when they are half cooked 125 g ($4\frac{1}{2}$ oz) blanched diced belly of pork and 100 g ($3\frac{1}{2}$ oz) chopped lean ham.

Finish cooking together then arrange in a dish with the pork and ham and coat with the reduced cooking liquor finished with butter.

4049 Endives à la Bourgeoise

Wash and drain the Belgian endives, arrange in a well buttered shallow pan, season with a little salt, cover with a lid and cook very slowly on the side of the stove.

By the time they are tender the butter should be clarified and the outside leaves slightly coloured.

4050 Endives à la Crème

Cook the Belgian endives in the usual manner keeping them slightly firm. Finish in the same way as for all vegetables prepared *à la Crème*.

4051 Endives au Jus

Cook the Belgian endives in the usual manner, cut in half, fold over and arrange in a dish. Coat with a good gravy obtained from a braised joint of veal.

4052 Endives Mornay

Arrange the cooked Belgian endives on a layer of Sauce Mornay in a dish. Cover with more sauce, sprinkle with grated cheese and melted butter and glaze quickly.

CHOUX—CABBAGE

In culinary terms, cabbages may be divided into seven different types:

1) White cabbage which is almost exclusively used for making Sauerkraut (Choucroute).
2) Red cabbage which is used as a vegetable, as an Hors-d'oeuvre and as a pickle.
3) Round green cabbages which are best when plain boiled or braised.
4) Scotch kale and spring cabbage which are usually plain boiled.
5) Cauliflower and broccoli of which only the flower part is normally used; the leaves may, however, be plain boiled when they are tender.
6) Brussels sprouts.
7) Kohlrabi and swedes of which the tender young leaves can be cooked but usually only the bulbous root is used in the same way as turnips.

4053 CHOU BLANC—WHITE CABBAGE

White cabbage may be braised in the same way as green cabbage but this is not usual as it is generally too firm. It is best suited for preparing a Sauerkraut.

4054 Choucroute—Sauerkraut

If the sauerkraut is too old it may be necessary to soak it in cold water for several hours before cooking; but wherever possible it is better to avoid this measure and use fresh sauerkraut.

Drain the sauerkraut if it has been soaked and squeeze it to remove all the water; carefully separate any tightly packed parts, season with salt and pepper and place in a braising pan lined with slices of bacon fat.

For 5 kg (11 lb) of sauerkraut add 3 carrots, 3 onions each stuck with a clove, a large Bouquet garni, 100 g ($3\frac{1}{2}$ oz) juniper berries tied in muslin, 200 g (7 oz) goose fat or lard and a 500 g (1 lb 2 oz) piece of blanched streaky bacon. Moisten to barely cover with White Bouillon, cover with more bacon fat, place on the lid, bring to the boil and cook gently in the oven for 4 hours; remove the piece of bacon after 1 hour.

To serve: remove the vegetables and flavourings, drain the sauerkraut well and arrange it in a timbale or on a dish. Surround with thin slices of ham, square pieces of the bacon and poached Frankfurt or Strasburg sausages.

CHOUX ROUGES—RED CABBAGE

4055 Chou Rouge à la Flamande
Cut the cabbage into quarters, discard the outside leaves and stumps and slice the rest into a fine Julienne. Season with salt and grated nutmeg, sprinkle with vinegar and place in a well-buttered earthenware Cocotte.

Cover with the lid and cook gently in a moderate oven. When three-quarters cooked, add 4 peeled and sliced pippin apples and 1 tbs of brown or caster sugar. Take care that the cooking is gentle from start to finish and that no other liquid except the vinegar is added.

4056 Chou Rouge à la Limousine
Cut the red cabbage into a fine Julienne, season and cook in the oven in an earthenware casserole with a little Bouillon, pork dripping and 20 shelled and broken raw chestnuts for 1 medium-sized cabbage.

4057 Pickled Red Cabbage for Hors-d'oeuvre
Cut 1 medium-sized red cabbage into a fine Julienne, place in a china bowl, sprinkle with fine salt and leave to macerate for 6–8 hours turning it over frequently. Then drain and place in a glazed earthenware jar together with 1 clove of garlic, a few peppercorns and 1 bayleaf. Cover with ordinary vinegar or preferably, cold boiled vinegar and leave to pickle for 1–2 days.

Note: Pickled cabbage is an excellent accompaniment for boiled beef.

CHOUX VERTS—GREEN CABBAGE

4058 Chou à l'Anglaise—Cabbage, English Style
Cut the cabbage into quarters, discard the stumps, and thick stalks from the leaves and wash well.

Cook in boiling salted water then drain well; press between two plates to remove the water. Cut into the shape of squares or diamonds etc. and place in a dish.

Prepared in this way the cabbage may be served as a vegetable or as a garnish.

4059 Chou braisé—Braised Cabbage
Cut the cabbage into quarters, discard the stumps, wash and blanch well then refresh and drain well.

Separate the leaves, cut out any large stalks and discard them. Season with salt, pepper and grated nutmeg and place them in a pan lined with slices of fat bacon. For each 1 kg ($2\frac{1}{4}$ lb) of cabbage, add 1 carrot cut in quarters, 1 onion stuck with a clove, a Bouquet garni, 4 dl (14 fl oz or $1\frac{3}{4}$ U.S. cups) white Bouillon and 3 tbs unclarified Bouillon fat.

Cover with more fat bacon and with a lid and bring to the boil. Place in the oven to braise slowly for 2 hours.

4060 Chou Farci—Stuffed Cabbage
Blanch and refresh a small whole cabbage then remove the centre stump. Place the cabbage on a cloth, carefully separate the leaves starting from the outside and season lightly. Starting from the centre this time, insert between the leaves, layers of well seasoned stuffing made from chopped cooked or raw meat, chopped onion and chopped parsley.

Re-form the cabbage to its original shape by pressing each layer to the next, cover completely with thin rashers of fat bacon and tie up.

Place in a pan with some Bouillon and some of its fat. Cover and braise very slowly for 3 hours. *To serve:* untie the cabbage and discard the fat; drain the cabbage, place it on a dish and coat with the braising liquid which has been skimmed of fat, reduced and thickened with Sauce Demi-glace.

Serve the remainder of the sauce separately.

Note: A useful variation of the above recipe and one to be recommended, is to remove the centre of the cabbage leaving just two or three outer rows of leaves. Chop the inside leaves, add to a meat stuffing and fill the cabbage with the mixture; braise in the usual manner. An improvement to this is to add a quarter part of Riz Pilaw and the same of foie gras fat to the stuffing.

4061 Sou-Fassum Provençal
Blanch and refresh a whole green cabbage; remove the large outer leaves and lay them out on a piece of fine net cloth. On this layer of leaves place the following mixture: 250 g (9 oz) blanched shredded beetroot leaves, 750 g (1 lb 10 oz) sausage meat, 200 g (7 oz) fried diced lean bacon, 1 onion chopped and fried in butter, the chopped flesh only of 2 tomatoes, 1 crushed clove of garlic, 100 g ($3\frac{1}{2}$ oz) blanched rice and 125 g ($4\frac{1}{2}$ oz) fresh peas in season—all these ingredients to be mixed well together.

Pull the corners of the netting over so as to re-form the cabage, tie it up and place to cook in the stock pot, for preference one being made with mutton and allow to cook gently for $3\frac{1}{2}$–4 hours.

When cooked, remove the netting and present the cabbage on a suitable dish.

4062 Small Cabbages for Garnishing
This may be prepared in any of the following ways:

A) Blanch, refresh and well drain a whole cabbage and remove as many large leaves as the number of garnishes requires. If some leaves are not large enough, put two together. Season the remainder of the leaves with salt and pepper, and share them out among the large leaves, wrap these around and squeeze into small balls. Arrange in a buttered pan and cover with thin slices of fat bacon.

Braise in the usual manner for braised cabbage.

B) Prepare small cabbages as above but place a small ball of stuffing in the middle of each.

C) Blanch the required number of large leaves of cabbage, refresh them, drain and spread them out. Place a spoonful of Riz Pilaw mixed with some foie gras purée inside each and fold over the outside leaves to form small packets.

Braise in the usual manner.

Note: Whether for ordinary braised cabbage, whole stuffed cabbage or balls of cabbage for garnishing, goose liver fat if available, may be used with advantage in the braising process.

4063 CHOUX FRISES—SCOTCH KALE; CHOUX DE PRINTEMPS—SPRING CABBAGE; LEAVES OF BROCCOLI, KOHLRABI, TURNIP AND SWEDE

All of these different leaves may be prepared *à l'Anglaise*, i.e. boiled in salted water, or cooked with butter as for Brussels sprouts (4074). These are the only suitable methods of cooking.

CHOUX-FLEURS—CAULIFLOWER; BROCOLIS—BROCCOLI

Broccoli differs from cauliflower by the colour of its flowers which are a deep violet and also in the arrangement of the flower which is not so massed as the curd of the cauliflower.

English broccoli never attains as large a size as the French varieties of the Midi; some of them do not even form a head, the flowers being only the size of a hazelnut and widely distributed in the interstices of the leaves.

The following recipes are equally suitable for cauliflower and broccoli.

4064 Chou-fleur à l'Anglaise—Cauliflower, English Style

When served à l'Anglaise, the cauliflower should be left whole with the first two rows of tender leaves which surround the head, attached.

Trim and wash the cauliflower and, if necessary, leave to soak in cold salted water. Cook in boiling salted water; when tender, cool slightly, drain and arrange it on a serviette or on a thick slice of toasted bread to absorb any moisture.

4065 Chou-fleur à la Crème

Divide the cauliflower into bouquets discarding all the leaves and cook in boiling salted water.

Drain well, re-form into shape in a deep dish and serve accompanied with a sauceboat of Cream Sauce.

Note: If desired, the cauliflower can be three-quarters cooked in the water, then drained and finished cooking in the Cream Sauce.

4066 Fritots de Chou-fleur

Divide the cauliflower into bouquets and cook in boiling salted water. Drain, season and marinate with oil and lemon juice for 20 minutes.

Dip each piece in frying batter and deep fry in hot fat at the last moment. Drain well.

Arrange on a serviette on a dish, garnish with fried parsley and serve accompanied with Tomato Sauce.

4067 Chou-fleur au Gratin

Cook a cauliflower divided into bouquets in the usual manner, drain well and heat in a little butter to dry out any remaining moisture.

Arrange the bouquets in a suitable-size round bowl to re-form it to its original shape, filling the centre with a few tablespoons of Sauce Mornay.

Coat the bottom of a gratin dish with Sauce Mornay and demould the cauliflower on top. Cover completely with more sauce, sprinkle with a mixture of grated cheese and fine dry white breadcrumbs, and with melted butter, and gratinate.

4068 Chou-fleur à la Milanaise

Place the cooked and well drained cauliflower in a buttered dish sprinkled with grated cheese.

Sprinkle the cauliflower also with grated cheese, add a few small pieces of butter and gratinate in the oven. On removing from the oven coat the cauliflower with a little brown butter and serve immediately.

4069 Chou-fleur à la Polonaise

Drain the cooked cauliflower well and place in a buttered dish; sprinkle with mixed chopped hard-boiled egg yolk and chopped parsley.

At the moment of service, coat with brown butter in which 30 g (1 oz) fine white breadcrumbs per 125 g ($4\frac{1}{2}$ oz) butter, have been fried to a golden brown.

4070 Cauliflower with Various Sauces
Cook the cauliflower whole in boiling salted water; drain well and arrange in a dish.

Serve accompanied with a suitable sauce such as: au Beurre, Hollandaise, Mousseline or with melted butter.

4071 Purée de Chou-fleur, also called Purée à la Dubarry
Cook the cauliflower in boiling salted water, drain it well but do not refresh. Pass through a sieve, add a quarter its quantity of slightly firm creamed mashed potato, mix together and reheat.

Finish with a little butter away from the heat and serve in a deep dish.

CHOUX DE BRUXELLES—BRUSSELS SPROUTS

4072 Choux de Bruxelles à l'Anglaise—Brussels Sprouts, English style
Cook the prepared sprouts in boiling salted water, drain them well and serve in a dish or on a vegetable grill on a dish.

4073 Choux de Bruxelles à la Crème—Creamed Brussels Sprouts
Cook the sprouts in the usual manner and drain them well without cooling. Heat in butter for a few minutes to become dry then chop them.

Mix in as much cream as they will absorb and serve.

4074 Choux de Bruxelles à la Bonne Femme
Cook the sprouts in boiling salted water keeping them firm; drain but do not cool them.

Place in a shallow pan with 50 g (2 oz) butter cut into small pieces per 500 g (1 lb 2 oz) sprouts; season with salt and pepper, cover and cook in the oven for 15 minutes.

4075 Choux de Bruxelles au gratin
Cook and drain the sprouts; heat in butter for a few minutes to become dry, season and mix in a little well buttered Sauce Béchamel.

Place in a suitable dish, coat with Sauce Mornay. Sprinkle with grated cheese and gratinate quickly.

4076 Choux de Bruxelles à la Milanaise
Proceed as indicated for cauliflower of the same name.

4077 Choux de Bruxelles à la Polonaise
Proceed as indicated for cauliflower of the same name.

4078 Choux de Bruxelles Sautés
Cook the sprouts in the usual manner, drain them well, then place into a frying pan containing some very hot butter. Sauté until lightly browned then place in a deep dish and sprinkle with chopped parsley.

4079 Purée de Choux de Bruxelles, also called Purée à la Flamande
Plain boil the sprouts until three-quarters cooked. Drain well but do not cool them, then finish cooking with a little butter.

Pass through a sieve and add one-third its quantity of mashed potato. Reheat and finish away from the heat with butter.

4080 CHOU MARIN—SEAKALE

Seakale is one of the finest and best of English vegetables. It should be trimmed very carefully, tied into bundles of 4–6 pieces and plain boiled in salted water.

All of the recipes for cardoons and all of the sauces served with asparagus are suitable for seakale.

4081 CHOU DE MAI

This kind of cabbage is used a lot in Belgium. It is similar to English Spring Cabbage and should be cooked whole in the same way.

CONCOMBRES—CUCUMBERS; AND COURGETTES

Although differing in shape and size, these two vegetables when cooked can be served in exactly the same way. They are used most frequently as a garnish.

4082 Concombres à la Crème
Peel the cucumber, cut into pieces and trim olive shape. Blanch and drain them, then stew in butter until almost cooked. Moisten with boiling cream and finish cooking whilst the cream reduces.

At the very last moment, add a little Sauce Béchamel to slightly thicken then serve in a deep dish.

4083 Concombres farcis—Stuffed Cucumber
This may be prepared in either of the following ways:

A) Peel and cut the cucumbers into sections 5 cm (2 in) long; blanch and drain them. Hollow out the centre of each piece to form a round case then place them side by side in a shallow pan and stew together with a little butter until three-quarters cooked.

Fill dome shape with raw chicken forcemeat using a piping bag and tube; replace in a moderate oven to cook the forcemeat and finish cooking the cucumber at the same time.

B) Peel the cucumber, cut in half lengthways and remove the centre with a vegetable scoop. Blanch and drain them without cooling. Fill each half level with chicken and frangipane panada forcemeat containing one-third its quantity of dry Duxelles. Fit the two halves together, wrap around with slices of salt pork fat and wrap each cucumber thus in a piece of muslin.

Braise the cucumbers in the usual way for vegetables; when cooked, untie them, cut into round slices of a thickness determined by the size of the item they are to accompany.

4084 Concombres Glacés—Glazed Cucumber
Peel the cucumbers, cut into pieces and trim to the size of large garlic cloves. Blanch them quickly then cook as for Carottes Glacées, reducing the cooking liquor to a syrupy consistency in which to roll and glaze the cucumbers.

4085 Courgettes à la Provençale
Cut the courgettes into slices and cook in butter. Add one-third its quantity of Riz Pilaw and a few tablespoons of Sauce Béchamel. Place in an earthenware dish, sprinkle with a mixture of grated Parmesan and breadcrumbs then with melted butter and gratinate in a hot oven.

Note: In Provence, courgettes are also cooked in the same way as eggplants, e.g. stuffed, fried, sautéed etc.

4086 CROSNES DU JAPON OR STACHYS—JAPANESE ARTICHOKES

For whatever way they are to be cooked, Japanese artichokes must first be cleaned before being blanched, keeping them slightly firm. They should then be heated in butter to dry but without colour.

Japanese artichokes should be very fresh as otherwise it is difficult to clean them properly and obtain a white colour. The best way to remove their skins is to rub them with coarse salt in a thick cloth, then to wash them to remove any particles of skin still adhering.

4087 Beignets de Crosnes
Cook the artichokes in salted water keeping them firm. Drain well, mix with sufficient very well reduced Sauce Allemande, spread on a buttered tray and allow to cool.

Take spoonfuls of this mixture, dip in frying batter and deep fry in hot fat. Serve arranged on a serviette on a dish garnished with fried parsley.

4088 Crosnes à la Crème
Blanch the artichokes then cook them in butter until three-quarters cooked; moisten with cream and finish cooking whilst the cream reduces. Add a little thin Sauce Béchamel at the last moment and serve in a deep dish.

4089 Croquettes de Crosnes
Mix some nearly cooked artichokes with very well reduced Sauce Allemande allowing $3\frac{1}{2}$ dl (12 fl oz or $1\frac{1}{2}$ U.S. cups) sauce per 500 g (1 lb 2 oz) artichokes. Spread on a buttered tray and allow to cool.

Divide into approximately 60 g (2 oz) pieces, mould into balls, flat round cakes or pear shapes etc.; flour, egg and breadcrumb them and deep fry in very hot fat 5–6 minutes before being required.

Drain on a cloth, sprinkle lightly with salt and arrange on a serviette on a dish; garnish with bouquets of very green fried parsley.

4090 Crosnes à la Milanaise
Blanch, drain and dry the artichokes then stew them together with a little butter for 12–15 minutes. Arrange in layers in a timbale sprinkling each layer with mixed grated Parmesan and Gruyère cheese. Moisten with a little very good gravy from braised beef, sprinkle the top with grated cheese and gratinate.

4091 Crosnes Sautés au Beurre
Cook the artichokes in the usual manner keeping them fairly firm. Drain and dry them well then toss in hot butter over a good heat to colour and finish cooking. Serve in a deep dish sprinkled with chopped parsley.

4092 Crosnes au Velouté
Cook the artichokes in salted water until tender. Drain and mix together with sufficient mushroom-flavoured Velouté.

4093 Purée de Crosnes
Cook the artichokes in salted water together with 125 g ($4\frac{1}{2}$ oz) quartered potatoes per 500 g (1 lb 2 oz) artichokes, keeping them a little firm. Drain well, pass through a sieve then dry out in a pan on a hot stove.

Add sufficient hot milk to give a good consistency and finish away from the heat with a little butter.

Note: Japanese artichokes may also be served au Gratin, à la Polonaise etc. proceeding in the same way as for Brussels sprouts of the same name.

EPINARDS—SPINACH

4094 To cook Spinach

Where possible, spinach should always be cooked at the last moment.

Cook the picked and washed spinach in plenty of boiling salted water, refresh, drain and squeeze out all the water. According to requirements it may be chopped or passed through a sieve. For leaf spinach there is no need to refresh or squeeze; it is only necessary to lay it out on a sieve to drain well.

4095 Epinards à l'Anglaise

Cook the spinach in plenty of boiling salted water, drain well but do not refresh it. Serve in a deep dish.

4096 Epinards à la Crème

Cook the spinach, then either chop or pass it through a sieve after refreshing and squeezing it. Place in a shallow pan with 60 g (2 oz) butter per 500 g (1 lb 2 oz) spinach and heat to dry out.

Add a quarter its volume of Cream Sauce and allow to simmer gently for 10 minutes. Turn into a deep dish and coat the surface with a little hot cream just before serving.

4097 Epinards au Gratin

Dry out the cooked and prepared spinach as above, using 100 g (3½ oz) butter per 500 g (1 lb 2 oz) spinach. Mix in 75 g (2½ oz) of grated cheese, place in a buttered earthenware dish, sprinkle well with grated cheese and melted butter and gratinate in a hot oven.

4098 Epinards Mère-Louisette

Wash the spinach, drain and dry, then roughly chop it. Place in a shallow pan with 100 g (3½ oz) butter per 500 g (1 lb 2 oz) spinach and cook over a hot stove, stirring frequently.

When cooked, add 50 g (2 oz) very small diced lean ham and 25 g (1 oz) diced Croûtons of bread fried in butter.

Place in a vegetable dish and serve immediately.

4099 Epinards à la Viroflay

Lay out flat on a piece of clean cloth, some large blanched leaves of spinach. In the centre of each place one Subric of Spinach made from the usual mixture but containing some small Croûtons of bread cut in small dice and fried in clarified butter.

Wrap up the Subrics in the leaves of spinach to the shape of small round packets. Arrange them in a buttered gratin dish, coat with Sauce Mornay, sprinkle with grated cheese and melted butter and gratinate in a hot oven.

4100 Subrics d'Epinards

Coarsely chop some cooked spinach and heat in it butter to remove most of the moisture. Remove from the heat and mix in 1 dl (3½ fl oz or ½ U.S. cup) well reduced Sauce Béchamel, 2 tbs double cream, 1 egg and 3 yolks beaten together and a little salt, pepper and grated nutmeg—these amounts are for 500 g (1 lb 2 oz) cooked spinach.

Heat sufficient clarified butter in a frying pan until very hot; take a tablespoonful of the mixture and drop in the butter, pushing it off with the finger. Continue with the formation of the Subrics taking care that they do not touch each other.

Cook to colour for 1 minute, turn over with a palette knife or a fork and colour on the other side. Drain, arrange on a flat or in a deep dish and serve accompanied with Cream Sauce.

Note: Another way of making a subric mixture is to mix an equal quantity of fairly thick pancake batter with the spinach after it has been dried with the butter.

4101 Crêpes aux Epinards

Cook the spinach in the usual manner and drain and squeeze it. Chop it roughly then add to an equal quantity of Yorkshire pudding batter.

Cook in butter as for pancakes using a small frying pan, or cook in the oven in deep tartlet moulds.

Note: These pancakes are a very good garnish for Relevés of beef, veal and ham.

4102 Soufflé aux Epinards

Prepare a mixture as for Soufflé de Chicorée but using spinach.

Arrange 2–3 layers of the mixture in a buttered soufflé mould alternating each with well washed, dried and trimmed fillets of anchovy arranged trellis-fashion. Finish with a layer of soufflé mixture, smooth dome shape and decorate with two rows of anchovy fillets arranged trellis-fashion.

Cook as for an ordinary soufflé.

Note: Thin slices of ham may be used instead of anchovies.

4103 Soufflé aux Epinards aux Truffes

This is prepared as in the preceding recipe replacing the anchovies with nice slices of truffle.

Note: The above spinach soufflés can, if desired, be served as a vegetable by cooking them in a timbale or deep dish; they can also be served as a garnish by cooking in small *Cassolettes* of a suitable size.

4104 FENOUIL TUBEREUX—TUBEROUS FENNEL

This vegetable is not used very often which is a pity since it is of an excellent and delicate flavour. It may be prepared in any of the ways given for celery and cardoons after first being cooked or well blanched in salted water.

FEUILLES DE VIGNE—VINE LEAVES

Young tender vine leaves may be used as a garnish after being prepared as in the following recipe.

4105 Feuilles de Vignes Farcies, or Dolmas—Stuffed Vine Leaves
Remove the stalks then blanch and drain the leaves well. For each portion place three or four leaves together in the form of a circle; place 1 tbs of Riz Pilaw bound with foie gras purée in the centre of each and enfold to the shape of even-sized balls.

Turn them over and place closely together in a shallow pan previously lined with thin slices of salt pork fat. Cover with more slices of the fat, moisten with White Bouillon and braise slowly in the usual manner.

Serve with a little of the braising liquid.

4106 FEVES—BROAD BEANS

Broad beans should only be shelled just before cooking and except when they are to be served à l'Anglaise it is essential to remove the inner skin after the beans have been cooked.

Broad beans are cooked in boiling salted water with a bunch of savory of a size in keeping with the quantity of beans. When cooked and drained, the beans should be sprinkled with chopped savory.

Do not forget that savory is an indispensable ingredient in the flavouring of broad beans.

4107 Fèves à l'Anglaise—Broad Beans, English Style
Cook the beans in boiling salted water, drain and serve in a folded table napkin accompanied with butter.

4108 Fèves au Beurre—Buttered Broad Beans
Plain boil the beans, drain well and toss in butter to dry them thoroughly. Finish with 100 g (3½ oz) butter per 500 g (1 lb 2 oz) beans, adding it away from the heat.

4109 Fèves à la Crème—Creamed Broad Beans
Plain boil the beans, drain well and dry in butter. Add 3 tbs double cream per 500 g (1 lb 2 oz) beans and toss over to mix.

4110 Purée de Fèves
This is prepared in the same way as mashed potato. It makes an excellent garnish particularly for serving with ham.

GOMBOS—OKRAS

This vegetable is much used in the Americas and the Far East but is not in general use in Europe despite attempts to popularize it.

There are two kinds, the long thin finger-like ones, and the round ones which are also known as Bamia or Bamies.

The following recipes are suitable for both kinds.

4111 Gombos à la Crème—Creamed Okras
Cut off the tops and tails of the okras; blanch well in salted water, drain them and cook in butter until tender.

Mix with a little Cream Sauce just before serving.

4112 Gombos Etuvés
Trim the okras and blanch them lightly. Place in a heavy pan with some onions cooked in butter and some blanched squares of lean bacon; moisten with a little water and cook slowly.

When cooked, arrange the pieces of bacon overlapping in a circle on a dish and place the okras in the cente.

4113 Okras for Garnishing
Trim the okras and two-thirds cook them in salted water. Drain them well and finish cooking them in some of the braising liquid from the joint with which they will be served.

If to be used as a garnish with Poulet Sauté their cooking should be finished in a thin veal gravy.

4114 Gombos Janina
Use round okras and soak them for 24 hours if they are the dried kind; they are about the size of a haricot bean. When obtained commercially in the dried form they are usually threaded on a string in the same way as dried morels.

Cook 125 g (4½ oz) chopped onion in mutton tail fat, add the roughly chopped flesh of 4 tomatoes, and 250 g (9 oz) diced cooked mutton and cook together for 7–8 minutes.

Add the well drained okras, moisten with a little water, cover and cook gently together. They should be highly seasoned and served as they are.

JETS DE HOUBLON—HOP SHOOTS

4115 Jets de Houblon—Hop Shoots
The edible part of the hop is separated from the fibrous part by breaking it off like asparagus.

Wash in several waters and cook in salted water with the juice of half a lemon per 1 litre (1¾ pt or 4½ U.S. cups) water. They may then prepare *au Beurre*, *à la Crème* or *au Velouté*.

When served as a vegetable it is usual to place a circle of poached eggs alternating with cockscomb-shaped Croûtons of bread fried in butter, either on top or surrounding the hop shoots.

HARICOTS BLANCS—HARICOT BEANS

4116 Haricot Blancs à l'Américaine (*Lima Beans*)
Cook the beans in water with the usual vegetables and a Bouquet garni plus a 500 g (1 lb 2 oz) piece of streaky bacon per 1 litre (1¾ pt or 4½ U.S. cups) of dried beans.

When cooked, drain them well and mix together with the bacon cut in dice and sufficient good Tomato Sauce.

4117 Haricots Blancs au Beurre—Buttered Haricot Beans
When the beans are cooked, season with salt and pepper and add 80–100 g (2¾–3½ oz) butter per 1 litre (1¾ pt or 4½ U.S. cups) of cooked beans. Serve in a deep dish, sprinkled with chopped parsley.

4118 Haricots Blancs à la Bretonne
Cook the beans in the usual manner, drain and mix with 2 dl (7 fl oz or ⅞ U.S. cup) Sauce Bretonne per 1 litre (1¾ pt or 4½ U.S. cups) of cooked beans. Serve in a deep dish and sprinkle with chopped parsley.

4119 Haricots au Gratin
Cook the beans in the usual manner, drain and mix in a little fatty gravy from roast mutton. Place in a buttered dish, sprinkle with dry white breadcrumbs and melted butter and gratinate in a hot oven.

4120 Haricots à la Lyonnaise
Cook 125 g (4½ oz) finely sliced onion in butter until lightly coloured and add to 1 litre (1¾ pt or 4½ U.S. cups) of the well drained cooked beans. Serve sprinkled with chopped parsley.

4121 Purée de Haricots Blanc, also called Purée Soissonaise
Pass the cooked beans through a sieve whilst still hot. Add 100 g (3½ oz) butter per 500 g (1 lb 2 oz) of purée and dry out by mixing on a hot stove. Add sufficient hot milk to give the consistency of mashed potato.

4122 HARICOTS FLAGEOLETS—FLAGEOLET BEANS

These are mainly used in the fresh state but when out of season, canned or dried ones may be used.

They may be prepared in any of the ways given for haricot beans. When made into a purée this excellent dish is known as Purée Musard and is used mainly as a garnish for mutton.

Flageolet beans are also suitable as the thickening agent when preparing a purée of French beans, indeed nothing is more suitable for this purpose because not only does it give smoothness to the purée but its flavour marries very well with that of French beans.

HARICOT ROUGES—RED BEANS

4123 Haricots Rouges—Red Beans
These beans are cooked in water with the addition of a quarter its volume of red wine, 150 g (5 oz) piece of streaky bacon, 1 carrot, 1 onion stuck with a clove, 1 Bouquet garni and a little salt and pepper, all per 1 litre (1¾ pt or 4½ U.S. cups) dried beans.

When the bacon is just cooked remove it, cut it into dice and place aside. By the time the beans are cooked the cooking liquor should be just sufficient to barely cover them. Thicken this with Beurre Manié and finish by adding the bacon which has been fried in butter until brown.

HARICOTS VERTS—FRENCH BEANS

4124 The cooking of French Beans
French beans are one of the finest of all the vegetables but they need to be prepared with the greatest possible care. Their quality is such that they are nearly always good in spite of the faulty preparation they so often receive.

French beans should be used very fresh and must not be cooked for too long in boiling salted water. They are best when still a little firm to the bite but not, of course, the least bit hard.

They should not be refreshed after cooking, it being sufficient to toss them in a pan on the stove to evaporate excess moisture. After seasoning with salt and pepper, add 100 g (3½ oz) small pieces of butter per 500 g (1 lb 2 oz) beans and toss over to coat them.

Note: Chopped parsley should not be used on French beans unless it is very tender, freshly picked and chopped at the last moment.

4125 Haricots Panachés
This is composed of equal quantities of French beans and flageolet beans tossed together with butter.

4126 Haricots Verts à la Tourangelle
Cook the beans in boiling salted water, drain them well and mix into sufficient buttered Sauce Béchamel. Place in a deep dish and sprinkle with a little freshly chopped parsley.

4127 Purée de Haricot Verts
Cook the beans in salted water, drain them well and dry them by cooking further with a little butter for 8–10 minutes.

Pass through a fine sieve and mix in half its quantity of a creamy purée of flageolet beans.

LAITUES—LETTUCE

4128 Laitues Braisées au Jus
Wash, blanch and refresh the lettuce; squeeze out the water, tie together in twos or threes and braise in the usual manner.

When they are cooked, untie and cut off the extremities of the leaves. Cut in half, fold them over then arrange in a circle in a dish alternating with heart-shaped Croûtons of bread fried in butter.

Alternatively, they may be served without the Croûtons but in both cases they should be coated with the reduced braising liquid with the addition of some Jus lié.

4129 Laitues à la Crème
This prepared in the same way as Chicorée à la Crème.

4130 Laitues Farcies—Stuffed Lettuce
Blanch the lettuce, refresh them and squeeze out all the water. Cut open down the centre without going through the stump. Place a piece of stuffing in the centre made of 2 parts good forcemeat and 1 part dry Duxelles.

Reshape, tie with string and braise in the usual manner; serve as for Laitues braisées au Jus.

4131 Stuffed Lettuce for Garnishing
Braise the lettuce as for Laitues braisées au Jus; cut them in half and trim.

Spread each half with a small tablespoon of either plain chicken forcemeat or, according to requirements, the same forcemeat containing one-quarter its volume of either Duxelles, chopped ham or finely chopped truffle. Fold over, place in a shallow pan with a little of the braising liquid and a few tablespoons of Bouillon, cover and place in the oven for long enough to cook the forcemeat.

Arrange in a dish and coat with some Jus lié containing the well reduced cooking liquid.

4132 Laitues à la Florentine
Blanch, refresh and drain the lettuce; remove the leaves; for each portion place 5–6 of them together to form a sort of round base. In the centre of each of these, place 1 tbs Riz Pilaw mixed with a little gravy and grated Parmesan then fold over the leaves to enclose the rice forming into the shape of balls.

Turn them over and place into a shallow pan lined with slices of salt pork fat, barely cover with fatty Bouillon, bring to the boil and cook gently in the oven for 30–35 minutes.

To serve: drain the lettuce, arrange in a deep dish, place a slice of poached bone marrow on each, sprinkle with grated Parmesan and coat with reduced tomato-flavoured veal gravy.

Note: By making them in different sizes these lettuces can be used as a garnish for soup, small Entrées such as Noisettes and Tournedos, and for Relevés of meat.

4133 Laitues à la Moelle
Braise the lettuce in the usual manner; arrange in a circle on a deep dish and place a slice of poached bone marrow on each. Coat with some lightly buttered Jus lié.

4134 Laitues à la Serbe
Braise the lettuce in the usual manner, trim the ends of the leaves and open them out through the length. Place a tablespoon of Riz à la Grecque in the centre of each and fold back and reshape them.

Arrange in a deep dish and lightly coat with some good tomato-flavoured Jus lié.

4135 Soufflé de Laitue
This is prepared in the same way as Soufflé d'Epinards.

4136 LENTILS

Lentils are cooked in the same way as indicated for dried vegetables at the beginning of this Chapter.

4137 Lentilles au Beurre—Buttered Lentils
Drain the cooked lentils, place in a pan and dry out by tossing over a hot stove adding 50 g (2 oz) butter per 500 g (1 lb 2 oz) lentils.

Place in a deep dish and sprinkle with chopped parsley.

4138 Purée de Lentilles, also called Purée Esaü
Proceed in the same way as indicated for Purée de Haricots Blancs.

MAIS—MAIZE

4139 The Cooking of Maize
Heads of maize should be selected very fresh and with their grains still milky in appearance. Cook them on the cob with the outer leaves still attached, either by plain boiling or steaming.

When required for serving whole, turn back the leaves so as to present the cob with the grains uncovered. Arrange on a serviette and serve accompanied with a dish of fresh butter.

To grill maize, place the cobs on a grid in the oven until the grains are fully swollen and golden brown in colour. Remove the grains and present on a serviette or serve as it is on the cob.

To serve maize as a garnish or accompaniment the grains should be removed from the cob when cooked and tossed in butter or cream in exactly the same way as for peas.

When fresh maize is unobtainable, the canned commercial product which is excellent, may be used instead.

4140 Croquettes de Maïs
Steam or boil the maize, drain and remove the grains. Dry out in a pan over a hot stove and stir in a little thick Sauce Béchamel. When the mixture is sufficiently reduced, thicken it with egg yolks as for a Chicken Croquettes mixture and spread it on a tray to cool.

Mould round, rectangular or cork shape, flour, egg and breadcrumb and deep fry them when required in clean very hot fat.

Note: These are mainly used as a garnish.

4141 Soufflé de Maïs à la Crème
Steam or boil the maize, drain and remove the grains. Pass these quickly through a sieve, place in a pan with a little butter and dry out on the stove.

Mix in sufficient cream to form a soft paste; add 3 egg yolks per 500 g (1 lb 2 oz) of purée then fold in 4 stiffly beaten egg whites. Fill into a buttered soufflé mould and cook in the usual way for soufflés.

4142 Soufflé de Maïs au Paprika
Before passing the maize through the sieve, add 2 tbs chopped onion cooked in butter and a good pinch of paprika per 500 g (1 lb 2 oz) grains of maize; proceed as indicated in the preceding recipe.

Note: Both the above soufflés can be used as a garnish by cooking them in moulds of the required size; they make an excellent garnish for whole poached poultry.

MARRONS—CHESTNUTS

4143 To shell Chestnuts
To prepare chestnuts make a shallow incision in the shell on the round side and place on a tray with a little water. Place in a hot oven for 7–8 minutes then remove both the outer shells and inside skins without breaking the chestnuts.

Another way to skin them is to cut them as before then place a few at a time into hot deep fat for a few moments then shell them whilst still hot.

4144 Marrons étuvés
As soon as the chestnuts have been shelled, place them in a shallow pan with sufficient Bouillon to just cover; add half a stick of celery per 500 g (1 lb 2 oz) of chestnuts and cook until tender keeping them whole.

If required for a stuffing for goose or turkey they should be only two-thirds cooked.

4145 Braised and glazed Chestnuts
Choose nice large chestnuts, make an incision in the round side then dip them into hot fat and remove the shells and inside skins.

Arrange them one row deep in a shallow pan, barely cover with well flavoured veal stock, place on the lid and cook gently in the oven without shaking or moving them. If they are heaped in the pan they are likely to become damaged.

When three-quarters cooked, remove the chestnuts from the cooking liquid, reduce this to a glaze, replace the chestnuts and roll them so as to cover with a glossy coating.

These are mainly used as a garnish.

4146 Purée de Marrons—Purée of Chestnuts
Shell the chestnuts in the usual manner and cook them in White Bouillon with a stick of celery and 15 g (½ oz) sugar per 500 g (1 lb 2 oz) of chestnuts.

When they are sufficiently cooked for them to break easily, drain and pass through a sieve. Replace in a pan and mix in 100 g (3½ oz) butter over a hot stove then add sufficient hot milk to give the purée the consistency of mashed potato.

4147 NAVETS—TURNIPS

Both for use as a vegetable and as a garnish, turnips are prepared in the same way as carrots, e.g. Glacés, à la Crème etc. They may also be stuffed as in the two following recipes.

4148 Navets farcis—Stuffed Turnips
These may be prepared in either of the following ways:

A) Choose some round even-sized turnips and peel them to a nice shape, then make a cut through the root end with a suitable plain round cutter, to about three-quarters of the way through.
Blanch them well, empty the insides and make this into a purée with an equal quantity of mashed potato.
Refill the turnips with this purée smoothing it dome shape, place in a shallow pan, add some butter and finish cooking, basting them frequently.

B) Empty the turnips as above and fill with a mixture made of semolina cooked with White Bouillon and flavoured with grated Parmesan. Cook then finish as above.

Note: In the same way turnips can be stuffed and cooked with spinach, chicory or rice. As a garnish they are pleasing to the eye and make excellent eating.

4149 Purée de Navets—Purée of Turnips
Peel and slice the turnips and cook in a little water with some butter, salt and sugar. When cooked, pass through a sieve and mix with just sufficient good mashed potato to obtain the right consistency.

4150 Pousses or Feuilles de Navets—Turnip Tops
The young shoots and leaves of turnip are much appreciated as a luncheon vegetable in England. It is prepared in the same way as boiled cabbage.

OIGNONS—ONIONS

4151 Oignons farcis—Stuffed Onions
Peel some medium-sized Spanish onions, cut off the tops and blanch them well.

Empty them leaving 8 mm (⅓ in) thick cases; chop the centre parts and finish cooking in butter. Mix this together with an equal amount of Duxelles and fill into the cases.

Braise in the usual way for vegetable and at the last moment, remove the lid from the pan so as to glaze the onions and gratinate the stuffing.

Note: Onions may also be stuffed with spinach, Risotto or a semolina mixture prepared as for stuffed turnips. They can also be filled with a soufflé mixture made with spinach, tomatoes or chicory etc. There is plenty of scope for other varieties of little known and excellent fillings.

4152 Oignons Frits—Fried Onion Rings
Peel the onions and cut them into ½ cm (⅕ in) thick rounds; separate the rings, Season with salt and pepper, flour them and deep fry in very hot oil. Drain well and season lightly with salt.

Note: When prepared in this way they are usually served as a garnish.

4153 Glazed Onions
White glazed onions: Peel even-sized button onions without damaging the outer layer and place them in a pan with sufficient White Bouillon to barely cover together with 125 g (4½ oz) butter per 1 litre (1¾ pt or 4½ U.S. cups) of Bouillon.

Cook on the stove until tender then remove the onions; reduce the cooking liquid to a glaze, replace the onions and roll them in the pan so as to coat with the glaze.

Brown glazed onions: peel the onions as above and cook them very slowly in a pan with butter and a pinch of sugar so that they colour and cook together at the same time.

4154 Purée d'Oignons, also called Purée Soubise —Purée of Onions
See Coulis d'Oignons Soubise (151).

OSEILLE—SORREL

4155 Oseille—Sorrel
Remove the stalks from the sorrel, wash several times then cook very slowly in a very little water until soft. When cooked, drain on a sieve.

Make a blond Roux with 60 g (2 oz) butter and 30 g (1 oz) flour per 1 kg (2¼ lb) of sorrel, then add 7½ dl (1⅓ pt or 3¼ U.S. cups) White Bouillon, a little salt and a pinch of sugar. Mix until it boils then add the sorrel, cover with the lid and braise gently in the oven for 2 hours.

When ready pass the sorrel through a sieve and mix in 3 eggs or 6 egg yolks beaten and passed through a fine strainer. Reheat until it thickens and finish with 1 dl (3½ fl oz or ½ U.S. cup) cream and 150 g (5 oz) butter.

Place in a deep dish and coat the surface with a little well flavoured veal gravy.

4156 OXALIS—WOOD SORREL

Pick and wash the oxalis, cook in plenty of boiling salted water and drain. It may then be prepared à la Crème, au Gratin or stuffed.

A purée of oxalis is known as Purée Brésilienne and is made in the same way as other purées of vegetable.

4157 PATATES DOUX—SWEET POTATOES

Sweet potatoes are usually cooked by baking them in their skins in the oven and serving them with butter.

They can be cooked in any of the ways as for ordinary potatoes particularly *Sautées*, *Gratinées* and *Duchesse* etc.

They are also very good when cut into pieces and deep fried but in this case they must be served as soon as they are ready as they tend to become soft very quickly.

They can also be made into a soufflé in the same way as Soufflé de Pommes de Terre.

Note: A purée of sweet potato is an excellent accompaniment with venison and can be served in place of a purée of chestnuts.

PETITS POIS—PEAS

Whichever way they are to be cooked and served, peas should be very green, freshly gathered and shelled at the last minute. This is one of those vegetables which easily lose their quality if not cooked carefully. When prepared with care the flavour of peas is of incomparable delicacy but the slightest negligence will result in a vegetable of poor flavour and little value.

4158 Petits Pois à l'Anglaise—Peas, English style

Cook the peas quickly in boiling salted water, drain them and dry by tossing in a pan on a hot stove.

Serve in a dish accompanied with pats of fresh butter.

4159 Petits Pois au Beurre—Buttered Peas

As soon as the peas are cooked, drain and toss in a pan on a hot stove to dry them. Add a pinch of caster sugar and 150 g (5 oz) butter per 1 kg ($2\frac{1}{4}$ lb) cooked peas and toss over again to mix.

4160 Petits Pois Bonne-Femme

Lightly colour 12 button onions and 125 g ($4\frac{1}{2}$ oz) blanched diced salt belly of pork in butter; remove from the fat and mix 15 g ($\frac{1}{2}$ oz) flour into the remaining fat to make a Roux. Cook for a few moments then mix in 3 dl ($\frac{1}{2}$ pt or $1\frac{1}{4}$ U.S. cups) White Bouillon and bring to the boil.

Add 650 g (1 lb 7 oz) peas, the onions and pork and a bouquet of parsley; cook until the sauce is reduced by half and the vegetables are tender.

4161 Petits Pois à la Flamande

Prepare 250 g (9 oz) new carrots as for Carottes Glacées. When half cooked, add 250 g (9 oz) freshly shelled peas and continue to cook so that both are finished at the same time.

At the last moment, remove from the fire and finish with a little butter.

4162 Petits Pois à la Française

Take a pan a little larger than the total of ingredients it will contain and place in it 650 g (1 lb 7 oz) freshly shelled peas, 12 button onions, 125 g ($4\frac{1}{2}$ oz) butter, 10 g ($\frac{1}{3}$ oz) salt, 20 g ($\frac{3}{4}$ oz) sugar and a Bouquet garni comprised of a nice heart of lettuce, 2 sprigs of parsley and 2 sprigs of chervil.

Mix these ingredients well together to form a compact mass and keep in a cool place until required for cooking.

When it is time, add 3 tbs water to the peas, cover the pan tightly with the lid and place to cook slowly.

When cooked, remove the Bouquet, thicken the peas with butter away from the heat and place them in a deep dish. Cut the lettuce in quarters and arrange on top of the peas.

Note: The lettuce can be shredded and cooked in with the peas but as it may not be to everybody's taste it is advisable to cook it as above.

4163 Petits Pois aux Laitues

Cooked the peas as for Petits Pois à la Française or Petits Pois au Beurre adding some blanched and tied whole lettuce to cook in with the peas.

When cooked, trim the lettuce and cut them into two or four pieces; place the peas in a deep dish and arrange the lettuce on top in a circle or a cross.

4164 Pois Princesse or Mange-touts—Sugar Peas

Cut the Mange-touts into two or three pieces and cook as for any of the recipes for ordinary peas.

4165 Petits Pois à la Menthe

Cook the peas in boiling salted water together with a bunch of fresh mint. Serve *à l'Anglaise* or *au*

Beurre, arranging a few blanched whole leaves of mint on top.

4166 Pois à la Paysanne
Use very large fresh peas and cook as for Petits Pois à la Française shredding the lettuce and cutting the onions into quarters. When cooked, thicken with Beurre Manié made with 30 g (1 oz) butter and 10 g ($\frac{1}{3}$ oz) flour per 650 g (1 lb 7 oz) peas.

4167 Purée de Pois Frais, also called Purée Saint-Germain—Purée of Fresh Peas
Cook the peas in just sufficient boiling water to cover them together with a pinch of sugar, 10 g ($\frac{1}{3}$ oz) salt per 1 litre ($1\frac{3}{4}$ pt or $4\frac{1}{2}$ U.S. cups) water and 1 lettuce tied together with a few parsley stalks.

When cooked, drain and pass the peas through a sieve whilst the cooking liquid is left to reduce. Add 125 g ($4\frac{1}{2}$ oz) butter per 1 litre ($1\frac{3}{4}$ pt or $4\frac{1}{2}$ U.S. cups) of this purée and mix in the cooking liquid which should be reduced almost to a glaze.

4168 PIMENTOS OR PIMENTS DOUX—PIMENTOS OR SWEET PEPPERS

There are several different kinds of pimentos used in cookery; some of them such as chillis and the Cayenne pimento are so hot and strong that they can be used only as a condiment.

Large pimentos or capsicums as they are sometimes called, can be green, yellow or red in colour; there is a slight difference in the quality of the three but it is not readily noticeable.

Although the big Spanish pimentos are best, other varieties can be prepared in the same ways. They are generally used as a garnish.

In whatever way pimentos are to be prepared they must first be skinned either by grilling under the salamander or by plunging into hot deep fat. The skin should be removed as quickly as possible and the seeds removed by cutting the pimento open at the stalk end.

4169 Pimentos farcis—Stuffed Pimentos
Choose small green pointed pimentos similar in shape to a carrot. Skin them, cut off the stalk end and remove the seeds.

Half fill them with half-cooked Riz Pilaw, place in a shallow pan, add some good beef or veal stock and braise until tender.

4170 Pimentos for Garnishing
For this use, select large red or green Spanish pimentos.

After peeling and brasing them cut them according to requirements.

4171 Pimentos for serving with cold meat
Chop 1 large Spanish onion and cook in 1 dl ($3\frac{1}{2}$ fl oz or $\frac{1}{2}$ U.S. cup) olive oil until a golden colour. Add 500 g (1 lb 2 oz) skinned and de-seeded red pimentos and allow to cook together for 15–20 minutes.

Add 3 dl ($\frac{1}{2}$ pt or $1\frac{1}{4}$ U.S. cups) good quality vinegar and reduce by half; season with salt and pepper then add a touch of garlic, $2\frac{1}{2}$ dl (9 fl oz or $1\frac{1}{8}$ U.S. cups) tomato purée, and 100 g ($3\frac{1}{2}$ oz) sultanas.

Cover with a lid and cook very gently for $1\frac{1}{2}$ hours. Serve cold.

4172 Purée de Pimentos
Braise some large red pimentos together with two-thirds their weight of rice.

When well cooked, drain well and pass through a sieve; mix in 60 g (2 oz) butter per 1 kg ($2\frac{1}{4}$ lb) purée.

Note: This purée is particularly suitable for serving with poached chicken and boiled white meat. It should not be too thick.

POMMES DE TERRE—POTATOES

4173 Pommes de Terre à l'Anglaise—Plain Boiled Potatoes
Trim the potatoes barrel shape and cook by boiling in salted water or by steaming.

These potatoes are often used to accompany boiled fish. In keeping with the English style they should be cooked without salt.

4174 Pommes de Terre Anna
Trim the potatoes cylindrical shape then cut them into thin slices; wash and dry in a cloth.

Arrange the slices overlapping in a thickly buttered Pommes Anna mould or a thick-bottomed sauté or omelette pan, arrange another layer on top going in the opposite direction to the first then season and spread with butter. Continue in this way until there are 5 or 6 layers of potatoes.

Cover the pan and cook in a hot oven for 30 minutes turning it in the mould if necessary so that it colours evenly all over.

Turn out on to a lid, allow the excess butter to drain off, then slide the potato on to the serving dish.

4175 Pommes Anna for garnishing
Baba or dariole moulds are usually used to prepare

these but wherever possible these moulds should be made of tinned copper. After well buttering the moulds, fill them with thin slices of seasoned potato of a diameter in keeping with the size of the mould.

Place the moulds in a deep tray with sufficient hot fat to come half-way up their sides and cook in a very hot oven for 25 minutes.

Demould just before being required.

4176 Pommes de Terre à la Berrichonne
Trim the potatoes to the size of large olives and place them in a shallow pan together with 250 g (9 oz) blanched, diced, streaky bacon and 100 g ($3\frac{1}{2}$ oz) chopped onions which have been fried and coloured in butter. These quantities are for 1 kg ($2\frac{1}{4}$ lb) potatoes.

Barely cover with White Bouillon, add a Bouquet garni and cook in the oven allowing the liquid to reduce by half.

Arrange in a deep dish and sprinkle with chopped parsley.

4177 Pommes de Terre Berny
To 1 kg ($2\frac{1}{4}$ lb) potato croquette mixture (4182), add 120 g (4 oz) chopped truffle. Divide into approximately 60 g (2 oz) pieces and mould to the shape of apricots. Dip into beaten egg then into very finely shredded almonds.

Deep fry in hot fat 5–6 minutes before serving.

4178 Pommes de Terre à la Boulangère
The recipes for this preparation can be found in the Chapter on Entrées and Relevés, most suitably Epaule de Mouton Boulangère (2783).

4179 Pommes de Terre Byron
Prepare the required amount of a Pommes Macaire mixture and cook it in a small frying or omelette pan until nicely coloured.

When ready, turn out on to a round dish, coat well with cream, sprinkle with grated cheese and glaze quickly.

4180 Pommes de Terre Château
Trim the potatoes to the shape of large olives, place them in a shallow pan, season and cook slowly in clarified butter until very soft and golden brown.

Arrange in a deep dish and sprinkle with chopped parsley.

4181 Pommes de Terre à la Crème
Either *Vitelotte* potatoes or a firm non-floury type such as new kidney potatoes should be used for this preparation. Cook them in salted water, peel them whilst still hot then cut into fairly thick slices.

Place in a shallow pan, cover with boiling cream, season them and cook on a hot stove to reduce the cream, shaking the pan frequently.

Finish with a little more cream at the last moment.

4182 Croquettes de Pommes de Terre
Cut the potatoes into pieces and cook them quickly in salted water keeping them slightly firm.

Drain, dry out in the oven then pass them through a sieve. Replace in the pan and add 100 g ($3\frac{1}{2}$ oz) butter per 1 kg ($2\frac{1}{4}$ lb) potatoes; season with salt, pepper and grated nutmeg and mix well on the stove. Remove from the heat and mix in 4 egg yolks and 1 whole egg.

Divide the mixture into 60 g (2 oz) pieces and mould round, cork or pear shape using flour. Egg and breadcrumb them and deep fry approximately 5 minutes before serving.

4183 Croquettes de Pommes de Terre Dauphine
Prepare a potato croquette mixture and add 300 g (11 oz) very stiff Chou Paste (325) per 1 kg ($2\frac{1}{4}$ lb) of potato mixture.

Divide into 50 g (2 oz) pieces, mould cork shape using flour, then egg and breadcrumb and deep fry in very hot fat approximately 5 minutes before service.

4184 Pommes de Terre Dietrich
See under this name in the section on Hot Hors-d'oeuvre.

4185 Pommes de Terre Duchesse
Prepare a potato croquette mixture and mould into the form of small *Brioches à Tête*, bread rolls or flat cakes; or pipe out with a piping bag and star tube on to a buttered tray.

Brush with beaten egg and place in a hot oven to colour, some 7–8 minutes before serving.

4186 Pommes de Terre Duchesse au Chester
Prepare a potato croquette mixture adding 100 g ($3\frac{1}{2}$ oz) grated Cheshire cheese per 1 kg ($2\frac{1}{4}$ lb) of potato mixture.

Mould into small round flat cakes, place on a buttered tray and brush with beaten egg. Place a thin slice of Cheshire cheese on each and place in the oven for approximately 7–8 minutes before serving.

4187 Pommes de Terre Fondantes
Trim the potatoes to the shape of large elongated olives weighing approximately 90 g (3 oz) each.

Cook slowly in butter or lard in a shallow pan

turning them frequently; when they are soft, flatten them slightly with a fork without breaking them.

Drain off the fat and replace it with 100 g (3½ oz) fresh butter per 1 kg (2¼ lb) potatoes. Cover and leave on the side of the stove until the potatoes have absorbed all the butter.

4188 Pommes de Terre Frites en Allumettes
Cut the potatoes square at the ends and sides then cut into thin batons half-way between the size of a Pommes Pailles and a Pommes Pont-Neuf.

Deep fry in hot fat allowing them to become very crisp. Drain and serve.

4189 Pommes de Terre Chatouillard
Trim the potatoes to the shape of a large cylinder; push a thin trussing needle through the centre of the length and cut spiral fashion using the needle as a guide for the knife to peel off long ribbons of an even 3 mm (⅛ in) thickness.

Deep fry as for Pommes Soufflées.

4190 Pommes de Terre Chip—Game Chips
Cut the potatoes into very thin round slices using a vegetable slicer. Leave them in cold water for 10 minutes then drain and dry them in a cloth; deep fry until very crisp.

They may be served hot or cold and are generally used to accompany roast game prepared and served in the English style.

4191 Pommes de Terre Collerette
Trim the potatoes to the shape and size of corks then cut into slices using a special grooving knife. Cook as for Pommes Chips.

4192 Pommes de Terre en Copeaux
Cut the potatoes into thin irregular ribbons by turning them between the fingers and following with the point of a small knife.

Deep fry in hot fat until crisp and dry; serve arranged in a pile on a serviette on a dish.

4193 Pommes de Terre Fraise
These are prepared with a special tool consisting of a cutting blade which rotates on a thin screw thread which is pushed in the centre of a cylindrical-shaped potato.

This will produce a continuous ribbon of potato in the form of a spring. Cook as for Pommes Soufflées.

In reality these are a variation of Pommes Chatouillard.

4194 Pommes de Terre en Liards
These are the same as Pommes Collerette but without being grooved.

4195 Pommes de Terre Pailles—Straw Potatoes
Cut the potatoes into long thin Julienne, wash them well then dry in a cloth.

Deep fry for a few minutes then drain in the frying basket. When required for serving, plunge into very hot deep fat to fry until very crisp; drain on a cloth and season with a little salt.

4196 Pommes de Terre Pont-Neuf
Cut the potatoes square at the ends and sides then cut into batons of 1 cm (⅖ in) wide sides. Deep fry until crisp on the outside and soft in the centre.

This is the basic type of fried potato.

4197 Pommes de Terre Soufflées
Cut the potatoes square at the sides then cut into rectangular-shaped slices of exactly 3 mm (⅛ in) absolutely even thickness. Wash well and dry.

Place in hot deep fat and immediately turn up the heat so as to bring the fat quickly back to its original temperature; maintain this temperature until the potatoes are cooked which is when they float to the surface of the fat.

Remove to a frying basket, drain them then immerse immediately in fresh, very hot deep fat; the sudden contact of the heat should cause the potatoes to puff up; fry until dry and crisp. Remove, drain on a cloth, lightly season with salt and arrange on a serviette on a dish.

4198 Potato Nests for the presentation of Fried potatoes
Line the inside of a special nest-shaped frying basket with washed and dried potatoes cut as for Pommes Pailles, placing them together well and trimming the top level.

Place the smaller basket inside then deep fry until golden brown; turn out as soon as cooked.

Arrange on a serviette and fill with any kind of fried potato.

4199 Pommes de Terre Georgette
See under this name in the section on Hot Hors-d'oeuvre.

4200 Gratin de Pommes de Terre à la Dauphinoise
Thinly slice 1 kg (2¼ lb) Dutch potatoes. Place in a basin, season with salt, pepper, and grated nutmeg and add 1 beaten egg, 7½ dl (1⅓ pt or 3¼ U.S. cups) boiled milk, and 125 g (4½ oz) grated fresh Gruyère cheese.

Mix well together then fill into well-buttered dishes which have been rubbed with garlic. Sprinkle the surface liberally with more cheese and butter and cook in a moderate oven for 40–45 minutes.

4201 Pommes de Terre Gratinées

This may be prepared in either of the following ways:

A) Make some mashed potato and place in a buttered earthenware dish. Smooth the surface, sprinkle with a mixture of grated cheese and dry white breadcrumbs, and with melted butter and gratinate in a hot oven.

B) Bake some nice well washed Dutch potatoes; when cooked, cut them in half lengthways and scoop out the insides. Pass this through a sieve whilst still hot and make into an ordinary mashed potato.

Refill the empty skins with this potato, sprinkle with grated cheese, dry white breadcrumbs and butter, and gratinate in a hot oven. Arrange on a serviette on a dish and serve immediately.

4202 Pommes de Terre à la Hongroise

Cook 100 g ($3\frac{1}{2}$ oz) chopped onion in butter and sprinkle with 1 tsp of paprika; add the coarsely chopped flesh only of 2 tomatoes, 1 kg ($2\frac{1}{4}$ lb) thick round slices of potato, and barely cover with White Bouillon.

Cook in the oven until the liquid is almost completely reduced; sprinkle with chopped parsley when about to serve.

4203 Pommes de Terre au Lard

Fry 250 g (9 oz) blanched and diced streaky bacon and 12 button onions in butter until coloured brown. Remove from the pan and place aside; add 30 g (1 oz) flour to the fat in the pan and cook for a few minutes then moisten with $7\frac{1}{2}$ dl ($1\frac{1}{3}$ pt or $3\frac{1}{4}$ U.S. cups) White Bouillon and season with a little pepper.

Add 1 kg ($2\frac{1}{4}$ lb) medium-sized potatoes cut in quarters and slightly trimmed, replace the bacon and onions and add a Bouquet garni. Cover and cook gently.

When cooked, place in a deep dish and sprinkle lightly with chopped parsley.

4204 Pommes de Terre Lorette

Prepare 500 g (1 lb 2 oz) Pommes Dauphine mixture, add 30 g (1 oz) grated cheese then divide into 50 g (2 oz) pieces.

Mould crescent shape, using flour and deep fry in hot fat approximately 6 minutes before being required.

4205 Pommes de Terre à la Lyonnaise

Cut some boiled, peeled potatoes into slices. Toss them over and over in butter in a frying pan until golden brown; at the same time sauté a quarter of their amount of sliced onions also in butter.

When the onions are nicely brown, mix the potatoes and onions together, season with salt and pepper, place in a deep dish and sprinkle with chopped parsley.

4206 Pommes de Terre Macaire

Bake some Dutch potatoes. When they are cooked, cut them in half and scoop out the insides. Season this with salt and pepper and mash with a fork adding 200 g (7 oz) butter per 1 kg ($2\frac{1}{4}$ lb) potato.

Spread it in the form of a flat cake in a thick-bottomed frying pan containing very hot clarified butter and well colour on both sides.

4207 Pommes de Terre Maire

This is another name for Pommes à la Crème.

4208 Pommes de Terre à la Maître d'Hôtel

Cook some medium-sized Dutch potatoes in salted water, peel them and cut into slices whilst still hot.

Place in a shallow pan, cover with boiling milk and season with salt and pepper; cook until nearly all the milk has been evaporated. Add a liberal amount of butter, turn into a deep dish and sprinkle with chopped parsley.

4209 Pommes de Terre Marquise

To 500 g (1 lb 2 oz) Duchesse potato mixture, add 5 tbs well reduced very red tomato purée. Pipe out on to a greased tray spiral fashion or in the shape of grooved meringues using a star tube, lightly brush with beaten egg and place in the oven to colour 7–8 minutes before serving.

4210 Pommes de Terre Ménagère

Bake some large Dutch potatoes, cut off a slice from the top of each and scoop out the insides. To each 1 kg ($2\frac{1}{4}$ lb) of this potato, add 150 g (5 oz) diced raw ham cooked in butter together with 100 g ($3\frac{1}{2}$ oz) chopped onion; mix together and moisten with $1\frac{1}{2}$ dl (5 fl oz or $\frac{5}{8}$ U.S. cup) boiling milk.

Fill the empty skins with this mixture, smooth the surfaces level and sprinkle with dry white breadcrumbs and melted butter. Gratinate in a hot oven.

4211 Pommes de Terre à la Menthe

Plain boil some medium-sized new potatoes together with a bunch of mint. When cooked, drain them, arrange in a deep dish and place a blanched mint leaf on each potato.

4212 Pommes de Terre Mireille

Cut some medium-sized potatoes into slices, season

and sauté them in butter. When cooked, add 250 g (9 oz) sliced artichoke bottoms sautéed in butter and 100 g ($3\frac{1}{2}$ oz) sliced truffle per 1 kg ($2\frac{1}{4}$ lb) of potatoes.

Toss over to mix well and serve in a deep dish.

4213 Pommes de Terre Mirette

Cut the potatoes into 3 mm ($\frac{1}{8}$ in) dice and cook them in butter keeping them somewhat soft. Add 60 g (2 oz) Julienne of truffle and 3 tbs melted meat glaze per 500 g (1 lb 2 oz) of potatoes and toss over to mix together.

Place in a gratin dish, sprinkle with grated Parmesan and melted butter and gratinate quickly.

4214 Pommes de Terre Monselet

Cut some nice Dutch potatoes into 2 cm ($\frac{4}{5}$ in) thick slices, season and sauté them in butter. When cooked arrange overlapping in a circle in a deep dish and fill the centre with sliced mushrooms cooked in butter. Sprinkle some Julienne of truffle cooked in Madeira on top of the mushrooms.

4215 Pommes de Terre Mousseline, or Mousse Parmentier

Quickly prepare a fairly stiff mashed potato and mix in 100 g ($3\frac{1}{2}$ oz) grated Parmesan and 6 tbs whipped cream per 1 kg ($2\frac{1}{4}$ lb) of potato. Fold in 5 stiffly beaten egg whites, turn into a buttered and floured timbale or deep dish, sprinkle with grated Parmesan and cook as for a soufflé.

4216 Pommes Nana (*for garnishing*)

Cut the potatoes into Julienne. Season them and press into well buttered dariole moulds. Place in a deep tray with very hot fat to come half-way up and cook as for Pommes Anna.

On removing from the oven, turn them out and coat with Sauce Chateaubriand.

4217 Pommes de Terre Ninon

Bake some potatoes and scoop out the insides as soon as they are cooked; place into a basin. Mix the potatoes with a fork and add and mix in a third its quantity of truffled foie gras.

Fill this mixture into tartlet moulds containing a little very hot clarified butter; place in a hot oven until the outside is crisp and of a nice brown colour.

Turn them out, arrange in a circle on a dish and coat with Sauce Chateaubriand.

4218 Pommes de Terre Noisette

Cut out balls of potato the size of large hazelnuts using a round spoon cutter. Season them and fry in butter taking care that they are golden brown outside but still soft inside.

4219 Pommes de Terre Normande

Cook in butter without colour 100 g ($3\frac{1}{2}$ oz) chopped white of leek and 50 g (2 oz) chopped onion. Sprinkle with 1 tbs flour, mix together then moisten with $7\frac{1}{2}$ dl ($1\frac{1}{3}$ pt or $3\frac{1}{4}$ U.S. cups) boiling milk. Season with salt, pepper and grated nutmeg and add 1 kg ($2\frac{1}{4}$ lb) potatoes cut as for Pommes en Liards, and a Bouquet garni.

Allow to cook gently until tender then turn out into a deep dish and gratinate the surface.

4220 Pommes de Terre Parisienne

Prepare the potatoes as for Pommes Noisettes, cutting them a little smaller.

When cooked, roll them in melted pale meat glaze and serve sprinkled with chopped parsley.

4221 Pommes de Terre au Parmesan

These potatoes are prepared in the same way as Pommes au Chester using Parmesan cheese instead of Cheshire cheese.

4222 Pommes de Terre Persillées

Plain boil some even-sized potatoes; when cooked, drain and roll them in melted butter and chopped parsley.

4233 Pommes de Terre Robert

Prepare the potatoes as for Pommes Macaire adding 6 egg yolks and 1 tbs chopped chives per 1 kg ($2\frac{1}{4}$ lb) potato mixture.

Cook in a frying pan as for Pommes Macaire.

4224 Pommes de Terre Roxelane

Bake 6 large Dutch potatoes and when cooked, scoop out the insides. Mash this with a fork and add 150 g (5 oz) butter, 4 egg yolks and sufficient fresh cream to make a soft mixture, then fold in 2 stiffly beaten egg whites.

Fill the mixture into small cases made from emptied small Brioches.

Sprinkle with chopped truffle and cook in a moderate oven as for Soufflés.

4225 Pommes de Terre Savoyarde

Proceed as indicated for Gratin de Pommes de Terre à la Dauphinoise but using White Bouillon instead of milk.

4226 Pommes de Terre Saint-Florentin

Prepare a potato croquette mixture adding 125 g ($4\frac{1}{2}$ oz) chopped lean ham per 1 kg ($2\frac{1}{4}$ lb) of mixture.

Mould cork shape with flour, dip into beaten

egg then broken vermicelli. Flatten into rectangles and deep fry in very hot fat.

4227 Pommes de Terre Schneider
These potatoes are made in the same way as Pommes à la Maître d'Hôtel using White Bouillon instead of milk. When cooked, finish with a little butter and melted meat glaze. Serve sprinkled with chopped parsley.

4228 Pommes de Terre Suzette
Trim some Dutch potatoes to the shape of an egg cutting one end level; stand them upright on a tray and bake in the oven.

When cooked, cut off the tops and empty out the insides leaving cases. Season the pulp and mash it together with 125 g (4½ oz) butter and 4 egg yolks per 1 kg (2¼ lb) of potato. Mix in a few tbs double cream and a little fine dice of white of chicken, salt ox tongue, mushrooms and truffle.

Fill the cases with this mixture, replace the tops and place in the oven for 10 minutes. When ready, arrange them in a deep dish and brush with melted butter.

4229 Pommes de Terre Voisin
These potatoes are prepared in the same way as for Pommes Anna except that a thin layer of grated cheese is sprinkled between the layers of potato. They are cooked in the same way.

4230 Purée de Pommes de Terre—Mashed Potato
Peel some Dutch potatoes, cut them into quarters and cook them quickly in boiling salted water. When cooked, drain and dry them out in the oven for a few minutes then pass them quickly through a sieve.

Replace in a pan and vigorously mix in 200 g (7 oz) butter per 1 kg (2¼ lb) purée; now add approximately 2½ dl (9 fl oz or 1⅛ U.S. cups) boiling milk a little at a time until the right consistency is reached. Reheat but do not allow to overheat.

Note: The potatoes cooked for mashing should be only just cooked. It should be borne in mind that if left a long time before serving, mashed potato will lose all its qualities.

4231 Quenelles de Pommes de Terre
Prepare a Duchesse potato mixture with the addition of 3 whole eggs and 150 g (5 oz) flour per 1 kg (2¼ lb) of mixture.

Divide into 50 g (2 oz) pieces, shape as flat cakes or corks, or mould with tablespoons, placing them on a floured rimless lid.

Lower them into boiling salted water and allow to poach gently. Drain them well and arrange in a buttered dish previously sprinkled with grated cheese. Sprinkle with more cheese and melted butter and gratinate quickly in the oven.

On removing from the oven, coat with a little brown butter.

4232 Soufflé de Pommes de Terre
Make 500 g (1 lb 2 oz) fairly stiff mashed potato finished with a little cream. Mix in 3 egg yolks then fold in 3 stiffly beaten egg whites.

Turn the mixture into a buttered soufflé mould or into small china dishes and cook as for soufflés.

RIZ—RICE

It is essential to choose the right type of rice for the preparation of Riz Pilaw and Risotto. Patna or long grain rice is preferable for Riz Pilaw although if not available, Carolina type can be used instead. Carolina rice is the most suitable for sweet dishes and salads.

Italian rice in particular the Piedmont variety, is the most suitable for the preparation of Risotto.

4233 Riz au Blanc (*for eggs, chicken and salads*)
Wash 250 g (9 oz) Carolina rice and cook for 18 minutes in 2 litres (3½ pt or 9 U.S. cups) boiling water containing 15 g (½ oz) salt. When cooked, drain, wash in warm water, drain again then spread out on a hot cloth to dry.

Serve in a deep dish sprinkled with melted butter.

Note: If this rice is to be used for a salad it should be seasoned with oil and vinegar whilst still warm. If left to get cold the rice will not absorb the flavour of the dressing.

4234 Riz à la Créole
Wash 250 g (9 oz) Carolina rice and place in a pan with 5 dl (18 fl oz or 2¼ U.S. cups) water, a pinch of salt and 75 g (2½ oz) butter. Cook fairly quickly for 18 minutes then separate the grains with a fork adding an extra 75 g (2½ oz) of butter.

Note: In Creole cookery, lard is used instead of butter. Goose fat or chicken fat may also be used.

4235 Riz au Currie—Curried Rice (*for eggs, fish and chicken and for serving on its own*)
Cook 1 large tbs chopped onion in 50 g (2 oz) butter and add 1 tsp curry powder and 250 g (9 oz) picked but not washed Patna rice. Mix on the stove until the rice is well coated with the butter and curry powder, then moisten with 5 dl (18 fl oz

or 2¼ U.S. cups) White Bouillon. Cover with the lid and cook in the oven for 18 minutes.

When cooked, separate the grains with a fork adding 50 g (2 oz) butter.

4236 Riz au Gras (*for boiled and braised poultry and meats*)
Blanch and refresh 250 g (9 oz) rice; place in a pan with 6 dl (1 pt or 2⅝ U.S. cups) fatty Bouillon and cook gently together for 25–30 minutes.

4237 Riz à la Grecque (*for joints of meat, poultry, quails etc.*)
This is prepared in the same way as Riz Pilaw; a few minutes before serving carefully add 25 g (1 oz) fairly fatty sausage meat cooked gently together with 25 g (1 oz) shredded lettuce, 3 tbs peas à la Française and 25 g (1 oz) skinned and diced red pimento.

Care should be taken when mixing in the garnish not to break the grains of rice.

4238 Riz à l'Indienne (*for any dish prepared à l'Indienne*)
Cook 250 g (9 oz) Patna rice in 2½ litres (4⅘ pt or 2¾ U.S. qt) boiling water containing 25 g (1 oz) salt; stir frequently.

Allow to cook for 16 minutes from the time the water comes back to the boil, then drain, wash well in plenty of warm water then drain again. Spread on a warmed cloth on a tray and dry for 15 minutes in a warm oven.

4239 Riz Pilaw (*for fish, shellfish and poultry etc.*)
Cook 50 g (2 oz) chopped onion in the same amount of butter until golden in colour. Add 250 g (9 oz) unwashed Patna rice and mix on the stove until it takes on a milky appearance.

Moisten with 6 dl (1 pt or 2⅝ U.S. cups) White Bouillon, cover with a lid and cook in a moderate oven for 18 minutes. As soon as it is cooked, turn into another pan and carefully fork in 50 g (2 oz) butter cut in small pieces.

Note: When prepared in this way Riz Pilaw can be kept hot for several hours without losing its flavour, an important point to be borne in mind for restaurant service.

4240 Riz Pilaw for stuffing poultry
The recipe for this will be found in the Chapter on Garnishes (328).

4241 Riz Portugaise (*for various uses*)
Prepare the rice as for Riz Pilaw but before moistening with the liquid add 150 g (5 oz) roughly chopped flesh only of tomatoes and 2 peeled and diced red pimentos.

Finish with butter in the same way as Riz Pilaw.

4242 Riz à la Turque
Prepare the rice as for Riz Pilaw adding approximately 2 grammes of saffron with the Bouillon.

When the rice is cooked, mix in 150 g (5 oz) Tomato Fondue.

4243 Riz à la Valenciennes (*for garnishing poultry, pigeons, quails etc.*)
Cook 50 g (2 oz) chopped onion in butter until golden in colour; add 250 g (9 oz) Carolina rice and stir on the stove until it takes on a milky appearance.

Moisten with 7½ dl (1⅓ pt or 3¼ U.S. cups) White Bouillon and add 60 g (2 oz) lean raw ham (Bayonne for preference) cut in dice; cover with a lid and cook in the oven for 25 minutes.

When cooked, separate the grains with a fork then mix in 60 g (2 oz) cooked sliced mushrooms, 2 small artichoke bottoms, sliced and cooked in butter, 40 g (1½ oz) butter and a touch of Spanish red pepper. Instead of the pepper a small red pimento, skinned and cut in dice may be cooked in with the rice.

Note: This dish may be served in its own right accompanied with cooked chipolata sausages.

4244 Risotto à la Florentine
This is prepared in the same way as Risotto Italienne but finish with 4 tbs cullis from a Daube of beef (Stuffato). Arrange in a deep dish and surround with a *cordon* of the same cullis.

4245 Risotto à l'Italienne
Cook 100 g (3½ oz) chopped onion in butter to a golden colour; add 250 g (9 oz) picked Piedmont rice and stir on the stove until it becomes well impregnated with the butter.

Moisten with 5 dl (18 fl oz or 2¼ U.S. cups) White Bouillon, cover and cook in the oven for 18 minutes.

When cooked, mix in 60 g (2 oz) grated Parmesan cheese and 40 g (1½ oz) butter. Arrange in a deep dish and sprinkle with grated Parmesan.

Note: In principle, the term Risotto implies the use of Parmesan cheese only; if not available, Gruyère cheese may be used instead.

4246 Risotto maigre
This is prepared in the same way as Risotto Italienne but moisten with Fish Bouillon or with a mixture of two parts of decanted mussel cooking liquor to one part of water.

4247 Risotto à la Milanaise

This is prepared in the same way as Risotto Italienne with a final addition of a Milanaise garnish. Serve with a *cordon* of Sauce Demi-glace well flavoured with tomato.

Note: In giving the above recipe it should be borne in mind that this book is a guide; it is felt necessary therefore to point out that it is generally accepted that Risotto à la Milanaise is simply a Risotto Italienne flavoured with saffron.

4248 Risotto à la Piémontaise

Cook 50 g (2 oz) chopped onion in 50 g (2 oz) butter to a golden colour; add 250 g (9 oz) Piedmont rice and stir on the stove until it is well impregnated with the butter.

Moisten with twice its quantity of White Bouillon or approximately 5 dl (18 fl oz or $2\frac{1}{4}$ U.S. cups), adding it in three stages as each previous one is absorbed by the rice. When adding the Bouillon, stir it in with a wooden spoon then cover the pan with the lid as in this way a creamy result will be obtained.

Finally, add 60 g (2 oz) grated Parmesan cheese and 40 g ($1\frac{1}{2}$ oz) butter. White truffle cut into shavings or cooked ham cut in dice may be added to complete this dish.

Note: It is possible to prepare this rice by adding all the Bouillon at once but in this case it should not be stirred at all. It is a strict rule that the rice should not be stirred during the actual cooking as this could displace the liquid and cause the rice to stick to the bottom of the pan.

4249 SALSIFIS—SALSIFY OR OYSTER PLANT

There are two varieties of salsify used in cookery—the white and the black; the black variety is also called Vipers' Grass (Fr. *Scorsonère*).

The same recipes are applicable to both kinds. In whatever way they are afterwards to be finished the salsify should first be carefully scraped then washed before being cooked in a *Blanc*.

4250 Salsifis à la Crème

Cook the salsify keeping it slightly firm, drain and cut into 4–5 cm (2 in) lengths; the thicker pieces can be divided into two or four lengthways so that all the pieces are roughly the same size.

Place them into very thin Sauce Béchamel and cook so that by the time the salsify is tender the sauce is almost completely reduced.

Finally, add a few tablespoons of fresh cream sufficient to bring the sauce back to its normal consistency.

4251 Salsifis Frits—Fried Salsify

Cut the cooked salsify into 7–8 cm (3 in) lengths and place on a tray. Season with salt and pepper and sprinkle with a little lemon juice, oil and some chopped parsley. Allow to marinate for 25–30 minutes taking care to turn them over occasionally.

Drain the salsify, dip into light frying batter and deep fry in very hot fat until the batter is dry and crisp. Drain and arrange on a serviette and garnish with fried parsley.

Note: The marinating is optional but is to be recommended.

4252 Salsifis au Gratin

Prepare some salsifis à la Crème but with a minimum amount of sauce. Add some grated Gruyère and Parmesan cheese and a little grated nutmeg.

Place in a timbale or deep dish, sprinkle with grated cheese, dry white breadcrumbs and melted butter and gratinate quickly.

4253 Salsifis Sautés

Cut the cooked salsify into 5 cm (2 in) lengths and sauté them in butter in a frying pan until nicely coloured. Season, place in a deep dish and sprinkle with a little chopped parsley.

TOMATES—TOMATOES

4254 Tomates à la Bressane

These are prepared in the same way as Tomates Sautées à la Provençale. On removing from the oven, place in each a nice chicken's liver sautéed in butter.

4255 Tomatés Grillées—Grilled Tomatoes

When possible use whole tomatoes; brush them with oil, season and grill them gently.

4256 Tomates Farcies—Stuffed Tomatoes

If the tomatoes are large, cut them in half horizontally, if medium or small, cut a slice off the stalk ends. In either case carefully remove the seeds and juice, season the insides with salt and pepper and place them on an oiled tray. Place in the oven until half cooked then fill them with the selected stuffing as indicated by their description on the menu.

4257 Tomates Farcies à l'Ancienne

Select some medium-sized tomatoes, cut off a slice at the stalk ends and remove the insides without damaging the tomatoes.

Season the insides of the tomatoes with salt and pepper, sprinkle with a little oil and cook in the oven for 5–6 minutes. Drain and fill with Duxelles containing a touch of garlic and some finely diced ham. Replace the covers which have been cut round with a plain cutter, brush with oil and cook in the oven for approximately 12 minutes.

On removing from the oven, arrange in a dish and surround with a little Sauce Demi-glace well flavoured with tomato.

4258 Tomates Farcies à la Carmelite
Empty the tomatoes as in the above recipe and fill them with a mixture of chopped hard-boiled eggs bound with Sauce Béchamel.

Sprinkle with grated cheese and a little oil and place under the salamander to gratinate the surface.

Arrange in a dish and surround with a *cordon* of Tomato Sauce.

4259 Tomates Farcies au Gratin
Empty the tomatoes in the usual way then fill them with a fairly stiff Duxelles. Sprinkle with dry white breadcrumbs and a few drops of oil and gratinate in a hot oven.

On removing from the oven, arrange in a dish and surround with a *cordon* of thin tomato-flavoured Sauce Demi-glace.

4260 Tomates Farcies à la Hussarde
Empty some large halves of tomatoes as indicated for Tomates Farcies and fill them with a mixture of scrambled eggs, mushrooms and diced ham. Sprinkle the surface with breadcrumbs fried in butter, and arrange in a dish.

4261 Tomates Farcies à l'Italienne
Cut a slice off the stalk end of firm medium-sized tomatoes, empty them carefully then fill them with Risotto containing $\frac{1}{2}$ dl (2 fl oz or $\frac{1}{4}$ U.S. cup) meat glaze and 1 dl ($3\frac{1}{2}$ fl oz or $\frac{1}{2}$ U.S. cup) well reduced tomato purée per 1 kg ($2\frac{1}{4}$ lb) of Risotto.

Arrange on a tray and cook in the oven. On removing, arrange them carefully on the serving dish, coat sparingly with thin Tomato Sauce and finish with a pinch of chopped parsley on each.

4262 Tomates Farcies à la Provençale
Cut some large tomatoes in half, empty them of seeds and place them, cut side down in a frying pan containing very hot oil. Cook them slightly then turn over to cook the outsides; arrange in an earthenware dish and fill them with the following mixture.

For 6 tomatoes, cook 2 tbs chopped onion in oil until lightly coloured; add the coarsely chopped flesh only of 4 tomatoes, a pinch of chopped parsley and a little crushed garlic. Cover and cook for 12 minutes. Finish by adding 4 tbs breadcrumbs soaked in Bouillon then passed through a sieve; 2 anchovies also passed through the sieve; and a little fatty gravy from a Daube of beef.

Sprinkle the stuffed tomatoes with mixed breadcrumbs and grated cheese, and a little oil; gratinate under the salamander.

These tomatoes may be served hot or cold.

4263 Tomates Farcies à la Portugaise
Empty the tomatoes in the usual way then fill them dome shape with Riz à la Portugaise.

Arrange in a deep dish and sprinkle with chopped parsley.

Note: In addition to the above recipes for stuffed tomatoes, other fillings may be used such as *Hachis* of chicken or lamb, or scrambled egg which is then sprinkled with grated Parmesan and glazed quickly under the salamander.

4264 Tomates Frites—Fried Tomatoes
Select some firm medium-sized tomatoes and cut them into 1 cm ($\frac{2}{5}$ in) thick slices. Season with salt and pepper then dip into light frying batter and deep fry in very hot fat as required.

Drain, arrange on a serviette on a dish and serve immediately.

4265 Mousse de Tomates—Mousse of Tomato
Cook 1 tbs chopped onion in butter until golden. Moisten with 1 dl ($3\frac{1}{2}$ fl oz or $\frac{1}{2}$ U.S. cup) dry white wine and reduce by half. Add 300 g (11 oz) coarsely chopped flesh only of tomato, salt, pepper, a pinch of paprika and a sprig of parsley. Cover and cook very gently for 25 minutes.

Add 4 dl (14 fl oz or $1\frac{3}{4}$ U.S. cups) Velouté and 3 tbs calf's foot jelly or, failing this, 3 soaked leaves of gelatine. Allow to boil for 2 minutes then pass through a fine sieve; adjust the seasoning bearing in mind that there is cream to be added.

When the mixture is almost cold, mix in 5–6 tbs half-whipped cream, pour into the mould from which it will be served and place on ice or in a refrigerator to set.

4266 Tomates Sautées à la Provençale
Cut some large tomatoes in half, remove the insides then season them and place cut side down in a frying pan containing some hot oil. When half cooked, turn them over and sprinkle with chopped parsley mixed with a little crushed garlic and some breadcrumbs.

Place in a slow oven to finish cooking; remove and arrange on a dish to serve.

4267 Tomates à la Rivoli (*cold*)
Select some small very red tomatoes and empty

them completely without damaging them. Place one skinned cocks' kidney cooked in butter inside each and fill up with Mousse of tomato; allow to set.

Arrange the prepared tomatoes in a deep dish and cover completely with Chicken Aspic Jelly.

4268 Purée de Tomates—Tomato Purée
See Sauce Tomate in the Chapter on Sauces.

4269 Soufflé de Tomate à la Napolitaine
Prepare 3 dl (½ pt or 1¼ U.S. cups) well reduced tomato purée; add 50 g (2 oz) grated Parmesan cheese, 2 tbs thick Sauce Béchamel and 3 egg yolks.

Fold in 3 stiffly beaten egg whites then place alternate layers of this mixture and freshly cooked macaroni, mixed with butter and grated Parmesan cheese, in a buttered soufflé mould. Finish with a layer of the soufflé mixture.

Cook as for an ordinary soufflé.

TOPINAMBOURS OR ARTICHAUTS DE JERUSALEM—JERUSALEM ARTICHOKES

4270 Topinambours à l'Anglaise—Jerusalem Artichokes, English style
Trim the artichokes to the shape of large olives and cook them slowly in butter. Season and mix with a little thin Sauce Béchamel.

Note: The artichokes can be cooked in water or milk but the best way is to cook them in butter as above.

4271 Topinambours Frits—Fried Jerusalem Artichokes
Peel the artichokes, cut into thick slices and cook them in butter. Allow to cool then dip each slice in frying batter and deep fry in hot fat at the last moment.

Arrange on a serviette and garnish with fried parsley.

4272 Purée de Topinambours, also called Purée Palestine
Peel, slice and cook the artichokes in butter. Pass them through a sieve then mix the resultant purée on the stove with 50 g (2 oz) butter per 500 g (1 lb 2 oz) purée.

Add sufficient mashed potato to give a good consistency and finish with a few tablespoons of boiling milk.

4273 Soufflé de Topinambours
This is prepared in the same way as Soufflé de Pommes de Terre (4232).

TRUFFES—TRUFFLES

Truffles are used almost exclusively as a garnish but they can be prepared as a vegetable or as an Hors-d'oeuvre.

For these they should be prepared in a very simple fashion since they have no need of refinement to be perfect.

4274 Truffes sous la Cendre
Select some very nice fresh truffles, clean them well but do not peel them. Season lightly with salt and sprinkle with good brandy.

Wrap each truffle in a thin slice of salt pork fat then in a double thickness of buttered or greased paper; dampen the outer paper.

Arrange the truffles thus prepared on a bed of hot cinders. Cover with more cinders and spread on top a bed of charcoal to be renewed as necessary.

Allow 40–45 minutes for medium-sized truffles of 55–60 g (2 oz) in weight and 50–55 minutes for large truffles weighing from 70–75 g (3 oz) each.

When cooked, remove the outer layer of paper, arrange the truffles in a folded serviette on a dish and serve accompanied with very fresh butter.

4275 Truffes au Champagne
Select some nice large truffles, clean them well and peel carefully. Season them, place in a pan, moisten with Champagne and add 1 tbs Mirepoix à la Bordelaise per 500 g (1 lb 2 oz) truffles; cover with a lid and cook.

When ready, place the truffles in a deep dish or in small silver pans. Reduce the Champagne almost completely, add a little well flavoured thin veal gravy and pass through a fine strainer over the truffles.

Keep them on the side of the stove for 10 minutes without allowing them to boil, then serve.

4276 Truffes à la Crème
Cut 500 g (1 lb 2 oz) raw peeled truffle into thick slices; season with salt and pepper and cook very gently together with 60 g (2 oz) butter and a little flamed brandy.

Separately, reduce 3 dl (½ pt or 1¼ U.S. cups) cream and 3 tbs Sauce Béchamel until very thick then add the cooking liquor from the truffles, a sufficient quantity of cream and finish with 60 g (2 oz) butter.

Mix in the slices of truffle and serve in a deep dish or a Vol-au-vent case.

Note: This same preparation can be used as a garnish for Suprêmes of chicken or game by arranging the truffles and sauce in small *Croustades*.

4277 Truffes à la Serviette
This is prepared in the same way as Truffes au Champagne using Madeira instead of Champagne and presenting the truffles arranged in a timbale which is placed in the centre of a serviette folded in the form of a lily.

It is, of course, more logical to serve under this name, truffles cooked as for *sous la Cendre*, arranging them inside a folded serviette in the same way as for boiled jacket potatoes.

4278 Timbale de Truffes
Line a buttered Timbale mould with ordinary short paste and cover this with thin slices of salt pork fat.

Fill the inside with raw peeled truffles, season with salt and pepper and add 1 dl ($3\frac{1}{2}$ fl oz or $\frac{1}{2}$ U.S. cup) Madeira and 2 tbs pale veal or chicken glaze. Cover with a round of the same fat, close up the mould with a layer of paste and finish in the usual manner. Brush with eggwash and bake in a hot oven for 50 minutes.

Demould the Timbale at the last moment and place on a serviette on a dish.

Note: Raw truffles for use as a garnish or as part of a dish should be carefully peeled before being cooked; however, when they are to be served in their own right as a special dish, the general rule is that they should not be peeled no matter how they are going to be cooked.

FARINACEOUS PRODUCTS

FONDUS AU PARMESAN

This type of Fondu is popular in Belgium where it is frequently served as a hot Hors-d'oeuvre. It has nothing in common with the Fondue au Fromage of Switzerland and of the region of Bresse in France.

4279 Fondus au Parmesan
Make a white Roux with 60 g (2 oz) each of butter and flour; add 5 dl (18 fl oz or $2\frac{1}{4}$ U.S. cups) hot milk and season with salt, pepper and grated nutmeg. Bring to the boil and cook in the oven without a lid for 25 minutes.

When ready, remove the crust which has formed on the surface of the sauce, pour the sauce into a clean pan and mix in 5 egg yolks and 100 g ($3\frac{1}{2}$ oz) grated Parmesan cheese. Spread on a buttered tray, butter the surface and allow to cool.

When cold, turn out on to a floured table and cut out 3 cm ($1\frac{1}{4}$ in) diameter rounds; egg and breadcrumb them and deep fry in very hot fat.

Arrange on a serviette on a dish and garnish with fried parsley.

GNOCCHI

4280 Gnocchi au Gratin
Prepare a Chou Paste with the following ingredients: 5 dl (18 fl oz or $2\frac{1}{4}$ U.S. cups) milk, a pinch of grated nutmeg, 100 g ($3\frac{1}{2}$ oz) butter, 250 g (9 oz) flour and 6 eggs. When ready, mix in 125 g ($4\frac{1}{2}$ oz) grated Parmesan cheese.

Divide the mixture into pieces the size of a walnut, drop them into boiling salted water and allow to poach gently. When they rise to the surface and are resilient to the touch, remove them and drain on a cloth.

Place a layer of Sauce Mornay in an earthenware dish, arrange the gnocchi neatly on top and coat with more sauce. Sprinkle with grated cheese and melted butter and gratinate in a moderate oven.

4281 Gnocchi à la Romaine
Place 1 litre ($1\frac{3}{4}$ pt or $4\frac{1}{2}$ U.S. cups) milk in a pan and bring to the boil; rain in 250 g (9 oz) semolina, season with salt, pepper and grated nutmeg and cook slowly whilst stirring, for 20 minutes.

Remove from the stove, add and mix in 2 egg yolks then spread the mixture 1 cm ($\frac{2}{5}$ in) thick on a moistened tray.

When cold, cut into rounds 4–5 cm (2 in) in diameter using a plain cutter and arrange them overlapping in a shallow buttered earthenware dish. Sprinkle with a mixture of grated Parmesan and Gruyère cheese and with melted butter and gratinate in a hot oven.

4282 Gnocchi de Pommes de Terre
Cook 1 kg ($2\frac{1}{4}$ lb) of potatoes in salted water; drain them as soon as they are cooked and pass quickly through a fine sieve. Replace in a pan and whilst still hot, mix in 50 g (2 oz) butter, 2 egg yolks, 2 whole eggs, 150 g (5 oz) flour, and a little salt, pepper and nutmeg.

Divide the mixture into pieces the size of a walnut, roll them into balls and flatten them slightly with the prongs of a fork to give them a grill pattern. Poach in boiling salted water then drain them on a cloth.

Arrange the gnocchi in layers in a deep buttered earthenware dish, sprinkling each layer with grated cheese; sprinkle the surface with cheese and plenty of melted butter and gratinate in a hot oven.

4283 Noques au Parmesan
In a warmed basin place 250 g (9 oz) of butter which has been mixed until soft and smooth; mix in

a little salt, pepper and grated nutmeg, then gradually mix in 2 egg yolks and 2 whole beaten eggs, 150 g (5 oz) flour and 1 stiffly beaten egg white.

Take pieces of this mixture the size of a hazelnut, drop them into boiling salted water and poach them until cooked.

Drain the noques on a cloth, arrange in a deep dish and sprinkle well with grated cheese and brown butter.

KACHE

The various recipes for this can be found in the section on 'Various Preparations for Hot Garnishes' in Chapter 2.

POLENTA

4284 Polenta

Rain 250 g (9 oz) coarsely ground maize into 1 litre (1¾ pt or 4½ U.S. cups) boiling water containing 15 g (½ oz) salt, stir with a wooden spoon, allow to cook for 25 minutes then mix in 60 g (2 oz) butter and 75 g (2½ oz) grated Parmesan.

If the Polenta is to be used as a garnish or a vegetable, spread it on a moistened tray and allow it to become cold then cut out into round or diamond shapes.

Shallow fry them in butter to colour on both sides, arrange in a dish and sprinkle with grated cheese and brown butter.

4285 Soufflé Piémontaise

Rain 60 g (2 oz) of maize flour into 5 dl (18 fl oz or 2¼ U.S. cups) of boiling milk seasoned with 6 g (¼ oz) of salt, stirring with a wooden spoon. Mix well, cover and place to cook in a moderate oven for 25 minutes.

When cooked, place in a basin and mix in 50 g (2 oz) each of butter and grated Parmesan then 3 egg yolks and 1 whole egg. Finally, fold in 3 stiffly beaten egg whites and pour the mixture into a soufflé mould which has been buttered and sprinkled with grated Parmesan.

Cook as for an ordinary soufflé.

4286 Timbale de Polenta

Make the polenta as indicated above, fill into a deep round buttered mould and allow to become cold.

When cold, turn out, cut a line around the top to the size and shape of the lid then egg and breadcrumb completely.

Deep fry to a golden brown, remove the lid and hollow out the centre carefully so as to leave an empty case.

Use as a Timbale case.

LASAGNES

Lasagnes can be prepared in any of the ways as given for Macaroni and Noodles thus it is not felt necessary to give separate recipes for them.

MACARONI

Under this heading are included all the different types of Italian pastas of cylindrical shape ranging from Spaghetti which is the name of large size Vermicelli, to Canneloni which is approximately 1 cm (⅖ in) in diameter.

4287 The Cooking of various Italian Pastas

All these pastas are cooked by boiling in salted water containing 8–10 g (⅓ oz) salt per litre (1¾ pt or 4½ U.S. cups) of water. They should not be cooled.

If it is necessary for any reason to stop the cooking, this can be done by adding cold water and drawing the pan to the side of the stove. Reheated pastas can only give a bad result.

4288 Canneloni farcis

1) Prepare the following filling: 250 g (9 oz) Gratin Forcemeat A (293) made with a little extra fat; 100 g (3½ oz) each of panada, ham and foie gras; 150 g (5 oz) cooked brain; 50 g (2 oz) small dice of truffle and 2 egg yolks. Pound the ham and foie gras together then mix in all the other ingredients.
2) Cook the canneloni, drain them and cut into 8 cm (3 in) lengths; cut them open along the side and lay out flat as rectangles. Lay some of the filling to one side, roll them up and arrange side by side in a gratin dish which has been buttered and sprinkled with grated cheese.

   Sprinkle the canneloni with a mixture of grated cheese and breadcrumbs and with melted butter and gratinate in a moderate oven for 15 minutes.

   Serve surrounded with a *cordon* of beef gravy.

Note: This is the general method of preparing canneloni but the fillings may be varied by including cooked beef, poultry or game.

4289 Macaroni au Gratin

Prepare a Macaroni à l'Italienne adding a little Sauce Béchamel; place in a buttered gratin dish previously sprinkled with grated cheese.

Sprinkle the surface with a mixture of grated cheese and dry white breadcrumbs and with melted butter; gratinate in a hot oven.

4290 Macaroni Crème Gratin aux Truffes
Cook 500 g (1 lb 2 oz) macaroni in boiling salted water for 14–16 minutes; drain well, place in a shallow pan with 2 dl (7 fl oz or $\frac{7}{8}$ U.S. cup) cream and allow to cook for 5 minutes.

Season with a pinch each of pepper and grated nutmeg then add 250 g (9 oz) grated Gruyère cheese, 100 g (3½ oz) butter and 20 slices of truffle; mix well together.

Tip into a gratin dish coated with butter and grated cheese; sprinkle the surface with a mixture of grated cheese and dry white breadcrumbs and with melted butter; gratinate quickly in the oven or under the salamander.

4291 Macaroni à l'Italienne
Cook the macaroni in boiling salted water, drain well and dry out on the stove. Season with salt, pepper and grated nutmeg and for each 500 g (1 lb 2 oz) macaroni add 75 g (2½ oz) each of grated Gruyère and Parmesan cheese and 60 g (2 oz) small pieces of butter.

Toss over to ensure that it is completely mixed and serve in a deep dish.

4292 Macaroni au Jus
Cook the macaroni in boiling salted water keeping it slightly firm. Drain well then place in a pan with some of the gravy from braised beef and allow it to simmer until it has been almost completely absorbed by the macaroni.

Place in a deep dish and sprinkle with a few tablespoons of the same gravy.

4293 Macaroni à la Milanaise
Cook the macaroni in the usual manner, drain and cut into sections; mix with grated cheese, some tomato-flavoured Sauce Demi-glace and the items of a Milanaise garnish (418).

Alternatively, simply prepare some Macaroni à l'Italienne and arrange it in a deep dish, making a hollow in the centre. In this hollow place the Milanaise garnish mixed with some tomato-flavoured Sauce Demi-glace.

4294 Macaroni Nantua
Cook, drain and dry the macaroni on the stove. Mix with some crayfish cream (Page 33 see Notes on Compound Butters), then for each 500 g (1 lb 2 oz) macaroni, add 24 crayfish tails.

Place in a deep dish and sprinkle with a Julienne of very black truffle.

4195 Macaroni à la Napolitaine
Prepare an Estouffade of beef (2467) with the addition of red wine and tomatoes; it should be cooked for 10–12 hours so that the meat falls to a purée; it is then passed through a sieve.

Cook some large-sized macaroni keeping it slightly on the firm side, drain it well and mix with butter.

Sprinkle the bottom of a deep dish with grated cheese, add a layer of the Estouffade purée then one of macaroni and continue to fill the dish in this way finishing with the purée. Serve as it is.

4296 Macaroni à la Sicilienne
Cook the macaroni in the usual manner, drain it well and mix with cheese as for Macaroni à l'Italienne, then add a quarter its volume of a purée of cooked chicken livers, mixed with a little Velouté.

4297 Macaroni aux Truffes Blanches
Prepare some Macaroni à l'Italienne and add 200 g (7 oz) thin shavings of white Piedmont truffles per 500 g (1 lb 2 oz) of macaroni.

Cover and keep warm for 5 minutes before placing in a deep dish to serve.

4298 NOUILLES—NOODLES

These are usually purchased ready prepared. If, however, it is necessary to prepare them on the premises the ingredients and method are as follows:

Ingredients:
500 g (1 lb 2 oz) flour
15 g (½ oz) salt
5 egg yolks
4 whole eggs

Method:
Mix together in the usual way for pastes, knead twice then allow to rest for 1–2 hours before rolling and cutting.

All the recipes given for macaroni can be used for noodles.

For Nouilles à l'Alsacienne it is usual to sprinkle the noodles when arranged in the dish, with some raw noodles sautéed in butter until very crisp.

RAVIOLIS

The preparation of Raviolis is always the same no matter which filling is being used. The following fillings are those which are most commonly used.

4299 Ravioli Filling A
Mix together 250 g (9 oz) finely chopped cooked chicken, 150 g (5 oz) mashed cooked brains, 100 g ($3\frac{1}{2}$ oz) pressed white cheese, 100 g ($3\frac{1}{2}$ oz) cooked, squeezed and chopped spinach, 100 g ($3\frac{1}{2}$ oz) cooked green borage, a pinch of green basil, 150 g (5 oz) grated Parmesan, 2 egg yolks, 2 whole eggs, salt, pepper and grated nutmeg.

4300 Ravioli Filling B
Mix together 300 g (11 oz) finely chopped, well cooked meat from a Daube of beef, 300 g (11 oz) cooked, squeezed and chopped spinach, 150 g (5 oz) mashed cooked brains, 2 whole eggs, 40 g ($1\frac{1}{2}$ oz) grated Parmesan, salt, pepper and grated nutmeg.

4301 Ravioli Filling C
Toss and fry in butter, 250 g (9 oz) chicken livers together with 2 chopped shallots, a pinch of chopped parsley and a touch of crushed garlic. Finely pound the livers then add the following one after the other—250 g (9 oz) cooked, refreshed and squeezed spinach, 2 fillets of anchovy, 100 g ($3\frac{1}{2}$ oz) butter, 3 whole eggs, salt, pepper and grated nutmeg and a pinch of basil. Pass the filling through a sieve before using.

4302 The Preparation of Raviolis
Raviolis can be made in several different shapes and ways as follows:

1) Roll out a piece of noodle paste very thinly indeed; cut into rounds using a 6–7 cm ($2\frac{1}{2}$ in) plain cutter. Moisten the edges, place a piece of the chosen filling the size of a hazelnut in the centre, fold over like a turnover and seal the edges well.
2) Roll out a piece of noodle paste very thinly indeed to a long rectangle 10 cm (4 in) wide. Place small pieces of the selected filling the size of a walnut at equal distances along one half of the paste. Moisten around all of the edges, fold the remaining paste over to cover the filling then cut the raviolis crescent-shape using a fancy round pastry cutter.
3) Roll out a piece of noodle paste into a square and pipe pieces of the chosen filling in lines leaving 5 cm (2 in) intervals between each. Moisten between the lines, cover with a second sheet of paste, press to seal then cut in 5–6 cm (2 in) squares using a pastry wheel.

Note: Noodle paste is normally used for making raviolis but the true ravioli paste is made with flour and water with the addition of 1 dl ($3\frac{1}{2}$ fl oz or $\frac{1}{2}$ U.S. cup) oil per 250 g (9 oz) flour.

4303 The Poaching and Serving of Raviolis
Having made the raviolis of whatever shape, place them into a pan of lightly salted boiling water and allow them to cook gently for 10–12 minutes.

Remove with a perforated skimmer and drain on a folded cloth so as to absorb all the moisture. Butter a deep dish, sprinkle it with grated cheese and add a few tablespoons of gravy from a Daube of beef, or some tomato-flavoured Sauce Demi-glace. Place in a layer of raviolis and fill the dish in alternate layers with grated cheese, some gravy or sauce and small pieces of butter; finish with a layer of sauce and butter.

Cover the dish with the lid and keep hot for a few minutes so that the cheese and sauce become blended together.

4304 Timbale de Raviolis à la Phocéenne
Fill the Timbale with equal quantities of raviolis and cockscombs plus some slices of truffle and flap mushrooms. Use a tomato-flavoured Sauce Demi-glace.

4305 Timbale de Raviolis à la Génoise
Fill the Timbale with equal quantities of raviolis and braised lamb's sweetbreads plus some slices of truffle and Cèpes. Use a Sauce Demi-glace prepared with the cooking liquid from braised veal.

CHAPTER 14

SWEETS, PUDDINGS AND DESSERTS

This chapter deals only with those sweet dishes which are normally made on the premises.

It should be noted that the composition of many of these may not be in accordance with the particular tastes of a country; it is therefore necessary to subordinate the style of preparation to the tastes of those to whom they will be served. Thus delicate *Entremets* of the kind served in France are not suited to English and American tastes; the people of these countries much prefer the more substantial kinds of sweet dishes to which they are more accustomed.

From this it can be seen how important it is for a cook to have some knowledge of foreign sweets, especially those derived from the English kitchen.

BASIC AND ANCILLARY PREPARATIONS FOR SWEET DISHES

THE VARIOUS PASTES

4306 Puff Paste

Sift 500 g (1 lb 2 oz) flour and 10 g ($\frac{1}{3}$ oz) salt together, make a well in the centre, add $2\frac{1}{2}$–3 dl (9–10 fl oz or $1\frac{1}{8}$–$1\frac{1}{4}$ U.S. cups) of cold water according to the type of flour used, and make into a paste. Roll into a ball without working it too much then leave to rest for 20 minutes.

Roll out the paste evenly to a 20 cm (8 in) square and of an even thickness; place 500 g (1 lb 2 oz) well kneaded butter in the centre and fold over the edges of the paste to enclose it completely, so forming a square block.

Allow to rest for 10 minutes then roll out the paste and give it two turns. The operation of giving it a turn consists of rolling out the paste to a sheet 60 cm (24 in) long by 20 cm (8 in) wide and approximately $1\frac{1}{2}$ cm ($\frac{3}{5}$ in) thick, then folding it in three. This constitutes one turn. The second turn must be given in the opposite direction to the first. Four more turns should be given making six in all but only two at a time with an interval of approximately 10 minutes between each two. The paste must be turned in the opposite direction for every turn.

The reason for giving these turns to the paste is to spread the layers of butter evenly throughout.

After receiving six turns it is ready for use.

Notes on the making of puff paste:

1) In order to obtain perfect puff paste the two main ingredients of butter and dough must be of exactly the same consistency.
2) The butter must be kneaded before being placed inside the dough; this is especially important in cold weather.
3) The paste must be kept in a cool place whilst it is resting but not on ice; although this may not have much effect on the dough it will harden the butter thus causing it to break into pieces under the pressure of the rolling pin and the two elements will not blend smoothly together.
4) To ensure even spread of the butter throughout the paste, the rolling out must be done geometrically, i.e. keeping the sides and ends parallel and the thickness even.
5) The time allowed for resting between turns should not be shortened as this will result in the paste remaining elastic and thus difficult to cut. It will also result in shrinkage during cooking.
6) When the paste is finished it should not be kept for too long a period before being used.

4307 Puff Paste Trimmings

The trimmings left after puff paste has been cut for use in various dishes can be utilized in many ways for pastry work. They are especially suitable for making tartlet and Barquette cases for garnishes and for Croûtons on which to serve eggs etc.

After the puff paste has been used for its particular purpose the cuttings should be assembled into a ball and kept in a cool place for further use. They should be used during the next two days in warm weather and within four days in cold weather.

4308 Ordinary Short Paste

Ingredients: 500 g (1 lb 2 oz) sifted flour, 10 g ($\frac{1}{3}$ oz) salt, 250 g (9 oz) butter, 2 dl (7 fl oz or $\frac{7}{8}$ U.S. cup) water.

Method: Make a well in the flour and place the salt, the softened butter and the water in the centre; mix the flour gradually into the water and butter until it is all incorporated and forms a paste. Mix for a moment then knead it twice, form into a ball and keep in a cool place wrapped in a cloth.

Notes:
1) The method of kneading this kind of paste consists of pressing it firmly between the palm of the hand and the table pushing it away in small pieces thus assuring the complete blending of the ingredients and giving a perfectly smooth paste.
2) As far as possible kneaded pastes should be made several hours in advance so that its elasticity has disappeared before it is used.

4309 Fine Quality Short Paste (*for flans and fruit tarts*)

Ingredients: 500 g (1 lb 2 oz) sifted flour, 10 g ($\frac{1}{3}$ oz) salt, 50 g (2 oz) caster sugar, 300 g (11 oz) butter, 1 egg, $1\frac{1}{2}$ dl (5 fl oz or $\frac{5}{8}$ U.S. cup) water.

Method: Make a well in the flour, place the salt, sugar, egg, the softened butter and water in the centre; mix the flour gradually into the other ingredients until it is incorporated and forms a paste. Mix for a moment then knead it twice as for ordinary short paste; roll in a ball and keep in a cool place wrapped in a cloth.

4310 Galette Paste

Ingredients: 500 g (1 lb 2 oz) sifted flour, 10 g ($\frac{1}{3}$ oz) salt, 15 g ($\frac{1}{2}$ oz) caster sugar, 375 g (13 oz) butter, $1\frac{1}{2}$ dl (5 fl oz or $\frac{5}{8}$ U.S. cup) water.

Method: Make the ingredients into a pastry as for ordinary short paste but do not knead it; keep in a cool place for at least an hour then give it three turns as for puff paste resting it for 8–10 minutes between each. After the last turn allow the paste to rest for a few minutes at least before using.

4311 Sweet Paste

Ingredients: 500 g (1 lb 2 oz) sifted flour, 200 g (7 oz) butter, 150 g (5 oz) caster sugar, 3 eggs, $\frac{1}{2}$ tsp orange flower water.

Method: Make the ingredients into a paste as for ordinary short paste; knead twice, roll into a ball and keep in a cool place covered with a cloth.

4312 Paste for Small Tea-cakes (*Petits Gâteaux*)

Ingredients: 500 g (1 lb 2 oz) sifted flour, 300 g (11 oz) butter, 300 g (11 oz) caster sugar, 1 whole egg, 4 egg yolks, 1 tbs orange flower water.

Method: Make the ingredients into a paste as for ordinary short paste; knead twice, roll into a ball and keep in a cool place covered with a cloth for at least 1 hour.

Roll out the paste 1 cm ($\frac{2}{5}$ in) thick and cut out into various fancy shapes using special pastry cutters. Place on a baking tray and brush with beaten egg. Decorate with halves of almonds, halves of glacé cherries, diamonds of angelica, crystallised orange peel, currants etc. then bake in a hot oven.

Brush with gum as soon as they come from the oven.

Note: The reason for glazing with gum is to give a brilliant shine to the biscuits; it must be done immediately they come from the oven. A solution of gum arabic is used for this and it is brushed on after they are baked.

For some items milk and sugar boiled to a syrup is used for glazing instead of gum arabic.

4313 Suet Paste

Ingredients: 500 g (1 lb 2 oz) sifted flour, 300 g (11 oz) very dry beef kidney suet, 15 g ($\frac{1}{2}$ oz) salt, 2 dl (7 fl oz or $\frac{7}{8}$ U.S. cup) water. (If the paste is to be used for fruit puddings add 50 g (2 oz) sugar).

Method: Separate the suet into pieces, remove any connective tissue, chop finely and place in a well in the flour. Add the salt and water and mix together bringing in the flour a little at a time. Roll into a ball; do not knead it and keep in a cool place until required.

4314 Brioche Paste

Ingredients: 500 g (1 lb 2 oz) sifted flour, 250 g (9 oz) butter, 6 eggs, 12 g ($\frac{1}{2}$ oz) yeast, 15 g ($\frac{1}{2}$ oz) salt, 25 g (1 oz) sugar, 1 dl ($3\frac{1}{2}$ fl oz or $\frac{1}{2}$ U.S. cup) lukewarm water.

Method:
1) Take a quarter of the flour and make a well in the centre; place in the yeast and dissolve it with a little of the water. Add a little more water, mix into the flour and make it into a soft paste. Roll in a ball, cut a cross on top, cover and allow to prove in a warm place until doubled in size.
2) Make a well in the remainder of the flour, place 2 tbs lukewarm water or milk and 4 of the eggs in it and mix to a dough kneading and beating it vigorously on the table. Add the other eggs one at a time continuing to knead the paste well. When it is very smooth

and elastic add the salt and sugar dissolved in a little water, then spread on top the butter, softened to the same texture as the paste; knead small portions of the paste and butter together and successively, then gradually re-assemble the whole together.

3) At this stage place the first dough which should be doubled in size on top of this paste and mix in small amounts at a time until all is amalgamated.

Place the paste in a basin, cover with a cloth and keep in a fairly cool place to prove for 12 hours. After 5 or 6 hours arrest the fermentation of the paste by beating it with the palm of the hand then allow it to prove again for the remaining time.

Note:

1) By increasing the amount of butter a finer paste can be obtained; up to 500 g (1 lb 2 oz) may be used but usually 400 g (14 oz) is sufficient.
2) The more butter there is in a brioche paste the less it must be kneaded.
3) This paste is used for certain fruit timbales. In this case it is placed to prove in a tall Charlotte mould and cooked in the same mould.

4315 Mousseline Brioche Paste

Take the required amount of fine brioche paste made with extra butter and add a further 60 g (2 oz) softened butter per 500 g (1 lb 2 oz) of paste. Roll in a ball and place into the mould in which it is to be cooked ensuring 1) that the mould is well buttered, and 2) that the mould is only two-thirds filled so that there is room for it to rise when proving.

Keep the mould in a moderate temperature to rise to the top, brush the top with melted butter then bake in a moderately hot oven.

4316 General Purpose Brioche Paste

Ingredients: 500 g (1 lb 2 oz) sifted flour, 200 g (7 oz) butter, 4 eggs, 15 g (½ oz) salt, a pinch of sugar, 15 g (½ oz) yeast, 1 dl (3½ fl oz or ½ U.S. cup) lukewarm milk.

Method:

1) Prepare the leaven using a quarter of the flour, the yeast and milk.
2) Make a paste with the remainder of the ingredients and continue as for Brioche Paste.

Notes:

1) This paste can be used for various Rissoles, Pâtés à la Dauphine etc.; the amount of sugar it contains is only to give it the required colour when cooked.
2) The paste must be kept firm enough so as to be able to roll it out.
3) When it is made specially for a Coulibiac the ingredients are as listed but the sugar is omitted.

4317 Paste for Beignets Viennois

Ingredients: 500 g (1 lb 2 oz) sifted flour, 200 g (7 oz) butter, 6 eggs, 20 g (⅔ oz) yeast, 15 g (½ oz) salt, 25 g (1 oz) sugar, 1 dl (3½ fl oz or ½ U.S. cup) milk.

Method: Prepare in the same way as for Brioche Paste.

4318 Savarin Paste

Ingredients: 500 g (1 lb 2 oz) sifted flour, 375 g (13 oz) butter, 8 eggs, 20 g (¾ oz) yeast, 15 g (½ oz) salt, 25 g (1 oz) sugar, 1 dl (3½ fl oz or ½ U.S. cup) lukewarm milk.

Method: Place the flour in a bowl and make a well in the centre; place in it the yeast and dissolve it with the milk. Add the eggs and make into a paste mixing it well for several minutes; detach the particles from the side of the bowl and incorporate in the paste then spread the mixed and softened butter in small pieces over the surface.

Cover with a cloth and place in a fairly warm place to prove until doubled in size.

Now add the salt beating it in by hand and continue until all the butter is absorbed and the paste takes on sufficient body to be lifted in one piece.

At this moment, add the sugar mixing well for a minute until it is incorporated in the paste.

Note:

1) The sugar should not be added until last otherwise it will inhibit the cohesion of the paste, making it a longer process of preparation.
2) Whether the savarin is for immediate soaking or for keeping in a dry state for use as *Croûte aux Fruits*, the mould should only be one-third filled with the paste; the paste will rise to the top of the mould as it proves.

4319 Baba Paste

Ingredients: 500 g (1 lb 2 oz) sifted flour, 300 g (11 oz) butter, 7 eggs, 20 g (¾ oz) yeast, 15 g (½ oz) salt, 20 g (⅔ oz) sugar, 1 dl (3½ fl oz or ½ U.S. cup) lukewarm milk, 100 g (3½ oz) mixed currants and sultanas.

Method: Proceed as for Savarin Paste adding the dried fruit at the same time as the sugar. In the same way as for a Savarin the moulds must not be more than one-third filled.

4320 Mazarine Paste

Prepare half the required amount of Brioche Paste and add to it a little at a time, an equal amount of Baba Paste; fill into plain Genoise moulds.

4321 Chou Paste
Ingredients: 1 litre (1¾ pt or 4½ U.S. cups) water, 375 g (13 oz) butter, 15 g (½ oz) salt, 25 g (1 oz) sugar, 500 g (1 lb 2 oz) sifted flour, 16 medium eggs, 1 tbs orange flower water.
Method: Place the water, salt, sugar and butter in a pan and bring to the boil.

Remove from the fire, add the flour and mix it in with a wooden spoon. Replace on the stove and continue to mix until the paste leaves the spoon clean and small beads of moisture appear on the surface of the paste.

Remove from the heat and mix in the eggs one at a time mixing each in thoroughly before adding the next. When the eggs have all been incorporated, finish with the orange flower water.

4322 Paste for Beignets Soufflés
The recipe for this is to be found in the Chapter on Garnishes under the title General Purpose Chou Paste (325). The only difference is that 25 g (1 oz) sugar should be added whilst making it.

4323 Ramequin and Gougère Paste
This paste is the same as Chou Paste (4321) with the following modification: 1) Use milk instead of water and omit the sugar and flavouring, and 2) after adding the eggs, add 250 g (9 oz) fresh Gruyère cheese cut in small dice.

4324 Genoise Paste
Ingredients: 500 g (1 lb 2 oz) caster sugar, 16 eggs, 375 g (13 oz) sifted flour, 200 g (7 oz) melted butter and flavouring to taste which can be: 1 tbs vanilla sugar, the grated rind of 1 lemon, or ½ dl (2 fl oz or ¼ U.S. cup) of a selected liqueur.
Method: Mix the sugar and eggs in a copper bowl, place over a gentle heat so that it becomes slightly warm and whisk until the mixture reaches the ribbon stage. Remove from the heat and continue to whisk until it is cold. Now add the chosen flavouring, the flour and the melted butter from which the liquid and sediment has been removed. The flour should be folded in lightly and the butter added in a thin stream so that the mixture does not become heavy.

According to requirements the mixture can be baked in various moulds or spread on a buttered and floured tray.

Note: The ribbon stage of a Genoise is reached when the mixture becomes thick and when lifting the whisk or spoon from the bowl, some of the mixture adheres and drops back in the form of a ribbon which disappears only slowly beneath the surface.

4325 Finger Biscuit Paste
Ingredients: 500 g (1 lb 2 oz) caster sugar, 16 eggs, 375 g (13 oz) sifted flour, 1 tbs orange flower water.

Method: Whisk the sugar and egg yolks in a basin until it becomes thick and white and reaches the ribbon stage. Add the flavouring, then rain in the flour, then the stiffly beaten egg whites, folding and cutting in with a spoon so as to keep the mixture light.

Place the mixture in a piping bag with a plain 1½ cm (⅗ in) diameter tube and pipe it out on to sheets of thick paper; sprinkle all over with caster sugar then shake off the surplus by holding the paper by the two ends. Spray a few drops of water over the biscuits to help them to become pearly, then bake in a very moderate oven.

4326 Biscuit Manqué Paste
Ingredients: 500 g (1 lb 2 oz) caster sugar, 18 egg yolks, 400 g (14 oz) sifted flour, 300 g (11 oz) butter, 16 stiffly beaten egg whites, 3 tbs rum.
Method: Whisk the sugar and egg yolks in a basin until the mixture becomes white and light.

Add and mix in lightly the rum, the flour, the stiffly beaten whites and lastly the melted butter from which the sediment and liquid has been removed. Fill into buttered and floured moulds and bake in a moderate oven.

4327 Punch Biscuit Paste
Ingredients: 500 g (1 lb 2 oz) caster sugar, 12 egg yolks, 3 whole eggs, 8 stiffly beaten egg whites, 375 g (13 oz) sifted flour, 300 g (11 oz) butter, ½ tbs each of orange sugar and lemon sugar and 3 tbs rum.

Method: Whisk the sugar, egg yolks and whole eggs in a basin until the mixture is very frothy. Add the orange and lemon sugars, the rum, flour, and fold in the stiffly beaten whites and the melted butter, taking care not to overmix.

Bake in buttered moulds, cases or flan rings according to requirements.

4328 Savoy Biscuit Paste
Ingredients: 500 g (1 lb 2 oz) caster sugar, 14 egg yolks, 185 g (6½ oz) each of very dry flour and fecula, sifted together; 14 stiffly beaten egg whites and 1 tbs vanilla sugar.
Method: Whisk the sugar and yolks until the mixture reaches the ribbon stage. Add the vanilla sugar, flour and fecula then fold in the stiffly beaten whites.

Fill into carefully buttered and sugared, or buttered and fecula-dredged moulds filling them only two-thirds full. Bake in a warm to moderate oven allowing the temperature to decrease regularly until they are cooked and dry.

VARIOUS PASTRY CASES

4329 Bouchée Cases
Roll out some well rested puff paste which has received the full number of turns to 8 mm (⅓ in) thickness. Cut out 7 cm (2¾ in) diameter rounds with a fancy pastry cutter. Place upside down on a moistened baking tray, brush with eggwash and mark the centre for the lids with a 3½ cm (1½ in) cutter, dipping it in hot water. Score a pattern on the lids.

Bake in a hot even, remove the lids as soon as they come from the oven and remove the soft centre of the pastry.

4330 Small Bouchée Cases (*Bouchées Mignonnes*)
These bouchées which are used as an item of garnish are made in the same way as in the preceding recipe but rolling out the paste slightly thinner and cutting them out with a 5 cm (2 in) diameter round fancy cutter.

Finish as indicated in the preceding recipe.

4331 Flan Cases
To make a 20 cm (8 in) diameter pale-baked flan case, roll 200 g (7 oz) short paste into a ball then roll it out to approximately 24 cm (10 in) in diameter. Butter a flan ring and place on a tray; pick up the paste in the hands, place over the ring and lower it in gently. Press it well into the sides of the ring then roll the pin across the ring to cut off the surplus paste.

Press the edge with a small ball of paste until it projects above the edge of the flan ring and pinch with pastry tweezers to form a decorated crest. Prick the bottom of the flan with the point of a small knife to prevent deformation, then line with a round of buttered thin paper; fill with split peas, rice or dried cherry stones and bake in a moderate oven for approximately 25 minutes.

Remove the paper and filling, brush the top and inside with eggwash and return to the oven for a few minutes so as to dry out the inside.

4332 Tartlet Cases
These are used a great deal in cookery and can be made in plain or fancy moulds of various sizes according to requirements. Either short paste or puff paste trimmings may be used.

Roll out the paste 2½ mm (⅛ in) thick, cut out with a fancy round cutter of a size in keeping with the tartlet tins; butter the moulds and line them with the rounds of paste. Prick the bottoms with the point of a small knife to prevent any deformation; line with a round of thin buttered paper and fill with split peas. Bake in a moderate oven for 12–15 minutes.

Remove the paper and split peas, demould, brush the insides and around the edges with eggwash and return to the oven for a few minutes to dry them out.

4333 Small Timbale Cases
Butter the moulds; roll out the paste as for tartlet cases and cut out with a fancy cutter of a size proportionate to that of the moulds. Mould these pieces of paste around the end of a floured rolling pin pressing the edges to the pin without any pleats so as to obtain a kind of pocket. Lower into the mould, remove the rolling pin and press with the fingers so that the paste takes the exact shape of the mould. Line with a piece of paper, fill with split peas then cook in the same way as for tartlet cases.

4334 Large Timbale Cases
Butter a Charlotte mould and if the timbale is going to be used as an Entrée, decorate the inside with small shapes cut from noodle paste. If the timbale is for a sweet dish there is no point in putting any decorations on at this stage; this is best left until afterwards. If the mould is decorated with noodle paste, moisten the cut shapes so that they will stick to the lining paste.

Roll the selected paste into a ball then roll out to a circle 20 cm (8 in) in diameter; sprinkle with flour and fold it in half bringing the edges to the centre so as to form a kind of skull cap without any joins. Roll out again to an even thickness of 8 mm (⅜ in) and place into the mould pressing it well into the bottom and sides.

Line with a piece of buttered thin paper; fill with split peas and cover with a round piece of paper. Place a thin round of the same paste on top sealing it well to the edges and pinch the edges together bringing it above the level of the mould. Decorate the inside and outside of this crest with pastry tweezers. Moisten lightly with water and arrange on top several superimposed circles of overlapping leaf shapes of paste. These may be cut with a pastry cutter or knife. Place three or four fancy rounds of paste in graduated sizes on top of each other in the centre and make a hole right through the middle of them to let the steam escape when cooking. Brush with eggwash and bake in a moderately hot oven.

When the timbale is baked, cut around the inside edge to remove the lid, empty out the peas, remove the paper and brush the inside with eggwash. Replace in the oven for a few minutes to dry out. Alternatively the timbale can be demoulded and dried in a cool oven.

4335 Croûte de Tourte à l'Ancienne

Roll a piece of ordinary short paste into a ball and roll out 6–7 mm ($\frac{1}{3}$ in) thick and to a diameter to suit the mould. Place this paste into the moistened Tourte mould, fill the centre with a pad of paper and cover with a thinly rolled layer of the same paste; seal the edges together.

Moisten a strip around the edge and cover it with a 1 cm ($\frac{2}{5}$ in) wide band of puff paste cut to the length calculated to encircle the Tourte. Seal the two ends together when they meet and knotch it around the edge using the point of a knife. Brush the top of the Tourte and the band of puff paste with eggwash, score with a knife and bake in a moderate oven.

When cooked, cut out the lid and remove the paper.

4336 Vol-au-vent Cases

Roll out a piece of puff paste which has had six full turns, to an even thickness of 2 cm ($\frac{4}{5}$ in). Place on top a template such as a pastry cutter, plate or a lid of the required size and cut out, slanting outwards and following the edge with a small knife. Turn the piece of paste over and place on a lightly moistened baking tray. Knotch the edge, brush the top with eggwash and trace a circle 3–4 cm ($1\frac{1}{5}$–$1\frac{3}{5}$ in) from the edge with the point of a knife so as to outline the lid. Score the lid trellis-fashion, score the sides then bake in a hot oven after allowing it to rest for a while.

As soon as the Vol-au-vent is cooked, remove the lid and remove the soft centre from inside.

VARIOUS CREAMS, MERINGUES AND PRALINS

4337 Crème à l'Anglaise—English Egg Custard

Ingredients: 500 g (1 lb 2 oz) caster sugar, 16 egg yolks, 1 litre ($1\frac{3}{4}$ pt or $4\frac{1}{2}$ U.S. cups) boiling milk and flavouring to choice, e.g. vanilla pod or orange or lemon zest infused in the milk or $\frac{1}{2}$ dl (2 fl oz or $\frac{1}{4}$ U.S. cup) of a liqueur which should be added when the custard has cooled.

Method: Place the sugar and yolks in a basin and whisk together until they reach the ribbon stage. Add the boiling milk—with or without the infusion—a little at a time. Place on the stove and stir with a wooden spoon until the yolks thicken the mixture and coats the back of the spoon.

Do not allow the custard to come to the boil as this will cause it to separate.

As soon as it is cooked, pass through a fine strainer or cloth and keep in a Bain-marie if for immediate use hot, or in a basin if it is to be used cold; in this case it should be stirred until it becomes completely cold.

Note: When mixing the sugar and yolks, 1 tsp of arrowroot may be added; this not only helps in obtaining a perfectly smooth blend but prevents the custard from separating if it gets too near boiling point.

4338 Crème à l'Anglaise collée—Jellied Egg Custard for Cold Sweets

Make the custard in the same way as for Crème Anglaise and when it is almost cooked, add 20–25 g ($\frac{3}{4}$–1 oz) or 8–10 leaves of gelatine previously soaked in cold water. Pass through a fine strainer into a basin and stir until it is completely cold.

The soaked and well drained gelatine may be added to the mixture when it is first placed to cook.

4339 Egg Custard Sauce (*for serving with hot or cold stewed fruits*)

This is prepared in the same way as Crème à l'Anglaise but using only 10 yolks per 1 litre ($1\frac{3}{4}$ pt or $4\frac{1}{2}$ U.S. cups) of milk.

Pass through a fine strainer into shallow silver or china dishes, sprinkle the surface well with icing sugar and mark trellis-fashion with a red hot iron.

4340 Butter Cream

Prepare a Crème à l'Anglaise, remove from the heat and stir until it is barely lukewarm. Add 450 g (1 lb) good quality butter per 6 dl (1 pt or $2\frac{5}{8}$ U.S. cups) of custard, whisking it in a little at a time. Add a little vanilla sugar if the vanilla flavour of the custard is not sufficiently pronounced.

Note: This butter cream can also be prepared with a syrup as in the following recipe and it can be flavoured and perfumed with a liqueur or any flavouring essence.

4341 Butter Cream made with sugar syrup

Prepare 5 dl (18 fl oz or $2\frac{1}{4}$ U.S. cups) of sugar to 28° on the saccharometer and infuse in it the required flavouring such as vanilla, lemon zest, flower petals etc. If using a liqueur this should be added when the syrup is just lukewarm using $\frac{1}{2}$ dl (2 fl oz or $\frac{1}{4}$ U.S. cup) of liqueur. It is, however, preferable to use an essence for the flavouring.

Whisk the flavoured or unflavoured syrup slowly on to 12 whisked egg yolks, place over a low heat and cook in the same manner as Crème à l'Anglaise until it thickens. Pass through a fine strainer and whisk in 450 g (1 lb) good quality butter.

Note: There are a very large number of different butter creams so it is impossible to give the full list. The two main types given above should be sufficient to provide the desired variations.

4342 Crème Chantilly—Whipped Cream

Keep some thick and very fresh double cream chilled for 24 hours before being required. When required, whisk it until it has doubled in quantity and is fairly stiff. Stop whisking at this stage as otherwise it will break down and turn into butter. Add 125 g (4½ oz) caster sugar of which 25 g (1 oz) should be vanilla sugar, per 1 litre (1¾ pt or 4½ U.S. cups) cream; if not for immediate use, keep in a cool place.

Note: The addition of a small amount of gum tragacanth in powder or solution form helps produce a more aerated result; however, it will have a less fresh and perfect taste unless it is incorporated into a sweet dish or an ice-cream mixture.

4343 Frangipane Cream

Ingredients: 250 g (9 oz) sugar, 250 g (9 oz) flour, 4 whole eggs, 8 egg yolks, 1½ litres (2⅝ pt or 6½ U.S. cups) milk, 1 vanilla pod, a small pinch of salt, 50 g (2 oz) crushed macaroons and 100 g (3½ oz) butter.

Method: Bring the milk to the boil and infuse with the vanilla.

Place the sugar, flour, eggs, yolks and salt in a pan and mix together with a wooden spoon. Pour on the milk slowly, mixing well. Place on the stove and bring to the boil stirring all the time; allow to boil for 2 minutes then pour into a basin.

Add and mix in the butter and macaroons, then smooth the surface with small pieces of butter to prevent a skin forming.

4344 Crème Pâtissière—Pastry Cream

Ingredients: 500 g (1 lb 2 oz) caster sugar, 12 egg yolks, 125 g (4½ oz) flour, 1 litre (1¾ pt or 4½ U.S. cups) milk infused with vanilla.

Method: Prepare in the same way as for Frangipane Cream.

4345 Crème à Saint-Honoré

Prepare the Pastry Cream as in the preceding recipe and whilst still boiling fold in 15 stiffly beaten egg whites.

Note: If this cream is not going to be used immediately it is advisable to add 4 leaves of gelatine (12 g or ½ oz) per 1 litre (1¾ pt or 4½ U.S. cups) milk; this also applies in warm weather.

4346 Mixture for Crème Renversée

Ingredients: 1 litre (1¾ pt or 4½ U.S. cups) boiling milk, which may be infused with vanilla or lemon zest, 200 g (7 oz) caster sugar (or loaf sugar dissolved in the milk), 4 eggs and 8 egg yolks.

Method: Mix the eggs and yolks together in a basin for a few seconds then add the sweetened and infused milk little by little whilst whisking it. Pass through a fine strainer then carefully remove any froth from the surface.

Note: When using a liquid flavouring such as coffee essence, tea etc. the quantity should be taken into account and a lesser amount of milk used so as to keep the proportions correct.

4347 Ordinary Meringue

Whisk 8 egg whites until they become as stiff as possible. Rain in 500 g (1 lb 2 oz) fine caster sugar mixing lightly with a spoon so that the egg whites do not lose their lightness.

Note: The proportion of whites used in the making of meringues is variable and it is possible to use as many as 12 egg whites for 500 g (1 lb 2 oz) sugar. It should be noted, however, that the lighter the meringue the lower the cooking temperature should be; they should be dried rather than cooked.

4348 Italian Meringue

Place 500 g (1 lb 2 oz) fine caster sugar and 8 egg whites into a copper bowl and mix together. Place over a gentle heat so as to warm the mixture slightly and whisk until it is thick enough to hold its shape between the wires of the whisk.

If not for immediate use, place the meringue in a small basin and keep in a cool place covered with a round of paper.

4349 Italian Meringue made with cooked sugar

Whisk 8 egg whites until very stiff whilst 500 g (1 lb 2 oz) sugar is cooking to the hard ball stage.

Pour the sugar on to the whites in a continuous thin stream whisking vigorously until it has all been absorbed.

4350 Soft Almond Paste

Place 250 g (9 oz) almonds in the crushing machine and crush to a very fine paste; transfer this paste to the mortar with the selected flavouring such as vanilla sugar or a small glassful of a good liqueur. Add a little at a time, 500 g (1 lb 2 oz) sugar cooked to the hard crack stage mixing vigorously and continuously with the pestle so as to produce a very smooth paste.

4351 Pistachio Paste for infusion

Skin 100 g (3½ oz) pistachios; wash them then crush in the mortar to a very fine paste. Add this paste to 1 litre (1¾ pt or 4½ U.S. cups) boiling milk flavoured with a third of a vanilla pod.

As the colour of the pistachios will not be sufficiently pronounced a few drops of vegetable green colour should be added. A little vanilla essence should also be added so as to bring out the flavour of the pistachios.

4352 Soft Pistachio Paste

Place 250 g (9 oz) skinned pistachios and 50 g

(2 oz) freshly skinned almonds in the crushing machine and crush to a very fine paste. Transfer to the mortar; first add 2 tbs of well flavoured vanilla syrup, then 250 g (9 oz) sugar cooked to the hard crack stage adding and mixing it in a little at a time. Turn it out on to a marble slab and add 3 tbs icing sugar, working it in by hand.

4353 Royal Icing Pralin (*for Gâteaux and various sweets*)
Whisk 2 egg whites and 3 heaped tbs icing sugar in a basin until it reaches the ribbon stage.

Mix in the required amounts of finely chopped almonds according to whether a stiff or soft paste is required and so indicated by its ultimate use.

4354 Pralin (*for soufflés, creams and ices*)
Melt 500 g (1 lb 2 oz) sugar very slowly in a copper bowl and cook it to a light caramel colour. Alternatively, the sugar may be cooked in the ordinary way and stopped when it reaches the required temperature. Mix in 500 g (1 lb 2 oz) very dry whole almonds or hazelnuts, or equal quantities of each, according to requirements.

Pour on to an oiled marble slab and allow to go cold. Crush in the mortar then pass through a fine sieve; keep in a tightly closed container in a dry place if required for future use.

4355 THE COOKING OF SUGAR

From the first stage of being a simple syrup to the last stage when it becomes a caramel, sugar passes through six distinct stages of cooking which are known as: the small thread 103 °C (218 °F), the large thread 107 °C (225 °F), the soft ball 115 °C (240 °F), the hard ball 121 °C (250 °F), the soft crack 141 °C (285 °F), the hard crack 157 °C (315 °F) and caramel 182 °C (360 °F).
Method: Place the required amount of sugar in a very clean copper pan with 1 tbs glucose per 500 g (1 lb 2 oz) sugar; add just sufficient water to ensure that the sugar dissolves. Bring it to the boil, and skim carefully; any impurities in the sugar could cause the sugar to crystallize later on.

When the boiling action starts to show a restricted bubbling this indicates that the water has been evaporated. From this moment on the sides of the pan must be cleared of any sugar which may crystallize on it, using the moistened fingers or a moistened brush; if this is not done it can result in the rest of the sugar turning.

The stages of cooking are reached very quickly and it is necessary to follow the progress closely for assuring the different degrees.

The sugar has reached the small thread stage when a little taken between the thumb and index finger forms a thin thread with no resistance when the fingers are parted.

The large thread stage is reached when the fingers are dipped in a few seconds later and the sugar forms threads which are longer and harder. It is now necessary to dip the fingers into cold water before using them to test the sugar and then to dip them immediately in the water afterwards.

The soft ball stage is reached when the sugar which attaches to the end of the finger forms a soft ball.

It is at the hard ball stage when it rolls more easily into a ball but offers some resistance.

It has reached the soft crack stage when the piece attached to the finger is flexible when plunged in the water but sticks to the teeth when tried.

It has reached the hard crack stage when a piece taken on the finger cracks cleanly like glass when plunged into water.

At this stage the sugar should be taken off the stove and kept warm whilst it is being used; only a few seconds more of cooking will bring it to the caramel stage.

SAUCES FOR HOT SWEETS

4356 Sauce Anglaise
This is the same as Crème à l'Anglaise.

4357 Sauce au Chocolat—Chocolate Sauce
Dissolve 250 g (9 oz) chocolate in 4 dl (14 fl oz or 1¾ U.S. cups) water; add 1 tbs vanilla sugar and allow to cook gently for 25 minutes. Finish at the last moment with 3 tbs cream and a walnut-sized piece of best butter.

4358 Sabayon
Place 250 g (9 oz) caster sugar and 6 egg yolks in a well-tinned basin and whisk until it reaches the ribbon stage. Mix in 2½ dl (9 fl oz or 1⅛ U.S. cups) dry white wine; place in a pan of very hot water on the side of the stove and whisk the mixture until it becomes thick and frothy.

Flavour to taste with vanilla sugar, orange sugar, lemon sugar, or 3 tbs of a good liqueur such as Kirsch, Kümmel or Rum.

Note: Sabayon can be made with other kinds of fine wines such as Madeira, Sherry, Marsala, Asti, Champagne etc. In this case the selected wine replaces the white wine and there is no need for any other flavouring.

4359 Fruit Sauces
The most suitable fruits for making sauces are apricots, redcurrants and mirabelle plums.

Note: Other fruits such as peaches, soft pears, apples etc. can also be used to make sauces but in the form of a very light purée. The fruit is prepared in the same way as when making jam but without reducing it so much. It is then passed through a sieve and finished at the last moment with a flavour such as Madeira, Kirsch, Maraschino, bitter almond milk etc.; and a little very fresh butter.

4360 Sauce à l'Abricot—Apricot Sauce
Pass some very ripe apricots or well drained stewed apricots through a fine sieve; thin out this purée with syrup made to 28° on the saccharometer. Bring to the boil skimming carefully, then remove from the stove when it coats the back of the spoon; flavour to taste with almond milk, Madeira, Kirsch or Maraschino.

Note: If this sauce is to be used for a Croûte aux Fruits a little good quality butter may be added.

4361 Sauce aux Cerises—Cherry Sauce
Prepare some stewed cherries; reduce the syrup, add an equal quantity of redcurrant jelly and flavour it with Kirsch.

4362 Sauce aux Fraises—Strawberry Sauce
Pass some strawberry jam through a fine sieve; thin it out with sugar syrup and flavour with Kirsch.

4363 Sauce Framboises—Raspberry Sauce
This is prepared in the same way as Strawberry Sauce.

4364 Sauce Groseilles—Redcurrant Sauce
Dissolve some redcurrant jelly and flavour it with Kirsch.

It may be lightly thickened with arrowroot.

4365 Sauce à l'Orange—Orange Sauce
Pass some orange marmalade through a fine sieve; add a third its quantity of Apricot Sauce and flavour it with Curaçao.

4366 Sauce Noisette
Prepare 5 dl (18 fl oz or 2¼ U.S. cups) Crème Anglaise and add 1 tbs fine Pralin (4354) made with hazelnuts and a little vanilla sugar.

4367 Thickened Syrups
These accompaniments for sweet dishes which are widely used in countries of northern Europe have the advantage of being economical to make but they should be used sparingly.

To make them, a syrup of 15° on the saccharometer is thickened with arrowroot, coloured according to its use and flavoured at the last moment with any suitable essence.

It is this kind of sauce which is used in these northern countries to glaze all kinds of flans and tartlets.

HOT SWEETS

BEIGNETS—FRITTERS

The various kinds of fritters can be grouped into five main types as follows: 1) fritters of fruit and flowers, 2) cream fritters, 3) Viennese fritters, 4) soufflé fritters, 5) those other fritters which resemble the preceding categories but do not completely fit into any single one of them.

4368 Frying Batter (*for fritters of fruit and flowers which are finished by dredging with caster sugar*)
Ingredients: 250 g (9 oz) sifted flour, 5 g (⅙ oz) salt, 2 tbs melted butter, 1½ dl (5 fl oz or ⅝ U.S. cup) beer, 2 dl (7 fl oz or ⅞ U.S. cup) lukewarm water, 1 tbs brandy and 2 stiffly beaten egg whites.
Method: Place the flour, salt and melted butter in a basin; mix in the beer and water without working it too much and add the brandy. Finish by folding in the stiffly beaten egg whites.

4369 Frying Batter (*for fruit fritters which are finished by glazing in the oven*)
Ingredients: 250 g (9 oz) sifted flour, 2 tbs melted butter, a pinch of fine salt, a pinch of sugar, 1 egg, 1½ dl (5 fl oz or ⅝ U.S. cup) beer and a little lukewarm water.
Method: Mix all the ingredients together using a spoon but without working it too much. Leave in a fairly warm place to rise then re-mix it again before using.

TYPE 1) FRITTERS OF FRESH FRUIT AND FLOWERS

This type of fritter is subdivided into three categories, A) fritters of fruits which have firm flesh such as apples, pears, bananas, apricots etc; B) those of soft watery fruits such as strawberries and cherries; C) those made with the flowers of plants such as acacia, elder, lily, marrow etc.

Category A:

4370 Beignets d'Abricots—Apricot Fritters
Choose apricots which are not too ripe; cut them in

half, sprinkle with sugar and place to macerate for 1 hour with Kirsch, brandy or rum.

Dry the half apricots, dip them into the frying batter and deep fry in hot fat.

Drain the fritters, place on a tray, dredge with icing sugar and glaze in a hot oven or under the salamander.

Note: Apple, pear, peach and banana fritters are prepared in the same way as apricot fritters.

Category B:

4371 Beignets de Fraises—Strawberry Fritters
Choose large firm strawberries, sprinkle them well with sugar and macerate with Kirsch, keeping them on ice for 30 minutes.

When required for serving, dip the strawberries in the frying batter and deep fry in hot fat. Drain, arrange on a serviette and sprinkle with caster sugar.

Notes:

1) It is important that the strawberries are very well coated with sugar so that it will penetrate whilst they are macerating; if not well sugared the heat of the fat will cause the strawberries to lose much of their own sweetness and thus become sour to taste.
2) Cherry, raspberry, redcurrant and orange fritters are prepared in the same way as strawberry fritters. For orange fritters it is advisable to use skinned segments rather than round slices.

Category C:

4372 Beignets de Fleurs d'Acacia—Acacia Flower Fritters
Select bunches of flowers which are in full bloom; pick off the flowers, sprinkle them with sugar and macerate with brandy for 30 minutes.

When required for service, dip the flowers in the batter and deep fry in hot fat; drain and sprinkle with caster sugar. Serve arranged on a serviette.

TYPE 2) CUSTARD FRITTERS

If the creams for the fritters are coated with a frying batter they are classified as fritters. If they are coated with egg and breadcrumbs as is sometimes the case they come within the category of Croquettes.

4373 Crèmes Frites—Fried Creams
Ingredients: 500 g (1 lb 2 oz) flour, 250 g (9 oz) caster sugar, 1 pinch fine salt, 24 egg yolks, 8 whole eggs, 2 litres ($3\frac{1}{2}$ pt or 9 U.S. cups) milk infused with either vanilla, lemon, orange or Pralin, (4354), 100 g ($3\frac{1}{2}$ oz) butter.

Method: Prepare the cream with the above ingredients and as indicated for Frangipane Cream. Spread the mixture evenly, $1\frac{1}{2}$ cm ($\frac{3}{5}$ in) thick on a buttered tray and allow to cool, then cut out with a knife or pastry cutter into rounds, rectangles, diamonds etc.; either dip into a frying batter or coat with flour, egg and fine breadcrumbs before deep frying in hot fat.

If the creams have been breadcrumbed they should be simply sprinkled with caster sugar; if fried in batter they should be dredged with icing sugar and glazed in a hot oven or under the salamander. Arrange on a serviette for serving.

4374 Beignets de Crème Fine
Prepare a Crème Renversée mixture increasing the number of eggs so as to give a firmer texture; cook *au Bain-marie* in a large mould in the usual manner.

Allow to become completely cold and well set, then cut into pieces of the desired shape; dip into frying batter and deep fry in hot fat. Drain, dredge with icing sugar and glaze quickly. Arrange on a serviette for service.

TYPE 3) BEIGNETS VIENNOIS—VIENNESE FRITTERS

4375 Beignets Viennois Chauds—Hot Viennese Fritters
Roll out the required amount of Viennese Paste to an even thickness of 5 mm ($\frac{1}{5}$ in).

Place on top and at equal distances apart small portions of well-reduced purée of fruit cooked with sugar; leave sufficient space between each portion.

Moisten the exposed parts of the paste lightly, then cover the whole with a second sheet of paste of the same size and thickness as the first. Press well together between the fillings to seal and cut out the fritters with a 6 cm ($2\frac{1}{2}$ in) diameter plain round cutter.

Place these rounds on a floured cloth on a tray and allow them to prove for 30 minutes. Deep fry in hot fat, drain, sprinkle with caster sugar and serve arranged on a serviette.

Note: Viennese fritters may be served with a light sauce such as Sabayon à la Crème flavoured with vanilla, lemon, orange, coffee or Kirsch etc.

4376 Beignets Viennois Froids or Krapfuns—Cold Viennese Fritters
Roll out a piece of fairly soft Viennese Paste and

cut it into 6 cm ($2\frac{1}{2}$ in) rounds with a plain round cutter.

Place half the number of pieces on sheets of buttered paper placed on trays; place a small amount of fairly thick jam or well-reduced purée of fruit cooked with sugar in the centre of each round; moisten the edges and cover with the other rounds of paste. Seal well around the edges and allow to prove for 30 minutes.

Pick up a sheet of the fritters by the two ends, immerse in hot deep fat and pull out the paper as they float free. Remove the fritters as soon as they are coloured on both sides. Drain them well and place immediately to soak in a light hot syrup flavoured to choice. As soon as they have absorbed a little syrup, remove, allow to cool and serve them cold.

Note: Both the above fritters are also known as Beignets à la Dauphine; they may both be filled with a Salpicon of fruit or with any kind of prepared cream.

TYPE 4) BEIGNETS SOUFFLES—SOUFFLE FRITTERS

4377 Ordinary Soufflé Fritters
Prepare Chou Paste (4321) and flavour it to choice. Take pieces the size of a walnut and place into moderately hot deep fat; fry them, gradually increasing the heat so as to ensure they swell in size and become dry and crisp on the outside.

Drain, arrange on a serviette and sprinkle with caster sugar.

4378 Beignets Soufflés en Surprise
Prepare the fritters as in the preceding recipe. On removing from the fat, drain them well, cut a small incision at one side and fill them with either some well reduced purée of fruit cooked with sugar, jam, a Salpicon of fruit or any kind of prepared cream.

Note: The cream known as Saint-Honoré is particularly suitable for these fritters.

TYPE 5) VARIOUS OTHER FRITTERS

4379 Beignets d'Ananas Favorite
Cut a pineapple into 8 mm ($\frac{1}{3}$ in) thick round slices; cut each slice in half and remove the centre core. Sprinkle with sugar and macerate with Kirsch for 30 minutes.

Dry the pieces of pineapple, dip into nearly cold thick Frangipane Cream containing chopped pistachios, place on a tray and allow to become cold.

Remove them from the tray carefully, dip each into light frying batter and deep fry in hot fat. Drain, dredge with icing sugar and glaze. Serve arranged on a serviette.

4380 Beignets à la Bourgeoise
Cut a stale Brioche made in the form of a crown, into 8 mm ($\frac{1}{3}$ in) thick slices and dip them into fresh cream which has been sweetened and flavoured to taste. Drain, dry lightly, dip into thin frying batter and deep fry them in hot fat.

Drain, sprinkle with caster sugar and arrange on a serviette.

4381 Beignets Grand'Mère
Sprinkle some round slices of stale Brioche with Kirsch or Rum; coat each with some well reduced purée of fruit cooked with sugar. Dip in frying batter and deep fry in hot fat.

Drain, dredge with icing sugar and glaze in a hot oven or under the salamander.

4382 Beignets Mignons
For each fritter take two soft round macaroons; make a depression in the centres, fill with apricot jam and stick them together. Saturate with Kirsch.

Coat with egg and fine breadcrumbs and deep fry in hot fat. Drain, arrange on a serviette and sprinkle with caster sugar.

4383 Beignets Régina
Pipe out some Finger Biscuit mixture (4325) in the form of dome-shaped macaroons. Bake in a moderate oven and allow to cool.

Make a depression on the flat side of each, fill with apricot jam and place two together. Soak in cream flavoured with maraschino. Coat with egg and breadcrumbs and finish as for Beignets Mignons.

4384 Beignets Suzon
Pass some Prepared Rice (4470) through a fine sieve and spread it in a thin layer on a buttered tray; allow to become cold.

Cut into rounds with a 8 cm ($3\frac{1}{4}$ in) diameter cutter and coat each with a layer of very firm Salpicon of fruit. Dip in thin frying batter and deep fry in hot fat.

Drain, arrange on a serviette and sprinkle with caster sugar.

4385 Beignets Sylvana
Empty some small round Brioches keeping the tops to use as lids. Lightly dip in thin sweetened and flavoured cream then fill with a Salpicon of fruit flavoured with Kirsch; replace the tops.

Dip into thin frying batter and deep fry in hot fat. Drain, arrange on a serviette and dredge with icing sugar.

CHARLOTTES

4386 Charlotte de Pommes—Apple Charlotte
Well butter a 1 litre ($1\frac{3}{4}$ pt or $4\frac{1}{2}$ U.S. cup) Charlotte mould. Line the bottom with slightly overlapping slices of bread cut heart shape and dipped in melted butter. Line the sides with slightly overlapping rectangles of bread exactly the height of the mould and also dipped in butter. The bread should be cut 4 mm ($\frac{1}{6}$ in) thick.

Meanwhile, peel and cut 12 large pippin apples into slices. Place in a shallow pan with 30 g (1 oz) butter, 2 tbs caster sugar, the grated zest of half a lemon and a little ground cinnamon. When the apple is cooked and reduced to a very thick purée, add 3 tbs of apricot jam.

Fill this mixture into the prepared mould bringing it above the top in a dome so as to allow for shrinkage. Cover with a thin round piece of bread dipped in melted butter then cook in a fairly hot oven for 30–35 minutes.

On removing from the oven, allow the Charlotte to rest for a few minutes on the serving dish before removing the mould. When required for service, remove the mould and serve accompanied with apricot sauce.

4387 Charlotte de Pommes Emile Giret
Prepare a Charlotte as in the preceding recipe.

When it is turned out for serving cover it completely with some very stiff pastry cream 1 cm ($\frac{2}{5}$ in) thick, smoothing it to the shape of the Charlotte.

Dredge well with icing sugar then brand it neatly trellis-fashion with a red hot iron.

Finish by piping small balls of Pastry Cream around the base of the Charlotte.

4388 Various Other Charlottes
Pear, peach, apricot and other Charlottes are made in the same way as an Apple Charlotte. The main point to bear in mind preparing them is that the purée of fruit being used must be very stiff; if it is too liquid the bread lining will become soft and the almost inevitable result will be a Charlotte that will collapse as soon as it is demoulded. It is also important that the mould is filled as full as possible with the fruit mixture because this will shrink during the cooking process.

HOT CREAMS

4389 Crèmes Frites
See Beignets de Crème.

4390 Crème Meringuée
Prepare a Crème Régence mixture as in the following recipe; pour into a tall buttered border mould and cook it *au Bain-marie.*

Demould on to a round dish and fill the centre with Italian meringue containing a Salpicon of crystallised fruits macerated with Kirsch.

Decorate the top of the cream border with the same meringue but without any Salpicon and piping it with a star tube; place in a moderate oven to colour.

Serve accompanied with orange-flavoured Sauce Anglaise.

4391 Crème Régence
Saturate 200 g (7 oz) Finger Biscuits (4325) with Kirsch and Maraschino then place them in 1 litre ($1\frac{3}{4}$ pt or $4\frac{1}{2}$ U.S. cups) boiled milk.

Pass through a hair sieve; add 10 egg yolks, 8 whole eggs, 300 g (11 oz) caster sugar and a small pinch of fine salt. Pour into a tall buttered Charlotte mould and cook *au Bain-marie* for approximately 35 minutes.

Allow the cream to rest for a few minutes then turn out on to the serving dish and surround its base with a circle of stewed halves of apricots placing a glace cherry on each. Coat with thickened apricot syrup flavoured with Kirsch and Maraschino.

4392 Crème Villageoise
Saturate 150 g (5 oz) dry Finger Biscuits (4325) with Kirsch and Anisette. Arrange them in layers in a deep dish alternating with layers of well reduced purée of fruit cooked with sugar; any fruit in season such as pears, apples etc. may be used.

Cover with a mixture made from: 200 g (7 oz) caster sugar mixed with 4 egg yolks and 8 whole eggs, and 1 litre ($1\frac{3}{4}$ pt or $4\frac{1}{2}$ U.S. cups) milk. Cook *au Bain-marie* in the oven until set.

4393 Custard Pudding
This is made with the same mixture as Crème Renversée using an average of 6 eggs and 180 g (6 oz) sugar per 1 litre ($1\frac{3}{4}$ pt or $4\frac{1}{2}$ U.S. cups) milk. Pour into a pie dish and cook in the oven *au Bain-marie*, or in the steamer. The mixture can be cooked on the stove in the same way as Crème Anglaise and served in special glasses.

According to whether a more or less light custard is required, the number of eggs should be increased or decreased. The amount of sugar used should be in accordance with the taste of the guests. If necessary the sugar can be replaced with Saccharin or with glycerine if for a diabetic person.

Custard pudding is usually flavoured with vanilla but any suitable flavouring for sweet dishes can be used.

CREPES—PANCAKES

4394 Mixtures for Pancakes and Pannequets

Mixture A:

Ingredients: 500 g (1 lb 2 oz) sifted flour, 200 g (7 oz) caster sugar, a pinch of fine salt, 12 eggs, $1\frac{1}{2}$ litre ($2\frac{5}{8}$ pt or $6\frac{1}{2}$ U.S. cups) milk.
Method: Place the flour, sugar and salt in a basin, add the eggs and the milk little by little, whisking it well to form a smooth batter. Flavour with 1 tbs vanilla sugar or orange or lemon sugar which should be included in the weight of sugar given above. The mixture may be flavoured with 3 tbs of Kirsch, brandy or rum.

Mixture B:

Ingredients: 500 g (1 lb 2 oz) sifted flour, 150 g (5 oz) caster sugar, a pinch of fine salt, 10 eggs, 3 dl ($\frac{1}{2}$ pt or $1\frac{1}{4}$ U.S. cups) cream, $\frac{1}{2}$ dl (2 fl oz or $\frac{1}{4}$ U.S. cup) brandy, 80 g (3 oz) melted butter, 1 litre ($1\frac{3}{4}$ pt or $4\frac{1}{2}$ U.S. cups) milk, $\frac{1}{2}$ dl (2 fl oz or $\frac{1}{4}$ U.S. cup) Orgeat syrup and 100 g ($3\frac{1}{2}$ oz) crushed macaroons.
Method: Place the flour, sugar and salt in a basin; add the eggs and mix well together then add the milk, cream, melted butter and brandy. Whisk well to a smooth batter, pass through a fine strainer and finish with the Orgeat syrup and crushed macaroons.

Mixture C:

Ingredients: 500 g (1 lb 2 oz) sifted flour, 150 g (5 oz) caster sugar, a pinch of fine salt, 10 eggs, $5\frac{1}{2}$ dl (19 fl oz or $2\frac{3}{8}$ U.S cups) cream, 5 dl (18 fl oz or $2\frac{1}{4}$ U.S. cups) milk, flavouring to choice.
Method: Place the flour, sugar and salt in a basin. Add and mix in the eggs then the milk and 3 dl ($\frac{1}{2}$ pt or $1\frac{1}{4}$ U.S. cups) of the cream. Whisk well to a smooth batter and finish with the remainder of the cream and the selected flavouring.

Mixture D:

Ingredients: 500 g (1 lb 2 oz) sifted flour, 150 g (5 oz) caster sugar; a pinch of salt, 4 egg yolks, 6 whole eggs, 12 dl ($2\frac{1}{10}$ pt or $5\frac{1}{4}$ U.S. cups) milk, 6 egg whites and flavouring to choice.
Method: Place the flour, sugar and salt in a basin. Add the eggs, egg yolks and milk little by little and whisk to a smooth batter. Gently mix in the egg whites which should be stiffly beaten and finish with the selected flavouring.

4395 Crêpes du Couvent

Pour a little Pancake Mixture A into a hot pan containing a little butter; sprinkle with a little diced pear and cover with a little more of the pancake mixture. Toss over to cook the other side, arrange on a serviette and serve very hot.

4396 Crêpes Georgette

These are prepared in the same way as Crêpes du Couvent replacing the pear with very thin slices of pineapple which have been macerated with Maraschino.

4397 Crêpes Gil-Blas

Prepare the following filling: Mix 100 g ($3\frac{1}{2}$ oz) butter in a basin until soft and smooth then add and mix in 100 g ($3\frac{1}{2}$ oz) caster sugar, 3 tbs brandy, a small piece of Hazelnut Butter (225) and a few drops of lemon juice.

Make the pancakes using Mixture C, spread them with the above filling, fold in four and serve arranged on a serviette.

4398 Crêpes à la Normande

These are prepared in the same way as Crêpes du Couvent replacing the pears with very thin slices of apple which have been lightly cooked in butter.

4399 Crêpes à la Parisienne

These are made using Mixture B; they are served plain and ungarnished.

4400 Crêpes à la Paysanne

These are made using Mixture B without the cream and macaroons; flavour with some orange flower water.

4401 Crêpes à la Russe

To Mixture C add a quarter its amount of biscuit crumbs saturated with Kummel and brandy; make into pancakes in the usual manner.

4402 Crêpes Suzette

These are prepared with Mixture A flavoured with Curaçao and tangerine juice.

Spread the pancakes like Gil-Blas pancakes with softened buttered flavoured with Curaçao and tangerine juice.

CROQUETTES

4403 Croquettes de Marrons—Chestnut Croquettes

Shell the chestnuts in either of the ways as indicated (4143) and cook them in a light vanilla-flavoured syrup. Reserve one small whole chestnut for each Croquette and pass the remainder through a sieve.

Dry the purée on the stove and mix in 5 egg yolks and 50 g (2 oz) butter per 500 g (1 lb 2 oz) purée. Allow to cool.

Divide the mixture into walnut-sized pieces and roll them into balls enclosing a whole chestnut in each. Coat with flour, egg and fine breadcrumbs, deep fry in hot fat and serve arranged on a serviette.

Serve accompanied with a vanilla-flavoured Apricot Sauce.

4404 Croquettes de Riz—Rice Croquettes
Divide some Prepared Rice (4470) into 60 g (2 oz) pieces; mould to the shape of any fruit such as a pear, apple, apricot etc. Coat with egg and fine breadcrumbs and deep fry in hot fat.

Serve accompanied with Apricot Sauce or vanilla-flavoured Sabayon.

4405 Various Croquettes
Sweet Croquettes can be made from tapioca, semolina, vermicelli, fresh noodles etc. cooking it in the same way as for Prepared Rice for sweet dishes (4470). Currants and sultanas may be added to these mixtures.

Note: Sauces for Croquettes are optional. Sauce Anglaise, Sabayon or a fruit sauce can be served if desired.

CROUTES AUX FRUITS

The use of bases and Croûtons for the presentation of Croûtes aux Fruits has largely been discontinued. Nowadays they are presented in the form of a turban or crown which is a satisfactory simplification.

4406 Croûte Dorée or Pain Perdu
Cut a Brioche or a stale loaf into slices 1 cm ($\frac{2}{5}$ in) thick and soak them in cold vanilla-flavoured milk.

Dip them in sweetened beaten egg then shallow fry in hot clarified butter until coloured on both sides. Drain them well, arrange on a serviette and sprinkle with vanilla sugar.

4407 Croûte aux Fruits
Cut a dry stale Savarin into slices 5 mm ($\frac{1}{5}$ in) thick, allowing 2 slices per person. Lay the slices on a tray, sprinkle with caster sugar and place in the oven to dry out and glaze at the same time.

Arrange them closely overlapping in a circle on a dish alternating with thin slices of pineapple of exactly the same size.

On this turban arrange poached quarters of apple and pear, the pear cooked in a pink syrup, if desired, so as to make the whole appear more attractive. Decorate with glacé cherries, diamonds of angelica and crystallized segments of yellow and green *Chinois* oranges. Coat with Apricot Sauce flavoured with Kirsch.

4408 Croûte à la Lyonnaise
Prepare some slices of Savarin as in the preceding recipe then spread them with a layer of vanilla-flavoured chestnut purée. Coat with Apricot Sauce, cooked to the small thread stage. Sprinkle with finely shredded toasted almonds and arrange them in a circle on a dish.

Fill the centre with chestnuts cooked in syrup, seedless raisins, sultanas and currants which have been soaked in warm water to swell them and drained—all mixed with some apricot purée thinned with a few tablespoons of Malaga wine.

4409 Croûte au Madère
Glaze some slices of Savarin as for Croûte aux Fruits and arrange them in a circle on a dish. Fill the centre with a mixture of equal amounts of crystallized fruit cut in large dice and seedless raisins, currants and sultanas soaked to swell in warm water—all mixed with apricot syrup flavoured with Madeira.

4410 Croûte Maréchal
Cut some elongated triangles 5 mm ($\frac{1}{5}$ in) thick from a stale Mousseline Brioche and spread them with Royal Icing Pralin (4353). Place on a tray, dredge with icing sugar then place on a slow oven to dry out the Pralin.

Deep fry a centre piece cut 10 cm (4 in) high from a loaf of bread; set it in the centre of a dish and surround with a Salpicon of pineapple, cherries, grapes and crystallized orange peel mixed with a little apricot purée. Arrange the triangles of Brioche upright around the Salpicon and leaning against the centrepiece; surround with poached halves of pears—half of them cooked in ordinary syrup, the others in pink syrup.

Place a small whole poached pear cooked in pink syrup on top of the centrepiece and fix it in place with a small decorative skewer.

Surround the circle of pears with a *cordon* of thin vanilla-flavoured apricot purée and serve a sauceboat of the same purée separately.

4411 Croûte à la Normande
Prepare some slices of Savarin as for Croûte aux Fruits; coat one side of each with a very thick purée of apple cooked with sugar and arrange them overlapping in a circle on a dish.

Fill the centre with some apple cooked as for

Charlotte de Pommes; arrange poached quarters of apples—some cooked in ordinary syrup, the others in pink syrup, in a pyramid on top of the apple.

Coat the apples with the syrup from the apples after reducing and thickening it with some fine apple purée, and flavouring it with Kirsch.

4412 Croûte à la Parisienne
Prepare some round slices of Savarin and coat with Royal Icing Pralin (4353) as explained for Croûte Maréchal; arrange them overlapping in a circle on a dish.

In the centre arrange a circle of thin slices of pineapple arranging them so that the top edges are resting on the Croûtes. Fill the centre with a mixture of fruits mixed with Madeira-flavoured apricot purée; coat the Croûtes with a lightly thickened apricot syrup flavoured with Madeira.

4413 Croûtes aux Abricots au Marasquin
Cook some Savarin paste or ordinary Brioche paste in buttered tartlet moulds. When cooked, hollow out the centres from the top leaving a fairly wide border.

Coat the insides with Royal Icing Praline (4353) and place them to dry in a slow oven; fill the centres with Frangipane Cream flavoured with Hazelnut Pralin (4353).

On top of each Croûte place a whole stoned apricot poached in Maraschino flavoured syrup and surround each apricot with small halves of glacé cherries and diamonds of angelica.

Serve accompanied with Maraschino-flavoured Apricot Sauce.

4414 Croûte Victoria
Prepare the Croûtes as for Croûte au Madère; arrange them overlapping in a circle on a dish and fill the centre with whole candied chestnuts and glacé cherries.

Serve accompanied with rum-flavoured Apricot Sauce.

Note:
1) A range of Croûtes aux Fruits can be made, using the name of the main fruit to describe them on the menu, e.g. Croûte aux Cerises or *Croûte Montmorency*; Croûte aux Pêches or *Croûte Montreuil* etc.
2) Slices of Savoy Biscuit, Genoise or Punch Biscuits can be used instead of Savarin to make these Croûtes.

OMELETTES

There are four distinct types of omelette. They are:

1) omelettes made with a liqueur,
2) jam omelettes,
3) souffléed omelettes,
4) surprise omelettes.

TYPE 1) OMELETTES AUX LIQUEURS

4415 *Example:* Omelette au Rhum—Rum Omelette
Add a little sugar and a touch of salt to the eggs and make the omelette in the usual manner.

Place it on an oval dish, sprinkle with caster sugar and pour a little warmed Rum around the omelette. This should be set alight when bringing the omelette to the table.

Note: Kirsch omelette, brandy omelette etc. are made in the same way.

TYPE 2) OMELETTES AUX CONFITURES—JAM OMELETTES

4416 *Example:* Omelette à l'Abricot—Apricot Jam Omelette
Add a little sugar and a touch of salt to the eggs; make the omelette in the usual way and when about to roll it, fill the centre with 2 tbs apricot jam for an omelette of 6 eggs.

Place it on an oval dish, sprinkle with caster sugar and either mark trellis-fashion with a red hot iron, or glaze it under the salamander.

Note: Omelettes using other jams such as greengage, plum or strawberry etc. are made in the same way.

4417 Omelette de Noël—Christmas Omelette
Add a little sugar and a touch of salt plus 2 tbs cream and a pinch of grated lemon rind per 6 eggs.

Just before rolling the omelette, fill the centre with as much mincemeat as it will hold and complete in the usual way. Turn on to an oval dish, pour a little warmed Rum over the omelette and set it alight when bringing it to the table.

TYPE 3) OMELETTE SOUFFLE

4418 *Example:* Omelette Soufflé à la Vanille
Whisk 250 g (9 oz) caster sugar and 6 egg yolks together until they become white and form a ribbon.

Fold in 8 stiffly beaten egg whites mixing them in gently with a spoon.

Mould nearly all this mixture in a high oval shape in a buttered and sugared oval dish. Smooth with a palette knife then decorate it with the remainder of the mixture using a piping bag and star tube. Cook in a moderate oven for the amount of time as determined by the size of the omelette. Remove from the oven 2 minutes before it is ready, and dredge with icing sugar. Replace in the oven so that the sugar will melt and cover the omelette with a caramelized coating.

Note: These omelettes can be flavoured to taste with vanilla, grated lemon or orange zest, Rum, Kirsch etc. The selected flavour should be added before folding in the egg whites although when a liquid flavour is being used it is best to add it in the form of small pieces of macaroons or finger biscuits previously soaked with the chosen flavouring. This idea is also applicable when making soufflés.

TYPE 4) OMELETTE SURPRISE

4419 *Example:* Omelette Norvégienne
Place an oval-shaped base of Genoise 2 cm (⅘ in) thick on a silver dish; the length of the oval should be proportionate to the size of the omelette.

Place either a cream or a fruit ice of the selected flavour on the Genoise, forming an oval pyramid.

Cover the ice with a layer of either ordinary meringue or stiff Italian meringue and smooth with a palette knife so as to give an even coating 1½ cm (⅗ in) thick. Decorate with some of the same meringue using a piping bag and tube; place in a very hot oven to cook and colour the meringue rapidly but without the heat penetrating to the ice inside.

4420 Omelette en Surprise Elizabeth
Cover the base of Genoise with vanilla ice-cream. Sprinkle with crystallized violets, cover with meringue and decorate the surface with whole crystallized violets. Finish as indicated for Omelette Norvégienne and just before serving cover the omelette with a veil of spun sugar.

4421 Omelette en Surprise aux Mandarines
This is prepared in the same way as Omelette Norvégienne using tangerine ice.

On removing the omelette from the oven, surround it with tangerine segments which have been dipped in sugar cooked to the hard crack stage.

4422 Omelette en Surprise Milady, also called Pêche Milady
This surprise omelette is made in the usual way but with excellent quality raspberry ice in which are set some nice peaches which have been poached in vanilla-flavoured syrup.

Cover with Italian meringue flavoured with Maraschino but leave the tops of the peaches showing through.

Decorate with some of the same meringue using a piping bag and tube; dredge with icing sugar and glaze quickly in the oven.

4423 Omelette en Surprise Montmorency
Cover the Genoise base with a cherry ice mixed with a few glacé cherries which have been macerated with Kirsch.

Continue as for Omelette Norvégienne and serve accompanied with a timbale of Cerises Jubilée (4523).

4424 Omelette en Surprise Mylord
This is prepared in the same way as for Omelette Norvégienne but covering the base of Genoise with alternate layers of vanilla ice-cream and poached pears. Cover with meringue and finish in the usual way.

4425 Omelette en Surprise à la Napolitaine, or Bombe Vésuve
Cover the base of Genoise with layers of vanilla ice and strawberry ice alternating with layers of broken candied chestnuts. Cover with Kirsch-flavoured Italian meringue shaping it long and flat. On top place a boat-shaped meringue case of a size in keeping with the omelette.

Cover with some of the same meringue to hide the join with the boat. Place in the oven to cook and colour the meringue quickly.

When about to serve, fill the boat with Cerises Jubilée (4523) and flame them when bringing the omelette to the table.

4426 Omelette en Surprise Néron
Cut a round base of Genoise and place it on the service dish; cover it to the form of a truncated cone using any kind of ice. Cover with meringue and place on top a previously dried round meringue case as for Omelette Napolitaine. Decorate with some of the same meringue, covering the join.

Place it in the oven to colour and cook the meringue. When about to serve pour a glass of warmed Rum into the case and set it alight when bringing the omelette to the table.

4427 Omelette des Sylphes
Soak a freshly baked Savarin in Maraschino-flavoured syrup; drain and attach it to a cooked flat pastry base of exactly the same size. Place on a dish.

Place a round of Genoise in the centre of the Savarin, thick enough to come half-way up the Savarin.

When required for serving place on the Genoise an iced strawberry Mousse moulded in a Madeleine mould of the same size as the piece of Genoise.

Cover the Mousse with a layer of Kirsch-flavoured Italian meringue forming it like a cone, the base resting on the savarin. Quickly decorate the cone and the Savarin with some of the same meringue using a piping bag and small tube; place in a hot oven to colour and serve immediately.

4428 Various Surprise Omelettes
Using the basic recipe for Omelette Norvégienne it is possible to produce an almost infinite number of variations of this type of omelette by altering the kind of ice used inside.

The exterior remains the same but the changes in the inside filling must be indicated in the title of the dish.

PANNEQUETS

4429 Pannequets aux Confitures
Prepare some very small thin pancakes, coat them with any kind of jam and roll them up. Trim both ends on the slant and cut each pancake into two diamond-shaped pieces.

Place these pieces on a tray, dredge with icing sugar and glaze in a hot oven. Serve arranged on a serviette.

4430 Pannequets à la Crème
Coat the pancakes with Frangipane Cream and sprinkle with crushed macaroons.

Finish in the same way as for Pannequets aux Confitures.

4431 Pannequets Meringués
Coat the pancakes with Kirsch and Maraschino-flavoured Italian meringue.

Roll them up, cut into diamond shapes as before and arrange them on a tray.

Decorate with some of the same meringue using a piping bag and tube, dredge with icing sugar and glaze quickly in a hot oven.

PUDDINGS

English puddings are almost innumerable, but although most of them are prepared in the pastry department rather than in the kitchen it is felt that a complete listing of them would serve no useful purpose.

The name pudding is also given to a large number of preparations which are actually creams, such as Custard Pudding.

Leaving aside those puddings which are made in the kitchen and also the creams, the hot sweet puddings can then be divided into six main types. These are:
1) cream puddings, 2) English fruit puddings, 3) plum pudding, 4) bread puddings, 5) puddings made with rice and other cereals, 6) soufflé puddings.

Nearly all English puddings can be served with an accompaniment of stewed fruits, Melba Sauce or Crème Chantilly.

CREAM PUDDINGS

4432 Pouding aux Amandes—Almond Pudding
Prepare a soufflé pudding mixture with almond milk instead of ordinary milk.

Pour into well buttered moulds which have been sprinkled with toasted flaked almonds and cook them *au Bain-marie*.

Serve accompanied with a white wine Sabayon flavoured with Orgeat syrup.

4433 Pouding aux Amandes à l'Anglaise—English Almond Pudding
Cream smoothly together 125 g ($4\frac{1}{2}$ oz) butter and 150 g (5 oz) caster sugar. Add 250 g (9 oz) very finely chopped almonds, a pinch of salt, $\frac{1}{2}$ tbs of orange flower water, 2 egg yolks, 2 whole eggs and 1 dl ($3\frac{1}{2}$ fl oz or $\frac{1}{2}$ U.S. cup) cream.

Pour this mixture into a buttered pie dish and cook *au Bain-marie* in the oven.

Note: All English puddings should be served from the dish in which they are cooked.

4434 Pouding de Biscuits—Biscuit Pudding
Crush 250 g (9 oz) Finger Biscuits (4325) in a pan; pour on 6 dl (1 pt or $2\frac{5}{8}$ U.S. cups) boiling milk sweetened with 150 g (5 oz) sugar. Place on the stove, mix until hot then add 5 egg yolks, 125 g ($4\frac{1}{2}$ oz) melted butter and 150 g (5 oz) diced crystallized fruit including some currants all previously macerated with Kirsch.

Fold in 3 stiffly beaten egg whites away from the heat then pour into buttered moulds sprinkled with browned breadcrumbs and cook *au Bain-marie* in the oven.

Serve accompanied with Apricot Sauce.

4435 Pouding de Cabinet—Cabinet Pudding
Saturate some Finger Biscuits (4325) with any suitable liqueur. Fill a round buttered mould with alternate layers of these biscuits and crystallized fruit including some currants, macerated with Kirsch; place a little apricot jam here and there in the mould. Fill the mould slowly with a Crème

Renversée mixture (4346) flavoured to choice then cook *au Bain-marie* in the oven.

Turn out the pudding at the last moment and coat it with Sauce Anglaise or Sabayon.

ENGLISH FRUIT PUDDINGS

4436 Apple Pudding
Prepare some Suet Paste (4313), allow it to rest for 1 hour then roll it out 8 mm (⅓ in) thick. Line a well buttered pudding basin with the paste and fill with sliced apples sweetened with sufficient sugar and flavoured with chopped lemon zest and a little ground cinnamon.

Cover with a round piece of the same paste sealing it well to the edges. Cover with a cloth and tie tightly.

For a 1 litre (1¾ pt or 4½ U.S. cups) capacity basin, steam or boil for approximately 2 hours.

Note: This type of fruit pudding can be made with other soft fruits and certain vegetables such as pumpkin.

PLUM PUDDING

4437 Plum Pudding
Ingredients:
500 g (1 lb 2 oz) chopped beef kidney suet
500 g (1 lb 2 oz) white breadcrumbs
250 g (9 oz) flour
250 g (9 oz) peeled and chopped apple
250 g (9 oz) mixed seedless raisins, sultanas and currants
250 g (9 oz) brown sugar
120 g (4 oz) chopped almonds
60 g (2 oz) each of crystallized orange, lemon and cedrat peel
60 g (2 oz) ground ginger
12 g (⅓ oz) mixed spice, containing a large quantity of cinnamon
3 eggs
2 dl (7 fl oz or ⅞ U.S. cup) stout
1½ dl (5 fl oz or ⅝ U.S. cup) Rum or Brandy
The juice and chopped zest of ½ lemon and ½ orange

(If possible the dried fruit should be macerated in the spirit beforehand).

Method:
Mix all the ingredients together and fill into buttered white pudding basins having projecting rims. Press the mixture in lightly then cover with a buttered and floured cloth. Tie up tightly under the rims with string and tie the cloth into a knot on top. Cook in boiling water or steam for 5–6 hours.

When cooked, turn out on to a dish, sprinkle with warmed brandy or rum and set this alight when bringing it to the table.

Instead of setting the pudding alight it can be served accompanied with rum-flavoured Sabayon, Brandy Butter or Sauce Anglaise thickened with a little arrowroot.

Note: If pudding basins are not available the pudding can be cooked in a buttered and floured cloth, tied and cooked in boiling water.

4438 Pouding à l'Américaine
Place in a basin 75 g (2½ oz) white breadcrumbs, 100 g (3½ oz) brown sugar, 100 g (3½ oz) flour, 75 g (2½ oz) each of chopped bone marrow and chopped beef kidney suet, 100 g (3½ oz) diced crystallized fruits, 3 egg yolks, 1 egg, a pinch each of chopped orange and lemon zest, a pinch of grated nutmeg, a pinch of ground cinnamon and ¼ dl (1 fl oz or ⅛ U.S. cup) Rum or Brandy.

Mix all the ingredients well together, pour into a buttered and floured mould or dish and cook *au Bain-marie* in the oven.

Serve accompanied with rum-flavoured Sabayon.

4439 Pouding à la Moelle
Melt 250 g (9 oz) bone marrow and 50 g (2 oz) chopped beef kidney suet in a Bain-marie; allow to cool slightly until lukewarm.

Add 200 g (7 oz) caster sugar and mix well together then add and mix in 80 g (3 oz) breadcrumbs soaked in milk and squeezed, 8 egg yolks, 3 eggs, 200 g (7 oz) diced crystallized fruits, 80 g (3 oz) sultanas and 50 g (2 oz) seedless raisins.

Place this mixture in a buttered and floured, deep plain mould and cook *au Bain-marie* in the oven.

Serve accompanied with rum-flavoured Sabayon.

BREAD PUDDINGS

4440 Pouding au Pain à l'Anglaise—Bread and Butter Pudding
Spread small thin slices of bread with butter and sprinkle with currants and raisins which have been previously soaked in warm water to swell them, then well drained.

Arrange these overlapping in a pie dish, cover with a Crème Renversée mixture (4346) and cook *au Bain-marie* in the oven.

4441 Pouding au Pain à la Française—French Bread Pudding
Soak 300 g (11 oz) white breadcrumbs in 1 litre

(1¾ pt or 4½ U.S. cups) boiled milk flavoured with vanilla and sweetened with 250 g (9 oz) sugar. Pass through a sieve and mix together with 6 egg yolks and 4 whole eggs, then fold in 4 stiffly beaten egg whites.

Pour this mixture into a deep border mould which has been buttered and sprinkled with fine breadcrumbs and cook *au Bain-marie* in the oven.

Serve accompanied with Sauce Anglaise, vanilla-flavoured Sabayon or a fruit sauce.

4442 Pouding au Pain à l'Ecossaise—Scotch Bread Pudding

Prepare this pudding in exactly the same way as for French Bread Pudding adding to the mixture 150 g (5 oz) of any sliced fruit in season. Pour into a deep border mould which has been buttered and sprinkled with fine breadcrumbs and cook *au Bain-marie* in the usual manner.

Serve accompanied with a raspberry flavoured Redcurrant Sauce.

RICE AND OTHER CEREAL PUDDINGS

4443 Pouding au Tapioca—Tapioca Pudding

Rain 250 g (9 oz) tapioca into 1 litre (1¾ pt or 4½ U.S. cups) boiling milk containing 125 g (4½ oz) sugar, a pinch of salt and 100 g (3½ oz) butter.

Place in the oven and cook gently for 25 minutes. Transfer the preparation to a clean pan and mix in 6 egg yolks, 75 g (2½ oz) butter, and 4 stiffly beaten egg whites.

Pour the mixture into a buttered Charlotte mould sprinkled with tapioca and cook *au Bain-marie* in the oven until set and resilient to the touch.

Allow to rest for 7–8 minutes then demould on to a dish and serve accompanied with Sauce Anglaise, Sabayon or a fruit sauce.

4444 Pouding au Sagou—Sago Pudding

This is made in the same way as for Tapioca Pudding using sago and sprinkling the buttered mould with sago.

The method of cooking and accompaniments are the same.

4445 Pouding à la Semoule—Semolina Pudding

This is made in the same way as for Tapioca Pudding using semolina and sprinkling the buttered mould with semolina.

4446 Pouding au Vermicelli—Vermicelli Pudding

This is made in the same way as Tapioca Pudding using vermicelli and sprinkling the buttered mould with roughly broken vermicelli.

4447 Pouding aux Nouilles Fraîches—Noodle Pudding

This is prepared in exactly the same way as for Tapioca Pudding. The noodles should be cut very thinly.

4448 Tapioca, Sago and Semolina Puddings—English Style

All these puddings are made by cooking the cereal in lightly sweetened milk, flavoured to choice.

Thicken with 4 eggs per 1 litre (1¾ pt or 4½ U.S. cups) of pudding then pour into a buttered pie dish and cook *au Bain-marie* in the oven.

Note: All English puddings of this type are made in the same way and should be served in the dish in which they are cooked.

4449 Pouding Brésilien

Prepare some tapioca pudding mixture, pour into a mould previously lined with sugar cooked to the caramel stage and cook *au Bain-marie* in the oven.

Serve without any accompaniment.

4450 Pouding à la Chevreuse

This is semolina pudding with the addition of diced crystallized fruits previously macerated with Kirsch. Serve accompanied with Kirsch-flavoured Sabayon.

Note: These cereal puddings lend themselves to a large number of variations either by the addition of crystallized fruits or by filling the mould with layers of the mixture which have been variously flavoured and coloured.

4451 Pouding au Riz—Rice Pudding

Make some Prepared Rice for sweet dishes (4470) and fold in 15 stiffly beaten egg whites per 500 g (1 lb 2 oz) of raw rice. Pour into a buttered and floured mould and cook *au Bain-marie* in the oven.

Serve accompanied with Sauce Anglaise, Sabayon or a fruit sauce.

4452 Pouding de Riz à l'Anglaise—English Rice Pudding

Make the pudding with 180 g (6 oz) rice, 1 litre (1¾ pt or 4½ U.S. cups) milk, 50 g (2 oz) sugar and 80 g (3 oz) butter keeping the grains of rice whole and the mixture milky.

Thicken with 3 eggs, pour into a buttered pie dish and cook *au Bain-marie* in the oven. On removing from the oven sprinkle the surface with icing sugar.

4453 Pouding de Riz au Chocolat
Add 50 g (2 oz) melted chocolate per 1 litre ($1\frac{3}{4}$ pt or $4\frac{1}{2}$ U.S. cups) of Prepared Rice for sweet dishes (4470). Fold in 2 stiffly beaten egg whites, pour into a buttered pie dish and cook in the oven.

Serve accompanied with a Chocolate Sauce mixed with an equal quantity of whipped cream.

Note: This pudding may be served hot or cold.

4454 Pouding de Riz à la Crème—Rice Pudding with Cream
This pudding makes an excellent accompaniment for hot or cold stewed fruit. Make the rice pudding in the usual manner and with a suitable flavouring. Add 4 egg yolks and 1 dl ($3\frac{1}{2}$ fl oz or $\frac{1}{2}$ U.S. cup) cream per 1 litre ($1\frac{3}{4}$ pt or $4\frac{1}{2}$ U.S. cups) pudding. Place in the serving dish and glaze quickly in the oven.

4455 Pouding de Semoule à la Crème
This is prepared in the same way as in the preceding recipe using semolina instead of rice.

SOUFFLE PUDDINGS

4456 Pouding Saxon
Mix 100 g ($3\frac{1}{2}$ oz) butter in a pan until soft and smooth. Mix in 100 g ($3\frac{1}{2}$ oz) each of caster sugar and sifted flour then add 3 dl ($\frac{1}{2}$ pt or $1\frac{1}{4}$ U.S. cups) boiling milk; bring the mixture to the boil stirring well and dry it in the same way as for Chou Paste.

Remove the pan from the stove, mix in 5 egg yolks then carefully fold in 5 stiffly beaten egg whites. Pour this mixture into well buttered moulds and cook *au Bain-marie* in the oven.

Serve accompanied with Sauce Anglaise or a Sabayon flavoured to choice.

4457 Pouding Soufflé Denise
Finely pound 125 g ($4\frac{1}{2}$ oz) skinned and well washed almonds to a smooth paste adding a few drops of cold water from time to time. When the almonds are ready as a fine paste, add sufficient water to give 5 dl (18 fl oz or $2\frac{1}{4}$ U.S. cups) almond milk. Squeeze through a muslin twisting it lightly so as to express all the milk.

Mix together in a pan, 100 g ($3\frac{1}{2}$ oz) each of flour and rice flour; add the almond milk mixing well so as to avoid any lumps. Pass through a strainer and add 150 g (5 oz) sugar, 100 g ($3\frac{1}{2}$ oz) melted butter and a pinch of salt.

Place on the stove and bring to the boil, mixing vigorously with a wooden spoon until the mixture is thick and dry like a Chou Paste and does not adhere to the spoon.

Place the paste into a basin and mix in 50 g (2 oz) butter a little at a time, then 8 egg yolks and 50 g (2 oz) finely pounded almonds flavoured with 1 tbs each of Kirsch and Maraschino. Finally fold in 5 stiffly beaten egg whites.

The pudding can now be cooked *au Bain-marie* and finished in any of the following ways:

1) in a buttered pie dish; in this case when it is cooked, dredge the surface with icing sugar and mark trellis-fashion with a red hot iron,
2) in a shallow buttered and floured Charlotte mould,
3) in a medium-height, buttered dome-shaped mould which has been lined with 2 cm ($\frac{4}{5}$ in) round pieces cut from a sheet of Genoise or Finger Biscuit mixture, 1 cm ($\frac{2}{5}$ in) thick.

In the last two methods the puddings should be coated with almond-flavoured Apricot Sauce and serve accompanied with a sauceboat of the same sauce.

4458 Pouding Soufflé au Citron—Lemon Soufflé Pudding
Prepare a soufflé pudding mixture as for Pouding Saxon and flavour it with grated lemon zest.

Cook in the usual manner and serve accompanied with lemon-flavoured Sauce Anglaise.

4459 Pouding Soufflé à l'Orange, au Curaçao, à l'Anisette, à la Bénédictine etc.
All these puddings are made in the same way as for Pouding Saxon adding the chosen flavouring or liqueur.

The accompaniment for all of them is a Sauce Anglaise flavoured with the same liqueur as used in the making of the pudding.

4460 Pouding Soufflé à l'Indienne
Add 50 g (2 oz) ground ginger and 150 g ($5\frac{1}{2}$ oz) diced candied ginger to a Pouding Saxon mixture and proceed in the usual manner.

Serve accompanied with ginger-flavoured Sauce Anglaise.

4461 Pouding Soufflé aux Marrons
Cook 1 kg ($2\frac{1}{4}$ lb) shelled chestnuts in a light vanilla-flavoured syrup. Pass them through a sieve and add 150 g (5 oz) caster sugar and 100 g ($3\frac{1}{2}$ oz) butter to the purée; dry out on a hot stove. Add 8 egg yolks then fold in 6 stiffly beaten egg whites.

Cook in buttered moulds *au Bain-marie* and serve accompanied with either Sauce Anglaise or a vanilla-flavoured apricot syrup.

4462 Pouding Mousseline
Mix together 125 g (4½ oz) butter and 125 g (4½ oz) caster sugar until soft and smooth. Add 10 egg yolks one at a time mixing well, then cook over a low heat mixing continuously until the mixture coats the back of the spoon. Immediately fold in 7 stiffly beaten egg whites and half fill tall buttered moulds with the mixture so as to allow room for it to rise.

Cook *au Bain-marie* in the oven for approximately 30 minutes then allow to rest for 10 minutes before demoulding.

Serve accompanied with a light Sabayon or fruit sauce.

4463 Pouding Soufflé Régence
Prepare a Pouding Saxon mixture flavoured with vanilla. Pour it into moulds which have been lined with sugar cooked to the caramel stage then cook in the usual manner.

Serve accompanied with a caramel-flavoured Sauce Anglaise.

4464 Pouding Soufflé à la Reine
Prepare a Pouding Saxon mixture flavoured with vanilla. Butter a funnel mould and sprinkle the inside with a mixture of chopped pistachios and crushed macaroons. Add the pudding mixture in layers alternating with layers of chopped pistachios and crushed macaroons.

Cook in the usual manner and serve accompanied with a pralin-flavoured Sauce Anglaise.

4465 Pouding Soufflé à la Royale
Line the inside of a buttered Charlotte mould with thin slices of a small diameter Swiss roll layered with apricot jam. Fill with soufflé pudding mixture and cook *au Bain-marie* in the oven.

Serve accompanied with a Marsala-flavoured Apricot Sauce.

4466 Pouding Soufflé Sans-Souci
Well butter a mould and sprinkle the inside with well-washed and dried currants. Fill with a soufflé pudding mixture made with the addition of 250 g (9 oz) peeled and diced apple cooked in butter, per 1 kg (2¼ lb) of mixture.

Cook in the usual manner and serve accompanied with a rum-flavoured Apricot Sauce.

4467 Pouding Soufflé Vésuvienne
Prepare a Pouding Saxon mixture and add 50 g (2 oz) each of tomato jam and seedless raisins. Fill into a buttered funnel mould and cook *au Bain-marie* in the oven.

When cooked, turn out the pudding on to a dish and surround with Apricot Sauce; pour a little warmed Rum into the centre and set it alight when bringing the pudding to the table.

ROLY-POLY PUDDING

4468 Roly-Poly Pudding
Prepare a Suet Paste (4313) and allow it to rest for 1 hour. Roll out the paste into a rectangle 5 mm (⅕ in) thick and spread it with any kind of jam. Roll up to the shape of a long sausage.

Place it on a buttered and floured cloth and tie up. Cook in boiling water or steam for 1½ hours.

To serve, cut the pudding into round thick slices 1 cm (⅖ in) thick, arrange in a circle on a dish and serve accompanied with a fruit sauce.

4469 RISSOLES

The preparation of sweet rissoles is the same as for those savoury ones served as an Hors-d'oeuvre, the only difference being that jam, purées of fruit cooked with sugar, Salpicons of fruit, stewed fruits or ordinary pralin-flavoured creams are used for the mixture.

For preference, puff paste trimmings are used for making these rissoles. Their shape can be varied and they can be made crescent-, round-, oval-, or turnover-shape.

Sweet rissoles are frequently made with General Purpose Brioche Paste (4316) in which case they become a variation of a *Beignets Viennois*. They are then invariably called *Beignets à la Dauphine* with the addition of a name denoting the mixture used.

RICE FOR SWEET DISHES

4470 Prepared Rice for Sweet Dishes
Ingredients: 500 g (1 lb 2 oz) Carolina rice, 300 g (11 oz) sugar, a pinch of salt, 2 litres (3½ pt or 9 U.S. cups) milk, 12 egg yolks, 1 vanilla pod or the zest of lemon or orange for flavouring and 100 g (3½ oz) butter.
Method: Wash the rice, blanch and drain it then re-wash in warm water. Drain again then place it into the milk which has been brought to the boil with the flavourings, sugar and butter and strained.

When it reboils, cover with the lid and place to cook gently in the oven for 25–30 minutes without stirring; any displacement of the liquid will cause the rice to stick to the bottom of the pan.

When cooked, remove from the oven and add the egg yolks mixing them in quickly and carefully with a fork so as not to break up the grains of rice which must remain whole.

SOUFFLES

Although soufflés are generally served without any accompaniment they may be served accompanied with a dish of any kind of stewed fruit in season, or with a Macédoine of fresh fruit where appropriate.

There are two types of soufflé mixture:

1) that made with a cream-type mixture; these can be used for all kinds of soufflés; 2) that made with a fruit purée; this allows of a more pronounced flavour of the fruit than when the fruit is combined with the cream-type mixture.

4471 Cream-type Soufflé Mixture (*for 4 persons*)
Ingredients: 1 dl (3½ fl oz or ½ U.S. cup) milk, 35 g (1¼ oz) sugar, 1 tbs flour, 10 g (⅓ oz) butter, 2 egg yolks and 3 stiffly beaten egg whites.
Method: Bring the milk and sugar to the boil, mix in the flour which has been diluted with a little cold milk and cook on the stove for 2 minutes.

Remove from the stove, mix in the butter and egg yolks and then fold in the stiffly beaten egg whites.

4472 Cream-type Soufflé Mixture (*for large numbers*)
Ingredients: 250 g (9 oz) sugar, 250 g (9 oz) flour, 8 yolks, 4 eggs, 1 litre (1¾ pt or 4½ U.S. cups) milk, 1 vanilla pod, 125 g (4½ oz) butter and 12 egg whites.
Method: Mix the sugar and flour with the eggs and 3 of the egg yolks. Whisk in the boiling milk, return to the pan, add the vanilla and cook as for Frangipane Cream.

Remove from the stove, add the butter and the remaining egg yolks and finish by folding in the stiffly beaten egg whites.

4473 Fruit Purée Soufflé Mixture
Ingredients: 500 g (1 lb 2 oz) sugar, 400 g (14 oz) of the selected purée of fruit, 10 stiffly beaten egg whites.
Method: Cook the sugar to the soft crack stage and add the purée of fruit which will dilute the sugar down below the hard crack stage. Now recook the mixture to the hard crack stage. Pour into the stiffly beaten whites and fold in.

Note:
1) If the addition of the fruit purée dilutes the sugar to below the hard crack stage it must be recooked until it attains the required degree.
2) It should be remembered that if a liquid flavouring is to be added to the soufflé it is preferable that it be in the form of small squares of finger biscuits or macaroons which have been soaked in the selected liqueur.

4474 The Moulding and Cooking of Soufflés
The soufflé mixture is placed in a soufflé mould or deep silver timbale or in a special false-bottomed dish—in all cases these should be buttered and sugared inside. They are cooked in a moderately hot oven so that the heat may reach the centre of the mixture by degrees. Two minutes before removing the soufflé from the oven, dredge the surface with icing sugar which will caramelize and form the required glaze when replaced in the oven.

The decoration of soufflés is optional but in any case it should be kept to a minimum.

4475 Soufflé aux Amandes—Almond Soufflé
Prepare a cream-type soufflé mixture replacing the milk with almond milk and adding 50 g (2 oz) chopped and lightly toasted almonds per 1 dl (3½ fl oz or ½ U.S. cup) milk. Pour into the mould and cook in the oven in the usual manner.

4476 Soufflé aux Amandes fraîches—Fresh Almond Soufflé
Proceed in exactly the same way as in the preceding recipe, replacing the toasted almonds with shredded fresh almonds.

4477 Soufflé aux Avelines—Hazelnut Soufflé
Prepare a cream-type soufflé mixture using milk in which 60 g (2 oz) Hazelnut Pralin (4354) per 1 dl (3½ fl oz or ½ U.S. cup) milk has been infused. Pour into the mould and cook in the usual manner.

4478 Soufflé Camargo
Prepare a hazelnut soufflé mixture as in the preceding recipe and also a tangerine soufflé mixture. Arrange these in the dish in layers, alternating with finger biscuits saturated with Crème de Curaçao. Cook in the usual manner.

4479 Soufflé aux Cerises—Cherry Soufflé
Prepare a Soufflé au Kirsch (see Liqueur Soufflés) and serve accompanied with a dish of stoned poached cherries mixed with a purée of raspberries.

4480 Soufflé au Chocolat—Chocolate Soufflé
Prepare a vanilla soufflé mixture made with milk in which 50 g (2 oz) chocolate per 1 dl (3½ fl oz or ½ U.S. cup) milk has been dissolved.

4481 Soufflé au Curaçao
Prepare a cream-type vanilla soufflé mixture flavoured with orange zest and containing ¼ dl (1 fl oz or ⅛ U.S. cup) Curaçao per 1 dl (3½ fl oz or ½ U.S. cup) milk.

4482 Soufflé Elizabeth
Prepare a vanilla soufflé mixture and arrange in the mould in layers alternating with layers of small pieces of macaroon saturated with Kirsch, and crystallized violets.

On removing the soufflé from the oven cover it with a veil of spun sugar and serve immediately.

4483 Soufflé aux Fraises—Strawberry Soufflé
This is a Soufflé au Kirsch which is served accompanied with a dish of chilled strawberries macerated with orange juice.

4484 Soufflé aux Fraises à la Moscovite
Prepare a cream-type soufflé flavoured with Curaçao. Serve accompanied with a dish of large very cold strawberries which have been mixed into a purée of wild strawberries flavoured with sugar and Kirsch.

4485 Soufflé aux Fruits en Croustade
Take a well buttered shallow mould similar in shape to a soufflé mould and line it with a very thin layer of Sweet Paste.

Cover the bottom with a layer of a stiff purée of apples cooked with sugar and flavoured with vanilla; on top of this arrange a varied garnish of fresh stewed fruits in season, cut into quarters if too large. The mould should by now be half full. Finish filling with a cream-type soufflé mixture flavoured with vanilla then cook in a moderate oven for approximately 25 minutes.

On removing from the oven, remove very carefully from the mould and slide it on to the serving dish.

To serve: surround the base with a few tablespoons of heated rum and light it on presenting it at the table.

4486 Soufflé aux Grenades à l'Orientale
Prepare a cream-type soufflé mixture lightly flavoured with vanilla. Arrange it in layers alternating with layers of Finger Biscuits saturated with Grenadine and Kirsch.

Cook in the usual manner.

On removing the soufflé from the oven cover it with a veil of spun sugar and sprinkle this with very small boiled sugar sweets flavoured with Grenadine and of a shape and size to imitate the grains of a pomegranate.

4487 Soufflé Hilda
Prepare a lemon-flavoured cream-type soufflé; serve accompanied with a dish of chilled strawberries coated with a purée of fresh raspberries.

4488 Soufflé Idéal
Prepare a cream-type soufflé mixture made with Hazelnut Pralin (4354) and containing some very small soft macaroons saturated with Noyau liqueur. Pour this mixture into a special square, white porcelain soufflé mould and cook in the usual manner.

4489 Soufflé Javanais
Prepare a cream-type soufflé mixture but replace the milk with the same quantity of an infusion of tea; add 50 g (2 oz) chopped pistachio nuts per 1 dl ($3\frac{1}{2}$ fl oz or $\frac{1}{2}$ U.S. cup) tea.

4490 Soufflé Lérina
Prepare a cream-type soufflé mixture containing some small cubes of Finger Biscuits (4325) saturated with Lérina liqueur.

This liqueur is similar to Chartreuse and is made in the St. Honnorat Islands.

Cook in the usual manner.

4491 Various Liqueur Soufflés
These soufflés may be made with either of the two soufflé mixtures—the cream type or the fruit purée type as indicated at the beginning of this section.

Soufflés made with the cream-type mixture are flavoured with liqueurs such as Rum, Curaçao, Anisette, Crème de Vanille, Crème de Cacao, Chartreuse etc.

Those made from a base of fruit are flavoured with Kirsch, Noyau etc.

4492 Soufflé Lucullus
On a suitable dish place a Savarin which has been soaked in Kirsch-flavoured syrup. Surround it with a band of paper tied in place with string to prevent it drying during the cooking of the soufflé. Prepare a fruit purée soufflé mixture from a fruit to choice and pour it into the centre of the Savarin.

Cook in the usual manner, remove the paper and serve immediately.

4493 Soufflé à la d'Orléans
Prepare a cream-type soufflé mixture containing small pieces of Jeanne d'Arc biscuits (these are similar to a Reims biscuit) saturated with peach liqueur and Kirsch; and 25 g (1 oz) each of glacé cherries and angelica cut in small dice.

Cook in the usual manner.

4494 Soufflé Palmyre
Prepare a cream-type soufflé mixture flavoured with vanilla and arrange in the mould in layers alternating with Finger Biscuits (4325) saturated with Anisette and Kirsch.

Cook in the usual manner.

4495 Soufflé Paulette
Prepare a cream-type soufflé mixture flavoured with vanilla and containing very small macaroons saturated with Kirsch. Cook in the usual manner.

Serve accompanied with a dish of chilled strawberries covered with a purée of fresh raspberries.

4496 Soufflé Praliné
Prepare a cream-type soufflé mixture flavoured with vanilla and made with 60 g (2 oz) of Almond Pralin (4353) which has been infused in advance in the milk.

When the mixture has been placed in the soufflé mould sprinkle the surface with either chopped toasted almonds or crushed Almond Pralin then cook in the usual manner.

4497 Soufflé Rothschild
Prepare a cream-type soufflé mixture containing 80 g ($2\frac{1}{2}$ oz) crystallized fruits cut in dice and macerated in Danziger Goldwasser (Danzig brandy) containing plenty of flecks of gold leaf; cook in the usual manner.

When about to serve, surround the top of the soufflé with a border of nice fresh strawberries or glacé cherries when strawberries are unobtainable.

4498 Soufflé à la Royale
Prepare a cream-type soufflé mixture flavoured with vanilla; arrange in layers in the mould alternating with layers of Finger Biscuits (4325) saturated with Kirsch which are then sprinkled with small dice of crystallized fruit such as pineapple, cherries and angelica also macerated in Kirsch beforehand.

Cook in the usual manner.

4499 Soufflé à la Vanille—Vanilla Soufflé
Prepare a cream-type soufflé mixture using milk which has been infused beforehand with a vanilla pod. Cook in the usual manner.

4500 Soufflé aux Violettes—Violet Soufflé
Prepare a cream-type soufflé mixture flavoured with vanilla and containing some crushed crystallized violets.

When the mixture has been placed in the mould, arrange a circle of large crystallized violets on top.

Cook in the usual manner.

SWEET SUBRICS

4501 Sweet Subrics
Place in a pan 5 dl (18 fl oz or $2\frac{1}{4}$ U.S. cups) milk and 100 g ($3\frac{1}{2}$ oz) sugar, flavour with vanilla and bring to the boil. Rain in 125 g ($4\frac{1}{2}$ oz) semolina and mix well; add 50 g (2 oz) butter and a few grains of salt and mix in. Cover with a lid and cook in a moderate oven for 25 minutes.

On removing from the oven, add and mix in 6 egg yolks then spread the mixture on a buttered tray approximately 2 cm ($\frac{4}{5}$ in) thick. Coat the surface with a little butter to prevent a skin forming and allow to cool.

Cut the mixture into rounds 6 cm (2 in) in diameter; heat some clarified butter in a frying pan, place in the rounds of semolina and colour them golden brown on both sides.

Arrange in a circle on a dish and in the centre of each Subric place a spoonful of firm redcurrant or quince jelly.

TIMBALES

4502 Timbale d'Aremberg
Line a buttered Charlotte mould with a layer of fairly firm Brioche Paste. Fill it with layers of quarters of pears cooked in vanilla-flavoured syrup and kept a little firm, alternating with layers of a fairly stiff purée of apricots cooked with sugar.

Close up the timbale with a layer of the same pastry, moisten the edges and seal well together. Make a small hole in the top for the steam to escape and bake in a moderate oven for approximately 40 minutes.

On removing the Timbale from the oven, turn it out on to a dish and coat with Apricot Sauce flavoured with Maraschino.

4503 Timbale Bourdaloue
Prepare a dry Sweet Paste containing 125 g ($4\frac{1}{2}$ oz) finely chopped almonds per 500 g (1 lb 2 oz) flour. Use this paste to line a buttered timbale mould and fill it with alternate layers of various stewed fruits alternating with layers of Frangipane Cream. Cover the timbale with a layer of the same paste, seal the edges well, make a hole in the top for the steam to escape and bake in a moderate oven.

When cooked, demould the Timbale on to a dish and coat with a thickened vanilla-flavoured apricot syrup.

4504 Timbale Favart
Cook a Brioche in a Richelieu mould. Hollow it out to form a Timbale as explained in the recipe for Timbale Marie-Louise. Glaze the outside with apricot jam and decorate with crystallized fruits.

The filling of this Timbale is comprised of whole or halves of fruit and nice vanilla-flavoured candied chestnuts; these are bound together with

Kirsch-flavoured apricot syrup containing a quarter its volume of puréed remnants of candied chestnuts.

This prepared filling should be placed in the timbale just before being served.

4505 Timbale Marie-Louise

Take a stale Genoise which has been cooked in a Charlotte mould; trim the ends neatly then remove a thick slice from the bottom. Slide the blade of a thin knife 2 cm ($\frac{2}{5}$ in) in from the top outside edge and cut completely round from top to bottom so as to remove the inside in one piece in the shape of a cylinder—so leaving a barrel-shape open at both ends. Coat the bottom slice with apricot jam and place it in the centre of the serving dish coated side upwards; place on top the emptied Genoise. Fill with quarters of peaches mixed with a purée of strawberries flavoured with Kirsch. Cover the top of the filling with meringue and place in the oven to colour.

To serve: surround the Timbale with crescent shapes cut from the removed piece of Genoise, sprinkled with icing sugar and glazed in the oven. Arrange these overlapping and alternately with slices of pineapple of the same size and shape. On this border set a circle of large strawberries.

4506 Timbale Montmorency

Cook a Brioche in a Charlotte mould of the required size.

When it is quite cold, remove the inside leaving a case of a thickness at the bottom and sides of 1½ cm (½ in.). Brush the outside with apricot jam cooked to the small thread stage and decorate it with pale baked shapes of puff pastry such as crescents, diamonds, small rounds etc.

To serve: Fill this Timbale with stoned cherries cooked in a light syrup then drained and mixed with some raspberry-flavoured redcurrant jelly.

4507 Timbale à la Parisienne

Cook a Brioche in a Charlotte mould and when it is quite cold remove the inside as in the preceding recipe; brush the outside with apricot jam and decorate with crystallized fruits.

To serve: pour into this Timbale a filling composed of the following: peeled apples and pears, peaches and apricots all cut in quarters and cooked in vanilla-flavoured syrup; pineapple cut in large dice; diamonds of angelica; halves of almonds; fresh grapes and seedless raisins soaked and swollen in warm water. This filling should be mixed with a Kirsch-flavoured apricot purée before being poured into the Timbale.

HOT FRUIT DISHES

ABRICOTS—APRICOTS

Whether fresh, canned or bottled, apricots should always be skinned for sweet dishes. When using canned or bottled apricots it is advisable to re-cook them if necessary as they are sometimes inclined to be a little too firm.

4508 Abricots Bourdaloue

Prepare a lightly baked flan case and cover the bottom with a layer of thin Frangipane Cream containing crushed macaroons. On top arrange halves of apricots poached in vanilla-flavoured syrup then cover these with a layer of the Frangipane Cream.

Sprinkle the surface with crushed macaroons and melted butter and glaze quickly.

Note: The above method is the usual procedure, but fruits *à la Bourdaloue* may be prepared in either of the following ways:

1) Arrange the fruit in a shallow timbale between two layers of Frangipane Cream, the top layer should then be lightly gratinated.
2) Arrange the fruit in the centre of a border of rice or semolina, cover it with the Frangipane Cream and gratinate as before.
3) Arrange the fruit in the centre of a border of Genoise coated with apricot jam; cover the fruit with the Frangipane Cream and gratinate.

4509 Abricots Colbert

Poach some very nice halves of apricots in a sugar syrup keeping them firm. Drain and dry them well; fill the cavities with Prepared Rice for sweet dishes (4470) and place together in pairs to re-form as whole fruits.

Flour, egg and breadcrumb them using very fine breadcrumbs then deep fry them at the last moment and drain. Stick a small piece of angelica into each apricot so as to imitate the stalk then arrange on a serviette.

Serve accompanied with Kirsch-flavoured Apricot Sauce.

4510 Abricots Condé

On a round dish prepare a border of vanilla-flavoured Prepared Rice for sweet dishes (4470) containing some diced crystallized fruits which have been macerated with Kirsch. This border may be moulded by hand or prepared in a buttered plain border mould.

On this border arrange apricots poached in syrup; decorate with crystallized fruits and coat with Kirsch-flavoured thickened apricot syrup.

4511 Abricots Cussy
Cover the flat side of soft macaroons with a layer of very finely cut Salpicon of fruit mixed with apricot purée. Place a nice half of poached apricot on each, coat with Italian meringue and arrange in a circle on a dish. Place in a warm oven for a few minutes to dry the meringue but without colouring it.

Serve accompanied with a Kirsch-flavoured Apricot Sauce.

4512 Abricots Gratinés
On a dish place a layer of thick purée of apples cooked with sugar, or a layer of semolina prepared in the same way as for Prepared Rice for sweet dishes (4470); the layer should be 2 cm ($\frac{4}{5}$ in) thick.

Arrange nice halves of apricots poached in sugar syrup on top and cover all over with Royal Icing Pralin (4353); dredge with icing sugar and place in a warm to moderate oven to lightly colour the pralin.

4513 Abricots Meringués
On a dish place a layer of vanilla-flavoured Prepared Rice for sweet dishes (4470); arrange halves of poached apricots on top. Cover with ordinary meringue and fashion dome or Charlotte shape; decorate with some of the same meringue, dredge with icing sugar and place in a warm oven to cook and colour the meringue.

On removing the dish from the oven, garnish the decoration with redcurrant jam and apricot jam.

4514 Abricots Sultane
Prepare a Genoise in a deep border mould. Using a little apricot jam stick it on to a base of cooked short pastry of the same size. Coat the outside with ordinary meringue and decorate it with some of the same meringue using a piping bag and small tube. Place in a moderate oven to colour.

When ready, fill the centre of the border with a vanilla-flavoured Prepared Rice for sweet dishes (4470), mixed with a little Frangipane Cream and some shredded pistachios; keep this mixture somewhat firm and mould it dome shape.

On this rice place some nice halves of apricots poached in vanilla-flavoured syrup and sprinkle them with chopped pistachios.

Serve accompanied with an almond-milk syrup finished with a hazelnut-sized piece of good butter.

ANANAS—PINEAPPLE

4515 Ananas Condé
Macerate some half slices of pineapple with Kirsch and sugar.

Arrange them overlapping in a circle on a border of Prepared Rice as indicated for Abricots Condé (4510). Decorate with glacé cherries and diamonds of angelica and coat with a thickened Kirsch-flavoured apricot syrup.

4516 Ananas à la Créole
Cook a peeled pineapple in a Kirsch-flavoured sugar syrup; cut in two halves vertically then cut each half across into thin even slices. Use these slices to line a dome-shaped mould and fill with vanilla-flavoured Prepared Rice (4470), leaving an empty space in the middle. Fill this with the trimmings of the pineapple, some custard apple and bananas, all cut in dice and cooked in syrup.

When set, demould on to a round dish; decorate the top with large leaves of thinly cut angelica and surround the base of the mould with bananas poached in Kirsch-flavoured sugar syrup.

Serve accompanied with thickened Kirsch-flavoured apricot syrup.

BANANES—BANANAS

4517 Bananes Bourdaloue
Skin the bananas and cook them gently in vanilla-flavoured syrup.

Finish as indicated for Abricots Bourdaloue (4508).

4518 Bananes Condé
Cook the bananas in vanilla-flavoured syrup then finish as indicated for Abricots Condé (4510).

4519 Bananes Flambées
Skin the bananas, cut them in half lengthways and sprinkle with caster sugar. Dip in flour then in beaten egg and again in flour then cook them in clarified butter.

Arrange the bananas side by side on an oval dish; sprinkle with sugar, pour over some warmed Kirsch and set it alight when bringing to the table.

4520 Bananes Meringuées
Cook the bananas in vanilla-flavoured syrup. Finish as indicated for Abricots Meringués either leaving the bananas whole or cutting them into slices.

4521 Bananes à la Norvégienne
Cut a slice lengthways from the top of the unpeeled bananas and remove the inside without damaging the skin.

Fill the emptied skins with banana ice and cover this quickly with rum-flavoured Italian meringue using a piping bag and tube.

Arrange the prepared bananas on a serving dish; place this in a shallow tray of crushed ice and place in a very hot oven to quickly colour the meringue.

4522 Bananes Soufflées
Cut the top quarter off the length of unskinned bananas and remove the insides without damaging the skins. Pass the flesh through a sieve and add it to a cream soufflé mixture; fold in the required number of stiffly beaten egg whites and fill this mixture into the empty banana skins.

Arrange in a circle on a dish and cook in the oven for 6 minutes.

CERISES—CHERRIES

4523 Cerises Jubilée
Remove the stones from some nice large cherries then poach the cherries in syrup; remove and place them in small silver timbales. Reduce the syrup and thicken it with diluted arrowroot using $\frac{1}{2}$ tbs per 3 dl ($\frac{1}{2}$ pt or $2\frac{1}{4}$ U.S. cups) syrup. Instead of the syrup, redcurrant jelly may be used.

Coat the cherries with the sauce, pour $\frac{1}{2}$ tablespoon of warmed Kirsch into each timbale and set alight when bringing them to the table.

4524 Cerises Valéria
Prepare some tartlet cases using Sweet Paste. When cooked and cold, fill each with vanilla ice-cream and cover with vanilla-flavoured Italian meringue using a piping bag and tube.

On top of the meringue arrange some stoned cherries previously cooked in sweetened Bordeaux wine.

Arrange the tartlets on a dish, place this on a shallow tray of crushed ice and place into a hot oven to dry the meringue.

As soon as they come from the oven, coat the cherries with redcurrant syrup, sprinkle with chopped pistachio nuts and serve arranged on a serviette.

4525 Flan de Cerises à la Danoise
Line a buttered flan ring with good Short Paste (4309). Fill it with stoned fresh cherries when in season or well drained canned cherries; in either case the cherries should previously be sprinkled with spiced sugar.

Place in a basin, 60 g (2 oz) sugar, 60 g (2 oz) softened butter, 60 g (2 oz) ground almonds and 1 egg; mix together well.

Cover the cherries with this mixture filling it to the top of the flan then cook in a moderate oven. Allow to cool.

Brush the surface with redcurrant jelly then glaze it with some rum-flavoured water icing.

4526 Flan de Cerises Meringué
Line a buttered flan ring with good Short Paste (4309); prick the bottom and fill with stoned cherries as for an ordinary flan. Cover with uncooked egg custard mixture and bake in the usual manner.

When cooked, allow to cool then cover the top with ordinary meringue; decorate by piping with meringue and replace in the oven to dry and colour the meringue.

Note: All the other kinds of fruit flans can be finished as meringued flans excepting those where the fruits are not cooked in the flan case, such as strawberries etc.

4527 NECTARINES

Nectarines can be prepared in accordance with any of the recipes given for peaches, thus it is not considered necessary to give any special ones here.

ORANGES AND TANGERINES

4528 Oranges, or Mandarines à la Norvégienne
Cut off the tops of the oranges or tangerines and remove the fruit by means of a spoon. Fill the skins with orange or tangerine ice according to which fruit is being used, then cover the ice with a small decoration of Italian meringue using a piping bag and tube.

Arrange on a dish and place this on a tray of crushed ice. Colour the meringue quickly under the salamander.

4529 Mandarines à la Palikare
Cut off the tops of the tangerines; carefully remove the fruit in segments and trim them of all skin and pith.

Fill the emptied skins with Prepared Rice for sweet dishes (4470) lightly coloured and flavoured with saffron; put some of the same mixture into a small dome-shaped mould. When set, turn out the mould on to a sculpted rice base placed in the centre of a round dish.

Cover the mould of rice with the segments of tangerine, coat with lightly thickened apricot syrup and surround with the filled tangerines, rice side upwards.

4530 Soufflé d'Oranges, or Soufflé de Mandarines en Surprise
Empty the oranges or tangerines without damaging the skin.

Half fill the emptied skins with either orange or tangerine ice according to which fruit is being used; cover this with a soufflé mixture of the same flavour.

Arrange the filled fruit on a dish and place it on a tray of crushed ice. Cook in the oven for 6 minutes for oranges or 4 minutes for tangerines.

PECHES—PEACHES

4531 Pêches Bourdaloue
Cut the skinned peaches in half, poach them in vanilla-flavoured syrup and finish in the same way as for Abricots Bourdaloue (4508).

4532 Pêches Condé
Proceed as indicated for Abricots Condé (4510).

4533 Pêches Cussy
Proceed as indicated for Abricots Cussy (4511).

4534 Pêches Flambées
These can be prepared in either of the following ways:

A) Poach the whole skinned peaches in vanilla-flavoured syrup and arrange them in a timbale. Thicken the syrup with diluted arrowroot and pour over the peaches. Add a little warmed Kirsch to the dish and set alight when bringing it to the table.

B) Poach the peaches as above and arrange them on a purée of fresh strawberries. Add a little warmed Kirsch and set alight when bringing it to the table.

4535 Pêches Gratinées
This is prepared in the same way as for Abricots Gratinés (4512).

4536 Pêches Impératrice
Cover the bottom of a timbale with Prepared Rice for sweet dishes (4470) flavoured with Kirsch and Maraschino.

Arrange halves of skinned peaches poached in vanilla-flavoured syrup on the rice and cover them with a thin layer of the same rice. On this spread a layer of Apricot Sauce and sprinkle with crushed macaroons.

Place in a warm to moderate oven for 10–12 minutes but do not allow the surface to gratinate.

4537 Pêches Meringuées
Prepare a lightly-baked flan case. Cover the bottom with Frangipane Cream mixed with some Pralin (4354) and arrange whole or halves of poached skinned peaches on top.

Cover with ordinary meringue and finish as indicated for Abricots Meringués (4513).

4538 Pêches Maintenon
Bake a Finger Biscuit mixture (4325) in a dome-shaped mould and allow to cool. Cut it into thin slices horizontally and coat each with Frangipane Cream containing a fine Salpicon of crystallized fruits and some toasted chopped almonds.

Place the slices back in the same order so as to re-form it, coat all over with Italian meringue and decorate with some of the same meringue using a piping bag and tube. Place in the oven to dry the meringue.

Place on a dish and surround with a circle of nice halves of skinned peaches poached in vanilla-flavoured syrup.

4539 Pêches à la Vanille
Cook some whole or halves of peaches in vanilla-flavoured syrup and arrange them in a timbale. Cover them half way up with the syrup which has been thickened with arrowroot, lightly coloured pink and flavoured with Crème de Vanille liqueur.

Surround with slices of a Brioche cut in the shape of a cockscomb and glazed with Royal Icing Pralin (4353).

The best way to poach peaches is as follows: select peaches which are just ripe, dip them into boiling water then immediately plunge them into ice water. If they are at the correct stage of ripeness the skin can be easily removed by the simple pressure of the fingers.

Now place them into a shallow pan and cover with hot syrup at 28° on the saccharometer. If they are to be served hot, leave them on the stove but do not allow to boil.

If the peaches are to be served cold, take them out of the syrup when they are ready and drain on a sieve.

For restaurant service where the peaches will be needed for a quick service it is sufficient after they have been skinned to place them on an enamelled or similar tray, then sprinkle them with sugar and keep in the refrigerator.

For peaches which are to be served sugared, the dipping into ice water after removing from the boiling water has the effect of keeping them fresh for several hours and prevents discoloration. It is this point which is so important for service in large *à la Carte* restaurants.

POIRES—PEARS

4540 Poires Bourdaloue
If the pears are of medium size, cut them in half; if

they are large they should be cut into quarters and well trimmed. They are cooked in vanilla-flavoured syrup then prepared in exactly the same way as for Abricots Bourdaloue (4508).

The notes given at the end of that recipe are equally applicable to pears as to all other kinds of fruit which are suitable for this preparation.

4541 Poires Condé

Very small pears which are carefully peeled and shaped are most suitable for this preparation. Those of medium size should be cut in half. Cook them in vanilla-flavoured syrup then proceed as for Abricots Condé (4510).

4542 Poires à l'Impératrice

Cut the pears in quarters, trim them neatly and poach in vanilla-flavoured syrup.

Arrange them in a shallow timbale between two layers of vanilla-flavoured Prepared Rice for sweet dishes (4470) and finish as for Pêches Impératrice (4536).

4543 Poires à la Parisienne

Cook some Genoise mixture in a flan ring and when it is cold, saturate it with Kirsch-flavoured syrup.

Mould some Prepared Rice for sweet dishes (4470) dome-shape in the centre of this Genoise base and surround it with halves of pears cooked in vanilla-flavoured syrup, standing them upright against the rice.

Encircle each half of pear with a piped border of meringue using a star tube, and pipe a nice rose shape of the same meringue on top of the rice; colour in a hot oven.

On removing from the oven, brush the pears with fairly thick apricot syrup and surround them with a circle of glacé cherries.

4544 Poires Sultane

Cut the pears in halves or quarters, trim them neatly and cook in a vanilla-flavoured syrup.

Finish in the same way as indicated for Abricots à la Sultane (4514).

4545 Timbale de Poires à la Valenciennes

Fill a buttered Charlotte mould two-thirds full with Savarin Paste. Allow to prove then bake in a hot oven.

When cold, cut off the top to serve as a lid and place it aside. Hollow out the centre leaving only the crust and brush the outside with thickened apricot syrup.

Decorate the outside of the Timbale with alternate lines of sugar crystals and very green pistachios. Brush the lid with thickened apricot syrup.

Cut some ripe pears such as Duchesse, Beurre, Doyenne or other similar variety, into quarters; peel them, then cut into fairly thick slices and cook them in butter in the same way as for an Apple Charlotte. When soft, mix in a quarter their quantity of apricot purée and flavour it with Crème de Vanille liqueur.

Fill the Timbale with this mixture, cover with the lid and place on a hot dish.

Serve accompanied with Kirsch-flavoured Apricot Sauce.

POMMES—APPLES

4546 Beignets de Pommes—Apple Fritters

Take some pippin apples which are the best variety for making fritters; remove the core and pips with a $1\frac{1}{2}$ cm ($\frac{3}{5}$ in) corer or column cutter. Peel the apples then cut them into round slices 7–8 mm ($\frac{1}{3}$ in) thick. Sprinkle with caster sugar and either Brandy or Rum and allow to macerate for 20 minutes.

A few minutes before being required, dry the slices lightly, dip them into a thin frying batter and deep fry in hot fat. Drain, place on a tray and dredge with icing sugar. Glaze quickly and serve arranged on a serviette.

4547 Pommes au Beurre

Remove the core from some Calville or pippin apples; peel them and place in boiling water containing a little lemon juice, for 2 minutes. Remove them and arrange in a shallow buttered pan; add a few tablespoons of vanilla-flavoured syrup, cover with a lid and cook gently in the oven.

When ready, arrange each apple on a small round of Brioche dredged with icing sugar and glazed in the oven.

Mix together equal amounts of softened butter and caster sugar, flavour with Brandy and fill the empty centre of each apple with this butter.

Coat with the cooking syrup which has been lightly thickened with apricot purée.

4548 Pommes Bonne-Femme—Baked Apples

Remove the core from pippin apples using a corer or column cutter; cut a small incision through the skin around the middle of the apples.

Arrange them on a tray, fill the centre of each with a mixture of butter and caster sugar, add a little water to the tray and cook the apples gently in the oven.

Serve these apples as they are.

4549 Pommes Bourdaloue

Cut the apples into quarters and peel them; trim

neatly then cook them in vanilla-flavoured syrup keeping them slightly firm. Finish in the same way as indicated for Abricots Bourdaloue (4508).

4550 Pommes en Charlotte
See Charlotte aux Pommes.

4551 Pommes Châtelaine
Select some medium-sized apples, peel them then cook as for Pommes Bonne-Femme.

When cooked, place them on a buttered tray, fill the centres with diced glacé cherries mixed with apricot purée.

Cover with thin Frangipane Cream, sprinkle with finely crushed macaroons and biscuits, then sprinkle with melted butter and gratinate in a hot oven.

4552 Pommes Chevreuse
Mould a base of Semolina Croquette mixture (4405) on a dish. Arrange on top, close together as a border, quarters of apple cooked in vanilla-flavoured syrup. Fill the centre with a Salpicon of crystallized fruit and seedless raisins mixed with apricot purée and cover this with a thin layer of semolina mixture.

Cover the whole dome shape with ordinary meringue; sprinkle with chopped pistachios, dredge with icing sugar and colour in a moderate oven.

On removing from the oven, decorate the top with a rose-shaped circle of elongated diamonds of angelica. Place a small apple cooked in pink syrup on top and surround the dish with quarters of apple—half of them cooked in ordinary syrup and the others in pink syrup; alternate the colours.

4553 Pommes Condé
Poach some large peeled and trimmed quarters of apples in vanilla-flavoured syrup.

Arrange on a border of rice and decorate with glacé cherries and angelica in the same way as for Abricots Condé (4510).

4554 Pommes Gratinées
Arrange some quarters of apple poached in vanilla-flavoured syrup on a base of apples cooked as for an Apple Charlotte and kept fairly stiff. Cover with a layer of fairly thin Royal Icing Pralin (4353), dredge with icing sugar and place in the oven to dry and lightly colour the pralin.

4555 Pommes Impératrice
This is prepared in the same way as Pêches Impératrice (4536) using quarters of apple poached in vanilla-flavoured syrup.

4556 Pommes Irène
Peel some nice apples and half cook them in a light syrup. Allow to become cold then scoop out the insides carefully leaving them in the shape of cases.

Pass the insides of the apples through a sieve, sweeten it with vanilla sugar and place a layer of this purée in the bottom of the emptied apples. Fill with vanilla ice-cream mixed with a third its volume of a cooked purée of plums.

Cover with Kirsch-flavoured Italian meringue; colour the meringue quickly in the oven and serve immediately.

4557 Pommes Meringués
Arrange some quarters of apple poached in vanilla-flavoured syrup on a base of Rice Croquette mixture (4404). Instead of the rice, a base of apples cooked as for Apple Charlotte may be used.

Cover with ordinary meringue smoothing it dome shape or in the form of a Charlotte; decorate with some of the same meringue using a piping bag and tube. Dredge with icing sugar and colour in a moderate oven.

4558 Pommes à la Moscovite
Choose some nice even-shaped apples; peel them three-quarters of the way from the top then cut out the centres so as to form a kind of case.

Poach these cases in a light syrup keeping them slightly firm then drain them well and arrange on a dish.

Fill the apple cases one-third full with a purée made from the insides, then fill to the tops with a soufflé mixture made from apples and flavoured with Kümmel.

Cook in a moderate oven for 20 minutes.

4559 Pommes à la Parisienne
Preceed in exactly the same way as indicated for Poires à la Parisienne (4543).

4560 Pommes à la Portugaise
Prepare the apples as for Pommes à la Moscovite. Fill them with a stiff Frangipane Cream mixed with some grated orange zest, crushed macaroons, and washed currants and sultanas, soaked to swell in lukewarm Curaçao-flavoured syrup, then drained.

Arrange the apples thus prepared on a base of Semolina Croquette mixture (4405) and place in the oven for 10 minutes. Finish by coating the apples with melted redcurrant jelly containing some well blanched Julienne of orange zest.

4561 Rabottes de Pommes, or Douillons Normande—Baked Apple Dumplings
Prepare the apples as for baking (4548) then en-

close each in a square piece of good Short Paste. Place a fancy round of the same paste on top, brush with eggwash and score with the point of a small knife.

Bake in a hot oven for 15 minutes.

4562 Flan de Pommes à la Batelière
Line a flan ring with good Short Paste and half fill with apples prepared as for an Apple Charlotte.

Cover this dome shape with some very soft Prepared Rice for sweet dishes (4470) into which has been carefully mixed 4 stiffly beaten egg whites per 500 g (1 lb 2 oz) of the cooked rice.

Bake the flan in the usual manner; when cooked, dredge it well with icing sugar and glaze with a red hot iron.

4563 Flan de Pommes Chaud Ninon
Prepare a lightly-baked flan case and fill it dome shape with apples cooked as for an Apple Charlotte. On top, arrange quarters of apples, half of them cooked in ordinary syrup and the others in pink syrup. Lightly brush the apples with reduced white syrup.

4564 Various Apple Flans
By slightly altering the previous recipes it is possible to obtain a large variety of flans and tarts which are generally served as luncheon sweets.

They are usually prepared by one of the following methods:

A) Cover the bottom of the case with apples cooked as for an Apple Charlotte. Cover with a layer of fresh fruit such as apricots, plums etc, either on their own or mixed. The flans can then be finished in the usual manner by either coating with a layer of apricot syrup or with melted redcurrant jelly; by covering with meringue and completing in the same way as other meringued flans, or by dredging with icing sugar and colouring in a hot oven.

B) Cover the bottom of the lightly-baked flan case with apples cooked as for an Apple Charlotte and then cover this with a purée of candied chestnuts flavoured with Rum. Garnish with fruit and finish as before.

C) Proceed as in B above but replace the purée of chestnuts with a cold Mousse of candied chestnuts.

These variations can be extended and the few directions given should suffice for an intelligent and adaptable cook. There is no need to specify for example, that the apple purée can be replaced by a purée of pears or other such fruit.

MISCELLANEOUS HOT SWEETS

4565 Mince Pies
Line some large buttered straight sided tartlet cases with Ordinary Short Paste or with Puff Paste trimmings. Place a little mincemeat in each, cover with a thin round of puff paste having a small hole in the centre and seal well to the sides. Brush with egg-wash and bake in a hot oven.

Preparation of Mincemeat:
Ingredients: 500 g (1 lb 2 oz) chopped beef kidney suet, 600 g (1 lb 5 oz) diced cold cooked fillet of beef, 500 g (1 lb 2 oz) seedless raisins, 500 g (1 lb 2 oz) each of currants and sultanas, 500 g (1 lb 2 oz) mixed peel, 250 g (9 oz) peeled and chopped apple, the grated rind and juice of 1 orange, 25 g (1 oz) mixed spice, 1 dl (3½ oz or ½ U.S. cup) each of Brandy, Madeira and Rum.
Method: Mix all the ingredients together, place in a stone jar, cover tightly and allow to macerate for one month.

4566 Omelette Célestine
Prepare a 2 egg omelette filling it with either a cream such as Frangipane Cream, a fairly stiff purée of fruit cooked with sugar, or with jam.

Make a second, slightly larger omelette, fill it with a different filling than that used in the first, then place the first omelette inside the larger and fold over in the usual manner.

Dredge with icing sugar and either glaze in the oven or mark trellis-fashion with a red hot iron.

4567 Oeufs à la Religieuse
Lightly bake a tall-sided flan case of a size appropriate to the number of portions of eggs to be placed inside. Coat the inside with Royal Icing Pralin (4353) and place to dry in a moderate oven.

In the meantime poach the required number of fresh eggs in boiling milk sweetened with 250 g (9 oz) sugar per 1 litre (1¾ pt or 4½ U.S. cups) of milk. Whilst the yolks are still soft, remove them and drain, then arrange them in the prepared flan case. Between each egg place a small slice of pineapple cut to the shape of a cockscomb.

Thicken the milk in which the eggs were poached with 6 egg yolks and 5 eggs per 1 litre (1¾ pt or 4½ U.S. cups) of milk. Pass through a fine strainer and pour it over the eggs in the flan.

Place in a warm oven to cook and lightly colour the custard.

4568 Schâleth à la Juive
Line a well greased iron pan with a thin layer of ordinary Noodle Paste. Fill three-quarters full

with the following mixture, which is sufficient for a 2 litre ($3\frac{1}{2}$ pt or 9 U.S. cups) capacity pan.

800 g ($1\frac{3}{4}$ lb) thick apple purée cooked with sugar, 200 g (7 oz) seedless raisins, 300 g (11 oz) currants and sultanas previously soaked and swollen in warm water, $\frac{1}{2}$ tbs each of chopped lemon and orange zest, a pinch of nutmeg, 125 g ($4\frac{1}{2}$ oz) caster sugar, 6 egg yolks, 4 eggs and $1\frac{1}{2}$ dl (5 fl oz or $\frac{5}{8}$ U.S. cup) Malaga wine: mix all these ingredients well together.

Cover the pan with a round of the same paste sealing it well to the edges. Make a hole in the centre for the steam to escape and cook in a moderate oven for 50 minutes.

When cooked, remove from the oven and allow to rest for 10 minutes before demoulding.

4569 Suprême de Fruits Gabrielle
Prepare 1) some apples cooked as for Apple Charlotte and mixed with whole eggs. Pour this into a buttered fancy border mould and cook *au Bain-marie* in the usual manner; 2) prepare a mixture of fruit, sufficient to fill the centre of the mould and composed of the following: cooked quarters of pears, cubed pineapple, glacé cherries, angelica cut into leaves with a cutter and currants and sultanas previously soaked and swollen in syrup; place all these fruits in a shallow pan.

To each 5 dl (18 fl oz or $2\frac{1}{4}$ U.S. cups) of syrup from the pears, add 500 g (1 lb 2 oz) sugar and cook it until it reaches the hard ball stage; at this time add 1 dl ($3\frac{1}{2}$ fl oz or $\frac{1}{2}$ U.S. cup) very thick almond milk to prevent the sugar cooking any further. Pour it over the fruits then place on the stove to simmer very gently for 10 minutes.

Demould the apple border on to a suitable dish and surround it with a circle of crystallized cherries.

Finish the fruit away from the heat with a little very good butter then pour it into the centre of the mould; sprinkle with finely shredded skinned pistachios.

4570 English Fruit Pies
These are made in pie dishes.

Whatever kind of fruit is being used, clean and peel them as necessary. Some need to be sliced, some cut into quarters, and others can be left whole.

Place the fruit in the pie dish filling it more or less according to the kind of fruit. Sprinkle with caster sugar and if a firm fleshed fruit such as apples is being used, add a few tablespoons of water. This is optional and in any case is not necessary when using soft fruits.

Surround the dampened edge of the pie dish with a band of short paste 1 cm ($\frac{2}{5}$ in) wide. Cover with a sheet of the same paste and seal it to the band which has been moistened. Brush the top with water, sprinkle with sugar and bake in a moderately hot oven. Puff paste trimmings can also be used to cover the pie and in this case the surface should be brushed with eggwash.

All English fruit pies are made in this way and all kinds of fruit can be used even when they are still green such as unripe grapes and green gooseberries. Often two kinds of fruit are mixed to make a pie such as apple and cranberries, apple and rhubarb, apple and loganberries, apple and redcurrant, apple and blackcurrant etc.

These pies are served accompanied with a sauceboat of cream or custard.

COLD SWEETS

SAUCES AND ACCOMPANIMENTS FOR COLD SWEETS

Cold sweets allow of the following sauces:

1) Sauce Anglaise which can be flavoured to choice.
2) Syrups—apricot, plum, greengage, redcurrant etc. the flavour of which should always be enhanced by the addition of a liqueur in keeping with the fruit base of the syrup. Kirsch and Maraschino are particularly suitable for this purpose.
3) Purée of fresh fruit such as strawberries, raspberries, redcurrants etc. with the addition of a little caster sugar. These purées can be used on their own or mixed with an appropriate amount of whipped cream.
4) Crème Chantilly, flavoured to choice.

Finally, some cold sweets may be served with cherry sauce as in the following recipe.

4571 Sauce aux Cerises—Cherry Sauce
Slowly melt 500 g (1 lb 2 oz) raspberry-flavoured redcurrant jelly; pour it into a cold basin and add to it an equal quantity of the liquid from some freshly cooked stewed cherries, the juice of 2 blood oranges, a little ground ginger and a few drops of red colour sufficient to give the sauce a bright colour. Finish by adding 125 g ($4\frac{1}{2}$ oz) glacé cherries softened in a little lukewarm Kirsch-flavoured syrup.

BAVAROIS

The chilled cream sweet referred to under the name of Bavarois in various books on cookery used to be described as Fromage Bavarois on menus. It was subsequently shortened by eliminating the word Fromage since this was considered slightly coarse and unnecessary, but it still remains understood though not included.

The title Bavarois, although sanctioned by usage seems illogical; the title Moscovite appears more logical and suitable. As a result of this, instead of writing Bavarois au Café etc. on the menu, it could be Moscovite à la Vanille, Moscovite au Café etc.

Bavarois are made in two ways: 1) by using a cream mixture; 2) by using a fruit mixture.

4572 Cream Bavarois Mixture
Mix together in a pan, 500 g (1 lb 2 oz) caster sugar and 16 egg yolks and moisten with 1 litre (1¾ pt or 4½ U.S. cups) boiling milk in which a vanilla pod has previously been infused. Add 25 g (1 oz) soaked and drained gelatine, place on the stove and cook it gently until the mixture coats the spoon but without it coming to the boil.

Pass through a fine strainer into a basin and allow to cool stirring from time to time. When the mixture starts to thicken, mix in 1 litre (1¾ pt or 4½ U.S. cups) whipped cream, 100 g (3½ oz) caster sugar and 25 g (1 oz) vanilla sugar.

4573 Fruit Bavarois Mixture
Mix 5 dl (18 fl oz or 2¼ U.S. cups) fruit purée together with an equal quantity of syrup at 30° on the saccharometer. Add the juice of 3 lemons, 30 g (1 oz) soaked and drained and melted gelatine passed through a cloth and 5 dl (18 fl oz or 2¼ U.S. cups) whipped cream.

Fruit Bavarois mixtures may contain some of the same fruit as used for the purée. The fruit in this case is added raw when it is strawberries, raspberries or redcurrants etc. or poached in syrup when it is a fleshy fruit such as pears, peaches, apricots etc.

4574 The Moulding and Presentation of Bavarois
Bavarois are usually moulded in funnel moulds which have been lightly coated inside with almond oil. When full they should be covered with a round piece of paper and allow to set either in crushed ice or in a refrigerator.

When required for serving the mould is plunged quickly into lukewarm water, dried, then turned out on to the serving dish.

Instead of oiling the mould a thin coating of light-coloured caramel can be used to line it; this gives an excellent appearance and taste to the Bavarois.

There is another way of presenting a Bavarois which can be recommended, this is to mould it in a timbale or deep silver dish which is then surrounded with crushed ice. In this case the Bavarois is not demoulded for serving thus the mixture can be made with less gelatine and therefore it becomes more delicate.

When made by this last method it is sometimes served accompanied with a dish of stewed fruit or fresh fruit salad. However, these accompaniments are more suitable for serving with certain cold puddings which have much the same appearance as a Bavarois.

Finally, whether the Bavarois is made in a mould or not it can be finished be decorating it with white or pink Crème Chantilly using a piping bag and tube or a paper cornet.

4575 Bavarois Clermont
Add 200 g (7 oz) of a purée of candied chestnuts to 1 litre (1¾ pt or 4½ U.S. cups) of vanilla Bavarois mixture and mould in the usual manner.

When it is demoulded surround the Bavarois with a circle of nice candied chestnuts.

4576 Bavarois Diplomate
Line a timbale mould with vanilla-flavoured Bavarois mixture; fill the centre with alternate even layers of chocolate and strawberry Bavarois.

4577 Bavarois My Queen
Line the Bavarois mould with a layer of fresh cream which has been slightly sweetened and mixed with a little melted gelatine. Fill with strawberry fruit Bavarois mixture containing some large strawberries which have been macerated with Kirsch.

When set, demould on to a dish and surround with a circle of large strawberries previously macerated with sugar and Kirsch.

4578 Bavarois à la Normande
Make a fruit Bavarois mixture from a fine purée of apples cooked with sugar and flavoured with rum adding 100 g (3½ oz) diced apples cooked in butter per 500 g (1 lb 2 oz) of purée. Finish with the required amount of very fresh, half whipped cream.

When set, demould on to a dish and surround with quarters of apples which have been poached in vanilla-flavoured syrup.

4579 Bavarois à la Religieuse
Line the mould with a mixture made by dissolving some chocolate in a well jellied syrup. Fill the

inside with vanilla-flavoured Bavarois mixture made with ordinary cream instead of whipped cream.

4580 Bavarois Rubanné
This kind of Bavarois is made with a mixture of several different coloured and flavoured mixtures arranged in the mould in separate layers. There are no precise rules to follow when making this Bavarois and it can be varied to include any of the various kinds of Bavarois mixtures.

4581 Various Cream Bavarois
Bavarois of almonds, Anisette, hazelnuts, coffee, chocolate, Kirsch, walnut, orange, violets etc are made in the same way as indicated for cream Bavarois. It is only the flavouring which alters.

4582 Various Fruit Bavarois
Following the recipe given for fruit Bavarois it is possible to make pineapple, apricot, strawberry, raspberry and melon Bavarois.

BLANC-MANGER—BLANCMANGE

Blancmange is very rarely made nowadays which is to be regretted because when well made it can be one of the best sweets served.

The blancmange which is served in England is entirely different from the kind that is made in other countries, but can be equally as good and it makes an excellent and wholesome sweet dish as may be seen from the recipe given below.

Correctly speaking and to be in accordance with its title, a blancmange should always be of a brilliant whiteness. However, for a long time now this composite name has lost its original significance; the adjective and the verb which comprise the name have become merged into one and it now represents only a general term which is applied equally to coloured blancmanges. The mistake in so far as the French language is concerned, is very old, since the verbal error dates from before the time of Carême; perhaps it should be forgotten and allowed to fade away.

4583 Blanc-manger à la Française—French Blancmange
Remove the skins from 500 g (1 lb 2 oz) sweet almonds and from 4 or 5 bitter almonds; place them to soak in cold water so as to whiten them.

Pound them as finely as possible, adding 8 dl (1 pt 8 fl oz or 3½ U.S. cups) of filtered water a spoonful at a time. Strain it through a cloth twisting it firmly.

Dissolve 200 g (7 oz) loaf sugar in this almond milk which will be approximately 7 dl (1 pt 4 fl oz or 3 U.S. cups); add 30 g (1 oz) gelatine which has been soaked, drained and dissolved in a little lukewarm syrup. Pass through a piece of muslin and flavour it to choice.

To mould the blancmange pour it into an oiled funnel mould, allow it to set then demould in the same way as for a Bavarois.

Note: In the preparation of almond milk the modern method to replace that given above, which is that of the kitchen of long ago, is to pound the almonds with just a few spoonfuls of water and some very thin cream.

4584 Fruit Blancmanges and Liqueur Blancmanges
All kinds of fruit reduced to a purée can be used in the preparation of these blancmanges. Use equal quantities of the fruit purée and the mixture as given for French Blancmange, and keeping the amount of gelatine the same.

These blancmanges take the name of the fruit used e.g. strawberry, raspberry, apricot or peach blancmange.

Blancmanges with liqueur are made in the same way using ½ dl (2 fl oz or ¼ U.S. cup) of the selected liqueur per 1 litre (1¾ pt or 4½ U.S. cups) blancmange mixture. The most suitable liqueurs are Kirsch, Maraschino and Rum. Chocolate blancmange and coffee blancmange are made in the same way as above but the aroma of the coffee does not go so well with that of the almonds as do the other flavourings.

4585 Blanc-Mangers Rubannés—Ribboned Blancmanges
These are prepared in the same way as Bavarois Rubanné by placing alternate layers of plain, and various colours and flavours of blancmange in the mould, arranging them in neat, even layers.

Note: These blancmange mixtures can also be poured into silver timbales, fine porcelain dishes or in deep dishes; by doing this it is possible to reduce the amount of gelatine used which is solely for setting the mixture. This will result in a finer and more delicate result and is quite easy to do since when prepared in this manner they do not have to be demoulded.

In this book *Le Cuisinier Parisien*, Carême recommends adding a quarter its volume of very good and fresh half whipped cream to the blancmange mixture just as it is beginning to thicken. This recommendation is quite valuable and is worth following.

4586 Blanc-manger à l'Anglaise—English Blancmange
Place 1 litre (1¾ pt or 4½ U.S. cups) milk to boil with 125 g (4½ oz) sugar; pour this on to 125

g (4½ oz) cornflour which has been diluted with 2½ dl (9 fl oz or 1⅛ U.S. cups) cold milk. Mix with a whisk to make it smooth then place on the stove and stir continuously for a few minutes.

Remove from the stove and flavour to choice. Whilst the mixture is still very hot, pour it into a mould which has previously been rinsed out with a light syrup—this is used to give a smooth shiny appearance to the blancmange when it is demoulded.

Allow to set and when very cold, turn out and serve either as it is or accompanied with a dish of stewed fruit.

CHARLOTTES

4587 Charlotte à l'Arlequine

Place a round piece of white paper in the bottom of a Charlotte mould; line the sides with finger-shaped pieces of Genoise glazed with pink, white and green pistachio coloured fondant, arranging them alternately and placing them very closely together with their glazed sides to the mould. Meanwhile, prepare four different Bavarois mixtures—strawberry, chocolate, pistachio and apricot—and set them in flan rings placed on oiled sheets of paper. When set, cut them into cubes and mix them into some slightly liquid ordinary cream Bavarois mixture. Pour this into the prepared mould and allow to set in the refrigerator.

When about to serve the Charlotte, demould it on to a dish, remove the piece of paper and replace it with a thin round piece of Genoise previously glazed with fondant and decorated with crystallized fruits.

4588 Charlotte Carmen

Line a Charlotte mould with ice wafers then fill it with the following mixture; 250 g (9 oz) purée of tomatoes cooked with sugar, 125 g (4½ oz) purée of red pimentoes cooked with sugar, a small pinch of ground ginger, 100 g (3½ oz) diced candied ginger; the juice of 3 lemons, 3 dl (½ pt or 1¼ U.S. cups) hot syrup at 32° on the saccharometer; 10 leaves of soaked and melted gelatine. Mix all the ingredients together, leave to thicken then mix in 1 litre (1¾ pt or 4½ U.S. cups) whipped cream.

4589 Charlotte Chantilly

Prepare the Charlotte by attaching ice wafers standing up and around a cooked short pastry base, with either apricot syrup cooked to the soft ball stage or with sugar cooked to the hard crack stage. To assist in doing this it is possible to use a Charlotte mould placing it on the piece of pastry and removing it when the wafers are firmly attached.

Fill with sweetened whipped cream flavoured with vanilla moulding it pyramid shape. Finish by decorating with some of the same cream coloured pale pink, using a piping bag and tube or paper cornet.

4590 Baquet and Panier Chantilly

The *Baquet* is a tub which is made by attaching well trimmed Finger Biscuits (4325) standing up and around a cooked short pastry base; use sugar cooked to the hard crack stage to attach the biscuits. At opposite sides place one biscuit which is taller than the other and with a round hole cut into the top with a small pastry cutter. Surround the tub with thin bands made of chocolate marzipan to imitate the iron hoops encircling the tub.

The *Panier* is a basket made in the same way but with biscuits all of the same height and without any bands of marzipan encircling it. Use sugar cooked to the hard crack stage to affix a plaited handle made of pulled sugar and decorated with some flowers made of pulled sugar.

Both the tub and basket are filled with whipped cream sweetened with sugar and flavoured with vanilla then decorated with pink whipped cream in the same way as the Charlotte Chantilly.

4591 Charlotte Colinette

Line the bottom and sides of a Charlotte mould with thin paper then cover this with very dry and very small meringues. Fill with Crème Chantilly flavoured with vanilla and containing some crystallized violets.

When the Charlotte is demoulded, decorate the top with some nice crystallized violets, sticking them on with sugar cooked to the hard crack stage.

This sweet should be served cold but not frozen.

4592 Charlotte Montreuil

Line the bottom and sides of a Charlotte mould with Finger Biscuits (4325) and fill with a Bavarois mixture made of 4 dl (14 fl oz or 1¾ U.S. cups) peach purée per 1 litre (1¾ pt or 4½ U.S. cups) cream Bavarois mixture, and the usual amount of whipped cream.

Add some sweetened slices of ripe peaches to the mixture when about to pour it into the mould.

4593 Charlotte Normande

Line a Charlotte mould with meringues of the same size and shape of finger biscuits. Fill with well reduced apples cooked as for Apple Charlotte.

Demould on to a dish, coat completely with Crème Chantilly and decorate with some of the same cream.

4594 Charlotte Opéra
Line a Charlotte mould with ice wafers and fill with a vanilla Bavarois mixture containing a quarter its amount of a fine purée of candied chestnuts and a Salpicon of crystallized fruit previously macerated with Maraschino.

4595 Charlotte Plombière
Line a Charlotte mould with either Finger Biscuits (4325) or ice wafers.

When required for serving, fill the mould with Plombière ice (4771) and turn out on to a serviette on a dish.

4596 Charlotte Renaissance
Cover the bottom of a Charlotte mould with a circle of white paper and line the sides with rectangular pieces of Genoise of the same height as the mould. Half of them should be glazed with white fondant, the others with pink and they should be arranged alternately with the glazed sides placed towards the mould.

Fill the mould with vanilla Bavarois mixture containing some sliced peeled apricots and peaches, diced pineapple and wild strawberries—all these fruits having been previously macerated with Kirsch. Place in the refrigerator to set.

After demoulding the Charlotte, peel off the paper and replace it with a slice of pineapple cut from the thickest part of the fruit and decorate it with crystallized fruits.

4597 Charlotte Russe
Line the bottom of a mould with Finger Biscuits (4325) cut heart shape and line the side with whole trimmed Finger Biscuits standing upright and close together.

Fill the centre with vanilla Bavarois mixture or with Pralin, coffee, orange or chocolate Bavarois. Fruit Bavarois such as apricot, pineapple, banana, peach or strawberry etc. can also be used for this Charlotte.

The actual flavour of the Bavarois or the main ingredient which characterizes the Charlotte must be included in the name used on the menu, e.g. Charlotte Russe à l'Orange, Charlotte Russe aux Fraises etc.

CREAMS

The creams which are served as cold sweets are divided into two separate types:

1) the cooked creams which are really only a variation of Crème Anglaise;
2) the creams derived from whipped and sweetened fresh cream of which Crème Chantilly is the example.

The cooked creams are prepared in either special dishes known as *Petits Pots* or in small silver or china dishes. They can be prepared in moulds in which case they are demoulded when very cold; these are known as Crèmes Renversées because they are turned out as against the first method where they are served in the dishes in which they were cooked.

However, the term Crème Renversèe has fallen into disuse and nowadays the term Crème Moulée (Moulded Cream) is generally used. Cream caramel is a perfect example of this type of cream.

The creams which are served in the dish in which they are cooked are more delicate than those which are turned out; this is because they do not require so many eggs. All the same, they are hardly ever served other than in the home like an English custard. For a more important lunch or dinner the moulded creams are to be preferred.

4598 Crème Moulée à la Vanille
Dissolve 200 g (7 oz) sugar in 1 litre (1¾ pt or 4½ U.S. cups) boiling milk; add a vanilla pod and allow to infuse for 20 minutes.

Beat 8 egg yolks and 4 eggs together in a basin then pour in the milk little by little whisking well. Pass through a fine strainer and allow to rest for a few minutes then remove all the froth which has formed on the surface. Pour into buttered moulds or into the special dishes.

Cook the creams *au Bain-marie* in a moderate oven covering the dish in which they are cooking. The water in the Bain-marie must not be allowed to boil at any time during the cooking. If this is allowed to happen, the high temperature will cause the air mixed in with the mixture to expand and form a mass of small bubbles; when the creams have cooled, this leaves them riddled with small holes and thus greatly mars the appearance. So to sum up, the creams must be poached, which means that they will coagulate due to the temperature of the water in the Bain-marie. This should be maintained at a constant 96 °C (205 °F).

As soon as the creams are cooked, they should be removed from the Bain-marie and allowed to cool.

When the creams are being served in the dishes in which they have been cooked 8 egg yolks and 1 whole egg are sufficient to set 1 litre (1¾ pt or 4½ U.S. cups) of milk. When cold, the dishes must be thoroughly cleaned on the outside then arranged on a serviette on a dish for serving.

If the creams have been made for demoulding, turn over the mould carefully on to the serving dish, leave for a few minutes then remove the mould.

Both these creams allow of any of the flavourings as used for sweet dishes but the most suitable ones are vanilla, almond milk, Pralin—both almond and hazelnut, coffee, chocolate etc. Fruit flavourings, unless they are used in the highly concentrated form of an essence, are not so suitable.

4599 Crème Moulée au Caramel—Cream Caramel
Line the bottom and sides of the moulds with sugar cooked to a light caramel. Fill up with mixture as for Crème Moulée à la Vanille then cook and demould as explained in the preceding recipe.

4600 Crème Moulée à la Florentine
Prepare some pralin-flavoured Crème Moulée mixture; fill into moulds and cook in the usual manner.

When very cold, demould on to the service dish, decorate with Kirsch-flavoured Crème Chantilly and sprinkle the surface with chopped pistachios.

4601 Crème Moulée Opéra
Prepare some pralin-flavoured Crème Moulée mixture and cook it in a fancy border mould.

When cold, demould on to the service dish and fill the centre dome shape with Crème Chantilly flavoured with crystallized violets.

Arrange a circle of large strawberries macerated with Kirsch-flavoured syrup around the edge and cover with a veil of spun sugar.

4602 Crème Moulée à la Viennoise
This is the same as Cream Caramel except that the lightly caramelized sugar is added to the hot milk instead of being used to line the moulds. It is then finished in the same way as Crème Moulée à la Vanille.

CREAMS MADE WITH WHIPPED CREAM

4603 Crème Chantilly
Take some very fresh, fairly thick cream and whisk it until it becomes stiff enough to stand on the whisk.

Add 250 g (9 oz) caster sugar per 1 litre (1¾ pt or 4½ U.S. cups) cream and flavour with vanilla or a fruit essence.

As far as possible and no matter what its use, the cream should be prepared only at the last moment.

4604 Crème Chantilly aux Fruits
This cream is prepared in the proportions of one-third purée of the selected fruit to two-thirds Crème Chantilly. The amount of sugar to use and the flavouring to adopt will vary according to the kind of fruit.

It is usually served as an accompaniment with a sweet but it can be served on its own as a sweet, decorated with some of the same cream or some of the fruit used. Serve accompanied with finger biscuits.

4605 Crème Caprice
To 5 dl (18 fl oz or 2¼ U.S. cups) Crème Chantilly add a quarter its amount of roughly broken meringues.

Fill into into a Madeleine mould previously lined with paper, seal tightly and chill well in ice for 2 hours until set.

Turn out at the last moment, remove the paper and decorate with a pink Crème Chantilly containing some strawberry or raspberry juice. Use a piping bag and star tube to make the decoration.

4606 Brise de Printemps
Add some violet essence to the Crème Chantilly then slightly chill it. Arrange it by the spoonful in fancy glass dishes and decorate with a few crystallized violets.

GELEES—JELLIES

As far as the method of preparation is concerned there are two types of jelly. They are 1) wine or liqueur-flavoured jellies, 2) fruit jellies. The base is the same for both of them—it is gelatine dissolved in a predetermined amount of water.

The gelatine can be produced by the cooking of calvers' feet; this gives the best kind of gelatine but the method of making it is quite complicated. Usually commercially manufactured gelatine is used to simplify the making of jellies and it is used in accordance with the proportions as follows.

4607 Calf's Foot Jelly
Take some nice large calves' feet, soak them well to remove any blood and blanch them well. Place to cook in 1 litre (1¾ pt or 4½ U.S. cups) water for each foot, skimming as completely as possible. Cover with a lid and allow to cook very gently for 7 hours.

At the end of this time, strain off the liquid and remove every trace of fat from it. Test the strength of its gelatine by placing a little on ice; if necessary, correct it by adding sufficient filtered water then test it again.

For each 1 litre (1¾ pt or 4½ U.S. cups) calf's foot jelly, add 250 g (9 oz) sugar, a touch of ground cinnamon, the zest of half a lemon and half an orange and the juice of half a lemon and 1 orange.

For the clarification of the jelly proceed as indicated in the following recipe.

4608 Jelly (*made with gelatine*)
Dissolve 35 g ($1\frac{1}{5}$ oz) gelatine in 1 litre ($1\frac{3}{4}$ or $4\frac{1}{2}$ U.S. cups) water. Add 250 g (9 oz) sugar and the rind and juice of half a lemon and half an orange. Bring to the boil then allow to stand for 10 minutes off the stove.
Clarification: whisk $1\frac{1}{2}$ egg whites in a clean pan together with $\frac{1}{2}$ dl (2 fl oz or $\frac{1}{4}$ U.S. cup) white wine. Add the gelatinous liquid little by little and whisking vigorously.

Place on the stove and whisk continuously until it almost reaches the boil. Pull the pan to the side of the stove and allow it to simmer very gently for a further 15 minutes; there should hardly be a discernible movement of the liquid.

When the clarification has taken place by the end of this time, pass the jelly through a jelly bag into a clean basin. If the jelly is not absolutely clear the first time it should be passed through the bag again until it is perfectly clear. Allow to become three-quarters cold before adding the flavouring.
The addition of the flavouring: whether the jelly is made with gelatine or from calves' feet the result of the above preparations is nothing more than a jellied syrup; the addition of a flavouring will give it its particular character as a sweet jelly.

The complementary items for jellies are liqueurs, fine wines or fruit juices; the amount of water used in making the jelly must be reduced by the quantity of liquid flavouring that will be added at the last stage of its making.

So, all jellies which will include a liquid flavouring will be made of 9 dl (1 pt 12 fl oz or 4 U.S. cups) of jelly and 1 dl ($3\frac{1}{2}$ fl oz or $\frac{1}{2}$ U.S. cup) of the chosen liqueur such as Kirsch, Maraschino, Rum, Anisette etc.

A jelly being made to have an addition of a fine wine such as Champagne, Madeira, Sherry, Marsala etc. will be composed of 7 dl ($1\frac{1}{4}$ pt or 3 U.S. cups) of jelly and 3 dl ($\frac{1}{2}$ pt or $1\frac{1}{4}$ U.S. cups) of the chosen wine to make 1 litre ($1\frac{3}{4}$ pt or $4\frac{1}{2}$ U.S. cups) of finished jelly.

For fruit jellies the method differs according to the kind of fruit used.

When making red fruit jellies such as strawberry, raspberry, redcurrant, cherry or cranberry the fruit should be very ripe; pass it through a sieve adding from 1–3 dl ($3\frac{1}{2}$ fl oz—$\frac{1}{2}$ pt or $\frac{1}{2}$—$2\frac{1}{4}$ U.S. cups) water per 500 g (1 lb 2 oz) fruit according to the proportions of juice in the fruit.

Filter the resultant juice and add it to double its quantity of a jelly made with twice the usual amount of gelatine—this is necessary to maintain the correct consistency of the jelly in spite of the addition of the juice.

When the fruits are over-juicy they should be passed through a sieve and the juice then allowed to ferment for a few hours. Only the clear juice produced by the fermentation should be filtered for use.

Jellies of watery fruits such as grapes, oranges, lemons, tangerines, are made in the same way. The filtering of their juices is done very easily and except for grape juice there is no need for them to be allowed to ferment.

If the fruit is not fully ripe it is possible to add their juice to the jelly before it is clarified; this method has the advantage of destroying the excess acidity. The proportions of the juice of these fruits is approximately the same as those of red fruits.

As regards stone fruit such as apricots, peaches, plums etc., these are frequently used as a garnish with or in fruit jellies but are not often used as the basic flavouring ingredient. When it is required to make a jelly of this kind of fruit, they should be dipped into boiling water so as to remove the skin. They are then cooked in a syrup and allowed to cool in it which should afterwards be used for making the jelly.

The resultant jelly after clarifying and cooling it until it is near setting point, should be flavoured with a little Kirsch or Maraschino to help bring out the flavour of the fruit used.

4609 Garnishes and Accompaniments for Jelly
Jellies are usually served on their own. Sometimes, however, they are garnished with fruit cut in various ways then poached before being arranged very neatly in the jelly, varying the colours.

A jelly made in this way is given the name of Suédoise de Fruits.

Note: This jelly is also described on the menu as *Gelée Macédoine* plus an indication of the flavour of the jelly.

4610 Gelées Rubannés—Ribonned Jellies
These are jellies of different colours and flavours placed in the mould in alternate layers of even thickness.

4611 Gelées à la Russe—Russian Jellies
These are ordinary jellies whisked on ice until they begin to set. They are then moulded as quickly as possible.

By using two or three different colours and flavours of jelly and skilfully mixing them just before moulding, it is possible to obtain very effective marbled jellies.

4612 Gelées à la Moscovite
These are ordinary jellies filled into moulds which can be tightly closed with a lid; to ensure that the moulds are hermetically sealed a layer of butter is spread over the joins with the lid.

They are then buried in ice and freezing salt like an ice-cream sweet, left until the lowering of the temperature causes the formation of a thin layer of frosting around the outer part of the jelly, so giving it a pretty effect.

It is important to remove the moulds from the ice as soon as the contrasting layer is formed and the jelly set, as a prolonged stay in the ice will transform the jelly into a block of uneatable ice.

Note: Modern practice has enormously simplified the service and presentation of jellies. Nowadays they are set in special coupes or deep silver dishes and moulding has largely been abandoned. The bottom of these utensils may be garnished with stewed fruit or fruit salad then covered with the jelly. As the jelly is served from this dish the amount of gelatine used in making it can be decreased by half thus resulting in a more delicate texture.

All these fruit jellies and others, served in coupes can be made nowadays from a base of apple jelly since it is now possible to obtain canned and bottled apple juice of good quality at a low price.

4613 Gelée Miss Helyett
To some Kirsch-flavoured jelly add a third its quantity of filtered juice of fresh raspberries. Pour into a wide border mould and allow to set.

Turn out on to a round base of cooked sweet pastry, fill the centre with Crème Chantilly and decorate this and the edge of the pastry base with any cold poached fresh fruit. Finish by sprinkling with coarsely crushed Pralin (4354).

COLD PUDDINGS

These cold puddings have much in common with the Bavarois and more often than not, their base is the same.

The main difference between the two is that a Bavarois is usually served without either a sauce or a garnish whereas the pudding is always served with either one or the other and very often with both.

The sauces suitable for serving with these puddings are as listed at the beginning of this Section. The garnishes are always composed of fruits either served separately in the form of stewed fruit, or added to the mixture in crystallized form when making the pudding.

4614 Pouding d'Aremberg
Prepare a Kirsch-flavoured Bavarois mixture and add to it an equal amount of a purée of ripe raw pears.

Decorate the bottom of a Madeleine mould with quarters of pears, half of them poached in ordinary syrup, the others in pink syrup and also some small shapes of crystallized fruits. Line the sides of the mould with Punch Biscuits (4327) saturated with Kirsch.

Fill the mould with the Bavarois and pear mixture and allow to set.

4615 Pouding Bohémienne
Make some very small thin pancakes and cover them with a Salpicon of crystallized fruits and soaked and drained seedless raisins, mixed with a thick purée of apple and pears cooked with sugar. Fold the pancakes into small balls or rectangles and arrange them in a buttered border mould.

Fill the mould with a Crème moulée à la Vanille mixture (4598) made with extra eggs, and cook *au Bain-marie* in the oven.

When cooked, allow to become cold in the mould; turn out at the last moment and coat with a Sabayon flavoured to choice.

4616 Pouding Clermont
Prepare a rum-flavoured Bavarois mixture and add a quarter its amount of a purée of candied chestnuts and 150 g ($5\frac{1}{2}$ oz) small pieces of candied chestnuts per 1 litre ($1\frac{3}{4}$ pt or $4\frac{1}{2}$ U.S. cups) of Bavarois mixture. Finish in the usual manner for a Bavarois.

4617 Pouding Diplomate
Decorate the bottom of a deep oiled border mould with small shapes of crystallized fruit.

Fill with vanilla Bavarois mixture arranged in layers and alternating with layers of Finger Biscuits (4325) saturated with Kirsch and sprinkled with soaked and drained currants and sultanas. Add a few tablespoons of apricot jam here and there.

Allow to set in the refrigerator and demould at the last moment.

4618 Pouding Diplomate aux Fruits
Prepare the pudding in the same way as in the preceding recipe adding a layer of thin slices of peeled fresh fruit such as ripe pears, peaches or apricots, macerated in a sweet liqueur.

When the pudding is demoulded surround the base with some stewed fruit, either the one used or a mixture.

4619 Pouding Malakoff
1) Prepare a Crème à l'Anglaise Collée (4338) and add 5 dl (18 fl oz or $2\frac{1}{4}$ U.S. cups) fresh

double cream per 1 litre ($1\frac{3}{4}$ pt or $4\frac{1}{2}$ U.S. cups) of mixture.

2) Prepare some apples and pears cooked as for an Apple Charlotte, currants and sultanas swollen in lukewarm syrup, fresh shredded almonds, diced preserved orange peel, slices of stale biscuit or Finger Biscuits saturated with a liqueur.

Lightly oil a Charlotte mould with almond oil; pour in a 1 cm ($\frac{2}{5}$ in) thick layer of the prepared Crème à l'Anglaise mixture and on top of this set a layer of the biscuits which have been spread liberally with the purée of fruit. Sprinkle with the diced fruit, add another layer of the cream, then the biscuits and repeat until the mould is full.

Allow to set; turn out at the last moment and coat with Kirsch-flavoured Sabayon.

4620 Pouding Nesselrode

To 1 litre ($1\frac{3}{4}$ pt or $4\frac{1}{2}$ U.S. cups) Crème Anglaise made without gelatine (4337), add 250 g (9 oz) fine purée of candied chestnuts and 125 g ($4\frac{1}{2}$ oz) soaked and drained currants and sultanas, diced preserved orange peel and diced glacé cherries; all these fruits should be in equal quantities and macerated with sweet Madeira wine.

To this mixture add 1 litre ($1\frac{3}{4}$ pt or $4\frac{1}{2}$ U.S. cups) whipped cream flavoured with Maraschino.

Line the bottom and sides of a Charlotte mould with greaseproof paper, fill with the mixture, cover with a tight-fitting lid then seal hermetically with a layer of butter over the join with the lid. Bury the mould in ice and freezing salt and chill well until set.

When required for serving, demould on to a dish, remove the paper and surround the pudding with a circle of large candied chestnuts or balls of purée of candied chestnut dipped in chocolate.

Note: The Crème Anglaise can be chilled by turning it in the ice-cream freezer, adding the whipped cream when the mixture is nearly stiff then moulding it quickly.

4621 Pouding Reine des Fées or Crème Reine des Fées

Make 4 egg whites into Italian meringue adding 250 g (9 oz) quince jelly to the sugar whilst it is cooking; finish the meringue by adding 50 g (2 oz) of diced crystallized fruit previously macerated with Kirsch and carefully drained. Pipe the meringue in the form of large button shapes on a sheet of paper just large enough to fit into a pan.

Pour 4 litres (7 pt or $8\frac{3}{4}$ U.S. pt) water into this pan and add 1 kg ($2\frac{1}{4}$ lb) sugar and $1\frac{1}{2}$ dl (5 fl oz or $\frac{5}{8}$ U.S. cup) Kirsch. Bring to the boil then slide in the sheet of paper and withdraw it as soon as the meringue buttons have detached themselves.

Allow the meringues to poach then drain them on a cloth and allow to cool.

Separately prepare two different Bavarois mixtures—one left white and flavoured with vanilla, the other coloured pink and flavoured with Curaçao. In both cases the mixtures should be finished with twice the usual amount of whipped cream; only half the usual amount of gelatine should be used.

Arrange the two Bavarois in alternate even layers in a lightly oiled Madeleine mould, placing some of the meringues between each layer. When full, cover with a piece of paper and the lid and chill in ice for 2 hours. Demould when required on to a serviette placed on a dish.

4622 Pouding Rizzio

This is prepared in the same way as Pouding Diplomate but garnishing the interior filling with crushed soft macaroons saturated with Rosolio liqueur and Kirsch, and with fresh fruit poached in syrup.

Serve accompanied with Apricot Sauce flavoured with almond milk and Kirsch.

4623 Pouding de Riz à la Crème—Rice Pudding with Cream

This pudding can be served as it is or as an accompaniment with cold stewed fruits. It is prepared in the same way as hot Rice Pudding with Cream (4454) but instead of placing it in the oven to glaze after adding the eggs, the mixture should be allowed to cool before adding a little whipped cream, 4 sheets of soaked and melted gelatine and 125 g ($4\frac{1}{2}$ oz) roughly crushed soft macaroons saturated with Kirsch, per 1 litre ($1\frac{3}{4}$ pt or $4\frac{1}{2}$ U.S. cups) rice mixture.

Pour the mixture into the service dish, allow it to set then dredge with icing sugar and mark trellis-fashion with a red hot iron.

4624 Pouding de Semoule à la Crème

This is prepared in the same way as the preceding recipe using semolina instead of rice.

COLD FRUIT DISHES

ABRICOTS—APRICOTS

4625 Abricots Mireille

Cut some nice, ripe peeled apricots in half. Arrange

them in a timbale together with the skinned kernels of the apricots; sprinkle with sugar and keep on ice for 1 hour. When about to serve, sprinkle with Kirsch, cover with sweetened whipped cream flavoured with vanilla and sprinkle this with crystallized jasmin and violet flowers.

4626 Abricots à la Parisienne
Cut some apricots in half and poach them in vanilla-flavoured syrup. Allow to cool; drain and place two halves together around a walnut-sized piece of vanilla ice-cream.

Place each re-formed apricot on the flat side of a large macaroon; cover cone shape with vanilla-flavoured Crème Chantilly and sprinkle with fine hazelnut Pralin.

4627 Abricots à la Royale
Poach some nice large halves of apricots in vanilla-flavoured syrup. When cold, place each half in a fairly deep tartlet mould and fill completely with very clear Kirsch-flavoured jelly.

Prepare a not too high border of Genoise, glaze it with redcurrant jelly cooked to the small ball stage and sprinkle with chopped pistachios. Place on a round dish.

Demould the jellied apricot tartlets and arrange them in a circle on the border; fill the centre with chopped pink Anisette-flavoured jelly.

ANANAS—PINEAPPLE

4628 Ananas Georgette
Choose a large whole pineapple and remove the centre leaving a case 1 cm ($\frac{2}{5}$ in) thick; keep the top slice with the leaves attached.

Fill the pineapple case with a pineapple Iced Fruit Mousse mixture (4901) into which has been mixed the inside of the pineapple cut into very thin pieces. Allow to set in the refrigerator.

Place on a dish on a serviette and cover with the top so that the pineapple resumes its normal appearance.

4629 Ananas Ninon
Line the inside of a soufflé mould with vanilla ice-cream bringing it from a point in the centre at the bottom, and level to the top edge so as to make a hollow centre in the shape of an inverted cone.

On this place two or three lines of overlapping thin slices of fresh pineapple in such a way that those on the top overlap the edge of the dish. In the centre arrange a pyramid of wild strawberries, cover them with a purée of raspberries and sprinkle with chopped pistachios.

4630 Ananas à la Royale
Cut the top off a fresh pineapple with its leaves, and keep it on one side. Remove the inside of the pineapple, leaving a case approximately 1 cm ($\frac{2}{5}$ in) thick.

Fill the pineapple case with fresh fruit salad macerated with Kirsch then place it in the middle of a glass bowl. Surround the base of the pineapple with a circle of nice Montreuil peaches poached in vanilla-flavoured syrup and place a large strawberry macerated with Kirsch, between each peach.

Replace the top of the pineapple with its leaves.

4631 Ananas Virginie
This is prepared in the same way as Ananas Georgette replacing the pineapple Mousse with a strawberry Mousse containing the flesh of the pineapple cut in dice.

BANANES—BANANAS

4632 Bananes en Salade
Choose bananas which are just ripe but still a little firm. Remove the skin and cut the fruit into round slices. Place these in a dish, sprinkle with sugar mixed with orange sugar and allow to macerate for 15 minutes.

When required for serving, arrange the sliced banana in a salad bowl, sprinkle with Kirsch and lightly mix, so as not to damage the slices.

Note: The orange sugar can be replaced by a fine Julienne of orange zest, blanched then cooked in syrup for a few minutes.

4633 Bananes Trédern
Cut some fairly ripe bananas in half lengthways; remove the flesh and keep half of the skins.

Cook half of the bananas in vanilla-flavoured syrup then drain and cool them. Coat them with apricot purée cooked to the small ball stage and decorate with shapes of crystallized fruit.

Pass the other half of the bananas through a sieve and add the purée obtained to a Kirsch Bavarois mixture in the proportion of one-third banana purée to two-thirds Bavarois mixture. Fill the banana skins with this mixture and place in the refrigerator to set. Arrange on a serviette on a dish and place one of the decorated half bananas on each of the halves filled with the Bavarois.

CERISES—CHERRIES

4634 Cerises Dubarry
Line a flan ring with good short paste and prick the bottom to prevent it rising during cooking.

Sprinkle it with caster sugar then fill it with nice stoned cherries placing them closely together.

Bake in the usual manner then allow to cool.

When very cold, cover the cherries with Crème Chantilly mixed with either almond Pralin or crushed macaroons.

Smooth the top and sides of the cream and coat all over with powdered macaroons. Finish by piping a decoration of pink and white Crème Chantilly.

4635 Cerises au Claret
Choose some nice cherries and cut off the ends of the stalks. Place them into a timbale and pour over sufficient sweetened Claret flavoured with a little cinnamon to just cover. Cover with a lid and place on the side of the stove for 10 minutes to poach the cherries.

Allow them to cool in the syrup then drain off the syrup; reduce it by a third and add 1 tbs redcurrant jelly per 6 tbs reduced syrup—this will thicken it slightly.

Pour the syrup back over the cherries and serve them very cold accompanied with Finger Biscuits (4325).

FIGUES—FIGS

Both raw and cooked, fresh figs can provide the means of some excellent sweets such as the following.

4636 Figues à la Carlton (*raw*)
Peel some fresh ripe figs, cut them in half, place in a timbale and keep on crushed ice.

Separately prepare some sweetened raspberry purée and keep it chilled.

To serve: mix twice the amount of Crème Chantilly into the raspberry purée and pour over the figs so as to cover them completely.

4637 Figues à la Carlton (*cooked*)
Poach some peeled fresh figs in vanilla-flavoured syrup and allow them to cool. Drain them well, place in a timbale and cover with raspberry-flavoured Crème Chantilly made as in the preceding recipe.

4638 Figues à la Crème
Peel the figs, cut them in half and place in a timbale. Sprinkle lightly with sugar, add a few tablespoons of Noyau liqueur and surround with crushed ice.

When about to serve, cover with vanilla-flavoured Crème Chantilly.

Note: After having been cooked, fresh figs can be served on a bed of rice or semolina, or Frangipane Cream etc.

Dried figs can be prepared by cooking in vanilla-flavoured syrup or in red wine and can then be served accompanied with rice pudding, semolina pudding etc.

Fresh figs can be cooked in the oven in an earthenware dish with a few tablespoons of water and a sprinkling of sugar. Figs cooked in this manner are more delicate than those cooked in the ordinary way.

FRAISES—STRAWBERRIES

4639 Fraises Cardinal
Arrange some large chilled strawberries in a timbale, coat with either Melba Sauce or a purée of fresh raspberries and sprinkle with either shredded fresh almonds or pistachios.

4640 Fraises à la Créole
Macerate equal quantities of nice strawberries and diced pineapple with caster sugar and Kirsch.

Macerate some slices of pineapple with Kirsch and arrange them closely overlapping in a circle on a dish.

Place the strawberries and diced pineapple in the centre of the dish arranging them pyramid shape and sprinkle well with Kirsch-flavoured syrup.

4641 Fraises Fémina
Choose some nice strawberries, sprinkle them with caster sugar and macerate with Grand-Marnier for 1 hour, keeping them chilled.

When about to serve, cover the bottom of a glass bowl or silver timbale with a layer of orange ice to which the liquid from the maceration has been added; arrange the strawberries neatly on top.

4642 Fraises Lérina
Cut a round piece from the stalk end of a small black Carmes melon. Remove the seeds and filaments from inside it, then remove the flesh with a spoon and sprinkle this with sugar.

Macerate sufficient wild strawberries with Lérina liqueur—if wild strawberries are not available, use cultivated ones.

Fill the melon case with the prepared strawberries and melon; replace the top and chill it on ice for 2 hours.

When required for serving, present the melon on a serviette placed on a dish.

4643 Fraises Marguerite
Macerate some small wild strawberries with caster sugar and Kirsch. Drain them well then mix into an equal quantity of pomegranate Sorbet; arrange in a previously chilled silver timbale.

Cover with Crème Chantilly flavoured with Maraschino and decorate with some of the same cream.

4644 Fraises Marquise
In the bottom of a chilled timbale, place a layer of Crème Chantilly mixed with half its quantity of a purée of wild strawberries. Cover this cream completely with nice medium-sized strawberries which have been macerated in Kirsch and rolled at the last moment in caster sugar to coat them.

4645 Fraises Melba
Place a layer of vanilla ice-cream in the bottom of a chilled silver timbale. On top of this arrange a layer of nice strawberries and coat them with a thick, slightly sweetened purée of a raspberries.

4646 Fraises Monte-Carlo
Select some nice strawberries, place them in a timbale and sprinkle with caster sugar and white Curaçao; keep in the refrigerator. With some other strawberries of poorer quality prepare a purée and mix this together with a third its quantity of vanilla-flavoured Crème Chantilly.

Have prepared in advance 1) a well-chilled Curaçao-flavoured Mousse moulded in a dome-shaped mould; 2) for each guest, one meringue shell surrounded with some spun sugar to give it the shape of a small nest.

To serve: demould the Mousse on to an oval dish; place the nests at both ends. Fill each nest with a tablespoon of purée of strawberries mixed with cream, and place three or four strawberries macerated with Curaçao on top.

Coat the Mousse with some of the same strawberry purée and cover with a veil of spun sugar. Finish by sprinkling the veil of sugar with crystallized violets.

4647 Fraises Nina
This is prepared in the same way as Fraises Marguerite but using pineapple Sorbet.

Place in the timbale and coat with Crème Chantilly mixed with sweetened raspberry purée.

4648 Fraises Rêve de Bébé
Cut off the top slice of a medium-sized ripe pineapple and remove the inside without damaging the skin.

Prepare a square piece of Genoise 2 cm ($\frac{4}{5}$ in) thick and make a hollow in the centre large enough to fit the pineapple. Attach the Genoise to a sheet of cooked short pastry of exactly the same size.

Coat the Genoise with pink fondant, decorate with royal icing and set a large strawberry at each corner.

Cut half of the removed pineapple flesh into thin slices and macerate them with sugar, Kirsch and Maraschino. Pound the other half and squeeze out the juices; use this to macerate sufficient wild strawberries to three-quarters fill the pineapple case.

When about to serve, fill the pineapple with alternate layers of slices of pineapple and strawberries, and vanilla-flavoured Crème Chantilly.

Place the pineapple thus prepared on the Genoise base and serve very cold.

4649 Fraises à la Ritz
Arrange some chilled sweetened strawberries in a timbale and cover with the following mixture: pass 250 g (9 oz) wild strawberries through a sieve, add sufficient Sauce Melba to give a nice pink colour then mix in an equal amount of stiffly whipped Crème Chantilly flavoured with vanilla.

Chill well before serving.

4650 Fraises Romanoff
Place some nice strawberries to macerate with orange juice and Curaçao. Arrange them in a chilled timbale and cover with Crème Chantilly using a piping bag and large star tube.

4651 Fraises Sarah Bernhardt
Choose some nice strawberries and macerate them with Curaçao and brandy.

When about to serve, place a layer of pineapple ice in the bottom of a timbale, arrange the strawberries on top and cover with Curaçao Mousse.

4652 Fraises Wilhelmine
Macerate some nice large strawberries with caster sugar, orange juice and Kirsch. Arrange in a timbale and serve accompanied with vanilla-flavoured Crème Chantilly.

4653 Fraises Zelma Kuntz
Arrange some nice chilled strawberries in a timbale and cover with a mixture of equal amounts of raspberry purée and Crème Chantilly.

Decorate with some of the same cream using a piping bag and tube and sprinkle with powdered hazelnut Pralin.

GOOSEBERRIES

4654 Gooseberry Fool
Cook 500 g (1 lb 2 oz) small green gooseberries in a light syrup. When cooked, drain them well and pass through a fine sieve.

Place the purée in a shallow pan and mix well on

ice, working in the necessary amount of icing sugar according to the acidity of the fruit and the strength of the syrup used to cook them in.

Mix in an equal amount of stiffly whipped cream, fill dome shape in a timbale and decorate the surface with Crème Chantilly; serve very cold.

Note: It is not absolutely necessary to pass the fuit through a sieve when making this English sweet. It suffices to mash them by whisking vigorously.

MANDARINES—TANGERINES

4655 Mandarines Almina
Cut out a round piece from the stalk end of the tangerines using a plain cutter 2 cm ($\frac{4}{5}$ in) in diameter. Remove the fruit then fill the skins with violet-flavoured Bavarois containing some Finger Biscuits (4325) saturated with Maraschino and broken into very small pieces.

Allow to set, replace the top when about to serve and arrange on a serviette on a dish.

4656 Mandarines à la Crème
Empty the tangerines as above; fill the skins with tangerine Bavarois made slightly stiffer than usual and finished with a third its quantity of fresh unwhipped cream.

Keep very cold until required for serving.

4657 Mandarines en Surprise
Proceed as indicated for Oranges en Surprise but replacing the orange ice with tangerine jelly.

MELONS

4658 Melon frappé—Chilled Melon
Choose 2 medium-sized ripe melons; pass the flesh of one, freed of all skin, seeds and filaments, through a sieve and prepare a Granité (4913) with the purée obtained.

Cut around the stalk end of the other melon and remove the piece; remove the seeds and filaments from inside. Scoop out the flesh in small pieces and place in a dish on ice to macerate with a little sugar and a wine or liqueur such as Port, Curaçao, Rum or Maraschino. Place the empty skin in the coldroom for 1 hour.

When required for serving, place the melon case on a sculpted block of ice; fill the inside with alternate layers of the Granité and the macerated melon. When full, replace the top.

Note: This dish is served with a spoon on to very well chilled plates; it is sometimes served at the end of a dinner instead of an ice.

4659 Melon à l'Orientale
Choose a melon that is just ripe; cut a round incision in the top and remove the piece.

Remove the seeds and filament; scoop out the flesh with a silver spoon and cut it into cubes. Sprinkle the inside of the melon with plenty of icing sugar and refill it with alternate layers of wild strawberries and the diced melon, sprinkling each layer with sugar.

Pour in 1 dl ($3\frac{1}{2}$ fl oz or $\frac{1}{2}$ U.S. cup) Kirsch, close the melon with the reserved top and seal the join with a line of butter. Keep in a cold place for 2 hours.

Arrange on a serviette and serve accompanied with wafer biscuits.

4660 Melon en Surprise
Empty the melon as in the preceding recipe and refill it with fresh fruit salad containing the diced flesh from the melon—all mixed with sweetened raspberry purée flavoured with Kirsch.

Replace the removed top piece and keep very cold for 2 hours before serving.

ORANGES

4661 Oranges au Blanc-Manger
Cut off the tops of the oranges at the stalk end and remove the flesh as described for tangerines. Fill with French Blancmange (4583) and allow to set.

Replace the tops and arrange the oranges on a dish on a serviette.

4662 Oranges Rubannées
Empty the oranges and refill the skins with several different colours and flavours of blancmange placed in even layers. Instead of blancmange, jelly can be used.

When required for serving, cut the oranges into quarters.

Note: These quarters of orange are sometimes used for garnishing other cold sweets.

4663 Oranges en Surprise
Cut off the top quarters of the oranges and remove the flesh.

Fill the skins with orange ice, cover over with Italian meringue and place on a tray of crushed ice. Place in a hot oven to colour thc meringue quickly.

On removing from the oven, replace the tops to which have been fixed a leaf on a stem made with pulled sugar.

Serve arranged on a serviette.

PEACHES AND NECTARINES

Nectarines are smooth-skinned peaches and they may be prepared in any of the ways as indicated for peaches—it is thus unnecessary to give separate recipes for them.

4664 Pêches Adrienne
Choose tender ripe peaches allowing one per person. Blanch them and peel in the usual manner; place them on a tray, sprinkle with sugar and keep in the refrigerator.

Make some ice-cream with wild strawberries and fresh cream and flavoured with vanilla. Prepare the same number of meringue shells as there are peaches.

Place the ice-cream in a shallow glass bowl and set the meringues on top.

Place a peach on each meringue and coat thinly with a Curaçao Mousse at almost setting point.

Cover the whole with a veil of spun sugar, sprinkle with crystallized rose petals and set the bowl on a sculpted block of ice.

4665 Pêches Aiglon
After peeling the peaches, poach them in vanilla-flavoured syrup and allow them to cool in the syrup.

When cold, drain the peaches well.

Place a layer of vanilla ice in the bottom of the inner case of a double timbale—the outer case should be filled with crushed ice.

Arrange the peaches on top of the vanilla ice and sprinkle them with crystallized violets.

Place the timbale on a block of ice sculpted to represent an eagle standing on a rock with its wings outstretched. Cover the dish of peaches with a veil of spun sugar.

4666 Pêches à l'Aurore
Peel the peaches, poach them in Kirsch-flavoured syrup and allow them to cool in the syrup.

When cold, drain the peaches well, arrange on a layer of Mousse Glacée aux Fraises (4903) set in the bottom of a timbale and coat them with cold Curaçao-flavoured Sabayon.

4667 Pêches Alexandra
Poach the peaches in vanilla-flavoured syrup and allow them to become very cold.

Arrange them in a chilled timbale on a bed of vanilla ice-cream coated with strawberry purée. Sprinkle the peaches with red and white rose petals and cover with a veil of spun sugar.

4668 Pêches Cardinal
Poach the peaches in vanilla-flavoured syrup. When they are very cold, arrange them in a timbale on a bed of vanilla ice cream and coat with very red, sweetened raspberry purée flavoured with Kirsch. Sprinkle the surface with very white, shredded fresh almonds.

4669 Pêches au Château-Lafitte
Blanch the peaches so as to remove the skins; cut them in halves and poach in sufficient Château Lafitte wine to cover them. Sweeten the wine with 300 g (11 oz) sugar per $7\frac{1}{2}$ dl ($1\frac{1}{3}$ pt or $3\frac{1}{4}$ U.S. cups) wine.

Allow the peaches to become cold in the wine, then arrange in a silver timbale. Reduce the wine by three-quarters and thicken it with a little red-currant and raspberry jelly. When this sauce is very cold, coat the peaches with it.

4670 Pêches Dame-Blanche
Poach the peaches in vanilla-flavoured syrup and allow them to cool in the syrup. Place a layer of vanilla ice-cream in a timbale and cover it with thin slices of pineapple macerated with Kirsch and Maraschino. Arrange the peaches on top. Decorate with points of Crème Chantilly between each peach and in all the spaces between, using a piping bag and star tube.

4671 Pêches Eugénie
Choose peaches which are exactly ripe; remove the stones carefully and skin the peaches. Arrange them in a timbale together with some wild strawberries in the spaces between.

Sprinkle with a few tablespoons of Kirsch and Maraschino; cover the dish and place on ice for 1 hour.

When about to serve, coat the peaches with very cold Champagne Sabayon.

4672 Pêches à l'Impératrice
Cut the peaches in half and poach them in vanilla-flavoured syrup; allow to cool. Drain and dry the peaches and cover the cut side with a half ball of vanilla ice-cream so as to give each the size and shape of the whole peach.

Brush the peach side with thick apricot sauce then roll the whole in toasted shredded almonds.

Arrange the peaches on a round base of Genoise saturated with Kirsch and Maraschino and which has been placed in turn on a base of cooked short pastry, glazed with raspberry syrup.

Cover the whole with a veil of spun sugar.

4673 Pêches Isabelle
Choose large peaches which are just ripe, skin them, cut in half and remove the stones. Arrange the halves in layers in a timbale and sprinkle each

layer with sugar and a little old Clos des Papes wine. Keep on ice for 2 hours.

Serve accompanied with vanilla-flavoured Crème Chantilly.

4674 Pêches Melba
Poach the skinned peaches in vanilla-flavoured syrup. When very cold, arrange them in a timbale on a bed of vanilla ice-cream and coat with raspberry purée.

4675 Pêches Mistral
Choose peaches that are ripe to the point where the stone comes away from the flesh cleanly. Skin them, arrange in a timbale and sprinkle with sugar. Coat with a fine strawberry purée, place skinned fresh almonds on top and at the last moment cover the peaches with vanilla-flavoured cream.

Serve accompanied with Finger Biscuits (4325).

4676 Pêches Petit-Duc
Prepare the peaches as for Pêches Dame-Blanche replacing the points of cream with redcurrant jelly.

4677 Pêches Rose-Chèri
Poach the peaches in vanilla-flavoured syrup and allow them to cool in the syrup.

When cold, arrange the peaches in a timbale on a bed of pineapple ice and coat with very cold Champagne Sabayon to which a few tablespoons of whipped cream has been added. Sprinkle the surface with crystallized rose petals.

4678 Pêches Rose-Pompon
Blanch and skin some nice large peaches; poach them in vanilla-flavoured syrup and allow them to cool in the syrup.

Take out the stones without opening the peaches too much and take care not to break them. Replace the stones with a small ball of firm vanilla ice.

Arrange the peaches in a timbale on a bed of raspberry and vanilla ice cream; cover with Crème Chantilly flavoured with Pralin (4354) and place in the refrigerator for 30 minutes before serving.

When about to serve, cover the dish with a veil of pink spun sugar.

4679 Pêches Sultane
Poach the peaches in vanilla-flavoured syrup and allow them to cool in the syrup.

Arrange them in a timbale on a bed of Pistachio ice and coat with very cold thickened syrup flavoured with rose essence.

Cover with a veil of spun sugar and set the dish on a sculpted block of ice.

4680 Pêches Trianon
For preference use some very ripe Charmes de Vénus peaches; skin them and sprinkle with sugar.

Arrange them on a crown of vanilla Mousse containing pieces of macaroon saturated with Noyau liqueur. Lightly coat with a purée of wild strawberries.

POIRES—PEARS

4681 Poires Alma
Peel the pears and cook them in a light syrup made from 1 litre ($1\frac{3}{4}$ pt or $4\frac{1}{2}$ U.S. cups) water, $2\frac{1}{2}$ dl (9 fl oz or $1\frac{1}{8}$ U.S. cups) Port wine, 250 g (9 oz) sugar and the chopped and blanched zest of 1 orange.

Allow the pears to cool, arrange them in a timbale, sprinkle with powdered Pralin and serve accompanied with Crème Chantilly.

4682 Poires Cardinal
Poach the pears in vanilla-flavoured syrup then proceed as for Pêches Cardinal.

4683 Poires Félicia
Peel and cut some ripe pears into quarters; poach them in vanilla-flavoured syrup and allow to cool. At the same time, cook some very small halves of pears in pink coloured syrup.

Arrange the quarters of pears in the centre of a border of Crème Viennoise. Cover the pears with Crème Chantilly flavoured with vanilla smoothing it pyramid fashion and sprinkle with crushed crystallized rose petals.

Surround the outside of the border with the pink halves of pears.

4684 Poires à la Florentine
Fill an oiled border mould with a Bavarois mixture thickened with semolina; allow it to set.

When required for serving, turn out the border on to a dish and fill the centre with poached halves of pears mixed with vanilla-flavoured apricot purée.

4685 Poires Hélène
Poach the pears in vanilla-flavoured syrup and allow them to cool in the syrup.

When required for serving, arrange the pears in a timbale on a bed of vanilla ice-cream and sprinkle with crystallized violets.

Serve accompanied with hot Chocolate Sauce.

4686 Poires Mariette
Peel and trim some small pears and poach them in a light vanilla-flavoured syrup. When cold, arrange

them in a deep dish on a bed of vanilla-flavoured purée of candied chestnuts.

Coat with reduced Apricot Sauce flavoured with old rum.

4687 Poires Marquise

Poach the pears in vanilla-flavoured syrup; drain them well and allow to cool. When quite cold, coat them several times with fairly thick redcurrant jelly and immediately sprinkle with toasted nibbed almonds.

Arrange the pears on a Pouding Diplomate made in a shallow mould and turned out on a round dish. Surround the pudding with neatly cut triangles of apple jelly.

4688 Poires Mary Garden

Poach the pears in a syrup; allow to cool then arrange on a deep dish on a layer of Melba Sauce containing some poached cherries.

4689 Poires Melba

Poach the pears in vanilla-flavoured syrup then proceed in the same way as for Pêches Melba.

4690 Poires Pralinées

Poach the pears in the usual manner and allow them to cool.

Arrange them in a timbale and coat with Frangipane Cream softened with the addition of a little ordinary cream.

Place a nicely moulded tablespoon of Crème Chantilly between each pear and sprinkle the whole with coarsely crushed almond Pralin (4354).

Serve accompanied with either hot or cold Chocolate Sauce.

4691 Poires à la Religieuse

Poach the pears in a syrup and when cold arrange them in a timbale. Thicken the syrup with diluted arrowroot, colour it a light pink and flavour with Rum. Pour over the pears and allow to become cold.

Note: This dish can also be served hot by proceeding in exactly the same way except that the Rum should be poured over the pears at the last moment and set alight just before serving.

4692 Poires Richelieu

Prepare a Flamri mixture (4701) and pour it into a plain border mould decorated with crystallized fruits. Cook *au Bain-marie* in the oven and when cold, demould it on to a round dish.

In the centre of the border, arrange pyramid shape, some quarters of pear poached in vanilla-flavoured syrup; coat them with Frangipane Cream to which has been added a quarter its quantity of crushed dry macaroons and twice its amount of stiffly beaten Crème Chantilly.

Decorate the top with Crème Chantilly using a small piping tube and serve accompanied with Kirsch-flavoured Apricot Sauce.

POMMES—APPLES

4693 Pommes Félicia

Cut the apples into quarters and poach them in vanilla-flavoured syrup. Finish in the same way as for Poires Félicia (4683).

4694 Pommes à la Royale

Peel some small apples, remove the cores with a column cutter and poach them in vanilla-flavoured syrup.

When very cold, drain, dry and coat with redcurrant jelly, Place each apple on a tartlet case filled with blancmange, then arrange them on a round dish.

Garnish the centre of the dish with chopped Maraschino jelly.

VARIOUS COLD SWEETS

4695 Biscuit Monte-Carlo

Cover a slightly moistened tray with a sheet of greaseproof paper; place on top 5 flan rings and fill each half-way up with meringue. Cook the meringues, then place them in a very slow oven for 24 hours until they are completely dry.

Sandwich the rounds of meringue on top of one another with Crème Chantilly, sprinkling each layer of cream with grated chocolate. Glaze the top with melted chocolate and decorate around the sides with Crème Chantilly, using a piping tube or cornet.

Pipe small rosettes of Crème Chantilly around the top edge of the biscuit and place a crystallized violet on each rosette.

4696 Croûte Joinville

Saturate some slices of freshly baked Savarin with Kirsch-flavoured syrup. Arrange in a circle on a dish with alternate rings of pineapple macerated with Kirsch.

Fill the centre with a pyramid of Crème Chantilly and with grated chocolate. Surround with Kirsch-flavoured apricot syrup.

4697 Croûte Mexicaine

Cut some oval slices from a stale Genoise 6 cm ($2\frac{1}{2}$ in) long by 8 mm ($\frac{1}{3}$ in) wide. Coat with

Royal Icing Pralin (4353) and place to dry in a moderate oven.

When ready, arrange the slices in a circle on a round dish and fill the centre with Plombière ice (4771) moulding it rock shape.

4698 Croûte Normande à la Chantilly

Prepare the Croûtes as for Croûte à la Normande (4411). Arrange in a circle on a dish and coat with a syrup thickened with some very cold purée of apple cooked with sugar.

Fill the centre with some cold apple cooked as for Apple Charlotte and cover with vanilla-flavoured Crème Chantilly moulded to the shape of a truncated cone.

4699 Diplomate aux Fruits

Prepare 1) a round base of Genoise made with the addition of some mixed dried fruit; glaze the top surface with Apricot Sauce cooked to the small ball stage, 2) a Fruit Bavarois, moulded in a Charlotte mould.

To serve: demould the Bavarois on to the Genoise base and surround it with some of the same fruit poached in syrup, as used for the Bavarois mixture.

4700 Eton Mess

This is prepared by crushing some cleaned strawberries with a fork then adding an equal quantity of whipped cream.

It may be presented according to taste, but for preference as simply as possible.

4701 Flamri

Place 5 dl (18 fl oz or $2\frac{1}{4}$ U.S. cups) each of water and white wine in a pan and bring to the boil. Rain in 250 g (9 oz) fine semolina, mix well and cook slowly for 20 minutes. Now add 300 g (11 oz) caster sugar, a pinch of fine salt and 2 eggs and finally fold in 6 stiffly beaten egg whites. Pour into buttered deep moulds and cook *au Bain-marie* in the oven.

When cold, demould on to a dish and coat with a sweetened raw purée of any fruit such as strawberries, redcurrants, cherries etc.

4702 Ile Flottante

Cut a stale Biscuit de Savoie (4328) cooked in a deep round mould, into thin slices; saturate each slice with Kirsch and Maraschino, spread with apricot jam and sprinkle with currants and nibbed almonds.

Place the slices on top of one another in their original order and coat the whole neatly with Crème Chantilly.

Sprinkle the cream with finely shredded pistachios, then with soaked, drained and dried currants. Place in a deep glass dish and surround with either cold vanilla-flavoured Sauce Anglaise or with raspberry syrup.

4703 Milk Junket

Heat 1 litre ($1\frac{3}{4}$ pt or $4\frac{1}{2}$ U.S. cups) milk to blood heat—35 °C (98·4 °F); remove from the stove and add 50 g (2 oz) sugar, flavouring to choice, and 6 drops of rennet, or 2 rennet tablets dissolved in a few drops of water.

Pour into a deep dish and allow to set.

Note: This simple and delicate sweet is really only sweetened and flavoured milk which is coagulated by means of the warmth and the rennet.

4704 Macédoine de Fruits Rafraîchis—Fresh Fruit Salad

Take any fruits in season such as ripe pears and peaches, apricots and bananas all of which should be peeled and sliced, together with some large or small raspberries, red and white currants, skinned fresh almonds etc.

Arrange the well mixed fruits in a chilled timbale and add sufficient syrup at 30° on the saccharometer, flavoured with Kirsch or Maraschino; allow to macerate for 1–2 hours turning it over carefully from time to time.

4705 Eugénia-Crème à l'Italienne

Choose some very ripe Eugenias; peel them, cut into slices and macerate with Maraschino-flavoured syrup.

Arrange the slices on a bed of vanilla ice-cream in a deep dish; decorate the top with Crème Chantilly and sprinkle with crystallized violets.

4706 Marquise Alice

Prepare a Pralin-flavoured Bavarois mixture (4581) and pour it into a mould lined with Finger Biscuits (4325) saturated with Anisette.

When set, demould on to a dish and coat evenly all over with stiff vanilla-flavoured Crème Chantilly.

Pipe some straight parallel lines of redcurrant jelly across the top, using a paper cornet and feather them by drawing the point of a small knife across them and in the opposite direction.

Surround the base with small triangular shapes of puff pastry which have been baked then coated with Royal Icing Pralin (4353) and dried in the oven.

4707 Meringues Germaine

Mash 3 small fresh, Gervais cream cheeses in a bowl with a wooden spoon. Mix in the same amount of fresh thick cream, 3 tbs caster sugar and 3 tbs purée of wild strawberries. If the colour of this mixture is not sufficiently pink a few drops of red colour may be added. It may be flavoured to choice with vanilla, Kirsch or grated orange zest.

Sandwich the mixture between nice dry meringue shells.

4708 Mont-Blanc aux Fraises

Macerate some small wild strawberries with vanilla-flavoured syrup; when cold, drain them well. Add them to some stiffly beaten Crème Chantilly in the proportions of 125 g (4½ oz) strawberries to 1 litre (1¾ pt or 4½ U.S. cups) cream.

Place in a deep dish and smooth dome shape; surround the base with large strawberries which have been rolled in granulated sugar and decorate the surface with some very red, large half strawberries.

4709 Mont-Blanc aux Marrons

Cook some shelled chestnuts in sweetened vanilla-flavoured milk. When cooked, drain them well and pass through a sieve, directly into a border mould in such a way that it falls in the form of vermicelli and fills the mould naturally.

Fill with the rest of the chestnut purée but without crushing that which went in first. Demould on to a dish and fill the centre with Crème Chantilly forming it into a rugged, irregular shape.

4710 Mont-Rose

Prepare a Charlotte Plombière (4595) in a shallow Madeleine mould.

When set, demould it on to a dish and cover with tablespoons of Crème Chantilly mixed with a purée of fresh raspberries placing them on top in the form of a rocky pyramid.

4711 Mousse Monte-Carlo

Whip 5 dl (18 fl oz or 2¼ U.S. cups) very fresh cream until it is firm and frothy. Lightly mix in 80 g (3 oz) caster sugar, 20 g (¾ oz) vanilla sugar and 50 g (2 oz) dry meringues broken into small pieces.

Place in the top part of a double silver timbale, the bottom part filled with crushed ice and allow to chill for 1 hour.

4712 Mousseline d'Oeufs Réjane

Using a piping bag and plain tube, pipe out Ordinary Meringue in the shape of large macaroons on to sheets of greaseproof paper. Slide the sheets into sweetened boiling milk which has been flavoured with vanilla and withdraw them when the meringues have floated free.

Poach them until firm, remove and drain.

Place the meringues in twos in small china or silver egg dishes, set a nice cooked half of apricot in the middle and coat with a few tablespoons of thick Crème Anglaise.

Serve very cold.

4713 Oeufs à la Neige

Mould some Ordinary Meringue into egg shapes, using two spoons and dropping them as ready into a shallow pan of sweetened, vanilla-flavoured boiling milk. Turn them over when half cooked so that they are poached evenly; when firm, remove them and drain on a sieve.

Strain the milk through a piece of muslin and make it into a Crème Anglaise using 10 egg yolks per 1 litre (1¾ pt or 4½ U.S. cups) milk. Arrange the cooked meringues in a glass bowl and coat with the cold custard. Serve very cold.

4714 Oeufs à la Neige Moulés

Prepare the meringues and sauce as in the preceding recipe adding 5–6 soaked leaves of gelatine to the sauce.

Arrange the cooked meringues in an oiled border mould, cover with the almost setting Crème Anglaise and allow to set. Demould on to a round dish for servicing.

4715 Riz à l'Impératrice

Make some Prepared Rice for sweet dishes (4470). Allow it to cool then add 125 g (4½ oz) Salpicon of crystallized fruit and 4 tbs apricot purée per 250 g (9 oz) raw rice. Mix in an equal quantity of Kirsch Bavarois, or 5 dl (18 fl oz or 2¼ U.S. cups) each of Crème Anglaise Collée (4338) and whipped cream.

Pour the mixture into a deep border mould, the bottom of which has been previously set with a layer of redcurrant jelly; allow to set in a cool place or packed in ice. Turn out on to a serviette placed on a round dish for serving.

4716 Riz à la Maltaise

Prepare a rice mixture as in the preceding recipe flavouring it with grated orange zest instead of the apricot purée and omitting the crystallized fruits. Mix in an equal amount of orange Bavarois, pour into a dome-shaped mould and allow to set in a cool place or packed in ice.

Demould on to a round dish and cover with orange segments free from skin and pith and macerated in a syrup flavoured with orange zest; these should be arranged in alternating rows.

4717 Rôd Grôd *(Denmark)*

Place 500 g (1 lb 2 oz) redcurrants and 250 g (9 oz)

raspberries in a copper pan with 8 dl ($1\frac{1}{3}$ pt or $3\frac{1}{2}$ U.S. cups) water. Boil for a few minutes then pass the whole through a fine sieve. This should yield about $1\frac{1}{2}$ litres ($2\frac{5}{8}$ pt or $6\frac{1}{2}$ U.S. cups) liquid to which should be added 380 g (14 oz) sugar, 35 g ($1\frac{1}{4}$ oz) each of potato flour and ground sago—both diluted in a little water, 2 dl (7 fl oz or $\frac{7}{8}$ U.S. cup) red wine and a quarter of a vanilla pod. Replace on the stove and boil for 2 minutes whilst stirring well. Remove the vanilla.

Pour into dampened special china moulds which have been sprinkled with caster sugar and place in the refrigerator for 48 hours.

When required for serving, demould on to a dish and serve accompanied with a little fresh cream and some milk.

4718 Suédoise de Fruits

A Suédoise of fruits is a jelly set in an aspic mould with layers of poached fruit; the colours of the fruit and their arrangement should be as varied as possible.

4719 Tivoli aux Fraises

Line a fancy funnel mould with a thick layer of very clear Kirsch jelly. Fill with a Bavarois mixture containing a good amount of a purée of wild strawberries and allow to set.

Demould at the last moment and surround it with some very clear chopped Kirsch jelly.

CHAPTER 15

ICES

Ices and the petits fours that normally accompany them, bring the dinner to a close, at least as far as the kitchen is concerned. When they are well made and presented, they can be the epitome of finesse and delicacy. In no other area of cookery is there more opportunity for the creative artist to produce culinary fantasies and masterly presentations than this. If Italy was the birthplace of the ice-cream confectioners' art, and if the Neapolitans maintained a well-deserved reputation as practitioners of this skill, it was the innovations of French chefs that carried this important branch of culinary expertise to its greatest perfection.

4720 The Preparation of Ices
Whichever kind of ice is being made it is essential to start making it well in advance, and certainly as far as ordinary ices are concerned, it is impossible to prepare them at a moment's notice.

There are two separate and distinct stages in the making of ices; they are:

1) the preparation of the mixture, and
2) the freezing and moulding of the ice.

Taking the second stage first, which is the same for all kinds of ordinary ices whatever their composition—the essential operation is that of freezing.

Freezing the mixture means surrounding the container of prepared mixture with crushed ice to which is added freezing or sea salt and saltpetre, in the correct proportions. The action of these two salts on the ice causes a big drop in the temperature of the freezing media and thus the rapid freezing of the preparation subjected to it.

According to the kind of ice being made, the mixture is either placed directly into moulds—these ices being the Biscuits Glacés, Soufflés Glacés, Ice Puddings, Mousses, Parfaits, Bombes etc.—or are first churned in the ice-cream machine which is known as a *Sorbetière*, and then moulded and frozen in the moulds. The cream ices or rich ices containing butter and those made from a sugar syrup or water ices are both made by this last process.

The machine in which the mixtures are solidified are usually operated by hand either directly or by means of a cog-wheel mechanism. The inner section or churn is made of pure tin and has an outer central pivot incorporated in the base—this embeds itself in a small hole made in the bottom of the outer wooden container in which the churn is fixed.

When the churn is hermetically covered it is surrounded just up to the edge of the outside container with crushed ice containing 3 kg ($6\frac{3}{4}$ lb) freezing salt and 500 g (1 lb 2 oz) saltpetre per 20 kg (45 lb) ice. The central container must come above the level of the ice by a third of its height to prevent any of the salty ice accidentally getting into the container whilst it is being churned. The ice should be strongly packed around the container using a special wooden pestle. This preparation for freezing the ice should be done at least 10 minutes before being required.

The freezer now being ready, the ice mixture for freezing is poured in, the container covered with the lid and the utensil is turned backwards and forwards by means of the handle on top; or if using a machine the handle is turned to put it in motion either doing it in the same direction all the time or in each direction for a short time. In either case the mixture is swished against the sides of the churn where it quickly solidifies. These layers are removed as they solidify by means of a special spatula as the mixture freezes and gradually the whole mass becomes completely frozen and forms a smooth homogenous consistency. The care with which this operation is conducted has a great bearing on the smoothness and delicacy of the finished product.

Preference is given these days, however, to modern ice-cream machines which have two mixers with floating blades attached to the central pivot; these work in the opposite direction of the turning container and skim the mixture constantly from the sides as it freezes. At the same time the mixture receives a firm and regular mixing which cannot be obtained by hand.

4721 The Moulding of Ices
The mixture when frozen and ready can be scooped out in round shapes and arranged on a serviette as was once the custom, or placed in glass dishes. But more often it is filled into special moulds which have a lid that can be sealed hermetically. These moulds must be filled carefully and banged gently on a folded cloth so as to pack it closely and remove any air which would otherwise leave holes in the mixture. The filled mould is covered with its lid and then sealed by spreading a line of butter around the outside, over the join, so as to prevent any contact with the salted water coming from the melting ice. Finally, the mould is placed in a suitably large container for it to be surrounded with salted crushed ice, as for freezing in the ice-cream machine. The mould must be left in the ice for at least one hour for an ordinary ice, or at least 2 hours if it contains a light ice mixture that has not been frozen beforehand, such as for Bombes, Parfaits etc.

When ready, remove the mould from the ice at the last moment, quickly wash it under cold water to remove any trace of salt then plunge it into lukewarm water for a moment so as to warm the mould causing the ice to detach itself from the inside; turn the mould over and slip out the ice on to a folded serviette placed on a dish.

4722 Ordinary Ice Mixtures
There are two kinds of ordinary ice mixtures—those made with a custard mixture and those made with a syrup the latter being mainly used for the making of fruit ices. The amount of eggs and sugar used in making these mixtures being so variable, the following recipes are given as being the average.

If a richer kind of ice is required all that is necessary is to increase the proportions of egg yolks and sugar per litre of milk. On the other hand, if a less rich ice-cream is required the proportions should be decreased.

To give an idea of the big difference that exists between the contents of these mixtures, it is worth noting that the proportion of egg yolks to milk can vary from 7 to 16 per 1 litre (1¾ pt or 4½ U.S. cups) and the sugar from 200–500 g (7 oz–1 lb 2 oz) per 1 litre. As regards water ices and fruit ices, their strengths range between 15°–17° on the saccharometer right up to 30°–32°.

4723 Ordinary Ice-Cream
Mix together in a basin 300 g (11 oz) caster sugar and 10 egg yolks until the mixture becomes thick and white. Gradually mix in 1 litre (1¾ pt or 4½ U.S. cups) boiling milk, place over gentle heat and cook until the mixture coats the spoon well; stir continuously and prevent it from boiling which would cause the mixture to break down.

Pass the mixture through a fine strainer into a basin and stir occasionally until it is completely cold.

VARIOUS FLAVOURED ICE-CREAMS

In these compositions the proportion of sugar and egg yolks as well as the method for making them is the same for each. The only difference between them is the flavouring or infusion which gives the particular character of the preparation.

4724 Glace aux Amandes—Almond Ice-Cream
Finely pound 100 g (3½ oz) freshly peeled sweet almonds and 5 bitter almonds, slowly adding a few tablespoons of water to help bring out the aroma.

Add this paste to the boiled milk and allow it to infuse for 20 minutes, then proceed to make the custard as explained above using the same amount of sugar and egg yolks.

4725 Glace aux Asperges—Asparagus Ice-Cream
Blanch 180 g (6 oz) green asparagus tips for 2 minutes. Drain them well and pound quickly whilst adding a few tablespoons of milk. Place the resultant paste to infuse in the milk then proceed in the usual manner.

4726 Glace aux Avelines—Hazelnut Ice-Cream
Lightly toast 100 g (3½ oz) hazelnuts then pound them finely, adding a few tablesppons of milk. Place the resultant paste to infuse in the milk then proceed in the usual manner.

4727 Glace au Cafe—Coffee Ice-Cream
Add 50 g (2 oz) freshly roasted and ground coffee beans to the milk and allow to infuse for 20 minutes.

Alternatively, use the same amount of ground coffee and 2½ dl (9 fl oz or 1⅛ U.S. cups) boiling water to make a strong infusion then strain it and add to 7½ dl (1¼ pt or 3⅛ U.S. cups) boiled milk.

Proceed in the usual manner.

4728 Glace au Chocolat—Chocolate Ice-Cream
Dissolve 250 g (9 oz) grated chocolate in 2 dl (7 fl oz or ⅞ U.S. cup) water then add it to 1 litre (1¾ pt or 4½ U.S. cups) boiled milk in which a vanilla pod has been infused.

If using sweet chocolate, 250 g (9 oz) sugar and 7 egg yolks are sufficient for 1 litre (1¾ pt or 4½ U.S. cups) milk.

4729 Glace aux Noix—Walnut Ice-Cream
Finely pound 100 g (3½ oz) well peeled fresh walnuts then add this paste to the boiled milk and allow to infuse for 20 minutes before proceeding in the usual manner.

4730 Glace aux Pistaches—Pistachio Ice-Cream
Pound 30 g (1 oz) sweet almonds and 70 g (2½ oz) freshly skinned pistachios adding a few drops of milk. Place this paste to infuse in the boiled milk for 20 minutes then proceed in the usual manner.

4731 Glace au Praliné—Pralin Ice-Cream
Pound 125 g (4½ oz) almond Pralin (4354) and pass it through a sieve. Add this to 1 litre (1¾ pt or 4½ U.S. cups) prepared vanilla ice-cream mixture and freeze it in the usual manner.

4732 Glace au Thé—Tea Ice-Cream
Make 3 dl (½ pt or 1¼ U.S. cups) of a very strong infusion of tea and add it to 7½ dl (1¼ pt or 3⅛ U.S. cups) boiled milk. Proceed to make the ice-cream in the usual manner.

4733 Glace à la Vanille—Vanilla Ice-Cream
When the milk has come to the boil, place in it a nice vanilla pod and allow it to infuse for 20 minutes. Then make the ice-cream in the usual manner.

Note: If it is wished to increase the creaminess of these various mixtures the milk may be replaced either wholely or partly by fresh cream. It is also possible to add 1 dl (3½ fl oz or ½ U.S. cup) whipped cream per 1 litre (1¾ pt or 4½ U.S. cups) of finished ice cream.

4734 VARIOUS FRUITS AND ICES MADE WITH ESSENCES AND LIQUEURS

The basic ingredient of these mixtures is a syrup of 32° on the saccharometer, to which is added the purée of fruit, essence or the particular liqueur which characterizes the name of the ice.

All these mixtures contain an addition of lemon juice, the amount of which varies according to the acid nature of the fruit being used. But this is never less than that of the juice of 1 lemon per 1 litre (1¾ pt or 4½ U.S. cups) of the mixture no matter how acid the fruit might be.

The juice of an orange is also suitable, mainly in mixtures made from red fruits. By using the combined juices of both a lemon and an orange the flavour and aroma of the fruit is brought out to advantage.

When in season the fruit juices used for making fruit ices are obtained from fresh fruits which are squeezed then passed through a cloth or fine strainer. When the fruits are out of season it is possible to use bottled or canned fruit juice.

All ices made of red fruits particularly strawberry and raspberry, can be improved by the addition of 2½ dl (9 fl oz or 1⅛ U.S. cups) very fresh unwhipped cream per 1 litre (1¾ pt or 4½ U.S. cups) of the mixture, adding it to the ice during the freezing process.

4735 Fruit Ice Mixtures
These can be made in either of the two following ways:

A) Pass the fruit through a cloth or fine sieve after having pounded it previously if the texture of the fruit requires it. Mix this purée with an equal quantity of cold syrup at 32° and add the requisite amount of lemon juice as determined by the acid nature of the fruit being used. These two parts should always be mixed in the cold state and be checked on the saccharometer.

   If the saccharometer shows higher than the required degree the mixture can be brought to its correct degree by adding a little water. On the other hand, should the required degree not be attained, more syrup should be added until the required level is reached.

B) Pound the fruit with approximately 300 g (11 oz) sugar per 500 g (1 lb 2 oz) of fruit. This amount of sugar can only be stated approximately and must be adjusted up or down by taking into account whether the fruit used is more or less sweet.

   Pass the purée through a cloth or fine sieve and add the necessary quantity of filtered water to bring the mixture to the desired degree.

4736 Liqueur Ice Mixtures
These are obtained by the addition of the determined quantity of the required liqueur to the fruit or cream ice mixture. The liqueur is usually added when the mixture is cold.

About 1 dl (3½ fl oz or ½ U.S. cup) of liqueur is the average amount for 1 litre (1¾ pt or 4½ U.S. cups) of syrup. In certain cases the flavour and aroma of the liqueur is enhanced and brought out by the addition of an infusion such as tea for rum ice, orange zest for Curaçao ice, the crushed kernels of fresh cherries for Kirsch ice etc.

These mixtures should always have lemon juice added to them. The required degree of those made with syrup is the same as for fruit ice.

VARIOUS MIXTURES FOR FRUIT ICES

4737 Glace à l'Abricot—Apricot Ice
Use 5 dl (18 fl oz or 2¼ U.S. cups) each of purée of fresh apricots and syrup plus the juice of 2 lemons.

The mixture should be at 18°–19°.

4738 Glace à l'Ananas—Pineapple Ice
Place 5 dl (18 fl oz or 2¼ U.S. cups) grated or pounded pineapple to macerate in an equal quantity of Kirsch-flavoured syrup for 2 hours. Pass through a sieve and test that the mixture is at 18°–20°.

4739 Glace aux Bananes—Banana Ice
Place 5 dl (18 fl oz or 2¼ U.S. cups) pounded banana flesh in an equal quantity of Kirsch-flavoured syrup and allow to macerate for 2 hours. Add the juice of 3 lemons then pass through a sieve.

The mixture should be at 20°–21°.

4740 Glace aux Cerises—Cherry Ice
Crush the flesh of 5 dl (18 fl oz or 2¼ U.S. cups) stoned cherries and pound the stones. Place all to macerate for 1 hour in 5 dl (18 fl oz or 2¼ U.S. cups) Kirsch-flavoured syrup. Pass through a sieve and add the juice of half a lemon.

The mixture should be at 21°.

4741 Glace au Citron—Lemon Ice
Place the zest of 3 lemons to infuse in 5 dl (18 fl oz or 2¼ U.S. cups) cold syrup for 2 hours. Add the juice of 4 lemons and 2 oranges then pass through a fine strainer.

The mixture should be at 22°.

4742 Glace aux Fraises—Strawberry Ice
Mix together 5 dl (18 fl oz or 2¼ U.S. cups) each of strawberry purée and syrup; add the juice of 2 lemons and 2 oranges.

Alternatively the mixture can be made by pounding 1 kg (2¼ lbs) strawberries with 500 g (1 lb 2 oz) caster sugar then adding the juice of 2 oranges and 2 lemons and passing through a fine sieve. Add sufficient filtered water to bring the mixture to 16°–18°.

4743 Glace aux Framboises—Raspberry Ice
This is prepared in either of the ways as for strawberry ice.

4744 Glace à la Groseille—Redcurrant Ice
Add 5 dl (18 fl oz or 2¼ U.S. cups) redcurrant juice to the same quantity of syrup and mix well. Because of the acidity of the currants the lemon juice should be added sparingly.

The mixture should be at 20°.

4745 Glace aux Mandarines—Tangerine Ice
Place the zest of 4 tangerines into 7½ dl (1⅓ pt or 3¼ U.S. cups) boiling syrup. Allow to cool then pass through a strainer and finish with the juice of 6 tangerines, 2 oranges and 1 lemon.

The mixture should be at 21°.

4746 Glace au Melon—Melon Ice
Mix together 5 dl (18 fl oz or 2¼ U.S. cups) pulp of ripe melon, the same quantity of syrup, the juice of 2 oranges and 1 lemon, and 1 tbs orange flower water. Pass through a sieve.

The mixture should be at 22°.

4747 Glace à l'Orange—Orange Ice
Place the zest of 4 oranges to infuse in 1 litre (1¾ pt or 4½ U.S. cups) boiling syrup. Allow to cool then add the juice of 4 oranges and 1 lemon; pass through a fine strainer.

The mixture should be at 21°.

4748 Glace aux Pêches—Peach Ice
This is prepared in the same way as Apricot Ice.

4749 Glace aux Poires—Pear Ice
Peel the pears and remove the pips. Pound the flesh with 500 g (1 lb 2 oz) caster sugar per 500 g (1 lb 2 oz) fruit. Add the juice of 1 lemon per 500 g (1 lb 2 oz) pears. Pass the purée through a sieve and add sufficient filtered water to bring the mixture to 22°.

4750 Glace aux Prunes—Plum Ice
This is prepared in the same way as Apricot Ice; the mixture should be at 20°.

4751 Glace aux Raisins—Grape Ice
To 7½ dl (1⅓ pt or 3¼ U.S. cups) juice squeezed from sweet grapes add the juice of 3 lemons and the necessary amount of sugar to bring the mixture to 20°. Pass through a fine strainer.

4752 Glace aux Violettes—Violet Ice
Pick 250 g (9 oz) violet petals, wash them and place into 7½ dl (1⅓ pt or 3¼ U.S. cups) boiling syrup. Allow to infuse for 10 minutes, pass through a strainer and allow to cool. Add the juice of 3 lemons.

The mixture should be at 20°–21°.

VARIOUS ICES

4753 Glace Alhambra
Line a Madeleine mould with vanilla ice cream and fill the centre with Crème Chantilly containing strawberries which have been macerated with Noyau liqueur for 2 hours; the liqueur used in the macerating should also be added to the cream.

Note: When strawberries are not in season, strawberry Mousse can be used instead of the cream.

4754 Glace Carmen
Fill a deep mould with distinct vertical alternate layers of the following ices: strawberry, coffee and vanilla.

4755 Glace Comtesse-Marie
Use a special square mould—either plain or with fancy sides. Line it with strawberry ice and fill the centre with vanilla ice-cream. When demoulded decorate it by piping with vanilla ice-cream using a star tube.

4756 Glace Coucher de Soleil
Choose 500 g (1 lb 2 oz) very ripe large strawberries, place them in a silver timbale and sprinkle with caster sugar and 1 dl ($3\frac{1}{2}$ fl oz or $\frac{1}{2}$ U.S. cup) Grand Marnier. Cover with the lid and place on ice for 30 minutes. Pass the strawberries through a sieve and make the resultant purée into an ice proceeding in the usual manner.

When the ice is starting to set, mix in 5 dl (18 fl oz or $2\frac{1}{4}$ U.S. cups) Crème Chantilly; replace the lid, continue to freeze then allow it to stand for 35–40 minutes.

Arrange the ice pyramid-fashion in glass coupes.

Note: This ice takes its name from its colour which should be that of the western sky at sunset.

4757 Glace Dame-Jeanne
Line a Madeleine mould with vanilla ice-cream and fill the centre with Crème Chantilly containing crystallized orange flowers.

4758 Glace Dora
Line a Madeleine mould with vanilla ice-cream and fill the centre with Kirsch-flavoured Crème Chantilly containing some diced pineapple and redcurrants.

4759 Glace Etoile du Berger
Line a star-shaped mould or a Madeleine mould having a star-shape moulded in its base, with raspberry ice. Fill the centre with Bénédictine liqueur Mousse.

Allow to chill well then demould on to a roughly shaped round bed of white spun sugar, arranged on a dish.

The spun sugar will throw the ice into relief making it resemble the beams that radiate from the points of a star.

4760 Glace Fleurette
Fill a square mould with alternate even layers of strawberry ice and pineapple ice.

When frozen, demould on to a dish and decorate by piping with lemon ice.

4761 Glace Francillon
Line a square mould with coffee ice-cream and fill the centre with brandy-flavoured ice-cream.

4762 Fromages Glacés
These ices are generally made in plain oblong moulds using two different colours and flavours of ice arranged vertically along the length of the mould.

4763 Glace des Gourmets
Line a bombe mould with Pralin-flavoured vanilla ice-cream; fill the centre with alternate layers of candied chestnut ice-cream flavoured with Rum, and vanilla-flavoured Crème Chantilly.

When frozen, demould and coat the ice with pralined shredded almonds.

4764 Glace des Iles
Line a Madeleine mould with vanilla ice-cream and fill the centre with pineapple ice.

4765 Glace Madeleine
Fill a Madeleine mould with vanilla ice-cream mixed with half its amount of Crème Chantilly and containing crystallized fruits which have been macerated with Kirsch.

4766 Moulded Ices
These ices can be made in large or small moulds. The large moulds are lined with tin and have hinged lids and are made to represent various objects. The small ones are also lined with tin and are made in the form of flowers, fruits, birds, corn sheaves etc.; these are served mainly for ball suppers or for garnishes around a large ice.

Any variety of ice may be used to make them but as a rule the colour and flavour of the ice should match the shape of the mould.

The small moulds can be kept frozen until required or be demoulded in advance and kept frozen until required.

4767 Mandarines Givrées—Frosted Tangerines

Cut around the top of the tangerines with a plain round cutter and remove it with the stalk to which two leaves should be attached.

Remove the fruit from the skin and with it prepare a tangerine ice in the usual way as for fruit ices.

Refill the skins with the ice, replace the tops then using a brush, sprinkle some water in a fine rain over the skins; place them immediately into the freezing cabinet.

As soon as the skins are rimed with frost arrange them on a serviette on a dish; serve immediately as the frost will melt quickly.

4768 Mandarines Glacées aux Perles des Alpes

Empty the tangerines as in the preceding recipe. Fill the skins with tangerine Mousse to which has been added some very small boiled sweet drops which have been flavoured with Chartreuse liqueur.

Replace the tops, sprinkle with water and finish as described in the preceding recipe.

4769 Glace Marie-Thérèse

Line a Madeleine mould with chocolate ice-cream and fill the centre with vanilla-flavoured Crème Chantilly.

Demould and decorate by piping with pineapple ice.

4770 Meringues Glacées

Garnish meringue shells with any kind of ice moulded with a spoon, or using a little less ice, place it in between two meringue shells.

Serve arranged on a serviette.

4771 Glace Plombière

Fill a Parfait mould with layers of vanilla ice-cream containing crystallized fruit which has been macerated with Kirsch, and a stiff purée of apricots cooked with sugar and a little water.

COUPES

As the name implies, this section deals with Coupes which are garnished ices, or a mixture of ices of different colours and flavours, or ices which are served with Crème Chantilly or with fruits.

The coupes in which these ice sweets are served are usually of cut glass.

4772 Coupes Adelina Patti

Fill the coupes level with vanilla ice-cream; place in a circle on top 6 brandied cherries, which have been drained and rolled in caster sugar; decorate with a rosette of Crème Chantilly.

4773 Coupes d'Antigny

Three-quarters fill the coupes with strawberry ice made with *des Alpes* or the *Quatre Saison* variety of strawberries, to which has been added some very light and scented cream such as *Fleurette Normande* or *Crème Niçoise* from the Midi in France. Place a cooked half peach on top of each and cover with a small veil of spun sugar.

4774 Coupes Bohémienne

Fill the coupes to a peak with vanilla ice-cream containing pieces of candied chestnuts previously sprinkled with Rum; coat lightly with rum-flavoured Apricot Sauce.

4775 Coupes Châtelaine

Place some raspberries in the bottom of the coupes, the raspberries having previously been macerated with sugar, Curaçao and Brandy. Finish with a small shape of Crème Chantilly on top of each.

4776 Coupes Clo-Clo

Place in the coupes some vanilla ice-cream mixed with a debris of candied chestnuts macerated with Maraschino. Place a whole candied chestnut in the centre of each and surround with a border of Crème Chantilly mixed with raspberry purée, piping it with a star tube.

4777 Coupes Dame-Blanche

Three-quarters fill the coupes with almond milk ice-cream. On this place a half peach poached in vanilla-flavoured syrup its cut side uppermost; fill the cavity of each peach with Bar-le-Duc white currants.

Surround the peach with a circle of lemon ice using a piping bag and star tube.

4778 Coupes Denise

Place some coffee ice-cream in the coupes; sprinkle with a few small liqueur sweets, for preference rum-flavoured ones. Cover the surface with small spoonsful of Crème Chantilly.

4779 Coupes Edna May

Place vanilla ice in the bottom of the coupes and on top of each arrange some very cold cooked cherries. Cover completely with pink coloured Crème Chantilly made by adding raspberry purée to the cream, and smooth to a point.

4780 Coupes Elizabeth

Ice is not used for this coupe. At the bottom of the coupes place some very cold stoned Bigarreaux cherries which have been poached in a cherry brandy-flavoured syrup.

Cover with spoonfuls of Crème Chantilly and sprinkle with a little mixed spice of which cinnamon is the predominating flavour.

4781 Coupes Emma Calvé
Place Pralin-flavoured vanilla ice-cream in the bottom of the coupes. On top of each, arrange a layer of stoned cherries poached in Kirsch-flavoured syrup and cover these with raspberry purée.

4782 Coupes Eugénie
Place vanilla ice-cream containing pieces of candied chestnuts in the coupes.

Cover with Crème Chantilly and sprinkle with crystallized violets.

4783 Coupes à la Favorite
Place a ball of vanilla ice-cream and a ball of Kirsch and Maraschino ice in the coupes. Surround with pineapple ice and fill the centre with Crème Chantilly coloured and flavoured with raspberry purée.

4784 Coupes Germaine
Place vanilla ice-cream in the bottom of the coupes. Arrange a few glacé cherries macerated with Kirsch on top of each and cover with candied chestnuts pressed through a coarse sieve so that it looks like vermicelli. Surround with a border of Crème Chantilly.

4785 Coupes Gressac
Place vanilla ice-cream in the bottom of the coupes. On top of each arrange either 3 small or 1 large macaroon saturated with Kirsch and on these place a poached half peach the centre of which is filled with Bar-le-Duc redcurrants. Pipe a border of Crème Chantilly around the peach.

4786 Coupes Hélène
Fill the coupes level with vanilla ice-cream. Decorate with a circle of crystallized violets, place some Crème Chantilly dome shape in the centre and sprinkle this with grated chocolate.

4787 Coupes Jacques
Fill one side of the coupes with lemon ice and the other side with strawberry ice leaving a space in the centre in which to place a spoonful of fresh fruit salad macerated with Kirsch.

4788 Coupes Jeannette
Fill the coupes with vanilla ice-cream and surround with a border of Crème Chantilly. Fill the centre with grated chocolate.

4789 Coupes Madeleine
Fill the coupes with vanilla ice-cream containing a Salpicon of crystallized pineapple. Coat with a thin layer of Kirsch and Maraschino-flavoured Apricot Sauce.

4790 Coupes Malmaison
Fill the coupes with vanilla ice-cream containing some peeled and depipped muscatel grapes.

Cover with a veil of spun sugar.

4791 Coupes Mexicaine
Fill the coupes with tangerine ice containing pineapple cut in very small dice.

4792 Coupes Midinette
Half fill the coupes with vanilla ice-cream. On top place a small round meringue and a small cooked half peach. Pipe a border of Crème Chantilly around the edge.

4793 Coupes Mireille
Fill the coupes with half vanilla ice-cream and half redcurrant ice-cream.

In the centre place a nectarine which has been poached in vanilla-flavoured syrup, the stone removed and replaced with some Bar-le-Duc white currant jam. Decorate with Crème Chantilly and cover with a veil of spun sugar.

4794 Coupes Monte-Carlo
Fill the coupes with vanilla-flavoured Crème Chantilly containing some small strawberries and small broken pieces of meringue.

4795 Coupes Petit-Duc
Fill the coupes with vanilla ice-cream. Place in each a poached half peach cut side uppermost; fill the centre of these with Bar-le-Duc redcurrants. Surround with a border of lemon ice.

4796 Coupes Rêve de Bébé
Fill the coupes half with pineapple ice and half with raspberry ice. Between the two ices arrange a line of small strawberries which have been macerated with orange sugar.

Surround with a border of Crème Chantilly and sprinkle this with crystallized violets.

4797 Coupes Madame Sans-Gêne
Line the bottom and sides of the coupes with a layer of vanilla ice-cream. Fill the centre of each with Bar-le-Duc redcurrants and cover with small spoonfuls of Crème Chantilly.

4798 Coupes Stella
Half fill the coupes with vanilla ice-cream. On top

of each arrange a small meringue and a peeled poached half apricot coated with Kirsch-flavoured Apricot Sauce. Surround with a border of Crème Chantilly.

4799 Coupe Thaïs
Half fill the coupes with vanilla ice-cream. Place a half peach on top of each and surround with a border of Crème Chantilly. Sprinkle the cream with chocolate shavings.

4800 Coupes Tutti-frutti
In the bottom of the coupes place a layer of mixed diced crystallized fruits macerated with Kirsch and Maraschino. Fill with alternate layers of strawberry, lemon and pineapple ice with a layer of the diced fruit between each.

4801 Coupes Vénus
Half fill the coupes with vanilla ice-cream. Place a small peach, poached in vanilla-flavoured syrup, in the centre of each and place a small very red strawberry on top. Surround the peaches with a border of Crème Chantilly.

4802 Coupes Victoria
Place small pieces of candied chestnuts macerated with Kirsch, in the bottom of the coupes. Fill each with vanilla ice and strawberry ice and place a whole candied chestnut in the centre.

LIGHT ICE-CREAMS

This kind of ice-cream is different from those dealt with up until now in that the mixture is placed into the moulds and frozen without first being churned in the ice-cream machine. Some of the nicest and most popular ices such as *Biscuits glacés*, *Bombes*, *Mousses*, *Parfaits*, *Poudings* and *Soufflés glacés* come into this category and because no special equipment is required they can be made in most establishments. These ices are all very much alike and the derivation of their different names are for most of the time quite puzzling and more often than not mere flights of fancy.

BISCUITS GLACES

4803 Biscuit glacé Mixture (*old method*)
Previously the mixture for Biscuits Glacés was a custard made with 500 g (1 lb 2 oz) sugar, 12 egg yolks and 1 litre ($1\frac{3}{4}$ pt or $4\frac{1}{2}$ U.S. cups) flavoured milk.

When ready, the custard was passed through a strainer into a basin and allowed to cool whilst stirring from time to time. The basin was then placed on ice and the custard whisked until it thickened.

Originally, the custard, without further addition, was placed into the mould; now it is usual to add 1 litre of whipped cream which makes it a mixture similar to that for Bombes which in turn is often confused with the mixture for Mousses.

4804 Biscuit glacé Mixture (*modern method*)
Place 12 egg yolks and 500 g (1 lb 2 oz) caster sugar in a copper bowl and whisk over a pan of hot water until the mixture becomes thick and white. Remove the bowl from the heat and continue whisking until the mixture is cold. Finally, mix in 250 g (9 oz) Italian meringue and 1 litre ($1\frac{3}{4}$ pt or $4\frac{1}{2}$ U.S. cups) whipped cream.
The Moulding of Biscuits Glacés: These are moulded in oblong tins of the shape of a brick. They have two lids—one for the top, the other for the bottom. Usually the mixture moulded in the two lids is of a flavour and colour different to that placed in the middle of the mould.

So, for example, one of the lids would be filled with strawberry mixture and the other with violet, whilst the centre compartment would be filled with vanilla mixture. When cut into vertical slices after being frozen and demoulded, these Biscuits Glacés show the distinctly marked different colours.

These rectangular slices are placed into special paper cases and the surface decorated as required for the particular presentation; they are then placed in the freezer until required for service.

Most of the Bombe mixtures can be used as a basis for Biscuits Glacés using the same name to indicate its composition.

4805 Biscuit Glacé à la Bénédictine
Fill the bottom part of the mould with a vanilla-flavoured mixture, the centre with a strawberry-flavoured mixture and the top with a Pralin-flavoured mixture.

4806 Biscuit Glacé Marquise
Fill the mould with two alternate layers of Kirsch-flavoured and strawberry-flavoured mixtures.

4807 Biscuit Glacé Mont Blanc
Fill the bottom part of the mould with a Rum-flavoured mixture, the centre with chestnut mixture and the top with vanilla-flavoured mixture.

4808 Biscuit Glacé à la Napolitaine
Fill the bottom part of the mould with a vanilla-flavoured mixture, the centre with a strawberry-flavoured mixture and the top with a Pralin-flavoured mixture.

4809 Biscuit Glacé Princesse
Fill the mould with a Pralin-flavoured mixture. When frozen, turn out and coat with toasted shredded almonds. Cut into slices and decorate each slice with piped vanilla ice-cream and tangerine ice.

4810 Biscuit Glacé Sigurd
Fill the mould half with strawberry mixture and complete with a pistachio mixture. Freeze, cut into slices and sandwich each slice between two wafers.

BOMBES

Bombes were originally made with ordinary ice mixtures and were moulded in round moulds, hence the name. This name was the more justified by the interior arrangement of concentric layers one on top of the other with only a very thin outer covering.

Nowadays Bombes are moulded in plain conical-shaped moulds with a round dome. The bombe mixture is a much finer one than it used to be.

4811 Bombe Mixture
Gradually mix 1 litre ($1\frac{3}{4}$ pt or $4\frac{1}{2}$ U.S. cups) syrup at 28° on the saccharometer into 32 beaten egg yolks.

Place over a low heat and whisk as for a sponge cake mixture until it becomes thick and white. Remove from the heat and continue whisking until the mixture is cold.

Now add the chosen flavouring and mix in $1\frac{1}{2}$ litres ($2\frac{5}{8}$ pt or $6\frac{1}{2}$ U.S. cups) stiffly whipped cream.

4812 The Moulding of Bombes
Firstly, line the bottom and side of the bombe mould with the ice as indicated by its name. This lining, the thickness of which can vary according to the size of the mould, should preferably be a thin one and should be ordinary ice mixture rather than Bombe mixture; ice-cream lends itself to this use far better than anything else.

The centre is then filled with a Bombe mixture of the correct flavour, or with a cold Mousse preparation. This is then covered with a round of paper and the mould is hermetically sealed with the lid. It is then frozen for at least 2 hours.

To serve the Bombe, remove it from the ice, wash the mould in cold water then dip into hot water; dry it, then demould on to a dish or on to a carved block of ice.

4813 Bombe Aboukir
Line the mould with pistachio ice-cream and fill with Pralin-flavoured bombe mixture.

4814 Bombe Abricotine
Line the mould with apricot ice and fill with alternate layers of Kirsch-flavoured bombe mixture and apricot purée cooked with sugar.

4815 Bombe Africaine
Line the mould with chocolate ice-cream and fill with rum-flavoured apricot bombe mixture.

4816 Bombe Aïda
Line the mould with strawberry ice-cream and fill with Kirsch-flavoured bombe mixture.

4817 Bombe Alméria
Line the mould with Anisette ice-cream and fill with Grenadine-flavoured bombe mixture.

4818 Bombe Alhambra
Line the mould with vanilla ice-cream and fill with strawberry bombe mixture; demould and surround with a circle of large strawberries macerated with Kirsch.

4819 Bombe Américaine
Line the mould with strawberry ice-cream and fill with tangerine bombe mixture; when demoulded decorate with pistachio ice-cream.

4820 Bombe Andalouse
Line the mould with apricot ice flavoured with Noyau liqueur and fill with vanilla bombe mixture.

4821 Bombe Batavia
Line the mould with pineapple ice-cream and fill with strawberry bombe mixture containing diced crystallized ginger.

4822 Bombe Bourdaloue
Line the mould with vanilla ice-cream and fill with Anisette-flavoured bombe mixture; demould and decorate with crystallized violets.

4823 Bombe Brésilienne
Line the mould with pineapple ice-cream and fill with vanilla and Rum-flavoured bombe mixture containing diced pineapple.

4824 Bombe Camargo
Line the mould with coffee ice-cream and fill with vanilla bombe mixture.

4825 Bombe Cardinal
Line the mould with redcurrant and raspberry ice-cream and fill with vanilla and Pralin bombe mixture.

4826 Bombe Ceylan
Line the mould with coffee ice-cream and fill with Rum-flavoured bombe mixture.

4827 Bombe Chateaubriand
Line the mould with chestnut and rum ice-cream and fill with vanilla bombe mixture.

4828 Bombe Clarence
Line the mould with pineapple ice-cream and fill with violet bombe mixture.

4829 Bombe Colombia
Line the mould with Kirsch ice-cream and fill with pear bombe mixture; when demoulded decorate with glacé cherries.

4830 Bombe Coppélia
Line the mould with coffee ice-cream and fill with Pralin-flavoured bombe mixture.

4831 Bombe Czarine
Line the mould with vanilla ice-cream and fill with Kümmel-flavoured bombe mixture; when demoulded decorate with crystallized violets.

4832 Bombe Dame-Blanche
Line the mould with vanilla ice-cream and fill with almond milk bombe mixture.

4833 Bombe Danicheff
Line the mould with coffee ice-cream and fill with Kirsch-flavoured bombe mixture.

4834 Bombe Diable rose
Line the mould with strawberry ice-cream and fill with Kirsch-flavoured bombe mixture containing glacé cherries.

4835 Bombe Diplomate
Line the mould with vanilla ice-cream and fill with Maraschino-flavoured bombe mixture containing crystallized fruits.

4836 Bombe Duchesse
Line the mould with pineapple ice-cream and fill with pear bombe mixture flavoured with Kirsch.

4837 Bombe Fanchon
Line the mould with pralin ice-cream and fill with Kirsch-flavoured bombe mixture containing coffee bean bonbons.

4838 Bombe Fauvette
Line the mould with pistachio ice-cream and fill with banana bombe mixture flavoured with Kirsch.

4839 Bombe Favorite
Line the mould with vanilla ice-cream and fill with strawberry Mousse. When demoulded decorate with large strawberries.

4840 Bombe Fédora
Line the mould with orange ice and fill with pralin bombe mixture.

4841 Bombe Florentine
Line the mould with raspberry ice-cream and fill with Pralin bombe mixture.

4842 Bombe Formosa
Line the mould with vanilla ice-cream and fill with strawberry bombe mixture containing large crystallized strawberries. When fresh strawberries are available omit the crystallized variety in the bombe mixture but place a circle of the fresh ones around the Bombe when it is demoulded.

4843 Bombe Francillon
Line the mould with coffee ice-cream and fill with brandy-flavoured bombe mixture.

4844 Bombe Frou-Frou
Line the mould with vanilla ice-cream and fill with Rum-flavoured bombe mixture containing crystallized fruits.

4845 Bombe Georgette
Line the mould with pralin ice-cream and fill with Kirsch-flavoured bombe mixture.

4846 Bombe Gismonda
Line the mould with pralin ice-cream and fill with Anisette-flavoured bombe mixture containing some Bar-le Duc whitecurrants.

4847 Bombe Grande-Duchesse
Line the mould with pear ice-cream and fill with Chartreuse-flavoured bombe mixture.

4848 Bombe Havanaise
Line the mould with coffee ice-cream and fill with vanilla and Rum-flavoured bombe mixture.

4849 Bombe Hilda
Line the mould with hazelnut ice-cream and fill with Chartreuse-flavoured bombe mixture containing hazelnut Pralin.

4850 Bombe Hollandaise
Line the mould with vanilla ice-cream and fill with Curaçao-flavoured bombe mixture.

4851 Bombe Jaffa
Line the mould with Pralin ice-cream and fill with orange bombe mixture.

4852 Bombe Japonaise
Line the mould with vanilla and Rum-flavoured ice-cream and fill with tea-flavoured Mousse.

4853 Bombe Jeanne d'Arc
Line the mould with vanilla ice-cream and fill with chocolate bombe mixture containing Pralin.

4854 Bombe Josephine
Line the mould with coffee ice-cream and fill with pistachio bombe mixture.

4855 Bombe Madeleine
Line the mould with almond ice-cream and fill with vanilla and Kirsch-flavoured bombe mixture containing crystallized fruits.

4856 Bombe Maltaise
Line the mould with blood orange ice and fill with vanilla-flavoured Crème Chantilly.

4857 Bombe Maréchal
Line the mould with strawberry ice-cream and fill with layers of pistachio, vanilla and orange bombe mixtures.

4858 Bombe Margot
Line the mould with almond ice-cream and fill with pistachio bombe mixture; when demoulded decorate by piping with vanilla ice-cream.

4859 Bombe Marie-Louise
Line the mould with raspberry ice-cream and fill with vanilla bombe mixture.

4860 Bombe Marquise
Line the mould with apricot ice cream and fill with Champagne bombe mixture.

4861 Bombe Mascotte
Line the mould with peach ice-cream and fill with Kirsch-flavoured bombe mixture.

4862 Bombe Mathilde
Line the mould with Kirsch-flavoured ice-cream and fill with apricot bombe mixture.

4863 Bombe Médicis
Line the mould with Brandy-flavoured ice-cream and fill with raspberry bombe mixture.

4864 Bombe Mercédès
Line the mould with apricot ice-cream and fill with Chartreuse-flavoured bombe mixture.

4865 Bombe Mignon
Line the mould with apricot ice-cream and fill with hazelnut bombe mixture.

4866 Bombe Miss Helyett
Line the mould with strawberry ice-cream and fill with vanilla bombe mixture.

4867 Bombe Mogador
Line the mould with coffee ice-cream and fill with Kirsch-flavoured bombe mixture.

4868 Bombe Moldave
Line the mould with pineapple ice-cream and fill with Curaçao-flavoured bombe mixture.

4869 Bombe Montmorency
Line the mould with Kirsch-flavoured ice-cream and fill with cherry bombe mixture; when demoulded surround the Bombe with halves of glacé cherries.

4870 Bombe Moscovite
Line the mould with Kümmel-flavoured ice-cream and fill with bitter almond bombe mixture containing crystallized fruits.

4871 Bombe Mousseline
Line the mould with strawberry ice-cream and fill with Crème Chantilly containing small pieces of macaroon saturated with Curaçao.

4872 Bombe Nabab
Line the mould with Pralin ice-cream and fill with Brandy-flavoured bombe mixture containing crystallized fruits.

4873 Bombe Nélusko
Line the mould with Pralin ice-cream and fill with chocolate bombe mixture.

4874 Bombe Néro
Line a dome-shape mould with caramel-flavoured vanilla ice cream and fill with vanilla Mousse containing truffle-shapes of chocolate the size of hazelnuts.

When ready, turn out the bombe on to a round piece of Punch Sponge Biscuit (4327) of the same diameter as the mould and set in the middle of a round dish. Cover the whole with a thin coating of Italian meringue, set a small baked pastry case brushed inside with very well cooked apricot jam on top, and cover round the sides with piped meringue; glaze quickly in a hot oven.

On removing from the oven, pour some hot Rum into the pastry case and set it alight as it is taken into the dining-room.

4875 Bombe Nesselrode
Line the mould with vanilla ice-cream and fill with Crème Chantilly mixed with a fine purée of chestnuts.

4876 Bombe Odette
Line the mould with vanilla ice-cream and fill with Pralin-flavoured bombe mixture.

4877 Bombe Odessa
Line the mould with apricot ice and fill with strawberry bombe mixture.

4878 Bombe à l'Orientale
Line the mould with ginger ice-cream and fill with pistachio bombe mixture.

4879 Bombe Patricienne
Line the mould with vanilla ice-cream and fill with coffee bombe mixture.

4880 Bombe Petit-Duc
Line the mould with strawberry ice-cream and fill with hazelnut bombe mixture containing some Bar-le-Duc redcurrants.

4881 Bombe Pompadour
Line the mould with pale pink strawberry ice-cream and fill with Curaçao-flavoured Mousse containing crushed meringues.

4882 Bombe Prophète
Line the mould with strawberry ice-cream and fill with pineapple bombe mixture.

4883 Bombe Richelieu
Line the mould with Rum-flavoured ice-cream and fill with coffee bombe mixture. When demoulded, decorate with crystallized coffee grains.

4884 Bombe Rosette
Line the mould with vanilla ice-cream and fill with Crème Chantilly containing some Bar-le-Duc redcurrants.

4885 Bombe à la Royale
Line the mould with Kirsch-flavoured ice-cream and fill with chocolate and Pralin bombe mixture.

4886 Bombe Santiago
Line the mould with Brandy-flavoured ice-cream and fill with pistachio bombe mixture.

4887 Bombe Sélika
Line the mould with Pralin ice-cream and fill with Curaçao-flavoured bombe mixture.

4888 Bombe Skobeleff
Line the mould with Vodka-flavoured ice-cream and fill with Crème Chantilly flavoured with Kümmel.

4889 Bombe Strogoff
Line the mould with peach ice-cream and fill with Kirsch-flavoured bombe mixture.

4890 Bombe Succès
Line the mould with apricot ice-cream and fill with Kirsch-flavoured Crème Chantilly containing diced crystallized apricots.

4891 Bombe Sultane
Line the mould with chocolate ice-cream and fill with pistachio bombe mixture.

4892 Bombe Suzanne
Line the mould with pink-coloured Rum-flavoured ice-cream and fill with vanilla bombe mixture containing some Bar-le-Duc redcurrants.

4893 Bombe Tortoni
Line the mould with Pralin ice-cream and fill with coffee bombe mixture containing crystallized coffee beans.

4894 Bombe Tosca
Line the mould with apricot ice-cream and fill with Maraschino-flavoured bombe mixture containing diced fruit; decorate with piped lemon ice when about to serve.

4895 Bombe Trocadéro
Line the mould with orange ice containing some finely diced crystallized orange peel; fill with alternate layers of Crème Chantilly and round slices of almond-flavoured Genoise; these should be cut into graduated sizes, saturated with Curaçao-flavoured syrup and sprinkled with some diced crystallized orange peel.

4896 Bombe Tutti-frutti
Line the mould with strawberry ice-cream and fill with lemon ice containing diced crystallized fruit.

4897 Bombe à la Valencay
Line the mould with Pralin ice-cream and fill with Crème Chantilly containing raspberries.

4898 Bombe Vénitienne
Line the mould half with vanilla and half with

strawberry ice-cream and fill with Kirsch and Maraschino-flavoured bombe mixture.

4899 Bombe Victoria
Line the mould with strawberry ice-cream and fill with Plombière ice (4771) containing pieces of candied chestnuts lightly macerated with Kirsch and Maraschino.

4900 Bombe Zamora
Line the mould with coffee ice-cream and fill with Curaçao-flavoured bombe mixture.

MOUSSES GLACES—ICED MOUSSES

These Mousses can be made either from a *Crème Anglaise* mixture or from a syrup. The syrup method is most suitable for making iced fruit Mousses.

4901 Iced Fruit Mousse Mixture
This is a cold syrup at 35° on the saccharometer to which is added an equal amount of a purée of the appropriate fruit and twice that amount of fairly firm Crème Chantilly.

4902 Iced Cream Mousse Mixture
Make a Crème Anglaise (4337) using 16 egg yolks, 500 g (1 lb 2 oz) caster sugar and 5 dl (18 fl oz or 2¼ U.S. cups) milk. Allow to cool, stirring occasionally and when very cold mix in 5 dl (18 fl oz or 2¼ U.S. cups) unwhipped cream, 20 g (⅔ oz) gum tragacanth in powder form and the selected flavouring. If making a fruit Mousse by this method, add 5 dl (18 fl oz or 2¼ U.S. cups) of a purée of the appropriate fruit.

Place the mixture on ice and whisk until it becomes light and frothy then fill into moulds lined with greaseproof paper. Seal hermetically and freeze thoroughly for 2–3 hours according to the size of the mould.

4903 Various Iced Mousses
Using the same methods as given above, Mousses can be made in the following flavours. Mousse Glacée à l'Anisette, au Café, au Chocolat, au Kirsch, au Marasquin, au Rhum, au Thé, à l'Abricot, aux Fraises, aux Oranges, aux Mandarines, aux Noix Fraîches, aux Pêches, à la Vanille, aux Violettes, etc.

PARFAITS

4904 Parfait Mixture
Mix 32 egg yolks with 1 litre (1¾ pt or 4½ U.S. cups) cold syrup at 28° on the saccharometer and pass through a strainer.

Place on the stove and cook gently and stirring constantly until the mixture coats the spoon well.

Place on ice and whisk until it is completely cold.

Add 1 dl (3½ fl oz or ½ U.S. cup) Brandy or Rum and mix in 1 litre (1¾ pt or 4½ U.S. cups) whipped cream. Fill into parfait moulds and freeze thoroughly for 2–3 hours.

Note: The name Parfait which used to apply solely to a *Parfait au Café* has now become the usual name for iced sweets of a single flavour Bombe mixture, without lining the mould. This is quite logical seeing that a Bombe mixture, apart from a few minor details, is exactly the same as a Parfait mixture.

It is therefore perfectly possible and only natural to make Parfait à la Vanille, au Chocolat, Praliné etc. as well as au Café.

ICED PUDDINGS

The preparations known under this heading do not follow any rigid rules and, strictly speaking, are not ice-cream sweets. They are in reality, iced sweets, the basis of which is usually a Crème Anglaise with the addition of gelatine as used for making a Bavarois.

The following recipes are exceptions to the above.

4905 Pouding Glacé de Castries
Line a Bombe mould with a thin lining of vanilla ice-cream. Fill the centre with very thin alternate layers of two different Bombe mixtures.

One of these mixtures should be vanilla and on each layer of it sprinkle some diced Finger Biscuits previously saturated with Anisette. The second mixture should be tangerine.

Also between each layer of Bombe mixture, sprinkle a little grated chocolate. Finish with a top layer of vanilla ice-cream.

Seal the mould hermetically and freeze the pudding for 2 hours; demould and sprinkle the top with crushed red *Pralines*.

Serve accompanied with very cold tangerine syrup.

4906 Pouding Glacé Marie-Rose
Line a Charlotte mould with rolled Gaufrette wafers placing them very closely together. Using a piping bag and small tube fill each wafer with some firm strawberry ice.

Fill the centre of the mould with vanilla bombe mixture flavoured with Pralin.

Seal the mould hermetically and freeze for 2

hours. When required for serving, demould on to a serviette on a dish and decorate the top with pink Crème Chantilly and ordinary Crème Chantilly.

Serve accompanied with a very cold chocolate sauce.

4907 Pouding Glacé Miramar
Line a Madeleine ice mould with Finger Biscuits saturated with Chartreuse, alternating with thin slices of fresh pineapple macerated with Kirsch, and peeled and depipped segments of tangerine. Fill the centre of the mould with pomegranate juice Bombe mixture flavoured with Kirsch.

Close the mould, freeze for 2 hours and demould on to a serviette on a dish for serving.

Serve accompanied with very cold vanilla-flavoured syrup.

4908 Pouding Glacé Seymour
Cut a mousseline Brioche into thin slices and place them to soak in cream which has been sweetened with sugar and flavoured with Kirsch.

Peel some peaches, slice them very thinly and poach in vanilla-flavoured syrup. Peel and thinly slice some very ripe pears.

Prepare a pink Bombe mixture flavoured with Kirsch and Orgeat.

In a dome-shaped mould arrange alternate layers of the slices of Brioche, the slices of peaches and pears, adding some Bar-le-Duc redcurrants, and the Bombe mixture.

Seal the mould hermetically, freeze for 2 hours then demould the pudding on to a serviette on a dish.

SOUFFLES GLACES—ICED SOUFFLES

The mixtures for iced soufflés are different according to whether the soufflé is a fruit one or a flavoured one such as vanilla, coffee or chocolate etc.

The flavoured soufflés are made with the Iced Cream Mousse Mixture; this can also be used to make an iced fruit soufflé but the following mixture is preferable.

4909 Iced Fruit Soufflé Mixture
Whisk 10 egg whites until stiff then whisk in 500 g (1 lb 2 oz) sugar cooked to the soft crack stage. Place in a basin and allow to become cold then mix in 5 dl (18 fl oz or 2¼ U.S. cups) each of fruit purée and stiffly whipped cream.

The Moulding of Large and Small Iced Soufflés:
Large soufflés are moulded in ordinary soufflé moulds which have a band of stiff paper tied around the outside coming 2–3 cm (1 in) above the edge of the dish so that when the mixture is set and the paper removed it gives the impression of a risen soufflé.

Individual soufflés are moulded in paper cases or in small silver dishes also surrounded with a band of paper to bring the mixture up above the edge of the dish.

Immediately they are filled the dishes are placed to freeze.

When required for serving, carefully peel away the band of paper which has now served its purpose. Arrange the soufflé or soufflés on a serviette on a dish or on a sculpted block of ice.

Iced soufflés may be varied in the same way as Bombes and Biscuits Glacés.

SORBETS

GRANITES, MARQUISES, PUNCHS AND SPOOMS

The Sorbets and those other preparations which are derived from them are very light ices, barely frozen, and which are served after the Entrée at a formal dinner.

Their role is that of refreshing the palate and to prepare the stomach for the roast course which will be served following the Sorbet.

In fact a Sorbet is both an aperitif and an aid to digestion.

4910 Sorbet Mixture
Sorbets are made with any of the liqueur-flavoured ice mixtures which should be regulated to 15° on the saccharometer; they may also be prepared as follows:

For 1 litre (1¾ pt or 4½ U.S. cups) of Sorbet: the juice of 2 lemons and 1 orange, 5 dl (18 fl oz or 2¼ U.S. cups) Port, Samos wine, fine Sauternes or other fine wine and sufficient cold syrup at 22° to bring the mixture to 15° on the saccharometer.

For liqueur Sorbets: It is usual to allow on average 1 dl (3½ fl oz or ½ U.S. cup) of liqueur per 1 litre (1¾ pt or 4½ U.S. cups) of the above finished mixture, according to the kind of liqueur used. In this case a syrup of 18°–19° is used and the addition of the liqueur will bring it to the required degree.

Whatever liqueur is being used, it should not be added until the Sorbet is completed and frozen, almost, so to speak, at the last moment before it is going to be served.

Fruit Sorbets: these are mainly made with clear fruit juice or fruit syrup; fruit purées are not very suitable for this preparation and it is only in exceptional cases that they can be used.

The freezing of Sorbets: pour the mixture into the previously chilled container and set the freezing machine in motion scraping down the sides as it freezes against them and placing it back with the rest. Once it has become frozen, stop turning.

When it is sufficiently firm add a quarter its amount of Italian meringue or stiffly whipped cream and mix in slowly and carefully. Finish by adding the liqueur.

To Serve Sorbets: take spoonfuls of the mixture and arrange it in Sorbet glasses or delicate wine glasses bringing the sorbet up to a point.

For a wine Sorbet, after placing it in the glass, pour a spoonful of the same wine as used in its preparation.

The consistency of all the various kinds of Sorbets must be such that they can almost be drunk from the glass.

4911 Various Sorbets

Having stated that Sorbets can be made from all kinds of fruit juices such as pineapple, cherries, strawberries, raspberries, redcurrants, etc. and with all kinds of liqueurs and wines such as Port, Samos wine, Marsala, Rhine wines, Rum, Kirsch, Brandy etc., and that the method of preparation is the same for all of them, it is judged to be unnecessary to give a separate recipe for each.

4912 Sorbet à la Sicilienne

Place a very green water melon in the refrigerator for 3 hours. One hour before it is required for serving, cut out a round section from the top and remove the seeds and filaments as indicated for Melon en Surprise.

Scoop off the flesh, using a silver dessertspoon but do not remove it from the inside of the melon. Sprinkle it with Maraschino and replace in the refrigerator.

Arrange the melon on a dish of crushed ice or on a sculpted block of ice, then present and serve it in Sorbet glasses in front of the guests.

4913 Granités

On the menu, Granités play the same role as the Sorbets; they also occur as adjuncts in several other preparations.

Granités have as a base, a very thin syrup of not more than 14° on the saccharometer. They are made entirely of a syrup without the addition of Italian meringue or of any other kind of ingredients.

Even more so than with Sorbets, Granités must not be worked too much during the freezing process as this will cause them to break down. When it is properly frozen it should form a lightly granulated mixture.

4914 Marquises

Marquises are prepared particularly with strawberries, pineapple and with Kirsch.

The mixture is similar to that of a Kirsch sorbet but marking only 17° on the saccharometer. They are frozen in the same way as the Granités but the result should be a little firmer.

When about to serve, mix in 4 dl (14 fl oz or 1¾ U.S. cups) Crème Chantilly flavoured with strawberry or pineapple purée, per 1 litre (1¾ pt or 4½ U.S. cups) of the frozen mixture.

4915 Punch à la Romaine

Mix the required quantity of dry white wine or dry Champagne into 5 dl (18 fl oz or 2¼ U.S. cups) of syrup at 22° to bring it to 17° on the saccharometer.

Add the juice of 2 oranges and 3 lemons, a thin strip each of orange and lemon zest, cover and allow to infuse for 1 hour. Pass through a strainer and adjust it to 18°.

Freeze the punch in the machine until it is fairly stiff then mix in a quarter its quantity of Italian meringue made in the proportions of 2 egg whites to 100 g (3½ oz) sugar.

When about to serve, finish the Punch with 1 dl (3½ fl oz or ½ U.S. cup) Rum added a little at a time.

Serve the Punch in glasses in the same way as for a Sorbet.

Note: For all these Sorbets and Punches the yield from 1 litre (1¾ pt or 4½ U.S. cups) of finished mixture is 15 portions.

4916 Spooms

Spooms are Sorbets made with a syrup at 20° on the saccharometer. Italian meringue is added to it using twice as much as for ordinary Sorbet because it must be very light and frothy.

Spooms are made with fruit juice, but more often with a wine such as Champagne, Samos, Muscat, Zucco etc.

They are served in glasses in the same way as a Sorbet.

CHAPTER 16

SAVOURIES

It is suggested that the inclusion of a savoury in the menu goes against all the rules of gastronomy and that they have no right to be included in a classical menu. Despite this the following recipes for savouries are given, these being chosen from amongst the most acceptable from a gastronomic point of view and those most commonly used. There is a relationship between Hors-d'oeuvre and savouries and many of the hot Hors-d'oeuvre given in that chapter can be served as savouries by merely heightening the seasoning. Amongst those worth noting are the various tartlets and Barquettes, Frivolités, Eclairs Karoly and Allumettes aux Anchois etc. The only difference between the hot Hors-d'oeuvre and savouries is that the latter should be more highly seasoned, particularly with Cayenne.

4917 Allumettes
Roll out some puff paste trimmings into a band 8 cm ($3\frac{1}{4}$ in) wide and 5 mm ($\frac{1}{5}$ in) thick and as long as required. Spread with well reduced Sauce Béchamel containing grated Gruyère cheese and seasoned with a touch of Cayenne. Sprinkle with grated Parmesan and press this on to the sauce with the blade of a knife. Cut into oblong shapes 2 cm ($\frac{4}{5}$ in) wide and place on a damp baking tray. Bake in a fairly hot oven for 12 minutes.

4918 Anges à Cheval—Angels on Horseback
Take some nice large oysters and roll each in a thin slice of bacon. Impale them on a skewer, season them and grill. Arrange on toasted bread and at the last moment, sprinkle with fried breadcrumbs and a touch of Cayenne.

4919 Beignets Soufflé—Soufflé Fritters
Prepare some Chou Paste (325) and add to it 150 g (5 oz) small dice of Gruyère cheese per 500 g (1 lb 2 oz) paste. Mould into pieces the size and shape of a walnut and deep fry in the usual way as for soufflé fritters.

4920 Beurreks à la Turque
See this recipe in the Chapter on Hot Hors-d'oeuvre (1105).

4921 Brochettes d'Huîtres Lucifer
Poach some large oysters in their own juices. Remove the beards then dry the oysters and dip them into some thin made mustard. Egg and breadcrumb, place six of them on each skewer and deep fry at the last moment.

Serve arranged on a serviette.

4922 Choux au Fromage
Pipe some Chou Paste (325) into small balls a little larger than those used for Gâteau Saint-Honoré. Brush with egg and bake in a moderate oven until very dry.

When cold, cut off a slice from the top of each and fill the insides by means of a piping bag, with melted cheese seasoned with Cayenne and mixed with whipped cream and grated Parmesan.

4923 Camembert Frit
Cut off the rind of a Camembert then cut the cheese into long diamond shapes.

Sprinkle them with Cayenne, pass twice through egg and breadcrumbs then deep fry in hot fat at the last moment.

4924 Canapés or Toasts
These are nothing more or less than pieces of toast. That is to say, slices of bread cut to any shape, toasted, spread with butter and covered with any suitable food or mixture.

4925 Canapés Cadogan
Prepare some oval pieces of bread with a shallow depression in the centre. Shallow fry them in butter and place some buttered spinach in the hollows. Arrange 2 oysters on the spinach, coat with Sauce Mornay and glaze quickly.

4926 Canapés à l'Ecossaise
Prepare some round slices of buttered toast and cover them dome shape with a purée of smoked haddock.

Glaze quickly.

4927 Canapés des Gourmets
Cut some very thin slices of bread, fry them in butter and cover with melted cheese.

Place two together with a grilled rasher of bacon between them.

4928 Canapés de Haddock
Finely slice the flesh of a smoked haddock and lay on a tray which has been spread thickly with butter mixed with a little Cayenne.

Place the tray in the oven until the butter is hot by which time the fish should be cooked. Arrange on squares of buttered toast at the last moment.

4929 Canapés Ivanhoe
Cover some round slices of buttered toast with a purée of smoked haddock and place a small grilled mushroom in the centre of each.

4930 Canapés aux Oeufs Brouillés
This may be prepared in either of the following ways.

A) Arrange scrambled egg dome shape on slices of toast, sprinkle with grated Parmesan and glaze quickly.
B) Arrange scrambled egg dome shape on slices of toast and decorate on top with strips of anchovy fillet arranged trellis-fashion.

4931 Canapés Rabelais
Prepare some squares of buttered toast and cover them generously with a mixture of chopped smoked tongue and lean ham mixed with mustard butter and a touch of Cayenne.

Sprinkle with grated horseradish.

4932 Canapés de Saumon
These may be prepared in either of the following ways.

A) Cover some oblong pieces of buttered toast with thin slices of smoked salmon.
B) Coat some round slices of buttered toast with a purée of poached salmon.

4933 Canapés Saint-Antoine
Prepare some oblong pieces of buttered toast and whilst still very hot, cover them with a purée of Roquefort cheese mixed with a third its weight of butter and seasoned with a touch of red pepper.

Gratinate under the salamander and place a grilled rasher of bacon on top of each when about to serve.

4934 Chicken Carcasses
Choose the carcasses of chickens which have been boiled. After trimming them, spread with some made mustard seasoned with Cayenne then grill.

4935 Champignons sous Cloche
Trim some medium-sized mushrooms, season with salt and pepper and fill the cavities with a walnut-sized piece of Maître d'Hôtel Butter and half a teaspoon of cream.

Place each mushroom on a round piece of toasted or fried bread 5 cm (2 in) in diameter and arrange them in egg dishes. Cover with special glass domes 10 cm (4 in) in diameter and 6–7 cm ($2\frac{1}{2}$–$2\frac{3}{4}$ in) high; the bottom edges should just fit into the bottom of the egg dishes.

Place the dishes on the side of the stove and allow to cook slowly for approximately 25 minutes.

4936 Condés au Fromage
Roll out some puff paste trimmings to the same dimensions as for Allumettes.

Spread with a thick layer of a mixture of well reduced Sauce Béchamel thickened with egg yolks and seasoned with Cayenne; and mixed when cold with some Gruyère and Parmesan cheese cut in very small dice.

Cut into rectangles and bake in a fairly hot oven for 12 minutes.

4937 Crème Frite au Fromage
Mix together 100 g ($3\frac{1}{2}$ oz) flour, 50 g (2 oz) rice flour, 3 eggs and 2 egg yolks. Add and mix in 5 dl (18 fl oz or $2\frac{1}{4}$ U.S. cups) milk and season with salt, Cayenne and grated nutmeg. Bring to the boil and cook for 5 minutes over a good heat, stirring all the time.

Add 125 g ($4\frac{1}{2}$ oz) grated Gruyère then spread the mixture on a buttered tray. Allow to cool then cut into rectangles.

Coat with beaten egg and breadcrumbs mixed with grated Gruyère; deep fry at the last moment and serve on a serviette.

4938 Croquettes de Camembert
Place 60 g (2 oz) each of flour and rice flour into a basin and mix in 2 dl (7 fl oz or $\frac{7}{8}$ U.S. cup) milk. Add 500 g (1 lb 2 oz) diced Camembert cheese without any rind, 150 g (5 oz) butter, and season with salt, Cayenne and grated nutmeg.

Cook this mixture until thick stirring continuously, then spread on a buttered tray and allow to cool. Cut into small rounds, egg and breadcrumb twice and deep fry at the last moment.

4939 Délices de Foie gras
Stud a fresh goose liver with truffle, season it well and wrap it in thin slices of salt pork fat. Cook in

an earthenware terrine with Champagne or Hock-flavoured aspic jelly. When ready, allow to cool for 24 hours.

Remove the fat from the jelly first by means of a spoon then by rinsing the surface briefly with hot water.

Serve the foie gras as it is, very cold and accompanied with slices of hot crusty toast.

4940 Diablotins
These are small poached and drained Gnocchi, sprinkled with grated cheese mixed with a very little Cayenne and gratinated at the last moment.

4941 Diablotins d'Epicure
Butter some very small round slices of toast and whilst still very hot coat them with a mixture of two parts Roquefort cheese, one part butter and one part chopped walnuts and seasoned with a touch of Cayenne.

4942 Fondants au Chester
Mix together 250 g (9 oz) each of flour, butter and grated Cheshire cheese with a pinch of salt, a touch of Cayenne and a few tablespoons of water. Divide the mixture and mould into small flat cakes 5 cm (2 in) in diameter; brush with beaten egg, mark with the prongs of a fork and cook in a moderate oven.

Allow them to cool and when cold, sandwich them together in twos with a Fondant cream made as follows.

Mix 6 egg yolks together with 3 dl (½ pt or 1¼ U.S. cups) cream and season with salt and Cayenne. Cook as for a Crème Anglaise and allow to cool. When nearly cold, mix in 5 g (2 oz) very good quality butter and 150 g (5 oz) grated cheese.

4943 Galettes Briardes
Mix together as a paste, 500 g (1 lb 2 oz) flour, 150 g (5 oz) butter, 300 g (11 oz) very ripe Brie cheese without any rind, 4 egg yolks and season with salt, Cayenne and grated nutmeg. Allow the paste to rest before rolling it out 7–8 mm (⅓ in) thick.

Cut out rounds with a fancy cutter 6 cm (2½ in) in diameter, brush the tops with milk, mark with the prongs of a fork and bake in a moderate oven.

4944 Laitances à la Diable
Poach some soft roes with butter, season with a touch of Cayenne then arrange on pieces of buttered toast at the last moment.

4945 Omelette Berwick
Sprinkle some fresh soft herring roes with salt, chopped chives, parsley and chervil and wrap each in a thin slice of smoked salmon; poach them gently with butter.

Place them on the slant in the middle of a small Omelette aux Fines Herbes before it is rolled in the usual manner. Serve sprinkled with melted butter containing a little Cayenne.

4946 Os Grillés—Grilled Bones
Use bones from a roast sirloin of beef with some meat left on them. Trim them, sprinkle with Cayenne, spread with made mustard and grill.

4947 Paillettes au Parmesan—Cheese Straws
Make some puff paste using three-quarters of the usual amount of butter. Give it ten turns using plenty of grated Parmesan mixed with a little Cayenne to roll it out; make sure that it picks up as much of the cheese as possible.

Roll out the finished paste 10 cm (4 in) wide and 3 mm (⅛ in) thick; cut into 3 mm (⅛ in) strips, place on a buttered tray and bake in a very hot oven. Serve arranged on a serviette.

4948 Pannequets Moscovite
Make some ordinary pancakes omitting the sugar and cut them into oblongs 7 cm (2¾ in) long by 4 cm (1⅗ in) wide.

Spread with caviare seasoned with a little Cayenne, roll up in the shape of cigarettes and arrange in glass dishes.

4949 Pouding de Fromage au Pain
Spread some slices of stale bread with butter, sprinkle with cheese and arrange them in a pie dish. When three-quarters full, cover with a custard mixture made by whisking 1½ dl (¼ pt or ⅝ U.S. cup) White Bouillon into 4 egg yolks; this will be suitable for a dish of 5 dl (18 fl oz or 2¼ U.S. cups) capacity.

Sprinkle well with grated cheese, cook in the oven *au Bain-marie* and glaze at the last moment.

4950 Sardines à la Diable
Remove the skin and bones from some sardines, spread with made mustard containing a little Cayenne, lightly grill them and arrange on pieces of very hot toast.

4951 Scotch Woodcock
Toast a long slice of bread 1 cm (⅖ in) thick. Cover it with some very thick English Butter Sauce (169) containing plenty of capers and anchovy purée.

Sprinkle with grated Parmesan, glaze quickly under the salamander and cut into small oblong pieces. Serve very hot.

Note: The sauce can be replaced by scrambled eggs and fillets of anchovy.

4952 Tartelettes Agnès
Line some fancy tartlet moulds with fine short paste and fill with a cheese Quiche mixture (1230) flavoured with Cayenne. Cook at the last moment and on removing them from the oven, place on each a poached slice of bone marrow dipped in melted meat glaze containing chopped parsley.

4953 Tartelettes à l'Ecossaise
Prepare some lightly-baked tartlet cases and fill them at the last moment with a purée of smoked haddock mixed with a little Sauce Béchamel.

4954 Tartelettes Kitchener
Fill some lightly-baked tartlet cases with a small dice of poached smoked haddock mixed with curry-flavoured Sauce Mornay.

Glaze quickly under the salamander and serve arranged on a serviette.

4955 Tartelettes à la Florentine
Fill some lightly-baked tartlet cases with Parmesan soufflé mixture containing some grated truffle, diced crayfish tails and well seasoned with coarsely ground pepper.

Place in the oven to cook for 3 minutes.

4956 Tartelettes Marquise
Line some tartlet moulds with fine short paste; cover the bottom and sides with Gnocchi mixture (4280) using a piping bag and a tube of the diameter of a stick of macaroni.

Fill the centre with Sauce Mornay flavoured with Cayenne, sprinkle with grated cheese and bake in a hot oven.

4957 Tartelettes Raglan
Fill some lightly-baked tartlet cases with a purée of smoked soft herring roes.

Cover this with a smoked haddock soufflé mixture in the shape of a hive using a piping bag and large fancy tube. Cook in the oven for 6 minutes and serve immediately.

4958 Tartelettes Tosca
Fill some tartlet cases with crayfish tails cooked *à l'Américaine*.

Cover with Parmesan Soufflé mixture and cook in the oven for 3 minutes.

4959 Tartelettes Vendôme
Line some tartlet cases with fine short paste; prick the bottoms then fill them with the following mixture. *For 12 tartlets:* lightly cook 50 g (2 oz) chopped shallot in butter and add 100 g (3½ oz) finely chopped and sautéed flap mushrooms, 50 g (2 oz) raw bone marrow cut in dice, 1 chopped small hard-boiled egg, 30 g (1 oz) breadcrumbs, salt, Cayenne, a little lemon juice and 3 tbs melted meat glaze. Mix all these ingredients well together.

Place a large slice of bone marrow on top of each filled tartlet and cook at the last moment.

4960 Welsh Rarebit
This can be made in either of the following ways but should always be on square or oblong pieces of buttered toast 1 cm (⅖ in) thick.

A) The easiest method consists of covering the toast with a thick layer of grated Gloucester or Cheshire cheese, sprinkling with Cayenne and placing in the oven to melt the cheese and glaze the surface.

B) The original method consists of melting the diced or sliced cheese with a few tablespoons of pale ale and a little English mustard.

When the cheese has melted, pour the mixture on to buttered toasts and smooth quickly with the blade of a knife. Sprinkle with Cayenne and cut into small pieces if desired.

4961 SANDWICHES

There are two main kinds of sandwiches, those made with ordinary bread and those made with toast.

Ordinary sandwiches are made by spreading thin slices of bread with butter containing seasoning and made mustard then filling them with thinly sliced ham or tongue.

The usual shape is rectangular, approximately 8 cm (3¼ in) × 4 cm (1½ in) but for buffets they should be only half this size and it is advisable to use finely chopped fillings made of equal amounts of the main ingredients and seasoned butter flavoured with mustard. When sandwiches are made in advance they should be kept pressed between the crusts of the loaf so as to prevent them drying and the corners turning up.

Sandwiches can also be made by toasting thick slices of bread, cutting them through horizontally then filling them to choice in the usual way.

The most common fillings for sandwiches are, ham, tongue, beef, pressed beef, chicken, foie gras, egg, caviare, tomato, cucumber, mustard and cress, and watercress.

In his book *La Cuisine Anglaise*, M. Suzanne indicated the type of sandwich which follows and which merits inclusion here.

4962 Bookmaker's Sandwich

This substantial sandwich is favoured by people attending race meetings; after perusal it will be seen that such a snack could on occasion take the place of a full meal.

Cut off the crusts from the ends of a sandwich loaf leaving at least 1 cm (⅖ in) of bread on them. Grill a thick steak, well seasoned with salt and pepper; allow it to cool then spread it with mustard and sprinkle with grated horseradish. Butter the crusts, put the steak between them and tie up with string. Wrap it in several sheets of clean absorbent paper, place in a press and tighten it gradually before leaving it for 30 minutes. When removed it will be seen that the inside of the sandwich is saturated with the meat juice which the outside crust has prevented from escaping. The string and paper are removed and the sandwich is then wrapped in greaseproof paper or placed in a box with a lid.

CHAPTER 17

POACHED FRUITS (COMPOTES), JAMS AND DRINKS

COMPOTES

4963 Single Fruit Compotes
Fruits for Compotes can be left whole or cut in halves or in quarters; they are then poached in a syrup flavoured in keeping with the type of fruit. The fruit is served in fruit dishes or in small glass bowls, covered with the syrup which can either be left as it is or reduced by boiling. For some kinds of fruit the syrup can be lightly thickened with arrowroot.

Poached fruits which are referred to in French as *Compotes* can be served either warm or cold. For preference the fruit used should not be too ripe.

4964 Compote of Apricots
Cut the apricots in half and place them into a boiling syrup at 11° on the saccharometer so as to loosen the skins. Skin the apricots and replace then in the syrup to poach. Crack the apricot stones, remove the kernels and place these to macerate in Kirsch-flavoured syrup.

Arrange the apricots in a dish with half a kernel on each half and cover with some of their syrup together with some syrup from the kernels.

4965 Compote of Pineapple
Peel a fresh pineapple, cut it into slices and remove the hard centre; poach in vanilla-flavoured syrup. If using canned pineapple drain and place the slices in a syrup for 1 hour beforehand.

Arrange the slices overlapping in a dish and cover with the syrup.

4966 Compote of Bananas
Peel the bananas and poach them for 5 minutes in a syrup well flavoured with Kirsch.

Place in a dish and cover with the syrup.

4967 Compote of Cherries
Stone the cherries without breaking the flesh. Place them in a sugar syrup cooked to the hard ball stage made from 300 g (11 oz) sugar for each 1 kg (2¼ lb) of cherries. Cover with a lid and allow to stand for 8 minutes on the side of the stove shaking the pan from time to time to ensure that the sugar dissolves.

Arrange the cherries in a dish, flavour their syrup with Kirsch and pour over.

Note: The cherries can also be prepared by poaching them in Claret which has been sweetened and flavoured with a little cinnamon.

4968 Compote of Strawberries
Cook 250 g (9 oz) sugar to the soft ball stage, add 1 kg (2¼ lb) choice strawberries, cover with a lid and allow to stand for 10 minutes.

Arrange the strawberries in a dish; lightly thicken the syrup with redcurrant jelly, flavour with vanilla and pour over the fruit.

4969 Compote of Raspberries
Dip the raspberries into a hot raspberry juice syrup for a few seconds only. Arrange in a dish and cover with the syrup.

4970 Compote of Mirabelle Plums
Remove the stones from the plums, then poach the fruit for 10–12 minutes in vanilla-flavoured syrup at 18°. Arrange them in a dish and cover with the syrup.

4971 Compote of Nectarines
Peel the nectarines and poach them whole in a vanilla-flavoured syrup at 18°. Arrange them in a dish and cover with the syrup.

4972 Compote of Peaches
Peel the peaches and poach them whole or cut in halves in a vanilla syrup at 18°.

4973 Compote of Pears
If the pears are small, peel them neatly leaving them whole. If they are medium size cut them in half and if large cut into quarters; peel them and remove the pips. If the pears are soft and ripe place them immediately in a vanilla-flavoured syrup and poach quickly. If they are a cooking variety of pear rub them over with lemon and blanch them in plenty of

water for a few minutes to keep them white, then poach them in a vanilla syrup at 12°.

Very often pears for a compote are poached in a syrup made with red wine flavoured with lemon zest and cinnamon.

4974 Compote of Apples
If for cooking whole, the apples should be cored and peeled neatly and evenly, then rubbed with lemon and placed in cold water as they are being prepared. Poach them carefully in vanilla-flavoured syrup at 12° and remove from the heat as soon as they are ready.

As a variation apples may be poached in a pink-coloured syrup.

4975 Compote of Prunes
Soak the prunes well in advance then cook them gently in a syrup at 12° made from half water and half red wine, sweetened with sugar and flavoured with cinnamon.

4976 Compote of Greengages
Choose fairly firm greengages and remove the stones. Poach them in vanilla syrup at 18° without allowing it to actually boil.

4977 Compote of Rhubarb
Cut the rhubarb stalks into sections 6–7 cm (2½ in) long; peel them and place in a shallow dish. Only half cover them with very sweet syrup because the rhubarb contains a vast amount of water. Cover with a lid and poach very gently without stirring so that they remain whole.

4978 Mixed Compotes
The mixed compotes are a kind of fruit salad made of several different kinds of cooked fruits, arranged in a dish on a bed of a purée of fruit cooked with sugar, or on a purée of any fresh fruit. Cooked fruit jellies such as redcurrant jelly, quince jelly, apple jelly play a part in these dishes being used either to coat the cooked fruit or to surround it in the form of fancy shapes, or chopped.

A variety of crystallized or preserved fruits are nearly always added to these mixed compotes.

JAMS

Under this general heading two different types of jam are included: 1) the kind where the fruit is cooked together directly with the sugar, and 2) the kind made only from the juice of a fruit and where, because of the large amount of pectin in the fruit, the juice in combination with the sugar produces a jelly-like jam.

The amount of sugar used in the making of jam is governed by the nature of the fruit and whether the fruit is more or less sweet. Nevertheless, for all acid fruits and acid fruit juices the amount of sugar required is approximately equal to that of the fruit.

If too much sugar is used it will impair the aroma of the fruit and after a short time, cause the jam to crystallize. If insufficient sugar is used the cooking time will have to be extended in order to reach the required degree of setting which will also impair the aroma by over-evaporation. If the jam is not cooked to the exact degree necessary it will soon start to ferment and become bad.

In the making of jams the best guide to the amount of sugar required is the quality of the fruit itself.

4979 The cooking, bottling and covering of jams
The amount of time required for cooking any kind of jam, marmalade or fruit jelly can only be roughly determined. It is a mistake to try to fix the exact time, since the duration of the cooking time depends solely on the degree of heat applied and consequently the rate of evaporation of the water contained in the fruit. As a general rule, the quicker the jam is made, the better the result, because the fruit will keep its colour better.

However, unless constant care and attention is given to a jam in which there is a high proportion of fruit, it should not be cooked over a fierce heat because of the risk of it burning. On the other hand, when making a jelly in which only the juice of the fruit is used, it should be cooked on a very hot stove so as to reach as quickly as possible, the stage which indicates that the cooking has reached its correct degree.

This degree is the same for all jams and can be recognized as follows. When the steam being given off becomes less dense and the jam shows a thick bubbling movement then the evaporation is completed and the cooking proper has commenced. From this time on, remove any scum as it rises. The jam which sticks to the skimming spoon at this stage runs off quickly; after a few more minutes it will be seen to run off much more slowly in larger spaced out drops. This stage is referred to as the coating stage (Fr. *Nappe*) and is a sure indication that the jam has reached the desired degree of cooking.

When this is reached, the jam must be removed from the stove, the heat allowed to subside for 7–8 minutes and then the jam should be poured gradually into warmed jars.

The next day the jam should be covered with rounds of white paper, well brushed with rectified glycerine which is infinitely more preferable to sugared Brandy; these rounds of paper should be placed directly in contact with the jam. Cover the jars with a double sheet of greaseproof paper and tie tightly. Store in a dry place.

4980 Apricot jam

For preference use very ripe apricots; cut them in half, break open the stones and remove the skin from the kernels; divide these into halves.

Allow 375 g (14 oz) of sugar per 500 g (1 lb 2 oz) of fruit. Place the sugar in a pan with 2 dl (7 fl oz or $\frac{7}{8}$ U.S. cups) water per 1 kg ($2\frac{1}{4}$ lb) fruit and when it has dissolved bring to the boil for a few minutes and skim carefully.

Add the apricots, reduce the heat slightly and stir almost continuously, being especially careful about this towards the end when there is the risk of the jam sticking to the bottom of the pan.

Remove from the stove as soon as the required stage of cooking is reached, mix in the kernels and pour the jam into the pots.

4981 Cherry Jam

Remove the stones from the cherries; weigh out 750 g (1 lb 10 oz) loaf sugar per 1 kg ($2\frac{1}{4}$ lb) fruit or equal quantities of sugar to cherries if the fruit is not very sweet.

Place the sugar in a pan, moisten with a little water to dissolve it and boil for 5 minutes skimming carefully. Add the cherries and 5 dl (18 fl oz or $2\frac{1}{4}$ U.S. cups) redcurrant juice and cook quickly until the required degree is reached.

Notes:

1) The addition of redcurrant juice is recommended for this jam as it ensures that it will set well and helps by cutting the cooking time.

   For red fruits the quicker the jam is cooked the more the fruit retains its colour.

2) When the fruit starts to boil it is important that the scum which is produced is removed immediately, if not it will solidify quickly and interfere with the end result; it can and often does cause the jam to ferment.

4982 Strawberry Jam

This is one of the most demanding of jams to make; it can be made in several different ways of which the following is the quickest and most simple.

Remove the hulls from strawberries which have just reached the exact stage of ripeness; do not wash them unless absolutely necessary.

Weigh out 375 g (14 oz) sugar for each 500 g (1 lb 2 oz) of strawberries; place in a pan, add sufficient water to dissolve it and cook to the hard ball stage stage taking care to skim it carefully when it starts to boil.

Add the fruit, then take the pan off the direct heat but keep it hot for 7–8 minutes until the juice from the strawberries has dissolved the sugar and turned it into a syrup.

Drain the strawberries on to a sieve; cook the liquid rapidly until it begins to reach the setting stage then at this moment, replace the fruit and cook for a further 5 minutes until the required degree.

Fill the jam into warmed jars a little at a time so as to distribute the strawberries evenly throughout and prevent them coming to the surface in a mass; this will happen if the pots are filled too quickly.

4983 Orange Marmalade

Select oranges of the same size, of a good colour and with soft, thick but unblemished skins. This is important because the thicker and softer the skins the more tender they will be and the easier they will cook.

Prick the oranges all over with a thin wooden skewer so as to speed up the cooking and place them into a pan of boiling water. Allow to boil steadily for 30 minutes then drain them, refresh them and place in cold water for 20 hours, changing it frequently. This is to soften the skins and to remove any bitterness from them.

Cut up the oranges into small pieces, remove the seeds and membrane and pass through a coarse sieve.

Weigh out an equal amount of sugar as there is orange pulp, dissolve this sugar in a pan and boil for 5 minutes skimming carefully.

Now add the orange pulp and $1\frac{1}{2}$ dl (5 fl oz or $\frac{5}{8}$ U.S. cup) apple juice per 500 g (1 lb 2 oz) of pulp. Place to cook and during the first stage skim very carefully indeed. Stir almost continuously during the second stage until it reaches the required coating stage.

Note: A proportionate amount of well blanched very fine Julienne of orange zest is usually added at the last moment.

4984 Plum Jam

Weigh out 375 g (14 oz) sugar per 500 g (1 lb 2 oz) stoned plums.

Dissolve the sugar, bring to the boil and skim; allow to boil for 7–8 minutes then proceed as for Apricot Jam.

Note:

1) It is bad practice to place the plums to macerate with the sugar several hours in advance as the acid contained in the fruit will cause them to darken and impart a disagreeable colour to the jam.

2) To obtain a nice green colour when making greengage jam do not try to make more than 3–4 kg (9–10 lb) at a time and cook it as quickly as possible.

4985 Rhubarb Jam

This jam is one of the longest to make and requires a lot of attention because of: 1) the large amount of water contained in the rhubarb, and 2) the ease with which it burns; it tends to stick to the pan especially towards the end of the cooking time.

If a green jam is required, select the green stalks; for a red jam use only the centre stalks with red skins, or use forced rhubarb. Whatever kind is used do not try to make more than approximately 2½ kg (5–6 lb) at any one time.

Discard the leaf ends of the stalks, remove the skin with a small knife from all round the stalks and cut into 5 cm (2 in) lengths.

Weigh out 400 g (15 oz) sugar per 500 g (1 lb 2 oz) of rhubarb; place in a pan with a little water to dissolve it, allow to boil for 7–8 minutes then add the sliced rhubarb. Cover with the lid, remove from the stove and allow to stand for 15 minutes during which time the rhubarb will disintegrate and be reduced to filaments.

Replace the pan on the stove and cook rapidly and stirring continuously until the required stage of cooking is reached.

4986 Tomato Jam

This jam can be made in several ways, the following, however, is the easiest and quickest.

It is necessary to realize that the net weight of usable tomato pulp will be on average only a fifth of the total weight of tomatoes. This is subject to such variations as the type of tomato being used, its ripeness and size etc. In order to obtain 500 g (1 lb 2 oz) of pulp it is necessary to start with 2½ kg (5½ lb) of tomatoes.

Slice the tomatoes thinly and pass them through a sieve. Place the purée in a pan, bring to the boil and boil for 5 minutes whilst stirring. Pour it into a cloth stretched over a jelly stand and allow to drain through. When this is completed only the pure tomato pulp will be left in the cloth.

Weigh out the same amount of sugar as there is pulp, place it in a pan with a little water and allow to dissolve. Now cook it to the hard ball stage and skim carefully after it has come to the boil.

A vanilla pod may be added to the sugar when placing it to cook or the jam can be flavoured with a tablespoon of vanilla sugar when being taken off the stove. In any case the jam should be flavoured with vanilla.

When the sugar has reached the stage indicated above, add the tomato pulp and 1½ dl (5 fl oz or ⅝ U.S. cup) redcurrant juice per 500 g (1 lb 2 oz) of pulp. Since the tomato pulp contains no pectin the addition of redcurrant juice is essential.

Place the pan on the stove and cook rapidly stirring constantly until the required stage of setting is reached. It is even advisable to continue to cook the jam for a few minutes after it has reached this stage.

Note: Apple juice can be used instead of redcurrant juice.

FRUIT JELLIES

4987 Blackcurrant Jelly

Choose very ripe blackcurrants, remove the stalks and place the blackcurrants in a pan with 1 dl (3½ fl oz or ½ U.S. cup) of water per 1 kg (2¼ lb) fruit. Place on a low heat so that the fruit swells and breaks and their juices are released into the pan. Turn out on to a sieve and allow the juice to run into a basin; this obviates the need to squeeze it out through a cloth.

Weigh out 850 g (1 lb 14 oz) of sugar per 1 litre (1¾ pt or 4½ U.S. cups) of blackcurrant juice, place it into a pan with a little water and allow to dissolve then cook to the hard-boil stage, skimming it well. Add the blackcurrant juice together with 2 dl (7 fl oz or ⅞ U.S. cup) whitecurrant juice per 1 litre of blackcurrant juice.

Keep on a low heat for a few minutes to dissolve the syrup then cook the jam rapidly until it reaches the setting stage, skimming it carefully.

Note: The reason for adding the whitecurrant juice is simply to lighten the deep colour of the blackcurrants; its use is purely optional.

4988 Quince Jelly

Choose very ripe quinces and cut them in slices. Peel and remove the pips then place the fruit in a basin of cold water.

Transfer the fruit to a pan with approximately 1 litre (1¾ pt or 4½ U.S. cups) water per 500 g (1 lb 2 oz) of peeled fruit and bring to the boil without stirring. As soon as they are cooked tip on to a sieve and allow to drain.

Replace the juice in the pan, add 800 g (1¾ lb) of loaf sugar per 1 litre (1¾ pt or 4½ U.S. cups) juice, allow it to dissolve then boil rapidly until it reaches the setting stage, skimming very carefully.

As soon as it is cooked, pass the jelly through a muslin so as to give a crystal clear result.

4989 Redcurrant Jelly

Method 1:

Use two-thirds redcurrants, one-third whitecurrants, plus 100 g (3½ oz) raspberries per 1 kg

(2¼ lb) of both fruits; crush them in a basin and squeeze a little at a time through a strong cloth to extract the juices.

Place this juice in a pan with 1 kg (2¼ lb) loaf sugar per 1 litre (1¾ pt or 4½ U.S. cups) juice, allow to dissolve then cook rapidly and skim carefully especially at the beginning, until it reaches the required stage.

Note: The quantity of juice expressed from 1 kg (2¼ lb) of very ripe redcurrants is approximately 6½ dl (1⅓ pt or 3 U.S. cups).

Method 2:
Use the same proportions of fruit as for Method 1. Clean and wash them in cold water then place in a pan with 6 dl (1 pt or 2⅝ U.S. cups) water per 1 kg (2¼ lb) fruit.

Allow to cook very gently for 10–12 minutes then pour on to a sieve and allow to drain.

Replace the juice in the pan, add 1 kg (2¼ lb) loaf sugar per 1 litre (1¾ pt or 4½ U.S. cups) juice and cook as indicated for Method 1.

Method 3:
Use the same proportions of fruit as for Method 1. Remove the stalks from the currants and clean the raspberries; weigh out 1 kg (2¼ lb) sugar per 1 kg (2¼ lb) fruit.

Place the sugar in a pan with a little water and cook until it reaches the soft ball stage, skimming it carefully when it first comes to the boil.

Add the currants and raspberries, remove the pan from the stove and allow to stand for 7–8 minutes until the juices run out of the fruit. Cook rapidly, skimming carefully until it reaches the required degree of setting.

Turn on to a sieve to drain off the jelly and fill into pots.

4990 Whitecurrant Jelly
This is prepared using only very ripe whitecurrants plus 100 g (3½ oz) of very pale coloured raspberries per 1 kg (2¼ lb) of the currants.

Any of the three methods given for redcurrant jelly may be used although Method 3 is to be preferred as it gives a clearer jelly.

4991 Redcurrant Jelly *(cold method)*
Prepare the juice by squeezing the crushed fruits through a strong cloth as indicated for Redcurrant jelly, Method 1. Add to this juice 1 kg (2¼ lb) icing sugar per 1 litre (1¾ pt or 4½ U.S. cups) juice taking care to mix thoroughly together with a silver spoon to ensure that the sugar is dissolved.

Fill the jelly into pots and allow to remain uncovered for 2–3 days. Cover in the usual manner and place where they will be exposed to direct sun for 2–3 hours each day for 2 days.

Note: This jelly is as delicate as it it fragile and it must be stored in a very dry place. It is necessary to use very ripe redcurrants, only the red ones if possible; or to add only 100 g (3½ oz) whitecurrants per 500 g (1 lb 2 oz) red.

4992 Orange Jelly
To make 1 litre (1¾ pt or 4½ U.S. cups) orange jelly take 12 medium-sized oranges of 150 g (5 oz) each, 2 dl (7 fl oz or ⅞ U.S. cup) good apple juice, 500 g (1 lb 2 oz) loaf sugar, and 1 tbs orange sugar. If a garnished jelly is required add some finely shredded candied orange peel.

To make the jelly, squeeze the juice from the oranges and filter it. Place the sugar in a pan with a little water and dissolve it.

Add the orange juice and the apple and cook as in the preceding recipes. Allow to cool for 10 minutes then add the orange sugar and the shredded peel.

4993 Apple Jelly
This is prepared in exactly the same way as for Quince Jelly and passing the juice without pressure. Do not cook the apple too much as otherwise the juice will contain some of the pulp, in any case it will be necessary to decant the juice since there will inevitably be a small amount at the bottom.

Replace the juice in the pan with 900 g (2 lb) loaf sugar and a third of a pod of vanilla per 1 litre (1¾ pt or 4½ U.S. cups) juice. Cook as for Quince Jelly then pass through a muslin.

4994 Tomato Jelly
Method 1:
Prepare the tomato pulp in the same way as for Tomato Jam. 7 dl (1¼ pt or 3 U.S. cups) apple juice, 1 kg (2¼ lb) icing sugar and 1 vanilla pod are required for each 1 kg (2¼ lb) tomato pulp. Place all the ingredients into a pan, cook over a low heat for 5 minutes then cook rapidly until it reaches the required stage.

Method 2:
Using the same amount of tomato pulp as for Method 1, replace the apple juice with a juice prepared from two-thirds of whitecurrants to one-third of redcurrants and a little vanilla. Replace the icing sugar with the same amount of loaf sugar.

Place the sugar in a pan and dissolve it with a little water then cook to the small thread stage taking care to skim it carefully when it starts to boil.

Add the tomato pulp, the vanilla and currant

juice to this syrup, leave on the stove for a moment to dissolve then cook very quickly until the required stage is reached.

HOT AND COLD DRINKS

The amounts given in the following recipes are sufficient for 12 glasses.

4995 Bavaroise
Whisk together 250 g (9 oz) caster sugar and 8 egg yolks until the mixture becomes a pale straw colour and reaches the ribbon stage.

Add in sequence, 1 dl (3½ fl oz or ½ U.S. cup) Capillaire syrup and 5 dl (18 fl oz or 2¼ U.S. cups) each of boiling hot freshly made tea and boiling milk, whisking vigorously so that the whole becomes very frothy. Lastly, add 2 dl (7 fl oz or ⅞ U.S. cup) liqueur, either Kirsch or Rum, which will give its name to the Bavaroise.

If a vanilla, orange or lemon Bavaroise is required, infuse the flavouring in the milk 15 minutes beforehand. If a chocolate one is required melt 180 g (6 oz) of chocolate and add it to the milk together with a little vanilla. If a coffee Bavaroise is required infuse 100 g (3½ oz) freshly ground coffee in the milk, or flavour with 5 dl (18 fl oz or 2¼ U.S. cups) freshly made coffee.

Bavaroise is served in special glasses and it must be served whilst still frothy.

4996 Bischoff
Pour in a basin 1 bottle of Champagne and ½ dl (2 fl oz or ¼ U.S. cup) lime tea; add 1 orange cut in slices, half a lemon cut in very thin slices and sufficient syrup at 32° on the saccharometer to bring the liquid down to 18°. Leave in a cool place for 1 hour.

Strain the liquid through a fine strainer then freeze as for Granité and finish by adding 1 dl (3½ fl oz or ½ U.S. cup) of Brandy.

Serve in punch glasses.

4997 Iced Coffee
Gradually pour 7½ dl (1¼ pt or 3¼ U.S. cups) boiling water over 300 g (11 oz) freshly ground coffee and allow to filter slowly. Place in a pan with 600 g (1 lb 5 oz) loaf sugar and allow to cool. Now add 1 litre (1¾ pt or 4½ U.S. cups) boiled milk which has been flavoured with vanilla and allowed to cool, and 5 dl (18 fl oz or 2¼ U.S. cups) very fresh cream.

Freeze in the ice-cream machine but see that the mixture remains almost liquid. Serve in very cold cups.

4998 Lemonade
Dissolve 250 g (9 oz) loaf sugar in 1 litre (1¾ pt or 4½ U.S. cups) filtered water. Add the rind and juice of 2 lemons and allow to infuse in a cool place for 3 hours.

Pass through a fine strainer, add a syphon of Seltzer water and serve in glasses with a thin slice of lemon in each.

4999 Claret Cup
Place in a bowl, 30 g (1 oz) loaf sugar, the zest of 1 lemon, 3 slices of lemon, 3 slices of orange, a thin piece of cucumber rind, 1 tsp Angostura Bitters and ½ dl (2 fl oz or ¼ U.S. cup) each of Brandy, Maraschino and Curaçao. Now add 1½ bottles of red wine and 1 bottle of soda water.

Cover the bowl, allow to infuse for 2 hours then pass through a muslin. Add a few pieces of crushed ice and a few nice clean mint leaves.

5000 Pineapple Water
Finely chop 750 g (1 lb 10 oz) fresh or canned pineapple; place in a basin and pour on 1 litre (1¾ pt or 4½ U.S. cups) boiling syrup at 20° on the saccharometer. Allow to cool and infuse for 2 hours.

Strain it through a jelly bag then add some ice and sufficient soda syphon water to bring the liquid to 9°. Keep in a cool place for 20 minutes then finish at the last moment with 1 dl (3½ fl oz or ½ U.S. cup) Kirsch.

5001 Cherry Water
Remove the stones from 500 g (1 lb 2 oz) of very ripe cherries and pass the fruit through a sieve. Place this pulp in a basin with the crushed stones and allow to macerate in a cool place for 1 hour. Moisten with 1 litre (1¾ pt or 4½ U.S. cups) filtered water then pass through a jelly bag or double muslin.

Add a piece of ice, 180 g (6 oz) sugar and keep in a cool place for 20 minutes. Finish by flavouring it at the last minute with 1 dl (3½ fl oz or ½ U.S. cup) Kirsch. The drink should be at 9° on the saccharometer.

5002 Raspberry-flavoured Redcurrant Water
Extract the juice from 375 g (14 oz) mixed white and redcurrants and 125 g (4½ oz) very ripe raspberries by pressing on a fine sieve. To the juice, add 5 dl (18 fl oz or 2¼ U.S. cups) filtered water, 180 g (6 oz) loaf sugar and a piece of ice. Keep in a cool place for 20 minutes stirring occasionally with a silver spoon to ensure that the sugar dissolves. The drink should be at 9° on the saccharometer.

5003 Melon Water
Pass 500 g (1 lb 2 oz) barely ripe melon flesh through a sieve; place in a basin and pour on 5 dl (18 fl oz or 2¼ U.S. cups) of boiling syrup at 20° on the saccharometer. Allow to infuse for 2 hours then pass through a jelly bag or muslin.

Add a piece of ice and the required quantity of Seltzer water to bring the syrup to 9°. Keep again in a cool place for 20 minutes then finish at the last moment with 2 tbs orange flower water.

5004 Kaltchale
Peel and slice 250 g (9 oz) each of pineapple and very soft peaches; add 125 g (4½ oz) each of diced ripe melon flesh, and a mixture of raspberries and picked white and redcurrants. Place all these fruits in a silver bowl and keep on ice.

Infuse a small piece of cinnamon in half a bottle of white wine, add 650 g (1 lb 7 oz) of sugar and the zest of 1 lemon and allow to cool whilst stirring occasionally, then mix in 5 dl (18 fl oz or 2¼ U.S. cups) of a purée of strawberries and redcurrants.

Filter this carefully and finish by adding 1 bottle of Champagne.

Pour this over the fruit and serve very cold.

5005 Orangeade
This is prepared in the same way as Lemonade replacing the lemon rind with orange rind and using only the juice of half a lemon.

Serve in glasses with a very thin slice of orange in each.

5006 Kirsch Punch
Drop 20 g (⅔ oz) of tea into 1 litre (1¾ pt or 4½ U.S. cups) boiling water and allow it to infuse for 10 minutes.

Place 500 g (1 lb 2 oz) loaf sugar in a punch bowl, strain the tea over it and allow to dissolve stirring with a silver spoon.

Add 7½ dl (1¼ pt or 3¼ U.S. cups) Kirsch, set it alight and serve in glasses.

5007 Rum Punch
Make an infusion with 20 g (⅔ oz) tea and 1 litre (1¾ pt or 4½ U.S. cups) boiling water, allow to rest for 10 minutes.

Place 500 g (1 lb 2 oz) loaf sugar in a punch bowl and strain the tea over it. Allow it to dissolve then add a few thin slices of lemon and 7½ dl (1¼ pt or 3¼ U.S. cups) rum.

Set it alight and serve the punch in glasses with a slice of lemon in each.

5008 Marquise Punch
Pour 1 litre (1¾ pt or 4½ U.S. cups) Sauternes wine into a copper pan, add 250 g (9 oz) loaf sugar and the thin rind of 1 lemon with a clove stuck in it. Allow the sugar to dissolve then heat the wine until the surface becomes covered with a light white froth. Remove the lemon rind and clove and pour the punch into a bowl.

Add 2½ dl (9 fl oz or 1⅛ U.S. cups) warmed Brandy, set it alight and allow it to burn out.

Serve in glasses with a thin slice of lemon in each.

5009 Iced Punch
Prepare some Marquise Punch and when the wine is hot remove from the stove and sprinkle in 20 g (⅔ oz) of tea; cover and allow to infuse for 10 minutes.

Pass it through a fine strainer, add 1 peeled and sliced lemon, 1 peeled and sliced orange and 2 dl (7 fl oz or ⅞ U.S. cup) of warm Rum. Set alight, allow to cool and dilute to 15° on the saccharometer.

Freeze as for a Granité and serve in glasses.

5010 Mulled Wine
Pour 1 bottle of red wine over 200 g (7 oz) loaf sugar in a copper pan and allow the sugar to dissolve. Add the zest of 1 lemon, a small piece of cinnamon and mace and 1 clove. Heat until the surface is covered with a fine froth then pass through a fine strainer.

Serve with a thin slice of lemon in each glass.

5011 Mulled Wine with Orange
Pour 2 dl (7 fl oz or ⅞ U.S. cup) boiling water over 300 g (11 oz) loaf sugar. Add the zest of 1 orange and allow to infuse for 15 minutes. Remove the zest and add 1 bottle of heated Burgundy wine.

Serve in glasses with a thin slice of orange in each.

5012 Vin à la Française
Place 250 g (9 oz) sugar in a basin and sprinkle with a few tablespoons of water to dissolve it.

Add 1 bottle of good Claret or Burgundy wine and half a lemon cut into thin slices. Mix well with a silver spoon and serve in glasses with a slice of lemon in each.

Note: Always remove the pips from the oranges and lemons used in these drinks; if this is not done they impart a bitter taste.

GLOSSARY

This glossary gives an explanation of or additional information on certain words and technical terms used in this book where it has not been possible to describe them fully at the time. In addition it provides short descriptions of some of the lesser known items of food and equipment commonly in use when this book was first published.

Agaric: family of fungus some of which are edible, e.g. the Orange Agaric.
Agoursis: the Russian name for small ridge cucumbers pickled in salt.
Amourettes: the spinal marrow of the ox and calf.
au Bain-marie (to cook): to cook an item in a container in a pan of water in the oven so as to prevent it from reaching too high a temperature.
Barquette: a boat-shaped pastry case.
to Beard: to remove the frilly part of certain shellfish such as an oyster.
to Blanch: to boil a food so as to get rid of its acridity; to place a food into boiling water as a means of preserving its natural colour.
Bouquet garni: herbs tied in a bundle—usually parsley stalks, thyme, bayleaf and celery.
Brioche à tête: a small Brioche made with a ball of the same dough on top.
Brunoise: items of food cut into small regular dice.
Buckwheat: a cereal plant the flour from which is used in the making of Kache and Blinis.
Calvados: a spirit distilled from cider.
Canapé: a small piece of toasted or fried bread covered with another item of food (see the Chapter on Savouries).
Capillaire Syrup: a sweet syrup flavoured with an infusion of a variety of fern belonging to the Adiantum family; orange flower water is often added.
Carapace: the shell of any kind of shellfish after the flesh has been removed.
Casserole: an earthenware dish having a lid, usually used to cook in and serve from.
en Casserole (to cook): see Poêling (2178).
Cassolette: a small dish made in different shapes, of either pleated paper, fireproof china or silver and used for presenting certain small Entrées, Hors-d'oeuvre and Entremets.
Caul: the net-like membrane which covers the animal's intestines; pig's caul is the one normally used in cooking.
Cédrat: a variety of citron tree the fruit and oil of which is used in cookery.
Cèpe: an edible fungus commonly known as the flap mushroom.
Cervelas: short thick smoked sausage.
Chanterelle: the Cantherelus mushroom which is small and yellow and has a frilly edge.
Chinois: a candied small green orange.
Chipolata: a type of long thin sausage, usually pork.
Chorizos: highly spiced Spanish pork sausages.
Citron: a citrus fruit similar to, but larger than a lemon; the candied skin is used in mixed peel.
Cocotte: a shallow earthenware or porcelain dish with a lid.

en Cocotte (to cook): see Poêling (2178).
Cordon: a line of sauce or gravy poured around an item of food when it is placed on the serving dish.
Croûtons: bread cut to various shapes and fried in butter usually for use as a garnish.
Cuisine Bourgeoise: middle class cookery.
Cuisine Menagère: household cookery.
Cullis: the well reduced, highly concentrated essential flavours of a food, in either purée or liquid form.
Curaçao: a liqueur made from the rinds of bitter oranges, originally from the West Indies island of that name.
Danziger Goldwasser: also known as Danzig brandy, a liqueur made from citrus peel and containing very fine flecks of gold leaf.
to Decant: to pour off a liquid after allowing any particles contained in it to settle.
to Deglaze: to add a liquid such as wine or stock to the sediment left in a pan from the cooking of a food.
Dessert: the last course of a meal, usually fruit but nowadays the name is commonly used to describe the sweet course.
to Egg and breadcrumb: (Pané à l'Anglaise): to coat a food with flour, beaten egg and either white or dried breadcrumbs. The eggs are usually lightly seasoned with salt and pepper and mixed with half a tablespoon of oil per 2 eggs.
Entrée: originally this comprised the dishes of the first course of a meal, nowadays it denotes a dish that is served before the roast and usually consists of an individual portion lightly sauced and garnished.
en Entrée (to truss): a method of trussing by folding back the legs at the joint of the drumstick and introducing them through an incision made in the skin. The bird is then tied with string. This method is suitable for cooking en Cocotte, Poêlé etc.
Entremets: the name in French denoting sweet dishes.
Escalope: a thin round slice cut from fish, meat, poultry etc., usually flattened.
Eugenia: a cherry-like fruit.
Fecula: very fine starch obtained from potato, rice, maize etc.
Fines herbes: a mixture of chopped fresh herbs, usually parsley, chervil, tarragon and chives.
Foie gras: fattened goose or duck liver.
Fondue: 1) a vegetable such as tomatoes, cooked until it is reduced to a pulp, 2) a type of cheese preparation.
Fumet: a highly flavoured, fairly concentrated essence of fish, poultry, meat etc.
Garbanzos: chick peas.
to Glaze: 1) to coat a food with aspic jelly, 2) to colour under the salamander, 3) to sprinkle a sweet with icing sugar then to place it in the oven to melt so producing a glossy surface which may also be coloured.
Gombo: a pale green pod-like vegetable, also known as Okra or Ladies Fingers.
to Gratinate: to bake food so as to form a crust on the surface.
Gratin dish: an oval earthenware or porcelain dish used for cooking and presentation, especially of Gratins.
Gribouis: a variety of Cèpe. In Russia this kind of mushroom is frequently used in its dried form.
Gum tragacanth: the gum produced from the tragacanth plant, used in pastry work for glazing purposes.
Hachis: finely chopped cooked meat reheated in a suitable sauce.
Hâtelet: an ornamental silver skewer used for decorating foods.
to Infuse: to extract the flavour and aroma of an ingredient by placing it in a boiling liquid and allowing it to stand.
to Inset: to make small incisions in an article of food such as meat or fish then to insert a small slice of truffle, tongue etc. in each. (Fr: *Contiser*).
Julienne: items of food cut into regular strips of a thickness in keeping with the item and its ultimate use.

Kilkis: a small fish caught in Northern waters and prepared in a similar way to anchovies.
Kirsch: a distilled white spirit prepared from a base of wild cherries.
Kohl-rabi: a turnip-like vegetable.
Kümmel: a liqueur flavoured with carraway and cumin.
Lavaret: a species of fish of the salmon family found in deep lakes.
to Lard: to insert thin strips of a food such as salt pork fat, bacon, truffle etc., into a piece of meat or poultry.
Lenten: this usually refers to meatless dishes or preparations.
Liaison: this refers to certain items used for thickening soup, sauces etc.; most commonly a mixture of egg yolks and cream.
Macédoine: a mixture of various fruits or vegetables cut in dice.
Madeleine mould: a large or small scallop-shaped mould with a hinge.
Marc: a spirit distilled from the skins and pips of grapes left after the juice has been expressed from them.
to Macerate: to flavour foods by steeping them in an aromatic liquid such as a liqueur.
Malvoisie: Malmsey, a variety of Madeira wine.
Maraschino: brandy liqueur made from a type of small sour black cherry.
en Manchon: see Recipe No 1646.
to Marinate: a process of tenderizing and adding flavour to items of food, especially meat by placing it in a liquid such as wine together with herbs and flavourings.
Morels: a type of edible fungus of excellent flavour (Fr. *Morille*).
Mousserons: this is the St George's Agaric, a small white mushroom of excellent flavour.
Natives: English oysters.
Neige de Florence: a delicate variety of Italian pasta in the shape of very small flakes.
Nonats: very small fish similar to whitebait but from the Mediterranean.
Noques: the French name for Gnocchi.
Noyau: a liqueur made with cherry stone kernels.
Orgeat: a beverage or liqueur made from almond kernels.
Oronge: this is the Orange Agaric, a type of edible fungus.
Oxalis: a vegetable of South American origin.
Pané à l'Anglaise: see Egg and breadcrumb.
en Papillote: to cook food in a paper case.
Paysanne: vegetables cut into small square, round or triangular slices.
Perles du Japon: pearl-shaped pieces of a paste made of tapioca, in dried form.
Physalis: the Cape gooseberry.
Pluches: sprays of chervil or other fresh herbs used as a garnish.
Poutargue: a relish made from the roe of the mullet.
Pralin: see Recipes 4353 and 4354.
Praline: a sugared almond, a speciality of French confectionery.
Printanier: a name given to a garnish of new season's vegetables trimmed or cut into various shapes.
to Prove: to place a dough or paste made with yeast in the warm to increase in size.
Quince: a fruit resembling an apple and which has a very high pectin content.
Ramequin: 1) a small fireproof dish, 2) a type of cheese fritter.
Ravier: an hors-d'oeuvre dish.
to Refresh: to make cold usually by placing under running water.
Relevé: the second meat course of a formal dinner usually a large joint or whole bird.
Rennet: a secretion obtained from the stomach of a calf, used in the making of junket.
Rillette: a type of potted meat usually made of pork; of French origin. There are many regional varieties.
Rillon: a potted meat similar to a Rillette but the meat is not pounded.
Royan: a small fish similar to the sardine.
Rosolio: a red-coloured liqueur made from raisins.
Rubanné: describes a moulded dish made up of a number of different colours and flavours in well defined layers.

Saccharometer: instrument used for testing the density of syrup.
Saffron: this is obtained from the stamens of a species of crocus and is used for colouring and flavouring.
Salamander: a type of grill in which the source of heat is at the top.
Salpicon: items of food cut in small dice, usually mixed with a sauce or forcemeat to bind it.
Sauerkraut: salted shredded white cabbage.
Salep: edible substance obtained from the tuber of a species of Orchis indigenous to the East and Near East.
Seltzer water: carbonated mineral water originally from Neider Selters in Germany.
Sigui: a species of fish found in the Baltic Sea, its flesh is similar to that of the shad.
Spit: a rod on which meat etc. is impaled for roasting in front of an open fire.
to Stud: to insert small pieces of truffle, ox tongue etc. into items of food.
Terrine: a deep oval or round earthenware dish with a lid used for cooking poultry and game. By extension the word Terrine indicates the actual food cooked in the dish, e.g. a Terrine can be a coarsely chopped pâté cooked in this dish.
Timbale: See Chapter 10 Composite Entrées, for the many interpretations of this term.
Tourte: a round-covered pie or tart.
Turban: a method of presenting food where it is arranged in a circle on the dish or cooked in a shallow round border or Savarin mould.
Verjuice: the juice of unripe grapes.
Vésiga: the dried spinal cord of the sturgeon.
Vin de Samos: a sweet white wine from the island of that name.
Vrilles: vine tendrils.
Zakouskis: Russian Hors-d'oeuvre. See the Introduction to the section on Hot Hors-d'oeuvre on Page 120.
Zest: the thin outer rind of a citrus fruit.

MENUS

MENUS DE DEJEUNERS

Concombre mariné aux piments doux
Duchesse au Caviar
Œufs frits
Pieds de mouton poulette
Poulet Bonne femme
Pâté de foie gras
Pain grillé très chaud
Asperges à l'huile
Pêche Cardinal
Pâtisserie

Hors-d'Œuvre
Œufs Cocotte
Sole grillée Diable
Faisan poêlé au Céleri
Parfait de foie gras
Salade Rachel
Soufflé au Chocolat
Tartelette aux fruits

Kilkis. Olives de Lucques
Crevettes roses
Truite au bleu
Agneau de lait Boulangère
Terrine de Canard Rouennais
Cœurs de Romaine
Asperges vertes
Mousse à la Fraise
Mille-feuilles

Hors-d'Œuvre
Merlan à l'Anglaise
Fricassée de poulet à l'ancienne
Selle d'Agneau à la Broche
Petits pois Française
Soufflé au Kirsch
Fromage à la Crème
Confiture de groseille de Bar-le-Duc

Figues nouvelles glacées
Olives farcies
Omelette aux fonds d'Artichauts
Langoustine Ravigote
Queue de bœuf en Daube
Cardons au parmesan
Alouette à la casserole
Salade Lorette
Fraises et pêches au Maraschino
Pâtisserie

Fenouil à la Grecque
Salade de Salicoque
Turbotin au vin rouge
Pilaw aux ris d'Agneau
Caneton nouveau aux petits pois
Mousse de jambon à la gelée
Salade d'asperges
Coupe d'Antigny
Fruits

Anguille fumée de Kiel
Cerneaux au verjus
Œufs brouillés aux truffes
Homard Américaine
Poulet poêlé Ménagère
Selle de Pré-salé
Petits pois aux laitues
Riz Impératrice
Sablés Viennois

Artichauts à la Grecque
Sardines au Currie
Truite à la Meunière
Pudding de Bécassine aux truffes
Selle d'Agneau de lait
Haricots verts à l'Anglaise, Pommes Anna
Soufflé aux Écrevisses à la Florentine
Crêpes Suzette
Fruits

Colchester Natives
Œufs frits
Merlan sur le plat
Noisette d'Agneau Rachel
Pommes pailles
Perdreau à la Broche
Salade de céleri aux truffes
Bavarois au Chocolat
Petits Condés
Fruits

Cantaloup rafraîchi
Matelote de Sole
Risotto de Volaille
Râble de lièvre à la crème
Purée de marrons
Aspic de homard
Salade de légumes
Poire au vin rouge
Pâtisserie

Anchois de Collioure
Tomates marinées
Œufs à la Reine
Whitebait Diablés
Tournedos Béarnaise
Pommes soufflées
Faisan Casserole
Salade d'Endives
Pâté de foie gras
Charlotte de pommes
Crème Chantilly

Hors-d'Œuvre
Moules à la Marinière
Côtelette d'Agneau grillée
Purée de pommes de terre
Perdreau Périgourdine
Salade de Céleri
Soufflé au Paprika
Mont Blanc aux marrons
Pâtisserie Parisienne

MENU

Hors-d'Œuvre
Melon Cantaloup
Tortue Claire
Germiny
Consommé Madrilène
Truite d'Écosse au Vin du Rhin
Mignonnettes de Sole
Poularde Soufflée au Paprika Rose
Concombres au Velouté
Selle d'Agneau Rôtie
ou
Selle de Chevreuil à la Bohémienne
Suprêmes d'Écrevisses Moscovite
Neige au Clicquot
Cailles escortées d'Ortolans
Salade de Cœurs de Romaine
Jambon de Prague sous la Cendre
Soufflé d'Asperges Rothschild
Biscuit Glacé à l'Orientale
Mille-Feuilles, Petit-Duc
Diablotins
Pêches, Nectarines et Raisins Muscat

VINS

Sandringham Pale Vino de Pasto
Josefhofer Auslese 1900
Château Mouton-Rothschild, Grand Vin 1878
Pommery et Greno, Vin Nature 1889
Bouquet et fils, House of Commons Cuvée 1892
Dow's Port 1887
Château-Yquem de Lur-Saluces 1884
Grande Fine Champagne
Grandes Liqueurs
Café Double

*

29th June 1906

Menu of Dinner served on board the *Amerika*, under the direction of G. A. Escoffier, on the occasion of the visit of Kaiser Wilhelm II of Germany.

MENU

Hors-d'Œuvre Suédoise
Consommé glacé
Tortue Claire
Suprêmes de Sole au vin du Rhin
Selle de Pré-salé aux Laitues à la Grecque
Petits Pois à la Bourgeoise
Poularde au Paprika Rosé
Cailles aux Raisins
Cœurs de Romaines
Asperges Mousseline
Écrevisses à la Moscovite
Soufflé Surprise
Mille-Feuilles, Petit-Duc, Friandises
Pêches, Nectarines, Ananas, Muscat

VINS

1897 Eitelsbacher
1888 Château-Fourteau
1893 Kiedricher Berg Auslese
1878 Château-Rauzan Ségala
Veuve Clicquot-Ponsardin, rosé
1900 Heidsieck et Cie
La Grande Marque de l'Empereur

*

18th June 1906

MENUS DE DÎNERS

Hors-d'Œuvre Moscovite
Tortue claire
Germiny
Truite au Chambertin
Mignonnettes de Sole
Whitebait Diablés
Cailles à la Turque
Baron d'agneau de lait Soubise
Petits pois à l'Anglaise
Pommes Byron
Suprêmes de Volaille Jeannette
Nageoires de Tortue à la Maryland
Sorbet fleur de Pêcher
Caneton de Rouen à l'orange
Jambon de Prague sous la cendre
Fèves de Marais
Asperges d'Argenteuil
Biscuit glacé praliné
Feuillantine
Œufs de pluvier en Aspic
Diablotins
Fraises Chantilly

*

24th May 1905

MENU

Hors-d'Œuvre
Consommé Leopold
Bisque d'Écrevisses
Turbotin au Volnay
Whitebait Diablés
Poularde à la Diva
Concombres au beurre
Selle d'agneau Portugaise
Haricots verts à l'Anglaise
Faisan Périgourdine
Salade d'Endives
Pâté de foie gras
Biscuit glacé aux marrons
Savarin aux fruits
Friandises

*

23rd November 1905

MENU

Frivolités Orientales
Cantaloup au Maraschino
Figues Fraîches
Gelée aux Paillettes dorées

Consommé aux Nids d'Hirondelles
Velouté au Blé Vert

Sterlets du Volga à la Livonienne
Nonnats de la Méditerranée au Fenouil

Chapon Fin à la Mode du Couvent
Mousse de Mai
Jeune Venaison à la Châtelaine
Petites Mascottes Printanière
Sylphides Roses

FLEURS DE PÊCHER

Cailles escortées d'Ortolans Ste. Alliance
Cœurs de Romaine aux Pommes d'Amour

Asperges de France au Beurre d'Isigny
Suprêmes d'Écrevisses au Champagne

Belle de Nuit
Bénédictines—Mignardises
Huîtres Perlières en Surprise
Fruits de Serre Chaude
Café Turc

Vins du Rhin
Grands Crus de France
Grandes Liqueurs

*

May 1906

MENU

Caviar frais—Œufs de pluvier
Melon
Tortue claire
Rossolnick
Truite au Chambertin
Laitances Meunière
Poularde Soufflée à la Catalane
Morilles à la crème
Selle d'Agneau de Galles aux laitues
Petits pois à l'Anglaise
Pommes Nana
Suprême d'Écrevisses Moscovite
Punch à la Mandarine
Caneton de Rouen à la Rouennaise
Cœurs de Romaine
Asperges de France
Biscuit glacé aux violettes
Friandises
Barquettes à l'Écossaise
Fraises
Pêches de Serre

*

12th April 1905

MENU

Œufs de pluvier
Caviar frais
Consommé Henri IV
Bisque d'Écrevisses
Truite au Chambertin
Laitances Meunière
Filet de poulet au beurre noisette
Petits pois à l'Anglaise
Selle de jeune Chevreuil aux cerises
Terrine de Cailles à la Richelieu
Punch glacé
Caneton de Rouen au sang
Salade Royale
Asperges Sauce Mousseline
Soufflé au Parmesan à la Florentine
Bombe Algésiras
Biscuit Génois
Fraises Chantilly

*

11th May 1905

Menu of the Luncheon offered by the Members of both Houses of Parliament to Admiral Caillard and his Officers, on the occasion of the visit of the French Fleet to Portsmouth in August 1905.

MENU

Truite Froide Amiral Caillard
Filet de Sole à la Masséna
Mayonnaise de Homard
Baron de Bœuf d'Écosse
Bœuf pressé Parlement
Jambon d'York à la Gelée
Chaud-froid de Cailles à la Loubet
Poularde Edouard VII
Côtelette d'Agneau Maintenon
Salade à la Parisienne
Cœurs de Laitue
Macédoine de Fruits au Champagne
Meringue Chantilly
Pêches Cardinal
Pâtisserie Française
Soufflé Glacé Fraternel
Dessert
Café

*

Westminster Hall
12th August 1905

MENU

Caviar Blinis
Royal Natives
Velouté aux petits pois frais
Filets de Sole Marie-Stuart
Barquettes de Laitances Florentine
Suprême de poulet au beurre noisette
Cœurs d'Artichauts au velouté
Selle de Chevreuil Grand Veneur
Mousse d'Écrevisses au Champagne
Punch Napolitain
Faisan truffé—Brochette d'Ortolans
Salade Lorette
Asperges vertes
Parfait de foie gras
Biscuit glacé à l'Orientale
Mignardises
Diablotins
Pêches de Montreuil
Raisins Muscat

*

5th October 1905

MENU

Hors-d'Œuvre Moscovite
Melon Cantaloup—Figues fraîches
Gelée Madrilène en tasse
Tortue claire
Truite Régina
Mignonnettes de Sole
Côtelettes d'agneau de lait Maréchale
Petits pois à l'Anglaise
Jambon de Prague sous la cendre
Crème de Champignons
Poularde Suédoise
Punch Sicilien
Caille au Muscat
Brochette d'Ortolans
Salade d'Asperges à la Toulousaine
Mousseline d'Écrevisses
Soufflé Hélène
Gâteau Manqué
Pêches. Nectarines

*

29th June 1906

MENU

Melon Cantaloup
Tortue claire
Crème Marie-Louise
Truite de Rivière au bleu
Côtelettes de Volaille Edouard VII
Selle de Chevreuil Grand Veneur
Pommes en Croquettes
Haricots Verts
Cailles escortées d'Ortolans
Salade de Cœurs de Romaine
Mousse d'Écrevisses Moscovite
Pêches Melba
Friandises
Soufflé au Parmesan

*

26th July 1906

MENU

Melon Cantaloup
Caviar
Tortue Claire
Consommé froid en gelée
Truite au Champagne
Côtelettes d'agneau de lait Maréchale
Concombres au velouté
Jambon de Prague sous la cendre
Petits pois à la Française
Poularde Néva
Poulet Rose Marie
Caille au raisin
Cœurs de Romaine
Asperges d'Argenteuil
Soufflé au Parmesan
Pêches et fraises Melba
Friandises

*

2nd June 1905

MENU

Caviar de la Néva—Blinis
Royal Natives
Tortue claire
Stschy à la Russe
Suprême de sole au Château-Yquem
Caille au nid
Selle de Chézelles à la Broche
Purée de Céleri
Bécasse au fumet
Salade Lorette
Asperges vertes
Parfait de foie gras au Clicquot
Soufflé Rothschild
Biscuit glacé aux perles des Alpes
Corbeille de fruits

*

1st November 1905

MENU

Hors-d'Œuvre Moscovite
Royal Natives
Tortue claire
Crème d'asperges
Saumon au Coulis d'Écrevisses
Whitebait diablés
Poularde à la Piémontaise
Cèpes Rissolés
Baron d'agneau de lait
Haricots verts nouveaux à l'Anglaise
Pommes Noisette
Mandarines givrées
Bécasse au Chambertin
Salade d'Endive au Céleri
Jambon sous la cendre
Fèves de marais
Bombe Néro
Savarin au Kirsch
Barquette Vendôme
Pêches et fraises

*

20th February 1906

MENU

Caviar—Blinis
Tortue claire—Velouté Marie-Louise
Turbotin au Chambertin
Suprême de poulet aux truffes fraîches
Fonds d'artichauts au velouté
Selle d'agneau de Galles
Haricots verts à l'Anglaise
Tomate au gratin
Mousse d'Écrevisses
Bécassine rosée—Ortolans des Chasseurs
Salade Impériale
Asperges de France
Parfait de foie gras
Soufflé en surprise
Corbeille de fruits

*

21st November 1905

MENU

Hors-d'Œuvre Moscovite
Royal Natives
Consommé Henri IV—Velouté Rachel
Turbotin Newburg
Mignonnette de Sole au paprika
Timbale de Cailles Périgourdine
Purée de Céleri
Selle d'agneau de Behague
Petits pois à l'Anglaise
Pommes noisette
Suprême de poulet Rose de Mai
Neige au Clicquot
Perdreau et Grouse à la Broche
Cœurs de laitues aux fines herbes
Asperges vertes
Parfait de foie gras
Bombe Ste. Alliance
Biscuit Mousseline à l'Orange
Barquette Vendôme
Fruits

*

5th October 1906

MENU

Melon au Porto
Tortue claire
Velouté aux Pommes d'Amour
Filets de Sole au Château Yquem
Cassolette d'Écrevisses
Caille Judic
Baron d'agneau de lait à la Menthe
Petits pois Française
Poularde Rose-Marie
Sorbet au Clicquot
Caneton de Rouen à la Presse
Salade d'Orange
Asperges Anglaises
Soufflé glacé aux Pêches
Pain de Gènes
Barquette Vendôme
Corbeille de Fruits

*

10th June 1905

MENU

Hors-d'Œuvre Moscovite
Consommé Henri IV
Bisque d'Écrevisses
Truite saumonée Livonienne
Whitebait
Timbale de Cailles à la Royale
Baron d'agneau de lait Mireille
Haricots verts à l'Anglaise
Suprême de volaille à l'Ancienne
Caneton de Rouen au sang
Cœurs de Romaine
Asperges d'Argenteuil
Bombe Orientale
Biscuit Mousseline
Diablotins à la Moelle
Fraises au Porto
Crème Chantilly

*

20th May 1906

MENU

Frivolités Moscovite
Consommé à la moelle d'esturgeon
Velouté aux nids d'hirondelle
Sylphide à la crème de piment
Cailles pochées aux perles noires
Julienne de Céleri
Cochon de lait St Antoine
Pommes aigrelettes à la gelée de groseille
Bécasse au feu d'Enfer
Cœurs de Romaine aux pommes d'amour
Asperges de Provence
Suprême de foie gras au vin de Moselle
Belles de Nuit
Diablotins roses
Mignardises

*

27th October 1906

MENU

Caviar—Œufs de pluvier
Melon
Tortue claire—Velouté Marie Louise
Timbale de homard Américaine
Poularde Favorite
Concombres à la crème
Jambon de Prague à la Metternich
Petits pois aux laitues braisées
Suprême de Caneton à la Viennoise
Neige au Clicquot
Caille Alexandra
Salade Impériale
Asperges d'Argenteuil
Soufflé au Parmesan à la Florentine
Biscuit glacé praliné
Mille-feuilles au chocolat
Fraises Élizabeth—Mignardises

*

15th April 1905

MENU

Hors-d'Œuvre à la Russe
Tortue claire—Crème de concombre
Saumon Véronique
Whitebait
Caneton de Rouen Vendôme
Selle d'agneau de lait
Petits pois frais—Pommes nouvelles
Caille aux feuilles de vigne
Salade
Sorbet Pluie d'or
Jambon de Prague au Madère
Soufflé d'Epinard
Asperges d'Argenteuil
Œufs de pluvier en gelée
Omelette Surprise
Mousse d'Écrevisses
Fraises Chantilly
Friandises

*

3rd May 1905

MENU

Melon Cantaloup
Bortsch
Velouté Royale
Timbale de Sole Newburg
Caille Judic
Riz à la Grecque
Selle d'agneau Portugaise
Haricots verts à l'Anglaise
Suprême de volaille glacé au Paprika
Punch à l'orange
Caneton Bigarade
Cœur de Laitue aux œufs
Asperges Milanaise
Soufflé Lérina
Bombe Alexandra
Biscuit Mousseline
Fruits

*

5th June 1905

MENU

Caviar Blinis
Tortue claire
Velouté Dame Blanche
Filet de Sole Alice
Caille pochée au Vin du Rhin
Nouilles à l'Alsacienne
Selle de Chevreuil aux cerises
Purée de Marrons
Bécassine rôtie
Salade
Asperges vertes
Poire Melba
Biscuit Mousseline au chocolat
Fruits

*

25th October 1905

MENU

Hors-d'Œuvre Moscovite
Caviar de Sterlet—Blinis
Tortue verte
Consommé aux nids d'hirondelle
Truite saumonée au Vin du Rhin
Barquette de Laitance au Paprika
Poularde Royale
Timbale de Truffes Rossini
Selle d'agneau de lait Soubise
Petits pois nouveaux à l'Anglaise
Pommes Byron
Soufflé d'Écrevisses à l'Orientale
Mandarines givrées
Bécassine à la broche
Cœur de Romaine
Asperges d'Argenteuil
Pêche au Kirsch
Biscuit glacé aux Violettes
Mignardises—Marrons vanillés
Diablotins—Fraises—Raisins

MENU

Melon Cantaloup
Tortue claire
Consommé froid en gelée
Mousseline de Sole aux Écrevisses
Américaine
Filet de poulet au beurre noisette
Concombre au velouté
Jambon de Prague sous la cendre
Maïs à la crème
Terrine de Canard Rouennaise
Caille aux raisins
Salade de Cœur de Romaine
Asperges d'Argenteuil
Soufflé au Parmesan
Pêche et fraises Melba
Friandises

*

4th June 1905

MENU

Caviar—Melon
Consomme Alexandra—Velouté Royale
Saumoneau poché au Vin du Rhin
Mignonnette de Sole au Paprika
Poularde soufflé Alfred de Rothschild
Baron d'agneau de lait persillé
Petits Pois nouveaux à la Française
Mousseline d'Écrevisses au Champagne
Punch à la Romaine
Caneton de Rouen à la Rouennaise
Cœur de Laitue aux œufs
Asperges de France
Pêche Hilda
Gâteau Marie Brizard
Barquette de Laitance Florentine

*

5th May 1905

MENU

Hors-d'Œuvre
Consommé froid Napolitaine
Rossolnick
Truite Suzanne
Baron d'agneau de lait
Courgettes au gratin
Petits Pois à la Paysanne
Poularde Rose-Marie
Caille aux Raisins
Cœur de Romaine
Asperges d'Argenteuil
Soufflé au Parmesan
Pêche Melba
Friandises

*

4th June 1905

MENU

Hors-d'Œuvre
Consommé Rossini
Velouté d'Écrevisses
Truite froide à la Norvégienne
Mignonnettes de Sole Murat
Côtelette d'agneau de lait Maréchale
Concombres à la Crème
Jambon de Prague sous la cendre
Soufflé d'Épinard
Caneton Vendôme
Poussin en Casserole
Cœurs de Romaine aux Pommes d'Amour
Asperges Mousseline
Fraises glacées à la Vanille
Friandises

*

4th June 1905

MENU

Hors-d'Œuvre
Melon rafraîchi
Consommé froid Madrilène
Truite Joinville
Poularde Edouard VII
Artichauts farcis
Selle de Chevreuil à la Crème à la Normande
Caille en cocotte aux raisins
Cœurs de Romaine
Asperges d'Argenteuil
Biscuit glacé
Pêches et fraises à la Cardinal
Gâteau Bibesco
Friandises

*

19th May 1905

Menu served on the occasion of the visit of the President of the French Republic to London.

MENU

Caviar frais—Melon Cantaloup
Potage Béarnais
Consommé aux nids d'hirondelle
Filet de truite au Chambertin
Poularde aux Perles de Périgord
Nouilles au beurre noisette
Mignonnette d'agneau Clarence
Petits pois à la Française
Suprême d'Écrevisses
Neige au Champagne
Cailles escortées d'Ortolans
Cœur de laitue
Asperges Crème d'Isigny
Pêche Alexandra
Parfait aux trois couleurs
Mignardises

*

Carlton Hotel
6th July 1903

MENU

Melon Cantaloup à la fine Champagne
Caviar
Poule au pot Henri IV
Turbotin Véronique
Selle de Chevreuil à la Crème
Bananes au beurre
Pommes Duchesse
Poularde Vendôme
Salade de laitue
Asperges de Paris
Fraises à la Ritz
Friandises

*

21st May 1905

MENU

Hors-d'Œuvre Moscovite
Tortue claire—Okra
Truite au Vin de la Moselle
Mignonnette de Sole
Poularde Diva
Concombres au velouté
Selle d'agneau Portugaise
Petits Pois aux laitues
Terrine de Caille à la Richelieu
Punch Rose
Caneton de Rouen à la Rouennaise
Cœur de Romaine
Asperges Vertes
Bombe Pralinée
Mille-Feuilles
Barquette Vendôme
Fruits

*

10th May 1905

MENU

Melon
Consommé Messaline
Sole Toulousaine
Suprême de Volaille aux fonds d'Artichauts
Noisettes d'Agneau Fines Herbes
Petits Pois à l'Anglaise
Pommes Parisienne
Mousse de Jambon Moscovite
Grouse à la Broche
Caille aux feuilles de Vigne
Salade
Aubergine au gratin
Pêches et Framboises rafraîchies
Crème Chantilly
Friandises

MENU

Caviar
Consommé de Volaille à l'Ancienne
Germiny
Suprême de Sole au Champagne
Laitance Meunière
Filet de Faisan Périgourdine
Purée de Céleri
Selle d'Agneau à la Broche
Pommes Mireille
Haricots verts
Bécassine Chasseur
Salade Lorette
Asperges, Sauce Hollandaise
Poire Melba
Friandises

MENU

Caviar—Blinis
Consommé Henri IV
Paupiette de Sole Newburg
Filets de Poulet aux Truffes
Fonds d'Artichauts à la Crème
Selle d'Agneau de Lait à la Grecque
Bécassine à la Broche
Salade Lorette
Asperges vertes
Soufflé Rothschild
Mandarines Glacées
Friandises
Barquette de Laitance

MENU

Caviar—Blinis
Bortsch
Saumon Hollandaise
Caille à la Grecque
Selle de Chevreuil poivrade
Purée de Marrons
Croquette Duchesse
Mousse de Jambon Alsacienne
Poussin Périgourdine
Salade
Asperges vertes
Biscuit aux Violettes
Friandises
Fraises Wilhelmina
Fruits du Cap

MENU DU NOËL, 1906

Frivolités
Caviar frais
Blinis de Sarrasin
Oursins de la Méditerranée

Consommé aux nids d'Hirondelle
Velouté Dame Blanche
Sterlet du Volga à la Moscovite
Barquette de Laitance à la Vénitienne
Chapon fin aux Perles du Périgord
Cardon épineux à la Toulousaine
Selle de Chevreuil aux Cerises
Sylphide d'Ortolans Reine Alexandra
Suprême d'Écrevisses au Champagne

Mandarines Givrées

Terrine de Cailles sous la Cendre aux Raisins
Bécassine rosée au feu de sarments

Salade Isabelle
Asperges de France
Délices de Foie gras
Soufflé de Grenade à l'Orientale
Biscuit glacé aux Violettes

Mignardises
Fruits de Serre chaude

Grandes Liqueurs
Fine Champagne 1830

BON VOYAGE

MENU

Caviar frais—Blinis
Royal Natives
Tortue Claire
Rossolnick
Suprême de Sole Marie Stuart
Barquette de Laitance Meunière
Filet de Poulet au Beurre Noisette
Cœur d'artichauts aux Truffes
Selle de Veau Braisée
Purée de Châtaignes—Pommes Nana
Mousse d'Écrevisses au Champagne
Punch Sicilien
Bécassine à la Broche
Salade Lorette
Asperges Vertes
Pâté de Foie Gras
Biscuit Glacé aux Violettes
Mille-Feuilles
Diablotins
Corbeille de Fruits

VINS

Berncastler Doctor, 1893
Veuve Clicquot-Ponsardin, 1892
Château Mouton-Rothschild
Grand Vin Mise du Château, 1878
Grandes Liqueurs—Café

*

Carlton Hotel and Restaurant
London
19th October 1905

NEW YEAR'S EVE DINNER

MENU

Caviar de Sterlet
Royal Natives
Tortue claire
Velouté Régina
Suprême de Sole Clarence
Poularde Alexandra
Morilles des Alpes
Mignonnette d'agneau à l'Écossaise
Pommes Parisienne
Crême de haricots verts
Soufflé d'Écrevisses Moscovite
Mandarines givrées
Caille aux truffes
Salade d'Endive et Céleri
Asperges de France
Parfait de Foie gras
Plum pudding à la fine Champagne
Mousse glacée Aurore 1906
Friandises
Fruits

*

31st December 1905

CHRISTMAS DINNER

MENU

Crèpe aux œufs de Sterlet
Consommé Santa-Maria
Velouté aux Paillettes dorées
Paupiette de Sole sous la cendre
Caille à l'Orientale
Jeune Chevreuil aux Cerises
Crème de Marrons
Suprême de Foie gras au Champagne
Neige aux Perles des Alpes
Chapon accompagné d'Ortolans Ste-Alliance
Salade Nazareth
Asperges de France
Le plum pudding des Rois Mages
L'Étoile du Berger
Bénédictins Blancs

*

25th December 1905

GARDEN PARTY

LUNCHEON

Melon Cantaloup Glacé

Consommé froid Madrilène
Consommé de Volaille chaud

Truite d'Écosse à la Vénitienne
Œuf Glacé au Jambon

Noisette d'Agneau à l'Estragon
Petits pois Bonne Femme
Poulets nouveaux Mireille

BUFFET FROID

Filet de Bœuf Printanière
Chaud-froid de Caille à l'Alsacienne
Galantine de Volaille aux Truffes
Suprême de Caneton aux Cerises
Cœurs de Romaine
Pêche Melba
Glace Napolitaine
Biscuit Mousseline
Petits-Fours
Savarin au Kirsch
Panier de Nectarines, Raisins, Fraises

VINS

Brauneberger, 1900
Hock Cup
Champagne Cup
Boquet fils, extra dry, 1892
Perrier Jouet, extra dry, 1898
Grande Fine Champagne
Grandes Liqueurs
Café Double

*

Hampton-on-Thames
21st July 1906

VISITE DU PRÉSIDENT LOUBET

SOUPER

donné au
CARLTON HOTEL RESTAURANT
le 7 Juillet, 1903
après la soirée de gala à l'Opéra

Consommé en Tasse
Filet de sole Alexandra
Côtelette d'agneau au beurre noisette
Petits pois Anglaise
Caille glacée à la Toulousaine
Suprême de volaille Jeannette
Mousse d'Écrevisses
Salade Mignonne
Pêches et Fraises Ste. Alliance
Friandises

SUPPER MENU

Velouté Ecossaise
Filet de sole Meunière
Côtelette d'Agneau Maréchale
Pointes d'Asperges à la Crême
Mignonnette de Poulet glacée au Paprika
Buffet Froid
Salade Lorette
Pêche Melba
Friandises

*

Carlton Hotel
11th October 1906

SUPPER MENU

Caviar frais
Royal Natives
Consommé Madrilène
Paupiette de Sole Orientale
Côtelette de volaille à la Maréchale
Pointes d'asperges
Noisette d'agneau Rachel
Caille au raisin
Parfait de foie gras
Pêche Alice
Friandises

SUPPER MENU

Natives
Consommé de Volaille
Filet de Sole Américaine
Côtelette d'agneau grillée
Concombres à la crème
Mousse de Jambon au blanc de poulet
Parfait de foie gras
Perdreau Périgourdine
Salade Rachel
Macédoine de fruit glacée
Friandises

EXAMPLE OF A FANCY SUPPER MENU

Caviar de Sterlet
Crêpes Moscovite
Consommé aux Pommes d'Amour
Sylphides à la crème d'Écrevisses
Mignonnette de poulet Petit-Duc
Velouté Favori
Cailles dodues escortées d'Ortolans
Nymphes roses—Désirs de Mascotte
Pointes d'Asperges à l'huile Vierge
Charmes de Vénus voilés à l'Orientale
Plaisirs des Dames
Étoiles Filantes—Frivolités

VINS

Zeltinger Schlossberg, 1897
Bollinger, Extra Dry, 1898

*

Carlton Hotel
Saturday, 6th October 1906

MENU

Hors-d'Œuvre Moscovite
Melon Cantaloup
Tortue claire
Velouté aux Pommes d'Amour
Paupiette de sole à l'Ancienne
Timbale de Ris de Veau Toulousaine
Poularde Rose-Marie
Selle d'Agneau aux laitues à la Grecque
Petits pois à l'Anglaise
Punch glacé
Caille en cocotte
Salade Romaine
Asperges d'Argenteuil
Terrine de Canard Rouennaise
Bombe Néro
Friandises
Diablotins
Fruits

*

13th June 1906

MENU

Hors-d'Œuvre
Huîtres au raifort
Poutargue de Gènes
Figues fraîches
Cocky Leekie
Velouté aux fleurs de courgette
Truite au bleu
Nonnats de la Méditerranée au Fenouil
Poularde à l'Aurore
Selle de Chevreuil à la Bohémienne
Pommes aigrelettes à la gelée de groseille
Suprêmes d'Écrevisse au Champagne
Pastèque en Sorbet
Perdreau aux raisins
Salade Créole
Cœur d'artichaut Petit-Duc
Mousse Favorite
Délices au Caramel
Pêches Rose Chérie

MENU

Hors-d'Œuvre Moscovite
Melon Cantaloup
Consommé froid Madrilène
Tortue claire
Truite d'Écosse au Vin du Rhin
Mignonnette de Sole
Filet de poulet Alexandra
Concombres au Paprika
Selle de Chevreuil à la Bohémienne
Suprême d'Écrevisse au Clicquot
Neige aux Perles des Alpes
Caille au raisin
Salade d'Asperges vertes
Aubergine au gratin
Biscuit glacé Orientale
Marcelin Anisette
Diablotins
Corbeille de Pêches et Nectarines

*

28th June 1906

MENU

Hors-d'Œuvre
Caviar frais—Crêpes Moscovite
Nymphes roses
Consommé de faisan au céleri
Bisque d'Oursins
Mousseline de Lavaret au Vin de Savoie
Mignonnette de Sole au poivre noir
Salmis de perdreau à l'ancienne mode
Selle d'agneau à l'Orientale
Aubergine à la Grecque
Crème de piments au blanc de poulet
Coupe givrée au Suc de grenade
Caille de vigne au vert-jus
Salade des Capucins
Soufflé de pomme à la Chantilly
Parfait glacé aux Avelines
Mignardises
Paillettes Diablées
Corbeille de fruits

MENU

Hors-d'Œuvre Moscovite
Natives
Consommé Marie Stuart
Chicken Okra
Timbale de Sole Orientale
Poularde Favorite
Concombre au beurre
Baron d'agneau de lait
Riz à la Grecque
Laitues braisées
Bécasse au fumet
Salade d'asperges et d'artichauts
Parfait de foie gras
Biscuit glacé Alice
Mille-feuilles
Fruits

*

13th December 1906

MENU

Hors-d'Œuvre à la Russe
Caviar frais—Blinis
Tortue claire
Velouté de volaille au Paprika
Paupiette de sole au vin de Moselle
Barquette de Laitance Florentine
Filet de poulet au beurre noisette
Riz pilaw aux Piments verts
Selle de Chevreuil Bohémienne
Pommes aigrelettes aux Cerises
Mousse d'Écrevisses à la Moscovite
Sorbet aux Perles des Alpes
Suprême de perdreau Souvaroff
Ortolans au Clicquot
Asperges nouvelles
Pâté de foie gras
Bombe Alaska
Mignardises
Paillettes Diablées
Poires, Pêches, Raisins Muscat

*

24th September 1906

MENU

Frivolités Moscovite
Consommé à la moelle d'esturgeon
Velouté de volaille aux Pommes d'Amour
Sylphides à la crème d'Écrevisses
Filet de Perdreau au Chambertin
Purée de marrons
Jambon de Prague au Paprika rose
Soufflé aux asperges vertes
Caille Hilda
Cœurs de Laitues
Suprême de foie gras
Belles de Nuit
Mignardises

*

7th November 1906

SUPPER MENU

Frivolités
Consommé aux Pommes d'Amour
Mousseline de volaille aux nids d'hirondelle
Suprême d'Écrevisses à la Crème de piment
Mignonnette de Poulet Petit-Duc
Nymphes roses
Désirs de Mascotte
Sylphide de jeunes pigeons
Ortolans pochés au Clicquot
Truffes sous la cendre
Délices de foie gras au Vin de Moselle
Asperges à l'Huile vierge
Charmes de Vénus voilés à l'Orientale
Belles de Nuit
Huitres perlières en surprise
Les plaisirs de Dame
Friandises
Treilles de raisin Muscat

CHRISTMAS DINNER

Natives
Caviar frais
Tortue claire
Velouté de Poulet au lait d'Amande
Suprême de Sole à la Samaritaine
Dindonneau du Périgord
Crème de Marrons
Noisettes d'agneau à la moelle
Pointes d'Asperges au beurre
Caille au raisin
Salade Nazareth
Parfait de foie gras
Plum Pudding aux feux follets
Mandarines givrées
Gâteau des Trois Rois
Friandises

*

24th December 1906

CHRISTMAS MENU

Frivolités
Caviar frais—Blinis de Sarrasin
Oursins de la Méditerranée
Natives au Raifort
Les Délices de St Antoine
Tortue Verte
Velouté de Poulet aux nids d'hirondelle
Sterlet du Volga à la Moscovite
Barquette de Laitance à la Vénitienne
Chapon fin aux Perles du Périgord
Cardon épineux à la Toulousaine
Selle de Venaison aux Cerises
Crème de marrons
Jeune agneau piqué de sauge à la Provençale
Sylphides de Roitelets
Gelée de Pommes d'Amour aux Écrevisses
Fine Champagne, 1820
Mandarines givrées
Cailles sous la cendre aux raisins
Bécassines rosées au feu de sarment
Salade Isabelle
Asperges de France
Foie gras poché au Vin de Moselle
Bûche de Noël en Surprise
Plum Pudding—Mince Pie
Mignardises aux violettes
Étoile du Berger
Fruits de Serre chaude
Café Turc
Grandes Liqueurs

*

Christmas 1906

INDEX

(Bold figures on left of column denote recipe numbers and figures on right of column denote page numbers)

3277 Abattis à la Bourguignonne 392
3278 Abattis Chipolata 392
3279 Abattis aux Navets 392
4508 Abricots Bourdaloue 536
4509 Abricots Colbert 536
4510 Abricots Condé 536
4413 Abricots, Croûte aux, au Marasquin 526
4511 Abricots Cussy 537
4512 Abricots Gratinés 537
4513 Abricots Meringués 537
4625 Abricots Mireille 551
4626 Abricots à la Parisienne 552
4627 Abricots à la Royale 552
4514 Abricots Sultane 537
4372 Acacia Flower Fritters 521
913 Aceto-dolce 121
914 Achards 121
915 Agoursis 121
3382 Ailerons de Dindonneau Dorés à la Purée de Marrons 405
3282 Ailerons de Volaille Dorés à la Purée de Marrons 393
3284 Ailerons de Volaille Farcis Chipolata 393
3285 Ailerons de Volaille Farcis Grillés 393
3283 Ailerons de Volaille Farcis, Terrine d', à la Boulangère 393
3368 Ailerons de Poulet Carmelite 404
3369 Ailerons de Poulet Lady Wilmer 404
3286 Ailerons, Risotto d' 393
194 Aïoli 29
4917 Allumettes 577
916 Allumettes for Hors-d'Oeuvre 121
917 Allumettes aux Anchois 121
1077 Allumettes Caprice 133
1078 Allumettes aux Crevettes 133
1079 Allumettes, Various 133
224 Almond Butter 33
4350 Almond Paste, Soft 518
1573 Alose Farcie 185
1574 Alose Grillée 185
1575 Alose Grillée à l'Oseille 185
1576 Alose à la Provençale 186
Alouettes 449
3787 Alouettes, Pâté de 459
3730 Alouettes du Père Phillipe 450
2185 Aloyau de Boeuf 267
2186 Aloyau de Boeuf Froid 268
1028 American Relishes 130
2187 Amourettes (de Boeuf) 268
2188 Amourettes, Cromesquis d', à la Française 268
2189 Amourettes (de Boeuf) Cromesquis d', à la Polonaise 268
2190 Amourettes (de Boeuf) Cromesquis d', à la Russe 268
2191 Amourettes (de Boeuf) Croquettes d' 268
2192 Amourettes (de Boeuf) Fritot d' 268
2193 Amourettes (de Boeuf) Timbale d', à l'Ecossaise 269
2194 Amourettes (de Boeuf) Timbales d', à la Napolitaine 269
2493 Amourettes de Veau Tosca 301
2195 Amourettes, Timbales d', Villeneuve 269
4379 Ananas, Beignets d', Favorite 522
4515 Ananas Condé 537
4516 Ananas à la Créole 537
4628 Ananas Georgette 522
4629 Ananas Ninon 552
4630 Ananas à la Royale 552
4631 Ananas Virginie 552
1725 Anchois 205
937 Anchois, Canapés d' 123
1095 Anchois, Beignets d' 135
1171 Anchois, Dartois aux 142
918 Anchois, Filets d' 121
919 Anchois Frais Marinés 121
920 Anchois, Médaillons d' 121
998 Anchois de Norvége 128
921 Anchois, Paupiettes d' 121
992 Anchois aux Poivrons 121
1251 Anchois, Sausselis aux 150
923 Anchois des Tamarins 122
1725 Anchovies 205
Anchovy, see also under Anchois
917 Anchovy, Allumettes 121
223 Anchovy Butter 33
918 Anchovy Fillets 121
917 Anchovy Fingers 121
919 Anchovies, Fresh Marinated 121
920 Anchovy Médallions 121
998 Anchovies, Norwegian 128
922 Anchovies with Pimento 121
85 Anchovy Sauce 17
2984 Andouilles and Andouillettes 359
2985 Andouillettes à la Bourguignonne 359
2986 Andouillettes à la Lyonnaise 359
4918 Angels on Horseback 577
4918 Anges à Cheval 577
1577 Anguille à la Beaucaire 186
1578 Anguille Benoîton 186
1579 Anguille, Coulibiac d' 186
1582 Anguille Frite 186
1583 Anguille Frite à l'Anglaise 186
924 Anguille Fumée 122
1584 Anguille en Matelote 186
1585 Anguille à la Menagère 186
1742 Anguille de Mer 206
1586 Anguille à la Meunière 187
3778 Anguille, Pâté d' 458
1589 Anguille Pompadour 187
1591 Anguille à la Romaine 187
1590 Anguille à la Rouennaise 187
1592 Anguille à la Tartare 187
1593 Anguille, Tourte d', à la Saint-Martin 187
1594 Anguille au Vert 188
1595 Anguille au Vert à la Flamande 188
925 Anguille au Vin Blanc et Paprika 122
2754 Animelles de menton 331
Apple, see also under Pommes
540 Apples, Baked 540
4386 Apple Charlotte 523
4561 Apple Dumplings, Baked 541
4564 Apple Flans, Various 542
4546 Apple Fritters 540
4436 Apple Pudding 529
165 Apple Sauce 26
Apricots, see also under Abricots
4370 Apricot Fritters 520
4360 Apricot Sauce 520
3961 Artichauts à la Barigoule 477
3962 Artichauts Cavour 477
3963 Artichauts, Coeurs d', Clamart
3964 Artichauts, Coeurs d', Grand-Duc 477
3969 Artichauts, Croûte aux Fonds d' 478
3974 Artichauts Dietrich, Quartiers d' 478
3970 Artichauts, Fonds d', Cussy 478
3971 Artichauts, Fonds d', Farcis 478
926 Artichauts à la Grecque 122
3975 Artichauts à l'Italienne, Quartiers d' 478
Artichauts de Jerusalem, see also under Topinambours
3976 Artichauts Lyonnaise 479
3972 Artichauts aux Pointes d'Asperges, Fonds d' 478
3966 Artichauts à la Provençale 477
3973 Artichauts Sautés, Fonds d' 478
3967 Artichauts Stanley 478
Artichokes, Globe, see under Artichauts

3972 Artichoke Bottoms with Asparagus Tips 478
3973 Artichoke Bottoms, Sautéed 478
927 Artichoke Bottoms, Small garnished 122
3971 Artichoke Bottoms, Stuffed 478
3977 Artichokes, Globe, Cream of 479
3968 Artichokes, Globe, Cromesquis of 478
3968 Artichokes, Globe, Croquettes of 478
3977 Artichokes, Globe, Purée of 479
Artichokes, Japanese, see under Crosnes
4086 Artichokes, Japanese 490
Artichokes, Jerusalem, see also under Topinambours
4270 Artichokes, Jerusalem, English Style 507
4271 Artichokes, Jerusalem, Fried 507
3965 Artichokes with Various Sauces 477
3978 Asparagus 479
Asparagus, see also under Asperges
502 Asparagus Royale 72
3985 Asparagus Tips, Buttered 479
3984 Asparagus with Various Sauces 479
3978 Asperges 479
3985 Asperges au Beurre, Pointes d' 479
3986 Asperges à la Crème, Pointes d' 480
3979 Asperges à la Flamande 479
3980 Asperges au Gratin 479
3981 Asperges à l'Italienne 479
3982 Asperges Mornay 479
3983 Asperges à la Polonaise 479
336 Aspics 52
3760 Aspic de Bécasses 453
277 Aspic Jelly, Chicken 40
2038 Aspic of Fillets of Sole 236
3511 Aspic of Foie gras 423
278 Aspic Jelly, Game 40
280 Aspic Jelly, Red Wine Fish 41
276 Aspic Jellies, Ordinary 40
3737 Aspic d'Ortolans 451
3371 Aspic de Volaille Gauloise 404
3370 Aspic de Volaille à l'Italienne 404
279 Aspic Jelly, White Fish 40
1080 Attereaux 133
1081 Attereaux à la Genevoise 134
1084 Attereaux d'Huîtres à la Villeroy 134
1082 Attereaux au Parmesan 134
1083 Attereaux Villeroy 134
Aubergines 480
3987 Aubergines à la Bordelaise 480
3988 Aubergines à la Crème 480
3989 Aubergines à l'Egyptienne 480
3990 Aubergines Frites 480
3991 Aubergines au Gratin 480
3992 Aubergines à la Napolitaine 480
3993 Aubergines à l'Orientale 480
3994 Aubergines à la Provençale 480
3995 Aubergines à la Serbe 480
3996 Aubergines Soufflées 481

4319 Baba Paste 514
3451 Ballotines de Caneton 414
3287 Ballotines of Chicken 393
Bananas, see under Bananes
4517 Bananes Bourdaloue 537
4518 Bananes Condé 537
4519 Bananes Flambées 537
4520 Bananes Meringuées 537
4521 Bananes à la Norvégienne 537
4632 Bananes en Salade 552
4522 Bananes Soufflées 538
4633 Bananes Trédern 552
4590 Baquet and Panier Chantilly 546
1596 Barbeau à la Bourguignonne 188
Barbel, see also under Barbeau
1598 Barbel, Grilled Small 188
1600 Barbel, Roast Small 188
1597 Barbel with Various Sauces 188
Barbillon, see also under Barbeau
1598 Barbillon Grillé 188
1599 Barbillon à la Meunière 188
1600 Barbillon Rôti 188
1727 Barbue 205
1726 Bar de Mer 205
3882 Barding for Roasting 469
3890 Baron of Beef, Roast 471
3900 Baron of Lamb, Roast 472
3900 Baron of Mutton, Roast 472
1085 Barquettes 134
928 Barquettes, paste, fillings etc. 122
1086 Barquettes Chevreuse 134
1087 Barquettes de Crevettes 134
1088 Barquettes d'Ecrevisses 135
1089 Barquettes de Filets de Sole 135
928 Barquettes, fillings 122
1090 Barquettes de Homard 135
1091 Barquettes d'Huîtres 135
1087 Barquettes Joinville 134
1632 Barquettes de Laitances 192
1092 Barquettes de Laitances à la Florentine 135
1093 Barquettes de Laitances au Parmesan 135
1088 Barquettes Nantua 135
1091 Barquettes Ostendaise 135
928 Barquettes, pastes for 122
1090 Barquettes Victoria 135
302 Bases and Cases 48
316 Batter, frying, for fritters of brains, soft roes etc. 49
317 Batter, frying, for Vegetables 49
4575 Bavarois Clermont 544
4576 Bavarois Diplomate 544
4572 Bavarois Mixture, Cream 544
4573 Bavarois Mixture, Fruit 544
4574 Bavarois, moulding and presentation 544
4577 Bavarois My Queen 544
4578 Bavarois à la Normande 544
4579 Bavarois à la Religieuse 544
4580 Bavarois Rubanné 545
4581 Bavarois, Various Cream 545
4582 Bavarois, Various Fruit 545
4995 Bavaroise 587
4106 Beans, Broad 492
4122 Beans, Flageolet 493
4124 Beans, French, Cooking of 493
994 Beans, French, for Hors-d'Oeuvre 127
4123 Beans, Red 493
3760 Bécasses, Aspic de 453
3746 Bécasse de Carême 452
3764 Bécasse Cecilia 454
3763 Bécasse, Chaud-froid de 454
3765 Bécasse, Côtelettes de, Sarah Bernhardt 454
3766 Bécasse Esclarmonde 454
3748 Bécasse Favart 452
3747 Bécasse à la Fine Champagne 452
1177 Bécasse, Fondants de, Castellane 143
3767 Bécasse Marivaux 454
3745 Bécasse à la Mode d'Alcantara 452
3769 Bécasse, Pain de 454
3750 Bécasse, Pâté chaud de 452
3751 Bécasse à la Riche 452
3752 Bécasse, Salmis de 452
3770 Bécasse, Salmis Froid de 454
3753 Bécasse Sautée au Champagne 452
3754 Bécasse Sautée aux Truffes 452
3755 Bécasse, Soufflé de 453
3756 Bécasse Souvaroff 453
3757 Bécasse, Suprêmes de 453
3759 Bécasse, Timbale de, Saint-Martin 453
3758 Bécasse, Timbale de, Nesselrode 453
Bécasses 451
3761 Bécasses en Belle-vue 453
3762 Bécasses, Bengalines de 453
3788 Bécasses, Pâté de 460
Bécassines 451
Becs Figues 451
Beef, see also under Boeuf
2293 Beef, Bitokes 279
2423 Beef, Brisket 291
2459 Beef, Carbonades 296
2294 Beef, Chateaubriand 279
2412 Beef, Chuck 289
2461 Beef, Daube 297
2463 Beef, Emincés 297
2467 Beef, Estouffade 298
2297 Beef, Filets en Chevreuil 280
2296 Beef, Filets Mignons 279
2234 Beef, Fillet, see also under Filet de Boeuf 273
2280 Beef, Fillet, cold 277
2286 Beef, Derivations of the Fillet 278
2295 Beef, Fillet Steaks 279
2422 Beef, Flat Ribs 291
2469 Beef, Fricadelles 298
2471 Beef, Goulash 299
2474 Beef, Hachis 299
2233 Beef, Hampes 272
2413 Beef, joints from topside or aitchbone 289
2483 Beef, Olives 300
2483 Beef Olives, see also under Paupiettes de Boeuf 300
2233 Beef, Onglées 272
2454 Beef, Pie 296
2422 Beef, Plate 291
2491 Beef, Pressed 301
2456 Beef, Pudding 296
2231 Beef, Ribs 272
3890 Beef, Roast Baron of 471
3893 Beef, Roast Fillet of 471
3894 Beef, Roast Joints, English Style 471
3891 Beef, Roast Ribs of 471
3892 Beef, Roast Sirloin of 471

2440 Beef, Rump 293
2490 Beef, Salt 301
2473 Beef, Sauté of, Tolstoi 299
2214 Beef, Sirloin 270
2215 Beef, Sirloin, Cold 271
2185 Beef, Sirloin with Fillet 267
2186 Beef, Sirloin with Fillet, cold 268
2216 Beef, Sirloin Steaks 271
2489 Beef, Smoked 301
478 Beef Tea 68
2298 Beef, Tournedos 280
2288 Beefsteak à l'Américaine 278
2289 Beefsteak à Cheval 279
2291 Beefsteak à la Russe 279
Beetroot, see under Betteraves
924 Beetroot, cut shapes 122
930 Beetroot Salad, as Hors-d'Oeuvre 122
3803 Beetroot Salad 462
931 Beetroot Salad with Cream 122
Béguinettes 451
3742 Béguinettes à la Bonne-Femme 451
3743 Béguinettes à la Liégeoise 451
3744 Béguinettes à la Polenta 451
Beignets, sweet 520
1094 Beignets 135
4370 Beignets d'Abricots 520
4379 Beignets d'Ananas Favorite 522
1095 Beignets d'Anchois 135
1096 Beignets à la Bénédictine 135
4380 Beignets à la Bourgeoise 522
1097 Beignets Cardinal 135
1098 Beignets de Cervelle 135
4374 Beignets de Crème Fine 521
4087 Beignets de Crosnes 490
4372 Beignets de Fleurs d'Acacia 521
4371 Beignets de Fraises 521
4381 Beignets Grand'Mère 522
1099 Beignets à l'Italienne 135
1100 Beignets de Laitances 135
1633 Beignets de Laitances 192
1101 Beignets de Laitances Villeroy 136
1102 Beignets à la Mathurine 136
4382 Beignets Mignons 522
1095 Beignets à la Niçoise 135
4383 Beignets Régina 522
4919 Beignets Soufflé 577
4322 Beignets Soufflés, Paste 515
4378 Beignets Soufflés en Surprise 522
4384 Beignets Suzon 522
4385 Beignets Sylvana 522
4375 Beignets Viennois, Chauds 521
4376 Beignets Viennois, Froids 521
4317 Beignets Viennois, Paste 514
3762 Bengalines de Bécasses 453
3899 Best End of Lamb, Roast 471
3899 Best End of Mutton, Roast 471
3895 Best End of Veal, Roast 471
930 Betterave en Salade 122
931 Betterave en Salade à la Crème 122
222 Beurre d'Ail 33
224 Beurre d'Amandes 33
223 Beurre d'Anchois 33
225 Beurre d'Aveline 33
226 Beurre Bercy 33
227 Beurre de Caviar 33
228 Beurre Chivry 33
229 Beurre Colbert 33
232 Beurre de Crevette 34
233 Beurre d'Echalote 34
234 Beurre d'Ecrevisse 34
236 Beurre d'Estragon 34
237 Beurre de Hareng 34
238 Beurre de Homard 34
239 Beurre de Laitance 34
242 Beurre Marchand de Vins 34
241 Beurre Manié 34
240 Beurre à la Maître d'Hôtel 34
243 Beurre à la Meunière 34
244 Beurre de Montpellier 34
246 Beurre de Moutarde 35
247 Beurre Noir, for large numbers 35
248 Beurre de Noisette 35
249 Beurre de Paprika 35
250 Beurre de Pimento 35
251 Beurre de Pistache 35
252 Beurre à la Polonaise 35
194 Beurre de Provence 29
253 Beurre de Raifort 35
254 Beurre Ravigote 35
255 Beurre de Saumon Fumé 35
256 Beurre de Truffe 35
254 Beurre Vert 35
1105 Beurrecks à la Turque 136
257 Beurres Printaniers 35
932 Bigarreaux Confits 123
4996 Bischoff 587
4805 Biscuit Glacé à la Bénédictine 569
4806 Biscuit Glacé Marquise 569
4803 Biscuit Glacé Mixture (old method) 569
4804 Biscuit Glacé Mixture (modern method) 569
4807 Biscuit Glacé Mont-Blanc 569
4695 Biscuit Glacé Monte-Carlo 558
4808 Biscuit Glacé à la Napolitaine 569
4809 Biscuit Glacé Princesse 570
4810 Biscuit Glacé Sigurd 570
4326 Biscuit Manqué Paste 515
2293 Bitokes à la Russe 279
4987 Blackberry Jelly 585
Blackbirds 448
3946 Blackbirds, Roast 475
2181 Blanc, for Meat and Vegetables 263
1719 Blanchailles 203
2180 Blanching, method for 262
4583 Blancmange 545
4586 Blancmange, English 545
4584 Blancmange, Fruit and Liqueur 545
4585 Blancmange, Ribboned 545
2726 Blanquette de Veau à l'Ancienne 327
2727 Blanquette de Veau aux Céleris 327
2728 Blanquette de Veau aux Nouilles 327
3301 Blanquette de Volaille 395
1106 Blinis 136
1728 Bloaters 205
3925 Boar, Young Wild, Roast 474
933 Boeuf Fumé de Hambourg 123
2419 Boeuf à la Mode, cold 291
2418 Boeuf à la Mode, hot 290
4813 Bombe Aboukir 570
4814 Bombe Abricotine 570
4815 Bombe Africaine 570
4816 Bombe Aïda 570
4817 Bombe Alméria 570
4818 Bombe Alhambra 570
4819 Bombe Américaine 570
4820 Bombe Andalouse 570
4821 Bombe Batavia 570
4822 Bombe Bourdaloue 570
4823 Bombe Brésilienne 570
4824 Bombe Camargo 570
4825 Bombe Cardinal 571
4826 Bombe Ceylan 571
4827 Bombe Chateaubriand 571
4828 Bombe Clarence 571
4829 Bombe Colombia 571
4830 Bombe Coppélia 571
4831 Bombe Czarine 571
4832 Bombe Dame-Blanche 571
4833 Bombe Danicheff 571
4834 Bombe Diable Rose 571
4835 Bombe Diplomate 571
4836 Bombe Duchesse 571
4837 Bombe Fanchon 571
4838 Bombe Fauvette 571
4839 Bombe Favorite 571
4840 Bombe Fédora 571
4841 Bombe Florentine 571
4842 Bombe Formosa 571
4843 Bombe Francillon 571
4844 Bombe Frou-Frou 571
4845 Bombe Georgette 571
4846 Bombe Gismonda 571
4847 Bombe Grande-Duchesse 571
4848 Bombe Havanaise 571
4849 Bombe Hilda 571
4850 Bombe Hollandaise 572
4851 Bombe Jaffa 572
4852 Bombe Japonaise 572
4853 Bombe Jeanne d'Arc 572
4854 Bombe Josephine 572
4855 Bombe Madeleine 572
4856 Bombe Maltaise 572
4857 Bombe Maréchal 572
4858 Bombe Margot 572
4859 Bombe Marie-Louise 572
4860 Bombe Marquise 572
4861 Bombe Mascotte 572
4862 Bombe Mathilde 572
4863 Bombe Médicis 572
4864 Bombe Mercédès 572
4865 Bombe Mignon 572
4866 Bombe Miss Helyett 572
4867 Bombe Mogador 572
4811 Bombe Mixture 570
4868 Bombe Moldave 572
4869 Bombe Montmorency 572
4870 Bombe Moscovite 572
4871 Bombe Mousseline 572
4872 Bombe Nabab 572
4873 Bombe Nélusko 572
4874 Bombe Néro 572
4875 Bombe Nesselrode 573
4876 Bombe Odette 573
4877 Bombe Odessa 573
4878 Bombe à l'Orientale 573
4879 Bombe Patricienne 573
4880 Bombe Petit-Duc 573
4881 Bombe Pompadour 573
4882 Bombe Prophète 573
4883 Bombe Richelieu 573
4884 Bombe Rosette 573
4885 Bombe à la Royale 573
4886 Bombe Santiago 573

4887 Bombe Sélika 573
4888 Bombe Skobeleff 573
4889 Bombe Strogoff 573
4890 Bombe Succès 573
4891 Bombe Sultane 573
4892 Bombe Suzanne 573
4893 Bombe Tortoni 573
4894 Bombe Tosca 573
4895 Bombe Trocadéro 573
4896 Bombe Tutti-frutti 573
4897 Bombe à la Valençay 573
4898 Bombe Vénitienne 573
4899 Bombe Victoria 574
4425 Bombe Vésuve 527
4900 Bombe Zamora 574
4812 Bombes, Moulding of 570
4946 Bones, Grilled 579
Bone Marrow, see also under Moelle
63 Bone Marrow Sauce 14
4962 Bookmaker's Sandwich 581
303 Borders of Forcemeat 48
304 Borders of Noodle Paste 48
305 Borders of Vegetables 48
306 Borders of White Paste 48
2039 Bordure de Filets de Sole à l'Italienne 236
1634 Bordure de Laitances Mornay 192
1107 Bouchées 136
4329 Bouchée Cases 516
4330 Bouchée Cases, Small 516
1108 Bouchées à la Bohémienne 136
1109 Bouchées Bouquetière 136
1110 Bouchées Diane 136
1111 Bouchées Grand Duc 136
1112 Bouchées Isabelle 136
1113 Bouchées Joinville 136
1635 Bouchées de Laitances Monseigneur 192
1114 Bouchées Marie-Rose 136
1115 Bouchées Mogador 136
1117 Bouchées Monseigneur 137
1116 Bouchées Montglas 137
1118 Bouchées Nantua 137
1119 Bouchées à la Périgourdine 137
1121 Bouchées Petite-Princesse 137
1120 Bouchées à la Reine 137
1122 Bouchées Saint-Hubert 137
1124 Bouchées, small for garnishing 137
1123 Bouchées Victoria 137
2987 Boudins Blancs Ordinaire 359
2988 Boudins Blancs de Volaille 359
2992 Boudins Noirs à la Lyonnaise 360
2993 Boudins Noirs à la Normande 360
3289 Boudins de Volaille Carignan 394
3290 Boudins de Volaille Ecossaise 394
3291 Boudins de Volaille Richelieu 394
1722 Bouillabaisse à la Marseillaise 204
1724 Bouillabaisse de Morue 205
1723 Bouillabaisse à la Parisienne 204
477 Bouillon, Fish 68
476 Bouillon, game 68
474 Bouillon, white 67
Brains, see also under Cervelle
1098 Brain Fritters 135
2175 Braising of Meats 257
1805 Brandade de Morue 211
1806 Brandade de Morue à la Crème 211
1807 Brandade de Morue Truffée 211
4440 Bread and Butter Pudding 529
281 Bread Panada 42
1601 Bream 188
1727 Brill 205
269 Brine, Pickling, general purpose 38
268 Brine, pickling for Tongues 38
4314 Brioche Paste 513
4316 Brioche Paste, general purpose 514
4041 Brionne 485
4606 Brise de Temps 548
2423 Brisket of Beef 291
4108 Broad Beans, Buttered 492
4109 Broad Beans, Creamed 492
4107 Broad Beans, English Style 492
Broad Beans, see also under Fèves
Broccoli 488
4063 Broccoli Leaves 488
1602 Brochet au Bleu 189
1603 Brochet, Côtelettes de, à la Soubise 189
1604 Brochet, Filets de à la Régence 189
1605 Brochet, Grenadins de 189
1606 Brochet, Grenadins de, à l'Oseille 189
1607 Brochet à la Montebello 189
1608 Brochet, Pain de, à l'Ancienne 189
1609 Brochet au Persil 189
1610 Brochet, Sauce Persil 189
1611 Brochet, Quenelles de, à la Lyonnaise 189
1612 Brochet, Quenelles de, Morland 190
1614 Brocheton à la Martinière 190
1615 Brocheton en Matelote à la Rémoise 190
1616 Brocheton à la Normande 190
1617 Brocheton à la Tartare 190
1125 Brochettes 137
4921 Brochettes d'Huîtres Lucifer 577
1082 Brochettes de Parme 134
3315 Brochettes de Rognons de Coq 396
1 Brown Stock 3
490 Brunoises 70
Brussels Sprouts, see also under Choux de Bruxelles
4072 Brussels Sprouts, English Style 489
Buntings, see also under Ortolans
3947 Buntings, Roast 475
Buntings 450
Buntings, Cold 451
1649 Burbot 193
3771 Bustard 455
Butter, see also under Beurre
224 Butter, Almond 33
223 Butter, Anchovy 33
227 Butter, Caviare 33
Butters, Compound (notes on preparation) 33
234 Butter, Crayfish 34
4340 Butter Cream 517
4341 Butter Cream, with sugar syrup 517
222 Butter, Garlic 33
254 Butter, Green 35
231 Butter, Green Colouring 34
225 Butter, Hazelnut 33
237 Butter, Herring 34
934 Butter for Hors-d'Oeuvre 123
253 Butter, Horseradish 35
238 Butter, Lobster 34
243 Butter, Meunière 34
245 Butter, Montpellier 35
246 Butter, Mustard 35
249 Butter, Paprika 35
250 Butter, Pimento 35
251 Butter, Pistachio 35
230 Butter, Red Colouring 33
93 Butter Sauce 18
169 Butter Sauce, English Style 27
233 Butter, Shallot 34
232 Butter, Shrimp 34
255 Butter, Smoked Salmon 35
235 Butter for Snails 34
239 Butter, Soft Roe 34
236 Butter, Tarragon 34
256 Butter, Truffle 35
257 Butters, Printanier 35

Cabbage, see also under Chou
Cabbage 486
4059 Cabbage, Braised 487
4058 Cabbage, English Style 487
Cabbage, Green 487
4057 Cabbage, Red, Pickled for Hors-d'Oeuvre 487
4063 Cabbage, Spring 488
4060 Cabbage, Stuffed 487
4053 Cabbage, White 486
4062 Cabbages, small for garnishing 487
1729 Cabillaud, see also under Cod 205
1732 Cabillaud Bouilli 205
1730 Cabillaud Crème au Gratin 205
1731 Cabillaud à la Flamande 205
1734 Cabillaud Frit 205
1733 Cabillaud Grillé 205
1735 Cabillaud à la Hollandaise 206
1736 Cabillaud à la Portugaise 206
3670 Cailles 443
3671 Cailles en Caisses 443
3695 Cailles Froides en Caisses 446
3672 Cailles en Casserole 443
3696 Cailles Cécilia 446
3690 Cailles sous la Cendre 445
3673 Cailles aux Cerises 443
3697 Cailles au Château-Yquem 446
3675 Cailles aux Coings 443
3676 Cailles à la Dauphinoise 444
3677 Cailles Figaro 444
3698 Cailles Glacées Carmen 446
3699 Cailles Glacées Cerisette 447
3700 Cailles Glacées Maryland 447
3701 Cailles Glacées Reine Amélie 447
3702 Cailles Glacées au Romanée 447
3678 Cailles à la Grecque 444
3680 Cailles Grillées Julie 444
3679 Cailles Judic 444
3681 Cailles Lucullus 444
3682 Cailles, Mignonettes de 444
3683 Cailles à la Minute 444
3684 Cailles au Nid 445
3705 Cailles Nillson 447
3685 Cailles à la Normande 445
3703 Cailles, Filets de, aux Pommes d'Or 447
3686 Cailles aux Petits Pois à la Romaine 445

3687 Cailles aux Raisins 445
3688 Cailles Richelieu 445
3706 Cailles Richelieu, Cold 447
3709 Cailles, Roi de 448
3691 Cailles Souvaroff 445
3707 Cailles, Timbale de 447
3693 Cailles, Timbale de, Alexandra 446
3692 Cailles à la Turque 446
3708 Cailles à la Vendangeuse 447
1636 Caisses de Laitances Nantua 192
4607 Calf's Foot Jelly 548
2712 Calf's Head, see also under Tête de Veau 326
2505 Calf's Heart, see also under Coeur de Veau 303
Calf's Liver, see under Foie de Veau
2725 Calf's Udder 327
2492 Calves Brains, see under Cervelle de Veau 301
2608 Calves Ears, see also under Oreilles de Veau 314
2615 Calves' Feet, see also under Pieds de Veau 315
2579 Calves' Tongues, see also under Langues de Veau 311
4923 Camembert Frit 577
935 Canapés for Hors-d'Oeuvre 123
4924 Canapés, Savouries 577
937 Canapés d'Anchois 123
936 Canapés à l'Amiral 123
938 Canapés à l'Arlequine 123
4925 Canapés Cadogan 577
939 Canapés au Caviar 123
941 Canapés City 123
940 Canapés aux Crevettes 123
942 Canapés à la Danoise 123
943 Canapés à l'Ecarlate 123
4926 Canapés à l'Ecossaise 577
944 Canapés d'Ecrevisses 123
945 Canapés au Gibier 123
4927 Canapés des Gourmets 578
4928 Canapés de Haddock 578
946 Canapés de Homard 124
4929 Canapés Ivanhoe 578
947 Canapés Lucile 124
4930 Canapés aux Oeufs Brouillés 578
948 Canapés au Poisson 124
949 Canapés Printaniers 124
4931 Canapés Rabelais 578
950 Canapés Rochelais 124
4933 Canapés Saint-Antoine 578
4932 Canapés de Saumon 578
3772 Canard Sauvage 455
3932 Canard Sauvage à la Bigarade 474
3934 Canard Sauvage au Porto 474
3481 Caneton, Aiguillettes de, Saint-Albin 418
3480 Caneton, Aiguillettes de, à l'Ecarlate 418
3920 Caneton d'Aylesbury Rôti à l'Anglaise 473
3451 Caneton, Ballotines de 414
3458 Caneton Braisé aux Navets 415
3460 Caneton Braisé à l'Orange 415
3453 Caneton Chipolata 414
3454 Caneton à la Choucroute 414
3483 Caneton a là Cuiller 418
3452 Caneton Farci à la Bordelaise 414
3477 Caneton Farci à la Rouennaise 417
3482 Caneton Glacé aux Cerises 418
3485 Caneton Glacé aux Mandarines 419
3485 Caneton à la Japonaise 419
3484 Caneton Lambertye 419
3455 Caneton à la Lyonnaise 414
3457 Caneton Molière 415
3482 Caneton Montmorency 418
3459 Caneton aux Olives 415
3784 Caneton, Pâté de 459
3461 Caneton, Pâté Chaud de 415
3462 Caneton aux Petits Pois 415
3456 Caneton Poêlé à la Menthe 414
3469 Caneton Rouennais aux Cerises 416
3470 Caneton Rouennais au Champagne 416
3472 Caneton Rouennais à la Dodine au Chambertin 417
3471 Caneton Rouennais en Chemise 416
3486 Caneton Rouennais, Mousse de 419
3476 Caneton Rouennais à la Presse 417
3475 Caneton Rouennais au Porto 417
3478 Caneton, Salmis de, à la Rouennaise 417
3487 Caneton à la Sévillane 419
3479 Caneton Rouennais, Soufflé de 418
3488 Caneton, Soufflé Froid de, à l'Orange 419
3489 Caneton, Terrine de, à la Gelée 419
3490 Caneton, Terrine de, Voisin 419
3464 Caneton, Timbale de, Mirabeau 415
3463 Caneton, Suprême de 416
1128 Cannelons 137
1129 Cannelons à l'Ancienne 138
4288 Canneloni Farcis 509
3771 Canopetière 455
97 Caper Sauce 18
170 Caper Sauce (English) 27
3771 Capercaillie 454
3938 Capercaillie, Roast 474
3302 Capilotade de Volaille 395
3016 Capons, Preparation of 363
2459 Carbonades de Boeuf à la Flamande 296
3997 Cardoons, Preparation and cooking 481
4003 Cardon aux Fines Herbes, Coeur de 481
3998 Cardons au Jus 481
3999 Cardons à la Milanaise 481
4000 Cardons à la Moelle 481
4001 Cardons Mornay 481
4002 Cardons au Parmesan 481
4004 Cardoons with various sauces 481
1620 Carp with Beer 190
Carp Roes, Soft, see also under Laitances
1631 Carp Roes, Soft 192
1632 Carp Roes, Barquettes of 192
1619 Carpe à l'Ancienne 190
1621 Carpe au Bleu 191
1620 Carpe à la Bière 190
1622 Carpe à la Canotière 191
1623 Carpe Chambord 191
1624 Carpe à la Juive 191
1626 Carpe à la Juive à l'Orientale 191
1625 Carpe à la Juive au Persil 191
1627 Carpe à la Juive aux Raisins 191
1628 Carpe à la Polonaise 191
1629 Carpe, Quenelles de, Morland 192
1630 Carpe, Filets de, à la Royale 192
951 Carolines 124
4006 Carottes à la Crème 481
4009 Carottes, Flan aux 482
4007 Carottes Marianne 482
4008 Carottes à la Vichy 482
2846 Carré d'Agneau en Cocotte à la Bonne-Femme 343
2847 Carré d'Agneau à la Boulangère 343
2848 Carré d'Agneau Grillé 343
2849 Carré d'Agneau Limousine 343
2850 Carré d'Agneau Louisiane 343
2851 Carré d'Agneau Marly 343
2852 Carré d'Agneau Mireille 343
2853 Carré d'Agneau Printanière 343
2854 Carré d'Agneau Saint-Laud 344
2855 Carré d'Agneau Soubise 344
2856 Carré d'Agneau à la Toscane 344
2910 Carré de Porc à la Choucroute 350
2912 Carré de Porc aux Choux de Bruxelles 350
2911 Carré de Porc aux Choux Rouges 350
2913 Carré de Porc à la Marmalade de Pommes 350
2914 Carré de Porc à la Paysanne 350
2915 Carré de Porc à la Soissonaise 350
2918 Carré de Porc au Salade de Choux Rouges 351
1737 Carrelet 206
1738 Carrelet Grillé 206
1739 Carrelet à la Meunière 206
1740 Carrelet Rôti 206
4006 Carrots, creamed 481
4009 Carrot Flan 482
4005 Carrots, glazed, for garnishing 481
497 Carrot Royale 71
1127 Cases, Vàrious 137
1130 Cassolettes Aiglon 138
1131 Cassolettes Alice 138
1132 Cassolettes Suzanne 138
2828 Cassoulet of Mutton 339
Cauliflower, see also under Chou-fleur
Cauliflower 488
4064 Cauliflower, English Style 488
961 Cauliflower for Hors-d'Oeuvre 125
3806 Cauliflower Salad 462
4070 Cauliflower with various sauces 489
952 Caviare 124
227 Caviare Butter 33
939 Caviar, Canapés de 123
974 Caviar, Duchesses au 126
953 Céleri à la Bonne-Femme 124
4010 Céleri Braisé 482
954 Céleri à la Grecque 124
Celeriac, see also under Céleri-Rave
955 Celeriac for Hors-d'Oeuvre 124
4015 Celeriac, Purée of 482

3805 Celeriac Salad 462
955 Céleri-Rave for Hors-d'Oeuvre 124
4012 Céleri-Rave à l'Italienne 482
4013 Céleri-Rave au Jus 482
4015 Céleri-Rave, Purée de 482
Celery, see also under Céleri
4010 Celery, Braised 482
4014 Celery, Purée of 482
498 Celery Royale 71
3804 Celery Salad 462
171 Celery Sauce 27
4011 Celery, other preparations 482
4016 Cèpes 482
4017 Cèpes à la Bordelaise 482
4018 Cèpes à la Crème 483
956 Cèpes Marinés 124
4019 Cèpes à la Provençale 483
4020 Cèpes Rossini 483
492 Cereals for clear soups 70
4635 Cerises au Claret 553
4634 Cerises Dubarry 552
4523 Cerises Jubilée 538
4525 Cerises, Flan de, à la Danoise 538
4526 Cerises, Flan de, Meringué 538
4524 Cerises Valéria 538
957 Cerises au Vinaigre 124
958 Cerneaux au Verjus 124
959 Cervalas Sausages 125
1098 Cervelle, Beignets de 135
2196 Cervelle de Boeuf au Beurre Noir 269
2197 Cervelle de Boeuf au Beurre Noisette 269
2198 Cervelle de Boeuf à la Bourguignonne 269
2199 Cervelle de Boeuf, Coquille de, au Gratin 269
2200 Cervelle de Boeuf, Coquille de, à la Parisienne 269
2201 Cervelle de Boeuf, Cromesquis de 269
2201 Cervelle de Boeuf, Croquettes de 269
2202 Cervelle de Boeuf, Fritot de 269
2203 Cervelle de Boeuf, à l'Italienne 269
2204 Cervelle de Boeuf, Marinade de 269
2205 Cervelle de Boeuf, Matelote de 270
2206 Cervelle de Boeuf, Mazagran de 270
2207 Cervelle de Boeuf, Mousseline de 270
2208 Cervelle de Boeuf, Pain de, à la Bourgeoise 270
2209 Cervelle de Boeuf à la Poulette 270
2210 Cervelle de Boeuf à la Ravigote 270
960 Cervelle Robert 125
2211 Cervelle de Boeuf, Soufflé de 270
2212 Cervelle de Boeuf, Subrics de 270
2213 Cervelle de Boeuf Villeroy 270
2494 Cervelle de Veau Beaumont 302
2495 Cervelle de Veau au Beurre Noir 302
2496 Cervelle de Veau en Caisses 302
2497 Cervelle de Veau Maréchal 302
2498 Cervelle de Veau Montrouge 302
2499 Cervelle de Veau Sainte-Menehoulde 302
2500 Cervelle de Veau, Vol-au-Vent de 302
2502 Cervelle de Veau, Various Preparations 302
2501 Cervelle de Veau Zingara 302
4935 Champignons sous Cloche 578
4021 Champignons à la Crème 483
4022 Champignons, Croûtes aux 483
4025 Champignons Farcis 483
4026 Champignons aux Fines Herbes 483
4027 Champignons, Flan grillé aux 483
4023 Champignons Grillés 483
4024 Champignons Grillés à la Bourguignonne 483
4030 Champignons, Purée de 484
4028 Champignons, Tartelettes Grillés aux 483
4040 Chanterelles 485
1651 Char, Potted 194
4587 Charlotte à l'Arlequine 546
4588 Charlotte Carmen 546
4589 Charlotte Chantilly 546
4591 Charlotte Colinette 546
4592 Charlotte Montreuil 546
4593 Charlotte Normande 546
4594 Charlotte Opéra 547
4595 Charlotte Plombière 547
4386 Charlotte de Pommes 523
4387 Charlottes de Pommes Emile Giret 523
4596 Charlotte Renaissance 547
4597 Charlotte Russe 547
4388 Charlottes, Various 523
2294 Chateaubriand 279
337 Chaud-froids 53
3763 Chaud-froid de Bécasse 454
36 Chaud-froid, Brown 11
3694 Chaud-froid de Cailles en Belle-vue 446
3718 Chaud-froid de Grives en Belle-vue 448
3719 Chaud-froid de Grives en Caisses 448
3633 Chaud-froid de Faisan 440
3634 Chaud-froid de Faisan Buloz 440
3373 Chaud-froid de Volaille à l'Ecossaise 404
3374 Chaud-froid de Volaille Gounod 404
3375 Chaud-froid de Volaille Rossini 405
Chaud-froid Sauces, see under Sauce
4041 Chayotte 485
4947 Cheese Straws 579
Cherries, see also under Cerises
957 Cherries, pickled 124
932 Cherries, pickled White-heart 123
31 Cherry Sauce 10
4361 Cherry Sauce for hot sweets 520
4571 Cherry Sauce for cold sweets 543
5001 Cherry Water 587
Chestnuts, see also under Marrons
4143 Chestnuts, to shell 495
4145 Chestnuts, Braised and Glazed 495
4403 Chestnut Croquettes 524
4146 Chestnuts, Purée of 495
505 Chestnut Royale 72
3772 Chevalier 455
3522 Chevreuil, Civet de 425
3523 Chevreuil, Côtelettes de 425
3524 Chevreuil, Côtelettes de, Beauval 425
3525 Chevreuil, Côtelettes de, aux Cerises 425
3526 Chevreuil, Côtelettes de, Conti 425
3527 Chevreuil, Côtelettes de, Diane 425
3528 Chevreuil, Côtelettes de, au Genièvre 426
3529 Chevreuil, Côtelettes de, à la Minute 426
3530 Chevreuil, Côtelettes de, Sauce Poivrade 426
3531 Chevreuil, Côtelettes de, aux Truffes 426
3532 Chevreuil, Côtelettes de, Villeneuve 426
3535 Chevreuil, Cúissot de 426
Chevreuil, Filets Mignons 426
3536 Chevreuil, Filets Mignons de, au Genièvre 426
3538 Chevreuil, Filets Mignons de, Sauce Venaison 427
3533 Chevreuil, Noisettes de, Romanoff 426
3534 Chevreuil, Noisettes de, Valencia 426
3539 Chevreuil, Selle de 427
3540 Chevreuil, Selle de, Briand 427
3541 Chevreuil, Selle de, aux Cerises 427
3542 Chevreuil, Selle de, Cherville 427
3543 Chevreuil, Selle de, à la Crème 427
3544 Chevreuil, Selle de, à la Créole 427
3546 Chevreuil, Selle de, Grand-Veneur (Scottish method) 427
3537 Chevreuil, Timbale de Filets de, à la Napolitaine 426
Chicken, see under Poularde, Poulet, Poussin or Volaille
Chicken, Aspic, see also under Aspic de Volaille
277 Chicken Aspic Jelly 40
3024 Chicken, Boiled, English Style 365
3379 Chicken, Breast of, on Various Mousses 405
4934 Chicken Carcasses 578
3372 Chicken, Chaud-froid of 404
3378 Chicken, Cold Mousses and Mousselines 405
480 Chicken Consommé 69
3311 Chicken Cockscombs and Kidneys, see also under Crêtes de Coq 396
3309 Chicken Cutlets 396
299 Chicken or Game Forcemeat 47
486 Chicken Forcemeat, fine, for Quenelles for soup 70
Chicken Fricassée, see under Fricassée de Poulet
Chicken Giblets, see also under Abattis
10 Chicken Glaze 6
3254 Chicken, Grilled, English Style 390
Chickens Livers, see also under Foies de Volaille

3376 Chicken Mayonnaise 405
Chicken Mousse and Mousselines, see under Mousselines de Volaille
3783 Chicken Pie 459
3335 Chicken Pie, English Style 399
Chicken, Pilaw of, see also under Pilaw de Volaille
3352 Chicken Pilaw, using cooked chicken 401
3023 Chicken, Poached, English Style 365
Chicken Quenelles, see under Quenelles de Volaille
3909 Chicken, Roast (Queen) 472
3910 Chicken, Roast (Spring) 472
510 Chicken Royale 72
3380 Chicken Salad 405
3181 Chicken, Sautés of 381
3354 Chicken Soufflé, using cooked chicken 402
3353 Chicken Soufflé, using raw chicken 401
706 Chicken Soup 93
3 Chicken Stock, White 4
3130 Chicken, Suprêmes, Fillets and Cutlets, see also under Suprême de Volaille 376
3339 Chicken, Timbale à l'Ambassadrice 399
3341 Chicken, Timbale Bourbonnaise 400
3340 Chicken, Timbale Bontoux 400
3342 Chicken, Timbale Maréchal Foch 400
Chicken Winglets, see also under Ailerons
21 Chicken Velouté 8
Chicorée de Bruxelles 486
4042 Chicorée à la Crème 485
4043 Chicorée à la Flamande 485
4044 Chicorée, Pain de 485
4045 Chicorée, Purée de 485
4046 Chicorée, Soufflé de 485
483 Chiffonade 70
4658 Chilled Melon 555
4357 Chocolate Sauce 519
2460 Choesels à la Bruxelloise 297
4058 Chou à l'Anglaise 487
4053 Chou Blanc 486
4059 Chou Braisé 487
4054 Choucroute 486
4060 Chou Farci 487
4064 Chou-fleur à l'Anglaise 488
4065 Chou-fleur à la Crème 488
4066 Chou-fleur, Fritots de 488
4067 Chou-fleur au Gratin 488
4068 Chou-fleur à la Milanaise 488
4069 Chou-fleur à la Polonaise 488
4071 Chou-fleur, Purée de 489
4081 Chou de Mai 489
4080 Chou Marin 489
4321 Chou Paste 515
325 Chou Paste, general purpose 50
4055 Chou Rouge à la Flamande 487
4056 Chou Rouge Limousine 487
Choux 486
4072 Choux de Bruxelles à l'Anglaise 489
4074 Choux de Bruxelles à la Bonne Femme 489
4073 Choux de Bruxelles à la Crème 489
4075 Choux de Bruxelles au Gratin 489
4076 Choux de Bruxelles à la Milanaise 489
4077 Choux de Bruxelles à la Polonaise 489
4079 Choux de Bruxelles, Purée de 489
4078 Choux de Bruxelles Sautés 489
4063 Choux Frisés 488
4922 Choux au Fromage 577
Choux-fleurs 488
961 Choux-fleurs for Hors-d'Oeuvre 125
4063 Choux de Printemps 488
962 Choux Rouges for Hors-d'Oeuvre 125
4058 Choux Verts 487
963 Choux Verts, Paupiettes de 125
4041 Chow-chow 485
1133 Ciernikis 138
3522 Civet de Chevreuil 425
3556 Civet de Lièvre 429
3557 Civet de Lièvre à la Flamande 429
3559 Civet de Lièvre à la Lyonnaise 429
3558 Civet de Lièvre de la Mère Jean 429
4999 Claret Cup 587
1741 Coalfish 206
3015 Cochon de Lait Saint-Fortunat 362
1138 Cockscombs Demidoff 138
3317 Cock's Kidneys, Stuffed for Cold Entrées, Garnishes etc. 397
1729 Cod, see also under Cabillaud 205
1732 Cod, boiled 205
1734 Cod, fried 205
1733 Cod, grilled 205
1803 Cod, Salt, with Beurre Noir or Brown Butter 211
2506 Coeur de Veau Farci 303
2507 Coeur de Veau Sauté 303
3963 Coeurs d'Artichauts Clamart 477
3964 Coeurs d'Artichauts Grand-Duc 477
4997 Coffee, Iced 587
1741 Colin 206
3771 Colin (American Partridge) 455
1134 Colombines 138
3772 Coot 455
4974 Compote of Apples 583
4964 Compote of Apricots 582
4966 Compote of Bananas 582
4967 Compote of Cherries 582
4976 Compote of Greengages 583
4970 Compote of Mirabelle Plums 582
4971 Compote of Nectarines 582
4972 Compote of Peaches 582
4973 Compote of Pears 582
4965 Compote of Pineapple 582
4975 Compote of Prunes 583
4969 Compote of Raspberries 582
4977 Compote of Rhubarb 583
4968 Compote of Strawberries 582
4978 Compotes, Mixed 583
4963 Compotes, Single Fruit 582
4082 Concombres à la Crème 489
964 Concombres à la Danoise 125
4083 Concombres Farcis 489
965 Concombres Farcis for Hors-d'Oeuvres 125
4084 Concombres Glacés 490
966 Concombres en Salade 125
4936 Condés au Fromage 578
3443 Confit d'Oie 413
1742 Conger Eel 206
1742 Congre 206
Consommés, Clarification 68
3771 Coq de Bruyère 454
3771 Coq de Bruyère, Grand 454
3087 Coq en Pâté 371
2199 Coquilles de Cervelle au Gratin 269
2200 Coquilles de Cervelle à la Parisienne 269
2084 Coquilles de Crevettes Glacées 242
2085 Coquilles de Crevettes Garnies 242
1825 Coquilles de Foies de Raie 213
2114 Coquilles de Homard Mornay 248
1638 Coquilles de Laitances à la Parisienne 192
2092 Coquilles de Queues d'Ecrevisses Cardinal 244
2644 Coquilles de Ris de Veau au Gratin 318
2645 Coquilles de Ris de Veau à la Parisienne 318
2159 Coquilles Saint-Jacques au Gratin 254
2160 Coquilles Saint-Jacques à la Nantaise 254
2161 Coquilles Saint-Jacques à la Parisienne 254
1656 Coquilles de Saumon 195
2058 Coquilles de Turbot 239
3304 Coquilles de Volaille à l'Ecarlate 396
3305 Coquilles de Volaille au Gratin 396
3306 Coquilles de Volaille Joffrette 396
3307 Coquilles de Volaille Mornay 396
3308 Coquilles de Volaille Parisienne 396
3709 Corncrakes 448
967 Cornets d'York 125
2920 Côte de Porc Charcutière 351
2921 Côte de Porc à la Flamande 351
2922 Côte de Porc Grand'Mère 351
2923 Côte de Porc à la Milanaise 351
2924 Côte de Porc, Sauce Piquante 351
2509 Côte de Veau au Basilic 303
2539 Côte de Veau en Belle-Vue 306
2511 Côte de Veau Bonne-Femme 303
2510 Côte de Veau Bouchère 303
2512 Côte de Veau en Casserole 303
2513 Côte de Veau en Cocotte 304
2514 Côte de Veau en Cocotte à la Paysanne 304
2515 Côte de Veau à la Dreux 304
2516 Côte de Veau à la Fermière 304
2517 Côte de Veau Financière 304
2518 Côte de Veau aux Fines Herbes 304
2519 Côte de Veau au Jus 304
2520 Côte de Veau Maintenon 304
2521 Côte de Veau Maraîchère 304
2523 Côte de Veau Maréchal 304
2522 Côte de Veau Marigny 304
2524 Côte de Veau Milanaise 304
2525 Côte de Veau Montholon 304
2526 Côte de Veau Napolitaine 304
2527 Côte de Veau Orléanaise 305

2528 Côte de Veau Orloff 305
2529 Côte de Veau en Papillote 305
2530 Côte de Veau Périgourdine 305
2531 Côte de Veau Pojarski 305
2532 Côte de Veau Printanière 305
2533 Côte de Veau Provençale 305
2534 Côte de Veau Talleyrand 305
2535 Côte de Veau Vert-Pré 305
2536 Côte de Veau à la Vichy 305
2537 Côte de Veau à la Viennoise 306
2538 Côte de Veau Zingara 306
2858 Côtelettes d'Agneau à la Bergère 344
2859 Côtelettes d'Agneau à la Bretonne 344
2860 Côtelettes d'Agneau Buloz 344
2861 Côtelettes d'Agneau Carigny 344
2862 Côtelettes d'Agneau Charleroi 344
2863 Côtelettes d'Agneau Châtillon 345
2864 Côtelettes d'Agneau Choiseul 345
2865 Côtelettes d'Agneau en Crépinettes 345
2866 Côtelettes d'Agneau Cyrano 345
2867 Côtelettes d'Agneau Farcies Périgueux 345
2868 Côtelettes d'Agneau Henriot 345
2869 Côtelettes d'Agneau à l'Italienne 345
2870 Côtelettes d'Agneau Malmaison 345
2871 Côtelettes d'Agneau Maréchal 345
2872 Côtelettes d'Agneau Marie-Louise 346
2873 Côtelettes d'Agneau à la Minute 346
2874 Côtelettes d'Agneau Mirecourt 346
2875 Côtelettes d'Agneau Morland 346
2876 Côtelettes d'Agneau à la Navarraise 346
2877 Côtelettes d'Agneau Nelson 346
2878 Côtelettes d'Agneau d'Orsay 346
3765 Côtelettes de Becasse Sarah Bernhardt 454
1603 Côtelettes de Brochet Soubise 189
3674 Côtelettes de Cailles d'Aumale 443
3524 Côtelettes de Chevreuil Beauval 425
3525 Côtelettes de Chevreuil aux Cerises 425
3526 Côtelettes de Chevreuil Conti 425
3527 Côtelettes de Chevreuil Diane 425
3528 Côtelettes de Chevreuil au Genièvre 426
3529 Côtelettes de Chevreuil à la Minute 426
3530 Côtelettes de Chevreuil, Sauce Poivrade 426
3531 Côtelettes de Chevreuil aux Truffes 426
3532 Côtelettes de Chevreuil Villeneuve 426
3605 Côtelettes de Faisan 436
3494 Côtelettes de Foie gras 420
3560 Côtelettes de Lièvre 429
3561 Côtelettes de Lièvre aux Champignons 430
3562 Côtelettes de Lièvre Diane 430
3563 Côtelettes de Lièvre Morland 430
3564 Côtelettes de Lièvre Pojarski 430
3549 Côtelettes de Marcassin à la Flamande 428
3550 Côtelettes de Marcassin Saint-Hubert 428
3552 Côtelettes de Marcassin Saint-Martin 428
3551 Côtelettes de Marcassin à la Romaine 428
2779 Côtelettes de Mouton en Belle-Vue 334
2780 Côtelettes de Mouton Bergeret 334
2760 Côtelettes de Mouton à la Bretonne 331
2761 Côtelettes de Mouton à la Buloz 331
2762 Côtelettes de Mouton Carignan 332
2763 Côtelettes de Mouton Champvallon 332
2781 Côtelettes de Mouton en Chaud-froid 334
2764 Côtelettes de Mouton Financière 332
2765 Côtelettes de Mouton Laura 332
2766 Côtelettes de Mouton Maintenon 332
2767 Côtelettes de Mouton Montglas 332
2768 Côtelettes de Mouton Mousquetaire 332
2769 Côtelettes de Mouton Murillo 332
2771 Côtelettes de Mouton Panées 333
2772 Côtelettes de Mouton à la Parisienne 333
2773 Côtelettes de Mouton Pompadour 333
2774 Côtelettes de Mouton à la Provençale 333
2775 Côtelettes de Mouton à la Réforme 333
2776 Côtelettes de Mouton Sévigné 333
2777 Côtelettes de Mouton Valois 333
2778 Côtelettes de Mouton Villeroy 333
1347 Côtelettes d'Oeufs 162
1348 Côtelettes d'Oeufs Dauphine 162
1657 Côtelettes de Saumon 194
1658 Côtelettes de Saumon d'Artois 195
1659 Côtelettes de Saumon Clarence 195
1660 Côtelettes de Saumon à l'Italienne 195
1661 Côtelettes de Saumon Pojarski 195
1579 Coulibiac d'Anguille (A) 186
1580 Coulibiac d'Anguille (B) 186
1581 Coulibiacs d'Anguille, small 186
1851 Coulibiac de Sardines 215
1662 Coulibiac de Saumon 195
1663 Coulibiac de Saumon, small 196
1698 Coulibiac de Truite 201
151 Coulis d'Oignons Soubise 24
4772 Coupes Adelina Patti 567
4773 Coupes d'Antigny 567
4774 Coupes Bohémienne 567
4775 Coupes Châtelaine 567
4776 Coupes Clo-Clo 567
4777 Coupes Dame-Blanche 567
4778 Coupes Denise 567
4779 Coupes Edna May 567
4780 Coupes Elizabeth 567
4781 Coupes Emma Calvé 568
4782 Coupes Eugénie 568
4783 Coupes à la Favorite 568
4784 Coupes Germaine 568
4785 Coupes Gressac 568
4786 Coupes Hélène 568
4787 Coupes Jacques 568
4788 Coupes Jeannette 568
4797 Coupes Madame Sans-Gêne 568
4789 Coupes Madeleine 568
4790 Coupes Malmaison 568
4791 Coupes Mexicaine 568
4792 Coupes Midinette 568
4793 Coupes Mireille 568
4794 Coupes Monte-Carlo 568
4795 Coupes Petit-Duc 568
4796 Coupes Rêve de Bébé 568
4798 Coupes Stella 568
4799 Coupes Thaïs 569
4800 Coupes Tutti-frutti 569
4801 Coupes Vénus 569
4082 Coupes Victoria 569
4085 Courgettes à la Provençale 490
1550 Court-bouillon, Plain 180
1549 Court-bouillon, Red Wine 180
1552 Court-bouillon, Salted Water 180
1551 Court-bouillon, for Shellfish 180
1547 Court-bouillon, Vinegar 180
1548 Court-bouillon, White Wine 180
2083 Crab, Dressed 242
3772 Crake 455
172 Cranberry Sauce 27
Crawfish, see under Langouste
Crayfish, see also under Ecrevisses
234 Crayfish Butter 34
1174 Crayfish, Stuffed 142
4340 Cream, Butter 517
4341 Cream, Butter, with sugar syrup 517
4599 Cream Caramel 548
4343 Cream, Frangipane 578
4344 Cream, Pastry 518
499 Cream Royale 72
109 Cream Sauce 20
4342 Cream, Whipped 517
4373 Creams, Fried 521
968 Creams for Hors-d'Oeuvre 125
969 Creams, Moulded for Hors-d'Oeuvre 125
4337 Crème à l'Anglaise 517
4338 Crème à l'Anglaise Collée 517
4605 Crème Caprice 548
4342 Crème Chantilly 517
4603 Crème Chantilly, as a cold sweet 548
4604 Crème Chantilly aux Fruits 548
4937 Crème frite au Fromage 578
1637 Crème de Laitances 192
4390 Crème Meringuée 523
4599 Crème Moulée au Caramel 543
4600 Crème Moulée à la Florentine 548
4601 Crème Moulée Opéra 548
4598 Crème Moulée à la Vanille 547
4602 Crème Moulée à la Viennoise 548
4344 Crème Pâtissière 518
4391 Crème Régence 523
4621 Crème Reine des Fées 551
4346 Crème Renversée, Mixture 518
4345 Crème à Saint-Honoré 518
4392 Crème Villageoise 523
4373 Crèmes Frites 521
969 Crèmes Moulées for Hors-d'Oeuvre 125

4395 Crêpes du Couvent 524
4101 Crêpes d'Epinards 491
4397 Crêpes Gil-Blas 524
4396 Crêpes Georgette 524
4398 Crêpes à la Normande 524
4399 Crêpes à la Parisienne 524
4400 Crêpes à la Paysanne 524
4401 Crêpes à la Russe 524
4402 Crêpes Suzette 524
2901 Crépinettes d'Agneau à la Liégeoise 349
2997 Crépinettes Cendrillon 360
2995 Crépinettes, Ordinary 360
3649 Crépinettes de Perdreau 441
2996 Crépinettes Truffées 360
3310 Crépinettes de Volaille 396
1138 Crêtes de Coq Demidoff 138
3313 Crêtes de Coq Villeroy 396
3314 Crêtes et Rognons de Coq à la Grecque 396
1078 Crevettes, Allumettes aux 132
1087 Crevettes, Barquettes de 134
2085 Crevettes, Coquilles de, Garnies 242
2084 Crevettes, Coquilles de, Glacées 242
1163 Crevettes, Croustades de, Joinville 141
1355 Crevettes, Oeufs aux 163
1493 Crevettes, Omelette aux 175
1139 Cromesquis 139
Cromesquis d'Amourettes de Boeuf 268
3494 Cromesquis de Foie gras 420
1140 Cromesquis à la Française 139
3968 Cromesquis of Globe Artichokes 478
1351 Cromesquis d'Oeufs 162
1352 Cromesquis d'Oeufs à la Polonaise 162
2047 Cromesquis de Palais de Boeuf 289
1141 Cromesquis à la Polonaise 139
2646 Cromesquis de Ris de Veau 318
1142 Cromesquis à la Russe 139
1143 Croquets 139
1144 Croquettes 139
1146 Croquettes à la Bergère 140
1147 Croquettes à la Bohémienne 140
4938 Croquettes de Camembert 578
1148 Croquettes Chasseur 140
4403 Croquettes, Chestnut 524
4089 Croquettes de Crosnes 490
1149 Croquettes à la Dominicaine 140
3494 Croquettes de Foie gras 420
1150 Croquettes, Garnished 140
1151 Croquettes à la Gastronome 140
1152 Croquettes de Gibier 140
3968 Croquettes of Globe Artichokes 478
1153 Croquettes de Homard 140
1154 Croquettes à la Hongroise 140
1155 Croquettes a l'Indienne 140
1156 Croquettes Jean-Bart 140
4140 Croquettes de Maïs 495
4403 Croquettes de Marrons 524
1157 Croquettes à la Milanaise 141
1811 Croquettes de Morue à l'Américaine 211
1145 Croquettes de Morue à l'Américaine, for Hors-d'Oeuvre 139
1158 Croquettes à la Nantaise 141
1353 Croquettes d'Oeufs 162
2047 Croquettes de Palais de Boeuf 289
4182 Croquettes de Pommes de Terre 499
4183 Croquettes de Pommes de Terre Dauphine 499
2647 Croquettes de Ris de Veau 318
4404 Croquettes, Rice 525
4404 Croquettes de Riz 525
1159 Croquettes Savigny 141
1160 Croquettes Sully 141
1161 Croquettes de Volaille 141
4405 Croquettes, Various sweet 525
4086 Crosnes du Japan 490
4087 Crosnes, Beignets de 490
4089 Crosnes, Croquettes de 490
4088 Crosnes à la Crème 490
4090 Crosnes à la Milanaise 490
4093 Crosnes, Purée de 490
4091 Crosnes Sautés au Beurre 490
4092 Crosnes au Velouté 490
1162 Croustades 141
1163 Croustades de Crevettes Joinville 141
1164 Croustades Nantua 141
1165 Croustades de Ris de Veau Financière 141
1166 Croustade de Volaille Régence 142
4413 Croûte aux Abricots au Marasquin 526
4406 Croûte Dorée 525
3969 Croûte aux Fonds d'Artichauts 478
4407 Croûte aux Fruits 525
3712 Croûte aux Grives 448
4696 Croûte Joinville 558
4408 Croûte à la Lyonnaise 525
4409 Croûte au Madère 525
4410 Croûte Maréchale 525
4697 Croûte Mexicaine 558
1169 Croûte à la Moelle 142
4034 Croûte aux Morilles 484
4411 Croûte à la Normande 525
4698 Croûte Normande à la Chantilly 559
1170 Croûte à l'Oie Fumée 142
4412 Croûte à la Parisienne 526
4335 Croûte de Tourte à l'Ancienne 516
4414 Croûte Victoria 526
1167 Croûtes à la Champenoise 142
4022 Croûtes aux Champignons 483
1168 Croûtes aux Foies de Raie 142
485 Croûtes, for soup 70
308 Croûtons, general 49
485 Croûtons, for soup 70
1254 Crustacés, Soufflés de, small 150
Cucumbers, see also under Concombres
4084 Cucumber, Glazed 490
3808 Cucumber Salad 463
966 Cucumber Salad for Hors-d'Oeuvre 125
4083 Cucumber, Stuffed 489
965 Cucumbers, Stuffed for Hors-d'Oeuvre 125
3565 Cuisses de Lièvre 430
3553 Cuissot de Marcassin à la Mode de Tours 428
258 Cullises, various 35
111 Curry Sauce 20
112 Curry Sauce (Indian Style) 20
3199 Curried Chicken 384
3898 Cushion of Veal, Roast 471
4337 Custard, English Egg 517
4338 Custard, Jellied Egg 517
4393 Custard Pudding 523
4339 Custard Sauce, Egg 517
Cutlets, see also under Côtelettes
1347 Cutlets, Egg 162
1348 Cutlets, Egg, Dauphine 162
1349 Cutlets, Egg, Manon 162
Cutlets of Pork, see under Côte de Porc
3523 Cutlets of Roebuck 425
1137 Cutlets, various 138

1664 Darne de Saumon Chambord 196
1665 Darne de Saumon à la Danoise 196
1666 Darne de Saumon Daumont 196
1667 Darne de Saumon à la Dieppoise 196
1668 Darne de Saumon à l'Ecossaise 197
1669 Darne de Saumon Lucullus 197
1670 Darne de Saumon Nesselrode 197
1671 Darne de Saumon Régence 197
1672 Darne de Saumon à la Royale 197
1673 Darne de Saumon Valois 197
1171 Dartois aux Anchois 142
1172 Dartois aux Filets de Sole 142
1173 Dartois aux Sardines 142
2830 Daube à l'Avignonnaise 340
2461 Daube de Boeuf 297
2462 Daube de Boeuf à la Provençale 297
2184 Deep Frying, Method of 266
3316 Desirs de Mascotte 397
4940 Diablotins 579
3383 Dindonneau à l'Anglaise 405
3395 Dindonneau, Blanc de, Toulousaine 407
3384 Dindonneau à la Bourgeoise 406
3385 Dindonneau à la Catalane 406
3386 Dindonneau aux Céleris Braisés 406
3387 Dindonneau aux Cèpes 406
3388 Dindonneau aux Champignons 406
3389 Dindonneau Chipolata 406
3397 Dindonneau en Daube 407
3390 Dindonneau à l'Estragon 406
3394 Dindonneau Farci aux Marrons 407
3391 Dindonneau Financière 406
3392 Dindonneau Godard 406
3393 Dindonneau à la Jardinière 407
3914 Dindonneau Truffé 472
4699 Diplomate aux Fruits 559
4105 Dolmas 492
1743 Dorade 206
3771 Dotterel 455
2083 Dressed Crab 242
970 Duchesses 126
974 Duchesses au Caviar 126
975 Duchesses à la Norvégienne 126
971 Duchesses Nantua 126
972 Duchesses à la Reine 126
976 Duchesses au Saumon Fumé 126

973 Duchesses Sultane 126
3450 Ducks and Ducklings, see also under Caneton 414
3461 Duck Pie, Hot 415
3784 Duck Pie, Cold 459
3772 Duck, Wild 455
3930 Duck, Wild, Roast 474
3933 Duck, Wild, Roast with Cranberry Sauce 474
3931 Duck, Wild, Roast English Style 474
3482 Duckling with Cherries, cold 418
3462 Duckling with Green Peas 415
3459 Duckling, Braised with Olives 415
3460 Duckling with Oranges 415
3476 Duckling, à la Presse 417
3920 Duckling, Roast, English Style (Aylesbury) 473
3917 Duckling, Roast (Nantes) 473
3918 Duckling, Roast (Rouen) 473
3465 Duckling, Rouen, see also under Rouennais and Caneton Rouennais 416
3473 Duckling, Rouen – Escalopes, Fillets and Suprêmes of 417
3474 Duckling, Rouen – Mousses and Mousselines 417
3466 Duckling, Rouen, stuffing for 416
3485 Duckling with Tangerines, cold 419
3458 Duckling, Braised with Turnips 415
311 Duxelles à la Bonne-Femme 49
310 Duxelles, dry 49
312 Duxelles, for stuffed Vegetables 49
313 Duxelles for various Garnishes 49
977 Eclairs Karoly 126
2104 Ecrevisses, Aspic de Queues, à la Moderne 245
1088 Ecrevisses, Barquettes d' 135
2090 Ecrevisses à la Bordelaise 243
2091 Ecrevisses en Buisson 243
2105 Ecrevisses, Mousse d', 245
2106 Ecrevisses, Mousse d', Cardinal 246
1174 Ecrevisses Farcies 142
2093 Ecrevisses à la Liégeoise 244
2094 Ecrevisses à la Magenta 244
2095 Ecrevisses à la Marinière 244
2096 Ecrevisses, Mousselines d', Alexandra 244
2097 Ecrevisses, Mousselines d', Tosca 244
2107 Ecrevisses, Petits Soufflés, Froids 246
2099 Ecrevisses, Soufflé d', a la Florentine 244
2100 Ecrevisses, Soufflé d', Léopold de Rothschild 244
2101 Ecrevisses, Soufflé d', a la Piémontaise 244
2108 Ecrevisses, Suprêmes d', au Champagne 246
2102 Ecrevisses, Timbale de Queues, Nantua 244
2103 Ecrevisses, Timbale de Queues, à la Parisienne 245
3778 Eel Pie 458
1587 Eel Pie, Hot 187
1588 Eel Pie, Hot, English Style 187
924 Eel, Smoked 122
925 Eel with White Wine and Paprika 122
Eels, see also under Anguille
491 Egg, threads of, for Consommés 70
Eggplant, see also under Aubergines
3990 Eggplant, Fried 480
Eggs, see also under Oeufs
1346 Eggs, Boiled in the shell 162
1293 Eggs in Cocottes 156
1297 Eggs, Cold 157
1290 Eggs cooked in the dish 155
1347 Egg Cutlets 162
1348 Egg Cutlets Dauphine 162
1349 Egg Cutlets Manon 162
1294 Eggs, French Fried 156
1307 Eggs, Fried, and Bacon 158
1430 Eggs, Fried, Poached and Garnished 170
1295 Eggs, Hard Boiled 156
1377 Eggs, Hot for Luncheon Hors-d'Oeuvre 165
1013 Eggs, Lapwing, for Hors-d'Oeuvre 129
1292 Eggs, Moulded 156
Eggs, Plovers 178
1013 Eggs, Plovers, for Hors-d'Oeuvre 129
1291 Eggs, Poached 155
1293 Eggs in Porcelain Cases 156
1296 Eggs, Scrambled 157
1291 Eggs, Soft Boiled 155
1012 Eggs, Stuffed 129
2465 Emincé de Boeuf à la Clermont 298
2464 Emincé de Boeuf à l'Ecarlate 298
2466 Emincé de Boeuf Marianne 298
2831 Emincé of Mutton 340
3318 Emincé de Volaille Bonne-Femme 397
3319 Emincé de Volaille Maintenon 397
3320 Emincé de Volaille Valentino 397
2463 Emincés of Beef 297
2831 Emincés of Mutton 340
Endive 485
Endive, Belgian 486
4047 Endives, Belgian, to cook 486
4848 Endives à l'Ardennaise 486
4049 Endives à la Bourgeoise 486
4050 Endives à la Crème 486
4051 Endives au Jus 486
4052 Endives Mornay 486
2217 Entrecôte à la Béarnaise 271
2218 Entrecôte à la Bercy 271
2219 Entrecôte à la Bordelaise 271
2220 Entrecôte aux Champignons 271
2221 Entrecôte à la Forestière 271
2222 Entrecôte à la Hongroise 271
2223 Entrecôte à la Hôtelière 271
2224 Entrecôte à la Lyonnaise 272
2225 Entrecôte Marchand de Vins 272
2226 Entrecôte à la Marseillaise 272
2227 Entrecôte Mexicaine 272
2228 Entrecôte Mirabeau 272
2229 Entrecôte Tyrolienne 272
2230 Entrecôte au Vert-Pré 272
2880 Epaule d'Agneau Boulangère 346
2881 Epaule d'Agneau Florian 346
2882 Epaule d'Agneau de Pauillac Grillée 347
2883 Epaule d'Agneau Windsor 347
2782 Epaule de Mouton Bonne-Femme 334
2783 Epaule de Mouton à la Boulangère 334
2784 Epaule de Mouton Braisée 334
2785 Epaule de Mouton aux Navets 334
2786 Epaule de Mouton aux Racines 335
2787 Epaule de Mouton au Riz 335
2540 Epaule de Veau Farcie 306
2541 Epaule de Veau Farcie à l'Anglaise 306
2542 Epaule de Veau Farcie à la Boulangère 306
2543 Epaule de Veau Farcie à la Bourgeoise 307
1744 Eperlans 206
1745 Eperlans à l'Anglaise 206
1747 Eperlans au Gratin 207
1748 Eperlans Grillés 207
978 Eperlans Marinés 126
1749 Eperlans à la Meunière 207
1754 Eperlans sur le Plat 207
1755 Eperlans Richelieu 207
1756 Eperlans au Vin Blanc 207
2832 Epigrammes 340
2903 Epigrammes d'Agneau 349
1958 Epigrammes de Filets de Sole 226
3651 Epigrammes de Perdreau 442
4095 Epinards à l'Anglaise 491
4096 Epinards à la Crème 491
4101 Epinards Crêpes d' 491
4097 Epinards au Gratin 491
4098 Epinards Mère-Louisette 491
4102 Epinards, Soufflé aux 491
4100 Epinards, Subrics d' 491
4103 Epinards aux Truffes, Soufflé aux 491
4099 Epinards à la Viroflay 491
979 Escabèche 126
1746 Escabèche d'Eperlans 206
1674 Escalopes of Salmon 197
2599 Escalopes de Veau à l'Anglaise 313
2600 Escalopes de Veau aux Champignons 313
2601 Escalopes de Veau Milanaise 313
2602 Escalopes de Veau à la Viennoise 313
2167 Escargots, Beignets à la Vigneronne 255
2164 Escargots à la Bourguignonne 255
2165 Escargots à la Chablisienne 255
2166 Escargots à la Dijonnaise 255
2163 Escargots à la Mode de l'Abbaye 255
17 Espagnole, Fish 8
18 Espagnole, Lenten 8
8 Essence, Fish 5
314 Essence, Tomato 49
Essences 5
1 Estouffade 3
2467 Estouffade de Boeuf, Basic Preparation 298
2468 Estouffade de Boeuf à la Provençale 298
1642 Esturgeon, Fricandeau de 193
1643 Esturgeon à la Normande 193

1644 Esturgeon en Tortue 193
4700 Eton Mess 559
4705 Eugenia-Crème à l'Italienne 559
Faisan 435
3598 Faisan à l'Alcantara 435
3599 Faisan à l'Angoumoise 436
3600 Faisan Bohémienne 436
3632 Faisan à la Bohémienne, Cold 440
3601 Faisan en Casserole 436
3602 Faisan en Chartreuse 436
3633 Faisan, Chaud-froid de 440
3634 Faisan, Chaud-froid de, Buloz 440
3603 Faisan à la Choucroute 436
3604 Faisan en Cocotte 436
3605 Faisan, Côtelettes de 436
3606 Faisan à la Crème 436
3635 Faisan à la Croix-de-Berny 440
3636 Faisan en Daube 440
3607 Faisan Demidoff 436
1178 Faisan, Fondants de, Marly 143
3609 Faisan Galitzin 436
3610 Faisan à la Géorgienne 437
3608 Faisan Grillé à la Diable 436
3611 Faisan Kotschoubey 437
3613 Faisan à la Normande 437
3789 Faisan, Pâté de 460
3614 Faisan, Pâté Chaud de 437
3615 Faisan, Pâté Chaud de, à la Vosgienne 437
3616 Faisan à la Périgueux 437
3617 Faisan Régence 437
3618 Faisan à la Sainte-Alliance 437
3622 Faisan, Sauté de 439
3623 Faisan, Sauté de, aux Champignons 439
3624 Faisan, Sauté de, au Suc d'Ananas 439
3625 Faisan, Sauté de, au Suc de Mandarines 439
3626 Faisan, Sauté de, au Suc d'Orange Amère 439
3627 Faisan, Sauté de, aux Truffes 439
3628 Faisan, Soufflé de 439
3620 Faisan Souvaroff 438
3629 Faisan, Suprêmes de 439
3621 Faisan Titania 438
3942 Faisan Truffé 475
3906 Fattened Pullet, Roast 472
3907 Fattened Pullet, Roast, English Style 472
3908 Fattened Pullet, Truffled 472
Fattened Pullets, see also under Poularde
4104 Fennel 492
980 Fennel, for Hors-d'Oeuvre 126
980 Fenouil, Pieds de 126
4104 Fenouil Tubereux 492
1645 Féra 193
4105 Feuilles de Vigne Farcies 492
4106 Fèves 492
4107 Fèves à l'Anglaise 492
4108 Fèves au Beurre 492
4109 Fèves à la Crème 492
4110 Fèves, Purée de 492
Fig Peckers 451
3928 Fig peckers, Roast 474
Figs, see under Figues
4636 Figues à la Carlton (raw) 553
4637 Figues à la Carlton (cooked) 553
4638 Figues à la Crème 553
981 Figues for Hors-d'Oeuvres 126
982 Filet d'Anvers 982
2235 Filet de Boeuf à l'Andalouse 273
2237 Filet de Boeuf à la Berrichonne 273
2238 Filet de Boeuf à la Bisontine 273
2239 Filet de Boeuf Bouquetière 273
2240 Filet de Boeuf Bréhan 273
2240 Filet de Boeuf Bristol 273
2242 Filet de Boeuf Châtelaine 274
2281 Filet de Boeuf Chevet 277
2297 Filets de Boeuf en Chevreuil 280
2243 Filet de Boeuf Clamart 274
2282 Filet de Boeuf Coquelin 278
2244 Filet de Boeuf Dauphine 274
2245 Filet de Boeuf Dubarry 274
2246 Filet de Boeuf Duchesse 274
2247 Filet de Boeuf Financière 274
2248 Filet de Boeuf Frascati 274
2249 Filet de Boeuf des Gastronomes 274
2250 Filet de Boeuf Godard 274
2251 Filet de Boeuf à l'Hongroise 274
2252 Filet de Boeuf Hussarde 274
2253 Filet de Boeuf à l'Italienne 275
2254 Filet de Boeuf Japonaise 275
2255 Filet de Boeuf Jardinière 275
2256 Filet de Boeuf London-House 275
2257 Filet de Boeuf Lorette 275
2258 Filet de Boeuf Macédoine 275
2259 Filet de Boeuf Madeleine 275
2260 Filet de Boeuf au Madère et Champignons 275
2261 Filet de Boeuf Mexicaine 275
2284 Filet de Boeuf Mistral 278
2262 Filet de Boeuf à la Moderne 275
2283 Filet de Boeuf Montlhéry 278
2263 Filet de Boeuf Montmorency 276
2264 Filet de Boeuf Nivernaise 276
2265 Filet de Boeuf à l'Orientale 276
2266 Filet de Boeuf à la Parisienne 276
2267 Filet de Boeuf à la Périgourdine 276
2268 Filet de Boeuf Petit-Duc 276
2269 Filet de Boeuf à la Portugaise 276
2270 Filet de Boeuf à la Provençale 276
2271 Filet de Boeuf Régence 276
2272 Filet de Boeuf Renaissance 277
2273 Filet de Boeuf Richelieu 277
2285 Filet de Boeuf à la Russe 278
2274 Filet de Boeuf Saint-Florentin 277
2275 Filet de Boeuf Saint-Germain 277
2276 Filet de Boeuf Saint-Mandé 277
2277 Filet de Boeuf à la Sarde 277
2278 Filet de Boeuf Talleyrand 277
2279 Filet de Boeuf à la Viroflay 277
2545 Filet de Veau Agnès Sorel 307
2546 Filet de Veau Chasseur 307
2547 Filet de Veau à la Dreux 307
2548 Filet de Veau Orloff 307
2549 Filet de Veau au Paprika 307
2550 Filet de Veau Sicilienne 307
2551 Filet de Veau Talleyrand 307
918 Filets d'Anchois 121
3703 Filets de Cailles aux Pommes d'Or 447
1630 Filets de Carpe à la Royale 192
3720 Filets de Grives Cherville 449
3569 Filets de Levraut Montemart 431
3568 Filets de Levraut Mornay 430
3570 Filets de Levraut Sully 431
3571 Filets de Levraut Vendôme 431
3566 Filets de Lièvre 430
3567 Filets de Lièvre Dampierre 430
1769 Filets de Maquereau Bonnefoy 208
1770 Filets de Maquereau à la Dieppoise 208
1771 Filets de Maquereau aux Fines Herbes 208
1772 Filets de Maquereau en Papillote 208
1773 Filets de Maquereau au Persil 208
1774 Filets de Maquereau Rosalie 208
2296 Filets Mignons de Boeuf 279
3536 Filets Mignons de Chevreuil au Genièvre 426
3538 Filets Mignons de Chevreuil, Sauce Venaison 427
1072 Filets de Truites Marinées 132
2280 Fillet of Beef, Cold 277
2286 Fillet of Beef, Derivatives 278
3893 Fillet of Beef, Roast 471
2295 Fillet Steaks 279
Fillets of Sole, see under Sole
2038 Fillets of Sole in Aspic 236
4325 Finger Biscuit Paste 515
279 Fish Aspic Jelly, White 40
280 Fish Aspic Jelly, Red Wine 41
1175 Fish Balls 142
477 Fish Bouillon 68
1555 Fish, Braising of 181
106 Fish Chaud-froid Sauce 19
482 Fish Consommé, double 69
1556 Fish, Cooking au Bleu 182
1560 Fish, Cooking au Gratin 183
1558 Fish, Cooking à la Meunière 182
1553 Fish, Cooking in salted water 181
1561 Fish, Crimping of 183
1557 Fish, Deep Frying of 182
8 Fish Essence 5
1562 Fish Forcemeat for Mousses and Mousselines 183
3777 Fish Forcemeat for Pies 458
488 Fish Forcemeat, fine, for Quenelles for Soup 70
12 Fish Glaze 6
1559 Fish, Grilling of 183
338 Fish Loaf, cold 53
1025 Fish, Potted 130
507 Fish Royale 72
3865 Fish Salads 467
1554 Fish, Shallow Poaching 181
1260 Fish Soufflés, small 150
6 Fish Stock 4
7 Fish Stock, Red Wine 5
22 Fish Velouté 8
4701 Flamri 559
4009 Flan aux Carottes 482
4331 Flan Cases 516
4525 Flan de Cerises à la Danoise 538
4526 Flan de Cerises Meringué 538
4027 Flan grillé aux Champignons 483
4562 Flan de Pommes à la Batelière 542
4563 Flan de Pommes Chaud Ninon 542
4564 Flans, Apple, Various 542
Flap Mushrooms, see under Cèpes
956 Flap Mushrooms, marinated 124
2422 Flat Ribs or Plate of Beef 291
282 Flour Panada 43
3511 Foie gras, Aspic de 423

3521 Foie gras et Cailles Tzarine, Timbale de 424
3492 Foie gras en Caisses 420
3493 Foie gras en Cocotte 420
3491 Foie gras, to cook and present 419
3494 Foie gras, Cromesquis 420
3494 Foie gras, Croquettes 420
3494 Foie gras, Côtelettes 420
4939 Foie gras, Délices de 578
3514 Foie gras, Escalopes de, Maréchal 423
3496 Foie gras, Escalopes, Périgueux 421
3497 Foie gras, Escalopes, Ravignan 421
3498 Foie gras, Escalopes, Talleyrand 421
3499 Foie gras Financière 421
1179 Foie gras, Fondants de, Monselet 143
3512 Foie gras du Gastronome 423
983 Foie gras for Hors-d'Oeuvres 126
3520 Foie gras Lucullus, Pavé de 424
3500 Foie gras, Mignonettes de 421
3515 Foie gras, Mousse de 423
3516 Foie gras, Mousselines de 423
3517 Foie gras, Pain de 424
3518 Foie gras, Pain de, en Belle-vue 424
3501 Foie gras au Paprika 421
3513 Foie gras au Paprika, cold 423
3519 Foie gras, Parfait de 424
3502 Foie gras Périgord 424
3793 Foie gras, Pâté de 460
504 Foie gras Royale 72
3503 Foie gras à la Sainte-Alliance 421
3504 Foie gras, Soufflé de 421
3495 Foie gras à la Strasbourgeoise 420
1262 Foie gras, Subrics de 151
3506 Foie gras, Timbale de, à l'Alsacienne 422
3507 Foie gras, Timbale de, Cambacérès 422
3508 Foie gras, Timbale de, Cussy 422
3509 Foie gras, Tourte de, à l'Ancienne 422
3510 Foie gras Truffé au Madère 422
1168 Foies de Raie, Croûtes aux 142
2552 Foie de Veau à l'Anglaise 308
2554 Foie de Veau à la Bordelaise 308
2555 Foie de Veau à la Bourgeoise 308
2556 Foie de Veau, Brochettes de 308
2557 Foie de Veau à l'Espagnole 308
2558 Foie de Veau aux Fines Herbes 308
2559 Foie de Veau Frit 308
2560 Foie de Veau à l'Italienne 308
2561 Foie de Veau Lyonnaise 308
2562 Foie de Veau, Pain de 309
2571 Foie de Veau Poché à la Flamande 310
2564 Foie de Veau Provençale 309
2565 Foie de Veau, Quenelles de 309
2566 Foie de Veau, Quenelles de, à la Viennoise 309
2567 Foie de Veau aux Raisins 309
2568 Foie de Veau au Rizot 309
2569 Foie de Veau, Soufflé de 309
2570 Foie de Veau sous Croûte 309
3321 Foies de Volaille et Rognons Sautés au Vin Rouge 397
1176 Fondants 142
1177 Fondants de Bécasse Castellane 143
1178 Fondants de Faisan Marly 143
1179 Fondants de Foie gras Monselet 143
1180 Fondants de Grives à la Liégeoise 143
1181 Fondants de Volaille Louisette 143
3971 Fonds d'Artichauts Farcis 478
3972 Fonds d'Artichauts aux Pointes d'Asperges 478
3973 Fonds d'Artichauts Sautés 478
315 Fondue Portugaise 49
4279 Fondus au Parmesan 508
303 Forcemeat, borders of 48
299 Forcemeat, Chicken or Game 47
486 Forcemeat, fine chicken, for Quenelles for soup 70
288 Forcemeat, fine with cream 44
488 Forcemeat, Fine Fish, for Quenelles for soup 70
487 Forcemeat, Fine Game, for Quenelles for soup 70
3773 Forcemeats, for Galantines, Pâtés and Terrines 457
3777 Forcemeat, Fish, for pies 458
293 Forcemeat, Gratin A, for pies and borders etc. 45
294 Forcemeat, Gratin B, for game pies 46
295 Forcemeat, Gratin C, for Croûtons, game pies etc. 46
288 Forcemeat, Mousseline 44
1562 Forcemeat, for Mousses and Mousselines of Fish 183
286 Forcemeat, with Panada and Butter 43
287 Forcemeat, with Panada and Cream 44
291 Forcemeat, Pike with Cream 45
297 Forcemeat, Pork 47
300 Forcemeats, Special for stuffing fish 47
292 Forcemeat, Veal 45
298 Forcemeat, Veal and Pork 47
2573 Fraise de Veau Frite 310
2574 Fraise de Veau à la Lyonnaise 310
2575 Fraise de Veau à la Poulette 310
2576 Fraise de Veau à la Ravigote 310
4639 Fraises Cardinal 553
4640 Fraises à la Créole 553
4641 Fraises Fémina 553
4642 Fraises Lérina 553
4643 Fraises Marguerite 553
4644 Fraises Marquise 554
4645 Fraises Melba 554
4646 Fraises Monte-Carlo 554
4647 Fraises Nina 554
4648 Fraises Rêve de Bébé 554
4649 Fraises à la Ritz 554
4650 Fraises Romanoff 554
4651 Fraises Sarah Bernhardt 554
4652 Fraises Wilhelmine 554
4653 Fraises Zelma Kuntz 554
3771 Francolin 455
283 Frangipane Panada 43
4343 Frangipane Cream 518
French Beans, see under Haricots Verts
1014 French Rolls, filled 129
2470 Fricadelles de Boeuf, using cooked meat 298
2469 Fricadelles de Boeuf, using raw meat 298
1642 Fricandeau d'Esturgeon 193
3322 Fricassée de Poulet à l'Ancienne 397
3324 Fricassée de Poulet Demidoff 398
3323 Fricassée de Poulet aux Ecrevisses 398
3325 Fricassée de Poulet Printanière 398
2730 Fricassée de Veau 328
1827 Fritot de Raie 213
3326 Fritot de Volaille 398
1182 Fritots 142
4066 Fritots de Chou-fleur 488
1094 Fritters 135
Fritters, see also under Beignets
4372 Fritters, Acacia Flower 521
4370 Fritters, Apricot 520
1098 Fritters, Brain 135
4376 Fritters, Cold Viennese 521
4375 Fritters, Hot Viennese 521
4377 Fritters, Ordinary Soufflé 522
1633 Fritters, Soft Carp Roe 192
1100 Fritters, Soft Roe 135
4371 Fritters, Strawberry 521
984 Frivolités 126
Frog's Legs, see under Grenouilles
4762 Fromages Glacés 566
Fruit Dishes, Cold 551
Fruit Dishes, Hot 536
985 Fruits de Mer 127
4570 Fruit Pies, English 543
4704 Fruit Salad 559
316 Frying Batter for fritters of brains etc. 49
4368 Frying Batter for fritters dredged with sugar 520
4369 Frying Batter for glazed fritters 520
317 Frying Batter for vegetables 49
3774 Fumets for Pies and Terrines 457
3776 Galantine 457
4310 Galette Paste 513
Game, see also under Gibier
278 Game Aspic Jelly 40
3771 Game birds 454
476 Game Bouillon 68
4190 Game Chips 500
481 Game Consommé 69
3597 Game, feathered 435
487 Game Forcemeat, fine, for Quenelles for Soup 70
Game, furred 425
11 Game Glaze 6
Game Pies 459
501 Game Royale 72
5 Game Stock 4
3771 Ganga 455
341 Garnish à l'Algérienne 54
342 Garnish à l'Alsacienne 54
343 Garnish à l'Américaine 54
344 Garnish à l'Andalouse 54
345 Garnish à l'Arlésienne 54
346 Garnish à la Banquière 55
347 Garnish à la Berrichonne 55
348 Garnish à la Berny 55

349 Garnish à la Bizontine 55
350 Garnish à la Boulangère 55
351 Garnish à la Bouquetière 55
352 Garnish à la Bourgeoise 55
353 Garnish à la Bourguignonne 55
354 Garnish à la Brabançonne 55
355 Garnish Bréhan 55
356 Garnish à la Bretonne 55
357 Garnish Brillat-Savarin 55
358 Garnish Bristol 56
359 Garnish à la Bruxelloise 56
360 Garnish à la Cancalaise 56
361 Garnish à la Cardinal 56
362 Garnish à la Castillane 56
363 Garnish Chambord 56
364 Garnish Châtelaine 56
365 Garnish à la Chipolata 56
366 Garnish Choisy 56
367 Garnish Choron 56
368 Garnish à la Clamart 56
369 Garnish de Compote 56
370 Garnish Conti 56
371 Garnish à la Commodore 56
372 Garnish Cussy 57
373 Garnish Daumont 57
374 Garnish à la Dauphine 57
375 Garnish à la Dieppoise 57
376 Garnish Doria 57
377 Garnish Dubarry 57
378 Garnish à la Duchesse 57
379 Garnish à la Favorite 57
380 Garnish à la Fermière 57
381 Garnish à la Financière 57
382 Garnish à la Flamande 57
383 Garnish à la Florentine 57
384 Garnish Florian 57
385 Garnish à la Forestière 57
386 Garnish Frascati 58
387 Garnish à la Gastronome 58
388 Garnish Godard 58
389 Garnish Grand-Duc 58
390 Garnish à la Grecque 58
391 Garnish Henri IV 58
392 Garnish à la Hongroise 58
393 Garnish à l'Italienne 58
394 Garnish à l'Indienne 58
395 Garnish à la Japonaise 58
396 Garnish à la Jardinière 58
397 Garnish Joinville 58
398 Garnish Judic 58
399 Garnish à la Lanquedocienne 58
400 Garnish Lorette 59
401 Garnish Louisiane 59
402 Garnish Lucullus 59
403 Garnish Macédoine 59
404 Garnish Madeleine 59
405 Garnish à la Maillot 59
406 Garnish à la Maraîchère 59
407 Garnish Maréchal 59
408 Garnish à la Marie-Louise 59
409 Garnish à la Marinière 59
410 Garnish Marquise 59
411 Garnish à la Marseillaise 60
412 Garnish Mascotte 60
413 Garnish Masséna 60
414 Garnish Matelote 60
415 Garnish Médicis 60
416 Garnish à la Mexicaine 60
417 Garnish Mignon 60
418 Garnish à la Milanaise 60
419 Garnish Mirabeau 60
420 Garnish Mirette 60
421 Garnish à la Moderne 60
422 Garnish Montbazon 60
423 Garnish Montmorency 60
424 Garnish à la Moissonneuse 61
425 Garnish Montreuil 61
426 Garnish Montpensier 61
427 Garnish Nantua 61
428 Garnish à la Napolitaine 61
429 Garnish aux Navets 61
430 Garnish à la Niçoise 61
431 Garnish Nivernaise 61
432 Garnish à la Normande 61
433 Garnish of Noodles 61
434 Garnish Opéra 61
435 Garnish à l'Orientale 61
436 Garnish à l'Orléanaise 61
437 Garnish of Haricots Panachés 61
438 Garnish à la Parisienne 62
439 Garnish Parmentier 62
440 Garnish à la Paysanne 62
441 Garnish à la Péruvienne 62
442 Garnish à la Piémontaise 62
443 Garnish à la Portugaise 62
444 Garnish à la Printanière 62
445 Garnish à la Provençale 62
446 Garnish of Vegetable Purées 62
447 Garnish Rachel 62
448 Garnish of Raviolis 62
449 Garnish Régence 62
450 Garnish Renaissance 63
451 Garnish Richelieu 63
452 Garnish Rohan 63
453 Garnish à la Romaine 63
454 Garnish Rossini 63
455 Garnish Saint-Florentin 63
456 Garnish Saint-Germain 63
457 Garnish Saint-Mandé 63
458 Garnish à la Sarde 63
459 Garnish à la Sicilienne 63
460 Garnish à la Strasbourgeoise 63
461 Garnish Talleyrand 64
462 Garnish Tortue 64
463 Garnish Toulousaine 64
464 Garnish à la Tourangelle 64
465 Garnish à la Trouvillaise 64
466 Garnish à la Tyrolienne 64
467 Garnish Vert-pré 64
468 Garnish à la Vichy 64
469 Garnish à la Viroflay 64
470 Garnish Walewska 64
471 Garnish Washington 64
472 Garnish à la Zingara 64
340 Garnishes 53
339 Garnishing of cold dishes 53
3000 Gayettes, Pork 360
4613 Gelée Miss Helyett 550
4611 Gelées à la Russe 549
4612 Gelées à la Moscovite 550
4610 Gelées Rubanées 549
3771 Gelinotte 455
4324 Genoise Paste 515
945 Gibier, Canapés au 123
1152 Gibier, Croquettes de 140
1217 Gibier, Piroguis aux 147
1256 Gibier, Soufflés de, small 150
Giblets, see under Abattis
3280 Giblet Pie 393
2884 Gigot d'Agneau Chivry 347
2885 Gigot d'Agneau à l'Estragon 347
2886 Gigot d'Agneau à la Liégeoise 347
2887 Gigot d'Agneau à la Menthe 347
2888 Gigot d'Agneau Sous Croûte 347
2788 Gigot de Mouton à l'Anglaise 335
2792 Gigot de Mouton Bonne-Femme 335
2790 Gigot de Mouton à la Bordelaise 335
2791 Gigot de Mouton à la Boulangère 335
2789 Gigot de Mouton Braisé 335
2793 Gigot de Mouton à la Bretonne 336
2794 Gigot de Mouton Mariné en Chevreuil 336
2796 Gigot de Mouton Soubise 336
2795 Gigot de Mouton Rôti, Sauce Menthe 336
4737 Glace à l'Abricot 565
4753 Glace Alhambra 566
4724 Glace aux Amandes 563
4738 Glace à l'Ananas 565
4725 Glace aux Asperges 563
4726 Glace aux Avelines 563
4739 Glace aux Bananes 565
4727 Glace au Café 563
4754 Glace Carmen 566
4740 Glace aux Cerises 565
4728 Glace au Chocolat 563
4741 Glace au Citron 565
4755 Glace Comtesse-Marie 566
4756 Glace Coucher de Soleil 566
4757 Glace Dame-Jeanne 566
4758 Glace Dora 566
4759 Glace Etoile du Berger 566
4760 Glace Fleurette 566
4743 Glace aux Framboises 565
4761 Glace Francillon 566
4763 Glace des Gourmets 566
4744 Glace à la Groseilles 565
4764 Glace des Iles 566
4765 Glace Madeleine 566
4745 Glace aux Mandarines 565
4769 Glace Marie-Thérèse 567
4746 Glace au Melon 565
4729 Glace aux Noix 564
4747 Glace à l'Orange 565
4748 Glace aux Pêches 565
4730 Glace aux Pistaches 564
4771 Glace Plombière 567
4749 Glace aux Poires 565
4731 Glace au Praliné 564
4750 Glace aux Prunes 565
4751 Glace aux Raisins 565
4732 Glace au Thé 564
4733 Glace à la Vanille 564
4752 Glace aux Violettes 565
10 Glaze, Chicken 6
12 Glaze, Fish 6
11 Glaze, Game 6
9 Glaze, Meat 6
Glazes 6
2446 Gras Double en Blanquette à la Provençale 294
2447 Gras Double à la Bourgeoise 294
2448 Gras Double Frit 294
2449 Gras Double Frit à la Bourguignonne 294
2450 Gras Double Frit à la Troyenne 294
2451 Gras Double à la Lyonnaise 295
2452 Gras Double à la Poulette 295

4280 Gnocchi au Gratin 508
4282 Gnocchi de Pommes de Terre 508
4281 Gnocchi à la Romaine 508
290 Godiveau with Cream 45
289 Godiveau with Ice 44
291 Godiveau Lyonnaise 45
Gombos 492
4111 Gombos à la Crème 492
4112 Gombos Etuvés 492
4114 Gombos Janina 492
Goose, see also under Oie
Goose Liver, see under Foie gras
3921 Goose, Roast, English Style 473
4653 Gooseberry Fool 554
3922 Gosling, Roast 473
4323 Goujère Paste 515
1646 Goujons en Manchon 193
986 Goujons à la Russe 127
1961 Goujons de Sole 227
2471 Goulash of Beef à la Hongroise 299
2572 Goulash of Beef à la Hongroise, for restaurant use 299
4913 Granités 576
293 Gratin Forcemeat A, for pies and borders etc. 45
294 Gratin Forcemeat B, for game pies 46
295 Gratin Forcemeat C, for Croûtons, game birds etc. 46
4200 Gratin de Pommes de Terre à la Dauphinoise 500
2182 Gratins, Methods for 263
3885 Gravies, Roast 469
168 Gravy, Brown 27
59 Gravy, Thickened, Tomato-flavoured 14
58 Gravy, Thickened, Tarragon-flavoured 14
19 Gravy, Thickened Veal 8
Grayling, see under Char
231 Green Colouring Butter 34
2169 Grenouilles Frites 256
2170 Grenouilles au Gratin 256
2171 Grenouilles à la Meunière 256
2172 Grenouilles, Mousselines de 256
2173 Grenouilles à la Poulette 256
2168 Grenouilles Sautées aux Fines Herbes 255
3608 Grilled Devilled Pheasant 436
1738 Grilled Plaice 206
1748 Grilled Smelts 207
1886 Grilled Sole 219
2183 Grilling, Method of 264
3710 Grives Bonne-Femme 448
3711 Grives en Caisses 448
3719 Grives, Chaud-froid de, en Caisses 448
3718 Grives, Chaud-froid de, en Belle-vue 448
3712 Grives, Croûtes aux 448
3720 Grives, Filets de, Cherville 448
3713 Grives au Gratin 448
3714 Grives à la Liégeoise 448
3721 Grives, Medaillons de, à la Moderne 449
3715 Grives au Nid 448
3790 Grives, Pâté de 460
3716 Grives, Pâté Chaud de, à la Liégeoise 448
3717 Grives sous la Cendre 448
3771 Grouse 455
3771 Grouse, Black 454
3771 Grouse, Hazel 455
3771 Grouse, Pin-tailed 455
3771 Grouse, Prairie 455
3940 Grouse, Roast 474
1646 Gudgeon, see also under Goujon 193
3436 Guinea Fowl, see also under Pintade 412
3786 Guinea Fowl Pie 459
3916 Guinea Fowl, Roast 473

2474 Hachis de Boeuf 299
2475 Hachis de Boeuf à l'Américaine 299
2476 Hachis de Boeuf en Bordure au Gratin 299
2477 Hachis de Boeuf en Coquilles au Gratin 300
2478 Hachis de Boeuf à la Fermière 300
2479 Hachis de Boeuf Grand'Mère 300
2480 Hachis de Boeuf Parmentier 300
2481 Hachis de Boeuf à la Portugaise 300
2831 Hachis of Mutton and Lamb 340
1757 Haddock, smoked 207
2842 Haggis 342
2931 Ham, see also under Jambon 352
2939 Ham, Braised with Broad Beans 353
2941 Ham, Braised with Lettuce 353
2964 Ham, Cold 357
967 Ham, Cornets of 125
2967 Ham Mousse, Cold 357
2950 Ham Mousse and Mousselines, Hot 355
2951 Ham Mousselines, Hot 355
2952 Ham Mousselines, Alexandra 355
2953 Ham Mousselines, à la Florentine 355
2954 Ham Mousselines à la Hongroise 355
3781 Ham Pie 458
2946 Ham, Prague, with Farinaceous Items or Vegetables 354
Ham Soufflé, see also under Soufflé de Jambon
2956 Ham Soufflé, using cooked ham 355
2957 Ham Soufflé, using raw ham 356
1258 Ham Soufflés, small 150
3554 Ham, Wild Boar 428
2290 Hamburg Steak 279
Hare 429
Hare, Cold 433
3584 Hare, Cold Mousse 433
3572 Hare, Mousses 431
3791 Hare Pie 460
3944 Hare, Roast 475
3576 Hare, Saddle of 432
3580 Hare, Saddle with Cherry Sauce 432
3581 Hare, Saddle with Redcurrant and Horseradish Sauce 432
1758 Harengs à la Calaisienne 207
987 Harengs à la Dieppoise 127
1759 Harengs Farcis 207
1183 Harengs à l'Esthonienne 143
989 Harengs aux Haricots Verts 127
991 Harengs Lucas 127
990 Harengs à la Livonienne 127
1760 Harengs Marinés 207
1761 Harengs à la Meunière 207
1762 Harengs à la Nantaise 208
1184 Harengs en Papillote 143
1763 Harengs Paramé 208
1764 Harengs Portière 208
992 Harengs Roulés 127
993 Harengs à la Russe 127
2833 Haricot de Mouton 340
Haricot Beans, see also under Haricots Blancs
4117 Haricot Beans, Buttered 493
4116 Haricot Blancs à l'Américaine 493
4117 Haricots Blancs au Beurre 493
4118 Haricots Blanc à la Bretonne 493
4121 Haricots Blancs, Purée de 493
4119 Haricots au Gratin 493
4120 Haricots à la Lyonnaise 493
4125 Haricots Panachés 494
4122 Haricots Flageolets 493
4123 Haricots Rouges 493
994 Haricots Verts for Hors-d'Oeuvre 127
4127 Haricots Verts, Purée de 494
4126 Haricots Verts à la Tourangelle 494
3939 Hazel Grouse, Roast 474
237 Herring Butter 34
988 Herring Fillets for Hors-d'Oeuvre 127
989 Herrings with French Beans 127
1760 Herrings Marinated 207
1759 Herrings stuffed 207
2109 Homard à l'Américaine 246
2127 Homard, Aspic de 250
2129 Homard, Aspic de, à la Russe 250
1090 Homard, Barquettes de 135
238 Homard, Beurre de 34
2110 Homard à la Bordelaise 247
2119 Homard Bouilli à la Hollandaise 249
2111 Homard à la Broche 247
946 Homard, Canapés de 124
2112 Homard Cardinal 247
2129 Homard Carnot 250
2113 Homard Clarence 247
2114 Homard, Coquilles de, Mornay 248
2130 Homard, Côtelettes de, Arkangel 250
2115 Homard à la Crème 248
2116 Homard, Croquettes de 248
1153 Homard, Croquettes de, as Hors-d'Oeuvre 140
2117 Homard à la Française 248
2131 Homard Grammont 250
2118 Homard Grillé 248
2132 Homard Mayonnaise 250
2120 Homard Mornay 248
2133 Homard, Mousse de 250
2121 Homard, Mousselines de 248
2122 Homard à la Newburg 249
2123 Homard à la Palestine 249
2134 Homard, Pain de 251
2137 Homard, Petits Soufflés froids 251
2125 Homard, Risotto de, Tourville 249
2136 Homard, Salade de 251

2126 Homard, Soufflé de 249
2124 Homard Thermidor 249
4115 Hop Shoots 493
934 Hors-d'Oeuvre, butter for 123
Hors-d'Oeuvre, hot 133
1186 Huîtres à l'Américaine 143
1187 Huîtres à l'Anglaise 144
1091 Huîtres, Barquettes d' 135
1188 Huîtres Favorite 144
1189 Huîtres à la Florentine 144
1190 Huîtres au Gratin 144
1191 Huîtres Maréchal 144
997 Huîtres Marinées 128
1192 Huîtres Mornay 144
996 Huîtres Natives au Caviar 128
1193 Huîtres à la Polonaise 144
2147 Huîtres à la Reine, Quenelles de 253
1194 Huîtres Soufflées 144
1257 Huîtres, Soufflés aux, small 150
1195 Huîtres Villeroy 144
1084 Huîtres, Attereau, à la Villeroy 134
1196 Huîtres Wladimir 144

4737 Ice, Apricot 565
4739 Ice, Banana 565
4740 Ice, Cherry 565
4751 Ice, Grape 565
4741 Ice, Lemon 565
4746 Ice, Melon 565
4722 Ice Mixture, Ordinary 563
4903 Ice Mousses, Various 574
4747 Ice, Orange 565
4748 Ice, Peach 565
4749 Ice, Pear 565
4738 Ice, Pineapple 565
4750 Ice, Plum 565
4743 Ice, Raspberry 565
4744 Ice, Redcurrant 565
4742 Ice, Strawberry 565
4745 Ice, Tangerine 565
4752 Ice, Violet 565
4728 Ice-cream, Almond 563
4752 Ice-cream, Asparagus 563
4728 Ice-cream, Chocolate 563
4727 Ice-cream, Coffee 563
4726 Ice-cream, Hazelnut 563
4723 Ice-cream, Ordinary 563
4730 Ice-cream, Pistachio 564
4771 Ice-cream, Plombière 567
4731 Ice-cream, Praline 564
4732 Ice-cream, Tea 564
4733 Ice-cream, Vanilla 564
4729 Ice-cream, Walnut 564
4735 Ice, Fruit Mixtures 564
4902 Iced Cream Mousse Mixture 574
4901 Iced Fruit Mousse Mixture 574
4909 Iced Fruit Soufflé Mixture 575
4903 Iced Mousses, various 574
4909 Iced Soufflés 575
4734 Ices, Fruit 564
4736 Ices, Liqueur 564
4766 Ices, Moulded 566
4721 Ices, Moulding of 563
4720 Ices, Preparation of 562
4702 Ile Flottante 559
2834 Irish Stew 341

4980 Jam, Apricot 584
4981 Jam, Cherry 584
4978 Jam, cooking, bottling and covering 583
4984 Jam, Plum 584
4985 Jam, Rhubarb 585
4982 Jam, Strawberry 584
4986 Jam, Tomato 585
2932 Jambon à la Bayonnaise 353
2933 Jambon à la Bourguignonne 353
2934 Jambon à la Chanoinesse 353
2935 Jambon à la Choucroute 353
2936 Jambon aux Epinards 353
2939 Jambon aux Fèves de Marais 353
2937 Jambon Financière 353
2938 Jambon Fitz-James 353
2937 Jambon Godard 353
2941 Jambon aux Laitues 353
2942 Jambon à la Maillot 354
3554 Jambon de Marcassin 428
3555 Jambon de Marcassin à l'Aigre-Doux 428
2943 Jambon à la Milanaise 354
2968 Jambon, Mousse Froide de, à l'Alsacienne 357
2970 Jambon, Mousse Froide de, au Blanc de Volaille 357
2969 Jambon, Mousse Froide de, au Foie gras 357
2944 Jambon Monselet 354
3781 Jambon, Pâté de 458
2958 Jambon Soufflé 356
1258 Jambon, Soufflés de, small 150
2949 Jambon Sous Croûte 354
2946 Jambon de Prague, with farinaceous items or vegetables 354
2947 Jambon de Prague Metternich 354
2948 Jambon de Prague Norfolk 354
2945 Jambon de Prague Sous Croûte 354
2965 Jambon de Prague en Surprise 357
3287 Jambonneaux of Chicken 393
2577 Jarrets de Veau à la Printanière 310
4608 Jelly 549
4993 Jelly, Apple 586
4607 Jelly, Calf's Foot 548
4609 Jelly, Garnishes and Accompaniments 549
478 Jelly, meat 68
4992 Jelly, Orange 586
4988 Jelly, Quince 585
4994 Jelly, Tomato 586
4990 Jelly, White currant 586
4610 Jellies, Ribboned 549
4611 Jellies, Russian 549
4115 Jets de Houblon 493
1847 John Dory 214
490 Juliennes 70
4703 Junket 559
58 Jus lié à l'Estragon 14
59 Jus lié Tomaté 14
19 Jus de Veau Lié 8

318 Kache of Buckwheat 49
319 Kache of Semolina 50
4063 Kale, Scotch 488
5004 Kaltchale 588
1655 Kedgeree of Salmon 194
998 Kilkis 128
5006 Kirsch Punch 588
4063 Kohlrabi Leaves 488
4376 Krapfuns 521

1092 Laitances, Barquettes de, à la Florentine 135
1632 Laitances, Barquette de, Mornay 192
1093 Laitances, Barquettes de, au Parmesan 135
1100 Laitances, Beignets de 135
1101 Laitances, Beignets de, Villeroy 136
1634 Laitances, Bordure de, Mornay 192
1635 Laitances, Bouchées de, Monseigneur 192
1636 Laitances, Caisses de, Nantua 192
1638 Laitances, Coquille de, à la Parisienne 192
1637 Laitances, Crème de 192
1776 Laitances de Maquereau 208
1639 Laitances Maréchal 192
1640 Laitances à la Meunière 192
1641 Laitances, Soufflés de 192
4135 Laitue, Soufflé de 494
4128 Laitues Braisées au Jus 494
4129 Laitues à la Crème 494
4130 Laitues Farcies 494
4132 Laitues à la Florentine 494
4133 Laitues à la Moelle 494
4134 Laitues à la Serbe 494
2755 Lamb, Baron of 331
2845 Lamb, Best End, see also under Carré d'Agneau 343
2756 Lamb, Best End 331
2758 Lamb's Brains 331
2757 Lamb, Cold Best End 331
2797 Lamb, Cold Leg of 336
2829 Lamb, Curried 340
Lamb Cutlets, see also under Côtelettes d'Agneau
2857 Lamb Cutlets 344
2832 Lamb, Epigrammes 340
2843 Lamb, House and Young 342
Lamb Kidneys, see also under Rognons
2824 Lamb Kidneys, various other preparations 339
Lamb, Leg of, see also under Gigot d'Agneau
2826 Lamb, Loin and Fillet 339
2827 Lamb, Noisettes of 339
3900 Lamb, Roast Baron 472
3899 Lamb, Roast Best End 471
2795 Lamb, Roast Leg 336
3902 Lamb, Roast Leg (cooking time) 472
3901 Lamb, Roast Saddle 472
3903 Lamb, Roast Shoulder 472
2825 Lamb, Saddle 339
2905 Lamb, Sautés of, see also under Sauté d'Agneau 349
Lamb, Shoulder, see also under Epaule d'Agneau
2879 Lamb, Young, other suitable preparations 346
2891 Lamb's Sweetbreads, see also under Ris d'Agneau 347
Lamprey, see under Lamproie
1647 Lamproie à la Solognote 193

2138 Langouste Froide 251
2139 Langouste à la Parisienne 251
2140 Langouste à la Russe 251
2141 Langoustines au Paprika 252
2395 Langue de Boeuf à l'Alsacienne 288
2396 Langue de Boeuf à la Bigarade 288
2397 Langue de Boeuf à la Bourgeoise 288
2398 Langue de Boeuf aux Fèves de Marais 288
2399 Langue de Boeuf à la Flamande 288
2400 Langue de Boeuf Saint-Flour 288
2583 Langues de Veau Braisées 311
2580 Langues de Veau Grillées 311
2581 Langues de Veau Orloff 311
2582 Langues de Veau en Papillote 311
3588 Lapereau à l'Aigre-doux 433
3589 Lapereau en Blanquette 434
3590 Lapereau Bouilli à l'Anglaise 434
3594 Lapereau de Garenne, Pâté de, au Chasseur 434
3591 Lapereau de Garenne, Sauté aux Champignons 434
3592 Lapereau en Gibelotte 434
3593 Lapereau Grillé à la Bergère 434
3595 Lapin aux Pruneaux 434
Lapin and Lapereau 433
3772 Lapwing 455
3951 Lapwings, Roast 475
3787 Lark Pie 459
1016 Lark Pâté 129
Larks, see also under Alouette or Mauviette 449
3732 Larks, Cold 450
3945 Larks, Roast 475
Lasagnes 509
1648 Lavaret 193
503 Leek Royale 72
Leeks, see also under Poireaux
1020 Leeks, Stuffed 129
3902 Leg of Lamb, Roast 472
3902 Leg of Mutton, Roast 472
4998 Lemonade 587
4136 Lentils 495
4137 Lentils, Buttered 495
4137 Lentilles au Beurre 495
4138 Lentilles, Purée de 495
Lettuce, see also under Laitues
4130 Lettuce, Stuffed 494
4131 Lettuce, Stuffed for garnishing 494
Leverets 429
Levraut 429
3569 Levraut, Filets de, Montemart 431
3568 Levraut, Filets de, Mornay 430
3570 Levraut, Filets de, Sully 431
3571 Levraut, Filets de, Vendôme 431
Lièvre 429
3556 Lièvre, Civet de 429
3557 Lièvre, Civet de, à la Flamande 429
3558 Lièvre, Civet de, Mère Jean 429
3560 Lièvre, Côtelettes de 429
3561 Lièvre, Côtelettes de, aux Champignons 430
3562 Lièvre, Côtelettes de, Diane 430
3563 Lièvre, Côtelettes de, Morland 430
3564 Lièvre, Côtelettes de, Pojarski 430
3565 Lièvre, Cuisses de 430
3583 Lièvre Farci Beauval 433
3575 Lièvre Farci Périgourdine 431
3566 Lièvre, Filets de 430
3567 Lièvre, Filets de, Dampierre 430
Lièvre, froid 433
3585 Lièvre, Mousselines de 433
3573 Lièvre, Noisettes de, Mirza 431
3586 Lièvre, Pain de 433
3791 Lièvre, Pâté de 460
3574 Lièvre, Pâté chaude, Saint-Estéphe 431
3576 Lièvre, Râble de 432
3577 Lièvre, Râble de, à l'Allemande 432
3578 Lièvre, Râble de, au Genièvre 432
3579 Lièvre, Râble de, à la Navarraise 432
3580 Lièvre, Râble de, Sauce aux Cerises 432
3581 Lièvre, Râble de, Sauce Groseille au Raifort 432
3582 Lièvre, Soufflé de 432
Lobster, see also under Homard
Lobster, Spiny, see under Langouste
238 Lobster Butter 34
2135 Lobster, cold with Various Sauces 251
120 Lobster Sauce 21
3904 Loin of Pork, Roast 472
3896 Loin of Veal, Roast 471
3897 Loin of Veal, Roast, English Style 471
2488 Loose-Vinken 301
1649 Lotte 193
1726 Loup de Mer 205

4287 Macaroni 509
4290 Macaroni Crème Gratin aux Truffes 510
4289 Macaroni au Gratin 509
4291 Macaroni à l'Italienne 510
4292 Macaroni au Jus 510
4293 Macaroni à la Milanaise 510
4294 Macaroni Nantua 510
4295 Macaroni à la Napolitaine 510
4296 Macaroni à la Sicilienne 510
4297 Macaroni aux Truffes Blanches 510
4704 Macédoine de Fruits rafraîchis 559
998 Macédoine for Hors-d'Oeuvre 128
Mackerel, see also under Maquereau
1775 Mackerel, Fillets with various Sauces 208
1768 Mackerel, grilled 208
1000 Mackerel, marinated 128
1776 Mackerel, soft roes 208
61 Madeira Sauce 14
320 Maintenon Mixture 320
4141 Maïs à la Crème, Soufflé de 495
4140 Maïs, Croquettes de 495
4142 Maïs au Paprika, Soufflé de 495
Maize, see also under Maïs
4139 Maize, cooking of 495
4655 Mandarines Almina 555
3704 Mandarines de Cailles 447
4767 Mandarines Givrées 567
4768 Mandarines Glacées aux Perles des Alpes 567
3738 Mandarines d'Ortolans 451
4529 Mandarines à la Palikare 538
4656 Mandarines en Surprise 555
4164 Mange-touts 497
1765 Maquereau à l'Anglaise 208
1766 Maquereau à la Boulonnaise 208
1767 Maquereau à la Calaisienne 208
1768 Maquereau Grillé 208
1000 Maquereaux Marinés 128
3548 Marcassin 428
3549 Marcassin, Côtelettes de, à la Flamande 428
3551 Marcassin, Côtelettes de, à la Romaine 428
3550 Marcassin, Côtelettes de, Saint-Hubert 428
3552 Marcassin, Côtelettes de, Saint-Martin 428
3553 Marcassin, Cuissot de, à la Mode de Tours 428
3554 Marcassin, Jambon de 428
3555 Marcassin, Jambon de, à l'Aigre-Doux 428
264 Marinade, cooked, for mutton 'en Chevreuil' 37
262 Marinade, cooked, for butcher's meats and venison 36
265 Marinade, cooked, for mutton 'en Chamois' 37
266a Marinades, the keeping of 37
266 Marinade, notes regarding the uses of 37
261 Marinade, raw, for butcher's meats and venison 36
263 Marinade, raw or cooked, for large game 37
3326 Marinade de Volaille 398
260 Marinades, Quick 36
4938 Marmalade, Orange 583
4706 Marquise Alice 559
5008 Marquise Punch 588
4403 Marrons, Croquettes de 524
4144 Marrons Etuvés 495
4146 Marrons, Purée de 495
1565 Matelotes, Basic Preparation 184
1569 Matelote, called Meurette 185
1571 Matelote, called Pochouse 185
1615 Matelote, Brocheton en, à la Rémoise 190
1556 Matelote à la Canotière 184
1567 Matelote à la Marinière 185
1568 Matelote à la Meunière 185
1570 Matelote à la Normande 185
321 Matignon 50
Mauviettes 449
3722 Mauviettes à la Bonne-Femme 449
3723 Mauviettes en Caisses 449
3732 Mauviettes Froides 450
3724 Mauviettes au Gratin 449
3725 Mauviettes Mère Marianne 449
3726 Mauviettes à la Minute 449
3727 Mauviettes à la Normande 449
3728 Mauviettes, Pâté chaud de, à la Beauçeronne 449
3729 Mauviettes à la Paysanne 449
3731 Mauviettes à la Piémontaise 450
202 Mayonnaise 30
203 Mayonnaise, Jellied 30
1686 Mayonnaise de Saumon 199

3376 Mayonnaise de Volaille 405
204 Mayonnaise, Whipped, Russian Style 31
2206 Mazagran de Cervelle 270
Marzagran de Volaille 398
1197 Mazagrans, for Hors-d'Oeuvre 144
4320 Mazarine Paste 514
9 Meat Glaze 6
478 Meat Jelly 68
338 Meat Loaf, cold 53
2175 Meats, Red, Braising of 257
2176 Meats, White, Braising of 259
920 Médaillons d'Anchois 121
3721 Médaillons de Grives à la Moderne 449
1687 Médaillons de Saumon Froids 199
1705 Médaillons de Truite Saumonée Froides à la Moderne 201
3377 Médaillons de Volaille Rachel 405
1001 Melon, Cantaloup 128
1002 Melon Cocktail 128
1004 Melons Confits, small 128
4658 Melon Frappé 555
1003 Melon Frappé au Vins 128
4659 Melon à l'Orientale 555
1003 Melon, with various Wines 128
4660 Melon en Surprise 555
5003 Melon Water 588
1004 Melons, Small Pickled 128
1741 Merlan Noir 206
1791 Merlan Orly, Filets de 210
1792 Merlan, Pain de, à l'Ancienne 210
1793 Merlan, Paupiettes de 210
1796 Merlan, Quenelles de, à la Morland 210
1795 Merlan, Quenelles de, Soubise 210
1798 Merlan, Vol-au-Vent de Quenelles de, Cardinal 210
1777 Merlans à l'Anglaise 209
1778 Merlans Bercy 209
1779 Merlans Colbert 209
1780 Merlans à la Dieppoise 209
1781 Merlans aux Fines Herbes 209
1782 Merlans au Gratin 209
1783 Merlans à l'Hôtelière 209
1784 Merlans en Lorgnette 209
1785 Merlans en Lorgnette au Gratin 209
1786 Merlans à la Meunière 209
1787 Merlans Montreuil 209
1790 Merlans à la Niçoise 210
1794 Merlans sur le Plat 210
1797 Merlans Richelieu 210
4348 Meringue, Italian 578
4349 Meringue, Italian with cooked sugar 518
4347 Meringue, Ordinary 578
4707 Meringue Germaine 559
4770 Meringues Glacées 567
3710 Merles Bonne-Femme 448
3717 Merles sous la Cendre 448
3713 Merles au Gratin 448
3714 Merles à la Liégeoise 448
3715 Merles au Nid 448
1569 Meurette 185
3682 Mignonettes de Cailles 444
3293 Mignonettes de Poulet 394
908 Milk Punch 119
4565 Mince Pies 542
322 Mirepoix 50
323 Mirepoix à la Bordelaise 50
323 Mirepoix Fine 50
1169 Moelle, Croûte à la 142
3772 Moorhen 455
4708 Mont-Blanc aux Fraises 560
4709 Mont-Blanc aux Marrons 560
324 Montglas Mixture 50
4710 Mont-Rose 560
Morels, see also under Morilles
4031 Morels 484
4032 Morels, cooking of 484
4031 Morilles 484
4033 Morilles à la Crème 484
4035 Morilles Farcies à la Forestière 484
4036 Morilles à la Poulette 484
1244 Morilles, Rissoles aux 149
4037 Morilles Sautées 484
4038 Morilles, Timbale de, Châtelaine 484
4039 Morilles, Tourte de, Villeneuve 485
1006 Mortadella 128
1799 Morue à l'Anglaise 210
1800 Morue à la Bamboche 210
1801 Morue à la Bénédictine 210
1802 Morue Benoîton 210
1803 Morue au Beurre Noir 211
1803 Morue au Beurre Noisette 211
1804 Morue, Bouillabaisse de 211
1805 Morue, Brandade de 211
1806 Morue, Brandade de, à la Crème 211
1807 Morue, Brandade de, Truffée 211
1808 Morue à la Crème 211
1809 Morue à la Créole 211
1145 Morue, Croquettes de, à l'Américaine 139
1810 Morue aux Epinards 211
1729 Morue Fraîche 205
1812 Morue à la Hollandaise 211
1813 Morue à l'Indienne 211
1814 Morue à la Lyonnaise 212
1815 Morue à la Provençale 212
1816 Morue, Soufflé de 212
1818 Morue, Tourte or Vol-au-Vent de, Bénédictine 212
1819 Morue, Vol-au-Vent de 212
1817 Morue Valencia 212
1820 Mostelle 212
2585 Mou de Veau en Civet 311
2586 Mou de Veau à la Tripière 311
2152 Moules à la Catalane 253
2153 Moules Frites 254
1007 Moules, for Hors-d'Oeuvre 128
2155 Moules à la Poulette 254
2156 Moules, Rizot de, Toulonnaise 254
2157 Moules Villeroy 254
2835 Moussaka of Mutton 341
3584 Mousse of Hare, cold 433
3584 Mousse Froide de Lièvre 433
1788 Mousse de Merlans 210
5902 Mousse Mixture, Iced Cream 574
4901 Mousse Mixture, Iced Fruit 574
4711 Mousse Monte-Carlo 560
4215 Mousse Parmentier 502
3658 Mousse of Partridge 442
3612 Mousse of Pheasant 437
1846 Mousse of Red Mullet, Cold 214
1688 Mousse de Saumon Froide 199
4265 Mousse de Tomates 506
3749 Mousse of Woodcock 452
3768 Mousse of Woodcock, Cold 454
4315 Mousseline Brioche Paste 514
1750 Mousseline d'Eperlans 207
288 Mousseline Forcemeat 44
4712 Mousseline d'Oeufs Réjane 560
3612 Mousseline of Pheasant 437
331 Mousselines, cold 51
332 Mousselines, cold mixtures for 51
334 Mousselines, cold, Moulding of 52
1751 Mousselines d'Eperlans Alexandra 207
1752 Mousselines d'Eperlans Tosca 207
1563 Mousselines, Fish, Cooking of 184
3516 Mousselines de Foie gras 423
3572 Mousselines of Hare 431
3585 Mousselines de Lièvre 433
3658 Mousselines of Partridge 442
3637 Mousselines of Pheasant 440
1838 Mousselines de Rouget 214
1678 Mousselines de Saumon Alexandra 198
1689 Mousselines de Saumon Froides 199
1679 Mousselines de Saumon Tosca 198
1564 Mousselines of Shellfish 184
1988 Mousselines de Sole 230
1700 Mousselines de Truite Helvétia 201
1701 Mousselines de Truite Tosca 201
1699 Mousselines de Truite Alexandra 201
1789 Mousselines of Whiting 210
3327 Mousselines de Volaille Alexandra 398
3328 Mousselines de Volaille Florentine 398
3329 Mousselines de Volaille à l'Indienne 398
3330 Mousselines de Volaille Patti 398
3332 Mousselines de Volaille à la Sicilienne 398
3749 Mousselines of Woodcock 452
3768 Mousselines of Woodcock, cold 454
4040 Mousserons 485
331 Mousses, cold 51
332 Mousses, cold, Mixtures for 51
333 Mousses, cold, Moulding of 51
1563 Mousses and Mousselines of Fish, Cooking of 184
1562 Mousses and Mousselines, Fish Forcemeat for 183
3572 Mousses of Hare 431
3637 Mousses of Pheasant, Cold 440
1677 Mousses and Mousselines of Salmon 197
1008 Mulberries 129
1821 Mulet 212
5010 Mulled Wine 588
5011 Mulled Wine with Orange 588
1821 Mullet, Grey 212
1008 Mûres 129
2403 Museau de Boeuf 289
1009 Museau de Boeuf, for Hors-d'Oeuvre 129
4030 Mushroom Purée 484
32 Mushroom Sauce 10
99 Mushroom Sauce, White 19

Mushrooms, see also under Champignons
4021 Mushrooms, Creamed 483
4023 Mushrooms, Grilled 483
4025 Mushrooms, Stuffed 483
4029 Mushrooms, turned and grooved for garnishing 484
Mussels, see also under Moules
1007 Mussels, for Hors-d'Oeuvre 128
134 Mustard Sauce 22
2770 Mutton Chop 333
2836 Mutton Pie 341
3900 Mutton, Roast Baron 472
3899 Mutton, Roast Best End 471
3902 Mutton, Roast Leg 472
3903 Mutton, Roast Shoulder 472
3901 Mutton, Roast Saddle 472
2755 Mutton and Grass Lamb, Baron and Double 331
2806 Mutton and Grass Lamb, Breast 337
2756 Mutton and Grass Lamb, Best End 331
2757 Mutton and Grass Lamb, Best End, cold 331
2759 Mutton and Grass Lamb, Cutlets 331
2826 Mutton and Grass Lamb, Fillets 339
2806 Mutton and Grass Lamb, Kidneys 337
2788 Mutton and Grass Lamb, Leg 335
2826 Mutton and Grass Lamb, Loin 339
2827 Mutton and Grass Lamb, Noisettes 339
2825 Mutton and Grass Lamb, Saddle 339
2782 Mutton and Grass Lamb, Shoulder 334
Mutton and Grass Lamb, other preparations 339

1198 Nalesnikis 145
2837 Navarin of Mutton 341
2838 Navarin Printanier 341
4147 Navets 496
4148 Navets Farcis 496
4150 Navets, Feuilles de 496
4150 Navets, Pousses de 496
4149 Navets, Purée de 496
4527 Nectarines 538
3533 Noisettes de Chevreuil Romanoff 426
3534 Noisettes de Chevreuil Valencia 426
3573 Noisettes de Lièvre Mirza 431
3523 Noisettes of Roebuck 425
2588 Noix de Veau à la Briarde 312
2596 Noix de Veau à la Caucasienne 313
2589 Noix de Veau Chatham 312
2590 Noix de Veau Lison 312
2591 Noix de Veau Nemours 312
2592 Noix de Veau Renaissance 312
2598 Noix de Veau à la Suédoise 313
2593 Noix de Veau en Surprise 312
2594 Noix de Veau en Surprise à la Macédoine 312
1822 Nonnats 212
1720 Nonnats aux Epinards Gratinés 203
1517 Nonnats, Omelette aux 177
1721 Nonnats, various methods of preparation 204
3295 Nonettes de Poulet Agnès Sorel 395
304 Noodle Paste Borders 48
4298 Noodles 510
4283 Noques au Parmesan 508
4298 Nouilles 510
2174 Nymphes à l'Aurore 256

1298 Oeufs Alexandra 157
1299 Oeufs à l'Américaine 157
1300 Oeufs aux Anchois 157
1301 Oeufs à l'Andalouse 157
1302 Oeufs à l'Anglaise 157
1303 Oeufs Archiduc 158
1304 Oeufs Argenteuil 158
1305 Oeufs d'Aumale 158
1306 Oeufs à l'Aurore 158
1308 Oeufs Bagnolet 158
1309 Oeufs Balzac 158
1310 Oeufs Belle-Hélène 158
1311 Oeufs Bénédictine 158
1312 Oeufs Benoîton 158
1313 Oeufs en Berceau 158
1314 Oeufs Bercy 159
1315 Oeufs Bergère 159
1316 Oeufs au Beurre Noir 159
1317 Oeufs Bignon 159
1318 Oeufs Boïeldieu 159
1319 Oeufs Boitelle 159
1320 Oeufs Bonvalet 159
1321 Oeufs Bordelaise 159
1322 Oeufs à la Boulangère 159
1323 Oeufs à la Bourguignonne 159
1324 Oeufs à la Bretonne 160
1296 Oeufs Brouillés 157
1325 Oeufs à la Bruxelloise 160
1326 Oeufs Bûcheronne 160
1293 Oeufs en Caisses 156
1327 Oeufs en Cannelons 160
1328 Oeufs Cardinal 160
1329 Oeufs du Carême 160
1330 Oeufs Carignan 160
1331 Oeufs Cavour 160
1332 Oeufs au Chambertin 160
1333 Oeufs Chantilly 160
1334 Oeufs à la Chartres 160
1335 Oeufs Chasseur 161
1336 Oeufs Châtelaine 161
1337 Oeufs Chatillon 161
1338 Oeufs Chimay 161
1339 Oeufs Chivry 161
1340 Oeufs Clamart 161
1341 Oeufs Cluny 161
1293 Oeufs en Cocotte 156
1342 Oeufs Colbert 161
1343 Oeufs Colinette 161
1344 Oeufs à la Commerce 161
1345 Oeufs Comtesse 161
1346 Oeufs à la Coque 162
1347 Oeufs, Côtelettes d' 162
1348 Oeufs, Côtelettes d', Dauphine 162
1349 Oeufs, Côtelettes d', Manon 162
1350 Oeufs Crécy 162
1354 Oeufs à la Crème 162
1355 Oeufs aux Crevettes 163
1351 Oeufs, Cromesquis d' 162
1352 Oeufs, Cromesquis d', à la Polonaise
1353 Oeufs, Croquettes d' 162
1356 Oeufs Daumont 163
1357 Oeufs à la Diable 163
1358 Oeufs Diane 163
1359 Oeufs Duchesse 163
1295 Oeufs Durs 156
1360 Oeufs à l'Espagnole 163
1361 Oeufs à l'Estragon 163
1012 Oeufs Farcis Garnis 129
1362 Oeufs aux Fines Herbes 163
1363 Oeufs Flora 163
1365 Oeufs à la Florentine 164
1364 Oeufs Florial 163
1366 Oeufs à la Forestière 164
1294 Oeufs Frits 156
1297 Oeufs Froids 157
1367 Oeufs Frou-Frou 164
1369 Oeufs Georgette 164
1368 Oeufs Galli-Marié 164
1370 Oeufs Grand-Duc 164
1371 Oeufs Grand'Mère 165
1373 Oeufs au Gratin 165
1374 Oeufs Grillés à la Diable 165
1375 Oeufs Halévy 165
1376 Oeufs Héloise 165
1378 Oeufs à la Huguenote 165
1379 Oeufs à la Hussarde 165
1380 Oeufs Isoline 165
1372 Oeufs Jeanne Granier 165
1381 Oeufs Jeannette 165
1382 Oeufs Jockey Club 165
1383 Oeufs au Jus 166
1307 Oeufs au Lard 158
1384 Oeufs Léontine 166
1385 Oeufs Lili 166
1386 Oeufs Lorette 166
1387 Oeufs à la Lorraine 166
1388 Oeufs Lully 166
1389 Oeufs Magda 166
1390 Oeufs Maintenon 166
1391 Oeufs Malmaison 166
1392 Oeufs à la Maraîchère 166
1393 Oeufs Marinette 166
1394 Oeufs Marivaux 166
1395 Oeufs Masséna 166
1396 Oeufs Matelote 166
1397 Oeufs Maupassant 167
1398 Oeufs Maximilienne 167
1399 Oeufs Mexicaine 167
1400 Oeufs Meyerbeer 167
1401 Oeufs Mignon 167
1402 Oeufs Mirabeau 167
1403 Oeufs Mireille 167
1404 Oeufs Mogador 167
1405 Oeufs des Moissoneurs 167
1291 Oeufs Mollets 155
1406 Oeufs Montargis 167
1407 Oeufs Montmorency 167
1408 Oeufs Mornay 167
1409 Oeufs Mortemart 167
1410 Oeufs Mosaïque 168
1411 Oeufs à la Moscovite 168
1292 Oeufs Moulés 156
1412 Oeufs Nantua 168
1413 Oeufs à la Napolitaine 168
1414 Oeufs Négus 168
4713 Oeufs à la Neige 560

4714 Oeufs à la Neige Moulés 560
1415 Oeufs à la Niçoise 168
1416 Oeufs Ninon 168
1417 Oeufs à la Normande 168
1418 Oeufs Opéra 169
1419 Oeufs à la d'Orléans 169
1420 Oeufs Orloff 169
1421 Oeufs d'Orsay 169
1422 Oeufs à la Parisienne 169
1423 Oeufs Parmentier 169
1424 Oeufs au Parmesan 169
1425 Oeufs à la Pastourelle 169
1426 Oeufs à la Percheronne 169
1427 Oeufs à la Périgourdine 169
1428 Oeufs Petit-Duc 169
1429 Oeufs à la Piémontaise 170
1290 Oeufs sur le Plat 155
1291 Oeufs Pochés 155
1431 Oeufs Polignac 170
1432 Oeufs à la Portugaise 170
1433 Oeufs Princesse 170
1434 Oeufs Princesse Marie 170
1435 Oeufs Printanière 170
1436 Oeufs à la Provençale 171
1437 Oeufs Rachel 171
1438 Oeufs à la Ravigote 171
1440 Oeufs à la Reine 171
1441 Oeufs Reine Margot 171
1439 Oeufs Régina 171
4567 Oeufs à la Religieuse 542
1443 Oeufs Roland 171
1444 Oeufs à la Romaine 171
1446 Oeufs Rosita 171
1445 Oeufs Rossini 171
1447 Oeufs Rothomago 172
1450 Oeufs Rothschild 172
1448 Oeufs à la Rouennaise 172
1449 Oeufs Rougemont 172
1451 Oeufs Saint-Amand 172
1452 Oeufs Saint-Hubert 172
1453 Oeufs Sardou 172
1454 Oeufs à la Savoyarde 172
1455 Oeufs Senora 172
1456 Oeufs à la Serbe 172
1457 Oeufs Sevigné 172
1458 Oeufs Soubise 172
1459 Oeufs Stanley 172
1460 Oeufs Sultane 173
1461 Oeufs Toupinel 173
1462 Oeufs Toussenel 173
1463 Oeufs à la Tripe 173
1464 Oeufs Tripes à la Bourgeoise 173
1465 Oeufs aux Truffes 173
1466 Oeufs à la Turque 173
1467 Oeufs Vaucourt 173
1468 Oeufs Vauluisant 173
1469 Oeufs Verdi 173
1470 Oeufs Victoria 174
1471 Oeufs Villaret 174
1472 Oeufs Villeroy 174
1473 Oeufs Viroflay 174
1474 Oeufs des Viveurs 174
1475 Oeufs, Vol-au-Vent d' 174
1476 Oeufs Yorkshire 174
1477 Oeufs Yvette 174
1013 Oeufs de Vanneau 129
1536 Oeufs de Vanneau en Aspic 178
1199 Oeufs de Vanneau Christiana 145
1538 Oeufs de Vanneau à la Danoise 179
1539 Oeufs de Vanneau Gabriel 179
1540 Oeufs de Vanneau à la Moderne 179
1541 Oeufs de Vanneau à la Moscovite 179
1542 Oeufs de Vanneau dans un Nid 179
1544 Oeufs de Vanneau Petite-Reine 179
1545 Oeufs de Vanneau à la Royale 179
1546 Oeufs de Vanneau Troubador 179
3438 Oie à l'Alsacienne 413
3439 Oie à l'Anglaise 413
3440 Oie à la Bordelaise 413
3446 Oie Braisée aux Navets 413
3441 Oie Chipolata 413
3442 Oie en Civet 413
3443 Oie en Confit 413
3449 Oie en Daube 414
3445 Oie Farcie aux Marrons 413
3444 Oie à la Flamande 413
1170 Oie Fumée, Croûte à l' 142
3448 Oie à la Mode de Vise 413
1021 Oie, Poitrines Fumées 129
3447 Oie au Raifort 413
3921 Oie Rôtie à l'Anglaise 473
151 Oignons, Coulis d' 24
4151 Oignons Farcis 496
4152 Oignons Frits 496
4154 Oignons, Purée d' 496
2488 Oiseau sans Tête 301
Okras, see also under Gombos
4111 Okras, creamed 492
4113 Okras for garnishing 492
1010 Olives 129
1011 Olives, stuffed 129
Omble-Chevalier, see under Char
Omble-Commun, see under Char
4416 Omelette à l'Abricot 526
1478 Omelette Agnès Sorel 175
4416 Omelette, Apricot Jam 526
1479 Omelette Archiduc 175
1480 Omelette Bénédictine 175
4945 Omelette Berwick 579
1483 Omelette Bretonne 175
1481 Omelette à la Bouchère 175
1482 Omelette à la Boulonnaise 175
1484 Omelette Brillat-Savarin 175
1485 Omelette à la Bruxelloise 175
4566 Omelette Célestine 542
1489 Omelette aux Champignons 175
1486 Omelettes à la Chartres 175
1487 Omelette Chasseur 175
1488 Omelette Châtelaine 175
1490 Omelette Choisy 175
4417 Omelette, Christmas 526
1491 Omelette Clamart 175
1492 Omelette Crécy 175
1493 Omelette aux Crevettes 175
1494 Omelette Durand 176
1495 Omelette à l'Espagnole 176
1486 Omelette à l'Estragon 175
1496 Omelette à la Fermière 176
1497 Omelette aux Fines Herbes 176
1498 Omelette aux Fleurs de Courges 176
1500 Omelette aux Fonds d'Artichauts 176
1499 Omelette à la Florentine 176
1501 Omelette à la Forestière 176
1502 Omelette Grand'Mère 176
1503 Omelette Grandval 176
1504 Omelette Hongroise 176
1505 Omelette Jurassiene 176
1506 Omelette Lorraine 176
1507 Omelette Lyonnaise 176
1508 Omelette Mancelle 176
1509 Omelette Marie-Jeanne 177
1510 Omelette Masséna 177
1511 Omelette Maxim 177
1512 Omelette Mexicaine 177
1513 Omelette Mireille 177
1514 Omelette Monselet 177
1515 Omelette Mousseline 177
1516 Omelette Nantua 177
4417 Omelette de Noël 526
1517 Omelette aux Nonnats 177
1518 Omelette à la Normande 177
4419 Omelette Norvégienne 527
1543 Omelette d'Oeufs de Vanneau 179
1519 Omelette à l'Oseille 177
1520 Omelette Parmentier 177
1521 Omelette à la Paysanne 177
1522 Omelette aux Pointes d'Asperges 177
1523 Omelette à la Portugaise 177
1524 Omelette des Prélats 177
1525 Omelette Princesse 178
1526 Omelette à la Provençale 178
1527 Omelette à la Reine 178
4415 Omelette au Rhum 526
1528 Omelette aux Rognons 178
1529 Omelette Rossini 178
1530 Omelette à la Rouennaise 178
1531 Omelette à la Savoyarde 178
4418 Omelette Soufflé à la Vanille 526
1532 Omelette à la Suissesse 178
4420 Omelette en Surprise Elizabeth 527
4421 Omelette en Surprise aux Mandarines 527
4422 Omelette en Surprise Milady 527
4423 Omelette en Surprise Montmorency 527
4424 Omelette en Surprise Mylord 527
4425 Omelette en Surprise à la Napolitaine 527
4426 Omelette en Surprise Néron 527
4427 Omelette des Sylphes 527
1533 Omelette au Thon 178
1534 Omelette aux Truffes 178
1535 Omelette Victoria 178
Omelettes 174
Omelettes, Jam 526
Omelettes aux Liqueurs 526
Omelettes Soufflés 526
Omelettes Surprises 527
4428 Omelettes Surprises, Various 528
1707 Ondines aux Crevettes Roses 201
4152 Onion Rings, Fried 496
60 Onion Sauce, Brown 14
Onions, see also under Oignons
4153 Onions, Glazed 496
4154 Onions, Purée of 496
4151 Onions, Stuffed 496
4983 Orange Marmalade 584
4365 Orange Sauce 520
4661 Orange au Blanc-Manger 555
4528 Oranges à la Norvégienne 538
4662 Oranges Rubannées 555

4663 Oranges en Surprise 555
5005 Orangeade 588
276 Ordinary Aspic Jellies 40
2 Ordinary White Stock 3
2976 Oreilles de Porc à la Rouennaise 358
2977 Oreilles de Porc Sainte-Menehould 358
2609 Oreilles de Veau Farcies 314
2610 Oreilles de Veau Frites 314
2611 Oreilles de Veau Grillées à la Diable 314
2612 Oreilles de Veau à l'Italienne 314
2613 Oreilles de Veau en Tortue 314
4040 Oronge Agaric 485
Ortolans 450
3737 Ortolans, Aspic d' 451
3733 Ortolans en Caisses 450
Ortolans Froids 451
3734 Ortolans aux Questches 450
3948 Ortolans au Suc d'Ananas 475
3736 Ortolans, Sylphides d' 450
3739 Ortolans, Timbale, Rothschild 451
3741 Ortolans, à la Vendangeuse 451
4946 Os Grillés 579
4155 Oseille 496
2578 Ossi-Buchi 310
2150 Oursins, Crème d', Chaude 253
2151 Oursins, Sauce à la Purée d' 253
2403 Ox Cheek 289
1009 Ox Cheek, for Hors-d'Oeuvre 129
2432 Ox Kidney, see also under Rognon de Boeuf 293
1009 Ox Muzzle, for Hors-d'Oeuvre 129
2404 Ox Palate, see also under Palais de Boeuf 289
2402 Ox tongue, Cold 288
2394 Ox tongue, to cook (see also under Langue de Boeuf) 288
2401 Ox tongue with various garnishes and sauce 288
4156 Oxalis 497
Oxtail, see also under Queue de Boeuf
Oysters, see also under Huîtres
4249 Oyster Plant 505
122 Oyster Sauce 21
184 Oyster Sauce, Brown 28
183 Oyster Sauce (English) 28
1257 Oyster Soufflés, small 150
995 Oysters 127
996 Oysters with Caviare 128
997 Oysters, pickled 128
2147 Oysters, Quenelles à la Reine 253
2148 Oysters, other recipes for 253

1200 Paillettes au Parmesan 145
4947 Paillettes au Parmesan 579
3769 Pain de Bécasse 454
1608 Pain de Brochet à l'Ancienne 189
4044 Pain de Chicorée 485
3517 Pain de Foie gras 424
3518 Pain de Foie gras en Belle-vue 424
3586 Pain de Lièvre 433
3587 Pain de Lièvre en Belle-vue 433
1792 Pain de Merlan à l'Ancienne 210
4406 Pain Perdu 525
1014 Pains à la Française 129
1015 Pains à la Varsovienne 129
2405 Palais de Boeuf, Attereaux de 289
2407 Palais de Boeuf, Croquettes and Cromesquis 289
2406 Palais de Boeuf Dunoise 289
2408 Palais de Boeuf au Gratin 289
1009 Palais de Boeuf, for Hors-d'Oeuvre 129
2409 Palais de Boeuf à l'Italienne 289
2410 Palais de Boeuf en Paupiettes 289
2411 Palais de Boeuf, Sauce Poulette à la Paysanne 289
281 Panada, Bread 42
282 Panada, Flour 43
283 Panada, Frangipane 43
285 Panada, Potato 43
284 Panada, Rice 43
4394 Pancake Mixtures 524
Pancakes, see under Crêpes
484 Pancakes, savoury 70
4429 Pannequets aux Confitures 528
4430 Pannequets à la Crème 528
1201 Pannequets, for Hors-d'Oeuvre 145
4431 Pannequets Meringués 528
4394 Pannequet Mixtures 524
4948 Pannequet Moscovite 579
Partridge, see also under Perdreaux
3771 Partridge, American 455
3771 Partridge, Black 455
3669 Partridge, Cold 443
3658 Partridge, Mousse 442
3658 Partridge, Mousselines 442
3949 Partridge, Roast 475
3950 Partridge, Truffled 475
3519 Parfait de Foie gras 424
4904 Parfait Ice-cream Mixture 574
3294 Pascaline de Poulet 394
4287 Pastas, Cooking of 509
492 Pastas for clear soups 70
4319 Paste, Baba 514
4322 Paste for Beignets Soufflés 515
4317 Paste for Beignets Viennois 514
4326 Paste, Biscuit Manqué 515
4314 Paste, Brioche 513
4316 Paste, General Purpose Brioche 514
4321 Paste, Chou 515
325 Paste, Chou, general purpose 50
4309 Paste, Fine Quality Short 513
4325 Paste, Finger Biscuit 515
4310 Paste, Galette 513
4324 Paste, Génoise 515
4323 Paste, Goujère 515
4320 Paste, Mazarine 514
4315 Paste, Mousseline Brioche 514
4308 Paste, Ordinary Short 513
4351 Paste, Pistachio, for infusion 518
4306 Paste, Puff 512
4307 Paste, Puff, Trimmings 512
4327 Paste, Punch Biscuit 515
4323 Paste, Ramequin 515
4318 Paste, Savarin 514
4328 Paste, Savoy Biscuit 515
4312 Paste for small Tea-cakes 513
4350 Paste, Soft Almond 518
4352 Paste, Soft Pistachio 518
4313 Paste, Suet 513
4311 Paste, Sweet 513
3775 Pastes for Moulded Pies 457
4157 Patates Doux 497
3280 Pâté d'Abattis 393
1016 Pâté d'Alouettes, as Hors-d'Oeuvre 129
3787 Pâté d'Alouettes 459
3778 Pâté d'Anguille 458
3788 Pâté de Bécasses 460
3784 Pâté de Caneton 459
1587 Pâté Chaud d'Anguille 187
1588 Pâté Chaud d'Anguille à l'Anglaise 187
3750 Pâté Chaud de Bécasse 452
3614 Pâté Chaud de Faisan 437
3615 Pâté Chaud de Faisan à la Vosgienne 437
3337 Pâté Chaud Financière 399
3716 Pâté Chaud de Grives à la Liégeoise 448
3574 Pâté Chaud de Lièvre Saint-Estèphe 431
3728 Pâté Chaud de Mauviettes à la Beauçeronne 449
3661 Pâté Chaud de Perdreau 442
3415 Pâté Chaud de Pigeonneaux à l'Ancienne 409
3336 Pâté Chaud de Poulet à la Challonaise 399
3338 Pâté Chaud de Poulet Vallauris 399
2027 Pâté Chaud de Sole à la Dieppoise 233
3789 Pâté de Faisan 460
3793 Pâté de Foie gras 460
3790 Pâté de Grives 460
3781 Pâté de Jambon 458
3594 Pâté de Lapereau de Garenne au Chasseur 434
1016 Pâté, Lark 129
3791 Pâté de Lièvre 460
3792 Pâté de Perdreau 460
3785 Pâté de Pigeons 459
3786 Pâté de Pintade 459
3783 Pâté de Poulet 459
3779 Pâté de Saumon 458
3780 Pâté de Soles 458
3779 Pâté de Truite 458
3782 Pâté de Veau et Jambon 459
1202 Pâtés à la Beauceronne 145
1203 Pâtés for Bortsch 145
1204 Pâtés à la Bourgeoise 145
1205 Pâtés du Chanoine 145
1206 Pâtés Dauphine 145
1208 Pâtés au Jus, Petits 146
1207 Pâtés Manon 146
1208 Pâtés Mazarin 146
1209 Pâtés Nimoise 146
1210 Pâtés, Ordinary 146
1211 Pâtés à la Parisienne 146
3335 Pâté de Poulet à l'Anglaise 399
1212 Pâtés au Verjus 146
921 Paupiettes d'Anchois 121
2484 Paupiettes de Boeuf Fontanges 300
2485 Paupiettes de Boeuf à la Milanaise 301
2486 Paupiettes de Boeuf à la Piémontaise 301
2487 Paupiettes de Boeuf Savary 301
963 Paupiettes de Choux Verts 125
1753 Paupiettes d'Eperlans 207
1793 Paupiettes de Merlan 210
2000 Paupiettes de Sole 231
2045 Paupiettes de Sole en Timbale 237

2742 Paupiettes of Veal with various garnishes 329
2733 Paupiettes de Veau à l'Algérienne 328
2734 Paupiettes de Veau Belle-Hélène 328
2735 Paupiettes de Veau à la Brabançonne 328
2736 Paupiettes de Veau aux Champignons 328
2737 Paupiettes de Veau Fontages 328
2738 Paupiettes de Veau à la Hussarde 328
2739 Paupiettes de Veau Madeleine 329
2740 Paupiettes de Veau Marie-Louise 329
2741 Paupiettes de Veau à la Portugaise 329
3520 Pavé de Foie gras Lucullus 424
Peaches, see under Pêches
326 Pearl Barley for stuffed chicken 50
3017 Pearl Barley for stuffed Poultry 363
Pears, see under Poires
506 Pea Royale 72
Peas, see also under Petits Pois
4159 Peas, Buttered 497
4158 Peas, English Style 497
4167 Peas, Fresh, Purée of 498
4164 Peas, Sugar 497
3003 Pease Pudding 361
4664 Pêches Adrienne 556
4665 Pêches Aiglon 556
4667 Pêches Alexandra 556
4666 Pêches à l'Aurore 556
4531 Pêches Bourdaloue 539
4668 Pêches Cardinal 556
4669 Pêches au Château-Lafitte 556
4532 Pêches Condé 539
4533 Pêches Cussy 539
4670 Pêches Dame-Blanche 556
4671 Pêches Eugénie 556
4534 Pêches Flambées 539
4535 Pêches Gratinées 539
4536 Pêches Impératrice, Hot 539
4672 Pêches à l'Impératrice, Cold 556
4673 Pêches Isabelle 556
4538 Pêches Maintenon 539
4674 Pêches Melba 557
4537 Pêches Meringuées 539
4422 Pêche Milady 527
4675 Pêches Mistral 557
4676 Pêches Petit-Duc 557
4677 Pêches Rose-Chéri 557
4678 Pêches Rose-Pompon 557
4679 Pêches Sultane 557
4680 Pêches Trianon 557
4539 Pêches à la Vanille 539
1213 Pellmènes Sibériens 146
4168 Peppers, Sweet 498
1652 Perch 194
Perdreaux 441
3641 Perdreau Alexis 441
3642 Perdreau Bonne-Maman 441
3643 Perdreau à la Bourguignonne 441
3644 Perdreau en Casserole 441
3645 Perdreau en Chartreuse 441
3647 Perdreau à la Crapaudine 441
3648 Perdreau à la Crème 441
3649 Perdreau, Crépinettes de 441
3650 Perdreau en Demi-deuil 441
3647 Perdreau à la Diable 441
3651 Perdreau, Epigrammes de 442
3652 Perdreau en Estouffade 442
3653 Perdreau à la Fermière 442
3654 Perdreau Kotschoubey 442
3655 Perdreau Lady Clifford 442
3656 Perdreau Lautrec 442
3657 Perdreau Marly 442
3640 Perdreau à la Mode d'Alcantara 441
3659 Perdreau à la Normande 442
3660 Perdreau aux Olives 442
3792 Perdreau, Pâté de 460
3661 Perdreau, Pâté Chaud de 442
3662 Perdreau à la Périgueux 442
3663 Perdreau à la Polonaise 442
3664 Perdreau, Salmis de 442
3665 Perdreau Soubise aux Truffes 442
3666 Perdreau, Soufflé de 443
3667 Perdreau Souvaroff 443
3668 Perdreau, Suprêmes de, Véron 443
3950 Perdreau Truffé 475
3669 Perdreaux Froids 443
3646 Perdrix aux choux 441
4158 Petits Pois à l'Anglaise 497
4159 Petits Pois au Beurre 497
4160 Petits Pois Bonne-Femme 497
4161 Petits Pois à la Flamande 497
4162 Petits Pois à la Française 497
4163 Petits Pois aux Laitues 497
4165 Petits Pois à la Menthe 497
Pheasant, see also under Faisan
3605 Pheasant, Cutlets 436
3608 Pheasant, Grilled Devilled 436
3612 Pheasant, Mousseline 437
3637 Pheasant, Mousselines, Cold 440
3637 Pheasant, Mousses, Cold 440
3789 Pheasant Pie 460
3614 Pheasant Pie, Hot 437
3941 Pheasant, Roast 474
3942 Pheasant, Truffled 475
1017 Piccalilli 129
4057 Pickled Red Cabbage for Hors-d'Oeuvre 487
932 Pickled White-heart cherries 123
1017 Pickles 129
269 Pickling Brine, General purpose 38
268 Pickling Brine for tongues 38
3783 Pie, Chicken 459
3784 Pie, Duck 459
3778 Pie, Eel 458
3786 Pie, Guinea fowl 459
3781 Pie, Ham 458
3791 Pie, Hare 460
1587 Pie, Hot Eel 187
1588 Pie, Hot Eel, English Style 187
3787 Pie, Lark 459
3789 Pie, Pheasant 460
3779 Pie, Salmon 458
3780 Pie, Sole 458
2455 Pie, Steak and Kidney 296
3790 Pie, Thrush 460
3779 Pie, Trout 458
3782 Pie, Veal and Ham 459
3788 Pie, Woodcock 460
4570 Pies, English Fruit 543
Pies, Fish 458
Pies, Game 459
3795 Pies, Household 461
Pies, Meat 459
Pies, Poultry 459
2418 Pièce de Boeuf à la Bourgeoise 290
2414 Pièce de Boeuf à la Bourguignonne 289
2415 Pièce de Boeuf à la Cuiller à l'Ancienne 290
2416 Pièce de Boeuf à l'Ecarlate 290
2417 Pièce de Boeuf à la Flamande 290
2418 Pièce de Boeuf à la Mode 290
2420 Pièce de Boeuf à la Noailles 291
2421 Pièce de Boeuf Soubise 291
980 Pieds de Fenouil 126
2800 Pieds de Mouton en Blanquette 336
2801 Pieds de Mouton, Fritots de 336
2803 Pieds de Mouton à la Rouennaise 337
2804 Pieds de Mouton à la Tyrolienne 337
2616 Pieds de Veau Custine 315
2617 Pieds de Veau Frits 315
2618 Pieds de Veau Grillés 315
2619 Pieds de Veau à la Poulette 315
2620 Pieds de Veau à la Rouennaise 315
2621 Pieds de Veau à la Tartare 315
2622 Pieds de Veau en Tortue 315
2623 Pieds de Veau à la Vinaigrette 315
3011 Pig, Sucking 362
3414 Pigeon Pie 409
3398 Pigeonneaux à la Bordelaise 408
3399 Pigeonneaux en Casserole à la Paysanne 408
3400 Pigeonneaux en Chartreuse 408
3401 Pigeonneaux Chipolata 408
3402 Pigeonneaux en Compote 408
3432 Pigeonneaux, Côtelettes de, en Chaud-froid 412
3403 Pigeonneaux, Côtelettes de, à la Nésles 408
3404 Pigeonneaux, Côtelettes de, en Papillotes 408
3405 Pigeonneaux, Côtelettes de, Sévigné 408
3406 Pigeonneaux Crapaudine 408
3407 Pigeonneaux à l'Estouffade 408
3408 Pigeonneaux Financière 408
3409 Pigeonneaux Gauthier au Beurre d'Ecrevisse 409
3433 Pigeonneaux à la Gelée 412
3434 Pigeonneaux, Medaillons Laurette 412
3410 Pigeonneaux à la Minute 409
3435 Pigeonneaux, Mousse de 412
3411 Pigeonneaux, Mousselines de, à l'Epicurienne 409
3412 Pigeonneaux aux Olives 409
3413 Pigeonneaux aux Olives Noires 409
3414 Pigeonneaux, Pâté de, à l'Anglaise 409
3415 Pigeonneaux, Pâté Chaud à l'Ancienne 409
3416 Pigeonneaux, Pâté Chaud Périgord 409
3417 Pigeonneaux aux Petits Pois 410
3418 Pigeonneaux à la Polonaise 410
3419 Pigeonneaux à la Printanière 410
3420 Pigeonneaux Saint-Charles 410

3427 Pigeonneaux, Sauté de, des Sylvains 411
3422 Pigeonneaux au Sauternes 410
3423 Pigeonneaux, Suprêmes de, Marigny 410
3425 Pigeonneaux, Suprêmes de, Saint-Clair 410
3426 Pigeonneaux, Suprêmes de, Verneuil 411
3428 Pigeonneaux, Timbale de, La Fayette 411
3429 Pigeonneaux Valenciennes 411
3430 Pigeonneaux Villeroy 412
3431 Pigeonneaux, Vol-au-Vent de 412
Pigeons, see also under Pigeonneaux
3785 Pigeons, Pâté de 459
3421 Pigeons Ramiers en Salmis 410
3915 Pigeons, Roast 473
1104 Pignatelli 136
2919 Pig's Brains 351
Pig's Ears, see also under Oreilles de Porc
2975 Pig's Ears 358
2983 Pig's Head 358
2982 Pig's Kidneys 358
2928 Pig's Liver 352
2981 Pigs' Tails 358
2974 Pigs' Tongues 357
2978 Pig's Trotters, Breadcrumbed and Grilled 358
2980 Pig's Trotters, Truffled 358
Pike, see also under Brochet
291 Pike Forcemeat with Suet 45
1609 Pike, with Parsley 189
1610 Pike, with Parsley Sauce 189
1613 Pike, with Various Sauces 190
2839 Pilaw Caissi 342
2840 Pilaw de Mouton à la Turque 342
3348 Pilaw de Volaille à la Grecque 401
3349 Pilaw de Volaille à l'Orientale 401
3350 Pilaw de Volaille Parisienne 401
3351 Pilaw de Volaille à la Turque 401
3772 Pilet 455
4168 Pimentos 498
1018 Pimentos à l'Algérienne 129
4171 Pimentos for cold meat 498
4169 Pimentos, Farcis 498
4170 Pimentos for garnishing 498
4172 Pimentos, Purée de 498
4169 Pimentos, Stuffed 498
4168 Piments Doux 498
Pineapple, see also under Ananas
5000 Pineapple Water 587
3437 Pintade en Chartreuse 412
3786 Pintade, Pâté de 459
3772 Pintail 455
3935 Pintail, Roast 474
1214 Piroguis Caucasiens 146
1215 Piroguis en Croissants 146
1216 Piroguis au Fromage 146
1217 Piroguis au Gibier 146
1218 Piroguis aux Légumes 147
1219 Piroguis Livoniens 147
1220 Piroguis à la Moscovite 147
1221 Piroguis au Poisson 147
1222 Piroguis Polonais 147
1223 Piroguis de Smolensk 147
1224 Piroguis aux Truffes 147
4351 Pistachio Paste for infusion 518
4352 Pistachio Paste, Soft 518
1737 Plaice, see also under Carrelet 206
1737 Plie Franche 206
Plovers Eggs, see under Oeufs de Vanneau
3772 Plover, Golden 455
3951 Plovers, Roast 475
483 Pluches 70
4437 Plum Pudding 529
3772 Pluvier Doré 455
3771 Pluvier Guignard 455
2177 Poaching, Method of 260
1571 Pochouse 185
2178 Poêling, Method of 261
3985 Pointes d'Asperges au Beurre 479
3986 Pointes d'Asperges à la Crème 480
1020 Poireaux Farcis 129
1019 Poireaux à la Greque 129
4681 Poires Alma 557
4540 Poires Bourdaloue 539
4682 Poires Cardinal 557
4541 Poires Condé 540
4683 Poires Félicia 557
4684 Poires à la Florentine 557
4685 Poires Hélène 557
4542 Poires à l'Impératrice 540
4686 Poires Mariette 557
4687 Poires Marquise 558
4688 Poires Mary Garden 558
4689 Poires Melba 558
4543 Poires à la Parisienne 540
4690 Poires Pralinées 558
4691 Poires à la Religieuse 558
4692 Poires Richelieu 558
4544 Poires Sultane 540
4545 Poires, Timbale de, à la Valenciennes 540
4167 Pois Frais, Purée de 498
4166 Pois à la Paysanne 498
4164 Pois Princesse 497
948 Poisson, Canapés au 124
2807 Poitrine de Mouton à la Bergère 337
2808 Poitrine de Mouton à la Diable 337
2809 Poitrine de Mouton, with various purées 337
2810 Poitrine de Mouton Vert-pré 337
2625 Poitrine de Veau à l'Alsacienne 315
2626 Poitrine de Veau à l'Anglaise 315
2627 Poitrine de Veau aux Céleris 316
1661 Pojarski, Salmon Cutlets 195
3169 Pojarski, Suprême de Volaille 380
4284 Polenta 509
4286 Polenta, Timbale de 509
4547 Pommes au Beurre 540
4546 Pommes, Beignets de 540
4548 Pommes Bonne-Femme 540
4549 Pommes Bourdaloue 540
4386 Pommes Charlotte de 523
4387 Pommes, Charlotte de, Emile Giret 523
4551 Pommes Châtelaine 541
4553 Pommes Condé 541
4693 Pommes Félicia 558
4554 Pommes Gratinées 541
4555 Pommes Impératrice 541
4556 Pommes Irène 541
4557 Pommes Meringués 541
4558 Pommes à la Moscovite 541
4560 Pommes à la Portugaise 541
4694 Pommes à la Royale 558
4174 Pommes de Terre Anna 498
4175 Pommes de Terre Anna, for garnishing 498
4173 Pommes de Terre à l'Anglaise 498
1226 Pommes de Terre à l'Ardennaise 147
4177 Pommes de Terre Berny 499
4176 Pommes de Terre Berrichonne 499
4178 Pommes de Terre à la Boulangère 499
4179 Pommes de Terre Byron 499
4180 Pommes de Terre Château 499
4189 Pommes de Terre Chatouillard 500
4190 Pommes de Terre Chip 500
4191 Pommes de Terre Collerette 500
4192 Pommes de Terre en Copeaux 500
4181 Pommes de Terre à la Crème 499
4182 Pommes de Terre, Croquettes de 499
4183 Pommes de Terre Dauphine, Croquettes de 499
4200 Pommes de Terre à la Dauphinoise, Gratin de 500
1227 Pommes de Terre Dietrich 148
4185 Pommes de Terre Duchesse 499
4186 Pommes de Terre Duchesse au Chester 499
4187 Pommes de Terre Fondantes 499
4193 Pommes de Terre Fraise 500
4188 Pommes de Terres Frites en Allumettes 500
1228 Pommes de Terre Georgette 148
4201 Pommes de Terre Gratinées 501
4202 Pommes de Terre à la Hongroise 501
4203 Pommes de Terre au Lard 501
4194 Pommes de Terre en Liards 500
4204 Pommes de Terre Lorette 501
4205 Pommes de Terre à la Lyonnaise 501
4206 Pommes de Terre Macaire 501
4207 Pommes de Terre Maire 501
4208 Pommes de Terre à la Maître d'Hôtel 501
4209 Pommes de Terre Marquise 501
4210 Pommes de Terre Ménagère 501
4211 Pommes de Terre à la Menthe 501
4212 Pommes de Terre Mireille 501
4213 Pommes de Terre Mirette 502
4214 Pommes de Terre Monselet 502
4215 Pommes de Terre Mousseline 502
4216 Pommes de Terre Nana 502
4217 Pommes de Terre Ninon 502
4218 Pommes de Terre Noisette 502
4219 Pommes de Terre Normande 502
4195 Pommes de Terre Pailles 500
4220 Pommes de Terre Parisienne 502
4221 Pommes de Terre au Parmesan 502
4222 Pommes de Terre Persillées 502
4196 Pommes de Terre Pont-Neuf 500
4230 Pommes de Terre, Purée de 503
4231 Pommes de Terre, Quenelles de 503
4223 Pommes de Terre Robert 502
4224 Pommes de Terre Roxelane 502
4226 Pommes de Terre Saint-Florentin 502

4225 Pommes de Terre Savoyarde 502
4227 Pommes de Terre Schneider 503
4232 Pommes de Terre, Soufflé de 503
4197 Pommes de Terres Soufflées 500
4228 Pommes de Terre Suzette 503
4229 Pommes de Terre Voisin 503
1229 Pomponettes 148
Pork, Best End, see also under Carré de Porc
2916 Pork, Best End, with various purées 350
2917 Pork, Best End, with various sauces 350
3003 Pork, Boiled Salt, English Style 361
2940 Pork, Braised Leg 353
2994 Pork, Carbonade of 360
2918 Pork, Cold Best End 351
Pork, Cutlets 351
2998 Pork, Emincé of 360
297 Pork Forcemeat 47
2999 Pork, Fricadelles of 360
2909 Pork, Joints of 350
2927 Pork, Loin of 352
3001 Pork Pie, Hot, English Style 361
2912 Pork, Roast Best End with Brussels Sprouts 350
2913 Pork, Roast Best End with Apple Sauce 350
2911 Pork, Roast Best End, with Red Cabbage 350
2910 Pork, Roast Best End with Sauerkraut 350
3905 Pork, Roast, English Style 472
2940 Pork, Roast Leg 353
3904 Pork, Roast Loin 472
3002 Pork, Salt Neck 361
2926 Pork, Shoulder of 351
2925 Pork, Spare Rib 351
70 Port Wine Sauce 15
4230 Potato, mashed 503
4198 Potato Nests 500
285 Potato Panada 43
3810 Potato Salad 463
Potatoes, see also under Pommes de Terre
4173 Potatoes, Plain Boiled 498
4195 Potatoes, Straw 500
4157 Potatoes, Sweet 497
1651 Potted Char 194
1025 Potted Fish 130
1025 Potted Meats 130
4432 Pouding aux Amandes 528
4433 Pouding aux Amandes à l'Anglaise 528
4438 Pouding à l'Américaine 529
4614 Pouding d'Aremberg 550
4343 Pouding de Biscuits 528
4615 Pouding Bohémienne 550
4449 Pouding Brésilien 530
4435 Pouding de Cabinet 528
4450 Pouding à la Chevreuse 530
4616 Pouding Clermont 550
4617 Pouding Diplomate 550
4618 Pouding Diplomate aux Fruits 550
4949 Pouding de Fromage au Pain 579
4905 Pouding Glacé de Castries 574
4906 Pouding Glacé Marie-Rose 574
4907 Pouding Glacé Miramar 575
4908 Pouding Glacé Seymour 575
4619 Pouding Malakoff 550
4439 Pouding à la Moelle 529
4462 Pouding Mousseline 532
4620 Pouding Nesselrode 551
4447 Pouding aux Nouilles Fraîches 530
4440 Pouding au Pain à l'Anglaise 529
4442 Pouding au Pain à l'Ecossaise 530
4441 Pouding au Pain à la Française 529
4621 Pouding Reine des Fées 551
4451 Pouding au Riz 531
4452 Pouding de Riz à l'Anglaise 530
4453 Pouding de Riz au Chocolat 531
4623 Pouding de Riz à la Crème, cold 551
4454 Pouding de Riz à la Crème 531
4622 Pouding Rizzio 551
4444 Pouding au Sago 530
4456 Pouding Saxon 531
4445 Pouding à la Semoule 530
4624 Pouding de Semoule à la Crème, Cold 550
4455 Pouding de Semoule à la Crème 531
4459 Pouding Soufflé à l'Anisette 531
4459 Pouding Soufflé à la Bénédictine 531
4458 Pouding Soufflé au Citron 531
4459 Pouding Soufflé au Curaçao 531
4457 Pouding Soufflé Denise 531
4460 Pouding Soufflé à l'Indienne 531
4461 Pouding Soufflé aux Marrons 531
4459 Pouding Soufflé à l'Orange 531
4463 Pouding Soufflé Régence 532
4464 Pouding Soufflé à la Reine 532
4465 Pouding Soufflé à la Royale 532
4466 Pouding Soufflé Sans-Souci 532
4467 Pouding Soufflé Vésuvienne 532
4443 Pouding au Tapioca 530
4446 Pouding au Vermicelli 530
3088 Poularde Adelina Patti 371
3019 Poularde Albuféra 364
3020 Poularde Alexandra 364
3021 Poularde à l'Ambassadrice 364
3022 Poularde à l'Andalouse 365
3025 Poularde d'Aumale 365
3026 Poularde à l'Aurore 365
3027 Poularde Banquière 365
3028 Poularde Boïeldieu 365
3024 Poularde Bouillie à l'Anglaise 365
3029 Poularde Bouquetière 365
3030 Poularde Cardinalisée 365
3356 Poularde Carmelite 402
3031 Poularde aux Céleris 365
3357 Poularde au Champagne 402
3032 Poularde aux Champignons 365
3033 Poularde aux Champignons, white 365
3034 Poularde Châtelaine 366
3035 Poularde à la Chevalière 366
3036 Poularde Chimay 366
3037 Poularde Chipolata 366
3038 Poularde Chivry 366
3039 Poularde Cussy 366
3358 Poularde Dampierre 402
3040 Poularde Demi-deuil 366
3041 Poularde Demidoff 366
3042 Poularde Derby 367
3043 Poularde Devonshire 367
3045 Poularde à la Dreux 367
3044 Poularde Diva 367
3046 Poularde Duroc 367
3359 Poularde à l'Ecarlate 402
3047 Poularde à l'Ecossaise 367
3048 Poularde Edouard VII 367
3049 Poularde à l'Elysée 367
3050 Poularde en Estouffade 368
3051 Poularde à l'Estragon 368
3052 Poularde Favorite 368
3053 Poularde à la Fermière 368
3054 Poularde Financière 368
3055 Poularde des Gastronomes 368
3056 Poularde Godard 368
3057 Poularde Grammont 368
3058 Poularde Grand Hôtel 368
3060 Poularde à la Grecque 368
3059 Poularde au Gros Sel 368
3061 Poularde Héloise 369
3062 Poularde à la Hongroise 369
3063 Poularde aux Huîtres 369
3064 Poularde à l'Impératrice 369
3065 Poularde à l'Indienne 369
3066 Poularde Isabelle de France 369
3067 Poularde à l'Ivoire 369
3068 Poularde Lady Curzon 369
3360 Poularde Lambertye 402
3069 Poularde à la Languedocienne 369
3070 Poularde Louis d'Orléans 369
3071 Poularde Louisiane 370
3072 Poularde Lucullus 370
3073 Poularde Maintenon 370
3074 Poularde Mancini 370
3075 Poularde Maréchal 370
3076 Poularde Marguerite de Savoie 370
3077 Poularde Marie-Louise 370
3078 Poularde Ménagère 370
3079 Poularde Montbazon 370
3080 Poularde Montmorency 371
3081 Poularde Nantua 371
3361 Poularde Néva 402
3082 Poularde à la Niçoise 371
3084 Poularde à l'Orientale 371
3085 Poularde Paramé 371
3362 Poularde Parisienne, Cold 402
3086 Poularde à la Parisienne 371
3087 Poularde en Pâté 371
3089 Poularde à la Paysanne 371
3090 Poularde à la Périgord 372
3091 Poularde à la Périgourdine 372
3129 Poularde aux Perles du Périgord 376
3092 Poularde Petite Mariée 372
3093 Poularde à la Piémontaise 372
3023 Poularde Pochée à l'Anglaise 365
3094 Poularde à la Polignac 372
3095 Poularde à la Portugaise 372
3096 Poularde Princesse 372
3097 Poularde Princesse Hélène 372
3098 Poularde Printanière 372
3099 Poularde Régence 372
3100 Poularde à la Reine 373
3101 Poularde Reine-Anne 373
3102 Poularde Reine-Blanche 373
3103 Poularde Reine-Margot 373
3104 Poularde Reine-Marguerite 373
3105 Poularde Renaissance 373
3106 Poularde au Riz 373
3363 Poularde Rose de Mai 403
3364 Poularde Rose Marie 403
3107 Poularde Rossini 373
3907 Poularde Rôtie à l'Anglaise 472

3108 Poularde Saint-Alliance 373
3365 Poularde Saint-Cyr 403
3109 Poularde Santa-Lucia 374
3110 Poularde à la Sicilienne 374
3111 Poularde Soufflé 374
3112 Poularde Souvaroff 374
3113 Poularde Stanley 374
3114 Poularde Sylvana 375
3115 Poularde Talleyrand 375
3367 Poularde, Terrine de, en Conserve 403
3366 Poularde en Terrine à la Gelée 403
3116 Poularde Tivoli 375
3117 Poularde Tosca 375
3118 Poularde à la Toulousaine 375
3119 Poularde Trianon 375
3908 Poularde Truffée 472
3120 Poularde à la Valenciennes 375
3121 Poularde à la Vénitienne 375
3122 Poularde Vert-Pré 375
3123 Poularde à la Vichy 376
3124 Poularde Victoria 376
3125 Poularde à la Vierge 376
3126 Poularde Villars 376
3127 Poularde Washington 376
3128 Poulardes, other preparations for 376
3199 Poulet au Currie 384
3083 Poulet aux Nouilles 371
3783 Poulet, Pâté de 459
3257 Poulet de Grains aux Fonds d'Artichaut 459
3247 Poulet de Grains à la Belle-Meunière 389
3248 Poulet de Grains à la Bergère 389
3249 Poulet de Grains en Casserole 389
3250 Poulet de Grains en Cocotte 390
3251 Poulet de Grains en Cocotte Bonne-Femme 390
3252 Poulet de Grains en Compote 390
3253 Poulet de Grains à la Crapaudine 390
3255 Poulet de Grains Grillé Diable 390
3256 Poulet de Grains à la Fermière 390
3258 Poulet de Grains à la Grand'Mère 390
3254 Poulet de Grains Grillé à l'Anglaise 390
3259 Poulet de Grains à l'Hôtelière 390
3260 Poulet de Grains Grillé Katoff 390
3261 Poulet de Grains à la Limousine 391
3262 Poulet de Grains Mascotte 391
3263 Poulet de Grains Mireille 391
3264 Poulet de Grains aux Morilles 391
3265 Poulet de Grains Printanière 391
3266 Poulet de Grains à la Russe 391
3267 Poulet de Grains Souvaroff 391
3268 Poulet de Grains à la Tartare 391
3181 Poulets Sautés 381
3182 Poulet Sauté Algérienne 382
3183 Poulet Sauté Anversoise 382
3184 Poulet Sauté Archiduc 382
3185 Poulet Sauté Arlésienne 382
3186 Poulet Sauté à l'Armagnac 382
3187 Poulet Sauté d'Artois 382
3188 Poulet Sauté Beaulieu 382
3189 Poulet Sauté Bercy 383
3190 Poulet Sauté Boivin 383
3191 Poulet Sauté à la Bordelaise 383
3192 Poulet Sauté à la Bourguignonne 383
3193 Poulet Sauté à la Bressanne 383
3194 Poulet Sauté à la Bretonne 383
3195 Poulet Sauté à la Catalane 383
3196 Poulet Sauté aux Cèpes 384
3197 Poulet Sauté Champeaux 384
3198 Poulet Sauté Chausseur 384
3200 Poulet Sauté Cynthia 384
3201 Poulet Sauté Demidoff 384
3202 Poulet Sauté Doria 384
3204 Poulet Sauté Durand 384
3205 Poulet Sauté Egyptienne 385
3206 Poulet Sauté Escurial 385
3207 Poulet Sauté à l'Espagnole 385
3208 Poulet Sauté à l'Estragon 385
3209 Poulet Sauté Fédora 385
3210 Poulet Sauté au Fenouil 385
3211 Poulet Sauté Fermière 385
3212 Poulet Sauté aux Fines Herbes 385
3213 Poulet Sauté à la Forestière 385
3214 Poulet Sauté Gabrielle 386
3215 Poulet Sauté Georgina 386
3216 Poulet Sauté à la Hongroise 386
3217 Poulet Sauté aux Huîtres 386
3218 Poulet Sauté à l'Indienne 386
3219 Poulet Sauté à l'Italienne 386
3220 Poulet Sauté Japonaise 386
3221 Poulet Sauté Josephine 386
3222 Poulet Sauté Jurassienne 386
3223 Poulet Sauté Lathuile 387
3224 Poulet Sauté Madras 387
3225 Poulet Sauté Marengo 387
3226 Poulet Sauté Marigny 387
3228 Poulet Sauté à la Marseillaise 387
3227 Poulet Sauté Maryland 387
3229 Poulet Sauté Mathilde 387
3230 Poulet Sauté Mexicaine 387
3231 Poulet Sauté aux Morilles 387
3232 Poulet Sauté a la Normande 388
3233 Poulet Sauté à l'Orléanaise 388
3203 Poulet Sauté d'Orsay 384
3234 Poulet Sauté au Paprika 388
3235 Poulet Sauté Parmentier 388
3236 Poulet Sauté à la Périgord 388
3237 Poulet Sauté à la Piémontaise 388
3238 Poulet Sauté à la Portugaise 388
3239 Poulet Sauté à la Provençale 388
3242 Poulet Sauté Saint-Lambert 389
3241 Poulet Sauté Saint-Mandé 388
3240 Poulet Sauté au Samos 388
3243 Poulet Sauté Stanley 389
3244 Poulet Sauté aux Truffes 389
3246 Poulet Sauté Verdi 389
3245 Poulet Sauté à la Vichy 389
3016 Poultry, Preparation of Fattened Pullets and Capons 363
3018 Poultry, to serve quickly and hot 364
3911 Poussin, Roast 472
3269 Poussins Cendrillon 391
3270 Poussins Hermitage 391
3271 Poussins à la Piémontaise 391
3272 Poussins à la Polonaise 392
3273 Poussins à la Tartare 392
3274 Poussins, Tourte de, à la Paysanne 392
3275 Poussins Valentinois 392
3276 Poussins à la Viennoise 392
1023 Poutargue de Mulet 129
1024 Poutargue de Thon 130
1823 Poutine 212
4354 Pralin 519
4353 Pralin, Royal Icing 519
Prawns, see also under Crevettes
2089 Prawn Mousse, Cold 243
2088 Prawns in Aspic 243
2086 Prawns, Curried 242
2087 Prawns, Fried 242
493 Profiteroles for soups 71
327 Provençale Mixture 51
4432 Pudding, Almond 528
4433 Pudding, English Almond 528
4436 Pudding, Apple 529
2989 Pudding, Black 359
2990 Pudding, Black, English Method 360
2991 Pudding, Black, Flemish Method 360
4440 Pudding, Bread and Butter 529
4441 Pudding, French Bread 529
4434 Pudding, Biscuit 528
4435 Pudding, Cabinet 528
4393 Pudding, Custard 523
4447 Pudding, Fresh Noodle 530
4437 Pudding, Plum 529
4451 Pudding, Rice 531
4452 Pudding, Rice, English Style 530
4454 Pudding, Rice with cream 531
4468 Pudding, Roly-Poly 532
4444 Pudding, Sago 530
4448 Pudding, Sago, English Style 530
4442 Pudding, Scotch Bread 530
4445 Pudding, Semolina 530
4448 Pudding, Semolina, English Style 530
2456 Pudding, Steak 296
4443 Pudding, Tapioca 530
4448 Pudding, Tapioca, English Style 530
4446 Pudding, Vermicelli 530
3889 Pudding, Yorkshire 471
Puddings 528
Puddings, see also under Pouding
4306 Puff Paste 512
4307 Puff Paste Trimmings 512
3016 Pullets, fattened, preparation of 363
4327 Punch Biscuit Paste 515
5009 Punch, Iced 588
908 Punch, Milk 119
4915 Punch à la Romaine 576
5007 Punch, Rum 588
4093 Purée de Crosnes 490
4071 Purée à la Dubarry 489
4138 Purée Esaü 495
4079 Purée à la Flamande 489
4121 Purée de Haricots Blancs 493
4138 Purée de Lentilles 495
4272 Purée Palestine 507
4167 Purée Saint-Germain 498
4121 Purée Soissonaise 493
4154 Purée Soubise 496

Quails, see also under Cailles
3670 Quails 443
Quails, Cold 446
3929 Quails, roast 474

301 Quenelles 47
1611 Quenelles de Brochet à la Lyonnaise 189
1612 Quenelles de Brochet Morland 190
1629 Quenelles de Carpe Morland 192
2565 Quenelles de Foie de Veau 309
1796 Quenelles de Merlan à la Morland 210
1795 Quenelles de Merlan Soubise 210
4231 Quenelles de Pommes de Terre 503
494 Quenelles for Soups 71
3296 Quenelles de Volaille à l'Ecarlate 395
3297 Quenelles de Volaille à l'Estragon 395
3298 Quenelles de Volaille Morland 395
3299 Quenelles de Volaille à la Périgueux 395
3300 Quenelles de Volaille d'Uzes 395
2424 Queue de Boeuf à l'Auvergnate 291
2425 Queue de Boeuf Cavour 291
2426 Queue de Boeuf à la Charolaise 292
2427 Queue de Boeuf Chipolata 292
2428 Queue de Boeuf Farcie 292
2429 Queue de Boeuf Grillée 292
2430 Queue de Boeuf en Hochepot 292
2431 Queue de Boeuf à la Nohant 293
4988 Quince Jelly 585
1231 Quiche au Jambon 148
1230 Quiche à la Lorraine 148
3590 Rabbit, Boiled, English Style 434
3596 Rabbit, various preparations 434
Rabbit, Wild and Domesticated 433
3576 Râble de Lièvre 432
3577 Râble de Lièvre à l'Allemande 432
3578 Râble de Lièvre au Genièvre 432
3579 Râble de Lièvre à la Navarraise 432
3580 Râble de Lièvre, Sauce aux Cerises 432
3581 Râble de Lièvre, Sauce Groseille au Raifort 432
4561 Rabottes de Pommes 541
1026 Radis 130
1027 Radis Noirs 130
1026 Radishes 130
1027 Radishes, Black 130
2841 Ragoût de Mouton au Riz 342
1824 Raie au Beurre Noir 213
1824 Raie au Beurre Noisette 213
1825 Raie, Foies de, Coquilles de 213
1826 Raie, Foies de, Croûtes de 213
1827 Raie, Fritot de 213
1828 Raie au Gratin 213
3709 Râle de Genêt 448
4323 Ramequin Paste 515
1232 Ramequins 148
5002 Raspberry-flavoured Redcurrant Water 587
4363 Raspberry Sauce 520
1233 Rastegaïs 148
1234 Ravioles à la Sibérienne 148
4299 Ravioli filling A 511
4300 Ravioli filling B 511
4301 Ravioli filling C 511
4303 Raviolis, Poaching and Serving 511
4302 Raviolis, Preparation of 511
4304 Raviolis, Timbale de, à la Phocéenne 511
4989 Redcurrant Jelly 585
4991 Redcurrant Jelly, cold method 586
4364 Redcurrant Sauce 520
3807 Red Cabbage Salad 462
230 Red Colouring Butter 33
1829 Red Mullet, see also under Rougets 213
1832 Red Mullet with Fennel 213
1031 Red Mullet with Saffron 130
7 Red Wine Fish Stock 5
81 Red Wine Sauce 16
3891 Ribs of Beef 471
Rice, see also under Riz 503
4404 Rice Croquettes 525
4235 Rice, Curried 503
284 Rice Panada 43
4623 Rice Pudding with Cream 551
328 Rice for stuffed poultry, Method 51
3017 Rice for stuffed poultry 363
4470 Rice, prepared for sweet dishes 532
1029 Rillettes de Tours 130
1030 Rillons de Blois 130
3689 Risotto de Cailles 445
4244 Risotto à la Florentine 504
4246 Risotto Maigre 504
4247 Risotto à la Milanaise 505
4248 Risotto à la Piémontaise 505
1235 Rissoles 148
1236 Rissoles à la Bergère 148
1238 Rissoles à la Bohémienne 149
1237 Rissoles Bouquetière 149
1239 Rissoles à la Bressane 149
1240 Rissoles à la Dauphine 149
1241 Rissoles à l'Indienne 149
1242 Rissoles Joinville 149
1243 Rissoles Marly 149
1244 Rissoles aux Morilles 149
1245 Rissoles Nantua 149
1246 Rissoles à la Normande 149
1442 Rissoles d'Oeufs 171
1247 Rissoles à l'Ostendaise 149
1248 Rissoles Pompadour 149
1249 Rissoles à la Reine 149
4469 Rissoles, sweet 532
1250 Rissoles Victoria 150
2892 Ris d'Agneau, Pâté Chaud, à la Chevrière 348
2893 Ris d'Agneau, Timbale de 348
2894 Ris d'Agneau, Vol-au-Vent de, Soubise 348
2635 Ris de Veau, Attereau à la Villeroy 317
2636 Ris de Veau Bonne Maman 317
2637 Ris de Veau à la Broche 317
2638 Ris de Veau en Caisses 317
2639 Ris de Veau à la Cévenole 317
2640 Ris de Veau Chambellane 317
2641 Ris de Veau, Chartreuse de 317
2642 Ris de Veau Comtesse 318
2644 Ris de Veau, Coquilles de, au Gratin 318
2645 Ris de Veau, Coquilles de, à la Parisienne 318
2643 Ris de Veau, Crépinettes de 318
2646 Ris de Veau, Cromesquis de 318
2647 Ris de Veau, Croquettes de 318
1165 Ris de Veau, Croustades de, Financière 141
2673 Ris de Veau sous Croûte 321
2649 Ris de Veau Demidoff 318
2650 Ris de Veau, Escalopes de, Favorite 318
2651 Ris de Veau, Escalopes de, Grand-Duc 318
2652 Ris de Veau, Escalopes de, Judic 319
2653 Ris de Veau, Escalopes de, Maréchal 319
2654 Ris de Veau, Escalopes de, Rossini 319
2655 Ris de Veau, Escalopes de, Villeroy 319
2656 Ris de Veau Excelsior 319
2657 Ris de Veau Financière 319
2658 Ris de Veau au Gratin 319
2659 Ris de Veau Grillé 319
2660 Ris de Veau Grillé Châtelaine 319
2661 Ris de Veau Grillé Gismonda 320
2662 Ris de Veau Grillé Jocelyn 320
2663 Ris de Veau Grillé Saint-Germain 320
2664 Ris de Veau des Gourmets 320
2665 Ris de Veau Montauban 320
2682 Ris de Veau, Palets de, à l'Ecarlate 322
2666 Ris de Veau en Papillote 320
2667 Ris de Veau à la Parisienne 320
2668 Ris de Veau, Pâté Chaud de 320
2669 Ris de Veau Princesse 320
2670 Ris de Veau aux Queues d'Ecrevisses 320
2671 Ris de Veau Rachel 321
2672 Ris de Veau Régence 321
2680 Ris de Veau Richelieu 322
2681 Ris de Veau à la Suédoise 322
2675 Ris de Veau, Timbale de, Baloise 321
2676 Ris de Veau, Timbale de, Condé 321
2674 Ris de Veau à la Toulousaine 321
2677 Ris de Veau, Vol-au-Vent à la Nésles 321
2678 Ris de Veau, Vol-au-Vent Régence 321
2679 Ris de Veau, other suitable garnishes 321
4233 Riz au Blanc 503
4234 Riz à la Créole 503
4404 Riz, Croquettes de 525
4235 Riz au Currie 503
4236 Riz au Gras 504
4237 Riz à la Grecque 504
4715 Riz à l'Impératrice 560
4238 Riz à l'Indienne 504
4716 Riz à la Maltaise 560
4239 Riz Pilaw 504
4240 Riz Pilaw for Poultry 504
4241 Riz Portugaise 504
4242 Riz à la Turque 504
4243 Riz à la Valenciennes 504
3885 Roast Gravies 470
1740 Roast Plaice 206
Roast Poultry 472
3882 Roasting, Barding for 469
3884 Roasting, Oven 469
3883 Roasting, Spit 469
Roasts of Beef 471

Roasts of Feathered Game 474
Roasts of Furred Game 474
Roasts of Lamb 471
Roasts of Mutton 471
Roasts of Pork 472
3886 Roasts, Presentation and Accompaniments 470
Roasts of Veal 471
Roasts of Venison 473
4717 Rôd Grôd 560
Roebuck, see also under Chevreuil
Roebuck, Fillet 426
3535 Roebuck, Leg 426
3923 Roebuck, Roast 473
3539 Roebuck, Saddle 427
3547 Roebuck, Saddle, with various sauces 428
2434 Rognon de Boeuf Bercy 293
2435 Rognon de Boeuf aux Champignons 293
2436 Rognon de Boeuf Chipolata 293
2437 Rognon de Boeuf au Madère 293
2438 Rognon de Boeuf Marchand de Vins 293
2433 Rognon de Boeuf Sauté 293
2439 Rognon de Boeuf au Vin Blanc 293
2684 Rognon de Veau Bercy 322
2686 Rognon de Veau à la Berrichonne 322
2685 Rognon de Veau à la Bordelaise 322
2687 Rognon de Veau en Casserole 322
2689 Rognon de Veau en Cocotte 323
2690 Rognon de Veau, Croûtes de 323
2691 Rognon de Veau au Currie a l'Indienne 323
2692 Rognon de Veau Grillé 323
2693 Rognon de Veau à la Liégeoise 323
2694 Rognon de Veau Montpensier 323
2695 Rognon de Veau à la Portugaise 323
2696 Rognon de Veau au Rizot 323
2697 Rognon de Veau Robert 323
2688 Rognon de Veau Sauté aux Champignons 323
2698 Rognon de Veau, with various wines 324
2182 Rognons Brochette 337
2813 Rognons Brochette à l'Espagnole 338
2814 Rognons, Brochettes de 338
2817 Rognons au Gratin 338
2818 Rognons à la Hussarde 338
2819 Rognons Michel 338
1528 Rognons, Omelette aux 178
2811 Rognons Sautés à la Berrichonne 337
2815 Rognons Sautés Carvalho 338
2816 Rognons Sautés au Champagne 338
2820 Rognons, Turban de, à la Piémontaise 338
2821 Rognons Turbigo 339
2822 Rognons Vert-pré 339
2823 Rognons Viéville 339
992 Rollmops 127
1653 Rothel 194
3467 Rouennais, Aiguillettes de, à la Bigarade 416
3468 Rouennais, Aiguillettes de, aux Truffes 416
1830 Rougets à la Bordelaise 213
1831 Rougets en Caisses 213
1832 Rougets au Fenouil 213
1833 Rougets Francillon 213
1834 Rougets au Gratin 213
1835 Rougets à la Livournaise 213
1837 Rougets à la Marseillaise 214
1846 Rougets, Mousse Froide de 214
1838 Rougets, Mousselines de 214
1839 Rougets à la Nantaise 214
1840 Rougets à la Niçoise 214
1031 Rougets à l'Orientale 130
1841 Rougets en Papillote 214
1842 Rougets à la Polonaise 214
1031 Rougets au Safran 130
1843 Rougets à la Trouvillaise 214
1836 Rougets, Filets de, Maréchal 214
1844 Rougets, Filets de, Villeroy 214
14 Roux, Blond 7
13 Roux, Brown 7
15 Roux, White 7
4353 Royal Icing Pralin 519
495 Royales 71
502 Royale, Asparagus 72
497 Royale, Carrot 71
498 Royale, Celery 71
505 Royale, Chestnut 72
510 Royale, Chicken 72
499 Royale, Cream 72
500 Royale, Cream of rice and almond milk 72
497 Royale Crécy 71
499 Royale Deslignac 72
507 Royale, Fish 72
504 Royale, Foie gras 72
501 Royale, Game 72
506 Royale, Green Pea 72
503 Royale, Leek 72
496 Royale, ordinary 71
507 Royale, Shellfish 72
508 Royale, Tomato 72
509 Royale, Truffle 72
1032 Royans 130
4415 Rum Omelette 526
5007 Rum Punch 588
2440 Rump of Beef 293
2443 Rump Steak Grand'Mère 294
2441 Rump Steak, Grilled 294
2444 Rump Steak Mirabeau 294
2442 Rump Steak, Shallow Fried 294
3871 Russian Salad 467

4358 Sabayon 519
3887 Sage and Onion Stuffing 470
3576 Saddle of Hare, see also under Râble de Lièvre 432
2895 Saddle of Lamb 348
3901 Saddle of Lamb, Roast 472
2825 Saddle of Mutton or Grass Lamb 339
3901 Saddle of Mutton, Roast 472
3547 Saddle of Roebuck, with various sauces 428
2699 Saddle of Veal 324
3803 Salad, Beetroot 462
1047 Salad of Calf's Feet and Sheep's Trotters 131
3806 Salad, Cauliflower 462
3805 Salad, Celeriac 462
3804 Salad, Celery 462
Salads, Composed 463
3808 Salad, Cucumber 462
Salad Dressings 462
3799 Salad Dressing, Bacon 462
3797 Salad Dressing, Cream 462
3798 Salad Dressing, Egg 462
3801 Salad Dressing, Mayonnaise 462
3800 Salad Dressing, Mustard and Cream 462
3796 Salad Dressing, Oil and Vinegar 462
3810 Salad, Potato 462
3807 Salad, Red Cabbage 462
3871 Salad, Russian 467
1694 Salad, Salmon 200
3812 Salad, Tomato 462
3846 Salad, Vegetable 466
3809 Salad, Vegetable using dried vegetables 463
3813 Salade Aïda 463
3814 Salade Alice 463
3815 Salade à l'Américaine 463
3816 Salade à l'Andalouse 463
3817 Salade Aurore 464
3819 Salade Bagration 464
3818 Salade Beaucaire 464
3820 Salade Belle de Nuit 464
1034 Salade Bergerette 130
3803 Salade de Betterave 462
930 Salade, Betterave en 122
931 Salade, Betterave, with Cream 122
1035 Salade Brésilienne 130
3823 Salade Carmen 464
1036 Salade Castelnau 130
1037 Salade Catalan 130
3804 Salade de Céleri 462
3805 Salade de Céleri-rave 462
3806 Salade de Choux-fleurs 462
3807 Salade de Choux Rouges 462
3808 Salade de Concombres 463
966 Salade, Concombres en 125
3826 Salade Crémone 464
3827 Salade Créole 464
3828 Salade Cressonière 464
3829 Salade Danicheff 464
3830 Salade Demi-Deuil 464
1038 Salade Dorzia 130
3831 Salade d'Estrées 464
3833 Salade Eve 465
3834 Salade Favorite 465
3835 Salade à la Flamande 465
3836 Salade Francillon 465
3843 Salade aux Fruits à la Japonaise 465
3837 Salade des Gobelins 465
1039 Salade Hollandaise 131
3839 Salade Irma 465
3840 Salade Isabelle 465
1040 Salade Italienne 131
3844 Salade Jockey Club 465
3845 Salade Lakmé 465
3846 Salade de Légumes 466
3847 Salade Lorette 466
3848 Salade Maraîchere 466
3849 Salade Mascotte 466
1041 Salade Midinette 131
3850 Salade Mignon 466
3852 Salade Mikado 466
1042 Salade des Moines 131

1043 Salade Monte-Carlo 131
3855 Salade Montfermeil 466
3856 Salade Muguette 466
1044 Salade Nantaise 131
3858 Salade Niçoise 466
3859 Salade Noémi 466
3860 Salade des Nonnes 466
1045 Salade Normande 131
3862 Salade Opéra 466
3863 Salade d'Oranges 467
3864 Salade Orientale 467
1046 Salade des Pêcheurs 131
1047 Salade de Pieds de Mouton et de Pieds de Veau 131
1048 Salade de Pieds de Veau Clarens 131
1049 Salade de Pieds de Veau à la Hongroise 131
3866 Salade Polonaise 467
3810 Salade de Pommes de Terre 463
3811 Salade de Pommes de Terre à la Parisienne 462
1050 Salade Portugaise 131
1051 Salade Provençale 131
3868 Salade Rachel 467
3869 Salade Régence 467
1052 Salade Réjane 131
3871 Salade Russe 467
3872 Salade Saint-Jean 467
3873 Salade Saint-Sylvestre 467
3812 Salade de Tomates 462
3875 Salade Tosca 467
3874 Salade Tourangelle 467
3876 Salade Trédern 467
3877 Salade aux Truffes 467
3878 Salade aux Truffes Blanches 468
1053 Salade Vauclusienne 131
3879 Salade Victoria 468
3380 Salade de Volaille 405
3880 Salade Waldorf 468
3881 Salade Windsor 468
3865 Salades de Poisson 467
3865 Salads, Fish 467
3802 Salads, Green 462
1033 Salads for Hors-d'Oeuvre 130
Salads, Simple 462
1054 Salads, Various Rice 131
1055 Salami 131
3752 Salmis de Bécasse 452
3478 Salmis de Caneton à la Rouennaise 417
3770 Salmis Froid de Bécasse 454
3619 Salmis de Faisan 438
3664 Salmis de Perdreau 442
Salmon, see also under Saumon
1681 Salmon, Cold 198
1654 Salmon, Cooking of 194
1657 Salmon Cutlets 194
1685 Salmon Cutlets, Cold 199
1675 Salmon, Grilled 197
1655 Salmon, Kedgeree of 194
1685 Salmon Mayonnaise 199
1677 Salmon, Mousses and Mousselines 197
1688 Salmon Mousse, Cold 199
1689 Salmon Mousselines, Cold 199
3779 Salmon Pie 458
1060 Salmon, Smoked 132
Salmon trout, see also under Truite Saumonée
1708 Salmon-trout, Cold, on Mousse 202
329 Salpicons, various 51
4249 Salsifis 505
4250 Salsifis à la Crème 505
4251 Salsifis Frits 505
4252 Salsifis au Gratin 505
4253 Salsifis Sautés 505
4251 Salsify, Fried 505
Salt Cod, see under Morue
267 Salt curing, dry 37
3772 Sandpiper 455
3937 Sandpiper, Roast 474
4961 Sandwiches 580
4962 Sandwich, Bookmakers' 581
3548 Sanglier 428
3772 Sarcelle 455
1056 Sardines 131
1848 Sardines à l'Antiboise 215
1849 Sardines à la Basque 215
1850 Sardines Bonne-Femme 215
1851 Sardines, Coulibiac de 215
1852 Sardines à la Courtisane 215
1174 Sardines, Dartois aux 142
1853 Sardines, Dartois de 215
4950 Sardines à la Diable 579
1854 Sardines à la Havraise 215
1855 Sardines à la Hyéroise 215
1856 Sardines à la Ménagère 215
1857 Sardines à la Niçoise 215
1858 Sardines à la Pisane 216
1860 Sardines Saint-Honorat 216
1859 Sardines à la Sicilienne 216
1861 Sardines à la Toulonnaise 216
1862 Sardines à la Vivandière 216
4360 Sauce à l'Abricot 520
164 Sauce, Albert 26
83 Sauce Albuféra 17
23 Sauce Allemande 8
84 Sauce Américaine 17
195 Sauce Andalouse 29
85 Sauce Anchois 17
85 Sauce Anchovy 17
4356 Sauce Anglaise 519
165 Sauce, Apple 26
166 Sauce, Aromatic 26
86 Sauce Aurore 17
87 Sauce Aurore, Maigre 17
93 Sauce Bâtarde 18
88 Sauce Bavaroise 17
89 Sauce Béarnaise 17
91 Sauce Béarnaise à la Glace de Viande 18
90 Sauce Béarnaise Tomatée 18
25 Sauce Béchamel 9
92 Sauce Bercy 18
93 Sauce au Beurre 18
27 Sauce Bigarade 10
20 Sauce Blanche Grasse 8
196 Sauce Bohémienne 29
63 Sauce, Bone Marrow 14
94 Sauce Bonnefoy 18
28 Sauce Bordelaise 10
94 Sauce Bordelaise au Vin Blanc 18
29 Sauce Bourguignonne 10
3957 Sauce for Braised Vegetables 476
167 Sauce, Bread 26
30 Sauce Bretonne 10
95 Sauce Bretonne (for fish) 18
60 Sauce, Brown Onion 14
184 Sauce, Brown Oyster 28
93 Sauce, Butter 18
169 Sauce, Butter (English Style) 27
216 Sauce, Cambridge 32
96 Sauce Canotière 18
170 Sauce, Caper (English) 27
97 Sauce aux Câpres 18
98 Sauce Cardinal 19
171 Sauce, Celery 27
31 Sauce aux Cerises 10
4571 Sauce aux Cerises, for cold sweets 543
4361 Sauce aux Cerises, for hot sweets 520
32 Sauce aux Champignons 10
99 Sauce aux Champignons (white) 19
100 Sauce Chantilly 19
197 Sauce Chantilly (cold) 29
33 Sauce Charcutière 11
34 Sauce Chasseur 11
35 Sauce Chasseur, Escoffier's Method 11
101 Sauce Chateaubriand 19
103 Sauce Chaud-froid, Blond 19
37 Sauce Chaud-froid, Brown, for ducks 11
38 Sauce Chaud-froid, Brown, for game 11
36 Sauce Chaud-froid Brune 11
106 Sauce Chaud-froid, Fish 19
105 Sauce Chaud-froid, Green 19
104 Sauce Chaud-froid, Pink 19
39 Sauce Chaud-froid, tomato-flavoured 11
102 Sauce Chaud-froid, White 19
31 Sauce, Cherry 10
40 Sauce Chevreuil 11
107 Sauce Chivry 20
4357 Sauce au Chocolat 519
90 Sauce Choron 18
41 Sauce Colbert 11
172 Sauce, Cranberry 27
109 Sauce, Cream 20
173 Sauce, Cream (English) 27
109 Sauce à la Crème 20
110 Sauce aux Crevettes 20
217 Sauce, Cumberland 32
112 Sauce Currie à l'Indienne 20
111 Sauce, Curry 20
112 Sauce, Curry (Indian Style) 20
18 Sauce Demi-glace 8
42 Sauce, Devilled 12
174 Sauce, Devilled (English) 27
43 Sauce, Devilled, Escoffier 12
42 Sauce Diable 12
43 Sauce Diable Escoffier 12
44 Sauce Diane 12
113 Sauce Diplomate 20
45 Sauce Duxelles 12
114 Sauce Ecossaise 20
175 Sauce, Egg 27
176 Sauce, Egg and Butter 27
16 Sauce Espagnole 7
17 Sauce Espagnole Maigre 8
46 Sauce Estragon 12
115 Sauce Estragon (white) 21
177 Sauce, Fennel 27
47 Sauce Financière 12
48 Sauce aux Fines Herbes 12
116 Sauce aux Fines Herbes (white) 21

91 Sauce Foyot 18
4362 Sauce aux Fraises 520
4363 Sauce Framboises 520
178 Sauce, Fried Bread 28
4359 Sauces, Fruit 519
49 Sauce Genevoise 12
198 Sauce Génoise 29
218 Sauce, Gloucester 32
50 Sauce Godard 13
118 Sauce, Gooseberry 21
51 Sauce Grand-Veneur 13
52 Sauce Grand-Veneur (Escoffier's Method) 13
53 Sauce Gratin 13
199 Sauce Gribiche 30
179 Sauce, Gooseberry (English) 28
213 Sauce, Green 31
118 Sauce Groseilles 21
4364 Sauce Groseilles, sweet 520
200 Sauce Groseilles au Raifort 30
54 Sauce Hachée 13
55 Sauce Hachée (Lenten) 13
119 Sauce Hollandaise 21
120 Sauce Homard 21
121 Sauce Hongroise 21
180 Sauce, Horseradish 28
219 Sauce, Horseradish, Cold 32
208 Sauce, Horseradish with Walnuts 31
122 Sauce aux Huîtres 21
56 Sauce Hussarde 13
123 Sauce Indienne 21
57 Sauce Italienne 14
201 Sauce Italienne (cold) 30
124 Sauce Ivoire 21
125 Sauce Joinville 21
126 Sauce Laguipierre 22
127 Sauce Livonienne 22
120 Sauce, Lobster 21
181 Sauce, Lobster (English) 28
60 Sauce Lyonnaise 14
61 Sauce Madère 14
128 Sauce Maltaise 22
129 Sauce Marinière 22
62 Sauce Matelote 14
130 Sauce Matelote Blanche 22
202 Sauce Mayonnaise 30
203 Sauce Mayonnaise Collée 30
204 Sauce Mayonnaise fouettée à la Russe 31
205 Sauce Mayonnaise, various 31
220 Sauce, Mint 32
63 Sauce Moelle 14
131 Sauce Mornay 22
64 Sauce Moscovite 14
206 Sauce Mousquetaire 31
132 Sauce Mousseline 22
133 Sauce Mousseuse 22
134 Sauce Moutarde 22
207 Sauce Moutarde à la Crème 31
32 Sauce Mushroom 10
134 Sauce, Mustard 22
207 Sauce, Mustard and Cream 31
135 Sauce Nantua 22
137 Sauce Newburg (with cooked lobster) 23
136 Sauce Newburg (with raw lobster) 23
138 Sauce Noisette 23
4366 Sauce Noisette, sweet 520
139 Sauce Normande 23
182 Sauce, Onion (English) 28
4365 Sauce à l'Orange 520
140 Sauce Orientale 23
221 Sauce, Oxford 32
122 Sauce, Oyster 21
183 Sauce, Oyster (English) 28
141 Sauce Paloise 23
185 Sauce, Parsley 28
186 Sauce, Parsley (for fish) 28
66 Sauce Périgourdine 14
65 Sauce Périgueux 14
67 Sauce Piquante 14
165 Sauce aux Pommes 26
68 Sauce Poivrade 15
69 Sauce Poivrade (for game) 15
70 Sauce au Porto 15
70 Sauce, Port Wine 15
187 Sauce, Port Wine (English) 28
71 Sauce Portugaise 15
142 Sauce Poulette 23
72 Sauce Provençale 15
208 Sauce Raifort aux Noix 31
143 Sauce Ravigote 24
209 Sauce Ravigote, cold 31
200 Sauce, Redcurrant and Horseradish 30
81 Sauce, Red Wine 16
188 Sauce, Reform 28
73 Sauce Régence 15
144 Sauce Régence (for fish) 24
145 Sauce Régence (for poultry) 24
210 Sauce Remoulade 31
146 Sauce Riche 24
74 Sauce Robert 15
75 Sauce Robert Escoffier 15
189 Sauce, Roebuck 28
76 Sauce Romaine 16
77 Sauce Rouennaise 16
147 Sauce Rubens 24
211 Sauce Russe 31
190 Sauce, Sage and Onion 29
148 Sauce Saint-Malo 24
78 Sauce Salmis 16
191 Sauce, Scotch Egg 29
110 Sauce, Shrimp 20
192 Sauce, Shrimp (English) 29
149 Sauce Smitane 24
150 Sauce Solferino 24
151 Sauce Soubise 24
152 Sauce Soubise Tomatée 25
153 Sauce Souchet 25
215 Sauce Suédoise 32
24 Sauce Suprême 9
46 Sauce, Tarragon 12
115 Sauce, Tarragon (white) 21
212 Sauce Tartare 31
26 Sauce Tomate 9
79 Sauce Tortue 16
154 Sauce Tyrolienne 25
155 Sauce Tyrolienne à l'Ancienne 25
91 Sauce Valois 18
80 Sauce Venaison 16
157 Sauce Vénitienne 25
158 Sauce Véron 25
213 Sauce Verte 31
159 Sauce Villageoise 159
160 Sauce Villeroy 26
161 Sauce Villeroy Soubisée 26
162 Sauce Villeroy Tomatée 26
163 Sauce Vin Blanc 26
214 Sauce Vincent 32
81 Sauce au Vin Rouge 16
99 Sauce, White Mushroom 19
163 Sauce, White Wine 26
193 Sauce, Yorkshire 29
82 Sauce Zingara 17
3004 Saucisses Anglaises 361
3005 Saucisses aux Choux 361
3007 Saucisses à la Marmelade de Pommes 361
3008 Saucisses, Pouding de, à l'Anglaise 361
3009 Saucisses au Risotto 362
3010 Saucisses au Vin Blanc 362
4054 Sauerkraut 486
1655 Saumon, Cadgery de 194
1656 Saumon, Coquilles de 194
1657 Saumon, Côtelettes de 194
1658 Saumon, Côtelettes de, d'Artois 195
1659 Saumon, Côtelettes de, Clarence 195
1660 Saumon, Côtelettes de, à l'Italienne 195
1661 Saumon, Côtelettes de, Pojarski 195
1662 Saumon, Coulibiac de 195
1663 Saumon, Coulibiacs, de small 196
1664 Saumon, Darne de, Chambord 196
1665 Saumon, Darne de, à la Danoise 196
1666 Saumon, Darne de, Daumont 196
1667 Saumon, Darne de, à la Dieppoise 196
1668 Saumon, Darne de, à l'Ecossaise 197
1669 Saumon, Darne de, Lucullus 197
1670 Saumon, Darne de, Nesselrode 197
1671 Saumon, Darne de, Régence 197
1672 Saumon, Darne de, à la Royale 197
1673 Saumon, Darne de, Valois 197
1674 Saumon, Escalopes de 197
1682 Saumon Froid en Belle-Vue 198
1683 Saumon Froid au Beurre de Montpellier 199
1684 Saumon Froid au Chambertin 199
1692 Saumon Froid Riga 200
1690 Saumon Froid à la Norvégienne 199
1691 Saumon Froid à la Parisienne 200
1693 Saumon Froid à la Royale 200
1060 Saumon Fumé 132
976 Saumon Fumé, Duchesses au 126
1675 Saumon Grillé 197
1687 Saumon, Médaillons de, Froids 199
1676 Saumon à la Meunière 197
1688 Saumon, Mousse de, Froide 199
1689 Saumon, Mousselines de, Froides 199
1678 Saumon, Mousselines de, Alexandra 198
1679 Saumon, Mousselines de, Tosca 198
3779 Saumon, Pâté de 458
1680 Saumon Régence 198
1694 Saumon, Salade de 200
1059 Sausage, Chicken 132

1059 Sausage, Goose Liver 132
3008 Sausage Pudding 361
Sausages, see also under Saucisses
1058 Sausages, Arles 131
1058 Sausages, Bologna 131
3005 Sausages with Cabbage 361
959 Sausages, Cervelas 125
3004 Sausage, English 361
3006 Sausages, Frankfurt, Hot 361
1057 Sausages, Frankfurt, for Hors-d'Oeuvre 131
1058 Sausages, Lyons 131
1059 Sausage, Pheasant 132
1057 Sausages, Strasbourg, for Hors-d'Oeuvre 131
3006 Sausages, Strasbourg, Hot 361
1057 Sausages, Viennese 131
1251 Sausselis aux Anchois 150
1252 Sausselis aux Choux 150
1253 Sausselis de Filets de Sole 150
2179 Sauté, Method of 261
2906 Sauté d'Agneau Chasseur 349
2907 Sauté d'Agneau à la Forestière 349
2908 Sauté d'Agneau Printanier 350
2473 Sauté de Boeuf Tolstoï 299
3622 Sauté de Faisan 439
3623 Sauté de Faisan aux Champignons 439
3626 Sauté de Faisan au Suc d'Orange Amère 439
3624 Sauté de Faisan aux Suc d'Ananas 439
3625 Sauté de Faisan au Suc de Mandarines 439
3627 Sauté de Faisan aux Truffles 439
3427 Sauté de Pigeonneaux des Sylvains 411
2743 Sauté de Veau aux Aubergines 329
2744 Sauté de Veau Catalane 329
2745 Sauté de Veau aux Champignons 329
2746 Sauté de Veau Chasseur 329
2747 Sauté de Veau aux Fines Herbes 330
2748 Sauté de Veau à l'Indienne 330
2749 Sauté de Veau Marengo 330
2750 Sauté de Veau aux Nouilles 330
2751 Sauté de Veau à l'Oranaise 330
2753 Sauté de Veau à la Portugaise 330
2752 Sauté de Veau Printanier 330
Sautés of Chicken, see under Poulet Sauté
4318 Savarin Paste 514
4328 Savoy Biscuit Paste 515
4568 Schâleth à la Juive 542
4951 Scotch Woodcock 579
3772 Scoter 455
Scollops, see also under Coquilles Saint-Jacques
2158 Scollops, to Cook 254
1726 Sea Perch 205
2149 Sea Urchins, see also under Oursins 253
4080 Seakale 489
2896 Selle d'Agneau à la Grecque 348
2898 Selle d'Agneau de Lait Edouard VII 348
2897 Selle d'Agneau Washington 348
3540 Selle de Chevreuil Briand 427
3541 Selle de Chevreuil aux Cerises 427
3542 Selle de Chevreuil Cherville 427
3543 Selle de Chevreuil à la Crème 427
3544 Selle de Chevreuil à la Créole 427
3545 Selle de Chevreuil au Genièvre 427
3546 Selle de Chevreuil Grand Veneur (Scottish Method) 427
2700 Selle de Veau à la Chartreuse 324
2711 Selle de Veau Froide 325
2701 Selle de Veau Matignon 324
2702 Selle de Veau Metternich 324
2703 Selle de Veau Nelson 324
2704 Selle de Veau à l'Orientale 325
2706 Selle de Veau Orloff 325
2705 Selle de Veau à la Piémontaise 325
2707 Selle de Veau Renaissance 325
2708 Selle de Veau Romanoff 325
2709 Selle de Veau Talleyrand 325
2710 Selle de Veau Tosca 325
4624 Semolina Pudding, à la Crème 551
1574 Shad, Grilled 185
1575 Shad, Grilled with Sorrel 185
1573 Shad, Stuffed 185
2805 Sheeps Trotters, see also under Pieds de Mouton
Shellfish, see also under Crustacés
1564 Shellfish, Mousselines of 184
259 Shellfish Oil 35
507 Shellfish Royale 72
1254 Shellfish Soufflés, Small 150
4308 Short Paste, Ordinary 513
4309 Short Paste, Fine Quality 513
3903 Shoulder of Lamb, Roast 472
Shoulder of Mutton and Grass Lamb 334
3903 Shoulder of Mutton, Roast 472
2926 Shoulder of Pork 351
Shoulder of Veal 306
3772 Shoveller 455
232 Shrimp Butter 34
110 Shrimp Sauce 20
Shrimps, see under Crevettes
1061 Sigui Fumé 132
2185 Sirloin of Beef (with the fillet) 267
2214 Sirlon of Beef (without the fillet) 270
2215 Sirloin of Beef, Cold 271
3892 Sirloin of Beef, Roast 471
2216 Sirloin Steaks, see also under Entrecôte 271
Skate, see also under Raie 213
1824 Skate with Beurre Noir or Beurre Noisette 213
1744 Smelts, see also under Eperlans 206
978 Smelts, marinated 126
924 Smoked Eel 122
933 Smoked Hamburg Beef 123
Smoked Salmon, see also under Saumon Fumé
255 Smoked Salmon Butter 35
Snails, see also under Escargots
2162 Snails, to prepare 255
235 Snail Butter 34
3927 Snipe, Roast 474
Snipes 451
1100 Soft Roe Fritters 135
Soft Roes, see also under Laitances
1863 Sole Alice 216
1865 Sole à l'Amiral 217
1864 Sole d'Antin 217
1866 Sole à l'Arlésienne 217
1867 Sole Bedfort 217
1868 Sole Bercy 217
1869 Sole Bonne-Femme 217
1870 Sole au Chambertin 217
1871 Sole au Champagne 217
1872 Sole Cléopâtre 217
1873 Sole Colbert 218
1874 Sole Coquelin 218
1875 Sole Cubat 218
1876 Sole Daumont 218
1877 Sole Deauvillaise 218
1878 Sole à la Dieppoise 218
1879 Sole Diplomate 218
1880 Sole Dorée 218
1900 Sole à la Doria 220
1881 Sole Dugléré 218
1882 Sole à l'Espagnole 218
1883 Sole à la Fermière 219
1884 Sole à la Florentine 219
1885 Sole au Gratin 219
1886 Sole Grillée 219
1887 Sole Grillée aux Huîtres à l'Américaine 219
1888 Sole à la Hollandaise 219
1889 Sole à l'Hôtelière 219
1891 Sole Jouffroy 219
1890 Sole Jules Janin 219
1892 Sole Lutèce 220
1893 Sole Marchand de Vins 220
1894 Sole à la Marinière 220
1895 Sole à la Ménagère 220
1896 Sole à la Meunière 220
1897 Sole Meunière aux Aubergines 220
1898 Sole Meunière aux Cèpes 220
1899 Sole Meunière aux Champignons 220
1900 Sole Meunière aux Concombres 220
1901 Sole Meunière aux Morilles 220
1904 Sole Meunière à l'Orange 221
1902 Sole Meunière à la Provençale 220
1903 Sole Meunière aux Raisins 220
1905 Sole Montgolfier 221
1906 Sole Montreuil 221
1907 Sole Mornay 221
1908 Sole Mornay "des Provencaux" 221
1988 Sole, Mousselines de 230
1909 Sole Murat 221
1911 Sole Nantua 221
1910 Sole à la Niçoise 221
1912 Sole à la Normande 221
1913 Sole à la Parisienne 221
3780 Sole, Pâté de 458
2027 Sole, Pâté Chaud, à la Dieppoise 233
2000 Sole, Paupiettes de 231
2045 Sole, Paupiettes en Timbale 237
3780 Sole Pie 458
1915 Sole à la Portugaise 222
1916 Sole à la Provençale 222
1917 Sole Régence 222
1918 Sole Richelieu 222
1919 Sole à la Rochelaise 222
1920 Sole à la Rouennaise 222
1921 Sole à la Royale 222

1922 Sole à la Russe 223
1923 Sole Saint-Germain 223
1924 Sole Saint-Malo 223
1914 Sole sur le Plat 222
1925 Sole au Vin Blanc 223
1926 Sole au Vin Rouge 223
2036 Sole, Vol-au-Vent à la Marinière 235
2037 Sole, Vol-au-Vent à la Présidence 235
1926a Soles aux Grands Vins 223
1927 Sole, Filets de, à l'Americaine 224
1929 Sole, Filets de, à l'Andalouse 224
1928 Sole, Filets de, à l'Anglaise 224
1930 Sole, Filets de, à l'Armoricaine 224
1089 Sole, Filets de, Barquettes de 135
1931 Sole, Filets de, Belle-Meunière 224
1932 Sole, Filets de, Bénédictine 224
1933 Sole, Filets de, Bercy 224
1934 Sole, Filets de, Boitelle 224
1935 Sole, Filets de, à la Bourguignonne 224
2040 Sole, Filets de, Calypso 236
1936 Sole, Filets de, à la Cancalaise 224
1937 Sole, Filets de, Caprice 225
1938 Sole, Filets de, Cardinal 225
1939 Sole, Filets de, à la Catalane 225
1940 Sole, Filets de, aux Champignons 225
2041 Sole, Filets de, Charlotte 236
1941 Sole, Filets de, Chauchat 225
1942 Sole, Filets de, à la Chevalière 225
1943 Sole, Filets de, à la Chivry 225
1944 Sole, Filets de, Clarence 225
1945 Sole, Filets de, Condé 225
1946 Sole, Filets de, aux Courgettes 225
1947 Sole, Filets de, aux Crevettes 226
1948 Sole, Filets de, Cubat 226
1172 Sole, Filets de, Dartois aux 142
1950 Sole, Filets de, Daumont 226
1951 Sole, Filets de, à la Deauvillaise 226
1952 Sole, Filets de, Déjazet 226
1953 Sole, Filets de, à la Dieppoise 226
1954 Sole, Filets de, Diplomate 226
1955 Sole, Filets de, Doria 226
1956 Sole, Filets de, Dubois 226
1957 Sole, Filets de, à la Duse 226
1958 Sole, Filets de, en Epigrammes 226
1959 Sole, Filets de, Floréal 227
1960 Sole, Filets de, à la Florentine 227
1961 Sole, Filets de, en Goujons 227
1962 Sole, Filets de, Grand-Duc 227
1963 Sole, Filets de, au Gratin 227
1964 Sole, Filets de, Héléna 227
1965 Sole, Filets de, Héloise 227
1966 Sole, Filets de, aux Huîtres 227
1967 Sole, Filets de, à l'Indienne 227
1968 Sole, Filets de, Ismaïla 227
1969 Sole, Filets de, Jean-Bart 227
1970 Sole, Filets de, Joinville 228
1971 Sole, Filets de, en Julienne 228
1972 Sole, Filets de, Lady Egmont 228
1974 Sole, Filets de, Manon 228
1975 Sole, Filets de, Marcelle 228
1976 Sole, Filets de, Marguery 228
1977 Sole, Filets de, Marie-Stuart 228
1978 Sole, Filets de, Marinette 229
1979 Sole, Filets de, à la Marinière 229
1980 Sole, Filets de, Marquise 229
1981 Sole, Filets de, Mexicaine 229
1982 Sole, Filets de, Mignonette 229
1983 Sole, Filets de, Miramar 229
1984 Sole, Filets de, Mogador 229
1985 Sole, Filets de, Montreuil 229
1986 Sole, Filets de, Montrouge 229
2042 Sole, Filets de, à la Moscovite 236
1987 Sole, Filets de, aux Moules 230
1989 Sole, Filets de, Murat 230
1990 Sole, Filets de, Nelson 230
1991 Sole, Filets de, Nemours 230
1992 Sole, Filets de, Newburg 230
1993 Sole, Filets de, à la Normande 230
1994 Sole, Filets de, Olga 230
1995 Sole, Filets de, à l'Orientale 230
1996 Sole, Filets de, à la d'Orléans 230
1997 Sole, Filets de, Orly 230
1998 Sole, Filets de, à l'Ostendaise 231
1994 Sole, Filets de, Otéro 230
2001 Sole, Filets de, à la Paysanne 231
2002 Sole, Filets de, à la Persane 231
2003 Sole, Filets de, en Pilaw à la Levantine 231
2004 Sole, Filets de, Polignac 231
2005 Sole, Filets de, Pompadour 231
2006 Sole, Filets de, à la Portugaise 232
2008 Sole, Filets de, Rachel 232
2009 Sole, Filets de, Régence 232
2010 Sole, Filets de, Rhodésia 232
2011 Sole, Filets de, Riche 232
2012 Sole, Filets de, Rochelaise 232
2013 Sole, Filets de, Rosine 232
2014 Sole, Filets de, à la Rouennaise 232
2015 Sole, Filets de, Saint-Germain 232
1253 Sole, Filets de, Sausselis de 150
2016 Sole, Filets de, Talleyrand 232
2017 Sole, Filets de, Tivoli 232
2018 Sole, Filets de, Trouvillaise 232
2019 Sole, Filets de, d'Urville 233
2020 Sole, Filets de, Valentino 233
1973 Sole, Filets de, à la Vallière 228
2021 Sole, Filets de, Vénitienne 233
2022 Sole, Filets de, Verdi 233
2023 Sole, Filets de, Véronique 233
2024 Sole, Filets de, Victoria 233
2025 Sole, Filets de, Walewska 233
2026 Sole, Filets de, Wilhelmine 233
2038 Sole, Aspic de Filets de 236
2039 Sole, Bordure de Filets, à l'Italienne 236
2043 Sole, cold fillets on Mousse 237
2029 Sole, Timbale de Filets, Cardinal 234
2028 Sole, Timbale de Filets, Carême 234
2030 Sole, Timbale de Filets, Carmelite 234
2039 Sole, Timbale de Filets, Escoffier 237
2031 Sole, Timbale de Filets, Grimaldi 234
2032 Sole, Timbale de Filets, Marquise 235
2033 Sole, Timbale de Filets, Richepin 235
2034 Sole, Turban de Filets, Villaret 235
2035 Sole et de Saumon, Turban de Filets, Villaret 235
4910 Sorbet Mixture 574
4912 Sorbet à la Sicilienne 576
4911 Sorbets, Various 576
4155 Sorrel 496
4061 Sou-Fassum Provençal 487
152 Soubise Sauce, Tomato-flavoured 25
3772 Souchet 455
3772 Shoveller 455
4475 Soufflé, Almond 533
4475 Soufflé aux Amandes 533
4476 Soufflé aux Amandes Fraîches 533
4476 Soufflé, Fresh Almond 533
4477 Soufflé aux Avelines 533
3755 Soufflé de Bécasse 453
4478 Soufflé Camargo 533
4479 Soufflé aux Cerises 533
4479 Soufflé, Cherry 533
4046 Soufflé de Chicorée 485
4480 Soufflé, Chocolate 533
4481 Soufflé au Curaçao 533
4482 Soufflé Elizabeth 534
4102 Soufflé aux Epinards 491
4103 Soufflé aux Epinards aux Truffes 491
3628 Soufflé de Faisan 439
4483 Soufflé aux Fraises 534
4377 Soufflé Fritters, Ordinary 522
4919 Soufflé Fritters for savouries 577
4485 Soufflé aux Fruits en Croustade 534
4486 Soufflé aux Grenades à l'Orientale 534
4477 Soufflé, Hazelnut 533
4487 Soufflé Hilda 534
2126 Soufflé de Homard 249
4488 Soufflé Idéal 534
2959 Soufflé de Jambon Alexandra 356
2960 Soufflé de Jambon Carmen 356
2961 Soufflé de Jambon des Gastronomes 356
2962 Soufflé de Jambon à la Milanaise 356
2963 Soufflé de Jambon à la Périgourdine 356
2966 Soufflé, de Jambon Froid 357
4489 Soufflé Javanais 534
4135 Soufflé de Laitue 494
4490 Soufflé Lérina 534
3582 Soufflé de Lièvre 432
4492 Soufflé Lucullus 534
4141 Soufflé de Maïs à la Crème 495
4142 Soufflé de Maïs au Paprika 495
4530 Soufflé de Mandarines en Surprise 538
4471 Soufflé Mixture, cream type 533
4472 Soufflé Mixture, cream type for large numbers 533
4473 Soufflé Mixture, Fruit purée 533
4909 Soufflé Mixture, Iced Fruit 575
1816 Soufflé de Morue 212
4530 Soufflé d'Oranges en Surprise 538
4493 Soufflé à la d'Orléans 534
3666 Soufflé de Perdreau 443
4494 Soufflé Palmyre 534
4495 Soufflé Paulette 535
4285 Soufflé Piémontaise 509
4232 Soufflé de Pommes de Terre 503
4496 Soufflé Praliné 535
4497 Soufflé Rothschild 535
4498 Soufflé à la Royale 535
4483 Soufflé, Strawberry 534

4269 Soufflé de Tomate à la Napolitaine 507
4273 Soufflé de Topinambours 507
4497 Soufflé Rothschild 535
4499 Soufflé, Vanilla 535
4500 Soufflé, Violet 535
4500 Soufflé aux Violettes 535
3355 Soufflé de Volaille à la Périgord 402
335 Soufflés, Cold 52
1254 Soufflés de Crustacés, small 150
1260 Soufflés, small, Fish 150
1255 Soufflés à la Florentine, small 150
1256 Soufflés de Gibier, small 150
4909 Soufflés Glacés 575
1258 Soufflés, Ham, small 150
1257 Soufflés aux Huîtres, small 150
1258 Soufflés au Jambon, small 150
1641 Soufflés de Laitances 192
4491 Soufflés, Liqueur 534
4474 Soufflés, moulding and cooking 533
1257 Soufflés, Oyster, small 150
1259 Soufflés Parmesane, small 150
1260 Soufflés de Poisson, small 150
1254 Soufflés, Shellfish 150
1261 Soufflés à la Suissesse, small 151
Soufflés, sweet 533
866 Soup—Bennett 111
587 Soup—Birds Nest 79
667 Soup—Bisque of Crab 89
670 Soup—Bisque of Dublin Bay Prawns 89
665 Soup—Bisque d'Ecrevisses 88
666 Soup—Bisque d'Ecrevisses à l'Ancienne 88
668 Soup—Bisque of Lobster 89
669 Soup—Bisque of Prawns 89
669 Soup—Bisque of Shrimps 89
673 Soup—Celery 89
706 Soup—Chicken 93
898 Soup—Chicken Broth 116
873 Soup—Chicken Liver 112
661 Soup—Chicken Velouté, cold, for Suppers 85
894 Soup—Clear Oxtail 116
907 Soup—Clear Turtle 117
910 Soup—Clear Turtle, using commercial produce 119
511 Soup—Consommé aux Ailerons 73
512 Soup—Consommé Alexandra 73
513 Soup—Consommé à l'Ancienne 73
514 Soup—Consommé d'Aremburg 73
515 Soup—Consommé à l'Aurore 73
516 Soup—Consommé Belle Fermière 73
517 Soup—Consommé Bellini 73
518 Soup—Consommé à la Bouchère 73
519 Soup—Consommé à la Bouquetière 73
520 Soup—Consommé à la Brunoise 73
521 Soup—Consommé Carmen 73
522 Soup—Consommé Célestine 74
523 Soup—Consommé Cendrillon 74
524 Soup—Consommé Chancelière 74
525 Soup—Consommé au Chasseur 74
526 Soup—Consommé Châtelaine 74
527 Soup—Consommé aux Cheveux d'Anges 74
480 Soup—Consommé Chicken 69
528 Soup—Consommé Colbert 74
529 Soup—Consommé Colombine 74
530 Soup—Consommé Croûte au Pot 74
531 Soup—Consommé Cyrano 74
532 Soup—Consommé Dame Blanche 74
533 Soup—Consommé Demidoff 74
534 Soup—Consommé Deslignac 75
535 Soup—Consommé aux Diablotins 75
536 Soup—Consommé Diane 75
537 Soup—Consommé Diplomate 75
538 Soup—Consommé Divette 75
539 Soup—Consommé Dominicaine 75
540 Soup—Consommé Doria 75
541 Soup—Consommé Douglas 75
542 Soup—Consommé Dubarry 75
543 Soup—Consommé à l'Ecossaise 75
544 Soup—Consommé Edouard VII 75
648 Soup—Consommé à l'Essence de Caille 84
649 Soup—Consommé à l'Essence de Céleri 84
650 Soup—Consommé à l'Essence d'Estragon 84
652 Soup—Consommé à l'Essence de Morille 84
654 Soup—Consommé à l'Essence de Truffe 84
482 Soup—Consommé, double fish 69
545 Soup—Consommé Flavigny 75
546 Soup—Consommé Florial 75
547 Soup—Consommé Florentine 76
548 Soup—Consommé Florian 76
657 Soup—Consommé au Fumet de Perdreau 85
481 Soup—Consommé, Game 69
549 Soup—Consommé à la Gauloise 76
550 Soup—Consommé Georges V 76
551 Soup—Consommé Germinal 76
481 Soup—Consommé de Gibier 69
552 Soup—Consommé Gladiateur 76
553 Soup—Consommé Grimaldi 76
554 Soup—Consommé Hélène 76
555 Soup—Consommé Henriette 76
556 Soup—Consommé à l'Indienne 76
557 Soup—Consommé à l'Infante 76
558 Soup—Consommé Isabelle de France 76
559 Soup—Consommé Ivan 76
560 Soup—Consommé Jeanne Granier 76
561 Soup—Consommé Judic 77
562 Soup—Consommé Julienne 77
563 Soup—Consommé Juliette 77
564 Soup—Consommé Kléber 77
565 Soup—Consommé La Perouse 77
566 Soup—Consommé Lorette 77
567 Soup—Consommé Lucette 77
568 Soup—Consommé Lucullus 77
569 Soup—Consommé à la Madrilène 77
570 Soup—Consommé Maintenon 77
571 Soup—Consommé Messaline 77
572 Soup—Consommé Midinette 77
573 Soup—Consommé Mikado 77
574 Soup—Consommé Mireille 78
575 Soup—Consommé Mirette 78
576 Soup—Consommé Mistral 78
577 Soup—Consommé Monsigny 78
578 Soup—Consommé Montespan 78
579 Soup—Consommé Montmorency 78
580 Soup—Consommé Murat 78
581 Soup—Consommé Murillo 78
582 Soup—Consommé Nana 78
583 Soup—Consommé Nantua 78
584 Soup—Consommé à la Neige de Florence 78
585 Soup—Consommé Nelson 78
586 Soup—Consommé Nesselrode 78
587 Soup—Consommé aux Nids d'Hirondelle 79
588 Soup—Consommé Ninon 79
479 Soup—Consommé, Ordinary 68
589 Soup—Consommé à l'Orge Perlé 79
590 Soup—Consommé à l'Orientale 79
591 Soup—Consommé Olga 79
592 Soup—Consommé à la d'Orléans 79
593 Soup—Consommé Orloff 79
594 Soup—Consommé d'Orsay 79
595 Soup—Consommé Otello 79
596 Soup—Consommé Otéro 79
655 Soup—Consommé aux Paillettes d'Or 84
597 Soup—Consommé Palestro 80
598 Soup—Consommé with Italian Pasta or Cereals 80
599 Soup—Consommé Petite Mariée 80
653 Soup—Consommé aux Piments Doux 84
482 Soup—Consommé de Poisson, Double 69
601 Soup—Consommé Polaire 80
602 Soup—Consommé Pompadour 80
603 Soup—Consommé Portalis 80
656 Soup—Consommé à la Portugaise 84
604 Soup—Consommé Printanier 80
605 Soup—Consommé aux Quenelles à la Moelle 80
606 Soup—Consommé Queue de Boeuf à la Française 80
607 Soup—Consommé Rabelais 81
608 Soup—Consommé Rachel 81
609 Soup—Consommé aux Raviolis 81
610 Soup—Consommé Récamier 81
611 Soup—Consommé à la Reine 81
612 Soup—Consommé Renaissance 81
613 Soup—Consommé Rossini 81
614 Soup—Consommé à la Royale 81
615 Soup—Consommé au Sagou 81

616 Soup—Consommé Saint-Hubert 81
617 Soup—Consommé au Salep 81
618 Soup—Consommé Sapho 81
620 Soup—Consommé Séverine 82
621 Soup—Consommé Sévigné 82
622 Soup—Consommé Solange 82
623 Soup—Consommé Staël 82
624 Soup—Consommé Stanley 82
625 Soup—Consommé Suzette 82
626 Soup—Consommé Talleyrand 82
627 Soup—Consommé au Tapioca 82
628 Soup—Consommé Théodora 82
629 Soup—Consommé Toréador 82
630 Soup—Consommé Tosca 82
631 Soup—Consommé Toulousaine 82
632 Soup—Consommé à la Trévise 82
633 Soup—Consommé Tyrolienne 83
634 Soup—Consommé d'Uzès 83
635 Soup—Consommé Valromey 83
636 Soup—Consommé Vendôme 83
637 Soup—Consommé Verdi 83
638 Soup—Consommé Vermandoise 83
639 Soup—Consommé au Vermicelle 83
640 Soup—Consommé des Viveurs 83
480 Soup—Consommé de Volaille 69
641 Soup—Consommé Warwick 83
642 Soup—Consommé Washington 83
511 Soup—Consommé with Chicken Winglets 73
643 Soup—Consommé Wladimir 83
644 Soup—Consommé Yvetot 83
Soup—Consommés, clarification of 68
647 Soup—Consommés, Special for suppers, hot or cold 84
658 Soup—Consommés with Wine 85
665 Soup, Coulis d'Ecrevisses 88
666 Soup, Coulis d'Ecrevisses à l'Ancienne 88
706 Soup—Coulis à la Reine 93
722 Soup—Cream of Lettuce 95
727 Soup—Cream of Pearl Barley 96
728 Soup—Cream of Sorrel and Oatmeal 96
729 Soup—Cream of Sorrel with Barley 96
709 Soup—Crème Agnes Sorel 94
710 Soup—Crème Antonelli 94
711 Soup—Crème Argenteuil 94
712 Soup—Crème d'Artichauts à la Noisette 94
713 Soup—Crème Cérès 94
714 Soup—Crème Chevreuse 94
715 Soup—Crème Choisy 95
716 Soup—Crème Comtesse 95
717 Soup—Crème Divette 95
718 Soup—Crème Hamilton 95
719 Soup—Crème Judic 95
720 Soup—Crème La Fayette 95
721 Soup—Crème Lafitte 95
722 Soup—Crème de Laitue 95
723 Soup—Crème La Vallière 95
724 Soup—Crème Lison 96
725 Soup—Crème de Maïs 96
726 Soup—Crème Nivernaise 96
727 Soup—Crème d'Orge 96
728 Soup—Crème d'Oseille à l'Avoine 96
729 Soup—Crème d'Oseille à l'Orge 96
730 Soup—Crème Pérette 96
731 Soup—Crème Princesse 96
732 Soup—Crème Régence 96
733 Soup—Crème Reine Margot 97
734 Soup—Crème Sultane 97
735 Soup—Crème Suzanne 97
736 Soup—Crème Turbigo 97
699 Soup—Fresh Pea 93
700 Soup—Fresh Pea with mint 93
660 Soup—Gelée de Volaille aux Pommes d'Amour 85
659 Soup—Gelée de Volaille Napolitaine 85
864 Soup—Giblet 111
912 Soup—Green Turtle, using commercial produce 119
878 Soup—Hare 113
791 Soup—Invalid 103
902 Soup—Kidney 117
874 Soup—Leberknodeln 112
875 Soup—Leber-suppe 113
885 Soup—Mock Turtle 114
888 Soup—Mutton Broth 115
895 Soup—Oxtail, Thick 116
896 Soup—Oyster with Okra 116
698 Soup—Pea, with croûtons 92
892 Soup—Pearl Barley and Celery 115
475 Soup—Petite Marmite, Preparation 67
600 Soup—Petite Marmite, Service 80
772 Soup—Potage Ambassadeur 101
773 Soup—Potage Américain 101
864 Soup—Potage aux Abattis à l'Anglaise 111
774 Soup—Potage Bagration gras 102
775 Soup—Potage Bagration Maigre 102
776 Soup—Potage Balvet 102
865 Soup—Potage Batwinia 111
777 Soup—Potage Bohémienne 102
867 Soup—Potage Bortsch Koop 111
868 Soup—Potage Bortsch Polonais 111
874 Soup—Potage aux Boulettes de Foie 112
778 Soup—Potage Brunoise Lié 102
869 Soup—Potage Camaro à la Brésilienne 112
779 Soup—Potage Chabrillan 102
780 Soup—Potage à la Champenoise 102
781 Soup—Potage à la Chantilly 102
871 Soup—Potage Clam Chowder 112
872 Soup—Potage Cocky-Leeky 112
782 Soup—Potage Derby 102
783 Soup—Potage Emilienne d'Alençon 102
784 Soup—Potage Fanchette 102
785 Soup—Potage Faubonne 102
885 Soup—Potage Fausse Tortue 114
786 Soup—Potage Fémina 103
873 Soup—Potage aux Foies de Volaille à l'Anglaise 112
787 Soup—Potage Fontages 103
834 Soup—Potage Garbure à la Béarnaise 107
835 Soup—Potage Garbure-Cooper 107
836 Soup—Potage Garbure Crécy 107
837 Soup—Potage Garbure Dauphinoise 107
838 Soup—Potage Garbure à la Freneuse 107
839 Soup—Potage Garbure à l'Oignon 107
841 Soup—Potage Garbure à la Savoyarde 108
840 Soup—Potage Garbure à la Paysanne 108
788 Soup—Potage Gentilhomme 103
789 Soup—Potage Germiny 103
790 Soup—Potage Girondins 103
890 Soup—Potage aux Gombos 115
843 Soup—Potage Hochepot à l'Ancienne 108
877 Soup—Potage Hochepot à la Flamande 113
792 Soup—Potage Jack 103
793 Soup—Potage Josselin 103
776 Soup—Potage Jubilée 102
795 Soup—Potage Julienne Darblay 103
796 Soup—Potage Lamballe 103
878 Soup—Potage aux Lièvre 113
879 Soup—Potage Lithuanien 113
880 Soup—Potage Livonien aux Kloskis 113
797 Soup—Potage Longchamps 103
798 Soup—Potage Madelon 103
800 Soup—Potage Marcilly 104
799 Soup—Potage Marigny 103
881 Soup—Potage Mille-Fanti 114
882 Soup—Potage Mille-Fanti clair 114
883 Soup—Potage Minestra 114
884 Soup—Potage Miss Betsy 114
886 Soup—Potage de Mouton à la Grecque 115
887 Soup—Potage Mulligatawny 115
801 Soup—Potage Narbonnais 104
802 Soup—Potage Nicolini 104
889 Soup—Potage aux Noques 115
890 Soup—Potage Okra 115
891 Soup—Potage Olla-Podrida 115
892 Soup—Potage d'Orge au Céleri 115
893 Soup—Potage Ouka 116
894 Soup—Potage Oxtail-Clair 116
895 Soup—Potage Oxtail Lié 116
897 Soup—Potage au Pistou 116
803 Soup—Potage Polignac 104
898 Soup—Potage de Poulet à l'Anglaise 116
899 Soup—Potage Puchéro 117
875 Soup—Potage à la Purée de Foie 113
900 Soup—Potage à la Purée de Jambon 117
805 Soup—Potage Purée d'Oseille et de Tapioca à la Crème 104
804 Soup—Potage Purée d'Oseille et de Vermicelle à la Crème 104
806 Soup—Potage Queue de Boeuf à la Napolitaine 104
807 Soup—Potage Rabagas 104

808 Soup—Potage Réjane 104
902 Soup—Potage aux Rognons à l'Anglaise 117
901 Soup—Potage au Rognon de Veau 117
903 Soup—Potage Rossolnick 117
809 Soup—Potage Saint-Julien 104
810 Soup—Potage Saint-Marceaux 104
811 Soup—Potage de Santé 104
619 Soup—Potage Sarah-Bernhardt 81
904 Soup—Potage Selianka 117
812 Soup—Potage Simone 104
815 Soup—Potage Sport 105
905 Soup—Potage Stchy 117
906 Soup—Potage aux Terrapines, thick or clear 117
854 Soup—Potage Thourins 109
855 Soup—Potage Thourins Roumanille 109
907 Soup—Potage à la Tortue Claire 117
909 Soup—Potage Tortue Lié 119
912 Soup—Potage à la Tortue Verte 119
813 Soup—Potage Ursuline 105
814 Soup—Potage Valaisan 105
816 Soup—Potage Velours 105
817 Soup—Potage Verneuil 105
856 Soup—Potage Villageoise 109
818 Soup—Potage Waldèze 105
819 Soup—Potage Windsor 105
852 Soup—Potée Bourguignonne 109
671 Soup—Purée Bonvalet 89
672 Soup—Purée Bressane 89
673 Soup—Purée de Céleri 89
674 Soup—Purée Clermont 89
675 Soup—Purée Compiègne 89
676 Soup—Purée Condé 90
677 Soup—Purée Conti 90
678 Soup—Purée Conti à la Brunoise 90
679 Soup—Purée Cormeilles 90
680 Soup—Purée Crécy 90
681 Soup—Purée Crécy à l'Ancienne 90
682 Soup—Purée Crécy à la Briarde 90
683 Soup—Purée Crécy au Riz, aux Perles etc. 90
684 Soup—Purée Cressonière 90
685 Soup—Purée Dubarry 91
686 Soup—Potage Esaü 91
687 Soup—Purée de Fèves 91
688 Soup—Purée Freneuse 91
689 Soup—Purée Georgette 91
690 Soup—Purée de Gibier 91
691 Soup—Purée aux Herbes 91
692 Soup—Purée Malakoff 92
693 Soup—Purée Maria 92
694 Soup—Purée Marianne 92
695 Soup—Purée Palestine 92
696 Soup—Purée Parmentier 92
697 Soup—Purée Pastorelle 92
698 Soup—Purée de Pois aux Croûtons 92
699 Soup—Purée de Pois Frais 93
700 Soup—Purée de Pois Frais à la Menthe 93
701 Soup—Purée de Potiron à la Bourgeoise 93
702 Soup—Purée de Potiron à la Maraîchère 93
703 Soup—Purée Portugaise 93
704 Soup—Purée au Pourpier 93
693 Soup—Purée Québec 92
706 Soup—Purée à la Reine 93
707 Soup—Purée Saint-Germain 94
708 Soup—Purée Soissonaise 94
703 Soup—Purée de Tomate 93
906 Soup—Terrapin, thick or clear 117
707 Soup—Tomato 93
909 Soup—Turtle, Thick 119
911 Soup—Turtle, using dried turtle meat 119
737 Soup—Velouté Albuféra 97
738 Soup—Velouté à l'Andalouse 97
739 Soup—Velouté de Blanchailles au Currie 97
740 Soup—Velouté Carmen 97
741 Soup—Velouté Cardinal 98
742 Soup—Velouté Columbine 98
743 Soup—Velouté de Crevettes à la Normande 98
744 Soup—Velouté Dame Blanche 98
745 Soup—Velouté Dieppoise 98
746 Soup—Velouté Doria 98
747 Soup—Velouté Doris 98
748 Soup—Velouté d'Ecrevisses Joinville 98
750 Soup—Velouté d'Ecrevisses à la Normande 99
749 Soup—Velouté d'Ecrevisses Princesse 99
751 Soup—Velouté d'Eperlans 99
752 Soup—Velouté d'Eperlans Dieppoise 99
753 Soup—Velouté d'Eperlans Joinville 99
754 Soup—Velouté d'Eperlans Princesse 99
755 Soup—Velouté d'Eperlans Saint-Malo 99
756 Soup—Velouté Eugénie 99
757 Soup—Velouté Excelsior 99
758 Soup—Velouté Fédora 100
759 Soup—Velouté de Homard à la Cleveland 100
760 Soup—Velouté de Homard à l'Indienne 100
761 Soup—Velouté de Homard à l'Orientale 100
762 Soup—Velouté de Homard au Paprika 100
793 Soup—Velouté aux Huîtres 100
764 Soup—Velouté Isoline 100
765 Soup—Velouté Jouvence 100
766 Soup—Velouté Marie-Louise 100
767 Soup—Velouté Nelusko 101
768 Soup—Velouté d'Orléans 101
769 Soup—Velouté Rosemonde 101
770 Soup—Velouté Thermidor 101
739 Soup—Velouté of Whitebait with Curry 97
860 Soupe Aïgo Bouido 110
861 Soupe Aïgo Bouido aux Oeufs Pochés 110
859 Soupe Aïgo à la Menagère 110
858 Soupe Aïgo-Saou 110
857 Soupe à l'Ail 110
820 Soupe à l'Albigeoise 105
823 Soupe à l'Ardennaise 106
824 Soupe à l'Auvergnate 106
825 Soupe à la Beaucaire 106
826 Soupe à la Bonne-Femme 106
827 Soupe à la Brabançonne 106
828 Soupe à la Bûcheronne 106
870 Soupe aux Cerises 112
822 Soupe à la Choucroute à l'Ancienne 106
821 Soupe au Cresson Alénois 105
829 Soupe Cultivateur 106
830 Soupe à la Dauphinoise 106
860 Soupe à l'Eau Bouillie 110
831 Soupe de l'Estérel 106
832 Soupe à la Fermière 107
833 Soupe à la Franc-Comtoise 107
842 Soupe à la Grand'Mère 108
844 Soupe Jeannette 108
845 Soupe Julienne à la Russe 108
846 Soupe du Laboureur 109
862 Soupe de Mariage 110
831 Soupe des Maures 106
863 Soupe aux Nonnats 111
847 Soupe à la Nevers 109
848 Soupe à la Normande 109
849 Soupe à l'Oignon 109
850 Soupe à la Paysanne 109
851 Soupe Poireaux et Pommes de Terre à la Maraîchère 109
853 Soupe à la Savoyarde 109
Soups, Classical Provençale 110
473 Soups, classification 65
664 Soups, Cream 87
662 Soups, Purée 85
Soups, Special 101
Soups—Special Vegetable 105
Soups—Thickened Bouillons 101
663 Soups, Velouté 86
296 Spiced Salt 46
Spinach, see also under Epinards
4094 Spinach, to cook 491
2187 Spine Marrow of Beef, see also under Amourettes 268
4916 Spooms 576
1062 Sprats, Smoked 132
Spring Chicken, see under Poulet de Grains
4086 Stachys 490
4345 Saint-Honoré Cream 518
2454 Steak Pie 296
2455 Steak and Kidney Pie 296
2456 Steak Pudding 296
2457 Steak and Kidney Pudding 296
2458 Steak and Oyster Pudding 296
2292 Steak Tartare 279
1695 Sterlet 200
1 Stock, Brown 3
6 Stock, Fish 4
5 Stock, Game 4
2 Stock, Ordinary White 3
3 Stock, White Chicken 4
4 Stock, Red Wine Fish 5
270 Stock for Ordinary Aspic Jelly 38
274 Stock for Ordinary Fish Aspic Jelly 39
272 Stock for Chicken Aspic Jelly 39
275 Stock for Red Wine Fish Aspic Jelly 40
273 Stock for Game Aspic Jelly 39

271 Stock for White Aspic Jelly 39
2046 Stockfish à la Mode des Pêcheurs Niçois 237
4371 Strawberry Fritters 521
4362 Strawberry Sauce 520
Strawberries, see also under Fraises
3887 Stuffing, Sage and Onion 470
3012 Stuffing for Sucking Pig 362
3013 Stuffing for Sucking Pig, English 362
3017 Stuffing for Poultry, Rice and Pearl Barley 363
3888 Stuffing, Veal 470
Sturgeon, see under Esturgeon
4100 Subrics d'Epinards 491
1262 Subrics de Foie gras 151
1263 Subrics à l'Italienne 151
1264 Subrics Piémontais 150
4501 Subrics, sweet 535
3011 Sucking Pig 362
3012 Sucking Pig, Stuffing for 362
4718 Suédoise de Fruits 561
4313 Suet Paste 513
3355 Sugar, cooking of 519
3463 Suprême de Caneton 416
3131 Suprême de Volaille Agnès Sorel 377
3132 Suprême de Volaille Albuféra 377
3133 Suprême de Volaille Alexandra 377
3134 Suprême de Volaille à l'Ambassadrice 377
3135 Suprême de Volaille à l'Arlésienne 377
3136 Suprême de Volaille Belle-Hélène 377
3137 Suprême de Volaille Boitelle 377
3138 Suprême de Volaille aux Champignons 377
3139 Suprême de Volaille aux Champignons (brown) 378
3140 Suprême de Volaille Chimay 378
3141 Suprême de Volaille Cussy 378
3142 Suprême de Volaille Doria 378
3143 Suprême de Volaille à la Dreux 378
3144 Suprême de Volaille à l'Ecarlate 378
3145 Suprême de Volaille à l'Ecossaise 378
3146 Suprême de Volaille Elizabeth 378
3147 Suprême de Volaille Favorite 378
3148 Suprême de Volaille Financière 378
3149 Suprême de Volaille à la Florentine 378
3150 Suprême de Volaille aux Fonds d'Artichaut 378
3151 Suprême de Volaille Henri IV 379
3152 Suprême de Volaille à la Hongroise 379
3153 Suprême de Volaille a l'Indienne 379
3154 Suprême de Volaille Jardinière 379
3381 Suprêmes de Volaille Jeannette 405
3155 Suprême de Volaille Judic 379
3156 Suprême de Volaille Maréchal 379
3157 Suprême de Volaille Marie-Louise 379
3158 Suprême de Volaille Marie-Thérèse 379
3159 Suprême de Volaille Maryland 379
3160 Suprême de Volaille Mireille 379
3161 Suprême de Volaille Montpensier 379
3162 Suprême de Volaille Orly 380
3163 Suprême de Volaille à l'Orientale 380
3164 Suprême de Volaille en Papillote 380
3165 Suprême de Volaille Parisienne 380
3166 Suprême de Volaille au Parmesan 380
3167 Suprême de Volaille à la Périgueux 380
3169 Suprême de Volaille Pojarski 380
3168 Suprême de Volaille Polignac 380
3170 Suprême de Volaille Régence 380
3171 Suprême de Volaille Richelieu 380
3172 Suprême de Volaille Rimini 380
3173 Suprême de Volaille Rossini 380
3174 Suprême de Volaille Saint-Germain 380
3175 Suprême de Volaille Talleyrand 381
3176 Suprême de Volaille Valençay 381
3177 Suprême de Volaille Valois 381
3178 Suprême de Volaille Verneuil 381
3179 Suprême de Volaille Villeroy 381
3180 Suprême de Volaille Wolseley 381
3757 Suprêmes de Bécasse 453
3629 Suprêmes de Faisan 439
3630 Suprêmes de Faisan Berchoux 439
3638 Suprêmes de Faisan à la Châtelaine, cold 440
3639 Suprêmes de Faisan des Gastronomes, cold 440
3631 Suprêmes de Faisan Louisette 439
4569 Suprême de Fruits Gabrielle 543
3668 Suprêmes de Perdreau Véron 443
4063 Swede Leaves 488
2482 Sweet-Meat 300
Sweetbreads, See under Ris de Veau or Ris d'Agneau
4311 Sweet Paste 513
3736 Sylphides d'Ortolans 450
3333 Sylphides de Volaille 399
4367 Syrup, Thickened 520

1265 Talmouses 151
1266 Talmouses à l'Ancienne 151
4767 Tangerines, Frosted 567
115 Tarragon Sauce, white 21
4332 Tartlet Cases 516
928 Tartlets 122
1267 Tartlets 151
928 Tartlets, fillings 122
928 Tartlets, pastes for 122
4952 Tartelettes Agnès 580
1268 Tartelettes Châtillon 151
1269 Tartelettes Diane 151
4953 Tartelettes à l'Ecossaise 580
4955 Tartelettes à la Florentine 580
1270 Tartelettes à la Gauloise 152
1271 Tartelettes aux Gnocchi 152
4028 Tartelettes Grillés aux Champignons 483
4954 Tartelettes Kitchener 580
1272 Tartelettes Marly 152
4956 Tartelettes Marquise 580
1273 Tartelettes Olga 152
1274 Tartelettes à la Polonaise 152
4957 Tartelettes Raglan 580
1275 Tartelettes à la Reine 152
1064 Tartelettes de Thon 132
4958 Tartelettes Tosca 580
4959 Tartelettes Vendôme 580
3772 Teal 455
3936 Teal, Roast 474
1696 Tench 200
2632 Tendron de Veau en Chaud-froid 316
2629 Tendron de Veau à l'Estragon 316
2630 Tendron de Veau à la Turque 316
2631 Tendron de Veau, with various garnishes 316
2143 Terrapin, à la Baltimore 252
2144 Terrapin Maryland 253
2142 Terrapin, Preparation and Cooking 252
3795 Terrines, Household 461
3794 Terrine, Standard Recipe 461
3367 Terrine de Poularde en Conserve 403
2713 Tête de Veau à l'Anglaise 326
2714 Tête de Veau Financière 326
2715 Tête de Veau Frite 326
2724 Tête de Veau Froide à la Flamande 327
2716 Tête de Veau Godard 326
2717 Tête de Veau à la Poulette 326
2718 Tête de Veau à la Ravigote 326
2721 Tête de Veau en Tortue 326
2722 Tête de Veau à la Toulousaine 326
2720 Tête de Veau, Sauce Tomate 326
2719 Tête de Veau Tarentaise 326
2723 Tête de Veau à la Vinaigrette 326
2725 Tétine de Veau 327
2050 Thon, Aiguillettes Orly 238
2047 Thon à la Chartreuse 237
1065 Thon à l'Huile 132
2048 Thon à l'Indienne 238
2049 Thon à l'Italienne 238
1066 Thon Marinette 132
1533 Thon, Omelette au 178
2051 Thon à la Provençale 238
3790 Thrush Pie 460
Thrushes, see also under Grives
3943 Thrushes, Roast 475
1276 Timbale Agnès Sorel 152
3339 Timbale à l'Ambassadrice 399
2193 Timbale d'Amourettes à l'Ecossaise 269
2194 Timbale d'Amourettes à la Napolitaine 269
4502 Timbale d'Aremberg 535
3758 Timbale de Bécasse Nesselrode 453
3759 Timbale de Bécasse Saint-Martin 453
3340 Timbale Bontoux 400
3341 Timbale Bourbonnaise 400
4503 Timbale Bourdaloue 535
3707 Timbale de Cailles 447
3693 Timbale de Cailles Alexandra 446
3464 Timbale de Caneton Mirabeau 416
3490 Timbale de Caneton Voisin 419
4334 Timbale Cases, Large 516

4333 Timbale Cases, Small 516
4504 Timbale Favart 535
3537 Timbale de Filets de Chevreuil à la Napolitaine 426
2029 Timbale de Filets de Sole Cardinal 234
2028 Timbale de Filets de Sole Carême 234
2030 Timbale de Filets de Sole Carmelite 234
2044 Timbale de Filets de Sole Escoffier 237
2031 Timbale de Filets de Sole Grimaldi 234
2032 Timbale de Filets de Sole Marquise 235
2033 Timbale de Filets de Sole Richepin 235
3506 Timbale de Foie gras à l'Alsacienne 422
3521 Timbale de Foie gras et de Cailles Tzarine 424
3507 Timbale de Foie gras Cambacérès 422
3508 Timbale de Foie gras Cussy 422
3342 Timbale Maréchal Foch 400
4505 Timbale Marie-Louise 536
3343 Timbale Milanaise 400
3344 Timbale Milanaise à l'Ancienne 400
4506 Timbale Montmorency 536
4038 Timbale de Morilles Châtelaine 484
3739 Timbale d'Ortolans Rothschild 451
3740 Timbale d'Ortolans Tzarine 451
4507 Timbale à la Parisienne 536
3428 Timbale de Pigeonneaux La Fayette 411
4545 Timbale de Poires à la Valenciennes 540
4286 Timbale de Polenta 509
2103 Timbale de Queues d'Ecrevisses Nantua 245
2102 Timbale de Queues d'Ecrevisses à la Parisienne 244
4305 Timbale de Raviolis à la Génoise 511
4304 Timbale de Raviolis à la Phocéenne 511
2675 Timbale de Ris de Veau Bâloise 321
2676 Timbale de Ris de Veau Condé 321
4278 Timbale de Truffes 508
1277 Timbales Dessoliers, Small 152
1278 Timbales Maréchal, Small 152
1279 Timbales Médicis, Small 152
1280 Timbales Montargis, Small 153
1281 Timbales Païva, Small 153
1282 Timbales Régine, Small 153
1283 Timbales Reynière, Small 153
Timbales, Sweet 535
1284 Timbales Talleyrand, Small 153
1285 Timbales Villeneuve, Small 153
4719 Tivoli aux Fraises 561
4254 Tomates à la Bressanne 505
4256 Tomates Farcies 505
4257 Tomates Farcies à l'Ancienne 505
4258 Tomates Farcies à la Carmelite 506
4259 Tomates Farcies au Gratin 506
4260 Tomates Farcies à la Hussarde 506
4263 Tomates Farcies à la Portugaise 506
4261 Tomates Farcies à l'Italienne 506
4262 Tomates Farcies à la Provençale 506
4264 Tomates Frites 506
1067 Tomates à la Génoise 132
4255 Tomates Grillées 505
1068 Tomates à la Monégasque 132
4265 Tomates, Mousse de 506
1069 Tomates au Naturel 132
Tomates, Purée de, see Sauce Tomate
1070 Tomates en Quartiers 132
4267 Tomates à la Rivoli 506
4266 Tomates Sautées à la Provençale 506
4269 Tomates, Soufflé de, à la Napolitaine 507
489 Tomato, diced 70
314 Tomato Essence 49
315 Tomato Fondue 49
4265 Tomato, Mousse of 506
508 Tomato Royale 72
3812 Tomato Salad 462
26 Tomato Sauce 9
4264 Tomatoes, Fried 506
4255 Tomatoes, Grilled 505
1070 Tomatoes, Quarters 132
4256 Tomatoes, Stuffed 505
4270 Topinambours, à l'Anglaise 507
4271 Topinambours Frits 507
4272 Topinambours, Purée de 507
4273 Topinambours, Soufflé de 507
2413 Topside of Beef, see also under Pièce de Boeuf 289
2299 Tournedos à l'Andalouse 280
2300 Tournedos à l'Arlésienne 280
2301 Tournedos Armenonville 280
2302 Tournedos Baltimore 280
2303 Tournedos Béarnaise 280
2304 Tournedos Belle-Hélène 281
2305 Tournedos Benjamin 281
2306 Tournedos Berny 281
2307 Tournedos à la Bordelaise 281
2308 Tournedos Bouquetière 281
2309 Tournedos Bréhan 281
2310 Tournedos Castillane 281
2311 Tournedos à la Catalane 281
2312 Tournedos Cendrillon 281
2313 Tournedos aux Champignons 281
2323 Tournedos à la Chartres 282
2314 Tournedos Chasseur 281
2315 Tournedos en Chevreuil 281
2316 Tournedos Chevreuse 281
2317 Tournedos Choisy 282
2318 Tournedos Choron 282
2319 Tournedos Clamart 282
2320 Tournedos Colbert 282
2321 Tournedos Coligny 282
2322 Tournedos Dubarry 282
2323 Tournedos à l'Estragon 282
2324 Tournedos Favorite 282
2325 Tournedos à la Fermière 282
2326 Tournedos à la Florentine 282
2327 Tournedos à la Forestière 282
2328 Tournedos Gabrielle 282
2329 Tournedos Helder 283
2330 Tournedos Henri IV 283
2331 Tournedos à l'Italienne 283
2332 Tournedos Japonaise 283
2333 Tournedos Judic 283
2334 Tournedos Lakmé 283
2335 Tournedos La Vallière 283
2336 Tournedos Lesdiguières 283
2337 Tournedos Lili 283
2338 Tournedos Lorette 283
2339 Tournedos Madeleine 283
2340 Tournedos Maréchal 283
2341 Tournedos Marguery 284
2342 Tournedos Marie-Louise 284
2343 Tournedos Marigny 284
2342 Tournedos Marion-Delorme 284
2344 Tournedos Marquise 284
2345 Tournedos à la Marseillaise 284
2346 Tournedos Mascotte 284
2347 Tournedos Masséna 284
2348 Tournedos Massilia 284
2349 Tournedos à la Matignon 284
2350 Tournedos Ménagère 284
2351 Tournedos Mexicaine 284
2352 Tournedos Mignon 284
2353 Tournedos Mikado 285
2354 Tournedos Mirabeau 285
2355 Tournedos Mireille 285
2356 Tournedos Mirette 285
2357 Tournedos à la Moelle 285
2358 Tournedos Montmorency 285
2359 Tournedos Montmort 285
2360 Tournedos Montpensier 285
2361 Tournedos aux Morilles 285
2362 Tournedos Narbonnaise 285
2363 Tournedos à la Niçoise 285
2364 Tournedos Ninon 285
2365 Tournedos à l'Orientale 286
2366 Tournedos Opéra 286
2367 Tournedos Parisienne 286
2368 Tournedos Parmentier 286
2369 Tournedos à la Périgourdine 286
2370 Tournedos à la Persane 286
2371 Tournedos Petit-Duc 286
2372 Tournedos à la Piémontaise 286
2373 Tournedos Polignac 286
2374 Tournedos à la Portugaise 286
2375 Tournedos à la Provençale 286
2376 Tournedos Rachel 286
2377 Tournedos Régence 286
2378 Tournedos Richemond 286
2379 Tournedos Rivoli 287
2380 Tournedos Rossini 287
2381 Tournedos Roumanille 287
2382 Tournedos Saint-Florentin 287
2383 Tournedos Saint-Germain 287
2384 Tournedos Saint-Mandé 287
2385 Tournedos à la Sarde 287
2386 Tournedos Senateur 287
2387 Tournedos Tivoli 287
2388 Tournedos Tyrolienne 287
2389 Tournedos Valençay 287
2390 Tournedos Ventadour 287
2391 Tournedos Vert-pré 287
2392 Tournedos Victoria 288
2393 Tournedos Villaret 288
1593 Tourte d'Anguille a la Saint-Martin 187
4335 Tourte, Croûte de 517
4039 Tourte de Morilles Villeneuve 485
1818 Tourte de Morue Bénédictine 212

4333 Timbale Cases, Small 516
4504 Timbale Favart 535
3537 Timbale de Filets de Chevreuil à la Napolitaine 426
2029 Timbale de Filets de Sole Cardinal 234
2028 Timbale de Filets de Sole Carême 234
2030 Timbale de Filets de Sole Carmelite 234
2044 Timbale de Filets de Sole Escoffier 237
2031 Timbale de Filets de Sole Grimaldi 234
2032 Timbale de Filets de Sole Marquise 235
2033 Timbale de Filets de Sole Richepin 235
3506 Timbale de Foie gras à l'Alsacienne 422
3521 Timbale de Foie gras et de Cailles Tzarine 424
3507 Timbale de Foie gras Cambacérès 422
3508 Timbale de Foie gras Cussy 422
3342 Timbale Maréchal Foch 400
4505 Timbale Marie-Louise 536
3343 Timbale Milanaise 400
3344 Timbale Milanaise à l'Ancienne 400
4506 Timbale Montmorency 536
4038 Timbale de Morilles Châtelaine 484
3739 Timbale d'Ortolans Rothschild 451
3740 Timbale d'Ortolans Tzarine 451
4507 Timbale à la Parisienne 536
3428 Timbale de Pigeonneaux La Fayette 411
4545 Timbale de Poires à la Valenciennes 540
4286 Timbale de Polenta 509
2103 Timbale de Queues d'Ecrevisses Nantua 245
2102 Timbale de Queues d'Ecrevisses à la Parisienne 244
4305 Timbale de Raviolis à la Génoise 511
4304 Timbale de Raviolis à la Phocéenne 511
2675 Timbale de Ris de Veau Bâloise 321
2676 Timbale de Ris de Veau Condé 321
4278 Timbale de Truffes 508
1277 Timbales Dessoliers, Small 152
1278 Timbales Maréchal, Small 152
1279 Timbales Médicis, Small 152
1280 Timbales Montargis, Small 153
1281 Timbales Païva, Small 153
1282 Timbales Régine, Small 153
1283 Timbales Reynière, Small 153
Timbales, Sweet 535
1284 Timbales Talleyrand, Small 153
1285 Timbales Villeneuve, Small 153
4719 Tivoli aux Fraises 561
4254 Tomates à la Bressanne 505
4256 Tomates Farcies 505
4257 Tomates Farcies à l'Ancienne 505
4258 Tomates Farcies à la Carmelite 506
4259 Tomates Farcies au Gratin 506
4260 Tomates Farcies à la Hussarde 506
4263 Tomates Farcies à la Portugaise 506
4261 Tomates Farcies à l'Italienne 506
4262 Tomates Farcies à la Provençale 506
4264 Tomates Frites 506
1067 Tomates à la Génoise 132
4255 Tomates Grillées 505
1068 Tomates à la Monégasque 132
4265 Tomates, Mousse de 506
1069 Tomates au Naturel 132
Tomates, Purée de, see Sauce Tomate
1070 Tomates en Quartiers 132
4267 Tomates à la Rivoli 506
4266 Tomates Sautées à la Provençale 506
4269 Tomates, Soufflé de, à la Napolitaine 507
489 Tomato, diced 70
314 Tomato Essence 49
315 Tomato Fondue 49
4265 Tomato, Mousse of 506
508 Tomato Royale 72
3812 Tomato Salad 462
26 Tomato Sauce 9
4264 Tomatoes, Fried 506
4255 Tomatoes, Grilled 505
1070 Tomatoes, Quarters 132
4256 Tomatoes, Stuffed 505
4270 Topinambours, à l'Anglaise 507
4271 Topinambours Frits 507
4272 Topinambours, Purée de 507
4273 Topinambours, Soufflé de 507
2413 Topside of Beef, see also under Pièce de Boeuf 289
2299 Tournedos à l'Andalouse 280
2300 Tournedos à l'Arlésienne 280
2301 Tournedos Armenonville 280
2302 Tournedos Baltimore 280
2303 Tournedos Béarnaise 280
2304 Tournedos Belle-Hélène 281
2305 Tournedos Benjamin 281
2306 Tournedos Berny 281
2307 Tournedos à la Bordelaise 281
2308 Tournedos Bouquetière 281
2309 Tournedos Bréhan 281
2310 Tournedos Castillane 281
2311 Tournedos à la Catalane 281
2312 Tournedos Cendrillon 281
2313 Tournedos aux Champignons 281
2323 Tournedos à la Chartres 282
2314 Tournedos Chasseur 281
2315 Tournedos en Chevreuil 281
2316 Tournedos Chevreuse 281
2317 Tournedos Choisy 282
2318 Tournedos Choron 282
2319 Tournedos Clamart 282
2320 Tournedos Colbert 282
2321 Tournedos Coligny 282
2322 Tournedos Dubarry 282
2323 Tournedos à l'Estragon 282
2324 Tournedos Favorite 282
2325 Tournedos à la Fermière 282
2326 Tournedos à la Florentine 282
2327 Tournedos à la Forestière 282
2328 Tournedos Gabrielle 282
2329 Tournedos Helder 283
2330 Tournedos Henri IV 283
2331 Tournedos à l'Italienne 283
2332 Tournedos Japonaise 283
2333 Tournedos Judic 283
2334 Tournedos Lakmé 283
2335 Tournedos La Vallière 283
2336 Tournedos Lesdiguières 283
2337 Tournedos Lili 283
2338 Tournedos Lorette 283
2339 Tournedos Madeleine 283
2340 Tournedos Maréchal 283
2341 Tournedos Marguery 284
2342 Tournedos Marie-Louise 284
2343 Tournedos Marigny 284
2342 Tournedos Marion-Delorme 284
2344 Tournedos Marquise 284
2345 Tournedos à la Marseillaise 284
2346 Tournedos Mascotte 284
2347 Tournedos Masséna 284
2348 Tournedos Massilia 284
2349 Tournedos à la Matignon 284
2350 Tournedos Ménagère 284
2351 Tournedos Mexicaine 284
2352 Tournedos Mignon 284
2353 Tournedos Mikado 285
2354 Tournedos Mirabeau 285
2355 Tournedos Mireille 285
2356 Tournedos Mirette 285
2357 Tournedos à la Moelle 285
2358 Tournedos Montmorency 285
2359 Tournedos Montmort 285
2360 Tournedos Montpensier 285
2361 Tournedos aux Morilles 285
2362 Tournedos Narbonnaise 285
2363 Tournedos à la Niçoise 285
2364 Tournedos Ninon 285
2365 Tournedos à l'Orientale 286
2366 Tournedos Opéra 286
2367 Tournedos Parisienne 286
2368 Tournedos Parmentier 286
2369 Tournedos à la Périgourdine 286
2370 Tournedos à la Persane 286
2371 Tournedos Petit-Duc 286
2372 Tournedos à la Piémontaise 286
2373 Tournedos Polignac 286
2374 Tournedos à la Portugaise 286
2375 Tournedos à la Provençale 286
2376 Tournedos Rachel 286
2377 Tournedos Régence 286
2378 Tournedos Richemond 286
2379 Tournedos Rivoli 287
2380 Tournedos Rossini 287
2381 Tournedos Roumanille 287
2382 Tournedos Saint-Florentin 287
2383 Tournedos Saint-Germain 287
2384 Tournedos Saint-Mandé 287
2385 Tournedos à la Sarde 287
2386 Tournedos Senateur 287
2387 Tournedos Tivoli 287
2388 Tournedos Tyrolienne 287
2389 Tournedos Valençay 287
2390 Tournedos Ventadour 287
2391 Tournedos Vert-pré 287
2392 Tournedos Victoria 288
2393 Tournedos Villaret 288
1593 Tourte d'Anguille a la Saint-Martin 187
4335 Tourte, Croûte de 517
4039 Tourte de Morilles Villeneuve 485
1818 Tourte de Morue Bénédictine 212

271 Stock for White Aspic Jelly 39
2046 Stockfish à la Mode des Pêcheurs Niçois 237
4371 Strawberry Fritters 521
4362 Strawberry Sauce 520
Strawberries, see also under Fraises
3887 Stuffing, Sage and Onion 470
3012 Stuffing for Sucking Pig 362
3013 Stuffing for Sucking Pig, English 362
3017 Stuffing for Poultry, Rice and Pearl Barley 363
3888 Stuffing, Veal 470
Sturgeon, see under Esturgeon
4100 Subrics d'Epinards 491
1262 Subrics de Foie gras 151
1263 Subrics à l'Italienne 151
1264 Subrics Piémontais 150
4501 Subrics, sweet 535
3011 Sucking Pig 362
3012 Sucking Pig, Stuffing for 362
4718 Suédoise de Fruits 561
4313 Suet Paste 513
3355 Sugar, cooking of 519
3463 Suprême de Caneton 416
3131 Suprême de Volaille Agnès Sorel 377
3132 Suprême de Volaille Albuféra 377
3133 Suprême de Volaille Alexandra 377
3134 Suprême de Volaille à l'Ambassadrice 377
3135 Suprême de Volaille à l'Arlésienne 377
3136 Suprême de Volaille Belle-Hélène 377
3137 Suprême de Volaille Boitelle 377
3138 Suprême de Volaille aux Champignons 377
3139 Suprême de Volaille aux Champignons (brown) 378
3140 Suprême de Volaille Chimay 378
3141 Suprême de Volaille Cussy 378
3142 Suprême de Volaille Doria 378
3143 Suprême de Volaille à la Dreux 378
3144 Suprême de Volaille à l'Ecarlate 378
3145 Suprême de Volaille à l'Ecossaise 378
3146 Suprême de Volaille Elizabeth 378
3147 Suprême de Volaille Favorite 378
3148 Suprême de Volaille Financière 378
3149 Suprême de Volaille à la Florentine 378
3150 Suprême de Volaille aux Fonds d'Artichaut 378
3151 Suprême de Volaille Henri IV 379
3152 Suprême de Volaille à la Hongroise 379
3153 Suprême de Volaille a l'Indienne 379
3154 Suprême de Volaille Jardinière 379
3381 Suprêmes de Volaille Jeannette 405
3155 Suprême de Volaille Judic 379
3156 Suprême de Volaille Maréchal 379
3157 Suprême de Volaille Marie-Louise 379
3158 Suprême de Volaille Marie-Thérèse 379
3159 Suprême de Volaille Maryland 379
3160 Suprême de Volaille Mireille 379
3161 Suprême de Volaille Montpensier 379
3162 Suprême de Volaille Orly 380
3163 Suprême de Volaille à l'Orientale 380
3164 Suprême de Volaille en Papillote 380
3165 Suprême de Volaille Parisienne 380
3166 Suprême de Volaille au Parmesan 380
3167 Suprême de Volaille à la Périgueux 380
3169 Suprême de Volaille Pojarski 380
3168 Suprême de Volaille Polignac 380
3170 Suprême de Volaille Régence 380
3171 Suprême de Volaille Richelieu 380
3172 Suprême de Volaille Rimini 380
3173 Suprême de Volaille Rossini 380
3174 Suprême de Volaille Saint-Germain 380
3175 Suprême de Volaille Talleyrand 381
3176 Suprême de Volaille Valençay 381
3177 Suprême de Volaille Valois 381
3178 Suprême de Volaille Verneuil 381
3179 Suprême de Volaille Villeroy 381
3180 Suprême de Volaille Wolseley 381
3757 Suprêmes de Bécasse 453
3629 Suprêmes de Faisan 439
3630 Suprêmes de Faisan Berchoux 439
3638 Suprêmes de Faisan à la Châtelaine, cold 440
3639 Suprêmes de Faisan des Gastronomes, cold 440
3631 Suprêmes de Faisan Louisette 439
4569 Suprême de Fruits Gabrielle 543
3668 Suprêmes de Perdreau Véron 443
4063 Swede Leaves 488
2482 Sweet-Meat 300
Sweetbreads, See under Ris de Veau or Ris d'Agneau
4311 Sweet Paste 513
3736 Sylphides d'Ortolans 450
3333 Sylphides de Volaille 399
4367 Syrup, Thickened 520

1265 Talmouses 151
1266 Talmouses à l'Ancienne 151
4767 Tangerines, Frosted 567
115 Tarragon Sauce, white 21
4332 Tartlet Cases 516
928 Tartlets 122
1267 Tartlets 151
928 Tartlets, fillings 122
928 Tartlets, pastes for 122
4952 Tartelettes Agnès 580
1268 Tartelettes Châtillon 151
1269 Tartelettes Diane 151
4953 Tartelettes à l'Ecossaise 580
4955 Tartelettes à la Florentine 580
1270 Tartelettes à la Gauloise 152
1271 Tartelettes aux Gnocchi 152
4028 Tartelettes Grillés aux Champignons 483
4954 Tartelettes Kitchener 580
1272 Tartelettes Marly 152
4956 Tartelettes Marquise 580
1273 Tartelettes Olga 152
1274 Tartelettes à la Polonaise 152
4957 Tartelettes Raglan 580
1275 Tartelettes à la Reine 152
1064 Tartelettes de Thon 132
4958 Tartelettes Tosca 580
4959 Tartelettes Vendôme 580
3772 Teal 455
3936 Teal, Roast 474
1696 Tench 200
2632 Tendron de Veau en Chaud-froid 316
2629 Tendron de Veau à l'Estragon 316
2630 Tendron de Veau à la Turque 316
2631 Tendron de Veau, with various garnishes 316
2143 Terrapin, à la Baltimore 252
2144 Terrapin Maryland 253
2142 Terrapin, Preparation and Cooking 252
3795 Terrines, Household 461
3794 Terrine, Standard Recipe 461
3367 Terrine de Poularde en Conserve 403
2713 Tête de Veau à l'Anglaise 326
2714 Tête de Veau Financière 326
2715 Tête de Veau Frite 326
2724 Tête de Veau Froide à la Flamande 327
2716 Tête de Veau Godard 326
2717 Tête de Veau à la Poulette 326
2718 Tête de Veau à la Ravigote 326
2721 Tête de Veau en Tortue 326
2722 Tête de Veau à la Toulousaine 326
2720 Tête de Veau, Sauce Tomate 326
2719 Tëte de Veau Tarentaise 326
2723 Tête de Veau à la Vinaigrette 326
2725 Tétine de Veau 327
2050 Thon, Aiguillettes Orly 238
2047 Thon à la Chartreuse 237
1065 Thon à l'Huile 132
2048 Thon à l'Indienne 238
2049 Thon à l'Italienne 238
1066 Thon Marinette 132
1533 Thon, Omelette au 178
2051 Thon à la Provençale 238
3790 Thrush Pie 460
Thrushes, see also under Grives
3943 Thrushes, Roast 475
1276 Timbale Agnès Sorel 152
3339 Timbale à l'Ambassadrice 399
2193 Timbale d'Amourettes à l'Ecossaise 269
2194 Timbale d'Amourettes à la Napolitaine 269
4502 Timbale d'Aremberg 535
3758 Timbale de Bécasse Nesselrode 453
3759 Timbale de Bécasse Saint-Martin 453
3340 Timbale Bontoux 400
3341 Timbale Bourbonnaise 400
4503 Timbale Bourdaloue 535
3707 Timbale de Cailles 447
3693 Timbale de Cailles Alexandra 446
3464 Timbale de Caneton Mirabeau 416
3490 Timbale de Caneton Voisin 419
4334 Timbale Cases, Large 516

Tripe, see also under Gras Double
2445 Tripe 294
2453 Tripes à la Mode de Caen 295
Trout, see also under Truite
1071 Trout, Marinated 132
1072 Trout, Marinated fillets of 132
3779 Trout Pie 458
1710 Trout, Stuffed 202
Truffles, see under Truffes
4274 Truffes sous la Cendre 507
4275 Truffes au Champagne 507
4276 Truffes à la Crème 507
1534 Truffes, Omelette aux 178
4277 Truffes à la Serviette 507
4278 Truffes, Timbale de 508
256 Truffle Butter 35
509 Truffle Royale 72
3914 Truffled Turkey 472
1698 Truite, Coulibiac de 201
3779 Truite, Pâté de 458
1709 Truites au Bleu 202
1710 Truites Farcies 202
1072 Truites, Filets de, Marinées 132
1711 Truites Gavarnie 202
1712 Truites à l'Hôtelière 203
1713 Truites à la Hussarde 203
1714 Truites à la Mantoue 203
1071 Truites Marinées 132
1715 Truites à la Meunière 203
1716 Truites Persillées 203
1717 Truites à la Vauclusienne 203
1718 Truites au Vin Rouge 203
1702 Truite Saumonée en Belle-Vue 201
1697 Truite Saumonée Cambacérès 200
1703 Truite Saumonée Froide au Chambertin 201
1704 Truite Saumonée Froide au Champagne 201
1706 Truite Saumonée Froide à la Norvégienne 201
1065 Tunny Fish in oil 132
1064 Tunny Fish Tartlets 132
2052 Tunny Fish with various garnishes 238
2034 Turban de Filets de Sole Villaret 235
2035 Turban de Filets de Sole et de Saumon Villaret 235
2820 Turban de Rognons Piémontaise 338
2055 Turbot à l'Amiral 239
2053 Turbot, Boiled 238
2054 Turbot, Braised 239
2062 Turbot, Cold 240
2081 Turbot, Cold Young 242
2058 Turbot, Coquilles de 239
2057 Turbot Crème Gratin 239
2059 Turbot Daumont 239
2060 Turbot à la Parisienne 239
2061 Turbot Régence 239
2064 Turbotin à l'Amiral 240
2065 Turbotin à l'Andalouse 240
2066 Turbotin Bonne-Femme 240
2067 Turbotin au Chambertin 240
2067 Turbotin au Champagne 240
2068 Turbotin Chauchat 240
2069 Turbotin Commodore 240
2070 Turbotin Daumont 240
2071 Turbotin Dugléré 240
2072 Turbotin Fermière 241
2073 Turbotin à la Feuillantine 241
2074 Turbotin au Gratin 241
2076 Turbotin aux Huîtres 241
2075 Turbotin à la Mode de Hollande 241
2077 Turbotin à la Parisienne 241
2078 Turbotin Régence 241
2080 Turbotin à la Saint-Malo 242
2079 Turbotin Soufflé Reynière 241
4147 Turnips 496
4063 Turnip Leaves 488
4150 Turnip Tops 496
4149 Turnips, Purée of 496
4148 Turnips, Stuffed 496
Turkey, see also under Dindonneau
3386 Turkey with Braised Celery 406
3396 Turkey, Cold 407
3387 Turkey with Flap Mushrooms 406
3388 Turkey with Mushrooms 406
3383 Turkey, Poached 405
3912 Turkey, Roast 472
3394 Turkey, Roast, with Chestnut Stuffing 407
3913 Turkey, Roast, English Style 472
3914 Turkey, Truffled 472
2145 Turtle Flippers, à l'Américaine 253
2146 Turtle Flippers with Madeira 253
330 Twarogue 51

2725 Udder, Calf's 327
3334 Ursulines de Nancy 399

3772 Vanneau 455
1286 Varénikis Lithuniens 153
1287 Varénikis à la Polonaise 153
1073 Varientes 132
1288 Vatrouskis au Fromage 153
Veal see also under Veau
2504 Veal, Best End, cold 302
Veal, Blanquette 327
2624 Veal, Breast of, see also under Poitrine de Veau 315
2587 Veal Cushion, see also under Noix de Veau 312
2595 Veal Cushion, Garnishes 313
2508 Veal Cutlets, see also under Côte de Veau 303
2598 Veal Escalopes, see also under Escalopes de Veau 313
2603 Veal Fricandeau 314
Veal Fillet, see under Filet de Veau
292 Veal Forcemeat for borders, bases and Quenelles 45
2604 Veal Fricandeau, cold 314
19 Veal Gravy, thickened 8
2605 Veal Grenadins 314
2606 Veal Grenadins, cold 314
3782 Veal and Ham Pie 459
3895 Veal, Roast Best End 471
3898 Veal, Roast Cushion 471
2683 Veal Kidney, see also under Rognon de Veau 322
2731 Veal Loaf 328
2584 Veal, Loin 311
2732 Veal, Paupiettes, see also under Paupiettes de Veau 328
298 Veal and Pork Forcemeat 47
2633 Veal, Quasi and Rouelle 316
3897 Veal, Roast Loin, English Style 471
3896 Veal, Roast Loin 471
2699 Veal, Saddle of, see also under Selle de Veau 324
Veal, Sauté of, see under Sauté de Veau
Veal Shoulder, see under Epaule de Veau
2634 Veal Sweetbreads, see also under Ris de Veau 316
3888 Veal Stuffing 470
2628 Veal Tendons, see also under Tendron de Veau 316
2492 Veau, Amourettes 301
2726 Veau, Blanquette de 327
2503 Veau, Carré 302
2492 Veau, Cervelles 301
Veau, Coeur de 303
2508 Veau, Côtes de 303
Veau, Côtes de, Froides 306
Veau, Epaule de 306
2598 Veau, Escalopes de 313
2544 Veau, Filet de 307
Veau, Foie de 308
Veau, Foie de, Froid 310
2729 Veau, Fricadelles 328
2603 Veau, Fricandeau 314
2605 Veau, Grenadins 314
3782 Veau et Jambon, Pâté de 459
Veau, Jarrets de 310
2579 Veau, Langues de 311
Veau, Mou de 311
2587 Veau, Noix de 312
Veau, Noix de, Froide 313
2608 Veau, Oreilles de 314
2731 Veau, Pain de 328
2732 Veau, Paupiettes de 328
2615 Veau, Pieds de 315
2624 Veau, Poitrine de 315
2633 Veau, Quasi de 316
2634 Veau, Ris de 316
2683 Veau, Rognon de 322
2633 Veau, Rouelle de 316
1049 Veau, Salade de Pieds de, à la Hongroise 131
1048 Veau, Salade de Pieds de 131
Veau, Sautés de 329
2699 Veau, Selle de 324
2628 Veau, Tendrons de 316
2712 Veau, Tête de 326
2725 Veau, Tétine de 327
3952 Vegetables, Blanching 476
305 Vegetable Borders 48
3956 Vegetables, Braising of 476
3957 Vegetables, braised, Sauce for 476
3954 Vegetables, Cooking à l'Anglaise 476
3960 Vegetable Creams 477
3955 Vegetables, dried, Cooking of 476
3958 Vegetables, finishing with butter 476
3959 Vegetables, finishing with cream 476
3960 Vegetable Purées 477
3953 Vegetables, Refreshing of 476
3846 Vegetable Salad 466
3809 Vegetable Salad using dried vegetables 463
1005 Vegetable Stalks 128

21 Velouté, Chicken 8
661 Velouté, Cold Chicken, for Suppers 85
22 Velouté, Fish 8
20 Velouté, Ordinary 8
22 Velouté de Poisson 8
21 Velouté de Volaille 8
3924 Venison, Roast, English Style 473
80 Venison Sauce 16
Vésiga, Notes on 196
4376 Viennese Fritters, Cold 521
4375 Viennese Fritters, Hot 521
5012 Vin à la Française 588
209 Vinaigrette 31
4105 Vine Leaves, Stuffed 492
1074 Vine Tendrils 132
1289 Visnisckis 154
659 Volaille, Gelée de, Napolitaine 85
660 Volaille, Gelée de, aux Pommes d'Amour 85
1181 Volaille, Fondants de, Louisette 143
3326 Volaille, Fritot and Marinade 398
4336 Vol-au-Vent Cases 517
2500 Vol-au-Vent de Cervelle de Veau 302
2037 Vol-au-Vent de Filets de Sole Présidence 235
3345 Vol-au-Vent à la Financière 401
3346 Vol-au-Vent Frascati 401
2894 Vol-au-Vent of Lamb's Sweetbreads 348
1819 Vol-au-Vent de Morue 212
1475 Vol-au-Vent d'Oeufs 174
3431 Vol-au-Vent de Pigeonneux 412
1798 Vol-au-Vent de Quenelles de Merlan Cardinal 210
2894 Vol-au-Vent de Ris d'Agneau Soubise 348
2677 Vol-au-Vent de Ris de Veau à la Nésle 321
2678 Vol-au-Vent de Ris de Veau Régence 321
2036 Vol-au-Vent de Sole à la Marinière 235
3347 Vol-au-Vent à la Toulousaine 401
1074 Vrilles de Vigne 132

958 Walnuts, green with Verjuice 124
Warblers 451
3928 Warblers, Roast 474
3772 Water Fowl 455
1572 Waterzoï 185
2082 Weever 242
4960 Welsh Rarebit 580
1719 Whitebait 203
94 White Bordelaise Sauce 18
3 White Chicken Stock 4
306 White Paste Borders 48
163 White Wine Sauce 26
Whiting, see also under Merlans
3548 Wild Boar 428
Winglets, see under Ailerons
Woodcocks 451
Woodcocks, Cold 453
3788 Woodcock Pie 460
3749 Woodcock, Mousses 452
3768 Woodcock, Mousse, Cold 454
3749 Woodcock, Mousselines 452
3768 Woodcock, Mousselines, Cold 454
3750 Woodcock Pie, Hot 452
3926 Woodcock, Roast 474
4156 Wood Sorrel 497

3889 Yorkshire Pudding 471
2063 Young Turbot, see also under Turbotin 240
Young Turkey see under Dindonneau

2929 Zampino 352
2930 Zampino Cold 352
1073 Zampino, for Hors-d'Oeuvre 133